etropolitan

THE NATIONAL WEALTH

THE NATIONAL WEALTH

Who Gets What in Britain

DOMINIC HOBSON

HarperCollins*Publishers*

HarperCollins*Publishers*
77–85 Fulham Palace Road,
Hammersmith, London W6 8JB

Published by HarperCollins*Publishers* 1999
1 3 5 7 9 8 6 4 2

Copyright © Dominic Hobson 1999

The Author asserts the moral right to
be identified as the author of this work

A catalogue record for this book
is available from the British Library

ISBN 0 00 255913 7

Set in New Baskerville by
Rowland Phototypesetting Ltd,
Bury St Edmunds, Suffolk

Printed and bound in Great Britain by
The Bath Press, Avon

For My Father

CONTENTS

CHAPTER SIX: THE REDBRICK UNIVERSITIES

CHAPTER SEVEN: THE PUBLIC SCHOOLS

PART TWO: THE STATE

CHAPTER NINE: CENTRAL GOVERNMENT

PART THREE: PEOPLE

CHAPTER FOURTEEN: THE RICH

CHAPTER FIFTEEN: COMPANY DIRECTORS

CHAPTER SIXTEEN: THE PRIVATE SECTOR PROFESSIONALS

CHAPTER SEVENTEEN: THE PUBLIC SECTOR PROFESSIONALS

PART FOUR: BUSINESS

PART FIVE: FINANCE

CHAPTER TWENTY-SEVEN: BANKS AND BUILDING SOCIETIES

CHAPTER TWENTY-EIGHT: THE RISE OF INSTITUTIONAL INVESTORS

CHAPTER THIRTY-TWO: THE FUTURE OF OWNERSHIP

ACKNOWLEDGEMENTS

The author and publishers would like to thank the following for their assistance in the sourcing and securing of copyright permission for material quoted in this book:

ACNielsen Company Ltd; The Bank of England; The British Bankers' Association; The British Tourist Authority; British Venture Capital Association; The Certification Office for Trade Unions and Employers' Associations; Charities Aid Foundation; CIPFA; Citywatch Limited; The Directory of Social Change; DTZ Debenham Thorpe; The English Tourist Board; HESA; Hodder and Stoughton Limited; The Institute of Economic Affairs; The Institute of Petroleum; Jordan's Limited; Legal Business; Miller Freeman PLC; The National Association of Pension Funds Limited; NGO Finance; Oddball Publishing Limited; The Office for National Statistics © Crown Copyright 1999; PBI; Penguin Books Ltd; The Peters Fraser & Dunlop Group Ltd; Radius Works; Simon & Schuster UK Limited; The *Sunday Times*; The TAS Partnership Limited and The University of Chicago Press.

The author and publishers have made every effort to contact and trace the copyright holders of quoted material. They would, however, be grateful to hear of any omissions, so that future editions of this book can be amended.

FOREWORD

When at the first I took my pen in hand,
Thus for to write, I did not understand
That I at all should make a little book
In such a mode; nay, I had undertook
To make another, which when almost done,
Before I was aware, I this, begun.

JOHN BUNYAN, *Pilgrim's Progress*

This book is about money: who has it, who gets it, why they do, and how they do. Occasionally, it even discusses whether they should. But it is not a textbook of economics, or a work of morals. Rather, it is a reconnaissance of capitalism in Britain today. Like *Anatomy of Britain* and *Friends in High Places* before it, *The National Wealth* is about the workings of Britain. But its focus is economic and financial rather than political and bureaucratic. Where Anthony Sampson and Jeremy Paxman dissected the structure of power, this book explores the distribution of income and wealth. They answered one important question: Who runs Britain? *The National Wealth* answers another: Who owns Britain?

It is possible to answer this question directly. The earliest drafts of the book did exactly that. To some extent, the final version still does. But it soon became plain that an undergraduate adherence to the question would reduce the book to a catalogue. The intriguing challenge was not to find out who owned what, but to unravel the origin, dynamics and consequences of the present distribution of wealth. This is why the book now ranges beyond the narrow question with which it began. It explores history (how did this dispensation come about?), economics (is this the best use of scarce resources?) and politics (who? whom?). *The National Wealth* is not just about wealth. It is about power and status too.

This is one reason why it is a big book. The other is the sheer size of its subject matter. 'The mind shrinks,' wrote the Victorian statistician, Sir Robert Giffen, 'from the task of framing a catalogue or inventory of the nation's property.' Unfortunately, I did not chance upon his advice until this venture was well-embarked. It has taken a decade to turn the germ of an idea, first advanced by Christopher Sinclair-Stevenson in the waiting room of a firm of libel lawyers on 10 July 1989, into this book. His question ('Who really has the money?') had occurred to him the night before, at a reception hosted by the heirs to one of the great landed estates: the Church Commissioners. The location of his Archimedean moment was significant. Most people, asked who owns the country, think instinctively of Church, Aristocracy and Oxbridge.

They certainly have land, and money and securities too. All three appear, along with the other great estates of the past, in the first fifth of the book. But they are plutocratic pygmies now, undone by the long shift in the nature of wealth, from land to money and substitutes for money. In the twentieth century, power and wealth have shifted decisively from the great estates of the realm to the State itself. It now spends more than £2 in every £5 earned by everybody living and working in Britain today. Though privatisation has ended a failed experiment in ownership by the State, its power to tax and spend (and, increasingly, regulate) is undiminished and even expanding. The changing role of the State is covered in the second part of the book.

If the twentieth century saw a shift of power and wealth from Church and Aristocracy to the State, the long displacement of landed wealth by money and securities is now being overtaken by a third revolution in the nature of property. Trained minds, protected in some cases from competition, are replacing rents and dividends as the most valuable form of wealth. The Fat Cats, and their equally well-paid advisers in the City and the Law, are explored in the third part of the book. Their habitat is the PLC, which has become virtually the only form of social organisation which now stands between the family and the State. The enormous impact of corporate business, on how we shop and play as well as how we work, is told in the fourth section of the book.

The ubiquity of the PLC, and the spread of its techniques into areas previously immune or even hostile to commercial values, is the most obstinate of the themes which unite the five parts of this long book. In no age were British men and women more obsessed with the distribution of income and wealth than the twentieth century. Yet it is the PLC, and not the State, which ends it as the chief arbiter of production, consumption, distribution and exchange. Who owns the PLC can truly be said to own the country. This is why the closing chapters of the book are devoted to the institutional investors: the pension, insurance and mutual funds which channel the savings of millions of ordinary people into the great corporate enterprises which provide the work and goods and entertainment which fill our daily lives.

But the book is about people as well as organisations. It encounters them in public places (voters, taxpayers, patients, and undergraduates) as well as private lives (parents, church-goers, public schoolboys, and liverymen). The book visits them at work and asks what they are paid and why. In its pages, readers will come across Cabinet ministers, MPs, civil servants, judges, dons, bishops, clergymen, aristocrats, farmers, lawyers, bankers, accountants, architects, engineers, doctors and dentists, teachers, army officers, Fat Cats and plutocrats, middle managers, journalists, shopkeepers, publicans, sportsmen, and charity-workers. The book does not confine itself to their working lives. It observes people shopping, eating, drinking, gambling, saving, reading newspapers, and watching films and sport and television.

The comprehension of such diversity is one aim which has survived the alteration of the original purpose of the book. It remains an important attraction for its readers. But I have tried to balance its range and variety with a proper respect for interest and narrative. Though each chapter of each part is intended to be read as a piece of the whole, the book can also be read as a collection of self-contained essays on thirty-two different subjects. They are cross-referenced where necessary in the end-notes, so readers who relish some parts more than others need never lose their way. But some readers are bound to notice the people and the subjects which are excluded, as well as those which are included.

To some extent, omissions are unavoidable. A book which is so heavily populated with people and institutions, and which runs from the Norman Conquest to the takeover of Forte by Granada, is potentially unbound in both time and space. A text which sought to encompass literally everything and everybody would be unwieldy, and certain to fail in its ambition. Much has already disappeared during the process of preparing the book for publication, chiefly in order to maintain its readability (and portability). But some areas were omitted deliberately. The most obvious is the limited treatment of the poor and the State services on which they rely, like hospitals, schools, benefits and pensions. This is not because the poor are unimportant, or even because a book about the distribution of income and wealth necessarily excludes those who own little of either. On the contrary. It is because the poor and vulnerable are so numerous, and their difficulties so multifarious, particular and intractable, that a few pages culled from secondary sources in a book of this kind can neither comprehend nor appreciate them. They deserve a book of their own.

Some, and especially those who believe that the wealth of the few is purchased by the poverty of the many, may read the omission as a form of political testimony. If so, they are mistaken. Unlike some recent books on the State of the Nation, the book propounds no theory nor expounds any doctrine. What ties its disparate parts together is the fact that they were organised by a single intelligence. My preferences are obvious, but not I hope obtrusive. They lie with shoppers rather than voters; taxpayers, not tax-eaters; entrepreneurs over professionals; and with markets rather than institutions, especially of the political kind. If the book has any message for my countrymen at all, it is to trust themselves rather than self-appointed intercessors, be they great or good, politicians or life assurance salesmen, sports stars or cultural interpreters. Not everybody will be pleased by this approach. Some will reckon their livelihoods devalued, others their motives impugned. But getting money, like the sex and power for which it can be exchanged, is often the unacknowledged motive behind what is said and done in the name of something else.

My judgments, erroneous or not, must stand. But for errors of fact, of which there are bound to be some, apology is due. It is impossible to capture such a large picture exactly, even for an instant. It blurs constantly, as time advances and facts change. Facts and figures are invariably retrospective. Understanding lags events. But readers have the assurance that no word or figure in this book was checked later than January 1999. Of course, many of the prices and values in the text are historical rather than contemporary. Instead of cluttering the page with parenthetic conversions into modern prices on the page where they occur, a conversion table is reproduced at the back of the book.

In the composition of *The National Wealth*, I have incurred many debts. Although the book relies to a lesser extent on interviews than most books of its kind, many people gave freely of their time and knowledge. Others read chapters, or even braces of chapters. Their number includes Sir Douglas Lovelock and Ann Dickens of the Church Commissioners; Brandon Jackson and Rex Davis; Andrew Studdert-Kennedy; Robin Porteous; Ian Posgate; Lord Saye & Sele; Peter Virgin; Michael Wakeford; Robert Strick; Bernard Harty and the staff of the Corporation of London; Dr Keith Boyfield; Andreas Loizou; Ian Walter; Rupert Beeley; Christopher Forbes, late of Citywatch; George and Alastair Ross Goobey; Robin Gordon Walker; Daniel Phelan of NGO Finance; Gerard Riley of Lafferty Publications; Eric Carnell of Sewells International; Nigel Johnson of the Monks Partnership; David Nicholas of BP Oil; Iain Loe of CAMRA; Jonathan Heap of DTZ Debenham Thorpe; the staff of the library at Trinity House; Ian Sinclair; Chris Cheek; and Alec Cunningham.

Special thanks are due to Claire Gagneux, for her help in researching aspects of government; Martin and Jocelyn Broughton and Michael and Sue Prideaux, for their patronage as well as their hospitality and enthusiasm; my other friends at BAT, and especially Wendy Black and Heather Honour;

Susannah Fiennes, for postponing marriage; Matt Ridley, for those stimulating walks up and down the hill; and Iris Childs-Lindsey, for her insights into the world of gambling. Many more people read or commented on passages, or replied to my correspondence, even if the text or questions were unwelcome. That much-maligned apologist for the PLC, the public relations or press officer, was an invaluable source of information everywhere except in central government. I am grateful to them all. It is interesting to record that the only people who went out of their way to be rude or unhelpful were Oxbridge dons and City research analysts, and even among them there could always be found a handful yet to be warped by bitterness or pride.

My publishers and editors changed frequently (as if to remind me that I was portraying a world in flux) though only once at my behest. Happily, it eventually fell to Richard Johnson, Biddy Martin, John Thomas, Katie Fulford, Prue Jeffreys, Zoe Mayne and Marian Reid to bring the book to fruition. They recognised its unusual demands, and persuaded themselves and others to work in unorthodox ways to ensure it was up-to-date as well as publishable. Paul Boyfield updated many of the figures in the second half of 1998, giving way only in January 1999 to my mother and my sister Susan, who took to telephone canvassing with their usual energy and facility. Thanks are due also to my friends and colleagues at Asset International, publishers of *Global Custodian* and *Plan Sponsor* magazines, and especially to Charles Ruffel. Their patience and forbearance were exemplary.

Only two people have known *The National Wealth* intimately since the beginning. My father read and edited its earliest incarnation, never wavered in his conviction that the book was worthwhile, and sacrificed his own work to its completion. Accordingly, it is dedicated to him. The other is the Fearsome Uxor, who has spent much of the 1990s combining the roles of consultant radiologist, single mother, and Dorothea Brooke. It was not until the book was finished, and I returned from Mars to Venus, that she appreciated how lucky she was to play only three roles. Jamanda will never believe it, but there is not a word in this book which does not bear the weight of my gratitude and love.

London, February 1999

HOW TO USE THIS BOOK

Every author hopes that readers will devour his work in its entirety. This book was certainly written to be read as a continuous narrative (its character may be encyclopaedic, but it is not an encyclopaedia). However, a volume of this size and scope makes such unusual demands on the time of its readers that some advice on the spirit in which it should be read is not out of place. Many people will read it from cover to cover, while others will be taken by some subjects more than others. The best advice to readers is to tackle only those parts which intrigue immediately, in any order which they choose. It is given in the confident hope that the pleasure of the parts will draw the piecemeal reader ineluctably into the experience of the whole.

PART ONE

THE INHERITORS

CHAPTER ONE

THE CROWN

In spite of the hundreds of journalists who have hunted for royal stories, no one yet knows how life is led in the royal palaces, what private views the Queen holds, what she says to her visiting statesmen.

ANTHONY SAMPSON, 1962[1]

If the photographers weren't interested – that would be the time to start worrying.

PRINCE CHARLES, 1982[2]

Thank you for the enormous bill, which will take a little time to pay.

The Queen to HARDY AMIES[3]

The Monarchy is a labour-intensive industry.

HAROLD WILSON, 1977[4]

It is said that the Conqueror, disembarking with his army at Pevensey Bay on Thursday 28 September 1066, stumbled and fell as he landed. His companions, thinking this a bad portent of the impending engagement with the English army, were afraid. William rose slowly to his feet, both fists filled with sand. 'Look,' he said, 'I have seized England with my two hands.' It took him five years to make good that claim among the unreconciled English of the west and north. But, when the Conquest was done, it was indeed the one moment in history when all the power and wealth of England coincided in the rights and personality of one man. Seven hundred years before the Industrial Revolution, the wealth of England lay in nothing but its fertile fields and crowded farmyards, and the Conqueror seized them all. He then placed himself at the apex of a pyramid of feudal obligations in which all the land, and all the things which stood upon it, belonged ultimately to the king.

Though the present Queen can trace her ancestry back to the Conqueror, nobody could say the same of her. Far from owning everything, everybody owns her. Over nine hundred years, the people of Britain have steadily resumed the wealth and power which the Conqueror took, and reduced their sovereign to a pantomime. But even as it shed its greatness, the monarchy managed for the most part to retain the affection and esteem of its subjects. Now even they are gone. If the royal family in the reign of Queen Elizabeth II is remembered by historians at all, it will be for the speed and recklessness with which its members squandered their inheritance of popular respect and goodwill. In the last thirty years they have shed not only their morals but their dignity. The beginnings of this steady diminution in public respect are usually dated to June 1969. That summer, both the BBC and ITV broadcast *Royal Family*, a ninety-minute documentary about the life of the Queen and her family, intended (in the words of the director) to portray them as 'human'.[5]

The End of Remoteness

The one scene from the film which everybody who saw it can remember is the barbecue by the loch at Balmoral, in which the Duke of Edinburgh cooks the sausages while Prince Charles mixes the salad dressing. Its defiance of the warning of the Victorian political economist Walter Bagehot that 'above all things our royalty is to be reverenced, and if you begin to poke about it you cannot reverence it . . . Its mystery is its life. We must not let in daylight upon magic' was blatant.[6] Few remember now its homage to his belief that the appeal of monarchy lies in its ability to reduce questions of national allegiance and political obligation to the level of the individual and the familial. *Royal Family* was a mistake. It was a mistake not because it dispelled the mystique, or made the extraordinary seem ordinary. It was a mistake because it aroused public curiosity to know more, and invited the media to satisfy it.

The Queen was convinced of the need to court the press even before her private secretary, William Heseltine, persuaded her to agree to *Royal Family*. In 1967, she had knighted the round-the-world yachtsman Francis Chichester in a televised public ceremony at Greenwich, using the same sword Elizabeth I had used to knight Francis Drake. Like *Royal Family*, and the investiture of the Prince of Wales at Caernarvon Castle in July 1969, this was a conscious use of the media to promote the monarch. Her children absorbed the lesson, lacing it with a frivolity they had cause to regret. In the summer of 1987, *It's a Royal Knock-Out* – in which Prince Edward, Prince Andrew, the Duchess of York and Princess Anne took part in a television pantomime with celebrities such as Rowan Atkinson and Gary Lineker – was an embarrassing disaster.

The royal advisers had assumed they could control the terms and timing of the selling of the monarchy.[7] But by inviting the cameras to record the private lives of princes they conferred a spurious legitimacy upon the activities of the one group of journalists it was beyond the power of the Establishment to contain: the paparazzi. 'It would appear,' said Earl Spencer the day after Diana, Princess of Wales, was killed in a car accident in Paris, 'that every proprietor and every editor ... that has paid for intrusive and exploitative photographs of her, encouraging greedy and ruthless individuals to risk everything in pursuit of Diana's image, has blood on his hands today.'[8] A few days before her death, Diana herself had complained to her friend Rosa Monckton: 'It's a hunt, Rosa, it's a hunt.'[9] It was a hunt she did much to maintain, but her mother-in-law had started the chase.

The triumph of Diana was not to discover the mischievousness of the media. It was to turn the power of the press on her in-laws to such devastating effect that the monarchy may never recover. This was never more evident than in the hours and days which followed the death of Diana on 31 August 1997. As the mourners went about the streets of Kensington and St James's, the Queen was criticised for failing to share the grief of her subjects. She was forced eventually to fly down from her holiday retreat at Balmoral and mingle with the crowds. On the eve of the funeral, she was bludgeoned into making a special television broadcast indicating that she shared the verdict of her people on the dead princess.

'She was an exceptional and gifted human being,' the Queen intoned. 'In good times and bad, she never lost her capacity to smile and laugh, nor to inspire others with her warmth and kindness. I admired and respected her – for her energy and commitment to others, and especially for her devotion to her two boys.' It was still not enough. At the funeral, Earl Spencer was applauded by the congregation after launching an ill-mannered attack on the royal family. The prime minister, whose urge to please had already prompted him to dub Diana the People's Princess, became concerned. Over lunch at Balmoral Castle on the following day, he explained the need for change.[10]

The Diana Phenomenon

That 'dear paradise' on Deeside, which Victoria and Albert purchased and re-built, has hosted many of the seminal moments in the precipitate decline of the House of Windsor over the last twenty years. It was on the banks of the Dee in the late summer of 1980 that royal journalists first spotted Prince Charles alone with Diana Spencer. Twelve years later they were staying there again when the transcript of the celebrated 'Squidgygate' tape was published by the *Sun*, in which the Princess refers to 'this fucking family' and describes her marriage as 'torture'. A few months earlier, the *Sunday Times* had serialised *Diana: Her True Story*, which revealed that the Princess of Wales was so unhappy in her marriage that she had made five attempts on her life.

At one point in the Squidgygate tape, recorded as early as 1989, Diana warns that she will distance herself from the rest of the royal family. 'I go out,' she says, 'and . . . conquer the world.'[11] She accomplished this by giving a definitive answer to a question which has dogged kings and queens for over two hundred years: what is a constitutional monarch for? With some help from the Duchess of York, Diana showed that the monarchy was no more than the hereditary arm of show-business, whose players led (and were expected to lead) show-business lives. Diana knew that the media were happy to accept her at her own valuation – warm, caring, affectionate, vulnerable, all-too-human – without inquiring deeply into whether the image was contradicted by a taste for jet-setting, expensive clothes, exotic holidays, and international pleasure-seekers. She understood that television and tabloid newspapers are concerned with appearance not substance, with images rather than words, and value those who feel rather than those who think. She was a master of the gestures – a smile, a look, a touch – which could communicate the personality she wished to convey. By the time she appeared on *Panorama* in November 1995, to give her first and last television interview, Diana had even learned to talk in the confessional idiom of pop psychology and female journalism. When Prince Charles bared his soul on television, in a lengthy profile by Jonathan Dimbleby, it was judged a public relations disaster. Unlike his estranged wife, he did not know the argot ('there were three of us in this marriage') or how to fashion a soundbite ('queen of hearts').

Nobody outside the entertainment industry could rival Diana in her understanding of the demotic spirit of the age, and of the role of the media as its interlocutor. The mass culture of tabloids and television makes no attempt to lead or to instruct: it simply mirrors the lives of its consumers. Diana reflected contemporary behaviour so faithfully that people lived with and through her on a daily basis, in much the same way that they adopt the characters from television soap operas.[12] As the Queen admitted in her live telecast on the eve of the funeral, millions of people who never knew Diana personally felt close to her because they read the story of her life in words and pictures every day of the week. The Princess became an integral part of that self-referring system in which the tabloids feed off television, television feeds off tabloids, and it becomes hard to tell fact from fantasy. 'I still don't really believe she's dead,' said a visitor to St James's Palace before her funeral. 'Perhaps that's because I didn't really believe she was alive.'[13]

This ability to mirror ordinary lives, even fictionalise them, was a throwback to that earlier idea of kingship identified by Bagehot: the ability to reduce great questions to the level of the familial and the ordinary. From at least the time of Queen Victoria, the royal family was expected to mirror the domestic virtues of its subjects. In contracting a glittering marriage which went horribly sour, and portraying the royal family as dysfunctional, Diana did no more than update an earlier idea of the monarchy for the age of divorce and single parenthood. Much of the popular reaction to the death of Diana can be understood in the same way. Just as a royal wedding is a brilliant edition of a universal fact, so is a royal funeral. The near-religious veneration of Diana in the immediate aftermath of her death drew heavily on the popular superstitions which have flourished in the post-Christian era – astrology, diets, aromatherapy, therapeutic massage, counselling, colonic irrigation, crystals, meditation, working out – which the Princess herself did so much to promote.

Four years before Diana died, the American journalist Camille Paglia described her as 'the most powerful image in the world today, a case study in the modern cult of celebrity and the way in which it stimulates atavistic religious emotions'.[14] The queues, candles, messages, pictures and banks of flowers wrapped in cellophane which built up outside the royal palaces (and a department store) in the first week of September 1997 testified to a continuing need for spiritual encounter and religious ritual. Shrinking contact with organised religion meant that few of the mourners realised both were readily available in churches and chapels the length and breadth of the land. Untutored, they coped by copying what they had seen others do on television.

Anthony Sampson records that Prince Charles became fascinated during his anthropological studies at Cambridge and afterwards by the fact that the 'modern monarchy could still reveal unexpected yearnings among ordinary people, as if some spiritual element had been neglected'.[15] Perhaps some unconscious collective memory was at work in September 1997 too. Until the mid-seventeenth century Civil War, monarchs were thought to rule by Divine Right. Bagehot thought the monarchy 'by its religious sanction . . . gives now a vast strength to the entire Constitution, by enlisting on its behalf the credulous obedience of enormous masses'.[16]

Had she remained a member of the royal family, perhaps even had she lived, Diana might have refreshed that credulity sufficiently to secure the position of the monarchy for another generation or two. She might have re-invented for an age of mass culture the religiosity (through her beauty and New Age idealism) and intelligibility (through her failed marriage) Bagehot deemed so vital to popular appreciation of the institution. It is more likely that she would have ended up, as the historian Andrew Roberts predicted, married to a Californian billionaire and running a colonic irrigation clinic.

But it was long before her death on 31 August 1997 that the royal family lost its last, best hope of making publicity work for it.

Diana's chief legacy to her countrymen (apart from a ghoulish trade in memorabilia) is a massive charitable fund of a kind George III would have understood. As the historian of charity, Frank Prochaska, has pointed out, the monarchy has long since become a 'welfare monarchy' which seeks legitimacy by doing good.[17] In that respect, Diana was a glamorous version of a traditional royal. But when she was gone, she took not only the glamour but much of the goodwill.

The media caravan Diana boarded at the time of Squidgygate has moved on now. It cannot stay with anybody, or any subject, for longer than a soundbite or a punchline. What Diana proved was the emptiness of monarchy as celebritocracy. Celebrities are known not for their achievements, or even for their office, but for their personalities. When their personalities are annihilated, there is nothing left to celebrate, and because they cannot fill the gap which she has left, the royal family are now exposed for what they are. Like her, they are glorified charity-mongers and page-fillers, with no power which does not depend on others and no purpose beyond their own perpetuation. Now, only the odiousness of elected politicians stands between Britain and the declaration of a republic.

Modern Monarchy: Influence, Not Power

In January 1994 the Tory MP Michael Portillo made an attempt to burnish the tarnished crown. 'The point of the monarchy,' he said, 'is that it is a national focal point. It's the source of the authority and legitimacy of government, yet above politics. Above all, it is the personification of the nation. It's an institution vital to our national well-being.'[18] To explain the survival of the monarchy into the age of democracy, it is necessary to employ ingenious arguments. Portillo took most of his from the first chronicler of constitutional monarchy. Bagehot argued, with considerable cynicism, that the chief use of the monarchy was to muffle the dramatic changes and divisions of Victorian Britain with a strong dose of artificial continuity and stability. 'A Republic', he wrote, 'has insinuated itself beneath the folds of a Monarchy.'[19]

Since the Second World War a succession of left-wing writers have argued, in much the same vein, that the coronations, investitures and weddings of the House of Windsor have provided a damagingly agreeable cloak for a nation in retreat from empire and flight from economic reality. 'When there is no great social change, and the country is inclined to escape from harsh facts, while Britain is having to make the painful transition from imperial splendour to competitive trading,' wrote Sampson in 1962, 'the palace represents in most people's minds a feudal, uncompetitive haven of "it's not done".'[20] In *The Enchanted Glass*, published in 1988, Tom Nairn angrily refuted the Old Left idea of the monarchy as a jumble of harmless pageantry and meaningless flummery. He described it as the source and symbol of the British rejection of modernity, or what he called the Glamour of Backwardness.[21] Years later his ideas were transmitted to a much wider audience through *The State We're In*, where Will Hutton accorded monarchy-as-symbol a major role in his analysis of the origins of the City-Conservative hegemony.[22]

Since May 1997, *The State We're In* has not read so well. But there is something in the Nairn–Huttonite analysis of monarchy. It is obvious that an institution capable of attracting such intense and sustained interest as the royal family must influence its audience at least as much as its audience influences royalty. As Nairn presciently wrote in 1988:

> Only a deaf-and-dumb hermit with no TV set in remotest Shetland could hope to escape the Royal Touch. From the moment the daily paper drops on the mat until the end of late-night television the most casual observer cannot avoid bombardment by news of regal migrations, openings, hand-wavings, speeches, banquets, romances, plans for nursery and paddock, receptions and walkabouts amid touched and wondering crowds. Such items are rarely doleful or disturbing. The amazing health and longevity of the Windsor stock (a contrast to most past dynasties) tends in any case to keep funerals at bay. Were departures or illnesses more common, incidentally, they would probably serve to intensify the mass cult ... Even with this big gun in reserve ... royalty succeeds remarkably in pervading and colouring the British way of life. Give us this day our daily trance: near the conclusion of every other TV news programme the announcer's manner and tone of voice alters, a warm smirk replacing the customary asperity. 'Come with me', it implies, into the Ukanian land of reliably good news where the worst that can befall us is a princely chill or a presentation posy dropped in the mud. A kind of salve is gratefully administered after the usual ten minutes of jolts, truncated tragedies, MPs' pronouncements and tales of national failure. Most of the nation follows, like the victims of the alien intelligence in so many science fiction movies.[23]

The accuracy of this portrayal is undeniable, but Nairn could not have imagined a more striking affirmation of his thesis that princes are worth more dead than alive than the Cult of Diana which has now developed. But if the media-driven process of Give-Us-This-Day-Our-Daily-Trance has fossilised social attitudes, this is another reminder that monarchy has traded whatever *real* power it had for some ill-defined form of cultural influence.

Prince Charles would probably agree that it has no real influence. Unlike Diana, he has translated his enthusiasms (architecture, the environment, unemployment, ethnicity) into tangible achievements like books (*A Vision of Britain*), magazines (*Perspectives on Architecture*), model villages (Poundbury in Dorset) and venture capital funds (the Prince's Youth Business Trust). Even so, his achievements are much less interesting to the tabloid-reading and television-viewing public than his sex life. It would be pointless for him to hope – like George VI or Elizabeth II – that he could justify his position by emphasising the stability and continuity of an old country or the moral values and domestic virtues of a sturdy race. Neither monarch nor people have much of these left. There is probably a greater willingness to let members of the royal family air opinions about public policy today, precisely because we know they do not matter.

They do not matter because they are not monarchs any more, but celebrities. Prince Philip took up what he described as 'dontopedalogy' (opening his mouth, and putting his foot in it) as long ago as the 1950s.[24] The monarchy has survived his cracking jokes with General Stroessner,* and urging the government to recycle more waste; his daughter calling for more nursery school places; and his eldest son fretting about the plight of poorer pensioners and flirting with Islam. Shortly before she died, Diana described the Conservative government as 'useless'. Nobody, except a few Conservative backwoodsmen, cared. People accepted long ago that royal opinions are about as worthy of a hearing as their own.

The real powers of the monarch – to appoint and sack ministers and civil servants, make war and sign treaties – were forfeited three hundred years ago, and the royal prerogative has been subordinate to parliamentary sovereignty ever since. Journalists who fret about the residual political powers of Elizabeth II would do better to worry about the lack of limits on the executive power of the prime minister. The only rights of a constitutional monarch, set out by Bagehot in a famous passage in the *English Constitution*, are 'the right to be consulted, the right to encourage, the right to warn'.[25] No monarch has refused a dissolution of Parliament since before the Great Reform Act of 1832, and the present Queen has not participated in the choice of a prime minister, even peripherally, since 1963. Her intercourse with the incumbent of 10 Downing Street is limited to an informal chat each Tuesday evening, and his dutiful visits to Balmoral in the summer and Windsor in the winter. In political difficulties

---

* Prince Philip is supposed to have said to General Alfredo Stroessner, the Paraguayan dictator: 'It's a pleasant change to be in a country that isn't ruled by its people.' Pimlott, *The Queen*, p. 268.

(a government falls) and genuine crises (the Germans invade) the residual powers of the monarch might cease to be nugatory, but, in the meantime, the principal constitutional value of the monarchy is to separate the head of state from the chief executive: to keep the trappings of power separate from its exercise. 'The monarch is,' wrote Ferdinand Mount, 'by all the evidence of the twentieth century and most of the nineteenth, too, in the position of a marriage guidance counsellor who must be visited . . . to comply with some court ruling but whose words are totally unheeded by the unhappy couple.'[26]

How the Monarchy Unbalanced the British Constitution

It could be argued that the British people ought to be grateful for any restraint the Queen is able to place upon her prime minister, even if it may be to remind Tony Blair that Harold Wilson had many of the same ideas. Her right to warn is one of the few checks on the exercise of executive power which the constitution affords. But the truth is that the monarchy is cause rather than cure for a constitution dangerously short of checks and balances. It is unbalanced precisely because the prime minister has assumed on behalf of the people powers he once exercised on behalf of the monarch. The Glorious Revolution of 1689, in which Parliament gave the crown to William and Mary in exchange for control of taxation and the army, used to be seen as the beginning of that providential British progress from absolute monarchy to parliamentary democracy. In fact, it marked the end of a struggle between monarch and Parliament which stretched back to Magna Carta, and the beginning of a struggle between Parliament and prime minister in which Parliament has yet to win a round.

The earlier struggle was primarily fiscal. Powerful barons (and later the wealthy middle classes) resisted the imposition of taxes by the king. In the medieval political system, kingship was synonymous with government and the money raised from taxation was the principal way the power of government was felt. Magna Carta was not a 'charter of liberties', but a series of concessions extracted under duress from a tax-imposing king by reluctant taxpayers. In those days, 'liberty' meant principally the right to enjoy private wealth without excessive taxation and, as baronial resistance to taxation gathered pace in the thirteenth century, a convenient constitutional fiction developed. If the king was the government, he should finance government business out of the revenues he drew from his own estates. By the time of the Wars of the Roses (1455–85), the great fifteenth-century jurist, Sir John Fortescue, regarded it as axiomatic that the normal expenses of government be paid for out of 'grete lordshippes, maners, feeffermys and other such demaynes' of the king.[27] General taxation was for 'extraordinary' requirements only, of which war was the most obvious and frequent.

Repeated attempts were made to force kings to fund the 'ordinary' expenses of government out of their own (principally landed) wealth and income. The Middle Ages are replete with baronial demands that the monarch should, as the contemporary phrase had it, 'live of his own'. Medieval parliaments tried to prevent the alienation of crown lands, in the vain hope that a financially secure monarch would have less recourse to general taxation.* The modern mind struggles with the notion of a king paying for the government of the country out of his own pocket, but, when monarchy and government were indistinguishable, this was a perfectly comprehensible idea. The Treasury was originally no more than a chest containing the king's money, and seizing it was always the first act of a usurper. Titles still used today – first lord of the Treasury, chancellor of the Exchequer, lord privy seal, master of the rolls – stem from the time when the entire executive and judicial arms of government were members of the royal household, and paid from the royal revenues. The Houses of Parliament are known as the Palace of Westminster because royal palaces were the places from which the country was run.

The idea that the king should pay for the government of the country proved remarkably durable. During the seventeenth and eighteenth centuries Parliament emerged largely as a result of its resistance to the efforts of kings and queens to raise money by taxation. Today, it is hard to imagine Parliament as the friend of the taxpayer. The prime minister treats the House of Commons with contempt, MPs are so desperate to become ministers that they are prepared to rubber-stamp anything which the Cabinet proposes, and the area of prime ministerial patronage is larger than it was in the time of Walpole. But from the Plantagenets onwards, Parliament emerged as an institution whose chief responsibility was to negotiate the financial settlement between the king and his subjects.

It took a long time before the executive power of the Crown and the legislative power of Parliament finally became separate. It was not until 1830 that monarchs ceased to fund ministerial and civil service posts out of their own pockets. In theory, George III was responsible for paying the salaries of the chancellor of the Exchequer and the prime minister as well as ambassadors and judges; in practice, they supplemented trifling salaries by embezzling public money. But monarch and state were still so intertwined that George III had to secure special parliamentary legislation to own land in a private capacity.[28]

---

* In 1404, a parliamentary Act of Resumption on all lands alienated since 1366 was actually passed, and again in 1406. Acts of Resumption became the panacea Parliament adopted as the cure for heavy taxation and royal impecuniousness.

The slow dismantling of this 'Old Corruption', with the taxpayer gradually assuming responsibility for government salaries, was one of the main achievements of the first reformed Parliaments.[29] The prime minister and the Cabinet ceased to be a royal coterie, and were drawn from the leaders of the parties in Parliament. But reform had a price: the power and patronage of the monarch passed to the prime minister, and executive and legislative power were once again fused in the office and personality of one man, as they had been in the Conqueror. The wealth of the nation was prostrate before a government which had power to tax as well as to spend, and the advent of democracy meant it could claim the mandate of the people. Public expenditure and taxation have risen inexorably ever since.

Recovering Power Through Financial Independence

In an age when the state spends nearly half the national income, it is hard to subscribe to the Whig myth that the constitutional development of Britain was providential. The truth is that a series of historical accidents deprived the British constitution of that separation of powers which Mount has described as 'indispensable to liberty'.[30] The omnipotence of Parliament – or, more correctly, the concentration of power in the hands of the prime minister and the Cabinet – also left the monarchy essentially functionless, and with no prospect of being given anything meaningful to do. Even though the arguments for creating alternative centres of power to Downing Street and the Cabinet Office are overwhelming, it is still unthinkable to restore to an hereditary monarchy its traditional role as guardian of the liberties of the people. These days, that role is reserved for government-appointed judges.

Though the monarchy is said to be busy reconsidering its role, and the prime minister seems at times to have dispensed with every adjective but 'new' and 'modern', the royal family cannot count on Parliament to give them anything genuinely new or modern to do. In opposition, Mo Mowlam gave them a taste of what a New Labour Monarchy might be like, when she advocated transferring Buckingham Palace and Windsor Castle to the National Trust, and moving the Queen to a new People's Palace designed by top architects and furnished by Terence Conran.[31] In government, New Labour's reforms seem to amount to no more than an end to bowing and curtseying to Her Majesty, and a reduction in those entitled to use the prefix HRH. The truth is that politicians covet power, and an emasculated monarchy is a useful obstacle to its division. The prospect before the Queen and her successors is more of the same – charity-mongering and page-filling, but on a significantly smaller and cheaper scale.

The one way in which the monarchy could recover some measure of autonomy, if not power, is to be financially independent of the taxpayer. Prince Charles is openly in favour of this. He told the journalist Penny Junor in 1987 that he would prefer to swap the Civil List for the revenues of the Crown Estate (which George III swapped for the Civil List at his accession in 1760):

> The royal family must have money. If they have to look to the State for everything, they become nothing more than puppets, and prisoners in their own countries. That is what happened to the Japanese royal family. They can't even go on holiday without asking Parliament. That would be an intolerable situation; but I think it might be a good idea if the royal family stopped receiving money from the Civil List and lived instead on the income from the Crown Estate. That seems sensible to me, although I suspect I might get some opposition.[32]

This idea was considered seriously in the late 1980s, to the extent that the monarchy would be allowed to keep enough of the revenue to cover its official expenses, but it was eventually dismissed. According to Prince Charles, the yield from the Crown Estate would more than cover the cost of the monarchy, but this was probably untrue in 1987, once all the costs to the public purse were taken into account. However, it would certainly make financial sense for the royal family today. In 1997, the net revenues of the Crown Estate exceeded £102 million, while the net value of the Civil List was only £8.9 million. Even if the royal family were forced to bear the £20 million cost of running the palaces currently funded by the public, and to give up other official sources of income such as the Duchy of Lancaster and the travel grant from the Department of Transport, resuming control of the Crown Estate would leave them substantially better off. The total cost of the monarchy to the taxpayer in 1997 was about £45 million, excluding security – which is one reason why no government would ever allow the swap to happen.

Cutting the Cost of the Monarchy

Since the early 1990s, political pressures have argued for a smaller, cheaper and tightly controlled monarchy. Public hostility to a family judged too large and living too lavishly has spread hostility to its costs far beyond the ranks of republicans. An important explanation for the change in public mood is the burgeoning number of minor royals and their increasingly frivolous behaviour. But it also reflects the change in outlook engineered by the Conservative governments after 1979. The three administrations of Margaret

Thatcher were the first since Gladstone to absorb themselves shamelessly in the minutiae of public expenditure. Theirs was an ethos which could not be less conducive to the survival of the Georgian-cum-Victorian idea of monarchy as part-pageant, part-upholder of the social hierarchy and part-symbol of a bogus British national identity. The instincts of Thatcherites are English rather than British, liberal rather than conservative, individualistic rather than patriotic, and meritocratic rather than deferential. Above all, they are interested in the substance rather than the theatre of life. They were bound to ask whether the royal household was well-managed or value for money, and rapidly came to the conclusion that it was neither. This was not surprising – courtiers capable of laying on spectacles such as the royal wedding of 1981 are, by definition, ill-suited to looking after the cheese-parings and the candle-ends.

The Thatcherite search for efficiency led to substantial changes in the way the royal family was financed and managed. The government did not have to request changes: the royal household was alive to the need for reform. In 1984 the Earl of Airlie, newly appointed as lord chamberlain, identified a number of areas of royal finance and administration in need of change. Within two years, Sir Michael Peat, recruited from the royal auditors, was implementing these. In July 1990, Thatcher agreed to put the public funding of the monarchy on to a new footing. The Queen's income from the Civil List was raised by half, to £7.9 million a year, for ten years.[33] This was more than she needed immediately, but she was expected to save the surplus of the early years to cover rising costs as the millennium approached. (The calculations assumed an annual inflation rate of 7.5 per cent over the ten years, which has proved overly pessimistic.) The management of the occupied royal palaces was returned by the Department of National Heritage to the royal household, to be funded by an annual grant. Putting an end to headlines about the 'Queen's pay rise' at budget time every year and returning decision-making to the occupants of the royal palaces, explained Margaret Thatcher, was 'both appropriate for the dignity of the Crown and in tune with responsible financial management'.[34] It restored certainty to the royal finances, and introduced a strong incentive to be more careful with them. The cost of running the royal palaces fell from £30 million to 1991 to less than £20 million in 1997, as staff were fired, management and efficiency improved, and maintenance contracts put out to tender.[35]

The Conservatives were surprised when the public supported the idea of an economical monarchy. In November 1992 (at the end of *annus horribilis*, in which two royal marriages failed), the Heritage secretary was shocked when his proposal to use public money to repair fire-ravaged Windsor Castle was unpopular. The public were not impressed by the argument that they owned the castle, or that they were already paying for its maintenance. They thought the Queen should have insured her house and contents, as they insure theirs (although, in fact, no government buildings are insured).* In the end, the £37 million cost had to be met by throwing Buckingham Palace open to the public, and introducing an entrance charge at Windsor Castle.† The announcement that Buckingham Palace would be open to the public for eight weeks from the second half of August each year did not, as some argued, mark the admission of the royal family to the Heritage Industry. They were already members, having opened their private residences at Balmoral and Sandringham to the public. But it was the end of the illusion that the cost of the monarchy could be insulated from downward pressures on public expenditure and taxation.

For the royal finances, the Windsor Castle fire of 20 November 1992 could not have occurred at a more sensitive time. Just six days later the prime minister told the House of Commons that the Queen and the Prince of Wales would pay tax on their private incomes from 1993, and that the Queen would reimburse Civil List payments of £900,000 made to five minor royals. John Major disclosed that the Queen had volunteered to pay tax as early as August that year, and that negotiations between the Treasury and the Lord Chamberlain's Office had already taken place. Discussions on tax had begun in February 1992, but pressure on the Queen had little momentum until the royal family began to disintegrate and the Murdoch press took up the issue in the early 1990s. The man who actualised the changing public mood was Philip Hall. His research, unveiled in a *World in Action* programme in June 1991 (and published in a book the following year), changed the terms of the debate.[36] He showed that royal immunity from taxation was not a historic right, but a twentieth-century invention.

It was significant that, when the terms of the deal between the Treasury and the Lord Chamberlain were announced in February 1993, the tabloids denounced them as too generous to the royal family. Tax was not payable on public assets used by the monarchy, or on the use of the royal yacht (the annual cost was then £8.4 million), the royal train (£2.8 million) or aircraft of the Queen's flight (£9.2 million); money paid by the Queen to her mother and husband would be tax-deductible (when used to meet official expenses); and bequests to Prince Charles were freed from inheritance tax to avoid, as

* When the royal household assumed responsibility for running its properties in April 1991, it explored whether buildings should be insured, but was discouraged. The government self-insures all its buildings, on the grounds that asking the taxpayer to assume the risk for such a large estate is cheaper than paying insurance companies.
† The decision to open Buckingham Palace was spectacularly successful. In its first year, 380,000 visitors paid £5 million in just two months.

TABLE 1.1
The Cost of the Monarchy

Civil List: The Queen*	£7,900,000
The Queen Mother's parliamentary annuity	£643,000
The Duke of Edinburgh's parliamentary annuity	£359,000
Royal palaces in England: maintenance	£15,600,000
Royal palace in Scotland	£1,500,000
Royal travel†	£16,500,000
Post Office services	£500,000
Central Office of Information†	£500,000
Secondees from the armed services	£750,000
	£44,252,000

Source: Buckingham Palace, 1998.

* Since 1975 the Queen has reimbursed HM Treasury for annuities paid to the Duke of Glou-cester (£175,000), the Duke of Kent (£236,000) and Princess Alexandra (£225,000). Since April 1993, she has reimbursed those to the Duke of York (£249,000), Prince Edward (£96,000), the Princess Royal (£228,000), Princess Margaret (£219,000), and Princess Alice, Duchess of Glou-cester (£87,000). The Prince of Wales derives his income from the Duchy of Cornwall.
† Some of these grants are of recent provenance. The Ministry of Defence funded *Britannia* and the Queen's flight from 1952, but the taxpayer has funded the royal train only since 1960 (there was previously a subsidy to British Rail), the cost of overseas visits since 1961, state visits to Britain since 1971, and press and publicity costs since 1974.

John Major put it, 'the assets of the monarchy being salami-sliced away by capital taxation through generations, thus changing the nature of the insti-tution in a way few people in this country would welcome.'* Tax would be paid on private assets and income, and bequests to Prince Andrew, Prince Edward and Princess Anne would be subject to inheritance tax.

The royal yacht and the Queen's flight went next; the government announced that *Britannia* was to be decommissioned in 1997, rather than undergo a refit or be replaced at a possible cost of £50 million. In April the following year, the Queen's flight was disbanded and the aircraft and crew transferred to 32 Squadron RAF, Northolt, used by government ministers for business abroad. Although the planes can be used by any member of the royal family on official business, privately they can be used only by the Queen, the Duke of Edinburgh, the Queen Mother and the Prince of Wales. The

* It was perfectly reasonable not to pay tax on the use of the trains and aircraft on official business; ordinary people would not pay tax on business expenses.

royal train has survived, because it is said to be more efficient and convenient than paying for aircraft and hotels.

The royal family were clearly upset by the decision to scrap *Britannia*. The Queen wept openly at the decommissioning ceremony, and the Prince of Wales told Jonathan Dimbleby that 'we are classic geniuses at not valuing our assets . . . But I'm biased because I know her, I've known her all my life.' But when the Prince of Wales recommended sharing the glories of *Britannia* with the public during Cowes Week, Buckingham Palace pompously rejected a 'most interesting suggestion' on the grounds that the royal yacht was not for public entertainment but 'a secure base for the Royal Family to live on'.[37] The clinching arguments were financial, not political. *Britannia* cost £11–12 million a year, and would cost about five times that to refit or replace.

For once, finance prevailed over politics without political cost. The British people were as indifferent to the fate of the royal yacht as they were to the fate of Hong Kong, whose cession to China provided *Britannia* with its last official outing. The royal family have become a form of public entertainment the public is reluctant to pay for – partly because they believe them to be rich, but largely because of the cultural change effected by the unlikely combination of Thatcherism and the younger royals. In the sixties (the decade of the investiture of the Prince of Wales) and seventies (the decade of the Silver Jubilee) spending money on the monarchy was popular, except on the extreme Left. When the Queen found herself paying for her official duties from her private income, her husband could appeal directly to the public for an increase in official funding without ridicule. 'We go into the red next year,' Prince Philip told an American news organisation in November 1969, 'which is not bad housekeeping . . . We've kept the thing going on a budget which was based on costs of eighteen years ago . . . Now inevitably if nothing happens we shall either have to – I don't know, we may have to move into smaller premises, who knows? We had a small yacht which we've had to sell and I shall probably have to give up polo fairly soon, things like that.'[38]

A Select Committee on the Civil List started work under prime minister Edward Heath in May 1971, but investigating the private fortune of the Queen was specifically excluded from its remit. When soaring inflation forced the government to re-visit the issue in 1975, raising the Civil List to over £1 million for the first time, the House of Commons was treated to the sight of the Labour chancellor Denis Healey explaining to the Labour Left that this was the only way royal servants could be guaranteed the minimum rates of pay demanded by the trade unions. Under the Conservatives, the Civil List was increased steadily, and in 1990 political criticism was smothered by a ten-year funding deal with the royal household. But within two years the solecisms of the younger royals and a hard recession had whipped popular resentment of tax-privileged wealth to such a pitch that the tabloids were asking why the royal family needed the Civil List at all. By the end of 1992, even a Conservative MP argued that 'there is a feeling of unease about their enormous wealth. It would be enormously nice if she would consider living off her own income.'[39]

The Crown Estate

Nobody (except the Queen and her financial advisers) knows how rich she actually is. In its first list of the rich, published in 1989, the *Sunday Times* said she was 'the richest woman in the world'. Editorial enthusiasm for undermining the monarchy saw the newspaper push its estimates of her net worth from £5.2 billion in 1989 to £6.7 billion in 1990, and reach a peak of £7 billion in 1991. A year later came the admission that 'in the past we have not distinguished clearly enough between the Queen's wealth as head of state . . . and her personal wealth.'[40] Their first mistake was to assume that the Queen owns the Crown Estate. In fact, her great-great-great-great-grandfather, George III, had struck a Faustian pact with Parliament at his ascension to the throne in 1760. He agreed to surrender to the Treasury for his lifetime the revenues of the royal estates, in exchange for a fixed income of £800,000 a year.*

Although the surrender was personal and voluntary, each succeeding sovereign has reaffirmed his example. The price was the permanent alienation of a royal patrimony handed down since the Conqueror. Custom and precedent mean that the Crown Estate is now effectively a nationalised industry.† 'Ever since 1760,' as the historian of the Crown Estate wrote, 'the land revenues have been looked upon as a part of the income not of the sovereign but of the state.'[41]

The assets which George III gave up are today valued at £2,605 million,[42] made up of agricultural estates, forests, and a variety of commercial buildings in towns and cities around the country. But the composition of the Crown Estate is far removed from the portfolio George III inherited from

---

* The first King to be voted a fixed income by Parliament was Charles II, who agreed to surrender his feudal dues, in return for a fixed annual income of £1.2 million, to be paid out of the rents of the Crown Estate and revenue from Excise duties and Customs dues. The £1.2 million never materialised, and for William III in 1698 it was agreed that, if royal income fell below £700,000 a year, Parliament would make up the difference. The payment was called the Civil List because Parliament insisted on funding the military directly. What changed in 1760 was that George III turned the royal patrimony over to Parliament.

† By one of those meaningless formulations beloved of constitutional lawyers, the Crown Estate is not technically the property of the government or the private estate of the Queen. It is part of the hereditary possessions of the sovereign 'in right of the crown'.

TABLE 1.2
Crown Estate:
Agricultural and Forestry Holdings (acreage)

England

Bedfordshire	Chicksands	282
Berkshire	Windsor Great Park, Ascot Race Course	17,915
Cambridgeshire	Holmewood	5,125
Cheshire	Delamere	109
Cumbria	Aldingham, Muchland and Torver	3,425
Devon	North Wyke (Grassland Research Institute)	619
Dorset	Bryanston Estate and Portland Bill	5,679
Essex	Stapleford Abbots, including Hainault	3,752
Gloucestershire	Clearwell and Hagloe	1,942
Hertfordshire	Gorhambury and Putteridge	6,929
Humberside	Sunk Island, Swine, Derwent, Gardham	23,003
Kent	Bedgebury, Isle of Sheppey, Romney Marsh	10,070
Leicestershire	Gopsall	8,018
Lincolnshire	Billingborough, Ewerby, Friskney, Louth	48,646
Norfolk	Croxton, King's Lynn	13,288
North Yorkshire	Boroughbridge	3,226
Nottinghamshire	Bingham, Laxton	10,257
Oxfordshire	Wychwood	1,252
Somerset	Dunster, Taunton	20,091
Staffordshire/Shropshire	Patshull	3,853
Surrey	Oxshott	1,574
Sussex	Poynings	0.6
Wiltshire	Devizes, Savernake	20,483

Scotland

Central Region	Stirling	431
Dumfries & Galloway	Applegirth	17,493
Grampian	Fochabers, Glenlivet	70,990
Highlands	Lythmore, Scotscalder	1,535
Lothian	Whitehill	3,461

Wales

Monmouthshire	Tintern	472
Powys	Bronydd Mawr	567
Cardiganshire	Aberystwyth, Plynlimon	3,061
Waste and Common Land	Various	63,513

		371,061

Source: The Crown Estate: Commissioners' Report, 1997.

his predecessors. Though it retains what it calls 'ancient possessions' in a number of counties, as well as in the West End of London, many assets were acquired more recently. Some of its lands in southern England belonged to Edward the Confessor (1042–66) and more were added by the Conqueror, but none of its business and retail parks were bought before the mid-1980s.

The dissipation of the royal estates began almost as soon as the Conqueror was dead but they were augmented periodically as well. The estates of barons who died without heirs reverted to the crown as a matter of course,[43] and it still retains the right to lands escheated in this way. The Sussex village of Poynings and sixty-two acres of land, a fraction of which is still part of the modern Crown Estate, came to it by this route in 1797. The unforgiving nature of medieval politics was another source of royal augmentations: forfeiture of estates to the crown was not abolished until 1870.

The defeat of the rebel barons in 1321–2 enabled Edward II to confiscate and redistribute among his friends the lands of many of the great families of England – Clifford, Dayville, Mowbray, Mortimer, Audley – and of some minor ones too.[44] There were similar confiscations throughout the fourteenth century, which helped to turn the usurper Henry IV into the greatest land-owner in England since the Conqueror.[45] Edward IV added the appropriated lands of his enemies Warwick, Salisbury and Spencer. The fifteenth-century jurist Sir John Fortescue, who was driven into exile for a time by the king, estimated that one fifth of the land of England was at one time or another in the hands of Edward IV during his reign.[46] During and after the Wars of the Roses, English kings could count on an annual income of anywhere between £22,000 and £40,000 a year from the Crown Estate.[47] When the money ran out, Henry VIII turned to the monasteries. Of the thousands of acres of farmland he plundered, the Crown Estate has retained nothing but part of Stapleford Abbots in Essex.[48] But the most valuable properties it owns today do have their origins in his depredations.

The London holdings of the Crown Estate now account for more than half of its total capital value. It owns over twenty-five million square feet of office, retail and other commercial and residential space, mainly in prime central London locations. Its tenants include several government departments and ministerial residences, a string of embassies, several clubs, South Africa House in Trafalgar Square, and the Strand Palace Hotel.[49] Its most valuable parts are derived almost exclusively from the Tudor expropriations of the sixteenth century, coupled with astute purchases of adjoining sites during the early nineteenth century. Henry VIII took many freeholds from the Church, and bullied existing tenants into surrendering their rights. Whitehall was taken from Cardinal Wolsey on his disgrace and death in 1530 and, to provide a supply of water to his palace there, Henry acquired the fields to the north

TABLE 1.3
The Crown Estate: The Central London Holdings (square feet)

	Office	Retail	Misc.	Total
City of London	1,030,094	58,687	25,245	1,114,026
Fulham	–	–	Residential	–
Kensington	323,588	291,644	1,165	616,397
Lower Regent Street, Haymarket	1,333,037	375,475	56,942	1,765,454
Millbank	776,809	11,825	3,600	792,234
New Oxford Street, Wardour Street	439,202	79,005	–	518,207
Park Lane	53,949	17,279	–	71,228
Regent's Park	760,239	39,483	361,525	1,161,247
Regent Street	1,556,998	1,397,264	117,162	3,071,424
South of Pall Mall	794,212	10,452	293,426	1,098,090
St James's	695,936	222,602	240,094	1,158,632
Trafalgar Square, Strand	338,587	77,412	49,758	465,757
Victoria Park	27,668	1,936	Residential	29,604
Whitehall, Victoria	682,381	11,540	64,808	758,729
	8,812,700	15,169,604	1,213,725	25,196,029

Source: The Crown Estate: Commissioners' Report, 1997.

of Westminster Abbey.[50] Modern St James's was taken from Eton College, on terms which rankle to this day.[51] What is now Regent's Park was seized from the Benedictines of Barking Abbey, and laid out initially as a hunting-ground. But it is from the developed commercial properties to the south of the park that the Crown Estate now collects its fattest rents. For this, the taxpayer can be grateful to royal patronage.

The appearance of Regent's Park and Regent Street today is largely the work of John Nash between 1811 and 1828. Nash was a builder-cum-architect and property speculator, said to have married the mistress of the Prince Regent to provide a cover for the army of illegitimate royal children. This unexemplary favour earned him a senior post with the Commissioners of Woods and Forests, the precursors of the modern Crown Estate Commissioners; it was from this office that Nash persuaded the Prince Regent to secure money from Parliament to acquire additional land and develop this famous shopping parade. The Prince Regent was not wholly successful. The original plan was to run a road from Regent's Park to the royal residence at Carlton House Terrace to enhance the value of the down-at-heel parts of the Crown Estate around Pall Mall and Haymarket. But Parliament could not advance sufficient funds, so Regent Street lurched eastwards to escape expensive freeholds in the St James's area. Much of it was jerry-built too; Lower Regent Street had to be comprehensively redeveloped in the 1920s.

Regent Street was only completed through the device of selling commercial leases which entitled tenants to build in their own idiom. The original plan to scatter fifty-six villas across Regent's Park was reduced to just eight. Fortunately, in modern times, scarcity has boosted their value. A seventy-five-year lease on one, The Holme, was sold for £5 million in 1982. Another, St John's Lodge, went for £9 million five years later.[52] Grove House, a restored Decimus Burton villa, was bought by the Sultan of Oman for between £10 and £12 million in 1992.[53] In the late 1980s, greatly encouraged by rising prices, the Crown Estate asked Quinlan Terry to design six more villas for private sale. As the property market collapsed, the quantity was cut to three: the Villa Veneto, the Villa Gothick and the Ionic Villa. Veneto was first offered for sale in 1992 at £9 million. It sold for £5 million in 1993.[54] In 1994, Villa Gothick was bought by an Arab for £6.75 million.[55]

Nash died in disgrace in 1835, accused of peculation in the matter of bricks supplied to the rebuilding of Buckingham Palace, a project begun in 1826 with £250,000 of public money. It exceeded its budget two-fold within four years, and the Prince Regent had to redevelop Carlton House Terrace to pay for it. Their experience with Nash made the Commissioners of Woods and Forests more circumspect in their next development, but it proved equally unsatisfactory. The idea was to lease to speculative builders land in Kensington Gardens; unfortunately, the rents demanded by the Commissioners made the plots hard to sell and they were not fully let until 1852. Even now, Kensington Palace Gardens is lined with expensive mansions of the kind favoured by the embassies of countries too poor to feed their populations.

Kensington Palace Gardens and Regent Street are still the most valuable assets owned by the Crown Estate. Over 200,000 acres of farmland and forest account for less than a third of its rental income. Many of its tenant farmers are struggling financially, but, as the National Audit Office reported in 1988, the Board of Commissioners finds it awkward to break with the agricultural heritage.[56] The chairman of the Commissioners is a former chairman of ICI; the Board includes two former presidents of the Country Landowners' Association and a Scottish farmer. Its dominant figures – chief executive Christopher Howes and urban commissioner Sir John ('Jimmy') James – are both immersed at the heritage end of the property business through their involvement with the Duchy of Cornwall and the Grosvenor Estate. But the constraints they face are real.

Some are common to all nationalised industries. The Crown Estate is not allowed to buy shares – only land, government bonds or cash – or borrow

TABLE 1.4
The Crown Estate: Urban Holdings Outside London (square feet)

England

Berkshire	Ascot, Datchet, Windsor, etc.	Various	376,018
Cambridgeshire	Cambridge	Business Park	96,357
Cheshire	Chester	Chester Castle	14,760
Devon	Plymouth	Marine Biol. Building	41,878
Essex	Tibury to Gravesend	Ferry Rights Only	–
Gloucestershire	Cheltenham	Retail Park	223,228
Greater Manchester	Altrincham, Manchester	Retail Park Offices	253,952
Hampshire	Portsmouth, Gosport	Superstore	*
Herefordshire	Hereford	Superstore, Offices	71,470
Hertfordshire	Hemel Hempstead, St Albans	Business Parks	143,379
Isle of Wight	Carisbrooke, Osborne	Castle, Golf Course	†22,000
Kent	Dover	Residential	–
Greater London	SE and SW London	Commercial, Parkland	208,358
Norfolk	Norwich, Thetford	Business Park	‡322,530
Northamptonshire	Crick	Distribution Depot	§–
Oxfordshire	Oxford	Business Park	68,298
Somerset	Taunton	Commercial, Agric.	263,446
Surrey	Guildford, Horley, Oxshott	Business Pk, Resid.	¶385,766
Warwickshire	Leamington Spa	Retail Park	136,065
West Midlands	Birmingham	Office	35,776
Worcestershire	Worcester	CrownGate Centre	290,267

Scotland

Lothian	Edinburgh	Offices Retail	‖88,531
Strathclyde	Glasgow	Office	68,885

3,110,994

Source: The Crown Estate: Commissioners' Report, 1997.

* 3-acre site.
† Plus 7 acres of land at Carisbrooke Castle.
‡ Plus 173 acres at Thetford being sold for development.
§ 4-acre site.
¶ Plus 40 acres of nursery and grazing land at Gatwick. The Oxshott estate includes Claremont, left by the King of the Belgians to Queen Victoria in 1865.
‖ Plus 12 acres of amenity land around the castle.

money, which makes it difficult to change or grow rapidly. Like any other government department or public body, it comes under direct political pressure to give the public access to its land and properties; to provide social housing at low rents; to plant broad-leaf trees rather than faster-growing conifers; and to ensure that its developers, farmers and foresters make obeisance to environmentalism. It is expected to replace the railings in Kensington Park Gardens, and to keep medieval open-field farming alive at its Laxton estate in Nottinghamshire. The historical accident of its connection with the monarchy has also lumbered it with uneconomic ferry rights at Tilbury (where it has proved difficult to raise the licence fees) and the massive liability of maintaining Windsor Great Park (the only royal park not supported directly by the taxpayer).[57] London Zoo is another popular luxury subsidised by the Crown Estate. The thirty-six-acre Zoological Gardens, established in 1826, are leased for a peppercorn rent.

Not all the historic duties of the Crown Estate are onerous. Although King John ceded the exclusive right to fish in the sea nearly eight hundred years ago (in the Magna Carta) the Crown Estate retains full ownership of 1,699 miles of foreshore, over half the beds of tidal rivers, and almost the whole of the seabed out to the twelve-nautical-mile territorial limit around the United Kingdom. This is a more valuable piece of property than it sounds. The Crown Estate still derives nearly one seventh of its revenues from sales of sand and other aggregates, fish-farming, and the lease of moorings to fishing boats, oil rigs and private motor boats and yachts.* It also collects rents from oil and gas companies which lay pipelines on the seabed, and takes a cut of any minerals mined under the sea. (The owners of Wytch Farm, where British Gas found oil, were appalled to discover that the royalties went to the Crown Estate.)[58] On land, the Crown Estate owns the Mines Royal, giving it the benefit of any gold and silver finds. Among its assets is the St David's gold mine near Barmouth, which produced the gold used for the wedding rings of the Queen, the Queen Mother, Princess Margaret, Princess Anne and Princess Diana. Perhaps the mine is cursed.

---

* During the last century the Crown Estate discovered that the Earls of Lonsdale had for generations been mining coal under the sea off Whitehaven. It demanded the surrender of the mines, or at least their revenues, but the Earl stood firm. He argued that since the mine shafts were accessible only by trespass across his land, he should keep the proceeds. Thirty years of litigation followed; Lonsdale eventually paid the Crown Estate compensation of £50,000. See Douglas Sutherland, *The Landowners*, Anthony Blond, 1968.

The Duchy of Cornwall

It is not hard to see why the *Sunday Times* was tempted to name the Queen as the owner of the Crown Estate, or why Prince Charles thought his plan to resume control of the assets might lead to 'some opposition'. Even after two decades of privatisation at highly attractive prices, no democratically elected government could give away assets worth £2.6 billion and a host of important public duties to a monarch whose position is supposed to depend on popular consent. If any part of the Crown Estate is given away, the likeliest beneficiaries are local authorities, quangos and conservation groups rather than the Queen or the Prince of Wales. If the heir to the throne genuinely wants to 'live of his own', he will have to find the money elsewhere – much of it perhaps from the estates and other assets of the Duchy of Cornwall, from which he already draws his income. These were not handed over to Parliament by George III, largely because they were in such a dilapidated state, but they are now much improved; the Duchy values them at over £108 million.[59] This is undoubtedly low, since the properties are not regularly valued, but still places Prince Charles among the wealthiest two hundred people in the country in 1997.

Charles does not regard the Duchy of Cornwall as a personal possession: he sees it as a publicly accountable private estate, which he is managing for the benefit of his sons and their successors. It is true that its revenues revert to the monarch when there is no Prince of Wales, as they did under both Edward VIII and George VI, and as they have almost continuously since the Dukedom of Cornwall was established by Edward III in 1337. When the monarch is enjoying the revenues of the Duchy, the Treasury offsets them pound for pound against the cost of the Civil List. Even when there is a Prince of Wales, its revenues are used in lieu of a payment from the Civil List – not in addition to it. On the accession of the Queen, the Treasury agreed that she could retain one ninth of its revenues to provide for the heir apparent. By the time he was eighteen, this gave Charles an income of £21,000 a year. When he reached the age of twenty-one the entire income was handed over to him; it was then worth £248,000. Until his marriage, he surrendered fully one half of this income to the Treasury. From 1981, to cover the additional costs of the married state, the share taken by the Inland Revenue was reduced to a quarter.

For Charles, the tax measures agreed between the monarchy and the government in 1993 were beneficial. He stopped paying a quarter of the net revenue of the Duchy to the Treasury in return for paying income tax on his personal income net of administrative expenses. As part of the deal, the Duchy remained exempt from capital taxes on asset sales. The first year left him with £1 million of net income after paying expenses of £2 million and tax of £1 million. Improbably, he was marginally better off under the new system than under the old. By electing to pay tax, he has exposed himself to possible increases in tax rates, but he has also worked hard to increase the earning power of the Duchy.[60]

Since securing the passage of legislation in 1982 allowing him to buy and sell assets on its behalf, he has overseen a systematic programme of disposals and acquisitions designed to increase its income and raise its capital value. It has sold low-yielding farm and residential properties in Cornwall and London and re-invested the proceeds in a mixture of commercial and retail assets in London and the south-east, as well as higher-yielding arable land in Lincolnshire and Cambridgeshire, and built up a stock-market portfolio worth £45 million in 1997. The Duchy's gross income has risen from £1 million in the mid-1970s to £6.8 million, despite heavy reinvestment and expenditure on repairs and improvements. Charles may not own the assets of the Duchy, but they have helped him to assemble a modest private fortune. By investing unspent income, he had amassed personal wealth of £2 million by 1994.[61]

The bulk of this sum is earmarked for his sons, especially Prince Harry, who looked (until the death of his mother) as if he would have no other source of unearned income. When Diana died, her estate was valued at £21.7 million, of which £17 million had come from her divorce settlement with Charles. Most of the rest was left to her by her father; some £8.5 million in death duties and other taxes was paid on the total amount. The balance of £12.9 million net of costs went to the two young princes, William and Harry, and their mother will continue to contribute to their wellbeing from the grave through royalties charged on the use of her image and the manufacture and sale of goods bearing her signature-cum-logo.

By comparison with his predecessor, the taxpaying record of the present Prince of Wales is hard to criticise. After his investiture, he paid less tax than other rich people – for a time in the 1970s, the top rate of tax on unearned income was over 90 per cent – but by agreeing to give to the Treasury half the revenues of the Duchy, he more than doubled its contribution to the public funds. He was also among those who urged the Queen to pay income tax in the early 1990s, and was closely involved in the subsequent negotiations. By contrast, his immediate predecessor as Prince of Wales (Edward VIII) had in 1921 persuaded the Treasury to grant the Duchy total immunity from taxation. In return, he would pay the Exchequer '£20,000 p.a., subject to variation (either upwards or downwards) as might seem desirable'. In practice, this meant he paid between one fifth and one quarter of the net revenues to the Treasury until he became king. To avoid embarrassing revelations, the Duchy abruptly ceased publication of its accounts, while continuing to present accounts which implied that it was paying tax. (Duchy tenants continued to deduct tax at source, which the Inland Revenue later reimbursed to the Prince.) Phillip Hall believes that this congenial arrangement enabled Edward to accumulate a fortune of around £1 million by the time he became king in 1936.[62] Charles resumed publication of the Duchy accounts in 1982.

He has also brought to the management at its estates a greater energy than any prince since Albert. This matters. Unlike the Crown Estate, the wellbeing of the Duchy depends to a large extent on the enthusiasm or indifference of the Duke. The original endowments of the Dukedom of Cornwall, given by Edward III to the seven-year-old Black Prince on 17 March 1337, consisted of extensive estates in south-west England, the Welsh Marches, conquered parts of Wales and the environs of London, but these were frittered away – mainly by the Tudors. The present Prince of Wales did not inherit a single acre in the principality; he purchased 711 acres of south Glamorgan in 1984, largely for sentimental reasons. Few parts of the modern Duchy date back to 1337 either, though it is not surprising that Dartmoor, with its 70,000 acres, is among them. The bulk of Dartmoor is unenclosed scrub land, with less than one third of its acres let even today. The moor is popular chiefly with pony-trekkers and the military, which has paid handsomely for the privilege of manoeuvring its men and machines across its unwelcoming expanse. Its best-known tenant is the Home Office, where a prison built in 1809 to house French prisoners-of-war and the adjacent Princetown still covers 1,660 acres.

Nor does the modern Duchy own anything like the whole of Cornwall, and nearly half of the 20,000 acres it does own were acquired as recently as the reign of George VI. Other assets are also of surprisingly recent provenance: the main estate in Gloucestershire (Daglingworth) was acquired in 1959; Highgrove House was not purchased until 1980, and 3,000 acres of the most productive farmland in Cambridgeshire and Lincolnshire were also acquired in the 1980s. Only two farms in the entire estate, one at Bradninch in east Devon and the other at Mere in Wiltshire, had belonged to the Black Prince. Only Prince Albert prevented the Duchy from disappearing together. As a commissioner from 1840 and, from 1842, Lord Warden of the Stannaries – an archaic term for the chief executive, harking back to the tin mines which littered Cornwall in the Middle Ages – Albert transformed its estates. The income of the Duchy rose from £24,885 in 1838 to £60,753 in 1861, while costs remained steady, and, at a time of declining fortunes in agriculture, the surplus was invested in securities rather than land.

This transformation was an example which greatly influenced Prince Charles. When he first took charge in 1969, the Duchy was again contracting: rents had fallen and its costs were rising, through failure to invest in new techniques and machinery. Charles appointed Francis Gray, whose reputation

TABLE 1.5
The Duchy of Cornwall: Land Holdings (acreage)

Cambridgeshire	1,186
Cornwall	20,460
Devon	72,342
Dorset	3,361
Gloucestershire	1,636
Greater London	35
Herefordshire	1,885
Isles of Scilly	3,976
Lincolnshire	1,935
Nottinghamshire	714
Somerset	16,203
South Glamorgan	712
Wiltshire	3,744
	128,189

Source: Duchy of Cornwall.

was based on aggressive management of the historic endowments of Christ Church, Oxford, to work a miracle in the Duchy, and by the early 1990s it was once more financially secure. It has a rental revenue of about £10 million a year, and another £2 million from stockmarket investments valued at £45 million.

The Prince is alive to commercial considerations; one of his main purposes is to prove that environmental and social sensitivity is not incompatible with financial success. Organic beef and lamb from Highgrove sell at premium prices; the cereals, herbs and fruit grown on the Home Farm provide the raw material for a range of food and drinks (like 'Duchy Original' biscuits) which the Duchy manufactures for sale. 'Highgrove' is a registered trademark for a range of fudge, soaps, and seeds, and table mats are sold illustrated with the Prince's watercolours. He is a thoroughly post-modern entrepreneur, for whom salesmanship, charity and publicity-seeking are not antilogous but tautologous. He has chaired Business in the Community since 1985, a charity devoted to bridging the gulf between public and private sectors, and talks without irony of 'community entrepreneurs', in the way that modern charity-mongers describe themselves as 'social entrepreneurs'. He has spoken on television of a 'contributing monarchy', written about 'social cohesion', and uses words like 'giving', 'ethos', 'values' and 'duty' almost as carelessly as the prime minister. His religion is distinctly New Age. In many ways, Charles is a serious version of Diana.

The Public/Private Wealth of the Queen

It is impossible to predict the impact of these ideas and enthusiasms on the institution of the monarchy if and when Prince Charles becomes King. But as Charles III he will certainly be able to apply them to a much larger estate.

Though even the *Sunday Times* now concedes that the Queen is short of ready cash, she has a great deal of personal capital tied up in land, houses and securities.[63] She owns the Balmoral and Delnadamph estate in Aberdeenshire, the summer retreat of the royal family and a place whose castle and 50,370 acres are said to command the special affection of Prince Charles. Winter holidays are passed at Sandringham House in Norfolk, bought by Prince Albert in 1861, and which became the country house of the Prince of Wales. The future Edward VII nearly doubled the size of the estate before he became king in 1901, and it now extends to 20,456 acres.[64] Seven hundred of them were rescued from the sea, under the direction of Prince Philip. The *Sunday Times* reckons Balmoral and Sandringham are worth £110 million between them, thanks largely to the rising value of East Anglian farm land, but this is optimistic.[65]

Apart from the Studs at Sandringham, a small amount of land in Hampshire, West Ilsley Stables and Sunninghill Park (where Prince Andrew lives), the Queen owns no other land. The occupied royal palaces – Buckingham Palace, St James's Palace and Clarence House, Marlborough House Mews, the residential parts of Kensington Palace, Windsor Castle, Frogmore House, and Hampton Court Mews and Paddocks – are effectively the property of the state, maintained at public expense.[66] This means that the royal family lives for much of the time in large houses subsidised to the tune of £17 million a year by the taxpayer, but most people now accept that they are public buildings.[67] Not least because parts of Windsor Castle and Buckingham Palace are open to the public, the royal palaces have remained controversial only because they include 285 apartments occupied free or at minimal rents by assorted officials and hangers-on. This was discovered by the Public Accounts Committee in 1994, and was followed by a string of unsympathetic newspaper articles about the number of passengers the Queen was putting on the public payroll. The allegations were largely unfair, but undeniably effective. The vast majority of the apartments are occupied by employees and pensioners of the royal household, who saw free accommodation as part of the rate for the job, but as a result of the rumpus they now pay rents equivalent to 16.7 per cent of their salaries. Sixty apartments are earmarked for leasing at fully commercial rates, and several will be sold when they become unoccupied. The deeply unpopular 'grace-and-favour' apartments, long prized by impoverished courtiers, are being phased out. Only four are still occupied; the Queen has not bestowed her grace-and-favour since 1991.[68]

The division between her public and private assets is increasingly clear. In 1988 the *Sunday Times* counted the royal collection of art as a personal possession, but the collection belongs to her, as sovereign, not as a private individual. The profits of entrance fees to the Queen's Gallery at Buckingham Palace and other occupied and unoccupied royal palaces, and the proceeds of the associated publishing and retailing activities, accrue to the Royal Collection Trust rather than the taxpayer. The Trust is a charity set up in 1993 to ensure that earnings such as these were not subject to the income tax the Queen had agreed to pay. Its income is not trifling: in 1997 it was £17.3 million, though the net profit was rather lower.[69] It is used to cover the costs of preserving the collection, which receives no direct grants from the taxpayer, and the establishment of the trust did not mark much change in the status of the royal collection. It was accepted long ago that the vast assembly of pictures, enamels, miniatures, Old Master drawings, watercolours, prints, manuscripts, books, photographs, furniture, sculpture, ceramics, glass, porcelain, arms and armour, textiles, silver, gold, gems, clocks, Fabergé eggs and ornaments assembled by kings and queens down the centuries belonged to the monarchy as an institution rather than to a specific monarch.* ('By definition,' wrote the surveyor of the Queen's Pictures two years before the trust was set up, 'the royal collection is a private collection, held in trust by each monarch in turn for those who will succeed to the throne.'[70]) The royal family held back some items – the royal stamp collection and the assortment of vintage motor cars at Sandringham – but the fact that even these are frequently put on public display confirms their inalienable standing.[71] When Edward VIII wanted to take his father's stamp collection abroad as part of his pay-off after the abdication, he found that it was regarded as royal not private property.

Monarchs have for centuries distinguished between the crown jewels and their personal pieces, and sightseers have funded the upkeep and administration of the crown jewels for decades: they have been on permanent display at the Tower of London since 1838. But the border between public and private in the royal jewellery collection is otherwise hard to draw. Officially,

* The computer inventory of the Royal Collection Trust had recorded 9,560 pictures and miniatures, 154,437 works of art, 86,933 books and 114,326 prints and drawings by the end of the 1996–97 year. See *The Royal Collection Trust Annual Report 1996–97*, p. 29.

the jewels the Queen inherited from Queen Mary and others are 'heirlooms' which she is not at liberty to sell, but 'crown jewellery' she must pass on intact to her successor. This is a self-imposed category lying somewhere between the inalienable and the private, which may not impress the Inland Revenue when it comes to assess the liability of the Queen to inheritance tax.* Both the main investigators of the royal jewellery collection concluded that a majority of the pieces, being inherited, purchased privately or given by friends, belong to the Queen in a personal capacity.[72] Some of them are extremely valuable. Andrew Morton valued the private royal jewellery at £35 million in 1989, though he likened the assessment to 'landing a plane in fog without radar'.[73] It is clear that the Queen does own jewels, works of art and furniture which she could sell. But whether her collection is worth the tens of millions of pounds journalists like to claim will be impossible to establish until she dies.

The Duchy of Lancaster

The revenues of the Duchy of Lancaster fall into a category similar to the crown jewels or the Duchy of Cornwall. The Queen enjoys the revenue from the estates (via a figure known as the Keeper of the Privy Purse for Her Majesty's Use) but not the capital, and spends it on her public duties as well as her private interests. The Duchy is ostensibly run by a member of the Cabinet and obliged to submit accounts to Parliament, though none of its assets was surrendered to Parliament by George III or his successors. Unlike the Duchy of Cornwall, it makes no direct contribution to the public funds in lieu of taxation (though it is of course taxed as part of the income of the Queen). Like the Duchy of Cornwall, it retains income from the Lancastrian foreshore and river beds it owns and from *Bona Vacantia*, or the value of the estates of those who die within its boundaries. Earnings from *Bona Vacantia*, which amounted to £1.2 million in 1997, are now transferred to a charitable fund, and the Duchy surrendered its right to the proceeds of fines levied in the Lancastrian courts in 1967.

But the Duchy still collects the rents from over 48,500 acres of farm land scattered across seven counties and a number of valuable urban and commercial properties. Its most valuable possession is the 2.5 acres of central London

---

* Liability is determined by the status of the beneficiary rather than the category of asset. Assets owned by the Queen as sovereign can pass to her successor as sovereign without taxation, as assets of husbands pass tax-free to their widows. Any privately owned assets are liable to inheritance tax if left to anybody other than her successor as sovereign. See Hall, *Royal Fortune*, p. 182.

south of the Strand and adjacent to the Savoy Hotel. The landed estate as a whole yielded an income of well over £5 million in 1997, which implies its properties could easily be worth as much as £100 million.[74] But the Duchy has also sold land in recent years, and reinvested it in stocks and shares. Its portfolio, which produced £1.8 million in 1997, had a market value of over £44 million.[75] Custom dictates that the monarch has no access to the landed and financial capital of the Duchy, but the Queen will not resent this. The Duchy of Lancaster paid her £6.8 million in 1996–7.[76]

TABLE 1.6
The Duchy of Lancaster: Land Holdings (acreage)

Crewe & South	10,701
Needwood	7,532
Lancashire	11,839
Yorkshire	18,126
Urban Estates (London and Harrogate)	308
	48,506

Source: Duchy of Lancaster.

Her right to enjoy this income depends on a series of historical accidents possible only in a country like Britain, where legal and constitutional history runs unbroken from the Conquest to the present. The most important accident was the ruling that the Duchy Estates were held separately from the Crown Estate in 1760, when George III swapped the bulk of the royal estates for the Civil List. The Duchy estates were dilapidated and yielded precisely £16 to the Privy Purse that year. In each of the previous fifty-nine, they had yielded nothing. So the taxpayer made no sacrifice when the Duchy of Lancaster remained in the hands of the king in 1760, and Parliament did not press the point. It produced £15,500 through increased assets by 1830, when the Civil List was reduced to supporting the official duties of the monarch alone, but William IV pleaded successfully that the Duchy revenues were his last independent source of income.

Twentieth-century governments might still have nationalised the Duchy, had a second and earlier accident not confirmed that its assets are indeed the private property of the monarch, and not some remnant of the Middle Ages, when the king was synonymous with the state. In 1399, the usurper Henry IV declared by royal charter that they be held separately from the other property of the Crown, and descend to his male heirs. His descendants would at least enjoy some of the family wealth, even if his *coup d'état* did not endure. Confirmed by subsequent charters, it was honoured more in the breach than the observance by monarchs of the past, but the passage of time has given it a prescriptive strength which has so far proved impregnable.

Customs can of course be overturned by law, but the constitutional oddity of the Duchy of Lancaster has proved useful to governments wanting to reduce the cost of the monarchy without undermining its dignity. The Queen has relied on the Duchy rather than the Civil List to support her three cousins – the Duke of Gloucester, the Duke of Kent and Princess Alexandra – since 1975, when a Labour government needed a sop to throw to its republican backbenchers as it increased the value of the Civil List. As public demands for a slimmed-down monarchy have grown more vehement, the Duchy has also taken on the burden of the Duke of York, Prince Edward, the Princess Royal, Princess Margaret and Princess Alice. Although the sums which pass through the Keeper of the Privy Purse are now subject to taxation in the same way as the private income of the Queen, tax is payable *after* the deduction of official expenditure, which includes the sums paid to junior members of the royal family.

Tax Immunities of the Monarchy

The value of exemption from tax is at the heart of speculation about the real value of the wealth of the House of Windsor which remains genuinely mysterious: the private investments. Phillip Hall, the most diligent student of the royal finances, reckons the exemption of the private wealth of the royal family from taxation during the twentieth century has allowed the relatively modest fortune accumulated by Queen Victoria to multiply to around half a billion pounds today.[77] Elizabeth II, like the other four monarchs who have sat on the English throne during this century, has reason to be grateful to her great-great-grandmother. When Victoria became Queen in 1837, the monarchy was £50,000 in debt; at her death sixty-four years later she left her children and grandchildren over £4 million.[78]

Certainly Victoria had luck: the miser John Camden Neild, who died in 1852, left her practically all his fortune of £500,000.[79] Carefully invested, the Neild legacy had doubled in size by the turn of the century. A grateful Queen not only provided for Neild's servants, but built a chancel and window to his memory in his rural parish church in Buckinghamshire. But luck was less important than Prince Albert. Granted an initial allowance of £30,000 from the Civil List, and baulked by the prime minister in his bid to purloin the £100,000 a year enjoyed by Queen Adelaide until her death in 1849, the Prince Consort was forced to exploit other sources of revenue.[80] Albert proved an astute manager of the remaining Crown estates, multiplying the income the royal family drew from the Duchies of Lancaster and Cornwall. All the private residences were bought at his instigation. Osborne House on the Isle of Wight was bought in 1845 for £45,000, and renovated with the help of Thomas Cubitt for another £200,000. Balmoral was bought in 1853 for £31,500, and comprehensively re-built as a Scottish *schloss*. Osborne now belongs to the taxpayer and Balmoral will never pay its way, but by 1861 Albert could afford to spend £220,000 on Sandringham. Its 20,000 acres of forestry and farmland are still a paying proposition.

However, nothing Albert did helped the royal finances more than his premature death in 1861. The frugality of her prolonged widowhood enabled Queen Victoria to save a fortune from both the Privy Purse and the Civil List. During the first ten years after his death, she saved £509,000 out of the Civil List alone, despite her share of it remaining static at £385,000 throughout her long reign. (The convention of fixing the Civil List at the outset of a reign, natural to an era without inflation, was not abandoned until the 1970s.)[81] These savings prompted the radical MP, Sir Charles Dilke, to ask in 1871 whether the taxpayer was not being too generous. He also accused the Queen (inaccurately, as it happened) of reneging on her obligation to pay income tax. Victoria actually volunteered to pay income tax when it was reintroduced by Peel in 1842, just as George III had paid it during the prolonged Napoleonic crisis between 1799 and 1816.

It was Edward VII who asked the government to relieve him of the obligation when he became king in 1901. He was refused then, and refused again in 1904. His motives were not reputable. Even during his short reign he managed to save over £260,000 from the Civil List, and left £2 million in his will. (This led some to conclude that Edward VII must have augmented the Civil List with proceeds from the sale of honours and insider-dealing tips from his City friends.)[82]

George V achieved what his father had craved: in 1910 he persuaded Lloyd George (of all people) to exempt the Civil List from taxation, in return for a promise to pay for state visits. This bargain remained intact until 1971, when the cost of state visits was assumed by the Foreign Office. Hall estimates that tax exemption, inter-war deflation and economies in the royal household enabled George V to save £487,000 from the Civil List alone during his twenty-six-year reign, and possibly another half-million pounds from other sources. He was certainly worth at least £3 million by the time of his death, of which around £750,000 was inherited directly by George VI.[83]

A rush of further exemptions followed the lifting of income tax on the Civil List. In 1920 Queen Alexandra was exempted from tax on the first £50,000 of her £70,000 annuity, and this privilege was extended to the children of the king, who were relieved of taxation on four fifths of theirs. As Prince of Wales, the future Edward VIII secured exemption for his revenues from the Duchy of Cornwall in return for an annual payment to the Treasury set initially at £20,000.[84] In 1933, George V persuaded the government to relieve the Duchy of Lancaster of its liability to tax. By the time of the abdication, George VI could pay his exiled brother £300,000 for Balmoral and Sandringham, and guarantee him an annuity of £21,000 a year. The new king nevertheless asked the government to exempt his private investment income, and all taxation of the personal income of the sovereign was ended, without public knowledge, some time between 1937 and 1952.[85] The royal tax exemptions did not become generally known until the early 1970s, when inflation forced the Queen to ask Parliament to increase the value of the Civil List (Elizabeth II was the first monarch since George IV not to make a profit on the Civil List[86]). The deliberations and subsequent report of a Select Committee in 1971 lodged both the tax immunities and the existence of a large private fortune in the public mind for the first time: there had to be some connection between the value of the one and the size of the other.

How Rich is the Queen?

During the meetings of the Select Committee, newspapers began speculating about the value of the private assets of the Queen, and figures such as £50 million or £100 million were soon being bandied about. Sir John Colville – a former private secretary to the Queen who had become a director of Coutts, the royal bankers – wrote to *The Times* to suggest that £2 million was a more realistic figure.[87] The lord chamberlain, Lord Cobbold, told the committee:

> There is no foundation for the suggestions which have been made in some quarters that the Queen owns private funds which may now run into such figures as £50 millions or more. Your committee were assured that these suggestions are wildly exaggerated.[88]

Twenty years later, the debate reignited by public discussion of the royal tax immunities and the eventual decision to begin paying tax again, journalistic estimates of the royal fortune ranged from £100 million to £8 billion. Even respectable newspapers joined in. An Establishment-minded magazine, *Harpers & Queen*, was not beyond comparing the Queen with Imelda Marcos, and in January 1992 *The Economist* put her total wealth at £150 million.[89] A year later *The Times* identified a £45 million royal share portfolio held in nominee accounts at the Bank of England.[90] In 1993–4 the *Sunday Times*, still struggling to distinguish between public and private wealth, could not decide whether the Queen was worth £450 million or £5 billion.[91]

When details of the royal tax arrangements were made public in February 1993, the lord chamberlain, the Earl of Arlie, tried to put an end to the speculation. 'Her Majesty,' he said, 'has authorised me to say that even the lowest of these estimates is grossly overstated.'[92] Now that she pays tax on her investment portfolio, the Queen is no more obliged than any subject to divulge its contents and market value. A definitive assessment of her personal wealth must await the historians of the future. For now, Buckingham Palace is happy to encourage the belief that the Queen has private means of £50– 60 million, while Hall and the journalists of the *Sunday Times* haggle over whether her wealth is five or ten times that figure.

They agree that she is not short of capital. She makes a large annual investment in the turf, including a stud and stables to breed and train her horses, which cannot be remunerative.[93] In 1976 she paid Rab Butler £750,000 in cash for Gatcombe Park, which was given to Princess Anne (Butler later told his biographer, 'The Royal Family drive a very hard bargain'[94]). Mark Phillips now rents the adjacent property, Aston Farm, which the Queen bought to extend the Gatcombe estate. 6,700 acres were added to Balmoral in 1978, again at a cost of three quarters of a million pounds, apparently to secure a grouse moor. The Queen also met the considerable cost of the house Prince Andrew and his wife built at Sunninghill Park near Windsor. When they were divorced in 1996, the Queen settled £300,000 on the Duchess of York, and established a £1.4 million trust fund for her daughters Beatrice and Eugenie.[95] That same year, Princess Diana collected £17 million from her mother-in-law, plus her rooms at Kensington Palace, and generous expenses for her private office. Unfortunately, all the public remember of this generous settlement is that the Queen stripped the Princess of her royal title.

Monarchy into Heritage

The Queen is obviously rich; she does not live in a suburban villa and bicycle to work. She retains broad acres, lavish palaces, and a small measure of political influence. Her wealth, despite the imposition of taxation and a succession of expensive divorce settlements, is more likely to endure than her influence.

As a form of power, influence is often underestimated. The monarchy has survived the twentieth century chiefly because it provided a model of private virtue and public duty: its *raison d'être*. One of the curiosities of a constitutional monarchy, especially in an age of intense media scrutiny, is that the private lives and public duties of princes are no longer divisible. To a far greater extent than in the days of Good Kings and Bad Kings, the endurance of the monarchy depends on the personalities and characters of those who fill its offices. Without any real duties to perform, they stand or fall by their appetite for duty alone.

Elizabeth II has it in abundance. She learned it from her father, who became king only because his brother shirked his duty. But the new generation of royals, raised in a culture where liberty means freedom rather than duty, have found it impossible to sacrifice their personal happiness. 'I think this is what the younger members find difficult,' the Queen said in the television documentary *Elizabeth R*, broadcast during the *annus horribilis*. 'The regimented side'.[96] Between them, Diana, Fergie, Andrew and Edward have reduced the House of Windsor to the status of the House of Grimaldi: a trivialised, scandal-ridden celebritocracy, robbed of prestige and devoid of purpose. Even Diana, who claimed that she was trying to save the monarchy by bringing it closer to the people, did no more than reflect the babble of rival and often contradictory visions of the Good Life. She moved effortlessly between the worlds of the poor and the sick and of the rich and the tanned. Tony Blair, the inventor of the People's Princess, was impressed by her. He may think he can do for the Windsors what he did for himself: make the monarchy legitimate by popular endorsement. It was what Mirabeau tried to do for the Bourbons. In the absence of a proper constitutional role, and on behalf of a royal family drained of moral force, it is unlikely to work.

The royal family would be wiser to entrust its future to one of the great growth businesses of the second half of the century: the Heritage Industry. It is a field in which the remnants of the territorial aristocracy have found new wealth and fresh purpose. Mountbatten argued that the monarchy was different from the aristocracy – classless, unique. His views encouraged the House of Windsor to plunge downmarket, beginning with Prince Charles mixing the salad dressing, and ending with his wife confessing on *Panorama* that she had slept with her riding instructor. During the quarter-century which separated these events, the aristocracy was reinventing itself as the custodian of a shared national history and culture. It is conventional to see the aristocracy and the monarchy as dependent parts of a single hierarchy which cannot survive the eclipse of either. In fact, while the royal family was squandering money, goodwill and public respect on a succession of publicity stunts and ill-conceived marriages, the aristocracy was enjoying an unexpected renaissance.

CHAPTER TWO

THE ARISTOCRACY

I cannot stress too strongly, I've no power, except for here on the estate.

11th DUKE OF DEVONSHIRE, 1990[1]

After all, we've lived through the Civil War, the Revolution of 1688 and the Great Depression. We've had it all chucked at us. We're still here and we're going to be here for a long time yet.

SIR NICHOLAS BACON, 1989[2]

We had our revolution during the war. We did not cut off their heads, we only cut off their incomes.

MARGARET BONDFIELD[3]

I'd rather not have been born wealthy, but I never think of giving it up. I can't sell. It doesn't belong to me.

THE DUKE OF WESTMINSTER[4]

This man, who has over £100 million, won't write a little, tiny cheque to his wife.

SALLY ANN LASSON, former girlfriend of Lord Spencer[5]

When the *Sunday Times* published its first List of the Rich in 1989, it made a shocking discovery. The self-appointed mouthpiece of the meritocracy was appalled to find that nearly a quarter of the two hundred people listed were hereditary landowners. Twelve dukes, six marquesses, twelve earls, five viscounts, six barons and four members of the landed gentry – none with a first title dated later than 1814 – were between them worth over £7 billion. The Duke of Westminster, the richest person in the country when Gladstone raised the marquessate to a dukedom in 1874, was still the wealthiest man in Britain. In the subsequent ten years, well over a hundred members of the peerage and the landed gentry appeared in the *Sunday Times* lists of the rich, none worth less than £20 million.

The vast majority rely for their wealth not on their wit or energy but on the broad acreages, large houses and valuable art collections bequeathed them by their ancestors. Thanks to the rise in share prices, land values and art markets, the present Duke of Devonshire is probably richer than any of his ten predecessors, with enough unspent income to add modern works by Lucian Freud, Angela Conner and Elisabeth Frink to the collection of Old Masters at Chatsworth.[6] In 1985 the Duke gave evidence at the trial of three men who were later convicted of swindling him of £150,000. Under cross-examination, the Duke admitted that he frequently helped friends to furnish their flats and houses. 'I am a fortunate man and I am a rich man,' he explained, 'and I come across people who are not as fortunate as I am, and I have, over the years, helped a wide variety of people of all ages, not only ladies, but there have been men. The women have been all ages, though there were more young ones than old ones.'[7]

The 9th Earl Spencer is younger, but not richer than the 11th Duke. Yet when the Earl agreed in 1997 to settle a sum on his estranged wife, her initial bid was for £8 million. She eventually settled for a £1.8 million lump sum, a car, a house, school fees, medical insurance, nanny costs and £4,375 a year for each of the two children.[8] The 11th Duke of Northumberland left his successor £5,364,631 when he died in 1995. This immodest sum excluded Alnwick Castle and the family estates, which were held in trusts to protect them from his penchant for riotous living.[9] In reality, the 12th Duke is probably at least twice as rich as the 7th Marquess of Cholmondeley, who inherited £118 million in 1990. It was then the most valuable estate ever left in Britain.* (This surprised even the *Sunday Times*, which had marked the 6th Marquess down at a mere £45 million.)[10]

All over the country, aristocrats have benefited not only from rising land prices, and the flood of tax exemptions and subsidies given to farmers, but from lower rates of taxation on incomes and investments and a prolonged stock-market boom. Even the least wealthy have flourished. The land sales which sapped the wealth of the aristocracy for most of the twentieth century have either ceased or become part of a broader plan to rationalise estates and diversify wealth. The 6th Duke of Westminster actually owns more than the 1st. In Scotland, aristocratic ownership has survived on a massive scale. A recent study found that titled landowners own over 2.5 million acres or

---

* Even in the dark days of the mid-1970s, when rich men had greater incentives to conceal their wealth from the Inland Revenue, the 10th Earl Fitzwilliam and the 5th Earl of Leicester left estates of more than £11 million apiece.

13.4 per cent of Scotland.[11] Between them, the 95 richest landowners in the *Sunday Times* own 2.3 million acres, or 3.85 per cent of Britain. It was estimated in 1994 that the ten largest aristocratic landowners possess nearly 1.5 million acres.[12] Perhaps 1,600 great estates survive in England, 500 in Scotland and another 150 in Wales.[13]

If Margaret Thatcher created a generation of self-made entrepreneurs, she also liberated a great deal of Old Money. The value of land for development into housing estates or supermarkets increased massively in the 1980s. One visitor to a North Country estate found its rent roll had soared from £72,000 in 1979 to £200,000 ten years later. Lower taxes, rising incomes and higher share prices pushed up house and cottage rents, and the value of shooting and fishing rights. 'We'd never have seen the same rise in values under a Labour government,' Sir Francis Dashwood told a journalist in 1989. 'It's the fact that Mrs Thatcher has made the country so prosperous that has had a disproportionately beneficial effect on old money which happens to be in the right place.'[14] One observer, surveying the aristocratic scene in 1988, claimed that scarcely a grand house in the land was not renovating or repairing something, and that fifteen great estates were buying back cottages they had sold in the 1970s.[15] 'The great thing which the Thatcher years have given us is confidence,' the Earl of Shelburne told a Sunday newspaper in 1989. 'Right through the 1970s there was an innuendo that we shouldn't be allowed to exist, that people with big houses and estates rolled around with red faces and bottles of claret stuck in their mouths all the time. Now all that's gone and we've got the confidence to make decisions.'[16] A year later Jeremy Paxman found him smelling of post-prandial cigars and driving a top-of-the-range BMW. He referred to the family seat of Bowood House, where he has built a garden centre, restaurant, golf course and country club, as 'Bowood Inc'.[17]

The Nadir of Aristocratic Fortunes

No earthly resurrection is more remarkable. In 1955 the teenage Earl of Shelburne watched his father order the demolition of the larger part of Bowood House to save money.[18] In that same decade, Woburn Abbey was partially demolished, the bulk of Eaton Hall and Rufford Abbey were lost, Panshangar disappeared, and Lowther Castle was reduced to a shell. Perhaps 500 country houses were demolished in the ten years after the Second World War. Twice as many were sold, mostly for conversion into orphanages, golf clubs, schools and training centres, nunneries, colleges, hospitals and the prototypes of the now ubiquitous country house hotel. Aristocratic fortunes

TABLE 2.1
The Richest Landed Aristocrats

	Creation	Acreage c.1880	Income c. 1880 (£ est.)	Present Acreage	Present Wealth (£m est.)
Duke of Westminster	1871	19,749	325,000	148,300	1,700
Earl Cadogan	1800	–	–	7,300	500
Duke of Devonshire	1694	198,572	180,990	70,000	390
Viscount Portman	1873	33,001	100,000	3,100	260
Lord Howard de Walden	1597	–	–	3,110	250
Duke of Northumberland	1766	186,379	176,000	90,200	250
Marquess of Tavistock	1694	86,335	225,000	13,000	175
Marquess of Northampton	1812	23,501	23,870	30,000	150
Duke of Sutherland	1833	1,358,545	141,679	16,500	150
Marquess of Bute	1796	116,668	153,000	53,990	130
Duke of Beaufort	1682	51,085	56,266	52,000	120
Marquess of Salisbury	1789	20,202	60,000	13,000	120
Marquess of Cholmondeley	1815	33,991	41,288	12,000	100
Earl of Leicester	1837	44,090	59,578	26,000	100
Marquess of Normanby	1838	6,834	7,037	15,000	100
Viscount Petersham	1827	12,944	24,528	–	100
Duke of Rutland	1703	70,137	98,000	18,000	100
Sir Euan Anstruther-Gough-Calthorpe	1929	43,586	141,224	10,150	95
Lady Anne Bentinck	–	183,199	107,920	17,000	85
Earl of Pembroke	1551	44,806	77,720	14,000	80
Earl Spencer	1765	27,185	46,764	13,500	80
Earl of Radnor	1765	24,870	42,900	10,000	75
Duke of Roxburghe	1707	60,418	50,917	65,600	75
Earl of Yarborough	1837	56,893	84,649	27,000	75
Earl of Rosebery	1703	–	–	22,400	72
Simon Howard	–	78,540	49,601	13,000	65
Charlotte Townshend*	–	7,008	10,557	18,000	65
Sir Nicholas Bacon	1611	3,377	5,358	13,000	60
Earl of Jersey	1697	19,389	34,599	9,000	60
Earl of Halifax	1944	–	–	18,000	55
Earl of Mansfield	1776	49,074	42,968	33,800	55
Sir Tatton Sykes	1783	34,010	35,870	12,000	55
Baroness Willoughby de Eresby	1313	132,220	74,006	75,700	55
Lord Barnard	1698	104,194	97,398	53,000	50
Marquess of Bath	1789	55,574	68,015	10,000	50
Lord Egremont	1963	109,935	88,112	14,000	50
Duke of Buccleuch	1663	460,108	232,000	275,000	45
Lady Juliet de Chair†	–	115,743	138,800	–	45
Earl of Derby	1485	68,942	163,273	27,000	45
Earl of Portsmouth	1743	–	–	3,000	45
Lord Clinton	1299	34,776	32,613	26,000	40
Earl of Harewood	1812	29,620	38,118	–	40

TABLE 2.1 *cont.*

	Creation	Acreage c.1880	Income c. 1880 (£ est.)	Present Acreage	Present Wealth (£m est.)
Marquess of Lothian	1701	–	–	18,000	40
Earl of Airlie	1639	69,875	28,592	37,300	35
Earl Bathurst	1772	13,663	21,168	15,000	30
Duke of Grafton	1675	25,773	39,284	10,500	30
Duke of Marlborough	1702	23,511	36,557	11,500	30
Earl of Verulam	1815	–	–	2,500	30
Marquess of Zetland	1892	–	–	14,000	30
Lord Middleton	1714	99,576	54,014	14,000	28
Viscount Allendale	1911	24,098	34,670	20,000	25
Earl of Cawdor	1827	101,657	44,662	56,800	25
Lord Lambton (Earl of Durham)	1833	30,471	71,671	55,000	25
Lord Mostyn	1881	11,963	23,752	–	25
Lord Hotham	1797	–	–	–	24
Lord Braybrooke	1788	–	–	–	20
Earl of Caledon	1800	–	–	–	20
Earl of Carnarvon	1793	35,583	37,211	10,000	20
Viscount Downe	1680	–	–	–	20
Lord Feversham	1826	39,312	34,328	–	20
Earl Home	1605	106,550	56,632	33,000	20
Earl of Lichfield	1831	–	–	–	20
Earl of Lonsdale	1807	68,085	71,333	80,000	20
Earl of Moray	1562	–	–	–	20
Duke of Wellington	1814	19,116	22,162	7,000	20
Earl of Wemyss and March	1633	62,028	54,968	35,100	20
Sir Watkin Williams-Wynn	1688	145,770	54,555	–	20
Lord Hamilton	1886				18
Marquess of Ailsa	1831			10,000	15
Earl of Aylesford	1714				15

Sources: John Bateman, *The Great Landowners of Great Britain and Ireland*, Leicester Press, 1971; *Whitaker's Almanack*, 1998; The *Sunday Times* Rich Lists, 1989–97.

* Heiress to Viscount Galway.
† Heiress to Earl Fitzwilliam.

were at their nadir. Even the 2nd Duke of Westminster felt obliged to sell Grosvenor House.

In 1945 the country had elected a socialist government pledged to use the tax system to redistribute wealth from rich to poor. Aristocrats were already struggling financially: income tax had risen to unprecedented heights during the war; country houses, requisitioned to house evacuated schools or billet troops, were in poor repair. It took Lord Iliffe two years to make Basildon

Park habitable after its wartime occupation by the American 101st Airborne Division. Eaton Hall, the Cheshire seat of the Grosvenors, was left in such a bad state by the army that it had to be demolished. The compensation offered by the government for damage was rarely adequate.

The decision by the Duke of Devonshire to return to Chatsworth in 1959 was later portrayed as a vote of confidence in the future of the aristocracy, but it actually followed a refusal by the government to accept the house in lieu of death duties. The trustees of Castle Howard were so desperate that they tried to tempt back the schoolgirls who had nearly destroyed the house by fire during the war. The Earl of Leicester would have sold Holkham Hall if the terms of his settlement had allowed it. James Lees-Milne, invalided out of the army at the end of 1941, was invited by the National Trust to tour the country in search of country houses which might benefit from being taken over. During these journeys he composed his private diary, whose entries record the atmosphere of catastrophe and decline which pervaded the households of the landed aristocracy in the 1940s. At roughly the same time, Evelyn Waugh was composing *Brideshead Revisited*, a novel of aristocratic life similarly suffused with a sense of decline. 'It seemed then,' he wrote in the preface to the revised edition, 'that the ancestral seats which were our chief national artistic achievement were doomed to decay and spoliation like the monasteries in the sixteenth century. So I piled it on rather, with passionate sincerity.'[19] He had a point. By 1947 the 7th Earl Spencer was so hard up that he was reduced to ransacking the graves of his ancestors in search of jewels and land deeds. He found none, but stripped the lead from their coffins to repair the roof at Althorp.[20] In the early 1950s, the 13th Duke of Bedford declared 'there was no future for the aristocracy in England.'[21]

It was not surprising that he felt that way. In 1953 the 12th Duke had accidentally shot himself during a walk on his estate. He had attempted to avoid death duties by handing over the estate to his successor, but the Labour government had extended the qualifying period to five years before death. The accident occurred just months before they were up, and 13,000 rural acres, together with a large part of the Bedford Estate in Bloomsbury, had to be sold to pay duties of £5 million.[22] The hazardous workings of the 'qualifying period' also impinged on the Dukes of Devonshire. In 1950 the 10th Duke died of a heart attack after chopping wood on his Sussex estate, three and a half months short of the end of the five-year period. Everything the family possessed – land, houses, furniture, art, books – was liable to death duties at a rate of 75 per cent; £5 million was payable at once, and interest would accumulate at 8 per cent a year until the whole debt was paid. Rembrandt's *Philosopher*, Holbein's cartoon of Henry VII and Henry VIII, Rubens's *Holy Family*, Claude's *Liber Veritas*, and other national treasures had to be sold.

The ducal estates shrank through land sales from 120,000 acres to 72,000. It took the 11th Duke seventeen years to pay off the death duties; the deficit was not erased from the accounts until 1974.[23]

Since their introduction in 1894 by Sir William Harcourt, death duties had become progressively heavier and increasingly hard to avoid. Harcourt had levied them at a mere 8 per cent on estates of £1 million or more, but once the principle of taxing inherited wealth was admitted, death duties rose inexorably to 40 per cent in 1919, 65 per cent in 1940 and 75 per cent in 1948. Aristocrats struggled to avoid this dreadful arithmetic by passing their assets to a successor while they were still alive, and by setting up private estate companies. (In 1946, the 8th Baron Howard de Walden escaped death duties by turning his Marylebone Estate into a private company.) Valuations were harsh: from 1919 land was valued at its market price rather than its letting value, greatly over-valuing it at a time of agricultural depression.* Fittingly, Harcourt himself fell victim to death duties when he inherited Nuneham from his nephew in 1904. The estate never recovered, and shortly after the Second World War it was given to Oxford University, which converted the park into an arboretum.

Capital taxes were intended to have this effect. 'Death duties were designed', as Sir Roy Strong has observed, 'slowly to eliminate [aristocratic landowners], enabling the major contents to pass to the state in lieu of tax and the building to become redundant, be demolished or given over to a wider social use.'[24] But the rest of the tax system was no more congenial. Harcourt had also raised the standard rate of income tax to the then daring level of 3.33 per cent. When it was raised to 5.8 per cent to pay for the Boer War, revenues from direct taxes exceeded those from indirect taxes for the first time in British history. In 1907 Asquith pioneered a higher rate on unearned incomes and in 1909 his successor, Lloyd George, introduced a 'super-tax' on higher incomes.[25]

His People's Budget marked the first explicit use of taxation for social purposes, provoking the constitutional crisis which ended in the emasculation of the House of Lords by the Parliament Act of 1911. The four new land taxes, which outraged landed aristocracy the most, raised little and were repealed in 1920.[26] The real danger lay in income tax. The First World War raised the highest rate to 32.5 per cent, changing out of recognition political perceptions of the tolerable level of direct taxation. The standard rate rose to 50 per cent during the Second World War, and did not fall below 40 per cent again until 1960. In 1941 the highest rate was raised to 97.5 per cent.

The post-tax value of aristocratic rent rolls shrank. In 1949 the Duke of Northumberland paid over two thirds of an annual rent roll of £130,000 in

* For the agricultural depression, which lasted from the 1870s to World War II, see Chapter 18.

tax. After meeting other costs, he was left with £2,500 to meet the running expenses of Alnwick Castle (£7,000 a year) and Syon House (£4,000). But confiscatory levels of taxation were only the most obvious of the problems confronting the aristocracy in the 1940s and 1950s. The nationalisation of the coal mines (though the compensation was generous) deprived families such as the Devonshires, Lonsdales, Butes, Londonderrys and Durhams of an important source of income. The Agriculture Act of 1947, which gave agricultural tenants security of tenure, caused rental income to stagnate. The 1947 Town and Country Planning Act effectively nationalised land by imposing a 100 per cent levy on the profits of its development. This made it impossible for the largest landowners to sell or develop profitably, and denied them a role in the reconstruction of the cities devastated by the Luftwaffe. The graded listing of buildings deemed to be of agricultural or historic interest was placed on a statutory footing, lumbering their owners with a range of obligations they could not escape and which were only partially relieved by countervailing tax concessions.

The aristocracy was powerless to prevent any of these imposts. According to the so-called 'Salisbury Rules', the House of Lords agreed not to oppose any measures which had appeared in *Let Us Face the Future*, the 1945 Labour Party manifesto. 'We give clear notice', read one passage, 'that we will not tolerate obstruction of the people's will by the House of Lords.' In anticipation of resistance by the Upper House to the nationalisation of the iron and steel industry the Labour government had secured the passage of a new Parliament Act in 1949, reducing the power of the Lords to delay non-financial legislation from two years to two parliamentary sessions and one calendar year. The Parliament Act of 1911 had already eliminated the power of the upper house to resist financial legislation. 'Our ancestors were wise enough to keep the political power of the State in the hands of those who had property,' lamented the Duke of Northumberland after the passage of the Act. 'We have destroyed their systems, and placed power in the hands of the multitude, and we must take the consequences.'[27]

The Aristocracy Rediscovers Money

Nearly a century later, around eight hundred hereditary peers still had the right to sit in the House of Lords. Occasionally, they inflicted an embarrassing amendment on a careless government. Though their influence was rarely decisive, it could be powerful. The Poll Tax, War Pensions and War Crimes bills are all remembered, at least in part, because the House of Lords brought them to public attention. The Countryside March in the spring of 1998 bore impressive witness to the continuing influence of the territorial aristocracy. Properly organised, the peerage even secured legislative changes which benefited them directly. (Their amendments to the Wildlife and Countryside Bill of 1981 greatly enlarged the subsidies available to landowners.)

In 1997, as the Conservative Party endorsed plans by the New Labour government to abolish the voting rights of hereditary peers, one member of the House of Lords was bold enough to claim that an unelected aristocrat could still make a valuable contribution to democracy. Significantly, the 8th Marquess of Hertford claimed his right to participate in the legislature not on the basis of rank or birth but business experience. 'If, together with a peerage, you have inherited a large country estate, you have to learn a lot about farming, forestry, maintenance of houses and conversion of farm buildings,' he said. 'Many of us have learned a lot about the tourist trade. There is quite a variety of good jobs to be good at and, with all due modesty, I have been pretty successful at all of them.'[28] When the Marquess moved back into Ragley Hall in 1956, he occupied just two rooms, and the only eggs he ate were those which could not be sold because they were cracked.[29] Today, he lives in ten rooms, welcomes 90,000 visitors a year to his 6,000-acre estate, and is said to be worth £14 million.[30]

The Marquess borrowed money, and reinvented his stately home as a working farm and tourist destination. One of his biggest money-spinners was leasing the Great Hall for corporate dinners. Almost every leading peer now lets the family seat for concerts, balls, wedding receptions (even weddings, now 'approved premises' are allowed) and corporate entertainment. Syon House, conveniently located close to both central London and the Twickenham rugby ground, is a favourite venue of the antiques trade and London businessmen. It has a permanent banqueting and conference centre, as well as three shops, a garden centre, a trout fishery, an aquatic centre, a butterfly house, and an art centre. Blenheim Palace, Arundel Castle, Beaulieu and Althorp are all available for hire. The 9th Earl Spencer, whose years as a reporter for the NBC television network gave him a ready understanding of the value of publicity, has created a gaudy Shrine of Diana (with museum attached) at Althorp. The 7th Earl of Bradford runs a major farming, forestry and tourist operation from the family seat at Weston Park. He also owns a London restaurant called Porters, an interest which encouraged him to introduce a bill in the Lords outlawing tipping on the grounds that it is 'ridiculous to bribe someone for giving you food'.[31]

'The most important person in my life apart from the family', he admits, 'is my accountant.'[32] This view of the role of the aristocracy could scarcely be further removed from Bagehot's dictum that its main purpose was to prevent 'the rule of wealth – the religion of money . . . the obvious and natural idol of the Anglo-Saxon'.[33] But in the 1860s no aristocrat needed to have his possessions valued because he did not plan to sell them, and they were not worth much if he did. For income, most relied on rents rather than dividends. No major nineteenth-century landowner received more than half his income from stocks and shares or mineral royalties;[34] the average aristocrat was more likely to borrow money than to invest it. The large houses and ostentatious lifestyle of the average Victorian peer were ruinously expensive even without the additional hazards of shooting, gambling and the turf; the total indebtedness of the British aristocracy at the end of the nineteenth century was probably between £150 and £200 million.[35] Bagehot himself remarked in 1879 that 'a large part of the titles of our richest landowners are mortgaged . . . to insurance offices who have much money constantly to lend,'[36] but their power and prestige were intact, and rested on the possession of land, not money. Writing in 1881, the 15th Earl of Derby said, 'the objects which men aim at when they become possessed of land may be enumerated as follows: 1) political influence; 2) social importance, founded on territorial possession, the most visible and unmistakable form of wealth; 3) power exercised over tenantry; the pleasure of managing, directing and improving the estate itself; 4) residential enjoyment, including what is called sport; 5) the money return – the rent.'[37]

From the Glorious Revolution to the Third Reform Act of 1884, the biggest single obstacle to elevation to the peerage was lack of a substantial landed estate. 'It was land that was the key to riches and status,' writes David Cannadine of the Victorian aristocracy. 'From land to status to power the line ran, and rarely the other way.'[38] At the end of a century which has seen a sustained assault on their command of all three, the modern aristocracy is understandably obsessed with keeping what capital and other possessions they have. Alan Clark, heir to a thread manufacturing fortune which has given him Saltwood Castle, farms in Wiltshire and Devon, and 17,500 acres of Sutherland, declares himself 'totally unimpressed by the old convention that it's bad manners ever to talk about money. It's no more bad manners to apply your mind to the preservation of your wealth, and to discuss it, than to put on a raincoat in bad weather . . . I have great confidence in the future of old money, because the current generation are far tougher than their forebears. After all, we've had to look after our wealth through some dark days, so the toughness is inbred . . . Having seen what a close squeak we had in the years after the war, we're not going to let the new money take it off us. We're going to take it off them.'[39]

The maxim of the 11th Duke of Marlborough is that 'all our enterprises must have their budgets and wash their faces'. The 8th Earl Spencer and his second wife licensed a Japanese firm to manufacture and distribute products under the 'Royal Spencer' label.[40] Lord Brocket turned the family seat into a thriving conference centre, which has survived even his own incarceration for fraud. (His salesmanship is obviously undiminished by the experience, since he persuaded the prison authorities that an hour in bed with a woman was an urgent medical appointment.)[41] Aristocrats whose ancestors abjured income in the interests of personal prestige and social harmony now routinely weather local opposition to turn parts of their estates into gravel pits, super-markets or golf courses. The Earl of March has added a 1950s-style motor-racing circuit to his leisure businesses at Goodwood, and the heir to the 4th Lord Lovat used the family name to brand bottled water.

One reason the Grosvenor Estate lost its battle with the last Conservative government to prevent its tenants from buying their freeholds was popular resentment of its hard-nosed business methods. 'Forty years ago the Grosvenor Estate was very much more gentlemanly,' complained one tenant. 'Now it is run by people who have been to business school.'[42] Sentimental attachments have certainly been shed by the cadre of professional property men who run the 300 acres of Mayfair and Belgravia which created the Grosvenor fortune. In March 1998, they sold the freeholds of a large number of buildings on the London estate for the first time since 1952, when the embattled 2nd Duke was forced to dispose of the whole of the Pimlico Estate to pay for the redevelopment of Grosvenor Square.[43] The 240,000 square feet of space was sold for over £60 million.[44] Grosvenor Estate Holdings, which controls the web of private businesses owned by the Duke of Westminster, owns more foreign real estate than any other property company in Britain: it controls a business park in Vancouver, shopping malls in California and Texas, and offices in San Francisco and Sydney. Its property investments in Asia and continental Europe, where it is in partnership with the government of Singa-pore, are large and growing.[45]

Another wealthy duke, Devonshire, has turned Chatsworth into a business conglomerate, with museums, hotels, commercial forests, shops, farms and restaurants – and the house. The shop sells 'The Duke's Favourite Sausages', and the Duchess confesses she would 'love to be a Marks & Spencer tycoon'.[46] In London, the 8th Earl Cadogan and his heir, Viscount Chelsea, have at various times diversified into leasing, retailing, the travel business, wholesale clothing, furniture distribution, holiday camps and sheep farming in Aus-tralia. In 1989 the Duke of Beaufort lent his name and fortune to a highly controversial takeover bid for BAT Industries, masterminded by the late James Goldsmith and the Australian buccaneer Kerry Packer.

There are those who deplore the Thatcherisation of the aristocracy. Hugh Montgomery-Massingberd, a romantic chronicler and observer of the doings of peers past and present, told Nicholas Coleridge in 1988:

They seem to have lost their basic good manners. Everyone is treated in a more abrupt and disagreeable way, with plenty of *noblesse* but not much *oblige*. The Thatcherite 'I Want It Now' ethic has crept upwards. There is a feeling they just don't care for anyone but themselves any more. You can see it too in the breakdown of county society. Most grand people these days just import rich smart London friends for the weekend, and humbler locals are avoided at all costs. If they abandon chivalry, they'll lose everything. There's an unpleasant air of tough shits about the aristocracy at the moment, and if they're not careful they'll become like communist bosses, just richer than everybody else.[47]

But this is to make the same mistake as left-inclined critics, who see the aristocracy, like the monarchy, as little more than beneficiaries of a malign Culture of Backwardness. Hostility to material success, a preference for professional over entrepreneurial careers, the exaltation of the rural rather than the urban, and the British cult of the amateur, are all ascribed to the triumph of the 'gentlemanly values' of the British aristocracy. This is a staple of leftist critiques from *Anatomy of Britain* (1962), through *English Culture and the Decline of the Industrial Spirit* (1980), to angry polemics such as *The Enchanted Glass* (1988) and *The State We're In* (1995).*

If it exists, the Culture of Backwardness is a curious phenomenon to trace to the British aristocracy, which was always inquiring, cosmopolitan, highly commercial, and not at all antipathetic to new forms of wealth creation.† Aristocrats were financing international trading expeditions in the Middle Ages. Eighteenth- and nineteenth-century landowners were progressive farmers, enthusiastic stock speculators and property developers, mining magnates, road, rail and canal builders. Some owned industrial enterprises. Primogeniture obliged their second and third sons to work, and not always in the staple occupations of Church, Army or the Law. The aristocracy invented the Grand Tour. Some – the 8th Duke of Marlborough and the 3rd Marquess of

---

* Sampson, *Anatomy of Britain*; Martin Wiener, *English Culture and the Decline of the Industrial Spirit 1850–1980*, Cambridge University Press, 1981; Tom Nairn, *The Enchanted Glass*, Radius, 1988; Will Hutton, *The State We're In*, Jonathan Cape, 1995. Attempting in 1962 to sum up the message of his first *Anatomy of Britain* in a few sentences, Sampson wrote: 'The old privileged values of aristocracy, public schools and Oxbridge which still dominate government today have failed to provide the stimulus, the purposive policies and the keen eye on the future which Britain is looking for, and must have . . . The old fabric of the British governing class, while keeping its social and political hold, has failed to accommodate or analyse the vast forces of science, education or social change which (whether they like it or not) are changing the face of the country.' pp. 637–8.
† 'Gentlemanly values,' as Harold Perkin has rightly pointed out, were an invention of the professional classes rather than part of the aristocratic ethos, *The Rise of Professional Society: England Since 1880*, Routledge, 1989, pp. 119, 365.

Salisbury among them – were keen amateur scientists and engineers. Modern commercial law was largely invented by the Earl of Mansfield, who became lord chief justice in 1756: the reconciliation of property and liberty was the special mission of the Whig aristocracy. It was twentieth-century contempt for private property, not the mythical persistence of gentlemanly values, which was the true cultural catastrophe for the British economy. The modern, business-minded duke or earl is not an aberration, but an authentic representative of the aristocratic tradition. Like everybody else with energy or verve, they simply came out of the closet in the 1980s.

Milking the Heritage Industry

Yet it is not hard to see why people believe the aristocracy is part of a general Culture of Backwardness. Heritage is now an industry, and those who played a large part in the making of British history are bound to be part of it whether they like it or not. As early as 1959 Evelyn Waugh was marvelling at the grip the Cult of the Country House exerted on the national imagination. Today, the cult figures prominently in novels, films and television plays greatly inferior to *Brideshead Revisited*. Hundreds of country houses are open to the public, most of them no longer living organisms but time-capsules retrieved from an imagined past. In the conventional view, the cult is a mixture of snobbery and nostalgia stifling creativity and progress:

> The country house stands for a pre-war society of established values and social relations; its very fabric is the product of a uniquely English artistic tradition, and its occupants, in their family relationships, employment of servants, and ownership and rule over the surrounding countryside, reflect a secure social order. That the great days of the country house were over added a sealing touch of romantic nostalgia, so that it was admired with passive regret rather than as a positive image of life for the present . . . a symbol for all that Britain had lost.[48]

One of the chief ironies of British socialism is that its psychological roots are much more deeply buried in this imagined world of stability and security than the aristocracy ever were. This is why the Cult of the Country House tends to be seen as a cultural phenomenon, when it would be best understood in economic terms. It is the latest attempt by the aristocracy to safeguard the remains of its wealth and influence.

When the 6th Marquess of Bath opened Longleat to the public in April 1949, he was not seeking to bring British history to a halt. He was facing death duties totalling £700,000. He sold 8,600 acres around Longleat and another 4,500 acres of Wiltshire, Shropshire and Northamptonshire as soon as he returned from the war.[49] He reorganised and improved what remained, but to survive he needed additional sources of income. It was the steady stream of visitors to the Cheddar Caves, which he also owned, which persuaded him that the public would pay to look around his house. In its first twelve months, Longleat received 135,000 visitors. They paid 2s 6d each, generating nearly £17,000 for the house and estate. In 1966, a safari park was added, and the attractions now include boat trips, a miniature railway, a collection of dolls' houses, a Dr Who exhibition, a Victorian kitchen and a maze. The average annual attendance at Longleat is close to 400,000.[50] The 7th Marquess, who helped in the car park when the house opened to the public, absorbed the lesson; he has allowed the Dutch leisure company, Center Parcs, to build a 400-acre complex in the woods near the house.

Unlike Longleat, Beaulieu is neither architecturally impressive nor replete with art treasures. Yet the 3rd Lord Montagu of Beaulieu has created a string of attractions round his family seat which now draw nearly half a million visitors a year. They include the National Motor Museum, a museum of eighteenth-century shipping, boat trips, a model railway, cafeterias, an hotel, vintage car auctions, and many other attractions. When he took over the house in 1951, the costs of the estate exceeded its income one hundredfold. 'I had been brought up to believe that Beaulieu was the most important thing in my life,' he said. 'Whatever else I did, the property – house, estate, and the people who lived on it – had to be secured for the future. Quite clearly, however, there was not much money around.'[51] The ruins of the Cistercian abbey had been open to the public from the 1890s, but generated little cash; the establishment of the motor museum in 1952 transformed the economics of the Beaulieu Estate. Montagu had worked in public relations, and persuaded the motor manufacturers of the publicity value of adding to the single vintage car his motor-mad father had acquired. 'We must abandon the pretence that the world owes us a living,' he wrote in *The Gilt and the Gingerbread*, first published in 1967. 'We must adopt the attitudes and methods of the Impresario.'[52]

For a time he formed an unlikely double-act with the 13th Duke of Bedford, who also used professional sales techniques after opening Woburn Abbey in April 1955. They appeared on television together, singing 'The Stately Homes of England'.[53] Woburn is now not so much a stately home as a circus of popular delights. The Duke had returned from fruit farming in South Africa in 1953 after the deaths in rapid succession of his grandfather and father, to be greeted by death duties of £5 million. He rejected advice to give the estate to the National Trust, opened it to the public, and promoted it unstintingly.

'He pushed the financial assets of a title and estate to their legitimate conclusion,' wrote Anthony Sampson in 1962, 'opening up his eighteenth-century
mansion, Woburn Abbey, with every kind of ballyhoo and sideshow . . . two
million pounds' worth of pictures, a Chinese dairy, and occasional nudist
camps.'[54] Proximity to London ('just a quick run on the M1', the beaming
face of the Duke enthused in the advertisements) made Woburn easily the
most popular and lucrative of the early stately extravaganzas. 'I will not try
and pretend that I embarked on the idea primarily out of a sense of social
obligation,' he wrote in his autobiography, A Silver-Plated Spoon. 'The initial
drive was purely economic. I wanted to find some way of perpetuating Woburn
intact. Opening it to the public seemed the only way of doing it.'[55] The
enterprise is now run by his heir, the Marquess of Tavistock, who believes
that 'Disneyland sets the standard for everything else.'[56]

The prominence of the Duke of Bedford, Lord Montagu and the Marquess
of Bath in the Cult of the Country House is arguably unfair. The Earls of
Warwick had turned the family castle into a major tourist attraction in Victorian times, a century before Lord Brooke sold its contents and disposed of
the castle to Madame Tussauds. Lord St Levan and Lord De L'Isle opened
St Michael's Mount and Penshurst to the public on a fully commercial basis
several years before Longleat welcomed its first paying punters. By the early

TABLE 2.2
Most Popular Historic Houses in Private Ownership*

Property	Owner	Visitors	Admission Charge (£)	Income† (£m)
Beaulieu Abbey	Lord Montagu	506,352	8.00/2.80	3.40‡
Blenheim Palace	Duke of Marlborough	419,902	7.50	3.10
Chatsworth House	Duke of Devonshire	404,721	5.75	2.30
Harewood House	Earl of Harewood	254,000	6.00	1.50
Castle Howard	Simon Howard	200,000	6.50	1.30
Weston Park	Earl of Bradford	164,256	5.00	0.82
Bowood House	Earl of Shelburne	154,804	4.80	0.74
Hatfield House	Marquess of Salisbury	150,000	5.20	0.78

Source: The English Tourist Board, 1996.

* Longleat House and Woburn Abbey should undoubtedly be included in this table, but figures
are not available.
† These figures do not include revenues from sales of trinkets, ice-creams, teas and other
attractions.
‡ Income figures combine 386,382 visitors to Beaulieu (£8.00 admission) and 120,000 to Buckler's
Hard (£2.80 admission).

1960s, around 300 country houses were open to the public, of which about half were privately owned. Aristocrats like to pretend that they are continuing a long tradition of hospitality by opening their houses to the public, but the grand scale of the operations conceived by the 6th Marquess of Bath and his two best-known successors show how nonsensical that claim is.

It is true that eighteenth- and early nineteenth-century aristocrats allowed their servants to supplement their incomes by showing visitors around the house. But the extent of public opening was measured in dozens rather than tens of thousands. Nor did aristocrats open their houses to gain money, but to show off their taste, aesthetic sensibilities and cultural refinement. Most aristocrats found it cost money to entertain the public, but rich dukes like Westminster, Devonshire, Sutherland and Rutland would not stoop to charging for fear of loss of face. More modest families who sought to escape the costs could get into trouble with local shopkeepers and publicans if they closed the house; in 1883 an ugly mob marched on Knole, after Lord Sackville closed the house to the public.[57]

Even after the introduction of paid holidays, and the invention of the railway and the motor car, aristocrats still saw it as their duty to admit the public, and introduced charges to contain the numbers. The modern aristocrat who describes himself as the 'trustee' or 'custodian' or 'steward' of a precious national heritage has a self-image few of his forebears would recognise. If the Georgian and Victorian aristocracy were stewards or trustees of anything, it was to ensure that they handed their estate to their successor intact, if not enlarged and enriched. 'In [modern] house opening,' James Lees-Milne pointed out in 1968, 'money is ninety-nine times out of a hundred the prime motive.'[58] Safeguarding and sharing the national heritage is merely the sales pitch.

It was not until the eve of the First World War that the 1st Marquess of Curzon, collector of castles and cottages and barns, talked of them as 'part of the heritage of the nation, because every citizen feels an interest in them', and of men like himself being 'trustees to the nation at large'.[59] He not only bought and renovated Bodiam and Tattershall Castles, but used the fortune of his American wife to refurbish both Montacute and Kedleston, arguing that 'if you renovate a beautiful house, it does not matter that it will pass from your family. You are preserving a lovely thing for the nation.'[60] Though Bodiam and Tattershall Castles and Montacute House are all now owned by the National Trust, Curzon had hoped that Kedleston would remain in his family. It was not finally lost until 1987, when his nephew presented it to the National Trust, which bought the house and its contents with the assistance of the largest single grant (£13.5 million) ever made by the National Heritage Memorial Fund.

The grant was controversial. Though the Fund is ostensibly independent, it was dominated from its inception by leading members of the Cult of the Country House. *The Economist* pointed out in 1994 that the eleven trustees of the fund included one who lived in a castle, another who lived in a hall, and two whose family seats belonged to the National Trust.[61] It is scarcely surprising that over half of the £200 million the Fund has dispensed since its origin in 1980 has gone to country houses and estates.[62] Yet the fund was first established by a Labour government in 1946 to preserve landscape, not stately homes.

By the 1980s the aristocracy also controlled the National Trust, which had been set up by another group of socialists at the end of the nineteenth century to save medieval buildings and ancient landscapes. It was the 11th Marquess of Lothian who persuaded the National Government to allow impoverished aristocrats (like himself) to transfer their estates to the National Trust without paying tax, while continuing to live in their houses. Harold Nicolson – husband of Vita Sackville-West, whose family seat at Knole was given to the National Trust in 1948 – became vice-chairman of the National Trust in 1947, when he also became a wholehearted member of the Labour Party. 'We are getting more and more evidence', he admitted in 1949, 'that the present government (or rather their supporters) do not like the Trust because it is managed by aristocrats working on a part-time basis.'[63] Fifty years on, the National Trust owns 164 country houses and sixteen castles. In many cases, the family is still living in part of the house.[64]

Taming Old Labour

Most aristocrats would prefer not to be tenants of the National Trust. It is an important long-stop, but only when all else has failed.[65] The 7th Earl Brownlow made several attempts to run Belton commercially before it was finally rescued by the National Trust in 1983 (using an £8 million grant from the National Heritage Memorial Fund).[66] After succeeding to the title in 1978, he organised special events every weekend and at one time employed over seventy people, but the costs still dwarfed the income.[67] His experience was not unusual. By the 1970s many privately owned country houses were again in severe financial difficulties. When the Earl of Warwick finally sold his castle to Madame Tussauds in 1978, his cousin wrote to *The Times* to complain that 'many families have battled against hopeless odds, against punitive taxes and ungrateful governments'.[68]

Certainly, the Labour governments of the 1960s had resumed the attack on inherited wealth. They increased income tax; levied a selective employment tax on staff salaries; reintroduced land development tax at 40 per cent;

imposed a new 30 per cent capital gains tax; and extended from five years to seven the period for exemption from death duties. In 1967 a Land Commission was set up. Though it was designed to curb property speculation by effectively nationalising land with planning permission, landowners found that any agricultural land sold for development was liable to a swingeing levy or even expropriation. After a brief respite under the Heath government, which abolished or attenuated the most damaging tax measures and got rid of the Land Commission, the aristocracy was by February 1974 facing a socialist government committed to the most comprehensive attack on inherited wealth since the Second World War. The new chancellor, Denis Healey, declared openly that he wanted to reverse 'the unfair advantages enjoyed by generation after generation of the heirs and relatives of wealthy men'.[69] His principal weapon was the replacement of death duties with a new capital transfer tax aimed specifically at the loophole – lifetime gifts made at least seven years before death – through which landowners had passed their wealth to succeeding generations. Any transfer of wealth, except that between a husband and wife, was subjected to tax. It brought to an end the one relief from capital taxation even the Attlee government had conceded to landowners in their role as farmers.*

Development land tax was reintroduced at a rate of 80 per cent, eliminating the profitable development of agricultural land for the third time since the war. Discretionary trusts established abroad to hold family assets were denied to British residents. For nearly three years, the new government threatened to impose a wealth tax on land, works of art, securities and cash, which would be levied even if these assets were not sold, transferred or bequeathed. The Labour manifesto of February 1974 had promised it, and legislative options were set out in a Green Paper in August of that year. Even the recently introduced value added tax (VAT) damaged owners of historic houses: it was payable on all repairs, but not on the costs of demolition and construction. In tax terms, it was more sensible to knock a house down and replace it with a smaller one than to repair and maintain the existing structure.

In the face of this seemingly unstoppable assault, the British aristocracy displayed to the full their ruthless instinct for survival, transforming themselves from the overbearing élite of the past into the custodians of a shared national heritage. In the early 1950s, when they had last faced financial catastrophe, the aristocracy had refused to subscribe even £25 a year to support a proposal by Sir Harold Wernher (owner of Luton Hoo) that they form their own trade union. By 1974 they had set up the cunningly named Historic Houses Association, which joined forces with the Country Landowners Associ-

---

* The 1949 Agriculture Act had granted landowners a 45 per cent rebate of death duties on agricultural land.

ation to lobby Whitehall and Westminster for more sympathetic treatment by the tax system.[70] Two independent protest lobbies emerged, in the shape of Heritage in Danger (1974) and SAVE (1979), who linked the fate of the great country houses with the destruction of the natural environment and succeeded in collecting over one million signatures to a petition to Parliament.[71] There was black propaganda too. John Cornforth, editor of *Country Life* (house journal of the historic housing wing of the Heritage Industry) completed a report for the British Tourist Authority on the state of 950 country houses. It was entitled *Country Houses in Britain: Can They Survive?*

The Cornforth report drew a bleak picture of historic houses. Squeezed between soaring inflation and excessive taxation, more sales and demolitions were certain.[72] Its publication was timed to coincide with the opening of an emotive exhibition at the V&A entitled *The Destruction of the Country House 1875–1974*. Sir Roy Strong, then director of the museum, argued that 'the historic houses of this country belong to everybody, or at least everybody who cares about this country and its traditions.'[73] This was a voice, first articulated by Curzon, which chimed exactly with the needs of the beleaguered aristocracy. Houses and heirlooms were no longer private possessions; they became national treasures entrusted to the safekeeping of a small group of public-spirited families. 'We belong to our possessions, rather than our possessions belong to us,' Lord Montagu of Beaulieu, first president of the Historic Houses Association, said at the time. 'To us, they are not wealth, but heirlooms, over which we have a sacred trust.'[74]

Even the National Trust, an organisation then deeply disinclined to debate political matters, was persuaded to speak up for the private landowner, and under this barrage of negative publicity the government was forced to seek terms. In November 1976 Healey announced that the introduction of the wealth tax was postponed *sine die*. Houses open to the public for at least sixty days a year were to be exempt from capital transfer tax, as was agricultural land which owners farmed themselves. The establishment of private charitable trusts invested in land and securities, but dedicated to the support of country houses, was facilitated. The only measure the heritage lobbyists sought and did not win was the exemption from VAT of repairs to country houses.

The tax position of the aristocracy improved still further under the Conservatives between 1979 and 1997. The top rate of income tax fell from 83 per cent to 40 per cent. The investment income surcharge, on rents as well as interest and dividends, was abolished. Indexation of capital gains for tax purposes made it possible to sell land and other assets previously unsaleable because of the prospect of a massive tax bill on inflationary increases in value. (If land turned out to be worth less on the open market than the indexed value, a useful tax loss could be generated.) Capital transfer tax was moderated and then replaced by a gentler inheritance tax, which restored the right to make lifetime gifts.[75] Taken together, these changes made aristocratic estates more secure from destruction by the tax system than at any time since the Second World War.

Even where Labour governments had succeeded in separating a landowner from his money, it turned into a major propaganda coup for the Cult of the Country House. In May 1974 the 6th Earl of Rosebery died, leaving an estate of £10 million, on which death duties of £4 million were payable. Offered the family seat of Mentmore Towers at a discounted price of £2 million in lieu of the taxes, the government baulked for two years. A proposal from Sir Roy Strong to turn the house, with its rich collections of Victorian art and furnishings, into a country branch of the V&A was rebuffed. The Treasury refused to advance funds. The house and its contents were finally auctioned for £6.3 million in May 1977. Mentmore Towers lost its contents in the 'Sale of the Century'. The house was bought by the World Government of the Age of Enlightenment, a meditationist sect headed by Maharishi Mahesh Yogi. One room, scattered with mattresses, was used for the practice of 'cosmic flying', or levitation. It was presumably not quite the end which the 5th Lord Rosebery had in mind for his house when, as prime minister, he had introduced the first death duties.

The Mentmore débâcle (with some assistance from the Earl of Warwick, for allowing Warwick Castle to be vulgarised by Madame Tussauds) led directly to the formation of the National Heritage Memorial Fund in 1980. Since then, the Fund has pumped perhaps £100 million into the aristocracy by buying its unwanted or unviable art, furnishings, houses and land at full market prices.* Among the houses and contents the fund rescued in the 1980s were Canons Ashby (£1.5 million), Nostell Priory (£6 million), Weston Park (£7.75 million), Belton House (£8 million), Calke Abbey (£6.3 million), Fyvie Castle (£3 million), Chastleton House (£4 million) and several others, including Kedleston Hall (£13.5 million).[76]

By 1992 the Heritage lobby was so powerful that it had an entire Department of State named after it. When the National Lottery was set up in 1993, the 'national heritage' was one of five 'good causes' eligible for 5.6 per cent of every pound spent on lottery tickets. One of the first decisions by the Heritage Lottery Fund, which administers the heritage industry share of the lottery, was to spend £12.5 million on the acquisition from the Churchill family of the private papers of Sir Winston Churchill.

---

* Full market prices net of tax. Until the Fund was set up, the difference between high market prices and low probate valuations meant it was almost always better to sell a house and pay the tax rather than offer assets to the government at a lower price in lieu of taxation.

Selling the Family Silver

The National Heritage Memorial Fund is only one of a number of buyers which have pushed up the value of the art and furnishings of the aristocracy over the last twenty years. Untroubled by revolution or conquest, the British peerage has the largest collection of fine art and antiques in private hands anywhere in the world. The Earls of Radnor began selling their art collection in the 1890s, but had enough left a century later to charge Andrew Lloyd Webber £8 million for a Canaletto. In 1994 the Earl of Pembroke lost a Rembrandt worth £400,000 after burglars raided Wilton House. A year later, a Titian valued at £5 million was stolen from Longleat. The £100 million-plus valuations of peers such as the 6th Marquess of Cholmondeley, the 8th Earl Spencer and the 6th Marquess of Bute reflected mainly the rising value of their art collections. From the mid-1970s until the boom ended in the spring of 1990, prices rose more or less continually.[77]

At the top of the boom, the Duke of Beaufort got £8.6 million for the Badminton Cabinet, and a Bernini from Castle Howard raised £3 million. Prices were chased upwards by American, Australian and Japanese billionaires, and by a new breed of institutional buyer. Pension funds, banks, companies and consortiums, and the fabulously well-endowed Getty Museum, all bought art in the 1980s. Over the twenty years to 1990, the sale value of the Old Masters which dominate aristocratic collections matched stock market returns and outperformed bonds, precious metals and agricultural land.[78]

The 7th Marquess of Northampton is the deftest operator in the international art market.[79] His first disposal was a set of Greek vases from Castle Ashby, which fetched £1.34 million in 1980. A Dossi Dosso followed for £1.8 million in 1983. His sale of Mantegna's *Adoration of the Magi* for £8.1 million in 1985 was the highest price ever paid for a painting. The Marquess was so impressed by these returns that he began to job a little in the market himself. In 1990 he became embroiled in a controversy over the origins of the so-called Sevso hoard of Roman silver, which he had acquired for £9 million. The pieces, of unknown provenance, seemed to have passed through the Lebanon before being stored in a Swiss bank vault.[80] After a long legal battle in New York, where ownership was contested by both Croatia and Hungary, the courts decided that the coins belonged to the Marquess. They are thought to be worth at least £40 million.[81]

Northampton is unapologetic about selling in the dearest market. 'As far as the loss of heritage is concerned,' he says, 'I'm afraid I'm not very patriotic, because I believe we've got to think more globally. Art has shuffled around the world since the year dot.'[82] It is not a view which the Heritage lobby and its supporters in government share. Today, museums are given six months to match a foreign bid before a work of art is licensed for export. Despite the constraint, by the end of the 1980s art was being sold abroad at such a hectic pace that Britain ran a modest surplus on its balance of trade in art and antiques. Sales continue today. In 1995 the Howards of Castle Howard exported Gentileschi's *Finding of Moses* for £5 million, followed by a collection of Roman and ancient Egyptian artefacts.[83] The Marquess of Bute raised £10.7 million from an art auction in the summer of 1996. The trustees of Sudeley Castle sold Constable's *The Lock* to the Thyssen Foundation in Lugano for £10.78 million in 1990, and in 1997 a Poussin (*Temps Calme*) for £16 million.[84] Ironically, the embarrassment caused by using Lottery funds to buy the Churchill papers has made it easier for art to be exported, since no government wants to be seen to be using public money to make the rich richer.

Museums complain, and ministers fret, but the efflux of aristocratic artefacts continues. This is where the changed image of the aristocracy is at its most ingenious: the guardians of the National Heritage are not only selling it but using public money to prop up the prices as they do so. Asked in 1984 to explain why he had sold a collection of Old Master drawings from Chatsworth, the Duke of Devonshire replied that he thought it was 'morally wrong for someone with my resources to claim taxpayers' money for this house.' The truth is that the drawings fetched £21.2 million at auction, more than four times what the British Museum was able to muster.[85] The taxpayer can always expect to compete with private buyers if a work of art is important enough. In 1992 the National Gallery paid the Marquess of Bute £8 million for an Aelbert Cuyp landscape, and the 7th Marquess of Cholmondeley sold the gallery *Portrait of a Lady with a Squirrel*, by Hans Holbein, for £10 million.[86] In 1994, the Marquess of Zetland sold *A Calm* by Jan van de Cappelle to the National Museum of Wales for £3.85 million – below its market value of £5.5 million, but tax concessions made it a better deal for the Marquess.[87]

The Inland Revenue has accepted works of art in lieu of capital taxes ever since they were introduced. From 1956 the aristocracy was given a special concession: the right to offer works of art in direct payment of death duties. The 11th Duke of Devonshire settled part of the £5 million of death duties he inherited by offering Hardwick and half a dozen art treasures to the National Trust.[88] Even where the rules are unclear, it seems the Inland Revenue is always ready to negotiate. It is mainly paintings which are accepted in lieu of inheritance tax, but sculpture, furniture, musical instruments, steam engines, landscape and even geological specimens are all eligible – and there is no upper limit to the amount payable on an object which can be set against taxes. The 7th Marquess of Cholmondeley endeavoured to reduce his inheritance tax bill on the sale of *Portrait of a Lady With a Squirrel* by offering the nation a collection of furnishings (which would remain *in situ* at Hough-ton Hall).[89] The government declined his offer, but he was still able to sell £21 million of furniture, pictures and other works of art in exchange for a tax break on what remained in the house.[90] Even Old Labour governments were prepared to extend tax concessions to art, ostensibly in return for greater public access. Outstanding works of art were among the possessions exempted from capital transfer tax in 1975.[91]

Inheritance tax is waived on works put on permanent public display, even in the homes of their owners, provided they are good enough to be included in a national collection. This loophole has provoked considerable criticism, largely because owners do not advertise that the public has purchased an interest in their possessions. By the end of 1997, the Inland Revenue had no less than 19,716 items on its register of tax-exempt works of art.[92] Sensing the growth of a new tax-avoidance industry, Gordon Brown tightened up the rules of the exemption in his 1998 Budget to make sure that taxpayers are getting something for their money. But few people are insensitive enough to barge into private homes, even if they knew what they were entitled to view. Landowners can further reduce liability to inheritance tax by agreeing to allow the public access to land of 'outstanding scenic beauty' – the size of the tax break supposedly reflects the value of access gained. This is obviously difficult to measure, but the Duke of Devonshire has found it worthwhile. He has given the public access to his Bolton Abbey estate in the Yorkshire Dales (occupied by his heir, the Marquess of Hartington) in return for a cut in his exposure to inheritance tax.

Another useful source of income is the sale of redundant titles. Most aristo-cratic families have, in addition to their main title, a collection of obscure feudal honours attached to estates they no longer own. The Manorial Auction-eers Partnership, the trading arm of the Manorial Society of Great Britain, conducts regular auctions. In 1989, the Earl of Lonsdale raised £400,000 from the sale of thirty titles, and the Duke of Wellington £115,000 from ten. The lordship of Stratford-Upon-Avon went for £87,000, and five years later, the Earldom of Arran fetched £400,000.[93] The principal trade is in lordships of the manor; there are probably 20,000 in England and Wales and 4,000 in Scotland. Some have real economic rights, to graze or fish or extract minerals, but most are little more than pieces of vanity and rarely command substantial prices. Today they fetch between £5,000 and £8,000, but in the boom years of the 1980s the average price of a lordship of the manor rose to £10,000.[94] If the owner of Wallop Manor finds himself bidding against the resident of the Old Rectory for the same title, prices can still go as high as £20,000. Earl Spencer got £188,000 for the manorial lordship of Wimbledon in 1996.

Around one in three titles are bought by stereotypically gullible Americans and Canadians, but the Manorial Society reckons lordships of the manor are bought mainly by *nouveaux-riches* owners of old manor houses.[95] Feudal and Irish baronies – which have never entitled the holder to sit in the House of Lords, but allow him to call himself the 10th Lord Smith – are the most popular and can fetch as much as £50,000.[96] The entrepreneurial outlook of the Manorial Society, established in 1906 by a group of peers concerned to preserve manorial records, is itself a telling symptom of the attitude of the aristocracy towards those parts of the national heritage in its possession. The society publishes books and arranges exhibitions as well, with the express object of making money for its membership. All its members are titled, and a recent survey showed that they had net personal assets of £4.5 billion between them. 'We are here to make money out of the privatisation of history,' says the society chairman, Robert Smith. 'We make no bones about that.'

The aristocracy is also adept at milking the Ministry of Agriculture. Farming subsidies obviously benefit larger rather than smaller landowners, and the aristocracy has done well out of price support, grants to protect sites of special scientific interest, and payments for turning arable land into forest, or not grubbing up hedgerows or chopping down broad-leafed trees.[97] It was with the assistance of agricultural subsidies that the Grosvenors planted the pitiless landscape of their 133,000-acre estate in Sutherland with spruce, larch and pine. Among the aristocrats to have benefited from the notorious 'set-aside' scheme, in which farmers are paid to leave land fallow, are the Duke of Buccleuch, Viscount Leverhulme, the Marquess of Northampton, Earl Spencer and the Duke of Atholl.[98] The aristocracy has also picked up a share of grants paid to farmers who turn fields into country parks and golf courses, or convert redundant farm buildings into offices and farm shops.

Historic houses also attract subsidies. The Historic Buildings Council first began to offer repair and maintenance grants to owners of stately homes in the early 1950s, provided they were open to the public; its successor English Heritage has maintained the tradition. In 1996–7 it spent £36.7 million in historic properties.[99] The opening requirements for the beneficiaries were minimal, amounting to opening one day a week in high summer. (By avoiding publicity, Lord Walpole managed to collect his grants despite admitting only forty-six visitors a year to Wolterton).[100] European grants for owners of historic houses are now becoming available for the first time, via the so-called Raphael Fund. These days, peers find it is not just their houses but themselves which attract public largesse. The 6th Earl of Munster was carried to the House of Lords every day to collect his only form of income: the daily attendance allowance.[101] Latterly about £150 a day, it made the difference between solvency and misery for a number of impoverished aristocrats. Once travelling expenses were added, a peer who was reasonably diligent in attending, could clear £25,000 a year.

A Brief History of Aristocratic Greed and Ambition

None of this is a surprise. The aristocracy was always ruthless in defence of its economic interests. 'Many families who pride themselves on having always lived in a house,' as Nicholas Ridley unkindly pointed out to the annual conference of the Historic Houses Association in 1988, 'in fact married into it, bought it, or stole it at some point in their murky history, when they were robber barons, property speculators, or simply won the pools.'[102] Almost every wealthy aristocrat is the beneficiary of past acts of violence, greed, treachery, graft, or sacrilege. The Norman aristocracy, like its Saxon predecessors, took the land of England by force. By the time of *Domesday* in 1086 only two English nobles – Thurkill of Arden and Colswein of Lincoln – still held estates of baronial dimensions, and both had held on to their land only by grovelling before the Conqueror.[103] The Thurkills of Arden, who once held large estates in Staffordshire and Warwickshire, are the only family clinging on today. With a pedigree traceable to Aelfwine, sheriff of Warwickshire under the Confessor, they are one of just two families in England which can prove descent through the male line dating back beyond the Conquest. In 1962 Anthony Sampson found an Arden practising as a doctor at Windsor, the author of *Posterior Dislocation of Both Shoulders.**

The Ardens may have escaped, but the Conquest placed the rest of England in the hands of a small group of Norman *conquistadores*, many of whom had come from as far afield as Sicily in search of booty.† Of all the land described in *Domesday*, around 170 barons held roughly half.‡ The greatest of them was Robert of Mortain, half-brother of the Conqueror, who had holdings in

* Sampson, *Anatomy of Britain*, p. 5. Only the Borders family of Swinton, which can trace its lineage to Edulf, lord of Bamburgh, who administered the country between the Forth and the Tyne during the reign of King Alfred, has a longer genealogy than the Ardens.

† The Norman hierarchy was not installed immediately. The Conqueror attempted to govern England with the help of Saxon nobles who accepted his rule. William planted his followers only on the estates of those who had fallen at Hastings or refused to make their peace with him. It was not until after the suppression of the rebellions of the west and north that William completed the wholesale expropriation of the old English aristocracy. See Hugh Montgomery-Massingberd and Mark Bence-Jones, *The British Aristocracy*, Constable, 1979, pp. 138–9; H. R. Loyn, *Anglo-Saxon England and the Norman Conquest*, Second Edition, Longman, 1991, p. 328.

‡ The total annual revenue from land in 1086 – exclusive of the towns, and of the four northern shires excluded from its remit – was £73,000, of which the barons and their men got £35,400. Dr Elizabeth Hallam, Introduction to *The Domesday Book: England's Heritage, Then and Now*, Hutchinson, 1985, p. 14.

nineteen counties yielding rents of £2,500 a year.* But greater men take greater risks, and have left no lasting inheritance. 'And yet time has his revolution,' as Lord Chief Justice Sir Ranulphe Crewe expressed it in his famous adjudication on the De Vere claim to the lord great chamberlainship in 1625. 'There must be a period and an end to all temporal things, *finis rerum*, an end of names and dignities and whatsoever is terrene; and why not of De Vere? Where is Bohun, where's Mowbray, where's Mortimer? Nay, which is more and most of all, where is Plantagenet? They are entombed in the urns and sepulchres of mortality.'

In fact, Mowbray survived. A baron, familiar for his black eyepatch, sits in the Upper House as the 26th Baron Mowbray, the 27th Baron Segrave and the 23rd Baron Stourton; his earliest title dates from 1283.† Other names redolent of the multifarious struggles of the Plantagenet era – Clifford, Courtenay, Fiennes, Howard, Lumley, Manners, Nevill, Sackville, Stanley, Talbot, Willoughby – have also survived, not always with their wealth intact, and sometimes by sleight-of-hand rather than genuine tenacity. Ralph Percy, Duke of Northumberland, is ostensibly a descendant of the great medieval hero, Harry Hotspur. But his ancestors were named Smithson, a Yorkshire baronet called Sir Hugh Smithson having changed his name after marrying a Percy heiress in 1750.‡ The truth is that not one of the earliest medieval peerages has survived by direct descent through the male line. The Wars of the Roses were particularly prodigal of great men; its various conflicts reduced the total size of the peerage from a medieval peak of 57 to 44 by the time Henry VIII ascended the throne in 1509. His father, crowned on the field of the last battle, was understandably anxious not to enlarge their number.

The Wars of the Roses are best understood (even by non-Marxists) as a struggle for landed wealth between aristocratic families who recognised that violence was an effective alternative to litigation or arbitration by the King.[104] In the fourteenth and fifteenth centuries the aristocracy even managed to turn the Black Death, which raised agricultural wages and reduced the number of urban consumers, to personal economic advantage. The infamous Statute of Labourers in 1349, which attempted to cap wages and oblige men to work only the estates of their landlords, was arguably the first instance in which the aristocracy used its political power expressly to protect its economic inter-

---

* Only ten barons had annual incomes of more than £750, and ninety had to get by on less than £100 a year. Edward Miller and John Hatcher, *Medieval England: Rural Society and Economic Change 1086–1348*, 1978, pp. 15–16.

† He disputes the premier barony of England with the 28th Baron De Rose, a creation of the usurper Simon de Montfort in 1264, whose premiership is therefore considered illegitimate.

‡ His illegitimate son endowed the famous Smithsonian Institution in Washington DC. Montgomery-Massingberd and Bence-Jones, *The British Aristocracy*.

ests.[105] In the sixteenth century, it was no longer possible to seize that power by violence. Henry VII banned private armies, and began to run the country through lesser nobles and even commoners skilled in bureaucracy and pettifoggery rather than the martial arts. But the opportunities for personal aggrandisement, particularly after the Dissolution of the Monasteries, were even greater.

'When I consider and weigh in my mind all these commonwealths which nowadays anywhere do flourish,' wrote Thomas More in *Utopia* in 1516, 'so God help me, I can perceive nothing but a certain conspiracy of rich men procuring their own commodities under the name and title of the commonwealth.'[106] It was an accurate description of the realities of life at the Tudor court under Henry VIII. A late Victorian edition of Sir Henry Spelman's great *History of Sacrilege* (first published in 1698) suggested that four out of five members of the contemporary peerage had some former Church lands among their estates.[107] Among the wealthiest aristocratic families of today, the fortunes of the Cavendishes (Dukes of Devonshire), Thynns (Marquesses of Bath), Herberts (Earls of Pembroke), Russells (Dukes of Bedford), Stanhopes (Viscounts Petersham), Portmans (Viscounts Portman) and Manners (Dukes of Rutland) all rest directly or indirectly on the spoliation of the monasteries.

Careerism of this kind was not confined to the sixteenth century; it is perennial. William Marshal, the illiterate who rose to the Earldom of Pembroke and the lord protectorate of England and its boy-king Henry III, achieved wealth and power through royal patronage as early as the twelfth century.[108] The 4th Marquess of Reading is descended from Rufus Isaacs, son of a Jewish fruit merchant who rose from cabin boy to lord chief justice and viceroy of India. Despite involvement in the Marconi Scandal of 1912, he collected four orders of knighthood (and one for his wife), and in twelve years advanced from baron to viscount to earl to marquess.[109] The wealth of the Cecils (Marquesses of Salisbury and Exeter) was acquired through the systematic abuse of public funds and positions by Robert Cecil, chief minister to James I. Sir Nicholas Bacon, the wealthy East Anglian landowner, is descended from Francis Bacon, who re-invented himself as an essayist and philosopher after being impeached and fined for corruption during his time as lord chancellor to the same king. The Duke of Westminster is the beneficiary of a cynical marriage pact between two ambitious families during the reign of Charles II. The Lascelles' fortune (Earls of Harewood) was built on the Atlantic slave trade of the eighteenth century. By the end of the nineteenth century, businessmen were giving large sums to both major political parties in full expectation of receiving a peerage and, in the twentieth, the Inchcapes and the Vesteys used business fortunes to purchase hereditary titles from cash-strapped political parties.

The Secret of Aristocratic Survival: Exclusivity, Not Openness

These attempts to turn power into wealth and wealth into power are at least as familiar in the age of James Goldsmith and Mohamed Fayed as in the era of Wolsey (son of a butcher) and Thomas Cromwell (son of a tanner). All that has changed is the ease with which it can be done. One of the most enduring myths about the British aristocracy is that it survived because it was always open to new forms of wealth.[110] Anthony Sampson has argued that 'the British aristocracy has survived partly because it has never been very exclusive' and described it as a 'time-honoured machine for the conversion of money into prestige'.[111] Hugh Massingberd, a leading authority on the modern peerage, agrees that 'the British sort of aristocracy has managed to avoid becoming a closed corporation and has always recruited itself from the outside.'[112] But this is the chief characteristic of democratic, rather than aristocratic, systems of government. The secret of the survival of the British aristocracy was not its openness but its ability to concentrate wealth, power and status in the hands of a remarkably small number of people. Its survival was most at risk not when its ranks were closed but when they were open to outsiders. The peerage discovered this in the seventeenth century, and again in the twentieth.

It is true that nearly half the wealthiest peers when Elizabeth became Queen in 1558 were 'new men' enriched by her father. But Henry VIII expanded the peerage by only a dozen men, and Mary added a mere six. In 1559 there were still only 61 peers, and their number shrank by two during the reign of Elizabeth.[113] There was open relief among social climbers at the demise of Elizabeth, who was notoriously parsimonious in her distribution of honours.[114] At the beginning of 1603 Sir John Harington sent King James of Scotland, then waiting to take up the English throne, a New Year gift of a lantern, adorned with a crucifixion. On it were inscribed the words of the good thief: 'Lord, remember me when thou comest into thy kingdom.'[115]

But James knew the peerage was not anxious to share its wealth and power with men like Harington, so he invented a new hereditary title which was not part of the peerage at all. This was the baronetcy, a sort of hereditary knighthood, and it was a roaring success. James and Charles I sold so many to aspirant country gentlemen that the price fell catastrophically, and they were forced to start selling peerages as well. Sir William Cavendish (an ancestor of the current Duke of Devonshire) was the first to take advantage; he paid £2,900 to become a baron. But selling peerages weakened respect for aristocracy and aristocratic institutions. Exposing the artificiality of noble blood was a contributory factor to the Civil War, which concluded with the abolition of

the House of Lords, the execution of the king and the declaration of a
republic. More than 700 Royalist aristocrats had their lands confiscated and
sold.[116] The aristocracy did not experience a crisis of similar gravity again
until the passage of the 1911 Parliament Act, when a left-wing government
threatened to flood the Upper House with artificial creations.

The interregnum gave the aristocracy such a fright that blatant trafficking
in honours did not recur until the twentieth century. The English peerage
ended the seventeenth century with just 177 members.[117] Apart from en-
nobling his bastard children – the Dukes of Buccleuch (Lucy Walter), Grafton
(Barbara Villiers), Richmond (Louise Renée de Keroualle) and St Albans (Nell
Gwyn) are all descended from the illegitimate offspring of Charles II – the Merry
Monarch created or revived only ten peerages. In eighteenth-century Britain
there was one aristocrat for every 3,500 citizens. It is no coincidence that the
period between the Glorious Revolution of 1688 and the Third Reform Act
of 1884–5 was the golden age of the British aristocracy.

For two centuries, they remained an exclusive caste. Of the 25 non-royal
dukes, 35 marquesses, 195 earls, 125 viscounts, 464 barons, 5 countesses, 15
baronesses and just over 1,000 hereditary baronets that make up the modern
aristocracy, only 44 can claim a title older than the sixteenth century. One
in five members acquired theirs during the twentieth century. Although the
aristocracy today consists of slightly less than two thousand people (an astonishingly small proportion of a total population of nearly sixty million), it is
forty times the size of the peerage under Henry VIII.

The scale and rapidity of the expansion of the aristocracy during the twentieth century did much to discredit the whole idea of an hereditary nobility.
Until then it had taken time, patience and luck to buy an estate, build a
mansion, intermarry with the local gentry, establish a pedigree, educate the
next generation at Eton and Oxbridge, and perform the public service necessary for full integration into the British aristocracy. Few of the nabobs, brewers
and slavers of the eighteenth century managed it. In the first three quarters
of the nineteenth century only one *bona fide* industrialist – Edward Strutt,
created Baron Belper in 1856 – was raised to the peerage. But dozens of his
twentieth-century successors match his feat. It was democracy, not plutocracy,
which made the difference.

How Democracy Corrupted Aristocracy

Democratically elected politicians need money to fund their campaigns and
newspapers to support their causes, and they were happy to trade honours
and titles in return for both of these. From the 1880s the entire system of

honours took on its present debased form, in which knighthoods and peerages are awarded for contributions to party funds, long service on the back
benches, or the prolonged tenure of public office. Of course, money was
never irrelevant to social advancement in Britain, but opening the ranks of
the peerage to 'mere wealth' is usually dated to Disraeli's ennoblement of
the iron master, Sir Ivor Guest, as Baron Wimborne, and Sir Edward Guinness,
the brewer, as Baron Ardilaun, in 1880.

Superficially, these were orthodox elevations. Both men had acquired
estates, inherited baronetcies and married into the aristocracy. Guinness had
an impressive record of charitable work. But their rise to the peerage marked
the beginning of the plutocratic rush. Gladstone added the bankers Edward
Baring, Rothschild and Tweedmouth, the brewer Michael Bass, and the son
of the famous railway contractor, Thomas Brassey. Lord Salisbury ennobled
the brewer Henry Allsop and another Guinness. Between 1886 and 1914 two
hundred people entered the peerage for the first time, of which only a
quarter were scions of aristocratic families. The rest consisted of bankers,
businessmen, colonial administrators, lawyers, diplomats and soldiers.[118] The
'plebeian aristocracy' Disraeli ascribed to Pitt was, in fact, his own creation.[119]

In 1895 the first press baron, Algernon Borthwick, proprietor of the *Morning
Post*, was raised to the peerage as Lord Glenesk and Edward Levy-Lawson, the
owner of the *Daily Telegraph*, followed in 1903 as Lord Burnham. In 1905
Balfour raised Alfred Harmsworth to the peerage as Lord Northcliffe. But it
was Lloyd George who flattered the popular press most shamelessly to advance
his cause. Between 1918 and 1922 he showered honours of various kinds on
no less than forty-nine newspapermen of various ranks, ranging from editors
to proprietors.[120] In his contempt for the hereditary principle, his ruthless
pursuit of personal and party advantage and his cynical exploitation of the
popular press, Lloyd George was the prototype for modern democratic politicians. 'As to politics,' observed Lord Grey in 1921, 'I am not the sort of
person that is wanted now. Lloyd George is the modern type, suited to an
age of telephones and moving pictures and modern journalism.'[121]

Lloyd George stripped the award of honours of all pretensions to exclusivity.
He sold peerages, baronetcies and knighthoods at a hectic pace to anyone
who could pay. He did so mainly because, as a prime minister without a party,
he needed his own electoral war chest. In the eighteen months before the
general election of June 1922 he dispensed 26 peerages, 74 baronetcies and
294 knighthoods. There was a recognised tariff: £10,000 for a knighthood,
£30,000 for a baronetcy and £50,000 or more for a peerage, and he employed
brokers to tout the honours. From 1918 Maundy Gregory, a failed playwright
and inglorious war veteran, ran a full-time broking operation from an office
in Parliament Square, earning £30,000 a year from importuning socially

TABLE 2.3
The Aristocratic Plutocrats

Name	Origin	Creation	Acreage c. 1880	Present Acreage	Present Wealth (£m est.)
Viscount Rothermere	Publishing	1919	–	–	1,200
Lord Vestey	Imported meat	1922	–	70,500	650
Earl of Iveagh	Brewing	1919	15,000	25,270	600
Lord Cowdray	Constuction, oil	1917	–	87,800	475
Lord Rotherwick	Shipping	1939	–	–	285
Lord Rothschild	Banking	1885	15,378	5,500	260
Samuel Whitbread	Brewing	–	13,829	14,000	175
Lord Daresbury	Brewing	1927	–	–	170
Earl of Stockton	Publishing	1984	–	–	170
Lord Iliffe	Publishing	1933	–	25,853	95
Viscount Weir*	Shipping	1938	–	4,875	94
Viscount Hambleden	Retailing	1891	–	–	60
Earl of Inchcape	Shipping	1929	–	17,300	43
Viscount Bearsted	Oil Property	1925	–	1,085	40
Lord Margadale	Drapery	1964	106,900	49,500	40
Lord Ashcombe	Building	1892	6,789	–	30
Viscount Astor†	American Furs	1917		34,500	30
Viscount Leverhulme	Soap	1922	–	24,700	30
Viscount Wimborne	Steel	1918	83,500	20,200	30
Lord Burton	Brewing	1897	58,000	48,000	28

Source: *Whitaker's Almanack*; The *Sunday Times* Rich Lists.

* The 4th Baron Inverforth is also part of the Weir family.
† The Astors also have a Baron Astor (1956).

ambitious businessmen. The Conservatives complained that Lloyd George was pinching 'their men' by offering the same honour at a lower price, but he was quite unashamed, telling a Conservative fund-raiser who complained about his tactics:

> You and I know perfectly well it is a far cleaner method of filling the Party chest than the methods used in the United States or the Socialist Party ... Here a man gives £40,000 to the Party and gets a baronetcy. If he comes to the Leader of the Party and says I subscribe largely to

the Party funds, you must do this or that, we can tell him to go to the devil.[122]

Despite this ingenious defence, a number of embarrassments resulted. These culminated in the notorious Birthday Honours list Lloyd George submitted to George V in June 1922. Of the five men recommended for peerages, one was implicated in a business scandal and three were war profiteers.

By 1914 Edward and William Vestey were worth £10 million apiece. William was made a baronet in 1913, and in 1922 he paid Lloyd George £25,000 for a barony.[123] Publicly, he was recommended on the grounds that the family meat trading company had made available to the army its cold storage facilities in northern France. In fact, the government had paid for the privilege. Worse, Vestey had sacked several thousand British workers and moved his headquarters to Argentina to escape a tax liability of roughly £3 million. Sir Archibald Williamson, the great-grandfather of the present Baron Forres, had traded with the enemy in South America, and another new peer, Sir Samuel Waring, made his fortune from profiteering in military contracts. Sir Joseph Robinson, chairman of a South African mining company, had bought mining freeholds in his own name and sold them to his company at hugely inflated prices. His proposed elevation was contested vigorously in a lively debate in the House of Lords on 22 June 1922, and the King refused to entertain the idea (as comedians put it) of the Earl of Randfontein. Legend has it that an envoy, despatched to the Savoy Hotel to explain the decision to the disappointed magnate, was astonished to be asked: 'How much more?' But Robinson, who declined the peerage in a letter to Lloyd George a week after the debate in the Lords, is said to have boasted that the episode 'did not cost me a single penny'.

One result of the Robinson scandal was the creation of a royal commission to scrutinise the procedure by which the prime minister recommended honours to the king. This, in turn, led to the formation of the Political Honours Scrutiny Committee and the passage of the Honours (Prevention of Abuses) Act in 1925, which made it a criminal offence to traffick in honours. The only practical effect was a return to the more discreet methods of the Edwardian era, as became evident when Maundy Gregory was arrested in 1932 after attempting to sell a knighthood to a retired naval officer. A cover-up was arranged, Gregory was persuaded to plead guilty and got away with two months in jail and a £50 fine.[124] Lloyd George, meanwhile, when accused of selling honours, had sued successfully for libel.

The Golden Age

Lloyd George did not care what damage he did to the hereditary peerage. The son of a Pembrokeshire farmer, he was born when the power and wealth of the territorial magnates was at its zenith, and where the impact of both was keenly felt. He entered politics when the machinery of democracy made it possible for the first time in two hundred years to displace the aristocracy from the leadership of the country. The Glorious Revolution of 1688 had made them more powerful than the monarchy. The King was subordinated to Parliament, the House of Commons was controlled by the House of Lords, and the executive and legislative arms of the state were exercised almost solely on behalf of the landed interest. Nobody who lacked property could vote, let alone hold public office: membership of the House of Commons was not open to people with landed incomes of less than £600 a year in the shires or £300 a year in the towns.* The House of Lords could oppose all but financial legislation, and anyway dominated the House of Commons through a mixture of patronage, bullying and bribery. Some constituencies were uncontested, and the local aristocrat nominated the MP. Where elections were held, the outcome could be fixed by subsidising rents, paying campaign expenses, or bribing or bullying the voters (the ballot was not secret until 1872). As late as 1900 the Marquess of Hastings evicted a tenant who did not vote for his candidate.

The eighteenth- and nineteenth-century House of Commons was filled with the heirs and second sons of the aristocracy, and promising young politicians who could not meet the property qualification without an aristocratic subvention. (Gladstone sat first for Newark, a pocket borough of the 4th Duke of Newcastle.) As late as 1880, 394 of 652 MPs were either titled aristocrats or significant landowners.[125] Throughout the nineteenth century, the prime minister and foreign secretary were drawn more often from the Lords than from the Commons. The Marquess of Salisbury, who fought unavailingly against the extension of the franchise throughout his political life, was still prime minister at the turn of the century.

Until the invention of County Councils in 1888, the peerage *was* local government in the countryside.[126] Several nineteenth-century Scottish magnates owned getting on for half of some counties. The biggest English landlords, such as the Dukes of Bedford, Devonshire and Northumberland, often owned at least one tenth of the counties where they had their family seat.

---

* It is often forgotten that the abolition of the property qualification was one of the main aims of the Chartist movement of the 1840s.

Quarter Sessions, where local aristocrats adjudicated as justices of the peace (JPs) on a wide range of civil, criminal and administrative matters, did not lose their responsibility for serious criminal cases until 1842. (Their lesser judicial responsibilities were not abolished until 1971.) Until 1906 JPs, like MPs, had to satisfy a property test. 'Running like a red thread through all the local institutions of the eighteenth century,' complained Sidney and Beatrice Webb in 1922, 'was the assumption that the ownership of property carried with it not only a necessary qualification for, but even a positive right to carry on, the work of government.'[127] The power of the landowner to influence his locality was customary as well as formal. His country house was the seat of local government, and a reflection of his power and prestige elsewhere. He was expected to subsidise local houses, churches, schools and roads, dispense patronage and pensions, chair the Poor Law Guardians, and lead the community in its seasonal rituals of fox-hunting and cricket.

From the 1680s to the 1880s the landed aristocracy used its control of the political system to entrench and enlarge its wealth. The Corn Bounty Acts of 1672 and 1688 and the Corn Law of 1815 propped up the price by restricting imports of foreign grain.[128] Between 1730 and 1870, Parliament was persuaded to pass about 5,000 enclosure bills, enlarging further the size and productivity of farms owned by the aristocracy. Private legislation was also used to facilitate the building of canals, turnpike roads, railways and housing estates (the Duke of Bedford obtained a private Act of Parliament to begin developing Bedford Square in 1776) or to redirect unwelcome developments on to neighbouring estates. The entire apparatus of the law was geared to the defence of private property. The ferocious 'Bloody Code' of the eighteenth century, which greatly increased the number of capital offences, was at bottom no more than a determined defence of their property by the aristocracy. Crimes as petty as stealing a sheep carried the death penalty.[129]

Control of the government machine also gave the aristocracy control of the profits and perquisites of public office. In 1720 a quarter of the peerage had government jobs. The post of paymaster general was the most eagerly sought, for the opportunities it offered to collect commission on loans to the government and interest on cash-in-hand. It made the fortunes of the Earl of Ranelagh, Henry Fox, Robert Walpole and, most notoriously of all, James Brydges, the first Duke of Chandos. Between 1705 and 1713, Brydges embezzled £600,000 from the post.[130] No systematic attempt was made to reform this 'Old Corruption' until Burke and Pitt set about it at the end of the eighteenth century, and still it persisted deep into the nineteenth century. Earl Bathurst was receiving over £37,000 from five government posts as late as 1832.[131] On the passing of the Great Reform Act that year he cut off his pigtail, the mark of his superiority, and cried, 'Ichabod, for the glory is departed.'[132] But competitive examinations for entry into the civil service were not introduced until the 1850s, and the effects were slow to permeate.

The aristocracy also dominated the other institutions of the state: the Church and the Army. One effect of the Dissolution of the Monasteries was to give its members control of many of the livings of the Church of England, to which they naturally appointed their friends and relatives. Even today, they are still patrons of dozens of Church livings.[133] For junior members of the aristocracy who did not fancy the Church, soldiering was the main alternative, and they simply bought a career as an army officer. As late as 1875, half of all army officers were either titled aristocrats or members of the landed gentry.[134]

But it was from the land that the aristocracy ultimately drew its economic and financial power. The eighteenth century saw a series of improvements in agricultural techniques – crop rotation, animal feeds, more and better use of manure, improved stock-breeding, new root crops – which improved the output and profitability of the land. The owners enclosed open fields and waste land, drained and reclaimed other areas, recruited land stewards to help them manage their estates, and replaced small tenant-farmers with proto-typical grain barons. Even the infamous Highland Clearances, which replaced crofters with sheep and blackened the reputation of the Dukes of Sutherland for evermore, were initially conceived as an agricultural improvement. As rents rose (Coke of Holkham increased his rental income threefold in forty years), the value of land increased.[135] Between 1690 and 1790 values roughly doubled.[136] At the same time, the growing mass of consumers in the industrial towns meant that even the repeal of the Corn Laws in 1846 could not dent the buoyancy of food prices. The rents farmers paid to aristocratic landlords increased commensurately,[137] and carried on rising until the mid-1870s, when the great agricultural depression of the last quarter of the nineteenth century finally set in.[138]

Rising rents and land values made it easier for aristocrats to borrow money to buy and improve land, build houses, quarry sand and slate, mine coal, and develop their urban estates. The Bedfords quadrupled their London rents in the eighteenth century by developing Bloomsbury, and the Grosvenors raised theirs six-fold by developing Mayfair.[139] Industrialisation provided the aristocracy with the opportunity to create entire new towns. The Duke of Norfolk and Earl Fitzwilliam more or less shared the ownership of Sheffield, a booming industrial town. The discovery of iron ore near Barrow-in-Furness transformed the fortunes of the Dukes of Devonshire during the mid-nineteenth century, and turned a sleepy village into an industrial workshop.[140] The development of genteel residential areas and seaside resorts was equally lucrative. The Devonshires created modern Buxton and Eastbourne; the Calthorpes laid out

Edgbaston; the Haldons Torquay; the Ramsdens Huddersfield; the Radnors Folkestone, and the De La Warrs Bexhill. The growing industrial economy had a large appetite for coal, and the Dukes of Argyll, Devonshire, Hamilton and Northumberland all owned coal mines, as did the Earls of Durham, Lonsdale and Bute, and the Marquess of Londonderry.[141] The Earl of Durham – popularly known as 'His Carbonic Majesty' – had to spend £20,000 filling the workings beneath Lambton Castle as a result of his mining ventures,[142] but even those who lacked coal could make money by feeding the demand for building stone, slate, sand, brick-clay and timber.

The aristocracy entered the eighteenth century as the richest estate of the realm; they left it richer still. The average annual income of a peer rose from £7,000 to £10,000, at a time when a labourer could expect to earn £10 a year. The acreage of England and Wales owned by the aristocracy and gentry increased from two thirds to four fifths.[143] At the beginning of the nineteenth century fewer than 30,000 people controlled one seventh of the entire national income.[144] The aristocratic share of non-landed wealth – stocks, shares, cash, furniture, paintings – also went up, as rising rental incomes were re-invested in the banking system, the stock exchange, and the art markets.* As the economy industrialised, even the most lavish industrial fortunes could not keep pace with the rising wealth of the richest members of the aristocracy. In the 1870s, the 1st Duke of Westminster had an annual income of £290– 325,000, the Duke of Portland of £190–200,000, and the Duke of Bedford of £225–250,000.[145]

By the 1880s, eighteen aristocrats had incomes of £100,000 or more and seventy-eight were earning over £50,000. Despite its tiny share of the total population, the aristocracy supplied at least half the millionaires in Britain.† No plutocrat could match the income and wealth of the richest aristocrats until the fortunes of men such as Sir John Ellerman, Lord Nuffield, Viscount Leverhulme and the Rand lords Julius Wernher and Alfred Beit, emerged either side of the First World War.‡ More than a century after the Industrial Revolution began, the key to a truly sizeable fortune was not entrepreneurial

---

* According to one estimate, the average personal estate left by titled aristocrats (at constant prices) rose continuously from a low of £453 in 1700 to £9,855 in 1875, an impressive compound annual growth rate of 1.8 per cent. See Peter Lindert, 'Unequal English Wealth Since 1670', in *Journal of Political Economy*, Vol. 94, 1986, pp. 1127–56.

† Only seventy-seven businessmen were being taxed on incomes in excess of £50,000 in 1873. With the exception of a banker, elevated to the peerage as Lord Overstone, all those with incomes of more than £75,000 in the 1880s were longstanding members of the peerage. Rubinstein, *Men of Property*, pp. 195–6.

‡ Only eleven businessmen managed to amass fortunes greater than £2 million between 1809 and 1879, but there were eighty-three over the next sixty years. Rubinstein, *Men of Property*, pp. 40–3. See also Chapter 14.

energy or industrial innovation, but broad acres in good farming areas, the blessing of minerals beneath them, and the ownership of land in a booming industrial town or seaside resort. 'The property of the landowners, independent of minerals, yields an annual rent of sixty-seven millions sterling, and is worth a capital value of two thousand millions,' wrote James Caird, the chief Victorian analyst of the agricultural scene, in 1878. 'There is no other body of men in the country who administer so large a capital on their own account, or whose influence is so widely extended and universally present.'[146]

By then, Caird could draw on the most comprehensive analysis of land ownership carried out since Domesday. The idea of a new Domesday survey of land ownership originated in 1871, and was taken up by the Earl of Derby in a polemical rather than an inquiring spirit. His *amour propre* had been pricked by the radical MP John Bright, who had alleged (on the basis of the 1861 census) that the number of landowners did not exceed 30,000, and that 'fewer than 150 men' owned half of England. Derby was convinced this would be disproved by a census of land ownership, and persuaded the government to conduct an official survey of landholdings from the parish records of 1872.[147]

The Return of Owners of Land (1873) has provided endless delight for snobs and scholars ever since. But, as a weapon in a contemporary political controversy, it backfired badly. The survey showed that more than half of England, nearly two thirds of Wales, over three quarters of Ireland, and nine tenths of Scotland were owned in estates of over 1,000 acres, and that these were in the hands of just 10,911 people. One contemporary, reworking the figures to eliminate double counting, conjectured that four fifths of the British Isles was owned by just 7,000 people. No other country in Europe, with the possible exceptions of Austria–Hungary and Romania, had this concentration of land ownership.[148] *The Return* refuted Bright in detail, but confirmed the substance of his argument.[149]

It also confirmed that it was then, in the 1870s, that aristocratic power and wealth were at their zenith. They and their supporters among the landed gentry owned one in every two acres of the country. One in two millionaires, and eight out of twelve members of the Cabinet, were landed aristocrats. They governed the country with an irreproachable belief in their legitimacy and fitness for the task:

> Every community has natural leaders, to whom, if they are not misled by the insane passion for equality, they will instinctively defer. Always wealth, in some countries birth, in all intellectual power and culture, mark out the men to whom, in a healthy state of feeling, a community looks to undertake its government. They have the leisure

for the task, and can give it the close attention and the preparatory study which it needs. Fortune enables them to do it for the most part gratuitously, so the struggles of ambition are not defiled by the taint of sordid greed.[150]

In the age of sleaze and cash-for-questions, the argument that government is best undertaken by a rich and leisured class reads better than it once did. But in 1862, when the 3rd Marquess of Salisbury wrote these words, the British people had not tasted democracy. Once they did, they confirmed his earlier prediction that universal suffrage would reduce government and politics to 'a struggle between those who have, to keep what they have got, and those who have not, to get it'.[151]

A Fighting Retreat: The Twentieth Century

In the last quarter of the nineteenth century, the aristocracy endured the beginnings of the quadruple disaster which overtook them in the twentieth century: the prolonged agricultural depression, the haemorrhaging of political power, mounting legislative attacks on landowners, and a growing burden of taxation. Yet their ruthlessness and skill in defending their interests was as apparent in adversity as in the golden age. They sold their houses, let them, or knocked them down to save money. Their art collections were put up for auction. They resisted the reform of the House of Lords until the last ditch. Even land, the essence of the power and status of the territorial aristocracy since before the Conquest, was not sacred. Finally, they transformed themselves from the overbearing élite of history into the custodians of national heritage. As democratic politics in Britain subsides into a crypto-American mixture of opportunism and venality, the aristocracy might claim that their values are undergoing an unscripted renaissance, but for most of this century they have been in economic and political retreat.

Their first reaction to adversity was to sell anything but land. The Duke of Westminster sold Cliveden to William Waldorf Astor in 1893. Lord Carrington sold Wycombe Abbey to a girls' school, moved into a local farmhouse, and bought a cheaper family seat in Wales. Great houses, including Broughton Castle, Houghton Hall, Knebworth and Montacute, were let from the 1880s. The 8th Duke of Devonshire abandoned his palladian villa at Chiswick to a private lunatic asylum, and the Stricklands stripped the inlaid chamber out of Sizergh Castle and sold it to the Victoria & Albert Museum. There was a major sale of a country-house art collection almost every year from 1882 until the outbreak of war in 1914, and many paintings and other objects were sold to foreigners without demur. The auctions, however, gave the aristocracy the first glimpse of its subsidised future: at the art sales of the Edwardian period the Treasury made its first purchases on behalf of the nation.[152]

The second solution was to find a rich wife. The 8th Duke of Marlborough sold his art collection in 1886, raising half a million from the sale of books, manuscripts, enamels and Old Masters, but this was insufficient to maintain both Blenheim Palace and his enthusiasm for electrical experiments. The 9th Duke was obliged to marry the American railway heiress Consuelo Vanderbilt, whose commitment to the alliance of blood and money was even more reluctant than his. The marriage was unhappy, and ended in divorce, but was probably worth $10 million to the Churchills by the time it ended.[153] The 8th and 9th Dukes of Manchester also trawled the American market for rich wives and, between them, bagged the Cuban-American heiress Consuelo Yznaga, the railroad heiress Helen Zimmerman and eventually Consuelo Vanderbilt, then on the rebound from Marlborough. But even her legendary wealth was not enough to save the Dukes of Manchester from penury.[154]

The 11th Duke of Marlborough is more ruthless than his grandfather. In 1994 he placed the £30 million family fortune in the hands of trustees to keep it from his wayward heir, the Marquess of Blandford,[155] but even this was easier than the decision his grandfather had to make after the First World War: the sale of land.[156] There is no sterner test of the aristocratic instinct for survival than the willingness to sell land. For a territorial aristocrat, it is the most precious of assets, the source not only of wealth but of power and status. According to *Burke's Peerage*, land was the prime test of rank and position. More secure than cash or securities, it was also immovable, giving its owner a literal stake in the country. The alienation of any part of an estate was a catastrophe, marking not only a diminution in wealth but a shrinkage of status and loss of political influence.

Until the twentieth century, the chief obstacle to elevation to the peerage was lack of a landed estate, and it was not easy to obtain. Pitt the Younger, prime minister during the years when the British peerage expanded faster than at any time since the Stuarts, was accused by Disraeli of creating a 'plebeian aristocracy ... He caught them in the alleys of Lombard Street, and clutched them from the counting houses of Cornhill.'* In fact, Pitt was careful to choose most from junior or cadet branches of landed families. He refused a title himself, and only Robert Smith, the banker who became Lord

---

* Between 1780 and 1790 the peerage of Great Britain increased from 189 to 220, and over the next ten years to 267. The Irish peerage increased by a half in the same period. Overall, the peerage of the United Kingdom was enlarged by 166 new titles between 1780 and 1832. See Mingay, *English Landed Society in the Eighteenth Century*, p. 9; Beckett, *The Aristocracy in England 1660–1914*, pp. 30–1, 486–7.

Carrington, and Peter Thellusson, the merchant who became Baron Rendle-sham, corresponded at all to the epithet of financier.[157] The key to the elevation of both was their ownership of landed estates. Wealth was enough to secure a baronetcy but not a peerage.[158]

Even in 1832, when faced with the prospect of having to flood the House of Lords with supporters of his Reform Bill, Earl Grey did not contemplate dilution of the landed requirement. He proposed to call up eldest sons in their fathers' baronies, promote Scottish and Irish peers to the upper house and ennoble a carefully selected group of landed gentry.[159] When Gladstone urged Queen Victoria in 1869 to raise the head of the English branch of the Rothschild family to the peerage she replied that 'she cannot think that one who owes his great wealth to contracts with foreign governments, or to successful speculations on the stock exchange, can fairly claim a British peerage . . . This seems to her not the less a species of gambling because it is on a gigantic scale.'[160] By then, Anthony de Rothschild was already a baronet and had acquired a country estate at Aston Clinton in Buckinghamshire, but the Queen could still argue without fear of contradiction that he lacked that literal stake in the country which only ownership of land over several generations could confer. Rich men without land might place personal and party advantage ahead of the public good. It was astute anticipation of the corruption of the aristocracy in the twentieth century.

The Newcastle armaments manufacturer Sir William Armstrong, elevated to the peerage in 1887, felt obliged to assemble an estate of 16,000 acres and two country seats to support his new status. In the nineteenth and twentieth centuries, the Barings, Levers, Vesteys and Pearsons all understood that only the possession of land could dignify their newly acquired peerages. Between 1909 and 1924 Weetman Pearson, 1st Viscount Cowdray, spent over £1 million on land.[161] Most of the 'business peerages' of the late Victorian and Edwardian eras went to men who possessed at least 2,000 acres,[162] and this requirement persisted even when the honours system declined into a bazaar after the First World War. Only 53 out of 162 non-landed millionaires got a title of any sort between 1920 and 1939.[163]

Until the end of the nineteenth century, this binding of the aristocracy to the soil was given formal expression in law. Strict Settlement was devised in the seventeenth century to ensure that land could be sold only once in each generation, and then only if a landowner and his heir agreed.[164] By restricting the supply of land for sale, Strict Settlement made it hard for New Men to enter the ranks of the aristocracy. The passage of the Settled Lands Act of 1882 was a significant symptom of the multiple crises engulfing the aristocracy: it loosened restrictions on the alienation of land. Even so, it forbade the sale of the family seat to inhibit the alienation of the core of the estate.[165] The overall aim and effect of the Act was plain. The aristocratic share of the acreage of the British Isles fell from four fifths in the 1880s to no more than a quarter a century later.[166] Within eighty years of the passage of the Settled Lands Act, only one third of the peerage possessed any estate at all.[167]

The massive alienation of aristocratic estates was the biggest change in land ownership since the Norman Conquest, exceeding by far the confiscations of the Civil War or the Dissolution of the Monasteries. Yet this cataclysm is not etched on the collective memory of the British people in anything like the same way because the land did not come into the possession of conquerors, or New Men, or regicides. Most was sold to those who were farming it already: the tenants. As the *Estates Gazette* remarked in October 1918, the sales marked 'not so much the foundations of a new aristocracy as the foundations of a new yeomanry'.[168] It is from this period that the owner-occupying farmer can date his emergence as the main force for good and evil in the British countryside.* Some of the aristocratic wealth withdrawn from the land was reinvested in great estates abroad, but much was wisely reinvested in the faster-growing stock market. Between the wars, the whole of the Bridgewater estate was sold off and £3.3 million reinvested in equities. By the 1920s, the Duke of Devonshire was earning more from dividends than rents.[169] The great sell-off was not an entirely destructive event, but there is no doubt of its scale. By 1915, 800,000 acres of England alone had changed hands, for £20 million,[170] and there was a further boom in sales during 1919 and 1920 before the bubble burst in 1921. In the years immediately before and after the First World War between six and eight million acres of England, or one quarter of the country, was sold by the aristocracy.[171] 'We all know it now,' *The Times* lamented in 1919, 'England is changing hands.'[172]

The main cause was the prolonged agricultural depression. The railways had opened the American prairies, the Ukrainian steppes and the Argentinian pampas, and refrigerated steamships (many of them owned, ironically, by the title-hunting Vesteys) brought their grain and beef to British consumers for the first time since the repeal of the Corn Laws. The price of cereals, wool and meat fell, and agricultural rents and land values fell with them.[173] Agriculture did not begin to recover until the Second World War, and did not prosper until the government began to subsidise the industry heavily in the 1950s. At the time of the Festival of Britain in 1951, farmland was worth the same in real terms as in 1880.[174] But the causes of the crisis were not purely economic; when the 11th Duke of Bedford sold the Thorney estate to its tenants, he explained that he was deferring to 'the social and legislative tendencies of the day'.[175] The extension of the franchise meant that tenants'

* See Chapter 18.

passion for ownership could be translated into reality by political means. The systematic attack on the estates of the great aristocratic landowners, which began with the Irish Land Act of 1881, culminated in the Leasehold Reform, Housing and Urban Development Act of 1993.

Land was at the centre of political agitation in Ireland in the last decades of the nineteenth century, and it was in Ireland that the state first directed and financed the confiscation of aristocratic property. By granting tenants the 'three fs' (fair rents, fixity of tenure and free sale), the Irish Land Act of 1881 abrogated the right of a landlord to do as he wished with his property, and the taxpayer made public money available at generous rates of interest to enable tenants to buy their holdings. In just forty years, fifteen of the seventeen million acres of Ireland were transferred from landlords to tenants, at a total cost to the taxpayer of £150 million.[176]

Gladstone had recognised during the passage of the 1881 legislation that it presaged 'fundamental changes in the nature of property, which might . . . be . . . found difficult to confine to one country of this kingdom'. He was right. A Crofters Act, extending fair rents and fixity of tenure to the Highlands, followed in 1886. By the outbreak of war in 1939, one third of Scotland was owner-occupied. In Wales, change was accomplished without legislation, though landowners were encouraged to sell by Lloyd George's incessant threats of expropriation. Owner-occupation rose from a tenth of land holdings in 1909 to two fifths at the beginning of World War Two.[177] In England, the readiness of the aristocracy to sell both before and after the war reflected a genuine fear that land would be nationalised. Joseph Chamberlain's Unauthorised Programme of 1885 included the famous call for 'Three Acres and a Cow', and between 1912 and 1914 Lloyd George waged a relentless campaign against the landed interest. His plans to increase the taxation of landlords, fix rents and nationalise small holdings were averted by the war, but the aristocracy sold anyway. The owner-occupied acreage of England rose from 11 per cent in 1914 to half by 1960.[178]

The aristocracy also found their urban estates threatened. A Leasehold Enfranchisement Society was formed in 1884, to campaign for freehold ownership.[179] Leasehold (a form of land tenure shared only with Hawaii) played a vital part in the profitable development of the urban estates of the British aristocracy. Towns were developed by leasing land to speculative builders for a specified term, usually of 99 years. The builders then sold the leases to owner-occupiers. This meant the costs of construction were borne by the developer, while the costs of maintenance fell on the leaseholder, who was obliged to maintain the quality of the building and respect the architectural unity of the estate. These terms were obviously attractive to the landlord, who paid nothing toward construction and maintenance, and could renew leases at higher prices as they expired. It was not until 1967 that a Leasehold Reform Act gave leaseholders the right to acquire the freehold of their houses. Even then, the right was restricted to inexpensive houses, and did not apply to flats.* The exclusion of the more valuable properties followed an intensive lobbying campaign by the great private landlords which restricted but did not avert the impact of the legislation on the richest estates – the London holdings of the Westminsters, Cadogans, Portmans and Howard de Waldens.†

The Duke of Westminster was sufficiently angered by the attrition of his property under the 1967 legislation to take the government to the European Commission of Human Rights in 1980, protesting that the Act had deprived him of property against his will at prices well below market values. The Commission referred the case to the European Court of Human Rights, where it was heard in September 1985. The court ruled that the 'compulsory transfer of property from one individual to another might constitute a legitimate means for promoting the public interest. The enhancement of social justice within the community could properly be described as being in the public interest.'[180] This was a major defeat, in which a political definition of the public good triumphed decisively over the rights of private property. The Conservative Party, never slow to seize an opportunity to extend its vision of a property-owning democracy, and alive to the complaints of its supporters about excessive service charges levied by unscrupulous landlords, decided there were votes in a further extension of leasehold enfranchisement.

The Leasehold Reform, Housing and Urban Development Act of 1993 gave another three quaters of a million leaseholders the right to buy their free-hold.‡ The Duke of Westminster resigned his membership of the Conservative Party, and Earl Cadogan stopped his donations. Of around thirteen hundred householders on the Grosvenor Estate, less than four hundred had enfranchised by the spring of 1998; the remaining leaseholders are able to coax more generous terms out of their landlord.[181]

Leasehold enfranchisement provides the clearest illustration of how democracy, once it had deprived the aristocracy of control of the political system, could be used to rob aristocrats of their wealth. Enriching the many at the expense of the few is good politics. Even the Conservative Party was driven

---

* The 1967 Leasehold Reform Act allowed holders of leases of more than twenty-one years, whose rateable value did not exceed £1,500 in London and £750 elsewhere, to force landlords to sell them the freehold. It applied only to the *house* they were living in.

† Landlords with a high proportion of residential lettings, such as the Earl of Cadogan and the Duke of Westminster, were nevertheless forced to sell a number of leaseholds cheaply under the legislation. Robert Pearman, *The Cadogan Estate*, p. 122.

‡ It gave holders of leases of more than twenty-one years the right to force the landlords of their primary residence to sell them the freehold with certain provisions. The Act ws not a total success and had to be supplemented by additional measures in 1996.

by the quest for votes to extend ownership at the cost of the principles on which ownership was based: the right of the citizen to own and enjoy his private property, and the obligation of the state to uphold contracts negotiated freely and in good faith. This is the true measure of the impotence of a minority, and particularly an unpopular one. 'The "enlightened selfishness" of the modern artisan now fully understands that political power, like everything else, is to be taken to the dearest market,' warned the 3rd Marquess of Salisbury in 1860. 'He cares little enough for democracy unless it will adjust the inequalities of wealth.'[182]

The Third Reform Act of 1884–5, unlike the Great Reform Act of 1832 and its successor of 1867, tilted the balance of power from the aristocracy to the people. It extended the borough vote to the rural areas, doubled the size of the electorate, abolished two-member seats and redrew constituency boundaries to reduce the representation of the deferential countryside in favour of the populous cities and the hostile Celtic fringe. Legislative clashes between the House of Commons and the House of Lords increased, culminating in the rejection by the Upper House of the People's Budget of 1909. This provoked the prolonged constitutional crisis which ended in the Parliament Act of 1911, which was carried in the House of Lords by the votes of bishops and newly created peers, with an eventual majority of just seventeen votes.

Even its final passage was not so much a defeat as an astute tactical retreat. The House of Lords might have disappeared altogether in 1911. Instead, an hereditary peerage retained a place in Parliament into the twenty-first century. The 'Salisbury Rules' ensured that the House of Lords survived a threatening socialist administration – the Attlee governments of 1945–51 – with its powers of delay reduced by merely one year. The Life Peerages Act of 1959, introduced by a Conservative government to enable peerages to be granted for life, was also a clever defensive coup by Harold Macmillan. It prolonged the life of the hereditary element by making the Upper House more representative and providing a retirement home for superannuated Labour MPs.

The success of life peerages was reinforced by the Peerage Act of 1963, allowing hereditary peers such as Tony Benn, Quintin Hogg and Alec Douglas-Home to descend to the Lower House, and by the decision to admit women to life peerages. 'Working' peers were created by all three major parties, and made up one third of the House and more than half of the peers who attended regularly in the years before the voting rights of hereditary peers were finally abolished by the New Labour government.

A modified House of Lords gave the hereditary aristocracy a continuing ministerial power base throughout the twentieth century. In 1919 one in three members of the Cabinet appointed by Lloyd George was an aristocrat. Five years later, half the Cabinet formed by Stanley Baldwin consisted of members of the landed aristocracy, as did Neville Chamberlain's first Cabinet in 1937. There were still enough aristocrats in the Macmillan Cabinets of the early 1960s for Sampson, in his first *Anatomy of Britain*, to mock the prime minister for an antediluvian partiality to the peerage. Macmillan was succeeded – as that earlier neophile, Harold Wilson, mockingly pointed out – by the 14th Earl of Home. Under John Major, the leader of the Lords was Viscount Cranborne, one of four earls, two viscounts, and five hereditary barons to serve the self-professed prime minister of classlessness.[183] Cranborne later abandoned his party rather than sacrifice the chance of retaining an hereditary element in the Upper House for a few years more.

But the New Labour government is now committed to strip all hereditary peers of their right to vote and to the creation of a representative Upper Chamber of an indeterminate kind at some unspecified date in the future. One thing is certain: the process of constitutional reform cannot be confined to the Upper Chamber. A supine House of Lords has helped successive governments to treat Parliament with contempt. The present prime minister hardly ever appears there, preferring to address the country through the media rather than the House of Commons, but he will find his backbenchers much less indulgent if he attempts to create a representative second chamber. As Ferdinand Mount has pointed out, the House of Lords cannot become a proper legislative chamber until the House of Commons has become one too.[184] It is a remarkable testimony to the staying power of the aristocracy that, more than a century after it was ostensibly overtaken by democracy, there is no easy way to reform or replace the House of Lords.

The Nationalisation of the Aristocracy

The only justification for government by an hereditary caste was if they ruled out of a sense of public duty, pursued the national interest in an enlightened and disinterested fashion, and adhered to the highest standards of personal probity. Chief among the reasons why the Conservative Party lost the General Election of 1997 was the public perception that its leading figures were in politics for what they could get out of it rather than what they could bring to it; that its policies were dogmatic and narrowly partisan; and that its MPs and ministers were financially corrupt and sexually incontinent.

The truth is that democracy makes it exceptionally hard to govern honestly. Its appetite for money, to fund parties and fight elections, is prodigious. The need to court the popular press, the most important influence over the public mood, is unrelenting, and the demands and indignities of a modern political career dissuade all but those who can afford to pursue it to the exclusion of all else. This has emptied Parliament of the knights of the shires, and filled it with men and women who want ministerial office, but lack the personal wealth to guarantee their independence or honesty. Since the 6th Baron Carrington resigned as Foreign Secretary in 1982, no minister has resigned on a point of honour, and many have had to be chased from office by *The Sun* or the *News of the World* or the *Daily Mirror*. Yet it would be foolish to think that the indignation of tabloid newspapers could restore a high-minded governing class of any kind, let alone the aristocracy. Public distaste for professional politicians may vindicate Victorian Cassandras like the 3rd Marquess of Salisbury, but it cannot restore their successors to power.

The frivolous behaviour and pathetic enthusiasms of some junior members of the aristocracy are doing as much damage to the moral standing of the peerage as the antics of the younger royals to the royal family, and collateral damage of this kind makes a political comeback virtually impossible. But it matters economically too; the peerage has struck a new bargain with Demos, surrendering land for conversion into suburbs, and throwing open their houses and estates as the playgrounds of the suburbanites. Their enemies may deplore the re-invention of the aristocracy as the custodians of the national heritage. But the truth is that the aristocracy now has to earn its living in the marketplace along with everyone else, and tainted brands do not sell well.

As late as 1962 a survey of visitors to National Trust houses found that their 'enjoyment of the visit consisted chiefly in the thrill of direct contact with the past, particularly in thinking about the people who lived in the house.'[185] But the motives of visitors to country houses today are different. They are not the puppets of the élite, persuaded that stately homes are a worthier destination for their taxes and lottery tickets than the local scanner appeal. They are consumers, in search of latter-day Punch-and-Judy shows, not a shared national heritage. With rising incomes, increased leisure, and the greater mobility of the motor car, they visit country houses in much the same spirit as their forebears went to the music hall or the cinema. For the aristocracy, this dependence on the shifting tastes of the consumer is not a secure economic basis for long-term survival. It was not until after World War Two that the public was persuaded to divert resources into shoring up stately homes and historic estates, and it might one day withdraw its favour. Nor can the aristocracy count on its present raft of public subsidies and tax concessions to last indefinitely. If the Cult of the Country House loses its grip on the public imagination, subsidising a few hundred aristocrats and their houses is one market failure no politician will be hurrying to correct.

If the public does withdraw its favour, few aristocrats have much in reserve. The extent to which aristocratic wealth has burgeoned in recent years is often exaggerated. The chief beneficiaries are those members of the caste which had a lot of land and money in the first place. Of the thirty largest landed fortunes a century ago, nineteen are still substantial millionaires. Some are richer than their grandfathers and great-grandfathers were, and several own more land.[186] But there are plenty of impoverished aristocrats. This is especially true of the Irish peers, whose lands were expropriated by a reforming government. Many are struggling to maintain historic houses and estates. It costs £60–80,000 a year to run even a modest country house without dipping into capital, and many families cannot find it. The Historic Houses Association reckons about twenty-five houses a year change hands. Sale is usually a last resort, but the estates which supported great houses are being eroded. The Duke of Devonshire, one of the richest surviving landowners, reckons even the biggest estates will last no more than another generation. 'Unless matters change soon,' he said, 'we will see not just the splitting up of larger estates into smaller ones, but the total extinction of any sizeable holdings whatsoever. The day of the big estate – even of the fairly big estate – is nearly over.'[187] Large houses without land are not viable, except as theme parts or living museums of the kind supported by the National Trust or the taxpayer. Once a house becomes dependent on charity or state hand-outs, the ties which bind the family to the house and its contents are severed, and the house no longer evolves or adapts organically to changing economic circumstances. Though families often linger on in one wing, ownership effectively passes to the public. This is the price of public subsidy; it always was. When Warwick Castle was badly damaged by fire in 1871, the funds to restore it were raised by a public appeal. By subscribing to it, as the *Daily Telegraph* recognised at the time, people were 'restoring in a sense a piece of national property, and entrusting it again to Lord Warwick as before'.

But, wrote the 6th Marquess of Bath in 1952, 'it is imperative that nothing is done or appears to be done which may lead the public to think that these houses have ceased to be the absolute property of the owners.'[188] Longleat was big enough for him to refuse the Faustian pact proffered by the taxpayer. Others were not so lucky. For over a century, the aristocracy has fought a rearguard action against a host of enemies, chief among them the Inland Revenue. But the tax-eaters who ruined them have now become the tax-payers who support them. Despite the optimism of recent years, the likeliest fate of the stately homes of England is a complete takeover by the one nationalised industry which is still growing: the Heritage Industry.

CHAPTER THREE

THE HERITAGE INDUSTRY

A piece of massive impudence ... Fancy my not being able to make a necessary alteration at Haddon without first obtaining the leave of some inspector ... !

THE DUKE OF RUTLAND, 1911[1]

We have indeed almost become a museum in which are preserved here and there carefully selected and ticketed specimens of what England *was*. The National Trust is England's executor.

CLOUGH WILLIAMS-ELLIS, *England and the Octopus*, 1928[2]

Too often people have an image of Britain that is stuck in the past – good at pageantry, less good at new technology. That perception is wrong, and it is bad for business and bad for Britain.

TONY BLAIR, 1997[3]

The one good thing that society can do for the artist is leave him alone.

CLIVE BELL[4]

The Heritage Industry was invented by the Victorian art and social critic John Ruskin. In 1854 he proposed to the Society of Antiquaries that it compile an inventory of buildings threatened with demolition or collapse, and establish a conservation fund to protect them from the negligence of their owners:

I must not leave the truth unstated that it is no question of expediency or feeling whether we shall preserve the buildings of past times or not. We have no right whatever to touch them. They are not ours. They belong partly to those that built them, and partly to all generations of mankind who are to follow us.[5]

The fund was not a success. Ruskin was virtually the sole contributor, and it made only a few small donations to crumbling churches.[6] The rich and dominant aristocracy of the age was suspicious of public subsidies, and hostile to any truncation of the rights of private property. Three years after Ruskin spoke, the burghers of Birmingham financed the purchase of Aston Hall, the former seat of the Holte family, and turned it into a precursor of modern Woburn or Longleat. To the great aristocratic landowners, unacquainted as yet with heavy capital taxes, it was a direct threat to their claim that public ends were not incompatible with private ownership.

They were right to feel uneasy. Ruskin was the first thinker to articulate the belief that the buildings, landscapes and artefacts of the past were no longer entirely the property of their owners but part of a precious heritage which belongs to the nation as a whole. It is true that his vision of the public ownership of the National Heritage was far removed from the fetid masses of today, heaving through country houses, and picnicking on their lawns. He vehemently opposed public subscription to rebuild fire-ravaged Warwick Castle in 1871, arguing that 'if a noble family cannot rebuild their own castle, in God's name let them live in the nearest ditch until they can.'[7]

Rather, his vision was the natural fruit of the 'organic' society he idealised, with its Burkean partnership between the generations and its three orders of landowners, merchants, and aesthetes. It stemmed not from snobbishness but from an *aesthetic* rejection of the ugliness and acquisitiveness of industrial capitalism. Ruskin thought that true wealth was not the cheap commodities and private possessions of industrial capitalism but the 'intrinsic value' of beauty and usefulness. It was an outlook he extracted from the medieval world, whose just prices, static hierarchy, cathedral battlements and timbered cottages he juxtaposed against the rampant economic individualism, slums and factories of industrial civilisation.[8] Though Ruskin believed passionately that the past could be used to redeem the present, his was a backward-looking vision of a kind common to all forms of English socialism.[9]

The Origins of the Heritage Industry

William Morris was Ruskin's chief disciple. He injected the amorphous ideas of his mentor into a harder socialist creed ill-disposed to the rights of private property, and prepared to use the state to trample upon them. 'Apart from the desire to produce beautiful things,' he wrote in *How I Became a Socialist*, 'the leading passion of my life has been and is hatred of modern civilisation.'* He and the socialist thinkers who followed him, such as R. H. Tawney and G. D. H. Cole, imbued English socialism with a nostalgic vision of 'Merrie England' which was as hostile to the aristocracy of the golden age as it was to the industrial capitalism of the Victorian era. (A best-selling collection of the articles of the late-Victorian journalist Robert Blatchford, a prominent figure in socialist circles, was entitled *Merrie England*.)[10] The arts and crafts movement poured scorn on the grand country houses of the eighteenth century, contrasting them unfavourably with the cottages, churches, cathedrals and castles of the Middle Ages.[11] According to Morris's biographer, the inept restoration of a medieval church in the Cotswold village of Burford persuaded him to make a reality of the dream of Ruskin, and set up a public body to protect ancient and historic buildings from spoliation by their owners.[12] 'I think', he wrote to *The Times*, 'our ancient historical Monuments are national property.'[13]

The Society for the Protection of Ancient Buildings (SPAB) was the prototype of the many organisations which have since emerged to make their living out of the Heritage Industry. It met for the first time, with William Morris as secretary, on 22 March 1876. An immediate ambition was to halt the threatened 'restoration' of Tewkesbury Abbey by George Gilbert Scott, a particular *bête noire* of the arts and crafts movement.[14] The abbey, a medieval structure set in a town famous for its half-timbered cottages, was exactly the kind of building the society wished to save for posterity. But the campaign was unsuccessful, not least because it lacked numbers.

The SPAB never developed a mass membership. It had as few as 443 members in 1910, and its successes were confined to prodding Leeds municipality into buying Kirkstall Abbey in 1895.[15] The passage in 1882 of legislation to preserve ancient monuments and historical buildings, sometimes attributed to the SPAB, owed more to a Liberal MP and antiquarian, Sir John Lubbock, who had purchased Avebury Rings to save the site from destruction. Between 1873 and 1882 he introduced a series of bills to protect similar monuments from careless farmers. When he achieved success with the Ancient Monuments Protection Act of 1882, the Pentre Ifan burial chamber in Wales became the first ancient monument in Britain to be given the protection of the state. Fifty sites were scheduled for protection, under the supervision of a single inspector, who was entitled to examine them only if the owner of the land agreed. Landowners rightly suspected that government interest would restrict

* Quoted in Raymond Williams, *Culture and Society 1780–1950*, Penguin, 1975, p. 154. The Whig historian G. M. Trevelyan, a leading figure in the Heritage Industry before and after the Second World War, said almost exactly the same thing, telling A. L. Rowse that he 'disliked practically everything since the Industrial Revolution'. In David Cannadine, *G. M. Trevelyan*, Fontana, 1992, p. 223. See also p. 117.

their rights to dispose of their property as they saw fit; when the Historical Manuscripts Commission was established in 1869 to catalogue private holdings of important papers on a voluntary basis, it was denounced as 'an arbitrary interference with the rights of Private Property'.[16]

Lubbock worried about registering Avebury Rings under his own legislation for precisely that reason. When the Royal Commission on Historical Monuments was set up in 1908 to catalogue ancient monuments and historical buildings on a more systematic basis, landlords feared its inspectors were the Inland Revenue in disguise. So there is nothing retrospective about describing the Historical Manuscripts Commission, the Ancient Monuments Act of 1882 and the Royal Commission on Historical Monuments (still going, ninety years later) for what they were: the first of a long series of legislative measures by which the state has eroded the rights of private property to preserve the National Heritage.

Yet not even the gloomiest of Victorian landowners could have foretold the penetration and compass of the modern Heritage Industry. The event which turned a minority concern for beautiful objects into widespread state direction of private property was the near-destruction of Tattershall Castle shortly before the First World War. The fifteenth-century castle had already lost its chimneypieces by the time the 1st Marquess of Curzon organised a rescue of the structure. The spectacle of 450-year-old stone chimneypieces being hawked around the antique dealers of London led directly to the Ancient Monuments Act of 1913, which obliged the owners of historic buildings to notify the government if they planned to alter or demolish any part of the structure. It also allowed the government to issue preservation orders to prevent demolition, alteration or neglect.[17] This power, extended by the 1932 Town and Country Planning Act, was the first serious abrogation of the rights of private property by the Heritage Industry, and established the principle by which it has extended its reach (if not its grasp) to one in every thirty or forty buildings in the British Isles.

'It used to be said that an Englishman's house was his castle,' Lord Cranborne complained to *The Times* after the 1932 Act gave local authorities the power to instruct owners to preserve their houses. 'It seems that this is no longer the case.'[18] It was not. The graded listing of buildings familiar today was introduced in 1944, and three years later, the 1947 Town and Country Planning Act put the system on a statutory footing. The sixty-seven ancient monuments identified under the 1882 legislation have now expanded to over 29,000 separate sites across Great Britain, and the Royal Commission on the Historical Monuments of England and its satellite bodies around the Celtic fringe are busy adding to the list. There are now nearly 435,000 listed buildings, 8,758 conservation areas, 945 local and national nature reserves, 6,264 'sites of specific scientific interest', 37 Areas of Outstanding Natural Beauty, and 17 World Heritage sites. Work is going on to identify which of an estimated 600,000 archaeological sites in England alone are of sufficient importance to deserve the protection of the law. The work, once complete, is expected to double the number of scheduled ancient monuments,[19] and registers of historic parks, gardens and battlefields are also being compiled.

There are now so many museums and galleries housing the art and artefacts of the past in Britain that no one knows exactly how many. In 1987 Robert Hewison counted 2,131 museums in Britain, half created since 1971.[20] There could be as many as 2,500 museums today, with central government financing 16, local authorities at least another 800, and perhaps 1,500 or 1,600 privately owned. Almost nothing is allowed to disappear any more. At Preston North End football club there is a museum of football; near Oundle there is a National Dragonfly Museum, and 'Heritage Centres', inspired by the astonishing success of the Jorvik Viking Centre in York, are springing up to recapture the industrial past. The director of the Science Museum told Hewison that the number of museums in Britain was growing so fast that 'the whole country [will become] one big open-air museum . . . you just join it as you get off at Heathrow.'[21] Mrs Thatcher, returning from the airport after a flight to the United States, was sufficiently exasperated with her fellow-countrymen to allude to Britain as 'the museum society'.[22]

The Listing Frenzy

The reach of the museum society extends far beyond the corridors of the municipal museum; virtually every village and town in Britain has at least one building which has earned a place in the national pantheon. When listing began in 1947, no building created earlier than 1840 was considered. The formation of the Georgian Society in 1937 brought the historical reach of the Heritage Industry to the eighteenth century, whose architectural and artistic achievements had previously suffered from the disparagement of Victorian medievalists. In the 1960s the formation of the Victorian Society signified the conquest by the Heritage Industry of the nineteenth century. A Thirties Society followed, which later obviated the need for Forties, Fifties, Sixties and Seventies societies by renaming itself the Twentieth Century Society. (There is even a Bakelite Society, for the veneration of early plastic objects.) By 1992 English Heritage was touring the country with an exhibition devoted to post-war buildings called, appropriately enough, 'A Change of Heart'.

In the 1980s the National Trust was criticised for failing to recognise the architectural achievements of the modern movement. 'Modernism has been dead for ten years,' expostulated Sir Roy Strong in 1991. 'The Trust should have been getting examples of all twentieth-century building types – a super-market, an airport, a hotel, a department store, a cinema, a factory, even council housing.'[23] If this was a joke, it was one the National Trust failed to spot. That year it acquired 2 Willow Road, the Hampstead home of modernist architect Erno Goldfinger. It also spent £2 million on the restoration of Sutton House in Hackney (the much-altered house of a Tudor merchant but one of the Trust's few urban properties), which reopened as a community centre in 1994. In 1995 the Trust granted Sir Roy his wish and bought a brick-and-tile council house dating from the 1950s. Its distinction owes noth-ing to architectural merit, and little to ambition to hoard aspects of the past. The reason the National Trust bought it is that it was the childhood home of Sir Paul McCartney.[24]

The same is true of many other listed buildings. They are protected not because they have any historical or architectural merit but because they were designed (or merely admired or lived in) by a celebrity or offer a glimpse of How We Lived Then (even if Then was only Yesterday). Listing has become a hoarding of the past which in an individual would be neurotic. There are now more than twice as many listed buildings as there were in 1980, and three times as many as in 1970, when there were already 128,000. Their quality is deteriorating as the quantity is increasing. Pigsties modelled on the Bank of England, urinals in Liverpool, a Butlin's chalet, a Victorian gas works, a railway signal box, a bus garage, shelters for London taxi drivers, a reinforced concrete silo, a corrugated-iron church, bollards and telephone boxes – all have joined the ranks of protected structures. Infamous buildings like the Leicester University engineering faculty, the Roman Catholic cathedral in Liverpool (known locally as Paddy's Wigwam), the Centre Point building at the eastern end of Oxford Street, the Millbank Tower, the concrete barracks of the National Theatre – all have become listed buildings. In Scot-land, the listed structures now include the Finnieston Crane in Glasgow and Bennet's Bar, 'one of the best pub interiors in Edinburgh'. In 1993 the first petition to list a council tower block was submitted.[25]

Like everything which receives blessings or money from the Heritage Indus-try, most of these buildings are chosen by a self-appointed clerisy of art and architecture experts whom the founder-members of SPAB would recognise and applaud. The public, which meets the costs of preserving the past, cannot be trusted to make the right choices. Like the contents of an attic, the lists have become longer and less manageable. When, in the late 1980s, the National Audit Office visited English Heritage, the body ultimately respons-ible for listed buildings in England, the lists of buildings had grown to two thousand volumes. This, concluded the Audit Office, 'makes it difficult to identify and use the information they contain'.

English Heritage and the Royal Commission on Historical Monuments have since invested in a computerised Listed Building System, but the lists are still expanding too fast. A sample survey in 1991 of one tenth of listed buildings estimated that 36,700 buildings were at risk of collapse, and twice that number were in urgent need of repair.[26] Buildings in danger included 2,400 listed as Grades I or II*, a status accorded to less than 30,000 buildings the length and breadth of the land. Yet only three hundred repair notices were issued between 1984 and 1990, and between 150 and 200 listed buildings were demolished each year. There are now so many applications to alter listed buildings (English Heritage alone fields over 10,000 a year) that the system is in danger of imploding. The bodies responsible for approving planning applications for listed buildings – English Heritage, Historic Scotland and Cadw: Welsh Historic Monuments – are trying to reduce their work by devolving powers to local authorities.[27] Dressed up as far-sighted delegation and decentralisation, it is a confession that their responsibilities have become unmanageable.

Once a building is listed, it is an offence to demolish, alter or extend it without going through a complicated and time-consuming procedure involving the local authority, the public heritage agencies and ultimately the Department of Culture, Media and Sport. Even if consent is granted, the delays add to the costs and divert development activity into less troublesome areas like the London Docklands. A Grade I listed building (there are 8,684 of them in England) cannot be altered *at all* without permission from the secretary of state. Owners of Grade II* (19,909) and Grade II (335,320) properties can also face prosecution if they make alterations without authorisation. If the house burns down, the owner is legally liable to rebuild it exactly as it was. In 1995 the Conservative MP Teresa Gorman was prosecuted by Thurrock Council for thirty-three breaches of planning laws after making alterations to a Grade II listed farmhouse without permission. She and her husband faced a maximum penalty of six months in jail or a fine of £660,000.[28]

When permission to redevelop or alter a building cannot be obtained, many owners have no option but to let it fall to pieces. Some are houses or commercial buildings which cannot be converted to alternative uses;[29] others owners cannot use or inhabit, such as old farm buildings or flour mills, power stations, follies and tombs. But if repairs are not carried out, the state is entitled to confiscate the building. In 1992 North Shropshire District Council acquired Pell Wall Hall (a house designed by Sir John Soane) by compulsory purchase at a price of just £1.[30] Where land and property values are low, owners can experience real financial hardship. 'A listed building', says Jocelyn

Stevens, chairman of English Heritage, 'can seriously damage your wealth.'[31] But the costs spread far beyond the owners; if they cannot adapt it for rent or commercial use, incomes and jobs are lost.

These costs are only partly relieved by countervailing grants for repairs and maintenance or tax concessions. Yet rather than accept that dilapidation and destruction are the natural fate of redundant and uninhabitable structures, or that it is better to save the best at the expense of the good, the listing authorities continue to seek powers to compel owners to keep them in proper repair. They have demanded and got new authority (via the infamous PPG15 – Planning Policy Guidance Note No 15) to force anyone wanting to alter or demolish a listed building to make a positive case for demolition. In conservation areas, they have acquired powers to prevent owners using cladding, or plastic window frames, or adding satellite dishes. The village green, the pillar box, the lamps and the trees have to stay the way they are. Heritage is no longer just an industry; it is a bureaucracy.

The National Heritage Memorial Fund and the Heritage Lottery Fund

Owning a listed building has one advantage. It helps to get grants from English Heritage, Historic Scotland and Cadw (the trading arms of the Historic Buildings Councils) for painting, pointing and clearing the gutters as well as major rehabilitation. It is for this reason that owners of built parts of the national heritage often lodge a listing application. In 1997 English Heritage spent £41 million supporting the owners of historic houses and ancient monuments, and Historic Scotland and Cadw dispensed another £15 million.[32] Handsome one-off grants are available from the National Heritage Memorial Fund (NHMF), whose trustees also choose the beneficiaries of the much larger Heritage Lottery Fund. The introduction of heritage as one of the good causes supported by the National Lottery has massively augmented the funds available for preservation of the past. Since its inception in 1980, the NHMF has spent under £200 million; in its first two years, the Heritage Lottery Fund dispensed £686 million. If matching funds are added to the total, the National Lottery injected over £1 billion into the Heritage Industry in its first two years.[33]

For owners of listed buildings, the Heritage Lottery Fund has one disadvantage: it is democratically controlled. Unlike the trustees of the NHMF, which never felt the press of the crowd, the Heritage Lottery Fund is under constant pressure to spend its millions on refurbishing the parish church and the municipal park rather than repointing the brickwork of the big house on the hill. The NHMF had until recently an unashamed bias towards historic houses, spending between half and two thirds of its grants on country houses, their contents and surrounding estates. This partly reflected the fact that stately homes are the chief repositories of the national heritage, but it also reflected the tastes and backgrounds of the trustees of the fund.

The first chairman of the trustees of the Memorial Fund was Lord Charteris of Amisfield, a former private secretary to the Queen and brother to the Earl of Wemyss and March, sometime president of the National Trust for Scotland. Charteris was succeeded by Lord Rothschild, who has spent a large part of his personal fortune refurbishing Spencer House in London and is also responsible for the maintenance of Waddesdon Manor in Buckinghamshire. Commander Michael Saunders Watson, owner of Rockingham Castle in Northamptonshire and a former president of the Historic Houses Association, was a trustee of both Heritage Funds until 1996, and Sir Richard Carew Pole, scion of one of the leading landowning families in Cornwall, is still a trustee, as was the Marquess of Anglesey, who gave his family seat to the National Trust in 1976.

But it was events as well as men which conspired to favour the country house. The immediate causes of the establishment of the NHMF were the Mentmore débâcle of 1977, and the decision by Lord Brooke to sell the contents of Warwick Castle.[34] A skilfully contrived sense of bereavement allowed the Heritage Industry to demand the restitution of the National Land Fund (set up in 1946 by Hugh Dalton, then Chancellor, to honour the dead of two world wars) as the National Heritage Memorial Fund (NHMF). The Land Fund had been intended to finance the purchase of land rather than buildings. Yet in its first year as the NHMF, £1.5 million was used to rescue the Dryden family seat of Canons Ashby in Northamptonshire, and another £118,000 was spent on silverware and furniture from Kedleston Hall. Kedleston later became one of three country houses dramatically rescued by the NHMF in 1985, after it had appealed to the government for a special subvention of £25 million. (Of this sum, £13.5 million was spent on transferring Kedleston and its contents to the National Trust, £6 million on buying the Chippendale furniture at another Trust property, Nostell Priory in Yorkshire, and £1.75 million on endowing the charitable foundation which acquired Weston Park in Shropshire from the Earl of Bradford.)

But it was when the National Trust asked the fund to support its purchase of Calke Abbey in Derbyshire from Henry Harpur-Crewe, who was facing a Capital Transfer Tax bill of £8 million on the death of his brother, that the power and influence of the trustees of the NHMF became plain. A special approach was made to the chancellor of the Exchequer, Nigel Lawson, who included an extraordinary grant of £6.3 million to the fund in his 1984 budget. It was the first occasion on which the Heritage Industry had featured directly in the major economic event of the year. When its spokesmen returned a year later for £25 million, they were irresistible.

Grants towards the purchase of drawings, paintings, watercolours, manuscripts and furniture are a less obvious but equally valuable form of assistance to the owners of large country houses. The £825,000 paid in 1981 towards the purchase of Altdorfer's *Christ Taking Leave of His Mother* by the National Gallery, for example, assisted in securing the future of Luton Hoo. In 1992 the £3.5 million the fund gave to buy Holbein's *Portrait of a Lady With a Squirrel* from the Marquess of Cholmondeley made it the most expensive picture ever acquired by the National Gallery. The trustees of the Heritage Lottery Fund may be the same people, but have enjoyed much less discretion. Their decision in 1995 to pay £13.25 million for the Churchill archive was so controversial that it is now unthinkable that Lottery money will ever be used again to buy family papers.

Yet the partiality of the Memorial Fund towards large country houses in the 1980s was not as great a perversion of its original purpose as is sometimes portrayed. Certainly, Dalton was no friend of the aristocracy. He was a keen fell-walker concerned to preserve and provide access to the land for people like himself. The £50 million with which he endowed the National Land Fund was intended to purchase for public benefit the land released by the régime of capital taxation he was imposing on the great aristocratic landowners. 'This money,' he told the nation, 'will be used to buy some of the best of our still unspoiled open country, and stretches of coast, to be preserved for ever, not for the enjoyment of a few private landowners but as a playground and a national possession for all our people'.[35] But Dalton was also a supporter of the National Trust, which was by then becoming the owner-of-last-resort of doomed country houses. In the same year that he established the National Land Fund, he gave £60,000 to the fiftieth anniversary appeal by the National Trust.

The Trust complained with little cause that Dalton had a 'weakness for land'. The National Land Fund was used from the outset to reimburse the Inland Revenue for property accepted by the Treasury in lieu of tax, and the houses were passed to the National Trust free of tax liabilities.[36] The government had accepted land and buildings in lieu of tax since Lloyd George had been chancellor in 1910, but only two properties were acquired during the subsequent thirty-six years. Between 1947 and 1957, by contrast, the National Land Fund enabled the government to pass twenty-six properties to the National Trust, including a string of well-known houses – Sissinghurst in Kent, Penrhyn Castle in Wales, Saltram near Plymouth, and Shugborough in Staffordshire. Hardwick Hall in Derbyshire, now owned by the Trust, was accepted by the Treasury in lieu of £350,000 of estate duties on the death of the 10th Duke of Devonshire.

The resurrected National Heritage Memorial Fund received an endowment of only £12.4 million in its first year (1980), but was promised an annual grant of £3 million. Its powers were enormous. The trustees were completely independent, and free to arrive at their own definition of what constituted the National Heritage. They could provide cash endowments for any country house, and buy any land, building or work of art they fancied. The trustees also managed to increase the annual grant to £5 million, and, after their skilfully self-publicised failures to save either the Badminton Cabinet or the *Three Graces*, the grant was raised to £12 million.

In its first decade and a half, the NHMF spent barely £1 in every £8 on the landscapes Dalton had extolled. But the post-Lottery years are proving less kind to it and its clients in the stately homes business. It ended the Conservative term of office in the spring of 1997 with its annual grant back down to £5 million and just £24 million in the bank.[37] Despite pledging that Lottery funds would always be additional to normal public expenditure, the Conservative government used the occasion of its establishment to cut the funding of the Memorial Fund by one third in the first full year.

The New Labour government is even less sympathetic to the traditional beneficiaries of the Heritage Industry. They can be expected to alter the balance of the trustees of the NHMF Memorial Fund and the Heritage Lottery Fund. New Labour also has its own clientèle in the television, recording, performing arts and film industries to satisfy. It may even nationalise the Lottery, and divert its resources into the ordinary responsibilities of the government. After all, it has already added health and education as a sixth good cause.

English Heritage, Historic Scotland and Cadw: Welsh Historic Monuments

Fortunately for the owners of great country houses, the National Lottery Fund is not their only source of public money. Thanks, oddly, to the post-war Labour government, they can claim maintenance and repair grants directly from Whitehall. This was the work of Sir Stafford Cripps, who succeeded Hugh Dalton as chancellor in 1947. Unlike his predecessor, who cared not at all for the aristocracy, Cripps was concerned at the damage heavy taxation was inflicting on country houses.

In 1948 he invited Sir Ernest Gowers to chair a committee charged with exploring 'what general arrangements might be made for the . . . preservation, maintenance and use of houses of outstanding historical or architectural interest, which might otherwise not be preserved'. The report, *Houses of Outstanding Historic or Architectural Interest*, was published in 1950. It disclosed that, because of high taxation, no individual, no matter how great his means, would have more than £5,000 a year to spend. This was less than the running costs of even a relatively small country house. Gowers proposed that beleaguered landowners be offered additional tax relief. 'Owing to the economic and social changes,' he advised, 'we are faced with a disaster comparable only to that which the country suffered by the Dissolution of the Monasteries in the sixteenth century.'[38] Despite this apocalyptic warning, tax breaks were unpalatable to an Old Labour chancellor; only one of the recommendations was implemented.

This was the foundation in 1953 of three Historic Buildings Councils, one each for England, Wales and Scotland. The councils were empowered to make grants towards preservation. A number of country house owners had good cause to be grateful. When the 20th Baron Saye & Sele inherited Broughton Castle in 1948, water was pouring through the roof in several places. The National Trust refused the house because he could offer no endowment; it survived only because the Historic Buildings Council paid for a new roof.

Today, the Councils do not merely dispense grants. Their branded trading arms – English Heritage, Historic Scotland and Cadw: Welsh Historic Monuments – make every effort to make money by attracting hordes of paying tourists to their most attractive sites. In 1997, 11 million people visited the 409 historic properties owned by English Heritage; 3 million trailed through the 330 properties owned by Historic Scotland; and Cadw welcomed over one million tourists to its 131 ancient and historic monuments. English Heritage, Historic Scotland, and Cadw are no longer merely departments of government: they are 'executive agencies', armed with their own budgets and expected to generate income as well as wait for taxpayers' money to be showered upon them.[39] Between them, the three have well over 400,000 subscription-paying members. There are shops and audio-visual displays at all the major sites, and substantial publishing arms churning out titles such as *Talkin' Roman* and *Fortress Scotland and the Jacobites*. Intellectual property, like Saxon brooches and eighteenth-century wallpaper designs, are licensed to manufacturers. Not everything has changed at English Heritage: in 1996 Chris Green, the recently appointed chief executive, resigned, allegedly unhappy with public sector bureaucracy.[40]

Despite mishaps of this kind, English Heritage, Historic Scotland and Cadw are less producer-driven than their nationalised predecessors. They are probably the most consumer friendly organisations in the government machine. They have to be: their Treasury stipends were cut as soon as Thatcher took office, encouraging them to increase their trading income or shrivel. The

TABLE 3.1
Most Popular Tourist Properties: England
Scotland and Wales, 1996

	Visitors	Admission Charge (£)
English Heritage		
Stonehenge	747,644	3.50
Dover Castle	317,502	6.00
Tintagel Castle, Cornwall	193,042	2.50
Osborne House, Isle of Wight	192,036	6.00
Kenwood House, Hampstead	157,842	Free
Cliffords Tower, York	155,846	1.60
Battle Abbey, Sussex	146,433	3.50
Carisbrooke Castle, Isle of Wight	140,943	3.80
Whitby Abbey, North Yorkshire	115,327	1.60
Kenilworth Castle	85,099	2.50
Historic Scotland		
Edinburgh Castle	1,165,132	5.50
Stirling Castle	414,187	3.50
Urquhart Castle	242,786	3.00
St Andrew's Castle	63,955	2.00
Skara Brae, Stromness	61,634	2.50
Melrose Abbey	57,951	2.50
Fort George, Ardersier	56,003	2.50
Linlithgow Palace	41,435	2.00
Dryburgh Abbey, Melrose	33,194	2.00
Caerlaverock Castle, Dumfries	32,467	2.00
Cadw: Welsh Historic Monuments		
Caernarfon Castle	260,724	3.80
Conwy Castle	173,918	3.00
Caerphilly Castle	93,036	2.20
Beaumaris Castle	91,964	1.70
Tintern Abbey	80,750	2.20
Harlech Castle	79,123	3.00
Chepstow Castle	75,663*	3.00
Castell Coch, Cardiff	68,615	2.20
Raglan Castle	55,259	2.20
Caerleon Roman Baths	47,061	1.70

Source: The English Tourist Board, *Visits to Tourist Attractions*, 1996.

* 1995 figure.

reinvention of the Historic Buildings Councils as branded businesses was largely the work of Lord Montagu of Beaulieu, first chairman of English Heritage, who brought to the new organisation the flair for salesmanship he had used to re-launch his own stately pile. The number of visitors to fee-paying sites has increased from half a million when he took over to nine million today. Income from membership subscriptions rose from zero to £1.9 million by the time he left in 1992, and now stands at nearly £4 million a year. The membership roll totals 374,000, and English Heritage hopes to raise it to 750,000 by the end of the decade. Montagu also altered the balance of the property portfolio, shifting the emphasis from dull ruins to historic houses and castles.

English Heritage acquired Stokesay Castle in Shropshire, a thirteenth-century manor house, and Brodsworth in Yorkshire, described as 'a Victorian time capsule'. Three London properties – Kenwood House in Hampstead, the Ranger's House in Greenwich, and Marble Hill House in Richmond – were inherited from the Greater London Council in 1984, and are marketed relentlessly as a suitable backdrop for private and public functions. But Stonehenge remains far and away the most popular heritage site of any, and it is a measure of the new ethos at English Heritage that, despite the sensitivity of the site, it has not shrunk from seeking to accommodate the tourists. The agency has battled for years with the Ministries of Defence and Transport, and the National Trust, to create facilities worthy of the numbers by diverting the A303, building a proper visitors' centre and providing a decent car park. At one stage, the plans included an underground monorail from the visitors' centre to a sunken 'observation and interpretation centre' at the stones. This was too much for the government, but it has agreed to restore its primitive beauty by diverting the A303 into a tunnel. It will also fund the purchase of the surrounding land from local farmers, who have a habit of ploughing up the 450 monuments which surround the main site. A private consortium is building a visitor centre 2½ miles away, served by a free park-and-ride shuttle.

These ambitious plans were hatched not by Montagu but by Jocelyn Stevens, who succeeded as chairman in 1992. It was the year a House of Commons select committee described Stonehenge as a 'national disgrace' and the National Audit Office report condemned English Heritage for poor record-keeping, inadequate control of costs, and a huge backlog of maintenance work.[41] (Harry Orde-Powlett found he could complete repairs to his family seat of Bolton Castle at one fifth of the price quoted by English Heritage.[42]) Its mismanagement of the records of listed buildings had by then become a major public embarrassment. It is not surprising that the appointment of Stevens – the former owner–manager of *Queen* magazine, founder of Radio Caroline and managing director of Express Newspapers – was read at the time as a sign that the transformation of English Heritage from government department into businesslike agency had some way to go. Six months after taking office, he issued a twenty-point, five-year plan which envisaged English Heritage shedding responsibility for half its properties to local authorities and the National Trust, firing one in nine of its staff, and privatising the work of its 380 heritage craftsmen as 'uncompetitive'.

His plan succeeded in antagonising local government and trade union lobbies as well as the high priests of the Heritage Industry. It confirmed their belief that the Conservative government was irredeemably philistine as well as a Hammer of the Workers. A trade union leader complained, as the direct labour force was privatised, that 'the job of re-pointing Hadrian's Wall cannot be given to a bricklayer used to a three-bedroom semi.' (Even the lesser figures in the Heritage Industry have their snobberies.) Stevens seems to enjoy pricking the pretensions of the cognoscenti. In 1996 the Friends of Kenwood House called for his resignation after he dismissed their plea for the restoration of a full-time curator as an idea typical of people with 'too much spare time'.[43] By then, the five-year plan was too well advanced for even the Friends of Kenwood to halt it.

Of the 409 properties owned by English Heritage, 127 are now managed by someone else, usually a local authority or the National Trust. The number of employees at English Heritage has shrunk by five hundred. The regular jousts and open-air concerts at their properties are peppered with corporate logos and, at one stage, Stevens pondered whether to surround the Albert Memorial with hoardings. The major sites which English Heritage has retained are buzzing with lively museums, shops and tea-rooms, and the earning capacity of the organisation has more than doubled to over £20 million.[44] Neither Historic Scotland nor Cadw has experienced such rumbustious management, or as great a switch to commercial values, but their managers speak without embarrassment of 'key performance targets', 'efficiency gains' and 'income per visitor'. The heritage agencies, like every other kind of organisation in Britain today, want to be businesslike.

Heritage as Business: The National Trust

The National Trust has taken commercialism further. A visitor to any of its properties will see that it has 'branded' itself in much the same way as Marks & Spencer or McDonalds.[45] It now has over 2.5 million paying members, larger than the Transport and General Workers' Union in its heyday, and far larger than any political party. The members subscribe nearly £50 million a year, and admission fees of non-members are worth £8.5 million. Rental and property income, mainly from tenant farmers, produced over £19 million in 1996–7. National Trust Enterprises, the limited company which manages the commercial activities, was set up as long ago as 1973, and now turns over nearly £50 million a year, generating an income of around £12 million from over 200 shops, 130 tea rooms and restaurants, 220 holiday lets, and a variety of publishing, advertising and corporate sponsorship activities. Corporate donations have risen from a mere £37,000 in the early 1980s to £1.5 million today. In 1996–7 alone, 57 companies gave money to the National Trust. They included Esso, which sponsored tree-planting schemes and provided Land Rovers; Barclays Bank, which produced £500,000 from its Countryfocus promotion; RoyalSun Alliance, which gave £700,000 to the restoration of Croome Park in Worcestershire; and the Rover Group, which furnished the prizes for the annual £1 million National Trust Raffle.[46]

The National Trust is always happy to make its properties available for promotions, conferences and receptions for companies which make a judicious donation. Exceptionally generous corporate donors can expect the periodic use of a flat in some historic properties. In March 1987, for example, H. J. Heinz spent £70,000 on sixty-five acres at Cape Cornwall, which it then presented to the Trust.[47] Its executives received modest favours in return. While it abjures gaudy 'events' at its properties, theatre, opera, classical music and jazz concerts are an increasingly common feature of the night-life at the Trust's country houses. 'We take pride in our independence of government,' says Dudley Fishburn, a former Conservative MP who now chairs the finance committee. 'Like any private sector organisation, we must pay our way and not depend on the taxpayer.'[48]

This is a curious claim, though the National Trust never tires of making it. As soon as the Historic Buildings Councils were set up in 1953, the Trust applied eagerly for grants. (The £40,000 it got to refurbish Claydon was the biggest grant the Councils made in their first ten years.)[49] In the 1970s and early 1980s, when money was exceptionally tight, it did not hesitate to hire government-subsidised youth trainees as a form of cheap labour. (Projects costing a total of £11 million cost the Trust only £1.4 million.)[50] In an extraordinary year, like 1985, it can expect to receive a special allocation in the budget. But even in an ordinary year, like 1996–7, it collected £17.9 million from a variety of public sector bodies, ranging from the Heritage Lottery Fund and English Heritage, through the Ministry of Agriculture, to European Structural Funds, County Councils and the Forestry Commission. In the previous year, it collected £16.8 million.

More importantly, it enjoys all the tax privileges of charitable status on a lavish scale. It is now the largest and most successful charity in Britain; relegating Oxfam to second place in 1990.[51] It pays no tax on its income, however earned. Tax-advantaged legacies are now of such importance – producing £27 million in 1996–7, or one sixth of total income – that members are being invited to special 'Legacy Days', where they are told what the Inland Revenue can do to enhance the value of their contributions. Far from being independent of the state, at least one third of the Trust's total income is either subsidised by the taxpayers or comes from them directly. Yet when the government pondered revising tax breaks for charities in 1993, the National Trust was outraged by the idea that it should lose any privileges. 'It doesn't apply to us,' said a spokesman. 'It's inconceivable that it should; it's inconceivable that the government should even dare to ask the question. We have nothing to do with government.'[52]

The businesslike nature of the Heritage Industry can be exaggerated. At the National Trust for Scotland, membership is in decline, and its trading income is less than £1 million a year. More than £1 in every £5 comes from the taxpayer; tax-subsidised legacies are its third biggest source of income; and the financing of acquisitions has depended entirely on the generosity of the Heritage Lottery Fund.[53] The state heritage agencies are no more successful: English Heritage, Historic Scotland and Cadw get less than one third of their keep from the consumer. But they have retained important public policy responsibilities, as well as the duty to own or manage historic buildings and ancient monuments. Where necessary, they are empowered to send owners a large cheque; the National Trust is one of the largest clients of English Heritage and Cadw.

None of this stops critics complaining that the commercialisation of the Heritage Industry has gone too far. Just as William Morris lamented destructive renovation, there are now complaints about ersatz history, architectural pastiche and lifeless museumisation. Magnus Linklater has claimed that the Heritage Industry is robbing the public of the duty to use their imaginations, and turning reverence for the past into parody:

> The curse of old buildings is not benign neglect but malign attention. All over Britain, historic houses have suffered in the name of 'restoration', and the pursuit of authenticity – linked to the search for ever more visitors – has resulted in some awful examples: waxwork parlourmaids parodying the idea of a 'genuine' 19th century kitchen; piped harpischord music inviting you to 'experience' the elegance of a ducal drawing room; a 'water garden' or maze installed where none was ever meant to be; plastic chickens and farmyard smells at Robert Burns's cottage in Ayrshire. The National Trust calls this kind of thing a 'cultural sheep-dip': plunge the visitor into it and he comes up gasping for air, wondering what he's been through ... Observe the dead eyes of a

Japanese tourist clamped in earphones, stumbling from computer screen to virtual-reality display in some historic time-capsule and you begin to appreciate how far this 'fakelore' has gone and how far it trivialises our history . . . Once the greatest problem of protecting our heritage was a lack of funds as the owners struggled with near bankruptcy and leaking roofs. Now the enemy is too much money spent on the wrong things.[54]

The Trust has faced criticism of this kind for decades. As early as 1955, the Duke of Bedford withdrew his agreement to give Woburn Abbey to the National Trust after seeing how it had mummified Petworth House and Uppark.[55] In 1994 an American journalist, Paula Weideger, devoted an entire book to lambasting the Trust for its lack of authenticity.[56] The painstaking rehabilitation of Uppark after the disastrous fire of 1989 – the Trust went to the extent of using lime-and-horsehair plaster and lead-based white paint mixed to age approximately – certainly verged on the parodic.

Yet leaving houses like Chastleton House and Calke Abbey trapped in a timewarp is almost as bogus. Massingberd has pointed out that the National Trust has achieved 'art-historical museumisation'. In their heyday, the great country houses were not art and furniture galleries but living organisms, integrated with the surrounding countryside and its inhabitants. Ironically, visitors to National Trust properties are often grateful to find the family is still living in the house, though the families may find the experience less congenial. Lord and Lady St Levan, who stayed as tenants at St Michael's Mount after giving the castle to the Trust in 1954, have to put up with over 200,000 visitors a year. 'There is absolutely no check on numbers,' claimed Lord St Levan as early as 1981. 'Everyone, including visitors from abroad, can become members and visit every property as of right.'[57] In September 1990 Andrew Lyle, who leased Barrington Court from the National Trust, decided to stop people viewing the gardens because so many members got in free.[58] The following year he decided to surrender the lease.

In 1988 the Earl of Belmore moved out of Castle Coole near Enniskillen, where he had lived rent-free since it was acquired by the Trust in 1951, because he was so horrified by the results of a five-year restoration programme. 'They have done the equivalent of sending an elegant lady to California for a face job,' he fumed. 'They are interested only in historical and architectural purity, and are ignoring what the family actually did with their possessions. That is what makes most great country houses so special. People don't want to feel it has been arranged by an interior decorator.' His description of one room as being 'germolene pink' achieved wide currency.[59]

Lord Scarsdale objected to the removal of the furniture from Robert Adam's state rooms at Kedleston Hall on similar grounds.[60] But owners are reluctant to recognise their good fortune. Scarsdale still lives in relative luxury in one wing. In 1981 Lord St Oswald was displeased to be asked to move out of Nostell Priory because the Trust wanted to close an unprofitable house, yet they had earlier agreed to pay for a staff of eleven and cover some of his insurance costs.[61] 'It is a tragedy that more families do not stay on, not just to live in luxury, but actively to manage the property,' says the present Lord Saye & Sele, who still owns and runs the family seat at Broughton Castle. 'Generally, they could do it cheaper than the National Trust, and with a greater sense of commitment.'[62]

It is undoubtedly true that many landowners did too readily give up the struggle to maintain the family seat. In the 1980s, some, especially those who had reached agreements with the Trust when the tax régime was more punishing, thought they could afford to maintain their family seats once again. This confidence was sometimes misplaced – the Clive-Ponsonby-Fanes bought back Brympton d'Evercy from the school which owned it, but had to sell it again a few years later. However, Lord Camoys succeeded in buying back the family seat of Stonor in Oxfordshire after his father had put it on the market, but then he has enjoyed a successful business career.

Few families could maintain a great country house without *any* support from the taxpayer. Massingberd advocated listing families as well as their houses, along the lines of the 'living national treasures' venerated by the Japanese and *Country Life* magazine.[63] It would certainly be easier on the public purse to subsidise people rather than bricks and mortar (and green fields), and more suitable to give tax breaks to owners rather than charities like the National Trust. This is as true of the owners of great country houses as of the proud householders of Acacia Avenue or the denizens of Cold Comfort Farm.

But it is always hard to re-visit what has happened. The Trust is unable to sell important assets, even to their original owners, whether or not a sale made good economic sense. This is because properties were always given on the understanding that the gift was inalienable. Sir Francis Dashwood, whose father gave West Wycombe to the Trust in 1944, had his offer to buy back the house refused in the mid-1980s.[64] A similar request from Henry Strickland, who wanted to buy back the family seat of Sizergh Castle in Cumberland, was refused, again on the grounds of inalienability.[65]

The right to declare land and buildings inalienable is written into the National Trust Act of 1907. They cannot be sold, mortgaged or even compulsorily purchased by the state without parliamentary approval. (The similarity of this stipulation to the medieval practice of mortmain would surely have pleased John Ruskin and William Morris.)* Inalienability is helpful in the sense that it encourages people to give land, houses and other treasured possessions to the Trust, confident that they will not be sold, broken up or destroyed. But if the success of the National Trust is attributable to inalienability, so are many of its problems. 'In trying to preserve things for ever, you discover that what would be an asset in the ordinary commercial world cannot be sold,' admitted the finance director in 1989. 'In financial terms it becomes a liability.'

A glance at the balance sheet of the National Trust shows an organisation which has land and buildings worth just under £17 million.[66] It owns 603,265 acres, 164 historic houses, 19 castles, 47 industrial monuments and mills, 49 churches and chapels, 9 pre-historic and Roman properties, 13 farm buildings, 114 other historic buildings, 160 gardens, 73 landscape and deer parks and tens of thousands of valuable paintings and objets d'art.[67] The Trust does not even put a value on its buildings, though they are insured for £3.4 billion. Land, buildings, furniture and works of art which cannot be sold or mortgaged are not assets in the conventional sense. Even its genuine assets are inflexible: £4 in every £5 of its £500 million of cash and securities is restricted to particular causes or properties.[68] Funds cannot be transferred from well-endowed properties to those in need of support, which greatly complicates running a scattered estate devoid of economic or geographical coherence. This is bound to make the National Trust a less effective custodian of the National Heritage than a private landowner would be.

Even those who accept this fact believe there is no alternative. The sheer size and success of the National Trust has inhibited alternatives to private ownership, but some are now becoming visible. Kit Martin has made a career from converting stately homes into separate houses or flats. The Landmark Trust rescues, restores and conserves historic buildings by letting them for self-catering holidays. Founded by Sir John Smith and his wife in 1965, it now owns or leases 166 properties, ranging from Lundy Island to The Pineapple at Dunmore. Most of the money to buy properties comes from the Manifold Trust, which Sir John set up in 1963 with a loan of £8,000 to buy properties for commercial letting. It now has an income of over £1 million a year, and the Landmark Trust over £3 million.[69] Sir John is admittedly a wealthy man, but his ingenuity is undeniable, and not unique.

Ernest, the grandson of Thomas Cook, was another wealthy man who showed what could be achieved without the National Trust. He used his

---

* There is also a parallel with the early modern aristocratic device of Strict Settlement, best summarised in the motto of the Curzon family, whose seat at Kedleston in Derbyshire the Trust now owns: 'Let Curzon Holde what Curzon Helde'. See also Chapter 2, p. 78.

estates to endow a grant-making charitable trust which dispenses funds to various countryside and environmental projects.* Cook had earlier used his fortune to buy country houses and estates and give them to the National Trust, and established his own charity only after the Trust refused to declare the whole of his estate at Bradenham inalienable, on the grounds that much of it was of insufficient quality. 'Relations became strained,' as the official history of the Trust puts it. 'In 1951 Cook cancelled his proposed gifts except for those he was covenanted to assign, and announced his intention to found a separate charitable trust bearing his own name.'[70]

The Perils of Public Ownership

The strength of the National Trust lies in its impertubability, not its imagination. This is why it shares with the clearing banks the frequent but unfortunate distinction of being mistaken for a nationalised industry: it was once described as a quintessentially English way of nationalising the land. Inalienability gives the joke palpable force. 'For everyone for ever', as the centenary slogan had it. Though inalienability is not as immovable as its managers like to pretend – plenty of its properties are leased and it often sells land, especially to create endowment funds for properties – the National Trust is in many ways worse than a nationalised industry.† This is because it is rich in assets but perpetually short of income. As a result, it is forced continually to cede its autonomy in exchange for money.

The Trust has to insist that all substantial gifts are adequately endowed, tying most of its funds to particular places or buildings. It can rely to some extent on periodic public appeals and there are two permanent appeals – Enterprise Neptune and the Lake District Landscape Fund – which aim to acquire coastal sites and scenic parts of the Lake District. However, these too are tied to particular causes or places. For much of the rest of its income, it is dependent on the indulgence of the Inland Revenue and other state bodies. It earns barely £1 in every £10 in the marketplace, the only source where no favours are extracted. Above all, it has become over-reliant on retaining the loyalty of a mass membership. Given that they account for two fifths of its ordinary income, it is not surprising that some of the 2.5 million

---

* They cover about 17,000 acres in Gloucestershire, Buckinghamshire and Dorset, mostly of let farm land but also woodland and let properties.
† It is ironic that the National Trust should be discovering the value of leasehold just as Parliament is phasing it out on the great estates. 'I have no objections to using other people's money to achieve our aims,' the National Trust chief agent told the *Sunday Telegraph* (6 February 1994). For the enfranchisement of leaseholders, see Chapter 2, p. 81.

members think the National Trust belongs to them rather than to posterity.

Mass membership was not one of its original aims. It did not pass 1,000 until 1926, or 100,000 until 1960. No systematic campaign to recruit members was attempted until 1969, when the National Trust appointed its first director of public relations. 'You must realise', he was told by one old hand when he arrived at the office, 'that the Trust has nothing to do with people.'[71] Today, it has everything to do with people. Most members have a view on every subject, and many have awkward views on one subject. In the 1960s and 1970s, at the very time when the membership was starting to burgeon, they embarrassed the council of the Trust a number of times over the culling of seals on the Farne islands.[72]

In the early 1980s, a small but highly organised group of members protested against a decision to lease land at Bradenham to the Ministry of Defence, which used the site to build a nuclear bunker. The Trust countered that it would have faced a compulsory purchase order anyway, and that leasing the land would enable it to manage the development. But arguments of that kind carried no weight when the Campaign for Nuclear Disarmament was enjoying one of its periodic surges in popularity. An Extraordinary General Meeting was convened at the Wembley Conference Centre in November 1982 to debate the issue, at enormous cost to the Trust. Although management won the vote comfortably and won again in court, where they were taken by the Liberal peer Lord Beaumont for breaching their obligations on inalienability, the row was the first serious attempt by a significant minority of the membership to take control. The implications were not lost on other members, or on the leadership.

'The hijacking by special interest groups of institutions set up for entirely different purposes is a real danger,' admitted Dame Jennifer Jenkins (wife of Roy) in 1994. As chairman of the Trust between 1986 and 1990, it had fallen to her to deal with the re-emergence of an issue which has split the membership since the 1930s: hunting. Hunting was then allowed on about one acre in seven owned by the National Trust. In all, about thirty hunts crossed its territory, their rights in some cases enforced by covenants when the land was given.[73] The same members who championed the rights of donors at Bradenham were naturally happy to override them on the question of hunting, and a motion was put forward at the 1988 annual general meeting to ban all fox, stag and hare hunting on National Trust property. The decision eventually went against the anti-hunting lobby, but the motion attracted enough support to persuade the Trust to start issuing 'licences' to hunt.

This encouraged the antis to re-launch the motion two years later in the hope of further concessions, and the motion to ban stag-hunting was narrowly carried.[74] Only one in fourteen members had bothered to vote, but the antis were outraged to discover that Dame Jennifer had used her 50,000 proxy votes to save fox-hunting and hare-coursing.[75] Her action persuaded several militants to stand for election to the council at the 1991 meeting (an unprecedented act of defiance) on the issue of the abuse of proxy votes by the chairman. They were not elected, but the Trust decided to play for time. The ban on stag-hunting was referred to a working party, charged with deciding whether it was cruel or not.

It reported two years later that hunting did indeed cause suffering, and hunting with stag hounds was banned from April 1997, putting an end to the Quantock Staghounds in north Somerset, who hunted exclusively on National Trust property. Even if the working party had contrived to report that stags enjoy being hunted to death, the Trust would still have had to ban it, because it was losing tens of thousands of members and potential members over the issue, if not as many as the anti-hunt lobby liked to pretend. Similar protests against tree-felling and road-building, and in favour of organic farming, are now a routine feature of life, but there is no clearer instance of the influence the membership now exerts over policies than its decisive switch in acquisition policy during the 1990s – from large country houses and estates to what is now known as 'open space'.

The Battle for the Commons

In the 1980s the National Trust was criticised heavily on the left of British politics for its eagerness to buy grand houses rather than protect the environment. David Clark, who was chairman of the Open Spaces Society in the mid-1980s, contrasted the eagerness with which the Trust had saved Kedleston Hall with its refusal of a stretch of coastline offered by South Tyneside Council, on the grounds that it was under-endowed. 'It is obsessed with buying grand houses at the expense of protecting the countryside, though its membership's priorities are precisely the opposite,' Clark wrote in 1986. 'It is unhealthily biased towards the areas favoured by the southern middle classes. And it concentrates far too much effort on . . . maintaining the homes of excessively rich people in exchange for them granting the public the privilege of viewing a few days a week. It had strayed a long way from its original purpose.'[76]

This was fair criticism. The three founders of the National Trust were closely associated with the Commons Preservation Society, the precursor of the Open Spaces Society, and the establishment of the National Trust was delayed by a fear that the activities of the two bodies would overlap. The first chairman of the National Trust, Sir Robert Hunter, was honorary solicitor to the Commons Preservation Society, and as early as 1884 he had recommended the formation of a company to buy and hold land and buildings on behalf of the public, to protect them from spoliation.[77] Octavia Hill (1838–1912), the most famous of the Trust's three founders, was also a prominent member of the Commons Preservation Society. The third, Canon Hardwicke Rawnsley (1851–1920), was a Cumberland parson who fought the encroachment of the railways in the Lake District, where the intellectual fathers of the Heritage Industry, Wordsworth and Ruskin, patented the idea that beauty belongs to Everyman.

It is not surprising that the National Trust's earliest concern for Places of Historic Interest or Natural Beauty was to preserve land for the people rather than houses for the aristocracy.* This was precisely the agenda of the Commons Preservation Society, founded in 1865 to save several London commons then under threat of enclosure and development: Putney Heath, Wimbledon and Wandsworth Commons, Epping Forest and Hampstead Heath. Its moving spirit was George Shaw Lefevre, a Liberal MP of the old school who secured the passage of the Metropolitan Commons Act of 1866. This legislation, which outlawed the enclosure of Commons within a fifteen-mile radius of Charing Cross, was later extended to the rest of the country by the Commons Preservation Act of 1876.

Today, the battle to save the medieval commons is portrayed by the Open Spaces Society and the Ramblers Association as a defence of communal property against the demands of rapacious landlords. This is propaganda. Common land is not owned in common, or even by the common people. Just like any piece of land, commons have always belonged to someone. They were different from other pieces of land only in the sense that rights of ownership were conditional on respect for the rights of others. Others had the right to use the commons to graze sheep or cattle, fell timber, cut turf, catch fish, dig stones, pick berries or nuts, and so on.† 'In practice,' as Matt Ridley has pointed out,

> . . . an English medieval common was a complex spider's web of jealously guarded property rights held under the supposedly benevolent umbrella of the lord of the manor . . . As the manorial system broke down, commons came in effect to be owned jointly by those who possessed these rights in common, rights . . . extinguished, converted or trampled upon in the process known as enclosure. But commons were never free-for-alls

* Though its inaugural meeting in July 1894 took place, ironically, at the London home of the Duke of Westminster. Robin Fedden, *The National Trust*.
† Rights of pannage – the right to graze pigs on beech mast and acorns – are still exerted in the New Forest, and the grazing of sheep on the Pennine moors is governed by 'stints' designed to prevent overgrazing by limiting the number each shepherd can add to the flock.

... The old pre-enclosure English common as a genuinely egalitarian place open to all is a nostalgic myth.[78]

But it was exactly the kind of myth likely to appeal to John Ruskin and William Morris. Commons were a remnant of the Middle Ages, a symbol of the mythical reciprocity between landlord and tenant threatened by an encroaching industrial civilisation. It was bound to appeal to Octavia Hill too; she not only suffered from an unrequited love for Ruskin (she was later a lesbian) but was concerned throughout her life to alleviate the abominable housing conditions of the urban poor. She attributed much of their misery and degradation to a lack of access to the fresh air and flowers of the countryside.

By the second half of the nineteenth century, the commons were the principal means of access to fresh air for the residents of the great Victorian cities. But the easy profits to be made from rising urban land values tempted many owners of common land to sell or redevelop them for profit. The lowly townsmen of Wandsworth had successfully resisted a plan to enclose their common as early as the mid-eighteenth century, and the residents of Hampstead fought a series of battles throughout the nineteenth century with the owner of the heath, Thomas Maryon Wilson, and his plans to extract gravel and build houses on the greensward.

The friends of the commons failed more often than they succeeded. As the economy industrialised between 1750 and 1850, over two million acres

TABLE 3.2
Common Land in England and Wales

	Number of Commons	Area (Acres)
Northern England	851	375,600
North-west	275	25,452
Yorkshire & Humberside	859	227,831
Midlands	813	29,405
Eastern England	844	19,027
South-east	2,238	75,120
South-west	1,172	158,394
Wales	1,593	467,028
	8,645	1,377,857

Source: Countryside Commission; Welsh Office.

of common land were enclosed for ploughing, added to nearby farms, or built on through private Acts of Parliament.[79] As the industrial towns grew, another half million acres were enclosed between 1845 and 1865. Legislation obliging owners to prove the case for enclosure, and to set aside space for recreation and allotments, was ineffective. When a man and his two sons were jailed for two months for cutting timber in Epping Forest, and Earl Spencer tried to sell one third of Wimbledon Common and Putney Heath for development, the Commons Preservation Society began a series of lengthy battles to preserve them for the public. They also fought a four-year legal battle with Earl Spencer, which ended in 1876 with the surrender of Wimbledon Common to a Board of Conservators. (Spencer was compensated with an annuity of £1,200, and finally gained a lump sum of £22,500 in 1958).[80] But the society used force if the law failed. At Berkhamsted Common, where Lord Brownlow fenced off 430 acres of common land, they sent 120 navvies by special train to tear down the fences in the middle of the night.[81]

Though nearly 1.5 million acres of common land now survive, the battle to 'save the commons' still arouses a degree of militancy. There was outrage in 1976 when the Central Electricity Generating Board was allowed to build a nuclear power station on common land at Dee Marsh in north Wales.[82] Plynlimon Common, also in Wales, became another *cause célèbre* when the Crown Estate chose to commemorate the wedding of the Prince and Princess of Wales by fencing off four square miles of common land and planting it with conifers.[83] In 1993 the government was forced to scrap a plan to drive a motorway through Oxleas Wood in south-east London.[84]

In some cases, commoners agree to development. In others, private landlords buy out their rights and seek 'de-registration' as a common. Ironically, the 1965 Commons Registration Act, under which a central register of commons was drawn up for the first time, has facilitated enclosure and development of common land by providing landlords with the option of 'de-registration'.* Landlords have also managed to circumvent common land protected from development in law by selling the lordship of the manor, so separating rights of ownership from the obligation to keep the common uncultivated and open to the public.[85] This device is especially popular with the owners of grouse moors, who argue that they cannot afford to expose their investment in game birds to ramblers or poachers.

The overwhelmingly private ownership of common land has made it a

---

* A royal commission, invited in 1955 to investigate rural commons, recommended that a central register be drawn up, the remaining commons be preserved in perpetuity and the public be granted a general right of access. The 1965 Act implemented only the first of these recommendations.

natural cockpit of confrontation between landlords and the Open Spaces Society and Ramblers' Association, but both these bodies have now moved far beyond the battle for the commons. They are seeking a general Right to Roam across all privately owned land.* 'I am today putting the path-blocking, anti-access, criminal, land-owning community on notice,' announced the newly elected chairman of the Ramblers' Association, Kate Ashbrook, in 1995. 'The time has now passed when they can get away with excluding the public from huge tracts of the countryside. We are fed up with being kept out of our own backyards.'[86] Under the last Conservative government, the association persuaded the Countryside Commission to ensure that all 120,000 miles of public footpaths and bridleways were open and properly signposted.†

Militant Ramblers nursed a justifiable expectation that the New Labour government would give them a statutory Right to Roam across open mountain and moorland as well as common land. When thousands of walkers trespassed on hills and moors to demand the Right to Roam on Sunday 24 September 1995, a group crossing the Brontë Moors at Haworth was addressed by the shadow Environment Secretary, Frank Dobson. 'The next Labour government', he pledged, 'will make the right to roam a legal reality.'[87] But after the Countryside March in London on 1 March 1998, the government decided to stick with the policy of threatening landowners with legislation unless they agree to open their land voluntarily. Old Labour may yet have its way. In November 1998 over 200 MPs backed a parliamentary motion calling for a general right to roam.

The National Trust: Betraying the Vision of Its Founders?

The Right to Roam marks the return of the Heritage Industry to its roots. It was nature, not stately homes and old masters, which was its first captive. The pastoral ideal, with its connotations of innocence lost, has deep roots in English art and literature and assumed a political reality at the time of the migration to the towns in the late eighteenth and early nineteenth centuries which it has never lost. 'Almost every Englishman,' wrote Kenneth Clark in 1949, 'if asked what he meant by "beauty", would begin to describe a land-

---

* The Law of Property Act of 1925 gave the public right of access to urban but not rural commons. In rural areas only commoners have the right to use common land and others have access by invitation only. Privately owned commons are under no obligation to admit the public. The Department of the Environment estimated ten years ago that the public had the legal right to roam over only one fifth of common land, and were liable to prosecution for trespassing on the rest.
† This was offset by tougher laws against trespass to deter hunt saboteurs, rave enthusiasts and New Age travellers from camping on private property.

scape – perhaps a lake and mountain, perhaps a cottage garden, perhaps a wood with bluebells and silver birches, perhaps a little harbour with red sails and white-washed cottages; but at all events a landscape.'[88] The medievalism of John Ruskin and William Morris stemmed directly from their rejection of urban and industrial civilisation: the Commons Preservation Society was founded to resist its encroachment on the green fields of England.

The National Trust is now synonymous with country houses, but throughout the first half century of its existence it was almost wholly devoted to the defence of landscape. It was not drawn into the rescue of country houses until the 1930s, and not on a large scale until the 1950s. Its full title – the National Trust for Places of Historic Interest or Natural Beauty – describes exactly the main interests of its founders. The first donation it received was Dinas Oleu, a four-and-a-half-acre stretch of headland overlooking Cardigan Bay near Barmouth, donated by Fanny Talbot, an acquaintance of Ruskin and Hardwicke Rawnsley.[89] Other early donations were all of land. The first property purchased by the National Trust, in 1902, was Brandelhow Woods, bought to guarantee public access to the shore of Derwentwater.

The current control by the Trust of more than one fifth of Cumberland stems from the early efforts of Rawnsley to halt its spoliation by the railways.* It was a landscape romanticised by Wordsworth, the inventor of the pointless country walk, who composed 'I wandered lonely as a cloud' after a perambulation along the shoreline of Ullswater. Prefiguring the hostility to private property, he had described the Lake District as 'a sort of national property, in which every man has a right and interest who has an eye to perceive and a heart to enjoy'. Grange Fell on Derwentwater, Gowbarrow Park on Ullswater, Queen Adelaide's Hill on Windermere and Borrans Field on Ambleside were all acquired by the National Trust before the First World War. Scafell Pike and Castle Cray on Derwentwater were given to the Trust in memory of the dead of that war. These holdings were augmented in 1944 by gifts of land from Beatrix Potter, whose association with the area has encouraged the British Tourist Authority to name it 'Peter Rabbit Country'. Almost all the central fell area and major valley heads are now owned by the Trust, as are six of the main lakes and most of their shorelines. Fittingly, Ruskin (who built himself a house at Brantwood, on Coniston) and Rawnsley are commemorated at Friar's Crag on the north shore of Derwentwater.

The roots of the National Trust are embedded in landscape of this kind. As late as 1934 it still owned only two country houses – Barrington Court and Montacute, both in Somerset – and by the end of the Second World War this

* Ironically, disused railway lines and bridges in Cumberland are now venerated as an integral part of the landscape. See Chapter 11, p. 406.

had risen to just seventeen. Today, it owns 164 historic houses, and would own more if dozens of impoverished aristocrats had not failed to raise an endowment fund to accompany the transfer.[90] To be fair, the Trust has never actually bought a stately home. Rather, owners were driven by punitive taxation to give their houses, and the Trust was compelled to accept them by a series of tax reliefs from governments embarrassed at the effects of their handiwork.[91] Tax changes enabled the National Trust to take on the houses it did by allowing the owners to remain as tenants after transferring the family seat.

The Country House Scheme, as it became known, was largely the work of the 11th Marquess of Lothian, who had inherited four houses, of which he gave away three. He offered Blickling Hall in Norfolk to the National Trust, with an endowment of 4,500 acres, provided he could remain as a tenant until his death. But then he encountered an obstacle: the National Trust was not legally empowered to accept land or other gifts as an endowment.[92] Unabashed, Lothian campaigned successfully for legislation to enable the Trust to accept land and houses without paying death duties, even if owners stayed on as tenants.[93] These changes, completed in 1937, precipitated a flood of donations, and a special Country House Committee had to be set up in 1936 to filter applications.

The results of Lothian's work are in some ways ironic. 'Nothing is more melancholy', he told the National Trust annual general meeting in 1934, where he launched the Country House Scheme, 'than to visit these ancient houses after they have been turned into public museums, swept, garnished, dead, lifeless shells, containing no children's voices, none of the hopes and sorrows of family life, no procession of guests meeting to discuss politics or economics, literature or art, or the varied problems of contemporary life.'[94] Which is sadly what visitors to the average Trust property experience today. There is no doubt, however, that Lothian diverted the National Trust from saving the landscape to saving country houses. Of course, it had acquired buildings from the outset, but, in keeping with the predilections of Ruskin and Morris, they tended to be exclusively medieval in character. Taking on the stately homes of the beleaguered aristocracy on an industrial scale was an entirely new departure.

Curiously, it did not become controversial until the mid-1960s. Even then, the controversy was a by-product of a personality clash between the aristocrats who had taken control of the National Trust and the director of Enterprise Neptune, the public appeal to raise money to buy stretches of coast threatened with development. Commander Conrad Rawnsley, grandson of Hardwicke Rawnsley, had more or less insisted on being appointed director when Enterprise Neptune was launched in 1963. In the estimation of the historians of the National Trust, he was not a success. They record that he fell out with his superiors, embarrassing them publicly on several occasions, and spent on administration about £1 in every £5 he raised. As relations deteriorated, he began to attack the Trust in public as 'a protégé of the old landowning class' run by 'belted earls' and 'bedevilled' by the Country House Scheme. After he parted company with the Trust in October 1967, the attacks became increasingly intemperate. He organised a Members' Movement for the Reform of the National Trust, alleging that it had become 'part of the Establishment, an inert and amorphous organisation proceeding by the sheer momentum given to it by those who continued to bequeath their wealth and property to it, as often as not to escape death duties'.[95] This had a certain force, as did his denunciations of the Trust for restricting public access to much of its land, failing to agree reasonable opening hours for its country houses, and the excessive consideration it showed to former owners at many properties.

However, Rawnsley made his claims in such intemperate terms (among other things, that the Trust was run by clique of homosexuals) that he failed to get support for change. But he did prompt a thoroughgoing reform of the management, and secured much wider and easier public access to its properties. These modest changes did not allay the suspicion that Rawnsley was right to portray the National Trust as the plaything of a clique of country-house dwellers and art-lovers. When David Clark attacked the National Trust in 1986 for betraying the vision of its founders, he was writing at a time when a Conservative government had just allocated £25 million of public money to rescue three country houses. Four years later, his successor as chairman of the Open Spaces Society, Rodney Legg, was even more outspoken:

> From being an egalitarian access organisation promoting the public good, the trust has become an élitist club of art connoisseurs, and defensive in the protection of a prize collection of dinosaurs. The Trust has evolved into a safety net for preventing the decline and fall of the English stately home. In doing so, it has saved an important element of the leisured landscape of the privileged, and more than a handful of traditional land agents, from extinction.[96]

Legg advised the National Trust to let all farmland which is not accessible to the public revert to its primeval, semi-wooded state, so that bands of rambling town-dwellers could walk across it unimpeded by cash crops, farm implements and fertilisers. The Ramblers' Association backed the call.

'I do not myself see a conflict between open spaces and buildings, large or small,' countered Dame Jennifer Jenkins, then chairman of the National

Trust. 'Both are part of our inheritance, both benefit people of all sorts.'[97] But the National Trust has become increasingly sensitive to allegations of élitism and bias towards stately homes; in 1984, it set up a Lake District Landscape Fund to purchase more of Cumberland, and in 1985 Enterprise Neptune was relaunched. In the 1990s, as the economic and fiscal pressures on country houses have abated, this change of emphasis has become more marked. In 1996–7, the Trust spent nearly five times as much on acquiring coast and countryside (£5.75 million) as it did on historic buildings and art collections (£1.25 million).[98] It will never satisfy everybody. Enterprise Neptune is criticised for concentrating on fashionable (and well-protected) landscapes in Devon and Cornwall, rather than the threatened coastline of remote County Durham. It is criticised for buying too many dramatic cliffs and not enough mud flats and marshes.[99] Groups, such as the Open Spaces Society and the Ramblers' Association, have militant members who will not be silenced until all land is taken into public ownership.

The National Parks

Most of them have read their *Small is Beautiful*, where E. F. Schumacher calls for exactly that. 'It is argued by some owners of open country', said the director of the Ramblers' Association in 1995, 'that they are morally entitled to treat walkers as trespassers because the land is their property. They lay claim to a freedom not only to decide how their land is used but also who has access to it. But land is different from all other types of property. The owners did not make the land.'[100]

The Labour Party toyed with the idea of nationalising the land in the 1930s and early 1940s, proposing a land tax in 1931 which was implemented after the Second World War. In 1929 the Council for the Preservation of Rural England (founded by the famous town planner, Patrick Abercrombie) and the National Trust persuaded the prime minister Ramsay Macdonald to appoint an inter-departmental committee to look into the possibility of establishing National Parks. Its brief was not to explore the public ownership of land but the scope for achieving the same effect through planning.[101] It was a time of increasing unease about the future of the countryside: the great aristocratic estates were being broken up; towns and cities, with their electricity pylons and ribbons of houses along arterial roads, were devouring green fields and disfiguring hills and valleys with steel girders.

Between the wars, hikers, ramblers and even motorists yearned only to take possession of the land from the dispossessed aristocratic landlords. In 1932 a mass trespass on Kinder Scout, orchestrated by the Communist Party, ended with the imprisonment of five ramblers, who became the Tolpuddle Martyrs of the rambling movement. Three years later, the Ramblers' Association was formed to campaign for public access to private property. In 1936, it joined forces with several other lobbying groups in a standing committee to press for the creation of National Parks, where owners would swap subsidies for public access. The standing committee (which still exists as an independent charity, the Council for National Parks) produced a stream of propaganda throughout the late 1930s. Chaired by the barrister Norman Birkett, it made clever use of modern techniques of persuasion such as film shows and roving exhibitions. It also drew heavily on the eloquent pen of G. M. Trevelyan, the popular historian.

Trevelyan, raised in the Victorian landowning aristocracy, was one of a number of liberal landowners who helped to invent the modern Heritage Industry. His brother, Sir Charles Trevelyan, First World War peacenik and Labour MP, gave the family estate of Wallington in Northumberland to the National Trust in 1941 because he was a 'socialist and believes it would be better if the community owned such houses and great estates'.[102] But it was G. M. Trevelyan who became chief propagandist and a generous benefactor of the campaign to save the countryside from the 'march of bricks and mortar'. In 1930 he became the first president of the newly formed Youth Hostels Association, which offered cheap overnight accommodation for the new breed of nature-seeking hikers.

Among them was Hugh Dalton, who was an energetic walker, and sometime president of the Ramblers' Association. He was also a supporter of the National Trust, whose true character he guilelessly exposed as a 'typically British example of Practical Socialism in action'. (He promised that 'a Labour government should give it every encouragement greatly to extend its activities.')[103] Dalton intended the £50 million National Land Fund, which he created in 1946, to be spent entirely on the purchase of beautiful landscapes for ramblers, and Trevelyan reported that the post-war Labour government was 'very keen on exactly the right policy'.[104]

In the National Parks and Access to the Countryside Act of 1949, the government took sweeping powers to protect large areas of countryside from unsympathetic development by designating them as National Parks. The Act drew heavily on the work of John Dower, a rambling enthusiast who worked at the Ministry of Town and Country Planning. His definition of a National Park still stands:

An extensive area of beautiful and relatively wild country in which, for the nation's benefit and by appropriate national decision and action, (a) the characteristic landscape beauty is strictly preserved, (b) access

and facilities for public open-air enjoyment are amply provided,
(c) wildlife and buildings and places of architectural and historic interest
are suitably protected, while (d) established farming use is effectively
maintained.[105]

A list of twelve proposed National Parks was drawn up by a committee chaired
by Sir Arthur Hobhouse (its members included Clough Williams-Ellis, author
of the inter-war tirade against the spoliation of the countryside, *England and
the Octopus*). With the exception of the South Downs and the Norfolk Broads,
they all became National Parks. It fell to Hugh Dalton, as Minister of Town
and Country Planning in 1950, to create the first in Snowdonia and the Lake
and Peak Districts. The South Downs has failed repeatedly to become a
National Park (most recently in 1998), but the Norfolk Broads were placed
under a new Broads Authority in 1989 which made them effectively a National
Park. The New Forest enjoys similar protection.

The Countryside Commission took over responsibility for the parks from
the National Parks Commission in 1968.[106] It is also responsible for designating
Areas of Outstanding Natural Beauty and mapping National Trails and 'Heritage Coasts'. It is funding the 'Community Forests' springing up on derelict
land at the edge of cities, and planning the new National Forest which over
a ten year period will gradually cover 194 square miles of Staffordshire, Leicestershire and Derbyshire, at a cost of £50 million. Some of the land is being
reclaimed from disused sand and gravel workings, and worked-out mines, but
much is agricultural land now being taken out of production. None of the
land is being compulsorily purchased, though local farmers are anticipating
generous subsidies for making it available. The Commission is even dictating
the appearance of the forest: it will be planted with native broad-leaf varieties
rather than the ubiquitous conifer.

The National Parks of England and Wales now cover nearly one tenth of
the two countries, and the burgeoning responsibilities of the Countryside
Commission mean that much of the rest of the country might as well be a
national park. Only Scotland has escaped having any. This is partly an accident
of history, but there was no great pressure in Scotland for public access to
the countryside in the immediate aftermath of the war. When the standing
committee was created in 1936, the Association for the Preservation of Rural
Scotland disdained to join. There is no exact Scottish equivalent of the restrictive English law of trespass, and what powers landlords do have to restrict
access to their land are severely circumscribed by the scale and nature of the
terrain. In short, people are free to ramble all over Scotland anyway. Until
the arrival of the motor car, this did not matter, because many of the most
beautiful parts were virtually inaccessible.

TABLE 3.3
Land Ownership in the National Parks

Park	The State	Conservation Bodies	Private Owners	Total	Percentage Privately Owned
Brecon Beacons	87,619	13,165	245,644	346,428	71
Dartmoor	83,413	8,938	143,466	235,817	61
Exmoor	21,548	17,038	131,022	169,608	77
Lake District	59,362	140,069	366,261	565,692	65
Northumberland	109,324	2,976	146,815	259,115	57
North Yorkshire Moors	65,852	3,372	285,624	354,848	80
Peak District	23,302	35,131	296,985	355,418	84
Pembrokeshire Coast	13,816	6,751	123,819	144,386	86
Snowdonia	153,731	47,489	413,582	614,802	67
Yorkshire Dales	3,859	11,426	421,766	437,051	97
Broads Authority	3,620	1,977	69,256	74,853	93
Total	625,446	288,332	2,644,240	3,558,018	74

Source: Council for National Parks.

That has now changed, and the Highlands are swarming with motorists, ramblers, mountaineers and snow- and water-skiing enthusiasts. Footpaths are being eroded by legions of hill-walkers, and the lochs echo to the sound of motor-boats. Environmentalists have become increasingly concerned about unsympathetic farming and forestry practices, especially overgrazing by sheep and the clearance of natural woodland to make way for conifer plantations. These pressures led to the formation in 1991 of a Scottish Council for National Parks, funded mainly by the Ramblers' Association. It has pressed for areas of the Highlands such as the Cairngorms, Loch Lomond and Ben Nevis to be designated as National Parks. It has yet to succeed.

Natural Heritage Joins the Industry

What Scotland does have is a rapidly expanding group of voluntary conservation bodies which now own over 330,000 acres of the country. Easily the biggest is the National Trust for Scotland. It is the creation not of the National Trust (which failed to establish a branch or secure donations of property north of the border) but of the same Association for the Preservation of Rural Scotland which disdained to join the committee on National Parks. It set up the National Trust for Scotland in 1931 to take ownership of a 500-acre estate at Loch Dee in the Galloway Hills, offered to the Association two years earlier. (The Association was not empowered to own property.) Ironically, the Trust never did acquire the Loch Dee estate; the first property it took on was Crookston Castle near Paisley, the gift of Sir John Stirling Maxwell of Pollok, one of the vice-presidents of the Trust.

Though dominated initially by lairds like Sir John, the National Trust for Scotland never became absorbed in saving castles and tower houses. It bought its first stretch of countryside at Glencoe in 1935, and the adjoining Royal Forest of Dalness (which includes the peaks of Bidean nam Bian and Buachaille Etive Mor) followed two years later, through the benefactions of the mountaineering enthusiast Percy Unna. Unna also financed the acquisition of the Five Sisters of Kintail in 1944 and of Ben Lawers in 1950. Today, the National Trust for Scotland cares for 120 properties, including a large number of historic houses; it also owns 187,873 acres of Scotland, and manages another 62,638 acres under conservation agreements. Only the Duke of Buccleuch owns more of the country. Together with other voluntary bodies – the Royal Society for the Protection of Birds, the Woodland Trust and the Scottish Wildlife Trust – conservationists now control nearly 2.5 per cent of Scotland.[107] But the centuries-old controversy about land ownership north of the border continues.

Just as the Duke of Sutherland was denounced for preferring sheep to men, the emergence of this new class of conservation landowners is leading to allegations that plants and animals have become more important than

TABLE 3.4

National Trust for Scotland
Most Popular Tourist Properties, 1997

	Visitors	Admission Charge
Culzean Country Park and Castle	196,949	£3.50
Glencoe Visitor Centre	149,973	£0.50
Culloden Visitor Centre	126,181	£2.60
Inverewe Garden	125,645	£3.80
Crathes Castle	121,690	£4.10

Source: National Trust for Scotland Annual Report and Accounts 1996–7, p. 24; British Tourist Authority, *Visits to Tourist Attractions*, 1996.

people in the management of the modern Highlands. Similar criticisms are being voiced south of the border, where the Royal Society for the Protection of Birds now controls over 130,000 acres of England, Wales and Northern Ireland in addition to 115,000 acres of Scotland. A host of local and county naturalist trusts (loosely organised as the charitable Wildlife Trust, the public face of the Royal Society for Nature Conservation) is in charge of another 200,000 acres. The Woodland Trust, a relatively new charity founded by an agricultural businessman, Kenneth Watkins, owns and manages 913 woods, ranging from half-acre plots to the 1,726-acre Ledmoor and Migdale forest in the Scottish Highlands. Its total holdings amount to 40,269 acres. Private conservation charities are becoming significant landowners all over Britain.

But even the sizeable assets they have accumulated are trifling by comparison with the area of wild countryside now owned or protected by the state. One of the lesser-known effects of the National Parks and Access to the Countryside Act of 1949 was the establishment of a Nature Conservancy Council to identify and protect important wildlife and landscape sites. Fifty years on, each of England (English Nature), Scotland (Scottish Natural Heritage) and Wales (Countryside Council for Wales) has its own equivalent of a Nature Conservancy Council.[108] Between them, they protect no less than 945 local or national Nature Reserves and 6,264 Sites of Special Scientific Interest (SSSIs). They cover 5.1 million acres, or nearly one tenth of Great Britain, and are expanding continually. Any location which supports an interesting form of life – mammals, insects, plants, geological features – now risks being designated a conservation area.

The brunt of this interference falls naturally on farmers, though the National Trust owns 423 SSSIs and 31 Nature Reserves, and many of the rest are on Forestry Commission or Ministry of Defence land. Most are managed by voluntary groups of palaeontologists, ornithologists, lepidopterists, naturalists and environmentalists. Between them, they have taken the Heritage Industry across its final frontier. Just as English Heritage and its Celtic equivalents are subsidising and policing villages, towns and cities into a form of architectural stagnation, and the Countryside Commission and the National Parks Authorities are doing much the same to the stone walls and hedgerows of the countryside, so English Nature, Scottish Natural Heritage and the Countryside Council for Wales are striving to ensure that no flower, grass, insect, bird, or animal ever becomes extinct in Britain again. The preservation of the 'natural heritage' is now as much a part of the Heritage Industry as the listing system or the National Parks.

Yet integration will never be complete. The modern Heritage Industry was invented by Victorian aesthetes and socialists, and given its mass appeal by an inter-war marriage of convenience between impoverished aristocrats, town planning enthusiasts, and ramblers. There is a glaring contradiction between conserving the past and giving the public access to it. Between them, the National Trust, English Heritage, Historic Scotland, Cadw and the National Trust for Scotland entertain at least seventeen million visitors in their properties every year. Floors, walls, paths, landscapes, pictures and artefacts are all suffering. The Countryside Commission estimates that there are now more than 100 million 'visitor-days' per year to the National Parks, polluting them with motor cars, litter and water sports. According to the Commission, three quarters of the British public prefers to spend its leisure in the countryside, and over half of the urban and suburban population visits 'the country' at least twelve times a year. Paths are crumbling, walks are crowded and there is increasing pressure to accommodate, feed and water the millions of tourists who traverse the Parks. In the Derbyshire and Yorkshire dales, visitors from the nearby industrial cities are so numerous that the owners have had to lay the rambling equivalent of motorways along the most popular walks.

This growing contradiction between conservation and public access is now intensified by the anthropophobic tendencies of the guardians of the natural heritage. The Scottish Council for National Parks is pressing for the creation of National Parks in Scotland not because its members are demanding access to sites but because too many people are visiting them. The chairman of the English Tourist Board has demanded an end to 'destructive tourism with down-trodden landscapes'.[109] The ramblers may want the Right to Roam, but the naturalists will not let them have it if it means broken orchids and dead butterflies. Man is not the only enemy of the natural heritage: a pond rich in insect and amphibian life silts up if it is not dredged regularly, and trout do not thrive where pike are populous. The Cairngorms Working Party planned to re-create two giant forests at Strathspey and Mar, where sheep have eaten the primeval woodland, by replacing foreign trees like larch and spruce with native species. The idea was dropped when they realised that it would mean shooting all the red deer which would otherwise eat the saplings, putting an end to the venison trade and valuable stalking fees. The first thing the National Trust for Scotland had to do after buying Mar Lodge was to cull the deer population before it ate the surrounding forest.

The true madness of the entire Heritage Industry is that it abhors change, and man as the harbinger of change, yet it must make changes to keep everything the same. It is obsessed with freeze-framing a pleasing visual landscape or a pretty town, or an interesting ecology, passing on to future generations an unaltered artefact rather than a vital organism in which people can live and work as well as stop and stare. Town and Country are now locked in a deadly embrace, in which each is crushing the spontaneity and progress of the other. Towns and cities are surrounded by Green Belts and Swampies which asphyxiate their natural lines of growth. The countryside is packed with visitors and refugees from the towns and cities whose dreams of rural bliss are rooted in its constancy and not its vitality. The Heritage Industry has encouraged them to believe that it belongs to them as well as to those who live and work in it.

They have forgotten (if they ever knew) that man is the author of the landscape and its wildlife, just as surely as he is the author of the townscape. 'Not much of England,' wrote Professor Hoskins in his great *Making of the English Landscape*, 'even in its more withdrawn, inhuman places, has escaped being altered by man in some subtle way or other, however untouched we may fancy it is at first sight. Sherwood Forest and Wicken Fen are not quite what they seem.'[110] The country which the Heritage Industry is now trying to save is the fruit not of the conflict between Man and Nature but of the long dialogue between them.

Now that one in forty buildings is listed, one acre in ten is under some kind of conservation order, and perhaps one acre in fifty is *owned* by a conservation body like the National Trust or the Royal Society for the Protection of Birds, the dialogue is in danger of becoming a monologue. Virtually no part of the built or natural heritage can now be shaped to the will of its owner without deferring to an inspector or collecting a subsidy. Britain may have escaped the nationalisation of land, but it has achieved the same objective by other means.

Nationalisation of the Arts

It is not hard to predict the consequences. They include the pauperisation of the owners of the national heritage, who find the easiest way of earning a living is to lobby the government for grants. Costs will rise, standards will fall, and prices will increase, as the Heritage industrialists are robbed of the discipline of winning favour in the marketplace rather than Whitehall. All these effects are readily apparent in an industry which was nationalised over fifty years ago: the Arts. Not one of the national opera, ballet or theatre companies operates at a profit, and all are dependent to a greater or lesser extent on infusions of cash from the taxpayer. Local and regional musical, dance and theatre groups are even more dependent on public largesse. Like the Heritage Industry, they have their own governmental sugar daddy: the Arts Council, created in 1945 as the successor to the Council for the Encouragement of Music and Arts, founded five years earlier.

Its first chairman was Maynard Keynes whose love of the arts, nurtured by Bloomsbury, bore fruit in the Arts Theatre he built in Cambridge in 1935 and blossomed in his marriage to the ballerina Lydia Lopokova. Although the council was originally envisaged as propagandist rather than patron, its establishment led ineluctably to increased public expenditure, following the continental precedent, where state subsidisation of the performing arts was part of the authoritarian tradition. Split since 1994 into three bodies – the Arts Council of England, the Scottish Arts Council, and the Arts Council of Wales – they distributed another £225.3 million in 1996–7. The beneficiaries included Spartish groups such as Women in Music and the Black Disabled Project as well as national companies – the Royal Opera House, the National Theatre and the London orchestras. Any group which can commend itself to what Jeremy Paxman calls the 'arts tsars' can expect a cheque.

Not many can: nine out of ten applications are refused. The 'tsars' see this as confirmation that the arts are under-funded, but it confirms only that subsidies attract applicants and create a paralysing culture of welfare dependency. A financial crisis is now a perennial part of the political furniture, as the arts tsars and their friends in the press display what the Treasury calls 'bleeding stumps'. When the Conservative government implemented the first-ever cut in the Arts Council budget in 1994–5, the clique made it sound as if a 1.6 per cent cut would dim the lights on every stage in Britain, never to go on again.[111] The impresario Cameron Mackintosh warned that 'the whole fabric of the British theatre is under threat from government cuts,' and that he would not have any actors, directors or lighting technicians for his (highly profitable) shows if they were not trained at the public expense.[112]

Peter Palumbo, then chairman of the Arts Council, did not speak to the Heritage secretary, Peter Brooke, for months after the cut. 'He will go down in history,' Palumbo claimed, 'as the Secretary of State who instituted the first-ever cash cut in 48 years to the Arts Council.'[113] In 1997 Palumbo's successor, Lord Gowrie, resigned a year early in protest at the failure of New Labour to restore the 'Tory cuts' and its decision to switch Lottery funding from the arts to education and health.[114] That same year Sir David Puttnam warned that 'unless government, private sponsors and arts organisations themselves tackle this issue with real determination, we will slide inexorably towards a situation in which income rather than ability becomes the deciding factor for anyone choosing a career in the arts.'[115]

Yet the cuts in 1994 followed a forty-four-year period in which public expenditure on the arts increased *twentyfold* in real terms, a much greater rate of expansion than the threefold increase in public expenditure as a whole.[116] They were also made at the very time when the National Lottery was about to start, which would inject another £100 million into the arts over the next couple of years. The arts benefit not only from the tax-breaks given to other parts of the Heritage Industry (for example, exemption for gifts to artistic foundations) but from a host of related spending by central government and local authorities in the shape of grants to arts, drama and music students and routine expenditure on libraries, museums and theatres. In 1997–8 the Department of Culture, Media and Sport *alone* had a budget of £227 million for museums and galleries, £107 million for libraries, and £196 million for the arts.

Since 1984, the government has encouraged company support through the Business Sponsorship Incentive Scheme, by which the taxpayer matches donations made by corporate sponsors. This was the brainchild of the Association for Business Sponsorship of the Arts, formed in 1976. From just £600,000 in its first year, it managed to produce over £57 million even in a recessionary year like 1991. By the mid-1990s, it was yielding over £80 million. These are sizeable sums by any standards, yet they are greeted with undisguised disdain by the beneficiaries. Arts professionals complain that business sponsorship is the worst form of patronage – short-term, and with an ulterior purpose – though some corporate sponsors have agreed to long-term contracts. Bankers and industrialists who served on the boards of opera companies and museums were patronised as philistines, an indulgence which only those who have existed for decades on state largesse could afford.

Contempt for commercial values is endemic in the arts, as it was in the nationalised industries of the 1960s and 1970s, and the consequences are the same. The quality of subsidised art is low, the cost of producing it is high, and the prices charged to consumers are excessive. Difficult as it is to gauge Great Art without the benefit of hindsight, it is hard to believe that the artistic achievements of the second half of this century will bear comparison with previous epochs. It is no coincidence that this was the period in which art was most heavily subsidised. 'Experimental' artists know that the taxpayer is the best customer for tat (with a few well-known exceptions such as Doris Saatchi). Many remember *Equivalent VIII*, a pile of bricks arranged by Carl André at the Tate Gallery in the 1970s, and know that Damien Hirst makes a living out of pickling fish, offal and dead herbivores, and rearranging pharmaceuticals in a bathroom cabinet. Many equally ingenious hoaxes have now been forgotten. They include a pile of used nappies arranged by Mary Kelly, who wittily christened her creation *Post-Partum Document*; a £10,000 ton of lavatory paper, arranged by Bernard Jacobson; and *Mneme*, a room empty of anything except steam and sound, designed by Ann Hamilton.

They were all purchased with public money. The same syndrome is apparent in the performing arts, where directors and producers know that it is easier to get a grant for an 'experimental' play than to write and produce one which earns its keep at the box office. In 1993, the year when the National Youth Orchestra had its Arts Council grant cut by £4,000, a choir of Bulgarian grandmothers was given £6,000 to sing folk songs on a Northumberland beach.[117] 'The arts,' Lord Gowrie explained, 'are by definition oppositional and untidy, and . . . talent erupts in unlikely places at inconvenient times.'[118] It would be truer to say that a Gresham's Law of the Arts is now at work, in which bad but subsidised art is driving out good but unsubsidised work. This is most obvious in the case of orchestras.

London has four independent orchestras and seven in all, if the BBC, Covent Garden and English National Opera orchestras are included. Yet the music director of the Arts Council has admitted, 'we do not have a first-rate orchestra in London.'[119] The Arts Council has tried for thirty years to reduce the number, to create one orchestra to compare with the best in Europe. In 1993 the Council commissioned a judge, Sir Leonard Hoffmann, to decide which London orchestra should have its grant cut. After concerted lobbying by all four, he recommended increasing the grant to the London Philharmonic, in the hope that it would raise its standards while the others maintained theirs.

Even the Arts Council could spot a scam when it saw one, and decided to keep the grants to all four orchestras as they were. The taxpayers are rarely as lucky. Most of the art produced in Britain today is purchased by a self-appointed clerisy of experts who effectively decide what survives and what expires. In the plastic arts, they have encouraged artists to believe that any form of self-expression is art, and that the public has to learn to appreciate it. In the performing arts, they have created a super-class of operatic and thespian Fat Cats, who do not worry about attracting an audience. They think the state should ensure that tickets are priced at sub-market levels. By the time the Royal Opera House closed in 1996 for re-building, every seat was being subsidised by the taxpayer to the tune of £28 a night.

There is no clearer example of how subsidies have inflated costs, and it became starkly obvious to a large television audience when the BBC broadcast its fly-on-the-wall documentary series, *The House*, in 1996. The programme proved what many had long suspected: the Royal Opera House was a grotesquely over-staffed collection of dilettantes and experts utterly indifferent to costs. Viewers saw histrionic conductors flounce out of rehearsals, and unionised bullies intimidating managers. The head of sales and broadcasting, was filmed giving a box office manager the sack. The opera and ballet companies contrived to hire the same designer simultaneously. *The House* was a vivid illustration of the culture which Sir Jeremy Isaacs, general director of the Royal Opera House from 1988 to 1997, had to confront in his search for economies.

Yet he was at least as effective at raising money as cutting costs. Before handing over to Genista Mcintosh in December 1996, he secured £78.5 million of lottery funding to subsidise the £214 million cost of closing and redeveloping the theatre. This was a highly controversial use of National Lottery funds – not least because few buyers of lottery tickets ever go to the opera. Yet the company seems to have believed that the taxpayer would also fund (at a cost of £28 million) a temporary home for them while the works were carried out. When this second subsidised home did not materialise, Covent Garden had to split its activities between opera at the Barbican and ballet at the Labatt's Apollo in Hammersmith. Unsurprisingly, it proved difficult to attract people to such remote and restaurant-free parts of the capital, and certainly not at full prices. Within a year of Isaac's departure, the entire board of the Royal Opera House resigned, following a damning inquiry into its managerial and financial affairs by the parliamentary select committee on Culture, Media and Sport.

Both the Royal Ballet and the Royal Opera had clocked up huge losses, precipitating a financial crisis which saw Covent Garden on the brink of insolvency twice during 1997. An expensive production of *Macbeth* was cancelled, and two wealthy benefactors (Lord Sainsbury and Vivien Duffield) had to advance an emergency loan of £2 million. Yet the Opera House did not even know a crisis was looming. The management simply did not produce the monthly financial figures which would have warned of impending disaster. 'Decisions are often taken about performance without financial accountability,' admitted Mary Allen, the second chief executive to be appointed, after Genista McIntosh resigned unexpectedly. 'We don't want to put money first and art second, but we need to integrate the two.'[120]

Mary Allen left shortly afterwards, along with the rest of the management. Culture secretary Chris Smith asked Sir Richard Eyre, formerly artistic director at the National Theatre, to tell him what to do next. In the meantime, he installed one businessman (Gerry Robinson of Granada) in the chair of the Arts Council and a second (Sir Colin Southgate of Thorn EMI) in the chair at the Royal Opera House. Sir Colin asked Robinson to double the subsidy, and proposed shutting the House for the whole of 1999, mainly to save money. Staff were told that it would close forever unless dozens of them agreed to leave, and the remainder gave up broadcasting fees and holiday pay and agree to work part-time. Music director Bernard Haitink threatened to resign, and the ballet dancers refused to work part-time. Meanwhile, Sir Richard rejected both the radical answer (allow the House to sink or swim) and the economical alternative (merge it with English National Opera) in favour of a 'commitment to ... excellence, artistic integrity, accessibility, accountability and cost effectiveness.' His report read well, but solved nothing. Behind the verbiage, its answer was familiar: more subsidy.

Gerald Kaufman, chairman of the Culture Select Committee, complained acidly of 'the blended aroma of mendicancy and complacency' emanating from the house. Yet the Royal Opera House is only one of dozens of arts organisations which do not bother with financial controls. In 1992 the English National Opera persuaded the Department of National Heritage to give it £11 million to purchase the freehold of the Coliseum. Five years later it was back with a demand for £120 million to finance a move to a brand new opera house. (By the end of 1997, it was being rescued from bankruptcy by the Arts Council.) The Royal Shakespeare Company, despite the popularity of its productions and a raft of subsidies from the City Corporation as well as the Arts Council, is in perpetual financial difficulties.

There is no reason to suppose that any of these organisations would disappear if public subsidies were withdrawn. Plenty of regional theatres survive by the simple device of putting on plays at affordable prices which people want to see. Glyndebourne has thrived for decades without public subsidy, and recently rebuilt its opera house with £33.5 million of private money. Sir George Christie simply told the existing 230 corporate members that their supply of tickets would dry up unless they gave him at least £90,000 each. Those who did not were replaced by more accommodating clients on his waiting list. Production costs at Glyndebourne are half those of Covent Garden.

The 'arts tsars' reckon Glyndebourne is a special case, but its example is instructive. The Arts Council was set up specifically to support those art forms which could not survive, or maintain standards, without subsidy. This meant, essentially, traditional high culture: opera, ballet, and the fine arts. Yet it is by no means obvious that high culture cannot earn its keep. Its principal consumers are rich, well-educated people, and there are a great many more of them than before the Arts Council was invented.[121] However, the guardians of high culture seem to spend more time and money lobbying for larger subsidies than attracting new audiences by discounting ticket prices or putting on popular shows. Even art galleries recognise the value of laying on periodic blockbusters: the Cézanne exhibition in 1996 at the Tate Gallery attracted over 400,000 visitors at £5 a head.

It is obviously much easier to blame the government for failing to subsidise prices. 'There is this nonsense that the arts are élitist,' Sir Simon Hornby, chairman of the Association for Business Sponsorship of the Arts, has said. 'They are only élitist if they don't get government support.'[122] Nobody in the arts is willing to believe that ticket prices would fall, rather than rise, in the absence of subsidies, whose chief effect is to drive up costs. Without subsidies, or with subsidies geared to consumers rather than producers, arts organisations would have to supplement their work with commercial income (just as novelists have to supplement their work with journalism or copy-writing).

They would have to consider imaginative solutions to their financial problems, such as selling shares to theatre-goers or establishing endowment funds, and they would regain proper artistic freedom.

The guardians of high culture think that artistic freedom was what Keynes purchased for them when he set up the Arts Council. 'The arts flourish best when they are self-governing,' claimed William Emrys Williams, an early secretary-general, 'and self-government is not incompatible with the acceptance of state subsidies.'[123] This was an optimistic view. As Gerald Kaufman explained to Lord Chadlington, the chairman of the Royal Opera House, when he appeared before the select committee, 'you get £15 million of public money annually, which, with money from the National Lottery, approaches £100 million. Then you decide the way you conduct yourselves. Do you expect us to think that is satisfactory?'[124]

The arts are now living under a government hostile to high culture and sympathetic to film producers, television executives and Britpop artists. One of the first decisions of the new secretary of state for National Heritage was to rename his department to emphasise its demotic and forward-looking character. In its seminally titled White Paper, *The People's Lottery*, the government added health and education as a Sixth Good Cause to the list of activities funded by the National Lottery – another step towards eradication of its independence from government. Like the Road Fund and the National Insurance Fund, the National Lottery will eventually be nationalised. The proceeds of People's Lotteries tend to get spent on Politicians' Priorities, and these are unlikely to include opera, orchestras and live theatre.

In fact, the National Lottery, greeted by the arts establishment as a potential saviour, will probably be its executor. It provided the last Conservative government with an excuse to reduce the annual grant-in-aid, and it led to an increased emphasis on capital projects, without much thought of how to pay for what goes on inside the buildings. Birmingham has a new Symphony Hall, Manchester the Bridgewater Hall, and London will eventually get a third Imax cinema as well as a brand new opera house. Subsidisation of the arts, like subsidisation of country houses, is judged increasingly in economic terms. This began under Thatcher, who earned the undying enmity of the arts tsars for daring to ask why their claim on public funds was so unquestionable. 'The party is not over,' said Grey Gowrie in 1985, when he was an arts minister rather than an arts tsar, 'but the limits of hospitality have been reached.'

Now even the arts tsars are beginning to present their applications for subsidies in terms of jobs created, foreign currency earned, and investors attracted. 'Whoever would have thought,' asked Gowrie in his last year as chairman, 'that the Arts Council would in the 1990s be a major economic force in the regeneration of cities? Or that jobs related to the arts should be growing so rapidly ... Areas like Gateshead, Salford, Stoke-on-Trent and Sheffield are seeing growth and development as a result of the £804 million ... allocated to more than 1,500 capital projects ... The arts contribution to the cultural industries [is] now so important to earnings and jobs in the UK; within the Department of Culture, Media and Sport remit alone turnover is about £50 billion each year.'[125]

National and municipal museums and art galleries, which were among the first state-owned institutions, have all learned to market themselves aggressively to consumers and tourists. The national museums, whose boards were once no more than talking shops for disinterested aesthetes and experts, are now packed with businessmen charged with increasing income from admission fees, catering and shops. The advertising slogan for the V&A ('a nice museum with an ace caff attached') captured the mood of salesmanship which swept through museums and galleries during the 1980s. Scholarly inquiry at centres of excellence has given way to naked competition for the leisure pound. When Elizabeth Esteve-Coll succeeded Sir Roy Strong as director of the V&A, she promptly made a number of experts redundant. Between 1988 and 1994 she launched a string of popular displays and exhibitions, refurbished galleries to make them friendlier, actively encouraged school visits, and introduced a voluntary admission charge. In 1996 the V&A finally

TABLE 3.5
Principal State-Owned Museums and Galleries, 1996

	Visitors	Govt. Grant 1996–7 (£)	Admission Charges
British Museum	6,228,275	33,196	Free
National Gallery	5,000,000	18,726	Free
Tate Gallery	2,002,000	18,777	Free
Natural History Museum	1,607,255	27,449	Yes
Science Museum	1,548,286	20,633	Yes
Victoria & Albert Museum	1,300,000	30,762	Yes
National Portrait Gallery	807,545	4,915	Free
Imperial War Museum	444,279	10,678	Yes
National Maritime Museum	458,316	10,545	Yes
Merseyside Museums & Galleries	457,590*	13,123	Free

Source: Department for Culture, Media and Sport Expenditure Plans, 1998–9; British Tourist Authority, *Visits to Tourist Attractions, 1996*.

* Tate Gallery Liverpool only.

accepted that it was in the Heritage Business, and introduced a compulsory £5 admission charge. These charges, disparaged by Jeremy Paxman as 'the absurd expectation that people should pay to see things they already owned', are now routine at top museums and galleries.[126]

The New Labour government has declared an ambition to scrap all admission charges by 2001, but even it hopes to encourage the further commercialisation of state-owned museums and galleries by allowing them to borrow money. The cultural change at these great institutions is rich in historical ironies. Free educational institutions, founded (mainly) by the Victorians for the cultural nourishment of the working classes, are now commercialised leisure amenities for the middle classes. Institutions whose origins are traceable to the pinnacle of Victorian commercial supremacy are now charged with retrieving the industries of that period from the condescension of history, by opening 'heritage centres' in dockyards and cotton mills and saving 'industrial archaeology' from demolition or redevelopment. Yet displaced cultural mandarins disparage the philistinism of businessmen, and scoff at the vulgarity of funding the great national museums and galleries through the National Lottery. They forget that the British Museum – the first great cultural institution in Britain – was funded from the proceeds of a public lottery. Perhaps they did not know that the workings of state lotteries were devised by John Julius Angerstein, a leading businessman of the day – one whose own art collection formed the nucleus of the modern National Gallery.*

Are Consumers Philistines?

It is ironic that the arts tsars, contemptuous for so long of commercial values, should find that they can now get subsidies by preserving the artefacts of industry and commerce and by turning these organisations into ersatz PLCs. Yet they should not think that their *embourgeoisement* marks the end of high culture: it was the wealth of the commercial world which gave birth to the

---

* The first museum in Britain was probably the Ashmolean in Oxford, the nucleus of which was the collection bestowed on the university by Elias Ashmole in 1683. The British Museum was founded by Act of Parliament in 1753 with the collection of books and antiquities presented by the Cotton family in 1700, the manuscripts bought from the Earls of Oxford and the assembly of objets d'art, antiquities and natural history exhibits bought from Sir Hans Sloane. To raise the cost of purchase, housing and maintenance, £300,000 was raised by public lottery. The museum opened to the public in 1759, but as its collections were augmented by a series of royal and aristocratic donations – notably the Elgin Marbles – it was rebuilt between 1823 and 1857. The National Gallery was founded in 1824 when King George IV and Sir George Beaumont persuaded the government to buy the picture collection of John Julius Angerstein, a Russian-born Lloyds underwriter, merchant and philanthropist.

high art and learning of the Renaissance. The fortune of the Medicis was built on international banking. The golden era of Dutch painting coincided with the commercial pre-eminence of the Netherlands. Great art was never dependent on patrons, who were far less wealthy than the modern state. Much of it, like the plays of William Shakespeare, was produced for consumers not patrons; letting consumers decide which galleries, museums, operas and art survive will not necessarily create a kingdom of the Philistines.

The Heritage Industry would benefit from a dose of consumer sovereignty too. One of its curiosities is that it is seen largely as a *cultural* phenomenon with economic effects, and not as an *economic* phenomenon with cultural effects. On the left of British politics, commentators have long linked the reverence for the past to post-war economic failure. Nostalgia for an imagined past in which triumphs were greater and living was easier, runs the argument, has bred a collective unwillingness to face the challenge of the future. As early as 1962 Sampson was worried that the British people had 'lost that capacity for change and realism that has been their most remarkable characteristic'.[127] Twenty years later Martin Wiener found in modern English culture nothing but ennui, hatred of modernity and unwillingness to change, of which the Heritage Industry was merely an organised and explicit form.[128]

In *The Heritage Industry*, published in 1987, Hewison wrote that he called it 'the "heritage industry" not only because it absorbs considerable public and private resources, but also because it is expected more and more to replace the real industry upon which this country's economy depends. Instead of manufacturing goods, we are manufacturing *heritage*.'[129] In 1990 Paxman condemned 'the paralysing tendency of the Establishment to cling to the past'.[130] On the left, the Heritage Industry, like the monarchy, has become a symbol of the determined reluctance of the British governing classes to embrace change and modernity, a device for keeping the people in a perpetual state of childhood, and the economy in a permanent state of underdevelopment. The New Labour government believes this analysis, and has set about 're-branding' Britain as a vibrant, dynamic place characterised by design, software and cappuccino rather than pageantry, pork pies and pints of bitter. Progressives, surprised by the depth of popular resistance to their exciting plans for the future, are always apt to believe the people are suffering from false consciousness.

The truth is that the Heritage Industry is not a symptom of aristocratic hegemony, political reaction or economic decay. It has thrived largely because of the execrable quality of so much of the art and architecture which New Labour is keen to trumpet. But its success owes most to the billions of pounds which the state has pumped into the industry, particularly since the Second World War. Successive governments have created a vast new class of people who are making a good living out of the Heritage Industry – as inspectors, regulators, bureaucrats, naturalists, environmentalists, archaeologists, curators, arts tsars, pop historians, lobbyists and cultural commentators. They have every incentive to ensure it continues to grow.

But if the producers of Heritage are powerful – and they certainly are – it is patronising to argue that the people who buy their output are suffering from false consciousness. Borrowing culturally from the past is the norm. It is modernism, and fetishisation of the new, which is unusual. If the Heritage Industry is a plot by the ruling classes to maintain control over the masses, Cool Britannia is a plot by the chattering classes to achieve the same effect. It would be more rewarding to let the consumer decide between them, by cutting off the subsidies to the barons of stage and celluloid as well as the lords of broad acres.

CHAPTER FOUR

THE CHURCH

The Sea of Faith
Was once, too, at the full, and round earth's shore
Lay like the folds of a bright girdle furled.
But now I only hear
Its melancholy, long, withdrawing roar,
Retreating to the breath
Of the night-wind, down the vast edges drear
And naked shingles of the world.
                    MATTHEW ARNOLD, *On Dover Beach*

You couldn't pin anybody down to anything.
            THE BISHOP OF OXFORD, on the Church Commissioners[1]

Where is Elton John's piano?
        Commonest Question asked by Visitors to Westminster Abbey[2]

The great problem of the central Church of England is that no one,
repeat no one, is in charge.
        SIR DOUGLAS LOVELOCK, former First Church Estates Commissioner[3]

In 1997 the Church of England celebrated the 1400th anniversary of the
second coming of Christianity to the British Isles. Augustine and a band of
forty monks, despatched by Pope Gregory to preach the gospel of Christ to
the pagan Anglo-Saxons, landed in Kent in 597. In Canterbury, where the
monks raised their first church, a new museum and interactive audio tour is
now open at the ruined Abbey of Saint Augustine. It was the centrepiece of
the theme English Heritage had chosen for 1997: *England's Christian Heritage.*
Of the £1 million which it had sunk into the project, the Heritage Lottery
Fund contributed £686,500. A short walk away in Canterbury Cathedral, the
heart of the Canterbury World Heritage site, a special exhibition commemor-

ating the life and work of St Thomas à Becket drew many of the two million tourists who visit the seat of the primate of the English Church every year. The chief attraction was the Becket Chasse, purchased by the Victoria & Albert museum with the help of a £3.7 million grant from the National Heritage Memorial Fund (NHMF).

The Church of England Joins the Heritage Industry

For the Church of England, these were apt ways to celebrate the coming of Saint Augustine. The melancholy, long, withdrawing roar of the Sea of Faith may not yet be spent, nor the Church of England reduced, as its primate once described it, to an old lady muttering in the pew. It is still unlawful to schedule a working church as an ancient monument, and even cathedrals are still in use for worship as well as gawping. But the triumph of Heritage at Canterbury in 1997 offered a glimpse at the future which awaits the Church of England as a whole. Fourteen hundred years after the coming of Augustine, its membership was so low that it decided to stop publishing the figures. The best guess is that there are now less than one million churchgoing Anglicans. There are more Roman Catholics in England, far more Non-conformists, and may soon be as many Muslims, Sikhs and Hindus. Every year, more people visit Canterbury Cathedral as tourists than worship in an Anglican church. One in two dioceses have appointed tourist officers to show the tourists around, and tap them for money.

'I'm not in the business of being a museum director, and God forbid that the Church of England would ever slump to that,' the archbishop of Canterbury protested in 1994.[4] But he used the same interview to plead for more public money to maintain listed Church buildings, on the grounds that churchgoers alone could not maintain the ecclesiastical heritage. A report prepared for the Bishop of London had shocked the Heritage Industry by recommending the closure of two dozen churches in the City of London: their congregations were too small to sustain them. The Church of England is dying, and the undertakers are preparing to embalm the corpse. The vast majority of its 16,000 churches are already listed buildings, forty of them Grade I. It would be no surprise if the Heritage Industry took over the congregations as well as the buildings, to fill the stalls and pews with Living National Treasures.

In 1997 even the welcome news that the inherited wealth of the Church of England had recovered from notional losses of £800 million, incurred in disastrous property speculations in the 1980s, was tempered by the knowledge that the Church Commissioners could no longer afford the provision of clergy pensions. That burden, borne by the central funds of the Church since 1954, was from January 1998 transferred back to the dwindling congregations of the parishes. Every member of every congregation must now find an extra 50p a week if they wish to keep their vicar, on top of the sums they have had to find to pay clergy stipends.

Five years earlier, the Church had given up the struggle to maintain its estate unaided. In the first five years after it started giving repair grants to 'places of worship' in 1992, English Heritage dispensed £65.7 million to churches and cathedrals around the country. It expects to spend at least £90 million on them over a ten-year period – and probably more. Since the NHMF was set up in 1980, the stained-glass windows, ceilings, organs, wall paintings, memorials and statuary of dozens of parish churches up and down the country have also benefited from grants.[5] In its first two years, the Heritage Lottery Fund gave £25 million to 223 churches, and turned away many more. Another £4.5 million went to cathedrals.[6] Ecclesiastical demand for help was so heavy that in October 1996 the Heritage Lottery Fund and English Heritage joined forces to create a single source of funding for churches and other places of worship. It will be worth £20 million a year.

The forty-two Anglican cathedrals are the chief beneficiaries of this largesse. A grant of £30,000 towards the restoration of the Durham Cathedral bells was one of the first made by the NHMF. In 1990–1 Ely Cathedral was given over £400,000 towards restoring its octagon and lantern. But it was the near-loss of the *Mappa Mundi* which precipitated admission of the cathedrals to full membership of the Heritage Industry. The decision of the dean and chapter of Hereford to put the *Mappa Mundi* up for sale in 1990 did for the cathedrals what the auction of Mentmore Towers had done for stately homes: it gave the guardians of the national heritage a vital argument to secure public funding for the cathedrals.[7] The *Mappa Mundi* was 'saved for the nation' by a grant of £2.27 million from the NHMF (and a matching gift of £1 million from J. Paul Getty Jnr) and is now in the possession of a well-endowed trust and library at Hereford Cathedral.

The consequences of that episode reverberated far beyond the banks of the Wye. That same summer of 1990, Robert Runcie became the first Archbishop of Canterbury to submit a formal request to the government for public assistance for the cathedrals.[8] In October 1991 the government made available fresh funds for distribution to them.*

This was the first direct state aid given to any part of the established Church

---

* In October 1991 £11.5 million was promised over the three years to 1994. A further £8 million was promised in March 1993 for 1994–6. See *Heritage and Renewal: the Report of the Archbishops' Commission on Cathedrals*, Church House Publishing, 1994, p. 124.

since the Napoleonic Wars. Unlike the beleaguered aristocracy of the post-war period, cash-strapped cathedrals had long fought shy of accepting public money. They feared it would be used as an excuse to eradicate the last vestiges of their centuries-old independence from the rest of the Church, or even to nationalise and pass to the Church Commissioners what little remained of their once-vast and valuable assets. In the early 1990s, they protested vigorously to the Archbishops' Commission on Cathedrals that they were not ripe for museumisation but places of 'living worship' with a real part to play in elevating, educating and succouring the inhabitants of the cities which surround them.[9] The report of that commission, chaired by Lady Howe of Aberavon, was studious in its acknowledgement of the religious importance of the cathedrals. But the text, tellingly entitled *Heritage and Renewal*, was replete with marketing, commercial and management tips of the kind the Heritage Industry has made its own.

The sad fact is that cathedrals such as Durham will never be allowed to fall down, because they no longer belong to the people who worship in them or even to the established Church of England. Durham is now a 'World Heritage Site' which belongs to people everywhere. Barring Armageddon, their taxes, entrance fees and donations will keep it standing long after all trace of the Christian faith has fled from English hearts.

The Economics of Cathedrals

Ironically, this public ownership has made the cathedrals far more popular as places of pilgrimage than they ever were in the days when English people cleaved to the faith in all its purity and fullness. Perhaps fifteen million tourists visit them every year, though most go only to the great medieval cathedrals – Canterbury, York, Norwich and Salisbury. Almost every great cathedral now has to invest in the machinery to welcome them: guides, restaurants, visitor centres and lavatories, of which the last are notoriously vexatious and unrewarding. 'We had a lot of trouble . . . with vandalism, and really quite surprisingly bad behaviour in the lavatories, and found we were spending a lot of money just on trying to keep them clean,' says the receiver general at Canterbury. 'So we did a major refurbishment . . . and now charge 10p to go in, and have attendants there. They are now the pride of Kent.'[10]

The tramp of tourists around the nave of a great cathedral is also far from costless. Floors are damaged by the millions of pairs of shoes. Yet the most obvious way of reducing the numbers – admission charges – is one which most cathedrals deny themselves, although all cathedrals charged an entry fee until Victorian times and some did not abandon one until the 1930s.

TABLE 4.1
Cathedrals as Tourist Attractions: The Top Ten, 1996

	Visitors	Admission Charge
Westminster Abbey*	2,500,000	Yes
York Minster	2,200,000	Free
St Paul's	2,000,000	Yes
Canterbury	1,700,000	Yes
Chester	1,000,000	Free
Norwich	638,000	Free
Salisbury	600,000	Free
Durham	500,000	Free
Exeter	400,000	Free
Winchester	357,475	Yes

Source: The English Tourist Board, *Visits to Tourist Attractions*, 1996.

* Westminster Abbey is not strictly speaking a cathedral, but a "royal peculiar"; a standard entrance charge of £5 was introduced in 1996.

Salisbury was the first modern cathedral to introduce a voluntary admission charge, and Ely a compulsory one. But Ely was left with little alternative after a proposed redevelopment of properties around the cathedral was universally reviled. Its dean and chapter complained in 1987 that tourists were costing it 12p a head, and it needed additional income to subsidise the costs.[11] By 1991 it was earning a profit of £140,000 from admission charges, photographic fees and candles (its biggest source of income). Tours of the tower, which offers a splendid view of the Fens, cost extra and are managed by a private company.[12] St Paul's Cathedral, the most indebted as well as one of the most popular, finally introduced an admission charge for its two million sightseers in June 1991, and eliminated its overdraft.[13] Westminster Abbey charged for admission to some parts of the abbey for several years before it finally introduced a standard £5 admission charge in 1996.

Other popular cathedrals continue to resist anything explicit. But a visitor in high season to any of them can expect to be greeted by 'welcomers', one of whose functions is to embarrass tourists into making a donation (another is to deter thieves and vandals). Most cathedrals have found these more productive than glass or oak boxes with coin slots, plastered with supplicatory leaflets in several languages, or capped with notices suggesting £1 might be about right. But they are sensitive to intimations that the primary role of the welcomer might be to separate tourists from their holiday money. 'Our

welcomers really are there to welcome and we forbid them to ask for money,'
protests the Dean of Canterbury. 'If they are asked "How much?", they are
instructed to reply "Nothing."' At Wells, welcomers are instructed to talk
about money only if they are asked.[14] But their effect is potent nonetheless.
In the mid-1980s Canterbury was collecting £50–60,000 a year in its donation
boxes; the introduction of welcomers raised that to well over £250,000, but
it was still not enough. Canterbury introduced an admission charge in 1996.

Some cathedral officials refuse to be embarrassed. 'Ninety per cent of the
people who come to the Cathedral are coming to look at a chunk of heritage,
not . . . a place of worship or a house of God . . . there is no earthly reason
why they shouldn't be asked to pay a quid towards the maintenance, is there?'[15]
English Heritage is helping to persuade even those with a less cynical view
of the merits of introducing an admission charge: it takes into account the
income-producing potential of a cathedral when deciding on its grants for
fabric maintenance and repairs. In 1994, the Howe Commission identified a
collective 'net maintenance overhang' of £38.5 million,[16] so it is obvious that
this work cannot be accomplished without grants from the taxpayer. Though
cathedrals work hard to make themselves look as impoverished as possible
(lavish trust funds never appear in cathedral accounts) the Howe Report was
probably right to describe their finances as 'not at all comfortable'.[17]

Maintaining the fabric is the biggest single charge on the income of a
cathedral, but protection is also expensive. Canterbury spends £75,000 a year
on round-the-clock security, and £45,000 on insuring the most precious parts
of the interior. Another £18,000 a year goes on fire alarms. Irreplaceable
objects inside the cathedral, such as the 'Achievements of the Black Prince',
have to be insured for restoration in the event of partial destruction by fire
or flood. Theft and vandalism are genuine threats. At Westminster Abbey
unscrupulous tourists have snapped fingers off marble statues and stolen
carvings from monuments. The crowns of Henry V and Elizabeth I (with her
collar) were stolen, and mosaic has gone missing from the shrine of the
Confessor – among others.

Insuring a cathedral and its contents against theft and disaster is fiendishly
expensive, and there are no grants from English Heritage for this. Running
costs are the unglamorous side of the Heritage Industry, which nobody wants
to pay for. 'These are not very sexy things,' says the receiver general at
Canterbury Cathedral. 'If you try to raise money for a lightning conductor
or a fire alarm system people laugh at you. You can, with difficulty, raise
money for refurbishing the nave floor or a stained-glass window. It is the
easiest thing in the world to raise money for bells. People love bells. But they
are not interested in preventing a fire.' In fact, national monuments like
Canterbury Cathedral have little to fear from natural disaster. When York

Minister was struck by lightning and lost an entire transept to fire, money poured in from a sympathetic public and the insurance monies were not needed. 'I try not to think about it,' adds the receiver general, 'but if the worst happened at Canterbury Cathedral I have no doubt that money would flood in from all over the world. That doesn't mean you don't insure it.'[18]

To meet running costs, cathedrals are adopting a harder-nosed approach. Most now make sure that they are charging market rents for properties they own in and around the close.* Properties which used to be let on soft terms to the poor are now being run commercially. 'It has reversed the financial position here,' says the Dean of Canterbury. 'Rents now form a very large proportion of our income.'[19] By the early 1990s, Canterbury was receiving over £1.25 million in rents, or nearly half its total income. Like all but one of the other forty-two English cathedrals (the exception is Christ Church), Canterbury also has a shop. St Paul's has installed a shop and public lavatories in the crypt, better known as the last resting-place of Nelson and Wellington.[20] Twenty-six cathedrals also run a restaurant. The Howe Commission reckoned the retailing and catering arms of the cathedral business were turning over £10.5 million a year, and generating a net profit of £1.8 million.[21]

As with their equivalents at the National Trust, the shops and refectories are run mainly by volunteers, and membership schemes, made familiar by the National Trust and English Heritage, are developing out of the Leagues of Friends. The Howe Commission estimated that the cathedrals had 50,000 Friends in all, who raise over £1 million a year in total – not a large sum. Howe urged them to recruit new members, by having a 'presence' in the cathedral.[22] This was code for a membership sales outlet akin to the cabins in the car park at the National Trust, or the booths the RAC and the AA set up in motorway service areas. Such shameless salesmanship is no longer alien, even to members of the chapter familiar with Matthew 21.[23]

Corporate sponsorship is no longer spurned. The Bristol Cathedral Choir was sponsored to the tune of £25,000 a year for ten years by Nuclear Electric. Ely Cathedral has windows sponsored by Tesco, John Lewis, Lloyds and Barclays banks, Cambridge Electronic Industries and other large companies.[24] Salisbury reached agreement with McDonalds to offer a free Big Mac to every visitor who donated at least £1.50, but public outcry prevented it. St Paul's accepted £15,000 from Lockheed to stage a concert, and was disappointed to have to refuse the money after protests that the company manufactured arms.

* Like the National Trust and the Crown Estate, cathedral closes were exempted from right to buy given to leaseholders by the last Conservative government, largely at the behest of the bishops in the House of Lords. For the Leasehold Enfranchisement Act of 1993, see Chapter 2.

The promotion and marketing of cathedrals is increasingly undignified. In the summer of 1992 Ely Cathedral hosted the first 'rave in the nave', where rock groups performed for an audience of young people.[25] It was sufficiently successful to warrant a debate at the General Synod in York that summer, and to receive official blessing in the lamentably titled *In Tune With Heaven* report.[26] A second rock concert took place in Winchester Cathedral in May 1993. Coventry has used its nave to host celebrations of the invention of the motor car and of tractor manufacturing in the city. Even Southwark, the hearth and home of unreconstructed Anglican socialism, privatised its refectory by renting space to Pizza Express. The bishops' palaces at Lambeth, Wells and Auckland Castle are now available for hire as corporate dinner and conference locations.

Lincoln Cathedral took its Magna Carta – one of four surviving copies made at the time of the signing in 1215 – on a tour of the United States, where it earned a profit of £91,420. Suitably encouraged, the chapter was persuaded by the sub-dean and treasurer, Canon Rex Davis, to repeat the success by taking it to his native Australia, where it was displayed at the World Expo in Brisbane as part of the bicentennial celebrations in 1988. Davis assured his colleagues that ('on the most pessimistic forecasts') the project would yield a profit of £50,000. It was a disaster; the eventual loss realised was £56,000. It would have been more, had the Australian taxpayer not covered most of the costs. 'Quite obviously,' Canon Davis admitted to the *Church Times*, 'we burnt our fingers over this.' But he excused the financial disaster as a marketing success. 'The benefits accruing,' he said, 'my goodness, some corporations would have paid out millions for them.'[27]

This is the dilemma of the modern cathedral. Its possessions, like its buildings, music and worship, are at once its witness to the faith and a part of the Heritage Industry. To sustain both its real work and its custodianship of part of the National Heritage, it must descend to the marketplace to find the means. Because they cannot sell the heritage they possess (the *Mappa Mundi* proved that) cathedrals must *market* themselves and their assets to tourists, taxpayers and antiquarians. 'Tourism has to be an important factor for us,' wrote Sir Stephen Hastings of the economics of Peterborough Cathedral. 'A provincial new town . . . [is] bound to look a little wistfully at the problems created by mass tourism. But suppose it comes; how are we to protect the awe-inspiring and essentially uncluttered impact of the great nave, with its unique timbered roof, for the flow of visitors we so badly need? We plan a completely new visitor centre . . . we are bound to anticipate the forthcoming arrival of the Eurostar at Peterborough with some eagerness.'[28]

This is why all the essential features of the Heritage Industry can now be encountered, quite unvarnished, at the great cathedrals. There are the handsome subsidies from English Heritage, and the collections of listed and unalterable buildings in the close, where the state has ordained that the outward appearance be preserved. (Rex Davis describes the nineteen Grade I listed houses and twenty-two Grade II listed houses which surround Lincoln Cathedral as 'a necklace of pearls which has become a hangman's noose'.) In and around the cathedral lurk visitor centres, shops, restaurants, and public lavatories, and admission charges are levied for some parts of the building. Once inside the cathedral, the senses are bombarded by welcomers, pro-motional literature, public appeals, membership application forms, and news of fund-raising and congregation-boosting rock concerts and piano recitals. Cathedrals have even begun to argue (like the rest of the tourist industry and the arts) that they are an important force in the local economy. 'What would happen to the economy of towns like Canterbury, Ely, Durham and Lincoln if there were no cathedral?' asks Davis.[29]

Selling the Parochial Heritage

All the problems of belonging to the Heritage Industry are encountered at the humbler level of the parish church. Although only a handful of villagers cross its threshold on a Sunday, the parish church often *is* the national heritage at the local level. They may resent the bells which disturb their Sunday slumber, but nobody wants to lose the spire and everybody wants the church to be there for christenings, weddings and funerals. Appeals to repair it are conspicuously successful. 'Parish churches are rather like regimental flags,' a fund-raiser told English Heritage in 1997. 'They became rallying places in times of crisis.'[30] But the Church has to maintain them in ordinary times, as well as critical ones. Often, it cannot.

Between 1969 and 1997, the Church Commissioners raised £28.5 million from the disposal of 1,505 redundant churches.[31] The economic pressure to close churches, especially in urban areas, is mounting as church attendance declines and the population shifts from the cities to the suburbs. The most sensible solution – demolition and redevelopment – is rarely an option. There are more than 11,000 parish churches. Many are listed, and popular hostility to the destruction of a local landmark is usually intense. Demolition nearly always has to be preceded by a public inquiry. Of all the redundant churches placed at the mercy of the Church Commissioners over the last thirty years, less than one in four was sold or demolished.

Their likeliest fate is to become the property of the Heritage Industry. English Heritage meets more than two thirds of the costs of the Churches Conservation Trust, although it does little more than make sure the building does not collapse.[32] The Church Commissioners fund their share of the costs of the Conservation Trust by withholding some of the proceeds of sales, which can be substantial, if the site is good. Holy Trinity, on Kingsway in central London, fetched £5.2 million when the site was sold for redevelopment. The Church Commissioners are also selling a large number of listed Georgian and Victorian vicarages, many built in an era when clergymen were expected to ape the local gentry, with large families and several servants. Most are now too costly for modern pastoral purposes, when the average vicar earns just £14,610 a year and struggles to pay the heating bill. Rural vicarages are also being placed on the market as plunging congregations dictate that one parson looks after four or five parishes. They have proved popular with middle-class urban refugees, not least because the sales (thanks to the Ecclesiastical Residences Act of 1776 and the Parsonages Measure of 1938) are free of Stamp Duty.

The proceeds are reinvested in cheaper modern houses, around half of them purpose-built. Between 1988 and 1997 the Commissioners approved the sale of 1,301 parsonages, the purchase of 564 replacement houses and the construction of 436 new houses.[33] Although the Church of England has a legal duty to offer pastoral care to the nation, its applications to build clerical bungalows in the Green Belt are not always received sympathetically by the planning authorities or the local people.

Would Disestablishment Help?

This is the essence of the problem now confronting the Church of England. It is cherished, not as the conscience of the nation, but as an aspect of its past. Its beliefs, like its buildings, are seen as *belonging* to the past. The often bitter disputes between different denominations or the fierce battle within the Church of England over the ordination of women – 'vicars in knickers', as the *Sun* put it – speak to the great mass of the British people only of superstition and bigotry of a kind normally confined to museums. The prime minister, the most self-consciously modern figure in Britain today, is an Anglican who has taken communion regularly at Roman Catholic churches. He has said that he finds denominational distinctions 'bizarre'. Likewise, a bishop who declares himself in favour of 'gay rights' or 'a bias to the poor' is regarded as interesting (rather than glib), precisely because everything else he says and represents is an outrageous anachronism.

For the Church, unlike the aristocracy, there is no future to be found in the past. An increasingly influential body of opinion within the Church of England thinks the only way it can break with the past is by disestablishment from the state. Since Henry VIII nationalised the Church nearly five hundred years ago, runs the argument, it has not had to rely on its own moral force or missionary zeal but has depended instead on the official sanction of the state. Twenty-four bishops still sit in the House of Lords, and both the General Synod and the Church Commissioners are answerable to Parliament for their doings. The prime minister retains authority over the appointment of bishops and cathedral deans, although he is not expected to override the wishes of the Church. The Queen remains the supreme governor of the Church. Freed from this incubus of the past, say, the disestablishmentarians, Anglicanism could rediscover its evangelical vitality.

It is more likely that it would decay into one sect among many, with no guarantee that it would be among the more successful. Robbed of its presence in every parish and its seats in Parliament, and absent from the great occasions of state, the Church of England would not so much cease to dazzle as disappear. Since the state diluted its control of ecclesiastical appointments, forms of worship and the liturgy in the 1970s, their quality cannot be said to have improved. As the Church of England has become more autonomous, its leaders have ceased to be men of holiness (or even learning) and become spokesmen of the public sector employees with whom they now share the burden of social work. This is allied to an increasingly righteous introversion. The privilege of all English men and women to be baptised or marry in an English church, once seen as opportunities to minister to the uncommitted, is becoming the private sacraments of the committed.

Disestablishment would also put at risk the privileged financial position the Church has enjoyed since the Reformation. Unlike the Roman Catholics or the Methodists (or any of hundreds of Christian and pseudo-Christian sects ranging from Presbyterians to Mormons), Anglicans have never had to rely on their own generosity to keep their Church afloat. They are the beneficiaries of historic endowments, valued in 1997 at nearly £3.5 billion, which produce an investment income of over £140 million a year.[34] Whether the Church would be allowed to retain them after parting company with the state is one aspect of disestablishment proponents rarely discuss, because at least some of the assets (and possibly all of them) ultimately belong not to the Church but to the state. If the Church forfeited its membership of the state, it is unlikely that it would be allowed to keep its patrimony. No other privatised industry was granted that privilege.

When the Archbishops' Commission on the Organisation of the Church of England recommended in 1995 that control of the income from the historic endowments be transferred from the Church Commissioners (who are answerable to Parliament) to a new National Council of the Church of England (which would not be answerable to Parliament) it encountered fierce resistance in the House of Commons. The Social Security Select Committee issued a report arguing that this could not be done without parliamentary approval in the form of primary legislation. Its then chairman, Frank Field, who is also an Anglo-Catholic layman, even argued that the state would be justified in nationalising some or all of the assets and distributing them among other religions.[35] In a pluralist society governed by a state secular in all but name, a 'national' Church which lacks even the nominal assent of a majority of the population would have difficulty developing a case for retaining historic endowments if it was disestablished.

Field had in mind particularly the assets of Queen Anne's Bounty. These belong unequivocally to the state. In February 1704 Queen Anne agreed to return to the Church the revenues from First Fruits and Tenths, the taxes the clergy remitted to the Pope before the Reformation and which were nationalised by Henry VIII in 1535.* Other parts of the wealth also stem directly from the state: in 1809 Parliament made a grant of £100,000 to raise the pay of impoverished clergymen, and a similar sum was paid every year except one until 1820. Another £1.5 million was given to the Church in two tranches in 1818 and 1824, for the express purpose of building churches in the sprawling new towns of the early industrial era. In all, some £2.6 million of public money (well over £100 million in modern prices) was given to the Church. It did not enjoy such lavish support from the taxpayer again until the 1990s but, properly invested, £2.6 million would be more than sufficient to account for the inherited wealth of the Church Commissioners today.

The Church Commissioners themselves, and every asset they manage, are also the creatures of the state, created by legislation passed between 1836 and 1840. This equipped them with powers to seize and redistribute the income from the endowments which supported a wide variety of Church appointments, and especially the landed estates of the bishops and cathedrals. The aim was to use the wealth of the Church, then being squandered on placemen, to remunerate the vicars and build the churches in the new industrial cities. In the words of the Act of 1840, the money was intended to make 'additional provision . . . for the cure of souls in parishes where such assistance is most required, in such manner as shall . . . be deemed most conductive to the efficiency of the established Church'. About £2 in every £5 belonging to

---

* 'First Fruits' was a proportion of the first year's income from a clerical post, formerly paid to the bishop and, from the thirteenth century, to the Pope. They are sometimes known as 'annates'. 'Tenths' was the annual payment to the Pope of one tenth of the income from an ecclesiastical post. First levied at one fortieth by Pope Innocent III in 1199, it was raised to a tenth by Gregory IX in 1228. After the breach with Rome, the proceeds of both taxes were taken by the Crown, and paid to the Court of First Fruits and Tenths. In 1704 Queen Anne returned the revenue of First Fruits and Tenths to the Church, in what is known as Queen Anne's Bounty. The taxes were abolished in 1926.

the cathedrals was diverted to the Commissioners as a result. Even today the Dean and Chapter Act of 1840 is remembered as 'the cathedral-crushing act'.[36]

The Church had not expected to have to pay for its mission to the industrial cities; it wanted the taxpayer to stump up. In 1836 even the reforming Bishop of London, Charles Blomfield, had recommended a tax of 2d a ton on coal to build new churches in London. The government, for fear of offending Dissenters as well as taxpayers, favoured instead plundering the rich endowment of the cathedrals.[37] It is true that the state did not *nationalise* the assets of the bishops and cathedrals at the outset; rather, the government capped the incomes of bishops and cathedral clergy and kept the balance. It also pre-empted the income of the many jobs abolished; the assets remained – initially at least – in the hands of their former owners.

But the Commissioners soon found they were taking charge of the assets as well. Many cathedrals had made the mistake of leasing land for long periods at over-generous rents, and found they could increase their income by transferring estates to the Commissioners in return for a regular annual payment. Most expected to resume control of the property when the lease expired and a higher rent could be charged, but the great agricultural depression of the last quarter of the nineteenth century meant most were better off continuing to take a payment from the Commissioners. By the turn of the century, the bishops and cathedrals had ceded control of almost all their assets in exchange for a regular annual payment and, in 1931, ownership as well as control was vested in the Commissioners.[38] Much of the agricultural portfolio controlled by the modern Church Commissioners stems from the transfers of the nineteenth century. They still pay the salaries of all bishops, and contribute towards the cost of other cathedral clergy.

It would be difficult today to disentangle which of these assets belong to the Church, and which to the state. But there is no doubt that the state would be entitled to expropriate most if the Church was disestablished. The Archbishops' Commission concluded:

> The State has an interest in the origins of the assets, played a part in arranging for their surrender, and was the source of some of them. It is therefore appropriate that the assets should be managed by a body in which the historic partnership between the Church and State continues to be embodied. We hope the State as well as the Church will find these reasons persuasive.[39]

Partnership between the Church and the state is certainly historic. The Church in England has relied on state patronage since King Ethelbert gave

Augustine a ruined Roman church at Canterbury to establish his first episcopal seat and monastery.[40] Until the complete secularisation of the state in the
twentieth century, this was the essence of Establishment: the Church traded
divine endorsement of secular authority for endowments of land and treasure.

Ecclesiastical Corruption

Unlike its Celtic predecessor, the Roman Christianity Augustine brought to
England was as much concerned with this world as the next. Its hierarchy
and its teachings were designed to reinforce rather than challenge the secular
authorities. Its priests lived not in caves, but cathedrals, monasteries, abbeys
and churches.[41] Its material needs were immense, and the triumph of opulent
Roman Christianity over its ascetic Celtic rival at the Synod of Whitby in 663
impaled the Church in England on the contradiction between spiritual mission and material need. It also mired the Church in a relationship with the
state as much economic as political. The state supplied the material needs
of the Church and protected its property, but never left the Church in any
doubt that it would call upon its wealth whenever the need arose. State attacks
on ecclesiastical endowments were a regular feature of English political life
long before the Dissolution of the Monasteries.

The Conqueror looted Saxon churches and monasteries; Richard Coeur
de Lion and his brother John milked the wealthy Cistercians; and the expropriation of the assets of French ('alien') monastic orders was a regular feature
of the public finances in the Middle Ages. It is not hard to see why the Church
was attacked so regularly. As early as Domesday, it controlled a quarter of
the wealth of England, and greed and corruption were rife.[42] Stigand, Bishop
of Winchester under the Confessor and Archbishop of Canterbury at the time
of the Conquest, sold bishoprics and abbeys, and was excommunicated for
his misdemeanours by no less than five Popes. His was only an egregious
example of a universal pattern. At the time, three out of four bishops were
monks, ostensibly pledged to a life of self-denial, but all controlled large
private estates as well as the vast holdings of the cathedrals-cum-monasteries
where they had their episcopal seats. They ran them with the same attention
to profit as their secular counterparts, and were careful to collect additional
income: the profits of markets, fines levied in the courts, and the sale of
teaching posts and school buildings.[43]

In the eleventh century there was even an epidemic of body snatching,
because a relic which caught the popular imagination could make the fortune
of a cathedral or church. A canon at Durham stole the corpse of Bede. In
1023 the body of Saint Alphege was snatched from St Paul's by two monks

from Canterbury, who used a candlestick as a crowbar to break into his sarcophagus.[44] There was a roaring trade in parish churches, which offered buyers secure revenues from Church taxes, and usually a strip of land and a few beasts as well. Many monks lived openly with mistresses and slept with nuns. This inability to adhere to the spiritual life prompted periodic revivals of the ascetic traditions of medieval monasticism but even new orders soon succumbed to worldly temptations. Sodomy was included in a list of moral abuses drawn up by Anselm, Archbishop of Canterbury, in 1102.[45]

The decline of both the Cluniac and Cistercian monks was astonishingly rapid. By the twelfth century perhaps half of the Black Monks in England were engaged in rent collection, lease renewals, and the organisation of work in the fields.[46] Monasteries became very rich indeed. Within fifty years of the first Cistercian foundations in England, the White Monks were heavily engaged in jobbing churches, church taxes and appointments; buying, selling and developing land; and borrowing on a lavish scale to embellish their abbeys. Their example was readily copied by the Black Monks. The emergence in the thirteenth century of the itinerant Franciscan friars, pledged to absolute poverty, caused nothing but embarrassment to the established orders. Fortunately, the Pope decreed absolute poverty heretical.

The moral laxity and material splendour of the medieval Church cost it popular affection. In the late fourteenth and fifteenth centuries, John Wyclif and his Lollard followers, stern critics of Popish superstition and fierce enemies of monasticism, prefigured the Dissolution of the Monasteries by arguing that the wealth of the Church was secular and had no religious justification. A Bill to disinherit the Church was put before Parliament as early as 1410.[47] The Dissolution of the Monasteries, contrary to Catholic propaganda, was not enjoined at the whim of a King who wanted to get divorced.

The Dissolution of the Monasteries

The Dissolution was the biggest single redistribution of wealth and power in Britain until the privatisation of the state-owned industries in the 1980s and 1990s. Unlike privatisation, there was virtually no popular resistance. By the time Henry VIII came to the throne, the greed of the monastic orders had long since earned them the enmity of ordinary people. The monks had become increasingly remote from their tenants: contact was reduced to the collection of rents, disputation and ill-feeling. Gifts to the Church dried up, or were diverted to the parish church.

More importantly, the leasing of the great ecclesiastical estates altered the balance of power in the land. The gradual relinquishment by the great monasteries of direct control of their estates led to the emergence of a new class of gentry: the 'new men' who expropriated the monasteries under Henry VIII. The great secular landlords, who had stood foursquare behind the Church in its resistance to the Lollards, were reduced and enfeebled by the dynastic struggles of the Wars of the Roses. The wealth of the monasteries lay prostrate before a powerful and ruthless monarch and his allies among the socially ambitious.

Thomas Cromwell, the son of a wealthy tanner, was an archetypal New Man. The financial and administrative skills he deployed in the suppression of the monasteries were honed in the service of Cardinal Wolsey, the son of an Ipswich butcher, who embarked on the venture long before Henry VIII broke with Rome. Though he had concealed his illegitimate daughter with the Benedictines at Shaftesbury, Wolsey closed twenty-nine monasteries and nunneries between 1524 and 1529 on the grounds that 'neither God was served nor religion kept' in them.[48] It was done with full papal authority, ostensibly in the interests of reform, but nobody was fooled: the confiscated estates yielded £1,800 to the Crown.[49] Wolsey kept enough for himself to endow Cardinal College in Oxford (precursor of Christ Church) and a school in Ipswich.[50]

Cromwell, who had managed many of the possessions looted by Wolsey, lacked even the flawed sympathy for the old religion of the disgraced Cardinal. By the time he entered royal service, anti-clericalism in general and anti-monasticism in particular were rife. The Reformation was in train. The official investigators commissioned by Cromwell in 1535 to probe the monasteries had a rich storehouse of anti-monastic stories on which to draw.[51] Popular tales of illiteracy, idleness, drunkenness, and sexual misdemeanours in the cloisters were rarely completely true. But there was plenty of graft, conspicuous consumption and sybaritic living (Rievaulx was home to 22 monks, who had 100 servants) and much cynical exploitation of tenants and gullible believers.[52]

The monastic response to the break with Rome was equally unblushing. By the end of 1535 virtually all monks had acquiesced on oath in the Acts of Supremacy and Succession by which Henry repudiated Catherine of Aragon, married Anne Boleyn, secured the succession of their children, and replaced the Pope as head of the English Church. Compliance in these measures stripped the monks not only of their formal defences (appeals to Rome and to ecclesiastical law) but of moral authority. If the vainglorious wars and extravagant spending of the King had drained the secular estate of taxable income his officials knew they could replenish his reserves by plundering the Church without fear of popular opposition. At bottom, the Dissolution was driven not by moral outrage or reforming zeal but by economic necessity. This is why it was a piecemeal and protracted campaign of attrition which was still incomplete at the death of Elizabeth.

Nor was the assault confined to the monastic orders: it was directed at the wealth of the Church as a whole. As early as 1531 the clergy were called upon to pay £118,000 in five annual instalments, and many of the greatest prelates were 'fined' additional sums.[53] Three years later Cromwell took the First Fruits and Tenths of all benefices vacant after 1 January 1535.[54] This entailed a new valuation of Church property, from the greatest monastery to the meanest chantry. The *Valor Ecclesiasticus* of 1535 was the first assessment of the wealth of the Church since 1291. The first Act of Suppression of March 1536 confiscated the wealth of all monastic houses worth less than £200 a year. This alerted the larger monasteries to their likely fate and, between 1537 and 1540, 188 elected to surrender their wealth and buildings voluntarily. When the final Act of Dissolution was passed in May 1539, less than 200 monasteries were still holding out.

The destructive effects were mainly aesthetic and architectural. In the space of two or three years, a great part of the medieval artistic achievement was lost.[55] Bullion, plate, books, jewels, reliquaries and other medieval images and icons were seized and sent to the Royal treasury in London. In the iconoclastic phase of the English Reformation under Edward VI, much medieval artwork was destroyed. Illuminated missals and service books were prominent casualties. Cromwell ordered all monastic buildings razed to the ground, but complete destruction was usually uneconomic. The royal commissioners settled for making the buildings uninhabitable, or laying upon the new owner an obligation to complete the desecration. The New Men either sold the bricks and stone for cash, or used them to build on the site. It is to economics, and not to conscience, that we owe romantic ruins like Fountains and Rievaulx.

The transfer of wealth and power proved completely irreversible.[56] Bullion, plate and other valuables worth perhaps £1.5 million were destroyed or dispersed. Farmland which had produced rents of £200,000 a year was confiscated and redistributed among various classes of landowner. The Reformation simultaneously subordinated the Church to the Crown rather than the Papacy. Ecclesiastical taxes – First Fruits and Tenths valued at some £40,000 a year – were paid to the King in London. The most important change of all was the transfer into private hands of a large part of the landed wealth of the Church. It lost control of between one fifth and one third of the entire national wealth, two in every three Church jobs, and the tithes which supported them.*

* 'Tithe' is derived from the Anglo-Saxon word for a tenth, *teogotha*. It was an ecclesiastical tax, levied ostensibly on biblical authority, by which one tenth of the annual produce of the land was given to maintain the clergy, relieve the poor and pay for the upkeep of the Church. The last tithes ceased to be collected in 1926.

It lost not only its political independence but its economic independence. Establishment is perhaps better described as dependence.

The End of Clerical Poverty

In *Pride and Prejudice*, the obsequious behaviour of the Reverend Collins towards his patron was drawn from contemporary life. It reflected the utter dependence of post-Reformation clergy on local landowners for jobs and perquisites. Lay ownership of Church jobs did not originate with the Reformation, but the mass privatisation which accompanied the Dissolution gave the aristocracy and secular institutions such as Oxford and Cambridge a degree of influence which they did not shed until the late twentieth century. Church jobs were bought and sold to produce an income for a relative or friend, and jobs with a large income or an attractive house could fetch tens of thousands of pounds. Today, almost 3,000 church livings are still owned by people and organisations outside the Church, but none of them are bought and sold and all of them are effectively controlled by the local bishop. If clergy are no longer at the mercy of their patrons, they are at the mercy of their bishop. This is one of the ways in which the Church has managed to increase its autonomy without Disestablishment, though few would argue that the results are universally pleasing.

One reason why they are not is that clerical control of ecclesiastical appointments has eradicated the (often grotesque) inequalities in pay. In previous eras, the Church attracted gifted and ambitious men of both humble and ample means precisely because it offered them the chance of a large salary, a seat in the House of Lords, and the chance of living in style at an episcopal palace. Today, there is a deadening equality in clerical salaries, with nobody earning less than £13,480 (a salaried layworker) and nobody earning more than £51,020 (the Archbishop of Canterbury). The palaces of the bishops, and even the capacious rectories of the Georgian and Regency periods, are being sold. The Church no longer offers a financially secure career to learned intellects of the ancient universities, and its canvas is too small to attract the truly ambitious. The entire financial purpose of the modern Church of England is to ensure that a clergyman in a poor parish earns at least as much as a clergyman in a rich one. Few of them want to become bishops; for most Anglican clergy, the parish boundary is their horizon.

In only one sense has the Church of England gained from greater equality in pay: it has eliminated clerical poverty. The Church Commissioners now endeavour to achieve a level of remuneration which is 'adequate for a clergyman (with no private means or working wife) to do his job without unnecessary anxiety about paying the bills, and to be able with his family to enjoy modest comforts.'[57] Falling numbers of clergy – there are around 10,280 ordained ministers and lay workers today, against nearly 20,000 thirty years ago, despite the admission of women to the priesthood – and the shift in population from thinly-attended village churches to suburban 'worship centres' has facilitated an increase in annual salaries from around £1,500 a year to a national minimum of £14,340 for ordained clergymen.[58] Clergymen also enjoy free housing, non-contributory pensions, low-interest car loans, subsidised insurance, full payment of National Insurance contributions and council tax, and reimbursement of expenses. These take clerical pay to a real value of over £20,000 a year. As recently as the 1930s, many parish priests had to supplement their stipends with a teaching post or, if they were lucky, dividends from investment of past benefactions or the rent of glebe-land.* This led to vast inequalities in clerical pay, with the unluckiest earning less than manual workers and the luckiest matching Cabinet ministers and company directors.

These have now disappeared. The average salary of a bishop, which was sixteen times that of an ordinary clergyman in 1835, is today less than twice that of a parson. Nobody holds more than one post any more, except in an honorary sense, and the centralisation of endowments means greater equality in remuneration throughout the country. Bishops can of course expect a car, a chauffeur, a gardener and a secretary, and occasionally still a palace to live in. The Archbishop of Canterbury has one at Lambeth and another at Canterbury. In 1994, running his office and library alone cost the Church £835,000. Servicing Bishopthorpe, the seat of the Archbishops of York, absorbed another £142,000.[59] The palaces are worth millions of pounds.

But the most remarkable change in remuneration is not the elimination of clerical poverty; it is the provision of pensions. Throughout most of the history of the Church of England, clergymen could not afford to retire. Most died in harness. Today, they all collect a pension, whose value has risen steeply, from £300 in 1959 to £9,173 in 1998–99. Widows (and now widowers) receive a pension of £6,116. Clerical pensions fall just short of two thirds of the national minimum stipend, which is the level the Church has undertaken to achieve and maintain. Lump-sum retirement payments were reintroduced in 1967 at £1,000 and are now worth £27,520; clergy also benefit from cheap retirement housing. But these gains have come at a significant price. Expenditure on pensions by the Church Commissioners climbed from £1 million in

---

* 'Glebe' is derived from the Anglo-Saxon word for soil, and refers to the land devoted to the maintenance of the incumbent of the parish. In modern parlance it does not include the parsonage.

TABLE 4.2
Stipends of Anglican Clergy, 1998–99 (£)

	Annual Stipend
Archbishop of Canterbury	51,020
Archbishop of York	44,700
Bishop of London	41,660
Diocesan bishops	27,660
Suffragan bishops, deans and provosts	22,740
Archdeacons	22,610
Residentiary canons	18,600
Incumbents: national minimum*	14,340
Assistant staff (including curates)†	13,480–14,010

Source: The Church Commissioners for England Annual Report and Accounts, 1997.

* The national average for incumbents in 1997 was £14,610.
† Plus additional points for seniority and responsibility.

1959 to £82.1 million in 1997, a more than tenfold increase. Contrary to opinion in the pews, this was the main cause of the financial holocaust which overtook the Church of England in the early 1990s.

How the Church Commissioners Lost a Fortune

At the General Synod held in York in July 1992 an eagle-eyed member was perusing the 1991 accounts of the Church Commissioners for England. He spotted a property write-off of £186 million, and asked for an explanation. On the Saturday of the Synod, the *Financial Times* carried a story entitled 'The Unholy Saga of the Church's Missing Millions', alleging that heavy borrowing to finance speculative property developments in Britain and the United States had cost the Church Commissioners nearly £500 million.[60] Two days later, the Archbishop of Canterbury, Dr George Carey, who had earlier blamed falling investment values on inflation, conceded that serious problems had come to light. 'Over the last few days we have heard criticism of the Church Commissioners' stewardship of resources,' he said. 'Serious points have been made about the management of funds and about judgements on investments ... We haven't lost £500 million.'[61] The last comment turned out to be true, but only just. The actual losses by the Church Commissioners totalled over £400 million.[62]

In October 1992, the archbishop invited Coopers & Lybrand to investigate what had gone wrong, and appointed a nine-man committee of laymen (the Lambeth Group) to make recommendations on the basis of what they found. It emerged that the Commissioners had borrowed heavily, most of it from the National Westminster Bank at floating rates of interest, to fund speculative commercial property developments. Total borrowings climbed from £11 million in 1986 to a peak of £518 million by 1990, the year that base rates peaked at 15 per cent and the property market crashed.[63] 'It is undoubtedly true that we borrowed too much at the wrong time,' admitted Douglas Lovelock, First Church Estates Commissioner at the time the change of policy was made. 'I am not disputing that. But of course that is hindsight . . . Nobody knew that the interest rates would go up as high as they did. Given hindsight, we would not have borrowed so much and we would not have made the switch into commercial property as large as we did.'[64]

The Commissioners not only borrowed too much. They failed to manage the developments competently. Projects expected to cost £600 million ended up at over £1 billion, as construction problems arose, specifications were changed, and partners bought out or failed.[65] Risks were concentrated in a small number of large developments, such as the Gateshead Metro Centre (a joint venture with John Hall), the Marlowes Centre in Hemel Hempstead (developed with McAlpines and Martin Landau) and the St Enoch's Centre in Glasgow (a joint venture with Sears PLC). The Metro Centre, though undoubtedly a commercial success, was much less successful in financial terms. The investment made a loss, after disastrous cost over-runs totalling £142 million.[66] Investments in shopping malls and office blocks in the United States also performed poorly, but the biggest single disaster was Ashford Great Park in Kent, where the Commissioners bankrolled a clutch of property developers and agents in the hope of planning permission for a large development to profit from the Channel Tunnel. When planning permission failed to materialise, they lost nearly £88 million.[67] Ashford Great Park became the subject of a special inquiry ordered by the Archbishop of Canterbury.

But it is not hard to see why the Commissioners behaved as they did. Their funds are closed. Unlike a pension fund or a life assurance company, no new money comes in during the year. To increase the value of assets, the only option is to borrow in the hope of securing exceptional returns. In the 1980s, property appeared to offer precisely that. The Commissioners were also under intense pressure to increase their income; the Church as a whole expected them to fund anything its members considered important. 'Some parts of the Church,' as the subsequent inquiry put it, 'have perhaps expected too much from the central endowments.'[68]

Easily the greatest burden the Commissioners had to bear was clergy pensions, which they had funded since 1954 without contributions from the rest of the Church. In the 1970s, an annual pensions bill of £5 million absorbed about one seventh of the net income. It rose to one quarter in the 1980s and to well over one third by 1991.[69] In 1996 pensions cost the Commissioners over half their net income.[70] Yet they made no proper actuarial assessment of whether assets were sufficient to meet the rising costs of pensions. They were effectively spending capital to cover the shortage of income even before the property débâcle, making the actuarial shortfall worse. When an actuary's report was finally commissioned, it showed that by 2010 pensions would absorb the whole of the income of the Church Commissioners.[71]

This was only the most egregious of a series of omissions and misjudgments by senior figures at No 1 Millbank. Cost control was non-existent; profit measures were faulty; accounting methods were unreliable; senior staff were too easily seduced by a good dinner or a bottle of fine wine. In one extraordinary episode reported by Terry Lovell, the Commissioners paid Martin Landau a £7 million premium for the right to fund the Marlowes shopping centre at Hemel Hempstead. Although the payment was conditional on cost over-runs being met by the developers, the Commissioners failed to invoke their entitlement and ended up paying an additional £60 million.[72]

As with much of what happened, this omission owed more to incompetence than misconduct. 'The Church Commissioners proved such an easy target to developers,' concluded the House of Commons Social Security Committee Report, 'that fraud was probably superfluous.'[73] The Coopers & Lybrand Report criticised record-keeping and financial control in the commercial property department, where decisions on who got paid and when were not vetted by senior staff.[74] Michael Hutchings, director of commercial property, was given considerable latitude in investment decisions by the Assets Committee, although it was supposed to approve every disposition of funds. He was not questioned about cost overruns, because the Committee thought his past achievements were a guarantee of future success.

'The only criticism I would ever make of Michael Hutchings,' Sir Douglas Lovelock told Terry Lovell, 'is that it was very difficult to find out what he was doing.'[75] Lovelock was chairman of the Assets Committee at the time the property investments were made, and Lovell is not concerned to portray him in a flattering light. But it is probably true. Lovelock describes himself as a 'regular committee churchman', whose strength was his ability to chair a meeting effectively. His brief was not to second-guess the fund managers, but to arbitrate among their various enthusiasms. Sir Douglas was offered the post of first Church Estates Commissioner in 1982 by the then Cabinet secretary, Robert Armstrong, after suggesting lightheartedly over lunch that it sounded interesting.[76] He was then chairman of HM Customs and Excise, a post to which he had gravitated after long service in a variety of capacities at the Ministry of Defence – not the ideal preparation for running a £3 billion investment fund.

But then the post is not well-paid by commercial standards. The salary was just £63,695 in 1992, when Sir Douglas completed his final year in the job. As a result, it has tended to go to old Whitehall hands whose careers have stalled short of the top. Significantly, Sir Douglas was succeeded in March 1993 not by another superannuated civil servant but by Sir Michael Colman, the mustard baronet and former chairman of the family firm of Reckitt & Colman. Two months after he took office an advertisement was placed by the Church Commissioners for a finance director with experience of financial management 'at the highest level'.

Ethics: The Constraints of Ecclesiastical Investment

One member of the Assets Committee has entered a plea of mitigation. 'All the time this property thing was going sour, the Assets Committee was spending . . . at least half of their time with the law case,' David Hopkinson, chief executive of fund managers M&G and commissioner responsible for stock-market investments, told Lovell. 'All my experience in the investment world is that when you start publicly going for an investment manager, and that is what we were, he gets defensive and his eye gets taken off the ball.'[77]

The law case he referred to was brought against the Commissioners by one of their own: the Right Reverend Richard Harries, Bishop of Oxford. He is the most prominent member of the Christian Ethical Investment Group (CEIG), which emerged from the longstanding campaign for disinvestment from South Africa to promote 'a stronger ethical investment policy in the Church of England'. In March 1990 it launched an action in the courts, which it hoped would lead to a ruling obliging the Commissioners explicitly to endorse Christian values rather than financial gain as the aim of their investment policy.

Like the National Trust, the Commissioners are attacked regularly for unsympathetic treatment of tenants, investing in environmentally unfriendly companies, and for allowing foxes to be hunted on their land. The one constant refrain, at least until Nelson Mandela was released, was the call to disinvest from companies which invested in South Africa. Liberal bishops and prominent laymen had occasional successes. In 1984 the Commissioners ostentatiously sold their investment in Carnation, an American company accused of exploiting black labour in South Africa.

But it took the formation of the CEIG, and the energy of Richard Harries, to turn a general distaste for apartheid and arms manufacturers into a court case. The duty of the Commissioners, the CEIG lawyers argued, was not simply to pay the salaries and pensions of Anglican clergymen but to propagate the gospel in England. They should invest their assets in line with Christian values, as individual Christians ought to do. Harries made a public appeal for funds to finance the litigation, and announced that some £2 million of assets belonging to the Diocese of Oxford were being transferred to the Allchurches Amity Fund because the Board of Finance of the Church of England refused to comply with the ethical criteria of the CEIG. It was not a strong foundation for a case, and Douglas Lovelock made no secret of his belief that the CEIG was wasting time and money. 'I must be quite plain,' he explained. 'Making money is the paramount objective. It is only at the margin that we trim.'[78]

That margin cannot be measured exactly. For decades, the Church Commissioners have not invested in companies whose main business is in armaments, gambling, alcohol, tobacco or newspapers, the last of which are excluded because they are associated with particular points of view.[79] It recently sold shares in BSkyB, on the grounds that the satellite channel disseminates pornography.[80] The Commissioners estimate their exclusions cover about one eighth of the London stock market by capitalisation, the maximum their fund managers believe possible to excise from a portfolio without substantial erosion of investment performance. (The Lambeth Group reckoned ethical considerations cost the Commissioners 0.5 per cent per annum.[81]) The policy does not exclude participation in the profits of 'unethical' activities, since that would preclude some core shareholdings such as Shell. Lovelock says he was bothered by the much larger cost of being forced to adopt a purist approach: lower investment returns, and thus lower clerical stipends and pensions. Disinvestment from South Africa alone would preclude 37 per cent of companies listed in London. If badly performing companies were added to the proscribed list, the Commissioners faced the prospect of having to sell half their securities portfolio.

The CEIG, however, are purists, not pragmatists. Their case reached the Chancery Division of the High Court in October 1991, where the group sought a 'declaration' that the primary goal of the Commissioners was the evangelisation of England and not the maximisation of income. Harries had pressed on despite a letter from the Archbishop of Canterbury urging him to desist and a stream of black propaganda about the costs of the case to Church funds.[82] Predictably, the case against the CEIG proved overwhelming. Sir Donald Nicholls, a senior Chancery judge, passed a devastating judgment. He found the plea for a declaration non-specific, generalist, ill-defined and rooted in moral argumentation which is, by its nature, incapable of resolution. 'Investments,' he said, 'are held by trustees to aid the work of the charity in a particular way: by generating money. That is the purpose for which they are held. That is the *raison d'être* . . . They must not use property held by them for investment purposes as a means for making moral statements at the expense of the charity of which they are trustees.'[83]

The Commissioners sought to recoup their legal costs from the CEIG, at least to the extent that they were covered by the appeal fund Harries had set up, but he had spent the lot on legal fees. But at least the Commissioners had a definitive judgment on their most important legal obligation. It was, as Sir Douglas had pointed out, to make money; unfortunately, during his time as First Estates Commissioner, they were more adept at losing it.

The Wealth of the Church Commissioners

And not solely because Michael Hutchings was punting in property. Their entire portfolio was overweight in property and drastically underweight in equities even before he borrowed half a billion pounds to lend to various property developers. The mistake the Commissioners made in the late 1980s was to *increase* an already excessive exposure to property with borrowed money. In 1990, the year the real estate market crashed, commercial, residential and agricultural property accounted for nearly three quarters of their net assets. John Plender reckoned the failure of the Commissioners to sell property and reinvest in the equity markets during the 1980s cost the Church between £50 and £100 million a year.[84] Had they matched the performance of other large funds in the ten years to 1991, the Church would have been over £1 billion better off.[85]

One of the first decisions Sir Michael Colman made after succeeding Lovelock was to sell property and buy equities. By 1996 property accounted for a third of the portfolio, and equities a half. Today, the property portfolio (valued at £928.6 million) accounts for about a quarter of the net assets of the Church Commissioners. It consists of the Hyde Park and Octavia Hill residential estates in London (£205 million), various commercial properties (£459 million) and an agricultural estate (£264 million) which has shrunk from 300,000 acres at the end of the last war to less than 130,000 acres today. The last of the Commissioners' commercial property in the United States was sold in 1996. In 1995 the Marlowes Shopping Centre was sold for £45 million, and the Beechwood Place Shopping Centre in Cheltenham for £15 million. A 90 per cent stake in the Metro Centre followed for £324 million,[86] and the St Enoch Centre in Glasgow in 1996. Since Sir Michael Colman took over, the Commissioners have sold property worth over £1 billion, using the proceeds to repay debt as well as buy shares.[87] Borrowings were down from the £518 million peak of 1990 to £4.5 million in 1997, and the value of assets

TABLE 4.3
Assets of the Church Commissioners, 1987–1998 (£ m)

	Properties	Securities	Other	Borrowing	Net Assets
1987	1,296.9	915.8	206.0	(169.3)	2,249.4
1988	1,510.8	1,042.3	286.0	(314.6)	2,524.5
1989	1,883.8	1,248.6	258.3	(447.9)	2,942.8
1990	1,689.0	777.9	416.2	(518.0)	2,365.1
1991	1,411.9	953.1	309.5	(383.4)	2,291.1
1992	1,181.3	975.8	261.6	(280.1)	2,138.6
1993	1,231.6	1,217.7	237.1	(224.5)	2,461.9
1994	1,295.2	1,068.7	267.9	(190.7)	2,441.1
1995	992.6	1,448.5	360.5	(23.1)	2,778.5
1996	843.1	1,778.7	402.0	(5.2)	3,018.6
1997	928.6	2,238.6	346.0	(4.5)	3,508.7

Source: The Church Commissioners for England Annual Report and Accounts, 1997, p. 47.

owned overtook the £3.4 billion at which it had peaked in 1989. Five years after it burst into the consciousness of ordinary Anglicans, the property nightmare was over.

The Church of England Becomes a PLC

Its consequences are not. One of them, little recognised even inside the Church of England, is a creeping series of changes in the organisation and management of the Church as a whole. Between February 1994 and September 1995, a twelve-man commission under the new Bishop of Durham, Michael Turnbull, pondered every aspect of its structure and financing.[88] They discovered that Church House was servicing no less than 100 committees, and that decision-making powers were scattered uncertainly and incoherently across the two archbishops, the House of Bishops, the diocesan bishops, the diocesan Bishops' Councils, the General Synod, the Central Board of Finance of the Church of England, the Church of England Pensions Board, Church House and the Church Commissioners, to say nothing of dozens of other boards and councils at national and local level.

The Turnbull Report was unsparing in its criticisms of this morass of time-wasting and ineffectual bureaucracy. 'At present the system impedes leadership,' it concluded. 'Much of what goes on at the national level puzzles and dismays many in the parishes and dioceses ... people are dissatisfied with and lack confidence in the national performance of the Church ... [There is] confusion and wasteful duplication of effort ... much of the work of the national bodies is committee-bound ... While many people ... can stop things happening, few (if any) can make things happen. Power is negative rather than positive ... It absorbs energies rather than releasing them ... There is ... an emphasis on producing reports rather than securing practical outcomes ... [a] focus on activity rather than action.' In short, the Church of England was a labyrinthine bureaucracy where nobody was in charge.[89]

The reforms the Turnbull Commission proposed were predictable. They were designed to make the Church of England less like an institution obsessed with procedures and more like a PLC interested in practical outcomes. The dozens of committees, boards and councils will be reduced to four business divisions: finance, human resources, mission, and heritage and legal services. These will be answerable to a board of directors, to be known as the National Council. Its seventeen members will devise policy, allocate funds, and make executive decisions, to be carried out by the business divisions. Unsurprisingly, the chief victims of the Turnbull Report were the Church Commissioners. Their number was to be cut from ninety-five to fifteen; their staff and functions merged with the Pensions Board and the Central Board of Finance; No. 1 Millbank put up for sale, and responsibility for expenditure decisions to be transferred to the National Council.

The glacial pace of change in the Church of England means that none of the changes has yet happened, though most were approved by the General Synod in November 1996. Some prominent churchmen were shocked by the inattention of the Turnbull Report to spiritual, as opposed to structural, renewal. 'I hope,' commented the Archbishop of York, 'that we shall not pursue a ... managerial and organisational exercise simply as an end in itself.'[90] But the transformation of the Church of England into a PLC look-alike is probably unstoppable: the institutional changes are in train, and signs of an increasingly businesslike way of life are breaking out all over the Church. The management of the episcopal car fleet was contracted out; press, poster, and radio advertising is used shamelessly to promote churchgoing, particularly around the major festivals – 'Make Room for God This Christmas,' 'Christians Make Better Lovers' and 'This Sunday You Could Find Yourself in Church' were among recent efforts. The Cross is being developed as a 'corporate logo' or 'brand image'. Attempts are being made to build up mailing lists of people who visit a church at Easter and Christmas only.

Clergymen will soon be subject to annual 'appraisals', and can even go on a two-year Master in Business Administration (MBA) course at the university college in Lincoln. 'It is our job to extract the best that successful corporations have to offer and use it in our context,' explained a Lincoln Cathedral canon.

'We have to think in terms of exceeding customer delight. What we have to offer is the glory of God, and we have to give the very best service to our customers in terms of added value and value for money that we can. Our product is quite simply allowing people to come closer to God.'[91]

Cathedral Chapters: Men Behaving Badly

Similar businesslike changes were proposed by the Howe committee for the cathedrals. Its report of 1994, *Heritage & Renewal*, recommended turning bishops into chairmen, deans into chief executives and canons into directors, serviced by lay administrators and properly qualified finance directors. After exploring the management of all forty-two cathedrals, the Commission identified 'wasteful use of resources, duplication of effort, unnecessary isolation in the mission to the world', and an 'uneven pattern of responsiveness . . . to existing management techniques and structures'. This meant that deans and chapters are arrogant, remote and badly run. But *Heritage & Renewal* will be more difficult to implement than the Turnbull Report. Cathedral canons have complete security of tenure, and can defy outside interference for as long as they want.[92] Just how long a determined cathedral canon can defy the authorities of the Church has become starkly apparent at Lincoln over the last ten years.

The cathedral chapter at Lincoln was already an unhappy place when the sub-dean and treasurer, Canon Rex Davis, conceived the disastrous fund-raising trip to Australia with the Mappa Mundi in 1988. Most chapters are intensely political places – at St Paul's, rows followed the sacking of the choir school headmaster and the appointment of the first woman priest, Lucy Winkett.[93] Westminster Abbey had to call in a judge to arbitrate in a feud after the Dean sacked the organist and choir master for alleged financial irregularity.[94] In political worlds of this kind, Rex Davis is an acknowledged master; a colleague described him in 1989 as 'the only person in the chapter who is politically streetwise, and knows how to get things done'.[95] It was an assessment Rex Davis was happy to endorse: 'Whether or not money is put into this project rather than that project,' he told the journalist Danny Danziger in 1989, '[is] politics with a small p.'[96]

Oliver Fiennes, who retired as Dean of Lincoln in 1989, described a chapter as 'a fellowship held together with enormous effort against all the odds'. Members are chosen by the bishop (or, in more important cases, such as the dean, by the prime minister) without consideration as to whether or not they will get on with one another. Internecine strife is such a regular feature that Fiennes reckoned the system 'both wasteful and cruel'.[97] His own feud with the conservative precentor (which spanned all his twenty years at the cathedral) scandalised the city of Lincoln, but was little known beyond its boundaries.* The same cannot be said of the feud ignited by his successor, the Very Reverend Brandon Jackson, who was appointed dean by Margaret Thatcher with a brief to end the factional strife within the chapter. The advice of Robert Hardy, the Bishop of Lincoln, to his new dean was candid: 'Get rid of the buggers.'

Jackson began briskly, tackling the sub-dean directly over the losses incurred on the Australian expedition, which had become a source of controversy both in Lincoln and the wider Church. His blunt approach sparked a fresh round of squabbling within the chapter, ending in an invitation to the Bishop to 'visit' his cathedral in October 1990. The Bishop censured the Dean and issued an invitation to all the cathedral canons to 'consider their position'. Nobody did, humiliating the Bishop, isolating Jackson and resolving nothing. The feud simmered for another five years before bursting into life again, this time farcically. A verger alleged that the Dean had jogged to her house in October 1993, armed with a bottle of wine, with clear sexual intent. Unable to muster a sufficiently vigorous erection, he brought her to orgasm using his tongue. He allegedly repeated this feat a month later at the Deanery.

The allegations were manifestly absurd. But, for reasons comprehensible only to the squabbling personalities of the chapter at Lincoln, the Bishop refused to believe the denials of the Dean. After Jackson rejected his invitation to resign, the Bishop convened a consistory court to test the veracity of the verger's tale. Unsurprisingly, it cleared the Dean of any misconduct.[98] Understandably peeved, Jackson told a television interviewer that the Bishop had arranged the court case as part of a concerted attempt to get rid of him. Both Jackson and Hardy sought (and received) the support of the Archbishop of Canterbury. Absurdly, the Bishop then said that he would not return to his cathedral until both the dean and the sub-dean resigned. A year later, Lambeth Palace resolved to put an end to the feud. After receiving a report from his appointments secretary, the Archbishop asked both Brandon Jackson and Rex Davis to resign. Jackson waited a year before acceding to this request, but left as soon as suitable terms were agreed. Davis remained in post.[99] The Bishop of Lincoln still nurses the hope that he will leave too, but he cannot be forced to go until he is seventy.

---

* A precentor is the senior residentiary, and is responsible in some cases for overseeing the musical life of a cathedral. The feud between Oliver Fiennes and David Rutter, precentor at Lincoln, is recorded in Danziger, *The Cathedral*, pp. 100–4.

The Slow Suicide of the Church of England

The rejection of archiepiscopal authority by the sub-dean of Lincoln is a near-perfect vignette of the institutionalised absence of leadership and authority in the Church of England which the Turnbull Report identified. The inability of Bishop Hardy to exercise his authority makes a mockery of the main recommendation of the Howe Commission: to concentrate power in the hands of bishops at the great cathedrals of England. The squabbling at Lincoln is precisely the kind of humiliation which dismays ordinary churchgoers, struggling to keep the faith afloat in a sea of public indifference. In the last few years they have endured embarrassing newspaper stories about the sexually exploitative 'Nine O'Clock Service' in Sheffield; the alleged 'internal ministry' of a vicar in west London; a west country bishop touching-up a trainee monk; the revelation that a north country bishop had a conviction for indecency; a Sussex vicar converting aggressively to atheism; and repeated cases of paedophilia and small-scale embezzlement by parish priests.

On matters as central to Christian understanding as the Virgin Birth and the Resurrection and on most of the moral issues of the day – abortion, homosexuality, euthanasia, divorce – the views of the men and women in the pews are insulted by their leaders on a weekly basis. As with the leaders of another part of the Heritage Industry, the National Trust, the House of Bishops relies on the financial support of its members, but distrusts and despises their views. The Church may claim to be both catholic and reformed but it is closer to the despotism of the Catholics than the democracy of the Reformers.

Its synods, at deanery, diocesan and national level, are dominated by the clergy. The General Synod, in particular, is dominated by clergymen elected not by voters but as representatives of 'special constituencies'. The Turnbull Commission (itself dominated by clergymen) expressly rejected turning the General Synod into a democratically elected body, or giving it any decision-making powers:

> Quite clearly an assembly of some 566 members, drawn from all over the country and meeting twice (or occasionally three times) a year, cannot be an executive body. As a representative assembly, it must be able to question, to seek and obtain information, and to express opinions which will influence, often decisively, the formation of policies. But it cannot itself be the forum in which those policies are formulated . . . Its role is primarily reactive.[100]

A separate review of synodical government conducted by Lord Bridge of Harwich, a member of the Turnbull Commission, also rejected the idea of allowing everyone on the electoral roll of their parish church to vote in synodical elections. Bridge thought it would be too difficult 'to ensure that the electorate was sufficiently well-informed about the issues and candidates'.[101]

This active hostility to democracy is one of the many luxuries which the vast endowments of the Church of England have afforded its leaders when almost every other institution in the land has had to open its books and seek popular endorsement. So long as their salaries, pensions, offices and churches were financed by the invested assets of the past rather than the congregations of the present, the leaders of the Church paid no penalties for ignoring the views of the membership – that they were those most corrupted by the Anglican inheritance has not stopped senior clergymen complaining that the assets of the Church Commissioners are morally and spiritually corrupting. What they mean is that the investment income spares the ordinary man and woman in the pew the need to give them more of their wages and salaries to spend on the various enthusiasms of the clergy.

This is why some well-known Anglican clerics greeted the news of the financial calamities of the late 1980s with anything but alarm. For them, the loss of investment income was an opportunity, not a crisis. The Archbishop of Canterbury was among them. He told the General Synod at York in July 1992, where the news first became widely known:

> We should be grateful for our past but not enslaved by it. Grateful too for all the material resources which our Church has inherited from the past and for the care and skill of the Commissioners and many others. We as a Church have lived on the capital of that past, but we cannot do that much longer. The time has come to work energetically and confidently for a future which, under God, we can control and direct through sacrificial and faithful giving.[102]

Of course, there is an element of necessary hypocrisy in claims of this kind. All the leading figures in the Church of England double as Church Commissioners, and it was more agreeable to greet the losses with joy than to take the blame. It was also another measure of their contempt for their congregations.

The effects of the financial difficulties may not turn out to be as pleasing as they imagine. Certainly, the mismanagement of assets by the Church Commissioners has increased the burden on the ordinary churchgoer. Historically, the Commissioners met around two fifths of the cost of clerical stipends, the whole of the salaries and official expenses of bishops, deans, provosts and two cathedral canons, the total cost of clerical pensions, lump sums and retirement homes, and a large part of repairing and maintaining clerical housing, from the humblest parsonage to Lambeth Palace. Inevitably, the financial losses of the first half of the 1990s have reduced the sums available for these responsibilities. As early as 1990 the Commissioners halted all expenditure on the refurbishment of parsonages, and mortgage lending to clergymen was severely curtailed. In 1991 they cut over £4 million from their allocation to clerical stipends, and instituted a series of rolling cuts which trimmed £5.5 million from their contribution in each of the following four years. By 1997 the proportion of the clergy pay bill met by the Commissioners had fallen to 15 per cent.[103] The share met from giving by congregations had risen to 62 per cent.

As other financial pressures mount, this share is likely to increase. The losses coincided with a steep rise in expenditure, mainly on pensions, but also on compensation for clergymen who left the Anglican ministry following the ordination of women (paying them off cost £2.9 million in 1996 and another £2.4 million in 1997).[104] As an increasing number of clergy marriages break up, the Commissioners are also having to house estranged spouses. One result is that parishioners are already having to bear the burden of paying for pensions. Although the Commissioners continue to pay existing pensions, responsibility for all pensions earned after January 1998 is now borne by the parishes. The weight of these commitments is distributed in a way which means some parishes feel the impact more keenly than others. The endowment income is now being directed towards poorer parishes, forcing wealthier parishes to contribute more to churches and vicars other than their own.

The average Church of England clergyman is now dependent, to an extent unprecedented in history, on the generosity of the members of his congregation. The same is true of the Church as a whole. Giving by parishioners now covers nearly half the annual cost of running the Church of England, and much of the rest comes from appeals and fund-raising activities they organise. Endowments account for less than one third of overall income. Sanctimonious calls by archbishops for more 'faithful and sacrificial giving', or a reversion to the ancient practice of tithing, are based on serious misconceptions about how much ordinary churchgoers can or are prepared to give. Tithing harks back to an age before the Welfare State pre-empted two fifths or more of their personal incomes. It also belongs to an age when the local leadership of the Church was more far more unpopular than it is today; tithing and anti-clericalism were closely connected in the past. They will be again.

At the moment, most of the frustration of ordinary churchgoers is directed at the regional and national leadership rather than local rectors, vicars and curates. It is no longer uncommon for parishes to withhold money from dioceses after some egregious violation of their beliefs. 'We don't believe we should be funding other churches that do not preach the true gospel, what we regard as heresy,' explained Philip Hacking, an Evangelical vicar in Sheffield who withheld £20,000 of his diocesan quota in 1994.[105] 'We are unhappy with clergy who preach a non-biblical gospel – for instance, on homosexuality – and we do not want to give a blank cheque to dioceses to support a ministry of which we do not approve.'[106] In 1996 several parishes in Southwark refused to remit funds to the diocese after a special service had been held in Southwark Cathedral to celebrate the contribution made by homosexuals to the life and work of the Church. Anglo-Catholics, dismayed by the decision in 1992 to ordain women, threaten periodically to establish a church within a church which is independent financially as well as in terms of ministry.

Even where differences between laity and bishops are not theological in nature, there is growing resentment of the rising burden of ecclesiastical taxation, especially since its chief cause was the failure by the leaders to restrain the Commissioners. Many parishioners have bitter memories of the expropriation of their historic endowments of glebe-land, cash and securities, transferred compulsorily to Diocesan Boards of Finance by legislative fiat in 1976. (Nobody knows what the expropriated assets are worth now, but their value in 1980–1 was over £90 million.) Some parish churches still lose legacies and other endowments to the diocese if a will is badly worded. Wealthier parishes have noticed that an ever larger proportion of the money they raise is pre-empted by Diocesan Boards for redistribution to poorer parishes through a 'quota' system, and that the methods used to establish their 'quota' are increasingly insensitive.[107]

As they pay a rising proportion of the stipend of the incumbent, parishioners are taking a closer interest in his assets and activities. The incumbent owns the job, the parsonage, the church itself, the churchyard and the church hall as parts of his 'parson's freehold', but most of the costs are met by the congregation. The parson is not free to sell, lease, alter or demolish any of the assets of his church without the permission of at least the diocese and probably the Church Commissioners as well. The contents – pews, lecterns, plate, ornaments and the like – are formally owed by the churchwardens, who cannot dispose of them without the permission of the diocese. For the congregation, maintaining the parish church is tenancy rather than ownership. They meet all the running costs, but the benefits of their capital accrue to the Church. Torrents of clerical cant about 'stewardship' have long obscured this fact. The mismanagement of the Church Commissioners has finally exposed it.

The financial disaster of the early 1990s has ignited a slow revolution in

TABLE 4.4
Income and Expenditure of Church of England, 1993* (£ m)

Expenditure

Stipends and housing	205
Pensions	79
Worship and buildings	250
Community and charities	37
Training	7
National Church responsibilities	7
Administration (mainly dioceses and parishes)	30
	615

Income

Covenanted giving in parishes (including tax relief)†	157
Other giving in parishes	134
Other income in parishes	89
Church Commissioners	153
Pensions board	10
Cathedral and diocesan endowments	64
From reserves	8
	615

Source: *Working as One Body*: The Report of the Archbishops' Commission on the Organisation of the Church of England, Church House Publishing 1995, p. 114.

* These figures are approximations only, because the Church of England has no idea from one year to the next what its overall income and expenditure is. The information is not collated centrally on a regular basis, but compiled periodically for some purpose or other.
† Tax relief on covenanted income is the one form of assistance the state gives to the established Church as a matter of course.

Church government. It increased the financial sophistication and political confidence of ordinary churchgoers, giving the process of change a popular momentum it would otherwise lack. The leaders of the Church of England cannot expect parishioners to produce an ever-increasing share of the income without a larger say in how it is spent. 'Greater financial self-sufficiency need not mean the triumph of inward-looking congregationalism,' the Archbishop of Canterbury told the General Synod in 1993.[108] But it probably does: some parishes are withholding money over theological differences, and others are demanding the right to re-create and maintain their own endowment funds.

The House of Laity of the General Synod has voted for the abolition of the parson's freehold. In time, churches and parishes will demand the right to appoint their own ministers by free and open choice, and to set and vary the terms of their employment and the value of their stipends, in the hope of attracting energetic men and women of superior moral and intellectual calibre. Churches and even parishes which cannot afford priests may decide they can do without; non-stipendiary ministers, who stick to ordinary jobs during the week, are common. Even in middle-of-the-road Anglican churches, ordinary members are performing every priestly function except presiding at the Eucharist. Evangelical churches have dispensed with ordained ministry as a matter of choice.

Many traditional parish churches have made no such choice. The traditional structure of the church, in which one priest serves one congregation in one parish, is failing to survive the haemorrhage even of nominal members of the Church of England. In many families, two generations have passed since any member was baptised, married or buried according to Anglican rites. This is not because the Church of England has lost its gift for inclusiveness – what the Preface to the Book of Common Prayer calls 'the wisdom . . . to keep the mean between the two extremes.' The decision in the autumn of 1992 to ordain women, preceded by the adoption of entrenched positions on both sides and accompanied by dire predictions of exodus and financial ruin, was a triumph of the Anglican spirit of compromise. Relatively few priests and communicants left, and many of them have since returned, as the claims of reason were seen to outweigh those of scripture and tradition. The real problem for the leaders of the Church of England is that their perennial search for the mean, rooted in a distant past when religious beliefs were a matter of life and death, has no distinctive claim on the predominantly secular imagination of the age. Ordinary Anglicans – of every persuasion and none – know that the central problem of the Church of England is not a lack of money, it is a lack of members, and they believe that the parish priesthood and especially the bench of bishops do not help to recruit new members. Neither the Turnbull nor the Bridge Reports offered any democratic outlet for this growing discontent with the leadership. The price will be the gradual disintegration of the national Church into a species of congregationalism. Only those congregations which can support themselves will survive. Disestablishment, when it comes, will merely accelerate the process: the mission of the Church of England to the English people is over.

CHAPTER FIVE

OXBRIDGE

Oxford and Cambridge are the marshalling yards for the gravy train.
WALLIS ELLIS, The Oxbridge Conspiracy[1]

The question of feeling inferior to Oxbridge never arose ... The only time we came across Oxford or Cambridge was when Glasgow regularly beat them in the Observer Mace national debating competition.
ANDREW NEIL[2]

I have no objection to the Oxford domination of society ... I see nothing wrong in Oxford and Cambridge people getting the best jobs when they are obviously the best people.
CHRIST CHURCH UNDERGRADUATE, 1994[3]

A country of 57 million people is governed by 2 per cent of her graduate total.
ANDREW ADONIS and STEPHEN POLLARD, A Class Act[4]

Nobody would argue that Oxford and Cambridge have nothing to say to the English people. Their graduates dominate Parliament, the Civil Service, the Foreign Office, the City, the Law (especially the judiciary), the Boardroom, the Arts, the Media and even the moribund Church of England. The fact that Oxford and Cambridge provided nine out of ten permanent secretaries, three out of four Cabinet ministers, and two out every five MPs was the least surprising but one of the most significant facts Anthony Sampson uncovered in his first *Anatomy of Britain* in 1962. Thirty years later, nothing much had changed. Three out of four members of the Major Cabinet were Oxbridge graduates, as were more than two in five of his MPs. Around one sixth of the Labour MPs opposite them were also educated at Oxford or Cambridge. The present prime minister is an Oxford man, like half of his twentieth-century predecessors. Six members of his Cabinet and one in eight of his MPs were educated at Oxford or Cambridge. If New Labour is less dominated by the ancient universities than the Old Labour governments of the sixties and seventies, Oxbridge still holds the top job.

The Great Fees Crisis

The old networks operate as smoothly as ever. When his chancellor and his education secretary wanted to lop £36.3 million off grants to the Oxbridge colleges, the new prime minister was lobbied shamelessly by Oxbridge dons who had advised him in Opposition and by his political mentor Roy Jenkins, the Chancellor of the University of Oxford. The most important call came from Dr Eric Anderson. The former headmaster of Eton, now reincarnated as Master of Lincoln College, Oxford, had the additional advantage of having taught Tony Blair when he was at Fettes.[5] The planned cuts were revised and research funds augmented. The incident was an apt reminder of the adaptability of the Oxbridge mafia. As power has swung away from politics towards the capital markets, newspapers and television, Oxbridge has colonised them too. Its graduates even dominate popular literature and alternative comedy. The grip of the ancient universities on the English imagination, evident in the popularity of pursuits as diverse as the Boat Race and *Inspector Morse*, is as tight as its hold on the best jobs and the levers of power.

It is a remarkable achievement. Nearly eight centuries after a group of learned men fled Oxford for a new home in a small town on a river bank at the southern edge of the fens, Oxbridge has come closer than any other institution to domination of the English way of life. Yet the achievement is extraordinarily fragile. The members and graduates of the universities and colleges of Oxford and Cambridge have status, influence, and power. What they lack is the guarantor of their perpetuation: wealth. This is not widely believed. Like many other myths about the ancient universities and colleges, popular conviction of their fabulous riches is tenacious. The old canard that it is possible to travel from Cambridge to London without leaving land owned by Trinity College, Cambridge, and from Oxford to Cambridge without leaving land owned by Merton College, was repeated as recently as 1982.[6] The truth is more prosaic: Oxbridge is the last of the nationalised industries. It is not a conspiracy against the public, by influence or otherwise, but a state satrapy at the mercy of its political masters.

Eric Anderson may have persuaded Tony Blair to stay the executioners in 1998, but in each of the next ten years the colleges must endure successive reductions in the amount of money given to them by the government to cover the fees they charge to students. Nor will they be allowed to charge students more to make up the shortfall. The government has imposed a ceiling of £1,000 a year on the fees they can charge directly, and warned that any institution which breaches it will face the full rigour of the law. Far from being self-governing bodies conspiring against the public interest, the colleges of Oxford and Cambridge are no longer free even to make contracts to supply services. 'Oxbridge colleges have for centuries charged fees to their students,' says John Flemming, chairman of the conference of colleges at Oxford. 'It is not as if the universities were contemplating something new. The question is whether they should retain the power to charge fees they have always exercised, in the event that the government were to withdraw the reimbursement of these fees from public funds.'[7]

Is Oxbridge Being Dumbed Down?

Allowing the colleges to charge fees would, of course, price many able students out of an Oxbridge education. This would defeat the real ambition of New Labour, presently hidden behind the row over college fees. 'When at Oxford and Cambridge half the places go to private schools,' Gordon Brown told the Labour Party conference in October 1997, 'it is time to modernise and extend opportunity by redistributing resources.'[8] The Blair government hopes to break the stranglehold of the colleges over admission to Oxbridge in the same way that the Attlee government destroyed the aristocracy: by cutting off their incomes.[9] A government spokesman has admitted as much. 'We are not asking for a dumbing down of the colleges,' he said, 'just a fair representation of state school pupils. Some 65 per cent of pupils who achieve three A grades at A level attend state school, yet this is not reflected in Oxbridge admissions.'[10] The colleges, perhaps foolishly, are trying to oblige. Cambridge has undertaken to increase its intake from state schools to 68 per cent and to appoint a full-time 'access officer' to encourage comprehensive pupils to apply. Oxford has agreed to fund bursaries for poorer students.

Ironically, before Old Labour (and Old Tory) destroyed the grammar schools, entry to Oxbridge was gradually being democratised. Before the Second World War, almost every undergraduate at Oxford and Cambridge was educated at a public school. Colleges wanted undergraduates who could afford the fees. The state and local authority scholarships introduced in 1920, to provide for ex-servicemen who wished to study at the ancient universities, were lost to the cuts in public expenditure imposed two years later. Although in the 1930s as many as half of Cambridge undergraduates were receiving financial assistance of some kind, it was not until after the Second World War that state aid became available on a substantial scale. This gave the colleges the confidence to begin admitting candidates solely on the basis of intellectual ability. The results were striking, particularly in the heyday of the grammar schools in the 1950s and 1960s.

By the 1960s, the proportion of public school undergraduates had fallen precipitately. In 1962 Sampson found Oxbridge rapidly becoming a meritoc-racy, and feared this would make the two ancient universities even more exclusive than in the days when only the second sons of the aristocracy attended to prepare for a career in the Church.[11] By 1969, the public schools were winning only 38 per cent of places at Oxford. Thirty years later, the grammar schools have largely disappeared, and the proportion of privately educated undergraduates has reverted to the 40–50 per cent level which New Labour spokesmen and thinkers find so offensive. 'No society can call itself open, let alone classless,' write Adonis and Pollard, 'if entry to its great universities is de facto restricted to a tiny proportion of its citizens.'[12] The élitism is even worse than they imagine: most of the rest of the intake, though ostensibly drawn widely from state schools, comes from a small minority of good comprehensives in the English shires. Using cuts in grants to bludgeon the colleges into taking more comprehensive pupils is a faster and cheaper route to the classless society than the alternative of improving secondary education in the state sector. But it would be foolish to assume it can be achieved without lowering standards, or without penalising otherwise modest people who think the best way to capitalise on the talents of their children is to send them to a public school.

It is undoubtedly true that some able children at state schools do not apply to Oxbridge because they or their teachers think it too upmarket for them. As long ago as 1962 the master of Clare College told Sampson that 'many grammar schools would rather send their boys to a provincial university, which they know, rather than risk being turned down by Oxbridge.'[13] Andrew Neil, who was at Paisley grammar school in the 1960s, wanted to go to Oxbridge, and even took some A and S levels, with a view to sitting the entrance examination. ' "Why do you want to go there?" my French teacher asked sniffily one day,' Neil recalled. ' "Glasgow is as old as most of the Oxbridge colleges and you want to do economics; Glasgow is where Adam Smith wrote the *Wealth of Nations*" . . . It [was] drummed into all of us that we were privileged to be going to a very superior seat of higher learning.'[14] It is more likely, even allowing for the fact that Scotsmen are less overawed by Oxbridge, that his French teacher was more comfortable with Glasgow than Oxford or Cambridge. Thirty years on, some schoolmasters still feel the same.

Oxbridge colleges get only three or four applicants for every place, against six or seven at other top universities. Yet there is no objective reason for anyone to be deterred. Far from bending over backwards to admit Wykehamists and

Etonians, college admissions tutors at both Oxford and Cambridge are anxious to increase the proportion of undergraduates from the state sector. Both universities have all but abolished the entrance examination, which was thought to favour privately educated candidates, and the public schools have begun to complain of discrimination against *them*. 'Some factors now militate against Etonians,' Eric Anderson warned the Old Etonian Association in 1992, shortly before he was translated to the Mastership of Lincoln College. 'When it comes to filling the last few places each year, a number of those College heads who wrote to me admitted that, other things being equal, their colleges might well choose candidates from state rather than independent schools.'[15]

Universities Versus Colleges

Ironically, one reason Oxford and Cambridge can afford to warp the admissions procedure is that they *are* relatively rich. Cambridge University spends £1 million a year on bursaries to undergraduates on full maintenance grants.[16] Richer colleges might be persuaded to deploy more of their wealth in a similar way if the government were not so intent on redistributing it through the universities. Many Oxbridge college bursars think that the enemies of college endowments are actuated by factors other than the merits of the case. Some speak openly of defying the government; certainly, if they are not prepared to resist, they face a stark choice: make economies, or use their endowments to find the balance. Either outcome would suit the government, since both would advance its ambition of emasculating the colleges. This is because the most obvious economy would be to eliminate college tuition fees at source, by eliminating the one-to-one supervision of undergraduates by college-based dons.

Unlike American or European universities, where tuition consists of cramming into a vast auditorium with hundreds of other undergraduates, Oxford and Cambridge offer each of their students a weekly session with a lecturer or fellow. 'My friends at German universities are scrambling for floor space in lectures with 800 other people,' said a German undergraduate at Queen's College, Cambridge. 'Here, I get two hours' one-to-one contact with my professor every week.'[17] Unfortunately, personal tuition is not cheap. It costs an additional £2,000 per year for each undergraduate, or an extra £36.2 million a year for the Oxbridge colleges. If this sum were withdrawn completely or even reduced and additional fees capped at £1,000 a year, the poorer colleges would not be able to survive. It is estimated that twenty-two colleges at Cambridge and twelve at Oxford would go into deficit immediately. 'Pembroke is an excellent college and will survive,' says Robert Stevens, the

Master of one, Pembroke College, Oxford. 'But the present funding arrangements for the bottom third of colleges in Oxford cannot continue. Unless
there is a sudden urge on the part of the very wealthy colleges to give away
part of their patrimony, I can see no alternative to levying fees.'[18]

In fact, the richer colleges at both universities have shared their patrimony
with their poorer brethren for decades. According to a complex formula of
redistribution, the 21 richer colleges at Oxford gave £1.8 million to 15 poorer
colleges in 1996–7. Similarly, the 13 richest colleges at Cambridge gave £1.4
million to the 16 poorest. Scarcely lavish sums; they are about one fortieth
of the gross endowment income of the colleges at both universities. The
government hopes that by reducing its subsidies of college fees, it will persuade the richer colleges to share more. This would have the further pleasing
effect of enhancing the power of the universities at the expense of the colleges, reinforcing the effects of the reduction in support for college fees.

Once the colleges are denied their special subsidy, the distribution of state
support at Oxford and Cambridge will be determined by the same method
as it is everywhere else: by the quality of teaching and research.[19] These are
matters for which the universities, not the colleges, are responsible. With
their fee income truncated and capped, and their endowments redistributed,
the colleges would be reduced to the status of the halls of residence at other
collegiate universities like Durham, Canterbury and London. In the spring
of 1998 even Dr Stevens of Pembroke, a likely beneficiary of any redistribution,
warned that the changes would reduce the colleges to the status of 'glorified
dormitories' to the university.[20] In September that year the government duly
trimmed its support for college fees by £12 million (to be phased in over ten
years) but raised the Oxbridge share of research grants by £50 million.

How the Universities Ceded Power and Wealth to the Colleges

This transfer of power and wealth from the Oxbridge colleges to the universities of Oxford and Cambridge would reverse a momentum which has run
the other way for over five hundred years. Back in the thirteenth century,
when Oxford and Cambridge were founded as educational academies for
aspirant clergymen, colleges did not exist. The students lived and worked in
'halls' or 'hostels', which were little more than doss-houses rented from local
landlords. The earliest benefactors endowed funds for the support of students,
not colleges. There was certainly a great need for them – the life of thirteenth-
century undergraduates was dominated by poverty. The first degree, a Master
of Arts, might take four years to complete and cost between £24 and £32 a
year in living and tutorial expenses. The higher degrees – theology, canon

or civil law or medicine – took longer, and cost even more.[21] A doctorate might take eighteen years of study.

'I am studying at Oxford with the greatest diligence,' wrote one thirteenth-century undergraduate to his patron, 'but the matter of money stands greatly in the way of my promotion as it is now two months since I spent the last of what you sent me. The city is expensive and makes many demands; I have to rent lodgings, buy necessaries, and provide for many other things which I cannot now specify.'[22] His unspecified expenses doubtless included drinking, gambling and whoring as well as lecture and examination fees; the literary evidence suggests that pleasure as well as knowledge was sought in medieval Oxford. But this did not mean the scholars were affluent. The vast majority were ill-dressed, badly housed, malnourished and dirt-poor. Many relied on loans from the Jewish moneylenders who congregated in the city until they were expelled from the country in 1290.

It was not surprising that the first regular income earned by the university of Oxford was devoted entirely to the support of impoverished scholars. It was first paid in 1214, and was an annual fine imposed on the townspeople for the murder of two students five years earlier. In 1209 a scholar at Oxford had killed a prostitute with an arrow. Her outraged neighbours, unable to apprehend the murderer, had seized several of his colleagues instead. Two of these unfortunate passers-by were then lynched outside the city walls.* Humiliating terms of redress, including an annual payment to cover the living expenses of students and the cost of an annual banquet, were imposed. The final condition was the harshest: rents for student lodgings, most of which were owned by local businessmen, were halved for the next ten years. From 1240 the income from these fines was paid into a 'Common Chest' at St Frideswide's Priory, and reinvested to generate an income for the support of impoverished scholars.

By 1240 the revenues of the Common Chest had been greatly increased by the expropriation of an endowment left by one Alan Basset for the singing of masses for his soul after death.† This was the other reason benefactors

---

* It was the unrest following this incident which persuaded a group of scholars to decamp to Cambridge, where they formed a new university.

† Endowments to subsidise the saying of masses for the souls of the dead were common in the Middle Ages. Alan Basset (d.1233?) had left the sum of £133 6s 8d to pay for two chantry priests to sing masses for him and his wife. Invested in property in Oxford, this yielded an income of £5 6s 8d a year. In 1243 the Bishop of Lincoln, Robert Grosseteste, switched this sum from the support of chantry-priests to scholar-priests. The unknown scholar-priests were the beneficiaries of the first proper endowment income received by the University of Oxford. See *The History of the University of Oxford*, Volume 1: The Early Oxford Schools, ed. J. I. Catto, Oxford University Press, 1984, 'The Endowments of the University and Colleges to c. 1348', by T. H. Aston and Rosamond Faith, p. 268.

were keen to alleviate the plight of poor scholars: they were a much cheaper source of sung and said masses for the dead. When Ela Longespee – Dowager Countess of Warwick, and a substantial benefactor of Oxford University in its early years – established the first 'chest' to make loans to poorer students at Oxford, it secured her special commemorative arrangements. Her example was followed by, among others, Eleanor of Castile (the beloved wife of Edward I) and Henry Chichele (Archbishop of Canterbury under Henry V).* Similar loan-chests were established at Cambridge.[23]

By 1360, Oxford University had £1,300 in its chests (getting on for half a million pounds in modern terms).[24] From 1427, this cash was stored in a single Chest of the Five Keys, which could be opened only if all five keyholders were present. (The last word in medieval security, it is now reduced to an exhibit at the Ashmolean Museum, but the finance department of the Oxford University secretariat still calls itself the University Chest.) By then, the universities had also become substantial rentiers. The whole of £206 13s 4d left to Oxford by William of Durham, a graduate, was invested in rent-producing properties around the town. Local notables often left their houses to the university for use as a hostel or hall for scholars.†

The colleges did not begin to rival the universities until the fifteenth century. Although Merton College was founded, with lavish endowments, in the 1260s, only thirteen of the sixty-three Oxbridge colleges date from before 1400. Between 1450 and 1550, the vast majority of the halls and hostels of the two universities were closed, incorporated as a college, or amalgamated with a college. (The last of them did not disappear until 1957, when St Edmund Hall became a college.) The universities have trailed the colleges in the volume and value of their benefactions ever since. Colleges command loyalties in ways universities cannot, and offer donors a better prospect of immortality than a single appearance in a list of benefactors which may run to hundreds of pages. The Reformation, and the accompanying Dissolution of the Monasteries, produced a phalanx of New Men anxious to take advantage of precisely that.

A dozen Oxbridge colleges were founded in the sixteenth century, more than in any other until the twentieth. Beneficiaries of the redistribution of the riches of the monasteries are still among the wealthiest colleges at both places. The richest college at Cambridge (Trinity) and Oxford (Christ Church) was patronised by Henry VIII. Trinity College at Oxford was founded

---

* Chichele also founded All Souls College.
† It is estimated that by 1279 the seven academic halls of the university were enjoying a collective rental income of £20 a year, enough to make the university one of the richest landlords in Oxford. *History of the University of Oxford*, Volume 1, p. 273.

by one of the most notorious profiteers of the Dissolution, Thomas Pope. Much of the wealth of both Wadham and Exeter derives from Sir William Petre (1505?–72), a royal official who plundered such a vast array of estates from the monasteries that even he developed a sense of self-disgust. ('We,' he wrote to Robert Cecil in 1551, 'which talk much of Christ and His Holy Word, have I fear me used a much contrary way; for we leave fishing for men and fish again in the tempestuous seas of this world for gain and wicked mammon.')[25] The inheritances of Brasenose, Gonville & Caius, Magdalene, King's and Christ's colleges also owe something to sacrilege. The second richest college at Oxford (St John's) stands on the site of a dissolved monastery, as does its namesake and equally wealthy counterpart at Cambridge. Wadham and Worcester, at Oxford, and Queen's, Jesus, Emmanuel and Sidney Sussex, at Cambridge, also share this melancholy heritage.

The Dissolution and the Reformation were good for the Oxbridge colleges for reasons other than money. The secular colleges survived (their monastic rivals were stripped of assets and masonry for new foundations) to furnish the Tudor monarchy and administration with talented laymen. Henry VIII judged 'no land better bestowed than that which is given to our Universities, for by their maintenance our Realm shall be governed when we be dead and rotten.' Though the universities remained primarily training institutions for the Church, the colleges also became places to which the wealthy sent their sons to become gentlemen presentable at court. At Oxford or Cambridge they could acquire a smattering of law, which was useful when competing for lucrative offices in government.

The Age of Scandal and Corruption

At Oxford and Cambridge, the enrichment of the colleges also created a new class of scholar: one concerned to protect his wealth, place and privileges. At the Reformation, both universities entered a long period of senescence, scandal and corruption which it took the energy of the Victorians to extirpate. From the middle of the sixteenth century until the middle of the nineteenth, a college fellowship was not so much an intellectual accolade as a meal-ticket for life. Fellowships were bought and sold eagerly, not least because the salaries of fellows were augmented by regular 'dividends' from any surplus of income over expenditure. Similarly, the 'fines' levied on the renewal of leases, and one-off surges in income from the felling of timber or the discovery of minerals, were regarded as windfalls to be divided among the fellows.

Sums set aside by benefactors to pay for dinners, drink, or clothes, were commuted into cash payments to fellows. Resident fellows could further supplement their stipends with lecture or tuition fees, and perhaps a second college post such as bursar or dean. To enjoy the income of a fellowship it was not necessary to reside permanently in college. Rooms let to absent fellows were welcome; they could be re-let for extra income.

Even today, the seventy-odd fellows of All Souls are not expected to remain in residence or teach: the college has no undergraduates. Once elected, a fellow does not have to do anything at all but enjoy a suite of rooms, serviced by college servants, and taste the glories of the college dining room and wine cellars. The prize fellows, chosen by competitive examination, receive £9,000 a year for seven years. They can extend their stay but most depart, to enlarge the influence of intellect in the affairs of the nation by inhabiting Westminster, Whitehall, Fleet Street, the City and the Courts. This worldliness, often cited as the main justification of the institution, has its critics. The fellows of the college were long identified as the authors of the policy of appeasing Hitler, devised and pursued when the foreign secretary, the Archbishop of Canterbury and the editor of *The Times* all belonged to All Souls.* But All Souls has its successes: John Redwood, one of the inventors of privatisation, is a fellow.

Like him, most fellows of All Souls find it preferable to seek more remunerative work beyond the confines of Oxford. But in the eighteenth and nineteenth centuries one did not necessarily exclude the other. Fellows of all Oxbridge colleges could draw an income from the college estates without being in residence. This imbued fellowships with a market value for which men were prepared to pay handsomely, and wardens and masters took generous bribes at fellowship elections. Places were reserved for personal favourites or relations, or nominated successors, and often for the relations of a founder or other benefactor. Much ingenuity was expended on proving consanguinity; between 1750 and 1857 more than half of those elected to fellowships at All Souls claimed kinship with the founder, Archbishop Henry Chichele (1362?–1443).

A fellowship also introduced the holder to a variety of ecclesiastical posts of which the college was patron. It was said of New College in the seventeenth century that it was 'less a place of education than a club whose members competed among themselves for the benefices to which the governing body had the right of presentation'.[26] Virtually all dons were clergymen, and distant clerical posts were exploited as a source of income for resident fellows (who installed a curate to do the job). Only one form of wealth remained conspicuously immune to expropriation by the fellows: the various trust funds estab-

---

* Viscount Halifax, Geoffrey Dawson and Cosmo Gordon Lang. A. L. Rowse, another fellow of the college, wrote a book disputing the claim.

lished by benefactors to provide scholarships and exhibitions for poor scholars, whose income was also derived from landed endowments. Without scholarships, even the middling classes would have struggled to survive at Oxbridge until the real cost of a university education began to decline in the nineteenth century. In the mid-Victorian period, a year at Oxford or Cambridge was costed at about £150, well beyond the means of most. In 1922 a royal commission estimated the cost – in caution money, rents, lecture and supervision fees and personal expenses – at £145, but the undergraduates reckoned £236 was a fairer estimate. Expenses had risen to about £270 a year by the eve of the Second World War.[27] These fees were an important part of college income: there were insufficient scholarship funds for the fellows to risk admitting undergraduates on merit alone.

The effect of this reliance on fees and endowments was a university system which failed in its primary duty: to educate. Men of ability could not penetrate institutions where well-endowed fellowships were virtually hereditary and masters and wardens never retired. (In 1854 Dr Martin Routh died in harness, at the age of 99, in his sixty-fifth year as president of Magdalen). Undergraduate places were allotted not on the basis of ability but the ability to pay, or eligibility for a closed place or a scholarship. Standards of teaching and intellectual inquiry slipped as fast as the fees increased. At Cambridge in the 1730s, Horace Walpole was dismissed by a half-blind professor of mathematics as unteachable; he attended lectures on anatomy which gave him a lifelong distrust of doctors, and was enraged by the low-church posturing of his theology teacher. Like most intelligent young men of the age, he learned more from his Grand Tour than at university. Walpole was equally dismissive of Georgian Oxford, which he described as a 'nursery of nonsense and bigotry'.[28]

Oxford and Cambridge seem so unchallenged today, it is hard to believe that for nearly two hundred years nobody took either seriously. From the Restoration to the Victorian reforms, gifted Englishmen recognised the higher virtues of an education at one of the Scottish or continental universities. While the Scots and Europeans were pursuing the Enlightenment project, Oxford and Cambridge remained resolutely male, ostensibly celibate and wholly Anglican. As late as 1851, 349 of 542 fellows at Oxford were in holy orders and only the head of Merton was not ordained. (In the eighteenth century Lord Chesterfield had described contemporary Cambridge as an 'illiberal seminary'.) At Oxford religious tests were not rescinded completely until 1871, and Greek remained compulsory until 1919. Talented Jews, Roman Catholics and Dissenters were excluded until the repeal of the Test and Corporation Acts in 1829.

By the middle of the nineteenth century Oxford was admitting less than two hundred freshmen a year, under half the number it had admitted even in the 1630s. Most were gentlemen filling in time with desultory studies before receiving their inheritance. The rest were earnest scholarship boys seeking ordination and Church livings, for which the universities were the jumping-off point. The historian Edward Gibbon described his fourteen months at Magdalen in 1752–3 as 'the most idle and unprofitable of my whole life'. The lectures, which undergraduates had to pay to attend, were often atrocious. Written examinations were unknown at either university until the end of the century. John Scott (1751–1838), first Earl of Eldon and symbol of Tory reaction against the Reform Bill, took an examination in Hebrew and History at Oxford in 1770. It consisted of the following exchange:

Examiner: What is the Hebrew for the place of a skull?
Scott: Golgotha.
Examiner: Who founded University College?
Scott: King Alfred.
Examiner: Very well, sir, you are competent for your degree.[29]

Few students bothered to graduate anyway; as late as 1913, a quarter of Cambridge men went down without taking a degree. The buildings were deficient, especially in the laboratories demanded by the new scientific disciplines. The dons were underpaid; even where they were not, they owed their fellowships more to family connections than to a love of learning. High-earning positions (often entailing no teaching responsibilities) were bought and sold like any other asset, though usually among family and friends rather than in the open market. With no pensions being paid by the University until 1922, the poorer fellows hung on to their posts long after they were competent or useful.

Rescue and Reform

Demands for reform were first voiced in the 1830s by the 3rd Earl of Radnor, a Whig politician and friend of the radical essayist William Cobbett. But the colleges were powerful enough to ensure that his views were ignored. For good measure, Oxford elected the reactionary Duke of Wellington as chancellor in 1834, confident that he could be counted on to resist the pressure for change. In 1850 a Whig prime minister, Lord John Russell, was persuaded to appoint a royal commission to recommend reforms. The Liberal government wanted fully reformed universities, directed by professors rather than fellows, and organised on a departmental rather than a collegiate basis. W. E. Gladstone, MP for Oxford University, averted this eventuality by taking charge, and guiding a moderate University Reform Act through Parliament in 1854.

This legislation reduced the powers of heads of colleges by creating an elected council of the whole university. It weeded out non-resident fellowships, and allowed the university to open private halls to accommodate undergraduates who could not afford the steep college fees. (Many of them, especially the halls for women, who began the long process of admission to the universities in the 1870s, subsequently became colleges.) The reforms did not endear Gladstone to his electors, yet they were scarcely revolutionary: the political powers of the heads of colleges were truncated, but the core problem was untouched. So long as the colleges were richer than the universities, and the government refused to ask the taxpayer to redress the balance, reform of the system of admission, teaching, research and examination was an impossibility.

The commission had not probed the finances of the colleges, which remained deeply obscure. Only four Oxford colleges – All Souls, Balliol, Corpus Christi and Pembroke – had agreed to supply financial statements to the royal commissioners, and these were insufficient to attempt any estimation of their true wealth. The Dean of Christ Church would not even answer letters from the commissioners.* The colleges of Cambridge were more co-operative, claiming a collective revenue of £185,000, but the figure was a deliberate underestimate. Even such scanty and inaccurate evidence exposed the main obstacle to reform: the colleges were using their wealth not for the benefit of higher education in Britain as a whole, or even for the good of the universities of Oxford and Cambridge in particular, but to defray the expenses of the pampered fellows.

They enjoyed it for another twenty years before a second reforming government disturbed them again, provoked by the rampant Toryism which swept Oxford in the 1860s. In 1870, a Liberal government led by an increasingly progressive W. E. Gladstone secured legislation to abolish religious tests for university degrees. This was followed by the appointment of a second royal commission in 1871, charged with inquiring into 'the property and income belonging to, administered, or enjoyed by the Universities of Oxford and Cambridge, and the Colleges and Halls therein ... and also to report the uses to which such property and income are applied'.[30]

It is a striking commentary on the Victorian zeal for reform, and the ability of Oxbridge to resist it, that the report of the royal commission of 1872 remains the most up-to-date and comprehensive statement to be published

---

* The university was co-operative, but its figures were wrong. The report of the royal commission of 1852 estimated the annual income of Oxford University at £7,500, but the Commissioners were misled; the real wealth of the university was probably closer to £9,250 a year. *Victoria History of the County of Oxford*, Volume III, ed. the late Revd H. E. Salter and Mary Lobel: The University of Oxford, Oxford University Press, 1954, p. 32.

of the landed and financial assets owned by the Oxbridge colleges. The royal commissioners insisted the colleges submit full financial statements, which they subjected to rigorous scrutiny and analysis. This was not always easy. In 1871 Lincoln College was still keeping its accounts in Latin. Reactionaries at both universities continued to resent what they saw as unwarranted intrusion into private property. But only the fellows of Sidney Sussex refused to co-operate with the royal commission, and they were overruled by the master.[31]

The report of the commissioners, published in July 1874, confirmed what everybody knew: the colleges at Oxford owned twenty-four times as much land (184,748 acres) as the university (7,683 acres). At Cambridge the imbalance was even more marked. The college estates (124,820 acres) were over fiftyfold those of the university (2,445 acres). This meant that the colleges were far richer than the universities. At Oxford, they had a collective income (£366,254) nearly eight times that of the university (£47,589), and at Cambridge, the joint income of the colleges (£306,535) exceeded that of the university (£34,051) by a factor of nine.

These figures encouraged the commissioners to recommend that the universities construct many new buildings and laboratories, and recruit more academic staff, to be paid for out of a tax on the endowment income of the colleges. The Universities of Oxford and Cambridge Act of 1877 obliged the colleges to 'contribute more largely out of their revenues to University purposes'.[32] Amid great grumbling from the fellows, a gradually rising tax on college wealth was agreed with the universities at both Oxford and Cambridge.*

Unfortunately, the graduated increase in the tax rested on the assumption that college incomes would continue to increase. As it turned out, the royal commission had measured them at the height of their prosperity. Even now, the report provides a fascinating snapshot of the assets and revenues of the unreformed colleges at their nineteenth-century peak. Overwhelmingly invested in the broad acres, rents and tithes of the landed past, rather than the bonds and shares of the twentieth century, the wealth of the colleges was mired in the Middle Ages. This grave imbalance pitched them headlong into the great agricultural depression of the last quarter of the nineteenth century. The same prolonged agricultural depression which overwhelmed the other historic estates of the realm – Crown, Aristocracy and Church – did its deadly work at Oxbridge too.

---

* At Cambridge the tax was initially fixed at £1,000 a college, rising to a minimum levy of £25,000 a year from 1894. But, after complaints from the colleges, the levy was reduced to percentage payments up to a maximum total level of £30,000, which they would work towards over twenty years. At Oxford, where a Common University Fund was set up, a similar system was agreed.

It shrank the rental income of St John's College, Cambridge, so severely that the 'dividend' collected by the fellows shrank from £300 in 1872 to £80 in 1895. At Oxford, Oriel had to suppress a number of fellowships between 1881 and 1914. Desperate remedies, including a poll tax on undergraduates and an appeal to former members, were applied. In 1890 it was proposed to suspend college contributions to the university tax altogether, but in the end it was cheap bread for the masses, not the machinations of the fellows, which blunted the impact of the 1877 reform. By the time of the First World War, the unequal distribution of wealth was still the major brake on the expansion and reform of the two universities. 'The richer colleges,' claimed a book about Cambridge originally published in 1913, 'can buy the first-class men; the poorer colleges can only get them by a lucky chance. What can Magdalene, Corpus and St Catherine's do against Trinity, St John's, King's and Caius?'[33]

The Nationalisation of Oxbridge

At the end of this century, as at the beginning, the richer colleges are still getting the first-class men. The poorer colleges regularly find themselves at the foot of the Oxbridge examination league tables. With roomier accommodation, better libraries and facilities, and more and better dons on the premises, it is easy for wealthier colleges to poach the finest intellects. At both Oxford and Cambridge, there is a well-established correlation between college wealth and examination results. It has become so marked at Oxford that the Congregation voted in the early 1990s to discontinue publishing the colleges of candidates in class lists, in a bid to frustrate the compilers of the Norrington Table.* The accentuation of this inequality would be one of the unintended side-effects of the withdrawal of the public subsidy to college tuition fees. 'Ending college fees would be disastrous,' says Richard Benthall, treasurer of Christ Church. 'It may sound as if we are rich, but every penny is accounted for. The collegiate system is expensive to maintain and if we lose fees we will have to charge the students. That will make the colleges even more élitist.'[34] This is undoubtedly true, and is precisely why the government will never allow the colleges to resume their power to charge undergraduates directly, no matter how much they huff and puff about their right to govern themselves.

* The Norrington Table was devised in the 1960s by Sir Arthur Norrington, president of Trinity College, Oxford, as a method of comparing performance in final examinations of candidates from the various colleges. Candidates are awarded points for each class of degree, and a league table is prepared from the total points awarded to each college. The table has never been sanctioned by either the university or the colleges. Attempts to suppress it have proved unsuccessful.

The truth is that Oxbridge struck a Faustian pact with the state after the First World War, and neither the colleges nor the universities can recoup the independence they surrendered then.

By the time of the armistice both Oxford and Cambridge were in deep financial difficulties. During the war, the effects of the agricultural depression were exacerbated by the loss of fee-paying undergraduates and the great inflation which accompanied the war effort. At the end of the war, Cambridge reckoned it needed to spend £750,000 on buildings, and another £53,000 a year on academic salaries. But the University Chest was empty. Cambridge ran at a loss in the first three years after the war.[35] Finances were no healthier at Oxford. There was no alternative but to submit to the state for assistance.

In 1919 the vice-chancellors told the president of the Board of Education, the Oxford historian H. A. L. Fisher, that they needed a large infusion of taxpayers' money if they were to maintain academic standards and bring their facilities up to date. There was widespread resistance at both universities to the idea of taking the king's shilling, which it was felt would compromise their independence. But necessity prevailed. 'I dislike, and I suppose everyone here dislikes, the idea of receiving government money,' J. J. Thomson, master of Trinity, told the Cambridge Senate. '[But] I am convinced that the only alternative is to lose the efficiency of the University, and much as I dislike the receipt of money from the government I dislike still more the idea of an inefficient University.'[36] An initial grant of £30,000 a year was accepted by each university, and a decision on future funding was referred to a third royal commission, chaired by a Balliol man and former Liberal prime minister, H. H. Asquith. Fisher wanted it to make a grand inquisition into the assets and revenues of the colleges and universities, along the lines of the Cleveland inquiry of 1871, but this was opposed successfully.

This did not prevent the commissioners exploring extreme solutions to the problem of funding the ancient universities. They included complete expropriation of the endowed assets of the colleges by the universities, the appropriation of college surpluses by the universities, and giving universities a right of veto over college spending plans. A scheme for unifying the agricultural estates of the colleges of both universities under the single management of the Ministry of Agriculture was seriously considered. The commissioners had discovered how little difference the redistribution of wealth between the universities and the colleges under the Act of 1877 had made to the balance of wealth and power in Oxford and Cambridge. By 1920 the endowment income of the Oxford colleges (£560,766) had *increased* to ten times that of the university (£54,973). Their Cambridge equivalents (£400,139) had slipped a little, but enjoyed an income eight times as large as the university (£53,551).[37] At both Oxford and Cambridge, the colleges were giving the

universities barely a twentieth of their income. The Oxford colleges gave
£27,626 and the Cambridge colleges £23,613, of which a quarter came from
one college, Trinity.[38]

The expropriators were resisted successfully, and the taxation introduced
in the 1870s was not made more effective. Instead, the Asquith Report invited
the taxpayer to rescue the universities:

> The Universities and Colleges have at their disposal a very large revenue
> even without the State grants already paid to them. Nevertheless it is
> clear to us that the sums available are totally insufficient to meet the
> existing needs of the Universities and Colleges . . . It is essential, in our
> opinion, that the State should come to the relief of the Universities with
> increased grants forthwith.[39]

The Report recommended an annual state grant of £100,000 a year to each
university (plus another £10,000 for women's colleges), and a lump sum
to kick-start a pension scheme.[40] It did not materialise immediately. Public
expenditure constraints ensured that the annual grant did not clear £100,000
until the early 1930s, and the public subsidisation of Oxbridge did not really
take off until after the Second World War. However, the Asquith Commission
put state funding of Oxbridge on a permanent footing for the first time.

Between 1914 and 1918, state investment in the buildings, equipment and
teaching posts needed to support medicine and new sciences like biology,
physics, chemistry and engineering had been accelerated at both universities
by the pressing demands of the First World War. Afterwards, the grants committee set up to fund various military projects was adapted by Fisher as a
permanent University Grants Committee, the forerunner of the Higher Education Funding Council for England (HEFCE) and its Welsh and Scottish
counterparts, which is today only one of dozens of ways in which public
money reaches the ancient universities. In 1919 the taxpayer supplied about
3p in every £1 received by Cambridge and 1½p in every £1 received by Oxford.
Today, the state supplies 60.6p in every £1 received at Cambridge and 57.5p
for Oxford.

Government expenditure on the ancient universities rose without ceasing
from the 1940s to the 1980s. 'At no period have the universities and colleges
in fact been so prosperous,' wrote the Oxford historian V. H. H. Green at
the height of the spending boom in the 1960s. 'The only faint uneasiness
that may cross the mind arises from the relative loss of freedom which financial
dependence on the State must entail, no genuine danger in an age of benevol-
ently disposed governments, but not perhaps a threat which should be entirely
forgotten.'[41] The Conservative governments of the 1980s proved to be the

malevolent paymaster Green could not foresee. In 1980 the first Thatcher administration imposed cuts in university funding, trimmed research council budgets, and forced overseas students to meet the full cost of their tuition fees. These cuts were accompanied by a tripling of the numbers of university students, and a massive increase in the number of universities, obliging every university to make less money go further. Funding was also geared to assessments of the standards of teaching and research, and to the number of students each university attracted. For the first time, Oxbridge dons were exposed to serious competition for public money.[42]

They have to compete harder for research and teaching funds, and they have to teach more. Oxbridge dons are paid on the same scale as their contemporaries at the former polytechnics, and their jobs are no longer secure for life. In 1997 it became apparent that Oxbridge was likely to be the main victim of the review of university funding conducted by Ron Dearing, the former chief executive of the Post Office. The Dearing Report, delivered a few months after the New Labour government was elected in 1997, recommended that the government review the funding of the fees charged by the Oxbridge colleges to assess whether 'an exceptionally high level of funding . . . in relation to other funding needs in higher education . . . represents a good use of resources.'[43] This was to re-visit an issue the Conservatives had failed to resolve in favour of the taxpayer. New Labour was not so sensitive, provoking the uproar which ended with the Master of Lincoln calling on his former pupil at Number Ten.* For the first time, the colleges were brought face-to-face with the reality of dependence on the state.

Could Oxbridge Be Privatised?

The experience has caused deeper thinkers at both universities to re-examine the feasibility of financial independence. They have not forgotten how recently Oxbridge dependence on the taxpayer came about. Although state support was put on to a permanent footing in the 1920s, it did not become a dominant feature of Oxbridge finances until well after the Second World War. Taxpayers did not fund college fees at all until 1962, and did not meet the full cost until 1977. However, between them the two ancient universities now receive some £335 million a year from public funds. To replace a sum of this magnitude would require an endowment of £8–12 billion. It would

---

* From 1999, college fees were replaced by a new funding system which pays the colleges an additional sum to cover the cost of teaching and the maintenance of historic buildings. It will yield them £24.2 million a year, against £36.3 million via the old system of college fees.

be extremely difficult, though not impossible, to raise, but it is unrealistic to expect Oxbridge to forgo *all* public funding.

If the universities and colleges decided to forgo only their core funding from the HEFCE, and continued to benefit from publicly funded research and support for students, they would have to replace only £175 million a year.[44] This would require a capital endowment of £4–6 billion, or £2–3 billion at each university – a large but more manageable figure. Several American universities enjoy endowment funds of this size. In 1996, the capital value of the endowment funds at Harvard were put at $8.8 billion (£5.4 billion); Yale had $4.8 billion (£3 billion), and Princeton £4.5 billion (£2.7 billion).[45] Oxford and Cambridge cannot match these figures, but they are far richer than other universities in Britain, and considerably richer than they would like the outside world to know.

Between them, the colleges and universities enjoy an investment income of £174 million. It is reasonable to guess that they control physical and financial assets worth perhaps £3.8 billion, even before account is taken of the wealth residing in their inheritance of great art and artefacts. This is some way short of £4–6 billion, but in recent years both the universities and the colleges have proved adept at raising funds from private sources. In October 1988 the Campaign for Oxford was set up, with an initial target of £250 million from private benefactors. The chancellor, Lord Jenkins, said it aimed to provide 'the icing on the cake, not the cake itself'. By the time it closed five years later, the Campaign had raised £341 million. Cambridge followed suit in 1989, setting up the Cambridge Foundation, with a target of £250 million by the year 2000. By 1997, it had secured £184.5 million.[46]

Fund-raising is now a permanent feature of life at both universities, with development programmes run by professional fund-raisers, and the colleges have separate appeals. Lincoln College, Oxford, employed a professional fund-raiser called Howard Raingold, who solicited a total of £6 million from past members and major companies.[47] The support of foreign benefactors enabled even impoverished Pembroke to spend £4 million on a residential development in the late 1980s. The North Commission reckoned that Oxford as a whole raised over £700 million in the ten years to 1998, of which £500 million will support research and the balance will go on hiring dons, subsidising students and building new facilities.[48] At Cambridge, Downing and St John's have recently built lavish and expensive new libraries. Jesus thought raising £11 million for a new court and library by no means unachievable, and found the £2.1 million construction cost of the library without really trying.[49]

Institutions which can raise private funding at a rate of £50–60 million a year will take thirty years or less to raise the £2–3 billion they need to break

TABLE 5.1
Assets of the Universities of Oxford and Cambridge, 1997 (£ m)

	Oxford	Cambridge
Land & Buildings	*138.5	355.3
Restricted Endowments	291.2	362.2
General Endowments	42.9	117.8
Net Current Assets	67.5	128.0
Liabilities	(23.3)	(10.2)
Total Net Assets	516.8	953.1
Endowment Income	18.4	31.0

Sources: University of Oxford Financial Statements, 1997 and Abstract of Accounts for the Year ended 31 July 1997; Cambridge University Reporter, 19 December 1997.

* Stated at cost. Their real value is up to five times as high.

free of the HEFCE. Both universities can call on global networks of alumni who, if not wealthy in their own right, are running companies which have millions to spare. The American Friends of Cambridge University have raised over £20 million.[50] When the Oxford Union building was in danger of falling down, a Japanese bank was first among the contributors to the restoration appeal. Both universities now have full-time development directors, offices in the United States, and mailing lists of alumni who receive regular despatches in the shape of *Cam* and *Oxford Today*. Henry Drucker, the fund-raiser who ran the Campaign for Oxford, made such an impression that he was invited to advise New Labour on how to reduce its dependence on the trade unions. It proved much harder work.

Can the Colleges Survive?

'A return to private money is likely to mean a return to [the Oxbridge] duopoly of quality,' says Lord Jenkins. 'We, to put it bluntly, have richer alumni, greater treasures, more glamour, and therefore greater money-pulling capacity.'[51] But there is a familiar obstacle to capitalising on this pulling-power: most of the existing endowments belong to the colleges, not the universities. Of the total endowments, £3 in every £4 belongs to the colleges, where there are huge differences in wealth. At Oxford, two thirds of the endowments belong to the top twelve colleges, and the concentration is even narrower at Cambridge. This unequal distribution affects not only the academic performance of the poorer colleges; it makes it harder for them to generate income. Poorer colleges accommodate fewer students, so their fee income is smaller. Their rooms are less commodious, so their income from leasing college rooms for conferences is lower. A realistic plan for independence from the state would involve either centralisation of the endowments of the colleges or systematic redistribution of income from rich to poor colleges.

This was the ambition of the Royal Commission of 1871. It was also the ambition of the Commission of Inquiry into Oxford University, chaired by Sir Oliver Franks, between 1964 and 1966. Franks recommended a major overhaul of the college contributions scheme conceived in 1871, which would turn the tax into a mechanism for transferring money from wealthier colleges to poorer ones, not least by making the income of college trusts as well as endowments liable to the tax. The aim was to build up the permanent endowments of the poorer colleges 'to the point where they become economically viable and independent'.

Thirty years later, a second Commission of Inquiry chaired by Dr Peter North estimated that the Franks scheme had succeeded in transferring some £70 million from rich colleges to poorer ones,[52] but that the scale of the redistribution was still inadequate. 'The ultimate conclusion must be that they have certainly not succeeded in "solving the problem" of the poorer colleges,' read the Report. 'Disparities in levels of resources and concerns about their effects continue to exist.'[53] Chief among the North recommendations was an intensification of the contributions scheme, and its extension to five new colleges (Green, Harris Manchester, Kellogg, Mansfield and Templeton). But the most revolutionary recommendation was the reform of the presentation of the accounts of the colleges, so that they could be taxed by the university on the basis of accurate, up-to-date and comparable financial information.

The opacity of Oxbridge college accounts is legendary. Though college bursars prepare orthodox accounts for their own purposes, the financial information they share with the world is virtually impossible to understand. They claim that they are obliged by their statutes to present their finances in particularly obtuse ways, and obliged by numerous trusts to devote much of their endowment income to particular ends. It is hard to imagine a more convenient alliance of law and expediency. When public expenditure on the universities was rising, the colleges had a strong incentive to appear poor, in the hope of attracting a larger slice of the available funds. Public expenditure is now falling; the incentive is the same.

'If we were to sell all of St John's assets we would raise around £150 million, which would run the university for just over a year,' claimed the senior bursar at St John's, Cambridge, in 1990. 'The collegiate system is the whole foundation of the university. The colleges attract benefactors but if you add them to a soup called Cambridge they lose their specific appeal – colleges act as a sort of priming pump for the fund-raising process.'[54] But reformist spirits in the government, the universities and among the poorer colleges are not convinced: the independent wealth of the colleges is more threatened today than at any time since the Royal Commission of 1871.

Like the aristocracy, the colleges will not surrender without a fight. Their first defence is to plead poverty, their second to proclaim their independence of the university and the state. But their most effective is the legitimate but opaque nature of their financial accounts. Archaic methods of accounting for income make it difficult to assess their wealth accurately. Revenues are filtered through dozens of different accounts, and are not consolidated in a comprehensible way. The colleges produce no balance sheets itemising the market value of their assets. Like other institutional investors, they are skilled at turning income into capital, rendering attempts to assess and capitalise their income hazardous and easily discredited. (Though poorer colleges naturally have to pursue income at the expense of capital.) Assessments of wealth are further complicated by the conceit of continuing to distinguish between trust funds where revenue is available to the college to spend as the fellows see fit, and those where use is restricted to prescribed purposes. All these devices enable them to disparage external estimates as ludicrous exaggerations, without the need to contradict them in detail.

The Wealth of the Oxbridge Colleges

In July 1989 *The Economist* estimated that the value of the endowments of the Oxford colleges was £900 million. This was variously described by Oxford officials as 'grossly too high' and 'at least 50 per cent' too high.[55] Two years later, John Bradfield, then senior bursar at Trinity, the richest college at Cambridge, described a series of frivolous comments in the *Financial Times* about the size and management of its wealth as not only 'misleading' and a 'canard' but 'Wrong! . . . Wrong! . . . Absurd!'[56] But only five Cambridge colleges were prepared to comment on estimates of their wealth. At Oxford only two colleges were prepared to supply significant details additional to the published accounts, and a clear majority did not even acknowledge receipt of a request for further information.

'I would not wish to comment on the paper which you have produced,' replied the Treasurer of Oriel, 'other than state that in many instances it is highly inaccurate and therefore completely misleading.'[57] The response of the senior bursar of St John's College, the second richest at Cambridge, to a written request for financial information was typical. 'The published accounts of the College constitute the only material about the financial and property affairs of the College which is made generally available,' he wrote. 'These are considered together with a fuller report by the Governing Body of the College once a year, but the latter document is confidential to the Governing Body and I am afraid I am not at liberty to release this. I am sorry that I am not able to be of more assistance on this occasion.'[58]

The secrecy and paranoia which surrounds the finances of the colleges makes a generalised assessment of their wealth a dangerous undertaking, even without the hazards posed by the differing history and circumstances of each of the sixty-odd colleges at Oxford and Cambridge. As the last people to attempt a comprehensive valuation of the colleges – the Royal Commissioners of 1871 – rightly observed, 'the circumstances of each body are so various that no general remarks could explain the peculiarities of each, or be applicable to all.'[59] But some generalisations can be made. One is that new colleges (which means all those for women) tend to be poorer than the historic ones. A second is that poorer colleges are forced to seek income rather than capital growth from their endowments, which can make them seem richer than they are. A third is that some of the historic colleges are poorer today than at the time of the Royal Commission 120-odd years ago. Oxbridge as a whole is much less of a financial force in the land than it was in the Victorian period, largely because its inheritance was primarily landed, in a century when the chief sources of wealth are not broad acres but industry, commerce and finance.

The colleges were slow to adjust their assets to the new forms of wealth. This is scarcely surprising: even after the securities markets developed on a substantial scale in the eighteenth century, only the deep-delved earth was considered an appropriate repository for a collegiate foundation with no finite lifespan. A number of colleges were owners of South Sea stock at the time of the Bubble in 1720.[60] St John's, Cambridge was a major buyer of government bonds in the 1740s, but only as a temporary home for cash balances awaiting reinvestment in land. The material history of the colleges of Oxford and Cambridge between the Middle Ages and the First World War is largely a story of the accumulation and management of landed assets.

Though their income from fixed rents was hit badly by the inflation of the sixteenth century, they prospered in the agricultural boom of the eighteenth

TABLE 5.2
Estimated Wealth of the Oxford Colleges, 1997 (£ m)

College	Foundation	Acreage	Gross Endowment Income	Endowments*
Christ Church	1546	18,232	5.4	103.8
St John's	1555	4,821	6.1	101.6
All Souls	1438	15,668	4.0	81.2
Nuffield	1958	424	3.9	70.1
Merton	1264	13,689	3.2	63.6
The Queen's	1341	6,175	3.3	55.4
Magdalen	1458	5,215	2.6	51.1
Jesus	1571	4,357	2.8	50.7
University	1249	5,047	2.7	47.6
New College	1379	8,174	2.0	43.3
Corpus Christi	1517	6,110	2.2	42.1
Balliol	1263	–	2.0	38.1
Brasenose	1509	3,083	1.5	30.6
Trinity	1555	3,182	1.4	30.0
Lincoln	1427	1,987	1.8	28.0
Wadham	1612	2,583	1.3	25.0
Somerville	1879	–	1.2	25.0
Exeter	1314	2,986	1.1	24.2
Hertford	1740	–	1.0	21.8
St Catherine's	1963	–	0.9	20.0
St Anne's	1952	–	0.9	19.6
St Hilda's	1893	–	0.8	18.7
St Hugh's	1886	–	0.9	18.7
Lady Margaret Hall	1878	–	0.9	17.0
Oriel	1326	–	1.1	16.8
Wolfson	1966	–	0.8	16.4
St Edmund Hall	1957	–	0.8	16.1
St Antony's	1953	–	0.5	11.4
Worcester	1714	447	0.5	10.7
Pembroke	1624	17	0.5	10.7
St Peter's	1961	–	0.4	9.3
Keble	1868	622	0.4	8.6
Linacre	1965	–	0.2	4.4
Templeton	1984	–	0.4	2.5
Mansfield	–	–	0.1	2.2
Harris Manchester	1994	–	0.1	1.6
Total	–	102,821	59.7m	1,137.9m

Source: University of Oxford Accounts of the Colleges, 1996–7.

* Calculated by capitalising agricultural income at 4 per cent; urban rents at 7.7 per cent; dividend and interest income at 4.5 per cent.

century.* As the economy industrialised, and towns became cities, colleges with land in the right places did exceptionally well. The Universities and College Estates Act of 1858 allowed them to alienate land for the first time and to grant building leases. Green fields were turned into lucrative housing estates, factories, pubs and offices. Merton, already one of the richest colleges, gained markedly by this tactic. But, like other historic estates, the colleges made the mistake of granting long leases at fixed rents whose value was eroded by inflation. Like the aristocracy, Oxbridge colleges sold agricultural land aggressively before and after the First World War, and reinvested the proceeds in government bonds and shares.

The change of policy was most marked at King's, where Keynes was the presiding influence. By November 1920, he had sold a third of the college estates, reckoning he could obtain twice the yield in the stock market.[61] But his switch from land to securities in the 1920s was not as lonely or inspired as his followers have sometimes claimed.† Many rich colleges adopted the same approach. Between 1871 and 1920, university and collegiate income from securities increased by one half at Oxford and one third at Cambridge.[62] The Asquith Commission of 1922 found Oxford colleges had increased revenues by between 59 and 309 per cent by selling land and reinvesting the proceeds. Cambridge colleges raised income by between 64 and 479 per cent.[63]

The earnings of the fellows rose accordingly. At Christ's, they saw their salaries rise from £180 in 1900 to £450 by the end of the 1930s. These huge increases served only to underline the poverty of the previous policies of estate management. Few colleges had professional advisers. On one occasion, Keynes had to deal with a disgruntled tenant farmer himself over dinner at the college. The Asquith Commission stated bluntly that if a college was too poor or inept to manage its agricultural estates properly it should sell them and invest the proceeds in gilts.[64] But the scale of the land disposals can be exaggerated. The university and colleges of Oxford owned 191,891 acres in 1871 and 175,856 acres in 1920, a drop of only 8 per cent. The acreage owned by Cambridge fell by 11,738 acres in the same period – just 9 per cent. Many

---

* In 1576 Sir Thomas Smith, a Cambridge man, former Provost of Eton and Secretary of State to Elizabeth, piloted through Parliament an Act allowing one third of rents paid to Eton, Winchester and the university Colleges to be paid in corn and malt. Though some Colleges were slow to take advantage of the legislation – King's College, for example, did not adopt it until 1597–8 – it provided inflation-proofing as the century wore on. 'Without which happie helpe,' it was later written of the Cambridge colleges, 'the Colleges had, many of them, bene left forsaken by theire studentes long ere this.' *The Victoria History of the Counties of England*: Cambridge, p. 189.
† The same is true of his work in the City, where he chaired the National Mutual Life company. See Chapter 29.

TABLE 5.3
Estimated Wealth of the Cambridge Colleges, 1997 (£ m)

College	Foundation	Acreage	Gross Endowment Income	Endowments*
Trinity	1546	19,752	2.4	355.0
St John's	1516	20,105	7.5	127.3
Gonville & Caius	1348	2,499	4.2	74.6
Emmanuel	1583	2,254	2.8	54.6
Jesus	1496	1,789	2.9	50.5
King's	1441	–	2.1	45.8
Clare College	1317	10,734	1.8	42.5
Peterhouse	1280	2,717	2.2	33.7
Corpus Christi	1352	2,175	1.8	32.3
Downing	1807	–	1.7	30.6
Newnham	1871	–	1.4	29.3
Christ's	1505	3,475	1.5	29.1
Churchill	1961	6,000	1.1	25.3
Sidney Sussex	1589	–	1.5	24.8
Pembroke	1347	1,912	1.0	22.5
Trinity Hall	1351	549	1.2	22.0
Selwyn	1882	–	1.0	21.5
Girton	1873	–	0.9	20.3
Queen's	1448	569	0.9	17.9
Magdalene	1542	994	1.0	16.3
New Hall	1954	–	0.7	15.5
St Catherine's	1473	345	0.9	15.2
Fitzwilliam	1954	–	0.7	14.7
Robinson	1975	–	0.7	14.2
Clare Hall	1966	–	0.6	12.2
Darwin	1964	–	0.4	9.3
Lucy Cavendish	1965	–	0.3	7.6
Wolfson	1965	–	0.2	4.6
St Edmund's	1965	–	0.2	4.0
Hughes Hall	–	–	0.1	1.6
Total		75,869	64.7m	1,174.8m

Source: Abstracts of the Accounts of the Colleges for the Year Ended 30 June 1997,
Cambridge University Reporter, 18 May 1998.

* Calculated by capitalising agricultural income at 4 per cent; urban rents at 7.7 per cent; and
dividend and interest income at 4.5 per cent.

colleges re-entered the agricultural land market in the late 1920s and early 1930s.

Although the Oxbridge colleges have pursued a more balanced investment policy during the twentieth century than they did in the nineteenth, the resumption of chronic inflation after the Second World War finally forced them to shed historic estates in favour of stock market investments. Even then, they probably sold land too slowly to protect their wealth effectively. Today, dividends and interest payments still account for only half the endowment income at both universities. The colleges of Oxford continue to own about 100,000 acres, their counterparts at Cambridge own 75,000 acres. These are large estates by comparison with other institutional investors.

There are real arguments for keeping landed assets. Many colleges are sitting on long leaseholds which will be worth a fortune when they fall in. But the retention of large landed estates reflects the ties of sentiment and the pull of history as well: it gives palpable form to the collegiate preference for accumulating capital over generating income. 'You have to bear in mind the longevity of the liabilities. Here they are infinite,' was how the senior bursar at Trinity College, Cambridge, explained his apparently excessive land bank.[65] Institutions whose collective memory includes the Tudor inflation are not about to sell land wholesale because the second half of the twentieth century suggests equities are a better hedge against rising prices.

Oxbridge as Heritage

Of course, the burden of the past is imposed as well as self-imposed. Like the cathedrals, Oxbridge colleges are members of the National Heritage as well as part of a living university. One of them, Christ Church, has a cathedral on the premises, which cost the endowment £563,741 in 1996–7.[66] Even in years when the cathedral is not in need of major repairs or maintenance, Christ Church reckons to devote about £10 million of its investments to its needs. The college also has to protect Christ Church Meadow, a field in the heart of Oxford, from spoliation and development. Almost every college has historic and listed buildings to maintain to the exacting standards set by English Heritage. (Oxbridge colleges were among the earliest claimants from the Historic Buildings Councils in the 1950s.) Even the concrete and glass of St Catherine's College, Oxford – the work of the Danish architect, Arne Jacobsen – was listed Grade I in 1993. Trinity College, Cambridge, reckons to spend £1 million a year on the upkeep of its buildings alone.

New buildings cannot be erected without the laborious acquisition of planning consents. The libraries of the colleges are full of precious books, manuscripts, plate and works of art which have to be insured and protected against fire and theft. Emmanuel College at Cambridge owns enough material of historical and antiquarian interest for a benefactor to have offered to fund the creation of a museum. He was refused, on the grounds that the running costs would be too high. 'One is only too aware that what in the hands of a private individual amounts to wealth in the form of illuminated manuscripts, plate or even historic buildings, in the case of corporate bodies like ours become liabilities to be insured, cared for and maintained,' says the senior bursar of Gonville & Caius.[67]

But Heritage has benefits as well as costs: it is a crucial part of the Oxbridge sales pitch. 'Oxford was a good story,' recalls Henry Drucker of his time raising funds for the Campaign for Oxford. 'It wasn't a fake story, and it had a unique pull. Where else could you produce a fund-raising leaflet headed 'Oxford: The Next 800 Years?'[68] At Oxford there is now an interactive museum in Broad Street, called *The Oxford Story*. Partly owned by the university, it welcomed 172,000 visitors in 1996, each paying £4.50. Given that the 225,000 visitors to the Ashmolean did not have to pay a penny for the privilege, it can be judged a considerable commercial success. Cambridge welcomed 308,561 people to the Fitzwilliam Museum in 1996, but has yet to plunge downmarket in the same way.

Cambridge has preferred to draw on its intellectual heritage to sell itself. In 1995 the university organised an exhibition of its scholarly, scientific and creative achievements at Christie's in London, for the benefit of the Cambridge Foundation. It was a blatant attempt to raise money by flattering the visitors with accounts of the great minds the university has harboured and the intellectual achievements its colleges and faculties have incubated.[69] Oxford and Cambridge once regarded tourists as a nuisance; now they draw on their architecture and history shamelessly to extract money. The Bodleian applied recently to the Lottery Fund for £6.5 million to fund repairs. The application was refused, but it marked the admission of the ancient universities to full membership of the Heritage Industry.

How Oxbridge Touts for Money

The willingness of Oxbridge dons to solicit for money was one of the chief cultural changes identified by Jeremy Paxman in 1990, at the fag-end of the Thatcher era. 'Everyone,' he wrote, 'including the professors of Byzantine theology, had now heard the message from Whitehall: the State was no longer some ever-indulgent patron. The universities had to "get into the market-place" and find alternatives sources of finance . . . they dutifully took their cue, and began attempting to solicit money from industry.'[70] Dons like to pretend that this was revolutionary; in reality, it was simply a change of scale. Oxford and Cambridge relied for eight centuries upon private benefactions from wealthy public servants, landowners and ecclesiastics, not because they were particularly well-disposed towards higher learning but because State, Land and Church were the chief sources of money until the beginning of this century. As soon as industrial and commercial fortunes reached significant size, the colleges and universities tapped them too.

The Randlords were among the first to achieve the requisite scale.[71] The first Rhodes Scholars came to Oxford in 1903, subsidised by the enormous mineral fortune Cecil Rhodes had assembled in South Africa. The merchant bankers, Schroders, and the newspaper baron, Lord Rothermere (then still plain Sir Harold Harmsworth) also subsidised building programmes and professorial chairs at Cambridge before the First World War. In 1920 Rothermere turned to Oxford, endowing the Harmsworth Professorship of American History. Walter Morrison, who had inherited a large business fortune, gave the Bodleian Library £50,000 the same year. The Rockefeller Trustees donated £600,000 towards its expansion eight years later. In 1935 the 50 Shilling Tailor, Montague Burton, endowed a chair of international relations.

But the munificent gifts of the Oxford motor manufacturer William Morris, Viscount Nuffield, outshone them all. His first benefaction, given in 1926, was £10,000 to fund a chair of Spanish studies at Oxford. Four years later he bought the Radcliffe Observatory to house a new Institute of Medical Research.* Between October 1936 and October 1937, he gave no less than £2.5 million (about £73 million in today's money) towards the institution now known as the Nuffield Institute of Medical Research. His final benefaction was £1 million towards the foundation of Nuffield College, to which he left the whole of his personal wealth (including his house, Nuffield Place). Morris also gave generously to several impoverished colleges at Oxford, including St Peter's, Pembroke and Worcester.

Oxford was not the only beneficiary of the new commercial wealth. In 1919 the British oil companies endowed the Cambridge school of chemistry with £210,000. The biochemists got £165,000 from Sir William Dunn in 1922, and the school of agriculture £133,000 from the Rockefeller Foundation in 1923. The same Foundation was also responsible in October 1928 for one of the greatest benefactions ever given to Cambridge: £700,000 (about £19 million in today's money) towards the construction of the new University Library. In 1945

---

* The Radcliffe Trust, set up in 1714 under the will of Dr John Radcliffe, was directed to build a library in Oxford and employ a librarian. Any residual income was to be applied to such charitable purposes as the trustees saw fit. The trust is still functioning, and funds a variety of conservation, musical, craft and academic causes.

the Shell Oil Company endowed a professorial chair and a new department of chemical engineering at Cambridge with £1.5 million, and Cambridge had its own benefactor from the motor industry: Sir Herbert Austin (later Lord Austin of Longbridge) donated £250,000 to re-equip the Cavendish Laboratory.[72]

Both St Catherine's College, Oxford and Churchill College, Cambridge were created almost entirely with subscriptions from major industrial companies and corporate charities.[73] At Oxford, Green College is named after its main benefactor, Dr Cecil Green, the founder of Texas Instruments. Both universities have benefited from the largesse of the Wolfson Foundation: all the women's colleges at Oxford and New Hall at Cambridge have received donations from it, and both universities now have a Wolfson College for graduates. It is significant that both were founded in the mid-1960s, when Margaret Thatcher, far from telling the ancient universities to get into the marketplace, was an obscure Opposition MP.

Is Autonomy Compatible with the Marketplace?

Much of the snobbishness of modern Oxbridge dons about industrial and commercial benefactions stems not from a study of their financial history but from their detestation of the former prime minister, the first post-war premier to stanch the flow of public money into the universities. By 1985 Oxford hated Thatcher enough to deny her an honorary degree by 738 votes to 319 in Congregation, an honour among Oxford-educated prime ministers which she shares only with Zulfikar Ali Bhutto of Pakistan. She was not greatly admired at Cambridge either. 'It's inconceivable that Wittgenstein would be offered a lectureship today,' a Cambridge don told Paxman in the 1980s. 'I mean, what would his business plan look like?'[74]

Oxbridge dons argue that their growing reliance on private sources of funding has shifted the balance of their working lives from teaching (funded by the taxpayer) towards research (funded by big companies and charities as well as the taxpayer). The charities and companies which buy the best minds at Oxbridge are interested in practical results, not intellectual achievement. They want products to sell to consumers, and drugs to heal the sick. 'Cheque-book research', where dons are hired on short-term contracts to undertake projects for companies and charities, colours the working lives of thousands of Oxbridge dons (especially in medicine and the life and physical sciences). Even state-funded research is now measured for its effectiveness, in the quad-rennial Research Assessment Exercises orchestrated by the research councils. Continued funding depends on results.

Until the 1980s, Oxbridge dons nursed a belief that the taxpayer would always be willing to support their pursuit of knowledge for its own sake. In their view, the purpose of a university was to prevent scholars being distracted from their real work by having to earn a living; that real work is not 'teaching' or 'research', both of which can be measured by the government, but scholarship. The true scholar is the man or woman who pursues or perpetuates knowledge for its own sake, without regard to its usefulness. It is the 'idea of a university' expounded by John Henry Newman at Oxford in 1852, and its supposed destruction at the hands of Thatcher's utilitarian governments is almost the only belief which redbrick and Oxbridge dons of left and right hold in common.

Yet the university described by Newman was always an illusion, which bore no relation even to the Oxford he knew. It was sustained for a few decades after the Second World War by unconditional state subsidies, but could never outlast the vast expansion of the university system launched by the Robbins Report of 1963. When the number of university students doubled again in the ten years to 1995, it was inevitable that state spending would not increase at anything like the same rate. Instead, universities were invited to increase their 'efficiency' – a euphemism for taking more students on the same budget. It was not Thatcher who destroyed the idea of a university but a previous generation of Oxbridge dons, who sold the independence of the ancient universities to the government in 1919.

The state naturally looks to the universities to train managers, engineers and applied scientists, and to pursue research which adds to the national income rather than to public expenditure. These were precisely the conditions which the government attached to public funding when it was increased after the Second World War. Politicians are responsive to voters, and voters want the fruits not of scholarship but of economic growth.

The companies on which Oxbridge relies increasingly for research grants and endowments are responsive to a different audience: shareholders. 'Big business and universities will never share the same values,' says Quentin Skinner, Regius Professor of modern history at Cambridge. 'But in the past 15 years we have had to stop being so fastidious about taking their money because of the extent to which the state won't pay the bills. We can't afford to lose the chance of knowledge generation.'[75] In fact, knowledge generation (and perpetuation, in the case of useless disciplines such as Latin and Ancient Greek) is an idea which cannot survive a condition of financial dependence on anyone: taxpayers, companies, or charities.

Even rich individuals have an ulterior motive in patronising a college or university: immortality. Few are willing to give a substantial sum to a university or college unconditionally. The error is to think that there is anything modern about this direction of the lives of dons. The earliest benefactors at Oxford, like Ela Longespie and Alan Basset, were purchasing masses, not scholarship. Yet dons argue that many contemporary benefactions compromise the autonomy of the universities in a way that ancient gifts did not. In 1996 Oxford was mired in dispute over whether to accept £20 million from Wafic Said, a Syrian-born businessman with close links to the Saudi royal family, to build and endow a new school of business. The university was desperate for the money, but many dons disliked Said's background and his conditions. He wanted the right to appoint a majority of the trustees of the controlling foundation, and the power to veto the appointment of the director. Oxford dons, further incensed by a proposal to build the new school on one of the last greenfield sites in the centre of the city, voted against his offer by 259 votes to 214. Hasty and embarrassing negotiations ensued. Hostile dons were canvassed, and placated or compromised as best the university could manage. The school eventually opened in a refurbished suite of rooms at the Radcliffe Infirmary, with the intention of moving eventually to a new building in a car park opposite the railway station. Said agreed to forgo the right to appoint the majority of the trustees but retained the right to veto the director.

It is hard to see how such give-and-take can be avoided. In 1994 Rewley House, the centre of part-time education at Oxford, agreed to rename itself Kellogg College after accepting £12 million in grants from the Kellogg Foundation. That same year, Manchester College re-named itself Manchester Academy and Harris College after accepting £3.6 million from Sir Phil Harris, the carpet magnate.[76] The cash enabled Manchester to become a full college, and a change of name seemed a small price to pay. Templeton College would not exist without the £7 million furnished by Sir John Templeton.

The extent to which these benefactors interfere in the daily lives of their foundations is largely a matter of temperament. Lord Nuffield was sufficiently deferential to the dons of Oxford to abandon his plan to found a college for accountants and engineers. He disliked the design and appearance of the college itself, but never interfered and still left them everything in his will. At Cambridge, the television rentals millionaire, Sir David Robinson, gave £18 million to found a new college in the 1970s without insisting on anything except that it should be situated on a large central site.[77]

Paradoxically, colleges are more likely to compromise their independence or integrity when accepting funds to endow a chair or lectureship. Jesus College, Cambridge was once offered a fellowship in Child Abuse. It refused the offer, but the university accepted £2 million from Dennis Gillings to establish a Professorship of Health Management.[78] In 1990 Rupert Murdoch gave £3 million to endow a chair of Language and Communications at Oxford. The holder, Professor Jean Aitchison, shocked fellow-dons by devising a course on 'language, media and film' which allows undergraduates to study soap operas and horror films. 'Students are more visually literate than literate-literate nowadays, and we are working with that,' explained one of her colleagues.[79]

Cambridge was almost as shocked when the university accepted £1 million from the popular novelist, Susan Howatch, to endow a lectureship in theology and natural science. Five years later, there was further grumbling when it accepted £2 million from the Thatcher Foundation to finance a new Chair in Enterprise Studies.[80] When King Fahd of Saudi Arabia gave Oxford £20 million in 1997 to fund its new centre for Islamic studies, there was the usual row over where it should be built. But there was also justifiable concern that the new institution would lack intellectual independence.[81] 'It's a big minus that the money is so directly linked to one family,' said Professor Akbar Ahmed of Cambridge University. 'It means that there has to be a "line" on something when research is carried out.'[82]

There is obviously a danger, as universities and colleges become more reliant on private and corporate donations, that errors of judgment will be made. Much of the disquiet about Wafic Said had less to do with his demands for control of the new foundation than the popular belief that he made his fortune in arms-dealing. Exeter College has received generous benefactions from Stephen Merrett, the controversial Lloyds underwriter, and Robert Maxwell was allowed to endow a fellowship at Balliol. In 1996 the same college accepted £350,000 from Dr Gert-Rudolph Flick to endow a Chair in the History of European Thought. Once it became known that Flick was the grandson of a Nazi arms manufacturer who had used slave labour during the war, Oxford returned the endowment. There was a similar controversy at Cambridge the same year, when BAT Industries gave the university £1.5 million to endow a Chair of International Relations in the name of Sir Patrick Sheehy, its former chairman. Sir Patrick had earlier rescued the Royal Commonwealth Society library from ruin and transferred it to Cambridge, but this counted for nothing compared with his lifelong service to a tobacco company. The Cancer Research Campaign threatened to withdraw funds from various projects it was subsidising at Cambridge if the university accepted the BAT donation.

But BAT was undeterred and the Senate House, encouraged by another £100,000 to fund bursaries for poorer undergraduates, voted to accept the donation by a majority of two to one. No charity withdrew its funding from Cambridge scientists. Opponents of the donation were further embarrassed by the revelation that the medical faculty was already in receipt of money from an American tobacco company, Philip Morris. They settled for a statement of principles governing all future donations from industrial sources. But the episode was a reminder that the interests of the donors and the universities do not always coincide. Big medical charities like Cancer Research and the British Heart Foundation are important sources of funding for scientists, but they are often obliged to work to political as well as medical agendas.

The ideal benefactor is the one who has no past and seeks no reward but flattery or immortality. In the 1980s the Japanese fulfilled this role admirably, particularly at Oxford. A group of Japanese motor manufacturers endowed the Nissan Institute of Japanese Studies at St Antony's College with £4.5 million. Merton was offered £1.5 million by Takeshi Funahashi, a Japanese golf-course developer. The college used it to build a new Quad.[83] In 1990 St Catherine's College at Oxford established an 'Institute' in Japan in conjunction with a hundred-odd Japanese companies based in and around the city of Kobe, to teach Japanese graduates about the British way of economic and social life. It caused considerable ill-will in Oxford; the complaint was that it siphoned into a single project many millions of pounds which might otherwise have gone to Oxford.[84]

Not all benefactors are as accommodating as Lord Nuffield or as gullible as the Japanese. 'It would be excellent to acquire large sums of money from bibliophile retired clergymen living quietly in the country with their libraries,' says Lord Jenkins, the Chancellor of Oxford University. 'It would be a grave illusion to think there are such people with money freely available. The people with money . . . are people who have made it recently and sometimes with sharp shoulders. One has to live in the real world.'[85] When it comes to money, Oxford and Cambridge have never needed an invitation to live in the real world. A great many of the private benefactions they accepted over the centuries were of extremely dubious provenance.

John Balliol was a rapacious landlord who did time in prison, and founded the college as a penance for desecrating churches. Walter de Merton embezzled public funds and stole from Jews. William of Wykeham, founder of New College, was a notorious pluralist. John Radcliffe, who endowed both University College and the university, was a quack doctor. Cardinal Wolsey, founder of Christ Church, was an embezzler, a social climber, a drunk, a libertine, a nepotist, a pluralist, and the father of at least two bastard children. In modern times, both Cecil Rhodes and Alfred Beit were distinctly sharp-shouldered. At Oxford and Cambridge, *pecunia non olet* ('money has no smell') is a motto of longstanding.

Cambridge now has a Marks & Spencer professor of farm health, a Guinness professor of management studies, a BP professor of organic chemistry, a Price Waterhouse professor of financial accounting, a Hitachi Centre for Communications Systems Research,[86] a Glaxo Institute of Applied Pharmacology, a Rolls Royce advanced materials research centre, and a Bill Gates computer laboratory. In 1994, Oxford was hawking professorial chairs to other corporate sponsors at £1 million a time, according to *The Times*.[87] It now has a Fiat professor in Italian studies, a Squibb Corporation Institute of Pharmacology, and an Institute of Modern Chinese Studies endowed with £10 million by Sir Run Run Shaw, the Hong Kong businessman. All of these donors have worthy aims and ambitions, but they are not interested solely in the pursuit of knowledge for its own sake.

The corruption of scholarship by commercial values is nowhere more evident than at the new schools of management which both universities have now established. In the past, even those Oxbridge degree courses which did prepare undergraduates for a specific career, such as law or medicine, were taught with more respect for theory than practice. 'We are not in the business of conversion courses,' an Oxford law don told Walter Ellis. 'Our law undergraduates follow a three-year course designed to give them a deep understanding of the philosophy as well as the practice of law. It is not seen as a vocational qualification.'[88]

Management, if it is not completely a non-subject, is resolutely *practical* rather than intellectual. 'You don't have to be a great intellectual to be a good manager,' admitted the director of the MBA course at the Judge Institute of Management Studies at Cambridge.[89] Oxford, which did not establish even a sub-faculty for management studies until 1990, tried initially to resist this truth. When Colin Mayer was setting up the first MBA course at Oxford in 1995 he claimed it would be 'as intellectually challenging as anything in the curriculum'.[90] The idea was to link with other disciplines in the university – like economics and political sciences – to advance knowledge of business rather than to provide a purely practical training for a career. John Kay, the first director of the Said Business School, claimed that the new institution 'will be the most intellectually rigorous business school in Europe. That's what the Oxford positioning dictates.'[91] But he admitted that this claim was more ambition than reality. 'Management at the moment is at the pre-scientific stage medicine was at one hundred years ago,' he says. 'We know a lot about it, but we don't have the structure to put that knowledge together.'[92]

It is likely that the Said Business School will rediscover what the Judge Institute has already found. The lack of takers for its three-year MBA course saw it cut initially to twenty-one months, and eventually to just twelve. 'Educationally, it was a dream,' the MBA course director explained of the scheme devised by that most intellectual of management gurus, Charles Handy. 'For employers and students it was a nightmare.'[93]

Is Oxbridge Still the Enemy of Progress?

If engagement with the world of commerce has reduced the intellectual autonomy of Oxbridge, it has also eliminated the oldest criticism of the two ancient universities: their anti-industrial, anti-scientific bias. Until deep into the nineteenth century, the experience of the average Oxbridge undergraduate included minimal scientific instruction and no contact with business. In Victorian times, the universities were the preserve of aspirant clergymen and professionals. The sons of businessmen did not attend, except to lose their earthiness for a career in the church, the law or politics (both Peel and Gladstone used Oxford to shed their commercial backgrounds). T. H. Huxley told a parliamentary committee in 1868 that a man could win the highest academic awards at Oxford or Cambridge, and not know that the earth revolved around the sun.[94]

A hundred years later Sampson complained that Oxbridge was still 'quasi-aristocratic' and geared to gentlemanly professions such as law and the civil service. He noted contemptuously that Balliol had only just got around to appointing its first lecturer in management studies.[95] In 1980, in an influential book, Martin Wiener claimed that Oxbridge had equipped the country with successive generations of amateurs and generalists who not only knew nothing of economic, technological or business matters but imparted their culture to the entrepreneurial classes, turning them from industry towards the gentlemanly professions. 'Oxbridge', he wrote, 'institutionalised Victorian resistance to the new industrial world.'[96]

These criticisms were always unfair. Oxbridge did far more damage in the social and political fields (where its graduates achieved dominance) than in the commercial and industrial fields (where they did not). Science was never the Cinderella Oxbridge detractors have portrayed. Newton, Harvey, Babbage and Darwin were all Cambridge men, and, anyway, the success of a civilisation is not measured solely by economic criteria. Imperial Britain had need of able administrators and energetic clergymen. Even if Oxbridge did institutionalise a British preference for gentlemanly values over commercial success, an anti-industrial culture did not become problematic until it collided with incompatible material aspirations. This did not happen until after the Second World War.

Nor was it apparent that Britain was in a state of relative economic decline until the Great Exhibition of 1851. By then, the Cambridge Natural Sciences tripos was in its third year. The Cavendish Laboratory, where Rutherford split the atom and Watson and Crick unravelled the mystery of DNA, was established as early as 1871. Although all three complained of a lack of funding, this may even have assisted their work. 'We haven't the money,' Rutherford said, 'so we've got to think.' The Cavendish pioneered electrical measurement, gas discharges, atomic structure and radioactivity as well as nuclear physics and molecular biology. It even pioneered links with British industry. W. G. Pye, who set up an electrical manufacturing enterprise in Cambridge in 1910, was a technician at the Cavendish.

It is true that science–industry links of this kind were not always encouraged. In the 1930s two Oxford pathologists, Howard Florey and Ernst Chain, proved the therapeutic value of penicillin. But the university discouraged them from patenting their work, and the rewards were reaped by pharmaceutical companies in the United States. When Martin Wood left the Oxford physics faculty in 1959 to set up Oxford Instruments (now a major manufacturer of specialised medical equipment), he was treated as 'an absolute pariah and letting the side down'.[97] Such attitudes owed much to petty jealousies and personal rivalries even then; they now belong entirely to the past. In the 1960s Cambridge turned IBM away, but today its vice chancellor is a former IBM executive named Alec Broers, who succeeded David Williams in October 1996. He has brought in £7.4 million from Gordon Moore (founder of Intel) for a science and technology library; £12 million from Bill Gates to build a new computer laboratory; £13 million from Unilever to endow a centre for the study of molecular sciences; and £19.5 million for the BP Institute. 'If you do leading research, and you want that research to be influential,' says Broers, 'you have to look for partners in the corporate world – you just can't do it alone.'[98]

Cambridge is now such a hi-tech boom town that journalists have dubbed it Silicon Fen. Property men speak breathlessly of the Cambridge Phenomenon. Hundreds of companies in the computing, telecommunications and biotechnology industries have congregated in and around the city, drawing others in to work with them. Microsoft recently decided to build in Cambridge its first research centre outside the United States, at a total cost of £60 million.[99] Many of the new companies are located at the Cambridge Science Park, built by Trinity College as long ago as 1975 to encourage hi-tech companies and academics to work together. St John's opened an Innovation Park across the road in 1987. Magdalen has followed their example in Oxford, joining with the Prudential Assurance Company in the late 1980s to create a science park to the south of the city. Cambridge now wants to build a 'science campus' to rival that of MIT, where dons and corporate employees can work side by side, starting with the £32.5 million its vice chancellor has coaxed out of BP and Unilever.[100] A 'school of entrepreneurship' to teach PhDs the rudiments of cash flow and stock control is now being developed at the site.

It is already routine for both colleges and universities to purchase stakes in companies founded by entrepreneurial academics. In 1994 Cambridge University, in conjunction with Trinity and St John's, participated in the management buy-out of a computer software company, Cadcentre,[101] and took their profit when the enterprise was floated on the stock exchange. Oxford University made £5 million when it sold some of its shares in Oxford Molecular, a company specialising in drug design software. This is a massive cultural change. One of the founders of Oxford Molecular is a chemistry don named Graham Richards. At the time of its sale to the public in 1994, he explained that a plan to set the company up in the 1970s had foundered on the resistance of academic colleagues. 'It just wasn't the done thing for academics to be exploiting their ideas,' he said. 'When I became chairman of the university industry committee in 1978, the university would not even permit . . . consultancy work on laboratory notepaper.'[102]

The chief obstacle to the commercialisation of academic ideas in the 1970s was that they were nationalised. Any idea with a decent chance of finding an industrial application had to be surrendered to the British Technology Group to exploit. Thatcher changed the rules in 1987, and allowed universities to patent and commercialise scientific discoveries made in their laboratories. Oxford and Cambridge now have networks of scientists, entrepreneurs and venture capitalists looking to exploit academic ideas and expertise commercially. Oxford University has even set up a subsidiary company, Isis Innovation, to help dons make money from their discoveries. Oxford is already being called Silicon Spires, but embracing the world of commerce is not without its risks. There is an obvious danger, at the cusp where science meets business, that dons will exaggerate the economic potential of the work or come under pressure from their financiers to report encouraging results earlier than it warrants. The temptation to capitalise on work with commercial application may corrupt both dons and universities.[103]

Yet even as dons risk turning into Fat Cats, the belief is still strong in some quarters that Oxbridge is the architect and custodian of national economic backwardness. 'Oxbridge imparts to our élite values which, in their anti-commerce, anti-technology, anti-market snobbery, make them unfit to run a modern economy,' wrote Andrew Neil, as recently as 1994. 'It is the Oxbridge élite which has presided over the decline of this nation, and it lacks the ability or the temperament to reverse it.'[104] He wrote this in a review of *The Oxbridge Conspiracy*, where Walter Ellis argued that Oxbridge turns out conservative professionals rather than industrial managers and dynamic entrepreneurs. 'Look to Oxbridge for gifted advocates, astrophysicists, surgeons and administrators,' he wrote, 'but do not expect to find many who are willing to risk everything for a new idea . . . If Branson had gone to a decent college after Stowe, he would probably be a Lloyd's broker by now, or an accountant with

Goldman Sachs. But Virgin Airways would probably never have got off the ground.'[105]

Like Thatcher, Ellis was fascinated by the possibility that an Oxbridge education is an obstacle to entrepreneurial dynamism. Any university education probably is. People who have nothing to lose are more likely to take risks. But the picture of Oxbridge as the domesticator of restless minds seems increasingly inadequate. In 1996 Nick Corfield, a 35-year-old Cambridge maths graduate, returned to his alma mater not in search of recruits for the Bar or the City or the accountancy profession, but to give £1 million towards the foundation of a Centre for Mathematical Studies. He had made a fortune out of computer software in the United States. His example is striking, but not unusual. There is probably at least as high a proportion of entrepreneurs among Oxbridge graduates as there are Oxbridge graduates in the population as a whole.

Like every other institution in Britain today, from the monarchy to charities, the ancient universities are no longer establishmentarian: they are *businesslike*. Dons at both Oxford and Cambridge talk of the universities not as seats of learning but as 'centres of excellence' (occasionally as 'international centres of excellence'). 'Cambridge and Oxford are wonderful brand names, recognised all over the world, but they have never pushed themselves as much as the top American universities,' explained Nick Corfield after making his donation. He was away too long.

Nobody could accuse modern Oxford and Cambridge of failing to promote themselves: they have merchandising operations selling sweatshirts, baseball caps and mugs to tourists. The Oxford University Shop is now in the High Street, and top advertising gurus advise the universities on their 'brand image'. The Campaign for Oxford and the Cambridge Foundation have raised well over half a billion pounds, making full use of the marketing tools of the business world: direct mail and telephone canvassing. Oxford even invented a new order, the Chancellor's Court of Benefactors, to flatter the gullible rich.

Vice chancellors have ceased to be members of the Great and the Good and have become chief executives, touring the world in search of corporate contributions. The bursar of Brasenose, Dr Robert Gasser, has organised the colleges, theatres and museums of Oxford into a filming consortium to market their facilities to film-makers.[106]

There has been more new building at Oxford and Cambridge in the last ten or fifteen years than at any time since the nineteenth century. In the 1980s, colleges at both universities made systematic use of Business Expansion Scheme tax-breaks to build and buy additional property to let to undergraduates. Most of the new rooms include en-suite bathrooms, not to please the undergraduates but to impress conference delegates, to whom the rooms are rented during the vacations. Even the university presses, long a byword for conservatism, have discovered the rewards of popular publishing (Oxford University Press recently shocked the world of letters by dropping its poetry list). The Cambridge Examining Board, which exports school examinations to 100 countries, recently won a Queen's Award for Export Achievement. In 1995 Balliol was reported to have 'out-sourced' its night-portering to Group 4 Securitas.[107] Scullions manhandling vomit-stained undergraduates into their beds, like scouts and bedders, are part of a paternalistic Oxbridge which is passing rapidly away. Traditional casts of mind, preserved for a few post-war decades by the unquestioning generosity of the taxpayer, are going with them.

Has the Glory Departed?

The expansion of higher education over the last thirty years means that fewer of those who direct the fortunes of the country are drawn from Oxbridge. The ancient universities are now only two of well over a hundred universities in Britain. In the 1930s, Oxford and Cambridge produced one graduate in ten; today, they produce one in fifty. Their enemies are confident that the sheer weight of numbers will dilute their influence and power. Certainly, their denizens are increasingly indistinguishable from their provincial counterparts. Oxbridge dons, like Anglican clergymen, are now part of the chorus of public-sector complaint.

This becomes obvious in isolated acts of Spartism like denying Thatcher an honorary degree or voting against the Said School of Business. 'The objective of many was simply to give the university a bloody nose,' observed its director. 'They had forgotten that they were themselves the university; the nose they bloodied was their own.'[108] John Kay is a former Oxford don who escaped to London, to make a fortune by renting his brain to the private sector. He knew how much professors of Greek on £36,000 a year resent mere lecturers in business studies earning three or four times as much. When the plans for the new School of Business were settled, fifty-five dons still voted against them. 'There are fifty-five people in Oxford,' said Kay, 'who would oppose anything you put forward.'[109]

Oxford has become so concerned about lecturers grumbling at their lack of pay and promotion prospects that it has created 162 new professorships. Cambridge, confronting the same problem, created a new rank of senior lecturer at a slightly higher salary.[110] A majority of dons at both longed openly for a Labour government to fill their coffers and offer them jobs. Their efforts to attract more boys and girls from comprehensive schools, irrespective of the damage it may inflict on academic standards, is not a duty but a labour of political conviction.

The undergraduates whose characters they mould are a characteristically post-modern mixture of greed and frivolity. In 1993 Peregrine Worsthorne was baffled when told by the president of the Oxford Union that she would go into politics after making a pile of money in the City, but had not yet decided which party to support.[111] The Oxford Union is now more likely to debate the merits of smoking and unprotected sex than whether to die for king and country. A debate in 1993 was on the motion, 'This house believes that it is the duty of everyone to exploit their assets'. The case for the motion was opened by a super-model and seconded by an actress from a television soap opera.

Though the subjects and occasions have changed, Horace Walpole would find just as much nonsense and bigotry at Oxford and Cambridge today as he encountered in his own time. The shortage of women would not bother him much, but it is still striking among the fellows, if not among the under-graduates. Of 66 colleges, only Newnham, New Hall, Lucy Cavendish and St Hilda's continue to resist the opposite sex (with the predictable effect that the intellectual calibre of the men has risen, while that of women has fallen). There is as yet no comparable increase in the quotient of female dons. At Oxford, Walter Ellis found that only 9 out of 200 professors, 8 out of 126 readers, and 164 of 934 lecturers were women.[112] The lack of feminine influ-ence in the common room may be one reason why Oxbridge dons are so small-minded.

'Those connected with the academic world do not expect to do other people's academic work for them,' replies one college bursar to a request for assistance in understanding the college accounts. 'I should warn you that your letter may have got up the noses of some bursars in Oxford and Cam-bridge by implying that they should do so.'[113] The incestuous maleness of college life makes for a good deal of politicking and backbiting, rather like a cathedral chapter, which those from the real world often struggle to compre-hend.[114] The former BBC journalist John Tusa resigned in 1993 as president of Wolfson College after just six months, following an 'irreconcilable clash of cultures' in the common room. 'Sadly,' Tusa said afterwards, 'behind the rhetoric, there is a deep fear of real involvement with the outside world.'[115]

Even at Oxford, always more worldly than its Fenland rival, there are dons who interpret the world outside as a threat or a nuisance rather than an opportunity. There is much grumbling among the dons at Cambridge about the costs of economic success: rising house prices, traffic congestion and the loss of green fields. But the reactionaries are no longer in the ascendant at either university. Of course, there are still differences between Oxford and

Cambridge, and between the colleges within them. The imprint of centuries cannot be effaced. Oxford will always be frivolous, worldly and political, just as it was once Catholic and royalist. (Wolsey was an Oxford man.) Cambridge will stay platonic, solemn and scientific, just as it was once Protestant and Roundhead. (Cromwell was a Cambridge man.) Nearly all prime ministers went to Oxford; nearly all the great poets and scientists to Cambridge. Cambridge is still pursuing the Enlightenment project, and Oxford chasing the baubles of wealth and power. Yet the similarities between Oxford and Cambridge are now more striking than the differences. 'Our brands are very closely linked,' explains John Hendry of the Judge Institute, at Cambridge, in the fashionable argot of the business world. 'I hope Oxford is successful. If it is not, it will reflect on us.'[116] The contrast now is not between Oxford and Cambridge; it is between Oxbridge and Redbrick.

CHAPTER SIX

THE REDBRICK UNIVERSITIES

Universities now find themselves in such a pass because they have gradually, over the decades, become almost totally dependent on direct official subventions. The financial issue is, thus, crucial.

PROFESSOR ELIE KEDOURIE[1]

Today, many polytechnics yearn to become universities and, if the present system survives, one day some politician will be daft enough to let them.

SIR DOUGLAS HAGUE, 1991[2]

Why am I the first Kinnock in a thousand generations to be able to get to a university? Why is Glenys the first woman in her family in a thousand generations to be able to get to a university? Was it because all our predecessors were thick? Did they lack talent?

NEIL KINNOCK[3]

Oxford and Cambridge have dominated university education in Britain for 800 years. Even now, when they are only two out of well over 100 universities far from the banks of the Isis and the Cam, the Oxbridge idea is still the model which each new university aims to emulate.* Each wants to be a place where scholars gather not simply to teach or to do research, but to do both, in arts as well as science, for graduates as well as undergraduates. No university sees itself solely as a place where men and women are prepared for the world of work. 'Each time we create a new set of institutions intended (rightly) to be different from Oxford and Cambridge,' wrote Peter Hennessy, 'a slow unacknowledged process of status creep gets underway. It is almost as if the original DNA of the British university system . . . remains so potent a genetic

---

* The actual number of universities at the beginning of 1998 was 110. But the total fluctuates as mergers take place and new universities are founded or university status is extended to other institutions of higher education.

code that all successor institutions are marked by its characteristics.'[4] It is sometimes said that life exists to serve DNA, but the interplay of life and DNA gives rise to diversity. The British universities are homogeneous because all but a handful have come to depend on only one other form of life: the taxpayer.

The universities are now the greatest of the nationalised industries, and they exhibit all the vices of public ownership. Their capital, in terms of buildings, equipment and books, is overused, rundown and obsolescent. The workers, in the shape of professors and lecturers, are resentful and strike-prone. Many make ends meet by moonlighting in big business and the media while pretending to do their appointed jobs of teaching and research. The resources they have to work with are allocated not by price but by faraway bureaucrats in Bristol, Cardiff and Edinburgh, who deliver the quantities of money which they believe will enable the universities to recruit and process the requisite quantities of undergraduates.[5] If they exceed their quotas, they can expect to be fined. Their output of research is measured by numbers of publications and corporate contracts, and extra money given to those which produce most. The result is a system not unlike a Soviet car factory of the Brezhnev era: the workers are cynical and disillusioned; the output is largely a statistical illusion; the customers are obliged to put up with whatever is produced, and the state tries (in the words of Patrick Hutber) to turn donkeys into zebras by painting stripes on their backs. Competition, the only real spur to change, is absent: the universities have a monopoly of the right to confer degrees, no matter how worthless.

The Nationalisation of the Universities

The nationalisation of the universities is a twentieth-century phenomenon. Until the First World War, all universities lived on a mixture of student fees, endowments, donations and the sale of services. Oxford and Cambridge did not accept public money on a permanent basis until the 1920s. This lack of public support condemned the new universities of the nineteenth century to a level of stringency which makes their twentieth-century descendants seem ostentatious. In 1828 the founders of University College, London, formed a joint stock company to raise £100,000, with a promised dividend of 6 per cent, but only one third of the stock was taken up and no dividend was ever paid. The endowment of the college was inadequate, and the fees barely covered the miserably small emoluments of the lecturers. The Professor of English was paid £30 a year, his colleagues in Philosophy and German £21 and £11 10s respectively. Even so, few could afford the fees charged. It took the founders eighty years to reach their initial target of 2,000 undergraduates. University College is far from rich even today – its prime exhibit is the mummified corpse of Jeremy Bentham – but its beginnings were auspicious by comparison with some of the great provincial universities which opened later in the century.

The University of Leeds opened in 1874 in a disused bankruptcy court. Both Liverpool University (1881) and the University of Leicester (founded in 1921 as a municipal memorial to the war dead) began in disused lunatic asylums. It was not until 1903 that Liverpool acquired its first purpose-built accommodation, giving to the world a generic term for the new universities: redbrick. At all the so-called civic universities of Victorian England, the professors were underpaid, the laboratories poorly equipped, and the amenities limited. The students were unable to pay much by way of fees. In 1898 Firth College, the prototype for Sheffield University, was refused admission to a federation of northern university colleges on the grounds that its facilities were inadequate, its premises poor, its finances perilous and its pupils mediocre. Its total annual income in 1900, twenty years after its foundation, was £2,200, and more than half of that sum already came from the taxpayer.

Impecunious new universities had naturally to look to the state for salvation far earlier than wealthier Oxford and Cambridge. Owens College (which became Manchester University) had asked for a public subsidy in the year of its foundation, but it received no satisfaction until the end of the century. The first grants of public money were made to the universities in the 1880s, with one of those modest and apparently well-judged subventions with which every avalanche of public money is started. The beneficiaries were the impoverished universities of the Principality of Wales. The only university open to Welshmen for most of the nineteenth century was St David's College at Lampeter. It was an Anglican foundation established in 1822 by Thomas Burgess, the Bishop of St David's, to educate ministers for the Church in Wales, which had acquired a limited right to award degrees in 1852. It at least could count on the support of the Church. The same was not true of the non-denominational college which opened in a disused pub at Aberystwyth in October 1872. It could not have survived without the support of the taxpayer.

The Castle Hotel, acquired from a bankrupt speculator for £10,000, was only partly paid for when the first students were admitted. It is a tribute to the energy of its founding father, Sir Hugh Owen, that enough money to repay the whole of this sum and finance an endowment fund of £9,000 was collected solely by a house-to-house canvass in Wales and a series of public meetings. Owen, a London barrister of Welsh Methodist origins, is best remembered for reviving the moribund Eisteddfod, but his main work was promoting education in Wales. In 1880 he prompted a departmental inquiry, chaired by Lord Aberdare, into 'the condition of intermediate and higher education in Wales and Monmouthshire', to which he submitted a complete scheme for the reorganisation of higher education in Wales. It was enacted, almost unchanged, in legislation of 1889. Two other university colleges, in addition to that at Aberystwyth, were established at Cardiff in 1883 and at Bangor in 1884, and in 1894 the three colleges were united as the constituent parts of a new University of Wales.

They were publicly subsidised from the outset, though the initial grants were scarcely lavish. But Owen had established an important principle: the taxpayer had a stake in the expansion of higher education. The Welsh example encouraged the new English universities to lobby the Treasury for subventions. They hit upon an argument which has proved persuasive ever since: the threat of scientific and economic retardation. 'Higher education', read a government White Paper of 1987, 'has a crucial role in helping the nation meet the economic challenges of the final decade of this century and beyond.'[6] This assertion is now almost 150 years old; it was first voiced in 1853 by Dr Lyon Playfair, an industrial chemist who had helped to organise the Great Exhibition. In *Industrial Education on the Continent*, he warned that without radical changes in the system of higher education the nascent industrial economies of Europe were bound to erode British industrial supremacy.

The machinery of government soon began grinding out the reports and initiatives which have raised total public expenditure on higher education to its present level by £4.4 billion. A Select Committee on Scientific Instruction reported in 1868; the Devonshire Commission was appointed in 1872 to inquire into the scientific needs of the country; and in 1881 a royal commission on technical instruction began the analysis which led to the Technical Instruction Act of 1889, under which local authorities were empowered to levy a penny rate to organise technical education.

This process was driven almost entirely by economic considerations. In 1872 T. H. Huxley, the Victorian man of science, warned that 'we are entering now upon the most serious struggle for existence to which this country was ever committed. The latter years of the century promise to see us in an industrial war of far more serious import than the military wars of its opening years.'[7] Darwinism, it seemed, was not peculiar to nature. By the time Huxley joined the debate, Playfair had become MP for the Scottish universities. Like progressives of all parties ever since, it was a position he used to draw unflattering comparisons between British *laissez-faire* and continental planning. In Europe, the universities were appendages of the state. Frederick II, Napoleon and Empress Maria Theresa had created institutions whose explicit purpose was to increase social welfare and the national wealth; the British left such important competitive weapons in private hands. 'The experience of commercial nations throughout the world', said Playfair, 'is that the competition of industries is a competition of intellect. The difference between the policy of this and other countries is that, while in other countries the State recognises the fruits of education and acts upon their perception of them, we leave the first steps to the efforts of intelligent men in various localities.'[8] The kind of men he had in mind were John Owens, Josiah Mason, Mark Firth, Thomas Ferens, and Henry Robinson Hartley.

The New Civic Universities

In 1851 a legacy of £96,654 11s 6d from John Owens, a Mancunian currier, furrier, manufacturer and shipper, enabled a new university college to be opened in Manchester.* Owens College was the kernel of the modern University of Manchester, and inspired others by its example. Between 1875 and 1880, Sir Josiah Mason, a manufacturer of steel pens in Birmingham, invested over £200,000 to found Mason College in the town. It became the University of Birmingham twenty-five years later, under the enthusiastic patronage of another wealthy businessman, the steel-screw manufacturer and local-national politician Joseph Chamberlain, who was first drawn into politics through the Education Society and the National Education League. He raised half a million pounds to rebuild the college, and furnished it with an endowment fund of similar size. By the time he entered the Cabinet, Chamberlain was convinced that 'university competition between states is as potent as competition in building battleships.'[9]

Another steel manufacturer, Mark Firth, purchased the site and financed the building of Firth College, which became Sheffield University. In west Yorkshire, the threat of industrial competition from continental textile manufactures persuaded local businessmen to support the foundation of the Yorkshire College of Science in 1874. It became the University of Leeds after moving to its present site in the 1920s. Hull University was founded in 1926 with £250,000 from Thomas Ferens, managing director of Reckitts, a starch and washing-powder manufacturing business in the town. Newcastle University began as a college of physical science in 1871, and was later patronised by the arms manufacturer, Sir William Armstrong.

---

* Owens had wanted to leave his fortune to his friend and business associate George Faulkner (1790?–1862), a Manchester cotton magnate. Faulkner declined, arguing that he was already rich enough, and urged Owens to use the money to found a college of further education. The idea properly belongs to Faulkner.

Henry Robinson Hartley, who founded the University of Southampton, specified that his endowment be used to establish a scientific institution.* The Hartley Institution opened in 1862, and Southampton University has retained a strong reputation for science and engineering ever since. At Nottingham, the university college and technical school were founded by the city council, and survived initially by running classes for the local lace and hosiery industries. D. H. Lawrence, a student at its teacher training department from 1906 to 1908, described it as 'a little slovenly laboratory for the factory'.[10]

Pauperisation of the Universities

Laboratories for the factories were precisely what the first infusions of public money were designed to provide. The first grants to Oxford and Cambridge were given to scientific endeavours – agriculture, engineering, physics, chemistry and biology – accelerated by the appetite of the First World War for scientific munitions.[11] The first public subsidies to the new universities (a mere £15,000 dispensed in 1889) were also concentrated on the sciences, which it was thought could add to national security and economic efficiency. But by 1900 the total public grant to the universities was only £25,000, and just eleven colleges were receiving money.

According to the Fabian thinker and activist Sidney Webb (1859–1947), a keen advocate of public funding of the universities, they really needed at least twenty times as much, and he had good reason to know. Webb was the founder of the London School of Economics and Political Science (LSE), established in 1895 to promote the study of the newly fashionable discipline of economics (and associated social sciences, such as politics and sociology). The Fabians, who then ran the London County Council (LCC) ensured its Houghton Street site was funded by the ratepayers.

But it was the threat of devastating economic competition from Europe and the United States, not the arguments and actions of the Fabians, which finally persuaded the governing classes of the need to increase state aid to the universities. 'Among the many important national functions in which the university institutions will have a large share', read a Board of Education report for 1913–14, 'will be that of meeting the scientific needs of our indus-

---

* Hartley (1777–1850) inherited a great fortune from two generations of successful wine merchants, and bequeathed £103,000 to the Corporation of Southampton 'to promote the study and advancement of the sciences'. The family firm imported chiefly port. 'The firm of Robinson and Hartley', says the history of the University of Southampton, 'made a substantial and profitable contribution to the gout of eighteenth-century England.' See A. Temple Patterson, *The University of Southampton*, University of Southampton Press, 1962, pp. 10–12.

tries on a scale which will enable this country to compete on equal terms with the best equipped of its rivals.'[12] The first university college dedicated completely to the application of science to industry was founded in London as early as 1907, well before the war broke out.

The Imperial College of Science and Technology was created through the merger of the Royal College of Science, founded by Prince Albert in 1845, the Royal School of Mines (1851) and the City and Guilds College, founded in 1884 by the City Corporation and Livery Companies.[13] All three were accommodated on land at South Kensington, purchased over half a century earlier by the commissioners for the Great Exhibition with funds left over from the event. The merger was financed largely by the South African diamond magnates and the Rothschilds. Public money, again supplied by the LCC, was also forthcoming. The goal of the new college was 'to give the highest specialised instruction and to provide the fullest equipment for the most advanced training and research in various branches of science, especially in its application to industry'. It became a college of the University of London the following year.

The Great War provided many vivid illustrations of the military value of scientific inventiveness and, from 1916, a separate Department of Scientific and Industrial Research was established, taking over the National Physical Laboratory from the Royal Society. The war also raised to prominence the first of the six state-funded Research Councils (the Medical Research Council, established in 1911). This ensured that state-funded research became a permanent feature of government policy from the 1920s.[14] The six councils now pump £525.1 million a year into British universities.

Once the conflict was over, the reconstitution of the wartime University Grants Committee (UGC) – which had dispensed public funds to a variety of scientific projects during the war – was a formality. Its successors, the Higher Education Funding Councils for England, Scotland and Wales, are now responsible for annual grants worth £4.4 billion.[15] In 1919 the UGC was charged by the president of the Board of Education, H. A. L. Fisher, with inquiring into 'the financial needs of university education in the United Kingdom and to advise the government as to the application of any grants that may be made by Parliament towards meeting them'.

One third of the £1 million of emergency aid which Parliament agreed to advance was earmarked for capital expenditure on lecture halls and laboratories for the new scientific disciplines. But university expansion was pointless without increased numbers of students, and the establishment of the UGC coincided with a government decision to subsidise the studies of ex-servicemen through state scholarships and local government awards. In 1920 the government even offered a site in Bloomsbury to the University of

London, on condition that King's College would also move there. Unwilling as yet to be corrupted by taxpayers' money, King's refused.*

But resistance to the nationalisation of higher education was never intense, particularly at the newer and poorer universities. The provision of public money in the aftermath of the First World War was the signal for a massive inflation of public expenditure on the universities for the next six decades.[16] After the Second World War, it exploded. The budget climbed from £4 million in 1945 to £81 million in just twenty years.[17] The world of science, intoxicated by its wartime achievements, provided powerful arguments for university expansion. The British failure to turn inventions into saleable products was already a cliché in official circles: in 1944 the Association of Scientific Workers could demand a massive expansion of existing universities without provoking accusations of self-interest.

The following year a committee chaired by Sir Alan Barlow recommended an increase of 35,000 in the number of scientific and technological graduates, to 90,000. In almost every field of intellectual endeavour, there were calls for more graduates and more research, lest the country fall behind its former friends and enemies. Unfavourable comparisons were made with the United States, where it was believed there were sixteen times as many science graduates and ten times as much state spending on research and development.[18] The arguments now seem stale, but in 1953 they persuaded the government to invest £12 million in the enlargement of Imperial College alone. They held that the intellect, and particularly the scientific intellect, was the key to economic growth. In 1962 Sampson declared flatly that 'science is no longer simply an academic pursuit but, primarily, a matter of national survival.'[19] But science is expensive. Sampson learned from a government minister that 'you can buy a professor of Greek for three thousand a year . . . but a professor of science may need a million pounds worth of equipment.'[20] It was believed that only taxpayers could afford him. Even today there is no point on the political spectrum where direct connections between scientific research and economic prowess are questioned seriously.

They are in fact difficult to demonstrate, and there is an understandable reluctance among academics to investigate them. Public expenditure on the universities has increased nearly fifty-fold since the end of the war, in real terms, even before hidden public subsidies are taken into account (student fees paid by the government, research grants and services bought by the public sector). Only two of the top fifty-eight universities and colleges – the

---

* The land was later purchased from the Bedford Estates with a grant from the Rockefeller Trustees, and became the site of the Senate House, the university library and the School of Oriental and African Studies (SOAS) of the University of London.

London Business School and LSE – receive less than half their income from the state, the one close to industry and finance, the other popular with fee-paying foreigners. Although endowment income accounts for over one tenth of the total income of Cambridge University, none of the redbricks earns more than one twelfth of its revenue from invested income.* Even when the state did not pay for the initial endowment of a university or the construction of its buildings, public subsidisation on this scale has given the government effective ownership of all the assets of the redbrick universities. Over the course of the twentieth century, the universities were nationalised, their gaze fixed on the flow of easy money rather than the erosion of their independence.

The Golden Age: Robbins and After

As long as the public grant to the universities continued to rise, and the government did not seek a large say in its distribution, the universities had no cause to resent their dependence. For nearly four decades, successive governments were content to indulge them. The spiralling costs and ambitions of scientific endeavour and equipment ensured that the sum of public money dispensed was always less than the dons demanded. And more could always be extracted from reluctant taxpayers, under the twin threats of the 'brain drain' and economic and scientific retardation. The *locus classicus* of this self-serving doctrine is the Robbins Report of 1963.

It was prepared by a committee consisting largely of dons, and chaired by one of the most prominent of his time, LSE economics professor Lionel Robbins. Their Report concluded that unless there was an immediate and impressive expansion of the university system, and a concomitant increase in public expenditure on the universities, there was little prospect of 'this densely populated island maintaining an adequate position in the fiercely competitive world of the future'. This was familiar, but the Robbins Report added a new twist: individual entitlement. The 'Robbins principle', as it became known, held that higher education should be available to all who wished to pursue it, provided they could reach the requisite standard.

This removed the last constraint on expansion: that the standard of entry and quality of university education would fall. Robbins accepted that, while more undergraduates would drop out as a result, an untapped ocean of talent was being denied its opportunity. Its authors ignored the prescient warning,

* The top universities are those which enjoyed university status before it was granted to the former polytechnics in April 1992.

TABLE 6.1

Reliance of the Universities on the Public Purse (£ k)

	Private Income	Public Sector Income	Public Sector as % of Total
England			
Aston	15,459	26,817	63.43
Bath	21,787	47,523	68.57
Birmingham	66,567	143,026	68.24
Bradford	18,308	40,914	69.09
Bristol	49,089	109,618	69.07
Brunel	19,573	54,917	73.72
City	32,795	36,538	52.70
Durham	29,691	62,369	67.75
East Anglia	21,622	46,022	68.04
Essex	20,085	29,999	59.90
Exeter	27,510	47,384	63.27
Hull	30,828	44,773	59.22
Keele	19,080	34,058	64.09
Kent	28,980	39,588	57.74
Lancaster	23,828	49,114	67.33
Leeds	84,288	145,899	63.38
Leicester	34,699	77,673	69.12
Liverpool	44,275	112,648	71.79
London Business School	25,281	8,868	25.97
London*	72,243*	44,876*	38.32*
– Birkbeck College	5,254	27,803	84.11
– Goldsmiths' College	9,396	23,671	71.58
– Imperial College	79,875	130,137	61.97
– King's College	49,363	94,776	65.75
– London School of Economics	43,121	30,662	41.56
– Queen Mary & Westfield College	36,149	86,492	70.52
– Royal Holloway & Bedford College	191,347	29,291	60.22
– University College	112,053	182,905	62.01
Loughborough	33,772	58,705	63.48
UMIST	34,665	49,139	58.64
Manchester	96,688	158,768	62.15
Newcastle	49,446	103,282	67.62
Nottingham	67,350	115,272	63.12
Reading	37,683	67,227	64.08

TABLE 6.1 *cont.*

	Private Income	Public Sector Income	Public Sector as % of Total
Salford	37,414	73,412	66.24
Sheffield	62,028	120,770	66.07
Southampton	49,855	109,974	68.81
Surrey	39,400	53,270	57.48
Sussex	18,940	52,062	73.33
Warwick	68,929	69,778	50.31
York	27,693	52,914	65.64
Wales			
Aberystwyth	15,980	38,509	70.67
Bangor	15,502	48,171	75.65
Cardiff	35,377	84,921	70.59
Lampeter	2,536	7,813	75.50
Swansea	21,391	52,772	71.16
Scotland			
Aberdeen	32,919	66,417	66.86
Dundee	28,276	61,819	68.62
Edinburgh	69,901	156,153	69.08
Glasgow	57,649	133,334	69.81
Heriot-Watt	23,962	40,822	63.01
St Andrews	18,248	36,284	66.54
Stirling	21,921	32,430	59.67
Strathclyde	40,756	93,511	69.65
Northern Ireland			
The Queen's University of Belfast	24,931	99,543	79.97
Ulster	15,487	81,423	84.02
Total	2,089,232	3,926,843	65.27

Source: Higher Education Statistics Agency, *Resources of Higher Education Institutions* 1996/97.

* Institutes and activities of the University of London only. The Colleges of the University are treated separately.

put succinctly by Kingsley Amis, that 'more will mean worse'.* At the time of the Robbins Report there were 216,000 places in higher education, over half of them in the thirty-one universities, and the rest in colleges of further education. The Report recommended an increase in places by two and half times to 560,000 by 1980, and another six universities on top of the seven pledged by the Conservative government two years earlier (York, East Anglia, Brighton, Canterbury, Warwick, Lancaster and Essex). Expenditure on higher education would rise, from £206 million in 1962 to £742 million in 1980.

These increases were regarded as a minimum. 'The country would have to go a good deal beyond what is contemplated in our recommendations', reckoned the Report, 'before the returns in terms of social net product could be said to suggest general over-investment in this sector.' Lord Hailsham, minister of education when the Robbins Report appeared, approved its recommendations within forty-eight hours. The government, sensitive to allegations that as paymaster it was impinging on academic freedom, agreed that the expansion should not be accompanied by institutional reform. The distribution of money was left to the UGC, then an autonomous grouping of self-interested academics. The committee ostensibly mediated between the universities and the taxpayer; in reality, the universities received a massively increased subvention and complete discretion over how it was spent. By 1969 the historian of the universities could declare that 'at no period have the universities and colleges . . . been so prosperous.'[21]

The Labour government, elected a year after the Robbins Report, was even keener on its recommendations than the outgoing Conservative administration. In the very month it appeared, prime-minister-in-waiting Harold Wilson (another don) told the Labour Party conference that he was 're-defining and . . . re-stating . . . socialism in terms of the scientific revolution' and promised a new Britain 'forged in the white heat of this revolution'. A computer-salesman-turned-don, Dr Vivian Bowden, was the main articulator of the white-hot technological revolution: 'For the first time in recorded history,' he said, 'the survival of the country depends on the universities.'[22]

Each of the seven new universities projected before the Report adopted the collegiate model of their illustrious forebears (though genuine independence for the colleges was abjured as a potential obstacle to a progressive curriculum). The six new universities recommended by Robbins were not created. Instead, *ten* existing Colleges of Advanced Technology (CATs) were

---

* 'The delusion that there are thousands of young people about who are capable of benefiting from university training, but have somehow failed to find their way there, is . . . a necessary component of the expansionist case . . . More will mean worse.' Article in *Encounter*, 1960.

upgraded to university status. In 1956 three late Victorian technical colleges – Battersea, Birmingham and Salford – had been renamed Colleges of Advanced Technology, and it was easier to relabel them as the Universities of Surrey (1966), Aston (1965) and Salford (1967) than to start all over again somewhere else. Between 1957 and 1960 six more technical colleges metamorphosed into CATs – Bradford, Bristol, Chelsea, Northampton, Cardiff and Loughborough – as a first step towards university status (the Bristol CAT became Bath University in 1966).

Scotland and Northern Ireland also acquired new universities. The Royal College in Glasgow, a prestigious engineering school founded in 1796, re-emerged in 1964 under the unlovely name of Strathclyde University. A former collegiate affiliate of Edinburgh University, Heriot-Watt, relabelled a university in 1966, had started as a school of arts in 1822. Northern Ireland, which had made do with Queen's University in Belfast since 1845, got a new university at Coleraine, now called the University of Ulster. There was much jockeying between Catholic Londonderry and Protestant Coleraine to play host to the new foundation. It was a clear sign that university funding was not immune to the politics of the pork barrel. The dons, the independence of whose monkish ancestors had on occasion cost them their lives, moved with unprecedented speed from low dosages of public money to outright membership of the dependency culture. Naturally, they have found the process of detoxification a painful one.

The Conservative Cuts of the 1980s

In 1980 it fell to the education secretary in the Conservative government elected a year earlier to impose the first cuts on the universities since the Second World War. The budget was trimmed by 8.5 per cent over three years, but the cuts did not fall evenly. It was left to the UGC to decide where they should fall, and the UGC bodged it. The budgets of good but unglamorous institutions like Aston, Bradford and Salford, whose graduates found work, were cut (at Salford, the grant fell by 40 per cent). Those of older but less successful institutions were not touched. Expensive but useful science courses disappeared; cheaper but useless arts departments remained intact. Projected increases in student numbers were shrunk without accompanying reductions in university staff. Dons capable of securing employment in the private sector took advantage of a generous voluntary redundancy scheme, leaving behind a rump of second-rate academics. The pay of those who remained in post was allowed to fall behind inflation. Overseas students were charged full fees for the first time, and then expected to pay a premium for the privilege of a British university education. Wherever possible, capital rather than current expenditure was trimmed.

In the universities, the sense of shock was palpable. 'The academic establishment at the universities,' recalled Kenneth Baker, education secretary in the mid-1980s, 'was the first professional middle-class group whose practices and interests were challenged by the Thatcher government.'[23] For twenty years, dons had assumed they could have it both ways: complete independence of the state and painless funding by the taxpayer. James Joll said of the dons of those years that they 'work when they feel like it, get up late if they want to and have long holidays'.[24] This made the retrenchment of the 1980s even harder to bear.

Dons were introduced to novel experiences such as redundancy and early retirement. In November 1987 they were even deprived of security of tenure, though the end of the job-for-life was leavened with a generous appeals procedure. (The first don made compulsorily redundant – a philosophy lecturer at Hull University – got his job back as soon as he appealed.[25]) They were subjected to the indignity of regular performance appraisal for the first time. Short-term contracts and differential rates of pay, common in other careers, were a shocking innovation in the universities of the 1980s. Every institution was also required to produce an annual report, itemising expenditure and improvements in efficiency. They were instructed by ministers to seek more income from sources other than the taxpayer. The emphasis, in both teaching and research, was shifted from the arts to applied science and vocational courses. All this was bad enough. Worse was to follow in the early 1990s.

Democratisation

In 1988 the UGC was replaced by a new Universities Funding Council (UFC), dominated by hard-minded businessmen rather than the dons who had governed its predecessor.* Instead of dispensing block grants to spend as the universities saw fit, the Funding Council attempted to link the scale of public subsidy to the number of students and the quality of teaching and research. Linking subsidies to numbers gave universities a strong financial incentive to increase the number of students they accommodated.

It proved so compelling that they contrived to hit the target Baker set them in 1989 – raising the number of eighteen-year-old school leavers in higher education from 15 to 30 per cent by the year 2000 – seven years early. (This

* Four years later, the single body was divided into the three Higher Education Funding Councils.

prompted a cut in funding, and predictable complaints that the government was denying thousands the chance of a decent start in life.) The number of students at university had risen from 321,000 in the early 1960s to 671,000 by 1979. However, in the early 1990s the total doubled in five years. By 1996, it was heading for 1.5 million, far in excess of the target of 560,000 places set by Robbins thirty years earlier. At the Labour Party Conference in September 1997, Tony Blair promised another 500,000 places at university by 2002.[26]

This vast inflation in the teaching load was accompanied by a less relaxed approach to the distribution of research funds. 'How many universities have got research plans?' asked Robert Jackson, the parliamentary under secretary of state who masterminded the university reforms of the 1980s. 'How many even believe that it is important to have research plans?'[27] Crudely, the government was aiming to create two different types of university: those which taught, and those which researched and taught. If it could identify the universities that were good at research, it could give them more of the research budget. So-called 'research selectivity exercises' were pioneered by the UGC in 1986; the first results were published by the new UFC in 1989. By totting up the number of publications ('publicly identifiable output') and the value of the private and public sector research projects each university had attracted, the UFC ranked the quality of research at each university on a five-point scale. Those with the highest scores would get the most money.

The results were predictably perverse: the quality of both teaching and research went down. The value of the subsidies given to the universities did not increase at anything like the same rate as the number of students – funding per student fell by two fifths in real terms. This was deliberate policy. 'Britain', Baker wrote, 'was running a high cost education system with a relatively low level of output.'[28] More places at lower cost was an ambition which dated back to a White Paper of 1972, *Education: A Framework for Expansion*, but it was facile to believe it could be accomplished without a diminution in the quality of the graduates.[29] Deterioration became a certainty when the government refused to allow universities to charge fees directly to students. Tuition fees (and maintenance grants) had been nationalised in 1962, and the Conservative government was not about to offend middle-class voters by allowing universities to reintroduce them in the 1990s. Denied the right to charge fees, universities continued to bid for research funding. This defeated the aim of concentrating research budgets where they were most effective, without making more money available for teaching.

Homogenisation of the Universities

It is in the nature of plans that their implementation subverts the intended outcome. The man in Whitehall, even if he knows best, never knows *enough* to predict how dozens of institutions and thousands of people will respond to his incentives. But believing that ministers and civil servants can decide the size, quality and composition of the graduate population, and the price at which it is produced, is merely pathetic. The worst effects of the planned economy in university education lie in the homogeneity, rather than the perversity, of the outcome. Instead of creating many different types of university, offering a wide variety of courses and specialities, the country is now carpeted with facsimiles of the Oxbridge model.

The decision in 1992 to abolish the distinction between universities and polytechnics, and to create a joint system of admissions, has multiplied the number of Oxbridge look-alikes to over 100. Each offers much the same blend of research and teaching, graduates and undergraduates, arts and science. In the expansion of the universities, more has meant not only worse; it has meant more of the same. Despite a quadrupling of the number of institutions since the early 1960s, and a quintupling of the number of students, the nature of a university is virtually unchanged. The Oxbridge model, designed for the education of a tiny élite, is now universal. Eighteen-year-olds are plucked from school, and incarcerated for three years in lecture halls, libraries and halls of residence, before being released at the age of twenty-one to fill a forty-year slot in a large company or a professional partnership. University teaching, as Niall Ferguson has pointed out, is organised much as it was in ancient Greece:

> Fundamentally, British universities continue to perform their core activity of teaching by traditional – in many cases, medieval – methods. I give lectures and tutorials; my students then go off and read books in libraries. The majority sit down and write essays with a pen and paper, which I mark with another pen. Nearly all assessment takes the form of written examination.[30]

To attend a lecture or tutorial, use a library, or take an examination, an undergraduate has to be physically present. This infrastructure of student accommodation, lecture halls and libraries is what makes a university expensive. Yet the new technology of videos, computers, and cheap telecommunications could make thousands of books and hundreds of lectures available to millions of students.

Making great minds and books available in this way is not as revolutionary as it sounds. The University of Oxford is already planning to offer undergraduates certificate and diploma courses on the Internet. The Internet originated among university academics as a way of easing communication, and its extension to undergraduates is far from radical. Delivering material over the network amounts to no more than a modern refinement of the university extension lectures of the nineteenth century, a series of roving public lectures by academics initially conceived by a Cambridge astronomer named James Stuart. They proved so popular that Cambridge University formed a special syndicate to co-ordinate them. The lectures inspired the creation of new universities at Bristol, Sheffield, Nottingham, Reading and Exeter.

Bristol in particular owed much to Benjamin Jowett (1817–93), the famous and formidable master of Balliol, who was a great enthusiast for university extension as a cheap alternative to Oxford. He persuaded both Balliol and New College to contribute £300 a year for five years towards the establishment of the University College at Bristol in 1876. The Open University still uses a combination of extension lectures and new technology (in the shape of the wireless and television) to allow people to earn degrees without giving up their jobs for three years. The nascent University of the Highlands and Islands is planning to operate from eleven locations, using video and computer conferencing for tutorials and lectures.[31]

But making better use of new technology is not the only change the universities need to make. The convention that people learn before they work is obsolescent. The sheer quantity of human knowledge, and the pace at which it is accumulating, means that people can no longer expect to live for forty years off the intellectual capital they accumulate at university. The flexibility of the MBA courses offered by a number of universities and business schools is only the most obvious example of the growing interaction between the cerebral and the practical. Employees acquire new knowledge all the time, on courses organised by the company or on their own initiative.

In the United States, hundreds of companies have set up 'corporate universities', in some cases with a physical campus. General Motors set up an 'internal college' as long ago as 1955, but the most famous is now run by the hamburger chain, McDonald's. The Arthur D. Little School of Management in Boston, established by a firm of management and technology consultants, has earned the power to award degree-style qualifications.[32] The first corporate university is now starting up in Britain. In 1998 British Aerospace announced that it was setting up a 'virtual university', complete with a vice chancellor and a faculty of engineering and manufacturing technology. The company is investing £2 billion over the next ten years.[33]

Corporate universities will always lack the purity of the traditional variety.

Their interest lies in the application of knowledge as well as its acquisition. But universities no longer have a monopoly of knowledge or original research. Pharmaceutical companies have giant research laboratories which are not unlike university campuses. Investment banks employ economists to monitor and study every kind of phenomenon, from broad money to industrial restructuring. (Many are producing economic research which is at least as good as that provided by the universities.) In the multifarious 'think tanks' which pepper Whitehall and Westminster, clever people are generating and disseminating knowledge and ideas quite outside the university system, and many university academics find them more sympathetic and influential publishers than the established academic journals. The don-as-journalist and media pundit, pioneered by A. J. P. Taylor, is now commonplace. But nowhere has the erosion of the distinction between university (three years of pure study in secluded surroundings) and life (trained minds being brought to bear on practical problems) gone further than in the relations between the universities and the great commercial companies.

The ability of the American university system to spawn innovative products and entrepreneurs has long fascinated British ministers of education. (It is the truest expression of their belief that the purpose of the modern university is to help the economy grow.) In the science parks which now surround most major British university towns, dons work closely with corporate scientists to turn knowledge into new products. Many university biologists, chemists, physicists and engineers are engaged in research projects commissioned by large companies. The University of Reading has a Coopers & Lybrand professor of Accounting, and hosts the International Securities Market Association Centre for Education and Research in Securities Markets. The University of Nottingham has chairs sponsored by Boots and Norwich Union, and provides a home for the Centre for Management Buy-Out Research. Toyota sponsors engineering research at Sussex, and UMIST has a Centre for Grain Processing funded by the Satake Company of Japan. Loughborough has headed a consortium of multinationals and academics charged with designing environmentally friendly cars.

Not all corporate sponsorships are as easy to justify. There is a Travelbag chair of tourism at Bournemouth University, and an AT&T chair in gender relations at Dundee. Naturally, there are fears that corporate support will imperil academic freedom. But Sir Douglas Hague, formerly a professor of managerial economics at both Manchester and Oxford and sometime chairman of the Economic and Social Research Council, believes this greater 'permeability' between universities and the outside world needs to be encouraged:

The technological innovations of the information and communications revolution are bound to transform the way universities carry out traditional functions, like teaching ... These technologies, new ways of thinking and the consequent development of knowledge businesses engaged in activities like research, consultancy and training, will lead to increasing competition for the universities from competitors in such organisations. It will come both from the services they offer and from the salaries they pay. To compete, universities will have to organise and operate in ways more like those of the knowledge businesses themselves. Indeed, they will have to form alliances with these newcomers if they are to go on engaging in activities which they have supposed were their own, as if by right ... The best universities of the twenty-first century will bring together brainpower *where it is*, not where it can be institutionalised.[34]

Yet the reforms of the last ten years have left the universities unprepared to cope with these novel threats. Instead of setting them free to adapt, the government has used its control of funding to impose the traditional model on an expanded university system, and has protected it by denying any other institutions the right to award degrees.

The Need for Competition

Universities are not immune to the rule that insulation from competition is the surest route to stagnation and decline. Imperilled by greed at the Dissolution, by zealotry during the Civil War and by torpor in the Georgian age, the 600-year long domination of university education by Oxford and Cambridge in England owed more to the absence of rivals than to intrinsic merit. A new university gestated for a time in the Elizabethan foundation of Gresham College, endowed by City financier Sir Thomas Gresham with a portion of the rents from his Royal Exchange.[35] Although the college was described as the University of London as early as 1612, the prospect was never translated into reality.*

Only Scotland challenged the supremacy of the English universities, and

---

* Gresham College survives today as Sir Thomas envisaged: to fund regular public lectures. Plans were hatched in the nineteenth century to merge the college with the new University of London, but came to nothing. The college moved to Barnard's Inn Hall at Holborn in 1984 to resume its role as a convenor of public lectures. It still derives its income (about £190,000 a year) from the Royal Exchange rents collected by the City Corporation and the Mercers' Company.

even there no institutions comparable to Oxford and Cambridge emerged until the fifteenth century. Medieval Scotsmen traditionally gravitated to Oxbridge, or to the European universities of Paris or Bologna. The first university in Scotland, founded at St Andrews in May 1410 by a group of clerical graduates from the University of Paris, was an accidental consequence of ecclesiastical politics. The loyalty of Crown and Church in Scotland to the Avignon papacy during the Great Schism (1378–1417) drove Scottish teachers and pupils from France. A group reconvened at St Andrews and began to teach, securing papal authority from the exiled Avignon pope, Benedict. But the growth of the university was slow. The first college, St Salvator's, was founded in 1450. St Leonard's Hospital in the town was turned into a college in 1513 and the third college, St Mary's, was not established until 1538.

St Andrews was not alone. A College of the Arts was founded at Glasgow in 1451 and the College of St Mary in the Nativity – usually known as King's College, in honour of James IV – at Aberdeen in 1495. These developed in due course into the Universities of Glasgow and Aberdeen. None of the three provided serious competition to Oxford and Cambridge; each was as poor and remote as Scotland itself.[36] Growth was hampered by the meagreness of their endowments, and dissipated in the fruitless controversies over the episcopacy and royal supremacy which racked the Church of Scotland until the end of the seventeenth century.

Only in the eighteenth century did the Scottish universities surpass their English rivals. This was the age of Adam Smith, David Hume and James Watt, but the intellectual flowering was brief. They entered the Victorian age in as advanced a state of decay as Oxford and Cambridge. The lord advocate introduced the Universities of Scotland Act of 1858 by saying that 'the Scotch universities had lost sight of their proper objects; and their educational establishments had descended below the requirements of the age.'[37] The closure of the moribund St Andrews University was seriously considered. At Dundee a new university college was opened in 1881 and endowed handsomely by the Baxter family, the local sugar refiners, jam-makers and linen manufacturers. Subordinated to St Andrews until 1967, it was the last university foundation in Scotland until Stirling University was set up in 1964.

England did not acquire a university to compete with Oxbridge until 1828. Though Oliver Cromwell had projected a new university at Durham, the plan was dropped at the Restoration, and the idea was not revived seriously for another 165 years. Its authors were a group of Whig politicians and enthusiasts for the new doctrine of Utilitarianism. Wedded to the intellect, distrustful of established religion, and zealous for reform of all kinds, their first murmurings in favour of a non-sectarian university in London were heard in 1812, but nothing was achieved for another sixteen years.

The plan which led to the foundation of University College was conceived by Thomas Campbell, a Scottish poet, who had before him the example of the University of Berlin (the creation of Wilhelm von Humboldt, the figure generally credited with establishing research rather than teaching as the principal purpose of a university). The idea was taken up by two leading Whig politicians, Lord John Russell, and Henry Brougham, an advocate of popular education, and later lord chancellor. Campbell, though buried in Westminster Abbey, is not now much remembered; he described the foundation of the University of London as the 'only important act in his life's little history'.[38]

In 1828 the college opened on eight acres of wasteland at Gower Street under the ambitious title of 'The University of London'. Dons now refer to a 'golden triangle' linking the three collegiate universities of Oxford, Cambridge and London, but the new university took a long time to become established. Many years passed before Bedford (1849), Birkbeck (1866), Queen Elizabeth (1881), Westfield (1882), Royal Holloway (1886), Queen Mary (1887), Goldsmiths' (1891) and the LSE (1895) were even founded, and none became part of the University of London until the twentieth century.

More importantly, most of the new colleges were established not to compete with the older universities, but to educate women and people who wanted to work by day and study at night. But there was one sense in which the foundation of University College was highly significant. Fierce disputation between its Utilitarian backers over the nature of the religious instruction to be offered led to a decision not to teach divinity at all. This aroused the ire of the Tory government, whose links with the established Church were then so close that the Church of England was described as the Tory Party at prayer. Religious bigotry denied the new college the power to examine undergraduates until 1836, and to award degrees until 1850. It also provoked the foundation of a rival institution in the capital. Influential Churchmen and Tory politicians, including the prime minister the Duke of Wellington, and the home secretary, Robert Peel, feared that University College would develop on wholly secular lines. For this reason a new college was founded as an Anglican rival to 'the godless institution in Gower Street'. Of the 242 people who subscribed funds to its foundation, eighty-eight were clergymen.[39] The new foundation opened as King's College in October 1831.

Like University College, King's was dogged in its early years by religious controversies, small numbers of students and a consequent shortage of money. The poor quality of the underpaid staff, and the abandonment of religious tests at Oxbridge, led to a further drastic fall in undergraduate admissions. The college even had to sell its silver spoons, replacing them with electro-plate imitations. 'I understand', wrote the comical clergyman Sydney Smith, a pluralist fiercely opposed to evangelicalism and Church reform, 'they have already seized on the air pump, the exhausted receiver, and galvanic batteries, and that the bailiffs have been seen chasing the Professor of Modern History round the quadrangle.'[40]

What Is a University For?

Yet, however laughable the new institution seemed to Sydney Smith, the foundation of King's College joined a debate about the nature of a university which reverberates to this day: what is a university *for*? To the founders of University College, it was to set dons free to study whatever subjects they chose and to pursue knowledge wherever it took them. To the dons of Oxbridge, and the founders of King's College, academic freedom and the advancement of knowledge were secondary to the inculcation of Christian virtue and understanding.

These distinctions were not mere sophistries. In 1853 the Christian Socialist theologian F. D. Maurice lost his chair of divinity at King's College for lack of orthodoxy on the doctrine of everlasting punishment.[41] In 1893 the college lost its public subsidy for denying entry to non-Anglicans, and did not abolish religious tests for undergraduates until 1902. In 1831 the bishop and chapter of Durham threatened to withdraw the £80,000 they had pledged for the new college at Durham if the government insisted on the admission of non-Anglican undergraduates (it did not).* At Oxford and Cambridge, attendance at the college chapel was compulsory for all undergraduates; it took parliamentary legislation, in 1854, 1856 and 1871, to open the universities to undergraduates of any religion and none.

After the legislation was passed, Oxford (Keble) and Cambridge (Selwyn) saw the foundation of new colleges to ensure that the ancient universities had at least one exclusively Anglican foundation. Elections to professorial chairs of all kinds (especially at Oxford) were governed largely by the religious opinions of the candidates. The distinguished physiologist Michael Foster was not made a Fellow because he was a Non-Conformist, and Benjamin Jowett was deprived of his salary for ten years for the excessive liberality of his religious opinions. The ancient universities opposed granting University College, London, the power to award degrees because a degree was a badge of religious profession. A BA, argued one Victorian cleric at Oxford, was 'evi-

---

* The foundation of Durham University by the Cathedral Chapter in 1832 owed more to a desire to protect the assets of the Cathedral from expropriation by the state than to any urge to further the aims of the Church of England. In 1831 the wealthy cathedrals of England rightly feared that if their endowments were not used hurriedly they would be confiscated. See Chapter 4; see also Chadwick, *The Victorian Church*, pp. 39–40, especially p. 39, f.n. 3.

dence that a youth has been able to afford not only the money, but ... the time, to live three years among gentlemen, doing nothing, as a gentleman should'.[42]

The drive of the Non-Conformists to overcome this sort of thinking, and to abolish the religious test for entry to the old universities, turned an arcane discussion about the nature of a university into the national debate which rages still. Is the purpose of a university to train men and women to be engineers, lawyers, doctors and business executives? Or is it to enlarge and enrich their minds? The Non-Conformists of Victorian England brought to this debate a higher educational tradition of their own which emphasised the practical and scientific over the cultural and theological. The Dissenting Academies which mushroomed in the eighteenth century (Kibworth, Taunton, Daventry, Kendal, Hackney, Hoxton, Warrington and Mile End) flourished precisely because Non-Conformists were excluded from Oxbridge. They attracted even Anglican students through the quality of their teaching, which blended the classical disciplines of the Oxbridge curriculum with modern subjects such as geography, mathematics and science. The eighteenth-century pioneers of modern science – the chemists Joseph Priestley and John Dalton, and the physicist James Joule – emerged from the Non-Conformist milieu of the Dissenting Academies.

The founders of several of the provincial universities were drawn from outside the established Church. Mark Firth and Thomas Ferens were Methodists, as was Sir Josiah Mason, though he had Unitarian sympathies too. Unitarianism is notoriously agnostic about God, and emphatic about the amelioration of the human condition and the possibility of scientific progress. Joseph Chamberlain, whose passion for education first drove him into national politics, came from the most famous Unitarian family of all. The Wills family, who endowed Bristol, were originally Congregationalist. Jesse Boot, who paid for the rebuilding of the university college at Nottingham on a greenfield site outside the city, was a Methodist. The links between Protestantism, industrialisation, modern science and the secularisation of the universities, though still hotly disputed, seem unanswerable.

Since the 1850s, the Utilitarian-cum-Non-Conformist idea of a university as a place where academics advance knowledge through research, and train undergraduates for useful work, has contended with the Oxbridge ideal of the university as a place where teaching is more important than research and practical accomplishments are less important than cultural enrichment. In 1851, the year when John Owens opened his college to instruct young men in 'such departments of knowledge as are most generally subservient to the purpose of commercial life', the parliamentary commissioners were complaining that Oxford was still mired in theological controversies, unable and unwilling to contribute to the advance of scientific knowledge, and reluctant to give professors a larger say in the running of the university than the cantankerous theologians of the colleges.

A year later John Henry Newman, the former Oxford don and Catholic convert, began a series of lectures entitled *Discourses on the Nature and Scope of University Education*. They were an encomium to the Oxford he loved but had left for Rome. The aims and principles he outlined later became a book, *The Idea of a University*. It remains the most influential statement of the ideals of higher education in Britain.* 'If the intellect is so excellent a portion of us, and its cultivation so excellent,' wrote Newman, 'it is not only beautiful, perfect, admirable and noble in itself, but in a true and high sense it must be useful to the possessor and to all around him; not useful in any low, mechanical, mercantile sense, but as diffusing good, or as a blessing, or a gift, or power, or a treasure, first to the owner, then through him to the world.'[43]

For Newman, teaching was more important than research. But the teacher's role was not merely to diffuse information and ideas. It was to engage in a dialogue with the taught, in which undergraduates learn to think and to master the techniques to rise above the mere accumulation of facts and make judgments about what they have learned. 'This implies that its object', wrote Newman of a university education, 'is on the one hand, intellectual, not moral, and on the other, that it is the diffusion and extension of knowledge rather than the advancement.'[44]

At this point the debate was joined in the English universities between the self-made commercial aristocracy of Manchester, and the self-satisfied clerisy of Oxbridge; between Non-Conformity and Anglo-Catholicism; between the classicism of Oxbridge and the scientism of the Dissenting Academies; between Utilitarianism and High-Mindedness; between the value of discernment and the usefulness of practical skills; between the enlargement of the mind and the training of labour; between useful science and the elevating humanities; and between the creation of wealth and the pursuit of knowledge for its own sake.

For a time in the 1950s and 1960s it seemed resolved. In an economy where graduates-plus-science was the elixir of growth, the interests of the universities and the nation appeared to coincide. In the nineteenth century, the government sought to bolster the nation by subsidising the building of churches.

---

* Twenty years earlier, while still at Oxford, Newman had opposed granting university degrees to Non-Conformists. 'It does seem a little too bad', he wrote, 'that the dissenters are to take our titles. Why should they call themselves M.A., except to seem like us?' See Chadwick, *The Victorian Church*, Part One, p. 95.

In the twentieth, they have subsidised scientists at the universities instead. But by the 1980s there was not enough science and too many of the wrong sort of graduates. Margaret Thatcher, an Oxford-educated scientist from a Methodist family, told Professor Ralf Dahrendorf, a sociologist from Germany, that 'the universities have failed Britain. You have failed us.'[45] She meant that the universities had failed to help the economy to grow. Universities must now justify themselves as producers of trained manpower, providers of fee-earning services and manufacturers of innovative, profitable products.

More Means the Same, Except Worse

But if the utilitarian idea of the university has triumphed, the Oxbridge model of its organisation has proved more resilient. In 1965 Sampson thought the University of Sussex, which opened near Brighton in 1961, had achieved 'the breaking up, for the first time for seven hundred years, of the Oxbridge monopoly'. Its inter-disciplinary 'schools of studies' were designed specifically to blur the rigid faculties of Oxbridge, and to end the intellectual balkanis- ation which resulted.* The lay-out of the university buildings (by the fashion- able architect, Basil Spence) was intended to escape the cloistered approach of the ancient universities. In place of the subfusc of Oxbridge, Hardy Amies designed bright yellow gowns and birettas. In 1971 Sussex elected to drop undergraduate examinations in favour of continuous assessment.

'To have a child at the University of Sussex', *The Economist* argued in 1964, 'is beyond question the most absolutely OK thing in Britain now.' There was widespread hope in progressive circles that Sussex had shed the incubus of Oxbridge. It had certainly proved to Sampson's satisfaction that 'a sudden institution can be invented without laughable results'.[46] But who has heard now of Martin Wight, Roger Blin-Stoyle and Tibor Barna, the 'distinguished' academics he found on the downs thirty years ago? In 1998 the *Financial Times* placed Sussex thirty-seventh in its league table of the top 100 universities, 35 places adrift of Oxford and 36 places behind Cambridge.[47]

Sussex was the second progressive experiment which failed to dislodge the Oxbridge model. In 1949 Keele University was established in a Victorian mansion near Stoke-on-Trent. It was the brainchild of A. D. 'Sandie' Lindsay, a deeply religious Scottish academic and politician of pronounced left-wing views. As a controversial master of Balliol and vice chancellor of Oxford

* Noel Annan discloses in *Our Age* (Fontana, 1991, pp. 505–6) that hostility to faculties was in large part a bid by junior dons to break the stranglehold professors had over the size and direction of university departments.

University in the 1930s, he had championed the opening of Oxford to wider social classes.[48] Keele was intended to be classless and experimental. It was a palimpsest on which Lindsay wrote his educational and socio-political enthusiasms, forged in service to the left-wing clerisy, the Labour Party, popular writing, the Workers' Educational Association, and the Oxford tutorial classes and university extension lectures.

Its novelty was correspondingly brash. Keele offered four- rather than three-year degrees, and courses which jumbled the arts and sciences deliberately, with an emphasis on producing twentieth-century Renaissance men and women. It reflected Lindsay's dislike of academic specialisation in general and research in particular, as a self-indulgent diversion from the main task of teaching undergraduates. It also reflected the unsystematic nature of his mind. (Lindsay was apt to describe himself as a 'sociologically minded person' who favoured 'co-operative thinking'.[49]) Though it secured funding from the UGC, Keele was so poor that it was still using Nissen huts in the 1960s.

In 1962, the only kind thing which even Sampson could find to say about it was that it had 'no high table'.[50] His optimism about the potential of the new universities (which he distinguished from the older civic, or redbrick, universities) was otherwise boundless:

> The new universities seem to offer a real chance of breaking the social monopoly of Oxbridge; and it is likely that, lacking the dingy Victorian associations of the big civic ones, they may jump towards the head of the queue. Already three kinds of university are emerging – Oxbridge, Redbrick and New. The new vice chancellors have a missionary zeal . . . Oxford and Cambridge, in so far as they are geared to anything, are geared to the nineteenth century gentlemen's professions – the law, the civil service or diplomacy, which have adopted their old collegiate traditions. The powerful new professions which between them control the business corporations – accountancy, insurance, actuaries, engineering – have grown up largely outside this charmed circle . . . Oxbridge has refused to adapt its curricula to take note of them while Redbrick has found itself trammelled with specialist courses . . . Here is the most exciting challenge to the New Universities, . . . they are not trapped in any curricula, and they can construct courses which are both broad-minded and relevant.[51]

Hindsight has erected a barrier to optimism of this kind, but it illuminates the fallacies on which it was based. The first mistake was to assume that Oxbridge was the product not of experience but of unwillingness to experiment. The second was to assume, as Robbins did, that there were as many as

560,000 students in Britain who could benefit from a university education.

From the outset, the new universities had a stronger idea of what they wanted to avoid than what they wanted to achieve. Their concern was novelty, not excellence, and this found its chief expression in their architecture, which drew heavily on the skills of modernists such as Lasdun and Spence. Their buildings were intended to obliterate memories of the communal way of life of the ancient universities, a facet of Oxbridge considered distasteful by the self-obsessed society of the 1960s. To emphasise the discontinuity with the cloisters, the real world of shops, restaurants and banks was placed at the feet of the tower blocks where the undergraduates made love with fellow undergraduates, and read Carlos Casteneda through a haze of joints, joss-sticks, and the clash of disorganised minds.

Distributed carefully around the country in a parody of fairness to the regions, the exclusion of the new foundations from the inner cities was the only sign that even universities could not override economic reality. Greenfield sites on the edge of cathedral towns were much cheaper than the urban alternative. But the plan was clear: it was to create universities which owed nothing to the past. This contempt for what had gone before corrupted their methods of teaching and research; they specialised not in broad-minded and relevant courses in the new professions but in marginal disciplines in the social sciences, modish courses, and experimental teaching techniques which paid scant attention to the level of intelligence of their undergraduates. The students followed their own whims, and chose unexacting courses like sociology or psychology rather than the harder disciplines of, say, physics or chemistry.

The vast expansion of the universities in the eighties and nineties has reinforced these effects. A funding system which rewards those which attract the most students has led to a proliferation of non-courses such as media studies, environmental science and gender relations, and a lowering of entry requirements to scientific and mathematical courses. 'It's much more effective to address a subject like this through the genre of soap rather than through something like *Panorama*, because people know the characters,' is how a lecturer in Communication Studies at Westminster University explains why her students watch *Neighbours* and *East Enders* as part of their degree course.[52] This softening of standards has had a knock-on effect in schools, where the A-level examination is no longer used to sift the finest minds from the dross but to give as many students as possible an entrance ticket to a university education.

Many of the new universities admit people who have not taken A levels at all, running 'foundation courses' to help them catch up. Once they are at university, undergraduates no longer allow their fate to be decided by a set of gruelling final examinations after three years. They pick and choose between 'modules' and work at their own pace, passing or failing on course work. The pressure to fill places means that many students are lured into colleges and courses to which they are unsuited, and eventually drop out. According to the Higher Education Funding Council for England, the money wasted on teaching and accommodating undergraduates who drop out of university is now running at £180 million a year in England alone.[53]

Because drop-outs and re-sits cost money, there are courses which nobody is allowed to fail. Anecdotal evidence suggests that vice chancellors are urging colleagues to reduce pass marks to ensure the university is not penalised. According to a document leaked to *The Times*, a student at Heriot Watt graduated despite getting only 13 per cent in one of the most important papers.[54] The number of graduates with good degrees has mushroomed spectacularly. The proportion of Firsts has risen from 11 per cent of degrees in 1973 to 15 per cent today; the number of Thirds has halved, and Upper Seconds have increased from a third to nearly half of the total.[55] By 1995, the Major government was so concerned about declining standards that it created a new monitoring body – the Quality Assurance Agency for Higher Education – to despatch squads of external examiners into universities. But employers have already drawn their own conclusions. According to the chairman of the agency, many are switching to aptitude tests to recruit graduates because they can no longer rely on degrees to measure ability.[56]

A degree is no longer a passport to a job. According to the *Financial Times*, two thirds of the graduates of the top 100 universities enter a job or professional training course within six months of leaving university. One quarter of the graduates of Sussex University, the great educational hope of the early 1960s, fail to find a job, a training position, or even a second degree course.[57] It is not surprising that graduates are becoming disillusioned. Their expectations are raised, but they find they are under-qualified for the jobs they want and over-qualified for those they do not want. A graduate in environmental science from North London University told the *Sunday Times* in 1995 that she was taking a job as a customs officer on the Channel Tunnel. 'I'm going to have to search through people's suitcases, looking at knickers,' she said, 'and I've been to university for three years.'[58]

Many once-hopeful graduates are now stacking shelves, answering the telephone or filing their nails in reception. Some, if a psychologist is to be believed, have chosen permanent unemployment rather than endure the humiliation of stop-gap jobs as they wait to begin their real lives.[59] Professor Alan Smithers, director of the Centre for Education and Employment Research at Manchester University, tells the sad story of the nephew of a friend:

[He] was the first of his family to go to university. After three years of effort and sacrifice he emerged with a splendid upper second. He should have been delighted, but a year on he and his family are disillusioned. Since graduating from his new university he has been unable to get a job. He and his family are hurt and surprised, but the writing was on the wall because he could not say what his degree was *in* or *for*. The best he could manage was that it was a collection of modules about the sociology of the application of science.[60]

Thirty-odd years ago, Robbins argued that the universities were a perpetual growth machine: the more graduates an economy had, the faster it would grow. Today, far from solving Britain's economic problem, graduates are part of it.

Fees and Loans: The Missed Opportunities

There is only one way to reconnect the universities to the realities of the labour market: it is to place power in the hands of the consumers of higher education (the students) rather than the producers (educational bureaucrats and dons). Dons think this is happening already. In 1994 the *Independent on Sunday* invited Blake Morrison to return to Nottingham University, where he was a freshman in 1969. He encountered his old politics tutor, John McClelland, author of *A History of Western Political Thought*. McClelland read out some unflattering remarks about himself which a student had scrawled on a questionnaire before adding:

Now we're supposed to sell the subject as well as teach it. We have to wow the weenies. It wouldn't surprise me if before long some faculties don't set up customer care departments and re-name the lecturers 'marketing managers' . . . You lot were lippy. But at least you knew you were the pupils and we were the teachers. Now students are consumers: they want the subject served up for them. It's the era of customer feedback, and if the punters aren't happy it's our fault.[61]

His complaint is justified only to the extent that his students are filling in questionnaires rather than filing out of his lectures. They see their three years at university not as an expensive investment in their human capital but as a civic right, because they live in Britain in the 1990s. They place more value on it than they do on the right to vote.

The obvious solution is to charge the students fees, but this is not an option politicians relish. Free tuition and means-tested maintenance grants (first introduced in 1962) are aspects of the middle-class welfare state which are electorally dangerous to dislodge. In 1984 even Thatcher was forced to disown a proposal by Keith Joseph to let the universities charge a means-tested tuition fee. When the Labour spokesman on higher education proposed in 1993 that a possible option was to secure 'funds from individuals using and directly benefiting from higher education', he was sacked by the Party leader, John Smith.

That same year, John Ashworth, director of the LSE, floated the idea that the School should charge means-tested top-up fees, offset by bursaries and loans for poorer students. His fellow academics voted down the proposal, and two years later refused to renew his contract. Ironically, the LSE had already become the premier fee-charging university college in the country by importing more fee-paying foreign students (only one third of LSE students are now British). In 1996, the LSE court of governors voted by a majority of two to one to explore means-tested fees.[62] What had changed since 1993?

The shortage of money had got worse. In the budget of November 1995, Kenneth Clarke cut the capital expenditure budgets of the universities by one third. The vice chancellors then warned they were so short of money that they would have to charge every student a registration fee of £300 a year. After investigation by a committee chaired by Ron Dearing, the New Labour government agreed in 1997 to impose a means-tested annual tuition fee of £1,000 on each student from 1999. An important principle was breached: university tuition is no longer free.

This is one of the melancholy effects of the nationalisation of the universities. Events coax changes out of the system; the system itself does not initiate them. Fees were agreed, but not as a way to restore dignity and independence to the universities or to ensure that degree courses are broad-minded and relevant. They were advanced not on merit but as part of the solution to a financial crisis brought on by the rapid expansion of the number of university students in the last ten years, and accepted only after repackaging for political consumption.

The introduction of student loans was similarly distorted by the political process. In theory, loans offer young people the bridging finance to purchase a university education, and ensure that those who go to university are properly motivated. Yet when they were first proposed in 1985, Thatcher was implacably opposed, on the grounds that Conservative voters had got used to free university education for their children. It was not until free university education collided with another populist policy – a university place for virtually every eighteen-year-old school leaver – that a choice had to be made. The first student loans were introduced in the autumn when Thatcher was deposed.

But the terms reflected a continuing reluctance to choose between two ostensibly popular policies.

By the autumn of 1990, resistance to student loans was incompatible with the vast expansion in the number of university students which had been set in train, unless the government was prepared to let the standard of university education collapse. 'We had developed a system of funding higher education to suit a small and exclusive minority,' Kenneth Baker recalled. 'I wanted to expand the numbers without reducing standards, so that more young people would benefit and Britain would have a better-educated workforce.'[63] In other words, loans were introduced not to put purchasing power in the hands of students, but to bridge the gap between the size of the state subsidy and the size of the student population. The aim, as Nigel Lawson ingenuously wrote in his memoirs, was to 'enable a higher level of cash to be paid at a lower overall cost'.[64]

Financial considerations of this kind warped the loan scheme. Because the government would have to advance the money several years before any repayments began, student loans initially added to public expenditure. To limit the potential cost to the taxpayer, the Treasury imposed a ceiling of £420 a year on any one loan. This was not large enough to make a substantial difference, and the administration of the loans was chaotic. The private banks refused to act even as agents for advances and repayments, for fear that any role in such a controversial scheme would alienate customers who had graduated. Instead, the government had to set up a new Student Loans Company in Glasgow.

This was not a success. A report by the National Audit Office in 1995 discovered that one eighth of its loan book (or £142 million) was irrecoverable; the backlog of unpaid loans had risen to 17,000; the company had managed to answer only one in twenty-seven telephone inquiries during the autumnal peak; it had employed an assessor on a retainer of £8,000 a year who adjudicated only seven cases during his five years in the job, six of them in the final twelve months. The company also set a salary threshold so high that less than one in three borrowers began to repay loans when they entered work.[65] New ventures are invariably chaotic, but unnecessary embarrassment followed the loss of the chief executive for 'conduct which has brought himself and the company into disrepute'.[66] An attempt by the Major government to privatise its student loan book ended in humiliation; neither banks nor building societies would take on the losses or the stigma.[67]

The New Labour government (many of whose members were violently opposed to student loans in Opposition) now promises cheaper, longer, better and softer loans, but not because it wants to turn students into consumers. It wants to use loans to replace means-tested maintenance grants so that it can means-test tuition fees instead. This has the pleasing effect of softening the impact of the first tuition fees to be levied since the early 1960s. It also increases government control of the universities. Means-testing tuition fees and using loans to finance maintenance grants gives control of additional money for higher education to the government, not the students or the universities.*

It is not hard to see why the government wants to deny universities direct access to fee income. They might get a taste for it. The education secretary is fearful that giving the universities too much financial autonomy might end in differential fees being charged, with Oxbridge demanding a premium over the University of Redbrick and Suburbia University offering discounts and free haircuts to every student in media studies. A small group of top universities believe they could charge extra fees without losing customers. Since the number of universities was inflated in 1992, a British equivalent of the American Ivy League universities has emerged. Known as the Russell Group, after the London hotel where their officials meet to discuss matters of common interest, they are now taking a higher proportion of their undergraduates from the public schools.† But even if students are prepared to pay more, the government does not intend to let the top universities given them the chance. New Labour cleaves to the egalitarian view that the universities are separate but equal.

The Wilson government made a virtue of the indifference of the Robbins Report to academic standards. 'Let us move away from our snobbish caste-ridden hierarchical obsession with university status,' said Oxford-educated Tony Crosland, in 1965.[68] His ambition was not to create a new type of university for a new age, as Wilson had implicitly promised the Party conference in 1963, but to imbue the new universities and especially the polytechnics (test-beds for the promised relationship between the universities and industry) with the same measure of esteem as Oxford and Cambridge. The Open University, which started in 1969, was once the zenith of this egalitarian approach. It demanded no entrance qualifications at all. Now, thanks to John Major, there are dozens of universities which operate on the same principle.

---

* It was precisely to ensure that the universities, rather than the Treasury, benefited from additional expenditure on higher education that the Dearing Committee recommended a flat-rate tuition fee of £1,000 a year – which was not to be means-tested – coupled with the preservation of means-tested living-cost grants and the readier availability of loans to all qualifying students.
† The members of the Russell Group are Oxford, Cambridge, UCL, Imperial, LSE, Bristol, Edinburgh, Birmingham, Glasgow, Leeds, Nottingham, Sheffield, Southampton, Newcastle, Liverpool, and Warwick.

Universities as Businesses

So far, neither fees nor loans have reduced the dependence of the universities on the state, or their subjection to the political imperatives of their paymasters. Many of those academics reared in the golden age of the don – the thirty years of rising public esteem and expenditure after the Second World War – have yet to recognise the origin of their difficulties. But a growing number agree with Kenneth Minogue, Professor of Government at LSE, who has described the current prostration of the universities as

> . . . an object lesson in the perils of dependence on the State. In the course of the twentieth century, universities have lost, step by step, the considerable autonomy they had previously enjoyed. They lost it because they were bribed into becoming functionaries of national policy. In the wake of the Robbins Report, they were showered with gold, new universities were founded, jobs opened up and delightful prospects of power and importance unhinged the wits of simple academics . . . The result was to leave universities both financially and politically helpless before the next turn of Fortune's wheel.[69]

For a time the University Grants Committee could deliver public money without awkward questions being asked about its use, but it could not shield the universities from their paymasters for ever. Teachers and taught both failed to recognise that, if the taxpayers were footing the bill, society might one day begin to question the return on its investment.

For the universities, the only lasting means of escape from their present bondage is to achieve true financial independence. Thanks to the reforms of recent years, that possibility is no longer so remote. Over the last ten years they have learned how to cut costs and raise funds, and how to sell themselves and their services to students and companies. Thirty years ago, dons did not have to think about money at all; twenty years ago, the Association of University Teachers affiliated to the Trades Union Congress; even ten years ago, university lecturers were balloted on taking industrial action in pursuit of a pay claim. Today, they earn one tenth of their income from the sale of services to business, charities, and hospitals (not including government and research councils).

Several universities have fully fledged scientific and technological subsidiaries to generate extra income. Surrey Satellite Technology, a subsidiary of Surrey University, sells budget launching kits.[70] Sheffield set up a consultancy business in 1986, which now sells environmental auditing and land reclamation services to business. Robert Gordon University in Scotland has established strong links with the oil and gas industries, and has a commercial arm which generates sales of £10 million.[71] Other companies spawned by universities include UnivEd Technologies (Edinburgh), Filtronic Comtek (Leeds) and Aromascan (UMIST).[72] Under its go-ahead vice chancellor, Sir Colin Campbell, Nottingham has transformed itself from a provincial backwater into one of the biggest contractors to the private sector in the entire university system. In 1997, the Nottingham Law School was discussing incorporation and a public flotation with the venture capitalists, 3i. Heriot-Watt has already floated off its business school as a separate company.[73] Warwick, founded in 1965 as a university to service the metal-bashers of the West Midlands, now earns half its income from the private sector. Thirty years ago its buildings were occupied by students protesting about its links with local companies and its best known don – the romantic socialist, E. P. Thompson – had resigned to pen an anti-business polemic called *Warwick University Ltd*. Today, the archive of trade union history started by Professor Thompson is housed in a £4 million library sponsored by BP.

Assets are being sweated. Vivian Bowden complained in the early 1960s of the 'low utilisation factor' at the universities, reckoning their buildings were used for only 125 days a year (Sir Geoffrey Crowther joked that two universities could be accommodated within the same buildings if the dons were prepared to work a shift system).[74] Since the 1980s the universities have rented out their buildings for conferences and as film sets on a systematic basis. Several in historic market and cathedral towns have formed the British Universities Accommodation Consortium, run from Nottingham University. Aberdeen, Edinburgh, St Andrews, Bath, Norwich, and even Leeds, Manchester, Sussex and Surrey, have found they can attract tourists by undercutting local hotel prices. Some offer more than a room: Manchester has sold archaeology courses; Southampton tempts elderly tourists with a crash course in the culture and politics of Weimar Germany; visitors to Durham can choose choral training; and Nottingham has run a symposium entitled 'learning to love your computer'.

Every university now has a corporate plan. Some even have mission statements. Admissions tutors advertise for students on television and in the newspapers, tempting them with hot-line numbers and money-off vouchers for driving lessons and pizza restaurants. The Liverpool and Leicester Polytechnics have now 're-branded' themselves as Liverpool John Moore University and De Montfort University. De Montfort is run on ostentatiously businesslike lines, with the vice chancellor as the chief executive, his pro-vice chancellors as main board directors, and the governors as non-executive directors. Every service, from catering to the law faculty, is treated as a 'cost centre', and those which under-perform are axed. The vice chancellor told the *Financial Times* that in the past universities were 'too busy chasing Nobel Prizes instead of giving industry and the community the service they really need'.[75]

'Universities must become more entrepreneurial than ever,' says Kenneth Edwards, vice chancellor of Leicester University and a previous chairman of the Committee of Vice Chancellors and Principals. 'They must find more public and private investment to restructure and re-equip for new teaching and learning techniques.'[76] The LSE has a marketing arm, Enterprise LSE, which combs the private sector for research and consultancy contracts. At Gateshead, the University of Sunderland has opened a satellite campus at the Metro Centre. Called *Learning World*, it aims to introduce shop assistants and shoppers to the educational services it provides. 'Shopping and education maybe haven't mixed before', explains a spokesman. But they are certainly mixing now. Students are shopping around, and universities are selling their services.[77]

They are even selling them abroad. Ironically, the imposition of tuition fees for foreign students, met by the university establishment in 1981 as the educational equivalent of the sack of Rome, has created a thriving export business. Several universities market their services and degree courses abroad, in some cases establishing local distribution networks like the Kobe Institute in Japan or the British University of Thailand (where Exeter and Nottingham Universities administer the university and award degrees). Plans are afoot for a branch campus in Kuala Lumpur.[78] Franchise deals, which allow foreign students to complete most of their course at home before coming to Britain for a final year, are common in Asia. Shortly before the Asian economic crisis, British universities were earning a fee income of £300 million in south-east Asia.[79] The Department of Trade and Industry reckons educational exports are now worth £3.5 billion a year.

For the vice chancellors presiding over this transformation of the Grove of Academe into Acme PLC, a few good books and membership of the Great and the Good is no longer sufficient. They demand six-figure salaries, subsidised housing, and a car allowance as compensation for the hours they spend poring over business plans, winning research contracts and wooing corporate sponsors. The first signs of Fat Cattery are apparent, with vice chancellors muddling their expenses claims and demanding golden hellos and golden handshakes. In 1994 Huddersfield University was instructed by the Higher Education Funding Council for England not to pay a £400,000 golden hand-shake to its departing vice chancellor. The lucky man had just had his pay improved by 45 per cent and backdated four months (the award was later halved).[80] A few years later, Glasgow Caledonian University dismissed its principal after discovering that he was running a Saab and a Jaguar, taking holidays at the expense of the university, and giving vacant jobs to his friends.[81]

Can the Universities Be Privatised?

It is not clear whether this new breed of vice chancellor is yet ready to take his university into the private sector. Throughout the post-war period there was only one venture in university education wholly unsupported by public funds: the University College at Buckingham. Lord Beloff, one of its founding fathers, had no doubt that he was contesting the spirit of the age. 'I myself see the project', he wrote, 'not simply as an educational venture among others ... but as a piece of political litmus paper. It is a way of testing whether or not it is true that statism has made such gains in Britain since, say, the foundation in 1895 of the London School of Economics, the last great private venture in the field of higher education, that no further initiative is possible; that the dreary descent into egalitarian uniformity is irreversible.'[82]

When Sampson first considered the University of Buckingham, in 1982, he placed it in inverted commas.[83] It remains an isolated experiment, unless the Royal Agricultural College at Cirencester is counted as a university. Manchester Business School considered, and rejected, a proposal to go entirely private in the early 1990s.[84] The latest new university to be built, at Lincoln, abandoned its early hopes of private ownership in favour of joint funding by the private and the public sector. Of the £20 million raised to begin construction in 1995, nine tenths came from public sources.[85] The new University of the Highlands and Islands is also reliant on public funds.

A complete escape from the state's clutches is impossible without the freedom to determine the level of fees a university can charge students. This is politically awkward, but the economic case is hard to refute. The present system taxes the parents whose children are not at university to subsidise undergraduates whose earnings in later life will be considerably higher. 'Why', Kenneth Clarke asked in 1993, 'should bus drivers pay for the education of lawyers?'[86] It is a fair question. A better-educated workforce benefits bus drivers as well as lawyers, but free undergraduate tuition is still a regressive tax.

For people whose children do not go to university, investing public money in higher education yields much lower returns than investing it in primary and secondary schools. At present, the higher the level of education, the more the benefits accrue to the individual rather than to the economy or society. Even student loans have turned out to be a form of cheap borrowing for the middle classes; in 1994 the sub-market rates of interest charged on student loans were probably costing the taxpayer £250 million a year.[87] So far, the reality of loans and the prospect of fees does not seem to have put younger people off applying (mature students do seem to be deterred). This suggests that the decision to invest in a university education is still relatively painless. Still-higher fees might be a bonus, if they forced young people ill-suited to university life to think again.

A larger obstacle to privatisation is the likelihood that fee-charging universities would be penalised in the distribution of other forms of state funding, such as capital and research grants. As Dearing has said: 'To privatise yourself is to deny yourself public funding.'[88] Universities have already found it hard to raise funds elsewhere, except against income-producing projects like new halls of residence. In 1995 the University of Lancaster tapped the bond markets for £35 million but soon ran into cash-flow problems, which undermined the confidence of the City in the creditworthiness of the universities.[89] The hopes invested in the Private Finance Initiative, where private companies fund and design buildings which they then rent to the universities, have yet to be realised.[90]

One unforeseen side-effect of reliance on outside financial support is the need for universities to be willing to invest their funds in research contracts and technological subsidiaries. In recent years, this has plunged several universities into financial trouble. When difficulties occur, or new needs arise, asset sales are no longer unthinkable, but few universities have much that is valuable other than their principal sites. According to the Higher Education Statistics Agency, the total net assets of the universities (including Oxford and Cambridge) amounted to less than £12 billion in 1997. The bulk consists of buildings which cannto be sold.

In 1991 Homerton College in Cambridge seriously considered selling its entire site to a supermarket chain.[91] Royal Holloway College in London is luckier, having inherited a handsome collection of paintings from its founder, the patent pills dispenser Thomas Holloway. But at no university outside Oxbridge does endowment income exceed 8 per cent of total revenues. The total value of the endowment funds owned by all the universities outside Oxford and Cambridge is probably less than £3.5 billion. Spread across nearly 150 institutions, this does not amount to much. But most of the emerging Ivy League universities have reputations which are solid enough to sustain a fund-raising campaign like the Campaign for Oxford or the Cambridge Foundation, and several already have a computerised 'alumnus database' for appeals. The LSE appointed a professional to raise £50 million,[92] and another well-connected part of London University, the London Business School, has launched an appeal for £20 million.

Two recent observers of university life – Paxman in 1990 and Sampson in

1992 – report that modern dons are obsessed with money.[93] This is not surprising. The universities find themselves marooned between the old world and the new, neither wholly dependent on taxpayers nor wholly independent of them, but dependent enough to have little or no autonomy where and when it matters. In the 1980s the Conservative government finally resolved the long-running debate between justice and excellence in higher education and slayed the donnish dream of mind-expanding education for all. Rising student numbers – and the elevation of the polytechnics to university status – have given Britain a continental-style university system, with large numbers of students, less personal supervision, a high drop-out rate, lower standards of academic achievement, and an emphasis on processing people for work rather than the cultivation of the whole person.

Britain needed to educate more than the tiny élite of previous generations. The mistake was to democratise a system designed for an élite, blurring the distinction between academic and vocational studies and stimulating a proliferation of pseudo-academic degree courses for the less gifted. This was the unavoidable outcome of treating young people as citizens (with an equal right to university) rather than consumers (with the means to purchase the education they need). For all the talk of lifelong learning, investing in human capital and raising the quality of the workforce, the expansion of the universities was not in the end an economic phenomenon; it was a democratic one. Justice triumphed over excellence. The perspicacious don will have noticed that the one institution in the British system of education where excellence still counts for more than justice is privately owned. It is called the public school.

CHAPTER SEVEN

THE PUBLIC SCHOOLS

Their coded casualness, their expensive dictated hairstyles, their manner of walking, their ways of holding their mouths and lips, their swooping convoluted vowels, all were part of their unspoken but firm assumptions. It was peer-group stuff, of course; but it would survive and be recognised over time across large public rooms, board-room tables and at suitable dinner parties.

RICHARD HOGGART, on Pop[1]

I should have written a different book, she scolded, about the public schools, which were the real cause of Britain's ills.

WALTER ELLIS, *The Oxbridge Conspiracy*[2]

In England . . . money matters when it counts most: at school, from five to eighteen.

ANDREW ADONIS and STEPHEN POLLARD[3]

The age of the meritocrat – the flowering of those who left school in the 1950s and 1960s, and came to prominence in the 1970s and 1980s – may already be over . . . As the millennium approaches, we could be on the brink of the return of the dominance of the public-school pupil.

ANDREW NEIL[4]

The public schools produce most of the people who run most of Britain most of the time. Tony Blair was a public school boy, and so were two of his twenty-one Cabinet ministers. Under John Major, only five members of the Cabinet were not educated at public schools. A recent survey found that seven out of nine generals, one in two permanent secretaries, and eight and a half out of every ten judges were also at public schools.[5] Even today, the provost of Eton is not afraid to tell the boys that they are being educated 'to exercise authority'.[6] Britain is not alone in having an élite. In most countries the connections between wealth, status and power are easy to draw; in Britain, upward mobility is too great and status owes so little to money that the gradations of society are harder to gauge. Ultimately, they depend on subtle differences in dress, speech and manners which are notoriously complex for outsiders to parse. This is why the inverted snobs of Old Labour, the upwardly mobile meritocrats of New Labour and the economic liberals of the New Right hold one belief at least in common: that, in Britain, being gifted or successful is not enough.

'Almost insensibly they are still teaching their pupils to think of themselves as special by birth and opportunity; inheritors of influence and access, high on the British hog, they are giving above all a class-bound background to the education they so firmly value,' is how Richard Hoggart, an unreconstructed apologist for Old Labour, sees the modern public schools. 'We are still branded on the tongue. We have some innovations, particularly unattractive, which say without putting it into words: "Keep off, you horrible lower class person" . . . Those who cannot instantly decipher your class from your clothes or bearing tend to assume that you are a kind of nondescript.'[7]

Andrew Neil, more Thatcherite than the former prime minister herself, is not so old-fashioned. His hostility to the public schools stems from his belief in meritocracy. 'I have never been against people just because they were products of public school and Oxbridge, which would have been a stupid and self-defeating reverse snobbery, but I felt strongly that those who had benefited from such institutions did not have an automatic right to power and privilege in our society. They should have to prove their worth, in open and fair competition with everybody else, and be judged on their merits.'[8] Blairite writers, from Anthony Sampson to Andrew Adonis and Stephen Pollard, share this irritation that the public schools somehow confer on their charges an 'effortless superiority'.[9]

Bastion of Privilege or Service Industry?

It is the oldest criticism of the public schools, and one which has many dimensions. Judging by the way they advertise themselves, many parents of public school pupils are looking to purchase not a good education but a verbalising patina, an ethos, and a network of social connections which will help their children to succeed in a class-bound country.[10] Richard Hoggart writes with horror of a middle-class mother he saw on television, explaining that she had sent her son to a third-rate public school to acquire 'good bearing', the 'right sort of friends' and 'proper principles'.[11] In 1989, Adonis and Pollard were amazed to find the headmaster of Gordonstoun assuring the readers of *The Times* that his job was to 'instil in teenage boys and girls a real sense of decency, straightforwardness, common sense and loyalty'.[12] It was as if Dr Thomas Arnold, whose reinvigoration of Rugby launched the Victorian reforms, had returned to assure a new generation of public school parents that 'what we must look for here is, 1st, religious and moral principles: 2ndly, gentlemanly conduct: 3rdly, intellectual ability.'

The dictum of Dr Arnold is often cited as proof of the anti-scientific and anti-industrial ethos of the public schools, of their preference for character-building over education. Certainly the Victorian public schools worshipped the classics to the exclusion of the sciences (Dr Arnold stopped the scientific instruction being given at Rugby) and valued mental and moral training over preparing young men for careers or equipping them with useful knowledge. They also nurtured that strong belief, so well-expressed by Sir Henry Newbolt in *Vitai Lampada*, in the character-building nature of sport and schoolboy leadership. In his influential book, first published in 1980, Martin Wiener claimed that the manly, anti-intellectual ethos of the public schools was the chief mechanism by which the backward-looking, anti-business and anti-scientific values of the landed aristocracy were transmitted to the entre-preneurial and professional classes of Victorian England, robbing British industry of the trained scientific minds it needed to compete with Germany, France and the United States.[13]

It is a curious claim. Far from being antipathetic to industry, commerce and science, British aristocrats were among the most enthusiastic proponents and practitioners of all three.[14] The real explanation of the curriculum of the nineteenth century public school is not cultural, but economic. Then, as now, the public schools were not reactionary bastions of class privilege but businesses selling a professional service, whose end-product was a well-developed person capable of holding down a well-paid job. The public schools were not (and are not) a mechanism for the transmission of aristocratic values, but the means by which the middle classes reproduce themselves and their wealth. The businesslike ethos of the modern public school is well expressed by the present headmaster of Eton: 'interest in the individual and in that individual's personal growth and development'.[15] The Victorian professional classes, like their successors today, used the public schools not to turn their rough-and-ready sons into bogus gentlemen but to provide a good education at an affordable price. As Harold Perkin has pointed out, the terrible food, uncomfortable beds, unheated dormitories and rank bad teaching of many Dotheboys Halls reflected chiefly the need to keep the costs down.[16]

If they were anti-industrial or anti-scientific – and the hostility of the Vic-torian public schools to business and science is greatly exaggerated – the bias was an accidental by-product of their real purpose: training people for public service. Late Victorian Britain had a massive empire to administer, offering ample interesting, well-paid, pensioned work. A classical education, plenty of sport and flogging, lengthy and unnatural separation from women, and a stint as a prefect at a public school were a better preparation for life as a district officer or colonial governor than school certificates in mathematics, chemistry and physics or (had the Victorians known them) business studies. Haileybury, first established in 1805 by the East India Company as the Imperial Service College, was re-founded in 1862 specifically to produce a new generation of army officers and administrators. Yet as soon as the empire was dismantled, and the jobs disappeared, public schools such as Haileybury adapted their techniques to the rise of the professional and corporate economy of the twentieth century. They abandoned Latin and Greek and turned themselves into examination hothouses.

The public schools now win their pupils a disproportionate number of university places. These lead in turn to the best jobs in the City, the professions, the media and the multinationals. Their examination success is so formidable that universities, especially Oxford and Cambridge, now discriminate openly against public school pupils.[17] The clearest evidence of change is in the transformation of the girls' public schools. At West Heath in the 1970s, Princess Diana got no O levels, but won the school dancing competition.[18] Once-similar establishments – Downe House, Wycombe Abbey and St Mary's, Calne – are now in the top thirty.[19] Like any business, public schools have survived because they have changed, not because they have stayed the same.

Giving Parents What They Want

The failure of journalists and writers to appreciate the capacity for change in the public schools reflects their characteristic unwillingness to dispense with stereotypes. As recently as 1995 an entire book was devoted to the homosexual experiences of former public school boys.[20] Middle-class Englishmen seem to relish outdoing one another in tales of hardship and cruelty at public school. Jeremy Paxman prefaces his study of the British Establishment with unlikely tales about French masters being fired for failing to pass the marmalade to the headmaster's wife, and rugby-playing jocks beating him with a shoe while assuring him that 'the purpose of a public-school education, Paxman, is to teach you to respect people you don't respect.'[21] When the vice provost of Eton published a new history of the school in 1994, the reviews were dominated by allegations that Anthony Chenevix-Trench, the headmaster in the second half of the 1960s, was a drunken sadist with a fondness for beating the boys. Trench was in fact a reformer, who put an end to fagging and ritualistic public beatings. His mistake was to continue to beat the boys in private, allowing overheated imaginations to work.

Of course, modernity has not eliminated every facet of the past. Only the army or the navy can rival the public schools as an attraction for a certain type of homosexual. Nearly a century and a half has elapsed since C. J. Vaughan was forced to resign as headmaster of Harrow after his liaison with a pupil was exposed.[22] On the other hand, in 1997 the Boarding School Alliance had to postpone a marketing campaign to dispel the 'negative image' of boarding after detectives raided a number of schools, investigating a child pornography ring.[23] The music master at a Surrey public school leapt off Beachy Head, apparently after being exposed as a paedophile. Salacious reports of unfortunate public school masters caught abusing positions of trust are as much a staple of the popular and broadsheet press as ever they were.[24] But the two major public school sex scandals of recent years seem self-consciously modern. The Master of Dulwich College was forced to stand down for alleged sexual harassment of a secretary while they were on a marketing trip to Asia and the Middle East, and the headmaster of Charterhouse resigned the same year after being linked with a nineteen-year-old prostitute he met through an escort agency.[25] The girl had enjoyed a private education.

Girls now account for almost half the numbers at independent schools.[26] In 1993 a public school headmaster explained why his school was going fully co-educational. 'We're simply recognising where the markets are for our product,' he said.[27] The need to attract girls (and particularly mothers of girls) would make it hard for the public schools to maintain the traditional regimen of cold showers, chilly dormitories, incessant games-playing and hellenic encounters after lights-out, even if there were still a market for these things. The truth is that there is not. The number of full-time boarders has fallen dramatically since the war, plunging particularly rapidly in the 1980s and 1990s.

The post-sixties generation of parents is often sceptical about the character-building nature of the boarding experience, and schools have had to adapt their product accordingly. They now offer flexible régimes, in which pupils can opt for day-schooling, weekly boarding, and even periodic overnight stays. Economic pressures have reinforced the pressure for change and flexibility – boys' schools need girls to make up pupil numbers as the school-age population contracts, and parents find day fees more affordable than boarding. Parents have demanded and got more co-educational schools, better accommodation, more sympathetic pastoral care, more flexibility over boarding and, above all, higher academic standards.

'What the successful public schools offer now is a service industry, which they are happy to have judged not by their own standards, but by the agreed yardsticks of the rest of society,' wrote Paxman in 1990. 'In return for several thousand pounds, they say, we will give your child a better chance of gaining admission to university or to the profession of his choice.'[28] The ambition of the modern public school parent is rarely much broader than that: they want well-paid, not well-rounded children. In 1987 David Newsome, headmaster of Wellington, complained to a private audience of 'the shallow materialism of some of the homes from which our boys come, and the glib expectation that a school such as mine will provide the culture, sensitivity and spirituality that are so flagrantly inconspicuous in the domestic *mise-en-scène*'.[29] In 1994 Stephen Winkley, headmaster of Uppingham, told Adam Nicolson that the dominant characteristic of his pupils was docility. 'What they want is a quiet life,' he said. 'It's a suburban vision really . . . I am disappointed by what has happened to people, to the freedom of open discussion that one used to have. When you talk to them about their ambitions, their dreams, what they come up with is "Shall I become a solicitor?"' [30]

To become a solicitor today, it is necessary to go to university, and getting young people into university is the principal service the public schools provide. Naturally, it is also the chief measure by which they are judged. The entrance ticket to the better universities is the A level examination, where the public schools consistently do better than their state competitors. In the 1997 *Financial Times* league table, pupils at the top fifty public schools got an average score of one A and two Bs, two grades better than the top fifty state schools. Not a single secondary modern school was ranked by the *Financial Times*; there was no comprehensive school in the top 200; and the highest-ranking state school was a selective grammar school in Essex, in seventy-first place.[31]

Better A levels are not, of course, all that they seek. Public school children enjoy a wider curriculum than their state contemporaries, with music, drama, sport, and trips abroad; they all have science laboratories, a swimming pool, a sports hall, and a theatre. In 1997, independent schools spent £571 per pupil on new buildings and equipment, or about £273 million in total.[32] The average public school boy or girl spends eight to ten hours a week playing sport, and is often coached by nationally acclaimed figures who find teaching a handy way to make ends meet.

The willingness to organise school expeditions and supervise hours of sport is one measure of how much better paid, motivated and qualified public school teachers are by comparison with their counterparts in the state sector. There are also more of them. The pupil–teacher ratio at public schools is about 10:1, compared with 30:1 at state schools. Most parents believe that more teachers mean better results, not simply in terms of academic achieve-ment. At the foot of the *Financial Times* league table, a single A level grade separates the bottom fifty public schools from the bottom fifty state schools. The parents of wellborn blockheads are obviously still prepared to pay hand-somely for an education which gives a child the confidence to hold down a job as a chartered surveyor or a Lloyd's broker. But there is no doubt that most parents measure the return on their investment in the number of GCSEs and A levels their children secure.

The introduction of A level league tables in the early 1990s has given them the tools to distinguish between schools on that score. Parents now use league tables ruthlessly, to distinguish between schools and to weed out ineffective teachers once they have made their choice. The headmaster of Cheltenham College was dismissed in 1995 after a run of relatively poor results in the A level tables. 'There is no doubt that increasing competition has led to more short-termism,' said Anne Lee, ousted as head of Malvern Girls' College after less than two years as headmistress. 'A lot of heads believe their governing bodies respond too quickly to the league tables or changes in the roll.'[33]

It is, however, precisely this responsiveness which accounts for the success of the public schools. They have increased their share of the market to 7 per cent of children against 5.8 per cent twenty years ago, despite significant real increases in the cost of fees, year in and year out. Like the aristocracy, the English middle classes will take a lot of punishment, not only from the tax system and the trade cycle, before they surrender private education for their children.

Their perception of the value of a private education is shared even by those parents who cannot afford one. A MORI poll in August 1996 found only two in five who said they would stick with the state sector if they could afford to go private.[34] Cultural commentators such as Richard Hoggart may deplore the educational choices people make, and public school headmasters may despise those making them, but the only barrier to the displacement of state schools by the private sector is price. This is the precise reverse of the outcome predicted by Tony Crosland, who, as secretary of state for Education in the first Wilson government, greatly accelerated the comprehensivation of state secondary schools. 'The state sector must be strengthened so that it can match all but the very-best fee-paying schools,' he demanded. 'Once the state system is strong enough to compete, if parents want to send their children to some inferior fee-paying school for purely snobbish reasons, that's their affair. Why should they be denied the freedom to spend their money buttressing their egos?'[35]

The Destruction of the Alternative

One reason the comprehensive experiment failed to reduce the public schools to a rump, attended only by the children of snobs, is that public schools endure a harsh discipline quite absent in the state sector. If they fail to produce results, the price is bankruptcy. A state school, no matter how atrocious, can continue almost indefinitely. When government inspectors and local councillors recommended the closure of Hackney Downs Comprehensive in east London in 1994 because 'under-achievement among the majority of pupils . . . high levels of truancy . . . unsatisfactory teaching . . . staff absence . . . and poor parental support' meant it was 'failing to give its pupils an acceptable standard of education', the idea was shocking enough to become a national *cause célèbre*. (It closed shortly afterwards, though it is said that Hackney Downs was one of the best state schools in London before it went comprehensive in the 1960s.)[36] Similarly, the New Labour government was thought greatly daring when it threatened state schools with closure or takeover by the private sector if they could not explain their surplus places and poor results. When Leicester City Council announced plans to hold consultations on the closure of up to eight secondary schools with hundreds of spare places and a record of abysmal results, council officials described it as a 'very radical solution'.[37]

Even good state schools rarely offer a competitive alternative. Among the several fictional characters whom Peter Mandelson and Roger Liddle used to illustrate the horrors of Conservative Britain in *The Blair Revolution: Can New Labour Deliver?* were Ben and Laura Hodgson, two London yuppies who reluctantly send their children to a private school in a neighbouring borough:

> Ben and Laura had been reluctant purchasers of private education. They are not natural 'opters-out' who regard 'going private' as a sign of having made it . . . The decision on schools had been an agonising one. Ben and Laura had visited local primary schools before deciding to opt out. At one school they hadn't liked the atmosphere: the avoidance of any competitive spirit, and learning to read through 'real books' rather than a structured reading scheme. At another they liked the teachers, but the facilities were poor and undermaintained: the classrooms were dingy; the school roof was leaking. An additional worry was the number of children from disturbed backgrounds or whose English was virtually non-existent, as there was no effective support for children with special needs . . . In the state sector, quality largely depended on the luck of the draw . . . The local neighbourhood comprehensive had

a dismal reputation, and there was no certainty of entry to better state schools north of the river as other parents had arranged.

Ben was a first generation university graduate. He had won a scholarship to Oxford from a grammar school in the North of England in the 1960s. He wanted his children to have that same opportunity, but he knew there was no guarantee of this even if his children attended the best schools in the country. There was the fearful example of a colleague's eldest son – educated at a leading London day-school with one of the finest academic records in the country, but now gone off the rails, addicted to drugs and a drop-out . . . Ben harboured doubts about private education in its own terms, not just because of its divisive social effects. He worried that it was too pressured and too socially exclusive to produce balanced young adults. But, in inner London, he saw no acceptable alternative.[38]

The story of Ben and Laura is a near-complete description of the educational holocaust which has overtaken the state schools since the 1960s: the destruction of the grammar schools; the imposition of progressive methods of teaching; expenditure on salaries rather than books, equipment and buildings; the alienation of the natural leadership; the pre-emption of places at the few decent schools by articulate parents who know how to work the system to their advantage; the kicking-away of the ladders out of ignorance and poverty.

Ironically, it was the canting attitudes of people such as Ben and Laura which brought these things about. Back in the mid-1960s, a young journalist not unlike Ben Hodgson had an after-dinner drink with the then secretary of state for Education. 'I'd like to send my kids to a comprehensive school,' he told Tony Crosland, 'but as long as the public schools exist, my wife feels we'd be letting our kids down if we sent them anywhere else. If you would abolish public schools, we'd have no hesitation in sending our kids to a comprehensive.' Crosland was crushing. 'You really mustn't assume one's function is to ease the conscience of the middle classes,' he retorted. 'Why can't you and your wife take your own decisions?'[39] Thirty years later, Ben and Laura Hodgson are still waiting for the government to make their choices for them; their hopes now rest on its ability to raise the standards in state schools to those in the private sector.

One of their creators is now at Number 10 advising the prime minister on educational matters. Like the Hodgsons, his master has preferred excellence to justice for his own children. In 1994 Tony Blair decided to send his son to a grant-maintained school in another borough, where children are selected by interview, rather than risk his future in an Islington comprehensive. At the time Labour Party policy was to abolish grant-maintained schools. 'That's our choice as parents, and I wouldn't want to deny that choice to other parents,' the future prime minister explained.[40] Later, his secretary of state for Social Security, Harriet Harman, also sent her son to a selective, grant-maintained grammar school in a neighbouring borough, which prompted John Prescott to expostulate that he was 'not going to defend any fucking hypocrites'.[41]

In education, hypocrisy has a low political cost. Most parents are reassured rather than dismayed by politicians who refuse to lay down their children's lives for their own political ideals. The Blairs and Harriet Harman and her husband were doing what the articulate middle classes have always done: working the system to the advantage of their children. The good state schools tend to be in suburbs of the wealthier towns and cities. 'It is where most people live, that the state schools are worst,' write Adonis and Pollard. 'Middle class children now go to middle class comprehensives, whose catchment areas comprise middle class neighbourhoods, while working class children are mostly left to fester in the inner city comprehensive their parents cannot afford to move away from.'[42]

Ironically, it was to sever this connection between wealth and standards that the direct grant grammar schools were destroyed. The Donnison Report of 1970, which recommended their abolition, described them as 'predominantly middle class institutions ... Three out of four pupils come from the homes of white-collar workers: three out of five have fathers in professional or managerial occupations. Only one out of thirteen comes from a semi-skilled or unskilled worker's family.'[43] It was characteristic of the campaign for comprehensive education that these facts were thought to speak for themselves. The purpose of education was not learning, but social integration. The direct-grant grammar schools were particularly irksome to the progressive conscience because their parents paid modest fees. Most grammar schools were 'maintained' by local authorities but, since the early part of this century, a group of private grammar schools had qualified for 'direct grants' from central government in return for taking between a quarter and two thirds of their pupils from the local state primary schools. An increasing number of their pupils, all of them selected by examination, went on to university. Naturally, their clientèle was dominated by the aspirant middle classes: with a degree, their children could aspire to top positions.

The direct grant grammar schools were finally abolished in 1976. Faced with a choice of turning comprehensive or going independent, 59 opted to abandon selection and 119 chose independence. This was the final act of a campaign against selective education which went back over thirty years, and in particular against the dreaded 11-plus examination. The 1944 Education Act had introduced a tripartite system of secondary schooling in Britain: gifted children were to go to grammar schools, stupid ones to secondary moderns, and the manually dextrous to technical schools. Entry to the first or relegation to the second or third was dictated by an examination taken at the age of eleven – the notorious 11-plus – which made the tripartite system undeniably hierarchical and élitist. Few technical schools were set up, and four out of five children were condemned to secondary moderns; most of these squeezed children out of school at the age of fifteen, with few qualifications, leaving a grammar school élite to pit the accident of intelligence against the accident of wealth and birth.

Ultimately, the 11-plus was the undoing of the grammar schools. It ruthlessly reclassified three quarters of children as less intelligent than the rest, for most secondary moderns did not provide even for GCEs or O levels (what are now GCSEs). Many parents could not abide the finality of its verdicts, and the justification for selecting children at so young an age (the private sector has always preferred thirteen) was not convincing. The argument in favour of the 11-plus, recorded in the Hadow Report of 1926, now reads like an excerpt from a work of eugenics:

> There is a tide which begins to rise in the veins of youth at the age of eleven or twelve. It is called by the name of adolescence. If that tide can be taken at the flood, and a new voyage begun in the strength and along the flow of its current, we think that it will move on to fortune.

It was during the 1920s that the psychometric ideas of Sir Cyril Burt (who invented measurement of the Intelligence Quotient, or IQ) first achieved currency.[44] The case for the tripartite system was based in large part on his belief that the intelligence and aptitude of children could be measured, and they could then be given an education appropriate to their gifts.

It was a meritocratic rather than egalitarian strategy, which is why it was bound to fail. (In a democracy, only egalitarian strategies can succeed.) Principally because it offered a means of avoiding the stigma of failing the 11-plus, the comprehensive experiment was launched on a bipartisan basis, to widespread popular acclaim. By the outbreak of war in 1939 it was common wisdom among 'educationalists' and Board of Education civil servants that decisive selection at the age of eleven was, as the Spens Report of the previous year said, 'artificial and often mistaken'. Their alternative was what was then known as the 'multi-lateral' school, better known to subsequent generations as the comprehensive. In theory, comprehensives would still sift children by intelligence, but would make it possible to change streams after the age of eleven. However, their other justification – the ability to mix out of class with children who were cleverer or more stupid, and from different social backgrounds – quickly came to dominate. 'Although the comprehensives were invented by a coalition government,' wrote Sampson in 1962, long before the comprehensivisation of secondary education had begun in earnest, 'they have become firmly associated with socialism and egalitarianism.'[45]

The 1944 Education Act required local authorities to prepare and present schemes for turning their secondary schools into comprehensives. Ellen Wilkinson, the Labour education minister who implemented the legislation, directed that all newly built secondary schools were to be 'multi-lateral where possible'. But the comprehensivisation of education was sporadic under the 1944 Act. It was left to local authorities, whose ideas and resources varied widely, to decide whether they wanted them or not. Not many did. The number of comprehensive schools rose from 10 in 1950 to 175 in 1964, against 4,000 secondary moderns and 1,300 grammar schools. Of the 2.8 million children at secondary school in 1964, one quarter were in grammar schools and just 6 per cent at comprehensives.

It was only with the re-election of the Labour Party in 1964 that comprehensivation swept the country. In 1965 Crosland, who had moved to the Department of Education and Science after a brief stint at the Department of Economic Affairs, issued the notorious Circular 10/65 which 'requested' local authorities to go comprehensive, and set out a number of ways in which they might choose to do so. Crosland told his wife: 'If it's the last thing I do, I'm going to destroy every fucking grammar school in England. And Wales. And Northern Ireland.'[46] (The escape of Scotland, by virtue of the fact that it was under the control of the secretary of state for Scotland, was illusory: Scottish state schools were comprehensivised as well.) Ostensibly restricted to a request rather than a requirement, Crosland and his successors nevertheless found ways of blackmailing the recalcitrant.

In a second circular, 10/66, Crosland refused central government funding for new school buildings which did not fit a comprehensive pattern. From 1968 schools whose buildings were demolished were always rebuilt as comprehensives. The Donnison Report of 1970 urged the abolition of all remaining distinction and diversity in the state-subsidised sector:

> We are agreed that the conventional grammar school, selecting about 20 per cent of children at the age of 11, will not provide what the country or its most gifted children need ... Grammar Schools of the traditional kind cannot be combined with a comprehensive system of education: we must choose what we want. Fee-paying is not compatible with comprehensive education.[47]

By the time Labour left office in June 1970, the number of comprehensive schools had increased sevenfold, and covered more than one third of secondary schoolchildren. The incoming Conservative secretary of state for Education, Margaret Thatcher, dropped the legislation and annulled Circulars 10/65 and 10/66. But she did not reverse the drive towards universal comprehensivisation. She considered 3,600 proposals for the reorganisation of secondary schools, and rejected only 325; the vast majority were proposals to go comprehensive.[48]

In 1971, when the comprehensive experiment was at its height, Sampson visited what was the most avant-garde school in Britain: Countesthorpe College, outside Leicester. His account, though clearly intended to be taken seriously, reads now like a passage from a satirical novel:

> Countesthorpe College rises from a sea of mud in the midst of a middle-class housing estate, and two miles from a working-class estate: the two form the main catchment area. Local adults can use the school's facilities, and their community association is part of the buildings. The school is built in the shape of a big circle, of one storey only; the grey brick and stained woods, the curved walls, and the skylights dispersing soft light give a background of peaceful relaxation, and the windows look out on to greenhouses and fishponds. The school is made up not of rooms but of spaces and recesses – essential for the 'project' work on which the teaching is based. There are dramatic gyms, a huge art space, a black cube-shaped theatre workshop, and a stage. The lessons are equally unconventional: the courses have elaborate titles like 'Creative Expression in Two and Three Dimensions' or 'The Individual and the Group', reflecting the inter-disciplinary approach as in new universities. The children are only streamed for learning languages; the rest of the learning is through project work. There are special sessions for 'non-involved' children who go into a remedial group to work on motorbikes to satisfy their aggression. The children are encouraged to express themselves by using tape recorders: 'The spoken word is more important for most than the written word.' There is no headmaster at Countesthorpe, only a 'warden' called Tim: he has no proper office, but moves around, in a springy and speculative walk, from recess to recess. Tim McMullen is a genuine 'anti-head': he is a slim, complex man, whose own shape and style seem experimental. He came from a public school and hates the public school system . . . Experiments can't do worse than the existing schools, he maintains.[49]

But they could. Countesthorpe has struggled ever since to escape what the current principal calls 'ill-informed attention in the past'.[50] Yet Countesthorpe is a good school by the standards of many comprehensives. Its pupils and parents have not lost respect for the authority of teachers, or ceased to regard the buildings and equipment as an investment in their future, or set fire to them or cheered as the teachers went on strike. Some comprehensives, particularly in the inner cities, are not so lucky.

Hindsight makes it hard to understand why experiments such as this were intensified by the Labour government elected in 1974. However, the atmosphere at that time was deeply hostile to the idea that children need discipline, competition, examination and the skills of literacy and numeracy rather than personal freedom and social integration. (At some comprehensives in the late 1960s, the idea of a school was inverted, with the pupils establishing rules for the teachers and punishing those who broke them).[51] When Brian Cox published the first of the notorious Black Papers in 1969, questioning the wisdom of the progressive–comprehensive orthodoxy, he was vilified. Comprehensive teachers and polytechnic lecturers referred to him as an 'educational Powellite' and a 'fascist'. 'Within a few days in March 1969,' Cox recalls, 'I found myself the most hated professor in the country, nicknamed by left-wingers as the Enoch Powell of education.'[52]

Prime ministers were not immune to this treatment. When James Callaghan questioned the efficacy of progressive teaching methods, as late as 1976, he was accused of being tricked by the schools inspectorate and of 'selfish political motives' and 'political demagoguery'.[53] Despite his misgivings, comprehensivisation acquired new momentum in the year he became prime minister. It was the Education Act of 1976 which finally *compelled* local authorities to turn their schools into comprehensives. This prompted a crisis at Tameside in Greater Manchester, where the Conservatives won control in the local elections of May 1976 on a pledge to retain selective secondary schooling. Fred Mulley, the secretary of state, used powers available under the 1944 Education Act to direct Tameside to comprehensivise its schools and secured a court order compelling the Council to abolish its five grammar schools.

Mulley's successor, Shirley Williams, was even more zealous. A product of St Paul's School for Girls, she believed that 'the freedom to send one's children to an independent school is bought at too high a price for the rest of society.'[54] Threats of litigation, harsh deadlines and 'naming and shaming' were used to bully schools into becoming comprehensives. When Thatcher became secretary of state in 1970, one third of state secondary schools were comprehensive. By the time she became prime minister nine years later, only one tenth were not. The pressure exerted by central government in the 1970s marked the abandonment of the tradition that education was a matter for local government.

The success of the drive for comprehensives had a doubly ironic outcome. Not only did the Conservative governments of the 1980s intensify the centralis-

ation of education, in a vain attempt to redeem the inadequacies of comprehensive education. The failure of the comprehensive experiment saved the
public schools.

How the State Saved the Public Schools

By the early 1960s, the public schools were on the brink of extinction. In
1962 Sampson found the headmaster of Eton, Robert Birley, fretting about
competition from the grammar schools. 'The grammar schools realised quite
suddenly about three or four years ago that they could get as many boys into
Oxford or Cambridge as were clever enough, and that made things far more
competitive,' he told Sampson. 'Ten years ago half the boys at Eton went to
Oxford and Cambridge: now it's only a third.' A year earlier, Birley had tried
to persuade the Headmasters' Conference to accept public subsidies in return
for admitting boys from poorer backgrounds. He was thwarted not by his
public school colleagues but by the grammar school headmasters, who
thought the Birley scheme would cream off their brightest pupils at the time
when they were coming into their own.

In 1962 Sampson was confident that the grammar schools would 'creep
steadily up over the next ten years', and envisaged a Britain gradually taken
over by meritocrats. One grammar school headmaster assured him, 'We've
got the Establishment on the run.'[55] By the end of the 1960s, Sampson had
trouble telling the grammar and public schools apart, especially in terms of
academic results. 'The grammar schoolboys are making deeper marks on the
British power-structure,' he wrote in 1971, after another ten years of success.
'The grammar schools appear to be less prone to drop-outs, pot-smokers and
general ennui than the public schools; without boarders, they have a less
highly-charged atmosphere; and with fewer boys from rich homes, there is a
more straightforward ambition for success.'[56]

It was hard to dispute that the rising class of the sixties and seventies were
the grammar school men. One of the minor curiosities of the comprehensive
experiment is how many of the leading politicians associated with it during
those years were products of grammar schools. Harold Wilson, who went to
Wirral Grammar School, was reputed to have said that his alma mater would
be abolished over his dead body. (Typically, expedience overrode his commitment.)[57] Denis Healey attended Bradford Grammar, and Roy Jenkins was at
Abersychan Grammar, Margaret Thatcher at Grantham High, Ted Heath
at Chatham House Grammar in Ramsgate, and Anthony Barber at Retford
Grammar. Yet, in little more than a decade, they led or served in governments
which turned all the remaining grammar schools into comprehensives or

chased them into the private sector. 'The speed of the process needs emphasising,' write Adonis and Pollard. 'In the late 1960s the State grammar schools
and quasi-State direct-grant schools were intact, and together easily outclassed
the independent sector in terms of academic output. The proportion of public
school educated undergraduates at Oxford was . . . on a steady downward path
after the Second World War . . . Yet the next decade saw both these meritocratic pillars of the State school system collapse.'[58]

The public schools could scarcely believe their luck. The first half of the
twentieth century, unlike the second half of the nineteenth, was remarkably
inhospitable to the archetypal public school. By contrast with the Victorian
era, when dozens of public schools were founded as classical boarding establishments, only progressive private schools like Stowe (1923), Summerhill
(1924), Dartington Hall (1926), Bryanston (1928), Gordonstoun (1934) and
Millfield (1935) flourished.[59] The social exclusiveness and fee-paying status
of the old-style public schools made them a natural target of social and
political reformers. As early as 1919, a mixture of economic pressure and
socio-political insecurity had impelled the headmasters of Charterhouse, Eton
and Marlborough to offer to accept a percentage of state primary school
pupils if the state subsidised their fees. (The offer was refused.) During the
inter-war years many of the lesser public schools, their best pupils siphoned
off by the grammar schools and staff salaries rising rapidly to keep up with
tempting offers from the grammar schools, came close to bankruptcy. In the
1920s even Dulwich College had to accept London County Council scholarship boys to ease its financial problems. During the Second World War, public
school headmasters welcomed the recommendation in the Fleming Report
that the taxpayer fund a quarter of the places at the public schools. Even
leading establishments like Harrow and Tonbridge were close to collapse. In
the 1940s, local authorities did subsidise a handful of places at public schools,
but the experiment fizzled out. The Fleming scheme foundered not on the
opposition of public school headmasters, who were always eager to take the
taxpayers' money, but because neither the government nor the local authorities were prepared to pay and the grammar schools protested that they would
lose custom to a subsidised competitor. Far from rescuing the public schools
from the multitude, the 1944 Education Act created a formidable competitor
for them in the shape of the selective-entry grammar schools. For over-taxed
parents, the grammar school became the cheapest way of ensuring that their
children got a place at university. In fact, for a brief interlude in the 1950s
and early 1960s, it looked as if the grammar schools would reduce the public
schools to the status of their equivalents in Continental Europe: finishing
schools for the rich and stupid.

By the time Crosland became secretary of state for Education, the secondary school population educated at public schools had shrunk from 9 per cent to 5.5 per cent.[60] He was convinced that the public schools would disappear naturally, either as they became dependent on public subsidies or were forced to shut by competition from the state sector. In agreeing to set up a commission to investigate how public and direct grant schools could be integrated into the state system, he was doing little more than fulfilling a manifesto pledge. At the outset, he told its chairman – a former social worker and county education officer, Sir John Newsom – that the government would not endorse abolition of the public schools. It was estimated that £60 million would be needed to nationalise the public schools; there was also anxiety about the erosion of personal liberty which abolition implied. Crosland was convinced that their withering away would vindicate his comprehensive experiment.[61] Nothing needed to be done and – if abolition were ruled out – nothing could be done.

By the time the Newsom Commission reported in July 1968 that the public schools should surrender half their places to children from state schools who 'needed' a boarding school education (their entry to be lubricated by a £12 million grant), there was no chance that the government would take the idea seriously. But the public schools did not wither away because, by destroying the grammar schools, the advocates of comprehensive education had eliminated the only serious competition the public schools had ever faced. All the great grammar schools – Bradford, Bristol, Manchester, Birkenhead, Haberdashers' Aske's, Latymer Upper, the Royal Grammar School, Newcastle, King Edward's, Birmingham – elected to join the independent sector rather than undergo comprehensivisation. By intensifying competition for pupils, the irruption of the grammar schools into the private sector forced the traditional public schools to raise their standards.

During the 1970s middle-class parents began to appreciate that a university education was necessary for a professional career, including previously undemanding occupations such as stock-broking, Lloyd's and accountancy. They fled the comprehensives.

'The demands of the dispossessed metropolitan middle classes and the rich-must-have-degrees were at one, to be met by public schools targeting their resources on "academic value added", appropriating at least a modicum of the old grammar school ethos in the process,' write Adonis and Pollard of these years. 'The transfer of leading city grammar schools into the private sector, fleeing the same egalitarian tide, gave a powerful impetus to reform.'[62] By the 1980s, educating a child at a public school had ceased to be a social embarrassment, and had become a form of conspicuous consumption. The ability to pay remorselessly rising school fees out of fully taxed income has transformed private education from a social habit into the most jealously guarded form of private property this generation can display – and the next generation can inherit.[63]

In 1982 Eric Anderson, then headmaster at Shrewsbury, said that '60 per cent of the public schools would have gone under if the grammar schools had remained.'[64] Sixteen years later, the public schools are flourishing: about 2,400 independent schools are now educating 590,000 pupils in the United Kingdom. As prosperity has rolled across the country, the combination of rising middle-class incomes and plunging standards in the state sector has allowed the public schools to increase their share of the secondary education market while raising their fees significantly. The population educated at independent schools increased from 5.8 per cent in 1979 to a peak of 7.5 per cent in 1990, and it is still over 7 per cent.

Throughout this period, private school fees have increased at a consistently faster rate than retail prices. Increases averaged 10 per cent in the 1980s and are still averaging 5 per cent in the 1990s.[65] The expense of a private education is the most powerful confirmation of its value. Parents with three children at public school are paying £30,000 or £40,000 a year out of post-tax income, before the uniforms, riding lessons and piano tuition are added. It is the ironic result of an egalitarian policy – comprehensivisation – that access to the best education in Britain, which translates into the best jobs and the most fruitful contacts, is now the privilege of wealth, status and power to a greater extent than at any time since secondary education became universally available. The comprehensive school strengthened the social divisions it was designed to bridge.

Solving the Public School Problem

Characteristic of the direction that the educational debate has taken in Britain since the war is that social divisions are still treated as the primary problem rather than as a symptom of the malaise: the pitiful condition of state education, particularly at the secondary level. *Class Act: The Myth of Britain's Classless Society* describes how French and German politicians, even of leftish hue, have prevented the destruction of their state school systems because their own children attend them. The problem, its authors reckon, is 'the divorce of the professional classes from the State system'.[66]

It is a common view. Addressing the Headmasters' Conference in 1993, Andrew Neil (then editor of the *Sunday Times*) asked his audience to 'imagine how different things would be if top civil servants, television producers, managing directors, the royal family and even newspaper editors sent their children to state schools. The most powerful pressure groups within the

Establishment would be inside rather than outside the system . . . The future of the state system would be the stuff of dinner party conversations in Kensington, Chelsea and Westminster, not as an academic exercise but as something that directly involved their children. The lobby for increasing spending on education, or using resources more efficiently, would acquire new and powerful voices.'[67]

In 1996, George Walden, a former Conservative education minister, published a book entitled *We Should Know Better*, in which he gave vent to his longstanding conviction that the only solution to the national educational malaise was to make the middle classes use state secondary schools. 'The breakfast tables of Tory MPs like myself would be educational battlegrounds,' he has said, 'as our wives described in lugubrious detail the shortcomings of state schools and insisted we do something about them.'[68] The idea that the public schools have robbed state schools of their natural middle-class leaders is trivial as well as patronising. The problem in state education is structural, not sociological; working-class parents are just as capable as middle-class parents of distinguishing between good schools and bad. The difference is that they lack the means to make their preferences known. The middle classes have voted with their feet (by moving to the leafier suburbs) or their wallets (by buying a private education). People who lack money and mobility have to put up with whatever the Department for Education and Employment, the local education authority and the teachers are prepared to supply, no matter how much they complain about the shoddy standards. In this sense, state schools are no different from any other nationalised industry: they are run in the interests of the producers, not the consumers.

For over twenty years, governments have assumed that they can solve the problem by making the producers (the teachers) do what the consumers (the parents) want. By the mid-1970s, parental aversion to the progressive ideas of teachers and educationalists had begun to affect the political climate. In 1976, in one of his first speeches as prime minister, James Callaghan called for a Great Debate on education. Among the ideas he advanced was a 'core curriculum of basic knowledge'.[69] Twelve years elapsed before a Conservative government introduced the first national curriculum in the 1988 Education Act. It laid down both the 'core' (English, maths and science) and the 'foundation' subjects (technology, history, geography, music art, modern language and physical education) which teachers were expected to cover. It also set attainment targets, which were to be monitored by testing at the ages of 7, 11, 14 and 16. This was coupled with per capita funding and open enrolment, to allow successful schools to attract more money as they expanded.

These measures were not unlike the investment, output and productivity targets the governments of the 1950s and 1960s set for the nationalised coal and steel industries, which did not prevent their generating a negative return on capital.[70] The national curriculum was a straightforward attempt to force teachers to teach what politicians thought parents and employers wanted children to learn. Open enrolment and per capita funding were part of a subtler plan to simulate the workings of the market. Instead of giving parents the money to buy a place for their child at the school of their choice, it gave schools the obligation and the money to take their child. It gave consumers the illusion of choice but not the money to make their choices effective.

Teachers refused to implement the national curriculum or carry out the tests until they were modified to their satisfaction. But if teachers disliked the reforms, they were a gift to other producers: the Department for Education and Employment and the schools inspectorate, both of which have become far more powerful and important since funding of schools and determination of the curriculum were centralised. The publication of league tables, which began in earnest in 1990–1, has reinforced their influence. Paradoxically, the main result is a further diminution in educational standards, as schools struggle, not to get children into university, but to avoid being penalised by the Department for Education or stigmatised by the chief inspector of schools.

Meanwhile, the root cause of the problems remains untouched. The connections between the poor academic performance and grim physical condition of the average state school and its ownership and direction are raised only in facile comparisons of expenditure per pupil at state and private schools.* This is helpful to the producers, since it encourages the view that the problems stem entirely from a lack of resources rather than an unwillingness to embrace selection in any form, the lack of choice of schools, fundamental shortcomings in the quality of the teachers, and inadequate teaching methods.

The true solution to the low standards and crumbling buildings of the state sector is not to force parents who can afford a private education to buy a state one, but to give every parent the means to buy the education they want for their children. Parental vouchers, encashable at any school, are an obvious way to do this. Coupled with a restoration of the right to charge fees and a return to selective entry (though not of the 11-plus variety), this would give the consumers of education the power to create schools whose entrance requirements, organisation and curriculum are not dictated by the educational establishment. This is precisely why the Department for Education

* Independent school fees have to cover capital costs and administrative overheads as well as the cost of teachers, making comparisons of per capita expenditure between the public sector (where these costs are absorbed elsewhere) and the private sector misleading.

and Employment, local education authorities, the schools inspectorate and (less explicably) teachers have resisted these reforms so fiercely.

As secretary of state for Education in the first half of the 1980s, Keith Joseph proposed a voucher scheme. 'Schools policy remained the fiefdom of those officials brought up and bred in the DES tradition,' recalled Kenneth Baker, his successor. 'They had seen to it that key policy battles with Ministers had been won by civil servants. Keith's idea of education vouchers had been scuppered by them first delaying, and then proposing a 'super voucher' scheme which was so radical that it frightened the Cabinet and was rejected as unacceptable.'[71] The timid nursery voucher scheme introduced at the fag-end of the Major government was scrapped immediately by New Labour at the behest of the local education authorities and the teaching unions.

The Myth of State Education

There were many arguments against vouchers. One of the most telling was the cost of subsidising parents who would send their children to public schools anyway. But all the detailed objections were persiflage. The truth is that departmental officials did not believe (or could not afford to believe) that people can be trusted to make the right choices for their children. It is a belief which rests on the great historical myth that, until the state called schools into being and forced parents to enrol their children, there was no education worthy of the name.

Private schools have existed since the Dark Ages. By the middle of the nineteenth century the public schools were only part of a vast array of private, fee-paying schools. In 1818 – over fifty years before the state empowered local authorities to establish schools, fund them out of the rates and compel children to attend – a parliamentary select committee chaired by the educational reformer Henry Brougham estimated that about one in fourteen children was already attending a fee-paying school. The Anglican National Society for promoting the education of the poor in the principles of the Established Church was in its seventh year, and the Non-Conformist British and Foreign School Society was in its fourth. A second survey in 1834 indicated that the numbers in schools had tripled since 1818, to nearly 1.5 million pupils, without any direction from the state. In 1833, when the first state grant of £20,000 was handed to the National Society and the British and Foreign School Society, the government was (as Professor West puts it) jumping 'into the saddle of a horse that was already galloping'.[72]

The work of the denominational societies was part of a long tradition of voluntary educational institutions, dating back to the 'song schools' founded by the churches and cathedrals of the Dark and Middle Ages to teach choristers how to read and sing and train older boys for the priesthood. (King's, Canterbury, founded contemporaneously with the Cathedral by Augustine in 598, is, by that measure, the oldest public school in England.) Most, like Westminster, survived the Dissolution to become ordinary schools within the Established Church and, after the Reformation, there was a burst of secular foundations by wealthy businessmen. One authority reckons that between 1480 and 1660 rich London merchants endowed 153 schools in ten counties with assets worth a total of £216,939, providing an education for 8,000 poor children. Another £92,465 8s was invested in scholarships for them at the ancient universities, many linked to particular schools.[73]

These sums are equivalent to tens of millions of pounds today, and reflected the gratitude of many provincial Englishmen of humble origins for the wealth a little education had enabled them to amass. To this day, the livery companies of the City retain close connections with a number of public schools.

The Victorians were equally prolific: between 1840 and 1869 forty-one new boarding schools were founded to educate the children of the commercial and professional classes. Marlborough (1843) specialised in sons of the clergy, Wellington (1859) in those of army officers, Cranleigh (1863) in the scions of Surrey farmers and publicans. The seven schools founded by the Anglo-Catholic clergyman, Nathaniel Woodard (1811–1855) and the establishments set up by his liberal rival Joseph Brereton (1822–1901) were all funded by the public subscription of shares. Unlike the lavishly endowed foundations of the medieval and early-modern period, the Victorian public schools were expected to subsist largely on their fees and return 5 per cent to their shareholders. It gave them a strong incentive to give parents what they wanted. Many were sited near railway stations, specifically to allow them to recruit pupils as widely as possible. By modern standards, the fees were cheap; in the 1860s and 1870s those at a new public school ranged from £30 to no more than £60 a year. Marlborough set its early fees so low that overcrowding and uncontrollable numbers sparked a week-long riot by the boys in 1851.

The First Public Schools for Girls

The Victorians also founded the first private secondary schools for girls. Until the nineteenth century, girls were not educated, unless it was to learn Latin at a convent or attend a ladies' academy to master the social accomplishments (dancing, painting, sewing and the piano) which rich or well-connected husbands expected. Anything more was considered unnecessary.[74] Anyway, demanding subjects were reputed to impose a dangerous physical strain on the weaker vessel, especially if her knowledge was tested by examination.

It was not until 1848 that Queen's College, the first school to specialise in the secondary education of women, was founded in Harley Street, financed by the savings of a lady-in-waiting to Queen Victoria. Its goal – to improve the status and knowledge of governesses – was not ambitious, and it owes its place in history chiefly to the fact that it numbered Frances May Buss and Dorothea Beale among its earliest pupils. These formidable spinsters ('Miss Buss and Miss Beale Cupid's darts do not feel, How different from us, Miss Beale and Miss Buss,' as the late Victorian ditty went) became respectively headmistress of the North London Collegiate School and of the Ladies' College at Cheltenham. They were pioneers of a campaign against sex discrimination in education, and the institutions they ran marked the beginnings of serious secondary school education for women in Britain.

Miss Buss opened the North London Collegiate School for Ladies at 46 Camden Street in April 1850, but it has since moved to Canons at Edgware in Middlesex. The day-school attracted thirty-five daughters of professional men and 'the most respectable' tradesmen on its first day. Within a year, the number of pupils had more than tripled. Miss Buss set rigorous academic standards, and was an innovator in many other ways. Girls were expected to swim in the public baths at St Pancras, and her plan to make the girls 'really bold swimmers' by capsizing a boat full of them in open water was nearly implemented. In the interests of dress reform she organised a tug-of-war between girls wearing stays and those who were not, which the latter won. Girls who fainted were doused with cold water, and whole mornings might be passed erasing ink spillages from the classroom floor.

From 1944, the North London Collegiate was a direct grant grammar school, but was driven back into the private sector by Fred Mulley and Shirley Williams in the mid-1970s.[75] The school was never rich (it was poor enough in the nineteenth century for a £50 donation from Princess Louise to make survival possible), but is now one of the leading academic schools in the country *tout court*, and is regularly near the top in the *Financial Times* tables.

In June 1858 Dorothea Beale was chosen from fifty candidates as first principal of the Ladies' College, Cheltenham, the earliest proprietary girls' school in England. It had opened four years earlier, with 200 parents subscribing £10 each in exchange for a place. At the time she arrived there were only 69 pupils at the school and £400 in the bank.[76] By 1864 Miss Beale had stabilised its finances, and its academic success was forcing her to buy houses in the town to accommodate the rush of applicants. By the time the Ladies' College was incorporated as a company in 1880, 500 girls were at the school. Perhaps only Miss Beale, with her iron self-discipline, demonic energy and childhood dreams of running a school, could have created a great institution with such limited resources. Personal frugality, inspired by rigid High Church principles and reinforced by lack of a family, enabled her to spend her own money on the school and on its sister foundation at Oxford.*

Victorian Reform

The achievements of the Victorians were not confined to new foundations. They also renewed the ancient public schools. These had entered the nineteenth century in an advanced state of corruption and decay. The boys, who were essentially self-governing, learned little; they were also drunken, licentious, bullying and riotous. As late as 1818 two companies of soldiers were despatched to suppress a rebellion of pupils at Winchester, where the boys rose in 1770, 1774, 1778 and 1798. The first affray, in which pistols were discharged, was sparked by a publican attempting to eject some pupils from his alehouse at closing time. The last occurred in 1848, when the boys barricaded themselves in after being refused a bonfire party.[77] During the French Revolution virtually every major school experienced a riot demanding 'rights of boys'.

Few parents were willing to send their children to such establishments, leaving the masters to collect and spend the income from historic endowments on themselves, their friends and family. The earliest public schools, Eton and Winchester, were supposed to use the endowments to educate the poor, but the teachers had long since taken to admitting fee-paying pupils instead and pocketing the income from the endowments and the fees. When the members of a parliamentary committee chaired by Henry Brougham investigated the public schools in London between 1816 and 1818, they were so shocked by the peculation that they advocated confiscation of the endowments to fund a proper system of secondary education in the capital.[78] But nothing was done for more than forty years.

Finally, in 1861, the newspapers, led by the *Edinburgh Review*, began a public campaign for an official investigation into the abuse of endowments, and a royal commission was duly established. Chaired by the 4th Earl of Clarendon, it was charged with examining the revenues and management of nine schools judged as 'significant of the position that few schools had gained in the public eye': Charterhouse, Eton, Harrow, Merchant Taylors', Rugby, St Paul's, Shrewsbury, Westminster and Winchester. At each, the commissioners found

---

* Dorothea Beale was also the founder of St Hilda's College, Oxford. She established it to train teachers, to whose shortage and low quality she attributed the poor calibre of women's secondary education. The early undergraduates were mainly, but not exclusively, Old Cheltonians.

grave abuses of trust. They reckoned the annual income of the nine schools averaged £81,831 in the early 1860s (about £3.3 million in modern terms). It was not an enormous sum, but it was highly concentrated. Three quarters of it accrued to Eton, Winchester and Charterhouse, where the money was consumed by the fellows, reducing the staff to reliance on fees. Unsurprisingly, they had taken to overcharging parents, and lowering entry standards to keep numbers up. The commissioners' criticism was a masterpiece of discretion:

> It is but just to these great schools to say that there is not one of them, we believe, which would consciously submit itself to the level of a mere commercial speculation. The principle which they appear to recognise as the measure of the charges which they make is that of raising, not as much money as parents can be induced to pay, but as much as will maintain an adequate staff of highly qualified teachers, beside defraying other expenses. This principle has not perhaps been consistently observed in practice by the more prosperous schools, whilst the less prosperous ones, and those which draw their scholars chiefly from the less wealthy classes, have deemed themselves obliged to lower their standard in some degree in order to maintain their numbers; but it seems everywhere to be assumed as the true principle, and we trust that it will be kept steadily in view.[79]

Despite the widespread evidence of inefficiency and corruption they had uncovered, the Clarendon commissioners did no more than recommend that the schools direct their endowment income to its proper use.

The Taunton Commission: An Opportunity Missed

The Victorian conscience was not satisfied. If such nefarious practices were permissible at the great endowed schools, unthinkable defalcations must be in progress at lesser establishments. A second royal commission, chaired by the 1st Baron Taunton, was set up in 1864, and over the next four years conducted an industrious, detailed and scrupulous investigation more characteristic of Victorian reformers. The Taunton commissioners investigated the ancient foundations; the old grammar schools founded by City merchants and other wealthy patrons; the new public schools then springing up; the private schools run for profit – even the so-called 'proprietorial' schools, dedicated to the education of particular religious denominations.[80]

What is striking is the immense variety of the schools they investigated or uncovered. The commissioners reckoned there were around 3,000 endowed schools in Britain, each varying in wealth, curriculum, ambitions, and standards. Barely one in ten was offering a classical public school education (consisting largely of Latin and Greek) as preparation for a university place. Some were extremely rich; others dirt-poor. Many were providing a good education, but several were appalling. At Sedbergh in 1867, the visiting commissioner found the mastership held in common by two clergymen who had not spoken to each other for fifteen years, and the teachers of the upper and lower forms blaming each other for the uselessness of their charges. 'As to Sedbergh,' the commissioners concluded, 'I despair of putting it into any class at all . . . it simply cumbers the ground.'[81]

Of course, the endowed schools catered largely for the better-off, but a similar breadth and variety catered for the poorer sections of society. An earlier royal commission on 'popular education', chaired by the 5th Duke of Newcastle, had reported in 1861 that nearly all children of school age were receiving some kind of schooling, for an average duration of 5.7 years.[82] 'Wherever the Commissioners went,' concluded the report, 'they found schools of some sort, and failed to discover any considerable number of children who did not attend school for some time, at some period in their lives.'[83] All charged fees, but many were subsidised by the churches. Between 1820 and 1883 the Church of England raised £12.25 million to build and maintain Church schools. The commissioners were impressed; they recommended only better funding and more thorough inspection of the thriving private sector, not nationalisation.

W. E. Forster, who became education secretary under Gladstone in 1868, ignored these findings when he secured the passage of the Education Act of 1870. But he did accept the recommendation that school boards be established to fund schools out of local authority rates. His Act established the celebrated 'board schools', where attendance was compulsory for all children up to the age of thirteen. They were not free (only those parents who could not afford the fees were excused payment), but they were sufficiently subsidised to drive private schools out of business by undercutting their fees and paying higher salaries to teachers. The private schools were eligible for subsidies if they agreed to be inspected, but they found an inspection usually concluded with a demand for better facilities and higher salaries, which they felt unable to meet. In this way, new private schools were discouraged from starting up.[84]

Forster made no provision for secondary education. But the Taunton commissioners had outlined a scheme of immense potential for the provision of secondary schools by the private sector. Instead of deploring the chaotic mixture they had identified, the commissioners recommended taking the best elements of each type of school and using them to create a national system of non-sectarian secondary school education. To finance it, they proposed to confiscate the endowments of the corrupted public schools and redistribute them across a national network of secondary schools. The commissioners had discovered that although individual endowments were often quite small – two thirds of the 782 endowed schools examined had an investment income of less than £100 – the aggregate income of the endowed schools and associated charitable foundations was £336,201, or £13 million in modern money.[85] This was insufficient of itself to create a network of the size proposed but would be enough if coupled with fees and scholarships financed by the ratepayers. Only Eton, Harrow and the other 'great schools' identified by the Clarendon commissioners were to be excluded from the scheme. (It was argued that both types of school, new and old, would benefit from the competition.) Matthew Arnold, a member of the commission and chief advocate of the scheme, recommended that the new and reformed schools be known as 'Royal Schools'.

If there was a missed opportunity in secondary education in Britain, this was it. Contrary to popular perceptions, the error did not occur in 1944, when R. A. Butler failed to use the Fleming Report to nationalise the public schools. It happened in 1868 when W. E. Forster failed to privatise secondary education. The royal schools would have changed the entire course of English schooling by creating a national network of privately owned secondary schools and averting the disastrous experiment of comprehensivisation a century later. Forster was certainly familiar with the proposal: he was not only a member of the Taunton Commission, but brother-in-law to Matthew Arnold. He failed to translate it into legislation because the Church of England was unwilling to cede control of middle-class education to secular schools and because forward-looking public schools such as Marlborough, Uppingham, King's Canterbury and Wellington were unwilling to surrender their financial independence.[86] The headmasters of Uppingham and King's Canterbury masterminded a great agitation against the recommendations, in the process forming the Headmasters' Conference to present a united front to the government. The first achievement of this body (still the voice of the independent schools in England) was to castrate the Endowed Schools Act of 1869, which merely appointed commissioners to redress the grosser abuses of endowment income and re-found moribund schools.

In retrospect, Forster vies with Crosland for the mantle of the person who did most damage to education of the young in Britain. Forster said of his Education Act of 1870 that he aimed only to 'fill up the gaps' and that 'we must take care ... not to destroy the existing system in introducing a new one.' In fact, almost everything which has gone wrong with education began to go wrong from 1870. The board schools created under the Act were supervised by elected politicians, whose itch to interfere is a professional hazard. They were financed by a mixture of national and local taxpayers, giving both central and local government a say in what went on. The Act did not make schooling free but, by making it compulsory, made fees harder to collect.* By creating state-subsidised schools, it drove many private and Church schools out of business and prevented new schools being born, narrowing the range of choice available to parents, and suppressing the inventiveness and experimentation which is the preserve of the private sector.

It is true that Forster did not invent state intervention in education. The first public money was given to the denominational societies as early as 1833, on terms which gave them a perverse incentive to reduce their fee income. (Schools which accepted grants were restricted in the scale of the fees they could charge.) Government inspectors had visited schools since 1839, and a separate Department of Education, with its own budget, had existed since 1856. But Forster weakened the chief barrier to the nationalisation of education – fee-paying – and left schools at the mercy of the tidy minds of the twentieth-century bureaucratic state. In 1891 a special fee-grant of ten shillings a head was introduced, making education virtually free. By the Education Act of 1902 the board schools were nationalised and taken over by local authorities, which were empowered to fund secondary as well as elementary schools. Grants to denominational schools were made conditional on the surrender of one third of the seats on their governing bodies to local government officials.

By 1907, previously independent grammar schools were taking public money in return for providing a quarter of their places free of charge. Fee-paying in state-funded primary schools was abolished in 1918 and in secondary schools in 1944. This finally robbed parents of their ability to choose which school their child attended, and of their responsibility to decide between schools and curricula. It placed the system firmly in the hands of teachers, Whitehall and town hall officials and elected politicians: exactly what Robert Morant, the tidy-minded Wykehamist behind the Education Act of 1902, had intended.[87]

The eventual conversion of the tri-partite system of secondary education envisaged by the 1944 Act (grammar, secondary modern and technical) into the universal comprehensive, and the subsequent imposition of a national curriculum, were the logical culmination of the process Forster had launched and Morant had perfected. The gradual raising of the school-leaving age, coupled with denial of the right to charge fees, eliminated the last vestiges

---

* The Act did not make education to age 13 compulsory; it made provision for local authorities to frame by-laws making it compulsory. By 1876, half the population was under compulsion, and in 1880 school was made compulsory for all five to ten-year-olds. See Timmins, *The Five Giants*, pp. 68–9.

of financial autonomy at state schools by forcing them to apply for further funding to keep pupils for longer. Attempts by the Conservative government to give headmasters control of their budgets, and to receive their grants from Whitehall rather than the local education authority, have not altered their fundamental condition: complete financial dependence on the taxpayer.

Can the Public Schools Survive?

The public schools escaped absorption into this system more by luck than judgment. They came close to surrendering their independence to the state voluntarily in both 1919 and 1944, and were on the verge of economic defeat when the state rescued them by abolishing the grammar schools in the 1960s and 1970s. Wherever public subsidies are available, they have seized them eagerly. They have long relied on the taxpayer to fund a considerable number of places for the children of diplomats and military personnel based abroad.[88] When rolls fell during the severe recession of the early 1990s, the Independent Schools Information Service (ISIS) proposed to the government that public schools become eligible for grant-maintained status.[89]

By then, some had already become dangerously dependent on the Assisted Places Scheme, set up by the Thatcher government in 1981 to subsidise places at public schools for children from poorer homes. By the time New Labour abolished the scheme in 1997, 40,331 pupils were receiving assistance worth a total of £140 million. Even now, several local education authorities are funding over 3000 pupils at independent schools. But the chief effect of the abolition is to increase the dependence of independent schools on fees, making them more exclusive than they were already, in the same way that Old Labour made direct-grant schools more exclusive by chasing them from the public sector.

For the public schools, rising social exclusivity carries a big political risk, even under a government led by a public school man with children at a selective entry school. This is one reason why the schools publicise their expenditure on scholarships (financial support for brighter children) and bursaries (financial support for poorer children) so avidly. In 1998, according to ISIS, the parents of 88,394 public school pupils were receiving assistance from their schools with the fees, at a total cost of £125 million a year.[90] Although New Labour is making friendly overtures towards the public schools – in 1997 Stephen Byers, then a junior education minister, told the Girls' School Association that 'the time has come for old prejudices to be buried'[91] – the quiet voice could not conceal the big stick. He had earmarked £500,000 of public money for pilot projects intended to explore the scope for co-operation between state and private schools. The possibilities include sharing sports facilities, public schoolboys coaching their proletarian brethren in examination and interview techniques, and state school pupils taking some A level courses at the local Greyfriars. Those schools which form links will know that they are buying insurance, not a guarantee of survival; most public schools will be too terrified not to take part.

As recently as 1983, Labour promised to abolish the public schools. In opposition in 1995, the present education secretary, David Blunkett, recommended applying VAT to school fees (the idea had to be publicly disowned by Blair before it became too popular among the rank-and-file). In opposition, Labour also talked of tying the charitable status of public schools to a commitment to admit more state-educated pupils. More than four out of five independent schools enjoy the benefits of charitable status, which is worth over £60 million a year to them. The reassurance offered by Stephen Byers ('It is not part of this government's agenda to encourage the Charity Commission to withdraw charitable status from independent schools'[92]) seems too carefully phrased to be comforting. His pledge was not well-received on the Labour back benches either, where several senior Party figures have pressed the Charity Commission to investigate whether the public schools are still worthy of charitable status. They have also argued for public funding of university tuition fees to be withheld from undergraduates educated at public schools.[93] An influential Labour MP (Margaret Hodge) has called for the charitable status of the public schools to be linked to a 'duty to contribute to the common good'. The public schools counter that the parents of their pupils are paying for a state education service they never use. ISIS reckons this combination of fully taxed but unused school places is worth £2.5 billion a year to the taxpayer.

How Rich Are the Public Schools?

The willingness of the public schools to argue – even entreat – with the state is a measure of their weakness. Unlike those other ancient estates – Church and Oxbridge – the public schools are not yet corrupted by a vast patrimony or enfeebled by near-total reliance on public money. They are merely selling a service, in a market in which the state no longer offers serious competition, for which people are prepared to pay handsomely. And they have to pay handsomely, because few public schools have much unearned income; none is rich enough to provide the service free.

This is the chief source of the political difficulties of the public schools: they ration the best education in Britain by price. Their boarding fees, which average nearly £12,000 a year, are beyond the reach of all but the wealthiest sections of society. Two in three public school parents have incomes exceeding £40,000 a year. Unlike the monasteries at the time of the Dissolution, or the aristocracy of the early twentieth century, or the pension funds of today, politicians do not wish to devour the public schools because they are too rich. Their enemy is not the green-eyed monster thrown up by a populist democracy looking for loot. Their enemies are the Bens and Lauras, the conscience-stricken progressives who fret that excellence for the few is bought at the price of justice for the many.

Of course, some public schools have considerable private fortunes. But, with the possible exceptions of Winchester and Whitgift, they owe them not to the abuse of power but to serendipity. Those lucky enough to be endowed with land in or on the fringes of London made a fortune as the capital expanded, much of which they have now reinvested in the stock market. The wealth of Rugby, for example, stems from a codicil in the will of the founder which replaced a legacy of £150 with a field in what is now Holborn. Developed as housing in the seventeenth and eighteenth centuries, it originally provided the security for mortgages to build the school, which still owns a few acres of Lamb's Conduit Street. Most of the income is used to fund scholarships and bursaries.

Bedford School – or, more particularly, the Harpur Trust, which supports four independent schools in Bedford – has land in the same part of London, stemming from thirteen acres of meadow given to it by Sir William Harpur in 1566. Similarly, the investment income Etonians enjoy comes not from farms the school owns in Dorset and Oxfordshire but from the westward advance of London across its Thames-side estates, and especially from the Chalcot estate in north London. The last of it is now being sold; the sale of the freeholds to one batch of flats and houses in November 1995 yielded £4 million.[94]

Whitgift also had the luck to be founded in 1596, on a part of the archiepiscopal estates eventually eaten up by suburban London: Croydon. By the time the Elizabethan Archbishop of Canterbury, John Whitgift, died in 1604, his foundation controlled 700 acres there. The decisive move was transferring Trinity School to Shirley Park in the 1960s, freeing the site for the development of the Whitgift Shopping Centre, from which the Foundation now derives nine tenths of its income. It is rich enough to subsidise three schools and a collection of almshouses. Dulwich College, founded by the theatrical impresario Edward Alleyn (1566–1626) at the start of the seventeenth century, has also benefited from the encroachment of suburban London. Alleyn's College of God's Gift is rich enough to support several schools in south London.

TABLE 7.1
Most Expensive Public Schools, 1997

	Day fees £ pa	Boarding fees £ pa
Cheltenham Ladies' College	8.595	14,850*
Marymount	8,601	14,799
Winchester	10,908	14,544
Tonbridge	10,170	14,400
Westminster	9,930	14,400
Millfield	9,315	14,385
Bedales	10,851	14,328
Roedean	8,700	14,325
Bryanston	9,531	14,295
Harrow	–	14,295
Benenden	–	14,205
Stowe	9,930	14,175
King's, Canterbury	9,750	14,115
Marlborough	10,140	14,100
Haileybury	10,140	13,980
Eton College	–	13,947
Charterhouse	11,520	13,941
Oundle	–	13,920
Uppingham	9,000	13,920
Rugby	8,205	13,805
Malvern Girls' College	9,480	13,815
Heathfield	–	13,800
Sherborne	10,350	13,770
Cranleigh	10,140	13,710
Sevenoaks School	8,676	13,680
Radley College	–	13,650
Shrewsbury	9,600	13,650
Felsted	10,740	13,620
Brighton College	8,760	13,575
St Paul's	8,985	13,560
Downe House	9,786	13,500
Bradfield	10,068	13,425
Canford	10,080	13,425
St Edward's, Oxford	9,600	13,425
Dean Close	9,300	13,350
Malvern College	–	13,350
Wellington College	9,735	13,350
Lancing	10,020	13,335
Ampleforth	6,870	13,305
Gresham's	9,480	13,305
Walthamstow Hall	6,810	13,290
St Edmund's, Canterbury	8,589	13,260
Clifton College	9,105	13,245
Dulwich College	6,618	13,236
Cheltenham College	9,975	13,200
King's, Rochester	7,590	13,170
Bloxham	10,290	13,125
Frensham Heights	8,700	13,125
New College, Cardiff	7,875	13,125
St James's & The Abbey	7,722	13,095

Source: Financial Times 1,000 Schools, 1997.

* The Purcell School of Music in London charges £17,988 a year, and Chetham's School of Music in Manchester £16,425, but both are specialists with limited competition.

Other schools whose inheritance was generous, but far from the metropolis, have struggled to keep up with these. Winchester is older and more powerful – its alumni have exerted an influence over national affairs ever since it was founded by William of Wykeham in 1382 – but it is comfortable rather than rich, being heavily reliant on agricultural rents (some dating back to original endowments) rather than urban office blocks or a booming stock market.

Charterhouse, on the other hand, is still living off a City property deal concluded in 1609. That year, Thomas Sutton (1532–1611), one of the richest commoners in England, paid £13,000 for the buildings of a dissolved Carthusian monastery and bequeathed the school and almshouses he established in the abandoned cloisters a massive legacy: rents worth £5,000 a year and other assets valued at £60,410.[95] The school decamped to a hill-top site in Godalming in 1872 after a severe ticking-off by the Clarendon commissioners for the misuse of an investment income then averaging nearly £23,000 a year.[96] The only public school to subsidise the fees of a majority of its pupils, Christ's Hospital, also had the priceless advantage of beginning in the City. The rich merchants of the Square Mile put up over £4,610 for its original endowment and, although the school moved to Horsham in 1897, it still collects rent from the London estate.

Should the Public Schools Become PLCs?

Few schools are rich enough to do as Christ's Hospital does, and even it relies on fees to cover 15 per cent of its costs. The vast majority are overwhelmingly dependent on their fee income. Yet, like the Oxbridge colleges and merchant banks of old, reticence has allowed the financial myth-makers to endow them with fabulous riches. For decades, the inadequacies and inefficiencies of charities legislation and the limited powers of the Charity Commissioners allowed public schools to hide what wealth they had. Two relatively wealthy schools – Eton and Winchester – somehow escaped the purview of the charity commissioners altogether.

Like all charities, the public schools fear that a realistic valuation of their endowment income might deter potential benefactors, or lead to demands from parents that fees be reduced. But their principal objection to greater financial openness is that it could cost them the valuable tax advantages of charitable status. The present range of charitable activities eligible for tax relief happens to include education. But the definition was reached at the start of the seventeenth century, long before schools were run by the state, or for profit. There is no reason to suppose it would be included in a fresh definition of charitable activities which the more politically minded charity-mongers now seek.[97]

Genuine contradictions arise when public schools, whose charitable status originally depended on their commitment to educate the children of the poor, are found to be running an aggressive service business for the wealthy middle classes. This is an era in which schools employ marketing consultants to sell their facilities to consumers who expect the highest standards in teaching, accommodation, sports facilities, laboratories and examination results. There is a risk that endowment income may not be directed to the proper purposes of the charity.

The true nature of the public schools is increasingly at odds with their official status. Like a great many other charities, they have assumed the domi-

TABLE 7.2
Public Schools With Significant Private Assets (Est. £ m)*

	Investment Income	Investment Value
Christ's Hospital	11.5	190.5
Whitgift	10.0	160.5
Eton	5.9	154.5
Dulwich†	3.4	50.8
Bedford‡	3.1	38.4
Winchester	1.0	25.0
Tonbridge§	1.3	18.8
Rugby	2.1	18.0
St Paul's¶	0.4	11.0
Westminster	0.1	2.9

* These figures are for 1996–97. The table should include Harrow and Merchant Taylors, but reliable information is not available.
† These figures apply to the Dulwich Estate, which supports Dulwich College, Alleyn's, James Allen's Girls' School, the Central Foundation Schools of London and St Olave's and St Saviour's Grammar School as well as an almshouse charity. In 1995 the Dulwich Estate distributed capital of £20 million to these various beneficiaries, so the total value of the endowment funds was probably nearly £80 million by 1997, assuming the funds transferred matched the performance of the FTSE-100 index between 1995 and 1997.
‡ These figures apply to the Bedford Charity, which supports almshouses, flats and local charities as well as four schools (Bedford School, Bedford High School, Dame Alice Harpur School and Bedford Modern School) in Bedford.
§ These figures are for the Sir Andrew Judd Foundation, which supports the Judd School as well as Tonbridge School.
¶ These figures are for the St Paul's School Foundation, which supports St Paul's Girls' School and the Colet Court preparatory school, as well as St Paul's School.

nant organisational form of the age. Nearly two in five private schools are proprietary; the rest are companies in every respect except tax status. They are a major domestic business, generating fee income of perhaps £3.5 billion a year, and highly successful exporters. ISIS reckons the fees of foreign boys and girls are worth £161 million a year.[98] Dulwich has a sister school in Thailand; Harrow has opened an art gallery, and rents its buildings for conferences; Eton not only rents its buildings for corporate conferences and entertainment but – as the one public school famous enough for membership of the Heritage Industry – conducts guided tours, partly to control the 75,000 tourists each year. It even has a website.

Public schools have begun to use the media to sell their wares. A generous film about Eton was broadcast in 1995. Since Radley appeared on television, its status has improved from also-ran to one of the leaders. Schools are taken over or merged continually, with headmasters sometimes collecting a bonus for a successful deal. An educational entrepreneur has created a successful public company which now operates twenty schools in Britain and several more abroad.[99] In 1995, the Headmasters' Conference had to draw up a Code of Conduct to stop schools poaching pupils from each other by offering parents better deals on fees. Upmarket newspapers and magazines are full of advertisements for private schools. There is even an annual independent education exhibition at Olympia, where more than one hundred schools rent booths to sell their wares. Culturally, the transformation of the public schools from charities into PLCs would scarcely be a wrench.

Naturally, bursars are loath to surrender a subsidy from the Inland Revenue worth £60 million a year. They warn darkly that fees would have to rise commensurately, making access more exclusive still. But charitable status is a curse as well as an oblation. It gives the public an interest in the public schools, making them ultimately vassals of the state. In recent years politicians have threatened them with subjection to the national curriculum, as well as to income tax and VAT. Now New Labour is drawing them into a partnership to test their pliability. Becoming full-blown businesses might spare them lethal intimacy with the state.

The public-school-as-business would have real as well as political advantages. A lack of financial openness has allowed the public schools to increase their fees willy-nilly (since parents are not privy to the balance sheet), but it has also denied them knowledge of their inefficiencies. In particular, it has allowed the staff to enjoy automatic annual increments, otherwise unknown outside the public sector. Freed to compete openly, especially in a market where purchasing power was in the hands of the consumers of education rather than the producers, the public schools could revolutionise their management and the standard and variety of education in Britain. As real PLCs, rather than pseudo-charities, they could shed the burden of the past and sell a first-class service without unconvincing apologetics. Openness might even prove infectious, and confer similar benefits on those other medieval relics with which the public schools are so closely identified: the City livery companies.

CHAPTER EIGHT

THE MEDIEVAL CORPORATIONS

Every event, every action, was still embodied in expressive and solemn forms, which raised them to the dignity of a ritual. For it was not merely the great facts of birth, marriage, and death which, by the sacredness of the sacrament, were raised to the rank of mysteries; incidents of less importance, like a journey, a task, a visit, were equally attended by a thousand formalities.

J. H. HUIZINGA, *The Waning of the Middle Ages*[1]

We are the last bastion of formality. The ladies wear long dresses and we have to wear white tie. I'd describe the City as pomp without pomposity. You can't walk around the streets of the City in black tights and be pompous.

BERNARD HARTY, town clerk and chamberlain, Corporation of London[2]

You should be comfortable with the social aspects of the company's activities, in which you may well be expected to participate.

Advertisement for finance director, Drapers' Company[3]

On most nights of the week in oak-panelled rooms somewhere in the City of London large numbers of middle-aged men sit down to dinner at long, linen-covered tables decked with flowers, glass and silver candelabra. From the Gunmakers' Hall on Commercial Road to the home of the Master Mariners aboard the *Wellington* moored at Temple Stairs, there are no less than forty-three livery company dining halls scattered across the Square Mile. The diners dress formally, sometimes in white but more usually in black tie, but at the top table the garb of the master or prime warden might include a fur-lined gown and chains of office. If the lord mayor is there, or a sheriff has come, his guest of honour may well be wearing a lace-fronted shirt, breeches, and hose. Their entrance to the hall is often accompanied by a slow handclap, in these circles a sign of reverence not vexation. And as they feast on mulligatawny soup and loin of veal, there are toasts in claret to the Queen, the lord mayor of London, and the officers and benefactors of the company.

After the pudding, a rosewater bowl, used to clean the hands and face in the days before James I introduced the fork, is passed around. Eventually, a loving-cup is filled, and each diner takes a swig before passing it to his left. There are probably two or three speeches, before the diners are disgorged into the deserted streets of the City. As they slump in their seats on the last train home from Liverpool Street or London Bridge, none will reckon as money ill-spent the £60 or £70 which the evening cost.

The Quest for Status

The continuing appeal of the livery companies of the City of London is another of the minor curiosities of English middle-class life. They are likened sometimes to an upmarket Round Table or Rotary Club, in which philanthropic endeavours are lubricated with alcohol and canapés. This was the purpose the Victorians found for them. Until the reformers of the nineteenth century brought their zeal to bear, the companies were moribund, with shrinking memberships and no obvious purpose beyond pampering the dwindling 'livery' with the income of their historic assets. No new companies were founded between 1709 and 1930, and in the course of the nineteenth century a number of historic guilds – Combmakers, Fishermen, Hatbandmakers, Longbowstringmakers, Pinmakers, Silk Weavers, Silk Throwers, Soapmakers, Starchmakers and Woodmongers – disappeared altogether. It is only in the last 60 years that cataleptic companies awoke, and 23 new ones were created. There are now exactly 100 livery companies in all, 15 with histories of less than 20 years. The latest is the Worshipful Company of Information Technologists, formed in 1992. Waiting patiently for the 14-year probationary period to expire, and the necessary £300,000 for charity to accumulate in the company bank account, are the Water Conservators, the Fire Fighters, the World Traders, the Licensed Taxi Drivers and the Management Consultants.* With around 24,000 members, drawn from the professional and commercial classes of the southeast as well as the City itself, the livery companies are probably more prosperous now than at any time in the last 300 years. Half of them even admit women.

There are many explanations for the revival. As de Tocqueville observed, the club is the key to the English way of life: there is the element of snobbery,

---

* The City stipulates that a charitable fund of £300,000 be accumulated before it will grant livery status to a new company.

and the need to belong. Liverymen also play a minor part in the burgeoning Heritage Industry, giving expression to a quiet sense of history and patriotism through customs and ceremonies, invented at least as often as they are genuinely traditional.* A livery company dinner is also a useful forum for exchanging business cards. It is an astonishing fact that, of the 77 companies founded before 1929, 51 cannot think of a past or present member who would be instantly recognisable to an educated layman. They have an average lifespan of 450 years and an average livery of 228 members, but perhaps three dozen famous names between them. The Mercers can count Dick Whittington, William Caxton, Thomas More, Thomas Gresham and Lord Baden-Powell among their members (only the last of these was alive less than 450 years ago). Only the Goldsmiths, which count four twentieth century prime ministers – Asquith, Lloyd George, Baldwin and Heath – among their livery, can claim even a handful of contemporary men and women of distinction. It is a remarkable record of under-achievement, characteristic of ordinary men of business, but one which explains much of the continuing appeal of these extraordinary institutions. Membership of a livery company can charge with significance the life of the meanest office drudge.

This craving for status is strongest at the old companies, which guard their place in the hierarchy with intense devotion. Ranking does not depend on seniority, but on the importance and lucrativeness of the various trades during the Middle Ages. The Weavers, organised in 1130, possess the oldest royal charter but rank a mere forty-second in the Order of Precedence. The Saddlers, which rank twenty-fifth, claim to have emerged during the reign of Alfred. Most of the top dozen companies – known as the Great Twelve – rose to prominence in the fourteenth and fifteenth centuries, when London first emerged as a major international entrepôt. The Order of Precedence was finally settled in 1515 and has not altered since, except through amalgamations and disappearances, with new companies joining the bottom of the list as they receive their Letters Patent.†

---

* The ceremony of the loving-cup is a clear example. At some companies the diner passing the cup to his left is expected to turn his back to his neighbour on his right, ostensibly to shield the recipient from attack. In other companies, three diners are expected to stand at once, to protect the drinker from attack from either side. At the Turners' the loving-cup is launched by the clerk, who raises it in salutation to the master crying 'Master-Wass Heil', to which the Master is expected to reply 'Drink Heil'. These ceremonies are popularly traced to the fate of Edward the Martyr, slain at dinner at Corfe Castle in 978 when his head was buried in a cup.

† Letters Patent were open letters sent by the sovereign (as opposed to Letters Close, which were for the eyes of the recipient only) and were documents from the crown conferring rights, assets and privileges – such as the right to own land, or the exclusive right to manufacture playing cards – on a corporate body. It amounts to a patent; the 'letters' merely refer to the parchment on which the privilege is recorded and granted under the royal seal.

Ranking mattered because the Order of Precedence determined the place of a company in the many public processions which characterised the life of medieval London. The very term 'livery' (which today means no more than the company colour scheme) derives from the vivid costumes and banners displayed at public processions, not only by liverymen but by every class of society. The medieval mind was steeped in hierarchy. Every rank and station of life was assigned and proclaimed its place through costume and position in the public procession.

The Lord Mayor's Show is a last reminder of the central place processions once occupied in the life of the City. Companies staged their own, usually to and from their adopted church on the day of their patron saint. The profusion of churches in the modern City reflects the habit each company had of worshipping at a single church in the ward where the trade congregated. Poultry is the street where the poulters were found; Milk Street where the dairymen stood; and the Ward of Cordwainers where workers in Cordoba leather were gathered. Some companies had private chapels (the Mercers still do). Even now the master and company of the Vintners insist on processing to St James's Garlickhythe after the election of a new master every July, preceded by white-smocked wine porters pretending to sweep the rubbish and excrement of medieval London from their path. Its orderliness and ranks are an affirmation of status.

A man or woman can enter these curious worlds by one of four separate methods. The basic grade of membership is 'Freeman', a group usually 500 or 600 strong but often more. Most people become freemen by patrimony, where the only qualifications are to be at least twenty-one years old and born to a parent who was a freeman or woman at the time. (The Queen is a Draper because her father was; both Prince Charles and Princess Anne are Fishmongers because the Duke of Edinburgh is.) Once a year has elapsed, or they have turned twenty-five, a freeman or woman becomes eligible for election to the livery. Nobody is refused, making livery membership more like a family right than a distinction.

A less distinguished route to membership is available: redemption, or the purchase of a place for cash. If the richer companies are able to choose recruits by invitation only, the poorer will admit virtually anyone with money to spare. The 'fine' levied on new members is sometimes significant, but never excessive, and always larger for those without family or service connections. The Goldsmiths, for example, charge from as little as £5 (for freedom by service), through £50 (for freedom by patrimony) to £500 (for admission to the livery by redemption for people not in the craft).

Celebrities can count on membership of a livery company through 'presentation', reserved for those whose 'presence' might lend prestige to a company.

It explains why Margaret Thatcher is a Poulter, and why the Princess of Wales was a Grocer. Occasionally, in a xenophobic variant of presentation, distinguished foreigners are enrolled as associates of a company *honoris causa*. The rarest rite of passage into a livery was once the most common: servitude, or apprentice to the trade. Admission other than by apprenticeship was rare until the fifteenth century, when membership by redemption began to widen the interests of the medieval guilds and dilute their ties to a specific trade. Today, only the Goldsmiths still bind apprentices to the trade, though a number of other companies have token 'apprentices' who are merely candidates for membership.

All liverymen are also freemen of the City of London, since anybody who becomes a freeman of a company is automatically eligible for the freedom of the City. This takes place at a formal ceremony at the Guildhall, and is in most cases a quaint memorial of the ceremony by which an apprentice presented his 'master-piece' of finished work and was 'freed' to ply his trade in the City. Only Goldsmiths now have to produce an actual piece of work, and the freedom of the City is for most liverymen a meaningless privilege, but one for which a useful fee is paid to the chamberlain of the Corporation of London.

Unlike the Goldsmiths, patrimony and purchase have left most of the older liveries with only the most tenuous and artificial ties to their trade or profession. In some cases a trade has ceased to exist; in others, such as the Bowyers and Fletchers, it has become a sport. But many livery companies have forged new links with the modern successors to their medieval 'mysteries'. No Armourer or Brasier drives rivets or works in brass, but their company gives grants to further research and education in materials science and technology. They also have a joint scheme with the Cutlers to sponsor students at Sheffield City University. The Salters established an Institute of Industrial Chemistry in 1918, which funds the education of chemists and gives prizes to inspired teachers of chemistry. The Carpenters run a Building Crafts Training School, with the support of the Masons and the Tylers and Bricklayers.[4] The Gunmakers still proof small arms; the Spectacle Makers run examinations for opticians; the Vintners have examined Masters of Wine since 1953; the Fishmongers inspect 200 tons of fish a day at Billingsgate Market; and the Apothecaries set professional examinations for doctors.

Only the Goldsmiths still do what they have always done: test gold, silver and platinum at the assay office at their hall before applying a 'hallmark' as proof of its quality. Every spring they also welcome to Foster Lane the chancellor of the Exchequer, in his capacity as master of the Mint, to attend the Delivery of the Verdict in the Trial of the Pyx. This ceremony, at which the results of an impartial test of the coins produced at the Royal Mint are announced, was described by Nigel Lawson in his memoirs as 'a thoroughly surreal occasion'.[5]

How the Livery Companies Became Rich

The Delivery of the Verdict in the Trial of the Pyx, first held in 1282, is certainly a pantomime. The jury are laymen; the verdict is pre-established; the ceremony is pure theatre. But it is preceded by a genuine sampling of the coinage by skilled technicians: a dulled echo of the massive economic and political power once wielded by the City livery companies. In the Middle Ages, every town had guilds of craftsmen, merchants or like-minded citizens who banded together. The livery companies sought official backing for their trading monopolies from the outset, and English kings were quick to recognise that they could swap privileges for revenue. Henry II fined eleven guilds as 'adulterine' as early as 1179. By the end of the fourteenth century, guilds were routinely purchasing from the Crown exclusive rights to provide goods and services, so monopolising a trade within the City and sometimes further afield.[6] When the Mercer Dick Whittington (c. 1350s–1423) financed the invasion of Normandy by Henry V, which ended in the victory at Agincourt in 1415, he was rewarded with exclusive trading rights.[7]

The companies thrived in this primitive economy, in which the Crown sought revenue from the sale of patents and monopolies without regard to their impact on economic efficiency. In their power to escape taxes, fix prices, control entry into a trade by apprenticeship, regulate wages and hours of work, and repress bad workmanship, the medieval guilds were akin to trade unions rather than PLCs. Like most trade unions, they contributed to the economic stagnation of the Middle Ages by raising prices, lowering output, hampering investment and discouraging inventiveness and innovation. But it made the liverymen of the City of London, which then dominated the national economy to an even greater extent than today, extremely wealthy. The livery companies monopolised the trades and crafts which satisfied the City's consumers. The great markets – Billingsgate for fish, Smithfield for livestock, Southwark and Leadenhall for leather and Blackwell Hall for cloth – towered over the domestic economy, and spawned a host of ancillary industries around the City. Eventually, the livery companies took control of overseas trade as well. Most of the maritime commerce of the country passed through the port of London, which Parliament reckoned in 1604 was controlled by just 200 people.

The medieval and early modern City (like its modern successor) was the greatest concentration of commercial wealth in the kingdom, and its doors were open to the astute and ambitious as well as the well-connected. It attracted entrepreneurial talent like a magnet. Dick Whittington had no cat when he set out from Gloucestershire for the City in 1370, and he was not penniless either, but he made a fortune in London, and served four terms as lord mayor. He left assets worth £5,000 (about £2 million today), a significant sum, but well below the average for the time. The leading London merchants were at least as rich as the contemporary aristocracy and their wealth was far more liquid.[8] The father of stock-broking was a Mercer and the earliest bankers were the Goldsmiths.[9] Naturally, much of this wealth accrued to the livery companies, whose monopolies of manufacture and distribution enabled many men of humble birth to become extremely rich.

How the Livery Companies Declined

The medieval system of lucrative monopolies broke down gradually during the seventeenth century. The Stuarts sold monopolies openly to the highest bidder. Old and new livery companies were not excluded from this process – significantly, twenty-nine, nearly a third of the total, got their charters from Stuart kings – but it did raise costs, by introducing competition into the auction of trading rights. In 1624 a proper system of patent law replaced the auction and, from then on, the companies were on the defensive: trade was opened to allcomers.

The early Stuarts also made heavy claims on the personal and corporate wealth of the livery companies, in the shape of taxes (notably Ship Money), forced loans which were not repaid, and outright confiscation. The companies were forced to sell plate, levy members and even borrow to meet the exactions. In 1640 the Grocers had to pay Charles I £10,500 for a charter, which obliged them to mortgage property and sell plate.[10] James I used the wealth of the companies to finance the colonisation of Virginia and Ulster. Between January 1610 and October 1616 he bullied a total of £60,000 from 55 companies, and the Great Twelve ended up with 320,950 acres in Ulster, prompting the redesignation of the city of Derry as Londonderry.[11] The terrain was inhospitable, the Irish hostile, and the farming hard. In 1635 Charles I stripped the companies of their Irish lands and fined them £70,000 on the grounds of failing to develop them properly. They were restored under the Commonwealth and remained part of the corporate income of the wealthier livery companies until the last quarter of the nineteenth century, when the agricultural depression set in, violent attacks on English landlords were resumed and the government forced all Irish landlords to disgorge their estates to their tenants.

The exactions of the Stuarts placed the City firmly in the parliamentary camp during the Civil War. When Charles I tried to raise a loan in the Square Mile in 1640, only one man subscribed. But supporting Parliament seriously eroded the wealth of the companies. At the start of hostilities Cromwell was given £100,000. The City raised another £500,000 for the relief of Gloucester, and provided £10,000 a week at one stage to keep the train-bands going. At the Restoration, Charles II forced the companies to surrender their charters or prove their right to hold them, returning their privileges only on payment of a fine. Worse, the whole pattern of trade was turning against them: new industries, such as mines, escaped guild control; competitors set up in the countryside, beyond their reach; expanding industries needed labour, so barriers to entry were broken down. The guild system could not keep pace with consumer demand, and the state lacked the means to enforce their monopolies. The Tudors, especially Elizabeth I, had encouraged skilled foreigners to settle in England and teach their methods to the natives.

The pattern of trade shifted from the export of cloth and the distribution of foodstuffs and handicrafts, to an international trade in finished goods and luxuries. The Fellowship of the Merchant Adventurers in London – albeit a band of liverymen led by the Mercers – gradually displaced the livery companies. In 1564 Elizabeth granted them a monopoly of the cloth trade. Other joint stock trading companies emerged to take advantage of the maritime enterprise of sixteenth and seventeenth century England. Although these were usually dominated by liverymen, their activities marked a decisive shift in British trade. The various Navigation Acts (which attempted to ensure that all English imports were carried in English ships) symbolised not only the adoption of mercantilist policies but a massive shift in economic policy. Government now allowed businessmen to work out their own destiny within a national framework of rules. The Navigation Acts marked the beginning of the end of the medieval obsession with regulation and monopoly.

Eclipse of the Livery Companies

For much of the seventeenth and eighteenth centuries, the companies teetered on the verge of extinction. They were already in an enfeebled condition when the Great Fire of 1666 destroyed the property from which they drew most of their income: forty-four out of fifty-one company halls were lost in the Great Fire. The attractions of the City as a place to live and work were fading anyway, and as the Square Mile was gradually joined to Westminster, people settled in the larger and cheaper spaces to the west. The current reputation of the companies for feasting and entertainment stems not from the bacchanalia of Merrie England but from desperate attempts to attract new fee-paying members in the seventeenth century. Their fortunes did not begin to recover until the end of the eighteenth century, when the long building leases granted after the Great Fire began to expire. It was not until the nineteenth century, when the value of City property was massively inflated by national commercial and industrial success, that livery companies with land in the Square Mile became the wealthy institutions they are today.

Ironically, they came into this inheritance at the nadir of their fortunes in every other sense. The Reformation had robbed them of their religious duties to the dead; the capitalist economy had swept away their monopolistic and regulatory powers; the number of liverymen was dwindling, their role in local government was nugatory, and there was little to do but spend the increasing income from endowments on a mixture of entertainment and charitable works. This juxtaposing of wealth and redundancy was bound to attract the attention of Victorian reformers. Perspicacious liverymen warned their colleagues to make themselves useful before the state took too close an interest in their activities and assets; the companies hurriedly renewed an interest in their crafts, education and charitable work.

Scholarships to the universities were the first choice. The Goldsmiths' Company was funding seventy-five, worth £50 apiece, by 1882.[12] The late-Victorian enthusiasm for scientific and technical education saw the Drapers establish the East London technical schools (the precursors of Queen Mary and Westfield College) and finance libraries and laboratories at Oxford, Cambridge and Sheffield. The Goldsmiths founded Goldsmiths' College (originally a technical institute) and the Clothworkers funded the textile school at the new university college in Leeds. The Technical College at Finsbury and the South London School of Technical Art in Kennington were both funded by livery companies. In conjunction with the Corporation of London, sixteen Livery Companies set up the City and Guilds of London Institute in 1878.[13]

The Royal Commission of 1884

The main agent of change, however, was Joseph Firth Bottomley Firth, Liberal MP for Chelsea, who had campaigned vociferously against the livery companies since 1876. A Quaker of Yorkshire origins, Firth had conceived a passion for a single authority in the metropolis. In his book, *Municipal London*, he distilled his case against the Corporation of London and the companies. The ancient political rights and powers of the Corporation, whose deliberations were dominated by liverymen, were an obstacle, and its wealth would be a ready source of finance for a London County Council. He was the moving spirit behind the City Guilds Reform Association, whose ruthless propaganda persuaded even Gladstone that 'much of the revenue of these Companies is positively and utterly wasted, and very imperfectly and doubtfully bestowed.'[14] Disraeli was much less impressed, and his solicitor general dismissed the idea of a 'communistic enquiry' into the wealth of the livery companies. But when he was returned to office in 1880, Gladstone did not hesitate; a royal commission of inquiry into their wealth was set up almost immediately.

It was chaired by a Conservative turncoat, the Earl of Derby. Unlike the similar Victorian inquiries into the assets of the Church, Oxbridge and the public schools, expropriation was the declared purpose of several of the commissioners and of many who gave evidence before them. Firth, with another radical parliamentarian, W. H. James, and the working-class Liberal MP, Thomas Burt, were all members of the commission. There were calls for the livery company halls to be sold, their assets to be seized and pooled and the proceeds redistributed to worthy causes. The companies protested vehemently against the investigation as an abuse of their chartered privileges, and initially refused to disclose their corporate assets and income. Their supporters on the commission disdained to sign the majority report published in 1884, and composed a minority submission.

The key question was whether the state had any right to expropriate the assets of the livery companies, and the answer turned on the nature of the institution. If they were simply private fellowships without public obligations, state interference was difficult to justify. Nobody was surprised when Lord Chancellor Selborne told the commission that the livery companies were not public trusts but 'absolute and perfect masters of their own property'.[15] Selborne – as well as his male ancestors from his great-grandfather on – was a Mercer.

However, his comments had the imprimatur of the most senior law officer in the land, and the livery companies ensured they were given wide circulation. But they failed to persuade the hostile commissioners to abate their zeal. 'It appears to us obvious', ran the majority report, 'that the State has a right at any time to disestablish and disendow the Companies of London, provided the just claims of existing members to compensation be allowed.'[16] Its recommendations were less exciting: the companies were given five years to ensure officers did not abuse corporate assets for personal benefit and to redirect endowment income to charitable causes. The proposals never reached the statute book; the Liberal government fell before the legislation could succeed.

The Present Wealth of the Livery Companies

The commission established beyond doubt that the livery companies were wealthy. Their total income in 1879–80 was £750–800,000 (about £34–36 million in today's money) or nearly one fifth more than the combined annual income of Oxford and Cambridge Universities at the time.[17] The value of livery company capital – which consisted mainly of buildings in the City – was put at £15 million (£680 million today). This was an underestimate based on the view that City rents had peaked, and excluding valuable collections of plate, the Irish landholdings and some provincial estates. Only one quarter was trust income explicitly dedicated to charitable causes; the balance was private wealth, two thirds of which was spent on administration and entertainment.

In the end, the royal commission did not advocate expropriation, but it reminded liverymen how close they had come to disaster. The greedy outcasts of the 1870s set about transforming themselves into the exclusive charitable societies of today. New members were actively sought to bolster the Conservative vote in the City (liverymen then had a vote in parliamentary elections), and this produced a flow of new fees and fines which boosted the fortunes of even those companies which lacked a landed estate in the City. The companies redoubled their efforts to appear useful, and devoted more of their corporate income to charitable work.

Even now, the livery companies encourage the belief that their primary purpose is charitable, and that their charitable income is much larger than their corporate income. There is no means of checking this assertion. In law, they are private associations of individuals – just as Selborne said they were – and are not obliged to publish accounts any more than a private citizen is. Few bother to value regularly the City properties which make up the bulk of the wealth, even for their own purposes. The value of their real estate is known only to a handful of discreet City surveyors, and their corporate income only to the Inland Revenue. Their charitable income and assets are open to the world, but scattered across hundreds of different funds.

This selective openness is not merely a matter of law, or of habit; it is rooted in the culture and psychology of liverymen. As institutions, and as people, the liveries seem to be trapped in the era of Firth Bottomley Firth, defensively proffering charitable concerns as an antidote to the expropriators hammering at the door. It is a counter-productive riposte – their silence adds to the stock of tales about their Freemasonry, *Grandes Bouffes* and fabulous riches – but the prevailing mood of persecution and disdain affords them no other. The response of the clerk of one company to a request for an interview captures it perfectly:

I can see no point in agreeing to an interview because I would not be prepared to discuss the Company's Corporate finances in any way. However, in case you are interested in the broader functions of the . . . Company, I enclose a leaflet and the latest copy of the Company's Annual Review which will give you a perspective of our activities. I recognise that livery companies are from time to time a convenient target for journalists to tilt at. At the same time my experience is that however frank one is with journalists, in the end they will use any interview . . . to suit their own particular story line.[18]

Only weeks before Stella Shamoon of *The Observer* had interviewed the clerk, and her subsequent article failed to please. ('Why should we eat bread and cheese?' he asked her, in a Bourbonesque moment.)[19] For the clerks who run the companies day-to-day, openness is not part of their repertoire.

Like the majority at the older companies, the clerk is an ex-military man; he was an officer in the Scots Guards. A survey of the clerks of the other ninety-nine companies throws up two major-generals, two brigadiers, two colonels, three lieutenant-colonels, one major, four naval captains, five commanders, six group captains and two wing commanders. A 1992 advertisement for the post of clerk to the Drapers sought a man 'aged around 50 with a background in Civil Service, Law, property or armed services'.[20] At some companies the job is regarded as hereditary. The Goldsmiths were famous for a succession of clerks named Prideaux, the Ironmongers for several generations of Adams Becks. It will take a different generation of liverymen, or a drastic change in the law, to persuade the livery companies to open the books. Until then, it is possible only to guess at their corporate wealth.

Most of it lies in their property in the most valuable Square Mile of real estate in Britain: the City of London, and they probably own about one in twenty of its acres.* Much of the thirty or forty acres consists of the halls, which are liabilities rather than assets, though the better ones earn a modest income from hosting lunches, dinners and press conferences for City banks and brokers. A major disaster would have to overtake a company before it could be persuaded to sell its hall. Nor is large exposure to property, even

---

* Shirley Green estimated over a decade ago that the livery companies own 15 per cent of the Square Mile. If true, it would amount to a rental income of £500 million and property assets worth £6 or £7 billion if it were all prime office space. This is too high. The web of leases and sub-leases knitted by time and chance is so complex that it would involve primary legislation, search warrants and several man-years of work to assess the real value of the interest each company has in real estate. The Grocers, for example, own the whole of the west side of Princes Street, opposite the Bank of England, making it some of the most valuable land in the Square Mile. But it was let long ago on leases which do not expire for another half century. Shirley Green, *Who Owns London?*, Weidenfeld & Nicolson, 1986, p. 55.

in the City, a guaranteed investment; in recent years the Skinners' Company has incurred serious losses from fire, rent arrears, illegal sub-leasing and the collapse of the City office market.[21] On the other hand, a lease falling in or an adjacent freehold becoming available can provide a company with a massive windfall. The Leathersellers received a huge boost from the redevelopment of two City sites adjacent to their hall off Bishopsgate, after buying the freehold from the National Westminster Bank, and are now sitting on property worth perhaps £15 million.[22]

But no company has a more diverse City portfolio than the Mercers, who own large offices in prime streets such as Cheapside, Gresham Street and Moorgate, as well as valuable buildings in Holborn. The Drapers are also blessed with a handsome portfolio of City sites, owning all or part of several office blocks. The company's biggest asset is Drapers Gardens, a twenty-eight-storey tower block behind the current site of Drapers' Hall, built in the 1960s by the property developer, Harry Hyams. When it was let to the National Provincial Bank for £5 a square foot in the early 1970s, it was the most expensive office accommodation in the City.[23] The Drapers may well be sitting on charitable and corporate property assets worth well over £60 million.

A discreet brown tower block adjacent to Drapers Gardens is the source of much of the wealth of the Clothworkers, who developed Angel Court in partnership with the Morgan Bank in the 1970s. The Carpenters own those parts of Throgmorton Avenue which do not belong to the Drapers, and also have land in Lime Street and Fenchurch Avenue near the Lloyd's insurance market. The Merchant Taylors own almost all of the island site on Threadneedle Street where their hall stands – most of it is now office space – and another large office block on Bishopsgate. The Vintners developed handsome new offices above their hall at Southwark Bridge, and have other office blocks in nearby Upper Thames Street, Queen Street and Garlick Hill. The Salters have built offices, to an uncompromisingly contemporary design by Basil Spence, above their hall. The Plaisterers have an equally contemporary block above theirs at the west end of London Wall, which incongruously contains a fine Georgian plastered interior. The Bakers own a ten-storey office block above their hall in Harp Lane. Even the little-known Innholders have a valuable property on Moorgate, which they redeveloped in the 1980s.

Traditionally, livery companies did not dare to develop their own properties; they acted as ground landlords only, collecting a share of the rent-roll from the developer or institutional investor that held the lease. Only in the boom of the 1980s were they tempted to extract higher value from a building by developing it with property developers and institutional investors. In the property crash of the early 1990s, this lumbered several companies with unlet office space, draining cash in interest payments, maintenance costs and business rates. The Committee of Surveyors to the Twelve Great Livery Companies, an informal body which meets regularly to discuss common problems, was probably the source of this mistaken ambition (though the companies deny it influenced their decisions).

Property is not all that the livery companies own; the wealthier have valuable portfolios of stocks and shares. But it is in their moveable possessions that liverymen delight the most, and their medieval lineage is made explicit. The older companies have amassed large collections of furniture, paintings and silver, much given by past members, but some purchased. Their paintings are more notable for quantity than quality, but the Barber–Surgeons have a Holbein, the Grocers and the Ironmongers own Gainsboroughs, the Fishmongers have two Romneys, and the Merchant Taylors own a Brueghel (*A Flemish Festival*). The Drapers own Gobelin tapestries, the Skinners valuable Chinese porcelain, the Vintners a fifteenth-century Flemish tapestry.[24] The Armourers have a chair they believe belonged to Sir Francis Drake; the Grocers, Vintners and Bakers all have fine glass collections; and the Mercers have four silver spoons given to the company by Dick Whittington. A high proportion of livery company treasure is in precious-metal artefacts of this kind: in the Middle Ages, gold and silver plate was the commonest gift of a dying liveryman. Unsurprisingly, the Goldsmiths' Company has an especially fine collection, much of it acquired by shrewd purchases this century, but every piece a link in the unbroken chain binding the company to its medieval origins.

The Charitable Giving of the Livery Companies

The corporate wealth of the livery companies, in real estate, cash and securities and heirlooms, probably totals somewhere between £400 and £500 million, but the sole standard by which the companies wish to be judged is charity. Like the PR people at Camelot, who never fail to remind an audience of the 'good causes' which gambling serves, the clerks believe that the extraordinary organisations they run are justified by their charitable activities alone. Even these are not easy to disentangle.

The livery companies are trustees to literally hundreds of charitable trusts, almost all of them reported to the Charity Commissioners under the names of obscure benefactors. The Drapers have consolidated most of their welfare charities into the Drapers' Consolidated Charity, but the company is still trustee to another *eighty-seven* trusts listed separately. The Merchant Taylors administer sixty-five trusts devoted to seven different charitable objectives.[25] In 1978 the Haberdashers consolidated forty charities dating mainly from the sixteenth and seventeenth centuries, but were still left with forty-nine minor trusts.[26] The list of charities is not static either: the Drapers' Company were recently promised the entire estate of a woman, with a request that its income be devoted to the education of disabled musicians. Many years ago, the Company gave her a grant of £150 which enabled her to become a flautist. She was redeeming their gift.

This is the kind of story liverymen are always happy to share. Since the time of Firth Bottomley Firth, they have understood that charity is the *Danegeld* they pay to the spirit of reform. The cloak of charity allows even the richest companies to argue that only a modest proportion of their wealth is freely available to the members. 'Our corporate income is private and we are free to dispose of it as we will,' says a former clerk of the Drapers' Company, 'but we do not own the endowed charitable trusts, and can only allocate their income as directed. Even within our own company, people sometimes need to be reminded of that distinction.'[27]

The consolidation of charitable trusts, even those whose causes are now redundant, has not allowed the companies to overturn the wishes of past benefactors in their entirety. On Ash Wednesday the Stationers still serve cakes and ale after the sermon at St Faith's, as directed by John Norton in 1612. The Cooks' Company continues to distribute good black tea to the widow pensioners of the company once a year with the money left by W. S. Angell in 1842. Representatives of the Poulterers travel to Ilford and Barking once a year to give £1.50 to eighty old men and women, as specified by Thomas and Ann Neptun.

Of course, the direction of spending is not as unalterable as this suggests. Where the objective of a charity is completely redundant, rather than merely quaint, application can be made to the Charity Commissioners for its goals to be changed. Many companies have secured permission to amalgamate numerous small sums into a single large fund, allowing them to dispense money within the spirit of the benefaction uninhibited by the letter of the bequest. New companies have followed the example of the old in establishing charitable trusts, since these are a prerequisite of the grant of livery by the Corporation of London. The Air Pilots' Benevolent Fund, for example, was started long before the company received its Letters Patent in 1956.[28]

The charitable assets of most new companies remain small, but the combined giving by the amalgamated trusts of the richest twelve puts them among the top ten or twenty grant-making trusts in the country even before the minor ones are taken into account. The total sum dispensed to charities by the livery companies probably averages £15–20 million a year. This sum is not insignificant, and deluges their clerks in hundreds of begging letters from needy people and worthy causes every month. Though it is dwarfed by the charitable giving of the PLCs which have succeeded the livery companies as the main repositories of corporate wealth in the industrial age, a charitable income of £15–20 million a year requires possession of underlying property and financial assets worth £330–450 million. Roughly £4 in every £5 of that sum belongs to the dozen richest companies.

Housing the Poor and Educating the Rich

Liverymen like to think that charitable giving was always part of the purpose of a company, but it is of relatively recent origin. Charity was initially confined to members of the company, and benefactions were usually applied not to the relief of poverty or sickness but to the wellbeing of members beyond the grave. They ensured the singing of masses for the souls of the dead, and that the funerals of liverymen were always colourful and lavish occasions, accompanied by much processing and feasting.[29]

Only with the ousting of superstitious practices at the Reformation did the companies reduce their concern for the fate of members in the afterlife. Unlike their Catholic predecessors, Reformed liverymen were no longer indifferent to popular ignorance and poverty. Protestantism is pregnant with sound advice about the conscientious use of wealth and disparaging remarks about the wastefulness of hospitality and the singing of masses for the souls of the dead. (In 1550 the great Protestant preacher Thomas Becon denounced 'great monasteries for the bellied hypocrites, great colleges, chantries and free chapels for soul-carriers and purgatory-rakers'.[30]) Undoubtedly, political and other insecurities also played a part. Livery companies were favoured as trustees of charitable funds because other institutions were liable to abuse their trust, or expose the assests to confiscation by the government. Dean Colet, for example, left the endowments of St Paul's School in the hands of the Mercers because he did not trust the Church of which he was such a prominent member.

Ever since the Reformation, Catholic and Protestant propagandists have argued over whether the Reformation ignited the social conscience of wealthy men or became an excuse for hardness of heart. The great inflation of the sixteenth century makes it hard to discern whether charitable giving rose or fell in real terms, but it is certain that its nature changed radically.[31] Socially useful benefactions became much more common. Whereas before the Reformation nearly half of London benefactions went to religious institutions such as chantries and obits, from 1540 these fell to less than one fifth.[32] Instead, roads, bridges and municipal buildings, in provincial towns as well as in London, were built with fortunes made in the City, and liverymen funded apprenticeships and established loan funds to help tradesmen start up in business. Easily the greatest of the post-Reformation benefactions by liverymen was the £63,800 given and bequeathed by a Salter, Henry Smith (c. 1548–1626), for the relief of poverty. His benefactions were described by a contemporary as more like a 'romance or fiction than a thing really performed, because of the prodigious greatness thereof'.[33] Two years after Henry Smith's death, the trustees purchased as an investment a small farm in a village near London called Kensington. The farm – now a triangle between South Kensington, Sloane Square and Knightsbridge Underground stations – became some of the most valuable residential and commercial real estate in the world. Henry Smith's Charity has now sold the estate but controls assets of over £500 million, and enjoys an annual income of £21 million;[34] it is one of the wealthiest grant-making trusts in the country, giving millions of pounds a year to a variety of medical and other causes.[35]

The endowment of almshouses and schools first became popular in the sixteenth century. A string of well-known public schools – St Paul's and Abingdon (Mercers), Merchant Taylors, Oundle (Grocers), Tonbridge (Skinners) – and a number of lesser establishments owe their foundation to City merchants. All retain strong connections with the livery companies to which their founders belonged, in the shape of endowments, bursaries, scholarships and appointments to the board of governors. Nineteen livery companies still run almshouses, but the number fell consistently as the duty of housing the indigent passed to the state. In an effort to escape the restrictive covenants of its ancient almshouse charities, the Mercers have diverted some of their income into a separate housing association, which has built sheltered housing schemes for the elderly poor in Islington and Clerkenwell.

The Private Wealth of the Corporation of London

Housing the poor and educating the rich is an accidental contradiction of the kind history imposes on long-lived institutions. Since they have combined an opulent lifestyle with a charitable *raison d'être* for hundreds of years, the livery companies do not feel it too keenly. They have combined private life with public responsibilities for too long to detect any contrariness. Nor are they as impotent in the City as their clerks would have outsiders believer. They have retained their grip on formal power by informal means.

The unhealthy influence they exerted over the Corporation of London, the ruling local authority in the Square Mile, was one of the main targets of

Joseph Firth Bottomley Firth a century ago. But his ferocious attacks were counter-productive. They merely transformed the City from a Liberal stronghold into a Tory bastion. Since liverymen were entitled to vote in Parliamentary as well as civic elections, Conservative liverymen packed the companies with party supporters. They refused to yield this voting right until 1918, when it was restricted to those with business premises in London, and they did not lose it altogether until 1948. Even now, the City of London is one of the few inner city areas which the Conservative Party can count on for support. The City has not returned a Liberal member since 1880 and, though the parliamentary constituency is now amalgamated with part of neighbouring Westminster, even New Labour is unlikely to dent the Conservative supremacy in the Square Mile.

Not that the livery companies have allowed this to become too obvious. The City is the only local authority where elections are not fought on party platforms. The public face of the City today wears no party label at all. It is a reasonably safe assumption that most of the common councilmen (as Corporation councillors are known) vote Conservative; the overwhelming majority are also liverymen.* So are the lord mayor, the aldermen, and even the MP. Until 1742 the lord mayor was always chosen from one of the Twelve Great Companies (if only by transfer from a minor company), but he is now more likely to come from a lesser-known one. The two sheriffs are also elected by liverymen.[36] Their role is not purely ceremonial (they sit as judges, and accompany the lord mayor on foreign trips), and anyone who has served as sheriff is eligible for nomination for election as lord mayor.

It was not only the political privileges of the City which Firth Bottomley Firth failed to dislodge: he failed to rob the Corporation of its historic endowments. Uniquely among local authorities, the Corporation of London does not have to rely on the taxpayers alone. In 1998–9 it enjoyed a gross private income of over £81 million. The bulk of this sum comes in rents, service fees and charges the Corporation earns from its extensive and valuable property portfolio in the City. It owns roughly one fifth of the 717 acres of the Square Mile, but its 400 investment properties are scattered through the West End as well.[37] Some of these were conferred on the Corporation by history. A Charter of 1444 gave it rights of ownership over any waste ground, and it retained control of the areas either side of the Old City walls, mainly for defensive reasons (which is why much of its estate lies along the line of London Wall). There were also fourteenth- and fifteenth-century benefac-

---

* To stand for election to the Court of Common Council it is necessary to be a freeman of the City. Although it is possible to be a freeman without being a liveryman, the two are in practice more or less synonymous.

TABLE 8.1
The Private Wealth of the Corporation of London (£ k)*

Source	Gross Income (£ k)	Capital Value (£ k)
City's Cash		
Rent	35,986	506,300
Service Charges	4,789	–
Fees and Charges	20,884	–
Investment Income	16,008	295,716
Other	1,945	–
Sub-Total	79,612	802,016
Bridge House Estates		
Rents	16,459	201,383
Service Charges	863	–
Fees and Charges	1,794	–
Investment Income	15,796	253,267
Other	523	112
Sub-Total	35,435	454,762
Total	115,047	1,256,778

Sources: Bridge House Estates: The Trustees Annual Report and Financial Statements, Year
ended 31 March 1998, City's Cash Final Accounts, Year ended 31 March 1998.

* 1997–98 figures. The City's Cash is used to fund the City markets, open spaces and schools.
The Bridge House Estates still funds the bridges, but the substantial surplus is devoted to other
charitable causes.

tions, but the bulk of the Corporation's landed estate was acquired after the
Second World War.

In the Blitz, two fifths of the City was flattened by the Luftwaffe. Rather
than wait for private capital to resurrect the financial and trading heart of
the British empire, the Corporation used the powers of compulsory purchase
granted to all local authorities to acquire and redevelop 115 acres, mainly to
the north and south of what is now the west end of London Wall. After the
war £2.3 million (about £50 million today) was spent buying freeholds, and
rather less on building roads and restoring services. The site was then given
over to property developers, in return for one eighth of the rents.

The results were not always pleasing. Along London Wall, where pebbled pathways drive pedestrians up to the suspended walkways, rise six up-ended glass, concrete and steel slabs, punctuated at the western end by the brown toadlike structure of a 1980s office building, Alban Gate. On the walkways, where shoppers and lunchers were expected by the architect to gambol lightly, only commuters hurrying to the office or the station thread their way across the windy concourse. London Wall is one of the worst examples of sixties' office development to be seen in England. Though it did not build nor does it manage the buildings, as freeholder the Corporation is rightly embarrassed by them. But in 1998–9 it anticipates a rental and service charge income of £21 million from the City Fund estate, and one of the up-ended boxes (City Tower) is the most valuable building in the Corporation portfolio.

The Corporation is also heir to two private estates acquired over the centuries. The largest is City's Cash, a fund which in 1998–9 enjoyed a total rental, service charge and dividend income of over £50 million. It owns the freeholds to about thirty-five acres of the City of London, most stemming from the Corporation's historic right to acquire waste ground and ground close to the old City walls.[38] As a result, many of its properties are outside the old City walls, along Upper and Lower Thames Street, the Minories and Houndsditch, London Wall itself and Charterhouse Street. Subsequent bequests and benefactions added, among others, the freehold to the Central Criminal Court at Old Bailey. The fund also shares ownership of the Royal Exchange with the Mercers' Company, as stipulated by its founder, Thomas Gresham. The rents of three of the historic markets – Smithfield, Leadenhall and Billingsgate – go to City's Cash, and the fund also owns valuable retail property in the West End.

The second and smaller fund administered by the Corporation is the Bridge House Estates Trust, whose income maintains the four road bridges which connect the City to the south bank of the Thames. Its earliest revenue came not only from rents paid by the shopkeepers on the original London Bridge and the tolls levied on many travellers and pilgrims who used it but from hundreds of bequests by ordinary citizens on both sides of the river, leaving their money to 'God, St Thomas and London Bridge'. Until Westminster Bridge was opened in 1750, London Bridge was the only river crossing in the metropolis, and pilgrims en route to Canterbury made heavy use of it, for which they were duly grateful.

Many of the benefactions it received were tiny. Johanna de Bytheweye left the Bridge just twelve pence, and Margery Bacheler gave it her gold ring. Others were munificent. Henry II granted a tax on wool to build the medieval bridge, and Edward I gave the meat and fish 'stocks market' (where Mansion House now stands) to maintain it.[39] Bridge House Estates now owns an investment portfolio of property and securities valued at £454 million. Its income totals £345 million. The combined value of the City Fund (£259 million), City's Cash (£802 million) and Bridge House (£454 million) estates means the Corporation of London owns private assets valued at over £1.5 billion.

Who Runs the City of London?

The modern Corporation is careful not to flaunt its wealth. The reticence is understandable: over the last century and a half it has endured two major public inquiries into its wealth and privileges and survived repeated calls that it be drawn into the government of London as a whole. Reformers have long considered its medieval constitution an affront to the democratic conscience, and coveted its assets for schemes of municipal improvement. In Opposition, New Labour made clear that its plans for an elected mayor and assembly for London would necessitate a review of the anomalous position of the Corporation of London.

The shyness of the Corporation, like that of the livery companies and the Oxbridge colleges, is not purely the product of a long memory or contemporary political fears. It simply sees itself as above the clamour of party politics. The Corporation of London was founded so long ago that it is older than Parliament, and too old to have received a charter of incorporation from any English king. The lord mayor, the sheriffs, the aldermen, the common councilmen and even the officials of the Corporation see themselves not as councillors or local government officials but as temporary stewards of a historic trust.

It is now commonplace to complain that the financial markets have become more powerful than the government, but the ability of the Corporation to retain its medieval constitution is a reminder that governments have always fought shy of offending the City. In the seventeenth century, the Corporation was sufficiently important as a source of public finance for the City fathers to bully the government into paying for its reconstruction after the Great Fire. The Corporation had complained that it had 'no common stock, nor revenue, nor any capacity to raise within itself anything considerable towards so vast an expense' as rebuilding the City.[40] Parliament was forced to vote it £730,000 a year in coal tariffs, which sustained the Corporation until deep into the eighteenth century, but its financial difficulties were greatly increased by the failure to notice that it was lending money from its orphan accounts at a loss (the Corporation administered the personal estates of people who died, leaving children). Its failure to replenish the accounts meant Parliament twice came close to forcing the Corporation to sell its remaining assets, but it averted this unhappy fate by the judicious use of bribes and preferential leases for parliamentarians.*

The Corporation has since escaped the attempts of nineteenth- and twentieth-century reformers to get rid of its medieval constitution and subsume it in the government of London. Its governing body, the Court of Common Council, elected annually by the voters in each ward of the City, has its origins in the Saxon folk-moot of the pre-Conquest City. It consists of 132 common councilmen elected by the voters of the twenty-five wards of the City and their twenty-five aldermen. The Council is presided over by the lord mayor, a post the twenty-five members of the Court of Aldermen take it in turns to hold. The position of lord mayor used to guarantee a knighthood, and has at times taken on near-hereditary aspects. In 1996 Roger Cork, son of Sir Kenneth Cork, a lord mayor in the late 1970s, ascended to the post. Its holder represents the City abroad, but the post is now largely ceremonial. A tricorn hat and plumes, a scarlet or black and ermine-edged cloak, a mace and the odd sword and sceptre are the tools of his trade. His year begins with the Lord Mayor's Show, a procession of floats and bands through the streets of the Square Mile, echoing the countless processions which were an integral part of the life of every medieval city. Military victories are also celebrated with a march through the City.

Most of the year in office which follows is spent entertaining and being entertained at lavish lunches and dinners in the Guildhall, the Mansion House, livery company halls, and in foreign hotels. It is an expensive role to play. Although the Corporation meets the lord mayor's expenses up to £200,000 a year, he is still expected to contribute, and aldermen occasionally make it known that they are not interested in the post for that reason. There is a diplomatic purpose to the wining and dining. The lord mayor receives most visiting heads of state, and their receptions at the Guildhall are carefully co-ordinated with the Foreign Office and the palace. In June every year the chancellor of the exchequer makes a major economic policy statement after dinner at the Mansion House, and the prime minister visits the Guildhall each November to pronounce on foreign policy. The lord mayor also markets

---

* Running an unprofitable bank was not the only mistake the Corporation officials made at the Restoration. At the end of the seventeenth century they leased what are now their West End estates for 99-year terms, which lessees were allowed to renew automatically in perpetuity at the original rents. (The term was subsequently reduced to two thousand years by the Property Act of 1925, but the material effect is the same.) This enabled the leaseholders to reap the whole of the profits of their development into houses and shops during the eighteenth century. None of the profits accrued to the Corporation until the leases expired in 1765. Even today there are a number of Mayfair leaseholders paying eighteenth-century rents which do not even cover the costs of collection. They are also collecting the lavish market rents paid by the tenants. See Doolittle, *The City of London and Its Livery Companies*, pp. 10, 13–14.

the City, lobbying Westminster and Brussels for regulatory changes and public investment. When travelling abroad, he is said to have Cabinet rank, giving him access to decision-makers – a role he may have to cede to the new elected mayor of London.

The election of New Labour, with its grandiose plans for a London mayor and assembly, has created a pressure for change in the City constitution which the Corporation has found hard to resist. Unlike the lord mayor, the twenty-five-strong Court of Aldermen from which he is chosen is not part of a pantomime. The aldermen have a serious role as City magistrates, and play the Senate to the Common Council's House of Representatives. Like the common councilmen, they are elected by the voters of the twenty-five wards of the City. Unlike the councilmen, they are elected for life (in practice until the retirement age of seventy). There are no parallels for this kind of local government anywhere else in the country, but it is not the social exclusivity of the system which offends democratic sensibilities so much as the restricted electorate. The franchise is confined to residents, partnerships and sole traders in any or all of the wards where they pay local taxes. Just over 20,000 people are eligible to vote, and only 5,400 of them live in the Square Mile, mostly in the Barbican flats. (Only two of the twelve council estates run by the Corporation – at Petticoat Lane and Golden Lane – are in the City.) The rest of the electorate consists of the partners of unincorporated businesses such as legal and accountancy partnerships.

The election turnout is usually less than 100 voters, there are no political parties, and most seats are uncontested. The major banks, insurance companies, securities houses and listed companies which pay most of the rents, service charges and local taxes have no say at all in the government of the City, though it is not – it must be said – a right for which they have clamoured. But not everybody is indifferent. In 1994 there was a nasty row with the Smithfield Market Tenants' Association over the rent increases which the Corporation imposed to fund the £70 million cost of reburbishing Smithfield Market to comply with European hygiene regulations. The association managed to win two seats at a by-election simply by persuading its members to vote. The dispute was resolved quickly once the Smithfield traders threatened to pack every ward with its supporters.

A year later a wealthy telecommunications entrepreneur, Malcolm Matson, was shocked to find that election by the voters was not enough to secure him a seat at the Court of Aldermen. The other members blackballed him under an ancient rule which allows them to vet and reject elected colleagues. Matson took his case to the Court of Appeal, which ruled the Court of Aldermen should at least give reasons for their decision.[41] Its members explained that they had formed 'the overall impression' that Matson lacked the necessary 'experience, attainments and personal qualities'.[42] They were probably right to think that they might not get on with their new colleague. Matson has called for universal suffrage in the City and written a pamphlet for the Fabian Society calling for the Corporation to be abolished.[43]

By 1997 the Corporation was forced to make concessions to the growing clamour for reform. The New Labour government lent its support to the reformers, urging the Corporation to devise a constitution 'representing more accurately the various interests in the Square Mile'. A plan to give incorporated as well as unincorporated businesses the vote was approved by the Court of Common Council in late 1997. Aldermen will cease to serve for life; instead they will all stand for re-election every few years, and the number of common councilmen is to be cut to one hundred. In September 1998, the Common Council also agreed to abolish the right to veto elected members, and to introduce a proper business vote.[44]

The Corporation of London: Justification by Works?

The willingness of the government to accept such modest reforms is a reminder that, although the constitution of the Corporation is undemocratic, it works. By comparison with local government elsewhere, the Corporation is a model of sound municipal administration. This may not be unconnected to its lack of democracy and disdain for political partisanship.

'We have politics,' explains Bernard Harty, the town clerk and chamberlain of the Corporation of London, and a man with long experience of local government in the Midlands and the north of England. 'What we don't have is party politics.'[45] As the local authority, it runs the Central Criminal Court, a state primary school, a string of twelve council estates, three outstanding public libraries, and an 800-strong police force with a reputation for intelligence, discretion and integrity. Even its crematorium at Manor Park is the largest, busiest and most efficient in Britain.

In its stewardship of the historic London markets, the Corporation has effected radical change without undue controversy. Billingsgate decamped in 1982 from Lower Thames Street to an £8 million, thirteen-acre, purpose-built structure on the Isle of Dogs.[46] The old market building, refurbished as office space for National Westminster Bank, now shares the Billingsgate site with a blue-glass pyramid rented by Hong Kong and Shanghai Bank. The Spitalfields fruit and vegetable market was moved to a new location in Leyton over a single weekend in May 1991 without any interruption to trading. Leadenhall, once the market for 'foreigners' to sell their produce, is now treated by the Corporation as a characterful investment property rather than a working market. The exception was Smithfield, the last fully functioning market in the City. The traders have lost market share steadily, and resent the hefty rent rises the Corporation imposed to fund its £70 million refurbishment. But even at Smithfield the dispute was relatively short-lived, and the refurbished building now incorporates better accommodation and much-needed office space.

On the whole, the Corporation has handled the management and planning of a major financial centre with considerable aplomb. The rapid reconstruction of the post-war years rightly gave way to a period of concern about the City's historic character, but in the 1980s decades of tight planning controls were lifted as soon as it became clear that changing financial markets required a new kind of accommodation. The cautious city architect and chief planning officer of the first half of the 1980s, Stuart Murphy, gave way to his deputy, Peter Rees, a dynamic figure who had done time in the private sector as well as at Lambeth Council and the Department of the Environment. From 1986 – with the support of Michael Cassidy, who then chaired the planning committee – Rees persuaded the members of the Corporation to authorise the replacement of *one third* of the buildings in the Square Mile. Rees had grasped what the deregulation of the City at 'Big Bang' in October 1986 meant for office space long before he received his first planning application in May that year: huge floors to accommodate hundreds of deskbound traders and sales people.

'Big Bang changed the perception of what a City building should be,' recalls Cassidy. 'Not the Edwardian merchant bank, but a financial factory.'[47] He reckons Canary Wharf merely accelerated the revolution in the appearance of the City, by encouraging members of the Corporation to vote for major new developments such as Broadgate and London Wall without asking too many questions. It was not until 1995, after being rescued from a mountain of debt and the hands of the administrators, that Canary Wharf competed seriously with the City for prime tenants. That year, the Corporation took the unprecedented step of offering a Dutch bank the freehold of a development site at Spitalfields if it agreed to stay in the City rather than decamp to Docklands.[48] Cassidy was forced not only to adapt and accelerate the pattern of property development in the City but was said to have asked Sir Peter Levene, the chief executive of Canary Wharf, not to poach established City rent-payers.[49]

Banks and other financial institutions have additional reasons to be grateful for the slick administration of the Corporation. When an IRA bomb in St Mary Axe wrecked several buildings on and around Bishopsgate on a Friday evening in April 1992, the Corporation relocated every firm affected in time for the start of business on Monday morning. Security also had to be improved quickly, and the City police threw a tight security cordon around the Square Mile, reducing the number of access points and allowing the police to check every vehicle which entered. There were predictable disadvantages. The police used the opportunity of manned road blocks to arrest people for missing tax discs, drink-driving and the possession of drugs as well as explosives.[50] ('The police have to act in random fashion,' explained Cassidy, 'to create an impression of randomness.') But the plastic bollards gave way to permanent concrete barriers with remarkably little public opposition. City workers are said to appreciate the benefits of less traffic, reduced crime and greater pedestrianisation. The Corporation turned a potential disaster into a public relations coup.

'The principal purpose of having the Corporation in its present form is that we have to work closely with the business community,' says Cassidy, who as chairman of the policy and resources committee was the public face of the City from 1989 to 1996. 'The historical or ceremonial aspects don't even figure in most business people's checklists. They want us to look after people in the Square Mile, particularly after the bombs; do things well; and promote the City against competing cities. All of those functions are new. Even fifteen years ago we would not have done them.'[51]

This is a plausible defence of the undemocratic constitution of the Corporation of London. The City is a place where people work rather than live, its resident population of 5,400 multiplying more than fiftyfold during the working day as commuters pour into its offices, shops and restaurants. It is also the most successful segment of the British economy, paying far more in local and national taxes than it receives back in services, and pumping an estimated £20 billion into the rest of the country every year. It has to compete with other international financial centres like New York, Frankfurt, Paris and Tokyo in terms of transport links, restaurants and opera houses. It would be absurd if the residents of the Barbican and the Golden Lane and Petticoat Lane estates could dictate conditions of work in the Square Mile.

Under Cassidy, the Corporation set up an economic development team to attract business; invested £3.5 million in a comprehensive study of the relative strengths and weaknesses of the City; made joint bids for foreign investment with the London Docklands Development Corporation; launched a marketing service to sell City expertise to emerging markets; and persuaded the last Conservative chancellor, Kenneth Clarke, to sponsor the City Promotion Panel in 1995.[52] The Corporation has invested £19 million in the modernisation of the Barbican Arts Centre, to improve the City's cultural attractions. It campaigned to save St Bartholomew's Hospital, pledged £6 million to the Millennium Dome, and lobbied heavily for improved public transport in London.[53] Cassidy pressed the government remorselessly to invest in the

Underground and new rail links across London, and helped to form the London First lobbying group. But nobody pretends that this earns the City the affection of the country. This is *realpolitik*. The rest of Britain dislikes London in general and the City in particular, not only because it is so rich (the output of the capital is larger than that of four member states of the European Union) but because most people believe (fallaciously) that money-broking, insurance and securities-dealing are not real work. The Corporation has tried to counter this with a stream of propaganda about the importance of the City to wealth and jobs elsewhere. It also ensures that its wealth is disbursed in ways which please politically.

Of the £569 million City businesses paid in rates in 1997–8, all but £7.9 million was passed to the national pool for redistribution to less fortunate local authorities.[54] The money it keeps is used to fund national institutions such as the Central Criminal Court at the Old Bailey, and the Animal Quarantine Station at Heathrow airport. (The Corporation is the port health authority for London, making it responsible for protecting the capital from seaborne and airborne diseases.) It has also sought to lessen the stark contrast between the affluence of the City and the poverty and dilapidation of surrounding boroughs like Hackney, Islington and Southwark by making several joint bids for public money to refurbish the City fringes. It has funded a circus in Hackney, a school in Islington and a homeless project in Southwark.

But the most obvious way in which the Corporation sells itself to a sceptical public is its ownership and management of 10,000 acres of open spaces in and around London. They include Epping Forest and Chingford Golf Course (6,000 acres), Hampstead Heath (800), Burnham Beeches (540), Coulsdon Common (430), Highgate Wood (70), Queen's Park (30), Spring Park and West Wickham Common in Kent (552 acres in all), West Ham Park (77), Ashtead Common (500), the Wanstead Flats Playing Fields, and Shiplake Island in Oxford. In fact, the Corporation continues to buy land in Epping and Hampstead to protect it from spoliation, and took on Keats House, near Hampstead Heath, when Camden Council said it could not afford to maintain the building.

This motley collection of parks, commons and open spaces – acquired by a mixture of historical accident, purchase and public benefaction – was assembled mainly in the late nineteenth century, when the Corporation was anxious to appear useful by protecting green belt land around London from developers.* It agreed to assume control of Hampstead Heath after the

---

* Legislation was passed in 1878 empowering the Corporation to buy land for the citizens of London to enjoy.

abolition of the GLC, a political controversy it otherwise deftly ignored. None of the spaces makes money (there is a shell income from timber sales) and the City's Cash fund has to spend £12 million a year on maintaining them.

All four of the road bridges connecting the City to the south bank – Tower, London, Southwark and Blackfriars – are owned and maintained by the Corporation from its Bridge House Estates fund without recourse to the taxpayer. Three were built by the Corporation; the other was bought from private developers in the late nineteenth century. The original London Bridge, built in the Middle Ages, was not replaced until 1831. When it was rebuilt again in 1972, the Corporation persuaded an Arizona property company to pay £1 million for the old stone bridge. Blackfriars, built in 1769, was replaced by the present bridge exactly 100 years later. Southwark is the only London bridge to be built by a private company, and it was bought by the Corporation for £200,000 in 1868 – cheap by comparison with the gothic splendours of Tower Bridge, one of the chief international symbols of London but a highly controversial design when it was constructed in the 1890s. It cost £1.18 million, and has cost more since.*

The Bridge House Estates fund struggles to spend its massive endowment income. In 1994, it found a use for less than one third of an income of nearly £30 million. Rather than wait for ambitious politicians to expropriate a fund whose value was rising by nearly £20 million a year even before investment returns were added, the Corporation elected to devote the surplus to a wider range of charitable activities in the capital. With net assets up to £502 million in 1998–99, the new charity was able to give away £14 million to various charities. The Bridge House Estates Trust Fund is now one of the wealthiest charitable trusts in the country, on a par with Henry Smith Estates charities, the Leverhulme Trust and the Wolfson and Gatsby Foundations.[55]

It is surprising, in an egalitarian age, that the Corporation does not face more criticism for the £4.8 million in subsidies it gives to three private schools where it is the governing body. The City of London School for Boys, originally founded in 1442, was re-founded by the Corporation in 1837 and moved to its present site off Queen Victoria Street in 1987. The City of London School for Girls, established in 1894, was moved to handsome new premises in the Barbican in 1973, and the third independent school is the City of London Freemen's School, founded in 1854 for the education of orphans of freemen

---

* The Corporation planned a bridge to the east of London Bridge as early as 1876, and chose its site then. Not everybody was impressed by the Gothic bascule bridge design by the city architect, Horace Jones, produced in 1878. From *To God and the Bridge*, Exhibition Catalogue, 1972.

of the City. The world-famous Guildhall School of Music and Drama, founded by the Corporation in 1880, also receives £5 million a year from City's Cash in addition to its relatively new home in the Barbican.

The Barbican complex of schools, apartment blocks, theatres, concert halls, art galleries, libraries, shops and restaurants is (to date) the biggest architectural risk taken by the Corporation. Originally conceived as a 'gift to the nation', it was nevertheless intended to turn a profit, which it has never managed to do, mainly because the construction costs ran out of control. Almost every aspect of the development was mismanaged, from the number of car-parking spaces to the stage sizes, and the architects added indulgent touches like perspex spheres in the concert hall and hanging window shutters, which were practical disasters. It took a quarter of a century to build, being finally completed in 1982, by which time its cost, including the 44-storey tower blocks and 2,400 flats, had ballooned from an estimated £12 million to £45 million. The costs of the Arts and Music Centre had climbed tenfold, from £16 million to £161 million. The exhibition centre is too small and the 'Right to Buy', introduced by the first Thatcher government in 1980, has forced the Corporation to sell many of the Barbican flats at heavy discounts.

The Barbican has failed to win the affection of the theatre and concert-going public; despite having 123 separate entrances, its impenetrability is legendary. The steep grey walls and the proliferation of 'levels' were a depressingly literal translation of barbican – a fortified outwork or defence. The combination of gloomy illumination, colour-coded floor trails and lifts which often did not stop at each floor did nothing to dispel the gloom. However, with running and capital costs totalling over £22 million in 1997–8 – including subsidies of £1.3 million to the London Symphony Orchestra, and £2.1 million to the Royal Shakespeare Company – the Barbican Arts Centre makes the Corporation of London the third largest corporate sponsor of the arts (after the Arts Council and the BBC). In November 1995 it persuaded John Tusa, late of the BBC and Wolfson College, Cambridge, to take the job of managing director of the Barbican.

Trinity House

Like the monarchy, the Corporation of London is a wealthy medieval institution which has survived by being versatile and adaptable, but it is not the only wealthy medieval corporation to have survived by agreeing to fulfil public responsibilities.

The Corporation of Trinity House of Deptford Strond once enjoyed the exclusive right to pilot ships up the River Thames to the Port of London, and in its structure and habits it was indistinguishable from any other livery company enjoying the fruits of a monopoly. It had a master and wardens, an annual procession to St Olave's at Hart Street, a penchant for feasting and the ceremony of the loving-cup, regular prayers and supplications for the souls of dead members, almshouses and a funeral pall for hire. Even its origins are characteristically obscure.* It is certain only that Trinity House is the last representative of the dozens of societies, companies and guilds of shipowners and mariners in all the main ports of England in the fourteenth century.

Unlike most of the livery companies, Trinity House has retained a material rather than an honorary role. Its activities are now divided between the Trinity House Lighthouse Service (the general lighthouse service for England, Wales, the Channel Islands and Gibraltar) and a Homes and Pension Charity which uses the income from historic assets to house and support aged, sick or needy Merchant Navy officers, their widows and dependants. Today, the Lighthouse Service administers from its headquarters at Tower Hill no less than 72 lighthouses (including the famous Eddystone lighthouse off Plymouth), 11 lightships, 2 light float stations and 429 buoys (of which 318 are lighted). It also has responsibility for locating, marking and disposing of wrecks considered a danger to navigation. Its most important depot is Harwich, where control of all ships and stations is handled by a round-the-clock operations centre. These functions are funded not from endowments but from light dues levied on vessels calling at British and Irish ports.

This unusual status – a private company with a public purpose – has earned Trinity House a special place in the economics textbooks. Successive generations of economists, from Adam Smith through John Stuart Mill and A. C. Pigou to Paul Samuelson, have cited the lighthouse as the classic example of a 'public good' (something which has to be provided by the state because nobody can be made to pay for its benefits). For decades, it was retailed to economics undergraduates as proof that the market cannot supply all needs, and that even classical economists recognised that state intervention was sometimes justified. In fact, most lighthouses were originally built by private speculators licensed by Trinity House, and paid out of the light dues levied on shipowners, who therefore did pay for the benefits they enjoyed.[56] It was only when politicians encouraged it to take over the lighthouses and create an integrated national network that private initiative was excluded, and a corporatist system installed. Today Trinity House has to submit its budget to

---

* One supposition is that it derived from a Guild of Mariners known to have existed in the reign of Alfred the Great. Another theory is that it is the successor to a corporation founded by Archbishop Stephen Langton (d. 1228) for the suppression of looters who lured ships on to the rocks by lighting false beacons. See J. Grosvenor, *Trinity House*, Staples Press, 1959.

the Department of Environment, Transport and the Regions for approval, and negotiate its light dues with the Chamber of Shipping.

The dues are now paid into a General Lighthouse Fund under the trusteeship of the Department, but the right to tax shipping entering British ports was the foundation of the wealth of Trinity House. On 19 March 1513 the Guild of Mariners at Deptford, where Henry VIII built and maintained his navy, petitioned the king to grant them a charter of incorporation. The petition was the work of Thomas Spert, master of the newly built *Henri Grace à Dieu*. His petition lamented the lack of trained river pilots, and warned that the superior navigational skills of 'Scots, Flemings and Frenchmen' was exposing the royal dockyard and the City of London to attack. Half-finished cloth accounted for four fifths of English exports; and two thirds of the trade was conducted through the Port of London, so navigation of the lower reaches of the Thames was vital. The charter was granted in May 1514 to the 'Master, Wardens and Assistants of the Guild, Fraternity or Brotherhood of the Most Glorious and Undivided Trinity and of St Clement in the parish of Deptford-Stronde in the County of Kent'. This charter, renewed by subsequent monarchs, marked the inception of the Corporation of Trinity House.

A reliable income was not secured until 1593, when the rights of ballastage, beaconage and buoyage – the rent and sale of ballast to stabilise ships and the dues levied on ships for marking rocks and channels with beacons and buoys – were given to Trinity House by Lord High Admiral Howard of Effingham (hero of the defeat of the Spanish Armada). This transformed its fortunes; by 1604 James I raised the value of property it could hold from 20 marks (about £13) to £200, and granted it an exclusive right to license pilots on the Thames. This monopoly enabled the corporation to charge admission fees to new river pilots, fine interlopers and tax foreign ships, whether or not they used a Trinity House pilot.

By the 1670s the Corporation was rich enough for the diarist John Evelyn, who lived near Deptford, to be shocked when his father-in-law, a former master, gave land in Deptford to build a new hall and almshouses. He felt Trinity House was rich enough already.[57] Membership of the corporation certainly provided a handsome living in Stuart and Georgian times. In 1666 the 'Elder Brethren' split £850, and one or two members left fortunes of over £5,000.[58] It was mainly for the income that people such as the diarist Samuel Pepys (1633–1703), the colonist William Penn (1644–1718) and the prime minister William Pitt (1759–1806) agreed to serve as master. The corporation was then at the height of its powers: before the Navy Board or the Admiralty began to exert their influence there was virtually no maritime matter in which Trinity House did not have some authority or interest.

Like the livery companies, Trinity House attracted benefactions of plate, cash and real estate from masters and wealthy mariners. These were devoted to housing sick and poor seafarers or their widows and children. Seamen and their widows might get a place in the almshouses at Deptford or Stepney, on the north bank of the river where many seamen lived, or a pension from the corporation. (Trinity House has a letter from Nelson, written on board *Agamemnon* in April 1793, requesting a pension for a volunteer who had served on the ship.)[59] The corporation still provides rent-free accommodation for former mariners and their widows or spinster daughters at Walmer in Kent. The splendid headquarters building at Tower Hill, to which Trinity House moved in 1796, is the only asset of the corporate charity.

The main asset of the Homes and Pension Charity is the Newington (Trust) Estate, which consists of Trinity Church Square, Merrick Square and the surrounding streets between Borough High Street and Great Dover Street just south of London Bridge. The estate is mainly one of fine houses, but includes several office blocks to the north, Southwark crown court, two public houses, a BT engineering works and warehousing. It was valued in 1997 at over £19 million, of which two thirds was attributable to the residential portfolio. With other assets, the Homes and Pension Trust had a total value of just over £24.25 million in 1997.[60] The income of £2 million is spent mainly on the Trinity Homes at Walmer and on pensions and grants to mariners and their dependants.

Are Liverymen the Acceptable Face of Freemasonry?

Liverymen disclaim, usually with vehemence, the supposition that membership of a livery company is synonymous with Freemasonry. It is easy to see why the company and the lodge might attract the same type of personality. The similarities between them – mythical origins, secrecy, feasting, ritual, networking – are striking. The ceremony of the loving-cup is removed in detail but not in kind from apron-wearing police inspectors prodding naked, blindfolded estate agents with a sword at a masonic hall. Like liverymen, freemasons prefer to confine their public face to giving away money, and are puzzled and disappointed that the outside world does not emphasise their philanthropic side.

The Grand Charity of Freemasons gives away £3–4 million a year, and the Royal Masonic Benevolent Institution has upwards of £16 million to spend on housing and supporting destitute members and their relatives. There is a Royal Masonic Hospital at Hammersmith (whose attempted sale in 1984 was overturned by the rank-and-file after an embarrassing public row) and a Royal Masonic School for Girls at Bushey (a similar school for boys was closed in

1977, but the trust subsidises places at other schools instead).[61] The similarities with the charitable work of the livery companies are suggestive.

Of course, there are differences between the livery companies and the lodges, most obviously in terms of size. There could be as many as 750,000 freemasons in Britain, a membership eighty or ninety times the number of livery and freemen. Unlike liverymen, who tend to be relatively well-off, freemasons are drawn from all ranks of society, and the historic endowments of the brotherhood are not as large. The site of the masonic headquarters in Great Queen Street was acquired painfully, by subscription and annexation, between 1767 and 1899, and the present Freemasons' Hall was built as a memorial to masons killed in the First World War, with the proceeds of a £1 million appeal which took most of the 1920s to raise.[62] The Royal Masonic Benevolent Institution has net assets of just over £84 million.[63] There is the occasional valuable bequest (according to one account, a Midlands industrialist named Harry Ellard left £5 million to the Grand Charity in 1983), but ultimately masonic giving relies largely on lodge dues and special fund-raising events called 'Festivals'.[64] The power of Freemasonry lies in influence, not wealth. So it would be surprising, given the importance of the City of London, if Freemasonry had failed to penetrate the livery companies and the Corporation of London.

In 1983 Stephen Knight claimed both were infested with Freemasonry. He estimated that ten of the twenty-five wards were controlled by lodges, all the main salaried officers at the Corporation were masons, and senior wardens of the Guildhall Lodge routinely became lord mayor.[65] In a book first published in 1989, Martin Short repeated the claim that it is virtually impossible to become lord mayor of London without being a member of the Guildhall lodge, and that there are at least twenty-one livery company lodges.[66] Naturally, neither writer can produce any concrete evidence to back up his assertions, and livery company clerks treat them as insults rather than allegations to be taken seriously. It is impossible to say how much it matters: City men 'on the square' have escaped the critical scrutiny brought to bear on the police and the judiciary. 'There are so many competing bodies, especially in the City,' an alderman told Stephen Knight in 1983. 'What with Livery Companies, Rotary, Chamber of Commerce, Ward clubs, there are so *many* competing clubs. I would have thought that most people in the City attach much more importance to their Livery than they do to their Freemasonry.'[67] To the world outside, it is odd that they attach importance to either.

PART TWO

THE STATE

CHAPTER NINE

CENTRAL GOVERNMENT

We do not want to be in the same boat as the French – over-governed, but under-managed.

SIR JOHN BANHAM[1]

Businessmen are paid to operate the system rather than to understand or expound it, and nothing is more pathetic than to see politicians of either party coming cap in hand to industrialists or bankers for advice that the latter are not qualified to give.

SIR SAMUEL BRITTAN[2]

The Treasury is a very bad partner. They don't take any risks. They don't put any money up. But they expect a reward.

SIR JOHN EGAN, chief executive, BAA[3]

Public administration is not a private business. If it were, it would not be public administration.

SIMON JENKINS[4]

What is the state? Since the seventeenth century, the English have not pondered this question. It was left to continental metaphysicians to find the answer, while Englishmen got on with the business of government. The paradox of New Labour is that it has raised traditional English pragmatism to the status of an ideology. 'What counts,' says Tony Blair, 'is what works.' Like Heath and Thatcher before him, the prime minister has no experience of business, but he shares their messianic faith in its ability to get things done and make things happen. Business is, above all, a *practical* discipline. This is the secret of its appeal to a prime minister who has little interest in ideas, or personal or party allegiances, except as instruments in the unending battle for votes, influence and power.

'This government', explained a political lobbyist to a cod businessman from the *Observer*, 'likes to do deals.' Even in opposition, Blair was ready to cut deals with the chairman of British Telecom,[5] spoke of a 'compact with the customer', and despatched his shadow ministers to listen to lectures on 'quality management' and 'corporate leadership'. In office, he has talked of 're-branding' Britain as 'young' and 'modern', and styled himself as 'chief executive of Britain PLC'. His departmental ministers were set performance targets and threatened with annual appraisals. From now on, the 'share-holders of Britain PLC' will take delivery of annual reports on the progress the government has made towards fulfilling manifesto commitments.

The idea that a country can be run like a commercial enterprise is pre-democratic rather than modern. Victorian technocrats such as Chadwick and Kay-Shuttleworth, or their Edwardian successors Morant and Beveridge, would recognise it. The task of government, as they saw it, was the rational organisation of resources to deliver material benefits which everybody agreed were necessary, but which were denied by vested interest, intellectual error, or party dogma. It is government by technique rather than principle: the reduction of politics to questions of management. Technique and management are where businessmen excel. Within a year of taking office, Blair had 350 of them guiding him on aspects of government.[6]

The restaurateur Terence Conran was advising on 'competitiveness'; Peter Davis of the Prudential was heading a task force on the welfare-to-work pro-gramme; Brian Davis, chief executive of Nationwide Building Society, was being tapped for his thoughts on information technology; Martin Taylor, then of Barclays Bank, was chairing a group charged with the reform of social security; the chief executive of Vauxhall Motors was in charge of raising the standard of publicly funded training; and the television mogul, Greg Dyke, was rewriting the Patient's Charter. One senior businessman – the former chairman and chief executive of BP, Sir David Simon – was lured into the government itself as minister for Europe (the ultimate technocratic project). Big Businessmen are providing places on the welfare-to-work programme, subsidising specialist comprehensive schools, and taking over and reorganis-ing failing state schools in the same way they did with their ailing competitors.

Naturally, businessmen are flattered by the invitation to contribute to the public good. Most will hope for a knighthood, or even a peerage. But they have little choice: in a country where the government spends more than £2 in every £5 which people earn (and covers private life with rules concerning everything from the opening hours of shops to the age at which a teenager can smoke), the state is too rich a source of rents, patronage and contracts, and too threatening a source of laws and regulations, for large companies to shun an invitation from the prime minister. The major supermarkets enthused when they were invited to sell government-approved savings plans and install voting booths. Companies which spurned the Millennium Dome when it was being sold by a fading Conservative government greeted it enthusiastically when it was taken over by a new government with a massive majority.

There seems to be no end to the uses Blair can find for corporate Britain. When English football fans rioted in France during the 1998 World Cup, the prime minister looked not to the police or to the courts but to employers to give hooligans the sack. No one dared to point out that some of the worst offenders worked for a public corporation called the Post Office, but the proposal was not serious anyway. Its aim was to reinforce the prime ministerial brand: young, modern, decisive, innovative, and in touch with the mood of the pubs and clubs. Blair knows better than most that his elevation to No. 10 was the victory of an untried and untainted brand over a tested and tainted alternative. He has grasped that in a modern, media-driven democracy image counts for more than ideas. Voters, no longer trapped by class or ideology, can be treated like shoppers.

This is why government press officers are no longer the dry distributors of fact, but 'spin doctors' who place stories flattering to the governmental 'product' in the newspapers. It is also why New Labour psephologists monitor the reaction of the voters to every twist and turn of government policy. 'If you are running a company nowadays – suppose you are running Marks & Spencer or Sainsbury,' mused the prime minister, in a revealing interview a few weeks after taking office, 'you will be constantly trying to work out whether your consumers are satisfied with the product they are getting. I don't think there is anything wrong with government trying to do that in the same way.'[7]

Why Government is Different from Business

Government could scarcely be less like business is why. Companies provide tradeable goods and services which consumers purchase willingly from their income. Governments provide non-tradeable goods and services which taxpayers purchase unwillingly from expropriated earnings. In the marketplace, companies allocate resources to profitable activities; in government, resources are allocated by politicians and civil servants. Companies which fail to produce goods and services at prices consumers are willing to pay go bankrupt. Governments which provide services people explicitly reject, go on – for ever. Government, unlike business, is immortal.

It is also prodigal. The threat of bankruptcy prevents companies and consumers spending more than they earn. But in government there is no limit to the demands which politicians, civil servants and voters can make of the national income. They press demands without regard to the immediate impact (voters assume someone else will pay) or the wider economic consequences.* In the modern political marketplace, who gets what is determined not by benign competition on price and quality but by aggressive competition for public resources among vociferous interest groups. To govern democratically is to choose between them. Where a choice is invidious, the difference is split – one of the things that makes government different from business. Decisions, being political, are not fully rational. Shortly after taking office, Blair insisted that St Bartholomew's Hospital stay open. Economically, this was nonsensical; even retaining it as a specialist cancer and cardiac centre (rather than concentrating resources at the Royal London Hospital in Whitechapel) will cost an extra £23 million a year. But it made political sense. A vociferous interest group was silenced, the government appeared compassionate, the opposition heartless and penny-pinching.[9]

Irrationality and waste are characteristic of government activities, because the benefits of government decisions accrue to articulate interest groups (like the staff and their supporters at St Bartholomew's Hospital) while the costs fall on inarticulate taxpayers. The same is true, on a grander scale, of every task on which the government is engaged: raising of taxes; administration of justice; organisation of the national defences; provision of health, education and social security; subsidisation of agriculture, and the construction and maintenance of the transport system.

The Inland Revenue and Customs and Excise

No government activity bears the scars of trade-offs between interest groups more openly than procurement of the means to govern: the system of taxation. It is riddled with the oddities, exemptions and anomalies which betray what politicians have sought to encourage and discourage, penalise and reward. The Conservatives introduced tax reliefs for private health insurance and profit-related pay. New Labour took both away, but introduced a new tax break for film-makers. The Conservatives introduced PEPs and TESSAs, and several varieties of business start-up and expansion relief. New Labour has replaced PEPs and TESSAs with ISAs, and devised its own pet schemes for entrepreneurs. Both parties have gnawed at the tax privileges of home-owners, families and people who save for their retirement, but neither has dared abolish them, for fear of the electoral price Middle England will exact. Consumers pay VAT at 5 per cent on fuel, and 17.5 per cent on most

---

* The same phenomenon is observable inside companies, where resources are allocated by politics rather than price. The market stops at the entrance to the corporation.

other things; on orange juice, but not on caviar; on hot food, but not on cold; on CDs, but not on books or newspapers; on biscuits, but not on Jaffa Cakes.

Governments of both parties have only one fiscal achievement in common. They have both increased the overall burden of taxation, especially on families, while claiming to have done the opposite. In the 1940s and early 1950s, a married man on average earnings, with children, paid no income tax. Today, he pays it after earning less than one third of average earnings. This is the consequence of what economists call 'fiscal drag'. As incomes rise, the rate of tax has to be cut or the threshold at which it becomes payable has to be raised – otherwise, the tax burden will rise of its own accord. Naturally, successive governments have found hidden tax increases preferable to open ones. By allowing rising incomes to drag more people into the tax net (even though rising prices may mean their real incomes are not rising), they have increased taxation without paying a political cost.

Governments are adept at subterfuge of this kind. They have even discovered how to spend today the taxes of tomorrow. Since the early 1950s, the government has balanced its budget and repaid its borrowings in only five years out of forty, four them between 1987 and 1991. The National Debt, which is the accumulation of all past borrowing by governments, increased in every year but 1990. It is now equivalent to nearly half the national income. The payment of interest on the National Debt (£23.8 billion in 1997–8) is the fourth largest public expenditure programme, ahead of defence (£21.1 billion) but behind social security (£98.6 billion), health (£42.6 billion) and education (£36.7 billion). Borrowing, it can be seen, is not an alternative to taxation, it is a means of deferring taxation. This is the secret of its appeal to politicians. Even the self-consciously skinflint New Labour chancellor, Gordon Brown, who promised not to spend more than he raises in taxes and to borrow only to invest, tends to predict the repayment of debt tomorrow rather than deliver it today.

As voter resistance to high *rates* of income tax set in, governments resorted to less noticeable alternatives. They raised National Insurance contributions, and eroded or abolished additional tax allowances such as the married man's allowance, the child tax allowance and mortgage interest relief. In the last ten years, governments of both parties have attacked the tax privileges of pension funds, realising that people will not notice the rise in tax until they retire on a smaller pension decades from now (and perhaps not even then). They have also pretended that taxing companies is an alternative to taxing people, whereas companies are merely proxies for people in their guises as shareholders (who get lower dividends), employees (who get made redundant) and consumers (who pay higher prices).

TABLE 9.1
The National Debt (£ billions)

Instrument	
Fixed interest government stock	238.5
Index-linked government stock	51.7
NILO stocks	5.9
Treasury bills	7.6
National Savings	57.0
Certificates of tax deposit	0.9
Ways and means advances	31.5
IMF interest free notes	5.6
Temporary deposit facility	5.6
Total sterling debt	404.3
Government of United States loan	0.5
Government of Canada loan	0.1
US dollar bonds	3.1
US dollar floating rate notes	1.2
ECU bonds	2.0
ECU Treasury notes	3.9
ECU Treasury bills	2.7
Deutschmark Bonds	2.0
Assigned debt	0.1
Total foreign currency debt	15.6
Total National Debt	£419.9 billion

Source: *Bank of England Statistical Abstract*, 31 March 1997, Table 13.1.

Taxes ostensibly dedicated to particular purposes (e.g., National Insurance or Vehicle Excise Duty) were allowed to degenerate into general tax revenues. Onerous excise duties are lost in the astronomical prices of products which almost everybody is ashamed of consuming. Virtually nobody knows that four fifths of the price of a gallon of petrol goes to the government. Nor are governments averse to fiscal populism. The Conservatives imposed a windfall tax on the unpopular clearing banks; New Labour imposed one on the even more unpopular privatised utilities. Both exploited the indignation of taxpayers – as well as their ignorance and indifference.

They are able to do this because the system of taxation is of mind-boggling complexity. The laws of income tax run to 6,000 pages, and those on VAT extend the rules by another 1,000. There are thirteen principal reliefs from income tax – geared to age, marital status, physical condition, the size of the mortgage and a willingness to take in lodgers or invest in business start-ups. The size of the relief on pension contributions depends on a mixture of age and earnings, until they reach a ceiling or a cap. There are more ceilings and caps on the taxation of benefits-in-kind, including motor cars, relocation expenses and mobile telephones.

Surprisingly, VAT is not much better. When the tax was introduced in 1973, the chancellor of the Exchequer, Anthony Barber, described it as a simple tax. In its first year, it took three legal appeals to conclude that the big dipper at Blackpool was a chargeable form of fun not a zero-rated mode of transport. Ever since, people have argued what should be chargeable. The complexity of income tax and VAT has become self-fulfilling, with clever lawyers and tax accountants combing the law for loopholes to exploit, and equally clever tax officials drafting more laws to close them.

Politicians, ever prey to the special pleading of their supporters or the bright ideas of their policy advisers, have added further complexity by using the tax system to pursue their pet schemes of social and economic improvement. The reform of capital gains tax in the second budget introduced by Brown was a classic example of the genre. It replaced one complexity (indexation for inflation) with another (a rate which tapers away over ten years); introduced an artificial distinction between short- and long-term capital gains which owes nothing to economics or even to logic; and injected a bias against sales of assets which may well be necessary or sensible on other grounds. The reformed tax was not only perverse in its effects – Fat Cats in the City, a major target, turned out to be its chief beneficiaries – but too complex for software engineers to automate.

Even to operate unreformed parts of the system, companies and individuals have to employ an army of professional advisers. In 1996 the accountants KPMG estimated that the 2,000-odd listed companies spend £265 million a year complying with taxation.[10] In 1995, it was said that small, unlisted businesses spend a sum equivalent to 2 per cent of the national income (about £15 billion in 1997) understanding and compiling PAYE, VAT, and National Insurance returns. Yet the effects of the tax system in discouraging economic activity is little studied, except where its malign interaction with means-tested benefits prevents people working or ceasing to be poor.* Many activities which do not take place on a fully taxed basis happen instead in

* See Chapter 19.

the black economy, which is estimated at between 7 and 13 per cent of the national income, or as much as £100 billion a year. The amount of work not done at all is worth even more.

But these are not the measures the Inland Revenue and Customs and Excise use to measure their efficiency. They prefer to boast of how much they have cut the cost of collecting tax. The Inland Revenue employs over 52,000 people across 600 offices to collect more than £150 billion in taxes. Of each pound they collect, over 1.5p disappears in their own costs. HM Customs and Excise employs over 23,000 people to collect £82 billion in excise, import duties and VAT. Of each pound of excise duty they collect, 0.1p disappears in costs. This rises to 0.7 per cent for VAT, and 7.7p in the pound for import duties, where opportunities for bureaucratic empire-building are at their most lavish.[11] Millions more are squandered by Customs and Excise in its hopeless battles against the importation of drugs, pornography, firearms and contraband alcohol and cigarettes. Between them, the two revenue-raising organisations spend about £2.5 billion a year on running and capital costs.

Admittedly, these costs are much lower than they used to be. The Inland Revenue expense ratio is the lowest for twenty-five years. In 1979, it employed over 80,000 employees. Since then, it has invested in job-cutting technology, and awarded a ten year contract (worth £1.6 billion) to an American computer firm. Its management improved as the power of the Staff Federation waned. But the real economies have come not from new technology or better management but from transferring the burden of collecting tax to the taxpayers. Both the Inland Revenue and Customs and Excise are now using as unpaid tax collectors the individuals and businesses they tax.

Companies decide how much corporation tax they owe, and pay it quarterly in advance. If they pay too much, the Inland Revenue decides how much to pay back. In 1996 a system of self-assessment was introduced for the self-employed, higher-rate taxpayers and anyone else with complicated tax affairs. They now calculate their taxable income, and the Revenue calculates or checks tax payable on the figures they supply. Although the new regime was introduced with staggering incompetence – forms were sent late, to the wrong people, and a million taxpayers ended up with incorrect tax demands – the Inland Revenue was not inclined to apologise. Taxpayers who had paid in full received penalty notices and interest demands, and officials overwhelmed by errors simply threw away letters of complaint. While Hector the Inspector, a cuddly cartoon character in a bowler hat, underwent all manner of humiliations in his quest to help confused taxpayers, his real-life equivalents were levying instant fines of £100 (plus interest) on those who submitted a late return.

Employers have collected income tax on behalf of employees since the introduction of PAYE in 1944. Employers large and small have collected excise duties and VAT ever since the taxes were introduced. By relieving themselves of the burden of collecting tax from companies and the self-employed, the Inland Revenue and Customs and Excise merely completed the process, and allowed the government to claim it had cut the cost. Even top officials at Somerset House – who negotiate tax deals with lawyers and accountants, and devise ways to close loopholes – have reduced their work-load. The New Labour government has introduced a general anti-avoidance rule, saving them the time and trouble of proving that avoidance schemes are unlawful by making any form of tax-planning equivalent to evasion unless the courts decide otherwise.

Spending Money by Spending Capital

The government spent £312.6 billion in 1997–8. Running the government cost £6.4 billion. Yet until the 1990s government departments had no means of measuring costs or output (in terms of assets created or services delivered to the public). The only constraint on their spending was the cash limits imposed on departmental expenditure by the Treasury,* which measured the cost of inputs, but not the value of outputs. Nobody knew what it cost to run the government. The value of the capital assets government owned was unknown. Departments prepared no balance sheets, let alone consolidated accounts, and there was no real distinction between capital and current spending. There was no great pressure to know them either. Being insulated from the threat of bankruptcy, government departments did not have to worry about spending and borrowing. Their services lacked the test of profitability. Most were provided free at the point of use, so they had no price mechanism to tell them whether the public wanted more or less. Senior civil servants saw themselves as policy advisers not financial managers, and their job was to decide policy and persuade the Treasury to pay for it.

They did not want for success. Public expenditure increased by 3 per cent a year in real terms in the thirty-five years to 1998. There were wild swings around this mean both upwards (11 per cent was the high) and downwards (minus 3 per cent) but the overall trend was inexorable. In 1962 the government spent just over one third of the national income. By its post-war peak in 1982, public expenditure was getting on for half the national income. A

* The only other restraint was the Civil Service manpower targets. They were abolished in April 1988.

TABLE 9.2
Public Expenditure by Activity (£ billions)*

	Cost	% of total
Social Security	98.6	31.5
Health	42.6	13.6
Education	36.7	11.7
Debt Interest	23.8	7.6
Defence	21.1	6.8
Law and Order	17.0	5.5
Adjustments†	13.3	4.3
Personal Social Services	10.7	3.4
Other Environmental Services	9.7	3.1
Transport	9.1	2.9
Trade, Industry, Energy, Employment and Training	8.8	2.8
Central Administration	6.4	2.1
Agriculture, Fisheries and Food	5.2	1.7
Housing	3.5	1.1
International Development/Other International Services	3.4	1.1
Culture, Media and Sport	2.7	0.9
Total	312.6	100.0

Source: HM Treasury, Public Expenditure Statistical Analysis, 1997–8, Cm. 3801, Table 3.5.

* General government expenditure less privatisation receipts, National Lottery funded expenditure, and interest and dividend income.
† Including contribution to European Union budget.

mixture of economic growth and Treasury pressure has reduced the total to just under two fifths since then.

In his first year in office, Brown said he wanted to keep it there until the end of the present Parliament. But, after a 'comprehensive spending review', he decided he had another £100 billion to spend on the public services over the last three years of the Parliament. The public share of the national income will rise steadily beyond 40 per cent again to 2001 (more if the economy stops growing). Brown says he is shifting the balance of public expenditure from current spending (which merely keeps things going) to capital expenditure (which adds to national assets). Rather than allow public expenditure to be determined by an annual battle between spending ministers and the Treasury, he has also fixed departmental budgets for three years. Each now has a separate budget for capital and current spending, and extra money will go only to those which cut their costs or produce more services.

A shift from current to capital spending was certainly needed. A system which treated a £50 million investment in a motorway (which adds to economic growth) in exactly the same way as £50 million spent defending the pound against currency speculators (which does not) was deeply flawed. In a democratic political system, where the government is under constant pressure to increase its expenditure on all manner of interest groups, the failure to distinguish between current and capital expenditure encouraged governments to spend capital rather than cut current expenditure in sensitive areas such as social security or civil service salaries. Cutting capital spending on roads, for example, showed up in the national accounts as a cut in public expenditure but not as a capital cost in the shape of a deterioration in the value of the road network. It was always easier to cut the road-building programme than the salaries of Ministry of Transport officials.

Yet running assets down, as every car- and house-owner knows, is as sure a way of spending money as spending money. The effects can be seen everywhere – rundown schools and hospitals, crumbling roads, shabby social security offices. Nor did the effects stop there. The government accumulated a hoard of land and buildings (and works of art) which civil servants had no incentive to manage. If government bought a piece of land or a building, the whole purchase was written off at once. Any depreciation in value went unrecorded, making it impossible to say whether it should be refurbished or sold before it became worthless. Assets were simply hoarded – even unused land or unoccupied buildings were not put up for sale, so their market value was unknown. In most cases, departments did not have a record of what they owned. The Department of Output Statistics, in John Hadfield's novel *Love on a Branch Line*, which is allowed to continue in a splendid country house for years on end despite producing nothing, was parodic but true.

In November 1993 the chancellor of the Exchequer, Kenneth Clarke, announced that the government would be introducing 'resource-based accounting'. But another two years elapsed before reform began in earnest with the publication of the 1995 White Paper, *Better Accounting for the Taxpayers' Money*.[12] This technique will measure the capital and the current expenditure of the government for the first time; it becomes fully effective in the 1999–2000 financial year. Departments have spent the intervening years making lists of everything they own. The first National Asset Register itemising every piece of property the government owns – from roads and land and buildings, through intellectual property rights, to holdings of shares and bonds – was published in November 1997. Resource-based accounting is bringing commercial financial management to the heart of government for the first time. Its introduction was accompanied by new forms of control, consciously modelled on the practices of major PLCs. There is even talk of introducing to government a corporate governance régime of the kind the Stock Exchange now imposes on listed companies.[13]

The Rise of the Executive Agencies

This is not as preposterous as it sounds: most civil servants no longer work in bureaucracies along Whitehall or in the shabby provincial outposts of Whitehall departments. Three in four now work for the new breed of PLC look-alikes which have proliferated across Whitehall over the last ten years: the 142 Executive (or Next Steps) Agencies.* These mimic PLCs in every detail save shareholders. They have balance sheets and profit and loss accounts, boards of directors and chief executives, some of them appointed from business rather than the civil service. But every agency is still owned by the taxpayer and answerable to his representatives in Parliament through departmental ministers. 'The revolution achieved by Next Steps,' said David Clark, then chancellor of the Duchy of Lancaster, 'should be a managerial and not a constitutional one.'[14]

His comment echoes persistent accusations that ministers disown mistakes or embarrassing decisions made by chief executives of Next Steps Agencies. In 1995 the home secretary, Michael Howard, and the chief executive of HM Prison Service, Derek Lewis, argued publicly about who was responsible for a series of prison escapes. If escapes were a matter of policy, Howard was to blame; if they were an operational matter, Lewis was to blame. Lewis was sacrificed. He complained that he had 'responsibility without power'. Judge Stephen Tumim, the chief inspector of prisons, concurred. 'If you are dividing policy and operations,' he concluded, 'it means the Home Secretary is not responsible for anything at all.'[15]

Sir Robin Butler, the Cabinet secretary, was asked to pronounce. 'Agencies', he said, 'are not "hived off"'. Their chief executives are civil servants and the minister remains accountable to Parliament for everything they do, down to – to quote a phrase once used by Herbert Morrison – the last stamp licked on to an envelope . . . The question of who is to blame is often a very complicated one. I think we have been in danger over the last few days of criticising the agency structure in the civil service just because it does not

---

* Technically, there are only 138 Executive Agencies, but the Crown Prosecution Service, HM Customs and Excise, the Inland Revenue and the Serious Fraud Office all operate on Next Steps lines.

give an automatic answer in every case to the question: "who is to blame?"' In a modern, media-driven democracy, no question is more persistent or important, or harder to answer. In the days when the government made policy and civil servants carried it out, ministers took the blame. Today, when prisoners escape or the Child Support Agency fails, it is not the minister who resigns. A Next Steps Agency as Butler later observed, 'obscures and blunts the democratic accountability of ministers'.[16]

The original blueprint for the Executive Agencies, did not anticipate this difficulty. It supposed that the making of policy could be separated from its execution. This was the idea at the heart of *Improving Management in Government: The Next Steps*, a report by Robin Ibbs (a former ICI executive then heading the Efficiency Unit which Thatcher had set up when she took office in 1979). It led to the establishment of the first Executive Agencies in 1988. Ibbs's ideas did not seem revolutionary. Governments have always created agencies, authorities, commissions and corporations. Some were spun off from civil service departments because they required a particular expertise; others were created as freestanding bodies with the intention of distancing departmental ministers from their decisions. The Atomic Energy Authority, the Civil Aviation Authority, the Arts Council and the various research councils are all bodies of this kind. In the 1970s, the then powerful Department of Employment gave birth to three bodies – the Manpower Services Commission (MSC), the Health and Safety Executive (HSE) and the Arbitration, Conciliation and Advisory Service (ACAS) – which functioned as quasi-independent arms of the civil service. In addition to Executive Agencies, there are now over 1,000 quangos (quasi-autonomous non-governmental organisations) which have a variety of executive, advisory and judicial roles in the running of the country without being part of any civil service department or accountable to Parliament.*

Next Steps Agencies were meant to be different. They were to perform the core functions of government more efficiently without any diminution in their answerability to Parliament. Most have, and the gains are often striking. Coastguard, for example, has closed a quarter of its stations since becoming an agency. By replacing unionised officers with cheaper 'watch assistants', it cut its payroll by a seventh.[17] But the creation of Executive Agencies had larger

---

* Concern about quangos first surfaced in the late 1970s, when the Conservative Opposition portrayed them as a surreptitious extension of state control and an unhealthy source of government patronage. When Thatcher took office, Sir Leo Pliatzky got rid of 30 executive bodies (out of 489), 211 advisory bodies (out of 1,561) and a handful of tribunals. According to the Cabinet Office there were still 1,128 quangos in existence in 1997. They spent £22.4 billion a year; four fifths is met by the taxpayer. See Peter Hennessy, *Whitehall*, Fontana, 1990, p. 686 and Cabinet Office, *Public Bodies 1997*, HMSO p.(vi).

consequences: they raised searching questions about whether the government should be performing certain functions at all, and provided the financial information to answer them.

It did not take the government long to privatise some of the agencies; several of the earliest had operated as semi-commercial trading funds since the early 1970s.* These were natural candidates for sale to private buyers, and two were privatised by the Conservative government. The first was the Chessington Computer Centre, sold uncontroversially in 1998 to EDS, the US firm which runs the Inland Revenue computers. The privatisation of Her Majesty's Stationery Office (HMSO) was a different story.

The idea was unpopular with MPs on both sides of the House, who feared their free copies of Hansard and other government publications would be put at risk. Yet the case for privatisation was unanswerable: the organisation was badly overmanned. 'There were hundreds of people . . . who didn't seem to be doing very much, while the accountancy was all over the place,' according to one potential buyer[18]. 'When we announced redundancies,' said the new chief executive, 'we got 1,000 volunteers. That must say something about how a lot of people felt about the organisation and their contribution to it.'[19]

HMSO had relied for decades on its monopoly of government printing and publishing, and had failed to commercialise its output by selling official publications aggressively. Its management was inept. In 1996 it lost £3 million on sales to Uzbekistan because managers forgot to buy a letter of credit. In its first year in the private sector, HMSO lost over £10 million, and when it was eventually sold to a consortium of venture capitalists in September 1996, the price of £54 million was one third of what the government had originally hoped for.

Privatising agencies was bound to be difficult. Unlike nationalised industries, few are even half in the market economy. Almost all their work is on government contracts, and some activities – like the collection of tax – are too sensitive to privatise. But almost every agency makes as well as spends money. The government as a whole receives about £200 million a year from selling information. The Hydrographic Office collected £38 million from the sale of charts in 1996–7. The Driving and Vehicle Licensing Agency (DVLA) holds periodic auctions of personalised number plates, which are surprisingly lucrative: between 1989 and 1997 it raised £260 million at 41 auctions. The chemical and biological warfare plant at Porton Down (part of the Defence

---

* Trading funds were invented in the early 1970s. There were originally twelve which raised funds by selling goods and services in addition to their public expenditure allocation; used proper commercial accounting methods from the outset; and had the power to borrow. Some, like HM Land Registry, were fully self-financing and absorbed no public money.

TABLE 9.3
Privatised Executive Agencies

Agency	Date of Sale	Type of Sale	Name of Buyer	Price Agreed (£ million)
DVOIT	1993	Trade	EDS	5.5
National Engineering Laboratory	1995	Trade	Assessment Services Ltd	*1.95
Laboratory of the Government Chemist	1996	Share	LGC (Holdings) Limited	†0.36
Transport Research Laboratory	1996	MBO	Transport Research Foundation	3.1
Natural Resources Institute	1996	Transfer	Universities' Consortium	‡0.0
Chessington Computer Centre	1996	Trade	MEBO, Integris & Close Bros	§12.5
Occupational Health & Safety Agency	1996	Trade	BMI Health Services	0.35
HMSO	1996	Trade	Consortium led by Electra Fleming	54.0
Recruitment & Assessment Services	1996	Trade	Capita Group plc	7.25
Building Research Establishment	1997	MBO	MBO Team	¶1.7
PAYMASTER	1997	Share	EDS and Hogg Robinson PLC	22.81
ADAS‖	1997	MEBO	MEBO Team	23.5
DERA**	1997	Trade	Cinven	74.0

Source: Hansard, Written Answer, 23 July 1998.

* Price subject to adjustment.
† Baseline price subject to adjustments, payment of £1.96 million to LGC and a further possible payment of £0.3 million.
‡ The consortium consisted of the University of Greenwich, Edinburgh University, Imperial College and Wye College.
§ £1.25 million of price deferred until 31 December 1999.
¶ Price subject to adjustment.
‖ All consultancy, laboratory services and research and development work was privatised.
** Support Services Division privatised.

Evaluation and Research Agency) is opening a science park for commercial companies, in an effort to improve technology transfer to the private sector. The Historic Royal Palaces Agency, which manages Hampton Court and the Tower of London, has developed a sizeable corporate entertainment business.

But Executive Agencies have public duties as well as commercial prospects. In the first report published on this work, the National Audit Office pointed out that the Vehicle Inspectorate could not close under-used testing stations because policy demanded that owners of lorries have ready access to a site.[20] Ordnance Survey earns £50–60 million a year from the sale of maps, and faces commercial competitors ranging from Bartholomew's and the AA to companies providing satellite-based geographical positioning systems, but privatisation would be possible only if it was relieved of its statutory duty to draw maps. 'The government', explained the chief executive when its privatisation was first discussed, 'has to decide where commercial activities end and non-profitable exercises in the national interest begin.'

In the 1997 election, the Conservatives said they would privatise more Executive Agencies. The pledge was a measure of their limited progress. Plans to sell off the Insolvency Service were ditched after three private sector offers failed to convince ministers that they could offer better value; government-owned research laboratories were assessed for privatisation, but it was decided not to go ahead.[21] Had the Conservatives won the 1997 election, Companies House, HM Land Registry, Ordnance Survey, the Meteorological Office, the Valuation Office and DVLA would probably have found their way into the private sector. New Labour has yet to privatise an Agency, but their reluctance is not ideological. They agreed the sale of the Crown Agents, albeit to a charitable foundation. The obstacles are political. Defence ministers are keen to privatise the Defence Evaluation and Research Agency, on the grounds that the digital battlefield needs private sector expertise. But many Labour MPs are instinctively opposed. To mollify them, a defence minister has promised a solution 'somewhere in between' privatisation and public ownership. The true character of this 'third way' is already apparent at National Savings. Rather than asking private sector providers to increase its efficiency by installing better computers, New Labour will give the contract to the supplier who guarantees to preserve the most jobs.[22] It cannot afford to alienate its public sector clientele.

The Private Finance Initiative

Executive Agencies are not the prelude to the privatisation of government; they are part of a revolution in the idea of what government is for. They sharpen the distinction, which grew in the Conservative period, between government as policymaker, inspector and regulator, and government as purchaser or provider of goods and services. 'We are positioning ourselves', says the chief executive of the Highways Agency, 'away from being a road-builder to becoming a network manager and controller.'[23] His goal is to improve government cash flow by reducing costs and increasing the efficiency of asset usage.

This is what lies at the heart of every reform of the machinery at government in recent years: the drive to increase the flow of *cash* into Treasury coffers.

Where they cannot achieve it by increased efficiency, ministers are not above creative accounting. This is the chief purpose of the Private Finance Initiative (PFI), invented in November 1992 by Norman Lamont, then chancellor of the Exchequer. The aim was to increase capital investment by the government without having to raise taxes or borrow money. Private firms were invited to invest in projects (prisons, roads, railway lines and hospitals) which were once the sole preserve of the public sector.* In theory, this should enable the government to achieve political aims which are otherwise contradictory: lower public expenditure and better infrastructure.

Resolution of this contradiction is illusory. Contrary to political rhetoric, investment is a cost, not a benefit. By asking the private sector to raise the capital, the government forfeited its chief advantage: that it can always borrow more cheaply than anybody else. The purpose of the PFI is to transfer the risk of projects from the taxpayer to private financiers, but the greater the risk investors are asked to bear, the higher the premium they will demand for advancing funds. The cost of finance for PFI projects will always be higher than conventional government borrowing, and capital investments are not one-off events. People have to be hired to operate and maintain them, generating running costs which still have to be met by the taxpayer. These, of course, will not be apparent until the project is finished, and it is this which gives PFI projects a dreamlike quality for politicians. They can spend money on the infrastructure and cut public expenditure and taxation at the same time, because neither the higher cost of capital nor the running costs will be apparent until after the next election.

There is, however, a respectable argument for the PFI. Governments are not good at project management: cost overruns on public sector construction contracts have *averaged* 24 per cent, with major disasters costing even more. But private contractors will be no better unless they are bearing the full risk of a project. So far, they prefer to let the government take most of it. 'Shadow' toll roads have proved more expensive than building conventional roads, because the private contractors refused to bear the risk that traffic would increase faster than anticipated.[24] The taxpayer is also underwriting the risks associated with refurbishment of the London Underground; if ticket sales do not cover the costs of contracts, the government will meet any shortfall.

The contractors building the new prisons and hospitals which dominate

---

* PFI is being used extensively in the hospital-building programme. In November 1995 Stephen Dorrell, secretary of state for Health, promised one PFI hospital a month. The total value of PFI hospital-building contracts is £2.3 billion, with a priority list of fifteen sites worth £1.43 billion.

the PFI know the government will not allow them to collapse. When the private financing of the Channel Tunnel link collapsed, John Prescott, secretary of state for Environment, Transport and the Regions, provided a government guarantee for £3.8 billion of private funds. The link (a project of dubious value, which came close to collapse despite existing government guarantees of £1.5 billion) can scarcely be described as a private financing. Nor can any other. There is not a single PFI project which the government would allow to collapse. But private–public partnerships to build hospitals and railways play well in the newspapers, create jobs and sound sensible. They also improve immediate government cash flow, which is far enough ahead for most politicians.

Public and Private Prisons

One of the main beneficiaries of the PFI is the prison service. By the time the Conservatives left office in 1997, the private sector was engaged in the design, construction and management of six new prisons, and the government was about to commission twelve more. Jack Straw, the New Labour home secretary who in Opposition denounced privately managed prisons as 'morally repugnant', has moved from acceptance ('an urgent operational necessity') to enthusiasm. He inherited four privately built and managed prisons from the Conservatives (Blakenhurst, Bridgend, Fazakerley and the Wolds) and has approved two more (Agecroft in Salford and Pucklechurch near Bristol).[25] HM Prison Service has planning applications in hand for new privately financed prisons at Ashford in Middlesex, Maghull, Peterborough and Winnick.

Since the first privately managed prison opened in April 1992 (the Wolds on Humberside) under the management of Group 4 Security, the private sector has proved that it can build and run prisons more economically than the public alternative.[26] The running costs of privately managed prisons are 11 to 17 per cent cheaper, with no diminution in the quality of service. Richard Tilt, chief executive of HM Prison Service, is pleased the competition is driving up standards in the publicly managed prisons as well. They certainly needed to improve. Until recently, most prisons were run by the staff rather than the management. A 1986 government report reckoned that the restrictive practices of the Prison Officers Association (POA) meant the prison service squandered £1 in every £5. Lord Woolf, investigating the prison riots at Strangeways in April 1990, found the POA engaged in no less than twenty-four local disputes.

The government introduced reforms. Prison governors were given greater operational freedom, and flexible working practices were imposed on the POA. Between 1993 and 1995 the prison service was split between three separate Executive Agencies – HM Prison Service, the Scottish Prison Service and the Northern Ireland Prison Service – north and south of the border and in Northern Ireland. Derek Lewis, formerly chief executive of the Granada TV and leisure group, was hired to run the service in England and Wales, and immediately set about devolving responsibility to individual prisons and setting financial and other performance targets. Education, catering, health care and building work in prisons were all put out to tender.

Private competition to manage prisons was introduced gradually. Management of the illegal immigrant detention and deportation centre at Harmondsworth was handed over to a private company in the mid-1980s.[27] In 1990, private companies were allowed to tender for prison escort work, and the management of the new remand centre then being built. The government did not dare to expose established prisons or existing remand centres to competitive tendering, for fear of confrontation with the POA. This was why, when the Wolds opened in 1992, it was allowed to hold remand prisoners only. Group 4 began escorting prisoners to court for the first time in the east Midlands and Humberside a year later, but the POA was quick to tell the newspapers about 'customers' who had escaped from their care. In fact, the vast majority of escaped prisoners had still been in the custody of its own members.

The grip of the POA was not challenged until the government invited six private firms to tender for the management contract at the refurbished Strangeways Prison in Manchester, which was seriously damaged in the 1990 riot. It went eventually to the incumbent management and staff, but they had to make significant concessions on staff numbers and working practices. The winning bid was 20 per cent below the average cost of a publicly managed prison. The power of the POA was broken: the threat of privatisation was almost as effective as the reality.

It needed to be broken. Incarceration is now a £1.8 billion a year business, with 25,000 staff responsible for 66,000 inmates at 165 separate prisons. As crime has increased, and sentences have lengthened, the prison population has soared. If it continues to rise at the present rate, it will be over 90,000 by 2005, which will require 24 new gaols at a cost of £2 billion and another £300 million a year to run them. Yet the prison service has just completed the biggest prison-building programme since the Victorian era. At the time the Conservatives left office, they had constructed 22 new prisons and 6 more were being built, between them providing an extra 15,500 places. It was not cheap. The first 22 prisons, built between 1980 and 1994, cost over £1 billion. Between 1979 and 1997 expenditure on the prison service doubled in real terms to over £1.5 billion, and the courts spend another £500 million. Yet overcrowding is so great that the 'hulks' have made a return.*

At the 1993 Conservative Party Conference the home secretary, Michael Howard, made his famous claim that 'prison works.' It is difficult to share his enthusiasm. It costs more than £25,000 to keep somebody in prison for a year, and the money is almost entirely wasted. Despite the abolition of 'slopping out', more family visits, as well as less time in cells, increased work and study periods, an end to the censorship of letters, the installation of telephones, and a variety of educational and re-employment courses, prison is still, in the words of a 1990 White Paper, 'an expensive way of making bad people worse.' Incarceration is obviously awful (riots are commonplace and one prisoner a week commits suicide), but it still fails to deter. More than 50 percent of ex-prisoners re-offend within two years of release. Despite more prisons, more prisoners and longer sentences, notifiable offences doubled between 1979 and 1996. The worst crimes, such as grievous bodily harm and armed robbery, increased most.

Crime is an intractable problem, whose origins lie in a complex amalgam of social, cultural and economic causes. It would take decades to reconquer it in the way the Victorians did, even if the moral climate were kindly disposed to self-restraint.[28] No one wants to return to the ferocious punishments and public executions used to deal with criminals through most of history, but nobody any longer shares the Victorian belief that prison can make bad people better. Much of the helplessness about crime stems from this realisation: prison is useless, but there is no alternative. The taxpayer will have to go on paying for crime.

A New Conception of the State

Law and order, like defence, is one of the traditional functions of the state. Governments, particularly of the twentieth century, have added many more, but a change is taking place in the nature – if not the scope – of the modern state. John Major said it was 'right to think of government as an enabler'.[29] The architects of New Labour, anxious to part company with their nationalis-ing-cum-centralising past, are comfortable with this new definition of the state, even if their backbenchers are not. Gordon Brown talks easily of govern-

---

* In the eighteenth century, convicted felons were kept in privately-owned 'hulks', old ships moored along the Thames and elsewhere. 480 low-risk prisoners are now incarcerated in HMP *Weare*, which floats in Portland Harbour. See Frank McLynn, *Crime and Punishment in Eighteenth Century England,* Oxford University Press, 1991, p. 292.

ment as 'enabling and empowering, not centralising and controlling'. Paddy Ashdown also speaks approvingly of a state which 'commissions more but does less'.[30] But there is one aspect of the Conservative conception which centre-left parties, with their large number of supporters in the public sector, will never find congenial: market mimicry in the public services.

To break away from the uncosted, bureaucratic and producer-led approach to government which had prevailed since the war, the Conservatives tried to create pseudo-markets where they could not create real ones through privatisation. These so-called 'internal markets' worked by splitting the role of government-as-purchaser from the role of government-as-provider. In theory, if government-as-purchaser could find a supplier who was cheaper or better than government-as-provider, it would buy goods and services from the supplier.

The policy began modestly enough, with the issue of instructions to local authorities and NHS hospitals in the early 1980s to submit routine work such as dustbin collection, laundry and catering to competitive tender. In 1988 legislation made it compulsory for local councils to submit refuse collection, street-cleaning, grounds and vehicle maintenance, and school catering to private tenders.[31] The 1991 White Paper, *Competing for Quality*, sought to extend contracting out to central government. The Citizen's Charter, first published in July, was part of the same effort. It encouraged those services which remained in the public sector to improve their performance, by setting targets for service to the public and awarding Charter Marks to those Executive Agencies which achieved them. In theory, the agencies were contracted by the government to provide services in much the same way as private companies.

The Businesslike State in Practice: NHS Reforms

The National Health Service (NHS) was the laboratory for the most daring experiment in purchaser–provider splits. The creation of an 'internal market' was the centrepiece of the most far-reaching reform of the health service since its establishment in 1948. For decades, the divine status of the NHS in collectivist mythology had rendered it untouchable, even by a Labour government. Yet the NHS as originally conceived had two great flaws, each of which got progressively worse as the service aged and expanded.

The first was the persistent underestimation of its cost. In 1948 the NHS was expected to cost £134 million a year. Within three years of its foundation, a Labour government introduced prescription charges to contain its spiralling budget. By its fiftieth anniversary the NHS was costing £43 billion: fifteen times as much in real terms as at its inception. Its founders had assumed that medical knowledge would eradicate diseases and a healthier and better-fed population would make fewer claims on medical services. In practice, medical progress increased rather than reduced the costs of the NHS. Conditions which were once untreatable – ulcers, some cancers and heart and liver failure – can now be cured but only at formidable expense. The population is also ageing, and the elderly are susceptible to injury and disease.

The second flaw in the initial structure of the NHS was the impossibility of managing an organisation which employs more than a million people. The Health Service was from the outset the most centralised and politicised of all the public corporations created by twentieth century governments. 'When a bed pan is dropped on a hospital floor,' argued the minister who designed it, Aneurin Bevan, 'its noise should resound in the Palace of Westminster.' He wanted those who ran it to be 'the agents of my department'. For decades, the pursuit of a universal standard of health care extinguished any spark of managerial innovation in a torrent of circulars and layers of bureaucracy.

In practice, the NHS was unmanaged. The main beneficiaries were doctors. For decades, consultants ran the hospitals with no regard for the costs of treatment and great regard to their own empires. Nobody making a clinical decision in the NHS had any idea what it might cost. General practitioners (GPs) ran their practices with no incentive save the inflation of the patient list (they collected a cash bonus based on the number of patients). What financial incentives there were operated perversely. Unspent portions of a budget could not be carried forward, leading to wasteful spending blitzes at the end of every financial year on unwanted bedpans and sheets. A hospital which exhausted its budget for the year could close down in June, while an inefficient hospital doing half as many patients would plough on until December.

Machines were bought rather than leased, loading the NHS with capital costs it had no need to bear. NHS purchasing – especially of drugs and equipment but also of basic items like laundry and food – was decentralised to the point where the government's buying power was useless in securing better prices. In 1985 the NHS owned 450 storage depots, chiefly to accommodate the idiosyncrasies of particular clinicians. The burden of public expenditure rose steadily, as doctors embarrassed successive governments into ever-larger infusions of money under the threat of ward closures, lengthening waiting lists and dead babies.

By the time Norman Fowler became secretary of state for Health and Social Security in 1981, the problem he confronted was depressingly familiar: how to cut the cost of the NHS without causing the government fatal political embarrassment. He decided to make the same amount of money go further.[32]

Roy Griffiths, chief executive of J. Sainsbury, was invited to advise on how management could be improved, and found there was no management. 'If Florence Nightingale were carrying her lamp through the corridors of the NHS today,' he concluded, 'she would almost certainly be searching for the people in charge.'[33]

In retrospect, the Griffiths Report marked the beginning of the Cult of Managerialism in the NHS which the Labour Party was able to exploit so successfully in opposition. It led to the appointment in 1984 of the first non-medical chief executives to run regional and district health authorities. Armed with budgets from the Department of Health, their brief was to decide priorities and spend money on them, rather than allow doctors and nurses to drain the budget through a mixture of pay claims, careless clinical decision making and political infighting. In a highly politicised organisation, this was a vain hope. With or without chief executives, spending priorities were determined primarily by political sensitivities: the length of waiting lists, lobbying for cervical smears or breast screening, campaigns against local hospital closures, and periodic national health scares such as the AIDS panic of the 1980s or the contaminated blood and BSE-cum-CJD cases of the 1990s. Far from halting the rise in expenditure on health, the Griffiths Report was followed by further increases in real terms. The Conservatives raised expenditure every year; between 1979 and 1997, it increased by 75 per cent in real terms. But it soon became obvious that the reforms had changed nothing. After the 1987 election, in which the one bright moment for the Labour Party was a long-running tabloid story about a boy who had waited over a year for a life-saving heart operation, Thatcher decided that she would have to re-visit the question of how to run the NHS.

The internal market, invented by an American consultant in 1985, became the favoured option at an early stage in her deliberations.[34] In its worked-out form (unveiled in the soon-to-be-notorious White Paper of 1989, *Working for Patients*), a new type of fundholding GP would become the purchaser of acute medical services from a new type of self-governing hospital. What followed was a classic demonstration of Hutber's Law.[35] Self-governing hospital trusts gained well-paid chief executives with plush offices, company cars and boards of directors, but their budgets were still set by the secretary of state, and they had virtually no discretion over spending. NHS trusts were not allowed to charge patients for services, or to borrow to build facilities or buy equipment. They were obliged to provide certain services (accident and emergency), but were powerless to vary their biggest cost (salaries of doctors and nurses). Even their directors were appointed by the secretary of state. Deprived of real power, NHS Trust Hospital chief executives set about turning hundreds of clinical employees into 'managers', and subjecting every aspect of clinical activity to 'medical audit'. This turned doctors and nurses into resentful paper-shufflers, ready to furnish newspapers with stories of how the chief executive had recarpeted his office while grannies and children died on trolleys in the corridors.

GPs also failed to respond as expected. Though many were surprised to find themselves more powerful and better off as a result of becoming fundholders, ideological opposition to fundholding was strong. By the time the Conservatives left office, only half the population was served by a fundholding GP.* Health authorities remained the major buyers of hospital services. Even where GPs did become fundholders, they did not force NHS and private hospitals to compete for their patients; they maintained the comfortable relationships they enjoyed with local hospital consultants. They did not have the time or appetite for shopping around on behalf of their patients, few of whom could readily travel in pursuit of quicker surgery or better treatment. Even if fundholders had wanted to make a proper market, they lacked knowledge. There was no list of prices where they could find the cheapest or fastest supplier of hernia or hip operations. They could not tell whether a surgeon with time to spare at the other end of the country was an unrecognised genius or a bungling incompetent whose limitations were reflected in a lack of referrals.

One reason why reform of the NHS is ineffective is that doctors and bureaucrats can always rely on the next government to put it into reverse. One of the first decisions taken by New Labour was the abolition of the 'internal market' in the NHS. Fundholding by general practitioners was ended; money and powers were restored to the local health authorities. The NHS Trust Hospitals continue, but their boards are now filled with Labour rather than Conservative supporters. To emphasise the restoration of the centralised monolith, the new secretary of state, Frank Dobson, ordered a 're-branding' of the NHS. A new 'logo' is on all NHS stationery, to emphasise that tinkling bedpans can still be heard at the Ministry of Health.

Expenditure continues to climb. Dobson promised 'a lot more money' for the NHS, and the prime minister committed the government to 'sustainable year-on-year increases for the foreseeable future'. In the summer of 1998 the chancellor duly redeemed these promises, with annual increases of 4.7 per cent a year for three years, amounting to £21 billion by 2001. A week later the National Audit Office reported that one in two health authorities and one in eight NHS Trusts were in financial difficulties. 'We must be realistic about the impact of the new money . . .' said the chief executive of the NHS Confederation. 'It will take hundreds of millions of pounds to bring the budgets of health authorities and NHS trusts into line.'[36]

---

* By April 1997 there were 15,000 fundholders, serving 58 per cent of the population of England.

The Non-Management of the NHS Estate

Among the pledges made by Blair was the establishment of a special fund to refurbish hospitals and surgeries. More than any other government-owned organisation, the NHS bears witness to decades of under-investment. At its foundation, it inherited a large estate. In England and Wales alone, it acquired 1,771 hospitals belonging to local authorities, and another 1,334 from voluntary institutions. Political pressure to spend money on patients rather than plant meant that no government invested in assets, managed them imaginatively, or sold unwanted ones to raise funds for modern facilities. By the beginning of the 1990s, according to the Audit Commission, two in five NHS buildings were dilapidated. Up to £2 billion was needed to raise every hospital to an acceptable standard.

Most of the buildings were embarrassingly old. In the 1970s three in four NHS beds were in hospitals built before the First World War, and the average age of the existing stock was 70 years. The NHS entered the 1990s with 770 listed buildings on its books (11 listed Grade I) and over 150 historic workhouses, chapels and churches. It was, to adapt a phrase coined by Virginia Bottomley at the time, a reluctant arm of the Heritage Industry.[37] As the NHS began to dispose of unwanted Victorian hospitals and lunatic asylums, it became a target of the Heritage Industry. In 1995 SAVE Britain's Heritage warned that 121 large mental hospitals – including the splendid Friern Barnet Hospital, opened by Prince Albert in 1849 – were at risk of demolition, dilapidation or unsympathetic development.

The NHS owns buildings and equipment worth £29 billion. In its last ten years in office, the Conservative government approved seven hundred and fifty NHS capital projects of £1 million or more, and hundreds of smaller ones. Yet it was not until 1991 that the government began to manage these assets properly. An Executive Agency, NHS Estates, was established in April that year. At the time nobody knew what property the NHS owned, what it was worth, or what it cost to run. Government accounting conventions made it always cheaper to ask the Treasury for a new building or machine rather than sell or improve an old one (maintenance costs were chargeable while depreciation was not).[38]

The estate had not responded adequately to changes in clinical practice, such as day surgery and community care and the growing reluctance of doctors and nurses to live on-site. Over one third of the NHS estate in Scotland was not needed for operational purposes.[39] In England and Wales, the NHS owned 1,800 empty houses and flats, and had 11,400 vacancies in staff hostels.[40] After a cursory survey, NHS Estates concluded that 17,000 acres and 5 million square feet could be lost without losing operational effectiveness. The Audit Commission reckoned better management of property alone could release up to £400 million a year for clinical use.[41] Inside hospitals, new departments and equipment were put where there was space, rather than where they were needed, leading to predictable inefficiencies; one study found that junior doctors walked six or seven miles a shift, wasting three hours of productive time between departments. Porters walked twenty miles a day, keeping expensive consultants waiting. Nobody had thought about ease of maintenance when designing buildings or buying machines.

Commonsensical thinking was suppressed. The Audit Commission solved a bed shortage at one hospital by narrowing the space between existing beds by two inches.[42] In-house maintenance teams were large, but demoralised. In 1994 the Audit Commission said they routinely wasted nearly two fifths of the working day, and cost £180 million a year in absenteeism.[43] Hospitals fell short of statutory standards in fire precautions, waste incineration, the treatment of hazardous substances, food hygiene, and prevention of dangerous infections such as Legionnaire's Disease. But Crown immunity from prosecution (now lifted) meant hospitals could ignore the rules.

Corruption and Incompetence: the Property Services Agency

The NHS was not alone in its indifference to the cost of capital. Until 1994 the government did not bother to survey or value its buildings. It was not until 1990 that a sub-office of the Department of the Environment began to charge other departments and Executive Agencies a notional rent for the space they occupied. At the time, the government owned over 5,000 buildings (covering over 118 million square feet), half of them freehold.[44] Most were in appalling condition. In the Treasury, the basement flooded regularly, and the wiring caused a serious fire in 1996. Several departments were paid-up members of the Heritage Industry, with historical buildings which yielded nothing in rent and cost taxpayers a fortune to maintain. When Michael Portillo, then secretary of state for Defence, tried to sell or rent two unoccupied buildings (the Royal Naval College and Admiralty Arch) the idea was greeted with astonishment.* No one mentioned that the £1 million a year cost of three weekend retreats for ministerial Fat Cats – Chequers, Chevening and Dorneywood – could be unjustifiable.

---

* The Royal Naval College was eventually leased to the University of Greenwich. Admiralty Arch found temporary use as a shelter for the homeless.

One tenth of the Civil Estate was unoccupied, though the taxpayer was paying rent. When John Redwood bid for the leadership of the Conservative Party in 1995, nobody believed him when he said that the government owned enough unoccupied property to finance a programme of populist tax cuts. The civil service had, in fact, shrunk from 730,000 employees in 1979 to 596,000 in 1996 without shedding any office space, and the taxpayer was paying £120 million in rents for unoccupied government buildings. The leases were so unfavourable that it would have cost even more (£500 million) to buy them out. When it took office, New Labour decided to pay. It put 384 freehold and leasehold buildings with 8.9 million square feet of un-wanted space up for sale, at a cost of half a billion pounds in payments to landlords. 'This outcome,' reflected the National Audit Office, 'is a fitting commentary on the quality of the deals the government has struck in previous years.'[45]

Most of 'the deals' were struck by an organisation which was troubled by irregularities as well as by incompetence. Until 1988 the Civil Estate was run by the Property Services Agency (PSA), a semi-independent arm of the Department of the Environment set up by the Heath administration in 1972 to look after government property.* For the next twenty years the PSA mon-opolised the design, construction, management, maintenance, fitting and furnishing of all buildings for all government departments and public bodies. It was easily the biggest property business in the country. At the peak of its powers in the mid-1970s it commanded an empire of nearly 45,000 civil servants, a civil estate of 73 million square feet, a defence estate of 700,000 acres, and an annual budget of billions of pounds. Its responsibilities included state-owned museums and galleries such as the British Museum, the V&A, the National Gallery and the Imperial War Museum. It built sorting offices and telephone exchanges for the Post Office; supervised the building and management of embassies abroad; managed specialist facilities such as the National Physical Laboratory; and even ran the property side of the Alder-maston Atomic Weapons Establishment.

There was virtually no area of government policy – from Trident submarine bases to Kew Gardens – in which the PSA was not involved. Controlling this vast property empire demanded a preternatural degree of leadership and self-denial on the part of the officials who ran it. They did not have it. In

---

* The PSA descended directly from the Office of Works, founded in 1940 to cover the country with ammunition, tank and vehicle factories, power stations, pipelines, stores, hospitals, prisoner of war camps and other public works deemed essential to prosecution of the war. In due course it became the Ministry of Public Building and Works. Its activities were transferred to the new Property Services Agency when the Ministry was subsumed in the Department of the Environment in 1972.

1978 Leslie Chapman published *Your Disobedient Servant*, an account of his thwarted efforts to improve management of the PSA. The book (and its author) had a profound effect on Thatcher, then still in Opposition, and helped to shape her plans for reforming the Civil Service. By the end of the 1970s, it was a byword for runaway costs, labyrinthine bureaucracy and outright corruption. In 1986, a number of civil servants from the PSA and some of the building contractors they had used were sent for trial. Several were later convicted of corruption.[46]

The incompetence of PSA officials was almost as shocking: debts were uncollected; buildings were empty or dilapidated; the taxpayer was overpaying for office space. Its preference for expensive leaseholds over cheaper freeholds reflected the short-term thinking imposed by cash-based accounting.* But Thatcher had read and heard enough. In 1983 departments were allowed to take responsibility for minor property maintenance, and in 1988 were given full responsibility for their needs. PSA Supplies, which had monopolised the purchase of furniture and fittings for government offices, was re-launched as Crown Suppliers, but failed to survive without its monopoly.[47] The building and project management divisions of the PSA continued to get the bulk of public building contracts until they were broken up and privatised in the early 1990s. They had become a liability, and the government had eventually to pay buyers to take them on.[48]

The Great British Library Disaster

The most important of the project management contracts the PSA initially retained was the new British Library. When Colin St John Wilson was first invited to design it in 1962, he was told 'this may take some time'.[49] In June 1998 it was opened by the Queen, who joked that the invitation had sat in her in-tray longer than anticipated. After thirty-six years, only three of the eleven reading rooms were open, and six million books had yet to be transferred from the old building in Bloomsbury. A project which began as the biggest public works contract of the twentieth century ended as as the greatest public sector construction disaster of all time. The new British Library is the most expensive public building ever erected in Britain.

In the pre-digital sixties and seventies, the need for a new building to

---

* Despite extensive evidence that freehold office space is cheaper in the long run, the Government consistently failed in the 1980s to add to its freehold estate. In 1986 the PSA compared the cost of buying the freeholds of 120 government offices with the cost of rents. Over a 60-year period, rents exceeded the cost of purchase by £227 million. In London, less than a third of the properties are owned freehold. See NAO, *Property Services Agency*, pp. 23–4.

accommodate the national library was incontrovertible. The British Library had run out of space in Bloomsbury, and books were scattered across twenty depositories in various parts of London (including a disused Tube tunnel at Belsize Park) and a warehouse in Yorkshire. A new library would reunite the collections. But by the time it was complete, advances in computer technology meant that books could be distributed electronically, with no need for readers to sit and wait for them to be physically located and delivered.

The long delay was not entirely the fault of the PSA. It purchased a 12.5 acre site at St Pancras in 1976, and approved work on the first phase in 1978. This was meant to be finished by 1982, at a cost of £116 million. But the project was axed in the public expenditure squeeze which followed the 1979 election, and work did not begin in earnest until July 1984. The PSA did, however, bungle the management of the project, and failed to contain its costs. The Public Accounts Committee blamed 'serious management weaknesses' for the débâcle. The PSA failed to fix the price at the outset, and appointed a project manager who did not have control of the sub-contractors. The decision to build in phases wasted money on walls and entrances which had to be demolished.

As the costs mounted, the Treasury decided to cut the size of the library in half, so contractors refused to agree fixed price contracts with penalty clauses (because they did not know which parts were going to be built next). If newspaper accounts of the progress of the project are to be believed, the rising costs led to constant interference in its details, creating further problems and delays. It was reported that motorised shelving inadvertently threw books on the floor; supporting structures had to be protected against rust; electrical wiring required additional insulation; the air-conditioning and the sprinklers had to be adjusted and the ceilings raised. By the time the shrunken project was finished, twenty years behind schedule, it had cost £520 million.

It was lucky to be built at all. Total abandonment was twice considered. Writers and other users griped that it lacked the ambience of the round Reading Room. The design, chosen by the PSA at the fag-end of the modernist era, was described by a Commons Select Committee as 'an edifice that resembles a Babylonian ziggurat seen through a funfair distorting mirror'. The Prince of Wales denounced the new reading room as 'an assembly hall of an academy for secret police' and called the entire conception a 'dim collection of sheds groping for some symbolic significance'. Gerald Kaufman, chairman of the Commons Select Committee on Culture, Media and Sport, said the edifice was 'as glamorous as a public lavatory'.

The Ministry of Defence Estate

Much the same could be said of the new headquarters of the secret intelligence service (MI6) at Vauxhall Cross. Its cost of £230 million, coupled with the £245 million the government spent on the new London headquarters of MI5, means the taxpayer has spent almost as much on new housing for spies as on new accommodation for books. It is conventional to treat spies generously, on the grounds that they cannot lobby for extra resources in the usual way. But a taste for extravagance is assisted by the fact that MI5 (the domestic security service), MI6 (the secret intelligence service) and GCHQ (the monitoring complex at Cheltenham) do not have to justify their budgets in public. 'The security services, their establishments and their hardware, were one of the very few areas of public life virtually untouched by the rigours of the Thatcher era,' Nigel Lawson recalls. 'Most Prime Ministers have a soft spot for the security services, for which they have a special responsibility. But Margaret, an avid reader of the works of Frederick Forsyth, was positively besotted by them.'[50]

The New Labour government, despite its traditional hostility to a secret state which investigated many of its members, has found them similarly alluring. In October 1997 the Treasury announced that the secret services would be a special target of its comprehensive spending review. There were suggestions that the three services would be merged. But after the review was complete, the spooks had not merely blunted the threat, they had secured a small increase in their spending limit. The combined budgets of MI5, MI6 and GCHQ will rise from £743 million in 1999–2000 to £747 million the following year. They apparently convinced ministers that, although the Cold War was over, they had much to contribute to wars against terrorism, drugs, and the proliferation of dangerous weapons.

New Labour has proved equally timid over the defence budget. Mindful of the part its anti-American and non-nuclear defence policies played in the electoral defeats of the 1980s, the defence secretary, George Robertson, agreed to trim a mere £900 million off the defence budget for the last three years of the present Parliament. The chief threat has vanished, but the military chiefs have persuaded ministers that skills honed in the Cold War can be applied to policing the world. The British armed forces will now prepare to intervene further afield, and to that end the Royal Navy will get two expensive new aircraft carriers to carry a 'rapid reaction force' to faraway countries like Kuwait, Bosnia and anywhere else where states are collapsing or state-sponsored terrorism is thriving.

It is true that the armed forces have suffered genuine cuts in manpower and equipment since 1990, but these left the landed estate of the Cold War years strangely untouched. The Ministry of Defence sold three times as much property in the 1980s as it has since 1990. It owns one of the largest landed estates in Britain, consisting of 542,880 acres of freehold land, leasehold interests in another 45,690 acres, and the right to use a further 308,000 acres. This is an area equivalent to the whole of Northamptonshire. The majority is open country, used for infantry, armoured and artillery training, and these broad acres have not shrunk. Even the built estate – 48,000 buildings at 2,600 sites covering 198,900 acres – has shrunk by a mere 5 per cent since the end of the Cold War. Dozens of airfields, stores buildings, offices, supply depots, research laboratories, workshops and houses (nine tenths of them owned freehold) are now unoccupied. The Defence Estate is valued, even for accounting purposes, at £10 billion.[51]

Yet a strategy for managing the estate was not agreed until 1996. Another year elapsed before the Defence Estate Organisation, the Executive Agency which manages the assets, commissioned a survey and valuation. So far, the ministry has made no attempt to marry its shape and structure to the new military strategy. Two in three of the properties it owns are less than three acres in size, reflecting the recruiting priorities of years past, and inhibiting potential to concentrate at fewer and larger sites.[52] Even now, nobody at the ministry knows the optimum size and shape of the Estate, how much is used and when, or how much it costs to use. A computerised database of all properties was scheduled for completion at the end of 1998.

TABLE 9.4
Cuts in Defence Expenditure

	1980	1990	1997
RAF squadrons	15	11	6
RAF aircraft	1,320	898	572
RAF airfields	–	54	30
Defence personnel	469,000	351,000	271,00
Main battle tanks	640	699	388
Ships & submarines	242	235	153
Battalions & regiments	127	127	94
Net defence spending*	£27,083m	£28,645m	£21,183m
Built estate (acres)	242,904	209,545	198,920

Source: NAO, *Ministry of Defence: Identifying and Selling Surplus Property*, HC776, Session 1997–8, June 1998, p. 19.

* 1996–7 prices, excluding pensions.

It will take another decade to establish the extent of contamination of land by military use, which will have a significant impact on market values and sale costs. The Rosyth naval base, for example, was expected to fetch £9.5 million until it was discovered that the site was contaminated and lacked an independent supply of power. It was sold for £1 million. The few sales that have occurred have taken years to complete, with properties coming on and off market as officials dither or buyers fail to find the sum agreed. The delays add to sale costs, though nobody can say how much.

The prize transaction was the sale of four fifths of the married quarters' estate in 1996 for £1.7 billion. It left the taxpayer with the freeholds, an annual rent bill of over £100 million, and full responsibility for maintenance and allocation.[53] The purchasing consortium refused to buy any houses which could not be separated satisfactorily from the surrounding residential area, insisted the ministry invest £100 million in upgrading the rest, and disdained responsibility for building new houses. The NAO reckoned the sale proceeds were around £39 million below the value of retaining ownership. Earlier the Ministry of Defence squandered £7.6 million on an abortive plan to sell the estate to a housing trust.[54]

In 1987, two years before the Berlin Wall came down, the Public Accounts Committee complained that the Ministry of Defence had more training areas than it needed. They reiterated the complaint, with even more justification, in 1989. In the previous five years, the amount of training land at the disposal of the ministry had actually increased by over 15,000 acres, as the army continued to overestimate its needs.[55] Eight years later, the estate has not diminished. The armed forces have access to nearly 900,000 acres of the United Kingdom. There is not a single county in England, Scotland, Wales and Northern Ireland where the ministry does not own some land, and army commanders still claim it is not enough. In 1997 they asked for another 100,000 acres, the end of the Cold War having deprived them of some training areas in Germany.

Certainly the armed forces need large spaces where they can fire missiles, shells and bullets, fly aeroplanes, and drive tracked vehicles around without killing civilians. War and preparation for war have always obliged the state to aggrandise land and impinge on the natural landscape in this way. Defensive earthworks such as Offa's Dyke and Wansdyke – or, even earlier, Hadrian's Wall – are still in evidence. At the height of the Napoleonic invasion scare in 1803, the south-east coast of England was decorated with a string of forty-foot Martello towers. Another scare in 1859 occasioned Palmerston's Follies, the ring of forts surrounding Portsmouth and Plymouth.

But the Ministry of Defence estate today is largely the creation of a Cold War which ended ten years ago. Traditionally, Britain relied on naval power

TABLE 9.5
Uses of Ministry of Defence Land

	Acreage	*% of whole*
Airfields	66,718	7.4
Naval bases	3,212	0.4
Training areas and ranges	686,458	76.6
Barracks and camps	26,687	2.9
Storage and supply depots	26,934	3.0
Research establishments	54,363	6.2
Telecommunications establishments	17,742	1.9
Miscellaneous	14,597	1.6
Total	896,711	100.0

Source: Defence Estate Organisation, 1998.

rather than a standing army; the army did not acquire its first training areas, at Chobham and Aldershot, until the 1850s. Salisbury Plain was commandeered in the late 1890s. The other large training area at Otterburn in Northumberland – recently upgraded at a cost of £40 million (60 per cent over budget) after a lengthy public inquiry – was acquired in 1911.[56] Land was not requisitioned for military purposes until the First World War.[57]

It is the aircraft, tanks and long-range artillery of the twentieth century which necessitated the creation of large landed estate. During the Second World War the country became an armed camp, with the military controlling one acre in five. The Cold War was less greedy, but large open spaces were still needed to train infantry for tank battles. It also saw the establishment of American bases in Britain. The United States Air Force arrived at the time of the Berlin emergency, in July 1948. It was given the use of four airfields, after no more than a brief exchange of diplomatic letters, to enable B29s to drop atom bombs on Moscow.[58] They stayed nearly 50 years, their bases remaining the property of the Ministry of Defence until the Americans returned them to British control in the 1990s.

Beneath the shadow of nuclear Armageddon, the ministry had little cause to explain itself to the public. Large weapons establishments, such as Porton Down in Wiltshire, were hidden from public view.* They cannot now escape

* Gruinard Island in Wester Ross, contaminated with anthrax, was once a standing rebuke to the British military–industrial complex. It is now clear of contamination and has been returned to its former owner, who uses it to graze sheep.

the public gaze so easily: ramblers want access to their land, especially in the National Parks; archaeologists want the army to stop shelling neolithic sites; naturalists want to protect the landscape and its flora and fauna from unsightly buildings, flying projectiles and tank tracks; and the guardians of the national heritage want the taxpayer to preserve in aspic Georgian and Victorian military buildings.

The Ministry of Defence has abandoned its powers of compulsory acquisition, and now goes through the normal planning procedures. Training areas are often shut at weekends to allow the public access. (The Treasury was appalled to find that the Ministry of Defence had acquired 3,500 acres of Norfolk which it cannot use for half the year). The defence estate incorporates 141,000 acres of nature reserves. (Ironically, one of the most important is at Porton Down, whose secret enclosures have preserved varieties of wildlife long since destroyed elsewhere by factory farming.) The Ministry of Defence has disposed of much of its historical legacy of barracks, forts and docks, not always to the pleasure of the Heritage Industry, which criticises its emphasis on securing the best price. But for ordinary taxpayers it is a welcome change of emphasis.

Until the end of the Cold War, the Ministry of Defence was the most notorious spendthrift in government. Price was secondary to effectiveness; contracts were awarded on a cost-plus basis. 'Please go away and build this and send me the bill when you've finished,' was how Sir Peter Levene, head of arms procurement in the mid-1980s, described the practice to the House of Commons. Between 1959 and 1985, the Ministry spent £5 billion on torpedoes that did not work. (One, Spearfish, was prone to U-turns.) The Nimrod project took nine years, cost £1 billion, and failed to produce a serviceable aircraft.[59]

Waste on that scale has ceased. The Royal Ordnance and the Royal dockyards are in private hands. The Ministry of Defence has spawned forty-three Executive Agencies, and is starting to manage its vast estate. A new joint headquarters has been established; prices are being transferred from expensive and valuable city centre sites to out-of-town locations; regiments are being merged and the closure and sale of 87 of the 455 Territorial Army centres is expected to raise £40 million. The NAAFI has sold its financial services arm for over £100 million and entered a partnership with Spar to manage its 200 shops. Food distribution and the management of pubs and clubs are being transferred to the private sector.

Mercantilism Abroad: the Foreign and Commonwealth Office

The defence budget is still immense. Even after a cut in real terms of more than a quarter, and multiple initiatives designed to improve the efficiency of spending, the budget will remain over £20 billion until well into the twenty-first century. The chief argument for the expenditure is diplomatic: by participating eagerly in American-led wars Britain is able, in the words of Douglas Hurd, to 'punch above her weight' in world affairs. In this sense, the armed forces are an adjunct to the diplomatic service, whose 'fine minds', splendid buildings and contempt for financial control are said to provide a useful cloak for the geopolitical insignificance of the United Kingdom.

The Foreign and Commonwealth Office (FCO) is the one department of state which still offers gracious living at the public expense. It was not until 1990 that diplomats ceased to fly first class. Their Grade I-listed Whitehall headquarters, with its ornate Durbar Court, was until recently the best-kept architectural secret in the civil estate (in September 1997 Robin Cook opened it to the public for a day). The official residence of the foreign secretary, a Grade II-listed building at 1 Carlton Gardens, is intended chiefly for entertaining foreign dignitaries, and the Foreign Office retains three country houses – Chevening in Kent, Hanslope Park near Milton Keynes, and Wilton Park at Steyning – for house parties of foreign diplomats.

Around the world, the most minor ambassador or high commissioner can expect to welcome local power-brokers and British expatriates to a sizeable official residence. The FCO owns 1,440 properties, worth £800–£1,000 million, and leases almost twice as many. The most valuable and enticing is always the official residence; the Foreign Office admits that twenty-six of its buildings are of 'exceptional historic and architectural interest'. First among them is the Paris residence on the rue Fauborg St Honoré, but the residences in Cairo, Rome, Tehran and Tunis are also lavish. Nigel Lawson described the official residence in Washington as 'quite simply, the best hotel in the world for those fortunate enough to be able to stay in it ... the service is impeccable, the food and wine second to none.'[60] The Russians tried for years to recover the splendid British embassy building beside the river in Moscow.

To furnish its many buildings, the Foreign Office has accumulated a large and valuable collection of paintings, drawings, photographs and antique furniture, and has commandeered a large portion of the government art collection, which is valued at over £25¼ million.[61] Only the Ministry of Defence, with a handsome collection of paintings left by retired commanders or commissioned to commemorate historic battles, can rival it, and for decades both departments exploited the fact that nobody took much interest in the collection. No catalogue was prepared until the 1990s, when it was discovered that hundreds of paintings which art experts had assumed missing or lost were still owned by the government,[62] but 472 of them could no longer be found.

This indifference to public money and possessions allowed the FCO to carry on as it had when Britain ran an empire and the telephone had still to be invented. It was not until 1996 that the Foreign Office replaced the Corps of Queen's Messengers, who carried diplomatic bags around the world, with secure faxes and commercial couriers. Even now, the Foreign Office has diplomatic relations with 186 countries around the world, representation in 145 and physical representation in 123. This immense network of people and buildings was ridiculous even when Britain was a great imperial and industrial power, but it is now indefensible. There is no corner of the globe beyond the reach of the aeroplane and the telephone, so decisions do not have to be taken by a man-on-the-spot. There is no longer an empire to administer; since Hong Kong was returned to China in 1997, it has shrunk to 180,000 people in fourteen territories dotted around the world. Post-imperial oddities such as Gibraltar and the Falkland Islands are not strategically unimportant or cheap to maintain (the Falklands absorb £70 million a year), but are scarcely a convincing reason for the structure of the diplomatic service and its large landed estate.

Sensing this, FCO officials have re-invented themselves as commercial travellers. In the summer of 1998 Sir John Kerr, permanent secretary at the Foreign Office, begged the House of Commons to give him more manpower to deploy against his German and French competitors in eastern Europe, China and the United States. 'In countries like these,' he said, 'we do need to be out and about, spotting the opportunities for future business for British firms.'[63] Historians have argued for years about whether trade follows the flag or the flag follows trade, but the modern diplomatic mandarin would like his fellow countrymen to believe they are indistinguishable. He knows how susceptible politicians are to mercantilist modes of thought. Thatcher relished 'batting for Britain' in export markets. The British arms industry has survived for years on diplomatically assisted export orders and the aid budget was long ago captured as a hidden source of export subsidies. Despite the embarrassment which aid-for-trade arrangements can cause, as they did in the celebrated Pergau Dam affair is Malaysia, British jobs are always more important than British consciences.

New Labour understands this now, though it entered office with a different agenda. The Foreign Office was advertised as one of the chief targets of the comprehensive spending review. Robin Cook armed himself with an 'ethical' foreign policy and Clare Short, minister of overseas development, promised not to use the aid budget to subsidise British exporters. A year on, Cook has persuaded the Treasury to let the Foreign Office keep the proceeds of asset sales to increase its representation in markets sought by British companies – eastern Europe, the Caspian region, China and Latin America – and defeated plans to cut £117 million a year the taxpayer spends on free flights and school fees for diplomats posted abroad. He has invited businessmen to be 'occasional ambassadors for Britain'.[64] Employees of British Airways, BOC, ICL, Wimpey, British Aerospace, British Steel, BT, British Nuclear Fuels, HSBC and Glaxo Wellcome are all working on secondment to the Foreign Office. Cook has agreed to hire an extra fifty diplomats, most of whom will compete with their French and German counterparts in the oil-producing countries around the Caspian sea.

In 1997–98 the Foreign Office and DTI spent £220 million on export promotion, of which more than half was consumed by Foreign Office staff on the ground. These two departments have defeated plans for the creation of the single export promotion agency favoured by British business. 'The politics and the commercial work go together in so many countries, and it's the ambassadors, the political and diplomatic representatives of the UK, who can gain access,' claimed Derek Fatchett, Foreign Office minister for trade and investment. 'If there is another body, it does not necessarily follow that the political leadership in a country will talk to the other body in quite the same way as they talk to the ambassador.'[65] To deny this is to risk accusations of naiveté, but it remains unproven. Certainly, there is no economic rationale for retaining a cadre of diplomats as glorified salesmen. Meanwhile, the real sources of British influence – the BBC World Service, the British Council and tuition fees for overseas students – have all had their budgets cut.

Mercantilism at Home: the Development Agencies

Even after twenty years of privatisation, in which the state has transferred all but a fraction of its commercial activities to private ownership, central government is still mired in mercantilist-cum-interventionist thinking of this kind. The Victorians regarded the economy as a self-regulating mechanism, best left alone. But twentieth century governments (greatly encouraged by the emergent pseudo-science of economics) have interfered relentlessly – in the hope of creating wealth, jobs or power, or reducing prices or raising incomes, or a combination of all these. This form of state intervention was quite distinct from socialistic measures, such as old age pensions, which developed contemporaneously and were aimed at the alleviation of poverty. Intervention to stimulate growth and prosperity was new.

Its beginnings can be traced to a single year: 1909. This was when Winston

Churchill, president of the Board of Trade, secured the legislation establishing the first labour exchanges, and insisted that they be controlled by central government rather than the private sector or local authorities.[66] Renamed Job Centres, there are now over 1,200 dotted around the country. Their creation gave the Ministry of Labour, which began as a mere department of the Board of Trade, the bureaucratic momentum to become the first of the great economic departments of state. In the 1960s and 1970s, as the Department of Employment, it probably had more influence over economic conditions than the Treasury (it was the ministry for trade unions).

1909 was also the year when the government established the first of many public corporations. The brief of the Development Commission (it later gained an adjective) was to attract investment to the rural economy, moribund since the repeal of the Corn Laws began to bite late in the nineteenth century.[67] The Rural Development Commission has survived many changes of government and the partial eclipse of its original purpose. It now provides commercial space for businesses and gives advice and money to aspiring and established rural entrepreneurs in England.

It once covered the Celtic fringe as well, but both rural Scotland (Highlands and Islands Enterprise) and rural Wales (the Development Board for Wales) soon acquired similar bodies of their own. The rural development corporations are monuments to the inability of governments to defy the tyranny of distance. But a lack of success in rural Britain did not prevent the government trying similar solutions in urban areas. English Partnerships is the lineal successor to the English Industrial Estates Corporation (EIEC), a state-sponsored property developer set up in 1936 to attract light industry to the ravaged north east of England by providing factories at low rents. Similar agencies were established in the distressed areas of Wales and Scotland, and for a time in the 1970s they were among the chief beneficiaries of the *dirigiste* industrial policy of the Labour government. The two agencies were the representatives on the Celtic fringe of Tony Benn's ill-conceived National Enterprise Board (NEB). They were empowered to invest in private ventures; both did, and lost money, as propositions refused by the commercial sector tend to do.

In the 1980s, the Thatcher government tried to turn all the development agencies into entrepreneurial organisations. They were ordered to sell their factories to the tenants, stop backing half-baked propositions, and concentrate on working with private enterprise rather than trying to subsidise and direct it. After several near-death experiences and re-denomination as the catchier English Estates, the EIEC was finally subsumed into an Urban Regeneration Agency to co-ordinate government efforts to rescue the decaying inner cities. Re-named English Partnerships, it aims to encourage investment, by working with private investors to reclaim and redevelop derelict urban land.

In 1990 the Scottish Development Agency was merged with the Scottish Training Agency and re-named Scottish Enterprise. The bulk of its budget is spent on the difficult task of making the indigenous Scots entrepreneurial. It pursues this ambition by showering them with public money through a network of thirteen local enterprise and training agencies. The Welsh Development Agency, having survived allegations of impropriety in the use of public money, has concentrated on attracting inward investment, and is the most formidable of the many regional agencies pursuing foreign investors. By the beginning of 1997 it had secured 1,680 projects worth £11 billion.[68] In 1998 it absorbed the Development Board for Rural Wales.

Before it disappeared, the Development Board spent nearly £50 million a year on job-creation schemes in remote parts of the Principality. Between them, the six development agencies collected a total of £878 million from British and European taxpayers.[69] After eighteen years of Thatcherism, they covered only 13 per cent of their expenditure from private income. Despite their free market rhetoric, the Conservative governments never doubted the catalytic role of the state, particularly in the inner cities.[70] It merely swapped cash subsidies for tax cuts and deregulation, initially in the so-called Enterprise Zones, and later by replacing ineffectual local authorities with all-powerful Urban Development Corporations such as the London Docklands Development Corporation.[71]

The pre-war development corporations like EIEC were far more entrepreneurial. Though they were given cheap money by the Treasury, they remained private companies. It was not until 1960 that the EIEC and its Welsh and Scottish counterparts were nationalised and funded by a straightforward government grant. By then, the use of subsidy and regulation to make companies invest in a particular area was commonplace. The Board of Trade also took powers to prohibit private investment in 'over-developed' areas and veto tenants of the wrong sort.

New Labour has similar doubts about the allocative efficiency of the market economy. It has established eleven Regional Development Agencies (nine in England and one each in Scotland and Wales). They commenced their work in April 1999. The RDAs have absorbed the existing development agencies, creating a new class of super-agency. The chief rationale for the mergers is that public money is wasted as rival agencies bid against one another for inward investment projects or poach companies operating in another region. Eventually, they will be answerable to the regional assemblies the government has created in Wales and Scotland. Doubtless the pet schemes of regional politicians and civil servants, and their friends in business, will be treated generously.

MAFF: the Ministry for Farmers

There is no sphere of government activity where the interests of the producers do not dominate. But none has shown greater contempt for the consumer than the Ministry of Agriculture, Fisheries and Food (MAFF). 'The Ministry of Agriculture looks after farmers,' Norman Tebbit once said, 'and the Foreign Office looks after foreigners.' The various forms of subsidy, protection and regulation given to farmers adds £1,000 a year to the average family food bill.

Like every expansion of the state, the creation of a giant ministry began modestly. A Board of Agriculture was set up in 1889 as a sop to landowners griping about falling rent rolls. Its budget was mean; there was no junior minister; it had no departmental building. The only effective solution to the agricultural depression – reintroduction of agricultural protection – was beyond the realm of practical politics.

It took the German submarine blockade of 1915–18 to overturn seventy years of free trade in food, by obliging the state to maximise domestic production. The Corn Production Act of 1917 guaranteed farmers minimum prices for cereals, and gave the Board of Agriculture sweeping powers of inspection. A separate Food Production Department was set up within the board to enlarge areas under cultivation and increase productivity.[72] After the war, a brief interlude of free trade was followed by the resumption of subsidies in 1928 and the first protective measures in 1932. Price-fixing and quota-setting were institutionalised with the formation of the Milk and Potato Marketing Boards. By the outbreak of the Second World War, the modern structure of agricultural subsidy, protection and price-fixing had emerged. The war enlarged it, and it was not dismantled afterwards.[73]

Six years after the war ended, the government was still the sole purchaser of agricultural produce. The prices paid to farmers were costing taxpayers £410 million a year, while consumers endured rationing which was sometimes more severe than in wartime. But when rationing was abolished in 1951, price-fixing was not. The price to the farmer was fixed by MAFF, with the taxpayer making up any shortfall between the guaranteed price and the market price. Agricultural investment was subsidised, and producers of butter, bacon and cereals were protected by import quotas. The main reason why the National Farmers Union opposed British entry to the Common Market was the fear of losing this generous system of support. They need not have worried. The Common Agricultural Policy (CAP) proved an even bigger bonanza for British farmers, who could sell whatever they produced at guaranteed prices. Now, having produced too much in the past, they are being paid not to produce at all.[74]

CAP is one of the last relics of the planned economy; it attempts to bring supply and demand into balance by planning output. Inevitably, it fails. Governments then have to intervene directly in the marketplace, buying up the 'surplus' once the market price of any commodity falls to the minimum level guaranteed by European taxpayers. An entirely separate department of State, the Intervention Board, is obliged to buy all produce offered at the guaranteed price provided it meets minimum quality standards. Since it cannot sell it elsewhere until the European Commission agrees, the Intervention Board then has to store the surplus in giant warehouses. The government owns eight grain stores with a capacity of 500,000 tonnes, but otherwise relies on commercial providers. The European Commission later reimburses the cost of intervention, but only at standard rates. The British taxpayer meets the cost of any difference between the standard rates and the actual costs of intervention. In 1995–96 this amounted to £3.9 billion.

TABLE 9.6
The Food Mountains*

Commodity (subject to Intervention)	Stock (Tonnes)	Market Value (£m)
Barley	525,783	36.1
Rye	333	21.1
Wheat	0	–
Boneless Beef	99,653	62.9
Bone-In Beef	0	–
Butter	1,964	1.3
Skimmed Milk Powder	53,292	31.1
Total	681,025	152.5

Source: Intervention Board.
* At March 1998.

MAFF used to own farms as well as subsidise them. When Margaret Thatcher became prime minister, it owned 35,000 acres. Many were bought before 1914 to try to turn unemployed farm labourers into smallholders, and others after 1918 to settle returning soldiers.[75] Similarly, Land Settlement Association estates were acquired in the 1930s for the settlement of unemployed industrial workers. Experiments of this kind persisted until after the Second World War,[76] but all MAFF-owned estates were privatised in the 1980s and 1990s, mainly by sale to the tenants.[77] The less profitable estates owned by the Scottish Office (which owns over 280,000 acres of Scotland) have proved more difficult to sell. The crofters want further subsidies before they are prepared to assume the risks of ownership.

In *Whitehall*, first published in 1989, Peter Hennessy berated an ungrateful nation for criticising MAFF. It had, he wrote, 'presided for forty years over the most consistent and conspicuous success story in British industry . . . In terms of efficiency, manpower use, capital investment and output, farming has shown since the war what a mixed economy can do given the right circumstances and good management in both its public and private sectors.'[78] It is an odd view. Any industry will produce more for less if the state subsidises its investment, guarantees the price of its products, and excludes the threat of competition. The result is an over-capitalised monster, addicted to subsidy and methods of farming more destructive of the natural environment than any other economic activity. As taxpayers, ordinary people have funded the subsidies. As consumers, they have paid more for food. Their reward is factory farms and the spoliation of the landscape. 'We contrive at the same time,' concludes Oliver Rackham, historian of the countryside, 'to subsidise agriculture much more than any other industry, *and* to have expensive food, *and* a ravaged countryside.'[79]

The Official Reserves

The history of agriculture in Britain since the war proves that governments can defy economic reality, but only at ruinous cost and not for ever. Nothing demonstrates the vanity of the governing classes better than their refusal to accept this. But MAFF spent only £5 billion in 1997–8. In the late summer of 1992 the government spent almost as much in a single afternoon in a vain attempt to maintain the value of sterling. In the following four months, the value of assets accumulated for this purpose fell against the US dollar by 18 per cent and against the Deutschmark by 13 per cent.

The Bank of England has never disclosed the cost of this unsuccessful operation but, even in the short term, it was somewhere between £2 and £4 *billion*.* 'It was just as if,' a financial magazine commented at the time, 'Norman Lamont had personally thrown entire hospitals and schools into the sea all afternoon.'[80] The money Lamont threw at the speculators came from the official reserves, which are among the most valuable assets the country owns. In 1996, for example, their gross value was a quarter of the total net worth of the government. They are, however, trifling by comparison with the

---

* Until the value of the sterling assets is realised by selling them for foreign currency, the cost merely shows as an increased liability in the government balance sheet.

resources of the international capital markets. This means that, if an exchange rate parity is resisted without limit, the cost is always immense. The reason is simple. Daily turnover in the foreign exchange markets is over $1 trillion, and the total official reserves of the industrialised countries of the world amount to only $550 billion. If all the central banks of the developed world coordinated and used their reserves on a single day, they would still deploy only half the resources arrayed against them. Central banks do co-ordinate their intervention in the markets in a bid to steer exchange rates in particular directions. But even concerted intervention cannot work in isolation, or against economic realities, or defy the perceived trend in interest rates. All governments can hope to do is steer the speculative herd as best they can, by buying the currencies they want to go up and selling the ones they want to go down.

The management of the exchange rate remains the most pressing and intractable question in government. All governments want to avoid the twin extremes of recession and inflation, and the exchange rate is one of the main determinants of the balance between them. If it is too high, British goods will be relatively expensive, orders will be lost, and jobs will disappear. If it is too low, imports will become expensive, and inflation will start to rise. Ensuring that the rate of exchange is neither too high nor too low is hard to achieve, even if it was possible to agree on the 'correct' rate. Typically, British governments have sought fixed but flexible exchange rates, in which the value of the pound is kept at a competitive level by judicious adjustments to interest rates and periodic intervention in the market. Eleven member-states of the European Union have chosen a different option. By fixing the rates of exchange between their currencies, they have chosen not only to share a currency; they have chosen to share a rate of interest. It is a risky decision: the rate may be too low for countries with rising inflation, and too high for countries with rising unemployment.

This insidious choice is a modern dilemma. It was only when Britain abandoned the gold standard in 1931 that politicians took charge of the exchange rate and began to manipulate its value in the hope of encouraging growth. When the Second World War broke out, the government imposed exchange controls, which remained in force for forty years, and a new system of semi-fixed exchange rates against the US dollar was introduced.* But the war had left Britain with an intolerable burden of debt, and the pound came under chronic pressure. It was forced to devalue twice, within the system, in 1949

---

* This system, in which the US dollar remained convertible into gold at a fixed price of $35 an ounce, was agreed by the American, British and Canadian governments at a celebrated conference held at Bretton Woods, in the US, 4 July 1944.

TABLE 9.7
The Official Reserves*

	Assets† ($USm)	Liabilities‡ ($USm)
US Dollars	11,107	7,832
European Union Currencies	14,469	12,384
Japanese Yen	1,286	–
Other Currencies	190	161
Total Currencies	27,052	20,376
Special Drawing Rights§	439	2,646
IMF Reserve Tranche	2,935	–
Gold¶	5,082	–
Total Non-Currencies	8,456	2,646
Total	35,508	23,022

Source: Bank of England.

* At the end of March 1998 at parity rather than market rates. Non-US dollar assets are translated into US dollars at exchange rates (parity rates) which are fixed at the end of March each year, and apply for the whole 12 months.
† The assets are held mostly in the form of bonds issued by the governments of the relevant currencies.
‡ The liabilities are mainly foreign currency bonds issued by the British government.
§ SDRs are a synthetic currency which consists of a weighted average of five international currencies, invented in 1969 as an alternative reserve currency to the dollar. They form part of Britain's subscription to the assets of the International Monetary Fund (IMF), which lends them to member countries in need of foreign currency to pay for imports or to stabilise exchange rates.
¶ Gold reserves are a hangover from the gold standard, though they were later valued as a hedge against inflation. Central banks are increasingly reluctant to hold gold. It lost its formal role as the anchor of the international monetary system in 1971; its price is a quarter of its peak of $850 an ounce in 1980; it earns only minimal interest from being lent to producers and manufacturers to hedge market positions; at a time of low inflation worldwide, there is less need for a hedge against rising prices.

and 1967. In 1972, when it again came under pressure, sterling was allowed to float, and has floated ever since. But a floating rate of exchange proved to be a recipe for inflation. How to prevent this happening without the external discipline of a fixed exchange rate is one of the most interesting questions in economic management. The answers, of which there are many, are complicated by political considerations.

The New Labour government, which must decide whether and when to join the euro, is well aware of its complexities. They destroyed the Conservative Party as an effective force in government.

The Price of Publicly Financed Infrastructure: The Road Network

It is not surprising that politicians have sought economic nirvana in more tractable areas. Roads, as a glance at the promotional material issued by the development agencies reveals, are still seen as the fastest route from economic backwater to economic paradise: they are 'infrastructure', which brings jobs and prosperity. Certainly, an inadequate road system is a major constraint on economic growth. If raw materials take too long to reach the factory, and finished goods cannot reach their market, the division of labour which lies at the heart of economic growth is impossible. One of the main reasons the British economy took off in the eighteenth rather than the seventeenth century was the building of the turnpikes, the first attempt since the Romans to build a national rather than a local road network. In tandem with the canals, they allowed people, goods, raw materials and information to get around fast enough and cheaply enough to help the economy grow.

In the twentieth century, roads began to matter politically as well as economically. In 1978 Richard Marsh, a former transport minister who later chaired British Rail, complained that 'most ministers of transport have made their reputation out of the nation's strange obsession with the motor car.'[81] But the Marsh principle no longer applies. There is little talk of the freedom and prosperity roads and cars bring, and more of the costs they impose. 'Two cars in the drive,' says the present transport secretary, John Prescott, 'are not a symbol of prosperity, but of a failure of the public transport system.'[82] With twenty-eight million cars clogging the roads, the traffic jam is now as much a part of the British way of life as *Coronation Street*. Children once played I Spy and pub cricket in the back of the car – now a best-selling book encourages them to identify different cars in a traffic jam.

In 1997 Trafficmaster estimated that a typical day on the M25 cost half a million motorists the equivalent of twenty-nine years of life and liberty.[83] The Confederation of British Industry says traffic jams are costing British business £20 billion a year in wasted time and lost orders. Only advertisements for new motor cars, showing young people careering around empty mountain passes or deserted city streets, ignore this reality. For taxpayers, the cost of repairing roads damaged by SWOT (Sheer Weight of Traffic) is chronic, immense and perpetually in arrears. The maintenance backlog on local authority roads was estimated in 1997 at £3.5 billion. Many bridges on motorways and trunk roads are so dilapidated, they cannot bear the weight of the new 40-tonne lorries.[84] It was the delays caused by traffic jams which tempted the Major government to set up the notorious cones hotline, in the hope that it would speed up roadworks.

But roads waste more than time. Lives are lost. People are injured. Machinery is damaged or destroyed. Adults and children develop respiratory diseases. Policemen, firemen, ambulancemen, doctors and nurses are diverted from other work. Daily life is polluted by noise and fumes. The countryside is devoured by tarmac and concrete. Towns once constrained by bus routes and railways burst into open country. In every region, roads export as many jobs as they import.* By comparison with these costs, the benefits are nugatory. A bypass relieves a pretty market town. The verges of motorways are fertile habitats for wildlife (by 1994 the Department of Transport was planting more broad-leaved trees than the Forestry Commission). Motorists have a wider choice of jobs, shops and houses.

The costs of roads can be exaggerated. They are not as obtrusive as environmentalists allege: the metalled road network covers 723,000 acres, or 1.2 per cent of the total land area of the United Kingdom. Four in every five miles of road are in towns and cities, where they cause pollution but have little effect on landscape. The amount of new road-building is small, and proceeding slowly. In 1997 the Highways Agency had 220 projects in hand, and the majority were improvements to existing roads.

The £23 billion *Roads for Prosperity* programme, launched in 1989 as the 'biggest roads programme since the Romans', was the last road-building plan animated by the belief that traffic congestion was retarding economic growth. In 1992, as the first great anti-roads protest got under way at Twyford Down, the government promised to raise fuel duty by 5 per cent above the rate of inflation. A year later, John Gummer, the suddenly verdant environment secretary, imposed restrictions on the development of out-of-town shopping centres (thought to account for much of the recent surge in car journeys).

In 1995 Brian Mawhinney, the umpteenth Conservative transport secretary, declared an end to the Great Car Economy. Rather than say so, he called for a Great Transport Debate. The Green Paper which followed was *Transport: The Way Forward*. But it was actually about a single subject: how to reduce the incessant growth in motor traffic. In that sense, it was revolutionary. Since the first motorway was planned in the 1950s, the government had confined itself to prediction and provision; it had forecast the growth in motor traffic and built the roads to meet it. Now it was not going to build any more, and it was going to reduce the number of cars using the existing network. Only

---

* By eliminating the need for local sourcing and factories close to markets.

TABLE 9.8
The Road Network

	1982	1996	Increase		Acreage*
	Miles	Miles	Miles	%	
Motorways†	1,673	2,004	+331	19.8%	25,518
Trunk Roads	7,586	7,679	+93	1.2%	59,306
Principal Roads	21,562	22,280	+718	3.3%	64,719
Other Roads‡	182,895	197,210	+14,315	7.8%	572,864
Total	213,716	229,173	+15,457	7.2%	722,407

Source: *Annual Abstract of Statistics 1994 and 1998*, Table 10.3.

* Approximation. The standard width of a lane on any new road is 3.65 metres, though motorway hard shoulders tend to be narrower. Motorway central reservations are usually 4 metres wide. It is assumed that trunk roads have four lanes and a central reservation, and that principal roads have two lanes of 3.65 metres each. Though motorway hard shoulders are included at a width of 3 metres, grass verges are excluded.
† Including local authority motorways, which account for less than 3 per cent of the motorway network.
‡ Excluding unsurfaced roads and green lanes.

140 out of the 500-odd road schemes presaged in *Roads for Prosperity* survived the subsequent cuts.

The prescription lacked the spirit of the diagnosis. The obvious solution was to raise the cost of using the roads. But, in the age of 'Mondeo Man', the price mechanism is the one instrument of policy which is unutterable as well as unusable. There was talk of more parking restrictions and red routes for buses; higher taxes on cars; better management of traffic flows and road maintenance; more use of new technology; higher investment in buses, trains and cycle paths. Local authorities were left to devise traffic restrictions and bear the political consequences.

New Labour came into office pledged (like all its predecessors since the 1930s) to provide an 'integrated transport policy'. In the summer of 1998, this was unveiled by John Prescott, secretary of state for Environment, Transport and the Regions. The 'most radical transport policy in a generation' turned out to be more subsidies and regulation for the railways, extra bus lanes, bus timetables by telephone, combined bus-and-train tickets, and a spell at charm school for bus conductors. It was still up to local authorities to decide if they wanted to charge motorists for driving and parking in the centre of towns. (After full consultation and pilot schemes, of course, though the government would prefer it if these were postponed until after the next

General Election.) One radical idea which even the Conservatives were prepared to entertain – more use of toll roads – was abandoned.

Transport is the most vivid example of political perversity. After years of
under-investment in public transport, more than nine out of ten domestic
and commercial journeys take place on overcrowded roads. Yet instead of
taxing drivers for *using* their cars, the government taxes people for *owning*
them. By adding VAT, vehicle and fuel excise duty to the already heavy cost
of buying and owning a car (in depreciation and insurance), the government
encourages people to spread the burden over as many journeys as possible.
This fuels the demand for more and better roads.

But to accommodate the driver as parent and/or pedestrian, the government has to submit every proposal for a new or improved road to the planning
process. It now takes an average of fifteen years for a road to get from
conception to completion, infuriating supporters without appeasing detractors.* People who are prepared to bury themselves in tunnels and chain
themselves to trees are not influenced by the outcome of a planning inquiry.
Meanwhile, suburban planning restrictions are being relaxed, creating more
housing estates accessible only by road.

The only lasting solution to the incessant growth in car use is to make
drivers pay directly for the costs they impose. The technology exists to monitor
the whereabouts of a car, and deduct charges electronically. It is already in
use in Singapore and Norway, and will come into use in the Netherlands in
2001. A road-pricing pilot scheme in Leicester was encouraging.[85] Only politics
prevents pricing the use of roads. Drivers have the illusion that roads are free,
and no government is willing to pay the electoral price of their disillusionment.

Yet paying for road usage is scarcely novel. By the time Victoria ascended
the throne, the toll-charging turnpike trusts had created a national network
of roads 22,000 miles in length.[86] The Clifton Suspension Bridge has charged
a toll since it opened in 1864. The Severn and Humber Bridges also charge
tolls. The Dartford River Crossing, a toll-bridge and tunnel, was financed and
built entirely by the private sector. The Birmingham Northern Relief Road,
to be built by a private consortium called Midland Expressway, will charge
cars £2.50 and lorries £5 to avoid the busiest stretch of the M6.[87] But river

---

* One side-effect of the laborious planning process is to lumber the Department of Transport
with a sizeable estate as it buys up land and housing in anticipation of building a road. In 1997
the National Asset Register listed 1,932 surplus properties purchased 'in furtherance of road
building schemes'. Most are acquired by compulsory purchase ahead of road construction or
widening schemes, but the uncertainty means that the Department often has to buy more land
and housing than it needs, much of which has subsequently to be sold at a loss. See The National
Asset Register, pp. 175–180, and National Audit Office, *Department of Transport: Acquisition,
Management and Disposal of Land and Property Purchased for Road Construction*, HMSO, 16 June
1994.

crossings and five-star roads for Fat Cats and lorry drivers are not the same as roads for Everyman. It is impossible to charge piecemeal for road use. The system is a network, and charges in one part are likely to increase traffic flows in another unless charges are introduced throughout.

Universal charging would be a shock. It would also open the possibility of privatising the road network. Resentment might be reduced if motorists knew the charges would be invested in roads rather than child benefit and nuclear warheads (like the road tax fund before them). In 1995 the government pondered division of the network between regional corporations, to be funded by a direct charge on motorists or on fuel sales in each region. Estimates suggested the road network, sold in this way, might fetch up to £75 billion.[88] Others put it as high as £90–100 billion. But previous privatisations – the National Grid, the gas transmission system, British Telecom and Railtrack – suggest that networks are best kept intact, with users charged for access.[89] It is not impossible to imagine the state withdrawing from road provision. A privatised Highways Agency may yet become the tarmac equivalent of Railtrack or Transco.

*

To privatise or not to privatise? New Labour thinks it can avoid the choice by making government less like government and more like business. This is the Third Way: governing with the heart of a politician but the head of a businessman. It cannot be done. Government is different from business. It is driven by policy as well as judged by results. Unlike a PLC, the primary role of the state is political and juridical, not economic. It is a public institution, rooted in law and answerable to the voters, not a commercial organisation run by managers. Voters are not shareholders. They are interested in means as well as ends, and their ends conflict. After years of institutional upheaval, central government has ended up where the nationalised industries left off: neither wholly public, nor wholly private; surrounded by targets, with no incentive to hit them; the constant prey of here-today-gone-tomorrow politicians. In the end, as the nationalised industries found, there is no Third Way.

CHAPTER TEN

THE
NATIONALISATION
OF INDUSTRY

The theory of the Communists may be summed up in the single sentence:
Abolition of private property.
                    KARL MARX and FRIEDRICH ENGELS, 1848[1]

The evils that Capitalism brings differ in intensity in different countries
but the root cause of the trouble once discerned, the remedy is seen to
be the same by thoughtful men and women. The cause is private property;
the remedy is public ownership.
                                    CLEMENT ATTLEE, 1937[2]

No degree of prosperity could justify the accumulation of large amounts
of highly toxic substances which nobody knows how to make 'safe' and
which remain an incalculable danger to the whole of creation for historical
or even geological ages. To do such a thing is a transgression against
life itself, a transgression infinitely more serious than any crime ever
perpetrated by man.
                                        E. F. SCHUMACHER[3]

If any of you were any good you would be in private industry.
        MARGARET THATCHER, lunching with British Rail executives[4]

Few political ideas are further removed from the Third Way than nationalisation. It makes the state the owner and the controller, not the enabler or the
source of empowerment. Nationalisation is not a partnership between the
private and the public sectors, or even the subjection of private interest to
the public good, but the expropriation of private property by the state. It
is the quintessential socialist idea, largely untried before socialists acquired
political power, and one which stems directly from the governing ethic of
the Socialist creed.

This is why Tony Blair sought, as soon as he became leader of the Opposition in 1994, to expunge Clause IV from the constitution of the Labour Party. Nothing could signify the abandonment of traditional socialism more completely than dumping the historic commitment to 'the common owner- ship of the means of production, distribution and exchange'.* At a special conference on 29 April 1995 all but the Old Labour rump was persuaded to replace Clause IV with a 344-word 'statement of aims and values' – the media event which signified the birth of New Labour.†

'The all-embracing commitment to nationalisation in the infamous Clause IV', as the chroniclers of New Labour wrote a year later, 'gave the unfortunate impression that Labour favoured public ownership on principle.'[5] For decades, the Labour Party favoured it on nothing but principle. Emanuel Shinwell famously complained, when he became minister of Fuel and Power in 1945, that there were no blueprints to help him to nationalise the coal, gas and electricity industries. All he could find was a pamphlet by Arthur Greenwood and resolutions passed at Labour Party conferences.[6] At Transport House, a search uncovered 'two copies of a paper by Jim Griffiths, one of them a translation into Welsh'.[7] This was despite the fact that the nationalisation of coal was endorsed by successive Party conferences from 1913 onwards.

Earlier Labour governments offered no practical guidance. The first Labour administration, in office for just 9½ months in 1924, had no time to consider expropriation. The Land Utilisation Act of 1931 (the closest the Labour govern- ment of 1929–31 got to nationalisation) included full compensation for land- owners whose property was purchased compulsorily.[8] Once it was conceded that confiscation of private property without compensation was impolitic or inequi- table (it was impossible to distinguish between ordinary shareholders and the millionaire rentiers of socialist mythology), nationalisation became no more than ideological catharsis. The form it took was of little interest to its proponents.

Public Ownership: Moral Rather Than Economic Necessity

Nationalisation was a moral imperative, not a plan of action. Despite its pretensions to scientific status, socialism is primarily a doctrine of moral repugnance. Even the reconstructed socialists of New Labour, whose only

---

* Clause IV of the Labour Party Constitution, drawn up in 1918, committed it to 'secure for the workers by hand or by brain the full fruits of their industry and the most equitable distribution thereof that may be possible, upon the basis of the common ownership of the means of pro- duction, distribution and exchange and the best obtainable system of popular administration and control of each industry or service.'
† Ironically, Blair secured the support of the public sector trade unions for the abolition of Clause IV only by promising that a Labour government would re-nationalise the railways.

principle is pragmatism, are apt to moralise. ('Socialism to me', Blair told the Labour Party conference in 1995, 'is a moral purpose to life.') They yearn not for a higher standard of living, or greater economic efficiency, or even better forms of economic organisation, but to return to an economy of the imagination, in which human fellowship and social duty count for more than personal material gain. All of the early socialist thinkers in Britain – Thomas Carlyle, John Ruskin, William Morris, Robert Blatchford, R. H. Tawney, even George Lansbury – celebrated the Moral Economy of the Middle Ages. Its fair prices and reciprocal obligations compared favourably with the war-of-all-against-all under capitalism. In this sense, public ownership was not a vision of the future; it was a dream of the past.

The one truth universally acknowledged by traditional socialists was that the ills of capitalism could be traced to private ownership of the means of production, distribution and exchange. Private property was the irremediable obstacle to a return to the harmonious moral order of the Middle Ages. To that extent, the expropriation of private property through public ownership was not merely a means to Socialism; it was the essence, the soul, even the *end* of Socialism. The *means* by which it could be put into practice was a secondary matter. In government, the Labour Party was clear only that public ownership did not mean control by the workers. The ideas of the co-operative and syndicalist traditions, which envisaged control of industry by employees rather than politicians and civil servants, were never taken seriously. 'There is not yet a very large number of workers in Britain capable of taking over large enterprises,' argued Stafford Cripps, president of the Board of Trade, in October 1946. 'Until there have been more workers on the managerial side of industry, I think it would be almost impossible to have worker-controlled industry in Britain, even if it were on the whole desirable.'[9]

R. H. Tawney, the Christian Socialist thinker who portrayed the contest between capitalism and socialism as a battle between moral and immoral economic systems, left open the question of the way private property would be replaced by public ownership.[10] In *The Acquisitive Society*, he endorsed the public ownership proposals of revolutionists, guild socialists, syndicalists, co-operators and nationalisers alike – and dismissed choosing among them as a matter of little import. 'Which of these alternative methods of removing industry from the control of the property-owner is adopted is a matter of expediency to be decided in each particular case,' he wrote. '"Nationalisation," therefore, which is sometimes advanced as the only method of extinguishing proprietary rights, is merely one species of a considerable *genus* . . . it is a means to an end, not an end in itself . . . When the question of ownership has been settled the question of administration remains for solution.'[11]

The Municipal Precedent

As a result, the reality of nationalisation was shaped primarily by precedent. The examples available to the socialist administration of 1945 were of several kinds. The first was municipal. By the close of the nineteenth century town councils were providing roads, schools, hospitals, water and sewerage, gas and electricity, parks, police forces, free libraries, wash-houses, trams and buses; even art galleries and civic universities. Public provision was the natural accompaniment of expanding Victorian towns, and the displacement of private owners by the public authorities was pioneered by Liberal councils in cities such as Manchester, Birmingham and Leeds. The Birmingham Corporation bought out the city gas companies in 1875, though no powers of compulsory purchase were given to local authorities. By the time the gas and electricity industries were nationalised by the Labour government in 1948, local authorities already owned over one third of the gas industry and two thirds of the electricity industry.

The London County Council, dominated from its inception in 1889 by progressive Liberals and Fabian socialists, pursued a 'gas and water socialism' which ran far ahead of anything contemplated by previous generations of national politicians. It was municipal socialism which gave rise to the public corporation and the public utility, and made the nationalisation of electricity, gas and transport in 1947–8 relatively uncontroversial. But the creators of municipal socialism were not enthusiastic about the extension of public ownership beyond the utilities. Herbert Morrison, appointed to mastermind the nationalisation programme, was reared in its traditions. As minister of Transport under Ramsay MacDonald, he had invented a model public corporation (the London Passenger Transport Board) but he was notoriously lukewarm about nationalisation, even of the hospitals.

The Military–Strategic Origins of Nationalisation

His colleague, the chancellor of the Exchequer Hugh Dalton, did not regard gas and water socialism as socialism at all. 'We weren't really beginning our Socialist programme,' he confided to his diary in 1946, 'until we had gone past all the utility junk – such as transport and electricity which were publicly owned in every capitalist country in the world.'[12] The precedents for nationalisation by central government were equally far from socialism, owing more to militarism and imperialism. In late Victorian and Edwardian Britain, competition from continental Europe and the United States had fostered mounting political anxiety about the decline in 'national efficiency'. These themes have their echoes today, in debates about national economic performance, foreign investment and the role of the government in economic success. Similar worries can be found in every period of history, as the political mind struggles to separate commercial success from the wider ambitions of the state.

Such fears are valid, to the extent that military power depends on money. 'The triumph of any Great Power,' wrote Paul Kennedy in *The Rise and Fall of the Great Powers*, 'or the collapse of another, has usually been the consequence of the more or less efficient utilization of the state's productive economic resources in wartime, and . . . of the way in which that state's economy had been rising or falling, *relative* to other leading nations, in the decades preceding the actual conflict . . . There is a very clear connection in the long run between an individual Great Power's economic rise and fall and its growth and decline as an important military power.'[13] Military effectiveness depends on an economy capable of paying taxes. 'Our trade is our chief support,' Lord Carteret told the House of Lords in 1739, 'and therefore we must sacrifice every other view to the preservation of our trade.'[14] In the eighteenth century, the army and navy were deployed largely to protect commerce.

The ideas of the mercantilist school, which dominated economic thought until the close of the eighteenth century, provided powerful theoretical support. They favoured the intervention of the state in the economy because they believed it would enlarge national wealth. They contended that there was a fixed amount of wealth to go round, and that it was the task of government to secure as large a slice as possible. It could do so by sponsoring exports, protecting domestic manufacturers from foreign competition, ensuring goods were carried in British ships, protecting trading rights by force, subsidising domestic producers, and maintaining forts and garrisons along the trading routes. Offensive commercial wars were a constant possibility. The object of all three of the Anglo-Dutch wars of the seventeenth century was to destroy the commercial supremacy of Holland.[15]

Although over two centuries have elapsed since Adam Smith made a systematic case for complete freedom of trade, politicians have struggled ever since to abandon the mercantilism their predecessors adopted in the seventeenth century. Even in the Victorian heyday of *laissez-faire* at home and free trade abroad, the commercial policy of the British government was still primarily strategic: to magnify the wealth and power of the nation. The creeping nationalisation of the East India Company between 1784 and 1858, sometimes portrayed as the first instance of a private company being expropriated by the state, was in reality an attempt to secure the Indian empire and reduce its cost by breaking the Asian trading monopolies of the company.[16]

When Disraeli borrowed £4 million from Rothschilds in 1875 to acquire the bankrupt Khedive of Egypt's 44 per cent stake in the Suez Canal Company, he was pursuing the same objective. He was not pioneering the purchase by the state of shares in public companies, but ensuring that British business would continue to pay for India and its army. The vast majority of the trade which passed through the Canal was British, and Disraeli reckoned the stake was necessary to protect it from the French.[17] In 1914 Winston Churchill, then First Lord of the Admiralty, was persuaded to take a controlling stake in the Anglo-Persian Oil Company (later British Petroleum) to secure a supply of cheap fuel oil for the Royal Navy and deny the assets of the company to the Dutch (in the shape of Shell).[18]

After the Second World War, the nationalisation of steel was justified on strategic grounds. Military and strategic arguments remained familiar down to the last days of nationalisation in the 1970s, when Old Labour nationalised North Sea oil in the years following the first great rise in oil prices.* In the 1970s, shipbuilding companies and aeroplane engine and motor manufacturers were taken into public ownership on the grounds that British security and prestige would suffer if the country did not manufacture ships, aeroplane engines and motor cars. Even today, most of the manufacturing sector is viewed in this light.

The State and Technology

New technologies were particularly susceptible to nationalisation on strategic grounds. In 1914 the railways were nationalised, making use of reserve powers first assumed by government in 1871, in the wake of the Franco-Prussian war. The domestic telegraph system was nationalised as early as 1868, stifling the development of the telephone, whose trunk-line system was nationalised in 1892. The private telephone networks (with the famous exception of the municipal system in Kingston-Upon-Hull) were taken over by the state in 1911. In 1929, with government encouragement, the nine private telegraph companies which linked Britain to her imperial outposts in Africa, Australasia, India and the Americas were merged to form Cable & Wireless.[19]

Wireless stations were leased by the government to the company; by

---

* The British National Oil Corporation was established in 1976. It was given the right to buy up to 51 per cent of any oil produced in the North Sea, and first refusal over assets sold by private companies. It was equipped with £900 million of interest-free credit from the taxpayer and exemption from the special Petroleum Revenue Tax. It later acquired (at a price of £103 million) a majority stake in the North Sea oil operations of the Burmah Oil Company. Its operations were privatised in the 1980s.

exchanging the freehold to these for shares in the company in 1938 the government obtained its stake in the international telecommunications business. When the old dominions nationalised their share of the network in 1945, the British government bought the rump of the company for £32.2 million. Similarly, it was to secure air links with the empire, and enlarge the British share of the aviation market, that the Chamberlain government merged and nationalised the private airlines as the British Overseas Airways Corporation (BOAC) in 1939.[20]

No technology was more susceptible to political manipulation than nuclear power. Because it was unleashed as a weapon, atomic power was enmeshed from the outset in strategic considerations. The American decision to end its wartime collaboration with Britain over nuclear matters persuaded the Cabinet to authorise the construction of a plant to make plutonium at Windscale (now Sellafield) in Cumbria in December 1945. There was at the time an acute shortage of money and materials, but in matters of national security lack of resources was an invalid objection. When his Cabinet colleagues baulked at a budget of £100 million to build an atomic bomb, the foreign secretary, Ernest Bevin, told them: 'We've got to have this thing over here, whatever it costs . . . We've got to have a bloody Union Jack flying on top of it.' The cost was not disclosed to the full Cabinet – let alone to Parliament.[21]

The origins of the British nuclear industry warped its subsequent development. The civil nuclear power industry inherited the military indifference to cost and partiality to secrecy. When the United Kingdom Atomic Energy Authority (UKAEA) was set up in June 1954 to develop the military and commercial applications of nuclear power, it was given 24,000 staff and £50 million to spend. After a serious fire at Windscale in October 1957 contaminated dairy herds across the country, a critical report was suppressed.[22] By then, the strategic rationale was economic as well as military. Doubts about the technical competence of British nuclear scientists would harm export sales and deprive British industry of cheap electricity.

Ministers were so convinced of the importance of nuclear power that the race to build a reactor became the civilian equivalent of the Manhattan project. Being first mattered more than being the best, or even being practical. In that sense, the UKAEA succeeded magnificently. On 17 October 1956 the Queen opened the first civil nuclear reactor in the world at Calder Hall, next to the Windscale plutonium processing plant. The timing was propitious: Nasser had seized the Suez canal three months earlier, prompting panic about oil supplies. Two more nuclear power stations were ordered immediately.

Unfortunately, the Magnox design used at Calder Hall owed more to the need for weapons-grade plutonium than cheap electricity. The Berkeley and Bradwell power stations, both built to the Magnox design, were expensive.

The technology was an export failure. Just two Magnox reactors were sold – one to Italy and one to Japan. But the nuclear establishment did not give up or follow the French example and buy the cheap and efficient Pressurised Water Reactor (PWR) from the Americans. It invented the Advanced Gas-Cooled Reactor (AGR) instead. Seven were built, all of them ruinously uneconomic. The design of the AGR changed continually, and construction was invariably behind schedule.

Hartlepool took sixteen years to build, Heysham I fifteen years. Dungeness B, started in 1965, was not finished until 1985. No AGR was ever exported. In the 1970s, the chairman of the Central Electricity Generating Board (CEGB), Arthur Hawkins, described it as 'a disaster we must never repeat'. Nobody listened. Eric Varley, appointed energy secretary in the last Wilson administration in 1974, was persuaded to replace the AGR with yet another new design: a Soviet-style Steam-Generating Heavy Water Reactor. His successor, Tony Benn, reversed the decision and ordered two more AGRs.

Construction of the two new AGRs (Heysham B and Torness) was confirmed in 1979 by the incoming Conservative government. Persuaded that nuclear power was the way to defeat the inevitable miners' strike (and beat the rise in the price of oil) the new energy secretary, David Howell, ordered the first PWR as well. The CEGB had told him it would produce electricity far more cheaply than a coal-fired power station. After a four-year public inquiry, work began at Sizewell on the first PWR. Completed in January 1995, it was the first nuclear power station to be built in Britain on time and within budget. Ironically, it was also the last to be built.

Oddly, in view of the belated decision to abandon British technology in favour of a cheaper American alternative, the Conservatives continued to fund the most expensive of the many follies of the British nuclear establishment: the 'fast breeder' reactor project at Dounreay. In theory, fast breeder reactors were the energy equivalent of a perpetual motion machine. By extracting and burning uranium and plutonium from their own spent fuel, they would (in theory) produce more than they consumed. Convinced that UKAEA scientists were creating a world-beating technology (as well as providing much-needed employment in the north of Scotland) successive governments squandered billions of pounds on the prototype at Dounreay. It was abandoned in 1992.

By then, taxpayers had sunk over £100 billion into the nuclear power industry. Of the many ways governments have wasted scarce resources, none matched nuclear power for prodigality. Nor has the industry finished its sport with the taxpayer. Its chief legacy is a collection of contaminated sites, buildings and waste which will cost between £40 and £70 billion to clean up.[23] It was not until the government exposed the industry to the discipline of the marketplace that these costs were revealed. Working in secret, and insulated from the need to raise capital, the nuclear establishment built an empire of ash on a mountain of lies and self-delusion. Potential shareholders, invited to participate in the spoils of their secret wisdom, found them out.[24]

In 1989–90 the nuclear power stations were withdrawn from the privatis-ation of the electricity industry, because the cost of de-commissioning reactors was too great for shareholders to bear. These and the money and talents they consumed, are monuments to state planning, finance and ownership.[25] They testify to the perennial weakness of politicians for identifying and backing strategic industries and 'coming' technologies. Even now, politicians can be found who argue for nuclear power on the 'strategic' grounds that it frees the country from undue reliance on gas or coal or oil, protects jobs and generates exports, or is kinder to the environment. They will still be heard when the last nuclear power station in Britain closes in the second or third decade of the twenty-first century, leaving nothing but a pile of radioactive refuse too dangerous to handle for a hundred thousand years.

Invention of the Public Corporation

Because ministers saw nuclear power as an economic as well as a military weapon, the UKAEA was set up as a public corporation rather than a White-hall department.[26] Public corporations were intended to operate like private companies without being privately owned. The first of them was the British Broadcasting Corporation (BBC). From 1922 to 1938 it was run by John Reith, the first of the great nationalised industry managers. He later went to BOAC. His initial role at the BBC, however, was not so much commercial as political.

The inter-war state reacted to the invention of broadcasting in much the same way that the early modern state reacted to the invention of printing, or contemporary governments to the Internet. It was feared that the wireless might spread illiteracy, or drench the public in pornography and dross, or even foment sedition. During the First World War, the government banned communication between radio hams on grounds of national security. At first, like its inventor, the state saw the wireless as a useful alternative to the tele-graph or the telephone. It was only when ministers realised that wireless technology could be used to broadcast to the public that government became concerned. They decided that the dangers of subversion were better avoided by the creation of a broadcasting monopoly – at first a private one.

At the end of 1922 the British Broadcasting Company, financed by some two hundred British wireless manufacturers and independent shareholders, was granted an exclusive licence by the Post Office to broadcast. The company was commercial but regulated, and derived its revenues from the sale of licences to owners of wireless sets. Its independence was tested during the General Strike of 1926, when Churchill argued strongly for taking it over to disseminate government propaganda, but Stanley Baldwin persuaded his Cabinet that apparent autonomy would make the company a more effective tool of the state.[27] He was right. The company allowed itself to be used as the voice of the government during the strike, refusing even to broadcast a plea for reconciliation by the Archbishop of Canterbury.

But its independence was already at risk. In 1925 a Parliamentary committee decided that broadcasting was too important to be left to a private company:

> Broadcasting has become so widespread, concerns so many people, and is fraught with so many far-reaching possibilities, that the organisation laid down for the British Broadcasting Company no longer corresponds to national requirements or responsibility. Notwithstanding the progress which we readily acknowledge, and to the credit of which the Company is largely entitled, we are impelled to the conclusion that no company or body constituted on trade lines for the profit, direct or indirect, of those composing it can be regarded as adequate in view of the broader considerations now beginning to emerge.[28]

The 'broader considerations' were military, strategic, economic and technological, but mainly a fear that information selected by the market might imperil the security of the state and degrade the populace. In earlier centuries, the state had sought to control the Royal Mail for the same reason: to prevent the transmission of seditious messages.[29]

The British Broadcasting Company was duly dissolved and replaced by a new, publicly owned British Broadcasting Corporation in January 1927. Extraordinarily, the nationalisation aroused no controversy. The Conservative Party hoped to restrict the impact of broadcasting on the morals and opinions of the public, and the Labour Party preferred public ownership on principle. Financed by an annual 10s licence fee paid by the (mainly upper-middle-class) owners of wireless sets, the new BBC was run by a board of governors appointed by the prime minister. Under the director-generalship of John Reith, the former general manager of the private BBC, it became a byword for earnest programming and slavish devotion to reactionary cultural and social standards. Reith vowed to use the 'brute force of monopoly' to moralise the British people. 'To have exploited so great a scientific invention for the purpose and pursuit of entertainment alone,' he said, 'would have been a prostitution of its powers.'[30] For him, listeners were to be patronised. Driven

not by the profit motive but by public service, the new BBC was a foretaste
of the grander public corporations to come.

Natural Monopolies: an Invitation to Nationalise

This was not the only sense in which the BBC anticipated the future. One
of the arguments for a state broadcasting monopoly was the need to avoid
the 'chaos of the ether'. In the unregulated American broadcasting market
of the 1920s, too many stations competing for the same wavelength were
creating a cacophony of noise which had prompted calls for better licensing
and regulation. It made (and makes) sense for the state to decide allocation
of the broadcasting spectrum.

Economists identified another limit to the benefits of competition in broadcasting: the so-called 'natural monopoly', in which technical factors make it
inefficient for more than one producer to supply a service. The classic
examples are the gas, water and electricity industries, where it would be hard
to justify alternative networks of pipes and cables.[31] Regulation – or even
ownership – by the state was the obvious way to prevent exploitation of the
public.

The first natural monopoly to be nationalised was the road network. Its
haphazard development in the eighteenth century had created valuable local
monopolies rather than an effective national network. This was why the roads
were effectively nationalised by 1895, when the last toll was levied on the last
turnpike in the country. In the 1830s and 1840s, the railways threatened to
develop in a similarly haphazard way. Lines were built individually, rather
than as parts of a national system, and used different gauges, making it hard
to link them up. Owners resisted calls for different carriers to operate on the
same track, and the high costs of construction excluded competing lines
being built. The risk of monopolistic practices was obvious, but attempts to
regulate freight rates and fares proved ineffective or perverse.

By the mid-1840s, this had made the railways a candidate for nationalisation.
As president of the Board of Trade under Peel, Gladstone inserted into the
Railway Act of 1844 powers for the state to take over any railway, at the end
of a twenty-one-year period, if the public expressed dissatisfaction with the
cost or quality of service. When the option to buy became available twenty
years later, Gladstone proposed nationalisation to the prime minister. The
proposal was reviewed and rejected by a Royal Commission.[32] The attractions
of an integrated national network with co-ordinated prices and services were
not strong enough to counter the instinctive presumption in favour of private
ownership and against spending public money on buying assets.

But public ownership was not unthinkable, as the 1868 Conservative nationalisation of the telegraph network (which had developed along the railway tracks) showed. This was an astonishing event, occurring at the height of the Victorian faith in free trade and *laissez-faire*. Its rationale was the inefficiency of competition between private companies to provide telegraph services, which had led to a duplication of networks and a confusion of charges. J. L. Ricardo, founder and chairman of the Electric and International Telegraph Company, pressed the government to nationalise the industry in the interests of cheapness and efficiency, and the state paid £10.5 million to buy out the existing companies. A uniform charge, irrespective of distance, was promptly imposed.[33]

Another natural monopoly, the electricity industry, was slated for nationalisation almost as soon as it became commercially viable in 1878. Experience with private provision of gas, water and railways had persuaded late Victorian policymakers that public ownership of electricity generation and transmission was inevitable, but it did not happen until the Baldwin government set up the Central Electricity Board (CEB) in 1926. The Board did not take over the 600-odd generating stations, and distribution was left in the hands of local authorities and private companies, but it was given a monopoly over purchase of all electricity output. The aim was to concentrate generation at the most efficient power stations and link them via a single National Grid.

Similar arguments were used by Winston Churchill, then president of the Board of Trade, when he set up the Port of London Authority in 1908. Regarded then as a dangerous step towards socialism – it effectively nationalised the Thames from Teddington to the Nore – the Authority was advanced as an antidote to ruinous competition and under-investment by a string of private dock companies operating on the river. Significantly, control of the Authority remained in the hands of the private operators, its members being elected by the users of the river and its docks and harbours. Equally significantly, this arrangement was described by R. H. Tawney as 'a very bad constitution' of exactly the kind which nationalisation should avoid.

The architects of the BBC, the first of the modern public corporations, took his advice. The BBC was a different kind of organisation from either the CEB or the Port of London Authority or even the Post Office. (The Royal Mail was a department of government, and remained one until it too became a public corporation in 1969.) Its structure was designed to achieve political accountability without ministerial interference. It was run by an unelected board accountable to a minister answerable to Parliament, and the model was copied twice before the Second World War. The London Passenger Transport Board (LPTB), devised by Herbert Morrison as minister of Transport to nationalise the privately owned underground train and bus companies in the capital, adopted it. So did BOAC.

It was a bipartisan invention. The BBC (like the CEB) was established by a Conservative government. The legislation setting up the LPTB was initiated by the Labour government of 1929–31, but enacted by the National Government, which also created BOAC. Dual parentage has not prevented all public corporations becoming known, in an unjust slight to the former Labour lord president, as 'Morrisonian'. Although Morrison was sceptical about public ownership, and favoured a wide range of experiments, he was the one minister with a workable method of nationalising an industry. His mistake was to popularise the LPTB in *Socialisation and Transport*, published in 1933.

During the 1930s nationalisation finally moved beyond morals and pragmatism, and acquired intellectual clout. The catastrophic economic collapse and mass unemployment of the Great Depression persuaded collectivists that competitive capitalism was intrinsically prodigal, not only of labour but also of capital. Some socialists, and notably Oswald Mosley, became convinced that nationalisation was an integral part of the solution to the chaos and wastefulness of capitalism, enabling governments to affect investment, output and employment directly. Leading socialist economists such as G. D. H. Cole and Douglas Jay were convinced that capitalism was tending towards monopoly and that in the absence of competition, the profit motive and the price mechanism could not be relied upon to allocate resources efficiently. Nationalisation became an integral part of the alternative to monopolistic capitalism: economic 'planning'.

In *The Socialist Case*, published in 1938, Jay argued that public monopoly was the only sensible alternative to the certainty of private monopoly:

We must . . . accept the fact . . . that large-scale organisation of industry in a few units collaborating more or less openly in price and production policy has come to stay, and ought to stay, in modern conditions. This, however, establishes the overwhelmingly important conclusion that there is no justification for leaving such industries any longer in private hands. With the admission – by industrialists themselves – that competition has largely vanished, the justification for private ownership and control has vanished also . . . The choice in reality is not between competition and planning, but between planning by private profit-seeking groups, and planning by a Public Authority responsible ultimately to Parliament.[34]

By the time the second edition was published in 1946 the Second World War, in which all major private industries were subjected to state control, had put economic planning of this kind to a massive and seemingly successful test.

The Nationalisations of 1945–51

This was why nationalisation began in earnest with the election of the Labour government in 1945: at last, moral earnestness was harnessed to economic necessity. The only exception was the first nationalisation, of the Bank of England. The Bank had acquired a special status in socialist demonology, as the orchestrator of the 'bankers' ramp' which brought down the Labour government in 1931 and the author of deflationary policies which exacerbated the Great Depression. It was taken into public ownership as an act of exorcism rather than planning. The 17,000 private shareholders – the most important of which appointed the governor, the deputy governor and the directors – were bought out for holdings of gilt-edged stock, and the Treasury was empowered to give directions to the Bank. Otherwise, nothing changed. The conduct of monetary policy was unaltered. The governor, deputy governor, board and court all retained their positions.[35] Unlike France and Italy, private banks and insurance companies were untouched.

The nationalisation of the coal industry, despite a history of near-Irish passion and complexity, was easier to justify. They may have sung *Cwm Rhondda* in the voting lobbies and hung banners outside the pits on 1 January 1947 proclaiming, 'This colliery is now managed by the National Coal Board on behalf of the people,' but nobody was seriously opposed to the idea. The coal royalties belonging to landowners were nationalised, at a cost of £76.5 million, in 1938. The 800-odd private mining companies had been effectively nationalised during the war, and there was little public sympathy for coal-owners, who were widely blamed for running the industry down during the inter-war years. Churchill accepted nationalisation on behalf of the Conservative Party in August 1945, and his MPs voted against the measure only for the sake of opposing, not on grounds of principle. The Reid Report of 1945 had already recommended the public sponsorship of mergers between the private coal companies, the owners were begging for government aid, and the industry was popularly regarded as ripe for sweeping rationalisation. The spirit of the times argued that this was best accomplished by the state. The new National Coal Board was chaired by the former managing director of Powell Duffryn, the largest of the private coal-mining companies, who had long favoured nationalisation.

In the case of the electricity industry, the only heat generated by nationalisation stemmed from the feeling that it should have occurred years before. A Conservative government had nationalised electricity generation twenty years earlier, two thirds of the distribution companies were already in public hands, and a government report had recommended the nationalisation of the rest in 1936. Electricity, it was said, was in need of rationalisation. Supply was in the hands of a patchwork of 635 separate enterprises (there were seventy-five in London alone in 1947) using different voltages and currents, charging an array of tariffs, and governed by no less than 240 separate pieces of legislation. So the Electricity Act of 1947 did not mark the realisation of socialist aspirations. It reorganised the generation of electricity and unified public and private electricity distributors into 15 separate regional monopolies.

The nationalisation of the gas industry was also based more on industrial logic than socialist ideology. In the 1940s, the private gas-supply industry was fragmented across 700 separate undertakings, 334 of them capitalised at less than £20,000. The companies were widely judged to be badly run, and to supply sub-standard gas and maintenance. One third of the industry was owned by local authorities, which were equally fragmented. The Heyworth Committee, which reported on the industry shortly after the 1945 election, had recommended the formation of regional boards under public control to take over all existing undertakings. When the Labour government decided to nationalise the industry, the private owners did not even bother to oppose the plans. By the 1948 Gas Act, the industry was reorganised into twelve regional monopolies under a Gas Council.

The rail network was effectively nationalised during the First World War, and came close to actual nationalisation shortly after it. The Railways Act of 1921 had amalgamated the 119 separate companies of the Edwardian era into four regional monopolies, and their eventual amalgamation was anticipated by a royal commission in 1931. With government direction resumed during the Second World War, there was a general expectation that nationalisation would follow. The railway owners were disgruntled, particularly about the compensation they were offered, but found the Opposition unwilling to champion their cause. The leader of the Opposition, Winston Churchill, had advocated nationalisation for over forty years. In a famous speech in Glasgow in October 1906 – in which he claimed that 'the whole tendency of civilisation is towards the multiplication of the collective functions of society' – he first advanced a plan to nationalise the railways. He returned to the idea in 1908 and again in 1912, during his time as president of the Board of Trade, and argued for it strongly during the Coupon Election of 1918. 'I have never been shocked by the nationalisation of the railways,' he told Parliament in 1952. 'In fact, I believe I proposed it on my own before almost all members of the House had even thought about going into Parliament. I am by no means sure I have been right. It is no part of my case that I am always right. Anyhow, we have to face facts. The railways are and will remain nationalised.'[36]

Socialists hankered after an integrated national transport policy encompassing rail, road haulage and inland waterways, and nationalisation was a longstanding demand of the unionised railwaymen and transport workers. The Transport Act of 1947 created a new British Transport Commission, charged with providing 'an efficient, adequate, economical and properly integrated system of public inland transport and port facilities'. In practice, the integration and management of an empire consisting of 52,000 miles of railway track, 2,000 miles of canals, 450,000 lorries, 880,000 staff and a disparate collection of ports, harbours, warehouses, hotels and ferries was bound to be difficult to integrate. Dalton called it 'a poor bag of assets'. Five Transport Executives, covering railways, roads, waterways, London Transport and hotels had to be set up by the Commission for the day-to-day running of the industries. Trapped between ministers, the Commission and the trade unions, the Executives were never likely to realise the socialist dream of an integrated national transport network.[37]

Yet only the nationalisation of road haulage provoked ire. The government had taken control of both railways and canals during the war, and many canals were already owned by local authorities. Road passenger transport was also controlled mainly by local authorities (including the LPTB), and all bus and coach services had to be licensed by Area Traffic Commissioners empowered to set fares and timetables. It was decided to reserve powers to take them over but, apart from the bus interests of the railway companies, to leave them alone. Shipping was not tackled at all, so avoiding a potential source of controversy. Road haulage was different. Despite controls during the war, and subjection to Area Licensing Authorities after it, the road haulage industry consisted of thousands of private operators. Some carried only their own goods. Plans by the Attlee government to nationalise the entire industry, including one-man-one-lorry operations, created political uproar, and persuaded the government to restrict its ambitions to larger companies carrying goods, not their own, over distances greater than forty miles. This still resulted in a massive expropriation of private property: 432 haulage companies were purchased by voluntary agreement, 1,880 more by compulsory purchase, and 1,409 were bullied into selling by a government refusal to grant or renew an operating licence. The creation of British Road Services, as the new state enterprise was known, was undeniably unpopular.

The furore over road haulage was eclipsed by the row which accompanied the decision to nationalise the iron and steel industry. In the national pantheon, the ironmaster, unlike the coal-owner, was a heroic entrepreneur. To get the legislation through the House of Lords, the government had to reduce the delaying powers of the Upper House to one year. Debate in the Commons had to be guillotined. The issue split the Labour Cabinet and the parliamentary party, and one Labour MP crossed the floor of the House rather than vote in favour of nationalisation. The prime minister, Clement Attlee, was equivocal at best. Morrison and Bevin were opposed. Even the steel trade union did not press for public ownership.

Ideology was certainly a factor. Steel was, as the minister responsible for the nationalisation said, 'the citadel of British capitalism'.[38] The only real enthusiasts were left-wing Labour backbenchers such as F. S. Cocks, who dreamed that 'once we have nationalised steel we shall have broken the back of capitalist control of industry in this country and its domination for ever, and after that happens, whatever party is in power, we shall be a Socialist State.'[39] Backbench pressure secured the passage of the Iron and Steel Act of 1949, which nationalised all firms which had produced more than 50,000 tons of iron or 20,000 tons of iron and steel in 1946–7. There turned out to be 96 of them, to be merged or liquidated as seen fit by a new British Iron and Steel Corporation.

Yet ideology was not the only factor at work. The industry itself was persuaded of the need for rationalisation. The steel companies had already published a reconstruction plan to be subsidised by government, drawn up at the request of the wartime coalition, when Labour decided nationalisation was the answer. Protected from reality since the 1930s by a combination of tariffs and rearmament, and distorted by price controls, the industry was fragmented and in parts obsolescent, but it was not particularly inefficient, under-capitalised or unproductive – it even had a good record of industrial relations. But the importance of steel to the economy as a whole, and especially to the motor car, shipbuilding and armaments industries, was undoubted. At bottom, the decision of the Labour government to nationalise it was the closest it came to pure Jay-style economic planning.[40]

Method of Expropriation

Despite the conviction of ideologues like Cocks, and the absorption into the public sector of two million employees, the vast extension of public ownership which took place between 1946 and 1949 did not alter British ideas about private property in any fundamental sense. Nationalisation was ostensibly rooted in antipathy to private profit but, because the nationalised industries were to be run on commercial lines, profit was not completely unseated as a measure of success. Nor were the rights of property set aside. Just as the great Whig Ministry had paid slave-owners £20 million for deprivation of their human property when it liberated colonial slaves in 1833, so the equally radical Labour government of 1945–50 paid over £2.6 billion to private shareholders as 'fair compensation' for the expropriation of their property.

'Fair compensation' meant fair to the taxpayers as well as the previous owners. Inevitably, the two sides did not always find it easy to agree. The method chosen initially was that of 'net maintainable revenue', in which the current value of the assets was deduced from estimates of future earnings. But it proved awkward to apply to the nationalisations of the 1940s. Government negotiators and private owners naturally put a different price on the value of the assets. Even where a price could be agreed, it was unclear how it should be divided between thousands of shareholders and bondholders in hundreds of different companies. In the end, net maintainable revenue was used only to value the Bank of England and the coal industry. In every other case, the government paid the market price of the securities: this method was quick, cheap and easy.

Had the government paid the holders in cash, they would have had little cause for complaint. They could have reinvested the money in securities offering a similar, or higher, return. But they were paid in government bonds issued in the name of the industry. Electricity, Gas, British Transport and Iron and Steel bonds were issued, and only £80–90 million of the £2.6 billion was paid in cash.[41] If they sold the securities in the market, they incurred a capital loss if interest rates had risen. The sheer volume of debt being issued to buy the nationalised industries guaranteed that interest rates would rise, even without the economic difficulties which ended in the devaluation of September 1949.

The historian of the nationalised industries reckons the state achieved good value for money, with the exception of the railways, and secured a bargain in the case of the Bank of England. The use of the net maintainable revenue formula meant that the price took no account of the valuable gold reserves owned by the Bank. Only the railways, which suffered a catastrophic loss of traffic to the roads, looked expensive by the end of the 1950s.[42] Even there, government-generated inflation steadily eroded the real cost of the debt. John Redwood estimated that by 1980 inflation had wiped out 95 per cent of the value of the compensation paid to former owners.[43]

A paradoxical consequence of the method of nationalisation was that, in one sense, ownership of the industries (except coal and Cable & Wireless, where the owners were paid in cash) was not transferred to the state at all. Their capital continued to be owned by the former shareholders. Admittedly, since the securities were debt rather than equity they had no voting rights; equity capital disappeared from the balance sheets of the nationalised industries. Control rather than ownership had passed to the State.[44] The government could have assumed ownership as well, but the Treasury refused to consider taking equity stakes in the nationalised industries. Officials reasoned that ownership by the state would increase the pressure for subsidies and reduce the income received from those which were profitable, on the grounds

TABLE 10.1
The Cost of Nationalisation (£ million)

	Vesting Date	Payment	Cost
Bank of England	1946	Gilts	58.2
Civil aviation*	1946	–	–
Cable & wireless†	1947	Cash	32.2
Coal	1947	Cash and Gilts	392.0
Railways	1948	Transport Stock	927.3
LPTB	1948	Transport Stock	128.1
Canals and waterways	1948	Transport Stock	11.4
Private rail wagons	1948	Transport Stock	43.0
Road haulage	1948	Transport Stock	40.2
Electricity	1948	Electricity Stock	542.0
Gas	1949	Gas Stock	220.0
Iron and steel	1951	Iron/Steel Stock	245.8
Total			2,640.2

Source: Chester, *The Nationalization of British Industry*, HMSO, 1975, pp. 1009–25.

* BOAC was already publicly owned and other companies were acquired by private negotiation. No provision for compensation was made in the Civil Aviation Act.
† Cable & Wireless gave effect to a wartime agreement between Commonwealth countries to link public telecommunications utilities to the United Kingdom. The compensation paid to private shareholders excludes 2.6 million shares worth £3.3 million (9.5 per cent of the issued share capital) already owned by the Treasury.

that they needed to conserve resources. The nationalised industries were, in effect, unowned – and this was the source of their problems.

The Unowned Industries

In theory, every British citizen owned one fifty- or sixty-millionth of every nationalised industry. In practice, they owned nothing. Since their rights of ownership could not be realised in the marketplace, they did not correspond to normal rights of property at all. 'Ownership by the State,' as Thatcher pointed out in her memoirs, 'is just that – ownership by an impersonal legal entity: it amounts to control by politicians and civil servants.'[45] The ownership of the assets of the nationalised industries was vested in the corporations. They were not companies, governed by the Companies Acts and answerable to shareholders, but public corporations set up by Act of Parliament. The managers were not answerable to Parliament but to ministers who were answerable to the electorate. This meant that ministers intervened constantly in the management of the nationalised industries, chiefly to please the voters. Richard Marsh, a former Labour transport secretary who chaired British Rail in the early 1970s, said of his time at the railways that there was 'no planning beyond the next general election'.

Electorates dislike low pay, high prices, job losses and strikes. This gave ministers powerful incentives to disown the management in pay disputes, resist redundancy plans, and meet the cost of pay rises. Wage increases, which in a private business feed straight through to prices, tended in nationalised industries to be accommodated by an extra subsidy from the taxpayer. The electoral cycle also has a marked bias in favour of current spending over capital investment. Marsh was once instructed by ministers not to reduce long-term maintenance costs by replacing worn-out short rail with better quality long-welded rail because short rail was charged to the revenue account and long rail to the capital account. If new investment occurred, it was invariably directed to marginal constituencies or politically sensitive areas. The nationalised steel industry got two strip mills rather than one: the first in Wales and the second in Scotland. Politicians were unable to choose which group of supporters should benefit.

No industry was more politicised than coal. At first the National Coal Board (NCB) failed to raise output sufficiently to meet demand, but imports of cheap oil and gas, the growth of hydro-electric power and nuclear energy soon reduced the demand for coal. The NCB needed to close unprofitable pits and mechanise the profitable ones, which they did, but far too slowly, because pit closures were politically unacceptable. In 1965 the government began to bribe the CEGB to buy coal it did not want. By 1969, the Board was taking half of all coal mined in Britain, and stockpiling it at huge expense. Coal Board deficits were repeatedly written off. Heavy taxes were imposed on imports of oil. Where pits did close, regional development grants and redundancy payments were lavished on the area. It is not surprising that the leaders of the National Union of Mineworkers (NUM) became convinced they could defy economic reality indefinitely. They brought down one government in 1974, humiliated another in 1981, and entered the disastrous strike of 1984–5 demanding no pit closures, an import ban and a government pledge to underwrite 'loss without limit'.

The political pressure to 'buy British' and cross-subsidise loss-making public services was incessant. The CEGB was bullied into supporting nuclear power in the 1950s and 1960s on the grounds that it would create a new export industry. The Post Office was obliged in the 1970s to buy sub-standard British telephone technology, in the hope that it would encourage export sales. The Royal Mail was (and is) expected to use the profits of large urban post offices to subsidise rural sub-post offices. British Airways was expected to buy British aeroplanes rather than their cheaper and better American rivals. Just four years before it was privatised, British Gas told the Monopolies and Mergers Commission that it kept open unprofitable showrooms for 'public service and social reasons'.

One of the biggest obstacles to the privatisation of the railways was the maintenance by public subsidy of loss-making lines for social reasons. Another was the unwillingness of ministers to sanction increases in rail fares. Price-fixing of this kind was commonplace. Ministers held down the price of coal, gas, electricity and railway tickets to please the voter-as-consumer or reduce artificially the rate of inflation. If private industry complained about energy or steel or freight charges, the nationalised industries were ordered to reduce not their costs but their prices. 'It is clearly ridiculous', wrote a sympathetic analyst in 1971, 'to make the highest possible profit one can on behalf of the nation as shareholders if it is earned at the expense of these same shareholders in the guise of consumers or employees.'[46] But without profits, the industries were dependent on the taxpayer for investment. Natur-ally, ministers preferred to spend money on schools and hospitals. While the salaries of teachers, doctors, nurses, train drivers and telephone engineers went up, trains broke down, sewers crumbled, and telephones took months to install.

If a nationalised industry insisted on raising its prices, the Treasury used it as an excuse to cut its subsidy or borrowing limit. Inadvertently, this destroyed one of the main arguments in favour of nationalisation. The econ-omic planners had claimed that private owners could not be relied upon to invest without massive increases in prices. The government could always borrow more cheaply (they continued) so nationalised industry investment would always be more efficient than the private alternative. They also argued that investment by the nationalised industries was an essential weapon in reducing the amplitude of the trade cycle, since it could rise in recessions and fall in booms. 'Subsequent experience', as Alec Cairncross wryly observed, 'cast doubt on this attractive hypothesis.'[47] In the end, the main argument for privatisation was the need to give the nationalised industries access to the capital markets to invest in the re-equipment and refurbishment of their capital assets.

Privatisation de-politicised the decision to borrow. In the nationalised indus-tries, this was impossible. All decisions were political: ministers fixed prices, delayed or rewrote investment proposals, resisted redundancy plans, and rebuffed closures or cutbacks. Trade union leaders, suppliers and customers realised that it was more effective to negotiate with the minister than the management, but ministerial interference was not always overt. Political powers over appointments and access to finance gave them a constant, if subterranean, influence over nationalised industry decisions. These were known at the time as 'lunch table directions'.

The nationalised industries were the closest Britain has come to creating totalitarian-style bureaucracies, in which political and managerial decision-making is amalgamated. Deprived of autonomy, and insulated from the incentives and disciplines of the marketplace, nationalised industry managers valued neither efficiency nor profit. They enhanced their status and security by empire-building and the acquisition of personal comforts – a reduced workload, higher pay and a generous pension. The same temptations are present in large private companies, but their impact is blunted by the threat of bankruptcy or takeover. Nationalised industries neither go bankrupt nor get taken over.

Spiritual Failure of Nationalisation

It is sometimes argued that these problems were not foreseen, but they were all predicted by the opponents of nationalisation and ignored or mocked as out-of-date. Sir Charles Reid, chairman of the committee whose report preceded the nationalisation of the coal industry, resigned from the National Coal Board just a year after its formation, complaining of inattention to profits and costs. Nobody cared. Nationalised industries were not meant to be driven by financial disciplines but by the ethic of public service. The promise of nationalisation was a new moral order in which the mechanisms of the market economy – profits, prices, competition, and the like – would be replaced by new industrial spirit. 'The public corporation must be no mere capitalist business, the be-all and end-all of which is profits and dividends,' wrote Herbert Morrison in 1953. 'Its board and officers must regard themselves as the high custodians of the public interest.'[48]

As early as 1893 the socialist journalist, Robert Blatchford, was scoffing at critics who argued that socialism would not work because it destroyed the incentive of gain. Love of gain, he argued in Merrie England, was not a facet of human nature but a reflection of 'the state in which men live under a competitive commercial system.'[49] Once capitalism gave way to socialism, men would work for love of each other. R. H. Tawney argued that 'though British socialism is by no means indifferent to economic considerations, its foundations are ethical. Even if the way of co-operation did not yield all the economic advantages expected from it, we should continue to choose it. Both the type of individual character and the style of social existence fostered by it are those that we prefer.'[50] But he did not think it would come to that. 'By making the most fundamental of all industries a public service carried on in partnership between the State and the workers,' he wrote of the Sankey plan for the nationalisation of the coal industry, 'it will call into operation motives of public spirit and professional zeal . . . and which will raise the whole tone and quality of our industrial civilisation.'[51] Stafford Cripps told the House of Commons in 1949 that 'it is quite a false conception to consider that it is necessary to make a profit out of any industry except under a capitalist system.' In *The Socialist Case*, Douglas Jay argued that 'the British people . . . wish to feel themselves to be working for the community as a whole, and not for either private wages or private profit.'[52]

It is now obvious that nationalisation did alter the pattern of incentives in publicly-owned industries, but in quite the opposite direction to that anticipated. Within a year of nationalisation, the journal of the National Union of Railwaymen, *Railway Review*, was reporting widespread demoralisation, idleness and delinquency:

> Never was there a time when discontent was so rampant as it is today on British Railways. It is with the utmost difficulty that staff can be retained in the service, and . . . delinquency rears its ugly head in so many ways as to be a nightmare to very many of the supervisory staff; it has become a problem never experienced in days gone by . . . The first and most important thing that is wrong is the gradual development of a soulless, dehumanizing and individuality-killing atmosphere . . . Men – good, honest and trustworthy men – are leaving the railways every week in large numbers, all because of this soul-destroying system of remote control; a control that means nothing to them but a voice giving orders from out of the mouth of a telephone receiver.

The story was the same in the mining industry. One of the principal causes of the coal shortage in the harsh winter of early 1947 was absenteeism. Exactly two years after the formation of the National Coal Board, the Policy and Publicity Sub-Committee of the Labour Party reported to the National Executive Committee that 'we must recognize that the spiritual results of nationalization are not as good as we hoped.'[53]

They got steadily worse. On the nationalised docks, the trade unions persuaded the government to make it a criminal offence for a port to employ anyone who was not a 'registered' dock worker. The National Dock Labour Scheme, introduced in 1917, turned an already bloated payroll into a perpetual levy on the profitability of the docks. Its malign effects were enlarged by the Heath government, which obliged port employers to pay the wages of registered dockers even if there was no work for them to do. This was the price of settling the 1972 dock strike, sparked by the jailing of five dockers after a campaign against the containerisation of seaborne freight. The main effect was to divert container traffic to privately owned ports outside the scheme, like Felixstowe and Newhaven, or to continental ports such as Rotterdam and Antwerp. The National Dock Labour Scheme was abolished in July 1989. The government simply gave the registered dockers £35,000 to surrender their privileges. This cost the taxpayer £141 million.

By the time the Heath government caved in to the dockers in 1972, the nationalised industries had become the playthings of the militant and the workshy. Every nationalised industry workforce was unionised. Their leaders did not want a role in management, since any form of responsibility would have compromised their chief ambition of extracting more money for less work. Union officials could count on the management to provide them with office space and a ready flow of funds from closed shops and the automatic deduction of union dues.[54] At the Central Electricity Authority, one fifth of the board consisted of workers' representatives. But their primary loyalty was never in doubt. The trade unions turned the nationalised industries into cauldrons of industrial unrest. They became a byword for strikes, go-slows, overmanning, unwarranted pay rises, high prices, restrictive working practices, subsidies, import restrictions, waste and featherbedding.

This retrogressive transformation began almost immediately. The first step the National Coal Board took after nationalisation of the mining industry was to cut working hours and raise wages. By the 1970s the president of the NUM, Joe Gormley, was effectively running the industry in the interests of the workforce. The chairman of the Coal Board, Derek Ezra, did not dare to close a pit or appoint a manager without seeking Gormley's approval. A similar relationship developed at British Rail between Peter Parker, the chairman, and the leaders of Aslef and the NUR. Its legacy was mutual distrust. When Anthony Hidden reported on the Clapham railway disaster of 1989, he was struck by 'how obvious and how deep was the mistrust and suspicion employer had for union and union for employer.'

The Economic Failure of the Nationalised Industries

Idle, strike-happy workers were only part-authors of the dire performance of the nationalised industries. Managers following plans, rather than responding to prices, did the rest. Between the wars, a vigorous debate had taken place between market economists and their socialist counterparts over whether a publicly owned economy could be run efficiently. The Austrian market economist, Ludwig von Mises, had argued powerfully that nationalised industries were bound to be wasteful because they relied on bureaucrats rather than prices to allocate capital and labour between competing investments. He lost the argument to the socialists, who claimed that rational bureaucrats working for state-owned enterprises would allocate resources more efficiently than private companies. By sticking to textbook business practices, these paragons of reason were bound to out-perform the hunches of mere entrepreneurs.

Douglas Jay's *The Socialist Case*, which had a profound influence on the post-war Labour government, was imbued with this faith in the power of the rational bureaucrat. 'The case for socialism and planning in a free society,' he wrote in its closing pages, 'is . . . nothing more than a plea for the application of reason and intelligence to the job of producing and distributing the good things of life.'[55] (It drew him to conclude, in an infamous phrase, that 'the gentleman in Whitehall really does know better what is good for people than people know themselves.')[56] The disinterested expert in an office in Whitehall, rationally weighing the material needs of citizens and allocating resources accordingly, was a key part of the intellectual case for the nationalisations of the 1940s.

This prospect derived great emotional force from the longstanding Socialist critique of the inequalities, arbitrariness and apparent wastefulness of capitalism. Tawney, writing in 1922, before the possibilities of rational calculation under socialism became the stuff of academic dispute, described the idea that state management was inherently inefficient as 'hide-bound pedantry and irresponsible caprice'; he also dismissed the notion that competition is the friend of the consumer as 'cynically comic' and 'the precise opposite of the truth'. Was it unreasonable to suggest, he asked, that 'a combination of intellectual and moral training, professional pride, and organised knowledge would be at least as effective an economic engine as the struggle for personal gain which at present drives the wheels of industry? That question has hardly been discussed by economists.'[57]

In the next decade, economists did discuss the question of non-economic incentives, and armed the planners with a powerful new argument for nationalisation. Subsequently, practice proved less pleasing than theory. By the 1970s, economic planners had discovered that the rational calculator did not exist outside their imaginations. The politicians, civil servants, managers and employees responsible for the nationalised industries were pursuing self-interested strategies. With this discovery, they surprised no one but themselves. The popular rendition of what is now called Public Choice theory, *Parkinson's Law*, was first published in 1957.

It is a curious commentary on the self-absorption of the planners that the shortcomings of the nationalised industries were apparent to the public immediately, decades ahead of the same appreciation by academics and policymakers. The theory of rational calculation was still being applied as late as 1978, in the last of the three great White Papers on the nationalised industries. These documents (published in 1961, 1967 and 1978), attempted to put theory into practice by laying down financial techniques and objectives to ensure that prices matched costs and that subsidies for non-economic but socially desirable services (e.g., rural post offices and branch lines) were not excessive.[58]

Each reaffirmation of the doctrine of rational calculation was greeted enthusiastically by politicians, officials and academic commentators. As late as 1981 the Central Policy Review Staff reported that the performance of the nationalised industries could be transformed by setting strategic objectives, packing their boards with private sector managers, conducting regular efficiency audits, intensifying scrutiny by government, and forming 'business groups' within each sponsoring department. That same year, the scope for introducing private finance was explored enthusiastically, but with no practical effect.[59]

A year later the government tried to formalise its relations with the nationalised industries by agreeing written policy objectives with them. 'The value of this exercise was somewhat limited,' wrote Nigel Lawson of the agreement between the Department of Energy and the National Coal Board, 'by the need for the letter to take three forms: a list of general policy objectives, suitable for publication; an amplified version of the same, for private circulation; and a note of a frank meeting between Norman Siddall and myself, of which a single copy was kept locked in my office safe.'[60] The limited practical results of these experiments reinforced the case for a more radical approach. Privatisation began in earnest in November 1984, with the sale of 50 per cent of British Telecom.

Why did it take so long for policymakers to catch up with public opinion? Probably because the theory of rational calculation rested on unfavourable comparisons between an actual capitalist economy and an ideal socialist economy, which rendered it invulnerable to intellectual counter-attack until public ownership was discredited by practice over a prolonged period. The performance of the nationalised industries was not studied seriously during the first two decades of their existence. Most politicians, officials and economists subscribed to the conventional view that ownership was irrelevant to performance. Given the hostility of public opinion to further schemes of nationalisation, there was no political incentive to think any other way. For leading Labour politicians of the 1950s and 1960s, conscious of the electoral unpopularity of Clause IV, the irrelevance of ownership was a godsend.

The classic statement of the doctrine was written in 1956 by Tony Crosland, who argued that private companies owned by impersonal institutional investors were little different from nationalised industries:

> Efficiency has little to do with ownership because in the modern corporation ownership has little to do with control. Thus a change of ownership, by itself, makes little difference ... The basic fact is the large corporation, facing fundamentally similar problems and acting in fundamentally the same way whether publicly or privately owned. Its efficiency depends simply on the quality of its top management, and on whether the firm or industry is structurally well-adapted from a technical point of view.[61]

A year after *The Future of Socialism* was published, the National Executive Committee of the Labour Party rejected nationalisation as an end in itself. Public ownership lingered on as a policy aim only on the extreme left of the Party.

Rediscovery of the Relevance of Ownership

The irrelevance of ownership to economic performance remained the orthodox view on the soft left of British politics until the 1990s, when Blair excised Clause IV from the Labour constitution. In 1982, Peter Parker assured Sampson that 'the real problem is the relationship between governments and all industry; nationalised industry is only the sharp end of it.'[62] The SDP–Liberal Alliance, of which Parker was a prominent supporter, declared in 1987 that 'the real industrial issues are those of efficiency and responsiveness to the consumer rather than ownership.'[63] Denis Healey, the most important right-wing Labour figure not to join the SDP, remained an unrepentant Croslandite until he left Parliament. 'The central problems of private industry now concern management, organisation, and accountability rather than ownership,' he wrote in his memoirs. 'That is why privatisation is as much a red herring as nationalisation; the question is how an industry can best serve the people's needs, not ... the form of ownership.'[64]

Such views were shared by traditional Whitehall. Former Treasury civil servant Leo Pliatzky argued that the distinction between 'market' and 'non-market' sectors of the economy was more meaningful than that between public and private sectors: 'The question of ownership is less basic than the distinction between the commercial and the non-commercial ... From the point of view of a diversified pattern of ownership, control and patronage, there is a case for a degree of public ownership of industry, and there are some industries which fit naturally into a public sector.'[65] In 1989, Tony Blair was not embarrassed to advocate the re-nationalisation of gas, water and electricity, on strategic grounds. 'Their operations underpin the rest of industry,' he wrote. 'We believe that the great utilities must be treated as public services and should be owned by the public.'[66]

One reason that the intellectual foundations of public ownership remained undisturbed is that nationalisation seemed, at least for a time, to be working. Although the performance of the nationalised industries during the 1940s and 1950s was disappointing, this was attributed largely to the difficulties of massive industrial reorganisation. Their performance was bound to improve in the 1960s, and it did. When Pryke completed the first substantial study of the nationalised industries in 1971, he came to the (disputed) conclusion that they had out-performed the private sector at home and abroad, and that public ownership was the most significant factor in their success:

> What would have happened if they had remained in the hands of their former owners it is impossible to know and for the most part unrewarding to speculate, but in view of the quality of their performance it is difficult to believe that it would have been of the same standard had they not been transferred to public ownership . . . The belief that the nationalised industries have a mediocre record and that ownership is irrelevant to economic performance is a dogma which arose during the first and most difficult years of public ownership, and has lived on to become a serious obstacle to rational inquiry and rational conviction . . . The creditable way in which public enterprise performs is something more than a coincidence. The relationship between good behaviour and public ownership must henceforth be regarded as one of cause and effect.[67]

He attributed the success of the nationalised industries to managerial changes introduced as a consequence of nationalisation; rationalisation once they were taken into public ownership; the financial discipline imposed by the Treasury and by the regular interest payments of debt, rather than equity, finance; frequent parliamentary and press inquiries into their performance; the government imposition of rational pricing and investment appraisal techniques; and the motivating knowledge, common to nationalised industry managers and workers alike, that the great British public would pay the price of any inefficiency or failures on their part.[68]

Today, Pryke's book reads like a spoof. But it was not until the mid-1970s that there was a decisive change in both the political and intellectual appreciation of nationalisation, and in the conclusions supported by empirical evidence. Free market intellectuals had argued against nationalisation for decades, but in 1971 Pryke felt able to treat them as cranks. That same year, Sampson described Nicholas Ridley, one of the few politicians to demand de-nationalisation, as a 'throwback'. Eventually, it was the power not of ideas but of ideas married to popular disquiet which destroyed the consensus about the irrelevance of ownership to economic performance. Nationalisation was always unpopular with the general public, but in the 1970s unpopularity turned into contempt. Several established public sector industries – coal, rail, and especially steel – had begun to record huge and habitual losses, and nationalisation had come to mean the rescue of ailing private sector companies. The Heath government nationalised Upper Clyde Shipbuilders and Rolls Royce; the third Wilson administration rescued British Leyland and the shipbuilding industry.

British Leyland (BL) became a symbol of publicly owned industrial disaster. The government created the company in January 1968 by sponsoring the merger of Leyland Motors (Leyland buses and Rover cars) and British Motor Holdings (Austin, Morris and Jaguar cars), in the hope that a single company would revolutionise the design, production and marketing of cars in Britain. The effect was quite the reverse. The merger created a fragmented network of high cost factories which, between 1968 and 1974, made total pre-tax profits of just £104 million on cumulative sales of over £8 billion. By the end of 1974, BL was in such difficulties that the management approached the secretary of state for Industry for assistance from the taxpayer.

It helped that Tony Benn was an unreconstructed socialist, but not essential. No minister of the pre-Thatcher period would have allowed a 'strategic' industry such as motor manufacturing to collapse, or risked the subsequent political fall-out in the West Midlands. By 1974 BL was the only major British motor company still in business. Vauxhall was owned by General Motors; Ford had bought out its remaining British shareholders in 1961; and Rootes was in the hands of Chrysler. Benn agreed to inject an initial £100 million, and called for a report on the company from Donald Ryder, chairman of Reed International and an industrial adviser to the government. The Ryder report duly recommended nationalisation of BL and the investment of £1.4 billion of public money in new factories, machinery and models. Far from re-invigorating the company, nationalisation exacerbated its problems. Regular infusions of public money were used not to fund the investments and redundancies proposed by Ryder but to meet the wage demands of a workforce manipulated by militant trade unionists, who knew the government would not let the company fail. Between 1975 and its eventual privatisation in 1988 BL absorbed £2.9 billion of public grants and accumulated another £1.6 billion in government-guaranteed debt.

BL did more than any other nationalised industry to discredit public owner-ship, not least because the public could draw the connections between the abysmal quality of its cars and the cantankerous nature of its workforce. The 1970s was also a period of high inflation, and public resentment of rising coal, gas, electricity, post and telephone charges mounted. During the middle years of the decade, nationalised industry prices were rising anywhere between two and eight times as fast as prices generally, as the great public corporations passed the cost of pay increases to consumers in the form of higher prices. Strikes in pursuit of pay claims became the dominant image of nationalisation. The cost of the nationalised industries, in subsidies, capital grants and write-offs registered with taxpayers for the first time. By 1976 David Galloway could write: 'the difficulty in making any objective examination of the nationalised industries is the extent to which the issue is already prejudged: the very name now evokes inefficiency and can almost be guaranteed to cause a wry smile.'[69]

As real rates of return in the private sector fell to 3–4 per cent in the 1970s and early 1980s, the average rate of return in the nationalised industries fell to zero or worse. In a second study of the performance of the nationalised industries over the previous twelve years, Richard Pryke in 1981 reversed his earlier conclusions and argued that 'in general the nationalised industries' performance has been third-rate.' He backed his analysis with case studies of three nationalised industries – British Airways, British Rail ferry services and the Electricity and Gas Board shops – which were not monopolies, and which were manifestly less efficient than their privately owned competitors.[70]

The inescapable conclusion was that ownership did matter after all. It mattered because nationalised industries were free of the most basic financial and commercial discipline: the threat of corporate failure. In the final analysis, they could always borrow or beg from the taxpayer. They could overpay their workers, overcharge or undercharge their customers, squander their capital and shun all avenues of innovation, sure in the knowledge that the Treasury would enable them to survive.

Ironically, this was well understood by the man whose name will be for-ever associated with the nationalisations of the mid-twentieth century, Herbert Morrison. In *Socialisation and Transport*, he explained why he had decided against giving a state guarantee to the London Passenger Transport Board:

> The Government did not wish to do this for it might well have encour-aged a spirit of slackness, or even recklessness, on the part of the Board in matters of management, on the part of the travelling public in demanding lower fares and uneconomic facilities, and on the part of the work people in asking for big concessions as to conditions of labour;

all might be tempted to say 'Well, after all, the Treasury is behind us.' As I have shown from the Russian experience, this is a dangerous frame of mind.[71]

The obvious solution to the problems caused by non-ownership was to return the nationalised industries to private ownership. But it proved surprisingly difficult to achieve. Despite their unpopularity, privatisation was almost as unpopular as nationalisation. Ahead of every significant sale of the 1980s, public opinion was hostile. Even Thatcher proceeded cautiously at first. On the left, opposition to privatisation has never faltered. A dwindling band of Old Labour socialists still cling to the dream of worker self-management and 'industrial democracy', the last echo of the moral fervour which first brought public ownership to life. The dream, of an end to Property, masters them still.

New Labour is unlikely to shift the boundary between public and private sector it inherited from the Conservatives, except at the margin. This reflects its dislike of change, but also a refusal to accept that nationalisation failed because it destroyed property rights and that privatisation succeeded because it restored them. Instead, it plans to truncate them with tougher regulation of privatised companies.[72] But regulation is merely a temporary substitute for competition; what matters is ownership. Nationalisation, as much as privatisation, proved it.

CHAPTER ELEVEN

THE PRIVATISED INDUSTRIES

Public utilities like Telecom and Gas and essential industries such as British Airways and Rolls-Royce were sold off by the Tories in the closest thing, post-war, to legalised political corruption. What we all owned was taken away from us, flogged off at a cheap price to win votes and the proceeds used to fund tax cuts. In fact it was a unique form of corruption, since we were bribed with our own money.

TONY BLAIR, 1987[1]

What causes the inefficiency of common ownership is not that it is owned by many individuals but that individuals cannot trade their rights in the property.

CENTO VELJANOVSKI[2]

The first difference between running a privatised business and a nationalised business is that a privatised business can go bust. Once you have got that idea across to people, it is astonishing what effect it has.

ROBERT AYLING, CHIEF EXECUTIVE, BRITISH AIRWAYS[3]

Privatisation is not a process that has come to an end but a state of mind, which means it goes on and on.

IAN LANG, INDUSTRY SECRETARY, 1996[4]

It took the nationalised industries thirty years to forfeit the affection of the public. Their privatised successors will take at least as long to win it back. Today, the great water and energy utilities are the most unpopular institutions in the country. In summer, pipes burst, water is short and gardens shrivel. In winter, pensioners shiver in front of heaters they cannot afford to turn on, and the poor pay more to keep warm. On the railways, passengers are denied even a seasonal respite. Hot or cold, dry or wet, trains are always late or cancelled. But as workers are fired and prices go up, profits seem to rise inexorably, and boardroom salaries soar. This is the popular understanding of the biggest redistribution of wealth in Britain since the destruction of the great aristocratic estates.[5] Its grip on the public imagination owes much to ignorance, and more to misunderstanding, but it is rooted in the belief that water, light and warmth are too precious to life to be governed by truck, barter and exchange.

Ten years ago, Tony Blair shared this conviction. 'The major utilities – gas, water, electricity and the rail, postal and telecommunications networks – are uniquely important to the national economy,' he wrote in 1989. 'Their operations underpin the rest of the industry. We believe that the great utilities must be treated as public services and should be owned by the public – by the community as a whole.'[6] He was writing in the year that the water utilities were privatised. According to the opinion polls, only one voter in ten thought it was a good idea. Clear majorities were convinced that the newly privatised telephone service was less efficient and more expensive than its nationalised predecessor. The sale of British Steel, six months beforehand, remains the most popular privatisation; it was supported by less than two voters in five.[7]

In Opposition, Labour Old and New opposed every privatisation because they thought it won votes, not lost them. As late as the summer of 1996, the Labour Party was committed to the re-nationalisation of the railways. After three years of Blairism, it entered the 1997 general election bristling with promises to toughen regulation of every privatised enterprise. The privatised utilities were the victims of its only explicit pledge to tax and spend: the Windfall Tax. Introduced in the budget of July 1997, the tax raised £5.2 billion. Three quarters of it fell on the hated water and electricity companies. Much of the balance was levied on British Gas, alma mater of the archetypal Fat Cat, Cedric Brown.[8] The tax was retrospective, arbitrary and counter-productive (the cost was passed on to customers) but it was undeniably popular.

Were Public Assets Sold Too Cheaply?

By 1997, privatisation had become a part of the stock-in-trade of satirical comedians. Their efforts, and those of tabloid journalists, gradually reduced the public appreciation of privatisation to massive pay rises for bosses, higher prices for customers, and a pay cut or the sack for employees. Caricature has erased memories of what went before. At the time it was privatised, BT had 250,000 customers waiting for a telephone line to be installed. Three in a hundred telephone calls failed because of faults on the line. The public telephone boxes doubled as public lavatories. Electricity and gas prices went down before elections, and up after them. In the water industry, the sewers were crumbling, the beaches were a disgrace, the rivers were filthy, and water shortages were commonplace. The public image of British Rail, its timetables regularly undone by 'the wrong sort of snow' and 'leaves on the line', was of grubby trains and surly staff. Its public voice was the sepulchral croak of Jimmy Knapp announcing another series of one-day strikes.

Few remember these things now. After twenty years of privatisation, *how* public assets were sold matters more than *why*. The main criticism (and the chief justification for the Windfall Tax) is that they were sold for less than they were worth. This is incontrovertible: from 150 sales between 1979 and 1997, the government raised £90 billion in real terms, or about half the net value of the nationalised industries at the outset.[9] The size of this gap is the reason why shares in privatised companies almost always soared in value. A large part of the gain was usually made in the first few days after the sale, and shares in Amersham International, British Airways, British Telecom and Rolls-Royce were all worth a third more than the offer price within a week. Most privatisation issues continued to out-perform the stock market for years, at least until their monopolies were challenged.[10] A reluctance to sell shares in stages, or organise competitive auctions, usually denied the taxpayer any stake in the appreciation of the stock.

Though not deliberate, this underpricing was not unintended. The chief architects of privatisation, Margaret Thatcher and Nigel Lawson, have both admitted that they were prepared to sell nationalised industries cheaply to speed their exit from the public sector and to widen share ownership. In February 1982, Lawson was responsible for the privatisation of Amersham International, the radio-chemical company. Its shares soared to a premium of 35 per cent in early trading after being oversubscribed 25 times at the offer price. But the former chancellor is unapologetic. 'In retrospect, the serious underpricing of Amersham, though in no sense deliberate, may have been no bad thing,' he writes in his memoirs. 'The enormous publicity given to the profits enjoyed by subscribers . . . conveyed the clear message . . . that investing in privatisation issues was a good thing . . . Wider share ownership was an important policy objective and we were prepared to pay a price for it.'[11]

In this light, underpricing of state assets made sense. In Japan, where privatisation issues were consistently overpriced, the programme stalled because investors boycotted the sales. To attract ordinary people, privatisation shares also had to be sold at a fixed price rather than by auction, because they could not be expected to guess the right price to pay. The two sales priced by auction, Britoil and Enterprise, both flopped. But the subsequent performance of fixed price issues often made the initial valuation embarrass-ing. BT shares, which City advisers had insisted would flood the market, went to an immediate premium of 91 per cent. Under pressure from the National Audit Office (NAO) and the Public Accounts Committee, the government slowly got better at pricing privatisation issues. It appointed an independent adviser on pricing, and began to take a more sceptical view of City advice.

Nationalised assets were harder to value than subsequent stock market verdicts suggested. Many companies were privatised with excessively strong balance sheets, allowing them to move to more effective capital structures once they were in private hands. But most nationalised industries did not even prepare proper balance sheets until privatisation was a possibility. When George Jefferson became head of BT in 1981, he was unable to find out what assets the company owned, which were in use and which redundant, and whether either kind was depreciated.[12] At privatisation, nobody even thought to charge a premium for the public land under which BT cables were laid. A valuable asset was simply given away by the government, when it might have charged the company rent for the use of public land.[13]

The water companies left the public sector with a £5 billion golden handshake from the taxpayer, ostensibly to cover the cost of raising water quality. The NAO later believed the government had sold the English and Welsh water industry for £2.3 billion less than it was worth. The Medway Ports, bought by the management for £29.7 million in March 1992, were sold eighteen months later to the Mersey Docks and Harbour Company for £103.7 million. Ownership of the National Grid was transferred to the regional electricity companies at a valuation of £1 billion in 1991. Just four years later the companies themselves valued it for sale at four times this amount. Even the Conservatives were sufficiently embarrassed by this cheeky plan to threaten its owners with a windfall tax. But real assets are easy to undervalue. Royal Ordnance, sold to British Aerospace in April 1987 for £190 million, turned out to be a bargain. Within a year, unwanted factories sold by the taxpayer for £5 million were being sold to property developers for £450 million.

Happy memories of that bargain did not prevent British Aerospace returning to the government in 1998 with a threat to close what remained of Royal Ordnance unless it received a further subsidy. But then British Aerospace was used to periodic treats from the taxpayer. In 1988 the company bought the rump of British Leyland, the Rover car manufacturing business, for £150 million. A year later the NAO reckoned that British Aerospace had paid at least £56.5 million less than it should have done.*[14] Even this was an

---

* The Government was initially tempted to be even more generous. It agreed a net injection of £650 million to reduce the outstanding debts of Rover Group, and reduced this only when the European Commission rejected it as an unfair state aid to industry. The eventual net cost of the sale to the taxpayer was £460 million, including disguised subsidies in the shape of tax concessions and regional aid.

underestimate. Within a year, the company had recouped over four fifths of the purchase price by selling the Daf truck manufacturing venture and the Istel software house.[15] When Honda took a 20 per cent stake in 1990, the company was valued at £520 million, or three and a half times what British Aerospace paid. Just six years after Rover Group was sold by the government at a loss, BMW paid British Aerospace £800 million for it.

'Clawbacks', in which the government reserved the right to reclaim the proceeds of post-privatisation asset disposals, became a regular feature of sales as the programme matured. When electricity was privatised, the government reserved the right to clawback half of any profits made by the regional companies on the sale of surplus property, and withdrew the Central Electricity Generating Board (CEGB) headquarters (near St Paul's) and Bankside Power Station (in Southwark) from the sale rather than see them sold or redeveloped after privatisation.[16] When the bus companies were privatised, many of their most attractive city centre properties were withheld and sold separately.

The sale of British Coal, which put one of the greatest landed estates in the country on the market, was shaped by this growing awareness of the value of real estate. Though its land holdings were much reduced since the 1940s (at nationalisation, the 88 private companies and their 1,500 pits had owned a million acres of land) British Coal still owned around 250,000 acres and, in its last years of public ownership, earned £35 million a year from sales of unwanted property. R. J. Budge, which bought virtually the whole of the English coal industry, acquired a mere 14,000 acres of freehold land, and other buyers acquired negligible leaseholds. Any profits from property disposals by the new owners were clawed back fiercely, and the bulk of the estate was retained for separate sale. Between the privatisation of coal and the winding-up of the British Coal Corporation at Christmas 1997, all but 30,500 acres of the British Coal estate was sold separately, by the government.*

The privatisation of British Rail, sometime owner of an estate of over 200,000 acres, was accompanied by a similar division of the spoils. The operational assets of the railways – tracks, stations, signalling equipment and engineering works – now belong to Railtrack PLC. But non-operational land was retained by the British Railways Board. Its property subsidiary is now landlord to outmoded buildings, disused yards, vacant plots and disused viaducts and bridges too curious to be measured in acres or miles.† By 1998

---

* Letter from Coal Authority, 30 October 1998.
† British Rail did not know how much property it owned. In 1967, after Beeching had trimmed the network by 11,000 miles, Oliver Marriott put it at 280,000 acres. This had shrunk to about 200,000 acres by the time the industry was privatised. See Oliver Marriott, *The Property Boom*, Hamish Hamilton, 1967.

Rail Property Limited had raised £250 million for the taxpayer from over 2,000 individual sales, and valued what remained at £136 million.[17] Much of what remained had long since made that quintessentially English passage from working asset to heritage liability. The viaducts opposed by the founders of the Heritage Industry are now defended as fiercely by their modern successors as an integral part of the landscape. British Rail used to knock down redundant structures, or let them fall down (the Heritage Industry has not forgotten Euston Arch in 1962). Now it has to maintain them until a local authority, museum or group such as the Railway Heritage Trust agrees to take them on.

Leaving the national railway heritage in public ownership relieved the privatised industry of financial responsibility for it. But, in its anxiety to privatise the railways, the government allowed some gems to escape. One reason Railtrack shares rose from £3.90 on flotation in May 1996 to over £10 less than two years later was the over-endowment of the company with property. Railtrack owns a portfolio crammed with rent-producing assets and commercial sites ripe for redevelopment or disposal, including the surprisingly lucrative archway leases favoured by minicab firms and scrap-metal merchants. Most of the 2,500 stations are leased to the train operating companies, but Railtrack has retained the right to redevelop the most promising. The fourteen mainline stations, where the scope for commercial development is greatest, are managed directly already.[18] Railtrack will make over £1 billion from property rents, disposals and developments during its first years in private ownership.

A botched division of British Rail property was not the only reason rail privatisation proved a steal. The first train franchises to be sold had to be fattened with high subsidies. According to the NAO, the seven British Rail train maintenance depots were sold for only £32 million when they had £17 million of cash on their balance sheets.[19] The track maintenance units went cheaply too. A construction company called Jarvis bought the Northern Infrastructure Maintenance Unit for £11 million in 1995. A year later it was worth £50 million. These losses escaped public censure. But the underpricing of the rolling stock leasing companies (Roscos) was too large to lose in the financial pages. Assets valued at £3 billion were sold for £1.7 billion. The NAO reckoned that the government forfeited at least £700 million, but the market came up with an even higher figure.[20] Within two years, all three Roscos were sold to new buyers for an additional £790 million.[21] A Japanese bank made £330 million when one of them was sold. The management buyout team at another turned a joint investment of £300,000 into £83.7 million: a three hundred-fold increase in a matter of months. The managing director, Sandy Anderson, collected £33.6 million.[22] The rewards were so egregious that the transport minister, Gavin Strang, threatened the Rosco Fat Cats with a Windfall Tax of their own.

What changed between November 1995 and July 1996? The long answer is that rail privatisation had acquired an unstoppable momentum. When the initial sales were made, the first rail passenger franchises had yet to be awarded. An anti-privatisation group called Save Our Railways, made up of railway unions, local authorities and environmental groups, was contesting the entire privatisation process in the courts. Orders for new rolling stock had dried up, so the initial buyers were taking a substantial risk. 'If privatisation succeeds in improving the quality of rail services and attracting more passengers then the train operators will be clamouring for new rolling stock,' as the *Financial Times* put it in November 1995. 'If the government's gamble does not pay off the Roscos could be left with the finest collection of vintage trains outside a transport museum.'

But there is a shorter answer: Labour Party policy had changed. Between 1993 and 1996 four successive Opposition spokesmen on transport – John Prescott, Frank Dobson, Michael Meacher and Clare Short – promised to re-nationalise the railways. Tony Blair himself reiterated the message at his second conference as party leader in October 1995. 'If people look at Labour's policy and still want to buy, fine,' said Clare Short at the time. 'But lots of them think they are going to make lots and lots of money, like they did out of electricity, and they won't.' She was wrong. In the summer of 1996 re-nationalisation was abandoned, and the value of the Roscos soared. For their owners, the difference between Old Labour and New Labour was nearly £800 million.

Getting Rid of the Running Costs

Periodic threats by the Opposition did suppress sale prices. But low prices were not the only element which reduced the value of privatisation to the taxpayer; transaction costs were immense. The merchant bankers, lawyers, accountants, fund managers, institutional investors and advertising and public relations consultants employed by the government made a great deal of money out of the privatisation sales, even getting handsome 'completion bonuses' in addition to their fees. The full transaction costs of the privatisation programme will never be known because the information was not collated centrally, but the costs of thirty-one major privatisations between 1981 and 1994 totalled nearly £14 billion, or 34 per cent of the gross proceeds of the sales.

Marketing was one cost. Another was incentives to employees and small

TABLE 11.1
Proceeds of Major Privatisations, 1979–97

Company	Proceeds (£m)*
Amersham International	64
Associated British Ports Holdings plc	97
Atomic Energy Authority Technology	213
BAA plc	1,223
BBC Transmission Services	244
Belfast International Airport	47
British Aerospace plc	390
British Airways plc	854
British Coal	926
British Gas plc	7,791
British Petroleum plc	6,053
British Rail Hotels	75
British Shipbuilders Warship Yards	54
British Steel plc	2,425
British Sugar Corporation	44
British Telecommunications	16,138
Britoil plc	1,053
Cable & Wireless plc	181
Chessington Computer Centre	851
Electricity Industries	15,474
Enterprise Oil plc	384
Forestry Commission	199
General Practice Finance Corporation	67
Giroleasing and Girobank (Post Office)	451
International Aeradio (British Airways)	60
Jaguar	297
National Bus Company	149
National Enterprise Board Holdings	354
National Seed Development Organisation	65
National Transcommunications Ltd	70
Northern Ireland Electricity	765
Nuclear Power Industry	677
Privatised Companies Debt	4,134
Railtrack†	1,182
Residual Share Sales	1,310
Rolls-Royce plc	1,032
Rover Group plc‡	261
Royal Ordnance	201
Scottish Transport Group	49
Sealink (British Rail)	66
Water Companies	3,468
Wytch Farm	230
Miscellaneous	609
Total	£70,347m

Source: H.M. Treasury, Public Expenditure: Statistical Supplement to the Financial Statement and Budget Report, 1994–5 and 1996–7.

* These are gross proceeds, which were subject to large transaction costs; see p. 407.
† Proceeds from the sale of British Rail businesses, other than Railtrack, were treated as privatisation effects within the budget of the Department of Transport, and therefore did not count as privatisation proceeds.
‡ Includes Unipart (£52 million), Leyland Bus (£4 million), Istel (£48 million) and DAB (£7 million).

shareholders, in the shape of free shares, loyalty bonuses and vouchers. The NAO put the BT incentives at £111 million, and those of British Gas at £185 million, but easily the largest cost was fees to banks and institutional investors to buy shares if they were not fully subscribed by the public.[23] The initial sale of shares in the regional electricity companies, for example, was worth £53 million to the underwriters. But they were rarely called upon to perform. When they were, notably during the sale of shares in BP, they tried shamelessly to escape the commitment. This encouraged the government to reduce underwriting fees, and eventually to dispense with them altogether. Since privatisation issues were generously priced, underwriting was always a questionable investment.

However, the fees paid to underwriters and professional advisers were piffling by comparison with the cost of tidying up the ravaged balance sheets of the nationalised industries before they could be sold. The costs of thirty-one privatisations between 1981 and 1994 included £11 billion in debt write-offs and another £1 billion in cash injections.[24] These dowries and write-offs make the allegation that privatisation was driven by fiscal rather than economic necessity seem rather odd. 'Corporations such as British Telecom, British Gas and the water companies were being rushed to market to relieve public borrowing,' alleges Simon Jenkins. 'Little thought was given to the philosophy of their regulation and even less to injecting into them competition or other market disciplines.'[25]

Privatisation certainly raised revenue and reduced public borrowing. Without the £90 billion furnished by the privatisation programme, the government would have had to cut public expenditure, raise taxes, or increase public borrowing. In that sense, capital assets were sold to finance current expenditure. By dubbing privatisation proceeds 'negative public expenditure' (or one-off revenue gains) the government encouraged the view that it was running down its capital to pay for a spending spree. But in many cases the state was incurring a loss to shed a long term liability, rather than selling an asset to make a quick profit.

British Aerospace, British Steel, Associated British Ports, Short Brothers and Harland and Wolff were all transferred to private ownership at a net loss to the taxpayer, once debt write-offs were included. Overall, privatisation probably raised only £30–40 billion net of costs. But, as Nicholas Ridley pointed out: 'The sale proceeds were not what counted – it was avoiding the running costs.'[26] Between its nationalisation in 1975 and its final privatisation in 1988, British Leyland absorbed £2.9 billion of public money and accumulated government-guaranteed debts of another £1.6 billion.[27] At British Steel, £4.5 billion of debt had to be written off before the company could be privatised, turning sales proceeds of £2.5 billion into a net loss of £2 billion.

Contrary to popular belief, the privatisation programme was not an alternative to cutting public expenditure. It was a way of cutting public expenditure by ridding the taxpayer of the awesome financial liabilities incurred by bankrupt or semi-bankrupt nationalised industries. In extreme cases, the taxpayer paid buyers to take companies away. British Coal was the most extreme case of all. Between 1979 and 1994, the British taxpayer sank £20 billion into the industry. Yet its remaining assets were sold in 1994 at an overall cost to the taxpayer of £706 million. It looked as if the taxpayer had another bad deal, but by 1997 it was clear that paying the buyers to take on the burden of the coal industry was a bargain.

By the time it was privatised, it was close to death. Its markets were lost long before. Cheaper imports, changing industrial processes, anti-pollution legislation, fierce competition from oil and nuclear power, and chronic industrial strife saw to that. From 1990 it had also to compete with cheap and clean gas-fired power stations. Demand for coal fell precipitately. In December 1997 the government was forced to intervene once more. It imposed a moratorium on the construction of gas-fired power stations; the big generators were browbeaten into buying more from RJB; controls on open-cast mining were tightened; plans were laid to block imports of cheaper foreign coal. All the old arguments were rehearsed about the need to diversify sources of energy, and the government promised to warp the reform of the electricity market to increase the use of coal. 'We want,' said Tony Blair, 'to preserve as much of the deep-mined coal industry as we can.'[28]

Coal is poised to become part of the Heritage Industry. Pits in Wales and the north have become industrial museums already. Consumers will suffer while the rest of the industry catches up. But absorption into the national heritage is the only way the coal industry can hurt the taxpayer now, and heritage mines could scarcely be more expensive than real ones.

Coal is an exceptional case. Among the other privatised industries, only the railways will remain a direct charge on the taxpayer. The privatised companies are obliged to run 'socially necessary' services and (theoretically) the scale of the subsidy paid to them will diminish over the life of their franchises. This is the chief triumph of the privatisation programme: it has turned taxpayers from milch cows into rentiers. In 1980, the main nationalised industries cost the taxpayer £483 million in subsidies and loans. By 1996, the government had collected an average of £9 billion from privatised companies in each of the previous ten years. Only half came from the sales, the rest from dividends, interest payments on government loans and payments of corporation tax.[29] Harold Macmillan was wrong to liken privatisation to selling the family silver. 'We seem to have stumbled,' as Christopher Fildes puts it, 'on a way to sell the silver and still to collect the rent from it.'[30]

Does Privatisation Increase Efficiency?

It is true that selling the nationalised industries cheaply made it easier for their privatised successors to earn the profits which pay the taxes and dividends. But the profits also reflect genuine improvements in efficiency. These are difficult to demonstrate, mainly because the nationalised industries produced little financial information. But almost everybody who has studied the subject agrees that the productivity of labour in the former nationalised industries improved both before and after privatisation.[31] In every case, the spur was private ownership. The mere prospect of privatisation, and the personal rewards it promised, motivated managers and attracted talent from the private sector. Able men such as John King, Ian McGregor and Graham Day were recruited specifically to prepare companies for privatisation.

The largest problem they confronted was over-manning. The dramatic reductions in employment which ensued were guaranteed to make privatisation unpopular. But they are still the best measure of the inefficiency public ownership creates. The non-utility companies shed more than a quarter of their staff even before they were privatised. The effects were concentrated in three of the great nationalised disasters: British Coal, British Steel and British Airways. All suffered badly in the recession of 1980–1, and British Steel and British Coal were further damaged by long and ruinous strikes which cost them customers. Barely one in four steelworkers, and less than one in ten miners, was still at work by the time the industry was sold. The privatisation of British Airways was preceded by an equally ruthless reduction in over-manning.*

Unlike British Airways, the railway operating companies are not confronted by direct competition. But they do face an annual diminution in the value of their public subsidy. At first, this made them over-enthusiastic as cost-cutters. Within a year, National Express had shed one-fifth of its railway workforce. At South West Trains, Stagecoach lost so many people that it did not have enough drivers to maintain the service. At one stage, it was cancelling forty trains a day. Regional Railways North East, run by MTL Trust, ran into similar problems, and had to re-hire drivers it had made redundant.[32] Great Eastern Railway, short of guards, caused much hilarity by inviting passengers to do the job part-time in exchange for £5.25 an hour and free rail travel.[33]

---

* Litigation over the collapse of Laker Airways meant it was seven years before British Airways was privatised in February 1987. During that time, peripheral businesses were sold, unprofitable routes discontinued, overmanning reduced, productivity increased, and a more imaginative marketing campaign launched. Several subsidiaries were also sold while British Airways was still in public ownership.

TABLE 11.2
Employment in Privatised Industries

Company	1979	At Privatisation*	1994	1998
Amersham International	1,300	2,088	3,397	11,600
British Aerospace	73,000	80,000	46,500	44,500
British Airports Authority	7,070	7,462	8,498	9,000
British Airways	55,985	39,498	51,164	60,675
British Coal	297,400	30,880	30,880	15,000
British Gas	104,424	88,469	67,297	*37,314
British Rail	244,084	219,990	n/a	n/a
British Steel	186,000	53,720	41,300	52,900
British Telecom	233,447	238,384	165,700	129,200
Cable & Wireless	11,100	10,750	41,348	12,000
National Freight Corporation	34,549	24,305	33,989	38,526
Rolls-Royce	57,000	42,000	49,200	2,500
Electricity†				
Eastern Group	9,212	9,970	6,403	6,700
East Midlands Electricity	7,657	7,478	7,590	4,604
London Electricity	7,536	6,920	5,532	4,000
Manweb	5,185	5,551	4,634	2,151
Midlands Electricity	8,078	7,738	6,207	4,845
Northern Electric	5,113	5,439	4,714	3,417
Northern Ireland Electricity‡	4,057	3,851	3,329	2,350
Norweb	8,351	8,249	7,652	2,669
Seeboard	6,612	6,345	5,339	4,158
Southern Electric	8,344	8,233	7,391	6,499
Swalec	4,098	3,770	3,308	1,405
Sweb	5,715	5,641	4,733	3,142
Yorkshire	7,628	7,153	5,143	4,300
Total	87,586	86,338	71,975	50,240

The loss of jobs *before* privatisation in industries which had to compete, and the failure of the utilities to reduce their payrolls even after they were first privatised, has encouraged some critics (notably John Kay) to argue that *ownership* is irrelevant to efficiency. If state-owned industries have improved their efficiency, and privatised ones have not, ownership obviously changes nothing. What matters, it seems, is *competition* for customers. In the breezier days of Opposition, Blair was attracted by thinking of this kind. In one famous

TABLE 11.2 *cont.*

Company	1979	At Privatisation*	1994	1998
National Grid	N/A	6,512	5,127	3,689
National Power	N/A	15,221	6,955	4,348
PowerGen	N/A	8,682	4,782	3,456
Scottish Hydro-Electric	3,725	3,500	3,552	3,205
Scottish Power	9,699	9,850	7,778	4,748
Water§				
Anglian	5,404	5,098	6,031	5,333
Northumbrian	1,684	1,434	3,314	3,724
North West	7,864	7,561	8,103	4,106
Severn Trent	8,792	7,757	6,954	10,628
Southern	3,194	3,122	3,500	2,364
South West¶	1,949	1,876	3,060	3,420
Thames	8,972	8,977	10,141	10,995
Welsh	4,610	4,196	6,600	2,071
Wessex	1,940	1,844	1,852	1,460
Yorkshire	5,455	4,863	3,854	4,294
Total	49,864	46,728	‖53,409	48,395

Source: Privatisation Prospectuses; Annual Reports; Companies.

* British Gas divided itself in two in 1997. In 1998, 21,891 people were employed by BG plc and 15,423 by Centrica.
† Some companies have changed ownership. See Table 11.5.
‡ Northern Ireland Electricity has changed its name to Viridian; the privatisation figure is for 1991.
§ Some companies have changed ownership. See Table 11.4.
¶ South West Water has changed its name to Pennon.
‖ The apparent increase in employment by the water companies between privatisation and 1994 reflects their diversification into non-regulated activities, which complicates comparisons between the years.

speech he mused on the merits of a business which was not owned by anybody at all: the Stakeholder Company. This is an enterprise which responds to the needs of its customers, suppliers and employees as well as its shareholders.[34] Lasting economic success, the future prime minister argued, means 'moving beyond arguments about public versus private sector, market versus state, even regulation versus deregulation.'[35]

Certainly, competition is the chief spur to efficiency. Any market in which there is large number of companies competing to supply the same product, and which is cheap and easy for new companies to enter, is bound to increase efficiency. Competition will be so strong that excessive profits will be eliminated, and the firms which survive will be those which improve their efficiency most. But ownership is not irrelevant to this process; rather, it is integral. A privately owned company has to compete for capital as well as customers. If it is not run in the best interests of its owners, its shares will be sold.[36] Their price falls, the cost of capital rises, and profits decline. If the decline is not arrested, the company will be bankrupted or taken over by alternative management which shareholders believe will make better use of its assets.

Because they operate under this constant threat of financial disaster, loss of control, or even corporate extinction, managers of a privately owned company have to run it efficiently. That discipline is lost if capital is made available to them on any other terms. If the taxpayers supply it cheaply, or the customers are forced to pay more, or the suppliers are invited to charge less, or the pay of the staff is held down, the urge to efficiency wilts. The nationalised industries, which recruited capital from all of these sources, were insulated from the twin threats of bankruptcy and a catastrophic rise in their cost of capital. So they lacked the essential incentive to succeed.

Is There a Third Way?

New Labour is reluctant to believe this. It has recommenced the search for a Third Way between private and public ownership. London Underground, for example, will be neither privatised nor nationalised. Instead, the tracks and the tunnels will be split from the trains. The trains will stay in public ownership, but private companies will be invited to bid for long-dated concessions to refurbish and maintain the tracks and the tunnels.[37] This will change nothing. If London Underground cannot pay the concessionaires, subsidies and fares will continue to go up and investment will continue to be scrapped. The parliamentary transport select committee called the plan a 'convoluted compromise'.[38] The chairman of London Underground disliked it so much he resigned.[39]

The scheme's sole virtue is what it was not. 'It is not privatisation, nor nationalisation,' explained John Prescott, secretary of state for Transport, Environment and the Regions, 'but a radical new "third way" to generate £7 billion of long term investment while retaining a publicly owned, publicly accountable network.'[40] Getting private money into public assets is a perverse ambition (the government can always borrow more cheaply) but familiar. Prescott initially favoured transferring ownership of the Underground to a public service trust empowered to issue bonds funded by taxes as well as fares. Ironically, this is where privatisation started. In fact, if privatisation can be traced to a single event, it was the failure in 1981 and 1982 to devise a 'Buzby bond' which would have enabled British Telecom to borrow privately without the need for a change in ownership.

In the early 1980s, the nationalised industries were begging the government for the freedom to finance investment by borrowing privately. Since the mid-1950s they had not borrowed in their own name, but relied on advances from the government, which had enabled them to invest without regard to returns. They were now earning a negative return on capital, and, understandably, wanted the government to continue to guarantee their debts.[41] When the government refused, it altered the terms of the debate about their future. 'These instruments remained unreal, since the ownership of the company remained with the State and there was no real risk to the investor,' recalled the minister responsible for the Buzby bond. 'I was glad that the search for this Eldorado failed, because it was taking our eye off the ball.'[42]

The freedom to raise money in the markets became a major argument in favour of privatisation, especially in the boardrooms of the nationalised industries. Nowhere was release from Treasury bondage more keenly anticipated than in the water industry, where tight government control of capital expenditure had led to crumbling sewers and dirty water. By the mid-1980s, water authority chairmen were publicly restive about Treasury insistence that they should earn a decent return on investment by cutting costs and raising prices. In 1985 the government had to pass legislation to force them to increase charges to finance their investment plans.[43] The then chairman of Thames Water, Roy Watts, was outraged. He began to campaign publicly for privatisation. His enthusiasm was so great that in 1986 NALGO took Thames Water to court, alleging that the authority had acted *ultra vires* in preparing for privatisation without the backing of parliamentary legislation.[44]

Protecting Privatised Companies from Takeover

The government was more cautious. It adopted an Augustinian approach, selling companies to private investors without daring to create a genuine market in corporate control. In the earliest privatisations – British Aerospace, Cable and Wireless and British Telecom – less than half the shares were sold. Until it sold its last holding in BP the government retained the right, under the Bradbury–Bridges rules, to appoint to the board of the company two directors with a power of veto. In other privatisations, explicit restrictions on ownership were introduced. The government either retained a Golden Share (to block a takeover it considered unacceptable) for five or ten years or limited the size of the shareholding which a single investor could accumulate (usually to 15 per cent).

The water and electricity companies, AEA Technology, the British Technology Group and British Energy were all privatised with Golden Shares. Sealink ferries were sold with the proviso that ships would be surrendered to the state in an emergency. Privatised BAA was not allowed to sell airports. When Michael Ashcroft, chairman of the ADT Group, built up a 9 per cent stake in the company in 1989–90, he was strongly discouraged by the government from proceeding any further. Rolls Royce was lumbered not only with a ceiling on individual shareholders but a cap on the overall scale of ownership by foreigners, limits on asset disposals, and stipulations about the nationality of the directors. British Aerospace had similar limitations. When it bought Royal Ordnance, the company had to pledge that it would not sell the company to an overseas buyer. The same reasoning lies behind the New Labour pledge to keep a Golden Share in National Air Traffic Services after it is privatised.

Investment restrictions offer politicians control without ownership, but they are not costless. Both Rolls Royce and British Aerospace complained that the limitations raised their cost of capital, by denying them access to potential shareholders. Under pressure from the European Commission as well as the companies, the government was persuaded to raise the ceiling on foreign shareholders to 29.5 per cent in 1989 and 49.5 per cent in 1998.[45] The remaining restrictions are justified on 'strategic' and military grounds. It is more than coincidence that 'strategic' arguments were advanced in favour of nationalisation.[46]

There is a more respectable defence of ownership restrictions: they buy time for newly privatised companies to establish themselves. But Golden Shares are also a useful device for avoiding accusations that the country is being sold to Johnny Foreigner. Occasionally, plainer language is required. In 1990 the government told Tractebel of Belgium that its plans to acquire a stake in a regional electricity company were unwelcome. Five years later, even after the Golden Share had expired, the company was surprised to find it was still unwanted. In 1996 it announced that it had abandoned the idea of investing in the British electricity industry because the political risk was too great.[47] Around the same time, the Southern Company of the United States was banned from bidding for National Power.

Both decisions were arbitrary ones, based on the balance of political advantage. This is the chief disadvantage of ownership restrictions: they create opportunities for ministerial interference. In June 1984 the Government forced RTZ, the mining and industrial group, to sell most of the stake it had acquired in Enterprise Oil when the privatisation flopped. Yet BP was allowed to proceed with its bid for Britoil despite the fact that the company was protected by a Golden Share which entitled the government to appoint the board of directors even if the whole of the company was owned by a third party. The political pressure to use it against BP was immense. Britoil headquarters were in Glasgow, most of its assets were in Scottish territorial waters and, at a time when English predators had acquired several leading Scottish companies, there was considerable sensitivity north of the border over another passing into English hands. The problem was that more than half of the shareholders had sold their stock to BP.

Nigel Lawson, the chancellor, decided to use the Golden Share as a bargaining counter. He secured assurances from BP that it would increase North Sea exploration; move its North Sea headquarters to Glasgow; retain Aberdeen as the operational centre; transfer its research and development operations to Scotland; move dozens of executives north of the border; and endow research fellowships at the Scottish universities. These conditions loaded considerable costs on to a business transaction, purely for political reasons.* 'The Golden Share had been a useful device in making the original privatisation more acceptable . . .', admitted Lawson in his memoirs, 'but now it had become an embarrassment, obliging the Government to make choices that would have been far better left to the company's shareholders.'[48]

The effects of political arbitration are never benign. When it emerged in the spring of 1986 that the government was engaged in secret talks to sell the various parts of BL to General Motors and Ford, a wave of anti-American hysteria washed over the political world.[49] General Motors refused to accept limits on its control of Land Rover, and the negotiations collapsed as a result.[50] The reason British Aerospace eventually obtained the Rover Group so cheaply is that it was given exclusive negotiating rights: xenophobia had ruled out a sale to General Motors, Ford or Volkswagen. Ironically, British Aerospace sold Rover to the German car-maker BMW in 1994.

When the state-owned French port of Calais expressed an interest in acquiring the port of Dover, their chief antagonist was Dame Vera Lynn. The PR men persuaded her to demand that bluebirds, rather than the Tricolore, continue to fly over the White Cliffs of Dover. It was enough to postpone the sale, which has yet to take place. The Kuwait Investment Office (KIO) faced more substantial but equally misguided opposition, after using the opportunity of the failed BP flotation in October 1987 to buy 22 per cent of the company. Immense diplomatic pressure was brought to bear. When this failed, the

* The Britoil case is not an isolated example of the Scottish factor. When British Energy was privatised in 1996, the company had to move its headquarters to Edinburgh to reassure Scottish voters that control of Scottish Nuclear, which owned two privatised nuclear reactors at Hunterston and Torness, would not pass to England. Less than two years later, British Energy merged its English and Scottish nuclear power stations.

Government referred the KIO to the Monopolies and Mergers Commission (MMC). In September 1988 the MMC reported that the KIO holding in BP was against the public interest, because the government of Kuwait might become less friendly. The government promptly ordered the KIO to reduce its stake to less than 10 per cent. The Kuwaitis were understandably upset.

Less than a year later the government rewrote the legislation privatising the water industry rather than let even fellow-Europeans own too much of it. Several French water businesses had laid siege to the twenty-nine statutory water companies.[51] Compagnie Générale des Eaux (CGE), Société d'Aménagement Urbain et Rural (SAUR) and Lyonnaise des Eaux had acquired stakes or mounted bids for eighteen of them. They wanted to use the statutory water companies as vehicles for acquiring stakes in the ten major water authorities being privatised the following year, but public disquiet was intense. In January 1989 the government inserted into the Water Act a rule that any bid for a water company worth more than £30 million would be referred automatically to the MMC.

This was a more effective deterrent to takeover than the 15 per cent limit

TABLE 11.3
Ownership of the Statutory Water Companies

	Owner
Bournemouth & West Hampshire Water plc	Biwater PLC
Bristol Water plc	Générale des Eaux (30 per cent)
Cambridge Water plc	Independent
Dee Valley Water plc	Independent
Cholderton & District Water Company	Independent
Essex & Suffolk Water plc	Northumbrian Water (Lyonnaise des Eaux)
Folkestone & Dover Water Services Ltd	Générale des Eaux
Hartlepool Water plc	Anglian Water plc
Mid Kent Water plc	Générale des Eaux & SAUR (19.5 per cent each)
Mid Southern Water plc	SAUR Water Services plc
North Surrey Water Ltd	Générale des Eaux
Portsmouth Water plc	Independent
South East Water Ltd	SAUR Water Services plc
South Staffordshire Water plc	Générale des Eaux (30 per cent)
Sutton & East Surrey Water plc	Independent
Tendring Hundred Water Services plc	Générale des Eaux
Three Valleys Water plc	Générale des Eaux
York Waterworks plc	Independent

Source: Water UK.

TABLE 11.4
Ownership of the Public Water Companies

	Owner	Date of Purchase	Price (£m)
Anglian Water	Independent	–	–
Welsh Water	Hyder plc*	December 1995	872
Northumbrian Water	Lyonnaise des Eaux SA	November 1995	823
North West Water	United Utilities plc†	November 1995	1,800
Severn Trent Water	Independent	–	–
Southern Water	Scottish Power plc	June 1996	1,670
South West Water‡	Independent	–	–
Thames Water	Independent	–	–
Wessex Water	Enron	September 1998	1,360
Yorkshire Water	Independent	–	–

Source: *Financial Times.*

* Hyder plc was created by the merger of Welsh Water and South Wales Electricity.
† United Utilities plc was created by the merger of North West Water and Norweb.

on individual shareholdings the state retained in the major water companies at privatisation.* But it did not stop the French water companies buying stock aggressively when the major companies were floated in November 1989. It took an MMC investigation to stop CGE taking over Mid Kent Water in the summer of 1990. When CGE joined forces with SAUR and revived the bid five years later, it was eventually blocked.[52] However, Lyonnaise des Eaux was allowed to buy Northumbrian Water, and Enron of the United States bought Wessex Water without referral to the MMC.

In the electricity industry, the expiry of the Golden Share was followed by a blitz of bids from abroad. By 1998 American electricity companies had invested £13.8 billion in the British electricity industry, and left just four of the English regional electricity companies in native hands. Only the PacifiCorp bid for Eastern Group was referred to the MMC and even that was eventually allowed to go ahead.[53] Circumstances, as well as rules, can change. By the time it came to the privatisation of the railway industry, precluding foreigners had become a luxury a dying government could not afford. French companies, including CGE, acquired three passenger

---

* Nine of the ten water companies were privatised with a five year 15 per cent ceiling on individual shareholdings. Welsh Water was given even greater protection, in that the 15 per cent limit could be removed only by a 75 per cent vote of shareholders.

operating franchises. Wisconsin Central Transportation (WCT) of the United States acquired a virtual monopoly of railway freight operations.[54]

The immediacy with which bids emerge as soon as Golden Shares lapse illustrates the limits they place on the drive to increase efficiency. It was not until Hanson bid for PowerGen in 1990 that the company devised a capital structure adapted to life in the private sector. The same realisation did not dawn at Manweb until Scottish Power bid for the company in mid-1995. Northern Electric, finally exposed to a bid from Trafalgar House in late 1994, conjured up an extra £560 million for shareholders to fend it off. (The ease with which this bribe was financed was provocative enough to prompt a change in the regulation of electricity prices.) The failure of SWEB to cut its payroll was not exposed until Southern Company bid for it in July 1995. A counter-bid by Southern Electric promised to shave a further £60 million off operating costs. Similarly, invited to cut water bills by 20 per cent as a condition of taking over Northumbrian Water in 1995, Lyonnaise des Eaux did not baulk at the additional cost.

Private capital is always more demanding than its public equivalent. Private investors forced British Aerospace to change its management and its strategy by refusing to subscribe to a rights issue; proved that the Channel Tunnel rail link could not be built to the budget proposed by London & Continental Railways; and forced PowerGen and National Power to ensure new power stations were financed soundly. Their greatest triumph was to expose the bogus economics of nuclear power. Generating electricity from nuclear power looked like something-for-nothing until private investors included the costs of decommissioning reactors. The nuclear power stations had to be withdrawn from the initial electricity privatisation, and when eight of them were sold in 1996 (as British Energy), the total proceeds (£2.1 billion) amounted to less than the cost of Sizewell B (£2.3 billion).

Does Privatisation Change Employee Attitudes?

In public ownership, the nuclear industry was free to place technical perfection ahead of financial discipline. The need to compete for capital forces private companies to contain their costs. This also motivates managers and employees, by making the links between pay and performance more explicit. After privatisation, centralised, union-dominated wage-bargaining conducted under threat of a strike usually gives way to local agreements on pay and productivity. However, it would be wrong to believe that privatisation revolutionises industrial relations. Although one of the aims of privatisation was to improve attitudes by giving employees the chance to buy shares in their

TABLE 11.5
The Ownership of the Regional Electricity Companies

Company	Owner	Date of Purchase	Price (£m)
Eastern Group*	Texas Utilities	May 1998	4,450
East Midlands†	PowerGen	June 1998	1,900
London‡	Électricité de France	December 1998	1,900
Manweb	Scottish Power	July 1995	1,100
Midland	Avon Energy Partners (Cinergy & GPU)	May 1996	1,730
Northern	CalEnergy	December 1996	782
Norweb	United Utilities plc	September 1995	1,800
Scottish Hydro-Electric	Independent	–	–
Scottish Power*	Independent	–	–
Seeboard	§Central & South West Corporation	September 1995	1,600
Southern§	Scottish Hydro-Electric plc	September 1998	4,800
Swalec	Hyder plc	December 1995	872
South Western	Southern Company (75%) & PP&L Resources (25%)	September 1995	1,100
Yorkshire	¶American Electric Power & New Century Holdings	February 1997	1,500

Source: *Financial Times.*

* Eastern Electricity was acquired by Hanson for £2½ billion in July 1995. It was de-merged from Hanson in February 1997. In June 1997 Pacificorp offered £4.35 billion for the company, but its bid was capped by Texas Utilities, which paid £4.45 billion. Scottish Power acquired PacifiCorp for £4.2 billion in December 1998.

† East Midlands was acquired by Dominion Resources for £1.3 billion in December 1996, but it was sold to PowerGen in June 1998 for £1.9 billion.

‡ London was acquired by Entergy of the United States for £1.3 billion in December 1996. It was sold to Électricité de France two years later.

¶ The merged Southern Electric and Scottish Hydro-Electric is now called Scottish and Southern.

§ New Century Holdings and American Electric Power have taken over Central & South West Corporation.

employer (all privatised companies made special provision for staff to receive some blend of free, cheap or guaranteed shares) the most significant cultural change was not employee ownership but the breaking of trade union power.[55]

At first, the trade unions advised employees not to buy shares. At British Telecom, Associated British Ports, Amersham International and Cable and Wireless, nine employees in ten acquired them anyway. By the time electricity was privatised in 1990, the trade unions were arguing about the size of employee shareholdings. This is a reason to be pleased about employee share ownership. In 1919 R. H. Tawney thought that 'no scheme for reorganising the coal industry can be regarded as even approximately satisfactory which does not offer those engaged in it an effective voice in the control of its policy and administration.'[56] After fifty years in public ownership, the miners still did not have it. But when the remnants of the coal industry were privatised in 1994, two million shares were given to employees and another 890,000 reserved for them to buy. Even now, employees own 7 per cent of RJB. Two mines – the Tower colliery in South Wales and Monktonhall in Scotland – were bought by the miners who worked them.[57] Coal Products, the solid smokeless fuels subsidiary of British Coal, was also acquired by a joint management and employee buy-out team.[58]

In many cases management and employee buy-outs were the only feasible means of privatisation – and they were convenient for political reasons. The sale of the British Technology Group (BTG) to a management-led consortium in 1992 was driven largely by the need to thwart an American-led bid. Selling companies to staff, at prices which usually guaranteed a handsome return to the new shareholders, was also an easy way to circumvent trade union resistance to privatisation, which is why 6 of the 13 sales of subsidiaries of the nationalised British Shipbuilders; 36 of the 62 sales made by the National Bus Company; and 4 of the 25 rail operating franchises went to teams of managers and employees. But it would be naïve to believe that even such an extensive privatisation programme increased employee ownership significantly.

Employee shareholdings scarcely rose above a few per cent in any privatisation and, where the staff stake was large, the subsequent disillusionment could be crushing. At Monktonhall 150 miners invested £10,000 each to buy a pit which was virtually bound to fail. Five years later, after an abortive rescue attempt, the colliery went into liquidation.[59] Employee ownership could not overcome geological uncertainty or the economic realities of the market for coal, and it was mischievous to pretend that it could. Most buy-outs disappear quickly, in a lucrative sale to a PLC. Only *one* of the dozens of buy-outs of bus companies (Metroline) remained independent long enough to float on the Stock Exchange.

Even the spectacular success of the National Freight Consortium (NFC), bought by its staff and managers for a pittance in 1982 and floated on the Stock Exchange seven years later for £890 million, was more apparent than real. The legend has it that employees, monitoring the performance of their shares on charts posted at every depot, became obsessed with cutting their own costs. In fact, their early success relied not on the magic ingredient of worker-ownership but a familiar post-privatisation dowry: a portfolio of valuable but redundant properties ripe for sale and re-development and a string of fat, unexpired haulage contracts. Once these were spent, the company struggled.

Competition by Proxy: The Rise of the Regulator

Significantly, the weaknesses of NFC did not become apparent until it floated on the Stock Exchange in 1989. Nor did the company begin to tackle them until its share price came under pressure. In fact, when competition started to bite and customers demanded lower prices, an employee-dominated company like NFC found it hard to cut costs. Its short history proves that the only effective spur to efficiency is competition, for capital as well as for customers. For privatised companies operating in competitive markets, such as British Aerospace or British Airways, this did not need to be organised. The challenge was to find a proxy for competition when public sector monopolies – British Telecom, British Gas or the water industry – were transferred to private ownership.

The Conservative government found a solution in one of the great growth industries of the late twentieth century: regulation. The sale in November 1984 of British Telecommunications, the first public monopoly to be privatised, was accompanied by the creation of a new state agency charged with preventing the company from exploiting its dominant position. Called the Office of Telecommunications (Oftel), it is now one of seven regulatory agencies covering the former public utilities. Each of these industries has elements of natural monopoly, because distribution networks – gas pipelines, telephone lines, water pipes and sewers, the National Grid and the railway network – are expensive to duplicate. The regulators are a substitute for competition. Their task is to protect consumers by restraining the prices the monopolies charge and ensuring new entrants to the business have access to the distribution networks. This has to be done without damaging the ability of the privatised companies to fund investment and increase their output. It is not easy.

Regulators rely on the regulated utilities for information about their costs and prices. Naturally, the companies supply them with information which exaggerates their costs and minimises their resources. The regulators have to disentangle fact from fiction, and impose a cap on the amount by which companies can increase their prices. The cap is governed by a simple formula. Prices are allowed to rise by a fixed percentage a year for five-year periods, calculated by subtracting from the Retail Price Index (RPI) a figure (the X factor) designed to measure the room the company has to increase its efficiency. The regulator weighs up how much profit a company needs to maintain the value of its assets, and then selects an X factor which will divide that profit between cost savings and price rises. But the simplicity of the formula belies its limitations. It was easy for the regulators to underestimate the scale of the efficiency gains the privatised utilities could wring out of their operations, particularly in the early days. The X factors were initially set at too low a level, and shareholders enjoyed lavish returns.

This was not surprising. Everybody underestimated the inefficiency of state-owned industries. But mistakes could not be rectified quickly. Price caps were set for five-year periods, to allow shareholders to enjoy the fruits of greater efficiency before they were tightened again, and they could not be renegotiated without controversy. In March 1995, after the Trafalgar House bid for Northern Electric had exposed greater potential for efficiency gains at the regional electricity companies, the electricity regulator announced a review of the five-year price settlement he had reached with them seven months earlier. In one sense, it showed how flexible RPI minus X could be in redistributing efficiency gains between shareholders and consumers. But the regulator was nearly swept from office on the torrent of abuse from regional electricity managers.

Experience has made regulators more adept at identifying the information needed to set X at the right level, and they have toughened their stance on prices accordingly. They have also ventured into new areas such as quality of service and access to markets for new entrants, which were not part of their original remit. But RPI minus X has survived because nobody can think of a better alternative. The only practical option is to limit the profitability of the privatised utilities directly, by stipulating the rate of return they can earn on their capital. But experience in the United States, where private utilities are regulated in this way, suggests that the companies simply inflate the value of their assets. RPI minus X at least means they can increase their profits only by reducing their costs, which gives them an incentive to increase their efficiency, not their assets.

Regulated companies complain that regulatory regimes are driven as much by the ego of the regulator as the public interest, and that they have become arbitrary and opaque as a result. Relations between BT and the Office of Telecommunications (Oftel) became particularly strained, mainly because Oftel gradually expanded the range of services which were price-capped, from about half to four fifths of the activities of the company. The X factor became progressively more complex and was twice raised before the end of the five-year periods for which it was set. The regulator has also forced BT to disgorge the information to detect anti-competitive tactics such as cross-subsidisation and predatory pricing. Since 1993 Oftel has even dictated the price BT can charge other companies for connecting their customers to its network. By 1996 Sir Iain Vallance, chairman of BT, was in open conflict with the then director general of Oftel.

But no privatised company had as relentlessly acrimonious a relationship with its regulator as British Gas. It is said that Sir Denis Rooke, chairman of the company when it was privatised, refused to mention the first gas regulator by name. He referred to Sir James McKinnon among staff as 'the director general', Though Rooke stepped down in 1989, a culture of hostility to regulation survived. The relationship between McKinnon and senior executives of British Gas was notoriously combative, as the regulator sought to cut the price of gas and increase competition by eroding the strong market position inherited by British Gas or breaking the corporation up. Initial hopes on all sides that the relationship would improve when McKinnon was succeeded as director general of Ofgas by Clare Spottiswoode did not endure. By 1997 she was accusing British Gas of being 'really into this culture of game playing'.[60] The continuing tension indicated that the bitterness of the relationship had causes more fundamental than personality.

The real source of the difficulties was the shift in the focus of regulation in the 1990s from a limited objective (controlling prices) to a fundamental assault on the gas and telecommunications monopolies (increasing competition). BT and British Gas were bound to defend their position and their complaints are echoed periodically by the managers of the privatised electricity and water industries. The reform of the regulation of the privatised industries is now a cottage industry. New Labour has toyed with many ideas, including the appointment of panels of regulators; a clearer definition of their duties, greater answerability of regulators to Parliament; the amendment or replacement of the RPI minus X formula; and the merger or rationalisation of regulatory agencies.

Reforms of this kind have a natural appeal to New Labour, which sees regulation not as a substitute for competition but as a proxy for public ownership. This is why the government is replacing the Office of Passenger Rail Franchising (Opraf) and the Office of the Rail Regulator (ORR) with a Strategic Rail Authority, and subjecting the rolling stock leasing companies (which operate in a highly competitive market) to regulation for the first time. The gas and electricity regulators are being merged, with more reason, and the government is nursing a longer term ambition to extend the Oftel remit to broadcasting and information technology. A Green Paper on the regulation of the utilities as a whole canvassed several more ideas for reform. The prime minister is said to have overruled a plan to make consumers the sole beneficiaries of efficiency gains, but the Green Paper still threatened to force utilities to share with their customers any 'undeserved' profits stemming

from good fortune (like a fall in the price of gas) or their deliberate misleading of the regulator.

This is the continuation of nationalisation by other means. The chief weakness of regulation is not that it is unresponsive to voters, but that it allows
politicians to treat the privatised utilities as if they were publicly owned. Even
the Conservative government forced British Telecom to maintain telephone
boxes in rural areas and provide special telephone services for the deaf and
the blind. It allowed the company to overcharge for long-distance and international calls provided it kept the price of renting domestic lines down.
Similar obligations were laid on the gas, water and electricity companies to
maintain supplies to remote areas, conserve energy, improve the environment, and preserve the landscape. First among the ministerial 'guidelines'
to be issued to regulators by the New Labour government will be a similar
wish-list of the social and environmental objectives demanded by its supporters.

The regulators cannot ignore the politicians. They never could. The tighter
price controls and stronger emphasis on competition imposed by regulators
in the 1990s were a response to public disquiet about Fat Cattery in utility
boardrooms. After the water shortages of the summer of 1995, when one in
three consumers faced a hosepipe ban, Ofwat developed a sudden interest
in leaking water pipes. When the secretary of state for the environment,
transport and the regions, John Prescott, told the water industry to spend
less on dividends and more on repairing leaks, the director general of water
services hurriedly announced that he would now set annual (rather than
quinquennial) leakage reduction targets *and* impose a one-off price cut at
the next regulatory review. When the secretary of state went on to attack
Railtrack for profiteering in railway subsidies, the rail regulator promptly
announced a review of its access charges.

The quinquennial price review by an independent regulator, intended to
free privatised utilities from day-to-day interference by ministers, has proved
an unattainable idea. Regulation has merely replaced old forms of political
interference by new. When they were nationalised, ministers told the utilities
to put prices up (as a form of surrogate taxation) or down (to contain
inflation) before or after the next turn of the electoral cycle. The policies of
their privatised successors are even more susceptible to political manipulation.
Unlike its socialist predecessors, New Labour has grasped that control is no
longer synonymous with ownership.

Have Utility Prices Fallen?

New Labour also knows that there are votes in utility-bashing, in Parliament and the country. Old Labour backbenchers cleave to an uncomplicated detestation of privatisation in general and Fat Cats in particular. Regulation also gives ministers a tool for pursuing social policies without raising taxes. (The utilities have already volunteered a plan to overcharge rich consumers of energy in order to subsidise the poor). For a left-of-centre government which has denied itself the power to tax and spend openly, the temptation to make regulation a permanent feature of economic life is now overwhelming. It would be a mistake. Regulation is a temporary alternative to competition, not a permanent substitute for it.

Its goal is not to alleviate poverty, or save the environment, or satisfy the bloodlust of Labour backbenchers. It is to prevent monopolies exploiting consumers. In this limited aim, regulation can claim considerable success. The price of domestic gas has fallen dramatically. According to Oftel, the median domestic telephone bill fell consistently in real terms between 1989–90 and 1992–93, and started to fall in absolute terms in 1993–94.[61] The price of international calls took longer to fall, because of a series of cartels operated by the major telephone companies, but they are now cheap by historical standards. Domestic electricity prices fell slowly at first, because the generators were tied into expensive long term contracts to buy British coal, but they have tumbled since regulatory pressure was intensified in 1995.

One bill has failed to fall: water. This reflects two special factors. One was the poor state of the pipe and sewerage systems after years of under-investment; the other is the obligation to meet the high purity and environmental standards laid down by the European Union. Both were recognised at privatisation in 1989. Instead of forcing the water companies to reduce their prices by an RPI minus X formula, the Office of Water Services (Ofwat) allows them to raise their prices by RPI plus K. The K factor is different for each company, and depends on its estimated investment costs. Those with higher investment costs (such as South West Water, with its long coastline) can raise their prices by more. This has made investment costs the main influence over the price of water.*

---

* The fact that the cost of meeting higher environmental standards is the chief cause of rising water prices is generally unrecognised. The water industry is regulated by the Environment Agency and the Drinking Water Inspectorate as well as the Office of Water Services, and the two environmental regulators have no brief to increase competition. Their goal is to raise water standards, without regard to costs, to levels which are unjustifiably high. 'It would be cheaper', quipped Nicholas Ridley, environment secretary at the time the industry was privatised, 'to deliver free Perrier to every house in the land.'

TABLE 11.6
The Price of Utility Services to April 1998

At Privatisation	1998	Change	
		Nominal	Real
Domestic gas tariff*			
BG Price (KwH)	1.28p	1.413p	+10.4%	−33.5%
Cheapest	–	1.165p	−8.9%	−45.2%
BG Standing Charge	£32.49	£48.87	+50.4%	−9.4%
Cheapest	–	£25.00	−23.1%	−53.6%
Standard domestic electricity tariff†			
Eastern	6.50p	6.47p	−0.5%	−22.8%
East Midlands	6.62p	6.38p	−3.6%	−25.3%
London	6.78p	6.12p	−9.7%	−30.0%
Manweb	7.12p	6.68p	−6.2%	−27.3%
Midlands	6.89p	6.40p	−7.1%	−27.9%
Northern	6.89p	6.86p	−0.4%	−22.8%
Norweb	6.61p	6.41p	−3.0%	−24.8%
Seeboard	6.62p	7.26p	+9.7%	−14.9%
Southern	6.59p	6.22p	−5.6%	−26.8%
Sweb	7.28p	7.26p	−0.3%	−22.7%
South Western	7.15p	6.88p	−3.8%	−25.4%
Yorkshire	6.88p	6.14p	−10.8%	−30.8%
Scottish Power	6.24p	6.75p	+8.2%o	−16.1%
Scottish Hydro	6.13p	6.67p	+8.8%	−15.7%
Average annual household water and sewerage bill‡			
Anglian	£155.22	£288.00	+85.5%	+31.6%
Northumbrian	£102.16	£228.00	+123.2%	+58.3%
North West	£110.16	£234.00	+112.4%	+50.6%
Severn Trent	£107.31	£222.00	+106.9%	+46.7%
Southern	£124.36	£257.00	+106.7%	+46.6%
South West	£146.27	£354.00	+142.0%	+71.6%
Thames	£100.16	£201.00	+100.7%	+42.3%
Welsh Water	£149.70	£294.00	+96.4%	+39.3%
Wessex	£139.24	£266.00	+91.0%	+35.5%
Yorkshire	£121.57	£226.00	+85.9%	+31.8%

Source: Offer; Ofwat; Consumers' Association.

* This table records only the prices and standing charges levied by British Gas and its cheapest competitors on standard credit terms. In 1998 customers paying by monthly direct debit saw the price drop to 1.096 per kilowatt hour and the standing charge to a low of £15.
† The figures exclude standing charges, which on average have decreased from £9.24 at privatisation in 1990 to £8.61 in 1998, a fall in real terms of 28 per cent.
‡ The average household bill includes metered as well as unmetered customers and is for water supply, sewerage and environmental services. The balance between these varies from region to region. The 1998 figures do not include rebates in the case of North West, Severn Trent, South West and Welsh Water.

But they are hard to predict, and the initial estimates by Ofwat were too generous to the water companies. After battling in vain to persuade them to share the benefits of lower-than-estimated investment costs with customers rather than with shareholders, Ofwat has now imposed a one-off price cut in the year 2000.

Water: The Last of the Monopolists?

It is not a coincidence that water is the privatised industry where competition is least developed. Unlike gas or electricity, there is no substitute for water. People cannot stop drinking it or using it, or take their custom elsewhere. There are few new sources of supply. The water industry has developed no equivalent of the National Grid or Transco transmission network, making it impossible to move water from wet areas to dry ones, let alone allow competing firms to supply it across a single national network. It would be ruinously expensive to build one from scratch (the fifty-mile London Water Ring Main cost £250 million) and the present alternatives are as yet incomplete.[62]

But water and the present infrastructure of the industry are also poorly adapted to competition. Unlike gas or electricity, water is not fungible; its quality varies from place to place. The metering of water, unlike the metering of gas, electricity and telephone calls, is also rare and unpopular. Because it is the purest natural monopoly, water exhibits all of the problems of monopoly in vivid form. Prices are high and rising, and customer service is poor. The shareholders are getting rich, while the water mains are bursting and sewers are crumbling. The customers, meanwhile, are exhorted not to water the lawn or flush the lavatory, or clean their teeth with the tap on.

However, it is easy to exaggerate the degree of natural monopoly, even in an industry like water. Many people living on the borders between regional water companies already receive tap water from one company and sewage services from another. So-called 'inset appointments', in which companies compete to sign up unconnected consumers on new housing and industrial estates, have been allowed ever since the industry was privatised, and were further liberalised in 1992. But inset appointments were slow to catch on; it was not until 1996 that Anglian Water became the first water company to apply successfully for an inset appointment when it replaced Essex and East Suffolk Water as the supplier to a Buxted chicken factory.[63] RAF Finningley, near Doncaster, has replaced Yorkshire Water with Anglian, and the Ministry of Defence has requested bids to supply 140 military bases. Jeremy Bryan, running a company named Enviro-logic (in which South West Water took a 50 per cent stake in 1997), has made 'inset appointments' the basis of his business. In December 1997 Ofwat licensed the company to supply a customer of Welsh Water, and it has a number of other applications outstanding.[64] Bryan also hopes to supply low quality water, of the kind trapped in mines and under big cities, for industrial use. This would increase competition by segmenting the market, with a variety of providers delivering water of the appropriate quality to different types of customer.

In 1996, the Conservative government made the first serious attempt to break the monopoly of the regional water companies by denying them exclusive use of their local networks of pipes. It proposed that any water company should be free to use the pipes of another to supply any business consuming more than 250,000 litres of water a year.[65] In August 1998 Ofwat proposed reducing this so-called 'common carriage' threshold to 100,000 litres. The lower limit would raise the number of potential customers from a few hundred large companies to thousands of larger users, including hospitals.[66] But competition of this kind is bound to be localised, unless local pipe networks are linked into a single national system. Making use of the canals as trunk carriers would not be prohibitively expensive. Certainly, the technical arguments against the development of a national water grid are not convincing.[67]

The main obstacle is political rather than technical. Genuine competition in water supply means metering, since only the measurement of consumption would allow one water company to charge customers in the area of another. Just one in ten domestic consumers have chosen to have their water consumption metered. Most users rightly believe they are better off under the present system, in which bills are based on domestic rates. The unfortunate reputation of water metering is a pity. In the gas and electricity industries, it liberated consumers great and small from the tyranny of national and regional monopolists.

Gas: The Coming of Competition

In the electricity and gas industries, competition would never have developed if the suppliers had retained control of the distribution networks (as they have in the water industry). It was only when the national gas pipeline network and the National Grid were transferred to new owners that competition began in earnest. British Gas was in the private sector for ten years before it faced competition for domestic customers. This is because it was privatised in 1986 with a near-complete monopoly over the distribution and supply of gas. As early as 1982, the government had obliged British Gas to open its network to competitors supplying large industrial users, but competition was slow to develop.

The corporation was too dominant to be undercut on price, and it fixed the terms of access to its network. At privatisation, the government should have transferred ownership of the gas transmission network to a separate company and split British Gas into regional companies which could compete for customers. The chief obstacle to this was Sir Denis Rooke, then chairman of British Gas. He did not care who owned British Gas, but he opposed any attacks on its monopoly. He encouraged a successful trade union campaign against the privatisation of the high street showrooms in 1981, and frustrated a government order to British Gas to dispose of its oil assets. This opposition might have come to nothing had Rooke faced a more determined secretary of state for Energy. But Peter Walker thought the introduction of competition into the gas industry was a chimera, and was close to Rooke. He was welcomed on to the British Gas board when he left the Cabinet. But the close relationship between the minister and the company did neither party any good in the long term. Ultimately, the British Gas monopoly was indefensible.

The company was first referred to the MMC in 1988. The subsequent report obliged British Gas to publish its prices, which allowed competitors to undercut its tariffs, and gain market share. The obligation to publish prices was not lifted until March 1995, when the Office of Gas Supply (Ofgas) reckoned the business market was fully competitive. By then, British Gas was supplying less than one third. It took longer to set householders free to choose their gas supplier. After several years of wrangling over its monopoly with the Office of Fair Trading and Ofgas, the company requested a review of its position by the MMC in 1992. This signified a complete breakdown of relations between British Gas and Sir James McKinnon, then the director general of Ofgas. Self-referral was a high risk strategy, which was expected to end in a recommendation that British Gas be broken up, but the MMC report appeared to vindicate the risk. It allowed British Gas to keep its network, provided it sold its gas trading business. It also eased the RPI minus X formula to allow the company to rebuild its profits, and to keep its household monopoly until 2002.

But the then president of the Board of Trade, Michael Heseltine, used this timid report to good effect. Rather than force British Gas to disgorge its gas trading business, he ordered the company to transfer its trading *and* transportation activities into a separate (but wholly owned) company. He also opened the household monopoly to full competition from 1998. These measures, put into effect by the Gas Act of 1995, prompted British Gas to split itself in two. The assets of British Gas PLC are now divided between an international gas exploration and production business and Transco, which owns the national gas transmission and storage network. The gas supply, trading, retailing and service businesses which trade under the British Gas brand, including the witty and successful Goldfish credit card, are now provided by a separately listed company called Centrica. Splitting the pipeline network from gas supply threw the domestic gas market open to all-comers. Every domestic consumer in Britain can now choose their gas supplier.

A monopoly exposed to competition is bound to lose customers. Centrica was also handicapped by a string of long-term contracts British Gas had signed as monopoly supplier to the British market. With competitors buying gas in the spot market at less than half the price stipulated in the contracts, business and residential customers have flocked to change suppliers. Despite spending an estimated £1.5 billion renegotiating uncompetitive contracts, Centrica has lost between one in five and one in three customers wherever it has to compete. Only inertia prevents it losing more. Transco is under constant pressure from Ofgas as well as its customers to reduce its (price-capped) transmission charges. The company has also lost its monopoly of gas storage, Ofgas having forced it to auction its capacity in the expectation of driving prices down still further.[68] Some rivals, including Scottish Power, are acquiring storage capacity of their own.

The effects of competition on the monolithic corporation created by Sir Denis Rooke were immense. Twelve regional baronies, suffused with the ethos of technical excellence and public service, have given way to five businesses governed by a hard-nosed commercial culture. Nearly 50,000 of the people who worked for British Gas in 1993 have lost their jobs, at a cost of over £1.5 billion in redundancy payments. Half of its High Street showrooms are now shut. Shareholders, who knew nothing but rising dividends from 1987 to 1993, saw the market value of their company halve over the next three years. 'This used to be a rich company,' the British Gas chairman reflected in February 1997. 'But it isn't any longer.'

Electricity: A Long Wait for Competition

The losses shareholders suffered as British Gas disintegrated under the impact of competition proved that Rooke won a Pyrrhic victory in 1986. Its lessons were in the minds of ministers when it came to privatisation of the electricity industry. The idea of privatising electricity as a single enterprise was ruled out at the first presentation to Margaret Thatcher in 1987, and throughout competition was regarded as more important than the price or the timetable.[69]

The crucial break with the British Gas model was the decision to separate the ownership of the storage and transmission network (the National Grid) from the generators (the Central Electricity Generating Board) and the regional distribution companies. Two thirds of the conventional power stations owned by the CEGB were transferred to a new company named

National Power, and the rest to a second, PowerGen. The regional electricity boards in England and Wales were transformed into twelve privately owned regional monopolies, which initially shared ownership of the National Grid. They floated their holdings in 1996, and the National Grid is now an independent company.[70] Only in Scotland, where the South of Scotland Electricity Board (now Scottish Power) and the North of Scotland Hydro-Electric Board (now Scottish Hydro-Electric) have always generated electricity as well as distributed it, has the privatised electricity industry remained integrated.

The government hoped to privatise the nuclear power stations with their conventional counterparts, but they had to be withdrawn. The cost of decommissioning reactors was so immense that private investors refused to bear it. They were grouped instead into two new state-owned companies, Nuclear Electric and Scottish Nuclear, and guaranteed a 15 per cent share of the market. The costs of decommissioning were transferred to consumers, in the shape of a special 'non-fossil fuel levy' on all electricity bills,[71] which meant that the price of electricity rose in the early 1990s. By July 1996 the levy had covered sufficient costs for the government to merge the English and Scottish Advanced Gas-Cooled Reactors (AGRs) and Sizewell and privatise them as British Energy.

It is unlikely that the company will build any more nuclear power stations. The need for a special tax to cover the cost of shutting reactors down has made a mockery of scientific claims that nuclear fission offers limitless supplies of virtually costless energy. The only argument for nuclear power today is that it provides a valuable strategic alternative to fossil fuel. British Energy has allowed its planning consent for a third nuclear power station at Hinckley Point to lapse, and the sheer cost of the proposed Sizewell C (£3.5 billion) was sufficient to sink that idea. British Energy now plans to build non-nuclear power stations only, in conjunction with Southern Electric.[72] When Sizewell B closes in 2035, the British nuclear power industry will disappear, leaving only a large bill for decommissioning and a pile of radioactive waste too lethal to handle. By then British Energy will have transformed itself into a conventional power company.

This will give a much-needed boost to competition between the generation companies. Unlike conventional power stations, the nuclear variety cannot be switched off: nuclear power has to be guaranteed a slice of the electricity market, which means that British Energy (and the state-owned Magnox Electric) have no incentive to undercut the other generators.* The price of

* The ageing Magnox reactors which remain in state ownership were merged in December 1997 with British Nuclear Fuels Limited (BNFL), which is now a privatisation candidate. See Chapter 12.

electricity is still set by the heirs to the CEGB: National Power and PowerGen. They dominate the Pool, a half-hourly spot market run by the National Grid, which sets prices according to the price bid by the generator who brings supply into line with demand (electricity cannot be stored). Four times out of five, National Power or PowerGen sets the marginal price. Although most electricity is sold on long-term contracts between generators and distribution companies (the Pool accounts for only one tenth of sales), the price agreed in long-term contracts is influenced mainly by the Pool. Even big buyers cannot buy electricity separately from the generators. This has saddled electricity consumers with the cost of supporting the expensive long-term coal contracts which National Power and PowerGen were obliged to sign with British Coal. Despite falls in the market prices of coal, oil and gas, and a dramatic decline in the cost of building a power station, electricity did not begin to fall significantly in price until 1996.

The Pool has prevented the erosion of the National Power – PowerGen

TABLE 11.7
The Electricity Generators

Generator	Number of Power Stations	Declared Net Capacity (MW)	Share of Total Capacity (Per Cent)
National Power	22	17,033.5	23.2
PowerGen	12	14,803.0	20.2
British Energy	8	8,200.0	11.2
Independent Generators	15	6,414.2	8.7
Eastern Group	6	6,309.0	8.6
Scottish Power	24	4,244.1	5.8
Electricity Supply Board of Ireland	20	4,201.0	5.7
Scottish Hydro-Electric	53	3,723.1	5.1
Magnox Electric (BNFL)	6	2,949.0	4.0
Northern Ireland	5	2,207.0	3.0
First Hydro/Mission Energy*	2	2,088.0	2.8
BNFL	2	484.0	0.7
Others	22	654.2	1.0
Total	197	73,310.1	100.0

Source: OFFER, September 1998.

* Mission Energy bought the pumped storage businesses of the National Grid.

duopoly putting prices under downward pressure. Since privatisation, Offer has authorised dozens of independent generators to sell electricity to the National Grid. This has reduced the market share of National Power and PowerGen to less than half the domestic market, but even this degree of competition has had no impact. The two companies own most of the costly coal and oil-fired plants which are the last to be brought on stream as demand mounts. Since they usually set the price in the Pool, and it is always higher than the price bid by nuclear or gas-fired power stations, even their competitors have no incentive to undercut National Power and PowerGen. In the autumn of 1997 the government ordered an inquiry into the workings of the Pool,[73] and in the following year, National Power and PowerGen were invited by the regulator to sell up to 10,000 MW of plant. They will sell some, but their domination is unlikely to be tested until a genuine spot market in electricity develops, in which the buyers of electricity have as large a say in the price as the generators and regional companies.

That said, the regional electricity companies are scarcely familiar with competition. Until 1994, they enjoyed a monopoly of supply up to a ceiling of 1 MW, which was then lowered to 100 KW. Even the lower ceiling meant only 50,000 customers nationwide were free to choose their electricity supplier. As they were simultaneously cutting costs, the regional companies began to make embarrassingly large profits, and still managed to hoodwink the regulator into granting them over-generous X factors for the second five years from 1995 to 2000. Share prices rose, and there were bitter recriminations when the generosity of the Northern Electric defence against the Trafalgar House bid caused the director general to reconsider.[74]

It was not until the autumn of 1998 that the first of the 23 million domestic electricity users and two million small businesses actually experienced competition. Because it is not possible for different suppliers to sell *their* electricity to particular consumers (electricity flows throughout the network), competition for domestic consumers meant a computer system which allows the regional electricity companies to exchange billing information. The companies were in no hurry to build it. Despite having had eight years to prepare, they delayed the original starting date of April 1998 repeatedly because they were not confident that the systems worked. After the director general fined them £50 million apiece for lack of effort, competition eventually started in four provincial cities in September 1998. It will not be nationwide until the end of 1999, a decade after the electricity industry was privatised with a structure specifically designed to enhance competition.

Rail: Lowering Subsidies but Limiting Competition

Despite its failure to spark competition quickly, the electricity industry was the model for the privatisation of the railways. The government split the ownership of the network from the ownership of the trains and privatised them separately. This made sense. The railway network is a natural monopoly (it is not worthwhile to build a second one), leaving scope for competition to provide services on the same railway line.[75] Just as airlines do not own airports, and ships do not own ports, independent train companies can compete for customers on the same piece of infrastructure. Half a dozen privatised freight companies (all but one owned by an American company, EWS), a handful of private freight operators and twenty-five passenger train companies now tout for business across the old British Rail network.[76]

To gain access, they pay a fee to the owner, Railtrack Group PLC, privatised in a public flotation of May 1996. It earns over £2.25 billion a year from selling access to the rail network,[77] and is responsible for signalling and for the maintenance, renewal and upgrading of the track. It sub-contracts this work to a variety of regional and specialist track and train maintenance businesses spun out of British Rail and sold to trade buyers and management buy-outs in the mid-1990s.[78] Railtrack is also responsible for train timetables, in the hope that it can co-ordinate arrival and departure times, integrate rail services with other forms of transport, and identify what railway insiders call 'new journey opportunities'.

Railtrack is still a monopoly, its access charges regulated by the Office of the Rail Regulator, amid the usual chorus of threats to cut investment (by Railtrack) and complaints (by everybody else) about regulatory naivety. Competition occurs only in the right to maintain or use the network. The track maintenance and renewal companies were privatised, and compete for the right to service the network. Similarly, passenger services were divided into twenty-five separate franchises, each with a temporary monopoly over some part of the network, and auctioned to the highest bidder by the Office of Passenger Rail Franchising (Opraf). In theory, the bidder promising the best combination of price and service secures the franchise.

Practice is more complicated. Unlike other privatisations, the government was not prepared to let the market decide the level of output: when and how many trains run and what fares are charged. The holders of the railway franchises are obliged to guarantee a minimum level of service, which is laid down in considerable detail: frequencies, destinations, journey times, operating hours, and the number of carriages attached to the locomotive on each journey. Fares are tied to inflation for the first three years of each

TABLE 11.8
What Railtrack Owns

	Length Number	Value 1997–8 (£m)
Track		
Total track mileage*	23,000	2,484
Passenger & freight route mileage	7,839	–
Passenger route mileage only	1,057	–
Freight route mileage only	1,374	–
Total Mileage	10,270	–
Stations and signal boxes		
Passenger stations & depots	2,482	1,466
Signal boxes and control centres	1,160	†1,446
Other land and buildings	–	283
Bridges and tunnels		
Tunnels	984	–
Bridges	40,000	–
Other		
Electrification	–	788
Plant & machinery	–	316
Other infrastructure	–	641
Investment properties	–	252
Total	–	£7,676m

Source: Railtrack.

* The track mileage exceeds the route mileage because most routes have at least dual tracks.
† Total value of signalling systems.

franchise, and increases restricted to RPI minus 1 per cent in the subsequent four years. Opraf is under a statutory duty to ensure that fares are 'reasonable', that through-ticketing is maintained, and that discounts are offered to the young, the old and the disabled. The regulator also measures the punctuality and reliability of services, fining and rewarding companies according to performance.

Services and service standards of this kind cost money, and the government accepted from the outset that private railways would not supply the service the voters wanted without a subsidy. Perhaps one third of the revenues of the railway industry originate with the taxpayer,[79] but the train companies are expected gradually to reduce their appetite for subsidies by trimming costs. Official projections depict the aggregate subsidy declining steadily over the life of the franchises.

But the train operating companies and the government know that the real bargain is not subsidies-for-efficiency but subsidies-for-investment. Rail privatisation did not aim to cut the running costs of British Rail or even to raise money for tax cuts. The entire privatisation raised only £4.5 billion: a poor return on the £54 billion invested over the forty-eight years since nationalisation. The ambition was smarter trains and better services, partly to please Conservative-voting commuters, but mainly to get goods and people off the roads and into the trains.

So far, promises have outrun delivery. In 1997 Railtrack committed itself to invest £17 billion over the next ten years in brighter stations, better signalling and more tracks. EWS promised new locomotives, radiophones in the cab and better links to the ports. It is sampling new services (supermarket deliveries) and trying to win back the single-wagon and part-train freight shipments which British Rail abandoned as unprofitable. But much of the investment by the passenger franchise-holders is superficial. New liveries, logos and staff uniforms are universal. Marketing gimmicks familiar in the airline industry – 'free' meals and 'rail miles' and favours for frequent travellers – are spreading (though ticket pricing and sales remain as awkward and opaque as ever). Richard Branson, whose Virgin Rail controls two franchises, plans to install video screens in seats and fill the first-class departure lounge at Euston with table football games.[80] European Rail Catering (the new name of the old British Rail catering) has invested in a range of drinks trolleys which announce their arrival with a musical burst.[81]

However, new trains and carriages are being bought. According to Opraf, by the spring of 1998 fifteen railway companies had placed orders worth over £2 billion for 2,183 new pieces of rolling stock.[82] Hundreds of carriages are being refurbished. One of the rolling stock leasing companies has started speculative building of new stock, to standard specifications, for use anywhere on the network.[83] At privatisation, the average age of British Rail trains was eighteen years, most of it slam-door carriages rather than air-conditioned cabins with automatic doors. Their replacements will be faster as well as more comfortable; the tilting trains Virgin Rail has ordered for the soon-to-be-modernised West Coast line will knock 1½ hours off the London–Glasgow journey time by 2005.

TABLE 11.9
The Train Operating Companies and Their Franchises

Franchise	Franchisee	Years	Subsidy 1997–8* (£m)	Projected Subsidy final year (£m)
Anglia Railways	GB Railways†	7	36.2	6.5
Cardiff Railway Company	Prism Rail PLC‡	7	20.7	14.1
Central Trains	National Express PLC	7	134.6	97.3
Chiltern Railway	M40 Trains§	7	14.4	0.45
Connex South Central	Connex Rail Ltd¶	7	76.0	5.4
Connex South Eastern	Connex Rail Ltd	15	114.7	(1.6)
Cross Country	Virgin Rail Ltd‖	15	115.9	(10.6)
Gatwick Express	National Express PLC	15	(6.2)	(1.9)
Great Eastern Railway	FirstGroup PLC	7	28.7	(9.9)
Great North Eastern Railway	GNER Holdings Ltd**	7	55.1	0.14
Great Western Trains††	FirstGroup PLC	10	58.9	(2.8)
Island Line	Stagecoach PLC	5	1.9	0.98
LTS Rail	Prism Rail PLC	15	27.7	1.9
Merseyrail Electrics	MTL Trust Holdings Ltd‡‡	7	7.5	5.4
Midland Mainline	National Express PLC	10	8.2	(0.85)
North Western Trains	FirstGroup PLC	7	100.4	69.0
Northern Spirit	MTL Trust Holdings Ltd	7	141.7	93.7
ScotRail	National Express PLC	7	135.9	95.3
Silverlink§§	National Express PLC	7	49.4	16.3
South West Trains	Stagecoach PLC	7	62.6	36.9
Thames Trains	Go-Ahead Group PLC¶¶	7	2.5	3.9
Thameslink Rail	GOVIA Ltd‖‖	7	33.5	(29.4)
Wales & West	Prism Rail PLC	7	73.5	40.5
West Anglia Great Northern	Prism Rail PLC	7	54.6	(26.4)
West Coast Trains	Virgin Rail Ltd	15	76.6	(227.8)
Total			1,425.0	196.3

Source: Opraf.

* 1997–8 was the first full year of privatisation.
† GB Railways was a Management Buy-In (MBI).
‡ Prism Rail PLC was founded by four regional bus companies (Blazefield, EYMS; Lynton Travel and Q Drive Holdings). Floated on the Stock Exchange in 1996, it became the first quoted railway company since 1947.
§ M40 trains was a Management Buy-Out (51%) supported by the construction group John Laing (26%) and 3i (23%).
¶ Connex Rail is a subsidiary of Vivendi SA, part of the French utilities group, Compagnie Générale des Eaux (CGE).
‖ Stagecoach Holdings has a 49 per cent share in Virgin Rail.
** GNER Holdings is a subsidiary of Sea Containers Limited.
†† Great Western Trains was originally owned by FirstGroup management and staff (24.5%), but FirstGroup bought out its partner in 1998.
‡‡ MTL Trust Holdings is a bus group.
§§ Formerly North London Railways.
¶¶ Thames Trains was originally owned by Go-Ahead Group PLC (65%) and its management and staff (35%) but in March 1998 Go-Ahead bought staff and management holdings.
‖‖ GOVIA Limited is a joint venture between GTI of France and Go-Ahead Group PLC.

The operating companies say they would invest more if their franchises were not so short.[84] Trading franchises for investment was built into the auction process by the previous government, and several were not confirmed until the holders fulfilled commitments to invest in new trains. But official approval of changes of ownership – like the acquisition of the Great Western franchise-holder by FirstGroup – is already being used to extort promises of additional money and services. New Labour, with its congenital weakness for businessmen who promise to invest, is even more sympathetic to subsidy-for-rolling-stock swaps than its Conservative predecessor,[85] and there is every likelihood that the franchising system will degenerate into an auction of investment promises. Since it is the most promising source of competition in the privatised railway system, this is a temptation the government would be well-advised to resist.

The Buses: Order Out of Chaos

One reason rail privatisation succeeded in the unpropitious political circumstances of 1996–7 was the existence of a group of private businesses familiar with running subsidised transport services: the bus companies. Seventeen out of the twenty-five rail passenger franchises are now controlled by one of the enterprises which emerged from the disintegration and privatisation of the monolithic National Bus and Scottish Bus groups in the mid-1980s. One of them, Stagecoach, also has a half-share in Virgin Rail. Like National Express, MTL and FirstGroup, which also have railway franchises, Stagecoach is among the victors of the Darwinian struggle launched by the Transport Act of 1985. This legislation opened the bus market to genuine competition for the first time in over fifty years.*

After a brief free-for-all before and after the First World War, the buses were gradually taken over by the state, on the grounds that bus routes were a natural monopoly. Services were taken into public ownership by local councils or turned into temporary monopolies licensed for fixed periods to private operators. The private bus industry became the preserve of a handful of large combines, which were eventually nationalised, most by absorption into the British Transport Commission in 1948. The rest disappeared in 1968, when the second Wilson government established Passenger Transport Authorities

---

* The Transport Act of 1980 abolished price control. It also lifted licensing restrictions on long-distance express, excursion and tour services, and shifted the burden of proof in licence applications from applicants to objectors. The Transport Act of 1983 obliged local authorities to consider tenders from private operators who could offer services more cheaply.

(PTAs) in the major cities and set up the National Bus Company and the Scottish Bus Group to run services.

In the absence of competition, producers rather than consumers took control. Most bus services were controlled by unionised labour interested in less work for more money, and answerable to councillors uninterested in economy. They were inefficient, uncomfortable and relatively expensive. The numbers travelling by bus fell continually, and from 1968 the government was forced to subsidise the industry. To escape from this spiral of subsidised decline the 1985 Transport Act reduced the obstacles to starting a bus service to forty-two days' notice. It abolished blanket subsidies, forcing local authorities and PTAs to award bus routes to the private operator demanding the lowest subsidy. The National Bus Company, Scottish Bus Group and over half of the municipal bus companies were privatised.[86]

TABLE 11.10
The Consolidation of the Bus Industry

Company	Number of Vehicles	Market Share*
FirstGroup plc	9,721	23.1%
Stagecoach Holdings plc	8,236	16.4%
Arriva plc	6,307	13.9%
Go-Ahead Group plc	2,348	6.3%
National Express Group plc	2,239	6.7%
MTL Trust Holdings Ltd	944	2.1%
Traction Group Ltd	1,002	3.0%
Metroline plc	852	2.2%
Local Authorities	2,893	6.2%
Sub-Total	34,542	79.5%
Others†	41,358	20.1%

Source: Bus Industry Monitor 1998, published by the TAS Partnership Ltd.

* Based on 1996–97 turnover of UK bus operating subsidiaries owned at 1 October 1998.
† Total fleet includes coaches, though there are no statistics for turnover and market share in the coach business.

Now, 85 per cent of bus routes are run on a commercial basis. Costs are down, bus mileage is up, and passengers travel on newer, and often smaller buses. But, of the dozens of franchises created between 1985 and 1995, many sold to management teams, few remain independent. Eight major companies control three quarters of the market. In the transitional years, the larger companies were predators rather than competitors – running buses a few minutes ahead of their rivals, or concentrating their services in the urban rush hours, leaving less profitable times to their rivals.

There were periodic punch-ups between drivers employed by different companies. This was not surprising: they were often instructed to wait at lucrative stops, or race ahead to reach the busiest spots without stopping at the quieter points on the way. Travel cards became harder to obtain, and confrontations with the competition authorities became routine. Between 1987 and 1995 the Office of Fair Trading considered 267 complaints of 'predatory' pricing by rival companies. Many were against Stagecoach, now one of the biggest national companies. A 1995 MMC report accused it of behaviour which was 'predatory, deplorable and against the public interest' after it effectively bankrupted the municipally owned Darlington Transport.[87]

Is the Market Putting Together What the Government Put Asunder?

Many bus companies were too small and impoverished, or lacked the management, to survive all-out competition of this kind. Unlike larger groups, they could not cut costs by pooling overheads and purchasing power. But consolidation has created a risk that public monopoly will give way to private oligopoly. As competition recedes, collaboration beckons. In 1998 the Office of Fair Trading published evidence of collusion between ten bus companies operating in Merseyside and the Greater Manchester area. By carving up routes, they were able to drive up fares.[88] The fear of oligopoly intensified as the bus companies accumulated rail passenger franchises. Privatisation looks as though it may be delivering passengers to a handful of integrated transport companies. There are already complaints of revenue-raiding expeditions on the railways, with franchisees starting services a few minutes ahead of rivals on routes where they compete directly.[89] A graver danger is the emergence of regional transport monopolies, with rail-and-bus companies cutting services and raising fares, which was why the MMC insisted National Express sell some of its Scottish bus services before it was allowed to keep the ScotRail franchise.

This risk is mitigated because the bus-and-rail companies do not own the roads or the railway tracks. Provided these are owned separately by a body with an incentive to stimulate competition to use them, and the legal and regulatory barriers to starting a new service are low, a successful conspiracy against the fare-paying public is unlikely. In 1997, for example, FirstGroup was released from an earlier MMC direction to sell part of its Scottish operation after taking over Strathclyde Buses because Stagecoach had started a competitive service in Glasgow. Ensuring it is not too costly for new entrants to challenge the incumbent provider has enabled the bus industry to escape direct regulation altogether.

It is, however, relatively cheap to buy a bus and start a service. In the electricity industry, the costs of building a power plant or local distribution network are rather higher. In the twenty-first century, most consumers will probably buy all their energy needs from a 'multi-utility', which will sell gas (and perhaps water and telecommunications) as well as electricity. Companies of this kind are already emerging: United Utilities owns North West Water, Norweb, a telecommunications network, and an electricity and gas marketing business; Hyder PLC owns both Welsh Water and SWALEC, the electricity utility; British Gas is selling electricity, and the regional electricity companies are selling gas.

So far, they are enhancing competition. But some multi-utilities will reverse the verdict of privatisation, by generating as well as distributing electricity. When Scottish Power bid for Manweb in 1995, reuniting a generator with a distributor, the government did not object. The purchase was not even referred to the MMC. Encouraged, National Power bid for Southern Electric and PowerGen bid for Midland Electricity. They were surprised to find the bids referred to the MMC, and even more surprised when the president of the Board of Trade, Ian Lang, overruled its verdict that they be allowed to proceed. The disappointed bidders complained of arbitrariness and inconsistency, but the apparent contradiction is easily explained. Scottish Power had no generation capacity in England, but National Power and PowerGen then controlled two thirds of the market. Allowing the bids to proceed would have given them a captive clientele, releasing them from the need to compete for customers, and discouraging new entrants to the generation market.

There are now a number of companies which generate as well distribute electricity. Scottish Power (which owns Manweb) and Scottish Hydro-Electric (which owns Southern Electric) were both privatised as integrated companies. Eastern Group subsequently acquired several power stations from National Power and PowerGen. In 1998 PowerGen was allowed to buy East Midlands Electricity, provided it sold some of its generation capacity. Now it is not lack of competition for consumers but lack of competition among generators which is problematic. If government plans to force the regional electricity companies to open their local networks of wires and transformers to allcomers are implemented, even generators without distribution arms will be free to sell electricity directly to consumers.

BT: competition at last

It will take until the turn of the century before the competition to supply domestic electricity consumers is as intense as the competition consumers are already enjoying in telecommunications. Since the early 1990s, the number of telecommunications providers has exploded. As recently as 1981 British Telecom (BT) had a complete monopoly over the supply and installation of telephones (except in Kingston Upon Hull).[90] The first direct competitor to BT, Mercury Communications, was licensed in February 1982, but struggled to make an impact. Its chief problem, outside lucrative business markets such as the City, was reliance on renting lines from BT.[91]

Today, BT confronts 150 licensed competitors in its domestic market, of which ninety are cable companies armed with alternative networks of their own. For telephone services, consumers can now choose between BT, CWC (the successor to Mercury), the local cable television company, four mobile telephone networks, and a variety of Internet and callback providers.[92] The choice for business consumers is even wider and, as capacity has expanded, the price of calls has plunged. The number of fax, electronic mail, and Internet-based information and entertainment services available over the telephone are multiplying exponentially.

Competition was driven primarily by technology. The BT monopoly was built on its huge fixed investment in copper wire and mechanical switches. This network, valued at £14 billion, was too expensive for any competitor to reproduce. Unlike AT & T in the United States, the government decided not to break it into regional entities at privatisation or force the company to disgorge its network to a third party; this would have delayed the sale for five to ten years, and the government was not prepared to wait. This blunted the impact of the first cable television franchises, which were awarded as early as 1984. The enormous cost of building local networks, and the lack of personalised telephone numbers, meant they did not compete seriously with BT in telephone services until the mid-1990s.

In the end it was new technology, not the construction of alternative networks, which enabled new entrants to compete effectively with BT. Optical fibres, computerised switching and satellite and radio mast telephony gave new companies the weapons to disturb the BT monopoly. It allowed some providers to dispense with telephone lines altogether, and others to carry hundreds of thousands of calls on a single line. Since then, the cable operators have also passed millions of homes.[93] The National Grid has created a second national telecommunications network, Energis, by stringing fibre-optic cables between its pylons. Energis, floated on the Stock Exchange in December

1997, has since opened its network to Deutsche Telekom and France Telecom, which has brought foreign competition to local connections for the first time. Scottish Power has now copied its example, and the regional electricity companies are investigating technology which allows telephone calls to be carried across their copper wires.

The relentless rise of competition has reduced the price of telecommunications dramatically in recent years, but BT prices began to fall significantly only in 1993–4. As recently as 1995, BT still controlled 83 per cent of the business market, 93 per cent of the residential market, and 71 per cent of international calls. Because the markets continued to grow, it was not until the end of that year that BT experienced its first net loss of customers, and it did not suffer financial loss until 1997. Even today, only one in eight residential subscribers uses a supplier other than BT. The chairman of the company, Sir Iain Vallance, refers openly to his company as 'the world's best market defender'.[94] But the truth is less flattering.

TABLE 11.11
Real Percentage Change in BT Prices Since Privatisation

Year	Domestic Line Rental	Cheap Rate Local Call	Cheap Rate Regional Call	Cheap Rate National Call	International Call	Overall Weighted Average
1984–5	+7.1	+6.8	+23.1	+6.8	N/A	+2.0
1985–6	+8.5	+6.4	+6.4	+6.4	N/A	+3.7
1986–7	+3.7	−3.6	+2.7	−12.0	N/A	−0.3
1987–8	0.0	0.0	0.0	0.0	N/A	0.0
1988–9	0.0	0.0	0.0	0.0	N/A	0.0
1989–90	+10.0	+3.7	+3.6	0.0	N/A	+3.5
1990–1	+11.6	+10.1	+6.0	+7.1	N/A	+5.3
1991–2	+7.8	+4.6	+4.9	+4.9	−9.8	−0.7
1992–3	+5.9	0.0	0.0	0.0	−4.7	−0.5
1993–4	+3.2	0.0	−0.2	0.0	−5.5	−6.9
1994–5	+4.6	−1.2	−2.5	−6.9	−4.4	−7.3
1995–6	+19.8	−10.0	−10.0	−10.0	−10.0	−1.8
1996–7	+1.1	0.0	0.0	−19.8	−18.2	−4.9

Source: Oftel.

The government chose deliberately to protect BT from competition. It had lumbered the company with social obligations (such as telephone boxes in rural areas) and wanted to give BT time to prepare for competition.

Competitors were prevented from attacking the profitable part of the BT monopoly until the company had abandoned cross-subsidies and adjusted the price of each service to its actual costs. A single competitor was licensed in 1982, which did not manage to offer a service until 1986. It was also given time to establish itself. BT and Mercury enjoyed a local network duopoly until 1990, and an international one until 1996. For ten years the regulator was forced to concentrate on price control rather than competition.

It was not until 1995–6 that Oftel began to attack the dominant position of BT directly, and to seek powers to prevent the company acting anti-competitively. The market had already begun this work. Competitors still gripe that they pay too much for connection to the BT network, but with less cause than before. Its inter-connection charges are among the lowest in the world, and with good reason. For the first time since it was privatised in 1984, the company is facing genuine and constant competition in every area of its business. The volume of BT revenue subject to Oftel price control has fallen from nearly £4 in every £5 in 1993 to about £1 in every £5 now. In seeking additional powers to prevent BT abusing its market position, the director general of the Office of Telecommunications is advertising his own redundancy.

The Need to Break the Regulatory Habit

The ultimate aim of every utility regulator should be his own demise. If regulation is a substitute for competition, it should be disarmed as soon as competition is established, and any remaining functions transferred to the normal competition authorities. Of course, regulators are reluctant to accept this. In devising fresh responsibilities for themselves they have shown considerable ingenuity. They have also found a willing accomplice in the government, which has identified regulation as the post-socialist alternative to the re-nationalisation of the privatised industries. This is why the next director general of Telecommunication Services can look forward to adding Broadcasting and Information Technology to his title; his equivalents at Gas and Electricity to supervision of the entire energy market; and their counterpart at the Office of the Rail Regulator can set his heart on becoming the director general of the Strategic Rail Authority.

Nothing would undermine the purposes of privatisation more than perpetual regulation. Already, regulators have pushed the water companies and Railtrack into speeding up their investment programmes and halted the 'dash for gas'. Lists of extraneous social and environmental objectives are being prepared. Growing ministerial interference has prompted even sympathetic observers like Simon Jenkins to denounce privatisation as a fraud. ' "Denationalisation" was a sham,' he writes. 'The Office of Fair Trading and the statutory regulators may intervene in the electricity, gas, water, rail, air, media and telecommunication businesses. Government subsidies can be disbursed and cross-subsidies ordered. Railtrack is told to raise investment, water firms to clean rivers, power stations to use more coal. A command economy can be led as effectively in private as in public ownership.'[95]

This is to mistake beginnings for ends. Privatisation is not an end-state, but the beginning of a long process of liberation from direction by government towards government by competition. Change will not cease even then. Competition is a process of endless discontinuity, in which the shape and size and number of companies adjust without respite to the demands of consumers and the threats of competitors. Regulation is based on the belief that this process is imperfect, and needs correction. Yet regulators – even those armed, like Opraf, with 'extensive computer systems ... [to] extract data on train performance' – cannot hope to keep pace with the shifting realities of the marketplace.[96] Regulators are like observers in a physical experiment: the knowledge they need to ensure the market is competitive is known only to the market itself.

Perfect regulation, like perfect competition, is impossible. In competitive markets, it is also unnecessary; its retention can only create imperfections, not rectify them. Perverse effects are observable already, as regulated industries have tried to escape the downward pressure on regulated profits by diversifying into unregulated lines of business. BT lost $220 million on its first foreign investment, and has since formed a string of unproductive alliances in continental Europe. When BT agreed in 1996 to acquire MCI of the United States for $20 billion, it dithered for a year about paying too much, and was trumped by a rival who paid $37 billion. A decade and a half after release from state ownership, BT is still struggling to adapt to competitive markets. So are most privatised industries.

BAA made an ill-fated foray into hotels, before offloading them on Forte. The regional electricity companies wrote off a fortune in cable television and burglar alarms. Yorkshire Water had a brief flirtation with cable television, and Welsh Water dallied disastrously with hotels and road construction. In 1990 Severn Trent paid nearly £300 million for a pair of waste management businesses which turned out to be making serious losses.[97] In 1996 Thames Water wrote off £95 million on ventures abroad; two years later, it took charge of a water utility in Jakarta just before Indonesia was plunged into revolutionary turmoil. Across the straits, United Utilities had poured £90 million into the sewers of Bangkok.[98]

Of course, even the most well-adapted companies are not immune to error.

Nor do the benefits of competitive markets make them proof against the itch to interfere. But nor should regulators be endowed with superior wisdom, or granted the gift of immortality by default. Rightly used, regulation is a temporary expedient, employed to control the prices and behaviour of dominant enterprises until they can be subjected to the sterner disciplines of competition for customers and capital. This is not an argument for laissez-faire, but not yet. Where competition is weak, regulators should be directed to increase it.

The Airline Industry: More Competition Required

An obvious target is the civil aviation industry. British Airways[99] and the British Airports Authority (now BAA plc)[100] were privatised within months of each other in the first half of 1997. On the face of it, privatisation worked. British Airways entered the 1980s as a technical bankrupt, and the average BAA airport as a set for *Curry and Chips*. They leave the 1990s transfigured. British Airways, unlike its state-owned rivals around the world, is profitable and unsubsidised. BAA is so profitable that it has funded a lavish investment programme (including the whole of Stansted airport) with little borrowing and no subsidy. Its airports, now more like shopping centres than travel termini, are so well run that Indianapolis, Melbourne, Naples and Pittsburgh have invited BAA to show them how to manage theirs.

Much of this success is unmerited. It was built not on privatisation alone, but on lack of competition. British Airways controls two thirds of the civil aviation market in Britain, the Civil Aviation Authority (CAA) having failed consistently to nurture a serious competitor. British Caledonian, its chosen favourite, was acquired by British Airways in December 1987 after the CAA ordered an ill-judged exchange of routes between the two. (The merged airline promptly raised fares.) Virgin and British Midland are still in business, but handicapped by their lack of access to Heathrow. When British Midland applied for licences to operate from Heathrow to Scotland, objections by British Airways delayed the award for three years. It took Virgin five years to win slots to fly to Johannesburg.

Competitors who attack British Airways are given no quarter. The financial problems which brought down British Eagle, Air Europe, Dan Air and Laker Airways were caused in large part by the ruthless response of British Airways to competition. The transatlantic air fare cartel which undermined Laker ended in litigation which delayed the privatisation of British Airways for seven years, and cost the state-owned airline £8 million in damages. A decade later, the litigation stemming from its notorious 'dirty tricks' campaign against

Virgin Atlantic (which was competing on the profitable transatlantic and Japanese routes) ended in a £610,000 libel award to Branson and an out-of-court payment of £265,000 to his airline.[101] According to Virgin, the British Airways tactics included quadrupling service charges on Virgin aircraft; denying its pilots use of the night flight simulator at Heathrow; flooding the market with cheap tickets on Virgin routes; attempting to poach Virgin customers with special deals; unlawful use of Virgin computer data; and the dissemination of rumours about the weak financial position of Virgin Atlantic.

British Airways has not lost its ruthless streak. When discount and independent carriers like Ryanair, EasyJet and Debonair began to erode its share of European markets, British Airways set up its own low cost airline, Go. One reason it has to struggle to compete fairly with independent rivals is that it has too many staff earning too much money for too little work. Attempts to cut costs have provoked costly and embarrassing strikes, forcing the airline to sub-contract some work (holiday flights and baggage-handling) to cheaper suppliers. Its profitability depends on size and scale rather than efficiency and innovation. In recent years, it has reinforced its dominant position by forming alliances with foreign carriers like American Airlines.[102] These alliances yield some gains in efficiency, like joint ticketing, but their aim is not to cut costs. It is to gain access to markets which would otherwise be closed.

This is a forgivable ambition. International aviation is no longer the most overpriced, over-regulated and over-subsidised industry in the world. Fares are deregulated throughout Europe, and domestic markets are open to all-comers. But most state-owned airlines are still heavily subsidised by taxpayers, and virtually every airline is protected from takeover by foreign bidders on strategic grounds. This has precluded mergers – which would cut costs – in favour of cartels – which open markets rather than lower prices. British Airways and American Airlines account for two in every three flights across the Atlantic, and the alliance is bound to eliminate independent competitors, which will mean higher fares and poorer services.

The alliance has also illuminated the unhealthy nexus between British Airways, BAA and the CAA. In order to approve the alliance, the competition authorities have insisted that British Airways and American Airlines give up 267 landing slots at Heathrow. Nothing is more important to the prosperity of an airline than airports: popular ones guarantee a steady stream of passengers, and Heathrow is the busiest international airport in the world. London is a popular destination, and an entrepôt for flights elsewhere. In 1997, over 58 million passengers poured through the airport, one in three en route to somewhere else. British Airways, based at Heathrow, owns two in five of its landing slots.

This is a powerful competitive weapon. Every major airline wants to land at Heathrow, but the incumbent airlines can keep their slots as long as they want, provided they use them regularly. In any year, only one landing slot in fifty is surrendered; it cannot be bought in the open market. Airlines barter unwanted slots among themselves, sometimes for cash. (KLM is said to have recently earned £15 million from the sale to British Airways of eight daily slots at Heathrow).[103] This makes it hard for new entrants, such as Virgin and British Midland, to gain a foothold. They favour a proper market in landing slots, in which the right to land would revert to the airport which provides the runways. It would then sell the rights, for fixed periods, to the highest bidder.*

This would drive up the cost of landing at Heathrow. BAA frets that higher landing charges would drive airlines to alternative airports – Frankfurt, Paris or Schipol. It could just as easily divert them to Gatwick (which is quiet) or Stansted (which is virtually silent). Heathrow is hot, noisy and over-crowded with people and aeroplanes, and passengers like it much less than Gatwick or Stansted. But BAA likes it that way. The more well-heeled international travellers it can squeeze through the car parks, shops and restaurants, the richer it gets. This is why BAA wants to build a fifth terminal at Heathrow, and recently completed a £440 million fast rail link to Paddington Station in central London. It is now exploring faster rail links to the rest of the country, to tempt even more shoppers to visit the airport. Absurdly, they would further drive down the cost of using it. Landing charges are regulated by the CAA according to the usual RPI minus X formula, but with one curious twist. To the extent that BAA increases its revenues from unregulated commercial activities (mainly shopping, but also car parks and property development) the level of X is reduced. Under this formula, it is theoretically possible that airlines will one day be paid to land at Heathrow.

The only reason why BAA can afford to ignore popular dislike of Heathrow is that it is a monopoly. BAA services three quarters of British passenger traffic, and four fifths of air cargo. Ownership of Heathrow, Gatwick and Stansted gives it an effective monopoly of airports in south-east England, and control of Glasgow, Edinburgh and Aberdeen airports a genuine monopoly in Scotland. It does not have to compete for airlines and airline passengers against rival airports in either England or Scotland. This is why transport

---

* One problem is that nobody knows who owns landing slots, though airlines think they do. British Airways, for example, wants to sell its share of the 267 slots being surrendered as a condition of the alliance with American Airlines. The Office of Fair Trading was satisfied, but the European Commission says British Airways cannot sell what it does not own. Certainly, their only claim to ownership is the fact that they happen to be in possession. The logical owner is the airport, which provides the landing space.

economists, the MMC, parliamentarians and ministers have argued that BAA should be forced to sell Gatwick and Stansted. Competitors, not regulators, are the true friends of airline passengers.

*

This is the chief lesson of privatisation. It is competition, not a change of ownership or regulatory regime, which guarantees greater efficiency, better services, and lower prices. This has tempted some to conclude that privatisation was an exercise in futility. Tougher regulation, they say, could have achieved the same effects at lower cost. To some extent, like middle-period Mitterrand, when companies were neither privatised nor nationalised, this is the conclusion the government has reached. There will be neither nationalisation nor privatisation, but more regulation, a tougher competition policy, and greater commercial freedom for the Post Office. This will be an error: competition for customers depends on competition for capital. New Labour knows this, but its Old Labour supporters in the public sector do not want it. The result is the reduction of ownership to the balance of political advantage.

CHAPTER TWELVE

THE STILL-NATIONALISED INDUSTRIES

We are not in the business of reversing these [privatisation] reforms. I certainly believe that where there is no overriding reason for preferring the public provision of goods and services, particularly where those services operate in a competitive market, then the presumption should be that economic activity is best left to the private sector, with market forces being fully encouraged to operate.

TONY BLAIR, 1997[1]

Opposition to postal privatisation is motivated mostly by ignorance or by wilful misrepresentation.

FINANCIAL TIMES[2]

We are not selling the family silver. We are re-plating it.

GLENDA JACKSON, Transport minister, on London Underground[3]

The BBC is in business to be a public broadcaster, not to be a business.

CHRIS SMITH, Culture secretary[4]

The balance is struck in party not national terms. Under New Labour, privatisation is less predictable and more cynical. The ideological certainties of New Conservatism and Old Labour may have vanished, but the Old Labourites have not. Their misgivings ensured that decades of opposition to privatisation were not abandoned until the general election, when victory mattered more than conscience. The campaign was underway before New Labour conceded that the £1.5 billion hole in their spending plans would be filled by privatisation proceeds. A year in office was gone before the chancellor of the Exchequer listed any privatisations of his own. Even then, he abjured the 'P' word ('privatisation') in favour of the triple 'P' formula ('public-private partnership'). If the Conservatives discovered privatisation by chance (and pursued it as an alternative to retrenchment) New Labour adopted it by stealth (and pursued it as an alternative to raising taxes).*

This is not how ministers tell it. 'We must be prepared', Gordon Brown told the House of Commons in the summer of 1998, 'to break with old dogmas.' The Conservative benches hooted. They knew the dogmatics were behind him, not in front of him. Some were beside him: Old Labour Robin Cook and New Labour Gordon Brown had clashed publicly over whether to privatise the Tote. Backbench misgivings explain why the sale of shares in National Air Traffic Services (NATS) was limited to a majority stake and constrained by a Golden Share, and why the Royal Mint and the Tote might or might not be sold to private investors.[5] Only student loans, British Energy debt, motorway service areas and unwanted office blocks and car parks were certain contributors to the £4 billion the chancellor expected to receive from asset sales in each of the last three years of the Parliament.[6] Other assets were in pawn to the Old Labourites on the backbenches and the public sector trade unions.

This reliance on the shifting balance of power within the Labour movement has lent privatisation a randomness it lacked under the Conservatives. An Old Labour secretary of state for Transport, the Environment and the Regions (Prescott) stopped the sale of the Port of Tyne but a New Labour chancellor (Brown) disposed of the government stake in the Mersey Docks and Harbour Company.[7] A New Labour prime minister (Blair) told an Old Labour secretary of state for International Development (Short) to sell a majority stake in the Commonwealth Development Corporation.[8] An Old Labour trade secretary (Beckett) ruled out the sale of shares in the Post Office, but the New Labour prime minister (Blair) was unhappy.[9] Beckett was replaced with a New Labour alternative (Mandelson) but – to avoid provoking Old Labourites – he ruled out even partial privatisation in favour of an uneasy mixture of commercial freedom, regulatory control and a smaller government share of the profits.

Scottish Water: Old Labour Triumphs

The decision was apt. Privatisation is no longer a matter of principle, or even pragmatism dressed up as principle. It is party politics dressed up as the Third Way. In Scotland, the strongest redoubt of Old Labour, they do not bother

* The belief is common place that the Conservative government stumbled on privatisation, and used it to pay for tax cuts which were better funded from cuts in public expenditure, but the privatisation of British Aerospace, British Shipbuilders, NFC, the National Enterprise Board and the buses were promised in the 1979 Conservative manifesto, and privatisations worth £1 billion were in the first budget of the new government in June 1979.

to dress it up. North of the border, privatisation remains anathema. New Labour could enter the 1997 general election on a pledge to 'return Scotland's water service to local democratic control' without fear that it would cost votes. In government, it sacked the chairmen of two of the three Scottish water authorities, packed their boards with sympathetic councillors, and placed water and sewage services under the authority of a Scottish Parliament which is anything but New Labour. The independent Scottish Water and Sewerage Customers Council was replaced with a statutory regulator.

The changes were undeniably popular, but it is hard to see why. Like its counterpart in England, the Scottish water industry entered the 1990s with a formidable backlog of capital spending to meet higher environmental standards.[10] It still does: all three Scottish water authorities are in the bottom five for water quality. Because they cannot borrow privately, water bills are bound to rise. Ironically, the fear of higher bills was the main reason Scots opposed privatisation in the early 1990s. De-nationalisation was easier to resist north of the border, especially in the wake of the unpopular Poll Tax, because the service was provided by local councils rather than sellable regional water authorities.[11] But the Conservatives did not give up.

In 1992 Ian Lang, then Secretary of State for Scotland, used the reorganisation of local government to reopen the idea of privatisation. Just one in a hundred of the public responses was in favour,[12] and opinion polls confirmed this level of support. An impromptu referendum by Strathclyde Regional Council in 1994 tempted three in four voters to express an opinion. Only three in a hundred favoured privatisation. Lang was forced to defer to the preferences of the Scottish people. As the re-organisation of local government came into effect, water and sewage services were placed under the control of three publicly owned, regional water authorities. Any similarities with pre-privatisation arrangements south of the border were purely coincidental.[13]

The East of Scotland, West of Scotland and North of Scotland Water Authorities are old-fashioned public corporations; it will take a political earthquake to turn them into anything else. They were set up, as bodies independent of Scottish local government, in April 1996. Public ownership did not make them popular. Only Conservatives were willing to chair them or serve on their boards: both of the other main parties boycotted them on a principle. This made it easy for New Labour to be rid of the people running the authorities, but they decided to keep the new organisation. Returning Scottish water and sewage to 'local democratic control' was never taken seriously. After toying with Third Way solutions such as mutualisation and private-public partnership, largely for the sake of form, the Old Labour rump which runs Scotland decided the Morrisonian public corporation of ministerial appointees was the ideal solution after all.

Liberation of the Bank of England

In England, where New Labour has greater freedom to express itself, another public corporation has had its independence enlarged. In its first week in power, the government handed control of interest rates to the Bank of England. The level of interest is now set, without reference to ministers, by a nine-man monetary policy committee charged by the chancellor of the Exchequer with keeping retail price inflation at 2.5 per cent. Years after the general election, this one decision defines New Labour in government. It was not made solely because independence for central banks was fashionable (though it was, especially in soft left circles) and cosmopolitan (there is enthusiasm for it worldwide) or because it was (as the chancellor's press secretary put it at the time) a 'monster story.'*

Independence for the Bank of England marked the break with Old Labour in office in the same way that re-writing Clause IV had marked the break with Old Labour in Opposition. The Bank of England was the first institution to be nationalised by the Labour government in 1946; by making Eddie George the first independent governor of the Bank of England for fifty years, New Labour cut itself off from its past, delivering a deliberate shock to Old Labour.

An independent central bank is the quintessence of the Third Way: the Bank of England is now neither wholly public nor wholly private, but somewhere in between. Aspects of the decision to place it there were cynical, others naïve. Traditionally, the financial markets greet Labour governments with interest and exchange rate crises from which they never recover. By taking the politics out of interest rate decisions, New Labour believes it may increase its chances of re-election. Treasury ministers have also persuaded themselves that an independently administered inflation target will moderate wage demands, rather as Geoffrey Howe and Nigel Lawson used to believe that shop stewards would examine the permissible growth rate of the money supply before submitting a pay claim. Nor is this the only continuity with the Conservative regime: Lawson was one of three Conservative chancellors, together with Howe and Norman Lamont, to applaud the decision to give the Bank control of monetary policy.

The fashionability of independent central banks rests on the belief that

---

* Two journalists have recorded how Charlie Whelan, former press secretary to the chancellor, saw the decision. 'Economics arguments aside,' they write, 'he believed it would be a "monster story" and a political masterstroke ... He wanted Brown on a podium carrying the sign "HM Treasury" with the famous government crest "Dieu et mon Droit", well-lit and projecting the image of authority and control.' See Hugh Pym and Nick Kochan, *Gordon Brown: The First Year in Power*, Bloomsbury, 1998, pp. 8–9 and 15.

politicians cannot be trusted to make the right decisions on interest rates at awkward times. Yet it is questionable whether recent errors in the conduct of monetary policy were all the result of political interference. Subjection to ministerial control absolved the Bank of blame for bad mistakes in monetary management. 'At the Bank of England,' observed Rupert Pennant-Rea, a former deputy governor, 'we have the ability to mess things up – and our record shows that we have often used it.'[14] This is undeniable. In each of the last two economic cycles, Britain has suffered longer and deeper recessions than any other industrialised country. In the early 1980s, the scepticism of the Bank about the monetarist cure for inflation failed to persuade the government that the rates of interest and exchange were too high. In the late 1980s the Bank failed to notice that the economic boom had got out of hand, fuelled by oceans of credit created by the banks it was meant to control. It supported the insertion of the pound into the Exchange Rate Mechanism (ERM), at the wrong time and at a ruinously high rate which the Bank argued was too low. It remains to be seen if the Bank of England has misread the current economic cycle.

The record of the banking supervision department of the Bank of England is no better. It anticipated neither the secondary banking crisis of the mid-1970s, the collapse of Johnson Matthey in 1984, nor the demise of BCCI 1991. When NatWest Bank was embroiled in the Blue Arrow scandal, the Bank of England told the board to conduct an internal investigation rather than mount one of its own. Cynics noted that the then governor, Robin Leigh-Pemberton, was a former chairman of NatWest.[15] But it was the collapse of Barings which finally exposed the Bank of England as a securities market *ingenue*. Barings exported its entire capital to Singapore before Bank officials noticed anything wrong – and, even then, they had to be told.

No ministers were to blame for the Barings disaster. Two weeks after he had given the Bank of England control of interest rates, Brown stripped it of responsibility for the supervision of banks. That role has now passed to the new Financial Services Authority (FSA). The FSA, with 700 staff and a budget of over £150 million, succeeded the Securities and Investments Board (SIB) in October 1997. It has already absorbed the supervisory powers of the bank, and will eventually assume the duties of the various self-regulatory organisations which used to report to the SIB.[16] The chief argument for the new body, apart from a New Labour enthusiasm for regulation in general and statutory regulation in particular, was the inability of the Bank of England to keep pace with the vanishing distinctions between banks, fund managers and securities firms. The FSA is a standing rebuke to the Bank, and one which was well-advertised in advance.

Margaret Thatcher had toyed with stripping the Bank of England of its responsibility for banking supervision in the wake of the Johnson Matthey scandal. (And Nigel Lawson tried to persuade her to give the Bank full responsibility for monetary policy.) But hyperbolic claims have obscured the continuities. Gavyn Davies, a close associate of the chancellor, said in 1998, 'Gordon has implemented large chunks of his framework, and people haven't realised it yet! The depth and profound nature of what he has done to the macro-economic nature of this country is hardly realised. Macro-economic management, as understood by the Treasury for the last twenty years, has almost ceased to exist.'[17] In fact, it is the lack of radicalism which is most striking. The independence of the Bank is not entrenched by a written constitution or even by statute. The chancellor sets the inflation target; appoints four (arguably six) members of the monetary policy committee; expects it to take account of his economic and employment policies as well as the rate of inflation, and is free to rescind its decisions whenever 'extreme economic circumstances' or 'the national interest' demand it. When political pressure for a cut in interest rates became unbearable in the autumn of 1998, the chancellor publicly nagged the monetary policy committee.

It is naïve to imagine that the committee can be immune to political influences. Its unanimity did not last a year. The contradictory demands of manufacturing industry (being squeezed by a strong pound) and a consumer boom (which needed to be squeezed by higher interest rates) were evident. The contradiction itself stemmed from a political decision – the reluctance of the government to restrain the consumer boom by raising taxes – which the members of the monetary policy committee were powerless to influence. Regular appearances before the Treasury Select Committee of the House of Commons subject members of the committee to political pressure and, in deciding the rate of interest, they are neither subordinate to the politicians nor independent. This position is like that of a privatised utility, ostensibly above the political fray but forced to make its decisions in a charged political arena.

In every other sense, the Bank remains an unreconstructed nationalised industry. It may have lost responsibility for banking supervision, and the Treasury has resumed responsibility for the issue and management of government debt, but the Bank still monopolises the issue of money and (in its capacity of lender of last resort) insulates the banking system from the discipline of the marketplace. A truly radical reform of economic management would have re-examined both of these functions. After all, they are scarcely unshakeable. The Bank of England did not acquire its monopoly of the note issue until the Bank Charter Act of 1844, and it did not become the lender of last resort until the panic induced in the City in 1866 by the collapse of Overend, Gurney, then the greatest private merchant bank in

England. The Bank could shed both these responsibilities, as it once took them on.

They escape scrutiny because they confer valuable benefits on the government as well as the Bank. Since the Act of 1844 the Bank has divided itself into an Issue Department and a Banking Department. The Issue Department is responsible for issuing banknotes, and for investing in the securities the Bank holds to back the fiduciary note issue.[18] The issue of notes and coins at prices far above their intrinsic value as pieces of paper or base metals is highly profitable. The profit (known as seigniorage, after the tendency of medieval monarchs to claim it as their prerogative) runs at £1.25–1.5 billion a year, a sum equivalent to almost the total value of any new notes issued. This is a handsome margin by any standards, and the destruction of around £1 in every £5 in circulation in any year means the Bank can count on a regular contribution.[19] But the profit does not accrue to the Bank: the entire proceeds of the note issue are handed over to the Treasury. In fact, the Bank of England is not expected to make a profit at all. As a nationalised industry, it returns around half of its surplus income to the Treasury. (It keeps the rest to bolster its reserves.)

Seigniorage is one reason why the government is reluctant to surrender its monopoly of money, even to the European Union. But the Issue Department generates further income for the government from the gilt-edged bonds and other securities it holds to back the note issue. The Banking Department also has a small portfolio of income-producing financial assets. Since these are purchased largely with the interest-free cash deposits commercial banks are obliged to lodge with the Bank of England, they are the central banking equivalent of the free lunch.[20] The interest-free deposits are used to cover the costs of the Banking Department, whose activities generate no income. It is one of those unusual arrangements which suits both the tax-payer and the tax-eater. The Bank has a guaranteed income, and the banks are protected from competition by the cost of the tax.

This is one reason why its usefulness is rarely questioned. The other is the belief that a banking system needs a lender of last resort: a central bank willing to lend to banks which owe more than they own. All banks borrow short and lend long, taking in short-term deposits and lending the money long-term to others, so the system is inherently unstable. It is based on a confidence trick: a liquidity crisis is only as far away as a confidence crisis. A bank which loses the confidence of its customers will find its deposits disappear faster than its loans can be recalled. It is to prevent 'runs' developing into a general crisis of confidence in the banking system that the Bank of England stands ready to lend to banks in trouble.[21]

Runs are rarer than they were, but they still occur. In the 1970s the Bank

TABLE 12.1
Balance Sheet of the Bank of England*

Assets	£m	Liabilities	£m
Issue department			
Government securities	1,162	Notes in circulation	23,548
Other securities	22,388	Notes in Banking Department	2
Total assets	23,550	*Total liabilities*	23,550
Banking Department			
Cash	280	Deposits by central banks	1,060
Fixed assets	368	Deposits by banks	2,797
Advances to the market	11,336	Government bank accounts	8,211
Investment securities	1,363	Sums owed	301
Treasury bills	4	Capital and reserves	1,222
Shares in subsidiaries	82		
Other assets	158		
Total assets	13,591	*Total liabilities*	13,591

Source: Bank of England Annual Report and Accounts, 1998.

* At 28 February 1998.

organised a 'life-boat' to rescue a number of secondary banks which were in trouble; it cost the Bank around £100 million.[22] In 1991, the Bank organised another rescue of troubled fringe banks, which cost it £105 million.[23] The second rescue followed a mild run as depositors withdrew funds from lesser banks after the collapse of BCCI. Criticism has concentrated on the inadequate supervision of fringe banks and BCCI, but there is a deeper problem. By agreeing to act as lender of last resort, the Bank creates the 'moral hazard' that leads to periodic banking crises. Saving banks from their mistakes gives bankers and their customers little incentive to be prudent.

It might be cheaper and better to let some banks fail, and oblige all banks to publish enough information to enable their customers to distinguish between sound and unsound institutions.[24] Without a central bank to act as lender of last resort, commercial banks would increase their own reserves, reduce their exposure to banks they consider unsound, or purchase insurance against a run on the bank. Where runs occur, banks could lend their reserves to each other without the intermediation of a central bank.[25] Of course, lesser banks which got into trouble would go out of business without the Bank of England: no other bank would lend to them. But that would be the best outcome if it is only the central bank guarantee which keeps them in business. The other reason why banks agree to centralise reserves at the Bank of England is that the central bank monopolises the issue of money, which is the only form of legal tender. The virtues and vices of the state monopoly of money is one of the oldest controversies in banking. The Bank Charter Act of 1844 was preceded by a vigorous debate between the 'banking' and 'currency' schools. The banking school wanted private country bankers to retain their discretionary power to issue as many banknotes as they saw fit. The currency school wanted tight official control over the quantity of notes, and they won the argument. But the debate has reopened in recent years. In theory, there is no reason why competition should not confer the same benefits in the markets for money as it does in the markets for other goods and services. Competition between many different private and state 'brands' of money would not necessarily lead to chaos. Counterparties would conduct their business in the most reliable and stable currencies, and competing currencies might or might not be convertible into a basic form, such as gold or a basket of goods and services.[26]

It can be argued that money of the traditional sort is obsolete. Digital technology is replacing it with electronic balances stored on smart cards or computers (and transferred without the need for banks).[27] Electronic money is more efficient than ordinary money. Notes and coin are easy to forge and steal, and expensive to hold and use. The transaction costs of using cash may be as high as 2 per cent. Certainly banks are said to spend £2 billion a year handling cash on behalf of customers, which is why they are keen to replace cash with electronic forms of money like the debit and credit cards which are already outside the Bank of England monopoly. The credit card is, of course, an international currency already, though expensive to use.[28] Many businesses operate in more than one currency, and pay each other without bank intermediation. Multi-currency smart cards, which store balances electronically until they are spent, would eliminate seigniorage and check inflation automatically, because their owners would hold sound currencies only. If the check were effective, the last redoubt of the central bankers would fall. Their popularity depends entirely on keeping down inflation.

So the independent role of the Bank of England may not last. Facts change, and opinion changes with them. The nationalisation of the Bank of England was part of a backlash against the *deflationary* excesses of the central bankers of the 1930s. There are already signs of a backlash against the real authors of the monetary discipline of the 1990s: the international capital markets. The ebb and flow of capital has become the prime determinant of national rates of interest and exchange; governments and central banks which take risks with inflation are punished by an exodus of capital, which weakens the exchange rate and drives up the rate of interest.

Contrary to popular opinion, this power is not new. Market scepticism prompted the devaluation of the pound in 1949 and 1967; destroyed the Bretton Woods system of semi-fixed exchange rates in the early 1970s; precipitated the global stock market crash of October 1987; and buried the ERM in 1992–93. But the speed and scale of modern investment flows is unprecedented, and efforts by governments, central banks and international agencies have failed conspicuously to protect national currencies from their force. At some stage, a run on the pound is virtually certain to undermine even an independent Bank of England.

The markets are diminishing the influence of the Bank of England at home as well as abroad. Deregulation and innovation has made it easier for modern PLCs to insulate themselves from increases in interest rates, by raising equity rather than debt, borrowing at fixed rates, or hedging risks in the derivatives markets. Companies no longer rely for finance on the banking system, where interest rate changes have their most profound and immediate effects. Even homeowners are increasingly borrowing at fixed rates of interest, blunting the impact of increases in interest rates.

It was partly to restore waning authority over the markets that eleven European countries agreed to submerge their national currencies in the euro. This has created a single capital market throughout the greater part of the European Union, with a single structure of interest rates managed by a single central bank. If Britain joins the single currency, the Bank of England will become a regional satrap of the European Central Bank. The Old Lady of Threadneedle Street, reincarnated in 1946 as the Poodle of Westminster, should enjoy its spell as Watchdog of Lombard Street while it can. It may end its days as Running Dog of the European Central Bank.

The BBC: Free to Succeed?

The same forces (deregulation, innovation, competition) are having a profound effect on another great public institution. The British Broadcasting Corporation (BBC) does not think of itself as a nationalised industry. 'That implies an organisation wholly owned by the government, under the government's control and funded from general taxation,' snorts a spokesman. 'The BBC is a public corporation, with its independence guaranteed by a Board of Governors and largely funded by a specific licence fee.'[29] It is true that the director-general and governors of the BBC are answerable neither to Parliament (though they are appointed by ministers) nor to the usual regulatory authorities (the Independent Television Commission and the Radio Authority) and that the Corporation is funded by an earmarked poll tax.[30] But fine distinctions are no guarantee of independence.

In 1998 the BBC threatened to reduce its coverage of Parliament. 'I remind you', the Board was told by Gerald Kaufman, chairman of the culture select committee, 'that your charter is awarded by Parliament and your funding approved by the House of Commons.'[31] The charter obliges the BBC to achieve political 'balance' in its broadcasts, and the Corporation is under constant attack by politicians for failing to provide it.[32] More importantly, the BBC depends for the bulk of its income on the licence fee which the government could alter or abolish at any time. It has already explored the idea of charging a lower fee to pensioners. But misguided redistribution by the state is not the principal risk; the main danger to the BBC is competition from private broadcasters, fuelled by a mixture of deregulation and technology.

For sixty years, the state guaranteed the BBC a tax-funded monopoly and the BBC guaranteed the state immunity from political dissent. For decades, the BBC supported the government of the day instinctively. In the 1920s it supported Churchill during the General Strike. In the 1930s it supported appeasement by keeping him off the air. In the 1950s Henry Fairlie placed the BBC at the heart of what he called the Establishment. As late as 1962 Anthony Sampson was surprised by its 'reverent attitude to British institutions'. He wrote shortly after a BBC director general had banned Malcolm Muggeridge for daring to mock the royal family, and shortly before his successor took the first political satire (*That Was the Week That Was*) off the screens for fear that it might prejudice the outcome of the 1964 general election.

It was not until the 1990s that this bargain between the state and the BBC was tested. It is true that the BBC monopoly of broadcasting was broken in 1954, when commercial television was first authorised by the government, but the arrival of ITV merely replaced monopoly with duopoly. The ITV companies preferred a publicly funded BBC because it did not compete for advertising revenue. Competition for radio audiences was even slower to develop. It was argued for decades that a shortage of space on the radio spectrum made broadcasting a natural monopoly, and pirate stations broadcasting from rusting hulks in the North Sea were closed down by the government, which passed the Marine and Broadcasting Offences Act (1967) to outlaw their activities.

The first legal commercial radio stations were not established until 1973, and the current proliferation of stations happened only with further deregulation in 1990. The BBC–ITV television duopoly suffered no competition at all until 1984, when Channel Four (a public–private hybrid now ripe for privatisation) was set up. But the arrival in the late 1980s of cable and satellite television created a serious alternative to the terrestrial stations. The subsequent perfection of technology for digital transmission caused an explosion of alternatives.[33] When it launched its digital service in the autumn of 1998, BSkyB offered a choice of 140 channels. On Digital (a company owned by Carlton Communications and the Granada Group) started a service simultaneously, offering a further 30 channels. It was in 1994 that the BBC share of the broadcasting market fell below half of all viewers and listeners; it has since fallen to two fifths, and is bound to shrink further.

This presents the BBC with an existential problem. The licence fee, which currently accounts for 94 per cent of its income, is a regressive poll tax equivalent to a penny on the income tax, enforced only by the threat of fines and imprisonment.[34] It is levied on anybody capable of receiving BBC transmissions, whether or not they choose to watch them. So many different services are now available from cable, satellite and terrestrial broadcasters that many viewers and listeners claim not to watch or listen to any BBC programmes. This makes it implausible for ministers to argue that everybody should continue to pay the licence fee.

The problem of justifying the licence fee will become acute in 2001, when the current agreement on its value expires. But it is already problematic. Its value has not risen in real terms since the mid-1980s. It is indexed to inflation, but only until 1999. Two years later, it will need to be renegotiated. Its value was inflated for years by the prolonged switch from monochrome to colour licences, but that process is now complete. As a source of funding, the licence fee lacks the buoyancy of advertising or subscription revenue. It enables the BBC to compete, but investment yields no additional reward. When Martin Bashir interviewed Princess Diana in November 1995, 23 million people watched but it made no difference to the income of the BBC. Competitors are already out-bidding the Corporation for the right to broadcast major sporting events, feature films and new programmes. The BBC would have lost more had the government not reserved some key sporting events for terrestrial channels and ordered the commercial companies to allow the Corporation to broadcast highlights after the event.

The BBC cannot be accused of ignoring the competitive threats. In recent years, it has tried to cut its costs and increase its commercial income without jeopardising the licence fee. Michael Checkland, director-general until 1992, was the first in the history of the BBC to try to economise by eating into the corporate bureaucracy rather than axing programming or orchestras or sewing up hours of cheap repeats, snooker and darts. His successor, Sir John Birt, introduced an NHS-style internal market in which producers with fixed budgets were expected to shop around for the cheapest technical staff. In the process, he turned himself into a hate-figure for BBC traditionalists, who claimed that creative thinkers and programme-makers were being overrun by an army of accountants, management consultants and policy advisers. Mark Tully, the veteran BBC correspondent in India, attacked Birt in public. John Simpson, foreign affairs editor, joked that the last dictators worked at the BBC. The head of drama quit in May 1996, describing the Corporation as an 'Orwellian nightmare'. Inundated by leaks from resentful BBC staff, *Private Eye* started a fortnightly 'Birtspeak' column of extracts from office memoranda.

BBC producers and journalists have always believed that the management was starving them of resources and stifling their creativity, but the reality was different. The BBC John Birt joined as deputy director-general in 1987 was grossly inefficient. Its 25,000 staff exceeded the total employed by the rest of the broadcasting industry. It was also riddled with restrictive practices of the most egregious kind, its managers long since cowed by the National Union of Journalists (NUJ), the broadcasting union (Bectu), and a cadre of big-name presenters always ready to embarrass them in print. The BBC was a byword for jobs-for-life and bloated camera crews imposed by shop stewards under the constant threat of a broadcasting blackout. The idea that television and radio journalists should work jointly on stories – producing material for, say, *Newsnight* and *The World At One* as well as *Today* – was anathema; until 1998, each programme editor sent his own reporters and camera crew.

Birt has made a considerable impact on this luxurious regime. In the three years to 1997 he trimmed the costs by £281 million.[35] Over five years, the BBC expects to save £1 billion. But Birtism has sought to increase revenues as well as reduce costs. In May 1994 the Corporation established a wholly owned subsidiary, BBC Worldwide, to co-ordinate its commercial activities. The BBC had owned commercial businesses since the 1920s, when it launched the *Radio Times* and the now-defunct *Listener*. But BBC Worldwide has for the first time enabled the Corporation to establish joint ventures with commercial companies to create new broadcasting channels not funded out of the licence fee. In March 1997 BBC Worldwide formed UKTV, a joint venture with Flextech PLC, to produce eight new channels funded by a mix of subscriptions and advertising revenue. A year later, it reached a £338 million deal with Discovery Communications, a US company, to produce new programmes as well as channels on a fully commercial basis.

The venture with Flextech means that five of the nine digital channels the BBC launched in 1998 (UK Horizons, UK Arena, UK Style, UK FM and UK Gold) are funded by subscription rather than licence-payers.[36] BBC Worldwide has also acquired full control of European Channel Management, a global satellite broadcasting joint venture formed in 1995 with Pearson PLC and Cox Communications. It controls BBC World (funded from advertising revenues) and BBC Prime (a subscription channel). A three-year-old relationship with ICL (and its parent company, Fujitsu) has so far produced eight fully commercial Internet services. When magazine, book and video revenues and programme sales are added to the revenue from new channels, BBC Worldwide contributed £75 million to the BBC in 1997–98.[37] It aims to quadruple this sum by 2006.

However, rising commercial revenues have exposed the contradiction at the heart of the modern BBC. The Corporation has to increase its commercial revenues because the value of the licence fee is shrinking, but if they increase too fast there will be pressure to abolish the licence fee. To some extent, the contradiction is agreeable. The BBC can be commercial when it suits, and a public-service broadcaster when it does not. It broadcasts as much audience-grabbing sport, game shows and soap opera as the commercial channels (to ensure its market share continues to justify the licence fee), while using the licence fee to make the programmes advertisers and subscribers will not support. The fee cannot be used to subsidise BBC Worldwide, but commercial earnings can be used to subsidise the licence fee. Two terrestrial television stations, five national radio services and thirty-eight regional radio stations have no need to carry advertising. But they are used shamelessly to promote one another (and BBC branded products).

This privileged position is unsustainable. More than half of viewers and listeners have already switched to commercial providers. Competition is intensifying, but the BBC is unable to respond aggressively. It was allotted two satellite channels as early as 1982, but did nothing with them for more than ten years for fear of endangering the licence fee. Even today, the total commercial earnings of the BBC amount to barely a twentieth of their revenues. BBC Worldwide has made little impact in overseas markets and still generates over half its revenues in Britain. The Corporation cannot borrow, even against its assets, to fund investment. In the early 1990s, it found that the only way to comply with a government order to reduce its overdraft was to impose a moratorium on new programmes, and when it asked for permission to raise a loan in 1996, it was told to sell its transmitter network instead. This was sold to Castle Transmission Services, an American led consortium. The sale raised £244 million for investment in digital technology.[38]

Other parts of the BBC – like Radio One and Radio Two – could be privatised as easily. BBC Worldwide already operates like a PLC, and the technical and engineering operations of the Corporation are controlled by a second commercial business, BBC Resources. Both could be sold. Indeed, privatisation is a fate the Corporation should not disdain. It would free the BBC to borrow for investment, and to enlarge its commercial earnings with-

TABLE 12.2
Licence-funded BBC television
and radio transmissions

Station	Hours
Television	
BBC 1	7,611
BBC 2	8,264
Sub-Total	15,875
Network radio	
Radio 1	8,760
Radio 2	8,760
Radio 3	8,760
Radio 4	7,697
Radio 5 Live	8,760
Asian network	8,761
Sub-Total	51,498
Local radio	
Transmission by 37 BBC local stations	207,198
Total output	274,571

Source: BBC Annual Report and Accounts, 1997–8.

out limit. It could also make good the botched reforms of the Birt era, for the internal market has had perverse as well as beneficial effects. The accountants and lawyers in central administration expanded as technical and production staff shrank. Business units proliferated. There was too much paper, too many meetings, and too much pointless activity. Staff resigned, only to be rehired at higher rates. Defective pricing formulae wasted valuable production skills and studio space. The reform of the BBC showed (yet again) how hard it is to make a non-business businesslike.

There is plenty of fat still to cut at the BBC. A large and strongly unionised workforce remains in place, which struck against changes to working practices in 1994 and again in 1998 (in a dispute timed to coincide with the World Cup). Producers are over-indulged, and allowed to pursue the most whimsical ideas (like *El Dorado,* a disastrous soap set among British expatriates on the

Costa del Sol). Obliged by law to buy at least a quarter of its transmission time from independent producers, the BBC fills much of its quota with cheap, studio-produced flim-flam such as *Kilroy* and *Question Time*, leaving budgets free for expensive internal programme-making. The BBC also owns too much expensive property.[39] When BBC Resources totted up all the property the BBC used, it found the Corporation occupied (or did not occupy) over 7 million square feet at more than 500 sites around the country.[40] Unwanted property was subsequently sold or let, and staff had to abandon expensive locations, but it was not until 1998 that the Corporation formed a joint venture with a property management company.

A privatised BBC would be more than efficient. It would be free. Politicians can bully the publicly owned BBC in ways they could never deploy against privately owned broadcasters and newspapers. The duty to produce balanced and impartial political coverage, and to give equal access to all major political points of view, gives ministers and MPs a renewable licence to attack the BBC for bias. The Wilson governments were notorious for browbeating the Corporation and Wilson himself became so obsessed with BBC bias that he complained about an episode of *Steptoe & Son* in which Harold brought home a girl called Marcia.[41] In 1971 his complaints about *Yesterday's Men* provoked a crisis. Similar incidents erupted throughout the Thatcher years. Ministers effectively banned the broadcasting of *Real Lives* (a programme about Northern Ireland) and *Panorama* (an episode about the recession due to be broadcast just before the 1992 election). Even drama (*The Monocled Mutineer* and *Paradise Postponed*) was not immune to allegations of political bias.

Nobody except Will Hutton believes that the BBC is still the lackey of a right-wing Establishment.[42] John Birt described the BBC of the late 1980s as 'crudely, thoughtlessly, anti-Establishment,' and tried to persuade aggressive interviewers such as John Humphrys and Jeremy Paxman to be more emollient.[43] Ten years later, Broadcasting House and Television Centre echoed to the cheers of staff at Labour gains in the general election. In government, relations have proved less cordial. Alastair Campbell, press secretary to Tony Blair, is merciless with BBC reporters and producers who fail to please, and even in Opposition the Labour Party took the Corporation to court to prevent an interview with the prime minister from being broadcast on the eve of Scottish local elections.

The only release from political intimidation lies in the development of a proper broadcasting market, in which viewers and listeners could choose between the electronic equivalents of the *Guardian* and the *Daily Telegraph*; privatisation would be a prerequisite for the BBC to compete in it. 'If you either turned the BBC into a highly competitive advertising-financed channel . . . or if you simply abolished it,' counters BBC chairman Christopher Bland,

'who would contest that radio and television broadcasting, and indeed, without being too pompous about it, the cultural, educational, and information
life of the UK would be greatly diminished?'[44] There is no theoretical reason
to believe this: the invention of the printing press increased the volume of
books and diminished the quality of the average book, but the number of
quality books grew exponentially. Nor is there any practical reason to believe
it: new methods of payment – subscription, pay-per-view, pay-per-channel and
even pay-per-package – means the gutter is not the sole source of revenue in
broadcasting.

Dependence on the licence fee is a graver threat than privatisation. It forces
the BBC to compete for market share by broadcasting downmarket sport,
game-shows and soap operas – *and* obliges it to be democratic. The BBC
calls it 'providing something for everyone'. The Corporation is right to believe
that viewers and listeners expect a tax-funded broadcasting company to take
an interest in their lives, in the same way that they expect a tax-funded health
service to take an close interest in their illnesses. Twenty years ago, the Annan
Committee pronounced the ideal of a single, all-embracing, middle class
culture to be impossible.* It put an end to a Reithian vision ('few know
what they want and very few what they need') which had proved remarkably
durable.[45] As recently as 1962 the director-general of the BBC told Sampson
that 'commercially controlled television tends in the long run to undermine
the intelligence.'[46] The post-Annan BBC is not so high-minded. It believes
it must somehow 'represent' the whole nation.

Viewers and listeners can no longer be expected to graduate from the
Light Programme to the Home Service. Today, the BBC has to affirm the
lives of its viewers and listeners, not uplift them. Its directors and producers
fret continuously about whether they are making and broadcasting enough
programmes about the regions, women, the countryside, the young, the ethnic and sexual minorities and the arts. Unfortunately, this can be done only
by offending the educated, metropolitan audiences which have retained their
taste for traditional programmes. Alterations to programming on Radio Three
and Four have caused much grumbling without enlarging the market share
of the BBC. A privatised BBC could shed its self-imposed duty to 'represent'

---

* 'The ideals of middle class culture, so felicitously expressed by Matthew Arnold a century ago,
which had created a continuum of taste and opinion, always susceptible to change and able to
absorb the avant-garde within its own urban, liberal, flexible principles, found it ever more
difficult to accommodate the new expressions of life in the sixties. The new vision of life reflected
divisions within society, divisions between classes, the generations and the sexes, between north
and south, between the provinces and London, between pragmatists and ideologues. Sometimes
the divisions existed but were given new publicity: sometimes they were postulated and then
were brought about.' Quoted in Asa Briggs, *The BBC: The First Fifty Years*, Oxford University
Press, 1985, p. 358.

the nation and compete with commercial broadcasters in every sphere. It could concentrate on building an international multi-media business based on the strongest brand in broadcasting (and journalism) and quality programmes. In 1992 the BBC pledged to 'withdraw from programme areas or types in which it is no longer able or needed to make an original contribution.'[47] But the privatisation of the BBC is unlikely to happen soon. Its Charter does not expire until 2006, and a Labour government's attachment to public service broadcasting has survived the elevation of Tony Blair and the apostasy of Rupert Murdoch. New Labour thinkers have advanced their pet solution of mutualisation, which would free the BBC to raise private capital without jeopardising public ownership or the licence fee, but it would not set the Corporation free to compete with its rich commercial rivals. The BBC will survive until then; the same may not be true of another public corporation facing potentially ruinous competition: the Post Office.

Liberty or Death: the Post Office

Twenty years ago the Post Office had a monopoly of post and telephone communications in Britain. It now controls barely one sixth of the market, and its remaining business is under concerted technological and competitive attack. Telephones, fax machines, courier companies, direct debit, electronic mail and alternative advertising vehicles such as television, radio and newspapers are all taking business from the Post Office. Eight foreign post offices have taken advantage of European legislation to compete directly in its home market,[48] and its biggest earner (pre-sorted junk mail) is drifting to offshore locations, where rates are cheaper and businesses can still take advantage of the Post Office distribution network. Even where it still enjoys a monopoly, on mail costing less than £1 to send, the Post Office is losing custom.

Like the BBC, the Post Office needs access to private capital and the freedom to form alliances with commercial competitors. Unlike the BBC, it does not depend on a poll tax. The Post Office is consistently profitable. It has no debt. It needs no subsidies. Its costs are falling. There are no good reasons why the Post Office is still in public ownership, but there are plenty of bad ones. In every marginal constituency, as the former Post Office managing director Bill Cockburn once put it, there is a marginal post office. The threat of an end to the cross-subsidisation of uneconomic rural postal services and village shops by their profitable urban counterparts persuaded Conservative MPs to scupper a government plan to privatise the Post Office in 1994. It did not matter that the spectre was raised by the Union of Communications Workers (UCW).

The UCW campaign against the privatisation of the Post Office has become a case study in the techniques of public persuasion. It was masterminded by Alan Johnson, then its general secretary and now the Labour MP for Hull West. 'The Post Office's public service ethos would vanish with privatisation,' he warned. 'In many areas, postal workers collect and deliver prescriptions free of charge, fix cars, and help keep an eye on elderly people who are frail or infirm.'[49] In fact, the Post Office is staffed not by real-life Postman Pats but by 198,000 trade unionists who are now the last exponents of the old-fashioned public sector strike.[50] Local disputes, over matters as trivial as the employment of temporary staff, are endemic. Ruinous national strikes occurred in 1971, 1988 and 1996. In 1996–7, two in every three days lost to industrial action in the United Kingdom were in various parts of the Post Office. The Christmas postal strike, which coincides with its busiest time of year, is as much a part of the festive season as the holly and the ivy.

The national postal strike of 1971 gave birth to the private courier industry, depriving the Post Office of mail-order business it has not recovered. The strikes of 1988 and 1996 accelerated the use of fax machines and electronic mail; the Post Office was saved from complete destruction only by the unwillingness of governments to impose a permanent suspension of the monopoly of traffic costing less than £1.[51] The persistence of the monopoly has enabled the UCW to resist the introduction of new technology and working methods. Their reward is an industry characterised by overmanning, low wages, poor morale, high staff turnover – and theft. The credit card companies gave up using the Royal Mail: too many cards were being stolen. In 1991–2 (an average year) 796 Post Office employees were sacked for theft. In the sorting offices, even after a massive investment programme, much of the work is still done by hand. The UCW does not want its membership reduced by new technology, or seduced by new incentives. In 1998 the new general secretary of the union, Derek Hodgson, said of a government plan to give his members shares in a privatised Post Office: 'My members will not accept a bribe to destroy a good public service – they will not sell their souls to anybody.'[52]

This is an odd view of an institution whose chief characteristic is the queue. Instead of finding ways to shorten them, the Post Office has installed pens to make them more orderly, like sheep-dips. Vending machines are a rarity, and self-service weighing and stamping machines are unknown. The fast-service counter, a feature of the supermarkets even in the 1970s, has yet to be introduced to the Post Office. Pensions, benefits, tax discs and television licences are all dispensed by hand. The Post Office did not even let shop-keepers sell stamps until the late 1980s. The only technological innovation it has introduced recently is a television on a stick, to entertain the queue. The dowdy image of its average outlet has hampered the efforts of Post Office

Counters ('the biggest retail chain in Europe') to broaden its range of services. In recent years, it has forged joint ventures with the Alliance & Leicester, Lloyds TSB and the Co-operative Bank (to provide banking services) and with General Accident and Royal & SunAlliance (to provide travel and household insurance). It has tried cheap airline tickets, and even made a bid to run the National Lottery.[53]

But the core business of the Post Office remains the Royal Mail, and its most profitable parts are being ravaged by couriers, fax machines and electronic mail. To compete effectively, it needs the capital and commercial freedom to invest in new technology (like electronic mail sorting centres) and joint ventures with business partners (abroad, as well as at home). Without them, the Post Office will be battered, ineluctably, into a British equivalent of the United States mail service: the message-carrier of last resort. Yet neither capital nor commercial freedom is available to a publicly owned Post Office. 'As part of the public sector,' the chairman told the House of Commons trade and industry committee in 1993, 'it is inescapable that the Post Office is caught in the bizarre world of the cash-based PSBR which does not distinguish between a trading enterprise with customers and competition, such as the Post Office, and a spending government department like the DSS.'[54] As he rightly recognised, a publicly owned Post Office cannot borrow to invest.

Privatisation is unlikely to happen, but not because its opponents have a strong case. Their chief argument is that it would destroy subsidised sub-post offices and delivery services, especially in rural areas. The same argument was advanced in 1984 by opponents of a privatised BT but room was found to protect and even improve rural telephone services. Rural mail services could be protected too, by an auction (with the contract going to the bidder who required the lowest level of subsidy) or a levy (on competitors who do not deliver to outlying districts) or a tax (perhaps raised by local authorities). Any of these options would at least expose the true cost of the subsidy, which the Post Office does not yet know.* There might not even be need for a subsidy. The general secretary of the National Federation of Sub-Postmasters has admitted that there is 'no evidence whatsoever' that privatisation would lead to the closure of post offices.[55] Ironically, all sub-post offices are privatised already, and some post offices are franchised to private operators (mainly supermarket chains). The Post Office bank, Girobank, was sold to the Alliance & Leicester building society in July 1990, and Girobank now handles one pound in every three taken by British retailers.

---

* It is sometimes argued that people living in rural areas are too poor to pay a higher price for a postal service. There is no reason to believe that more poor people live in remote areas but, even so, postal charges exist to pay for a service, not to redistribute income.

TABLE 12.3
What the Post Office Owns

Directly operated post offices	601
Agency post offices	18,407
PostShops in post offices	217
Pillar boxes	112,000
Royal Mail sorting offices*	1,560
Parcel Force sorting offices	108
Royal Mail vans and lorries	29,300
Parcel Force vans and lorries	5,900

Sources: Post Office Annual Report and Accounts, 1997–8; Post Office.

* Royal Mail has 13 automated processing centres; 82 mechanised letter offices and 1,465 delivery offices. Parcelforce has 8 regional hubs and 100 delivery offices.

Girobank was the only part of the Post Office the Conservatives were able to privatise. A chance remark on the hustings by Margaret Thatcher during the 1987 general election, in response to a question on how the Queen would react to the sale of her silhouette, was enough to rule out privatisation of the Post Office for the whole of the next Parliament.[56] After the 1992 election, Michael Heseltine adopted a more robust approach. Parcelforce had been established as a separate business within the Post Office in 1986, and in July 1992 he launched a fresh inquiry into privatisation of the rest. Two years later a Green Paper advocated the sale of a 51 per cent stake, with statutory guarantees of a universal postal service at a single price policed by an independent regulator. To counter the threat of closures, post offices and sub-post offices would stay in state hands. The plan was too radical for Conservative MPs, especially those with rural seats.

But if they saved Mrs Goggins, the Conservative backwoodsmen lost the best manager the Post Office had. Bill Cockburn, who as chief executive had campaigned for privatisation, resigned. He had recognised that the Post Office could not compete effectively so long as it remained in state ownership, unable to borrow on its own account, with half its profits seized by the Treasury, and short of funds to make acquisitions. The UCW argues that the Post Office can raise capital and compete without a change in ownership, and New Labour, after a further inquiry, was persuaded to agree. 'Royal Mail, Post Office Counters and Parcelforce will remain in public ownership,' trade minister Ian McCartney told a cheering Labour Party conference in 1997. 'Our commitment is the maintenance of a universal, integrated, publicly owned, publicly accountable Post Office . . . [free of] unnecessary and damaging shackles.'[57]

However, after Tony Blair insisted the government retain the option to privatise the Post Office, a final statement on its future was delayed until he had appointed a trade secretary sympathetic to the idea. In December 1998, during his brief spell as Trade and Industry secretary, Peter Mandelson announced that the Post Office would not be privatised. Instead, it would be given greater commercial freedom within the public sector. Making a reality of this ambition is a key test for the Third Way.

Abjuring privatisation was a clear victory for the UCW (Mandelson had, in the words of its general secretary, 'earned our respect'). The Post Office management was more circumspect. In September 1998 chief executive John Roberts sent a blunt message to Mandelson. 'We want and need commercial freedom. Will we get it this time for real – or are we going to get another fudge?'[58] Only time will tell if he has got it for real, but a degree of scepticism is understandable: thirty years ago, another Labour government set the Post Office up as a public corporation (it had been a government department). In theory, it was free to develop post and telephone services outside the usual constraints of public finances. In practice, commercial freedom was overridden by the need to increase public spending without putting up taxes. History repeated itself in 1995. After his plan to privatise the Post Office collapsed, Michael Heseltine relaxed controls on its capital spending, freed it to pursue joint ventures, and fixed the Treasury levy at half of annual profits. Six months later, the Treasury tore the agreement up, imposed an arbitrary levy of £120 million on Post Office profits for 1996, and demanded another £400 million over the next three years. Predictably, the price of a stamp went up a penny in July 1996 (the additional revenue matched the levy more or less exactly). In the three years to 1998, the Post Office gave the Treasury as much money as it had in the previous ten. The share of profits devoured by the government rose to £4 in every £5.

This wrecked the investment plans of the Post Office. By 1998 the chairman reckoned he was £1 billion short, but the government had got its money without putting up taxes. Under New Labour the Treasury is promising to reduce its share of Post Office profits by half to 40 per cent over time. But experience suggests the Post Office will remain a backdoor tax machine as long as it is in public ownership. Interviewed by the *Financial Times* after he had become chief executive at W. H. Smith, Bill Cockburn did not take long to specify the difference between running a public enterprise and a private company. 'The Post Office is very vulnerable to being treated as a short term cash cow when the government needs the money,' he said. 'That might mean, for instance, that prices have to go up faster . . . So you get a managing-for-cash syndrome which can be damaging in the long term.'[59]

Getting Rid of the Nuclear Leftovers

One quirk of the triumph of the UCW is that British Nuclear Fuels Limited (BNFL), one of the hate-figures of the Old Labour past, may well be privatised before the Post Office. Despite its unhappy reputation, the nuclear industry is not a no-go area for investors: much of it is in private ownership already. The Radiochemical Centre at Amersham was separated from the United Kingdom Atomic Energy Authority (UKAEA), re-named Amersham International, and privatised in 1982. AEA Technology, the engineering arm of the UKAEA, was privatised in 1996. Eight nuclear power stations, now owned by British Energy, entered the private sector the same year.[60] Only the remains of the UKAEA, organised in the so-called Government Division, are unsellable. It continues to pursue the less unpopular forms of nuclear research at its Culham laboratory near Oxford, but the main task of the UKAEA Government Division is to wind itself up after decommissioning and cleaning up its five nuclear facilities. This will take at least 100 years. In the meantime, its activities will all cost money.[61]

This is not true of BNFL, the former fuel manufacturing arm of the UKAEA. It is organised as a PLC and has operated on a fully commercial basis since it was spun out of the Authority in 1971. In 1997–8 it made profits of £199 million on sales of £1.3 billion, enabling it to pay a dividend of over £50 million to the Treasury.[62] BNFL has long since expanded beyond fuel manufacturing (though it still makes nuclear fuel at a chemical factory near Preston) into fuel reprocessing, the decommissioning of nuclear reactors and cleaning up nuclear sites. Since the merger in December 1997 with Magnox Electric, the state-owned parent of seven aged Magnox nuclear reactors which could not be privatised, it has generated electricity as well. It supplies roughly one twelfth of the British electricity market. BNFL is also profiting from the slow dissolution of the nuclear industry at home and winning decommissioning contracts abroad.

Since it established an American sales subsidiary in 1990, the company has secured $2.5 billion worth of business in the United States. The US government has invited BNFL to advise it on managing the nuclear waste at an atomic weapons plant in Washington State. If it gets the job, the contract could be worth up to $6.9 billion. In 1998 BNFL shocked the government by joining forces with an American partner to pay £720 million for the nuclear services business of the US engineering company, Westinghouse.[63] To clinch

TABLE 12.4
Nuclear Facilities Still in State Ownership

Location	Type	Opened	Capacity
UKAEA			
Dounreay	Fast Breeder	1974	Decommissioned
Harwell/Culham	Research Facilities	–	–
Windscale	AGR	–	Decommissioned
Winfrith	SGHWR	–	Decommissioned
BNFL			
Berkeley	Magnox		Decommissioned
Bradwell	Magnox	1962	245MW
Calder Hall	Magnox	1956	244MW
Chapelcross	Magnox	1959	240MW
Dungeness A	Magnox	1965	440MW
Hinkley Point A	Magnox	1965	470MW
Hunterston A	Magnox	–	Decommissioned
Oldbury	Magnox	1968	424MW
Sizewell A	Magnox	1966	420MW
Trawsfynydd	Magnox	–	Decommissioned
Wylfa	Magnox	1973	950MW

Sources: UKAEA/BNFL/Offer.

the deal, the company was surprisingly ruthless. A plan to merge its fuel manufacturing business with a similar operation owned by Siemens, the German electrical company, was ditched summarily. It is not hard to see why: one in three of the 430 nuclear reactors around the world use Westinghouse technology, and most of the new plants being built in eastern Europe and Asia are also likely to adopt a Westinghouse design. For BNFL, the deal opens a new market in plant construction as well as fuel manufacturing and decommissioning.

The re-processing of spent nuclear fuel remains the biggest and most profitable business BNFL undertakes. It was always understood that nuclear energy was a Faustian compact. In exchange for abundant supplies of energy, one generation lumbered the next three thousand with a growing hoard of radioactive waste. One way of reducing its size is to 'reprocess' spent fuel, extracting the reusable uranium and plutonium from the waste material.[64] According to BNFL, only 3 per cent of the spent fuel becomes waste. The rest consists of uranium (96 per cent) and plutonium (1 per cent) which can be used to create more nuclear fuel. After overcoming a protracted Greenpeace campaign, BNFL opened its Thermal Oxide Reprocessing Plant (THORP) at Sellafield in Cumbria in 1994. It cost £2.9 billion to build, but will re-process an annual average of 700 tonnes of nuclear material in its first ten years, which will generate a profit of £500 million after decommissioning costs. Since the plant has an estimated life of twenty-five years, and business is already being placed for its second and third decades, THORP is likely to become more profitable as it ages.

Not all the spent fuel will be British. Two thirds of it will come from overseas. This has prompted allegations that BNFL is turning Britain into a laundry-cum-dump for radioactive waste. In fact, the lasting effects of importing spent fuel are confined to the radioactive discharges from Sellafield; all high-level waste is returned to its country of origin. Intermediate-level waste (contaminated cladding and equipment) and low-level waste (slightly radioactive material, like towels and overalls) does stay at Sellafield, but BNFL plans to swap it for equivalent amounts of high-level British waste. The company claims this will enable Britain to export all high-level waste in return for keeping low-level and intermediate-level waste from abroad. This makes sense, but it does not solve the problem of what to do with the waste. Finding a way of disposing of it safely is now the second biggest obstacle to the privatisation of BNFL.

Nuclear waste is stored in concrete bunkers in and around Sellafield. High-level waste will remain there for fifty years, until it cools down. For the foreseeable future, low-level and intermediate-level waste will stay there too. BNFL had hoped to bury the less dangerous material in a deep hole at the abandoned Longlands Farm near Sellafield, but planning permission for an underground laboratory was refused. An underground dump is now unlikely to be built until well into the twenty-first century, if at all. In the meantime, more concrete bunkers will be built at Sellafield.

Ministers are understandably reluctant to entrust a collection of bunkers filled with radioactive waste to a private company, but the lack of an underground repository is not the biggest obstacle to the privatisation of BNFL. The main hindrance, as in 1989 when the government first tried to privatise the nuclear industry, is the cost of decommissioning redundant nuclear power stations. BNFL refused to merge with Magnox Electric until the government provided an additional £3.7 billion to cover the cost of decommissioning the seven reactors, because the company was already bearing the burden of decommissioning its own Magnox reactors at Calder Hall and Chapelcross.

Had it managed without the subsidy, the deal would have pushed BNFL into technical insolvency. If BNFL is ever privatised, the Magnox reactors may well have to stay in public ownership. Shareholders want the profits of the nuclear clean-up, not the costs of the nuclear leftovers.

The profits are potentially immense, but hard to predict. The cost of defuelling the Magnox reactor at Berkeley was estimated at £64 million over five years, but BNFL completed the job in three years at a cost of £41 million. At Trawsfynydd, the same task took two years and cost £32 million. All that is clear is that the cost of decommissioning and cleaning up the nuclear facilities owned by British Energy, BNFL and UKAEA will run into billions of pounds. In 1997 the Science Policy Research Unit at Sussex University put the whole of this cost at £42 billion (and up to £70 billion if there are the usual cost over-runs). Although all three owners are setting aside sums, funded by the non-fossil fuel levy taxpayers have paid since electricity was privatised, the Sussex University researchers reckon these fall short by nearly £30 billion.[65]

The Forestry Commission

Costs of this magnitude are probably sufficient to ensure that a nuclear power station is never built in Britain again. Ironically, environmentalism is now the only force which can retrieve the nuclear industry from the condescension of posterity. Nuclear power may produce radioactive waste, but it does not exhale the carbon dioxide which environmentalists blame for warming up the planet. Over the last twenty years the Green movement has moved from the fringes of national life to become the successor to Christianity as a state-sanctioned religion. If its strategists ever do decide that trees are preferable to people, they might conclude that a dose from THORP is preferable to a shower of acid rain. It is a credit to the political nous of the Forestry Commission that it was among the first to anticipate and make use of this possibility.

The story goes like this: in the 1980s and early 1990s the Conservatives antagonised the entire Green movement (from the Duke of Somerset to David Bellamy and Greenpeace) with the steady privatisation of land owned by the Forestry Commission. Far from selling land owned by the Commission, objectors argued in a letter to *The Times*, the government ought to be buying more.[66] It would save trees from commercial exploitation, encourage the best silvicultural practices and (by reducing timber imports) stop the Brazilians and the Malaysians chopping down the rain forest. The letter marked the beginning of an unexpected transformation in the public image of the

Forestry Commission. From its foundation in 1919 until well into the 1980s, the Commission was the uprooter-in-chief of ancient landscapes and the principal enemy of the natural environment.

Established to make good the depletion of timber reserves during the First World War (which devoured a million acres of trees to make trench cladding, pit props, duckboards, ammunition boxes and coffins) the Forestry Commission was charged with doubling the national acreage of forest. It planted over 20,000 acres a year between the wars. Most were conifers rather than the broad-leaf trees of the aboriginal British forest. G. M. Trevelyan, propagandist for the National Trust, accused the Commission of turning the Lake District into a German pine forest.[67] But the policy did not change. By the 1950s pressure from the Treasury to reduce its reliance on public funds had persuaded the Commission to *replace* native trees with the faster-growing Alaskan sitka spruce.

In the 1960s and 1970s, naturalists grumbled that the tightly-packed conifer plantations were destroying wildlife. They exacerbated the effects of acid rain, poisoning fish, said some, and the Conservancy Council described the conifer plantations of Caithness and Sutherland as 'the most massive single loss of wildlife habitation in Britain since the Second World War'. David Bellamy called the coniferisation of the Highlands 'total vandalism'. By the beginning of the 1980s the Forestry Commission was being attacked by botanists, ornithologists, naturalists, biologists, farmers and fishermen – as well as the Heritage Industry. In his seminal works, *The History of the Countryside* (1986) and *The Last Forest* (1989), Oliver Rackham portrays the Forestry Commission as the arch-destroyer of ancient woodland. Now, many of the same people see it as saviour of the ozone layer *and* the British arboreal heritage.

It was the Green campaign to save and plant trees which rescued the Forestry Commission from obloquy. Targets were set. Saplings were planted. Grants were dispensed. Habitats were protected. Subsidies blossomed. A National Forest was planned, and virtually every tree in the countryside was nationalised. Anyone cutting down trees in the countryside without permission, or planting them with the aid of a grant, can expect a visit from the Forestry Commission to check that they have followed its rules. New trees which Commission officials consider aesthetically unpleasing or foreign to a particular part of the country have to be uprooted.

The belief that trees are not safe in private hands is curious. Certainly, farmers have cleared forests to plant crops since palaeolithic times. But throughout history (and pre-history) they managed their woodland as carefully as their arable land and pasture. Trees shelter the wildlife which men hunt to eat, as well as for sport, and supply the timber for tools and furniture. It is true that unscrupulous landowners have felled timber on their estates for short-term gain, or to escape their debts. But most landowners, even in the eighteenth and nineteenth century heyday of the great estates, regarded all of their land as assets held in trust for future generations. Trees were the chief expression of that long view. Many landowners were great planters as well as foresters. All the best-loved features of the modern arboreal landscape – fox coverts and spinneys, hedge-marked fields and copses – are usually the work of private landowners, and wildlife habitats are certainly safer in private hands than in public ownership. It was the state war machine which decimated the forests of Britain during the two great wars of this century, and it was the state-owned Forestry Commission which replaced the lost broad-leaf trees with 'carpets of Scandinavian gloom'.[68] Those conifers the Commission did not itself plant were subsidised by government grants and tax breaks so gener-ous that by the 1980s no self-respecting pop star was without a stretch of Scottish countryside. The promised benefits of quick-growing conifers (a stra-tegic timber reserve and well-paid jobs for those who harvest and process it) have not materialised either. Machines are cheaper than men, and the crop is suitable only for pulp. Britain imports nine tenths of her timber needs, as she has always done.

This is a measure of the scale of the failure of state-owned forestry. The Forestry Commission was established in 1919 specifically to create a reserve of five million acres of timber, of which it was expected to own almost two million directly. In 1945, after a second wartime attrition, the government decided the publicly owned timber estate should be more than doubled. Its successors in the 1960s thought of 7 million acres, because the deficit on the balance of payments was the main gauge and regulator of economic activity, and timber imports ranked third behind food and oil.[69] But the strategic

TABLE 12.5
Acreage Owned by the Forestry Commission*

	Conifers	Broadleaves	Coppice	Other†	Total
England	405,252	91,429	2,471	42,008	541,160
Wales	266,873	14,826	–	9,884	291,584
Scotland	1,144,096	14,826	–	69,189	1,228,112
Great Britain	1,816,221	121,081	2,471	121,081	2,060,856

Source: Forestry Commission, Forestry Industry Handbook, 1998.

* Area at 31 March 1998.
† Other woodland consists of areas where timber production is not the main objective, including those managed for amenity or recreational purposes.

arguments for state-owned forestry were never strong, and the economic argument was fallacious from the outset. Britain is too windy and cold, and land too short and expensive, for home-produced timber to compete with Scandinavian or Canadian imports. Subsidy does not alter the climate: it merely diverts resources. The Forestry Commission has lost money for eighty years. In 1996–7 its activities cost the taxpayer £48.5 million, and its losses have sometimes been twice this in recent years.[70] It plants trees which grow faster abroad, lacks the volumes to keep its mills going fulltime, and regularly makes expensive mistakes. In 1993 the National Audit Office reported that the Commission had wasted £10.8 million by failing to cut trees down at the right time.[71]

After the investment of hundreds of millions of pounds of public money, the Commission has accumulated a landed estate of over two million acres and nearly nine million cubic metres of wood. It is easily the biggest landowner in Britain. Yet its assets are worth only £1.65 billion, and state forestry is costing the taxpayer £50 million a year.[72] This is why the government told the Commission to sell assets in 1981, and it has sold land steadily since. Wholesale privatisation was considered by the Cabinet in 1986 and 1994, but rejected as too controversial. The Commission was adept at mobilising support for the status quo, because its hybrid nature allows it to call on private growers and timber merchants worried about the impact on timber prices as well as ramblers (who want guaranteed access) and naturalists (who fuss about the impact on wildlife). It was to break the ties between the Commission and this unlikely coalition of interests, as well as to ready the organisation for privatisation, that the Conservative government decided to split the regulatory responsibilities of the Commission from its commercial businesses.

In 1992 the Commission split itself between the Forestry Authority (which regulates the planting of trees and dispenses grants to landowners) and Forest Enterprise (the commercial timber and leisure businesses). A third division, Forest Research, became a Next Steps agency in 1997, but does no more than cover its costs.[73] Forest Enterprise is now profitable, and has also become a Next Steps agency, making it easier to privatise. It fells, processes and sells timber on a commercial basis, and the viable estates could continue to be sold piecemeal. The 'recreational facilities' built in and around state-owned forests since the early 1970s could certainly be privatised. The forests entertain perhaps a quarter of a million visitors a year, and the Commission now welcomes one in three with nature trails, picnic spots, cycling and riding routes, camping and caravan sites, log cabins and even the odd Centre Parcs-style resort.

Public access to commercial forests could be preserved by regulation. Plenty of privately owned forest land in Britain is open to the public already, and

TABLE 12.6
Facilities Owned by Forest Enterprise

	England	Wales	Scotland	Great Britain
Picnic Places	137	90	183	410
Forest Walks/Nature Trails	287	94	355	736
Cycle Trails	94	14	122	230
Horse Trails	41	2	56	99
Orienteering Courses	41	10	18	69
Visitor Centres	13	5	10	28
Car Parks	410	80	287	777
Forest Drives	8	1	5	14
Wildlife Hides	19	4	11	34
Lavatories	62	12	33	107
Play Areas	25	8	2	35
Forest Classrooms	20	0	4	24
Forest Cabin Sites*	2	0	2	4
Forest Cabins*	107	0	59	166
Camping/Caravan Sites*	18	1	6	25

Source: Forestry Commission Facts and Figures, 1997–8.

* Operated by Forest Enterprise Holidays.

people roam freely across the estates of the Duke of Buccleuch, the largest private landlord in Britain. The Forestry Commission could be reduced to a regulatory role, its assets divided between commercial foresters, charitable trusts, and private landlords prepared to open their estates to the public. It is a model of piecemeal privatisation which could also be applied to another organisation with a blend of heritage, environmental, commercial and leisure activities: British Waterways.

British Waterways

The British Waterways Board is part of the Heritage Industry. In common with other members of the industry, most of its assets are liabilities. Apart from clocks, the 2,000 miles of canals which it owns are the only eighteenth century structures still in working order. But, unlike clocks, their tow paths, embankments, locks and bridges are in constant need of maintenance and repair. British Waterways, as the Board prefers to be known, recently secured £32 million from the National Lottery towards the reopening of the Glasgow–Edinburgh canal. It is responsible for over 2,800 listed buildings and ancient monuments, including historic warehouses, a lighthouse, several aqueducts and a number of Georgian mileposts. It employs carpenters, stonemasons and bricklayers for authentic restoration work, and even cuts its hedges using traditional techniques. Its landed estate incorporates 66 SSSIs and 1,000 local wildlife habitats, rendering more than one in three of its 3,000 acres invulnerable to any form of commercial activity. More than half its income of £102.5 million comes from the taxpayer.[74]

The other half comes from a variety of leisure, tourism and property development businesses. By cutting its grant steadily in real terms, the Conservative government forced British Waterways to increase its commercial income. The Board has not yet found a way to tax all the 160 million visitors it entertains every year, but anybody who travels on its canals (or fishes in them) is expected to pay for the privilege. Commercial traffic pays freight tolls; anglers purchase licences; cruisers and narrowboats buy boating licences; and the private operators who rent passenger boats and hire cruisers to daytrippers and holidaymakers share some of their earnings with the board. It also sells water to farmers, factories and water companies, and rents space along its canal towpaths to electricity, gas, cable television and telephone companies. It has a profitable property development business too, refurbishing docks and dockside warehouses for residential and commercial occupation. In 1997–8 British Waterways earned £19.7 million from property, and another £11.8 million

TABLE 12.7
British Waterways Portfolio

	Listed	Unlisted	Total
Bridges	850	3,913	4,763
Tunnels	279	–	60
Aqueducts	–	–	397
Locks	563	986	1,549
Dwellings	408	628	1,036
Reservoirs*	–	–	89
Operational Land	–	–	291 acres
Non-Operational Land	–	–	2,996 acres
Canal network	–	–	2,102 miles

Source: British Waterways.

* The reservoirs cover 4,065 acres and include 600 miles of feeder channels.

from leisure.[75] It has a property investment portfolio valued at over £200 million.

Like the Forestry Commission, British Waterways is half-business and half-nationalised industry. It would like to be neither. Its commercial income will never be sufficient to meet the costs of maintaining its 200-year-old network, so British Waterways reckons its best bet is to become a charity like the National Trust. Without cutting it off from public subsidy, this would free the board to borrow for investment, maintenance and repairs, and give it access to a formidable range of grants forbidden to publicly owned bodies. The danger is that a charitable trust would concentrate on lobbying government for larger grants rather than increasing efficiency or finding ways of making money from its freight and leisure businesses through joint ventures, commercial sponsorship, membership schemes. This is why some observers argue it would be wiser to split the commercial activities from the subsidised ones, and sell or part-sell them to a private buyer, while leasing stretches of canal and other activities to a variety of heritage groups in exchange for declining levels of subsidy.[76] Regulatory responsibilities, such as water quality and pollution control, could be taken over by the Environment Agency.[77]

British Waterways cannot be sold as a single enterprise, because state ownership has starved the canals of investment.[78] In 1998, it reckoned it needed an additional £7 million a year for the next eight years to deal with the backlog of repair and maintenance work. This commitment is unlikely to appeal to a private buyer, even if it were sweetened with a share of the profits from property development. But there is no reason to despair of the canals generating more income, particularly under a government looking to reduce the volume of traffic on the roads. At their peak in the early nineteenth century, the 4,250 miles of navigable water carried thirty million tons of goods a year.[79] Today, the 2,000 miles of canal owned by British Waterways carry less than 4.5 million tons a year. Though it still owns the commercial docks at Sharpness, the board withdrew from the freight business in 1988.

This does not mean private freight companies could not make greater use of its network. Even today, large volumes of commercial freight are moved along the estuaries of the Thames, the Clyde, the Severn and the Humber, and around the coast by ship. The wider and deeper canals of the north-east are used by craft carrying up to 700 tonnes of bulky commodities such as coal, oil and aggregates. Even without fresh investment, waterborne carriers still account for a quarter of all freight movements in the United Kingdom. While it cannot compare with the two thirds carried by road, the waterways are still carrying four times the payload of the railways which drove them out of business in the nineteenth century.

In theory, they could carry more, but most canals are too narrow to accommodate modern traffic. British Waterways thinks only 338 miles of its canals are suitable for commercial freight transport; another 1,400 miles are suitable for cruising and fishing only, and the remainder are navigated only by canoeists. Through partnerships with restoration groups and local authorities, British Waterways has returned over 200 miles of derelict waterways to navigable standard, but its ability to restore more is restrained by government insistence that it reach long-term repair and maintenance agreements with (riparian) local authorities.

*

The few institutions which remain in public ownership after twenty odd years of privatisation are now the frontier where the role and limits of the state are debated. The Bank of England, the BBC and the Post Office – all in their different ways – are testing the limits of freedom within the public sector. New Labour is toying with semi-sales and private–public partnerships (and tougher regulation of privatised industries) in the hope that it can pocket the proceeds of privatisation without sacrificing the loyalty of Old Labour. But its best thinkers resort to mutualisation often enough to suggest that the Third Way has nothing original to say about the management of public property. New Labour is happier dabbling in the means of politics rather than its ends. Given that predilection, it is not surprising that the reform of the local and regional structures of government is the one area where the government has broken with the policies of its predecessor.

CHAPTER THIRTEEN

LOCAL GOVERNMENT

A government of national renewal requires a national renewal of government.

TONY BLAIR[1]

Least of all shall we preserve democracy or foster its growth if all the power and most of the important decisions rest with an organisation far too big for the common man to survey or comprehend.

F. A. HAYEK, *The Road to Serfdom*, 1944[2]

It is possible to argue that almost every local government function, taken by itself, could be administered more efficiently in the technical sense under a national system, but if we wish local government to thrive – as a school of political and democratic education as well as a method of administration – we must consider the general effect on local government of each particular proposal. It would be disastrous if we allowed local government to languish by whittling away its most constructive and interesting functions.

HERBERT MORRISON, 1945[3]

What has been clearly visible over recent years is a growing propensity for the government to determine, in increasing detail, the pace and direction in which local services should be developed, the resources which should be devoted to them and the priorities between them.

LAYFIELD REPORT, 1976[4]

The reform of local and regional government is the one area of policy where New Labour looks genuinely radical. A new assembly for Northern Ireland was elected in 1998. In September 1997 voters in Wales and Scotland approved plans for separate parliaments in Edinburgh and Cardiff. When the first elections to the new assemblies were held in May 1999, it marked the first shift of power from Westminster to the regions of the mainland since the

Act of Union in 1707. A year later, Londoners were scheduled to elect the first assembly for the capital since the abolition of the Greater London Council in 1986. It will be headed by the first full-time, salaried mayor to be elected in any city in Britain, and legislation will encourage other borough and county councils to replace traditional committee systems with similar executive mayors and Westminster-style cabinets.

From 1999, people will be able for the first time to vote in local elections at weekends, and at the supermarket and the railway station. Some local authorities are making use of the still-funkier ideas New Labour promised in Opposition – citizens' juries and panels, community forums and local referendums.[5] If the Scottish and Welsh precedents are promising, the various regions of England are likely to acquire directly elected assemblies during the next Parliament. The development agencies, which began work in nine regions at the beginning of 1999, already prefigure them. 'I believe this is a time in which we are renewing the whole of our political and national life,' the prime minister told the 1998 Local Government Association (LGA) conference. 'Local government can play a very, very big part in that.'[6]

The Centralisation of Power

The conference was not fooled. A few days later, the LGA told the government that, without greater financial autonomy, the promise of renewal was empty.[7] Central government supplies £4 in every £5 spent by local government. This gives Westminster and Whitehall a degree of control over the expenditure and activities of county and borough councils which emasculates local democracy. A council can spend money on its own priorities only after it has provided all the services laid down by central government, and discretionary spending is then restricted by law to a fixed amount per head of population. Modern councils have wide-ranging and onerous duties, but virtually no power to choose priorities, determine standards, or fix levels of funding. They have responsibilities, but no means or powers not dependent on central government.

Their responsibilities are awesome. Councils spent nearly £75 billion in 1996, mainly on schools, police, fire services, local transport, refuse collection and social services such as meals-on-wheels. They employed over 2.6 million people, and owned tangible assets (council houses, roads and sports centres) valued at £246 billion, which would cost perhaps four or five times as much to replace.[8] Yet councils have minimal control over the services they supply and the disposition of their assets. They are expected to house the homeless, and sell to tenants who wish to buy their council house, but are not free to

TABLE 13.1
Local Government: Sources of Income, 1997

	£ million	% of total
Government grant	60,064	77.7
Local taxes	10,631	13.8
Rents	4,271	5.5
Other	2,346	3.0
	77,312	100.0

Source: UK National Accounts Blue Book, 1998, Table 5.3.4.

decide how the proceeds will be spent. They are obliged to provide schools, but cannot open or close them, determine the curriculum, choose the examinations, or decide the pay of teachers. Standards are monitored by representatives of Whitehall. The same is true of the police and fire services.

The discretion councils enjoy is severely circumscribed. They can decide the frequency of a meals-on-wheels service. They can even decide whether to sub-contract it to a private caterer or a voluntary group, and whether to charge for the meals, but they cannot choose whether or not to provide a service. Decisions as important to a locality and as unimportant to the nation as a village bypass, or the exclusion of dogs from the municipal park, are talked through at ministerial level. Unlike ordinary people and organisations, local authorities cannot do what the government has not forbidden. They can do only what the law permits.*

If a local authority wishes to do something which is not permitted, it must either desist or secure a change in the law. To organise a motor race through Birmingham, for example, the city council had to procure a private Act of Parliament. It is not surprising that most councils are reduced to the sheep-like implementation of by-laws prepared by central government. It is to blueprints prepared in Whitehall that councils repair roads; inspect shops, restaurants, retirement homes and building works; license taxi-drivers, massage parlours and pawnbrokers; provide crematoria, cemeteries and ratcatchers; and enforce restrictions on noise and smoke. Increasingly, they also act as agents of the incipient European superstate in Brussels: town halls seethe with officials implementing European directives on weights and measures,

---

* In a famous case in 1991, the House of Lords declared a series of financial transactions entered into by Hammersmith and Fulham Council to be *ultra vires*; a number of banks lost large sums.

vehicle safety, and pollution control. Local government is no longer an expression of civic pride or a laboratory of democracy. It is reduced to the implementation of policies determined at national and supranational levels.

This satrapy is a post-war phenomenon. 'In few other European countries were the tasks of local authorities so wide and varied,' wrote A. J. P. Taylor, of Britain between the wars. 'For the ordinary British citizen, "they" usually meant the town hall, not an agency of central government.'[9] Nobody now thinks 'they' are in the town hall. Indifference to local government means that three out of five voters do not turn out in council elections. In some inner-city wards, less than one in ten people bother to vote. One third of seats are uncontested in the average local election, especially in remote areas. Voters see councillors for what they are: administrators, not politicians; inevitably, their fate is decided on national rather than local issues.

The reforms advanced by New Labour will do little to reverse this concentration of power at the centre. The Scottish Parliament and Executive will have the power to vary the rate of income tax by up to 3p in the pound. Any increase amounts to the ability to raise taxation by up to £450 million, or about 3 per cent of the Scottish Office budget. If Scottish taxes were raised, the Treasury would seek an equivalent reduction in the central government grant. Although the Scottish government will in theory control local authority spending and taxation, and be free to switch funds between budgets, neither will amount to much in practice. The vast majority of the money spent by Scottish local government will still come from London.

In Wales, the powers of the Welsh Assembly and Executive Committee are even less impressive. They have no right to vary rates of national or local taxation in the Principality, and their ability to switch money between programmes is even more tightly controlled than in Scotland. Devolved government will be funded from Westminster; the secretary of state for Wales will spend all but a fraction of the Welsh Office budget; and the Assembly and Executive lack even Scottish-style powers to raise revenue.

The new mayor and assembly for London will represent seven million people, but their spending power will total a mere £3.3 billion. Most of it will come from government grants, not local taxes, and Whitehall has retained the power to cap spending. 'The Government's overriding priority', said *New Leadership for London*, the 1997 Green Paper on the Greater London Authority (GLA), 'is the control of public expenditure within the planned totals.' The public–private partnership to attract capital to the London Underground was agreed directly by government before the GLA was elected.[10] The mayor will spend nothing on education, health or housing, and will not have power to switch money between programmes. Whitehall will continue to dictate minimum levels of service and spending on the Metropolitan Police, the

TABLE 13.2
What Local Authorities Own

	London Borough Councils	Metropolitan District Councils	English Unitary Councils	Welsh Unitary Councils	English County Councils	Scottish Unitary Councils	Total
Highways (miles)	8,037	24,373	15,204	21,978	131,659	30,893	232,144
Houses & flats	610,030	2,378,826*	368,203	129,070	–	594,331	4,080,460
Schools & colleges	2,628	5,394	1,332	2,011	14,912	3,719	29,996
Libraries†	2,559	3,093	834	731	13,534	1,437	22,188
Museums & galleries‡	259	1,620*	278	226	124	–	2,507
Cemeteries & crematoria	133	1,222*	–	76	–	–	1,431
Fire & police stations§	2,062	5,337*	–	626	1,130	387	9,542
Rubbish dumps	1,671	11,908*	316	187	–	–	14,072
Parks & allotments (acres)	26,114	237,744	30,167	13,048	–	+41	307,114
Sports facilities¶	147	1,343	128	211	17	–	1,846

Sources: CIPFA Highways & Transportation Statistics, 1997–8 Estimates and 1995–6 Actuals; CIPFA Housing Revenue Account Statistics, 1997; CIPFA Education Statistics, 1996–7, incorporating the Handbook of Unit Costs; CIPFA Public Library Statistics, 1996–7, Actuals; CIPFA Leisure & Recreation Statistics, 1997–8 Estimates; CIPFA Cemeteries Statistics, 1996–7 Actuals; CIPFA Fire Statistics, 1998, and Police Statistics, 1997–8, Estimates; CIPFA Waste Collections and Disposal Statistics, 1996–7, Actuals; CIPFA Leisure & Recreation Statistics, 1997–8, Estimates; CIPFA Scottish Branch Rating Review: Estimates of Income and Expenditure 1993–4 and 1998–9, and Actuals 1996–7; Scottish Transport Statistics, No 17, 1998 Edition.

* Includes non-metropolitan district councils.
† Service points, a definition which includes mobile libraries.
‡ Includes concert halls, theatres, community centres, public halls and arts centres.
§ Includes section houses.
¶ Includes indoor sports halls, leisure centres and golf courses.

London Fire Brigade and London Transport. The only new tax the mayor will be able to raise is traffic charges. Like other local authorities he is obliged to spend the proceeds on improving public transport. But the government has reserved the power to seize the proceeds of the new taxes anyway . Power, and especially the power to get and spend, are still centralised.

Who Centralised Power?

Many people believe the centralisation of power in Britain was the work of Margaret Thatcher. On this view, it was her repeated attempts to curb the spending of local authorities (culminating in the disastrous Poll Tax) which robbed them of autonomy:

> Margaret Thatcher detested local government as much as she detested the trade unions and the Labour Party. There is no reference in her memoirs which is not pejorative . . . She saw local councils as irresponsible, left-wing and profligate . . . holes not just in the public-spending bucket but in the whole Thatcherite political economy . . . councils needed punishing for being local and for being Labour. Her overspending rhetoric, the emphasis on 'hard-left' extravagance, the restless search for new controls, all indicated a resentment that a quarter of the public sector was beyond her direct control.'[11]

There is truth in this account, but it attaches too much importance to a brief episode in the long story of the centralisation of power in Britain. In the 1980s, Thatcher accelerated a momentum towards government by Westminster and Whitehall which began 160 years ago.

The localisation of power was doomed from the moment the state came under the sway of the utilitarian reformers of the 1830s. The utilitarian mind of the bureaucrat, with its faith in the power of rational men to devise practical solutions to people's needs, explains the encroachment of the centralised state more completely than the ideas of one prime minister. 'The only rational foundation of government,' the early Victorian political economist, Nassau Senior, argued, 'is expediency – the general benefit of the community. It is the duty of a government to do whatever is conducive to the welfare of the governed.'[12]

Senior was a member of the Poor Law Commission of 1833, which led to the New Poor Law of 1834. The New Poor Law was the first instance in British history of legislation designed to achieve uniform results throughout the country by using centrally-devised rules and centralised funding to eliminate local discretion. It shifted the distribution of poor relief from 15,000 separate parishes to unions of parishes run by Boards of Guardians enforcing regulations laid down by central government. It set a pattern. To reformers such as Senior and Edwin Chadwick, the chief advocates of reforms to improve public health, local control was synonymous with paralysis and disorder. In the question of sanitation alone, vestries, town councils, highway surveyors, health committees, commissioners of sewers, water and gas authorities, street commissioners, improvement commissioners, watch committees, poor law unions and turnpike trusts all had an interest. This was why bureaucratic reformers wanted to take social questions out of local politics; they were interested in efficiency, not democracy.

Remedies were devised at the centre, and implemented from the centre. The New Poor Law was governed by a central bureaucracy; responsibility for policing was shifted from parish constables to independent police forces from 1839; local health boards were set up under the Public Health Act of 1848; highways boards were established under the Highways Acts; school boards by the Education Act of 1870; and London was run by an unelected Metropolitan Board of Works until 1889. Permissive legislation designed to encourage local authorities to improve sanitation, housing and schooling gradually gave way to obligatory powers in the face of inactivity and backsliding. The unchecked Victorian boards of commissioners were the prototypes of the quangos of today. They were displaced by elected councils in the 1890s, but by then it was too late to recoup the local autonomy aggrandised by central government.

Central Growth and Local Government

By the time the system of democratically elected councils was formulated between 1888 and 1899, the utilitarian idea of local government was already dominant: local authorities were the agents of central government. The belief that the years between 1870 and 1945 were a golden age of local government is a Fabian myth. It is true that the burghers of Victorian cities like Birmingham, Bristol, Liverpool, Leeds and Manchester pioneered public health, housing and education, and public ownership of utilities such as water, gas, electricity and transport. But the real pressure for reform came from the centre. It was the power to act (granted by central government) which encouraged municipal leaders to implement reforms. If they failed, permissive powers gave way to statutory duties. This was the case with sanitation, housing and education. The 'gas and water socialism' of the Fabians was not the herald of the rising Welfare State, but its agent.

The replacement of unelected boards of commissioners by elected borough and county councils, which began with the County Councils Act of 1888, gave local government democratic legitimacy for the first time.[13] But the legislation also reflected the bureaucratic urge to impose symmetry and order on the chaos of traditional local government. Both the Georgian and the early Victorian reformers had appointed the boards of commissioners to bypass the corrupt morass of parish vestries, urban corporations and justices of the peace, which had administered local affairs since the Middle Ages. In terms of independence, the golden age of local government was not between 1870 and 1945, it was *until then*. In 1833 Lord Radnor told de Tocqueville that 'the central government has nothing to do with provincial matters, nor even their supervision.'[14]

The new system of county and borough councils, which persists to this day, was bent to the will of central government from the outset. Even before the First World War they were given social responsibilities, like secondary schools and free school meals, which they were entitled to subsidise from the rates. These responsibilities were too burdensome for local taxpayers to bear unaided, so grants from central government were significant. Inevitably, the power of the purse enabled the government to reduce local authorities to agents of national policy, without the need for more formal control. Whitehall and Westminster always disliked the lack of uniformity in standards of provision by local authorities, so some tasks were not entrusted to them at all. In 1909, the new old age pensions were paid through the Post Office. A year later, local authority labour exchanges were replaced by state-run and state-financed labour exchanges.

Creeping centralisation continued between the wars. In 1918, the government offered to replace primary school fees with grants, which became a reality by 1944. This robbed local authorities of financial control of schools, and exposed every aspect of education (including the curriculum) to eventual nationalisation. In 1991 control of teachers' pay, the largest item of local authority expenditure, was transferred to a new quango. In transport, the Road Traffic Act of 1930 removed responsibility for licensing buses from local authorities to centrally appointed road traffic commissioners. The building of main roads passed to central government by legislation of 1936 and 1946. Local authority ports and harbours were nationalised in 1947. In 1968 Passenger Transport Authorities were set up to run local buses and trains, robbing councils of direct responsibility for urban transport.

In health, legislation of 1929 empowered local authorities to turn infirmaries into municipal hospitals. Councils responded inadequately, making it easier to nationalise local authority hospitals and clinics in 1948. There was some argument within government over whether local authorities should continue to run hospitals, but they were eventually reduced to provision of residual health and social services such as old people's homes, children in care, immunisation and ambulances. Around 1,700 local authority hospitals were nationalised on the formation of the National Health Service in 1948. In 1973–4 all remaining local authority health services – vaccinations, health visitors, ambulances and health centres – were transferred to Regional and Area Health Authorities. Since 1990, local authorities have had no representation on these bodies.

Provision for the unemployed was transferred from local authorities to a centralised Unemployment Assistance Board in 1934. Local authorities continued to provide for the old, the sick and the widowed, but even these duties were taken over by central government after the Second World War. The main social service provided by local authorities today is meals-on-wheels. The gas and electricity utilities owned by local authorities, which supplied two thirds of electricity and one third of gas in 1945, were nationalised in 1948. Under the 1973 Water Act local authorities lost responsibility for water to the new regional water authorities.

Gigantism in Local Government

The engine of centralisation was the drive by government to achieve a uniform standard in public services. This is a potent enemy of local autonomy, arguing always for the reduction of diversity; the centralisation of financing; and the concentration of power in convenient units. Just as the utilitarian reformers were appalled by the chaos of unreformed local government in the 1830s and 1840s, so were their twentieth century successors. The Royal Commission on Local Government in Greater London, which deliberated between 1957 and 1960, deplored the fact that the capital was run by 7 county councils, 3 county boroughs, 28 London boroughs, the City Corporation, 71 urban and rural district councils and non-county boroughs and half a dozen *ad hoc* authorities. 'The machinery is untidy and full of anomalies,' its report declared. 'There is overlapping, duplication, and in some cases gaps.'[15]

Though the Commissioners admitted that this cumbersome machinery worked, its untidiness condemned it. The bureaucratic mind abhors anomalies, gaps, duplication and overlaps. In 1963, the seven county councils of London gave way to one (the Greater London Council) and the other bodies were replaced by thirty-two borough councils. The county of Middlesex disappeared, living on only as a cricket team. By the 1960s, the transfer of power from smaller units to larger ones was part of a well-established pattern. In 1944, district councils had surrendered education to county councils. Health and policing followed in 1946, and fire services and planning a year later. Mergers shrank the number of police forces from over two hundred and fifty in 1946 to fifty now.

This brand of thinking reached its apogee in the reconstruction of local government initiated by Peter Walker, who was secretary of state for the Environment in the early 1970s. He drew on a report of June 1969 which argued that the 1,210 separate local authorities in England bore little relation to modern patterns of life and work. The structure of boroughs and counties stemmed from an era before suburbs and transport allowed people to live in one place, work in another and send their children to school in a third. One large council was also thought to be cheaper than ten smaller ones: it has more clout with suppliers. Government grants are more equitable if they are spread over larger areas. The government also identified, and disliked, the apparently pointless rivalry between the various tiers of local government.

In the Local Government Act of 1972, the 58 county councils in England and Wales were reduced to 47; the 1,249 borough and district councils were slashed to 333; and six giant metropolitan counties – Greater Manchester, Merseyside, West Midlands, Tyne & Wear, South Yorkshire and West Yorkshire – were called into being as provincial equivalents of the GLC. Within them lurked 36 new district or borough councils. Scotland was given nine regional councils, sub-divided into fifty-three district councils. 'All the old and ancient boroughs were too small to meet modern requirements,' recalled Walker. 'Instead I went for districts with 40,000 or 50,000 electors. My guiding principle was to see that every function was as close to the people as possible.'[16] The twin aims of scale and intimacy were contradictory. Unsurprisingly, the reforms were not a success. Far from injecting democratic vitality into local government, they alienated voters from any allegiance or sense of identity.

The disappearance or disintegration of ancient counties, such as Rutland and Somerset, was keenly felt. The residents of artificial creations – Avon, Cleveland and Humberside – felt equal resentment. Undermining the ancient counties aimed, like the revolutionary regime in France, to destroy local and regional loyalties by dividing the country into *départements* of equal size, but the utilitarian nature of the reforms condemned them. Geography, not economics or demographics, gave the ancient counties of England their shape and meaning. The East Riding of Yorkshire and the northern part of Lincolnshire are divided by the Humber, and remained divided despite the construction of a bridge across the estuary and a change of name to Humberside. In Scotland, the reforms were unbalanced by the Strathclyde Regional Council. Ostensibly based on the regional economy of the city of Glasgow and its hinterland, it was a model of what the reforms were intended to achieve. But it was too big; it contained nearly half the Scottish population, or 2.5 million people, and it failed to command their allegiance. Scotsmen talked nostalgically of the city 'corporations' of the inter-war years.

The Banham Review

In 1986 the Conservative government abolished the GLC and the six metropolitan counties. In 1991, in the wake of the Poll Tax débâcle, it launched a review of the entire structure of local government. The Local Government Commission was chaired by a former director general of the Confederation of British Industry, Sir John Banham, who was told to take heed of local loyalties and preferences. His Commission was to decide 'whether a unitary structure would better reflect the identities and interests of local communities and secure effective and convenient local government'. It was a clear brief to get rid of pseudo-counties such as Avon, and replace two tiers with a single layer of local government, which Whitehall was convinced would be cheaper. The review took five years and (outside Scotland and Wales) the results were disappointing; the time lag gave county councils time to mount ferocious campaigns of self-preservation.

Only along the Celtic fringe were the results unequivocal. In Scotland, the regional and district councils were replaced by twenty-nine new unitary authorities,[17] and the giant Stratchclyde Regional Council was split between twelve separate authorities. The pattern was repeated in Wales, where eight county and thirty-seven district councils surrendered their powers to twenty-two unitary local authorities. The new structure restored many traditional county names, and returned to historic cities (such as Swansea and Cardiff) the autonomy they enjoyed before the 1974 reforms. In most parts of England, two tiers of local government survived (which has complicated New Labour plans for regional government). The reviled pseudo-counties disappeared, historic fiefs like Herefordshire, Rutland and the City of York were restored, and local government in England lost its neatness.

'Local government does not need to be neat,' the secretary of state for the Environment told the House of Commons. 'It needs to be effective.'[18] It sounded reassuring, but his was the authentic voice of central government: effectiveness, not pluralism or democracy, was what mattered. Even at the end of a review sparked by local resistance to central direction, Westminster and Whitehall were concerned with efficiency. Local government is now measured not by its ability to command the allegiance of local people, but by its economy and effectiveness in delivering services decided by central government.

The Rise and Rise of the Quango State

The temptation to dispense with the tiresome inefficiencies of local democracy in the delivery of public services is perennial. The Georgians invented the public commissioner to bypass municipal corruption. The Victorians perfected him to bypass municipal incompetence. Today, the quangos established by governments have more appointed members (70,000) than there are elected councillors (23,000). Colleges of further and higher education and grant-maintained schools were set free of local authority control in the 1980s. In the 1990s, regional training and economic development passed to 81 Training and Enterprise Councils and 22 Local Enterprise Companies, all run by appointees rather than elected councillors. Much public housing is now controlled by housing associations. Between them, local quangos now spend more than local authorities.[19]

The first of the modern breed of centrally appointed and centrally funded quangos were the New Town Development Corporations, set up by the government under the New Towns Act of 1946. They were equipped with sweeping powers to acquire land, create infrastructure and build factories, shops, homes, civic buildings and leisure facilities. Once a Corporation has completed the creation of a viable new town, its remaining assets (and liabilities) are handed over to another agency of central government: the Commission for New Towns (CNT). The Commission is charged with adding value to the assets and then selling them for the best price it can get. The New Labour government, despite a professed opposition to quangos, has decided not to pursue a Conservative plan to get rid of the CNT. It will be merged in AD 2000 with what remains of English Partnerships (when *its* regeneration activities have passed to the Regional Development Agencies).[20]

The concept of New Towns can be traced to Ebenezer Howard, whose 'garden city' idea was put into practice at Letchworth and Welwyn before the First World War, but the corporations were conceived exclusively by Whitehall. The Royal Commission on the Distribution of the Industrial Population, chaired by Montague Barlow, had reported in 1939 in favour of central government control of land use throughout the country. It advocated restricting factory development in the south-east, dispersing urban populations to new towns and garden cities around the capital, and subsidising industry to move to depressed areas. One of the members of the Barlow Commission, Patrick Abercrombie, produced a minority report in favour of a central ministry with strong executive powers.

Abercrombie got his strong executive ministry. The Ministry of Town and Country Planning and its successors built twenty-seven new towns, in two separate bursts of enthusiasm in the late 1940s and mid-1960s drawing heavily on the plans for the development of London which Abercrombie drafted in 1943 and 1944. It was always the intention to recoup the development costs of the new towns by selling the land and buildings, and the Development Corporations sold assets as they progressed. The last Corporation (Milton Keynes) was wound up in March 1992, and by 1998 CNT had sold enough remaining assets to repay the debt incurred in construction of the new towns. They are now turning a profit – for central not local taxpayers.

The New Town Development Corporations were the model for the Urban Development Corporations (UDCs) which the Thatcher administration set up in 1981 to bypass local government in the inner cities. The Labour governments of the 1940s and 1960s had preferred the Development Corporations to be run by civil servants; the Conservative governments of the 1980s packed UDCs with sympathetic businessmen instead. Like their predecessors, UDCs were fixed-term public corporations funded exclusively by central government, and armed with sweeping powers to acquire, reclaim, renovate and sell land. Established in the docklands of London and Merseyside in 1981, their work assumed a new urgency after the riots in the Toxteth area of Liverpool and other inner cities in July that year. A second and more substantial wave of UDCs followed the election victory of 1987, in which Margaret Thatcher pledged herself (on the stairs of Central Office) to reclaim the inner cities for Conservatism.

UDCs were under no obligation to explain their actions to local councillors, or even to consult them. 'We took their powers away from them because they were making a mess of it,' was how Michael Heseltine explained his preference for central rather than local government initiatives. 'They had advisory committees, planning committees, inter-relating committees and even discussion committees – but nothing happened.'[21] UDCs were known as Undemocratic Development Corporations, and opposed fiercely by local councils forced to cede control of large areas of the inner cities to them. By the time the last were wound up, and their remaining assets transferred to CNT, their reputation had improved, but they will always be seen as one-dimensional bodies which emphasised physical regeneration at the expense of people and democracy.

The UDCs were justified by results. At a cost of approximately £5 billion, they brought a quarter of a million jobs and £16.5 billion of private investment to some of the most derelict parts of the country. Even local councillors came eventually to appreciate the injections of energy and cash UDCs brought in their train. The same cannot be said of the attempt to repeat that success in one of the core responsibilities of local government: housing. Housing Action Trusts (HATS) were invented in 1988 to take over rundown council estates,

TABLE 13.3
The Achievements of the Urban Development Corporations*

UDC	Date Founded	Land Reclaimed (Acres)	Housing (Units)	Non-Housing Floorspace (000 Sq M)	Roads (Kms)	Jobs Created	Private Investment Attracted (£m)	Public Money Granted (£m)†
London Docklands	1981	1,984	24,046	2,324.9	290.5	80,022	7,658.2	1,860.3
Merseyside	1981	966	3,477	667.9	101.4	20,612	738.5	385.3
Black Country	1987	995	3,801	1,186.2	38.6	22,809	1,144.3	357.7
Teesside	1987	1,238	1,331	486.5	29.3	14,480	1,036.5	353.4
Trafford Park	1987	473	372	704.8	51.6	28,585	1,765.7	223.7
Tyne & Wear	1987	1,315	4,552	1,210.8	47.0	34,092	1,278.3	339.3
Bristol	1989	171	676	121.0	6.6	4,825	235.0	78.9
Central Manchester	1988	86	2,583	138.5	2.2	4,944	372.8	82.2
Leeds	1988	168	571	374.0	11.6	9,066	357.0	55.7
Sheffield	1988	610	0	494.7	15.0	18,812	686.4	101.0
Birmingham Heartlands	1992	348	803	314.0	49.3	4,808	370.2	36.7
Plymouth	1993	32	107	9.3	6.1	53	13.7	47.1
Cardiff Bay	1987	532	2,539	448.4	29.0	10,799	845.0	424.0
Total	–	8,918	44,858	8,481.1	678.2	253,907	16,501.6	4,348.4

Source: Department of the Environment, Transport and the Regions and Cardiff Bay Development Corporation.

* To March 1998. All 12 of the English UDCs are now wound up. The Cardiff Bay Development Corporation is scheduled to disappear in March 2000, by which time it expects to have reclaimed 1,139 acres of land, built 5,690 houses, 1,1356,383 square metres of commercial space and 51.8 kilometres of roads, created 31,1027 permanent jobs and attracted £1.7 billion of private sector investment, in exchange for total grant-in-aid of £500 million.
† Lifetime figures for grant-in-aid given to UDCs. Their total expenditure also included spending financed from capital receipts and European grants. The total lifetime expenditure of all UDCs exceeded £5 billion. The figure for London Docklands excludes grant-in-aid for the Docklands Light Railway, which totalled £485.2 million up to 31 March 1998.

refurbish them, and sell them on to new (and preferably private) landlords. Only six were set up; intimidation by local councillors ensured that few tenants voted in favour of a HAT unless the financial rewards were immense.[22]

That experiment is now over. Like the defunct UDCs, their residual assets pass to the CNT. It is fitting that they are united in death. At bottom, UDCs and HATs were expressions of Thatcherite exasperation with local government, of which she made no secret. This is why councils were forced to sell houses and flats to their tenants, and the burden of building new public housing was passed to housing associations. Thatcher wanted to strip councils of responsibility for schools as well: she enabled them to opt out of local authority control and receive funding direct from Whitehall. Both measures were resisted fiercely (though not universally) by councillors, cementing her reputation as the arch-destroyer of local autonomy. Yet she merely accelerated a process which, in the case of both housing and schools, stretches back to the origins of public provision.

The Centralisation of Housing

By the time the Conservatives left office in 1997, 1.75 million council tenants had bought their homes. The majority had purchased them under the Right to Buy legislation of 1980, which obliged councils to sell houses and flats to any tenant who wished to buy provided he had occupied his home for at least three years. Most were sold at discounts to their market value which averaged 50 per cent, but the Right to Buy was bolstered by other measures too. Council rents were allowed to rise, making a mortgage seem more afford-able. Shared ownership allowed tenants to buy part of the equity in a house and pay rent on the remainder. From 1989, cash grants were offered to council and housing association tenants wanting to buy a house on the open market. The rents-to-mortgages scheme, introduced in 1993, meant tenants could turn rents into mortgage repayments. In 1996 the Right to Buy was extended to housing association tenants.

Right to Buy was the prize exhibit in a recent analysis of the centralisation of power in Britain by Simon Jenkins, a former editor of *The Times*. 'Housing is one area of Thatcherism to which other commentators than myself regularly apply the word nationalisation,' he wrote in *Accountable to None: The Tory Nationalisation of Britain*. 'The primary reason is that Thatcher did not own the council houses she wanted to sell; councils did. She had to acquire sover-eignty over them to force their disposal . . . Right-to-buy meant the central government breaking a local contract between landlord and tenant, and turning the landlord into a forced seller. The 1980 Housing Act, followed by a housing act almost every year for a decade, asserted central power over local-authority housing sales. If an individual tenant had difficulty persuading a council to sell, or even found it dilatory in selling, section 23 of the Act gave Whitehall the right to take over the transaction.'[23]

It is true that councils owned the houses and flats. It is true also that section 23 was a coercive measure. Many councils resented the obligation to sell, and some actively resisted it. Councillors in Greenwich and Rochdale invited the government to despatch commissioners to undertake a task they would not complete. Norwich Council contested the legislation in the High Court, but lost. Around 200 councils had eventually to be forced by central government to sell. Leaseholders in council-owned blocks complained of massive increases in service charges and buildings insurance, and unsympathetic treatment of buyers who failed to maintain mortgage payments. In the 1996 Housing Act the government took powers to reduce service charges. It also offered local authorities financial incentives to return the purchase proceeds to buyers who could not keep up their mortgage payments.

Few councillors in urban Scotland were sympathetic to Conservatism. Most refused, as a matter of principle, to accept that any body could be a better landlord than the council. In the end, the government had to become a landlord itself. In 1986 it set up a quango, Scottish Homes, to build new houses for rent and sale, and gave tenants the right to switch their leases from the council to the new organisation. Between 1979 and 1997, 325,000 Scottish local authority tenants bought their council houses. But owner-occupation in Scotland, at 58 per cent, is still lower than in England.

But it is an exaggeration to describe the Right to Buy as an act of nationalisation. Many councils were selling houses to tenants before Thatcher became prime minister. Over 40,000 council tenants bought their homes in 1979, before the Right to Buy was introduced. The main obstacle to building more council houses was electoral: rate-payers were not prepared to pay for them. This was why council housing did not take off until central government agreed to subsidise. It subsidised construction directly from 1919, but councils were so slow to respond that the government extended the offer to the private sector. Of the four million houses built between the wars, less than two in five were built by local authorities. From the outset, the provision of public housing depended on subsidies from Whitehall, giving central government a stake in council housing which it has never surrendered. In fact, the level of subsidy grew heavier, because the government insisted on controlling rents as well.[24] Most rents remained at 1914 levels throughout the inter-war years and controls over private rents were not relaxed until the late 1980s.[25] The effects were predictable. Private companies stopped building new houses, and private landlords, who had supplied nine out of ten houses before the war, were driven from the market. The government had no choice but to get local authorities to build houses and, to ensure reasonable rents, to subsidise construction as well.

Council house rents became progressively less economic. The proportion of the cost of council housing which was covered by rents shrank steadily. In 1972, the Heath government forced local authorities to increase rents, but the long-term effect was a further increase in the central government subsidy. As rents rose, hardship was alleviated by an increase in means-tested cash benefits, paid by councils to poorer tenants, and reimbursed by central government. In the 1980s, the Conservative government used cuts in cash benefits as a tool to increase council rents, forcing poorer tenants on to housing benefit. Central government subsidies fell by two thirds in the 1980s, but expenditure on housing benefit doubled.

The Rise of the Housing Association

The shift from subsidising rents to subsidising people was sensible, but also part of a pattern of hostility to local authorities as landlords. The Conservative administrations of the 1980s and early 1990s sought openly to displace local government from the housing market by their favoured alternative: the housing association. In 1979 housing associations supplied one rented house in twenty-five; by 1997, when the Conservatives left office, their share had risen to one in seven. The key to their growth is the Housing Corporation, a central government quango which supplies them with cut-price finance they can use to attract additional funding from banks, building societies and institutional investors. The subsidy gives housing associations two advantages over local authorities: access to private capital and (because they do not have to recover the full cost of construction) the ability to set rents at attractive levels.

The new government allows local authorities to spend the proceeds of council house sales (on strict terms and conditions laid down by the Treasury). But under the Conservatives, only councils with no debt were allowed to spend sales proceeds as they saw fit. Local authorities which had debts were expected to devote 75 per cent of the money to the repayment of borrowing. This was a cause of serious complaint, but effective in squeezing local authorities out of house-building. In 1979 councils built nearly one new house or flat in every three. By the time the Conservatives left office, they were building less than one in 250. The Treasury argued that councils would use the capital windfall to raise current spending, and then argue for an increased annual subsidy. Nothing illustrates the nature of the relationship between central and local government at the end of the twentieth century better, except the tragic story of state education.

The Centralisation of Education

Since the Education Act of 1902, which abolished school boards and made the newly created borough and county councils responsible for both primary and secondary education, the overwhelming majority of British children have attended schools owned by local authorities. Local authorities still own around 30,000 schools and colleges in Great Britain.[26] But the buildings are all they

TABLE 13.4
Housing Tenure in Great Britain

Year	Owner Occupied (000)	Per Cent of Total	Privately Rented (000)	Per Cent of Total	Rented From a Housing Association (000)	Per Cent of Total	Rented From Council (000)	Per Cent of Total
1979	11,348	54.7	2,511	12.1	368	1.8	6,521	31.4
1980	11,618	55.5	2,410	11.5	401	1.9	6,499	31.1
1981	11,898	56.4	2,337	11.1	469	2.2	6,380	30.3
1982	12,270	57.7	2,318	10.9	483	2.3	6,180	29.1
1983	12,604	58.8	2,304	10.7	504	2.3	6,035	28.1
1984	12,913	59.6	2,290	10.6	525	2.4	5,924	27.4
1985	13,223	60.5	2,258	10.3	548	2.5	5,820	26.6
1986	13,565	61.5	2,205	10.0	564	2.6	5,724	25.9
1987	13,968	62.7	2,139	9.6	586	2.6	5,599	25.1
1988	14,424	64.0	2,077	9.2	614	2.7	5,412	24.0
1989	14,832	65.2	2,069	9.1	652	2.9	5,190	22.8
1990	15,099	65.8	2,123	9.3	702	3.1	5,015	21.9
1991	15,336	66.3	2,219	9.6	708	3.1	4,878	21.1
1992	14,466	66.3	2,286	9.8	773	3.3	4,788	20.5
1993	15,642	66.6	2,333	9.9	844	3.6	4,669	19.9
1994	15,813	66.8	2,395	10.1	937	4.0	4,528	19.1
1995	15,955	66.9	2,476	10.4	1,035	4.3	4,393	18.4
1996	16,100	67.0	2,534	10.5	1,103	4.6	4,299	17.9

Source: Housing and Construction Statistics, 1986–1996, Table 2.23, 1987–97,
Table 9.3, 1998.

do own. Central government decides how teachers are trained and what they are paid. It stipulates the age at which children join and leave school. The National Curriculum lays down what happens in the classroom at virtually every hour of every school day. The performance of teachers is monitored by state-imposed tests taken by all children at local authority schools at the ages of five, seven, eleven, fourteen, sixteen and eighteen.

The results are published, and organised in league tables, in order to help parents choose between schools. (Since the Conservatives introduced open enrolment, local authorities can no longer direct children to particular schools.) Standards are enforced from the centre. All schools and local education authorities are visited at least once every four years by OFSTED, a centrally-funded cadre of inspectors of schools which replaced local authority inspectors in 1992. Even the amount of money which local education authorities have to spend on schools is now determined in detail by Whitehall officials, largely on the basis of statistical measures of social deprivation rather than detailed knowledge of particular localities.

Most of these controls were introduced by the Conservative administrations of the 1980s and 1990s, which has encouraged the belief that the centralisation of power in education was another Thatcherite iniquity. But the Conservative reforms built directly on five acts of state centralisation between 1870 and 1976. The first two (1870 and 1902) laid on local authorities educational duties too onerous for a local tax base to support. The third (1944) used the financial power this conferred on Whitehall to eliminate the last possibility of local independence (the charging of fees) and to impose a uniform system (grammar, technical and secondary modern schools) based on selection by state examination (the eleven-plus).

The last acts of centralisation, which began with the notorious Circular 10/65 and ended with the Education Act of 1976, forced local authorities to turn secondary schools into comprehensives. Comprehensivisation was accompanied by the introduction of a progressive curriculum.[27] This matured into the national curriculum, which specifies exactly what schools teach, and when. By the time Margaret Thatcher came to power in 1979, the government had already taken control of the structure of schools and what was taught in them. Ironically, the centralising reforms which her governments introduced (they passed no less than *twelve* Education Acts) were rooted in parental dislike of the centralising reforms of the 1960s and 1970s, which were in turn dictated by the reform of 1944, which sanctified the unpopular eleven-plus examination.

In every reform of education since 1870, local authorities were expected to act as agents of central government. This gave them responsibility, but not power, making them the first target of parental ire. The post-1979 reforms began by removing the obligation on local authorities to turn their schools into comprehensives and replacing it with a duty to respect parents' preferences in the choice of school for their children. But the Conservative campaign against progressive education eventually developed into a crusade to excise local authorities from education altogether.

It began with the Assisted Places Scheme, which subsidised parents to remove their children from local authority schools and place them in the private sector. In 1984, the government took control of entry to the teaching profession by circumventing the local authority-controlled teacher training colleges. Ten years later, responsibility was passed to a centrally-controlled Teachers Training Agency. In 1986, the first parent and independent school governors were elected, with the intention of replacing local education authorities as the primary influence over discipline, the curriculum and the appointment of head-teachers. In 1987 the pay of teachers was taken away from the old machinery (the Burnham Committee) and given to the secretary of state (who later returned it to a centrally-appointed School Teachers' Review Body).

The first national curriculum was introduced in the Education Act of 1988. Open enrolment and per capita funding were introduced simultaneously, stripping local authorities of the power to limit the expansion of good schools to keep bad ones full. The Inner London Education Authority was abolished altogether. Governors and headmasters, rather than councillors, were given control of the school budget. The 1988 Education Act also set up City Technology Colleges (CTCs), a new breed of school independent of local authorities and funded by government grants and private sponsors. By the time the Conservatives left office, there were fifteen CTCs with over 11,000 pupils, and the idea was being extended to specialist technology, sports, art and language schools. In 1992, local councils were deprived of responsibility for sixth form and further education colleges: their funding was transferred to Whitehall, in the shape of the new Further Education Funding Council.

The most significant step (in symbolic if not practical terms) was to allow schools to opt out of local authority control altogether. If a majority of parents voted in favour, schools could elect to receive funding directly from Whitehall. Grant-maintained schools, as they became known, deprived local education authorities of ownership and control. If a local authority tried to set up a competitive school nearby, the government stopped it. This power was used for the first time in the London borough of Sutton in 1994. For the schools which opted out, the consequences were ambiguous. The governors and head-teacher took ownership of the school buildings and other assets, and were free to appoint staff and decide how to follow the national curriculum. But ministers retained the powers to appoint and dismiss governors and decide whether a school should expand or contract. In one controversial instance, at Stratford in east London, the ministry used its power to appoint a majority of the governors when the school failed its inspection.

Grant-maintained status aimed to do for schools what the Right to Buy did to the council house: persuade parents, like tenants, to escape local authority control. In her memoirs, Margaret Thatcher admitted that her reforms aimed at 'the unbundling of many of the LEAs' powers, leaving them with a monitoring and advisory role – perhaps in the long term not even that. It would have been a way to ease the state still further out of education, thus reversing the worst aspects of post-war education policy.'[28] Had it worked, grant-maintained status would have nationalised all but the worst state schools. But parents were indifferent, or unimpressed, and local authorities campaigned successfully to

TABLE 13.5
The Number of Grant-Maintained Schools in England in 1997

Local Authority	Grant-Maintained Primary Schools	Grant-Maintained Secondary Schools	Total Number of Schools*	Proportion of Schools Grant-Maintained
London Boroughs	66	119	2,543	7.3%
Metropolitan District Councils	46	80	5,226	2.4%
English Unitary Councils	4	2	1,303	0.5%
English County Councils	367	451	14,650	5.6%
Welsh Unitary Councils	5	12	1,960	0.9%
Total	488	664	25,682	4.5%

Source: CIPFA Education Statistics 1996–97 incorporating the Handbook of Unit Costs.

* Includes special schools and middle schools.

keep schools under their control. By the time the Conservatives left office, less than one in twenty had opted out.

The 1993 Education Act had attempted to revitalise the policy of opting-out, by allowing groups of schools to opt out, and setting up a funding agency for them which was not under the control of the Department for Education. It failed. The New Labour government has shunned the grant-maintained experiment, but made use of the coercive powers the Conservatives took: the right to appoint commissioners to take over failing schools or education authorities. In 1997, after a critical report by OFSTED, the government appointed a board of commissioners to take control of education throughout the London borough of Hackney. Education secretary David Blunkett has threatened several local education authorities with a similar fate, and incurred the wrath of the teachers' unions by backing the transfer of a failing comprehensive in Guildford to a private company.

The Enabling Authority

New Labour ministers make no secret of their admiration for the private sector, or of their preference for efficiency over democracy. But their Conservative predecessors were genuinely surprised to be accused of centralising power in education and housing. They embarked on reform to transfer power from councillors and bureaucrats to parents and tenants. The aim was to turn voters and ratepayers into consumers of local authority services instead. 'What I wanted to get across to the people at Westminster was that the place could be run like a business – that there was no difference between ratepayers and shoppers,' recalled Dame Shirley Porter of her time as leader of Westminster City Council. 'They had to be given value for money.'[29]

During the 1980s, local government was re-defined as 'the enabling authority.' Its task was to assess local needs and decide whether a private company or voluntary organisation could supply a better or cheaper service than the council. Even where they decided to continue to supply the service themselves, local authorities were expected to use the threat of competition to coax economies out of their workforce. The aim was to force councils to concentrate on delivering the best quality services at the lowest possible price.

The democratic legitimacy of this approach was questionable. But the transformation it has wrought in the management of council assets and the delivery of local authority services is not. Since 1983, the Audit Commission has monitored local government for signs of waste, encouraging all councils to deliver services more efficiently. The obvious way forward was privatisation – the 'enabling authority' is more interested in setting standards than owning assets. There are many assets to sell: leisure and shopping centres, empty houses and inner city and industrial estates. Since the nationalisation of their water, gas and electricity businesses, local authorities have provided few services on a commercial basis, but history has endowed them with assets which can earn a return. When the Conservatives came to office there were forty-two municipally-owned airports and forty-eight local authority bus companies. The county councils also owned 427,000 acres of arable land, much of it in their possession since before the First World War.[30] Disposals, encouraged by a measure which allowed councils to spend the proceeds, have reduced the size of the county council smallholdings by 37,000 acres since 1979 and the privatisation of the bus industry has reduced the local authority share of the bus market to 6.2 per cent.[31] Landfill sites, waste management operations, cemeteries and a dozen local authority airports have all gone to private buyers.

Compulsory Competitive Tendering

But privatisation was never the main objective of the 'enabling authority'. The forcible transfer of services to private providers was far more significant than the sale of assets. The Local Government, Planning and Land Act of 1980 was the first to oblige councils to justify providing a service (construction and maintenance) directly. By inviting private companies to bid for the work, councils found they could cut costs. The contracting out of refuse collection was pioneered by Southend in 1981, and became compulsory in the Local Government Act of 1988, which extended compulsory competitive tendering (CCT) to street and office cleaning, the maintenance of grounds and vehicles and school catering. The management of leisure and sports services, arts facilities, public libraries, security and car parking, and even professional services such as legal and architectural work, were added.[32]

CCT has transformed the culture of local government. Gaily painted dustbin lorries, covered in the logos and catchphrases of the new class of private contractor, are the most outward sign of its impact. Sports centres are now run by private companies, who make them livelier and more commercial. Policing unlawful parking on behalf of councils has become a lucrative business. It was run by the police, with the fines going to central government, but from July 1994 councils were freed to police parking themselves and keep the profits provided they are spent on local transport. (A surreptitious form of local taxation New Labour has unfairly claimed as its own.) Private capital has even invaded one of the last redoubts of old-style local government: in 1998 the government announced a plan to link municipal libraries electronically, with private companies supplying the technology.

The field where CCT has made the least impact is the best advertisement for it. For many people, municipal parks and gardens are the most visible symptom of local government in action. They are rarely encouraging. The ornamental gates and railings torn down in the Second World War were not replaced. The lavish floral displays of Victorian times have given way to sweeps of utilitarian grass, which are cheaper to maintain. Once-proud bandstands are vandalised, unpainted and graffiti-stained. Upended dustbins, refuse, excrement and vagrants are ubiquitous. The level of drunkenness is a constant rebuke to the Temperance Societies which filled municipal parks with water fountains. The statues of Victorian worthies, often paid for by public subscription, stand ravaged and unloved. Few citizens dare to venture into their local park after dark. Councils chip away continually at the periphery, by approving new housing schemes and roads. Local authority park managers, if they exist at all, have limited budgets. Revenue is raised only by renting space to circuses, or football teams. Money goes into swimming pools and tennis courts instead. In 1997, the National Heritage Lottery Fund announced that £57 million would be spent on refurbishing run-down parks in towns and cities. This was the first substantial investment in parks since the Public Health Act of 1875 empowered councils to spend public funds to create them, but private management might do more to revive them by raising revenue and cutting the costs of maintenance.[33]

Evidence that CCT reduces the cost of other local authority services is unequivocal.[34] This is why it is unpopular with the public sector trade unions, whose members either lose their jobs or learn to perform them at a lower price. In the 1980s and early 1990s they bullied councillors into retaining direct labour forces, and colluded with town hall managers to frustrate private rivals. One stratagem was to package several contracts into one, reducing the number of firms capable of bidding. Another was to reshuffle money or functions to get budgets below the threshold at which a tender was compulsory. Bidders were denied information on staff levels and wage rates, buried in paper, or set impossible targets (like collecting 101 per cent of rents). Onerous conditions, like requiring the service to be provided from a particular site or diesel-driven vans, were imposed. Short-dated contracts, excessive penalty clauses, over-ambitious performance criteria, and the prospect of zealous monitoring, all proved effective deterrents.

In some cases, direct labour forces were allowed to make absurdly low bids in exchange for an agreement to make additional payments later. In others, unions wrote to prospective bidders warning them to keep away. But the most effective obstruction was to insist that private contractors retain the existing workforce on the same terms and conditions, preventing bidders from cutting costs. This ploy was assisted by the Transfer of Undertakings (Protection of Employment) Regulations, or TUPE, imposed by the European Union in 1981. Intended to apply to corporate takeovers only, the regulations created a major barrier to competitive tendering after a group of Eastbourne dustmen made redundant by the privatisation of the council cleaning contract in 1990 claimed successfully for unfair dismissal and loss of earnings. By 1996, the public sector unions had persuaded New Labour to promise to end CCT. 'We will get rid of Compulsory Competitive Tendering,' Frank Dobson told the Labour Party conference in October 1995. 'CCT has had its day . . . It's not efficiency. It's exploitation. It's rotten and it's wrong and we'll end it.'[35]

In government, New Labour has yet to abolish CCT. Instead, they announced a review of it. By October 1997, the new government was applying the old rules fiercely enough to force Devon council to re-tender a landscaping contract.[36] In July 1998 Donald Dewar, the secretary of state for Scotland, ordered two Scottish councils to close down their direct labour organisations and invite the private sector to bid for their jobs.[37] But the government has promised to replace CCT by a legal duty on councils to ensure Best Value. This is intended to focus minds on the *quality* of the services as well as their price, with costs measured by comparisons between councils rather than competition between contractors. Judging by the enthusiasm with which it was greeted by local government officials, public sector trade unions and private contractors, all three see Best Value as an opportunity to inflate costs. It is hard to believe that a proxy will be as effective as competition itself.

Farewell Tammany Hall?

New Labour hopes that Best Value will put an end to the antagonism between business and local government which CCT created. 'What matters is what works,' Tony Blair told councillors and local government officials in 1998. 'The form of service delivery should not be determined by ideology. Both public and private sectors have important roles to play.'[38] The prime minister wants the Councillor to dwell with the Fat Cat, and the Unison official to lie down with the manager from Onyx. It is a dangerous strategy. One of the least-recognised benefits of CCT is a reduction in the scope for municipal corruption. For decades, local government (particularly in the cities) was synonymous with graft. This was why the Nolan committee on standards in public life turned its attention, after Westminster, to local government.

Poorly paid council officials are vulnerable to bribes from suppliers, and prone to collaborate with contractors to over-charge the council. In Hackney in the 1980s, council officials kept housing benefit for themselves, rented empty council houses for personal gain and stole student grant cheques. The borough of Brent suffered similar losses from its housing benefit and student grant allocations. In 1997–98 the Audit Commission discovered fraud worth £89 million in English and Welsh local government alone.[39] The DSS and NAO reckon housing benefit fraud is currently running at around £1 billion a year.[40]

Wherever councillors are electorally unchallenged, corruption is a way of life. The budgets they control and the powers they exercise (especially planning permission) are a constant source of temptation. When T. Dan Smith was leader of Newcastle City Council in the 1960s he expected 'one quarter of one per cent' of any money that passed through the Town Hall. He was later jailed for six years after admitting receipt of £156,000 from John Poulson, the architect. Not much has changed since in the north of England, where local government is still largely the preserve of a single party. Links between councillors, officials and local businessmen have caused embarrassment to the government recently in Bassetlaw, Doncaster and Hull. But some of the worst problems are in Scotland, where Labour has ruled unchallenged for decades.

Three constituency Labour parties in Renfrewshire were shut down after *Scotland on Sunday* exposed a web of drug dealing, money lending and vote rigging centring in Paisley. Monklands District Council was tarnished by allegations of nepotism and sectarianism. In 1997, nine members of Glasgow city council were suspended by the Labour party amid allegations of cronyism and votes-for-holidays. A year later, accountants found the direct labour organisation at North Lanarkshire council had run up a deficit of nearly £5 million by systematic under-bidding for contracts. (It also emerged that a council plumber was on £54,000 a year.) Three officials were suspended. Similar problems were uncovered at East Ayrshire council.

Problems of this kind are a by-product of domination. In local government, parties tend to control councils for long periods, and rarely face strong or intelligent opposition. Contempt for procedures, council officials and opponents develops, making it harder to distinguish between public and party interests. Supporters and sympathisers are given sinecures. Even relatively minor posts are often filled according to political affiliation. Both Labour and Conservative councils have used public assets to improve their prospects of election or re-election. In February 1995 Jeff Rooker, MP for Perry Barr, alleged that around £2 million in housing renovation grants was being given to Labour supporters by Birmingham City Council in a bid to win parliamentary nominations. The Labour Party later suspended its constituency parties in Ladywood, Perry Barr, Small Heath and Sparkbrook.[41]

In the 1980s Conservative councillors, who have long dominated Westminster City Council, were central figures in an alleged gerrymandering scandal. It was said that council houses in marginal wards were sold to middle-class families to increase the Conservative vote. After an investigation by the District Auditor, Dame Shirley Porter (former leader) and David Weeks (her deputy) were surcharged over £27 million. After prolonged litigation, the Auditor's decision was overturned by the Court of Appeal.[42]

The Nolan Committee has recommended the abolition of surcharging councillors, and its replacement by a new offence of misuse of public office. This is one measure of the scale of the problems in local government. Yet the main threat to its integrity is not corruption, but incompetence. In the 1980s the Audit Commission estimated local authorities were wasting £1¼ billion a year on unwanted school places, under-used property, and rent arrears. Neither officials nor councillors knew how to manage assets efficiently. The declining power and prestige of local government has made it difficult to attract men and women of talent and ability to serve as local government officers or councillors, turning some councils into little more than job creation schemes and propaganda platforms for political extremists.

'I have not the slightest doubt that there is an extensive network of nepotism and fraud in Hackney Council,' Ken Livingstone told the *Observer* in May 1995. 'The leadership knew full well that as soon as they tried to investigate it they would be accused of racism. This is not unique in London: there are other cases where the same thing is happening.' At Lambeth council in the 1980s, services collapsed while councillors plotted revolution in the chamber. Construction and maintenance contracts, which were not always fulfilled, were awarded to supporters at inflated prices. Benefits were embezzled, rent and rates went uncollected, and even the telephones were cut off when the council failed to pay the bill.[43] When Lambeth set its poll tax for the first time in 1990 it was the highest in England. But few were willing to pay it after councillors themselves said they would rather go to jail. When the council advertised for a new chief executive in 1995, the position was described as 'arguably the worst job in local government.'

A decade earlier, running Liverpool City Council was harder still. In 1985, councillors refused to set a budget at all in protest at central government control of local authority spending. When the council ran out of money, it delivered redundancy notices to its thirty thousand staff by taxi. Forty-seven councillors were surcharged and banned from political office for five years. 'You start with far-fetched resolutions,' Neil Kinnock told the Labour Party conference in 1985, 'and you end in the grotesque chaos of a Labour council – a Labour council – hiring taxis to travel round a city handing out redundancy notices to its own workers.' But Kinnock was only partially right. The way the councillors ran the city was grotesque and chaotic, but it was also entirely rational. The Spartacists of Liverpool, like their enslaved Roman predecessors, had nothing to lose.

The Nationalisation of Local Government

The irresponsibility of the councillors of Liverpool and Lambeth in the 1980s was a reflection of their powerlessness. They acted on what every councillor knows: political and financial power is now concentrated at the centre. They realised that they could over-spend freely, raise the rates and run up mountainous debts without incurring any of the normal political consequences. If the rates went up, or services were cut, the government could always be blamed for failing to provide sufficient resources. They had re-discovered Poplarism.*

Like the Poplarism of the 1920s, the confrontation between central and local government in the 1980s was a contest over the power to spend. As tactic and propaganda, neo-Poplarism was a brilliant success. As a strategy, it was a total failure. The 'loony left' councillors who ran large cities and bor-

---

* In 1921 Poplar Borough Council had protested against the inequality of rates in rich and poor London boroughs by refusing to pay its share of the expenses of the London County Council. Thirty councillors went to prison, a martyrdom which multiplied the number of councils prepared to defy Whitehall and Westminster. More councillors were surcharged and imprisoned, and in July 1926 the local authorities at West Ham, Chester-le-Street and Bedwellty were superseded by central government commissioners. Two years later, the government abolished Boards of Guardians, which had paid higher rates of poor relief than Whitehall rules allowed.

oughs in the 1980s and early 1990s gave central government all the excuses
it needed to drain local government of its remaining autonomy. They drew the
government, through a series of expedients designed to curb local authority
expenditure, into a final confrontation over the power of councils to get and
spend. The dénouement was the battle over the Poll Tax – an error from
which neither central nor local government gained. Westminster was forced
to underwrite a massive step-change in local government spending, and local
government was forced to cede control of all but one seventh of its income.

Political autonomy depends on financial independence, and local government has now lost virtually all independent sources of income. In 1890 three
quarters of all current expenditure by local authorities was met from the
rates. By the 1930s this had shrunk to just half, and by the 1950s to less than
half. The proportion of local authority expenditure funded by central grant
rose accordingly.[44] There were two reasons for this, and both originated in
central government.

The first was the range of duties laid upon local authorities by central
government. At the turn of the century councils spent about £100 million,
or perhaps 5p in every £1 of public spending. By the Second World War,
they spent about 10p in the pound. Today, they spend over £77 billion, or
about 25p in every £1 spent by the state, which reflects the continual expansion of the range of duties local authorities must fulfil. They are far too broad
to be supported from local taxes.

The second reason for the loss of financial independence is the emasculation of the local tax system. Rates were neutered in the 1930s by the derating
of farms and the partial derating of factories.[45] This robbed local government
of £24 million a year, equivalent to one fifth of their income from rates. The
government also deprived councils of local excise duties (so-called 'whisky
money'), insisting these be passed to the Treasury in exchange for grants
from central funds.

These were the first general grants given to local authorities. Most government grant continued to be allocated by Whitehall for specific purposes.
(The unallocated portion of government grant rarely exceeded one tenth of
the whole, so the freedom of action of councils to spend their income as
they saw fit shrank commensurately.)

But even general grants were irksome, in that they gave central government
a powerful influence over policies and programmes which were ostensibly
independent. From 1948 the government tried to concentrate the grant on
the neediest areas, with Whitehall devising increasingly complex formulae to
decide which councils needed the most money. Whitehall and Town Hall
became locked in a game of bluff, in which councils sought to be needier-
than-thou.

Councillors grew careless over spending, confident that they could persuade Whitehall to pay. The local government reforms of 1974 sparked an orgy of spending by town halls, conveniently attributed to the costs of the Whitehall-imposed reorganisation. There were rate rises of up to 30 per cent in 1974–5. In May 1975, the secretary of state for the Environment, Tony Crosland, had to warn local government that 'the party is over.' For the next three years, councils opted for discretion. Current spending remained roughly unchanged.

By the time Margaret Thatcher took office in 1979, the elements of the crisis to come were in place. Government grants were determined by a system which was bizarre, unpopular and unfair. Councillors had learned that they could overspend and overtax without risking defeat, by blaming government 'cuts' for their troubles. But Thatcher was determined to cut public spending, and local government was expected to bear its share. It was, said the new secretary of state for the Environment, Michael Heseltine, 'closing time'.

In the Local Government Planning and Land Act of 1980, the government took powers to determine the overall spending of local authorities. Authorities which spent in excess of their 'true needs' (as determined by government) received less money than those which showed restraint. This was described at the time by the chairman of the Association of Metropolitan Authorities as 'the biggest threat to the constitutional independence of local government in this country since the 19th century'.[46] The main effect of the Act was an explosion of supplementary rates, which devastated Conservative support in the local elections of 1980 and 1981. This shocked the government into action; in 1982, the right to set a supplementary rate was abolished.

Predictably, ordinary rates went up instead. This led in 1984 to the introduction of selective 'rate-capping' by central government. Rate-capping encouraged 'responsible' councils to spend right up to the government-imposed ceiling, while 'irresponsible' councils (such as Liverpool and Lambeth) either refused to set a budget at all or set one they knew would be 'rate-capped'. Prominent councillors – Derek Hatton of Liverpool City Council and 'Red Ted' Knight of Lambeth – were surcharged and disqualified from office. Further expedients were sought. In April 1986 the Greater London Council, which had raised a supplementary rate to subsidise fares on London Transport, was abolished (along with the other metropolitan counties).

Like Henry II, ministers had lost patience. They wanted a final solution to the problem of overspending by local authorities. They selected the Poll Tax. This was a flat-rate tax paid by every adult over the age of eighteen, alleviated only by rebates for the poor. It would cover all local spending not funded by central government grant or the uniform business rate (which was centralised simultaneously.)[47] In theory, by denying local authorities any subsidy from the business rates and imposing a personal tax linked directly to the cost of services, the Poll Tax would expose profligate councillors to the fury of the voters.

This, it was thought, would solve the problem of over-spending. 'Many people had no direct reason to be concerned about their council's overspending, because somebody else picked up all or most of the bill,' wrote Thatcher in her memoirs. 'This lack of accountability lay behind the continued over-spending.'[48] It was true that only half of local electors were liable to pay rates, and a third of them spending only partial rates or no rates at all. The household rate itself was subsidised by the business rate. But the reason the government thought the Poll Tax would succeed was precisely the reason it was bound to fail: many people had to pay a significant amount in local tax for the first time.

The anticipated reconnection of local spending to local votes failed to materialise. The Poll Tax provoked widespread non-payment and riots in many parts of the country. Councils greeted its introduction as a heaven-sent opportunity for a second orgy of spending, which could once again be blamed on the costs of reorganisation. Because it was levied at a flat rate, rather than on the ability to pay, the tax was easily portrayed as unfair. 'The Poll Tax was a flat rate tax,' wrote an organiser of the campaign against it. 'It was not based on ability to pay. Everyone over eighteen was liable. Rich and poor paid the same. The millionaire paid the same as the toilet attendant. The lawyer paid the same as the shop assistant. The prime minister Margaret Thatcher and her multi-millionaire husband paid the same as their gardener.'[49]

By the summer of 1990 the fiasco had forced the government to complete the centralisation of local authority financing, through blanket capping of poll taxes, and heavier use of central government grants to reduce the burden on those least able to pay. In the 1991 budget VAT was increased to 17.5 per cent to fund a £4.5 billion subsidy to local authorities. The Poll Tax was abolished and replaced by a council tax. This effectively restored the rates, after a property revaluation of the kind the Poll Tax was chosen to avert. In the legislation introducing the council tax, the secretary of state took powers to vary at will both the valuation bands and the amount of tax payable.[50]

The Poll Tax is now history, but its effects live on. Local government emerged from the débâcle more dependent on central government than ever before. The new government promised to abolish capping but has so far retained it. A plan to make the council tax more progressive by introducing higher and lower rate bands was dropped.[51] The business rate is still centralised. Ministers have begun to fret that the council tax is unfair, but their long-term solution to local government finance bears a worrying resemblance to the administrative machinations which led to the poll tax: they think annual elections will free them of the need to cap local government budgets.

Reforming Local Government: The Council as PLC?

Annual elections would be just another device to stop local authorities spending more than the government decides. Without a radical redistribution of duties or taxation, the problem at the heart of the troubled relations between central and local government (separating the power to decide from the power to tax) is insoluble. John Banham denounced the system of central funding and local spending as 'the worst of all worlds: most of the costs associated with centrally managed economies but few of the potential benefits'.[52] The centre lacks knowledge, while the periphery lacks means.

The hardest answer to the conundrum is to bring means into line with duties, for that was the ambition of the Poll Tax. 'The Community Charge offered a last chance of responsible, efficient, local democracy in Britain,' wrote Margaret Thatcher in her memoirs. 'Its abandonment will mean that more and more powers will pass to central government, that upward pressures on public spending and taxation will increase accordingly, and that still fewer people of ability will become local councillors.'[53] Perhaps a viable local tax base can be regained by some new mixture of property, business, indirect and income taxes levied at the local level. Unfortunately, the poll tax debacle has shifted the rejuvenation of the local tax base off the agenda of central government for a generation.

In truth, it is more likely that duties will be brought into line with means than means brought will be brought into line with duties. This approach was advocated by Nigel Lawson during his chancellorship in the 1980s, when he favoured centralising educational expenditure as the best way of bringing local responsibilities into line with local taxes. Until it happens, local government will continue to shrivel up. The calibre of councillor has declined for decades. 'Many councils tend to be dominated by a mixture of the retired or unemployed, small businessmen or trade unionists, plus in rural areas, farmers and landowners. It has not made for dynamic district councils,' writes one observer of the local government scene in Scotland.[54] It is no better in England or Wales. 'In a borough council now you might have only three or four councillors of talent and that isn't enough,' says Ken Livingstone, the former leader of the Greater London Council. 'Good councillors and officers have been driven out of local government.'[55] The government is openly concerned about the quality of local leadership, and hopes to raise it by encouraging councils to replace the committee system with cabinet-style 'ministers' led by an executive mayor.

It is difficult to be optimistic. After all, there is nothing to stop councils adopting executive mayors and cabinet government already. A Department of the Environment consultation paper first advocated directly elected mayors and a cabinet system as long ago as 1991. Simon Jenkins, the former editor of *The Times*, chaired a Commission for Local Democracy which endorsed the idea in 1995. A year later, a House of Lords report recommended legislation to encourage local authorities to experiment with new methods of decision-making. It was not until 1997, after a government-sponsored private member's bill failed, that Westminster promised to give elected mayors and cabinet-style government legislative impetus.

The need for legislative coercion is significant. Most councillors dislike the idea of abandoning the committee system. When the department of the Environment consulted local authorities on the idea of directly elected mayors in the early 1990s, not a single county, district, London or metropolitan borough council was in favour. 'Local government,' explained the then local government minister, David Curry, 'was much more interested in the structure of committees. It was more interested, perhaps, in some form of cabinet system for local government. It was also more interested in the idea of a council manager. It was especially interested, perhaps, in some form of cabinet system for local government. It was also more interested in the idea of a council manager. It was especially interested in councillors' allowances. It was not particularly interested in locally elected mayors.'

The modern council, unlike its Victorian predecessors, is not a forum for social and political experiment. Its members are resistant to new ideas and bogged down in the conservatism of the parish pump. The main reason for this is the law of triviality. Robbed of meaningful choices and the resources to implement them, councillors find political infighting and procedural wrangling in committee more congenial than executive action. Without a fundamental change in the nature of spending and revenue in local government, elected mayors would simply add another layer of complexity. The possibilities of deadlock between the salaried executive (mayor and cabinet) and the unsalaried legislative (councillors) arms of local government are infinite, especially if the mayor is not a member of the majority party.

A separation of the decision-making power from the representational function in local government is a characteristically Blairite prescription. It is drawn not from Montesquieu (author of the separation of executive and legislative power) but from the world of business. Its watchword is efficiency, not democracy. The council chamber is the boardroom; the mayor is the chief executive; and the members of the cabinet are the directors. In 1998, on publication of the Green Paper, *Modernising Local Government: Local Democracy and Community Leadership*, Blair told councillors flatly, 'If you're unwilling or unable to work to a modern agenda, the government will have to look to other partners to take on your role.'[56]

New Labour would like to see businessmen as heavily involved in local government as they are at the national level. Pilot projects, where councillors co-operate with business in procurement and staff training, are under way already. Private companies are running local schools. Twenty-five 'education action zones,' funded by business sponsorship and led by leading local businessmen, were operating by the beginning of 1999. Companies now sponsor street furniture and 'business improvement districts.' Ministers have considered allowing unelected businessmen to serve on council committees.[57] Labour-controlled Warrington Council has joined the Confederation of British Industry.

It is not hard to see why councils are keen to get close to business. The major PLCs are now the main source of wealth in Britain, and councils crave the investment, subsidies and jobs they can bring. But a willingness to entreat with business reflects the change in their personality. Eighteen years of ever-tighter financial control by Whitehall, growing familiarity with PLC-style quangos, and a new emphasis on efficiency rather than democracy, has made councils less like mini-Westminsters and more like the far-flung subsidiaries of a giant multinational. Local government entered the twentieth century as the pioneer of the welfare state. It leaves it as the copycat of the PLC.

PART THREE

PEOPLE

CHAPTER FOURTEEN

THE RICH

Wealth, as Mr Hobbes says, is power. But the person who either acquires, or succeeds to a great fortune, does not necessarily acquire or succeed to any political power, either civil or military. His fortune may, perhaps, afford him the means of acquiring both, but the mere possession of that fortune does not necessarily convey to him either. The power which that possession immediately and directly conveys to him, is the power of purchasing.

ADAM SMITH, 1776[1]

Of all classes, the rich are the most noticed and the least studied.

J. K. GALBRAITH, 1977[2]

My only mistake was in not holding Polly Peck Shares for ever and ever.

NIGEL WRAY, 1990[3]

It was very prettily said, that we may learn the little value of fortune by the persons on whom heaven is pleased to bestow it.

SIR RICHARD STEELE, 1710[4]

The richest 200 people in Britain probably own £1 in every £50 of the wealth of the nation. It is hard to be exact. Most rich people, as Paul Getty and Nelson Bunker Hunt have pointed out, have so much money that they do not know what they are worth.[5] A satisfactory definition of serious wealth is equally elusive. The self-appointed arbiter of these matters, the *Sunday Times Magazine*, has set its threshold below £20 million and as high as £50 million. One glib definition of a rich man is anybody who can sign a cheque for £100,000 without asking anyone else.[6]

It is clear only that the billion, or at least the tens of millions, has replaced the million as the true measure of wealth. In industry, and especially in the City, multi-million pound salaries, bonuses and golden handshakes are now commonplace. If the Inland Revenue is right in thinking that there are 42,000 people worth at least a million pounds living in the United Kingdom, roughly one in every thousand adults in the country is a millionaire.[7] Millionaires may not be ten a penny, but they are a penny a tenner.

Secrets of the Rich

The proliferation of millionaires is a measure of the falling value of money. It is also a measure of the unprecedented sums generated by a mature industrial economy. Not even the *Sunday Times* pretends its figures are accurate to the tenth digit, but the estimates by the newspaper are the best-informed and most comprehensive an outsider has made. Since even the Inland Revenue relies on them to some extent, they are unlikely to be bettered. This is because most rich people, like most ordinary people, work hard to keep their financial affairs a secret. Among British plutocrats, only a handful show their personal accounts, presumably because it is advantageous. It is said that Donald Trump persuaded *Forbes* magazine to grant him billionaire status because it made it easier to borrow money.

Rich people have every incentive to hide their wealth. Since the Second World War, governments have expropriated the rich by taxation, nationalisation and inflation. Taxation has created a handsome living for lawyers and accountants whose *raison d'être* is to keep the rich and their fortunes secret and together. The Vesteys, whose intricate tax avoidance schemes were the subject of a sensational exposé by the *Sunday Times* in 1980, began to organise their assets to minimise taxation as soon as death duties were introduced in the 1890s. As early as 1915, they shifted ownership of their operations abroad to escape the special wartime tax levied on overseas earnings. The scheme marked the beginning of a century-long battle by rich people to protect their wealth from the Inland Revenue.[8] As soon as one tax loophole was closed, others were found, which is why the Inland Revenue has persuaded the government to pass a general law against tax avoidance.

It is the variety of trust funds, private companies, offshore holdings, changes of residence and other legitimate tax avoidance schemes which make it impossible to calculate the wealth of the rich with any exactness. As tax planning has grown more sophisticated, probate figures have become a progressively less valuable guide to personal wealth. Even the *Sunday Times* cannot get at cash in the bank, or private equity portfolios. Important assets, like pensions, are impossible to identify and value. Shareholdings below 3 per cent of the issued capital of a company do not have to be declared, and may be further hidden in a nominee account. The value of a shareholding in a

TABLE 14.1
The Richest People in Britain in 1998

Name	Origin of Wealth	(£m)
Lord Sainsbury	Retailing	3,300
Hans Rausing	Food packaging	2,800
Lakshmi Mittal	Steel	2,000
Joseph Lewis	Finance	1,750
Duke of Westminster	Inheritance	1,750
Bernie Ecclestone	Motor racing	1,500
Garfield Weston	Food manufacturing	1,500
Sir Anthony Bamford	JCBs	1,300
Bruno Schroder	Banking	1,300
Sir Adrian Swire	Shipping	1,300
Mohamed al Fayed	Retailing	1,200
Sri Hinduja	Trading & finance	1,200
Tony O'Reilly	Food & inheritance	1,100
Richard Branson	Entertainment	1,000
Lady Grantchester	Pools & retailing	1,000
Viscount Rothermere	Newspapers	1,000
Robert Miller	Retailing	975
David Bromilow	Sports goods	800
Robin Fleming	Banking	770
Earl Cadogan	Inheritance	725
David & Frederick Barclay	Hotels & property	650
Earl of Iveagh	Brewing	650
Ken Morrison	Retailing	650
Lord Vestey	Food	650
Jack Walker	Steel	600
Brian Souter	Buses	560
Viscount Cowdray	Construction & oil	500
Sir Evelyn Rothschild	Banking	500
Gert-Rudolph Flick	Motor manufacturing	500
Bernard Lewis	Retailing	500

Source: The *Sunday Times* Rich List, 1998.

private company is notoriously hard to gauge; it is slightly less difficult to assess works of art, jewellery, land and buildings. Nor is it easy to calculate the present value of future earnings.

Does Money Mean Power?

Some find the lack of information worrying. 'A society where power is money and money is secret, is a society in which power is unaccountable and irresponsible,' wrote Nicholas von Hoffman.[9] This is an exaggeration. The power to spend, as Adam Smith pointed out, is difficult to translate into the power to rule.[10] The so-called nabobs, East India Company officials who pillaged India in the mid-eighteenth century, used their fortunes to obtain political influence. But their reputations worked against them. In late Victorian times, 60 out of 200 known millionaires were MPs, and a private fortune was the foundation of many a successful political career, like those of Robert Peel and William Gladstone.[11] But few were *nouveaux-riches*, and even fewer succeeded in the first generation. By the end of the nineteenth century, most rich men had to settle for a peerage.[12]

Not much has changed. Mohamed al Fayed has proved that MPs can be bought, but ministers deny him citizenship still. Both Octav Botnar (see footnote p. 542) and Asil Nadir found their generous support of the Conservative Party counted for nothing when their troubles began. Over the years the Labour Party has enjoyed the financial favours of Lord Kagan, Robert Maxwell and Owen Oyston and gave them nothing except one peerage. The alteration of policy on tobacco advertising by the New Labour government, following a donation of £1 million from the motor-racing entrepreneur Bernie Ecclestone, looked like a clear case of government-for-sale, but the Labour Party was sufficiently embarrassed to return the money (if not to reverse the policy). In Britain, the anti-Brussels duo, Sir James Goldsmith and Paul Sykes, discovered that great wealth can buy a man the time to indulge his political opinions, but not much else. Few of the modern rich pursue political careers: they lack the appetite for high levels of personal disclosure. Modern parliamentary life, in the words of former Conservative minister George Walden, is best suited to an impecunious eunuch.

In economic terms, the *power* of the mega-rich is equally diluted. Even a billionaire counts for little in a large and institutionalised economy such as Britain today. James Goldsmith understood this. '[Individual wealth] will never be as powerful as it was in the nineteenth century, nor should it be,' he told Anthony Sampson in 1989. 'It will always be a marginal personal thing compared to the major power of the State.'[13] Every year, the state spends one hundred times as much as the richest man in Britain, and beyond the state lie the hundreds of billions of pounds of institutionalised money controlled by the pension funds and multinational corporations. They are too large for any one man to have the whiphand. At the turn of the century a single fortune of £10–20 million, like those accumulated in South Africa by Alfred Beit or Julius Wernher, was equivalent to one hundredth of the total national income. Today, it is equivalent to one forty thousandth – or one two thousandth of the turnover of a large multinational.

Nabobs and the Old Corruption

The power of the rich has waned even as their fortunes have waxed. In the eighteenth and nineteenth centuries, half a million pounds was sufficient to place a man among the richest in the country. In 1688 Gregory King reckoned the great aristocratic landowners were the richest of all; they enjoyed an average income of £2,800 a year, a little more than £200,000 in modern money. It was not until the middle of the eighteenth century that tobacco barons, slave traders and owners, merchants, manufacturers and financiers began to accumulate business fortunes. But even the fabulously rich Hanoverian financier and government contractor, Sampson Gideon, left only £500,000. Josiah Wedgwood, the pottery magnate, left the same in 1795, and Sir Robert Peel, father of the prime minister, £1.5 million in 1830. Nathan Meyer Rothschild, by common consent the richest man on earth at his death in 1836, left £5 million.

The earliest banks and industrial companies were too small-scale to generate the gigantic fortunes they yield today. Men made more by plundering India. Robert Clive, who departed for the sub-continent a penniless clerk, returned in 1760 with £317,000 in precious stones and securities. He left behind landed rents worth £27,000 a year. On his return to Bengal in 1765, ostensibly to root out corruption, he picked up another £165,000. Other nabobs did almost as well. James Johnstone returned to Scotland with £300,000, and Richard Smith and Sir Thomas Rumbold extracted at least £200,000 apiece from land-grabs, loan-sharking, jewels, and various rake-offs from military contracts. In 1772 a committee of the House of Commons listed over £2 million taken in 'presents' by the British in Bengal in the eight years after the Battle at Plassey. Accused in Parliament of enriching himself, Clive replied that, in view of the booty available, he had acted with commendable restraint. 'By God, Mr Chairman,' he said, 'at this moment I stand astounded at my own moderation!'[14]

The other source of wealth in pre-industrial Britain was the network of pensions, sinecures and gratuitous emoluments known to the Victorians as the Old Corruption. Jobs in the Church of England, the armed forces, the law and public administration were used routinely by governments, to bribe, buy, reward or silence relatives, enemies and supporters. Walpole secured posts in the Exchequer for his sons worth £13,400 a year.[15] Such jobs yielded perquisites in bribes and commission payments from government contractors, and the opportunity for a turn on the sums of money passing through the public purse. Any of the top jobs in eighteenth-century government was worth £6–9,000 a year to its holder, even after expenses.

One in ten of the half-millionaires in the early decades of the nineteenth century (millionaires were rare) were beneficiaries of Old Corruption.[16] One of the best-known is John Scott, 1st Earl of Eldon and lord chancellor for twenty-five years until his death in 1838. The son of a Newcastle coal merchant, he bequeathed a fortune of £707,000. Alexander Adair, an army agent, left £700,000 in 1834. Lord Arden, brother of the assassinated prime minister, Spencer Perceval, and registrar of the Court of Admiralty for fifty years, was worth the same amount in 1840.[17] The Duke of Wellington, younger son of an impecunious Irish Earl, amassed over £600,000 from parliamentary and foreign grants by his death in 1852. These sums are all equivalent to over £25 million today. It is probable that the first millionaire in British history was not an aristocrat, banker, merchant or manufacturer, but an obscure Archbishop of Canterbury, John Moore. Skilful exploitation of Church posts and archiepiscopal estates meant he left £1 million in 1805.

Decline of Aristocracy, Rise of Plutocracy

The everyday millionaire is the product of a mature industrial civilisation. Landowners remained richer than financiers and industrialists until the long agricultural depression of the late nineteenth century. Rubinstein reckons that until 1880 at least half of the wealthiest people in Britain were land-owners.[18] The first self-made industrial millionaires, such as Charles Morrison and Henry O. Wills, died between 1899 and 1912. They were symptomatic of a decisive shift in wealth and power from country to town, land to money, and aristocracy to plutocracy. There was an absolute and relative decline in the value of land as a proportion of the national wealth during these years, from one quarter to less than one twelfth. The value of farmland fell further and faster still, while the growth of cities and industry increased that of urban and suburban land. The value of financial assets (owned mainly by businessmen) went up three to fourfold while land values halved.[19]

British business did not pioneer the billionaire.[20] The first were American, partly because every £1 was then worth nearly $5, but also because no British plutocrat could match a Mellon or Rockefeller. When J. P. Morgan died in 1914, worth over $100 million, John D. Rockefeller is reputed to have said, 'To think that he wasn't even a rich man'. Rockefeller, like Henry Ford and

Andrew Mellon, was by then a dollar billionaire. Vanderbilt, Astor, Duke and Carnegie all had fortunes measured in hundreds of millions of dollars, an unprecedented phenomenon in world history – large enough to alter the ethics of money-getting. The Robber Barons, as they were known, ascribed their wealth to the Darwinian ideas then achieving popular currency: competition, capitalism and (even) monopoly were proclaimed the 'survival of the fittest'. By eliminating their competitors, the billionaires proved that they were best fitted to their environment.

Sir James Goldsmith was fond of evolutionary metaphors for his success. But his tools, of money, and securities, are the inventions of men. As wealth shifted from land to money, the aristocrat (rooted to his ancestral acres and providing work for those who lived on them) gave way to the plutocrat (whose property is impersonal and highly mobile). The Vesteys made a fortune from shipping cheap food to the great industrial cities and, by buying up the aristocratic estates they had helped to ruin, used their money to mock the old order. William Vestey bought a peerage from Lloyd George for £25,000; a year later his son bought Stowell Park in Gloucestershire from an impoverished Lord Eldon, heir of the chief beneficiary of the Old Corruption.

It was an apt measure of the shift from old money to new. By the 1920s, the translation of commercial wealth into acres and titles was a well-established path to social prestige. Warren Hastings used his Indian winnings to refurbish the family estate at Daylesford, and Francis Sykes built Basildon Park in Berkshire. Peerages for rich industrialists did not, however, become commonplace until the close of the nineteenth century, when the brewers Henry Allsop (Lord Hindlip, 1880), Arthur Guinness (Lord Ardilaun, 1880) and Michael Bass (Lord Burton, 1886) became known as 'the beerage'.

The newly enriched appointed peers to the boards of their companies and took up aristocratic pursuits. (On the turf, the pools millionaire Robert Sangster now fills the role played by the Earls of Derby.) Some famous matrimonial alliances were contracted between blue blood and new money, especially of the American variety. Blenheim was restored with the railway stock Consuelo Vanderbilt brought to the Duke of Marlborough. Curzon needed two American wives to finance his estates and his political career. Between 1870 and 1914 over one hundred peers contracted marriages with American money.[21] But they took British money too. A niece of the Duke of Wellington married a Hull shipping magnate, Charles Wilson.[22] In the 1980s it was regarded as perfectly normal when the Marquis of Milford Haven married the daughter of a wealthy pugilist turned property developer.

The admission of great business fortunes to the ranks of the aristocracy is often portrayed as a triumph of aristocratic values, or as a merger of aristocracy with plutocracy. Yet few businessmen purchased landed estates of a size commensurate with their wealth. Most preferred a garden to an estate, and to keep their money in cash or securities. The popular belief that the *nouveaux riches* ape the life of their social superiors is a myth; business fortunes overthrew aristocratic conceptions of social status. In the aristocratic age, wealth, power and social status were virtually synonymous. Gladstone made the Marquess of Westminster a Duke because he was too rich to be anything else. Marlborough, Wellington and Haig were given the money to match their hereditary titles. But, in the twentieth century, money has acquired a status of its own.

Rise of Celebritocracy

The upper classes used to pretend that the pursuit of wealth for its own sake was an obsession exclusive to Jews.* The overwhelming majority of rich people in Britain, Harold Macmillan said, were 'Jews and Armenians'. Many of the great banking families – Rothschild, Goldsmid, Montagu and Samuel (and, later, Warburg) – were Jews. A second generation of retailing millionaires (Wolfson, Marks, Sieff, Cohen and Burton) sprang from the nineteenth-century influx fleeing persecution in Russia and Poland, and over two thirds of the 110 property millionaires identified by Oliver Marriott in 1967 were Jewish.[24]

Stephen Aris, in *The Jews in Business*, concluded there was no definitive explanation for the success of the Jews. The only specific traits he identified were a spirit of inquiry and a love of money (as a means to purchase prestige, usually through charity).[25] Otherwise, Jews shared with all immigrants the need to escape poverty, reliance on family and communal life, and a desire for financial independence in the face of repeated persecution. ('We have', John Cohen of Tesco said to Aris, 'to take up our bundle and run.') Asians, who have enjoyed a comparable degree of material success in Britain, share these traits. They sometimes ascribe their success to 'family loyalty'. Like Jews, exclusion from orthodox pursuits probably forced many Asians to go into business, but generalisation is facile: Jews and Asians are as omnipresent in the professions as in business.

But their success in business is undeniable. Jews loom disproportionately

---

* Or Non-Conformists. A lengthy controversy in economic history is the contribution of non-conformity to the Industrial Revolution. In Britain, its contribution was certainly significant. Dissenters were driven into money-making occupations by their exclusion from the professions, the universities, and Old Corruption. Protestantism is also a valuable source of economic virtue. Its rationality, diligence, appetite for work and respect for science and order is ideally suited to the process of industrialisation.[23]

large in any list of the richest in terms of their share of the population as a whole. The same is true of Asians. There are only 850,000 people of Asian origin in Britain, but they have produced dozens of millionaires. In 1997 *Eastern Eye* magazine identified 100 Asian millionaires in Britain, worth a collective £5 billion. The 1998 *Sunday Times Magazine* list of the rich included 43 Asian millionaires worth more than £20 million each. Many are from the Indian sub-continent – some heirs to established business empires; others were born in Britain. A fair number, like Manubhai Madvani (£150 million from industry) and Jasminder Singh (£150 million from hotels), were victims of the Kenyan and Ugandan persecutions.

But most rich people in Britain are neither Jewish nor Asian, and never were. The English majority, from the early Middle Ages, was as individualistic and capitalist-minded as any immigrant group.[26] The Scots minority could be said to have invented the Industrial Revolution. An enthusiasm for industry saved the Welsh, another minority, from the mass emigration which retarded the Irish economy for so long. Today, all four nationalities appear regularly in the *Sunday Times* lists. It is not surprising. Though historians and commentators have long blamed the failures of the British economy on a cultural hostility to the creation of wealth, everybody living in the United Kingdom has long shown an exaggerated respect for money-getting.

This is particularly true of the English. Journalists who quote Bagehot on the contradiction between money and status in England ('There is no country where "a poor devil of a millionaire is so ill off as in England." The experiment is tried every day, and every day it is proved that money alone – money *pur et simple* – will not buy "London Society"') tend to omit the opening sentences of the paragraph. There, Bagehot describes money as 'the obvious and natural idol of the Anglo-Saxon. He is always trying to make money; he reckons everything in coin; he bows down before a great heap and sneers as he passes a little heap. And within good limits the feeling is quite right. So long as we play the game of industry vigorously and eagerly . . . we shall of necessity respect and admire those who play successfully, and a little despise those who play unsuccessfully.'[27]

Great Landowners of Britain and Ireland, the popularisation of the official census of landowners, was issued ten years after Bagehot first published *The English Constitution* in 1867.[28] With its detailed accounts of the rent-rolls of the Anglo-Irish aristocracy, the book was a roaring success. The first survey of the commercial rich, *Fortunes Made in Business*, was published in 1883. The works of Samuel Smiles – *Self Help* (1859), *Lives of the Engineers* (1861–2), *Character* (1871) and *Thrift* (1875) – were not just bourgeois homilies; they were popular expositions of how to get rich, and sold in prodigious quantities.

British newspapers discovered the sales value of producing lists of the rich long before the *Sunday Times* published its first in 1989. The *Financial Times* ran a series on British millionaires in 1897. Unlike contemporary American journalism of the same kind (the *New York Tribune* distributed a list of 4,000 millionaires in 1892 and the *New York World* compiled an 'almanac' of millionaires in 1902) it was driven by prurience rather than public interest. American newspapers fretted about oligopoly and protectionism, but the British interest in wealth was purely salacious. The first *Sunday Times* list of the rich, consciously based on the *Forbes* and *Fortune* lists published in the United States, reflected the hostility of its editor towards the aristocratic, public school and Oxbridge Establishment he thought was running the country.* But its chief ambition was to sell newspapers.

Money, like sex, sells newspapers. The two are now often combined: even serious newspapers cover the sexual antics of a celebritocracy which draws no distinction between aristocrat and plutocrat. Newspapers cover the lives of dukes and marquesses in the same way they chronicle the lives and loves of millionaires, actresses, rock stars, sportsmen and television presenters. It is no longer quaint to find that James Hanson dated Audrey Hepburn, or that the daughter of James Goldsmith has married a Pakistani cricketer, or that Tony O'Reilly has married a Goulandris. Celebrities move in the same circles, doing much the same things. Wealth provides as sure an entry to the pages of *Hello!* as a title, Hollywood success, or an eye for a moving ball. The celebritocracy, like the aristocracy before them, are beyond parody; their purpose is to be prodigal, of both time and money.

The celebritocracy is not new. George Hudson rose from York draper to railway king and reigned as the toast of London society until he went spectacularly bankrupt in 1854. *The Theory of the Leisure Class*, in which Veblen dissects the social behaviour of the idle rich of the east coast of the United States, was published before the turn of the century. He took from Adam Smith the observation that 'the chief enjoyment of riches consists in the parade of riches' and turned it into a soundbite: conspicuous consumption. The early American millionaires turned money into social prestige by ostentatious displays of wealth. The massive houses and yachts, lavish parties, fast cars, visits to the casino, Scottish estates and regular appearances in the gossip columns of the modern British rich are the bathetic echo of Vanderbilt and Rockefeller.

Such trivial pursuits and banal pleasures do nothing to legitimise their

---

* *Fortune* published its first list of the rich in 1957. The *Forbes 400* list was started by Malcolm Forbes in 1982, but his father had published a list in 1918 with the headline 'America's Thirty Richest Own $3,686,000,000 – Rockefeller Heads List With $1,200,000,000.' Nicholas von Hoffman, *Capitalist Fools*, pp. 261–2.

existence, though it is hard to imagine what tabloid newspapers would do without them. Paradoxically, most of their readers are envious of the rich, or dislike them intensely. When *New Society* magazine conducted a poll on attitudes to the rich, they found that seven out of ten people thought the gap between rich and poor was too wide, two in five believed they owed their wealth to inheritance not effort; and a large majority was sure the rich were power-hungry, ruthless, snobbish and greedy. Less than one in five thought they created jobs or prosperity, and there was a two to one majority for redistribution from rich to poor. Yet over half the respondents also thought the rich were entitled to be rich.[29] The obverse of a low view of the rich is the realisation that anybody can be rich. Or can they?

Importance of Inherited Wealth

There are many ways to get rich; most of them are ordinary. Abstinence is not one of them. There is no British equivalent of the retired American tax clerk Anne Schreiber, who in half a century of frugal living converted her $5,000 nest-egg into a $22 million fortune by buying blue chip stocks and waiting fifty years.[30] It is harder to become rich by working and saving money than her example suggests. The power of compound interest is proverbially immense but, according to one estimate, it would take a person earning three times the national average wage his entire working life to assemble a capital sum equivalent to one hundred times his annual income even if he saved a quarter of it every year.[31]

Inheritance is a surer way to get rich, not least because it is easier to make money if you already have some. 'Broadly speaking,' writes Britain's premier historian of personal wealth, 'the most important qualification for achieving millionaire status in Britain has been to have had a wealthy father.'[32] In a detailed study of the period from 1809 to 1939, he found only fifteen truly self-made millionaires. They included the shipping magnate, Sir John Ellerman, who left £36.7 million, the Sainsburys (supermarkets) and the Flemings (merchant banking). When the *Sunday Times* published its first list in 1989, Andrew Neil was appalled to find that over half the people on it had inherited their money: a quarter were landowners rather than businessmen (they included 11 dukes, 6 marquesses and 14 earls). A decade on, Neil would be more encouraged. The number of self-made rich in the list overtook the inheritors in 1993, and have since increased to between two thirds and three quarters. Probably one British millionaire in three inherited his present fortune.[33]

Surprisingly few rich men start off with nothing. Lord Leverhulme, the founder of Lever Brothers, was lent £58,000 by his father; Sir Charles Tennant parlayed a £76,000 inheritance into a £3 million chemicals fortune; even Sir John Ellerman was left £600 by his father. Felix Fenston started his property empire in the 1940s with his demobilisation allowance; Jack Cotton set up in business with a £50 loan from his mother; Michael Heseltine left Oxford with a cheque for £1,000 from his maternal grandfather. Even a lost inheritance can have beneficial effects. Nigel Broackes inherited £25,000 from his grandfather, which he contrived to lose in a series of ill-conceived investments. This forced him to join a firm of estate agents, where he discovered the art of property development.

TABLE 14.2
Number of Self-Made Millionaires
Sunday Times, 1989–98

	Number	*% of Total*
1989	86	43
1990	96	48
1991	98	49
1992	145	48
1993	218	54.5
1994	360	72
1995	321	64.2
1996	323	64.6
1997	350	70.0
1998	656	65.6

Source: The *Sunday Times* Rich Lists, 1989–1998. The number of people listed increased from 200 in 1989 to 500 in 1994 and 1,000 in 1998.

Inheritance is a major determinant of subsequent financial success, which is one reason egalitarian tax systems seek to eliminate it. Inheritance tax is now payable at 40 per cent on £223,000 or more. Though the opportunities to avoid it have narrowed, the tax raises just £1.25 billion a year; the average rate of tax on personal estates is low.[34] For the rich, inheritance tax is voluntary, in that they can move abroad or make other arrangements to protect their assets. They are also able to give away their wealth to their families and friends well in advance of their demise. (The tax on alienated assets declines with each passing year; nothing is payable after seven years.) There are useful allowances for business and agricultural assets, and the risk of premature death can be covered in the insurance markets.

The one group of rich people who have found it hard to escape death duties is the aristocracy. Landed wealth traps them in their own country, and cannot be exported. The Dukes of Bedford and Devonshire were both hit hard by post-war death duties,[35] and the largest sum paid to the Inland Revenue at death remains the £11 million on the estate of the third Duke of Westminster in 1953. But his successors learned to work the system. On the death of the fourth Duke in 1967, the Westminster estate was liable to tax on assets valued at only £4 million. No tax was paid, because lawyers proved that the Duke was entitled to an exemption granted to those killed on active service (he died of cancer, but was disabled by war wounds received in 1942). The fifth Duke, who died in 1979, paid tax on an estate of £5 million, though his wealth was estimated at up to £400 million.[36] The sixth Duke is said to be the fourth richest man in the country; the wealth of the Grosvenors has survived.

Self-Made Millionaires: Inventors and Innovators

If inheritance is the easiest way to get rich, entrepreneurship is the hardest. Almost all the wealthy entrepreneurs listed by the *Sunday Times* have invested heavily in the businesses they created or control. They have usually acquired a substantial shareholding in the formative stages, retained a major interest as it expanded, and held on through the bad times. And because the risk of concentrated investment is much higher, the returns far exceed those of armchair investment. Of course, many who adopt the same techniques reap nothing but ruin, for the same reason, but those who succeed are treated relatively kindly by the tax system, as money accumulated through capital growth rather than earned income. Entrepreneurs can retain much of the wealth they create.

Some businesses produce more millionaires than others. One in seven of the fortunes listed by the *Sunday Times* were made in property development or building; one in eight from retailing; and one in fourteen from financial services. Property is prolific because of the gearing effect: developers invest little, but deal in large amounts (building with borrowed money works wonders in a rising property market, but wreaks havoc in a falling one.)[37] Shopkeepers have thrived in a nation of shoppers, and the retailers (especially the supermarkets) have long enjoyed excessive margins. The post-war retailing millionaires include Hugh Fraser of House of Fraser, Michael Kaye of Pricerite, Horace Moore of BhS, Simon Marks of Marks & Spencer, Sir Montague Burton of Burtons and Jacob Green of Evans Outsize, as well as the Sainsburys, Porters, Aspreys, Ashleys, Bentalls, Breninnkmeyers, Clores, Conrans and Currys.[38]

But great fortunes ultimately owe little to the shape of the British economy; they turn on the imagination, perseverance and courage of individuals. The most unusual entrepreneur invents or exploits a new product or technique. As Richard Arkwright made a fortune from his invention of the water frame, Hans Rausing has made billions from the Tetrapak drinks carton. But exploitation is more common than invention, partly because inventors are often inept at exploiting their own designs. Clive Sinclair succeeded initially, then failed, largely because he was more interested in the technology than the marketplace. James Dyson sold the rights to a wheelbarrow with a ball rather than a wheel for £10,000, then watched manufacturers sell half a million. He was careful to ensure that his next invention, the bagless vacuum cleaner, belonged to him. He is now worth an estimated £400 million, but insists that 'money on its own is vulgar. It's what you can do with it that matters.'[39]

Dyson invests heavily in research and development but, on the whole, innovation is a surer route to riches than invention. A variation to an existing product or service can yield handsome returns, without the risk of undiluted novelty. The source of the £560 million Fleming family banking fortune is

TABLE 14.3
Sources of Wealth, *Sunday Times,* 1989–98

Category	Number	Percentage
Industry	196	16.9 per cent
Building and Property	173	14.9 per cent
Retailing	148	12.8 per cent
Landowning	90	7.8 per cent
City, Finance and Insurance	81	6.9 per cent
Computers and Communications	79	6.8 per cent
Arts, Entertainment and Sport	76	6.6 per cent
Food and Drink	67	5.8 per cent
Printing and Publishing	56	4.8 per cent
Leisure	50	4.3 per cent
Miscellaneous	50	4.3 per cent
Distribution and Transport	46	3.9 per cent
Trade	31	2.7 per cent
Minerals and Oil	17	1.5 per cent
Total	1,160	100 per cent

Source: The *Sunday Times* Rich Lists, 1989–1998. The number listed increased from 200 in 1989 to 300 in 1992, 400 in 1993, 500 in 1994 and 1,000 in 1998.

the investment trust – a less risky method of buying shares devised by the son of a Dundee shopkeeper, Robert Fleming. Josiah Wedgwood invented the market for mass-produced crockery, coining brand names such as 'Queensware' with the objective of selling it to middle-class snobs. Peter Wood made £50 million by repackaging insurance for sale over the telephone. Direct Line spawned a horde of imitators, cutting the profits, but by then Wood had made his fortune.

Self-Made Millionaires: Serendipity

Another route to riches is to own a business operating in an industry, or a market, which is growing rapidly. The early cotton, shipping and railway fortunes were classic examples of this. Thomas Brassey, the railway contractor, left £3.2 million in 1870. The great Victorian shipping fortunes of the Cayzers and Weirs survive today. As the Industrial Revolution progressed, creating whole new classes of consumer in the cities, fortunes were made in the manufacture and distribution of food and drink. The Vesteys, Westons and Sainsburys prospered by making and selling food for mass consumption and all the great names in British brewing grew rich by slaking the thirst of the industrial classes. The Earl of Iveagh, head of the Guinness dynasty, was worth £13.5 million on his death in 1927.

William Morris was running a bicycle shop in Oxford when the motor car was invented. By moving into motor manufacturing, he made enough money to give away £30 million before his death in 1963. The first British oil fortunes (like that of Marcus Samuel, the founder of Shell Transport and Trading) also owed much to the invention of the internal combustion engine. Over the years, the *Sunday Times* lists have hosted more than a dozen who have made millions in motor distribution. Distribution accounts for about one third of the retail price of a car, and distributors have prospered mightily from fat margins in a booming market.

National Parking Corporation (NPC), founded on a London bomb site in 1949 by Donald Gosling and Ronald Hobson, was sold to an American company in 1998 for £801 million.[40] For thirty years NPC enjoyed a virtual monopoly of commercial car parking (being neither a product nor a service, it was outside the scope of fair trading legislation) and faced no competition until Stephen Tucker set up Europarks in the 1980s.

In the last two decades, the growth of the computer and telecommunications industries has spawned a number of British business fortunes. The Caudwell brothers of Stoke-on-Trent ditched a second-hand car business to start selling mobile telephones – just as the market took off. It is estimated that Robert Madge has made over £50 million out of computer networking in twelve years. Computers and telecommunications offer a rapid route to riches in exchange for a modest initial outlay. Madge started his business in a converted barn in Buckinghamshire.

Another market which has boomed is the City of London: the one sector where employees, as well as owners, can make a fortune. From the mid-1980s, a combination of lower tax rates, financial liberalisation and buoyant stock, bond and commodity markets delivered exceptionally high rewards to City bankers, traders and speculators. The *Sunday Times* reckons there are at least 1,000 millionaires working in the Square Mile. Plenty of them are the inheritors of Old Money. Between the death of Nathan Meyer Rothschild in 1836 and the outbreak of the Second World War, ten Rothschilds (including two women) left over a million pounds. Two Rothschilds still enjoy high rankings in the *Sunday Times* list, with over £1.25 billion between them, and Hambros, Flemings and Schroders litter its pages.

The holiday, leisure, entertainment and sports industries have also boomed; suppliers of cheap holidays, package tours and bargain-basement flights have thrived. Sir Michael Bishop of British Midland was worth over £100 million in 1998. There are at least three caravan park millionaires, and the De Haans of Saga Holidays have accumulated £60 million from holidays for the elderly. As the British have grown richer and more idle, they not only have more time to spend on holidays, but more money to spend on the popular pleasures of the age: movies, pop music, pulp fiction and spectator sport.

Thanks to the success of *Mr Bean*, Rowan Atkinson earned £11.25 million in 1997.[41] Sean Connery, Michael Caine and Roger Moore appear regularly in the *Sunday Times* lists, together with Paul McCartney and Mick Jagger. In 1998, the paper listed forty-eight popular music millionaires. Andrew Lloyd Webber (the composer of popular musicals) and Cameron Mackintosh (the impresario) are now among the fifty richest, and two popular novelists, Jeffrey Archer and Barbara Taylor Bradford, are said to be worth more than £50 million apiece. British sportsmen and women do not command endorsement incomes on the American scale, but boxers, golfers, racing drivers and even some footballers are earning millions of pounds a year.[42] Sport is a true winner-takes-all market, where differences in ability measured in hundredths of a second mark the difference between becoming a millionaire and a journeyman.[43]

Self-Made Millionaires: Having What Others Want

Land and property are a perennial source of wealth because land is unique. ('They don't make it any more,' as Mark Twain said.) Given a growing population, land will always increase in value. Even as the aristocratic estates shrank in the late nineteenth-century depression, the hunger for land to build houses and factories drove up the capital value of the land they retained. Several of the great aristocratic fortunes of today – Calthorpe and Radnor as well as Westminster and Devonshire – stem from owning the land on which cities and suburbs were built. London, Eastbourne, Folkestone, Sheffield, Birmingham and Cardiff were all built on land belonging to the British aristocracy. Those lucky enough to have coal deposits as well, such as the Butes and the Lonsdales, enjoyed a third source of income from the same assets. Agricultural and ground rents and mining royalties provided sums for reinvestment in the burgeoning industrial economy, and consolidated the financial strength of the great landowners.[44]

Land and property accounts for one in four of the fortunes identified by the *Sunday Times*. Those who did not inherit property developed it (or built on it). Oliver Marriott estimated thirty years ago that the property boom after the Second World War created 110 millionaires between 1945 and 1965.[45] Five of the most valuable wills published between 1940 and 1979 belonged to property developers.* Felix Fenston left his widow, Greta, one of the largest fortunes bequeathed in Britain. He had accumulated it by acquiring development sites with money borrowed from a bank, fixing the construction cost with a builder, selling the building on completion, and pocketing the difference between the development cost and the sale price. There was a second property boom in the early 1970s, and a third in the late 1980s. Both created fresh generations of property tycoons, like John Ritblat and Elliott Bernerd.[46]

Coal-owning produced ten millionaires and forty-one half-millionaires between 1809 and 1939 as the industrial cities consumed rising quantities of fuel. The best-known were David Thomas (Viscount Rhondda, worth over £1 million at his death in 1918) and James Joicey (first Baron Joicey, who left £1.5 million). Nationalisation did not disrupt their inheritance; pit-owners were handsomely compensated by the taxpayer. Other valuable minerals can still be found. Sean Quinn made his first fortune from selling the family farm in County Fermanagh as sand and gravel, but most have had to follow the

---

* Joseph Littman (£3.2 million), Bernard Sunley (£5.2 million), Howard Samuel (£3.8 million), Felix Fenston (£12.7 million) and Joseph Sunlight (£5.7 million). See Rubinstein, *Men of Property*, pp. 228–9, Table 8.1.

gold and diamond millionaires of the Edwardian era, and search abroad for lucrative deposits. Algy Cluff made a small fortune in North Sea oil, and sank much of it in African gold mines. Old-fashioned prospectors rarely make money but, according to the *Sunday Times*, a penniless one named Mark Creasy struck gold in the Australian Outback in 1994. After panning for twenty-five years in blazing temperatures, and surviving on (mainly) bread, porridge, onions and potatoes, he sold the rights to a mining group for £80 million.

Self-Made Millionaires: Luck

An easier way to strike it rich is to be lucky. The *Sunday Times* list acquired its first National Lottery winner, Mukhtar Mohidin, in 1997, and added another a year later. But it is more usual to get rich by being in the right business at the right time. In 1998 the Bartlett brothers made £7 million from the sale of a sandwich business they began in 1979. 'Since Margaret Thatcher, lunch has been cancelled,' they said. 'People don't stop for lunch. They eat a sandwich at their computer terminals.'[47] Twenty years earlier, Octav Botnar had no idea that Japanese cars would take such a large slice of the British market when he secured the licence to import Datsuns. Stephen Rubin bought a stake in a struggling company called Reebok as the craze for running shoes took off in America. In 1976 a Sussex garage proprietor, Ian McGlinn, invested £4,000 in a company called The Body Shop. At the end of 1997, he had multiplied his money 17,000-fold.

Governments can help by changing the rules. The legalisation of off-course betting in 1960 made the fortunes of Cyril Stein and Ladbroke.[48] Perpetual, the fund management business founded by Martyn Arbib, struggled until Nigel Lawson introduced the Personal Equity Plan, which was profitable and easy to sell. The brother-and-sister team of Anne Gloag and Brian Souter happened to found a bus company (Stagecoach Holidays) in Perth shortly before the government deregulated the industry. A decade later, they and others capitalised on the privatisation of the railways as well: Sandy Anderson was working for a leasing subsidiary of General Electric when the government put the rolling stock leasing companies up for sale in 1994, and many potential bidders were too nervous to buy. Within two years, Anderson had turned his investment into £33.6 million by selling his shares to Stagecoach.

Luck can rescue fortunes as well as make them. James Goldsmith claims he was saved from bankruptcy in his twenties by a bank strike, which meant his suppliers could not cash his cheques. Tony Clegg, one of the successful property magnates of the 1980s, was forced to diversify into property by a faltering textile business. 'Property chose me, I didn't choose property,' he said.[49] Chance plays a large part in getting rich, as it does in every other aspect of life, which is why it is fruitless to believe that the secrets of success in business can be studied, distilled and deployed. Luck is often retrospective too. An ability to take a large risk, without certainty of ultimate success, is a characteristic of the entrepreneurial personality. Rupert Murdoch nearly lost News International with his gamble on satellite television.

In business, strong nerves are more valuable than a trained mind. Arnold Weinstock is virtually the only British business tycoon with a university degree, and Alex Deas, who had a stake in a company which repaired damaged computer chips, is probably the only PhD ever to grace the *Sunday Times* list. A lack of formal education seems almost essential to business success, and it is not hard to see why. A poor education forces a person to survive on his or her wits and charm, rather than take their allotted place in an established hierarchy. It also frees the entrepreneur from competing attractions, intellectual or otherwise. People get rich from concentrating on one business. 'You can't diversify the human brain,' Jack Cotton told Sampson in 1962. 'I only know about one thing – property. I've been in the property business all my life.'[50]

Big fortunes can be made in prosaic businesses. Tony O'Reilly has talked, convincingly, of success in business as 'doing common things, uncommonly well'.[51] The *Sunday Times* lists include fortunes made in greetings cards, double glazing, funeral parlours, pornography, burglar alarms, pubs and nursing homes. 'Anybody interested in making money should go into property and odds are you'll make a lot of money', Michael Green told Jeffrey Robinson. 'There are a few people who do some good things in property, but for a lot of the people, the huge sums of money they make in property bears no relation to their talents. Yet society says they must be clever and special because they're very rich. There's something wrong about that.'[52]

What Makes a Millionaire?

Green is right. The most striking characteristic of the rich is their ordinariness. 'I don't do a lot,' Ronnie Frost, millionaire chairman of the Hays business services group, told the *Financial Times*. 'I don't spend a lot. I'm a really boring guy.'[53] As are most millionaires. But this has not stopped journalists, academics and management theorists searching for the essence of the plutocratic personality. If they could uncover what makes men rich, everybody could be rich. But their work has illuminated little of the psychology which persuades people (mostly men) to risk everything in pursuit of fabulous wealth. After talking to two dozen rich men, Robinson concluded that risk-takers have business acumen, strong personalities, strong personal ambitions, and an unusual ability to take a decision. He continued, '. . . to a man, they exhibit an above-average intelligence, a startling sense of individuality, remarkable memories, unnerving stamina, an uncanny ability to smell a deal, a certain kind of personal presence that tastes like money and tends to ensure confidence, and a native talent to spot the real risks, which they then proceed to minimise.'[54] Since his interlocutors included Asil Nadir, Robert Maxwell, Ian Posgate, Gerald Ronson and Gerald Ratner, they were obviously not able to spot all the risks. Perhaps the same traits which enabled them to succeed caused their downfall. What are those traits?

Greed is one, though few rich men will admit to making money for its own sake. 'Money has never been my God', John Cohen told Aris. 'I've never bothered about it.' His motivation was a craving for the respect of others.[55] James Goldsmith had another explanation. 'I started as a capitalist without capital and wanted to re-establish that for reasons of personal satisfaction,' he told Anthony Sampson. 'The drive was need, obviously the appetite recognising the need.'[56] Most rich men do not identify a need for money. They say money is merely the means of keeping a personal score in the game of business, and that competing with others is the real spur. Yet it is obvious that rich people enjoy making and spending money for its own sake. In some cases, it may be the only talent they possess. According to one biographer of Sir John Ellerman, he 'exercised his talent for making money largely for the pure joy of self-expression, and only incidentally for financial advantage. He was at heart an artist, but the financial wizard in him overwhelmed in the end every other creative impulse.'[57]

Money can also buy status and security. 'Here lies Jedediah Strutt,' reads the gravestone of an early self-made industrialist, 'who without Fortune, Family or Friends raised himself to a fortune, family and name in the world.'[58] Many rich men come from humble backgrounds. For those acquainted with genuine hardship, no fortune is large enough. Two of the richest men in Britain, John Hall and Donald Kirkham, are the sons of miners. 'I've got this burning desire,' Kirkham told the *Financial Times*. 'I'm not happy to be a multi-millionaire. I hear this talk of billionaires.'[59] Even outsize tycoons are often driven by insecurity or rootlessness. James Goldsmith, descendant of a Frankfurt banking family, was half-French and half-English and spent his childhood in Canada and the West Indies; he felt that he belonged nowhere. 'Dynamism is usually the result of disequilibrium. My disequilibrium comes from the very simple reason that I'm a foreigner over here. I'm a Jew to Catholics, a Catholic to Jews, an Englishman to the French and a Frenchman to the English. I've always been neither one nor the other – which is a very unsettling thing to be.'[60] Nigel Wray said: 'I think one is driven by a sense of insecurity, partly self-imposed, because obviously one borrows money to enable one to do more and the moment you borrow money you worry, how can I pay it back?'[61]

Nick Leslau, a business partner of Nigel Wray, told the *Financial Times* in 1997: 'Even though I'm worth £30 million on paper, I fear it could just disappear overnight.' Even in his last years, Sir James Goldsmith often woke from nightmares in which he went bankrupt. 'Being able to do it meant a lot of luck, a certain amount of skill, and a great deal of fear,' he told Anthony Sampson in 1988. 'I think you need all three.' Insecurity can express itself as hyperactivity. This is obvious in the case of Richard Branson. 'For Branson, running the business was not a way to make money for his own personal use, but an end in itself,' writes his biographer. 'He would often talk of giving it all up and retiring to Necker Island; but after two weeks, like Napoleon on Elba, Branson would be restless and unable to resist the lure of the fax and the telephone.'[62] Stephen Marks, who made a fortune from French Connection, admits: 'It never occurred to me where I wanted to go; I just wanted to keep it moving, keep going.'[63]

Anally Retentive Control Freaks?

Psychiatrists have identified in the rich a neurotic obsession with control, natural for those from poor or insecure backgrounds. Sir John Ellerman was an early control freak; obsessively secretive, he followed a rigid daily routine bordering on the ritualistic. His business empire was an 'intimate, tightly knit business concern, its numberless branches fitting with engineering precision into an organic whole.'[64] This need to be in control expresses itself in other ways too: many of the rich have allowed an understandable shyness to degenerate into an obsessive search for security. They shun publicity of any kind, and especially photographs. Some retreat into the palaces they have bought or built, and seek to exclude all forms of contact with the world outside. These gilded cages express a psychological need for privacy, order and security.[65]

Orderly, secretive and fastidious behaviour of this type is, in Freudian jargon, 'anal' or 'anally-retentive'. In 'Character and Anal Erotism' Freud argued: 'It is possible that the contrast between the most precious substance known to men and the most worthless, which they reject as waste matter ("refuse") has led to this specific identification of gold with faeces.'[66] This is hard to believe. Freud and his followers knew many wealthy people, and it would not be surprising if they had tailored their ideas to the needs of the rich. Their own love of money may have convinced the founding fathers of psychiatry that cash replaces faeces as the focus of attention when children grow up. If their rich clients were constipated, they had a ready explanation.

It is probably true that the rich need to believe money-lust is the product of uncontrollable psychological forces. It enables them to escape the moral responsibility which accompanies the possession of wealth. The Judaeo-Christian tradition is imbued with injunctions to abjure covetousness and use wealth responsibly. It was traditional Christian depictions of the evils of the love of money, such as the German *Dukatenscheisser,* or 'shitter of ducats', which alerted Freud to the usefulness of the connection. Bosch and Brueghel both equated coinage with excrement. The axiom of Francis Bacon, much quoted by the currency speculator and philanthropist, George Soros, was: 'Money is like muck, not good except it be spread.'

Even today, the wealthy are called 'filthy rich,' and a miser is known as a 'tight-arse.' Many of the rich are genuinely mean in trifling areas of expenditure, or psychologically incapable of spending their earnings. Michael Milken, who made hundreds of millions of dollars from the junk bond markets, was notoriously unwilling to spend them, and Paul Getty installed a payphone for his guests. 'Money is uncontrollable,' writes Martin Amis in *Money.* 'Even those of us who have it, we can't control it. Life gets poor-mouthed all the time, yet you seldom hear an unkind word about money. Money, now this has to be some *good* shit.'

Fragility of Riches

Amis is right. But so are the rich – insecure and greedy for more. Great wealth is fragile, especially when it is based on paper securities rather than real estate or hard cash. There is a lot of movement in and out of the *Sunday Times* lists, especially in the lower echelons. More than one in four of the people listed over the ten years to 1998 managed only one appearance. Even allowing for death, emigration and mistakes, it is a high rate of attrition. Of the fifteen tycoons in the first edition of *The Risk Takers* in 1985, two are dead (Gordon White and Tiny Rowland), another has endured serious difficulties (Gerald Ronson), a third is in exile (Asil Nadir), a fourth exiled from Lloyd's (Ian Posgate), a fifth disgraced and dead (Robert Maxwell), and a sixth less well-known than he was (Clive Sinclair).

The first list published by the *Sunday Times* in 1989 is equally illuminating. Octav Botnar, whose £1 billion made him then the ninth richest person in Britain, died in Switzerland in 1998, a fugitive from justice.* Arundbhai Patel,

---

* Botnar and his company, Nissan UK, committed the largest tax fraud ever uncovered in Britain. The Inland Revenue reckoned Nissan UK had escaped £92 million in corporation tax payments. Botnar and his company were raided by the Inland Revenue in June 1991.

worth an estimated £50 million in 1989, put his company into liquidation a year later. Nazmu Virani, ostensibly worth £83 million, went to jail. Sophie Mirman, worth £30 million in 1989, now runs two children's clothes shops in London. Among the property tycoons in the first list, Godfrey Bradman, Stuart Lipton, Trevor Osborne and John Whittaker were all undone (to a greater or lesser extent) by the squeeze of the early 1990s. George Walker lost his company to his creditors. The Lovats, then thought to be worth £55 million, were reduced by 1996 to selling the ancestral home.

Large business fortunes, as aristocratic ones, can survive for long periods. Guinnesses, Levers, Pilkingtons and Whitbreads still crowd the lists. Many of those in a list of the British rich published in the *Daily Express* in 1969 – Weston, Pilkington, Moores, Cowdray, Sainsbury, Cayzer, Schroder, Sangster, Rowland, Hyams and Clore – were still near the top nearly thirty years later, many having passed to the next generation. The Hoares have survived three centuries, and the Rothschilds two. The founder of the Morrison family fortune, James Morrison (1790–1857), was a contemporary of Nathan Meyer Rothschild. Just as Rothschild is reputed to have made a killing on the news of the British victory at Waterloo, so James Morrison made a killing in 1818 by buying up most of the available crêpe in anticipation of the death of Queen Charlotte. The £4 million he left was tripled by his son, and by the time his great-grandson died in 1996, the family fortune was far from its origins in drapery; it was also over £40 million.

But longevity and multiplication of this kind is unusual. Many of the great Victorian fortunes, which astounded contemporaries, have evaporated. The heirs to Lord Overstone, a famous banker who left £5 million when he died in 1883, had disappeared by the 1940s. The fortune amassed by Richard Thornton, the insurance broker and Baltic merchant who boasted that his signature was 'good for £3 million', is now barely a memory for his descendants. Victorian predictions that compound interest would transform contemporary business fortunes into twentieth-century behemoths stalking the markets of the world has not come to pass. It seems even great wealth is dissipated easily, and in unexceptional ways. Governments, by relieving gifts before death of tax, encourage its fragmentation. Charitable donations, riotous living and bad investment decisions do the rest. In 1994 Lord Palumbo was sued by two of his children, who alleged that he was mismanaging the family fortune. He was replaced by independent trustees. Family feuds of this kind, exacerbated in the Palumbo case by the offspring of a second marriage, can fragment even the largest fortune. Death, divorce, a lack of heirs, ill-feeling or personal preference can cause wealth to skip a generation, endow a charitable foundation, or go to the chauffeur.

One of the fastest ways for a woman to acquire a fortune is to marry a rich man. Bess of Hardwick, the founder of the fortune of the Dukes of Devonshire, was married and widowed four times.* Today, divorce can be as lucrative. Rich men tire easily of trophy wives. They are also subject to non-stop temptation, and are preyed upon by professional predators. However, the principal cause of the dissipation of wealth is having children. On the whole, rich businessmen divide their inheritance among all their children. The £21 million left by Henry Overton Wills III in 1911 was down to £9 million by the time Sir George Wills died in 1931, and his four sisters could muster barely £3 million between them as they died in the 1940s. Alice, the wife of Sir George, left only £73,000 in 1961.

Business fortunes tend to consist of cash and securities rather than land, making them less resistant to sub-division than the family seat of an aristocratic family. Many self-made men also prefer to nurture a new generation of entrepreneurs rather than add to the ranks of the idle rich. Peter de Savary has told his five daughters to expect nothing, and David Jones, who made a fortune in the Sharelink securities dealing business, will indulge his socialist beliefs by leaving little to his children. 'I will make sure they are well cared for and have every opportunity,' he told the *Sunday Telegraph*, 'but money does not buy happiness.'[67]

This is true: the often cold and intimidating personalities which guarantee success in business do not make for happy private or social lives. Many fabulously rich men – Paul Getty and Howard Hughes for instance – led miserable existences. Sir John Ellerman had no lasting interests outside his work and family; he lacked broad sympathies or social imagination, and even forced his wife to give up her friends.[68] The absorption of parents in business, or the prospect of inherited wealth, can lead to warped and tragic lives in the next generation. Two scions of the aristocracy, the Marquess of Blandford and the Marquess of Bristol, have squandered money and then reputations on drugs. In January 1999, the Marquess of Bristol was found dead in bed. He was forty-four.

But the reluctance of the *nouveaux-riches* to think dynastically is symptomatic of a new ethic as well a desire to free their children of the curse which can accompany great wealth. Michael Lewis has labelled it Conspicuous Production, as opposed to Conspicuous Consumption. The modern self-made businessman believes his children should work as hard as he did. Paradoxically, this hard-nosed sentiment may eventually rob personal wealth of its

* The co-heiress of John Hardwick of Derbyshire, Bess (1518–1608) married successively Robert Barlow, William Cavendish, Sir William St Loe and George Talbot, sixth Earl of Shrewsbury, inheriting all their estates. Her income was estimated at £60,000 a year. As Horace Walpole put it: 'Four times the nuptial bed she warmed/And every time so well perform'd/That when death spoil'd each husband's billing/He left the widow every shilling.'

legitimacy. 'The power of perpetuating our property in our families,' wrote Edmund Burke, 'is one of the most valuable and interesting circumstances belonging to it, and that which tends the most to the perpetuation of society itself. It makes our weakness subservient to our virtue; it grafts benevolence even upon avarice.'[69] If wealth is not accumulated for the sake of the family, it loses much of its purpose – what, people then ask, are the rich for?

What Are the Rich For?

An important function of the rich is to get richer. It is incumbent upon those who possess great wealth to create more of it, and provide pleasure and employment for others. 'It is the business of the wealthy man', as Hilaire Belloc wrote, 'to give employment to the artisan.'[70] Many wealthy men have no talent at all beyond the knack of making money. Felix Fenston returned to property development in 1963, bored after a two year sabbatical. After selling his first chain of carpet warehouses Phil Harris immediately set about creating a second. Michael Cannon, who collected £26 million for the Devenish chain of pubs, used the proceeds to create the chain of Magic Pubs, which he sold for £70 million before moving on to the Ambishus Pub Company. Sir Mark Weinberg has started three life assurance companies. As soon as Rocco Forte lost his family hotel chain to Granada, he set up a new one.

In each of these cases, the lure of the deal exceeded the love of money. Most rich men are not natural *rentiers*; they are serial risk-takers. 'If I had been a woman,' said Robert Maxwell, 'I would have been pregnant all the time.' For the same reason, the rich are often tempted by risky sports. Charles Church, the housing tycoon, was killed in 1989, flying a Spitfire. The furniture magnate, Donald Kirkham, flies Microlites and enjoys parachute-jumping. Richard Branson has crossed the Atlantic and the Pacific by boat and balloon. 'Speed has always been a fascination for me,' says the Irish millionaire, Michael Smurfit. 'I've never got over it.'[71]

But the rich have a duty to spend as well as to get. 'You cannot spend money in luxury without doing good to the poor,' thought Dr Johnson. 'Nay, you do more good to them by spending it in luxury than by giving it; for by spending it in luxury you make them exert industry, whereas by giving it you keep them idle.' The spending power of the rich within the national economy is not as powerful as it was two centuries ago, but it is not insignificant either. The importance of their spending habits is social rather than economic. There are many desirable objects and ideas which a market economy is not capable of producing, and which its bias towards mass-production for mass-consumption undermines. High culture survived in the well-educated but impoverished societies of communist Europe primarily because the mass market in which to buy the easier consolations of pulp fiction, sport and journalism. The fine arts, scholarship, education, even statesmanship, depend not on the market economy or the state or popular consensus but upon a class of individuals wealthy enough to fund the aims, ideas and institutions which cannot be delivered by politics or the price mechanism.

The thinking rich understand this. Ever since the Medicis erected public buildings with signs attached to advertise their beneficence, the wealthy have recognised that the best way to gain recognition is not accumulation but expenditure. Even the Old Corruption is not entirely to be despised: it bequeathed the lives and works of Edmund Burke, Samuel Johnson, Thomas Hobbes, John Locke, Samuel Taylor Coleridge, Adam Smith and Jonathan Swift. All were succoured, one way or another, by wealthy patrons. The wealth of the Robber Barons paid not only for Pinkerton's men, but for the Getty Museum, the Frick collection, the Morgan Library and the Metropolitan Museum of Art. In Britain, the nucleus of the National Gallery was assembled by the merchant and philanthropist John Julius Angerstein. The Gallery recently acquired a Sainsbury Wing. The sugar refiner Sir Henry Tate gave £80,000, 67 paintings and three sculptures to build and endow the Tate Gallery. The textile heir, Samuel Courtauld, used £300,000 of his money to assemble the collection of Impressionist paintings on display in Somerset House.

In the same way, only the rich can finance the generation and distribution of ideas uncongenial to the *zeitgeist*. Financial independence guarantees intellectual independence and, in politics, freedom from corruption. 'Cecils don't give a damn, and that makes a difference', as Clement Attlee once said of the greatest of political families. Similarly, it was the millionaire Heseltine who could afford to resign from the Cabinet on his own terms, while lesser men endured humiliation rather than lose their ministerial salaries. Financial independence, not rules about disclosure, is the best guarantee of probity in government. Similarly, dissidence, not consensus, is the source of progress. Dissidents are the mark of the free society. The campaigns for the abolition of slaves, prison reform, better housing, and the prevention of cruelty to animals, children and the mentally ill, and even socialism, were all financed privately.

Books, magazines, newspapers and even the broadcast media – vital to the dissemination of knowledge and ideas – cannot always survive in the marketplace. The Barclay twins bought *The European*. Tony O'Reilly rescued *The Independent*. The literary magazine, *Horizon*, was supported by the margarine heir, Peter Watson. A modern successor, *The Literary Review*, is funded by the Palestinian businessman and writer, Naim Attallah. The left-wing political monthly, *Prospect*, is funded by the industrial heir, Derek Coombs. More prosaically, dozens of football and rugby clubs are sustained by wealthy patrons.[72]

Hayek thought the cultural function of the rich was so important that if wealthy people did not exist it would be necessary to invent them.[73] His intellectual enemy, Maynard Keynes, was reproved by his friend, the French journalist Marcel Labordère, for advocating the 'euthanasia of the rentier', as part of his attack on excessive saving:

> The rentier is useful in his way not only, or even principally, on account of his propensity to save but for deeper reasons. Stable fortunes, the hereditary permanency of families, and sets of families of various social standings are an invisible social asset on which every kind of culture is more or less dependent. To entirely overlook the interests of the rentier class which includes benevolent, humanitarian, scientific, literary institutions and groups of worldly interests (salons) may, viewed in a historical perspective, turn out to have been a short-sighted policy. Financial security for one's livelihood is a necessary condition of organised leisure and thought. Organised leisure and thought is a necessary condition of a true, not purely mechanical, civilisation.[74]

Keynes conceded immediately that Labordère was right. Hayek recalled that Keynes had once expatiated on the 'indispensable role that the man of independent means plays in any decent society'.[75] Keynes decided to become financially independent to buy time to understand and impart ideas, and to invest in the authors and artists he valued. By 1936 stock market speculations had enabled him to amass £500,000. His monuments include the Arts Theatre in Cambridge, in which he invested £20,000.[76]

Other rich men have found it trickier to decide what causes to support. Bill Gates pointed out that 'giving away money effectively is almost as hard as earning it in the first place.'[77] But give the rich must. The Judaeo-Christian tradition emphasises the charitable duties of the rich, and many rich men accept its teachings. The Scottish-American steel magnate Andrew Carnegie claimed that 'the man who dies rich dies disgraced'. His giving was spectacular (the modern equivalent of $4.5 billion), and rivalled in modern times only by George Soros. 'I'm not spending as much as I'd like,' Soros told *The Guardian* recently, though he was already giving away £100 million a year. Unlike Carnegie, and most modern philanthropists, Soros finances ideas as well as institutions. He is said to spend two thirds of his time (and half of his income) on charitable works.

There is pleasure, too, in the philanthropy of the wealthy. The Anglo-

American banker George Peabody, who endowed the Peabody housing estates, admitted as much. 'For the first time,' he wrote, 'I felt a higher pleasure and a greater happiness than making money – that of giving it away for good purposes.' There is also vanity in giving, and it doubtless imparts a sense of power. When a millionaire is a commonplace figure, as he is today, a spectacular gesture makes one stand out from the crowd. Vivien Duffield, heiress to the Sears retail fortune of her father, Charles Clore, has fashioned a career for herself in philanthropy, giving away £90 million to a variety of charities, medical foundations, museums and arts organisations. 'If you're lucky enough to have money,' she says, 'it's your duty to give it away.'[78] But no one who saw her striding around the Royal Opera House in the TV documentary, *The House*, could doubt that she derives pleasure from duty.

Purists argue that any donation which gives pleasure to the giver lacks moral authenticity. Some observers also believe the modern plutocrat is less generous than his Victorian predecessors, but the Sainsburys and Westons, Paul Hamlyn and a host of lesser figures have all established charitable foundations. Few rival the great funds of the past – the Rowntree, Nuffield, Wolfson and Wellcome trusts – and there are fewer foundations than there were. This reflects declining rates of direct taxation, which have made giving to charity more expensive by reducing tax relief.[79] The authors of a recent study of the giving of the richest 500 people in Britain reckoned that they had given £175 million in all (or £75 million, when George Soros was excluded). As a proportion of their total wealth, this was less than some of the poorer members of society.

There are still many spectacular donations: Elton John gave the proceeds of his re-working of 'Candle in the Wind' to the Princess Diana fund, and George Michael donated the proceeds of one of his hit singles to AIDS research. But £75 million is trifling by comparison with the money the same 499 people spend on houses, cars, aeroplanes and parties. Carnegie argued that 'the duty of the man of wealth is first to set an example of modest, unostentatious living, shunning display and extravagance.' But even he found this advice impossible to follow. He bought 32,000 acres and a castle in Scotland, and built a palace on Fifth Avenue. Conspicuous Consumption will always outweigh Inconspicuous Charity – many donations are an aspect of Conspicuous Consumption anyway.

But it is short-sighted to deplore the vulgarity of the *nouveaux-riches*. It may take several generations for a wealthy family to develop the requisite sensitivities to make a contribution to civilisation. Sir John Ellerman filled his mansion at 1 South Audley Street with banal paintings and statuary. He delighted in telling visitors how he had haggled over the price of some vulgar artefact. But his son, the second baronet, became a world expert on African rodents. James Goldsmith pointed out:

> Vulgarity is to some degree a sign of vigour. It means that new people coming from nowhere are making it. It's the old American dream – anybody can be a millionaire. Now if we don't want vulgarity what is the alternative? Either generalised poverty, which I don't think anybody is seeking, or the protection of privilege, so there's no change. The Duke of Northumberland or the Duke of Buccleuch don't irritate anyone; but if we only want people who have had a hundred years to learn to use money to have money, we are clearly precluding change. So if we want change, if we want vigour, we are going to have vulgarity.[80]

During the course of the twentieth century, the concentration of personal wealth has diminished dramatically. The proportion owned by the richest one per cent has declined from roughly two thirds at the beginning of the century to less than one fifth now.[81] The rich have shed assets, to pay tax and avoid tax. The middling classes have acquired them, in the shape of owner-occupied houses and pension rights. With the broadening of the distribution of wealth has come a broader distribution of power. No modern millionaire can say with Cornelius Vanderbilt: 'Law! What do I care about the law? Hain't I got the power?' The most powerful determinant of the economic fortunes of the man in the street is not the plutocrat. There is no small class whose elimination would give rise to an age of universal plenty. It is the Fat Cats and other salaried rich, and the impersonal corporations for which they work and to which they entrust their savings, which now have the wealth and power in Britain.

CHAPTER FIFTEEN

COMPANY DIRECTORS

Today management has no stake in the company. Altogether those men sitting up there own less than 3 per cent of the company. You own the company. That's right, you, the stockholders, and you are being royally screwed by these bureaucrats with their stock lunches, their hunting and fishing trips, their corporate jets and their golden parachutes.

GORDON GEKKO in *Wall Street*[1]

Yes, it's the politics of envy. We're envious of their wealth. These people are stinking, lousy, thieving, incompetent scum.

FRANK DOBSON, on privatised utility 'Fat Cats', 1992[2]

Envy is a sad emotion to watch and demeaning to the people exercising it.

SIR JOHN BANHAM, 1991[3]

The administration of more and more of the world's capital is coming under the control of men who, though they enjoy very large incomes and all the amenities that this secures, have never on their own account and at their personal risk controlled substantial property. Whether this is altogether a gain remains to be seen.

F. A. HAYEK, 1960[4]

Modern capitalism is new. Unlike its aristocratic and plutocratic antecedents, its chief actors are not individuals. In terms of ownership, the land-owning economy described by Gregory King at the end of the seventeenth century is not very different from the mill-owning economy described by Karl Marx in the middle of the nineteenth century. Both were dominated by individuals in possession of large amounts of capital. Now, wealth is controlled by corporations and institutions. They are managed by individuals, but not owned by them. The great companies and savings institutions which control most of the wealth of the nation are the creatures of the rising scale of industrial organisation. But they are creatures also of the systems of progressive taxation by which twentieth century governments have sought to eliminate the wealthy man. One of the few authentically egalitarian aspects of New Labour is its continuing hostility to private accumulations of capital. Under a New Labour government (as under Old Labour), income from work is applauded; income from capital is condemned.[5]

This is one reason why New Labour, as with any revisionist form of socialism, is comfortable with Big Business. Large companies are the principal providers of income from work and, unlike the ducal estates and Satanic mills of the past, they are not owned and controlled by rich individuals. Their capital is supplied by faceless men at banks, pension funds and insurance companies, and their daily activities are determined by managers. The PLC appears to make ownership irrelevant, reducing capitalism to questions of organisation and technique.[6] It is also manipulated more easily by government, through changes in taxation, regulation and law. The government has already passed measures it believes will encourage companies to invest, employ, train and compete more, and is preparing measures to persuade them to charge, pay, pollute and take over one another less. The irony is that the corporate economy is also the incubator of the one kind of businessmen which even New Labour detests: the ones the popular press have dubbed 'Fat Cats'.

The 'Fat Cat' is a creation of the media, in which under-paid journalists have conspired with opportunistic politicians and trade union leaders to pander to the belief (well-expressed in a New Labour sound-bite) that many labour and few gain. First applied to the directors of the privatised utilities, 'Fat Cat' is now applied to any well-paid captain of industry. This is unfair. It is also unfortunate, since it obstructs public understanding of the most important question in contemporary capitalism: how to heal the fissure between ownership and control in Big Business. The destruction of individual wealth by progressive taxation was accompanied by the grant of tax privileges to pension funds. Anxious to spread their risks, they prefer to own small stakes in a large number of companies rather than large stakes in a small number. Since they cannot run companies directly, they rely on salaried managers. This has enabled the managerial classes to do just as well by administering the capital of others as by starting their own business – and at less risk. Once the value of bonuses, pension contributions and share options is added to an annual salary, a company director can become a millionaire.

Unsurprisingly, the majority of the wealth of the country is now controlled by salaried managers rather than risk-taking entrepreneurs. Old Labour would have welcomed such an outcome: Tawney predicted that the replacement of owner-managers by salaried office-holders would transform the ethics of capitalism.[7] Such an outcome required an alteration in human nature. Today, policymakers have a more modest ambition: to align the financial interests of managers and shareholders. But public perceptions are shaped by notions of legitimacy, not utility. The company director, unlike the aristocrat, performs no public duties. The company director, unlike the plutocrat, risks none of his own wealth. The rewards of the company director, unlike those of the employees, appear to be determined not by effort but by boardroom backscratching. It was because his rewards seemed unredeemed, unearned and undeserved that the well-paid company director ceased to be a Captain of Industry and became a Fat Cat.

It is hard to be sure when perceptions changed. Richard Giordano (latterly chairman of British Gas but then chief executive of the industrial gases company BOC) was probably the first director to attract attention for his earnings alone. His annual salary touched £1 million in the mid-1980s. Its size was the subject of comment as early as 1982, but he was American, and people expected it of Americans. Others thought he symbolised a change in public attitudes towards managerial rewards.

'The attitude of the British to wealth has changed,' claimed Geoffrey Mulcahy, chief executive of the Kingfisher retailing group, in 1988. 'There is a much greater appreciation of the responsibility borne by top management.'[8] This was optimistic. A year earlier Ralph Halpern, chairman of Burton Group, had granted himself share options worth £8 million. Amid public outcry, shareholders had insisted he make do with £2.5 million instead. Over the next decade, endless stories of company directors collecting large salaries and generous bonuses went a long way to elect the first Labour government for twenty-three years.

Tabloid newspapers ran features on The Ten Greediest Bosses. Even the *Daily Telegraph* ran a Tough At The Top column, salaciously itemising boardroom excesses for the delectation of its readership of disgruntled middle managers. Journalists staked out the homes of leading businessmen, in search of swimming pools, tennis courts and Bentleys. In 1991 the tabloids forced the BT chairman, Iain Vallance, to give a mid-recession bonus of £150,000 to charity. Three years later they discovered that the salary of Cedric Brown, chief executive of British Gas, had risen by 75 per cent to £475,000 a year. Brown made the crucial mistake of answering reporters as he climbed into a Mercedes-Benz in the drive of a large house in Buckinghamshire. The tabloids immediately declared him The Most Hated Man in Britain. At the annual general meeting of British Gas the following summer, the chief executive was greeted by a pig devouring a bucket of swill. His minders had renamed the pig Cedric.

MPs caught the popular mood. Cedric Brown was twice questioned by a committee of the House of Commons, which summoned him to Westminster to explain his earnings on television to the representatives of the British people. He stepped down shortly afterwards, and the focus shifted. In July 1996 a Labour Party spokesman attended the annual general meeting of United Utilities and, for the benefit of television crews outside, he crowned the company chairman King of the Fat Cats. The then chairman, who was a beneficiary of an executive remuneration scheme, which had attracted media attention, was played for the day by a plump, pin-striped, cigar-smoking man dressed as a cat.[9] Rising boardroom salaries were criticised from less predictable quarters: two Conservative prime ministers, a chancellor of the Exchequer and the director general of the CBI expressed disquiet. What had changed since Sir Geoffrey Mulcahy claimed the British people appreciated top managers?

The Privatised Utility Chiefs

The most important change, in terms of public perception, was the privatisation of the water and electricity industries between 1989 and 1991.[10] It was at the newly privatised utilities that some of the most startling increases in pay and perks were announced. Within four years, the average salary of the highest paid directors at regional electricity companies had almost quadrupled to £233,000. At the regional water companies, the average salary of the highest paid director more than doubled to £177,500. Salaries were only part of the story; for management, one of the principal benefits of translation from the public sector to the private was the opportunity to introduce share option schemes for top executives.

When the *Observer* investigated the value of the share options owned by the directors of the privatised electricity and water companies in 1995 their value was over £44 million, a sum equivalent to £364,000 a head. Four electricity company directors had become millionaires through shares and share options alone, and another twenty-one half-millionaires. In all, twelve water and electricity directors had become millionaires.[11] There was outrage in the press when a number of National Grid directors were granted and cashed share options before the company was even privatised, and one made a profit of over £350,000.[12] Newspapers filled with stories of privatised utility chiefs making large profits from share options.'[13] Other newspapers worked hard (without conspicuous success) to find directors who had broken the rules of option schemes.

New Labour worked hard to turn the issue to political advantage. In August 1994, four directors of PowerGen and National Power were named and

TABLE 15.1
Highest Paid Directors at Privatised Companies

	Salary at Privatisation	Salary, Bonus & Benefits, 1994*	Salary, Bonus & Benefits, 1997/8*
British Gas	50,000	492,602	†427,245
British Telecom	94,000	663,000	1,101,000
Eastern	62,270	296,000	376,000
East Midlands	62,270	331,712	‡458,000
London	75,950	201,145	180,000
Manweb	62,270	240,509	§487,345
Midlands	67,500	231,802	358,000
Northern	86,800	210,000	¶123,000
Norweb	62,270	215,274	‖238,400
Seeboard	65,100	184,000	407,000
Southern	62,270	258,000	**297,148
Swalec	65,375	203,420	††325,000
SWEB	70,525	213,000	269,000
Yorkshire	62,270	211,354	255,400
National Power	185,000	374,886	546,285
PowerGen	103,075	350,393	458,000
National Grid	N/A	330,000	355,000
Anglian	53,750	169,000	286,967
Northumbrian	54,800	135,000	175,000
North West	100,000	338,000	‖229,366
Severn Trent	75,250	224,200	239,800
Southern Water	100,000	169,000	§487,345
South West (Pennon)	70,000	130,000	198,000
Thames	150,000	247,000	277,000
Welsh	59,125	139,000	††325,000
Wessex	72,563	166,000	206,000
Yorkshire	54,825	156,000	298,000

Source: Privatisation Prospectuses; Companies' Annual Report and Accounts, 1994 and 1998.

* Bonuses and benefits exclude pension contributions and share and share options, both of which inflate remuneration shown by large amounts.

† Highest paid director at BG plc. British Gas split itself into BG plc and Centrica plc in 1997.

‡ Highest paid director at PowerGen, which acquired East Midlands Electricity in June 1998.

§ Highest paid director at Scottish Power, which acquired Manweb in July 1995 and Southern Water in June 1996.

¶ In 1997, the highest paid director received £430,000. Northern Electric was acquired by CalEnergy in December 1996.

‖ United Utilities acquired Norweb and North West Water in 1995. The highest paid director at United Utilities received £443,600 in 1998.

** Highest paid director at Scottish Hydro-electric, which acquired Southern in September 1998.

†† Highest paid director at Hyder plc, which was created by the merger of Swalec and Welsh Water in December 1995.

shamed by the shadow chancellor, Gordon Brown, as the 'share-option millionaires'.[14] Blair denounced the rises as an offence against the 'British sense of justice' and urged Major in the House of Commons to 'take a grip on these privatised utilities' because 'millions of people feel disgusted and outraged at this excess and greed.'[15] Politically, synthetic rage would not jeopardise the burgeoning relationship between New Labour and Big Business; even other directors were shocked by the goings-on at the electricity and water companies. 'There is little doubt that the remuneration committees of a number of companies in the privatised water and energy sectors have developed, perhaps unintentionally, remuneration packages that are richer than is required to recruit, retain and motivate quality managers,' concluded the Greenbury report on executive pay in 1995. It was commissioned by the CBI.[16] Several privatised companies scrapped their share-option schemes, and the about-to-be-privatised Railtrack decided not to set one up at all.

In office, New Labour has attacked the utility chiefs with impunity. Their shareholders were punished with a windfall tax in the first budget of the new government in July 1997, and culture secretary Chris Smith ordered three directors of Camelot to give up bonuses worth nearly £3 million.[17] A few months later the chancellor embarrassed the chairman of a water company after reading (inaccurate) newspaper reports which suggested he was going to be paid more for less work[18]. In the summer of 1998, Brown let it be known that he was considering giving regulators powers to penalise companies guilty of boardroom excess.[19] Periodically, other junior ministers threaten legislation to curb executive pay, but the leadership has denied them real retribution for people who earn too much – a rise in the rate of income tax.

Political hostility has somewhat cowed the privatised utility directors. Since 1995, their pay and perks have not risen so precipitously. By 1997, South West Water was struggling to attract a new chief executive because of its reluctance to offer a lavish salary.[20] Yet the utilities need better managers; a 1996 survey found one in two fund managers unable to name a utility management team they admired.[21] A shortage of talent was one reason salaries rose sharply after privatisation. 'I would never have come here for £40,000,' claimed Michael Hoffman, who was hired from Babcock to run Thames Water at a salary of £150,000, shortly before privatisation. 'And I would never have recruited top people into other positions if the company did not pay them proper competitive salaries.'[22] North West Water had to pay Robert Thian £100,000 to tempt him away from Novo, and Southern Water the same to tempt John Valentine from Fisons.

The appointments were not a lasting success: both Hoffman and Thian parted company with their new employers, at considerable expense to the shareholders, not long after they were appointed.[23] This was embarrassing, but the real mistake was not that they paid outsiders too much. It was that existing managers doubled their salaries, and turned themselves into million-aires because they were working for a private rather than a public company. According to Incomes Data Services, the average boardroom pay rise after privatisation averaged 70.3 per cent in the water industry and 105.8 per cent in the electricity industry. The chairman of one utility company told MPs in 1995 that he would have resigned if his pay had not increased after privatis-ation. Yet he had spent his entire career in the industry.

This was why the press was reluctant to believe a water company chairman when he argued in 1992 that 'we have to pay the market rates to get and keep the good people. These jobs are very demanding.'[24] After all, ran the argument, he had joined the company four years before privatisation. But he had a point. It is harder to run a privatised utility than a public one. The directors are answerable to regulators, shareholders, bankers and consumers as well as ministers and civil servants, which makes it awkward to raise prices, or cut fat. Expansion into unregulated businesses and foreign markets is necessary to offset downward pressure on regulated earnings.[25] Every utility except water now faces competition. But they have mismanaged all these challenges, despite soaring boardroom pay. The truth about the privatised utilities may well be that the Conservative government used the promise of lavish rewards to get management support for privatisation.[26]

Private Sector Directors

Unfortunately, privatisation coincided with a new spirit of openness about boardroom pay and perks. The main reason the Fat Cat was invented in the 1990s was that journalists learned for the first time what directors earned. Company directors are now expected to declare their remuneration in detail in the annual report to shareholders. The volume of data makes generalisa-tion difficult, but it is safe to say that no director of a FTSE-100 company is getting less than £180,000 a year. At the largest companies, no member of the board is taking home less than £230,000 a year, and the highest-paid directors are collecting well over £1 million. It is reasonable to assume that, in an average year, the highest-paid directors at FTSE-100 companies will be earning between £600,000 and £1.5 million a year. Most of these will be the executive chairman or chief executive of the company.

Earning over £1 million, commonplace in the City, is no longer unusual in industry and commerce. Table 15.3 is a random list of directors reported to have earned at least £1 million in pay and perks over the last decade. In

TABLE 15.2
Total Earnings of Directors at FTSE-100 Companies in 1998

Market Capitalisation (£m)	Full-Time Chairman or Chief Executive	Finance Director	Divisional Director
Less than 3,500	£304–509,000	£198–264,000	£184–276,000
3,501–5,999	£441–665,000	£272–374,000	£245–354,000
6,000–9,999	£534–820,000	£313–428,000	£233–390,000
More than 10,000	£795–1,089,000	£294–690,000	£230–496,000

Source: Monks Partnership: Board Earnings in FTSE-100 Companies 1998.

the last ten to fifteen years, boardroom pay has increased much faster than that of anyone else. A 1998 survey of the top 350 British companies identified forty-nine directors who earned more than £1 million.[27] Though they prefer euphemisms – 'remuneration' or 'compensation' – directors are now paid exceptionally well, and money has become their chief measure of status, especially against their peer group. They have, after all, spent time and sacrificed pleasures climbing to the top of the corporate dung-hill; this is the way of keeping score.

Once again, critics blame Margaret Thatcher for unleashing a culture of greed-is-good. Some businessmen undoubtedly did swallow a caricature of her beliefs, but more reinterpreted their duty in terms narrower than those which prevailed before she came to power: maximisation of the value of the company, not the creation of jobs or making a contribution to the balance of payments. But one reason businessmen now pay themselves a lot is that they can; directors of modern PLCs are in a uniquely favourable position. They do not own the company, but they control its resources. Like most people in charge of money which belongs to someone else, company directors are naturally tempted to bestow it on themselves. As J. K. Galbraith has observed, 'the salary of the chief executive of the large corporation is not a market award for achievement. It is frequently in the nature of a warm personal gesture by the individual to himself.'[28]

This truth is of seminal importance. The great debate about corporate governance – which erupted at the end of the 1980s and rages still – is not at all about how companies can best be run. It is a battle by proxy between the controllers of companies (the directors) and their owners (investors). Directors want to reduce the pressure from shareholders by stressing their responsibility to a wider constituency of employees, consumers, and communities. 'Management has never been so powerful, or so unaccountable,' Christopher Haskins, chief executive of Northern Foods, told Anthony Sampson

TABLE 15.3
Random List of Directors Reported to have Earned over £1m

	Company	Reported	Earnings £
Jim Fifield	EMI	1993	13,500,000
Jim Fifield	EMI	1997	5,768,200
Jim Fifield	EMI	1998	6,900,000
Sam Chisholm	BSkyB	1995	4,700,000
Ken Berry	EMI	1998	4,750,000
Archie Norman	Asda	1996	3,700,000
Jan Leschly	SmithKline Beecham	1995	3,516,940
Jan Leschly	SmithKline Beecham	1998	2,446,000
Rod Kent	Close Brothers	1998	3,400,000
Lord Hollick	United News & Media	1997	2,970,000
Martin Sorrell	WPP	1997	2,790,000
Bob Bauman	SmithKline Beecham	1993	2,782,132
Martin Bandier	EMI	1998	2,700,000
Greg Hutchings	Tomkins	1993	2,644,827
Greg Hutchings	Tomkins	1998	2,150,000
Terry Green	Debenhams	1997	2,600,000
John Browne	BP	1997	2,470,000
John Ritblat	British Land	1997	2,400,000
Hugh Collum	SmithKline Beecham	1998	2,300,000
Pierre Vinken	Reed Elsevier	1995	2,297,437
Sir Paul Girolami	Glaxo	1991	1,185,727
Sir Paul Girolami	Glaxo	1993	2,082,934
Henry Wendt	SmithKline Beecham	1989	1,998,000
Charles Brady	Amvesco	1996	1,440,000
Charles Brady	Amvesco	1997	1,950,000
Richard Oster	Cookson	1995	1,252,237
Richard Oster	Cookson	1997	1,700,000
Sir John Nott	Lazards	1989	1,562,959
Ken Berry	EMI	1998	1,504,000
Sir Christopher Lewinton	TI Group	1996	1,500,000
Sir Ian MacLaurin	Tesco	1991	1,482,000
Derek Bonham	Hanson	1994	1,040,000
Derek Bonham	Hanson	1996	1,480,000
Brian McGowan	House of Fraser	1994	1,450,000
Keith Oates	Marks & Spencer	1997	1,440,000
Robert Peel	Thistle Hotels	1997	1,400,000

TABLE 15.3 *continued*
Random List of Directors Reported to have Earned over £1m

	Company	Reported	Earnings £
Sir Ralph Halpern	Burton	1987	1,359,000
Robert Montague	Tiphook	1994	1,340,000
Sir Allen Sheppard	Grand Metropolitan	1994	1,340,000
Sir Geoffrey Mulcahy	Kingfisher	1994	1,310,000
Pierre Garnier	SmithKline Beecham	1998	1,300,000
Derek Hunt	MFI	1992	1,300,000
Peter George	Ladbroke	1997	1,280,000
George Simpson	GEC	1997	1,252,000
Lord Blyth	Boots	1996	1,180,000
Lord Blyth	Boots	1997	1,250,000
Sir Richard Greenbury	Marks & Spencer	1996	1,080,000
Sir Richard Greenbury	Marks & Spencer	1997	1,250,000
Richard Brown	Cable & Wireless	1997	1,240,000
Sir Clive Thompson	Rentokil	1998	1,230,000
John Hoerner	Burton	1996	1,120,000
John Clark	BET	1994	1,106,000
Michael Slade	Helical Bar	1989	1,106,000
Sir Peter Bonfield	BT	1998	1,101,000
Ann Iverson	Laura Ashley	1997	1,100,000
Henry Sweetbaum	Wickes	1994	1,100,000
Sir Richard Sykes	Glaxo Wellcome	1997	1,127,000
Mitchell Fromstein	Blue Arrow	1989	1,082,000
Richard Giordano	BOC	1992	1,047,741
Ken Hanna	Dalgety	1998	1,040,000
Sir Colin Chandler	Vickers	1997	1,070,000
Phil White	National Express	1997	1,050,000
Sir Alistair Grant	Argyll	1993	1,000,000

Source: *Financial Times*.

in 1995. 'Business isn't naturally democratic: the early owner-managers were all autocrats. But leadership is a dangerous concept: we need accountability. Capitalism has really failed to achieve it.'[29] Shareholders, on the other hand, seek ways to force managers to pursue shareholders' interests.

On the whole, the directors have had the best of it. This became starkly apparent in early 1998 when the proposed merger between Glaxo Wellcome and SmithKline Beecham was cancelled because the two boards of directors could not agree who would do which jobs after the merger. A combination worth £110 billion in total, and at least £20 billion to shareholders in the two companies, apparently foundered on a clash of egos. The day after the merger was abandoned, the decline in the share prices of the two companies amounted to £13.5 billion.[30] Within weeks of the débâcle, the five top directors at SmithKline Beecham collected pay and options packages worth £25 million, and those of the chief executive climbed to a new high of £66 million.[31] 'It must be a cause for public concern as well as concern to shareholders,' concluded an investigation by the House of Commons science and technology committee, 'that neither of the chief executives nor the boards of the two companies have been held publicly accountable for this course of events, nor have adequate explanations been forthcoming.'[32]

Corporate Governance: Bridging the Gap

Ironically, the débâcle occurred only weeks after the publication of the third in a series of reports intended to provide precisely this degree of accountability. In May 1991 the London Stock Exchange had sponsored the establishment of a committee under Sir Adrian Cadbury, chairman of Cadbury-Schweppes, to make recommendations on restoring public confidence in company reports and accounts following a series of spectacular financial collapses.[33] The committee was soon drawn into a broader examination of the ways directors run companies and reward themselves, and in 1992 it published a code of practice, recommending that the remuneration of directors be set by independent non-executive directors. It also advocated full disclosure of boardroom pay, including bonuses, pension contributions and share options. '[Managers]', declared the report, 'must be free to drive their companies forward but exercise that freedom within a framework of effective accountability.'[34]

In the years which followed, most directors declared their basic salaries, but there was reluctance to disclose the values of cash bonuses, share options and pension contributions, though these were often extremely valuable. A successful chairman or chief executive of a public company might retire on £500,000 or more a year, though he may not have worked at his last employer for more than a few years.[35] When actuaries Bacon & Woodrow surveyed 1,500 directors at over 200 companies one year after the Cadbury report, they found that the average director was paid a basic salary of a mere £92,306, but this was inflated by a further £62,428 by bonuses, pension contributions and other fringe benefits.[36] For chief executives, the comparable figures were

£157,706 and £103,621, with share options on top, worth an average of another £619,107.[37]

Pensions were especially contentious. Company accounts had long understated the value of executive pensions, though they were often more valuable than salaries. Because their value is linked to final earnings, they invariably exceed the contributions a director has made. A director who expects to retire on a pension of two thirds of his salary has a strong incentive to ensure his final years are his best-paid. In general, each additional £100 earned in the final year of employment means £1,000 extra in retirement; thus, a £100,000 pay rise at the end of a career can cost the company pension fund £1 million. In 1994, the chairman of a major public company was paid £2,185,000. But a footnote to the accounts showed an additional £2,270,000 set aside for an unfunded pension liability, to be financed by shareholders rather than the company pension scheme. The cost of the chairman to the shareholders was not £2.25 million. It was £4.5 million.

The Cadbury committee was unwilling to force companies to expose the true cost of pensions, but shareholders refused to let the issue die. The result was a four-year wrangle between directors and shareholders (advised by the actuarial profession) over the way to value boardroom pensions. Unsurprisingly, directors preferred a technique which produced a lower figure; shareholders preferred a technique which produced a higher one. But by the time the Cedric Brown controversy reignited public disquiet about boardroom pay in the autumn of 1994, companies were still revealing only the level of cash contributions. The Brown affair was a vivid reminder of how little the Cadbury committee achieved: it had improved disclosure about salaries and bonuses, but done nothing to halt the spiral in executive pay. The government threatened to legislate.

Directors recognised that their independence was in peril. Howard Davies, then director general of the CBI, warned that they might lose their 'licence to operate'. Iain Vallance, chairman of BT, admitted that 'public opinion may not, strictly speaking, constitute a legitimate stakeholder interest, but we ignore it at our peril. Justice must not only be done but be *seen* to be done.'[38] Tim Melville-Ross, then director general of the Institute of Directors, was even franker: 'This has the potential to undermine the capitalist system. We have to recognise that we have a very serious problem on our hands.'[39] Abashed, the CBI set up a second committee in January 1995, with the sole objective of making recommendations on boardroom pay.

The new committee was led by Sir Richard Greenbury, chairman of Marks & Spencer. He became a target of the press. His efforts to persuade the public that directors could regulate their behaviour was undermined by his decision to continue as both chairman and chief executive and to allow his pay to rise from £779,188 to £903,900, even before his inquiries were complete. Inevitably, the tabloid newspapers took an interest in Sir Richard's private life. Distressed by the level of intrusion, Greenbury vowed never to participate in public life again.[40] 'I think the level of personal disclosure is offensive and I don't like it,' he told the *Financial Times*. 'I don't think there should be any reason why ... people should know every penny I earn.'[41] The Greenbury Report was unlikely to revolutionise boardroom pay. It did little more than amplify the exhortations contained in the Cadbury report: that boardroom pay be set by remuneration committees consisting *exclusively* of non-executives; called for fuller disclosure and proper *justification* of pay, bonuses, pensions, share options and other fringe benefits; and conceded that, *in extremis*, companies should ask shareholders to vote on a pay package. The only surprising recommendation was that gains from exercising share options be taxed as income rather than capital gains – an embarrassing suggestion, hitting middle managers and ordinary employees harder than boardroom directors. The then chancellor endorsed the idea, but dropped it when he realised it would hurt the check-out girls at Asda more than the boardroom directors.

One field where the Greenbury Report had an impact was pensions. Company reports and accounts now carry analyses of the cost and value of boardroom pensions. Otherwise Greenbury made little difference. It was not until 1997 that the Siebe engineering company became the first to give its shareholders a direct vote on the remuneration of the board of directors. Elsewhere, shareholders still have to find duller methods of registering their displeasure, like voting against the re-election of a director on the remuneration committee. They rarely bother. Even as the Greenbury Report went to press, the remuneration committee at WPP was designing a package worth up to £35 million. It was, as one shareholder described it, 'beyond what any reasonable person would vote for'.[42]

But most shareholders did. Every listed company now follows the Cadbury–Greenbury code, in the slavish manner of people following the letter of the law rather than its spirit. Five years and two reports after it had begun, corporate governance had degenerated into box-ticking. But being formulaic was no guarantee of popularity. Two senior businessmen, Stanley Kalms of Dixons and Lord Young of Cable & Wireless, attacked the Greenbury report as over-prescriptive, and, in his valedictory address to GEC shareholders, Lord Weinstock complained that the Cadbury and Greenbury Reports had enabled shareholders to persecute directors. By then, directors were fed up with reading about their salaries and bored with the burgeoning output of the corporate governance industry. When it came to chairing a third committee, to gauge the impact of the Cadbury–Greenbury recommendations on

boardroom life and shareholder-company relationships, the business establishment had great difficulty finding a candidate.

Ronald Hampel, chairman of ICI, eventually agreed. His committee began
work at the end of 1995, and published its report two years later. Its main
achievement was merging the Cadbury Report on corporate governance and
the Greenbury recommendations on executive pay into a single 49-provision
corporate governance supercode. This is policed by the London Stock
Exchange as part of disclosure requirements for companies seeking a public
quotation. Annual reports now carry lengthy reports on corporate governance
and boardroom remuneration: dull texts, they confirm that the directors
conform with the recommendations of the supercode. In Britain, most companies separate the roles of chairman and chief executive; appoint independent non-executive directors to correspond with shareholders; give directors
contracts lasting no longer than a year; entrust boardroom pay to a remuneration committee made up of non-executives; and seek shareholder approval
for long term incentive plans such as shares and share options. These ideas
were all approved by Sir Adrian and Sir Richard.

But what do they amount to? More boxes are ticked. More is disclosed.
Boardrooms are crammed with non-executive directors. But boardroom pay
has risen relentlessly. Compliance with the Cadbury–Greenbury–Hampel
code can now be used to justify any package the remuneration committee
devises. British Gas cited Greenbury when Cedric Brown was attacked. Questioned at the 1996 annual general meeting about the £1.18 million salary paid
to the Boots chief executive, Lord Blyth, chairman Michael Angus reassured
shareholders that his package was 'clean-as-a-whistle Greenbury stuff'.[43] A
Trades Union Congress (TUC) study of 362 companies, published in 1998,
showed that boardroom salaries had risen not only in real terms but in relation
to the salaries of employees. According to the TUC, the average pay of the
highest-paid director (excluding fringe benefits and incentive plans) had
risen from £204,160 in 1994 to £312,910 in 1997: from twelve times the salary
of an average employee in 1994, to sixteen times its value in 1997.[44] In
FTSE-100 companies, the gap was wider still: the highest paid directors were
getting £970,000, forty-eight times the average pay of an employee.[45] At BP,
in 1997, the chief executive earned 60 times the average company salary. 'A
company director who takes a pay rise of £50,000 when the rest of the
workforce is getting a few hundred is not part of some general trend,' said
John Edmonds, general secretary of the GMB. 'He is a greedy bastard.'[46]
After eight years and three reports, corporate governance was back where it
started.

Rise of the Remuneration Committee

It is not hard to see why: the members of the three committees never addressed the question directly. The Cadbury committee discussed the way companies were run. The Greenbury committee discussed what to tell the public about the pay of directors, not how to cut it. The Hampel committee pasted its predecessors together. But the main reason boardroom pay has continued to rocket is that the chosen method of restraint is useless. All three committees placed faith in remuneration committees of independent non-executive directors. Their members well knew that an independent non-executive director is a fictional figure.[47] Non-executives are appointed not by shareholders but by executive directors and, in most cases, they receive a personal invitation from the chief executive. At Shell, retiring executives were made non-executives as a matter of course. In 1998 Cor Herkstroter created a sensation by refusing the honour.[48]

Non-executive directors know that recommending a pay cut for directors is not the best way to secure their seat on the board. The fees range from £15–30,000 a year to over £100,000 for a non-executive chairman of a major PLC, and these are often supplemented by a contribution to their pension plan. Few have a fixed term of office, or even a written job specification, and must agree their fees directly with the chief executive. This makes it hard to act independently.

One answer is to make the remuneration committee beholden to the shareholders, not the directors, and a way to do this is to pay them in shares. This is now common practice in the United States, and the Hampel committee hoped that companies would adopt it voluntarily. But even paying people in shares is no guarantee of independence. Most non-executive directors are executive directors elsewhere, and do not want to set an unfortunate example.

Few remuneration committees insist that directors meet their performance targets in full before collecting bonuses or cashing in share-option profits. When Stephen Walls, chairman of Albert Fisher, offered to forgo his £150,000 annual bonus because he had not achieved all his performance targets, the remuneration committee insisted he should have £60,000 of it.[49] Modern incentive plans are so complicated that the average member of a remuneration committee does not even try to understand them; they rely on specialist consultants to draw them up, and on their instincts when it comes to deciding performance-related pay. Their judgements are bound to be subjective, heavily influenced by their own remuneration, and to over-estimate the contribution made by an individual they know and like.

Even if they were not, there is no objective means by which they could decide how much a particular individual contributed to the success of the company. It is simpler to attribute magical powers to an executive than to examine his business and markets in detail, and far too complicated to speculate what it would cost to replace him. The usual solution is to check what people in similar positions are earning, and add 10 or 20 per cent.

This is what the trade unionists of the 1970s called 'comparability', and businessmen would normally deplore it, but it has the happy knack (provided a higher-paid group is chosen for comparison) of ensuring that salaries never shrink. Company directors never compare themselves to hospital doctors, army generals or Cabinet secretaries, who might exercise greater responsibilities for less money, but they point out how little they are paid compared with Snooks at Acme PLC or Snookerburger at Acme Inc. (A Bank of England spokesman explained a controversial pay rise for the governor on the grounds that he was 'in danger of being overtaken by Jeremy Paxman'.)

Where pay is set by comparability (rather than the market) a ratchet effect sets in. Differentials have to be maintained. The correct comparisons have to be chosen. No remuneration committee wants to pay its charges less than the average, so the average keeps rising. Comparability builds into the work of every remuneration committee a persistent tendency to err on the side of generosity. A study by Professor Brian Main of Edinburgh University reckoned that chief executives whose pay was set by a remuneration committee received 20 per cent more than companies without one.[50] Another study of 94 companies in the FTSE-100, published in 1998, found the effect was the same after six more years of corporate governance: companies with independent non-executive directors pay the most.[51]

Why Shareholders Cannot Stop It

It is natural to expect institutional shareholders to bring this agreeable process to a halt. (Retail investors worry about it more, but own too few shares to have influence.) Unfortunately, shareholders cannot vote directly on the remuneration of directors, and the Hampel committee rejected the idea of giving them the right. Only one of its members (the Labour-supporting Chris Haskins, chairman of Northern Foods) argued for it, though the National Association of Pension Funds urged the committee to endorse the idea. The New Labour government has threatened to make it a statutory requirement. Until it does, shareholders will not dispute the pay of directors regularly. They already vote on less than half the issues where they do have a direct say,[52] but since regular voting was one of the principal aims of the corporate governance movement ten years ago, it is naïve to hope that shareholders will improve that record until they are forced to change.

In 1996 shareholders in GEC did force the company to revise a package it offered George Simpson, the man they hired from Lucas Varity as managing director. Executive pay was the occasion rather than the cause of institutional disgruntlement. Protests about paypackages tend to occur at companies which shareholders dislike for other reasons. The poor performance of GEC in the last years of Arnold Weinstock had already alienated shareholders. By 1995, when Maurice Saatchi provoked institutional outrage (and his own resignation) with a performance-related share-option plan which might have yielded him £5 million, shares in Saatchi & Saatchi had tumbled from £50 in 1987 to less than £1.50. If he had met his performance targets over the following three years, as one shareholder said: 'We would only have lost 90 per cent of our money instead of 95 per cent. It was a red rag to a bull.'[53]

American shareholders in Saatchi & Saatchi had pressed for management changes at the advertising agency for years before their British counterparts joined them. But British investors deny they are boardroom doormats. They claim their best work is done *in camera*, and that they prevent many outrageous pay schemes taking off at all. This claim is, by its nature, hard to verify. But it is true that they do go public when the quiet approach fails. Institutional disquiet exposed the lavish boardroom perks at Marks & Spencer in the early 1980s. In 1982 the Post Office pension fund went to court to stop Lew Grade giving Jack Gill a £650,000 golden handshake.[54] In December 1989 institutional investors forced British Land to scrap a capital restructuring they considered too generous to management. In 1991, Norwich Union mounted a famous public attack on the management of the pollution controls group, Tace.[55]

But the issues, and especially the money, are rarely big enough to warrant a public fuss. A few hundred thousand pounds more for a director is neither here nor there at a company worth £10 billion (unlike an extra £3 a week for 10,000 workers on the shop floor, which is a material figure). 'Divided equally among the shareholders,' wrote Iain Vallance of his much-criticised salary, 'my pay would not buy much more than a postage stamp apiece.'[56] Under pressure to explain the 75 per cent pay increase to Cedric Brown, British Gas chairman Richard Giordano advanced a stronger version of the same argument. 'Shareholders have nothing to gain by paying Cedric Brown less than he deserves,' he wrote. 'The financial consequences of his success or failure will dwarf these events.'[57]

Nailing the future and fortune of the company to the retention of talent is an argument which impresses shareholders. But it works only because they are ignorant: institutional shareholders lack the information to decide what executives should be paid. Few employ staff to monitor boardroom pay, or corporate governance in general. They rely instead on the Association of British Insurers (ABI) and the National Association of Pension Funds (NAPF), and private corporate governance and proxy voting agencies like Pirc and Manifest, to keep them abreast of boardroom activities. In one case reported in the press, shareholders initially failed to notice that the directors had cancelled and reissued options at lower prices because the shares had halved since the scheme was introduced.[58] Even if they are persuaded to vote regularly, as the government is threatening to force them to do, shareholders are not convinced of their competence to determine boardroom pay. 'On the grounds of practicality,' wrote Iain Vallance, 'they have to trust these matters to the board's remuneration committee.'[59] Fund managers agree. Even if they all employed staff to monitor executive pay, the sheer quantity of data on thousands of different companies would swamp them.

Shareholders prefer to monitor corporate performance, not corporate governance. Directors know that they can settle their own remuneration provided the dividend rises and the share price is strong. In fact, there is evidence that companies with the best structures of corporate governance are not the most profitable; companies with small, tightly knit teams of managers often do better than boards packed with non-executives.[60] Shareholders also understand that directors cannot control everything: a downturn in the trade cycle or an adverse movement in the rate of interest or exchange, can have a larger influence on corporate performance than any number of supposed management triumphs or disasters.

Performance-Related Pay

All shareholders can do is try to ensure that boardroom pay is not out of joint with corporate performance, which is why tying the pay of directors to the company's financial performance is popular. Superficially, it aligns the interests of shareholders and directors. But no measure of financial performance is perfect. Traditional measures of profitability, such as Earnings per Share (EPS) or Return on Capital (ROC), are influenced by accounting techniques. Adjustments to debt and exceptional items, or share buy-backs, can make a bad performance appear a good one. Since the senior executives control the audit committee of the board (as well as the remuneration committee) they tend to ensure that the reported financial performance is as good as it can be made.

The solution favoured by the Greenbury committee was to replace traditional measures with broader, longer and more comparative measurements of financial performance. The chosen gauge was Total Shareholder Return

(TSR), to be measured over a three- to five-year period, and against other companies in the sector or in general. TSR measures return to shareholders in terms of dividend payments and increases in the value of the shares, and is therefore a measure of absolute and relative performance over time. These long-term incentive plans, which have acquired the unattractive sobriquet of 'L-Tips', are now the basis of executive pay at three out of four FTSE-100 companies. They reward directors with ever-larger packages of cash and shares as the company hurdles a succession of stiff performance targets. The rewards can be immense. In 1998 a mature, three-year L-Tip at BP yielded over £3 million for five directors, including £900,000 for chief executive John Browne.[61]

The L-Tip is an imperfect solution: the performance targets may be set too low, and a scheme introduced at the bottom of a recession is bound to be undemanding. Even the ABI-approved criteria demand no more than minimum real growth in TSR of 2 per cent, and several companies have not even aimed that high. The relative element in an L-Tip, designed initially to place a floor under boardroom pay, can have the opposite effect. The BP plan was lucrative because the company had outperformed seven other oil companies, which did not necessarily mean BP had performed well in absolute terms. Nor do L-Tips escape reliance on accounting measures. Share prices are set by the market, but the market relies on the accounts to measure profitability. In 1997 the former management of Wickes repaid £1.5 million in bonuses they had earned from an L-Tip scheme after the profits on which it was based were over-stated.[62] Share analysts and shareholders are increasingly sceptical of rising dividends and share prices as a measure of performance. But even fashionable measures like Economic Value Added (EVA) and Market Value Added (MVA) still rely on the work of the bean-counters.* There is no perfect measure of the financial performance of a company.

Even if one could be devised, the question of *how* to reward outstanding performance is equally intractable. A bonus is the obvious method, but bonuses have long since degenerated into part of the basic pay package, and cash does not align the interests of the directors with the shareholders as closely as shares. The Greenbury committee recommended paying bonuses in shares rather than cash. Some companies, like Glaxo Wellcome, now do this. But the average British company director prefers share options, which

---

* Economic Value Added (EVA) takes annual profits and subtracts the cost of capital. Market Value Added (MVA) takes market capitalisation and subtracts capital invested. EVA seeks to show net return to shareholders on an annual basis, while MVA aims to show net return in total. EVA is backward-looking while MVA, because it incorporates market capitalisation, embodies market expectations about future earnings. Both aim to arrive at the net increase in shareholder value by subtracting capital invested.

L-Tips were intended to replace. At the end of 1997, four out of five FTSE-100 companies still had executive share-option schemes. The proportion was higher still at smaller companies.[63]

Options to buy shares in the company at a pre-determined price, profitable only if the share price rises, have remained attractive for several reasons. For a start, they cost the directors nothing. If the share price fails to rise above the price at which the option can be exercised, all the director has lost is a potentially profitable opportunity. Options also remain attractive in tax terms. No income tax is payable on the grant of an option. In the 1984 budget, Nigel Lawson allowed share option gains to be taxed as capital not income. Within a decade, nine out of ten companies had an Inland Revenue approved share-option scheme.[64] Like cash bonuses, they have become a boardroom norm. It is not hard to see why. They enable executives to enjoy equity returns without putting up equity capital. A 1992 study reckoned directors typically make gains of 90 per cent on options after four years. The median profit in cash was £62,000, but in some cases directors made eight-fold gains and profits of over £200,000.[65] Averages can be misleading. By 1998, Jan Leschly, chief executive of SmithKline Beecham, was reported to own unexercised share option profits worth £52 million.[66]

Seven figure profits from share options are now commonplace though it helps to acquire options in a company facing disaster. Share options issued at a deeply discounted price of 0.1p in 1992 turned Archie Norman, saviour of Asda, into a multi-millionaire.[67] British Aerospace was another company where directors profited from the rescue. John Cahill made £3.2 million on his options in British Aerospace after helping to revive its fortunes, and Richard Lapthorne, his finance director, enjoyed a profit of £1.1 million on his share options in 1995.[68] Two years later his successor as chief executive, Richard Evans, realised £2.2 million from option sales and Mike Turner, the joint managing director, cashed options worth £1.5 million. But failure has its rewards, if a company is taken over at a price per share which exceeds the exercise price.[69]

Some companies have now introduced 'super options'. These are given to directors in multiples of their annual salary, provided they meet some easily measurable criterion (like beating EPS growth in the previous five years). Their advocates think them superior to L–Tips in aligning the interests of shareholders and managers. This is improbable: if the share price does not rise, the directors still lose nothing but a profitable opportunity; if it does, the shareholders have to meet the full cost of exercised options. The extent to which directors hold on to shares purchased through option schemes is unknown, but it is certain that they have not led to widespread share owner-ship by directors. Most directors trade them for cash.

It is increasingly obvious that performance-related pay is not the best way to get managers to pursue shareholders' interests. For a start, it does not work. Executive pay often appears to bear little or no relationship to corporate financial performance. This is partly a matter of timing. Because the rewards are based on accounting measures of *past* performance, it is not uncommon for directors to collect large sums in years when the company has performed badly. Uncertainties of measurement, especially in combination with time-lags, mean performance-related formulae can allow directors to take large pay rises in the same year that profits plunge, investments are written off, and staff are made redundant.[70] An academic study of the performance of 300 large companies between 1983 and 1991 found that directors bumped up their pay 20 per cent a year, which bore no relation to shareholder returns measured by TSR, EPS or ROC. The only strong link between pay and performance was growth in sales; *any* link between pay and corporate perform-ance broke down completely as the economy entered recession in 1988–91.[71] Executive pay did not fall as performance plummeted. In the matter of who gets what in British boardrooms, the role of performance is nugatory.

Some studies have identified an inverse relationship between pay and per-formance, with high-performing companies paying less. Certainly, perform-ance-related pay can have perverse effects: tying too much of the personal wealth of the directors to the fate of the company is bound to make them risk-averse, encouraging them to forgo profitable opportunities. Performance-related pay may also drive them to pursue short-term fixes rather than long-term strategies: firing a third of the workforce and slashing the R&D budget will increase profits and the share price in the short term, but it might not do much for the company in the longer term. Paradoxically, the most shareholder friendly manager may be one insulated from the risks of failure.

Paying for Failure: The Golden Handshake

Failure may not be as risky as it appears. A public company which gets into difficulty is usually taken over, but then the outgoing directors can profit by selling their shares and options to the bidder. John Clark was chief executive of BET PLC when the company was taken over by Rentokil in April 1996. He made a profit of £3.4 million from selling his shares to the bidder, on top of a salary totalling £1.1 million in the previous year.[72] Predictably, Clark was encouraged to resign by the new management. He launched a £5 million claim against Rentokil for compensation, and, after prolonged litigation, secured another £2.25 million.[73] When Guinness merged with Grand Metro-politan in 1997, after several years of poor performance, five directors seized the opportunity to cash their share options despite the company having fallen far short of the performance criteria set by the remuneration committee. Their justification was simple: the Grand Metropolitan directors were cashing in their options; Guinness directors were entitled to do the same.[74]

Directors are made redundant occasionally, but they rarely leave empty-handed. Golden Parachutes, as they are known, are sometimes written into their employment contracts. Most company directors are guaranteed a year's salary if the business is taken over; Jan Leschly, of SmithKline Beecham, would receive three years' pay.[75] For years, the key to a sizeable golden handshake was to insist on a rolling contract, whereby the job was always assumed to have the same number of years to run. Most senior directors were on three-year rolling contracts, guaranteeing them three years' pay if they lost their jobs, until the Greenbury committee recommended that no contract should run for more than one year. This followed complaints from shareholders that rolling contracts rewarded failure. In 1993 Alastair Ross Goobey, chief executive of Hermes Pensions Management, wrote a letter to every company in the FTSE-100 warning that the fund would vote against re-election of any director on a contract longer than twelve months. 'Too often recently we have read of senior executives who have been deemed to have failed in their role,' he wrote. 'But, as a consequence of their contract, [they] have been paid off with substantial sums.'[76]

Several cases were widely publicised. Sir Ralph Halpern, forced out of the top job at Burton Group in 1990, was given £1.6 million and a pension of £465,000 a year. His successor, Laurence Cooklin, lasted a year before fresh difficulties saw him leave with £773,000. Robert Horton, ousted in a board-room coup at BP in 1993 after the company registered its first-ever loss, got £1.5 million. Don McCrickard was given £763,000 by shareholders in the TSB, which was forced into a merger with Lloyds Bank after a difficult period following privatisation. Sir Kit McMahon collected £489,187 when he left the Midland Bank. Sir Derek Alun-Jones left Ferranti nearly half a million pounds to the good after fraud at a subsidiary cost the company £215 million.

It is not surprising that the Greenbury committee turned the twelve-month rolling contract into best practice, though companies can circumvent the time limit. Some cut contracts to a year but guarantee directors three years' pay if they have to leave unexpectedly. Others bump up salaries. In 1997 Granada, the media and leisure group, paid £374,500 to five directors to compensate them for cutting their notice period from three years to two. The shareholders were upset, and one in three of those who decided to vote opposed the payment.[77] But the company did not back down. Ian Martin, chairman of the remuneration committee, explained that the cut in the notice period was 'a significant loss of contractual value to the directors concerned

TABLE 15.4
A Random List of Payments to Departing Executives, 1989–1998

	Company	Year Paid	Amount* £
Jim Fifield	EMI	1998	6,400,000
Richard Oster	Cookson	1997	4,806,000
David Dworkin	Storehouse	1994	3,290,000
John Cahill	British Aerospace	1994	3,200,000
Ernest Mario	Glaxo	1993	2,700,000
Lord Young	Cable & Wireless	1996	c.2,400,000
John Clark	Rentokil	1997	2,250,000
Chris Greentree	Lasmo	1993	2,200,000
Peter Scott	Aegis	N/A	2,250,000
Peter Davis	Reed Elsevier	1994	2,022,000
Sir Ralph Halpern	Burton	1990	c.2,000,000
Ken Harvey	Norweb	1995	c.2,000,000
Robert Horton	BP	1993	1,552,740
Eric Parker	Trafalgar House	1992	1,300,000
James Ross	Cable & Wireless	1996	c.1,300,000
Alain Soulas	Arjo Wiggins Appleton	1996	c.1,300,000
Richard Young	Midlands Electricity	1994	1,235,000
Alastair Lyons	Abbey National	1997	1,200,000
Jim Maxmin	Laura Ashley	1994	1,200,000
Dermot McNulty	Shandwick	1998	1,200,000
John Conlan	First Leisure	1998	1,140,000
Philip Green	Amber Day	1992	1,130,000
Terry Bannister	Saatchi & Saatchi	1992	1,100,000
Stephen Brown	Tate & Lyle	1993	1,100,000
Roy Warman	Saatchi & Saatchi	1992	1,100,000
Brian Gilbert	Maxwell Communications	1991	1,007,125
John Brackenbury	Brent Walker	1997	1,064,000
Alan Michels	Telewest	1996	1,004,000
Michael Hepher	Charterhouse	1998	c.1,000,000
David Smith	Isosceles	1992	c.1,000,000

Source: *Financial Times.*

* Includes pension rights and shares or share options where appropriate, as well as compensation for loss of office.

which, if unsympathetically handled, might well be seen as a censure and becoming a demotivating factor'.[78] Gerry Robinson, chief executive of Granada and one of the beneficiaries of the payment, complained of 'an attempt, in an almost blackmailing way, to force people into a very narrow view of corporate governance'.[79]

Though institutions are usually more sanguine, retail shareholders do take a narrower view. When Michael Hoffman left Thames Water with a cash and share options package valued at £890,000, after the company had written off £95 million, shareholders asked angry questions at the AGM[80] But it was his contractual entitlement.[81] Shareholders forget that managers are also employees, who are entitled to be treated fairly. When John Gunn received a £1 million payment from the liquidators to British & Commonwealth, a company he once ran, outsiders were astonished. In fact, anybody who works for a company after it fails is entitled to claim benefits in lieu of notice.[82]

Corporate Aristocracy: Perks of the Job

But nobody can deny that directors are different from other employees. When shareholders at an AGM laughed at his defence of a £900,000 salary, Lord Sheppard essayed a joke. 'I agree it's laughable what they pay us,' he is reported to have said. 'My wife is working on that.'[83] If it fell flat, it was because many believe that executive remuneration is decided on a whimsical basis. Directors, like the trade union leaders of the 1970s, are in danger of losing touch with shareholders, employees and consumers.

The chief cause of remoteness is lifestyle. The average chief executive of a major public company is conveyed from his home to the office by chauffeur-driven car. The newspapers he reads on the way were not bought by him. Nor is the coffee awaiting him at his desk. His diary and correspondence are organised by a team of secretaries and personal assistants, whose duties may extend to paying his household bills. Lunch (and often dinner) are usually supplied by the company. If his duties necessitate foreign travel, the chauffeur will convey him to the first-class lounge at the airport. In remoter parts, he will probably travel by company jet, and while he is abroad, every imaginable expense will be met by the shareholders. He will not be able to remember the last time he paid for a ticket to Wimbledon, Goodwood, Lord's or Twickenham, or for the car to be serviced or insured or sold, or for the lawyers and the accountants who manage his personal legal and financial affairs. The shareholders will often pay for a London pied-à-terre as well as a country house, perhaps decorating them both, building the tennis court, tending the garden, and cleaning the swimming pool. The modern chief executive is rarely the hard-driving entrepreneur of his imaginings. He is usually no more than a peculiarly hard-working employee, but one insulated from the daily trials of life.

The public and private lives of some directors have become so closely entwined that it is increasingly hard to distinguish between them. Questioned in 1996 about a Golden Hello package worth nearly £5 million, the newly appointed chief executive of an engineering group explained that he had given up the chauffeur-driven car he enjoyed in his last job. 'I travelled on the tube for the first time in three years today, which I regard as a bit of a hardship,' he told the *Financial Times*. 'The Northern Line was bloody dirty.' Out of work for nine months after leaving Reed Elsevier, the chief executive of the Prudential has admitted that it was 'quite a shock at first, learning where the post box was, and writing your own envelopes.'[84] In the spring of 1996 Peter Robinson, chief executive of the Woolwich Building Society, said he was 'totally shocked' when the board asked him to resign after it was alleged that he had used corporate funds to buy a car and had invited Woolwich employees to decorate his house and mow his lawns. He was at the time earning £300,000 a year.[85]

As long ago as 1982, seven main board directors at Marks & Spencer were found to be leasing houses valued at £1.7 million from the company, with an option to buy at cost with interest-free loans from the shareholders.[86] In the same year, Jack Gill, managing director of Associated Communications Corporation, agreed to buy a house from the company at £109,000 below its market price. His boss, Lord Grade, had recently purchased a £405,000 Belgravia flat from the company for £1.[87]

Generous housing allowances are a common perk for company directors. The shareholders of Rio Tinto furnish the chief executive with a London house whose annual rental value is estimated at £270,000.[88] Jan Leschly was granted £850,000 in 'relocation expenses' by SmithKline when he moved from Princeton to Marlow.[89] Peter Aikens, chief executive of cider maker Matthew Clark, received a £127,000 'disturbance allowance' and £68,000 to cover the cost of selling his house at a loss when the company moved its headquarters from Guildford to Bristol. When the company had paid other expenses and associated tax, the shareholders had paid £431,000 to move the chief executive 105 miles.[90]

Fringe benefits take a variety of forms. In 1991 shareholders in Sun Alliance advanced a £500,000 interest-free loan to the chairman, Lord Aldington. He explained that he needed the money to pursue a libel action.[91] During his struggle to take over Forte in 1996, Granada chairman Gerry Robinson told journalists victory would be followed by the sale of the corporate jet. But once

Granada decided not to sell the Meridien chain, which owns a number of hotels abroad, he found it was the quickest way to reach them.

A director of EMI is reputed to have a contractual right to fly first-class.[92] (One of the oddities of executive travel is that air miles accrue to the traveller, not the company.) In 1998 the ousted chairman of a biotechnology company put in a claim for compensation. Apart from salary, pension, health and accommodation costs, the claim was reported to include membership of the Young President's Organisation (£42,400 a year); business-class air tickets to Australia for his family (£34,500); private school fees (£33,000); accountancy expenses (£13,000 a year); a Jaguar XJR (£22,000) and 'a second vehicle of equivalent status.'[93]

Market Value or Just Deserts?

Why do shareholders allow directors to treat the company as a personal sugar-daddy? In some cases, they know nothing of it. In most, they do not care: the sums are relatively small, and a few favours may help directors to do their jobs better. Shareholders also accept that they are part of the cost of talent. 'The people sitting on this board today can move to America or Europe and triple or quadruple what they earn,' Ian MacLaurin told irate shareholders in 1991, the year his reward for running Tesco rose to £1.5 million. 'The call has come many times to me and colleagues and we have stayed.'[94]

Certainly, the British boardroom is a model of restraint by comparison with its American counterparts. In 1994 Michael Eisner, chief executive of the Disney Corporation, took home $203 million after cashing in some of his stock options. Three years later, he cashed in another $100 million, and in May 1997 he was awarded a ten-year contract valued at $770 million. At Coca-Cola, chief executive Roberto Goizueta assembled a personal fortune of $1.4 billion in salary, bonuses and shares during his sixteen years at the top of the company, of which all but $100 million was taken in deferred stock. When he died in 1997, the Coca-Cola company took a $1 billion tax deduction for his pay alone.[95]

Americans such as Eisner and Goizueta make the remuneration of British company directors seem modest, and provide a reminder to shareholders of values in the international labour market. But the global market for executives is not as large and active as boardrooms would like their shareholders to believe. It is confined to a few dozen people renowned for their skill at running businesses, cutting costs and rescuing faltering companies. They operate in a handful of industries. One of them is motor cars; another is finance. In 1993, for example, Volkswagen hired Jose Ignacio Lopez de Arriortua from General Motors, at huge cost and risk, because they believed that only he could deliver the marginal reductions in costs which make for success or failure in the global car market.

If there were a truly global market in top executives for all industries, it would long since have eroded the huge differences in pay in one country rather than another. It would also have bid salaries down, rather than up. Not many British directors would travel well outside the United States. Their knowledge of languages is slim, and the cultural barriers to success in foreign countries are immense. In some markets, of which supermarket retailing is one, British managers anyway are paid more than their American counterparts.[96]

There is not even much of a national market in executive talent, partly because people are reluctant to move. When Brandon Gough became chairman of Yorkshire Water in 1996, shareholders were told he would continue to live in Hampshire.[97] The vast majority of executives, even at the highest level, are also promoted from within. According to one recent survey, the typical chief executive of a FTSE-100 company is a fifty-five-year-old man promoted six years earlier from a lesser job in the same organisation.[98] A survey of the 200 largest public companies found that the typical director was a fifty-six-year-old, Oxbridge-educated British male with an accountancy qualification – just as he was in 1970.[99]

But because the value of so few senior executives is tested on the open market, shareholders have to accept the valuation they place upon themselves. Asked how he knew Cedric Brown was worth £475,000 (in the absence of competing offers for his services) British Gas chairman Richard Giordano argued that the question was nonsensical. In a letter published in the *Financial Times*, he wrote:

> It is ludicrous to assume that the market pay for an executive can best be validated by his changing jobs. This view is often expressed by questions such as 'if he is underpaid why doesn't he leave?' or 'why hasn't he been poached?' If this view drives pay decisions, executive mercenaries will do well, but talented executives, whose experience is industry-specific or who value loyalty to their employers, will be put at a disadvantage. This would surely be a perverse outcome of the process of determining pay.[100]

Giordano was arguing that people who do not test their value in the marketplace deserve as much as those who do. Most boardroom defences of pay and perks are a variant of this argument for comparability.

Businessmen often cite the rewards conceded without controversy to pop stars and footballers. 'As a society we have adopted an odd set of priorities over remuneration,' complained Iain Vallance of BT at the height of the Cedric Brown furore. 'We put a high price on escapism (pop groups, footballers, film stars, lottery winners). Entrepreneurs and the well-heeled professions go largely beyond rebuke. But we quibble about the often much smaller sums that go to the bosses of the major companies which underpin our economy. And we tolerate the fact that our legislators and those who run the country are paid very little indeed.'[101] If a mere crooner or centre forward is worth £10 million, goes that argument, then surely a chief executive or an MP is worth at least a few hundred thousand. 'Other people at the top are paid huge sums of money, so why not businessmen?' asked Greg Hutchings, chief executive of Tomkins PLC, in response to press criticism of his salary, which was close to £1 million.[102]

He can be answered. In sport and entertainment, technology has created a global market in which the best squeeze out the second-best. Because television audiences want to see Alan Shearer rather than some third division journeyman, sponsorship has driven his capital value to £15 million.[103] Likewise, CD buyers prefer Pavarotti to any number of tenors who can sing almost as well; book buyers prefer Maeve Binchy or Jeffrey Archer to dozens of similar writers who lack the same brand recognition; and cinema-goers prefer a Hollywood star in almost anything to a bravura performance by an unknown actor in an art film. Recording, television and telecommunications technology has given consumers around the globe a choice of the best performers (or in some cases, the most popular), so they do not bother with second-best. A small and self-reinforcing clique of athletes, musicians, novelists and actors are reaping the rewards of massive global sales, which further enlarge the amount they will command when the next tournament, concert or film comes around.[104] The same forces are not at work in the markets for business executives. They are competing mainly against their colleagues for one of ten or twelve seats on the board of the company they work for.

In the absence of a market test of value, it is hard to identify an alternative criterion, though many have tried. In January 1995, just as the public storm over Cedric Brown was prompting the CBI to set up the Greenbury Committe, Iain Vallance penned an article for the *Financial Times* entitled 'Justice on Executive Pay.' In it, he wrote:

> The fundamental principle that properly underpins differentiation in levels of remuneration is justice – distributive justice. The central question is whether there is a just and fair reward for the job done. If we stick to that principle of justice, we can clear away much of the emotional

baggage surrounding the arguments and get down to the practical issue
of determining what is, or is not, a just reward.

Sir Iain was asking the right question. Public distaste for lavish salaries stems
largely from the popular belief that they are unfair, unjustified and devoid
of merit. But it is not surprising that he failed to arrive at a satisfactory answer
to his own question: 'What is justice?' Every philosopher since Plato first
posed the question has failed to find one. In the article, the search for
practical ways of deciding how and what to pay company directors quickly
overwhelmed the quest for principles of justice.

Degrees of Difficulty?

The practical tools Sir Iain identified were the size and complexity of the
job, its comparability with similar jobs, the demands it makes of the holder,
and the financial performance of the company. Certainly, executive jobs are
harder than they were, because even though directors are not competing in
a global market, their companies are. The barriers to the free flow of goods,
services and capital around the world have come down since the 1970s, exposing companies to competition for customers and capital. The value of a
company, and even its survival, depends to an unprecedented degree on the
ability and commitment of its management. According to the Institute of
Management, the *average* executive is working ten hours more a week than
he was twenty-five years ago. But senior executives are not paid to work hard;
they are paid to take decisions – good decisions. A bad decision by the
foreman may injure a workman, but a bad decision by the chief executive
can kill the company.

'The reality is that the skills of the man at the top do make the difference,'
says Sir John Harvey-Jones, 'and that such experience and abilities are rare.'[105]
To keep ahead of the competition (and the corporate predators) a chief
executive has to cut costs ruthlessly, bring new products to market quickly,
and anticipate and neutralise a range of competitive threats. Political, regulatory and legal risks have to be managed simultaneously, to ensure that consumers and citizens (and politicians and lawyers who claim to act for them)
are as happy as the customers. 'His contribution is not seven or ten times that
of the average worker,' says Tim Melville-Ross, of the Institute of Directors, of
the typical chief executive, 'it could be 5,000 times.'[106]

Iain Vallance let slip in 1995 that he might find it 'relaxing' to work the
hours of a junior doctor. Hard work and high risks warrant high rewards. Yet
few of the risks of running a business seem to be borne by the directors. The

entrepreneur who makes a fortune out of spotting a gap in the market and remortgaging his house to raise capital, deserves a reward for taking a risk. But a businessman who gets to the top of a company, as much by luck or by service as ability, does not. Sir Owen Green, a Black Country industrialist with a distaste for the trappings of corporate aristocracy, has pointed this out:

> There's absolutely nothing to be said against entrepreneurs or pop stars creating personal wealth through their own talent, direct from the general public. But in many large companies the people at the top are really a type of functionary – the culture and the strategy are already set. In any business which has not been created or distinctly improved by a single person, I can't see any justification for or any good example being set by trying to keep up with [people] who are entirely different animals.[107]

It is not a common view in the boardroom. In 1998 the chief executive of the Royal Bank of Scotland told the *Financial Times* that Peter Wood, who sold his Direct Line business to the Royal Bank, had taken no risk in setting it up: 'No one objects to the entrepreneur getting £100 million. But you are just as rare an animal if you can run a big company. Peter Wood didn't take any risk! No risk at all! I have no objection to Peter getting the money. But it is a myth to think that the qualities required to run a large business are easily available. How many in the Footsie-100 can do it? Not everybody. What matters in a company is the person who runs it.'[108]

Most top businessmen believe they are indispensable. When Greg Hutchings was asked if his talent was unique, his reply was an unequivocal 'Yes'.[109] In 1992 Robert Horton, the chairman of BP, told *Forbes* magazine: 'Because I am blessed by my good brain, I tend to get the right answer rather quicker and more often than most people.'[110] His colleagues disagreed; he was ousted in a famous boardroom coup later the same year. His successor, Lord Simon of Highbury, had inherited a company where the hard and unpopular work of reorganisation and rationalisation was over, the oil markets were picking up, and interest rates were coming down. As the profits of BP soared, he was fêted, well rewarded, and recruited as a government minister. There is no reason to believe that the outcome would have differed greatly if BP had stuck with Robert Horton instead.

Star executives such as Jim Maxmin and Ann Iverson could not reverse the fundamental problems at Laura Ashley by willpower alone. The company has changed its senior management five times in seven years without reviving its fortunes. Bill Cockburn, the best chief executive the Post Office ever had, could not rescue W. H. Smith. Leeds Permanent managed without a chief executive for eighteen months; its profits rose by 22 per cent. Most companies depend on a team of senior executives with different skills, not one man or woman, or even the chief executive and the finance director (who tend to attract the most publicity). As Arie de Geus of Shell observed in his book, *The Living Company*, the corporate machine is 'too complicated, too sophisticated to be in the hands of one individual. It is extremely dangerous for business. Yet companies are remunerating as if it is a beautiful thing.'

The error is understandable. Since the long recovery began from the near-collapse of capitalism in the mid-1970s, analysts and commentators have wanted to believe in the magical qualities of individual managers. Their faith works, to the extent that it drives up the share price of the companies whose managers they admire. Executives who have benefited from stock and stock options have begun to share it. But if stock markets fall, managers are certain to rebel against being paid in a depreciating currency. The cult of individualism in management will last only so long as it pays. Modern managers are not great leaders of men and businesses after all; they are like everybody else. Except that they are paid more money.

Is Management Different from Leadership?

This is the popular assessment of the boardroom now. Public cynicism about the character and morals of the average director was never more intense. When Nick Reilly, chairman of Vauxhall Motors, offered in April 1998 to forgo his £160,000 salary for a year if the workforce would agree to a pay deal, his gesture was attacked as a gimmick.[111] After years of adverse publicity about boardroom pay, nobody believed his offer was genuine: a Fat Cat, however unfair the caricature, makes an improbable Santa Claus. Yet Reilly had offered the one quality conspicuous by its absence in most discussions of executive pay – leadership.

Until the 1980s, executive pay was constrained by ideas of leadership which are now considered old-fashioned. The men who ran British business from the turn of the century to the 1970s had often fought in the wars alongside the men they managed. Just as the officer did not bed down until his men were comfortable, and went over the top first, the industrial manager was expected to set his employees an example of excellence and modesty. In *The Stagnant Society*, Michael Shanks described the characteristics of hundreds of industrial managers he had met:

> They want to make as much money as they can, certainly. But they want other things as well. They want to be loved by their fellow-men – not

least their workers. They want to be regarded as pillars of their local community, looked up to by their colleagues (and rewarded if possible by directorships and a place in the Honours List). They like to feel that they are doing a useful job and helping the country. They like to be able to relax from time to time, and not always to be bothered with office crises and problems. Besides the desire for profit, therefore, there is the desire for prestige, for self-satisfaction, for service, leisure, and a whole medley of other emotions – good, bad and indifferent. And the more secure financially and socially the industrialist is, the less large does the desire for profit loom in his calculations.[112]

The cosmopolitan businessman of today is different. Rightly obsessed with 'the bottom line', to the exclusion of all else, perpetually short of time, always on the move, and never beyond the reach of the telephone, the fax machine and the laptop, he is a getter of money rather than a leader of men. For him, money is not the route to social prestige; it is the source of it.

The archetypal modern manager is Al 'Chainsaw' Dunlap, an American who built a fearsome reputation for cutting costs on behalf of Kerry Packer and Sir James Goldsmith. 'If you're in business,' he once said, 'you're in business for one thing – to make money.' This is true, but some directors have taken it too personally. The few genuine Fat Cats are an accidental by-product of the otherwise commendable search for a new type of manager: energetic, profit-seeking, self-confident, well-paid. In the 1980s, corporatism gave way to individualism in the boardrooms of British business. Almost all that was shed was bad, but some good was sacrificed as well. Fat Cats undermine the morale of their employees. They have turned their middle managers into mercenaries, prepared to swap jobs every time someone offers more money.

Companies are finding it harder to attract talented graduates, who are put off by the caricature of business life which the hard-driving, job-slashing executive represents. It is a caricature which has taken hold beyond the confines of the boardroom, doing much to undermine capitalism by making business synonymous with large salaries and big cars for the few and the sack or long hours for the rest. Tales of Fat Cattery have done irreparable damage to the image of business among people who have no direct experience of it.

A burst of managerial exuberance was an understandable reaction to what had passed before. In the 1960s and 1970s, senior executive pay was constrained by bullying trade unions, prices and incomes policies, foreign exchange controls and high marginal rates of taxation. In 1970, the average director of a major PLC got £11,000 a year (about £100,000 today). He now earns up to five times as much, in real terms. Then, high earners were taxed at rates as high as 83 per cent on *earned* income. For the average manager, it made more sense to take a week off work to decorate his own house rather than to pay anyone else to do it for him. It was also during these years that companies developed those proxies for cash payment, like company cars, subsidised mortgages, and corporate entertainment, which have proved so awkward to excise, even in a more liberal tax regime.

But by the early 1990s a necessary release of managerial energy was in danger (in some quarters) of degenerating into a festival of personal aggrandisement. As Owen Green pointed out, boardroom excess cannot leave the morale of the workforce or the value of a company undamaged. 'How a director who has just had an 18 per cent rise dares to tell his workers to show restraint and accept less than 5 per cent I cannot understand,' he wrote. 'Perhaps those workers understand all too well. It suggests an almost papal separation of the leader from his flock. This distancing means executives lose touch with the people who actually do the work. It is not that the executives are objects of envy, though they may be. What they have lost is respect.'[113]

CHAPTER SIXTEEN

THE PRIVATE SECTOR PROFESSIONALS

All professions are conspiracies against the laity.

GEORGE BERNARD SHAW[1]

In every big transaction, there is a magic moment during which a man has surrendered a treasure, and during which the man who is due to receive it has not yet done so. An alert lawyer will make that moment his own, possessing the treasure for a magic microsecond, taking a little of it, passing it on.

KURT VONNEGUT[2]

The one great principle of the English law is, to make business for itself.

CHARLES DICKENS[3]

We are here to stay. Please trust us.

Investment banker, letter to clients, March 1998[4]

Goodbye for now.

The same investment banker, July 1998.[5]

Respect is what professionals crave. Unlike aristocrats or plutocrats, it is not from the possession of land or money that they derive their rewards. Their value rests on the esteem of others. Like Fat Cats, they are salaried employees. But unlike ordinary employees, they are not paid what is necessary to attract, retain and motivate them. In the market for highly paid professionals, price and competition are irrelevant. Unlike the itinerant labourer, the professional is not willing to accept the market valuation of his labour. It is not his ability to compete, but his status which determines his income – a status derived from a mind honed by education, raised to excellence by specialised training, and matured by long experience in its field. The professional demands that buyers accept *his* valuation of *his* talent, and invariably they do. 'If you want the best, you have to pay for the best,' a QC told the *Observer* in 1991. 'A lot of money is at stake in the sort of questions we have to decide.'[6]

If impudence is the first secret of the standard of living the professional enjoys, ignorance is the second. Denied the benefits of his trained intelligence, ordinary mortals cannot tell whether what they ask is simple and cheap or complex and expensive. A plaintiff does not know if his case is strong or weak; a borrower does not know if his credit is good or bad; and a patient does not know if he is sick or well. A *Sunday Times* correspondent who complained to the Law Society about the size of a legal fee was told that she had 'fallen into the trap of trying to analyse the fee charged from a scientific and arithmetic viewpoint. The assessment of a fair and reasonable fee is an art, not a science.'[7]

Companies who buy professional services often lack the information they need to make rational choices. Most seem to equate the most expensive with the most talented and, because company representatives are not spending their own money, cost is a matter of personal indifference. In most corporate transactions, the sums involved are so large that fees and commissions charged by professionals are trifling in the context of the whole. 'If you are doing a huge deal and you are going to make stacks of money as a result,' a City lawyer told the *Financial Times* in 1997, 'at the end of the day the professional fees are a minimal cost, and worth it.'[8]

Lawyers, accountants and investment bankers have turned the anxieties of their clients to advantage, transforming themselves into celebrities which every company wants to have on its side. At busy times, some clients are disappointed, but the lucky ones are prepared to pay even more for the privilege of working with the best. Once a transaction is under way, it is difficult for the buyers to know whether those they have hired are efficient or not. But it is obvious that anybody earning an hourly fee has a strong incentive to maximise the time the transaction takes.

The privatisation or public flotation of a company, or its merger or acquisition by another, or even its liquidation, is rich in opportunities for spending time. Winding up Brent Walker cost £50 million in professional fees, half of which went to the lawyers. The complicated refinancing of the Heron Corporation cost £60 million. By the end of 1995, the heavily indebted Eurotunnel project had spent £50 million on legal advice.[9] In boom years for mergers like 1996 and 1997, fees paid to City advisers amounted to well over £1.25 billion in each year. The incorporation and flotation of the Halifax building society cost £153 million, that of the Norwich Union £120 million.

Among the gifts to posterity of the late Robert Maxwell was a five-year bean feast for City professionals. To unravel his ruined business empire, the government appointed eight firms of professional advisers. By the time they finished, they had billed £100 million in fees.[10] Peter Phillips of Buchler Phillips, insolvency practitioners and receivers to the estate of Maxwell, was asked why his firm charged £167 an hour (the Official Receiver charged £49 an hour). He replied: 'If you want a Rolls-Royce job – and everyone I think wants the Maxwell case to be done thoroughly and well – then you need the appropriate Rolls-Royce drivers to do that job, and you get the miles per gallon that you'd expect.'[11]

Buchler Philips was singled out for criticism by the House of Commons Social Security Committee for recovering few assets at high cost, and later became the subject of a special report,[12] which alleged that Buchler Phillips had overestimated potential recoveries deliberately to 'maximise its fee income and to garner more publicity opportunities'.[13] Buchler Phillips origin-ally estimated the value of the Maxwell personal estate at £8.7 million.[14] In 1997 it emerged that, between them, Buchler Phillips and Nabarro Nathanson (the legal advisers) had recovered assets worth £1,672,500, but submitted invoices totalling £1,628,572. One pound in every £38 they recovered was left for the creditors.[15]

But professionals are not paid by results. They are paid by the hour, at a rate they decide for themselves. They may not even be spending money belonging to the end-client. Of the twenty-one firms of lawyers involved in the Maxwell investigations, only four were advisers to pension fund trustees whose property was stolen.[16] Banks involved in a major financial restructuring will bill the prostrate enterprise for their costs as a matter of routine. In 1993 the Heron Corporation announced it was no longer prepared to pay the fees of professional advisers not essential to the restructuring of the company.[17] Such threats are unusual; most of the time, professionals can charge whatever they like without fear of contradiction.

Rise of Human Capital

This enviable position signifies the triumph of Labour over Land and Capital. The professional, even more than the Fat Cat, is the true embodiment of a new form of wealth: human capital. Unlike land, labour or capital, it is inconceivable outside the context of a modern corporate economy. Human capital is the investment in education, training and experience which people add to their endowments of intelligence, application and energy. In a developed economy like that of Britain, its value is rising.[18] The balance of power in the labour market has shifted from hands to skills to brains. Lawyers, account-ants and investment bankers rent their brains – and the better the brain, the higher the rent. In 1995, when Maurice Saatchi left his advertising agency with several of the directors, the share price halved. Nothing but people had left, but they took their clients with them. The shareholders did not own all the assets of Saatchi & Saatchi – half of them had walked out the door.

The value of the mobile mind is linked to the value of what it produces, and it goes where the gap between the two is narrowest. Remuneration at investment banks, law firms and accountancy partnerships is determined by what the Americans call the EWYK principle: 'Eat what you kill.' What people kill is determined by what they know, and who they know. Firms will pay the price for an individual who can deliver the clients and the revenues to justify it. These professional superstars are the so-called 'rain-makers'. To attract the rain-makers the remuneration consultants invented the Golden Hello. These have now spread from the City to industry and the professions. To counteract the hello, employers have devised the handcuff. 'Our employees are a commodity,' an American investment banker told *The Spectator*. 'We simply look at what headhunters have recently been offering for employees with particular experience and talents, and then offer them a little more.'[19] In 1995 British Satellite Broadcasting was said to have paid David Chance, its deputy managing director, a special payment of £1 million (on top of salary and bonus worth £1.6 million) to stay.

The auction of the regional television franchises in 1991, in which success depended on the retention of human capital, was preceded by the issue of an armoury of Golden Handcuffs. Michael Grade was given a pair worth £500,000 to stay at Channel Four. At LWT, chairman Christopher Bland, chief executive Greg Dyke, arts controller Melvyn Bragg and others devised a share-option scheme which turned them into millionaires when they retained the franchise.[20] Lesser employees were consoled with a £50 Marks & Spencer voucher.[21]

'It was not a windfall, but a well-earned reward for a lot of genuine hard work,' protested Bland.[22] 'What matters most to me is that from next week I will own 1.5 per cent of LWT, the company of which I am chief executive and the company where I spend my working life,' said Dyke. 'This is very exciting.'[23] But it was not as exciting as the £800 million takeover offer by Granada less than six months later. The directors, who sold some stock when the option scheme matured in 1993, still owned enough to share another £50 million when the takeover went through.[24] For the more important among them, there were six-figure Golden Handshakes to share as well.[25]

A career is now viewed by the professional classes as any other investment decision: the net present value of future revenue streams. A taste of this view of the world (and a great deal of its self-image) was captured in a 1995 advertisement by the management consultants, McKinsey & Co.:

In investment banking, as in every industry, there are individuals whose performance is consistently above the norm. These people, used to being at the forefront of their peer group, are highly valued by their employers – and highly sought after by their competitors. At McKinsey, one of the world's most influential management consultancy firms, we're even more choosy. We're not looking simply for the best investment bankers, but for those who can apply their abilities to a far greater variety of business problems, at the top levels of management. This is your opportunity to expand considerably on your talents and experience with an international firm, and to influence the strategies of a wide range of businesses and institutions. As a member – or leader – of a team comprising both consulting colleagues and clients, you will be involved at every stage from defining objectives and initial concepts, to final execution. From the beginning, your contribution will have a direct – and often dramatic – effect on the performance of our clients' organis- ations. It's not a career for average thinkers. Nor for those with anything less than a consistently excellent record of progress, including at least a 2:1 degree and between three and seven years' blue-chip investment banking experience, with significant achievement at every step of the way. We're looking for those involved in top-level corporate finance, or the sale and trading of sophisticated financial products. You may well also have an MBA, accountancy or law qualification. The benefits of a career with McKinsey are manifold. Not only will you encounter a unique variety of intellectual challenges; you will also have the opportunity to broaden your skills across the full range of top management issues. As a strict meritocracy, we will ensure that you make the progress you deserve, as quickly as you deserve.[26]

McKinsey was looking for investment bankers with a high opinion of them- selves. Many of those who replied were already qualified as accountants, lawyers or MBAs. The switch to a new field – management consultancy – was little more than a matter of price.

Origins of Professionalism

Ironically, no firm finds it harder to retain its talent than McKinsey. Its alumni infest the boardrooms of British industry. They have infiltrated the CBI twice (Sir John Banham and Adair Turner), the FSA (Howard Davies), Oftel (Don Cruickshank) and even the Conservative Party (William Hague and Archie Norman). But they are rare in industry and commerce in regarding them-

selves as *professionals* rather than businessmen. Fat Cats are not, strictly speaking, 'professionals'; though many went to Oxbridge, the finishing school of
the professional classes, neither university had a business school until the
1990s.[27] Most Fat Cats have a professional qualification, but not one specific
to their trade or business. Even in modern Britain, anyone who calls himself
'businessman' or 'company director' is at risk of dubbing himself a crook.[28]

This is a snobbery of long standing. In pre-industrial Britain, when wealth
accrued mainly to owners of land, the low-born but ambitious man could rise
in the world through commerce: overseas traders were among the wealthiest
people. But throughout history, more humble Britons have improved their
status by acquiring a profession than by setting up a company. Besides, until
the Industrial Revolution, a successful clergyman, soldier, civil servant, tax
collector, lawyer or judge could expect to accumulate at least as much money
as a successful businessman – and at less risk. In medieval England, the chief
purpose of Oxbridge and the Inns of Court was to transform yokels into
gentlemen fit to take a plum job in the patronage of Church or State.

The Pastons, the great parvenus of the fifteenth century, rose entirely
through Oxbridge, the Inns of Court and the law (a profession which enabled
them to steal Sir John Falstolf's Norfolk estate by forging his will).[29] The
chief beneficiaries of the Dissolution of the Monasteries were all lawyers in
royal service – Thomas Cromwell (who lost his head), Richard Rich (who per-
jured himself at the trial of Thomas More) and Thomas Moyle (who strangled
the Abbot at Glastonbury). Nicholas Bacon and Edward Coke made fortunes
from the legal profession of the seventeenth century. The beneficiaries of the
patronage of Old Corruption[30] were the first true professionals. The 'living' of
the clergyman and the 'fees' of the lawyer owed nothing to competition for
customers, and everything to the value placed upon the office by its holder. The
Victorian reformers merely insisted that positions were distributed on the basis
of merit, rather than nepotism or politics. The placemen of the Old Corruption
were replaced by civil servants who passed an examination; the purchasers of
army commissions by officers trained at Sandhurst; the aristocratic JPs and corrupt officials of local government by administrators and public health officers;
the bachelor dons of the old universities by career academics; the charlatans
of the voluntary hospitals with trained doctors; the idlers of the circumlocation
offices with solicitors and barristers.

The Industrial Revolution spawned new professions: bankers, engineers,
commercial lawyers and accountants. By the end of the nineteenth century,
a modern professional class, selected on merit to provide services to government and the corporate economy, had come into existence. Like land and
capital, it earned a rent; unlike land and capital, it did not enjoy natural
scarcity, so its value was protected by restricting its supply. Aspiring pro-

fessionals were obliged to attend training courses, pass examinations and pay subscriptions to self-administered royal colleges, institutes and societies before they could sell their expertise to the general public.

The Royal College of Surgeons was established in 1800. The Civil Engineers set up an institution in 1818. The Law Society was created in 1825. The architects followed in 1837, the pharmacists in 1841, and the mechanical engineers in 1847. Writing on the professions in 1857, H. Byerley Thomson divided his subject into the 'privileged' and the 'underprivileged'. Entry to the first (which included the priesthood, the Bar and medicine) was regulated by law and closed to free competition. Entry to the second (which included architects, actuaries, and accountants) was subject to 'no legal restriction of entrance'.[31] But that was soon put right. The Institute of Chartered Accountants was founded in 1870, and the Institute of Actuaries in 1884; the Royal Institute of British Architects made examinations compulsory in 1887. The number of professional cartels rose from 27 in 1880 to 75 in 1918, and to 167 in 1970.[32] The Old Corruption gave way to professional trade unionism.

City v. State: Rise of the Super Class

Some of the professional trade unions are extremely large. The 1,470 accountants at work in 1881 have multiplied to nearly a quarter of a million.[33] However, within the professional classes, an élite (which Adonis and Pollard call a super class) has emerged.[34] A winner-take-all phenomenon – once confined to entertainment and sport, in which infinitesimal differences in ability translate into massive differences in rewards – now divides the professional class into the professional rich and the professional poor. Top barristers and accountants each much the same as Fat Cats, but fifteen times as much as a High Court judge, forty times as much as a hospital consultant, and seventy-five times what a university lecturer gets.

Senior civil servants, university professors, army generals, government ministers and physicians are all earning a fraction of the sums they could command at the equivalent rank in the private sector. The disparity is easily explained. The public sector professionals have a monopoly employer (the government) which has to answer to tax-payers as well as tax-eaters. Explaining the differences between the incomes of private sector professionals is harder. Finding them is not: almost all the highest-earning solicitors, barristers, accountants, investment bankers and other professionals are based in and around the City of London, as they were in the days of Dick Whittington and Henry V.

The great merchants of the medieval City were true professionals: they excluded competition from their 'mysteries' but they were open to those of talent from all over the country. In Tudor times, City merchants were four times as rich as their peers in the provinces.[35] The Industrial Revolution – said to have turned northern Britain into the workshop of the world – had an even greater impact on the City of London, transforming it into the centre of the international financial and commercial system. The City has always earned more money, produced more millionaires and paid more taxes than any other part of the country.[36] Which is why the City is still a magnet for talent, as it was for Dick Whittington. It is also why the Inland Revenue maintains a special unit for the City of London, to make sure the taxpayer gets his cut from the only tax district in the country where the *mean* taxable income is measured in six figures.[37] Hundreds of people in the City earn seven-figure sums year in, year out. How do they do it?

Big Swinging Dicks: Investment Bankers

The City is so studded with specialisms that it cannot be understood as a single entity. But outside the genuine professions like law or accountancy, almost everybody in the City makes money by clipping bits off large numbers. The trick is to buy things (such as aluminium, oil or coffee) or rights-to-things (shares and bonds) or rights-to-rights-to-things (futures and options) cheaply – and then sell them dearly. The City charges fees for underwriting the risk that nobody will buy the things or rights-to-things that some wish to sell, and the insurance markets charge premiums for things which may never happen. The commodity and financial futures markets sell protection against adverse movements in the price of commodities, money and markets.

The risks are real enough, but rarely large or imminent, so the cuts people take are correspondingly small. Even the fattest fees, paid for advice and underwriting of securities, rarely exceed 3 per cent, and are usually about 1.75 per cent. In the options and futures markets, a trader might expect 0.03125 per cent. The key to the wealth of the City is not the size of the toll, but the sums the toll is exacted from. In one study of international activity in the City, the average toll taken by financial traders was 0.28 per cent; this yielded over £11 billion a year in revenues *before* trading gains were taken into account.[38] When the foreign exchange market turns over $1–2 trillion a day, fractions as tiny as 0.004 per cent add up to billions of pounds.

Foreign exchange is a commodity business, dominated by large commercial banks. But the big banks are not where the highest incomes are earned. Senior clearing bankers are indistinguishable from ordinary Fat Cats, and rewarded in the same way. (In 1997, the total remuneration of the highest-paid directors at the clearing banks ranged from £437,000 at Bank of Scotland to £1.1 million at Standard Chartered.) The serious money, as City people call it, is earned in investment rather than commercial banking. Investment banking, familiar for sixty years or more on Wall Street, is a new phenomenon in the City, made up of what were once three separate industries: merchant banking, stock-broking and stock-jobbing. Increasingly, its practitioners are devouring even older City businesses, such as sugar and coffee broking, and breaking into relatively new markets like metals and oil and gas.

Investment bankers switch between markets relentlessly – in flight from assets which are falling, in pursuit of assets whose price is rising. They switch time zones, firms and businesses with disarming ease. In the City, unlike the corporate boardroom, there is an international market in talent. In 1986, the first million-pound salary was offered by an American bank in London to an Englishman working for an American bank in Hong Kong. Salomon Brothers is run from New York by an Englishman. A British investment bank hired its American finance director from a Canadian company. He had to commute to Paris every other weekend to see his wife. Communications and computer technology, and the abolition of artificial barriers to trade, have yoked the financial centres of the world together. The investment banker is the first of a new breed of international men and women, who make their living in the gaps which remain.

These are not many, or large. Financial markets come close to the ideal of perfect competition. They are characterised by maximum information, minimum transaction costs, and low barriers to entry. Inefficiencies are uncovered and exploited until they attract competitors, their profitability fades, and the search for new opportunities is resumed. In the 1970s, fortunes were made in Eurobonds and in the financing of North Sea oil. In the 1980s, they were made in property, mergers and acquisitions and Japanese equity warrants; and in the 1990s they were made in derivatives trading, international equity underwriting, emerging market debt, structured or principal finance, and mergers and acquisitions (again).[39] Anybody lucky enough to be working in a market which booms can expect to make a lot of money, not only because the market is booming but because new entrants will pay virtually anything to break into it.

In 1995 two mergers and acquisitions experts working at Deutsche Morgan Grenfell (DMG) poached two experts in international equity underwriting from a rival bank at a cost of £3.4 million each. A third expert in the same field, recruited as their boss, was guaranteed £5 million a year. In October 1996 BZW, the investment banking arm of Barclays Bank, recruited Bill Harrison from a rival (Flemings) in exchange for a guaranteed minimum of £5.8 million over two years. 'Anybody who wishes to participate in this business,' explained the chief executive of the bank, 'has to bid for the best talent.'

In the end, even the best talent could not make a difference at BZW. In the autumn of 1997, Barclays Bank sold or closed the various parts of BZW.[42] BZW began as it ended, with expensive human capital spinning in and out of the door. Created in 1984 through the purchase for £150 million of a stock-broker (De Zoete & Bevan) and a stock-jobber (Wedd Durlacher Mordaunt), its birth was accompanied by the departure of eight jobbers for better-paid jobs at a rival merchant bank. The price fell by £20 million, but it was a portent of the future.

The so-called Big Bang of October 1986, of which the creation of BZW was a part, caused a permanent alteration in the manners and morals of remuneration in the City of London. This extraordinary upheaval, whereby members of the Stock Exchange abandoned their monopoly of securities trading in London, was preceded by a scramble for talent. Foreign and domestic banks bid against each other for people they thought could help them to create a profitable investment bank. A huge weight of capital was brought to bear on a limited number of people as the member firms of the London Stock Exchange were bought by foreign and domestic banks. The total outlay, of roughly £1.5 billion, put a price of exactly £1 million a head on the 1,500 people who happened to be partners at the time.[43]

In the race to purchase talent, people doubled and trebled their salaries as they hopped from firm to firm. The eight jobbers who decamped from Wedd Durlacher Mordaunt to Kleinwort Benson left behind £8 million at BZW, confident that their new employers would pay it instead. During this period Golden Hellos and Handcuffs were invented to prise people away from firms or persuade them to stay. When the Golden Handcuffs placed on the 107 former stockbroking and jobbing partners at BZW expired in 1990, it cost Barclays' shareholders £111 million to buy them back.[44] In all, Big Bang created about 500 millionaires. It was a good time to be a partner in a stock-broking or jobbing firm. Decades of goodwill were sold by a single generation, at prices driven by a timetable nobody could halt.

Big Bang had permanent as well as transient effects. It transformed rates of pay, spreading the habit of massive rewards even to markets where pay was traditionally modest, such as fund management. In 1992 Leonard Licht left Mercury Asset Management for Jupiter Tyndall for a salary of £600,000 and a Golden Hello of £1 million.[45] He picked up another £8 million when Jupiter Tyndall was sold to Commerzbank in 1995.[46] By the time one of his protégées, Nicola Horlick, parted company with Morgan Grenfell Asset Management in January 1997, her earnings of £1.1 million no longer seemed exceptional. Two former colleagues, who had elected to stay at Mercury, made even £1 million look trifling; in 1997, Carol Galley was paid £5.44 million in salary, bonuses and deferred bonuses, and Stephen Zimmerman collected £5.33 million. The pay of the main board directors *averaged* £1.8 million.[47]

They became richer still when Merrill Lynch bought Mercury Asset Management in November 1997. Carol Galley collected £10 million for her shares. Chairman Hugh Stevenson made enough (£24 million) to warrant a place in the *Sunday Times* list of the rich. He was joined by George Magan, a former corporate finance executive at Morgan Grenfell who set up his own firm, then sold it to NatWest Bank at a price which netted him £15 million. Also on the list were Dr Kaveh Alamouti, a derivatives trader at Tokai Bank, who was paid £9 million in 1992, £14.5 million in 1993 and £2.25 million in 1994; and Guy Hands, who runs the principal finance division at Nomura International. Hands has bought pubs, Radio Rental shops, Ministry of Defence homes and leasing companies for cash, and then raised more than the purchase price by selling the right to enjoy the rental income from them. It earned him £40 or £50 million in 1997.

Rewards of this size are still unusual, but millionaires are now commonplace even at smaller merchant banks. In 1996 nine people at Lazards, seven directors of Flemings and four at Schroders earned over £1 million.[48] In 1983 Jacob Rothschild told Paul Ferris that the highest paid man in the City was paid £126,000.[49] In 1998 prices, that is less than a quarter of a million pounds. Today, thousands of people in the City earn the equivalent. In 1995, for example, the *average* remuneration of the directors of the Deutsche Morgan Grenfell group was £405,966; of the banking arm £558,585; and of the asset management arm, £380,711. The highest paid director in each case earned, respectively, £1.9 million, £1.2 million and £1.3 million.[50] It was not a particularly outstanding year.

It is true that merchant bankers were never underpaid. Kenneth Keith, one of the most successful of the 1950s and 1960s, made £1 million in his first decade after the war.[51] In the late 1970s, partners in member firms of the London Stock Exchange could expect £150,000 in a good year. But the markets were less competitive, and capital gains tax and laws against insider dealing were ineffective or non-existent. The top operators of the 1990s are working on a global canvas, against formidable competition. This has sharpened the inequalities in rewards between the best and second-best investment bankers, by tying pay more closely to individual performance in particular markets. It is said that Dr Alamouti, for example, joined the otherwise obscure Tokai Bank because they offered him 20 per cent of any profits he made. His arrangement was not that unusual: the head of emerging markets trading at DMG got 10 per cent of any profits he made.

In investment banking, salary is where remuneration begins rather than ends. City high-flyers can count on share options, generous pensions, free health insurance and a choice of expensive motor cars, and many also get cheap or subsidised mortgages. But it is from cash bonuses, linked to personal performance, that they derive the greatest rewards. In a good year, performance-related bonuses allow them to double, or even quadruple, their basic salary. Shigeru Myojin, head of proprietary trading at Salomon Brothers, was paid £19 million in 1996. Most of it was bonus payments.[52]

A derivatives specialist who can conjure transactions out of nothing, or a leading equity analyst judged essential to an underwriting mandate, or a corporate financier or fund manager or salesman with a valuable address book, will earn many times more than his or her colleagues. (Where income-producing clients are loyal to an individual rather than a firm, the individual can name his price.) Many use tempting offers from rival firms to improve their income without bothering to move. The best investment bankers, however, usually end up at the leading firms, sharpening further the differentials between pay packets at top-tier and second-division investment banks.

Even then, the divide between success and failure is large. Men and women of equivalent ability at different firms must compete for the same business, and not all of them can win. The one who secures an important privatisation contract, for example, will make a fortune for his firm and for himself. The one who fails may make nothing at all. But most investment bankers are not working at top firms; the vast majority are at one of the dozens of international banks which crowd the Square Mile. Though over twelve thousand are earning six-figure salaries, few are earning seven-figure sums. Truly massive earnings are the preserve of a minority who number five or six hundred.

No investment banker in London has ever earned as much as Michael Milken, the California-based American who invented the junk bond market: he took home $550 million in 1987. In 1995 another American investment banker, Henry Kravis, collected $76 million. He invented the leveraged buy-out. The creator of the modern hedge fund, George Soros, was making $1 billion a year in the early 1990s, and one of his London-based protégés, Nicholas Roditi, is said to have earned £50 million in 1995.[53] Steve Posford, chief executive at Salomon Brothers in London until September 1995, is thought to have earned $20 million in a good year. But exactly who earns exactly what at the leading investment banks is unknown; they can hide their earnings through directorships of obscure foreign subsidiaries. The most handsomely rewarded are often little-known corporate financiers who land massive transactions, or bond and derivatives traders whose luck, ingenuity or steady nerve has enabled them to earn millions for their firms. Most are employed by American banks, where a large domestic capital market gives them an advantage European rivals have failed to overcome.

TABLE 16.1

Investment Banking: A Sample of Jobs Paying Over £100,000 in 1998*

	Salary Range £	Average Bonus %
Senior Manager, Asset Finance	108,083–121,238	70.1
Deputy General Manager, Specialised Banking	115,000–159,667	131.3
Head of Structured Finance	100,000–114,154	219.0
Head of Principal Finance	107,750–120,545	92.8
Managing Director, Private Banking	120,000–150,000	63.2
Director, Treasury Products	106,500–128,556	186.1
Head of Capital Markets	140,000–236,400	62.5
Head of Eurobond Trading	103,750–132,661	134.0
Head of Bond Sales	105,000–145,000	107.6
Head of Bond Derivative Trading	122,500–163,750	163.8
Executive Director, Capital Markets New Business	100,000–124,500	54.2
Head of Equities Trading	110,000–136,500	97.5
Director, Illiquid Bonds	106,000–136,500	299.2
Head of Fund Management	119,625–197,750	45.8
Director, Corporate Finance	102,325–129,375	74.7

Source: Day Associates (PAS), *International Banks and Investment Houses Remuneration Guide*, published by the Monks Partnership in August 1998.

* Excludes the major British and American investment banks, where the very highest rewards are enjoyed.

Most American investment banks active in London pay seven-figure bonuses to a small number of employees every year. Goldman Sachs in particular revels in a reputation for high rewards, believing that it attracts talent. In 1993, seventy London employees received remuneration in excess of $1 million. The partners received $5 million or more each.[54] The firm repeated this feat for 33 partners and 20 high performers in 1995, and for 125 people in 1996.[55] Goldman Sachs is also the only major investment bank to remain a partnership; Morgan Stanley and Salomon Brothers abandoned partnership in the 1980s. The last merchant banking partnership in London disappeared in 1970, and all but one of its stock market equivalents vanished at the Big Bang.[56]

Over the last 25 years, the partners of Goldman Sachs have found it an increasingly irksome form of ownership. Their personal capital is tied up in the business until they retire, and older partners withdraw more capital than their successors are able to replenish. Having rejected the idea many times since the 1970s, the present generation of partners voted in favour of incorporation and public flotation in the summer of 1998. Each partner stood to gain about $120 million in cash and shares. The sale was postponed when the markets deteriorated, but some partners were opposed to selling from the outset. In their view, the lure of a partnership gave the firm an enviable capacity to attract and retain talented people. Even after the decision was made to go ahead with the flotation, the firm planned to reserve $6–8 billion of the proceeds of sale for distribution among the hundreds hovering just below partnership level.

It was a perfect illustration of the dilemma which confronts all professional firms: can shareholders own people? Modern investment banking poses this question in acute form. Without people, the business is worthless; with people, costs are high. When investment banking consisted of partnerships, this was not a problem. The partners were entitled to the profits. But investment banks with outside shareholders have employees collecting millions in profits without putting personal capital at risk. In theory, paying most of the rewards in bonuses is ideal: bonuses retain key staff, ensure pay adjusts to financial performance, and protects shareholders by ensuring that those who make the most get the most. In practice, they cause problems.

Bonuses create perverse incentives. The possibility of a large cash pay-out can make a risky strategy rational for a trader or fund manager. It can encourage them to concoct deals, perhaps using complicated derivative instruments, where the profits are short-term but the risks are long-term. If the strategy comes off, the trader gets a handsome bonus; if it fails, he gets his salary. Nick Leeson, the Barings derivatives trader, was expecting a bonus of £350,000 in 1994. To protect it, he was prepared to conceal losses sufficient to wipe out the bank's entire capital. Peter Young, the former Morgan Grenfell fund manager who sank millions into speculative technology investments, created a web of Luxembourg-registered companies to prop up the performance of his funds. It cost the parent Deutsche Bank over half a billion pounds in losses and compensation.

Equally, bonuses can encourage risk-aversion. Traders often withdraw from markets towards the end of the year, foregoing potentially profitable opportunities in order to protect a bonus from loss. For most investment bankers, habituation has transformed the annual bonus from an expectation into a right. It rises in good years, but does not fall in bad. Warnings of a fall in bonuses prompt threats to leave, forcing employers to set them by reference to a single criterion (will he/she leave?) rather than objective measurements of performance. This makes it hard to allocate costs and fosters tensions between successful and less successful parts of the same firm.

According to Nicola Horlick, the main concern of her colleagues at Morgan Grenfell Asset Management in the wake of the disastrous losses incurred by

Peter Young was that their annual bonuses would be cut. Several told her they would leave unless they were given more money. Later, after they realised that Horlick would not be reinstated, they disparaged her to their superiors in the hope of securing a share of her unclaimed bonus. When Swiss Bank Corporation took over S. G. Warburg, it had to pay £60 million to persuade key people to stay. When ING Bank bought the bankrupt Barings for a nominal payment of £1, ruined creditors were outraged to find staff bonuses totalling £100 million still being paid. In 1996 one former Barings employee (who was criticised for failing to supervise Nick Leeson) actually took ING to an industrial tribunal to claim an unpaid bonues of £500,000. Banks have now learned to use bonuses to get rid of people as well as to keep them, concentrating rewards among those they wish to keep. The bonus culture imposes a discernible seasonality on the City labour market. People change jobs as soon as their bonus is paid, usually in the New Year. They can be persuaded to defect earlier, but only if their new employer pays their antici-pated bonus and other deferred rewards. Deferred compensation now consti-tutes such a large proportion of City incomes that the earnings of a single year are no longer an accurate guide to the remuneration of individuals. Nicola Horlick may have earned over £1 million in her last year at Morgan Grenfell Asset Management, but another £2 million was locked in deferred compensation.[57] When Deutsche Bank bought Morgan Grenfell in 1989 it offered all share and share-option holders a choice of cash or interest-bearing loan notes. Most took loan notes because they could defer or even eliminate the possibility of capital gains tax. But many still left as soon as they could.

McKinsey have estimated that the average investment banker changes his job three times every six years. Investment bankers generate huge profits, and demand large rewards. If they do not get them, they defect. Individualism is now so extreme that people do not share their knowledge, for fear of reducing their own market value. They are reluctant to progress to manage-ment positions, in case they lose the clients which make them valuable. Invest-ment bankers are pioneering a new form of capitalism, in which the bulk of profits no longer accrue to those who put up the capital (the shareholders) but to those who use it (the employees). 'The traditional link between profit-ability and employee remuneration is getting broken,' complained Andrew Buxton, chairman of Barclays Bank, in 1996. 'Shareholders are getting less as employees are getting more, and that is a threat that shareholder banks need to recognise.' Aad Jacobs, chairman of the executive board of ING, the new owners of Barings, was at the same conference. 'If you want to work in Rome,' he said, 'do as the Romans do.' A day later, DMG had poached 44 staff from ING Barings, and a colleague was less sanguine. 'We totally disagree with these practices followed by Deutsche Morgan Grenfell,' said

Hessel Lindenbergh, chief executive of ING. 'I think there is growing resistance and irritation in the industry towards firms which deliberately poach whole teams. Poaching teams pushes up pay unduly.'[58] ING Barings sued DMG for $10 million, and won an agreement that the German bank would not approach any more of its staff for a year.

In 1995 Salomon Brothers discovered what happens if shareholders try to bring the interests of shareholders and employees into alignment. The largest shareholder tried to tie remuneration to the performance of the business as a whole rather than to particular individuals. He wanted to pay staff in discounted shares they could not sell for five years. The result was uproar. One in ten managing directors, including the head of trading, resigned. The plan was scrapped, but the problem has not disappeared: the shareholders are running the risks; the staff are reaping the rewards.

Upper-Class Bookies: Lloyd's of London

Lloyd's of London has wrestled for a generation with the embarrassment of running a market where the risks are tilted heavily towards the providers of capital and rewards to the users of it. No other financial market in Britain has failed so conspicuously to distinguish between the interests of insiders and outsiders. In 1983 Ian Hay Davison was invited by the Bank of England to serve as chief executive at Lloyd's, following a series of frauds, in which insiders had stolen millions of pounds from their backers. In a memoir, some years later, he referred to 'the ignorance and indifference of the Lloyd's community to its most basic legal and moral obligations'.[59] Lloyd's organisation and structure was designed to reward those who worked in it, often at the expense of those who funded it.

When ruined and angry Names plunged Lloyd's into near-terminal crisis in 1989, the fact that two thirds of the losses fell on one third of the Names was the least surprising revelation. Insiders had made sure the risks were concentrated on syndicates dominated by outsiders. This became starkly clear in the early 1990s, when outsiders bore most of the losses from the excess of loss (LMX) reinsurance spiral, where risks insured by one underwriter were reinsured with another. The continual and increasingly incestuous reinsurance of the risks was at the core of the financial crisis which swept Lloyd's in the early 1990s. The spiral was like a game of pass-the-parcel, where the value of the initial premium was eroded with each move and the basic principle of spreading the risk was discarded. But the LMX spiral was extremely profitable for the brokers who transacted the business. One, Bill Brown, shot to prominence after paying himself over £8 million (and several more in

dividends) from his family-owned company, Walsham Brothers, which specialised in reinsuring risks taken on by Lloyd's underwriters. With minimal overheads, no underwriting risk and a commission of 10 per cent on each
transaction, Walsham Brothers made a profit in 1990 of £35.6 million on
turnover of £36.3 million: a margin of 98 per cent.

But broking is the hard way to make a fortune at Lloyd's. Most brokers are
salary slaves, tramping the Room on behalf of the clients of giant insurance
companies. That said, boardroom rewards are not paltry. Directors of Lambert
Fenchurch Group and C. E. Heath collected salaries of £421,000 in 1998.[60]
Leading brokers like David Rowland of Sedgwick have become wealthy. 'We
are all barrow boys in pin-striped suits who like making money,' he once said,
a remark whose frankness did not debar him from chairmanship of Lloyd's.[61]
He collected a salary of £450,000 when he took the job at the beginning of
1993, and a £400,000 bonus three years later as a reward for pushing through
the long-awaited reconstruction.

But the serious money is made by underwriters. John Charman was valued
by the *Sunday Times* at £20 million in 1998, and Richard and Henry Lumley
were considered to be worth over £100 million. All of the top Lloyd's underwriters made money consistently throughout the crises of the late 1980s and
early 1990s. Much of their income stems from their own syndicates, though

TABLE 16.3
The Earnings of Lloyd's Underwriters in 1997 (£)

Syndicate	Remuneration
J. R. Charman	1,501,425
J. M. H. P. Wetherall	905,570
M. E. Brockbank	776,394
A. Shone	465,000
G. D. Gilchrist	460,000
N. C. Marsh	363,000
J. R. L. Youell	359,450
C. E. Dandridge	354,000
I. C. Agnew	328,000
T. J. Pepper	282,000

Source: Lloyd's Market Results and Prospects 1998, Financial Intelligence & Research Limited.

* The table gives figures for earnings from the syndicate in the name of the underwriter only.
It *excludes* earnings from other syndicates in which he participates; dividends from capital invested;
fees earned from managing agencies; and profit shares on managing agency fees. It is therefore
a considerable underestimate.

they also get a salary and a profit-related commission from the managing agents which run the syndicates. Even those whose syndicates lost millions continued to collect salaries in the hundreds of thousands while members of their syndicates were funding losses of the same magnitude.

Names have taken their revenge, and withdrawn their capital. The number underwriting at Lloyd's has shrunk from over 32,000 in 1988 to less than 10,000 now.[62] But the underwriters have turned even this to advantage. Since 1994 Lloyd's has admitted corporate as well as personal capital, which has entered the market through purchase of the managing agents, mostly owned by underwriters. This has allowed a single generation of underwriters to profit in much the same way that stock-broking and jobbing partners profited at the Big Bang. In 1997 Mark Brockbank, a leading underwriter, sold his agency to a Bermuda-based reinsurance company, collecting £19 million for his 22 per cent stake.[63] Other leading underwriters, such as Duncan Heath and Brian Smith, have also become multi-millionaires by selling their agencies.

The Shysters: Solicitors

The profession of law thrives under any circumstances. As early as the fourteenth century, the venality of lawyers made them a target of poetry and song.[64] One reason Shakespeare is replete with hostile references to them is that he lived through an age of plenty for the law, when the Dissolution of the Monasteries created a boom in land deals and litigation.[65] From one lawyer per 20,000 people in 1560, there was one for every 2,500 by 1640. 'Now all the wealth of the land dooth flow unto our common lawiers,' wrote an exasperated Elizabethan in 1587.[66]

Modern Britain, like Tudor England, has lived through the second great boom in the law.[67] There is now one lawyer for every 684 people in Britain. The modern economy has furnished them with opportunities to create new forms of property and contract, just as the Dissolution and the Industrial Revolution enabled their predecessors to create modern commercial law. Governments have added more: the Statute Book now consists of 50,000 public and 40,000 private Acts of Parliament. Despite heroic attempts to expunge redundant legislation from the statute book (17,000 Acts have disappeared) the work is unending. 'There is no hope,' admits a Law Commission official, 'that we will ever catch up with the volume of new legislation passed every year by Parliament.'[68]

But lawyers do not need to be judges or MPs to invent work for themselves. The humble solicitor can create a job for himself by chasing the right ambulance. Solicitors now advertise for potential litigants against doctors who misdiagnose patients, councils which fail to prevent pavement accidents, and companies which manufacture dangerous products. Advertising attracted 300 people suffering from lung cancer and other smoking-related diseases to launch an action against five tobacco companies.[69] An Association of Personal Injury Lawyers circulates details of legal precedents and advertising techniques in a regular newsletter; maintains a database of expert consultants; and runs regular training courses and conferences for lawyers keen to do personal injury work. The aim of the association is to 'promote full and just compensation for all types of personal injury'. The motives of its members may be less high-flown. The American legal experience, where plaintiffs have won spectacular pay-outs for trivial injuries, has persuaded many solicitors that fortunes can be made from injury and death. They have persuaded the Law Society to insure litigants who lose cases against paying the defendants' costs and to open a telephone sales line. Since conditional fee arrangements were introduced in 1995, solicitors have taken on over 34,000 personal injury claims on a 'no win-no fee' basis. If they lose, they get nothing; if they win, they get twice their normal fee.

Medicine, particularly in obstetrics and gynaecology, has become Elysium to legal bounty-hunters. According to the NHS, the cost of compensation for medical malpractice and clinical negligence rose from £50.5 million in 1991–2 to £149.1 million in 1995–6.[70] By 1997–98 it was over £300 million. In 1998 the National Audit Office (NAO) estimated that health authorities and NHS Trusts had set aside £1 billion to meet outstanding claims.[71] At the time, the NAO reckoned 28 health authorities and 74 NHS Trusts were in financial difficulties.[72] The medical negligence lawyers do not care. 'We take on cases we think we're going to win, or those which merit investigation,' says one. 'It isn't simply about financial compensation – money can only help to make it more bearable. Our work is about seeking improvements in medical standards.'[73]

Lawyers often argue that litigation is therapeutic for the defendant as well as the plaintiff. This is especially true of racial and sexual discrimination. Industrial tribunals, established as an informal way of adjudicating between employers and employees, have as a result become legal cockpits. Awards can be spectacular. In 1994 an industrial tribunal awarded £300,000 to an army major dismissed because she was pregnant. Even sport is no longer immune for events on the field of play. Paul Elliot of Chelsea lost his suit against Dean Saunders of Liverpool for a tackle that put him out of the game, but the solicitors collected £500,000. The lawyer who wrote *Sport and the Law* criticised England rugby player Phil de Glanville, who refused to take an All Black to court for stamping on his face: 'I'm afraid it's only this sort of litigation that shakes up the sports authorities. Governing bodies are failing to punish offenders adequately, and it's going to take the law to change that.'[74]

The best-known lawyer operating in personal injury litigation is Martyn Day of Leigh, Day & Co. His working methods were described by the *Financial Times*:

> This is how Day works. First, he tracks scientific and legal developments, especially in the US, attending legal conferences there and spending hours studying the legal and scientific press. He has built up a loyal support staff, most of whom hold both scientific and legal qualifications and can understand the implications of dry technical findings published in obscure academic journals. When a causal link is made between physical harm and, say, a certain industrial practice, he looks for clients on whose behalf he sues the company for damages. This well-established business in the US, where lawyers can bring cases on a no-win, no-fee basis, has been adapted by Day for the British legal system: he finances all his cases on State-provided legal aid.[75]

Day sued British Nuclear Fuels on behalf of leukaemia victims allegedly affected by radiation in their paternal sperm, having advertised for clients living near Sellafield in the local newspapers. He lost; the action cost the taxpayers £10 million in legal aid.

In 1996 he turned to tobacco. He agreed (on a no-win no-fee basis) to sue two tobacco companies on behalf of forty-nine former smokers suffering from lung cancer. It was the first occasion on which a conditional fee was agreed, the plaintiffs having failed to secure legal aid. Day estimated the costs of the case at £3 million, and the potential damages at £2 million.[76] If the action succeeds, the firm will take twice its normal fee.[77] If it fails, Day will lose nothing but time; the claimants will have to bear the defence costs, which may run to £20 million. Significantly, Leigh, Day & Co. threatened to withdraw when the tobacco companies asked the High Court to rule that they should bear the costs. But if it makes no sense for the lawyers to fund the action, it makes no sense at all for the ex-smokers to pursue the case. But it would undoubtedly encourage other people suffering from tobacco-related diseases. By securing compensation for his clients, Day would not bring litigation against tobacco companies to an end, but to the beginning. As he points out, victory for his clients would be 'determinative for all future tobacco cases'.[78]

Most personal injury work is funded by the taxpayer. The legal aid budget has doubled in size in six years. It is now running at £1.5 billion a year, and accounts for over one sixth of the gross income of solicitors.[79] Lawyers argue that legal aid keeps them poor, because it pays little and late. But in 1993–4, fifty barristers earned more than £100,000 from criminal legal aid fees and another 100 received the same amount again from the civil budget.[80] When the question was repeated in 1998, twenty barristers had received from

£190,000 to £320,000 in civil legal aid; another group had received between £329,000 and £500,000 from criminal legal aid. Solicitors had pocketed sums ranging from £1.6 million to £8.5 million in civil legal aid alone.[81]

In some cases, the payments covered several years and many cases, and costs are sometimes recovered from the defendant or his insurers. But it is undeniable that legal aid, designed specifically to give the poor access to justice, is being used by lawyers to fund speculative litigation.[82] Lawyers acting on behalf of victims of tranquilliser pills got through £35 million of public money before the case collapsed. This is why the lord chancellor wants to restrict legal aid to serious cases with a strong chance of success. Legislation introduced in the 1998–9 parliamentary session will ensure that most publicly-funded criminal work is performed by solicitors (rather than barristers) under fixed-price contract and that the civil legal aid budget is tilted away from ambulance-chasing and towards family and welfare cases. Legal aid will eventually be withdrawn from most claims for monetary compensation, with lawyers expected to work solely on a no win-no fee basis. The first to go will be personal injury cases.

Fixed-price contracts will put an end to the most notorious abuse of the legal aid budget, in which rich clients conduct complex and lengthy defences at the public expense. Advisers to Dr Jawad Harshim, an Iraqi businessman sued successfully by his employers for embezzling £333 million, received a total of £4 million in legal aid. This sum was not unusual. In the Barlow Clowes trial, also conducted on legal aid, four QCs and their juniors pocketed £1.7 million and the solicitors a further £1 million.[83] The prosecution of George Walker cost the Legal Aid Board £7.5 million; that of Kevin and Ian Maxwell nearly £5 million; and the case against Asil Nadir had cost £1 million by the time he fled to Cyprus.

The main sources of income for the humble solicitors of the suburbs and the provinces are conveyancing and the Legal Aid Board. Like most professions, the law is unequal. Two thirds of legal aid goes to solicitors working in large firms, and two fifths to the biggest of all. Virtually all of the largest firms are based in the south-east; two out of three of the largest firms are based in London. They generate fees worth well over £3.25 billion; even the lowliest partners earn £100,000 a year. But in the provinces and the suburbs, many solicitors are earning one fifth of this.

Some deserve less. When *Which?* tested eighty firms with straightforward legal problems, it found that clients were frequently given incorrect or even misleading advice.[84] Many solicitors are corrupt. Every year, the Legal Aid Board routinely investigates hundreds of exaggerated or fraudulent claims for legal aid, and found solicitors offering cigarettes, food and gifts to needy families in exchange for their signatures or a legally aided commission to write their will, pursue their social security claim, tackle their noisy neighbours or change their names by deed poll. Thefts of money belonging to clients are so common that the Law Society appointed a former fraud squad officer to its staff.

Since it was established by the Law Society, the Office of the Supervision of Solicitors has never received less than 11,000 complaints against solicitors in any one year; in 1997 the total reached nearly 25,000.[85] The Legal Services Ombudsman (who investigated over 1,500 complaints against solicitors in 1997) has warned that the OSS is in danger of being overwhelmed.[86] Yet the OSS is only the last resort; most valid claims are met by the Solicitors' Indemnity Fund, a compulsory scheme providing minimum cover of £1 million. By 1997 it had dispensed so much in compensation payments, it had an estimated deficit of £450 million.

Dozens of solicitors' firms have to be closed each year for malpractice. But corruption and incompetence are minor problems by comparison with price cartels and surreptitious overcharging. Most people avoid lawyers until they have to buy a house, get divorced, make a will, or bury a relative. Usually, no information is offered on the likely cost, or an agreed fee suddenly becomes inappropriate. By the time the true cost becomes apparent, it is too late to take the business elsewhere. The main determinant of cost is time, and solicitors all look to clock up as many chargeable hours per week as they can.

In the corporate sector, charging by the hour has made some commercial solicitors rich. In 1998, the top 100 law firms shared total fee income of £4.34 billion.[87] Over one quarter of this sum is generated by the five biggest firms, where profits per partner averaged £544,000. Companies have struggled to contain the cost of legal advice, mainly because lawyers refuse to abandon their time-sheets. They know that no system can match hourly billing in its scope for abuse.[88] It is easy to inflate the number of lawyers involved, and the hours they spend. Two clients can be charged for the same block of time, or one client can be billed for work done for another.

Hourly charging was once described by Lord Alexander as 'a charter for overcharging and inefficiency'.[89] It also gives lawyers a financial incentive to lose their sense of proportion. If they are paid by the hour, it pays to do every job perfectly, and reduces their willingness to use labour-saving devices such as computers to complete routine transactions. But the yuppification of the law has given this traditional indifference to consumers a sinister twist. Younger and greedier partners insist that their pay is linked to the fees they generate. Like their counterparts at investment banks, the division of the spoils no longer depends on age and seniority but on the EWYK principle.*

* 'Eat what you kill' (see p. 586).

TABLE 16.4
Highest Earnings at Major Law Firms

Firm	Gross Fees (£m)	Earnings per Partner (£)*
Slaughter & May	152.6	437–875,000
Allen & Overy	219.0	320–800,000
Freshfields	232.0	320–640,000
Linklaters & Paines	266.0	250–625,000
Clifford Chance	377.0	220–550,000
Herbert Smith	125.0	250–575,000
Macfarlanes	40.0	240–520,000
S. J. Berwin & Co	50.0	150–600,000
Lovell White Durrant	140.0	200–500,000
Dickson Minto	12.4	100–750,000
Gouldens	24.0	170–520,000
Richards Butler	57.4	130–650,000
Bird & Bird	20.1	255–395,000
Ashurst Morris Crisp	90.0	150–450,000
Olswang	18.2	150–505,000
Hammond Suddards	66.0	160–450,000
Baker & Mackenzie	41.7	150–450,000
Watson Farley & Williams	36.8	180–400,000
Barlow Lyde & Gilbert	41.5	185–370,000
Taylor Joynson Garrett	37.3	170–350,000

Source: The 1998 Legal Business 100.

* Partners are required to keep some capital in the firm. At some firms, partners are paid salaries plus a share of the profits, but the remuneration of most partners hinges on the amount of equity they hold.

This has sharpened the division between incomes at the same firms. A handful of partners at City law firms are earning well over £1 million in a good year. The most acquisitive partners hoard clients, denying colleagues access to protect their shares.

All but two of the top twenty firms are based in London. The City is the centre of the banking, securities, insurance and shipping markets of Europe, and English law is the idiom which most international business prefers. But the larger firms are following their multinational clients into foreign markets as well. Just as the American firms are expanding in London, City firms are expanding in Europe and the United States by opening offices, hiring indigenous lawyers and forming joint ventures. After liberty, language and the rule of law, the rule of lawyers could become the fourth great English gift to the world.

Gentleman Shysters: Barristers

Barristers have gained from the same forces. London hosts lucrative international litigation between companies. But the generous incomes available at the Bar owe more to old-fashioned restrictive practices. A top commercial Queen's Counsel (QC) or 'silk' will charge a 'brief fee' for taking on a case. Once work begins he will charge as much as £800 an hour, plus a daily fee ('refresher') of up to £3,750 for each day in court. If a case is complex or prolonged, he may charge a monthly retainer of between £40,000 and £100,000. Yet the opinion or skills in advocacy of a QC are rarely more valuable than those of a bright junior barrister. The sole purpose of the title of QC is to ensure that fees are set not by competition, but within the profession.

First appointed at the end of the sixteenth century to assist law officers of the Crown, a QC is now no more than an accolade granted by peers. Ostensibly awarded to the most able and experienced advocates in their late thirties or early forties, QCs are selected by a mysterious process which owes more to connections than skills. Becoming a QC gives a barrister no new rights, but he can charge considerably more for his services. There are less of them (just over one barrister in ten is a QC), which entitles them to charge a higher fee. Because they can also rely on a junior to do their research, the result is that a QC earns more money for less work. It is not easy to tell how much more.

Barristers are self-employed, so data about their earnings is patchy. The official survey of those who become judges suggests that leading barristers earn between £190,000 and £400,000 a year.[90] But the QCs who become judges are rarely the highest earners (though they are sometimes tempted towards the end of their careers by the generous pension).[91] David Pannick, an administrative law QC, assessed his daily fees at between £750 and £1,750 in 1993,[92] an income of between £195,000 and £450,000 a year. His fees have probably increased since.

It is at the commercial bar, however, that most money is made. Top commercial QCs would expect to earn at least £500,000 a year at the peak of their careers. But a group of fashionable barristers, all QCs, earn £1–1.5 million a year. For some reason, their number is usually put at ten. (In 1962, Anthony Sampson was assured that 'there are perhaps ten barristers earning over £20,000.')[93] Those privileged to have appeared in the Top Ten in recent years are Graham Aaronson, Michael Beloff, Michael Burton, Christopher Carr, Christopher Clarke, George Carman, John Chadwick, Terence Etherton, Michael Flesch, John Gardiner, Elizabeth Gloster, David Goldberg, Peter Goldsmith, Anthony Grabiner, Sydney Kentridge, David Oliver, Gordon Pollock, Kenneth Rokison, Peter Scott, Anthony Scrivener, Jules Sher, Nicholas Stadlen, Jonathan Sumption and Geoffrey Vos.

It is not surprising that barristers drift in and out of the list of legal millionaires. Like most self-employed people, their earnings fluctuate. Three or four years of work is sometimes paid in a single year. But out of a total profession of 9,698 barristers (in England and Wales) and 378 advocates (in Scotland), only 957 people are QCs. Rarity keeps their prices up. Criminal barristers working in the suburbs have long depended on a mixture of legal aid and restrictive practices. It allowed the profession to boom (the number of barristers has soared from just over 2,000 in the mid-1960s to nearly 10,000 today) but many are earning as little as £20,000 a year. It is only the celebrity briefs at the commercial bar, always among the highest earners in Britain, which rival the Fat Cats and investment bankers. What are their secrets? The first is the restriction of competition. Solicitors were long kept out of the higher courts, but clients had to go through solicitors to hire barristers. When the government proposed to allow solicitors to represent clients in the higher courts in 1989, the Bar was indignant. Lord Lane, lord chief justice, called the Green Paper 'one of the most sinister documents ever to emanate from government'. Lord Donaldson, master of the rolls, told the lord chancellor, to 'get your tanks off my lawn'. To his credit, Lord Mackay persisted, and the monopoly on advocacy in the higher courts was broken in December 1993. The first solicitor appeared there in February 1994.[94] He was a former barrister.

Four years on, only 630 out of 70,000 practising solicitors in England and Wales had joined him. Just two had become QCs or High Court judges. Solicitors seeking rights of advocacy had to prove they had 'relevant' skills. Judges continued to decide who could appear before them. Salaried lawyers were excluded from the courts, mainly because the salaried lawyers of the Crown Prosecution Service were the main source of briefs for junior barristers. It was not until the summer of 1998 that the new lord chancellor, Lord Irvine, announced that the government would remove all restrictions on advocacy in the higher courts. The legislation was introduced to Parliament at the start of the 1998–99 session.

The second secret of high incomes at the Bar is the inefficiency of the system of justice. A barrister receiving daily 'refreshers' of up to £3,750 a day has every incentive to maximise the time he spends in court, and the adversarial system is perfectly designed for that purpose. Most people experience its absurdities in divorce cases and contested wills, where lawyers waste millions of pounds a year litigating over the often limited assets of a divorcing couple or a dead relative. Death and divorce provide the perfect excuse for a protracted confrontation. Two brothers once got all the way to the High Court in a dispute over two toy trains left to them by their father. They eventually agreed to take one each. 'Suffer any wrong what can be done to you,' wrote Dickens after a visit to the High Court, 'rather than come here.' Many court cases – especially commercial litigation and fraud trials – still resemble Jarndyce *versus* Jarndyce. The system requires lawyers on both sides to disclose to each other everything relevant. They can then comb through acres of paper, at three-digit prices per hour, setting the pace of the case. The three Guinness fraud trials cost an estimated £20 million in legal fees; only one secured convictions. At the third trial in 1993, it took the court five weeks to decide whether a fee was dishonestly received.

Prolixity and procedural wrangling are the main problems. 'In the majority of cases,' wrote Lord Woolf in his interim report on the reform of the system of civil justice, 'the reasons for delay arise from failure to progress the case efficiently, wasting time on peripheral issues or procedural skirmishing to wear down an opponent or to excuse failure to get on with the case.'[95] Under the Conservatives, the lord chief justice proposed cutting the fees of barristers who failed to adhere to strict timetables, delivered long-winded speeches, or relied on oral rather than written submissions. But it is the adversarial system itself which encourages expensive wind baggery. Two barristers take the same facts, but one weaves them into a tale of unmitigated villainy while the other knits them into a tale of unblemished rectitude. The judge then dissects the arguments of both sides, and reassembles them for the benefit of the jury.

One of the main points of the report from Lord Woolf was the need to replace the adversarial system with a more constructive approach, in which court proceedings would be seen as a last resort. 'We have a very good system of justice,' Woolf thought, 'but no one can afford it – neither the state nor the public.'[96] Even in minor criminal cases, barristers may urge defendants to insist on their case being referred to a Crown Court, where the presence of a jury is thought more likely to end in an acquittal. The daily cost of a trial in a crown court is twice that of a magistrates' court.

In 1998 the government announced that it would curtail the right of defendants to choose trial by jury for a range of offences, including theft and grievous bodily harm. Predictably, lawyers said it would multiply wrongful convictions, and they have opposed ending jury trial in fraud cases for the same reason. Even the arcane practices and procedures of the court room, which would be risible if they were not so costly, are sacrosanct. Barristers may wear wigs and gowns, but judges have a choice of five different costumes, depending on the time of year or the nature of the case. In court, the use of new technology is negligible; documentation is always in paper form; the language is archaic; the jargon incomprehensible; the procedures inflexible.

No attempt is made to manage the workload or impose time limits. Cases are scheduled solely on the basis that the judge must never be kept waiting. (Lawyers clock up hours of fee-earning, waiting for entry to the court.) The late listing of cases is the main reason barristers are forced to drop a brief. A 1993 report by the Bar Council and the Law Society concluded that 'an air of Dickensian antiquity pervades the civil process.'[97] Three years later Lord Woolf denounced the court system for providing 'higher benefits to lawyers than their clients'. Yet any attempt to make going to court cheaper and more efficient is treated by barristers as equivalent to repealing the Magna Carta.

The Bean Counters: Accountants

Accountants are less pompous. Ironic self-deprecation is their hallmark. A 1995 poster campaign launched by the Institute of Chartered Accountants (ICA) said 'It's Easier to Sleep with a Chartered Accountant.'[98] They can afford to wear their learning lightly: the accountant, always popular in business, is now popular in government too. At times it seems as if nothing private or public can escape an 'audit'. As government has shifted from provision of services to regulation and supervision of services provided by others, and business has begun to make money rather than things, the auditor has come to embody the spirit of the age.

It is fitting, under a modernising government, that he belongs to the youngest of the professions. Although double-entry book-keeping was invented in Renaissance Italy, accountancy remained what an early president of the ICA called 'a semi-profession', until deep into the twentieth century. Unlike lawyers and doctors (both reviled in ancient Greece), the professional accountant emerged hesitatingly from the fog of nineteenth-century book-keeping. His technical methods were crude, and accountancy did not attract the élite in the same way as medicine and the law. It was synonymous with bores and number-crunchers, and did not even try to dispel its dreary image. When Sampson published his first *Anatomy of Britain* in 1962, the largest accountancy partnerships were unwilling to tell him how many staff they employed. The only joke he found was the telegraphic address of the ICA: Unravel.[99]

In the last twenty-five years the profession of accountancy has undergone a transformation. A training with a Big Five firm is now as valuable as an MBA, and success in the professional examinations presents a broad range of career choices. There are nearly a quarter of a million accountants active in Britain, or one for every two hundred and fifty people.[100] Accountancy is now the largest employer of professional labour outside the Civil Service. As President of the Board of Trade, Michael Heseltine (a failed accountant, but erstwhile publisher of *Accountancy Age*) deplored the fact that the brightest and the best were going into accountancy rather than starting their own business. In fact, a narrow majority of qualified accountants now go into business rather than staying in the profession.

Not all of those who remain pore over invoices, VAT receipts and cash books. Accountancy is now a multidisciplinary, multinational business conducted on a global scale. Andersen Worldwide, Deloitte & Touche, Ernst & Young, KPMG and Pricewaterhouse Coopers (PWC) compete with each other for clients in every market on earth. In 1997 the Big Five had a total fee income of £3.5 billion in Britain. (The total earnings from their collaboration with partnerships abroad are far higher, but British partners do not share in the earnings of colleagues based abroad.)

Globally, accountancy and related services were worth $50 billion in 1997. Often, the Big Five are competing for clients with merchant banks, lawyers and management consultants. No company looking to raise capital can afford not to appoint one of them as auditors. Between them, they audit all but a handful of the biggest companies listed on the London and New York stock exchanges – nine out of ten multinationals. This concentration of business reflects the amalgamations of recent years. Since 1990, the Big Eight have shrunk to the Big Five. Companies, stock markets and competition authorities on both sides of the Atlantic are worried that competition is now too attenuated to guarantee good service and fair prices.

The mergers have certainly undermined the independence on which the profession of auditor originally stood. Auditing company accounts still provides the profession with a steady income (company law obliges PLCs to have their books audited by qualified accountants) but the chief value of an auditing contract now lies in the opportunities it creates to sell other services to the same client – insolvency and management consultancy, tax advice, corporate finance, information technology advice and administration. This has created tensions within all the major accountancy partnerships.

Partners working in the faster-growing consultancy arms dislike subsidising colleagues on the audit side. KPMG has considered floating its consultancy business on the stock market, largely under pressure from its successful consultancy arm in the United States (though it would also allow the firm to lure talented staff from other professions by offering them share options). Andersen Worldwide has split its auditing business (Arthur Andersen) from its consultancy arm (Andersen Consulting), but retaining them both under a revenue-sharing umbrella has made the problem worse rather than better. Andersen Consulting resents the competition from Arthur Andersen, as well as the subsidy. After a failed attempt at amicable agreement, Andersen Consulting is now trying to secede from the partnership.

Regulators are worried: the price, thoroughness and reliability of company audits is being affected by the possibility of earning additional fees for other services. There is a suspicion that fee-hungry accountants may be colluding with managers keen to report ever-rising profits to their shareholders. None of the spectacular corporate bankruptcies of recent years, including Polly Peck, BCCI, Johnson Matthey and Baring Brothers, was anticipated by the auditors, who declared their accounts to be a 'true and fair view' of the state of the business. A survey found that shareholders were warned by auditors of an impending collapse at only one in seven companies which failed between 1987 and 1994.[101]

This has put at risk the right of accountants to regulate themselves. Recognising this, they are trying to reduce the scope for embarrassment. An Accounting Standards Board now sits in permanent session. Set up as a committee of the ICA in 1970, but raised to the status of a Board in 1990, it publishes regular Financial Reporting Standards (FRSs). To those who can understand them, FRSs have proved surprisingly controversial. A review panel in empowered to call for the withdrawal of accounts which do not comply with them, and auditors who play fast and loose with the rules can expect to find themselves in court. Despite these attempts to tighten self-regulation, New Labour is still pledged to subject the profession to independent regulation.[102]

Both the profession and the government are wasting their time: standards of work and professional ethics will never be perfected, particularly in a global economy. Even as the accountants presented their plans for a new self-regulatory regime to pre-empt government action, the World Bank was criticising the Big Five for putting their names to the accounts of Asian companies audited to local standards.[103] In the interests of fee-earning, bad accounting will always drive out good: the financial incentive to reform their behaviour is absent. Like other professionals, accountants making questionable decisions risk nothing but a lawsuit. They do not experience directly the pain of financial failure. In fact, accountants sometimes earn more from a bankrupt company than a thriving one. It was their work in winding up companies which first brought accountants to public attention in the late nineteenth century. Public testimony in prominent court cases – particularly Clarence Hatry in 1929 and the Royal Mail Steam Packet Company in 1931 – turned accountants into minor celebrities. Insolvency practitioners, such as Kenneth Cork, his successor Michael Jordan, and Christopher Morris and

TABLE 16.5
Partners' Earnings at the Top Twenty Accountancy Firms in 1997

Firm	Fee Income (£m)	Number of Partners	Fees Per Partner (£k)	Profit Per Partner (£)*
Andersen Worldwide	‡,§694.6	410	1,694	423,537
Deloitte & Touche	†440.9	335	1,316	329,029
Coopers & Lybrand (Now PWC)	766.0	596	1,285	321,309
Ernst & Young	†525.1	411	1,278	319,404
Price Waterhouse (Now PWC)	§,¶520.0	479	1,085	271,399
KPMG	575.2	561	1,025	256,328
Latham Crossley & Davis	12.5	18	694	173,611
Robson Rhodes	42.0	70	600	150,000
Grant Thornton	119.6	213	562	140,376
Smith & Williamson	38.4	69	556	139,130
BDO Stoy Hayward	106.4	197	540	135,025
Pannell Kerr Forster	72.7	136	535	133,640
Haines Watts	26.8	55	487	121,818
Nevill Russell	38.3	84	456	113,988
Macintyre Hudson	15.1	34	444	111,029
Morison Stoneham	7.5	17	441	110,294
Baker Tilly	¶30.4	69	441	110,145
Kidsons Impey	58.6	140	419	104,643
Kingston Smith	13.1	33	397	99,242
Moore Stephens	49.8	136	366	91,544

Source: *International Accounting Bulletin*, 1 December 1997, and *Accountancy Age*, 30 July 1998.
See also endnote 104.

* Author's estimates, by subtracting costs at 75 per cent of gross fee income.
† Gross Fee Income.
‡ Estimated by *International Accounting Bulletin*.
§ Figures include Arthur Andersen, Andersen Consulting and associated law firms, Garretts and Dorman Jeffrey & Co.
¶ Baker Tilly merged with Casson Beckman (London practices only) from 1 November 1997; combined revenue for 1997 is estimated to be in excess of £40 million.

Brian Smouha of Deloitte & Touche, remain famous because of their work winding up spectacular business failures like John Bloom, BCCI, Polly Peck and the Maxwell empire.

This does not mean the work is glamorous. Insolvency practitioners are upmarket debt collectors, who identify and sell the remaining assets of a failed business and divide the proceeds among the creditors. Like any form of debt collection, it requires a thick skin. Bossing about directors who have lost everything, fending off creditors who think they have lost everything, and sacking angry employees, is work suited to desiccated calculating machines. Abusive telephone calls, death threats and super-glued locks are routine events in a major insolvency. A practitioner working on winding-up Polly Peck was shot during an assignment in Istanbul.[105]

But it was worth it. The liquidation of Polly Peck yielded insolvency fees of £25 million.[106] Even that was nothing compared to the $232 million the liquidators collected between 1992 and 1998 for unravelling the remains of BCCI. When Christopher Morris of Deloitte & Touche attended a meeting of BCCI creditors in 1993, the questioners did not dissemble: 'Why don't you just go home and give us the rest of the money?' one asked. Spanning sixty-nine separate jurisdictions, BCCI is the most lucrative insolvency in the history of accountancy. It was also described as 'the largest professional assignment anywhere in the world, ever'.[107] Most would recoil from earning a living from the misfortunes of others, but the work is certainly lucrative. Top insolvency practitioners earn £250–350 an hour, and their work has proved remunerative enough to make millionaires of all the leading practitioners.

Nobody outside the firm knows exactly what they earn. The same is true, with rare exceptions, of other top accountants. Accountancy partnerships are not required to disclose financial information; they stopped revealing even their gross fee income in 1996. When KPMG published a full annual report detailing the earnings of its audit partners, the decision was not voluntary. (It was an obligation which followed incorporation of the audit arm, volunteered to protect the wealth of the partners from potentially ruinous litigation.) But it has afforded a definitive glimpse at what the wealthiest accountants are earning. The total remuneration of the senior partner, Colin Sharman, rose from £740,000 in 1995 to £771,000 in 1996. In 1998 he earned £904,000. But he is the highest-paid member of the firm; the majority of KPMG partners earn salaries of between £75,000 and £225,000 a year, with pension contributions and profit shares boosting these by one half to two thirds.[108]

Only Ernst & Young, of the Big Five, has followed the example of KPMG. Nick Land, the senior partner, took home £515,857 in 1997. Most of his fellow partners earned between £100,000 and £300,000 in salary only.[109] Earnings are undoubtedly smaller at middle-ranking firms. In 1996 BDO Stoy Hayward was the first to publish partnership earnings. They showed that the 158 partners earned an average of £92,000 each in the previous year, or about half the KPMG average. Four out of five partners earned less than £125,000, with most falling in the £75–100,000 range. Just six partners earned more than

£200,000. Average earnings have risen since to £130,000, with the senior partner earning somewhere between £325,000 and £350,000.[110] At other firms, it is possible only to guess at what the partners earn. But the best paid partners of any firm are agreed to be those at Andersen Consulting. They are understood to be averaging around £500,000 a year each.

Incorporation: The Twilight of the Professions

'We are not Fat Cats,' said the managing partner of BDO Stoy Hayward, after the firm published its first earnings figures in 1996.[111] But earnings of over £300,000 are getting on for twenty times the national average. The exorbitant remuneration of the professions is eroding public respect, even if professionals do not recognise this. It is true that some of their clients are indifferent (being Fat Cats themselves) but there is a genuine concern that professional costs are damaging the standard of living of others.

Economic activity cannot be costless. It consists of people exchanging goods and services for money, and it takes money to employ professionals to negotiate transactions, devise and enforce property rights, and uphold the sanctity of contract and the rules of the marketplace. These 'transaction costs' are now the biggest single expense of doing business. They are not investments in productive activity, but taxes on the activity of others. Many who gave to the Diana Memorial Fund were shocked to find her lawyers had charged £495,000 for three months' work.[112] Britain now has the slowest (if not the most expensive) housing market in the world, thanks to the involvement of professional intermediaries. Claims for personal injury pursued by bounty hunting lawyers have caused massive inflation of the legal aid budget. The spectre now haunting business is litigation on the American scale. In 1996 BAT Industries spent $100 million a year defending speculative lawsuits launched by American lawyers on behalf of ex-smokers. But it spent *five times as much* fending off lawsuits by their ambulance-chasing colleagues against its California-based insurance subsidiary.

These tolls add nothing to the stock of wealth; they merely redistribute it from owners to intermediaries. The chief effect of litigation against insurance companies, for example, is to raise insurance premiums. Costs are minimised where the parties to a transaction trust each other, and work to standardised rules and procedures. But professionals have created a business climate in which nobody trusts anyone, and the terms of major transactions seem designed to test accepted rules and procedures to the limit. Francis Fukuyama the Japanese-American writer, thinks a culture of trust is an essential ingredient of long-term economic success. It is the 'social capital' of trust and goodwill which balances the individualism of 'human capital', allowing businessmen to trade and collaborate without being surrounded by professional advisers. He describes litigation in particular as a 'direct tax imposed by the breakdown of trust in society'.[113]

It is because he has taken the caricature of economic man (what Fukuyama calls 'the rational utility-maximising individual') so seriously that the modern professional has lost his sense of the goodness of human beings and of the moral habits and tacit rules which govern their behaviour. Countless transactions do not happen because the professional-at-work undermines the personal trust of the principals. Alan Sugar says he had to ask the lawyers to leave the room so that he could reach an agreement with Rupert Murdoch to manufacture satellite dishes. 'I can guarantee that if Mr Murdoch had got out of the room, he would have got other advice and the deal might have fallen through.'[114]

People no longer go to a lawyer or an accountant when they are in trouble; they hire them to be told how to avoid getting into trouble in the first place. These things take time, and, for professionals, time is money. The public is well aware of it: it is the main reason professionals have forfeited their trust. People were never more willing to dispute the bill with their advisers. Corporate clients, under pressure from shareholders, have begun to do the same. This has for the first time provoked competition for fees *within* the professions. A professional can no longer demand that a client accept him at his own valuation. He must market himself, submit quotations, justify his bill and provide a high level of service, or lose the business. 'Public expectations of professions have changed. People will no longer accept mystique and remoteness,' wrote Lord Alexander of his chairmanship of the Bar Standards Review Committee. 'They want good-quality work and an all-round efficient service, backed by good client communication.'[115] When a firm of accountants surveyed 200 smaller companies on their attitudes towards the professions, comments like 'too many round figures for comfort', 'patronisingly expensive' and 'continually search for angles to overcharge' summarised popular cynicism.[116]

Clients now encourage competition for their business. Accountants in particular have noticed an intensification of rivalry. Predatory pricing (which accountants have dubbed, with professional hauteur, 'low-balling') is thriving as auditing contracts are put out to tender. Audit fees plunge by a third, say accountants, when a contract changes hands. In April 1995 BDO Stoy Hayward wrote to the members of the Royal Automobile Club, protesting that they had lost the contract to audit the club accounts because Price Waterhouse was guilty of 'low-balling'.[117]

This resistance to ever-rising fees is drawing the professions into compromising relationships and conflicts of interest as they struggle to retain or win business. City solicitors have ceased to be scriveners, brought in to write the documents after the deal is done; now, they are an integral part of the process of financial innovation. Their clients know that the legislation and self-regulatory codes which govern the City are open to reinterpretation by clever lawyers, who are expected to invent ways around legal or fiscal obstacles to the successful completion of a deal (or erect them). The first line of defence in a takeover is often to sue the bidder, or appeal for assistance to helpful laws or regulations. When BAT Industries was fighting off a hostile bid in 1989, it launched twenty-seven different law-suits against its foes. The bidder repaid in kind.

In the same spirit, companies no longer expect their accountants to plead ethical objections to adventurous tax arrangements, or doctorings of the profit and loss account. 'Accountants,' wrote Ian Hay-Davison of the offshore reinsurance business at Lloyd's in the early 1980s, 'were at the heart of the major misconduct at Lloyd's. Underwriters and brokers may have taken money . . . but in each case an accountant planned the arrangements and failed to warn his principal of the dangers of what they were doing . . . the dubious tax arrangements that were such a widespread feature of the Lloyd's of the 1970s were planned by accountants and audited or, to be strictly factual, *not* audited, by accountants.'[118]

Modern accountants do not fuss much about conflicts of interest. It is widely suspected that investigating accountants put companies into liquidation sooner than necessary in the expectation that they will be given the insolvency business. During the recession of the early 1990s, the Insolvency Service identified what it called 'significant compliance problems'.[119] Members of the Big Five were fined for hoarding money owed to creditors in a liquidation.[120] No accountant doubts that 'low-balling' bids for audit business are made on the assumption that losses will be outweighed by consultancy earnings from the same client. This is the main official anxiety about the independence of the audit (the 'true and fair view') and the ability of the profession to regulate itself.

The rising tide of successful litigation against auditors suggests that competition for audit business is discouraging the asking of awkward questions. Price Waterhouse and Ernst & Young spent $125 million settling a claim for negligent auditing of BCCI.[121] Coopers & Lybrand was sued for negligent auditing of Maxwell Communications and Barings.[122] Inadequate auditing of American thrifts cost Ernst & Young $400 million, KPMG $186.5 million and Deloitte & Touche $312 million.[123] In 1992 Price Waterhouse was ordered by an Arizona jury to pay $338 million to Standard Chartered over a faulty bank audit costing $300,000. A video was prepared by the prosecution, dubbed *The Titanic*, which alternated scenes from the movie *A Night to Remember* with figures and graphics showing how the auditors had failed to locate the financial icebergs beneath the accounts of the United Bank of Arizona.[124]

Accountants, architects, chartered surveyors, doctors and lawyers themselves are paying increasing sums for negligence and malpractice insurance. The Medical Defence Union reckons that litigation against doctors for negligence and malpractice is increasing at a rate of 15 per cent a year; its cable address, Damocles, says it all.[125] The rising cost of insurance, and the constant threat of financial ruin, has persuaded many professionals that partnerships with unlimited liability are a luxury they can no longer afford. Others, recognising that one major defeat will condemn the partners to penury, have considered incorporation as a limited liability company. In 1995, KPMG incorporated its audit arm, and in 1997 Price Waterhouse and Ernst & Young persuaded the States of Jersey to rewrite their company law to accommodate the American idea of partnerships with limited liability. These protect the personal wealth of partners – though not their professional assets – from litigants. The Jersey plan foundered on objections from the Inland Revenue, but the government has now promised to enact the necessary mainland legislation. In the meantime, accountants are trying to agree caps on their legal liability in any transaction where they are obliged to offer an opinion to clients.

Incorporation, limited liability partnerships and liability caps mark the end of the traditional idea of a profession. The willingness of all partners to take full responsibility for the actions and advice of one was a key factor in the rise of the professions. The transformation of partnerships into companies and company lookalikes, by obliging professionals to disclose full details of their income, confirms that they are as interested in money as anybody else. It proves that they are willing to take risks with the rules and endure previously insupportable conflicts of interest – even to perform work to a lower standard – in pursuit of greater fee income.

Resistance to incorporation is probably futile. Stockbrokers, merchant bankers and chartered surveyors have abandoned partnership structures; some have floated on the stock market. The scale of business is increasing, globally and nationally. Firms are establishing joint ventures with others in the United States and Europe. Provincial firms of lawyers and accountants are amalgamating to create new national networks. The mergers have created vast professional bureaucracies in which the traditional ethic cannot survive. No partner wants to be bankrupted by the incompetence or negligence of a partner they may never have met. 'Yesterday's law is totally unsuitable for today's business,' an accountant told the *Financial Times*. 'We can't expect an individual to put the future of their family on the line every time one of their fellow partners is accused of making a mistake.'[126]

These risks have exacerbated the tensions between the young 'rainmakers' and older colleagues who can remember the days of leisurely lunches. The younger partners want cash, not personal prestige, social standing or an agreeable way of life, and they want to kick passengers off the payroll. Dick Measelle, managing partner of Arthur Andersen, is an eloquent exponent of this new professional individualism:

> If I am really kicking ass in the American market and you're sitting at home taking holidays, we are going to fix that problem . . . This is not an egalitarian partnership from the standpoint that everyone makes the same amount of money. Partners are equal but some are more equal than others . . . We've got a lot of friction in this firm because we have got an open partnership.[127]

The sheer size of modern partnerships has diluted fellow-feeling, and made it impossible to manage a firm consensually. Younger partners are unhappy about pledging their wealth to senior partners whose competence they doubt, and whose histories they do not know. They think the people whose names appear first on the note paper are enjoying incomes they have not earned. If they do not get what they think they deserve, they leave.

Head-Hunters

Mobility, between as well as within professions, is characteristic of the modern professional. The marketplace in human capital is compered by another breed of professional, the recruitment consultant, or 'head-hunter', who was emerging as Sampson wrote his first *Anatomy of Britain*. 'For many of the old school,' Sampson wrote, 'the clamour from this market-place is horrifying; it cuts across two old industrial traditions – secrecy and lifelong loyalty.'[128] In the earliest phase of capitalism, ownership and control at both companies and partnerships were united in the same people. There were owner-managers and partners, who risked their capital in the venture and had long-term commitment to its success. The modern owners of human capital have recreated the pre-industrial labour market, in which most people sell their labour to the highest bidder.

Head-hunting is now a global industry generating fees the Economist Intelligence Unit put at $7 billion in 1996.[129] It is hard to describe executive search and selection (the term head-hunters use to distinguish themselves from employment agencies) as a true profession. It is completely unregulated, and there are no barriers to entry, save the cost of a telephone. The industry is dominated by partnerships of two to four consultants and sole traders, who turn over perhaps £500,000 a year. But if head-hunting is a relatively small business, it is a lucrative one. Historical accident has set the professional fee at 33 per cent of the first year's salary of every individual who agrees to change his job, giving head-hunters a strong incentive to demand exorbitant salaries for their clients. Annual incomes of six figures are common among head-hunters, and they rise to seven in a good year. David Norman and Miles Broadbent, proprietors of the most successful partnership in London until they split forces in 1996, were reported to pay themselves an average of £700,000 a year.

The biggest earners fill vacancies at the top of large PLCs, and move people between investment banks. Head-hunters have helped to turn investment banking into a business where people measure themselves by nothing but money. It is the perfect field of play for them: salaries are large, the turnover is immense and bankers are easily persuaded that it is cheaper to buy human capital than real capital. Twice in the last ten years the investment banking merry-go-round has alarmed the Bank of England sufficiently to warn that it was leading to a dangerous escalation of costs, a propensity to take excessive risks, and a lack of stability in employment and planning.

But the job-hopping habit is ingrained, and is spreading; there is an established trade in senior lawyers between British and American firms. In 1996 a partner at Clifford Chance moved to an American firm for a reported guarantee of £500,000 a year.[130]

Joint legal and accountancy partnerships are destroying the last barrier to mobility between the professions. The first multi-disciplinary professional practices, combining expertise in law, accountancy and management consultancy, are already being created. Arthur Andersen set up a firm of solicitors (Garrett & Co.), bought another (Dundas & Wilson) and tried to buy a third (Wilde Sapte). Coopers & Lybrand and Price Waterhouse both owned law firms even before their merger. Arthur Andersen owns the largest law firm in Spain, and KPMG the largest in France. The government has promised to eradicate all remaining barriers to multi-disciplinary professional firms. Only one professional divide now remains impermeable, or at least permeable in one direction only. It is that which separates the private sector from the public, which is now the last redoubt of the old professional ethic. Its adherents call it 'public service', but it is really something else.

CHAPTER SEVENTEEN

THE PUBLIC SECTOR PROFESSIONALS

As the struggle between lord and peasant was the master conflict in feudal society and the struggle between capitalist and wage earner the master conflict in industrial society, so the struggle between the public and the private sector professions is the master conflict of professional society.

PROFESSOR HAROLD PERKIN, 1989[1]

We live in a society that rewards City spivs and lawyers, car fleet managers and advertising touts, more than scientists, scholars and teachers. The Labour Party and the Liberal Democrats seem to have some values that rise above the level of the whelk-stall and the car-phone.

DR RICHARD DAWKINS, 1992[2]

If we were to channel more of the nation's talent into wealth-creating private business, this would inevitably mean reducing employment in the public sector.

MARGARET THATCHER, 1992[3]

The English judge ensures in a quiet but effective manner that his pay accords with his status.

DAVID PANNICK[4]

Michael Lewis was finishing a Master's degree at the London School of Economics when the letter arrived from Salomon Brothers, an American investment bank. He had got the job. The starting salary was $42,000 a year, with a guaranteed bonus of $6,000 after six months. At the dollar rate of exchange in 1985, Michael Lewis was about to start work on a salary of £45,000 a year. 'Receiving the news in England, the land of limp paycheques, accentuated the generosity of Salomon's purse,' he later recalled. 'A chaired professor of the London School of Economics, who took a keen interest in material affairs, stared at me bug-eyed and gurgled when he heard what I was to be paid. It was twice what he earned. He was in his mid-forties and at the top of his profession. I was twenty-four years old and at the bottom of mine. There was no justice in the world, and thank goodness for that.'[5] The gap which had opened between the economics student and his professor was not the modest fissure which separates the earnings of one profession from another. It was the chasm which separates the pay of the private sector professions from the pay of the public sector professions.

It was not always so. The most successful investment bankers, lawyers and accountants have always earned more than top civil servants or dons, but the *average* professional on both sides earned much the same. Judges, permanent secretaries, diplomats and chiefs of the defence staff enjoyed status which seems incredible today. In the 1970s, top Oxbridge graduates coveted jobs in Whitehall and medicine, not the City.[6] The money-minded graduates of today struggle to disentangle status from money. The gap which separates the professional classes of the private and the public sectors has a generational aspect, but it is mainly financial. The social historian, Professor Harold Perkin, has described the battle between the public and the private sector for a larger share of the national income as the 'master conflict' of modern Britain. In many ways, his own career traces the change since the 1970s. In 1967 he became the first Professor of Social History to be appointed in Britain, taking up the post at the new University of Lancaster, a creation of the redbrick boom of the 1960s.[7] By the mid-1980s, alienated by Thatcherism in general and its reduction in university staffing in particular, he took a job in the United States.[8]

In the Fifties and Sixties, the public sector professional (as Professor Perkin) and the institutions he ran (universities, the NHS, the nationalised industries) dominated the British way of life. In the 1980s, he and they became objects of scorn. Of course, the divide between private and public within the professional classes was never neat; it is still blurred. Judges move into the public sector late in life, mainly in pursuit of prestige and pensions, after making a pile at the Bar. Civil servants and army officers make the same journey, in the opposite direction. Hospital consultants drift in and out of the public sector on a daily basis, supplementing their public sector salaries with private practice. The craftier dons have fashioned a similar life, adding to their exiguous public sector pay cheques within journalism and consultancy. And, as architects and engineers can attest, there are poorly paid professionals in the private sector.

Professional Poor I: Architects

A full-time architect with decades of experience is lucky if he earns £45,000 a year. Despite a rigorous seven-year training, and in the middle of the biggest architectural boom since the late 1980s, the average architect was earning £27,000 in 1998. Only architects working in the largest practices can expect to work regularly; sole traders will work less than two in every three days in an average year – a rate of professional under-employment not dissimilar from acting. It takes a decade to establish a reputation which secures valuable commissions, and most architects never make it. There are only 30,000, and many cannot even afford the statutory registration fee to retain their licence to practise.[9] Architecture is a profession in decline.

It boomed briefly after the war, when central and local government carpeted bombed cities with schools and hospitals, universities, theatres and high-rise flats. 'We have not recovered from the trauma of having been so important in the 1950s and 1960s as handmaidens of the Welfare State,' said Francis Duffy, when he became president of the Royal Institute of British Architects (RIBA) in 1993. 'We haven't found a comparable commercial apparatus to get us into the 1980s and 1990s.'[10] Most architects are still rooted in the Modernist tradition, and despised the low-budget eclecticism of the commercial boom of the 1980s. They have enjoyed the pre-Millennium extravaganza more.

The resumption of publicly funded experiments, such as the Millennium Dome, suited a profession with a legendary disregard for public opinion. But the temporary patronage of the taxpayer cannot conceal the economic and

TABLE 17.1
Earnings of Architects, 1998

Private Practice	
Sole Principals	£15,000–35,000
Principals in Partnership	£25,000–50,000
Salaried	£20,000–28,879
In-House	£24,000–34,500
Public Sector	
Local Authorities	£24,000–32,000
Central Government	£26,400–35,917

Source: Royal Institute of British Architects: Architects' Employment and Earnings, 1998.

commercial failure of architecture and its self-image is beyond parody. A RIBA brochure describes the Institution as 'humming with conversation, wine, cakes and above all architecture'. Beneath an exquisite photograph of a *tarte aux fraises* is the mysterious phrase 'firmness, commodity and delight', which reads like a pun about tarts.[11] In the popular mind, the archetypal architect is a neophiliac poseur in a bow-tie and a crumpled crimson jacket. His visible contempt for the consumers who use his work, perhaps forgivable in an artist, is suicidal in a profession operating where Art meets Money.

Unfortunately for architects, the public has not forgotten the fifties and sixties either. Unlike a botched appendicectomy or a dodgy set of accounts, the architectural mistakes of those years cannot be hidden from view or confined to the inner pages of the broadsheet newspapers. The Modernist experimentation of the post-war period trapped two generations of urban poor in soulless high-rise council flats, and disfigured the commercial districts of our cities with steel and concrete boxes. Most of the architects responsible were working in the public sector on public contracts, who did not need to sell their vision to people, and they have not learned to do so since. 'My generation thought we were on the planet to make things better for everyone else,' says Francis Duffy.[12]

Professional Poor II: Engineers

Engineers have never shared that pretension. Less than one in forty admit that they went into the profession out of a 'desire to help society'.[13] This may be one reason why architects and engineers have never got on. Another is cultural. Engineers are earthy and provincial, while architects are a byword for pretentiousness. (Unlike some European countries, British engineers do not design buildings, and architects do not build them.) But the two professions do share a problem. They both have poor public images, making it hard to attract bright people – a new phenomenon for both, especially for engineers.

In Victorian times, Brunel, Naesmith and Telford were national heroes. Samuel Smiles published *Lives of the Engineers* in five volumes, to popular acclaim, and both *Self-Help* and *Thrift* were imbued with the idea that men such as Boulton, Watt and George Stephenson were important role models for the aspirant *bourgeois*. In the twentieth century, engineers were associated with commercial failures, like the VC-10, Concorde, Nimrod and the catastrophe of nuclear power, where technical excitement took precedence over profitability or even utility.

Engineering has yet to shed its association with the white-hot technological revolution promised by Harold Wilson in 1963, and put into effect by the planners and nationalised industries in the following years. Monty Finniston, who chaired an official committee of inquiry into the ills of the engineering profession between 1977 and 1979, told Anthony Sampson: 'In Germany or America engineers were regarded as right at the top, next to doctors, but here we found that engineers were rated below male models.'[14] One identified obstacle to raising their standing is the lack of a single public face: engineering is not a single profession, but a multiplicity of different disciplines. Ever since the Institution of Civil Engineers refused to admit George Stephenson to membership, the bridge-builders have distrusted the train-builders.

Now, as then, engineers and technicians of all kinds are obliged to work together on major projects. But computer technologists do not get on with foundrymen or welders, even in office hours. Forty separate professional organisations represent 290,000 chartered, incorporated and technical engineers. The only common thread is that CEngs, IEngs and EngTechs must all register with the Engineering Council. Established as a consequence of the Finniston Report, it was meant to raise the standard, status and influence of the profession. Nearly twenty years later, the Council has still to persuade the forty institutions to accept it as their public voice.

TABLE 17.2
The Earnings of Engineers, 1997 (£s)

Registration*	Average Incomes	Average Bonus†	Highest Earnings
Chartered Engineer	23,500–60,000	5,138	250,000+
Incorporated Engineer	19,540–41,397	3,774	90,000+
Engineering Technician	16,000–35,500	4,372	50,000+

Source: Engineering Council.

* 71.4 per cent of engineers are Chartered; 22.2 per cent Incorporated; and 6.4 per cent Technicians.
† Only 47.1 per cent of respondents to the survey received a bonus.

This persistent fissiparity has relegated engineering to the realm of the technical, allowing the bankers and the accountants to make more money from major engineering projects. Today, the highest paid engineer is the (usually Chartered) chairman or chief executive of a major engineering enterprise, but few get as far as the boardroom. Anecdotal and academic evidence suggests that engineers are too technically minded to run businesses.[15] A few dozen boardroom engineers earn over £250,000 a year, but the average in the top flight is a paltry £70,955[16] Their junior colleagues are making between

£25,000 and £40,000 a year. It will be a long time before the Michael Lewises of the world agree with Mike Heath, director general of the Engineering Council, that engineering is 'highly paid', the 'surest route to business success and a 'fascinating career'.[17]

Senior Civil Servants

Whitehall mandarins are the last professionals to believe that career satisfaction is an adequate substitute for money. In 1987 Peter Hennessy was told by a senior civil servant, surrounded at the time by bankers and lawyers, that he would never swap his job for a post in the City because it could not possibly yield as much interest and variety. The attraction of a career in the Civil Service is power – power without responsibility. 'Of all forms of power,' Hennessy wrote shortly after his illuminating encounter, 'private power is the most seductive for a certain sort of intelligent person.'[18]

Traditionally, senior civil servants use that power to frustrate the ambitions of their political masters. In *Yes, Minister*, a popular television comedy, senior civil servants were portrayed as lovable cynics, deflating the ambitions of their ministers, and the caricature embodied the self-image of the senior civil servant: the belief that his power is essentially benign. 'We felt public service was much more honourable and challenging than to dirty one's hands in trade,' a senior Treasury mandarin told Jeremy Paxman. 'Of course, I have a higher regard for the profit motive now, but we sincerely felt that it was a more proper use of one's talent to put it to the use of the community as a whole.'[19]

One of the many charges against Thatcherism is that it destroyed this ethos of public service, replacing disinterested Sir Humphrey Appletons with highly politicised, can-do merchants whose job was not to frustrate policy but to carry it out. On this view, the modern civil servant is little different from a business executive. No wonder so many are emigrating to the better-paid worlds of industry, commerce and the City, where their brains and experience command higher salaries. The best-known emigrant from the Treasury is Gerry Grimstone, a privatisation specialist who joined Schroders bank. But at the time of Big Bang in October 1986, no less than forty-four Treasury principals left the Civil Service for the richer pastures of the City.[20]

Both Deryck Maughan, chief executive at Salomon Brothers, and Peter Middleton, erstwhile chief executive at Lloyd's, set out as civil servants. Another Treasury official, Tim Parker, turned himself into a minor business celebrity by rescuing the Kenwood appliance business. Dame Pauline Neville-Jones became head of global business strategy at NatWest Markets. Many

retired civil servants top up their index-linked pensions with a sinecure in
the City. Lord Hunt, a former Cabinet secretary, agreed to chair both the
Prudential Assurance Company and the London operations of the Banque
Nationale de Paris. The former permanent secretary at the Treasury, Sir
Douglas Wass, was taken on by Nomura, the Japanese investment bank. The
National Westminster Bank has both Sir Charles Powell and Sir George Quig-
ley from the Northern Ireland Office.

It is argued that moves of this kind would never have occurred in the
pre-Thatcher civil service, but the purity of the Whitehall of the past is exaggerated. The first rules on civil servants taking jobs in the private sector were
introduced by the National Government in 1936, after a royal commission
had criticised the steady passage of senior civil servants from the War Office
to the boardrooms of arms manufacturers.[21] It fell to the last Wilson government to draw up a revised set of rules for civil servants in the wake of the
Poulson scandal of 1972 (Poulson had bribed civil servants to award him
contracts for twenty-five years). Within two years, the Commons Expenditure
Committee was warning that lucrative private sector jobs were once again
being dangled before senior civil servants.

Taking lucrative jobs in the City, or bribes from arms manufacturers, are
probably the least important ways in which civil servants pursue their own
interests rather than those of the public. What matters more is their interest
in Big Government. In this sense, modern civil servants do not differ from
their predecessors of any age. The administrators of Tudor and Stuart England used the machinery of the state to increase their personal power and
wealth. As the state expanded in the eighteenth and nineteenth centuries,
and the nascent civil service was drawn into the web of Old Corruption,
administrative posts were bought and sold precisely because public revenues
created plentiful opportunities to secure a generous income for minimal
effort.

In their seminal report on the reform of the Civil Service, published in
1854, Sir Stafford Northcote and Sir Charles Trevelyan declared:

> Admission into the Civil Service is eagerly sought after, but it is for the
> unambitious, and the indolent or incapable that it is chiefly desired.
> Those whose abilities do not warrant an expectation that they will suc-
> ceed in the open professions, where they must encounter the compe-
> tition of their contemporaries, and those for whom indolence of
> temperament, or physical infirmities unfit for active exertions, are
> placed in the Civil Service, where they may obtain an honourable liveli-
> hood with little labour, and with no risk.[22]

Their recommendation that civil servants be recruited from Oxbridge by competitive examination turned the civil service into a profession, complete with barriers to entry.

Traditionally, the Northcote–Trevelyan Report marked the beginning of a disinterested civil service. It also marked the beginning of a shift from Old Corruption to a new form of professional self-interest. An efficient body of permanent officers could not wax if government were allowed to wane. Though it took decades to supplant the placemen of the Old Corruption, the new breed of professional civil servants were at work on the expansion of government long before the inauguration of the Welfare State in 1945. However, the First World War prompted the major reorganisation which made a reality of the Northcote–Trevelyan Report. Sir Robert Morant, a little-known civil servant at the Board of Education before the First World War, could be said to have invented the Welfare State.[23] Beveridge too was bureaucrat first, and politician second. As the state expanded, so did the Civil Service. By the 1970s, the 16,000 civil servants of the mid-Victorian state had multiplied forty-fold.

The Civil Service expanded remorselessly until 1979, when Margaret Thatcher became prime minister, rising to power in part on the back of disillusion with the Mandarin state. In the 1980s, the private sector replaced the public as the vehicle of national aspirations. The new prime minister made no secret of her contempt for the 'negative attitudes' of the Whitehall elite[24] and teams of cost-cutters and efficiency-seekers were recruited from the private sector. The Civil Service Department (the original of the Ministry of Administrative Affairs) was abolished. The number of civil servants fell from 735,430 in 1979 to 492,000 by 1997, a decline of one third.

The philosopher–kings of traditional Whitehall were turned into business executives and ordered to prepare PLC-style accounts. Key administrative functions were hived off to independent Executive Agencies, headed by executives recruited in open competition and retained on short-term performance-related contracts. Three out of four civil servants now work in Executive Agencies.[25] The nationalised industries, from which entire departments had earned a living, were privatised. The government took on the Civil Service trade unions, resisting a five-month strike in 1981, and banning them from GCHQ, the listening station at Cheltenham. There were inquiries into the value of civil service pensions and attempts to relate civil service pay to merit, performance and local supply and demand, rather than the traditional measures of seniority, custom and comparability with the private sector.

The number of senior posts shrank as departments were closed, merged or rationalised. One fifth of top departmental jobs disappeared. At the Executive Agencies, most jobs went to incumbents, but the handful which went to outsiders inflicted serious damage on the morale of senior civil servants. The

TABLE 17.3
Senior Civil Service Pay in 1998

	No. in Band	Pay Band £
Cabinet Secretary & Head of the Civil Service	1	£130–134,999
Permanent Secretary to the Treasury	1	£130–134,999
Head of the Diplomatic Service	1	£125–129,999
Permanent Under Secretary, Ministry of Defence	1	£115–119,999
Permanent Secretary*	6	£110–114,999
Director of Public Persecutions	1	£110–114,999
Permanent Secretary†	2	£105–109,999
First Parliamentary Counsel	1	£105–109,999
Chairman of HM Customs & Excise	1	£105–109,999
Chief Executive of the National Health Service	1	£105–109,999
Director of International Finance, HM Treasury	1	£105–109,999
Permanent Secretary‡	3	£100–104,999
Chief Medical Officer	1	£100–104,999
Chief Scientific Advisers	2	£100–104,999
Director of Public Expenditure, HM Treasury	1	£100–104,999
Permanent Secretary§	4	£95–99,999
Head of the Secret Intelligence Service	1	£95–99,999
Director General of the Security Service	1	£95–99,999
Chairman of the Board of the Inland Revenue	1	£95–99,999
Director of the Office of National Statistics	1	£95–99,999
Head of the Government Accountancy Service	1	£95–99,999
Treasury Solicitor	1	£95–99,999
Chief of Defence Procurement	1	£90–94,999
Director, GCHQ	1	£90–94,999
Director of Finance, HM Treasury	1	£90–94,999
2nd Permanent Secretary, Ministry of Defence	1	£90–94,999

Source: Review Body on Senior Salaries, Report No. 40, Cm 3837, 1998.

* Education and Employment, Environment, Transport and the Regions, Home Office, Lord Chancellor's Department, Scottish Office, Department of Trade and Industry.
† Ministry of Agriculture, Fisheries and Food, Social Security.
‡ Culture, Media and Sport, International Development, Office of Public Service.
§ Health, Northern Ireland Civil Service, Northern Ireland Office, Welsh Office.

newcomers demanded private sector salaries: in 1991 an Australian statistician, Bill McLennan, was offered more than £100,000 to run the Office for National Statistics; John Chisholm nearly £150,000 to run the Defence Research Agency. These were levels to which Robin Butler, then Cabinet secretary and head of the Home Civil Service, could barely aspire. For the first time, the career of a mandarin seemed precarious as well as unrewarding. The rise of the Executive Agencies was a clear sign that public service had changed its meaning: it meant providing an efficient service to the public. Two permanent secretaries, Sir Clive Whitmore at the Home Office and Sir Geoffrey Holland at Education, announced that they were leaving partly in protest at the deification of the private sector. Senior civil servants have certainly lost self-esteem, and they believe they have lost public respect.

Much less has changed than they believe. Civil servants were figures of fun fifty years before the first episode of *Yes, Minister* was broadcast. The pay of senior civil servants (if not that of their staff) is still determined more by rank than performance. It is not as high as they would like, and Oxbridge graduates have developed a preference for the City, but bright people are still attracted by a career in Whitehall. The hundred-odd 'fast stream' places offered by the Civil Sevice every year are fifty or sixty times over-subscribed. Winners are still selected by the same mixture of competitive examination and interview invented by the Northcote–Trevelyan Report. A majority of permanent secretaries are still Oxbridge arts graduates, and few are sacked or retired early. The worst that can happen is failure to get promoted, and even failures can expect a gong and a comfortable retirement on a low-contribution, index-linked pension. Permanent secretaries are still chosen by the prime minister from a short list drawn up by permanent secretaries. Michael Bichard, feted by the government as the first genuine outsider to enter the upper echelons when he became permanent secretary at the Department of Employment in 1995, was actually a career civil servant with a background in local government and the Benefits Agency. Senior civil servants have so far escaped the Greenbury-style disclosure about pay and perks (and especially pensions) which created the private sector Fat Cat. Sir Humphrey is secure. From a personal point of view, a decade and a half of permanent revolution in Whitehall has meant little more than a higher salary.

Politicians

The danger of paying extra for the same people is more acute with another species of public servant: the politician. Sir Terence Higgins, a senior Conservative backbencher, spent much of the summer of 1996 touring radio and television studios to warn the public that only a massive pay rise for Members of Parliament could secure a continuing supply of representatives of his calibre. It is, however, more probable that the same people would be elected to the House of Commons, whatever they were paid. The modern politician is a member of a self-selected caste for whom politics is not a career choice but an addiction. The satisfactions it offers (power, publicity, self-importance, and, above all, the company of other addicts) cannot be fulfilled in any other way. Politicians are, as Peter Riddell writes, 'different from the rest of us ... They are abnormal.'[26]

Virtually every modern parliamentarian has spent his or her entire adult life either in the House of Commons or in jobs which allow them to pursue their ambition to be in the House. An aspiring politician must serve an apprenticeship as a party researcher, local councillor or constituency officer; stand for election in an unwinnable seat; battle against hundreds of hopefuls for a safe seat; do time as secretary to a backbench committee; serve a spell as a parliamentary private secretary; do a stint in the Whips Office; and then gradually ascend to the Cabinet via an under secretaryship and term as a minister of state.

In a sense, this career path is like any other: full-time, and the route to the top is rigid and hierarchical. The difference is that the financial rewards are pitiful, and the chance of success is remote.

'Why give up a six figure income for the risks of politics?' asked Sir Derek Spencer, the solicitor general, a political recidivist who returned to the House of Commons in June 1992 after five years. 'Basically, the excitement that comes from the uncertainty of it all. The feeling that you are at the centre of things. The opportunity to help individual constituents, which gives you a deep sense of personal satisfaction.'[27] The afterthought was significant. Politicians are as apt as civil servants to describe their primary motivation as 'duty', the 'desire to serve', or 'helping constituents'. In truth, this is often the least of their motives. The vast majority of politicians are fired by ambition: the pursuit of fame, or even the love of politics-as-a-game, ranks ahead of their desire to fulfil a public duty. Yet, when asked what he found most disagreeable, a Conservative MP replies unhesitatingly: 'The money'.[28]

Nobody sympathises with addicts who complain about the cost of their habit. The complaint is common only because most MPs know too little (and love the cabals and intrigue of politics too much) to supplement their incomes in the private sector. Politics has also become a full-time professional career. The rise in Parliamentary salaries, and the growth of ancillary political occupations like research for MPs, lobbying, think-tanks and special adviserships, means that a living can now be made out of politics. John Major spent £3.4 million a year filling Number 10 with political apprentices. Tony Blair is spending £4.9 million.[29] The typical Conservative MP of today is a former special adviser to a minister, a party researcher, or a public relations or political consultant. His typical counterpart on the Labour benches is a former party official or a trade union political officer, a university lecturer, or a local government official or councillor.

Full-time politicians have always existed, but their domination of the modern political scene is a post-war phenomenon. Previously only the rich, government ministers, or those sponsored by trade unions could afford to dedicate their working lives to politics. Now an overwhelming majority of MPs are professional politicians. To some extent, the job is the invention of its beneficiaries. People with time for politics tend to increase the need for political work. They encourage their constituents to approach them and inflate their expectations. The average MP receives at least 300 letters a week, takes up local issues with vigour, and is seen regularly in the place he or she represents. MPs charge newspapers, radio stations and television channels nothing to broadcast their views, and full-time politicians actively seek opportunities to propagate the gospel in books, articles and after-dinner speeches.

In a parliamentary version of Parkinson's Law, the number of paid ministerial jobs has expanded to meet the number of full-time politicians available to fill them. In 1900 Britain ran an empire covering one fifth of the globe with 69 ministers; now, there are 110. This places a formidable quantity of patronage in the gift of the prime minister, and it is the single most important means by which he controls his support in Parliament. The lure of office is used to silence malcontents and to emasculate the House of Commons. It can even be used in Opposition: the discipline of the Parliamentary Labour Party from 1992 to 1997 owed more to a longing for office than a lust for power. Once in government, the ambitions of even the lowliest and most incompetent backbencher cannot be defied with impunity. Parliamentary rent-seekers can be a serious problem if they are disappointed.

The back benches are littered with bitter rejects and grumpy misfits who feel their talents have gone unrecognised. In the last years of the Major administration, Alan Howarth, Emma Nicholson and Peter Thurnham changed parties in pursuit of preferment or to continue ministerial careers. It is not surprising that they felt insulted. The number of jobs available is so large that, once MPs too young, too old or too stupid are excluded, parliamentary competition for ministerial positions is virtually non-existent. Before 1830 there were no junior ministers. By 1914, there were 15. Clement Attlee ran one of the great reforming governments of the century with 32. Now there are 69. Modern governments offer 85 paid posts in the Commons and around 40 unpaid posts as parliamentary private secretaries to ministers. Perhaps 20 peers will be on the public payroll, putting almost 150 jobs in the patronage of the prime minister.

One reason MPs can afford to wait is that they are paid for being in Parliament. MPs were not paid at all until 1911, when £400 a year was given to those not serving in the government. David Lloyd George, who introduced the payment, explained: 'It is just an allowance, to enable men to come here, men who would render incalculable service to the State, and whom it would be an incalculable loss to the State not to have here, but who cannot be here because their means do not allow it. It is purely an allowance to enable us to open the door to great and honourable public service to these men.'[30]

Basic salaries were cut to £360 during the Great Depression of the early 1930s; in real terms, backbench salaries remained below the 1912 level until 1964, when they soared to £3,250. In 1957 Bill Deedes left ministerial office because he could not raise a family on £2,000 a year. Labour MPs of his acquaintance had to maintain two houses on a parliamentary allowance. Most had dinner at Lyons or ABC tea rooms: 'They ordered tea and two pieces of toast which were made into a step,' Deedes recalls. 'By perching the egg on the top step, they could enjoy two slices of toast impregnated with egg. For this they paid a few pence.'[31] Ministers were required to forgo their Parliamentary salary until 1946, when any minister earning less than £5,000 a year was allowed an extra £500 to cover constituency duties. From July 1996, ministers were entitled to take the full parliamentary salary, and this marked the final capture of the political process by full-time politicians.

The present salary of an MP is scarcely lavish, but it is supplemented by a generous range of expense allowances and other benefits. An annual allowance for office expenses was introduced in 1953. Free travel between Westminster and the constituency dates back to 1924, but secretarial allowances and free telephone calls had to wait until 1969, and London weightings and subsidies for overnight stays and second homes until 1972. The first pension scheme was introduced in 1965, and redundancy payments for MPs who lost their seats at a general election (equivalent to three months' salary) were added at the same time. They have risen since, and can be worth over £60,000 to a departing MP.[32] By 1983, when it was decided to increase annually the pay of MPs, in line with the Senior Principal scale of the Civil Service, all the main elements of the modern parliamentary pay package were in place.

It is never easy for MPs and ministers to increase their salaries. MPs usually reserve voting on any increase for the immediate aftermath of a general election, in the hope that it will be forgotten by the time they have to face the voters again. Shortly before the last general election, New Labour promised that ministers would not claim the pay rises agreed under the

TABLE 17.4
Total Pay Package for MPs, 1998

	£ Sterling
Salary	45,066
Allowances	
Office costs	49,232
Additional costs (Bed and Board) allowance for non-London MPs	12,717
Pension provision for staff	Up to 4,923
Motoring allowances (first 20,000 miles)	10,020
Motoring allowances (after 20,000 miles)	1,155
Free first-class rail travel on parliamentary business	Open-Ended
Free first-class rail travel for staff and family	Variable
Free stationery, post and inland telephone calls	c.2,000
Subsidised food and drink	c.2,000
Free parking at Westminster	c.5,000
One free journey to Brussels, Luxembourg or Strasbourg	c.700

Source: Fees Office, House of Commons; House of Commons Public Information Fact Sheet No. 17, May 1998; Review Body on Senior Salaries; author's estimates.[33]

Conservatives. In office, Blair ostentatiously declared that he would not accept his own increase. In 1995, he had declined an increase in his salary as leader of the Opposition, but in those days most of his front bench colleagues were not paid anything extra. In government, the same high-mindedness embarrassed Cabinet colleagues who needed the money more than he did. A madcap compromise, advanced by deputy prime minister Prescott, suggested that ministers accept the increases but give them to charity. Eventually, they decided not to take the money. This pleased backbench colleagues, several of whom are now reduced to stretching their allowances by padding out expenses claims and employing their wives or girlfriends as secretaries. The annual official income of an average MP will almost always exceed £130,000. But it is not enough.

Throughout the 1990s, Conservative politicians were dogged by allegations of financial impropriety, or what the tabloids dubbed 'sleaze'. In some ways, sleaze is a new word for an old habit. Businessmen first began to swarm around politicians in the eighteenth century, when rising public expenditure on wars against the French created opportunities for politicians to deliver public sector contracts in exchange for private sector emoluments. In an age when the government controls over two fifths of the national income, a politician can still be of use to a businessman in search of public sector contracts, investment allowances, export subsidies or a lighter touch on the legislative or regulatory tiller. Superannuated ones with Cabinet experience have proved especially valuable to private sector rent-seekers.

TABLE 17.5
Peers' Allowances, 1998

Daily subsistence allowance	£35.50
Nightly subsistence allowance	£80.50
Daily office and secretarial allowance	£34.50
Travel allowance per mile (first 20,000 miles)*	50.1p
Travel allowance per mile (after first 20,000 miles)*	23.1p

Source: Accountants' Department, House of Lords; Review Body on Senior Salaries.

* Payable whether by car, aeroplane or rail. Peers can also claim travel for their spouse twice a year.

A former Cabinet minister has time and contacts in Parliament and Whitehall, and a string of ex-ministers took jobs with companies they helped to privatise. The banks who underwrite privatisations and export contracts, finance major investment projects, and buy and sell cash and securities in overseas markets, paid handsomely for ex-ministers who knew those in government who could help them win business and licences. 'A big institution with international ambitions is involved in world politics and therefore it needs people who can tap into that,' explained Douglas Hurd, who joined the National Westminster Bank after leaving the Foreign Office in September 1995. 'They are part of its equipment. That is the way of the world.'[34] His earnings were reputed to exceed £200,000 in the first year.

Rewards of this magnitude are open only to the most successful politicians at the end of their careers. Ordinary backbenchers have to make do with more modest sums. Some are prepared, as the *Sunday Times* found out, to ask ministers questions in return for sums as paltry as £1,000. The ensuing row over 'cash for questions' forced John Major to invite Lord Nolan to chair a committee of inquiry into 'standards in public life'. It investigated MPs, jobs for ex-ministers, appointments to quangos and local government. Its successor, chaired by Patrick (later Lord) Neill, has extended its remit to party funding. Only the most priggish MPs were able to work up enthusiasm for the chief consequence of these ethical investigations: greater disclosure of their sources of income. The House of Commons committee charged with monitoring the work of the Nolan commission rejected the recommendation that MPs disclose their outside interests and earnings in bands of £5,000. The prime minister agreed with them. But the recommendations of the Nolan committee, published in May 1995, had eventually to be accepted by the government.

They included the establishment of an independent parliamentary commissioner for standards, reporting to a Commons committee; a ban on MPs taking paid work from parliamentary lobbyists; a requirement that MPs declare all extra-Parliamentary earnings; a two-year time limit on ministers taking jobs at companies where they had had official dealings; better scrutiny of appointments to quangos; and tutorials in ethics for new MPs. Sir Gordon Downey became the first parliamentary commissioner for standards: the first permanent guardian of parliamentary morals. In May 1996, the first of the new registers of MPs' interests was published. It was not illuminating; most MPs declared only those earnings they considered material to their work in Parliament. This had the ironic effect of promoting the former deputy leader of the Labour Party, Roy Hattersley, to the top of the extra-parliamentary earnings league in both 1996 and 1997.

It was ironic because the conduct of Conservative MPs was one of the main reasons for the scale of the Labour victory in May 1997. New Labour helped to secure the election of one of its friends in the media as the anti-sleaze candidate in the constituency of Neil Hamilton, a former minister at the heart of the cash-for-questions scandal, and chief subject of a disapproving report by Downey. Sleaze finally nailed the Conservatives as arrogant and corrupt, which is why Blair warned his MPs that they were not elected to enjoy the 'trappings of office'.

The gap between rhetoric and reality was soon exposed. Within weeks of the election, Lord Simon, a former chairman of BP, whom the prime minister had parachuted into government as minister for competitiveness in Europe, was forced to sell £2 million worth of shares he held offshore. A cheque for £1 million from the motor racing entrepreneur, Bernie Ecclestone, had to be returned by the Labour Party after it appeared to influence a decision on tobacco advertising. In December 1997 a plan to truncate middle-class tax relief was undone by its architect, paymaster-general Geoffrey Robinson, another close associate of the prime minister. It also emerged that the Robinson family fortune was protected from the Inland Revenue by complex off-shore arrangements. In December 1998 he was forced to resign, along with Peter Mandelson, the secretary of state for Trade and Industry, to whom he had advanced a large loan.

There was even a reprise of the 'cash-for-questions' scandal when one of the prime minister's staff told a journalist claiming to represent an American company that he could provide access to ministers. For many people, the sight of ministers and MPs prepared to corrupt their calling for a few thousand

pounds is evidence enough that Parliamentarians are underpaid. By the standards of comparable jobs elsewhere in the public sector – police superinten-
dents or medical consultants – £45,000 a year and a generous swathe of
allowances is a good living. The salary alone is the highest, in real terms, that
MPs have ever received. The allowances dwarf anything their predecessors
enjoyed. But ministerial salaries have fallen. The £17,190 the Duke of Wellington received as prime minister in 1830 is the equivalent of nearly £700,000
today.[35] The official prime ministerial salary was set at £5,000 for the next
100 years. It was doubled in 1937, the year Stanley Baldwin left office. He
was rich, but so was his successor, Neville Chamberlain, who took £10,000.
This was the modern equivalent of £300,000. Today, the prime minister takes
£60,167, and Cabinet ministers £45,201. In other words, the prime minister
has taken a pay cut of 80 per cent since the 1930s and Cabinet ministers of
70 per cent. When the review body on senior salaries compared ministerial
salaries with the private sector in 1996, they concluded that the prime minister
should be on £450,000, Cabinet ministers up to £485,000, ministers of state
up to £155,000, and even under secretaries of state on £96,000.[36]

But comparisons with the private sector are scarcely the right measure of
the rate for the job. Hundreds of hopeful applicants queue for every winnable
parliamentary seat, and no MP has not dreamt once of becoming prime
minister. If the market was the judge of parliamentary salaries, MPs and
ministers would not be paid for the privilege but pay for it. The constant
griping by MPs about their hard work and low salaries rests not on arguments
of history, justice or even of comparability. It merely reflects the kind of
people they are, and the type of job they have created for themselves. They
are addicts, not employees; they cannot quit the job for a better-paid one.
Most know nothing but politics anyway, and the demand for politicians in
other walks of life is limited. Even the handful of MPs who have private
businesses, or genuine professions, are too absorbed in parliamentary duties
to devote much time to them.

The work of anti-sleaze committees has made it harder for MPs to supplement their salaries with a clutch of non-executive directorships or political
consultancies. With the unintended blessing of Lords Nolan and Neill, professional lobbyists have taken over much of their work in securing access to
ministers. By comparison with past eras, few MPs have private means or
patrons; most ministers, let alone backbenchers, worry about money. Yet, as
politics becomes the preserve of fanatics, the financial pressures are intensifying. One authority reckons that in 1994 Conservative MPs were forced to
contribute around £250,000 to their local parties to keep their memberless
constituency associations afloat.[37] The same is true of many Labour MPs.
Unless the recommendation by the Neill committee for greater openness in

TABLE 17.6
Ministerial Salaries, 1998

	Entitlement	Salary Taken	MP's	Total Salary Drawn
Lord chancellor	148,850	148,850	–	148,850
Attorney general	65,509	65,509	45,066	110,575
Speaker of the House of Commons	61,650	61,650	45,066	106,716
Prime minister	102,750	60,167	45,066	105,233
Leader of the Opposition	56,513	56,513	45,066	101,579
Cabinet minister	61,650	45,201	45,066	90,267
Government chief whip	37,620	37,620	45,066	82,686
Lord advocate	80,219	80,219	–	80,219
Solicitor general	80,219	80,219	–	80,219
Minister of State	31,981	31,891	45,066	77,047
Government deputy chief whip	31,981	31,981	45,066	77,047
Opposition chief whip	31,981	31,981	45,066	77,047
Chairman of Ways & Means	31,981	31,981	45,066	77,047
Deputy chairman of Ways & Means	28,107	28,107	45,066	73,173
Under secretary	24,273	24,273	45,066	69,339
Solicitor general for Scotland	68,648	68,648	–	68,648
Assistant Opposition whip	20,580	20,580	45,066	65,646
Government whip/assistant whip	20,580	20,580	45,066	65,646
Cabinet minister in the Lords	80,107	60,495	–	60,495
Chairman of Committees in the Lords	53,264	53,264	–	53,264
Government chief whip in the Lords	53,264	53,264	–	53,264
Minister of State in the Lords	53,264	53,264	–	53,264
Deputy chairman of Committees in the Lords	49,052	49,052	–	49,052
Government deputy chief whip in the Lords	44,832	44,832	–	44,832
Leader of the Opposition in the Lords	44,832	44,832	–	44,832
Under secretary in the Lords	44,832	44,832	–	44,832
Government whip in the Lords	40,547	40,547	–	40,457
Opposition chief whip in the Lords	40,547	40,547	–	40,547

Source: House of Commons Public Information Fact Sheet No. 31, June 1998.

party funding creates mass-membership political parties (which seems unlikely) MPs will continue to need all the money they can get.[38]

This is why they are reluctant to resign even the lowliest of government posts, let alone a seat at the Cabinet table. 'If you talk', Robin Cook told his first wife after announcing that their marriage was over, 'I'll lose my job and go bankrupt and you'll lose the house.' Whether or not ministerial and parliamentary salaries rise, or the prime minister overcomes his reluctance to introduce the public funding of political parties, taxpayers and voters will pay a high price for the low principles of the *Sunday Times* and the high principles of Lords Nolan and Neill. MPs are already pressing for salaries to be given to the chairmen of major select committees, and to Opposition front-bench spokesmen. They will get them eventually, if only because it is up to MPs to decide what they pay themselves.

Public funding of political parties will probably follow, but it is difficult to believe the country will get better government as a result. When he became prime minister in 1924, Ramsay Macdonald accepted £40,000 in cash and dividend-yielding securities and a Daimler from his friend Alexander Grant, more or less openly, 'so that I may not require, whilst absorbed in public duties, to worry about income'.[39] Of all prime ministers, it can least be said of Macdonald that he sacrificed principle for personal or party advantage.

Judges

What made the works of Lords Nolan and Neill doubly unpalatable to MPs was the fact that both were lawyers. 'The House of Commons', thought Hazlitt, 'doesn't like lawyers.' Two centuries on, relations between judges and politicians are more hostile than ever. Politicians argue that the judiciary is usurping the elected representatives of the people with its official inquiries, judicial reviews and growing willingness to intervene in the public debate in speeches, articles and interviews. (The first news conference ever called by a lord chief justice took place in 1992.) For their part, judges claim that overpowering government is threatening the independence of the judiciary and the system of justice. In opposing ministerial demands for longer sentences and cuts in the legal aid budget, and in seizing opportunities to second-guess executive decisions and extend the reach of judge-made law, the judiciary has portrayed itself as the fearless defender of the man in the street.

The truth is more prosaic. Most judges are liberal progressives, reactionary only in defence of their status and standard of living. They persuaded the Conservative government that the backlog of court cases was due to the lack of judges, rather than the inefficiency of the court system. New Labour was persuaded to incorporate the European Convention on Human Rights into English law because it could reverse the loss of judicial power to administrative decision-makers. Judges have resisted cuts in legal aid because they threaten the viability of their profession. They have chaired official inquiries, and expanded the number of applications for judicial review, because both are lucrative sources of work. 'Judicial review', says Michael Beloff QC, 'has become a paying proposition for the profession.'[40]

Judges have even shed their traditional embarrassment about asking for a pay rise. For 200 years, their remuneration could be changed only by the consent of both Houses, and was designed to safeguard the political independence of the judiciary. However, it had the pleasing effect of ensuring that judges obtained regular pay rises without the need to argue their case. Unlike MPs, they saw off a government attempt to cut all official salaries by one fifth in the early 1930s, and undercover bullying persuaded even the Labour government of the 1970s (which contained several ministers who regarded the Bench as the seat of reaction) to heed Lord Denning when he complained that only a sizeable increase in pay would enable them to 'provide properly for the education of their children, their holidays and the like.'[41]

In the Top Salaries Review Board (TSRB), which has set judges' pay since 1973, the judiciary has found a reliable ally. 'Although the government could in theory refuse to implement what it considered excessive awards in full, it was always an awkward business,' recalled Nigel Lawson of his time as chancellor. 'Doubly so in the case of the Top Salaries Review Board, whose periodic fits of extreme munificence created a situation in which the awkwardness of rejecting an award was exceeded only by the acute political embarrassment of endorsing it.'[42] In 1992, the government plucked up the courage to reject the TSRB recommendation. At the nadir of a prolonged recession which had cost many people their homes and jobs, pay rises for judges *averaging* 21 per cent were beyond public and party endurance. Judges were asked to make do with 9.8 per cent over three years. What followed was a masterly display of judicial truculence.

Until 1993 no barrister had ever refused an invitation to become a judge, despite the fact that elevation to the bench has always led to a drastic reduction in earnings.[43] But in that year, six candidates refused to let their names go forward. Two more followed suit in 1994. The newspapers filled with articles and speeches by eminent barristers and judges recommending that judicial salaries be removed from the political arena before the calibre of the Bench deteriorated so badly that the courts were choked with re-runs of the Birmingham Six. The judges-in-waiting had, in a campaign orchestrated by those who had ascended before them, gone on strike.

In 1994 the government agreed to implement over five years the 1992 pay rises recommendation by the TSRB, as well as the regular upratings judges would have received. The effect was to guarantee the lord chief justice another £12,780 by 1999, on top of his usual annual increase, the law lords another £11,481; and the lords justices of appeal another £11,007.[44] By refusing a small number of judicial appointments, the Bar had persuaded the government that it was facing a massive recruitment problem. Yet many barristers continue to regard elevation to the Bench as the natural culmination of a career at the Bar. A moderately successful provincial barrister may indeed improve his earnings by becoming a district judge or magistrate. Self-employed barristers provide their own pensions. If they quit the Bar at fifty and serve twenty years on the Bench, they retire on a full and generous public sector pension.

This is why judges were outraged when the Conservative government altered in an unfavourable direction the terms on which pensions were granted. The staging of the 1992 pay increases meant some judges retired on less than the maximum final salary. In 1993, the government added further insult by raising the period of service for a full pension from fifteen to twenty years and lowered the retirement age from seventy-five to seventy. Economy was not the only objective: judges were staying on too long. Lord Widgery, a former lord chief justice, had carried on judging after he developed a degenerative nervous disease which made his voice inaudible and made him fall asleep in court. The recorder of London continued to adjudicate despite an advanced senility which killed him within a year of retirement.[45] The tightening of the retirement provisions was denounced nonetheless by one former law lord as an attack on the rule of law.

But the ability of the legal mind to equate its own comfort with the public

TABLE 17.7
Judicial Salaries, 1998

	Number in Post	Salary £
Lord chief justice	1	143,480
Lords of appeal in ordinary	12	134,192
Master of the rolls	1	134,192
Lord chief justice of Northern Ireland	1	134,192
Lord president of the Court of Session	1	134,192
Group 3 (including lords justices of Appeal)	47	127,553
Group 4 (including high court judges)	121	113,770
Group 5 (including recorders and senior circuit judges)	55	92,960
Group 6 (including circuit judges)	696	81,886–85,099
Group 7 (district judges in London)	226	72,452
Group 8 (district judges outside London)	456	68,452

Source: Review Body on Senior Salaries Report No. 40, Cm 3837, 1998.

interest was never more obvious than in the minor spat between the government and the Bench over the cost of lodgings for judges on circuit. These are typically comfortable houses in the centre of town, with a butler or housekeeper and one or two assistants, and a chauffeur-driven limousine.[46] When the government proposed a cut in the £4 million budget, Lord Ackner, a law lord, told an angry meeting of the Bar Council that 'to treat [judges] like commercial travellers and put them in hotels with doubtful security is not on.'[47] A retired senior judge, interviewed on the *Today* programme, explained that 'you can't be expected to make your own bed. You need a butler if you have a fairly substantial number of people in the house . . . You have on your mind, say, a difficult murder . . . like the murder of the little boy from Liverpool which lasted about six or seven weeks in Preston, and you are working in a bed and breakfast in Fleetwood. Do you think you would be able to do the job? Of course you couldn't . . . You couldn't do your job and work in a hotel.'[48]

The life of a judge is agreeable, and the Lord Chancellor's Department has never struggled to recruit them. Only at the lowest levels do judicial posts have to be advertised. Most judges are chosen from a tiny pool of talent by a process which David Pannick QC has likened to a cross between a Conservative Party 'Magic Circle' and a Papal Conclave.[49] Within months of taking office, New Labour was persuaded to abandon a long-standing plan to create an independent judicial appointments commission.[50] Yet the blackballing of able candidates, in a profession shot through with dormitory-style bitchiness and Freemasonry, is common. A catty note filed by a colleague with the lord chancellor is a serious impediment to preferment. It is not surprising that the people chosen by the system do not improve the public appreciation of the judiciary. Most are white, male and public school educated; there are no female law lords; there is one female judge in the appeal court; and seven women among ninety-six High Court judges.

The unrepresentative nature of the Bench helps to explin why four out of five people told the British Crime Survey in 1997 that judges were out of touch with the public. But once seated on the Bench, a judge is difficult to dislodge. No matter how stupid, lazy, rude, incompetent, insensitive or even ill they may be, a senior judge cannot be sacked without the assent of both Houses of Parliament. Judges of all grades have survived convictions for drink-driving. One caught smuggling whisky and cigarettes in his yacht was asked to step down, but kept his pension. Judge Pickles humiliated the judicial establishment for five years, lord chancellor Hailsham not daring to discipline him for fear that his decision might be subject to review. In 1998 Mr Justice Harman made history by becoming the first High Court judge to resign. By then, he had survived humiliation in the tabloids for professing ignorance of Gazza and Oasis, and kicking a taxi driver he mistook for a press photographer. He was undone by forcing the appeal court to order a retrial of a case in which he took twenty months to deliver a verdict, having lost documents and forgotten the evidence.

Provided he abjures egregious behaviour of this kind, a judge is master of his destiny. He has social status, comfortable travel and accommodation, good pay and a generous pension, and long holidays. High Court judges sit for only thirty-eight weeks a year. They rejected a suggestion by the lord chief justice that they sit for an extra ten days on the grounds that the long holidays were 'one of the few remaining attractions of the job'.[51] The judges were too modest. Unlike politicians, they do not have to defend their decisions in public, or convince the taxpayers they are worth their six-figure salaries. But they are rightly concerned about their public image. Lord Kilmuir thought silence essential to the judicial reputation for wisdom. The irreverent treatment of the Bench by the tabloids has long since robbed that silence of its dignity. Modern judges court the media, rather than endure it.

Armed Forces

Trial by media is not an ordeal the Top Brass has ever had to endure. Military men attract the respect of the public for their uncomplaining discretion and the unique hazards of the job. They play no part in politics, and few people know what they do between encounters in the Falklands and the Gulf, and civil wars in the Balkans. Even fewer could name the chief of the Defence Staff. Since the Second World War, this anonymity has guaranteed the armed services a slice of public money which only health, education and social security can rival. A low profile and a large budget have inhibited change: in professional terms, the armed forces end the twentieth century as they began it. The officers are still the public school-educated sons of the middle and upper-middle classes, and the rank and file the largely ill-educated sons of the working class.

It was the secretary for war in the first Gladstone administration, Edward Cardwell, who invented the professional army officer. He had already abolished flogging, when the German success in the Franco–Prussian War of 1870 persuaded Gladstone to increase the military budget. This gave Cardwell his opportunity for further reform. The payment of bounties to recruits was outlawed.[52] Units scattered across the Empire were brought home, to enabling the army to train on the modern scale. The powers of the commander-in-chief were increased, and short-service commissions, designed to increase the army reserve, were introduced in place of twenty-one-year contracts. A regimental system, based on recruitment in particular localities, was introduced.[53] The purchase of commissions was replaced by competitive examination.

In the Royal Navy, thoroughgoing reform had to await the appointment of 'Jacky' Fisher as First Sea Lord in 1904. He had risen through the ranks, and thought 'every fit boy [must] have his chance . . . irrespective of the depth of his parents' purse.'[54] He took them at age twelve by interview and examination rather than by nomination. By the time the First World War broke out, nomination had disappeared completely. The army did not change as rapidly, though the aristocratic element in the officer corps gave way to middle-class pupils of public schools. In 1939, four out of five army officers were public school-educated. Only the Royal Air Force, which did not establish an existence independent of the army until 1918, was untroubled by social conservatism.

TABLE 17.8
Pay of Officers and Men in the Armed Forces, 1998*

	£
Chief of the Defence Staff	130,000
Admiral/General/Air Chief Marshal	104,015–107,305
Vice Admiral/Lieutenant General/Air Marshal	77,065–79,500
Rear Admiral/Major General/Air Vice Marshal	68,115–69,605
Brigadier/Commodore in Royal Navy/Air Commodore	64,189
Colonel/Captain in Royal Navy/Group Captain	52,297
Lieutenant Colonel/Commander in Royal Navy/Wing Commander	44,997
Major/Lieutenant Commander in Royal Navy/Squadron Leader	31,894
Captain/Lieutenant in Royal Navy/Flight Lieutenant	25,152
Lieutenant/Flight Officer	19,728
Warrant Officer	25,539–29,437
Second Lieutenant/Pilot Officer	14,921
Scale A Marine/Private/Aircraftsman	10,187–10,486
Scale B Marine/Lance-Corporal/Senior Aircraftsman	12,753–13,998
Sergeant	20,641–22,652
Corporal	18,808–20,834

Source: Review Body on Senior Salaries Report No. 40, Cm 3837, 1998; Ministry of Defence; Public Sector Yearbook, 1997–98; Ministry of Defence.

* These were the rates in force from April to December 1998. They increased by 1.7 per cent in December 1998.

Twentieth century technology has accelerated the professionalisation of the other services. Modern warfare needs electronic engineers, not gallant cavalry officers. Its weapons are expensive to make, and their operators costly to train, so ability has overcome class. Collaboration among the three services is now crucial to military effectiveness, but some snobberies are ineradicable. It was the view of Earl Grey of Fallodon that 'the British Army should be a projectile to be fired by the British Navy', and the Senior Service has never accepted its diminished status. The Royal Air Force has always relied on upstarts rather than gentlemen, and suffers from a permanent suspicion that air power promises more than it delivers. In the army, most of those commissioned into the Household Division are still put forward at birth by their fathers. They are also expected, to a declining extent, to subsidise their lifestyle with private means.

But most members of the armed forces enjoy a degree of exemption from the economics of civilian life. Basic pay is supplemented by allowances to compensate for the less agreeable aspects of military life: unrelenting discipline, constant readiness, fearsome responsibility, and the periodic risk of being killed or maimed. Unpleasant duties – serving in Northern Ireland or aboard a submarine, for example – attract special allowances, and demanding skills command a premium. These allowances are balanced against the pleasant features of military life: frequent travel, generous leave, plenty of sport, useful training, guaranteed employment, cheap food, housing and furniture, and exemption from council taxes. The pension is handsome. An officer can expect to retire on an index-linked pension of roughly one third of earnings after sixteen years and half of earnings after thirty-four years. He makes no contributions to the scheme.

Military lives are harder than they were; the ending of the Cold War has delivered them into the hands of economy-minded politicians, and the number of military personnel is down by two fifths since 1980. Career opportunities and promotion prospects have shrunk. Rates of retention and recruitment are falling. A report recently recommended cutting the range of commissioned ranks in the army from twelve to eight, the goal being to make the job, not the rank, the primary determinant of pay. The army officer of the twenty-first century will fulfil more roles for more pay at the same rank. The jargon of corporate Britain, with its flat hierarchies and empowered employees, is finally washing over Tommy Atkins.

The Doctors

Soldiers are powerless to resist reform. They cannot strike, or run a poster campaign, or join a trade union. But doctors can. In recent years the British Medical Association (BMA) has emerged as one of the most militant and reactionary trade unions in Britain, its shop-steward for most of that time a gloomy Scot called Sandy Macara, the Jimmy Knapp of the professional classes. When the Conservatives introduced plans for the internal market in hospitals and fund-holding for general practitioners (GPs) in 1989, the BMA greeted them with a barrage of sanctimonious propaganda which cost its members £3 million. When the New Labour government partially reversed these reforms and introduced some new ideas in 1998, GPs complained about the loss of independence and hospital clinicians griped that only more money could save the National Health Service (NHS).

Doctors have never cared for change. 'The plain fact for the BMA,' one historian of the Welfare State has pointed out, 'was and is that it is always easier to make an impassioned speech against any proposal than a reasoned, and possibly complex one, for it.'[55] They treated the architects of the NHS, William Beveridge and Aneurin Bevan, in exactly the same way as they have treated Kenneth Clarke and Frank Dobson. In July 1945, delegates to the BMA conference cheered news of Beveridge's defeat at Berwick-upon-Tweed. Bevan was likened by one doctor to the recently deceased Führer; another agreed that he was planning a 'Hitlerite regime' for medicine. The minister, said a third, was 'rude, blustering and threatening'. When it came to a vote on whether or not to join the NHS, the members of the BMA voted against by a majority of nine to one.

To proclaim the irony of a profession which is prepared, in the space of forty years, to die in the last ditch both for and against the NHS is delicious, but unfair. Every profession is valiant in the defence of interest, not principle. It is also misleading. Far from opposing the nationalisation of medicine on principle in 1948, doctors have favoured it throughout the twentieth century – provided the price was right. Doctors enthused about the National Insurance Act of 1911, which made it compulsory for employers and taxpayers to contribute to the costs of medical treatment. Until then, those who could afford it paid the doctor or subscribed to a medical insurance scheme. This made it awkward for doctors to raise their fees. Taxpayers, as doctors well knew, are a readier source of cash.

By transferring the cost of treatment from patients (or their insurers) to taxpayers, the Act of 1911 doubled the income of doctors. 'We now resume our place as medical practitioners pure and simple, ready as sellers to give our services to the buyer, who is now not the poverty-stricken wage earner, but the solvent State Insurance Company,' one doctor confessed.[56] Likewise, the opposition of the BMA to the establishment of the NHS was not a matter of political or professional principle, but of money and power. In July 1942 BMA members voted in favour of a national health system. They relished the prospect of salaries instead of fees, but they wanted to keep their private patients as well.

Aneurin Bevan was forced to entreat. 'I stuffed their mouths with gold,' he later said. Hospital consultants were given salaries and allowed to keep their private patients. They could divide their time between the public and the private sectors as they saw fit, and keep their pay beds in the nationalised hospitals. Ordinary doctors who did minor surgery in cottage hospitals were put out of business. Lord Moran, personal physician to Winston Churchill and then president of the Royal College of Physicians, even talked Bevan into allowing consultants to give 'merit awards' to each other. (These payments, added annually to salaries, are still awarded today.) GPs, after their brief, hysterical campaign against nationalisation, did almost as well: salaries, capitation fees for each patient, and £66 million of compensation for loss of the right to sell their practices.

Almost at once, doctors began to exploit their position within the NHS. The number of doctors expanded rapidly.[57] GPs extracted their first big pay rise in 1952. In the 1960s, by threatening to resign from the NHS *en masse*, they secured a one third pay rise and a menu of loans, subsidies, allowances, and additional payments. In the 1970s, when Barbara Castle tried to abolish pay beds in NHS hospitals, consultants worked to rule. Pay beds were not abolished, but the dispute sparked a boom in private hospitals, where consultants could ply their trade in NHS time without the threat of NUPE nurses refusing to look after their patients.

But militancy exacted a price in public esteem: twenty years ago the BMA was known as 'the British Money Association'. In the 1980s, facing a government which wanted to economise rather than nationalise, it repositioned itself as a pressure group for the NHS rather than a trade union for doctors. Admittedly, this was due in part to a younger and more collectivist leadership.[58] But the change of stance owed more to *realpolitik*. The financial settlement extracted from the Labour government in the 1960s was generous, but made GPs utterly dependent on the taxpayer. If a doctor wants more money, it is easier to demand it under the guise of saving the NHS than of lining his own pocket. 'Patients will suffer,' as the joke goes, 'unless doctors get more.'

Most of the battles the BMA has fought since the 1970s were rooted in professional self-interest. They rejected the introduction of charges, fearful that asking patients for money would undermine their benign social image. Changes to the rules on deputising services used by GPs for night and weekend cover were resisted: they would have increased the GP's workload. Rules to prevent them prescribing expensive branded drugs were opposed, because they complicated relationships with patients. Changes to contracts with local health authorities, which had for years allowed doctors to exceed their budgets with impunity, were attacked on the most obvious of grounds.

In each and every case, the BMA portrayed these exercises in good housekeeping as attacks on the NHS. Norman Fowler described the BMA campaign against the list of branded drugs as 'as fierce and nasty a little campaign as I can remember'.[59] It was experience, not foresight, which led Kenneth Clarke to promise the Cabinet 'one hell of a campaign' by the BMA when he introduced his proposals for reform of the NHS in January 1989.[60] The BMA had set up a fighting fund to resist them before they were even published, to pay for advertising warning the public that the White Paper marked the beginning of the end of the NHS.

The true worries of doctors were far removed from saving the NHS. GPs were convinced that fund-holding would increase their workload, force them to compete for patients, and reduce their income by setting unrealistic targets for screening procedures. (Ironically, a major complaint of GPs in the 1960s was that they had no financial incentives to invest in equipment or preventative medicine.) Hospital consultants had different worries. They feared that the creation of self-governing NHS Trusts would tighten managerial and financial control of their activities, forcing them to spend more time on NHS work and less on private practice, or even to pay for the use of NHS equipment to diagnose and treat their private patients. Merit awards were thought to be at risk, and there were fears that their work would be audited for the first time.[61]

The fears of GPs were unjustified. Their hostility abated, as they discovered fund-holding made them better off. Between 1989 and 1996, the average remuneration of GPs increased by a half. New Labour, elected on a pledge to abolish fund-holding, was forced by its popularity among GPs to create fund-holding collectives rather than get rid of the practice altogether. Hospital doctors had a less happy experience. A new grade of semi-consultant – the specialist registrar – has intensified competition for money, work and jobs. Consultants are having to work harder, take training and refresher courses, and withdraw their charity from lazy or incompetent colleagues. Doctors know which of their peers is a danger to his patients, but professional *omerta* ensured they were not exposed. In 1995 the government secured an agreement with the BMA to make the monitoring of colleagues a contractual duty. The New Labour government has reinforced this discipline by forcing doctors to share the outcome of their work with colleagues, and death and complication rates at particular hospitals will be published.

Greater openness is opposed by consultants, who question its practicability and fairness. Their graver concern is the damage it will inflict on their fading reputation for competence. Public faith in the interchangeability of doctors was shattered in 1998, when the General Medical Council concluded that two heart surgeons had operated on children at the Bristol Royal Infirmary 'without regard to their safety'. Twenty-nine babies died between 1988 and

1995. Bereaved parents were amazed to learn that one of the surgeons had received an A merit award, one of the most valuable of the 'distinction awards' Moran agreed with Bevan in the 1940s. No doctor shared their surprise: clinicians know that merit awards are anything but meritorious. Rather, they are awarded by colleagues to colleagues in the same opaque way that barristers make other barristers QCs and judges.[62]

Losses of money and discretion have coincided with a loss of power. They can no longer run their departments without regard to the hospital as a whole. The Conservative reforms introduced a new class of NHS manager, charged with managing hospitals efficiently, but their reputation for lavish salaries and company cars has not endeared them to hospital clinicians. (In 1996 consultants at a Swansea hospital worked-to-rule until the chairman and the chief executive were dismissed.)[63] By private sector standards, however, hospital executives are not well paid. The highest-paid chief executive (probably at Guy's and St Thomas's Hospital) earned just over £122,000 in 1998.[64] But this is enough to upset hospital consultants, whose salary scale (though not their total earnings) peaks at less than £60,000.

By comparison with other professions, hospital doctors are overworked and underpaid. In 1993, junior doctors won the right to a maximum working week of 72 hours if on call, 64 hours on partial shift and 56 hours in a full shift. Even the most corpulent Fat Cat would not claim to work that hard, let alone take life-and-death decisions at the same time.[65] Hospital consultants claim long hours are essential to effective training (the longer a doctor is at work, the more conditions he will see) but it also frees them to spend more time with private patients. This is where they can make money. The world-famous heart surgeon, Magdi Yacoub, probably earns well over £500,000 a year, but few can aspire to one fifth as much. An official survey reckoned that only 1,500 doctors – out of a profession which numbers over 20,000 –

TABLE 17.9

Distinction Awards* 1998

Award	Number	Scale of Pay	Value £
A Plus	277	95 per cent	53,645–56,090
A	955	70 per cent	39,530–41,330
B	2,120	40 per cent	22,590–23,615

Source: Review Body on Doctors' and Dentists' Remuneration, 27th Report, Cm 3835, 1998.

* Formerly known as Merit Awards.

TABLE 17.10
Remuneration of NHS Trust Executives, 1998*

Position	Minimum	Median	Maximum
Chief executive	45,538	70,828	122,461
Board director	30,000	52,713	131,544
2nd Level non-board director	22,589	44,100	94,000
3rd Level non-board director	15,634	31,375	80,595
Director of clinical services (medical)	43,781	71,695	105,593
Director of clinical services (non-medical)	35,865	46,900	62,824
Director of contracting	30,900	49,516	69,745
Director of estates	34,593	52,630	70,500
Director of finance	37,386	54,482	100,426
General manager	36,225	50,994	75,804
Director of human resources	30,000	46,485	79,310
Director of medical policy	30,750	77,776	131,544
Director of nursing	30,522	47,248	76,002
Director of planning	41,003	51,736	75,141
All other executive posts	34,231	42,461	73,950

Source: NHS Salary Club Survey of Chief and Senior Executives, 7th Edition, February 1998, NHSP, Bristol.

* Including basic salary, performance-related pay, geographical and all other allowances.

are making more than £100,000 a year from private practice.[66] Given the weight of their investment in human capital, and the barriers to entry, doctors ought to earn a lot. Little more than a pleasing manner and a degree in English literature are sufficient for an investment banker. Lawyers' and accountants' examinations are trifling by comparison with the demands of the medical examiners. The average age of appointment to a hospital consultant post is thirty-eight.[67] By then, a doctor will have a BSc, an MBBS, Fellowship of a Royal College, and possibly an MD as well. This is the equivalent of taking three post-graduate degrees.

The reason hospital doctors earn such a paltry return on this massive investment of time and effort is that they have a single employer with a near-monopoly of jobs. In the United States, where the medical profession rejected President Truman's plans for British-style national health insurance, American doctors get the double bonus of selling their skills into an insurance-based system where the patient hires the doctor but does not foot the bill. The effect is to drive the cost of health care in the United States to over one tenth of the national income, enabling thousands of consultants to enjoy incomes of more than $500,000 a year. One consequence is that the cost of private health insurance is beyond the reach of millions of people, who have to rely on accident and emergency departments or the restricted benefits of the Medicare programme.

Unlike the American system, the NHS has succeeded in providing a high

TABLE 17.11
Doctors' Pay, 1998

Salary Scale (£)

Doctors Working in Hospitals

Hospital Consultant	*45,740–59,040
Associate Specialist	*27,120–47,175
Staff Grade Practitioner	24,465–40,465
Specialist Registrar	22,510–32,830
Senior Registrar	†25,930–32,830
Registrar	†22,510–27,310
Senior House Officer	†20,135–26,910
House Officer	†16,145–18,225

Doctors in Public Health Medicine and Community Health

Senior Clinical Medical Officer in Community Health	33,380–47,905
Clinical Medical Officer in Community Health	23,395–32,530
Trainee in Public Health Medicine	22,510–32,830

Doctors in General Medical Practice

Intended Net Average Remuneration	‡49,030

Source: Review Body on Doctors' and Dentists' Remuneration, 27th Report, Cm. 3835.

* With discretionary points, a hospital consultant can raise his salary to between £61,410 and £70,850, and an associate specialist to between £48,945 and £54,255.
† Doctors still in training increase their basic pay significantly by working additional duty hours on top of their basic working week. On full shift, each additional hour is reimbursed at the full hourly rate. Each partial shift is reimbursed at 70 per cent of the basic hourly rate, and on-call rotas at 50 per cent of the basic rate.
‡ The actual remuneration received by GPs depends on where they work, how many patients they have and how old they are, because the basic salary is supplemented by a vast range of allowances and fees to compensate them for elderly or deprived patients, vaccinating children, fitting IUDs, conducting cervical smears and so on. Essentially, a senior GP in an inner city practice with a lot of elderly patients will receive more than a young doctor in a leafy suburb with mostly young and healthy patients. The Intended Average Net Remuneration is also influenced by how effective a doctor is at controlling his costs.

standard of medical care for all. It is a success for taxpayers as well as patients. Thanks to the Bevan compromise of 1948, NHS patients obtain the services of the leading consultants for a fraction of their market value, in return for letting them top up their earnings in the private sector. The only losers are doctors. Despite a booming market in private practice (the value of private sector work to doctors was put at £600 million in 1992), its rewards are not spread evenly.[68] The distribution of the spoils is heavily concentrated among a small group of specialists working mainly in London, the west Midlands, the north west and southern Scotland.[69] Few of them spend more time in the private sector than the public.

Most consultants earn between £10,000 and £75,000 from private work.[70] The NHS Trust Federation reckoned in 1995 that the average consultant earned £28,000 a year from private practice. Most doctors either live in the wrong place or have the wrong skills to do private practice (a cardiologist obviously has more opportunity than a pathologist). The Monopolies and Mergers Commission found an élite group of 40–50 consultants was earning an extra £400,000 a year from private patients, and another group of similar size, earning an additional £300,000 a year.

Some doctors refuse private work on ideological grounds. A number of hospital managers discourage it, quoting the rule that full-time consultants should not earn more than one tenth of their total NHS remuneration from private practice. But most hospitals welcome it as a boost to revenues, making equipment and junior doctors available free of charge. Consultants could earn even more from private practice, but they have hampered the growth of the market by adhering rigidly to the BMA fee schedules, rather than competing for patients on price. This exposes them to constant downward pressure on fees from insurance companies, without increasing the volume of work. The BMA has opposed allowing GPs to charge for consultations, and the privatisation of primary health care as well. The main losers are its members.

Dentists

Patients are now tasting the alternative to free health care in the field of dentistry. Unless they are under 18, a student under 19, on income support, pregnant, or nursing a new-born baby, NHS patients are obliged to meet four fifths of the cost of any dental treatment they receive (up to a maximum of £330). Anybody who does not revisit their NHS dentist within fifteen months is dropped from the list, and it can be difficult to get back on. In some parts of the country, dentists are not interested in treating NHS patients at all. A fast growing minority of dental practitioners, particularly in London and the south-east of England, have opted out of the NHS altogether. Rather than charge the bulk of their fees to the patient, remit them to the government, and battle to coax the balance out of a state-funded payments bureaucracy in Eastbourne (the Dental Practice Board), they have concluded it is cheaper and easier to make the patient pay the full amount.

The first dentistry businesses, of which the privately owned Whitecross Group is the largest, are now creating chains of dentistry shops. Boots the Chemist is also entering the market. For the first time since the NHS was established in 1948, local health authorities in some parts of the country are finding it necessary to recruit salaried dentists to maintain an NHS service.

Dental services were never central to the NHS. To a greater extent than hospital consultants, dentists were free to decide how to divide their time between private and NHS patients. In the 1940s, their opposition to the NHS exceeded even that of GPs. Only half of the profession had agreed to treat NHS patients by the time it was inaugurated on 5 July 1948, and a matter of weeks before that the British Dental Association was urging its members to boycott the NHS. Unlike doctors, dentists have never become salaried employees of the state: they are self-employed professionals, who perform dental procedures for NHS patients in exchange for fixed fees agreed with the Department of Health.

Free dental care did not even survive the eclipse of the Attlee government. Charges for dentures were introduced by Hugh Gaitskell in 1950. A flat-rate charge for all dental treatment followed under Churchill in 1952. In 1968, under Wilson, the charge was raised to half the cost. It rose still further under the Heath and Thatcher governments of the 1970s and 1980s, until free dental check-ups were scrapped altogether in 1988. Today, a patient who does not qualify for an exemption has to pay for the consultation as well as the bulk of treatment. Adult patients, as a whole, now meet around two fifths of the cost of NHS dental treatment.[71] For all except pregnant women, free NHS dentistry has effectively ceased to exist.

As a result, they do not often go to the dentist, which matters less than it did. The fluoridation of water, improved diets, and widespread use of the toothbrush have more or less eliminated the need for traditional dentistry. Until the 1970s, the crumbling mandibles of the pre-fluoride generation created plenty of opportunities for dentists to drill and fill, pull teeth and issue dentures. As recently as the 1950s, it was not uncommon for poorer patients to have all their teeth removed rather than endure the expense and pain of repeated visits.

As dental health improved, the government woke up to the risk that paying dentists a fixed fee for each procedure was encouraging them to perform unnecessary work at the public expense. In 1997 a dentist who earned £1 million from unnecessary treatment for hundreds of NHS patients was struck off the register of the General Dental Council.[72] He had stopped practising in 1994, when changes were already in hand. In 1990, health ministers had persuaded dentists to accept a change in their method of remuneration. Fees-per-procedure were retained, but their value was reduced. The savings were diverted into new capitation fees for both adults (known as 'continuing care payments', to encourage dentists to think of themselves as health and prevention experts) and children.

The effect was to replace one set of perverse incentives with another. If fees-per-procedure encouraged dentists to perform unnecessary work, capitation fees discouraged them from performing any at all. The one positive financial incentive was to expand the number of patients on the register. Dentist wrote to anyone who had ever visited their practice and encouraged them to come and register as 'continuing care' patients. An economy measure turned into a bonanza for dentists. In 1991 their income exceeded the government target by an average of £15,000 each. Under the terms of the formula, the government was entitled to ask for the money back. To contain the cost to the taxpayers, and keep fees-per-procedure at levels which would not antagonise the voters, the Department of Health had devised what it called a Target Average Net Income (TANI) for dentists. If dentists undershot the target, the department made up the difference; if they overshot the target, they were supposed to make a refund. In 1992 the government asked for its £15,000 refund. After some robust negotiations, and a threat by the dental profession to withdraw en masse from the NHS, the government was defeated. It agreed to write the money off. Capitation fees were reduced. TANI became Notional TANI.

Only Whitehall could have devised a system of remuneration which subsidised lazy dentists and penalised industrious ones. TANI and its notional successor are, as one of the negotiators pointed out to the Department of Health during the recent dispute, a clear instance of negative performance-related pay. Yet they have proved formidably effective in containing the remuneration of the dental profession. Fixed fees for dental procedures rival branded medicines as the last example of retail price maintenance. Of the £1.25 billion a year the government spends on treating NHS dental patients, £400 million is recouped from patients. Dentists would prefer to sting the taxpayer rather than their NHS patients for more, but only one fifth of their income now derives directly from the Treasury.

Dentists claim that fluoridisation has not solved the dental problem, but increased its costs and complexity. As the life span of the average tooth increases, they say, the need for remedial and cosmetic work has grown. But nobody takes the claim seriously. Nor do they need to. Unlike doctors, a

TABLE 17.12
Dentists' Pay, 1998

	Salary Scale (£)
*Community Health and Salaried Posts Only**	
Consultant in dental public health†	45,740–59,040
Regional dental officer	52,805–56,040
District dental officer	46,940–49,700
Assistant district dental officer	36,250–52,890
Senior dental officer	32,940–47,175
Salaried dental practitioner	22,640–32,940
Dental officer	22,620–32,940
Trainee in dental public health	22,510–32,830
Dentists in General Practice	
Notional Target average net income (Notional TANI)‡	49,030

Source: Review Body on Doctors' and Dentists' Remuneration, 27th Report, Cm. 3835, 1998.

* Dentists working in hospitals are paid on the same scale as hospital doctors. See Table 17.11
† Consultants can raise their earnings to £70,850 through the discretionary points system.
‡ Notional Target Average Net Income is calculated by taking Department of Health estimates of the average gross income of dentists, and subtracting their estimates of expenses, to arrive at what the Department thinks dentists are entitled to earn. It is same as the figure for GPs.

strike or a total retreat by dentists into private practice would probably pass unnoticed by voters in marginal seats. The NHS employs just over 4,000 dental staff directly. Most are consultants and trainee consultants in NHS teaching hospitals. The rest are what used to be known as school dental inspectors, recast as peripatetic 'community' dentists. They are few in number and not much better paid than the teachers they meet on their daily rounds.

Teachers

In the age of global competition, and the third industrial revolution, every-body agrees that teachers were never more important. They are the managers and creators of human capital. Their work is at the heart of the professional ideal, with its belief in education, its worship of knowledge, its respect for experience, and its faith in selection by merit. Teaching is not, as Shaw had it, a job solely for those who cannot. The modern teacher has to teach children not only to read, write and add up but to interpret and analyse, to develop logical arguments as well as opinions, and to memorise and use complex mathematical techniques. Teachers are responsible for the socialisation of immigrants, the integration of the races, and the transmission to children of the moral values their parents left on the barricades.

To do all of these things in a country where growing numbers of children come from broken and violent homes, and where the only form of educational support is the television, makes teaching a demanding job. It requires people of outstanding talent. Unfortunately, it tends not to get them. In the inner cities, where some of the worst schools operate in the most testing social conditions, teachers and taught are now trapped in a 'conspiracy of the least'. A significant minority of teachers has a preference for agitation over cogitation, and the annual marches and conferences of the major teaching trade unions have become one of the primary targets of bourgeois dismay.

Middle-class anxiety about the teaching profession is intensified by the romantic belief that teachers were once well-paid and highly esteemed. In fact, school teachers were never much respected: teaching was always one of the 'lower' professions, not least because virtually anybody could get into it. A Teachers' Registration Council was not seriously discussed until the 1960s. For most children, until at least the Second World War, school was not a steady process of intellectual illumination by a caste of latter-day Platos but an unvarying diet of punishments and humiliations at the hand of misfits and sadists. Memoirs which contain happy memories of schoolmasters, and tales of intellectual fulfilment, are the exception: George Bernard Shaw (educated, admittedly, in Ireland) reckoned his teachers had equipped him for nothing but the life of a tramp.[73]

Teachers are now obsessed with an esteem that never was, and convinced they are paid less than they are worth. The truth is that teachers were never paid more than they are today. Throughout most of the twentieth century, a qualified male teacher was lucky to earn the modern equivalent of £10,000 a year. A qualified female teacher could not manage even that.[74] Fifty or sixty years ago, teachers were earning one tenth as much as solicitors. The incomes of female teachers were closer to those of shop girls and floorwalkers than to lawyers or accountants. Modern school teachers are doing at least as well as civil servants at the comparable level, and with more opportunities to enlarge their incomes by taking on extra responsibilities. (One reason New Labour wants to create a new class of 'Super Teachers' is to arrest the drift of talented teachers into better-paid administrative jobs.) There is no shortage of candidates for teaching posts.[75]

If the teaching profession has a weakness, it is size. It is the largest of the public sector professions. The 700,000-odd people who now teach in schools, colleges and universities are the beneficiaries of a growth industry. With periodic interruptions, public expenditure on schools and universities has grown continually since the first grants in 1833. Education is now the third largest arm of the Welfare State after social security and health, and the number of teachers has expanded commensurately. But size has spawned a fissiparity which only engineers can rival. It has proved impossible to find a commonality of interest between teachers in an education system split between large and small, public and private, primary and secondary, local authority and grant-maintained, and in which the echoes of historic antagonisms between Oxbridge and redbrick, polytechnics and universities, and grammar and secondary modern, can still be felt.

The largest professional body, the National Union of Teachers (NUT), is dominated by junior teachers at state primary schools and comprehensives. But at least five other unions, with ugly abbreviations like NAHT, PAT and NAS/UWT, claim to speak for some rank or political perspective within the profession. The NUT (led by Doug McAvoy, an old-fashioned public sector union leader) and the NAS/UWT (led by the telegenic Nigel de Gruchy) are locked in an unseemly but chronic battle for members. Until two unions merged recently, teachers in higher education were similarly split between the Association of University Teachers and the University and College Lecturers Union. During a protracted dispute over pay and conditions in colleges of further education in the mid-1990s four trade unions (NATFHE, ATL, ACM, and APC) were engaged in negotiations with employers. A second strike in the winter of 1996–7 involved eight unions.

It would be hard to describe this fragmented and squabbling occupation as a profession at all, were its members not so adept at excluding consumers of education from playing any part in their pay and patterns of work. Until the introduction of the national curriculum in 1990, teachers decided what was taught and how to teach it. When the government tried to involve parents in the management of schools in the mid-1970s, the general secretary of the NUT called it a '"busybodies" charter'.[76] In the 1980s its members waged industrial warfare against the National Curriculum. In the 1990s they demanded the abolition of the Office for Standards in Education.[77] Until the introduction of examination league tables, introduced by the Conservatives and refined by New Labour, teachers did not even have to show their worth by results.

Though it was funded by the taxpayer, pay was not discussed publicly. From 1919 to 1987 it was decided privately in the Burnham Committee, a colloquy of local authorities and teaching unions whose division of the spoils the government of the day was obliged to accept. As the Labour Party came gradually to dominate local government in the 1980s, Burnham became 'largely ... a matter of the NUT negotiating with the NUT'.[78] A similar arrangement obtained in the National Joint Council for Lecturers in Further Education, where unions met local authorities to decide what their members should be paid. Only universities escaped: the pay of university lecturers was agreed directly with the government by the vice chancellors, with noises offstage from the Association of University Teachers (AUT).

Even the Thatcher government was unable to break the power of the teaching unions, though it engaged them in a protracted dispute over pay between 1984 and 1987. At the end of it, the Burnham Committee was abolished. It was replaced in 1991 by a new School Teachers' Pay Review Body, akin to those for doctors, dentists and army officers. In theory, the new body would set the pay of teachers in the light of experience, performance and responsibility. This was coupled with a string of other initiatives designed to

TABLE 17.13
Teachers' Pay, 1998

	Salary Range £
Schools	
Headteachers and deputy headteachers	26,337–59,580
Qualified teachers	13,362–35,787
Unqualified teachers	11,235–17,769
Further Education	
Lecturer	12,915–25,014
Senior lecturer	22,593–29,859
Management staff	23,463–55,653
New Universities	
Lecturer	14,148–23,585
Senior lecturer	22,012–29,086
Principal lecturer	27,512–34,593
Researcher	10,218–22,797
Head of department (minimum)	26,304
Old Universities	
Lecturer	16,655–32,457
Senior lecturer	30,496–37,257

Source: School Teachers' Review Body 7th Report, Cm 3836, 1998; National Association of Teachers in Further and Higher Education; Association of University Teachers.

shift power from teachers to parents and from local authorities to central government. They included centrally funded city technology colleges and grant-maintained schools, open enrolment of pupils, the national curriculum, and regular testing and examination league tables.

Older teachers who were resistant to change were encouraged to retire early (inadvertently devastating the teachers' superannuation scheme) and plans were hatched to replace them with distinctly 'unprofessional' anybodies. In grant-maintained schools and city technology colleges, teachers were employed by the governing body rather than the local authority. This model was adopted wholesale for colleges of further education. In 1993 all colleges were removed from local authority control and turned into independent 'corporations', which are expected to agree pay and conditions with their staff. Funding comes from central government, via a new Higher Education Funding Council rather than the local authorities. The universities now derive their funding from the same source, the Universities Funding Council having disappeared when the distinction between polytechnics and universities was abolished.[79]

The teaching unions were not broken; they were powerful enough to defeat the government over the details of the national curriculum in 1993. New Labour, despite making education its top priority and promising to invest £19 billion in schools over three years, has found them just as awkward. Each of the reforms it has proposed (super teachers, education action zones, handing problem schools to private companies, and performance-related pay) has prompted the same response: a threat to go to slow or strike. The opening of the first conference season since the government took office saw the NUT agenda peppered with motions calling for campaigns and strikes. It does not improve the public image of the profession.

Education secretary David Blunkett told the hecklers at the NUT conference: 'Shouting won't make a difference. All you do is put off decent people who want to come into the teaching profession.'[80] Even Nigel de Gruchy has joked that teachers cannot bear to turn on television during an NUT conference because of the damage it inflicts on their image. But militancy has worked well for teachers. By generating a constant sense of crisis, it has ensured the profession is well-funded. It is only in higher education that the world of learning is genuinely in difficulties. As the undergraduate population has ballooned, the teaching workload has increased, and the pay of lecturers and professors has failed to keep pace. Policemen, nurses, train-drivers, even schoolteachers, are now earning more than some dons.

Unlike schoolteachers, judges, civil servants, doctors and dentists, dons have no pay review body to ransack the private and public sectors for suitable 'comparators'. As a result university posts are becoming harder to fill. Chairs in some disciplines have disappeared altogether for want of applicants. A number of well-known and mainly left-wing dons – like Bernard Williams, Alan Ryan and David Cannadine – emigrated ostentatiously to academic posts in the United States. Most claim to have trebled their salaries and halved their workloads. 'University professional staff are in a pay ghetto,' the AUT complained in 1996.[81] The mood in common rooms is one of militant despair.

The sourness of dons reflects the loss of less tangible rewards than money. Higher education was at the heart of the public sector professional ideal: trained minds, not blue blood, rising through the ranks by merit to solve the world's problems by the application of reason. Today, no government wanting answers puts the question to a royal commission made up of dons; that job goes to businessmen. Influence over public policy has passed to the board-room and the think-tanks which crowd the streets of Westminster. The idea of a university is corrupted by lack of money and the tide of numbers. Dons are reduced to begging for sponsorship to pursue their studies and research, and their output is subjected to the calculus of audit. The surging numbers of undergraduates, and the constant pressure to reduce the cost of processing them for their future tasks in industry and commerce, are reducing universi-ties to examination factories and dons to factory hands.

For dons, as for the public sector professions as a whole, universities filled with reluctant students are a daily reminder of the contradiction at the heart of their self-image. They want money, but they do not want to compete for it. They believe in their own merit, but consider it impertinent to measure it. When merit pay was introduced at Cambridge, one in six professors refused to accept any increment. 'Those of us against aren't any less greedy than the others,' explained one of the refuseniks, 'but American universities are poisoned by competitive relations over money, and I don't want it here.'[82] Every profession believes its existence is argument enough for its own rewards. Yet every profession is competing with every other profession for a larger share of the national income.

Beneath the cant about 'public service', civil servants, MPs and ministers, judges, army officers, doctors and dentists, teachers and dons are all in fierce competition with one another for a share of the two fifths of the national income the state has at its disposal. They are in competition also with Fat Cats, investment bankers, lawyers and accountants, whose interest is in reduc-ing that share. The divide between the private and the public sector pro-fessionals is far from exact. Accountants gain from consultancy contracts with government departments, and dons from consultancy contracts with private companies. But any latter-day Marxist searching for what Harold Perkin called 'the master-conflict of professional society' would find it here: in the battle between taxpayers and tax-eaters.

CHAPTER EIGHTEEN

FARMERS

Our farmers round, well pleased with constant gain,
Like other farmers, flourish and complain.
GEORGE CRABBE, 'The Parish Register', 1807

Telling farmers they must produce what their customer wants, not what
they want to produce, is a message that takes a bit of getting through.
DAVID NAISH, 1996, President, NFU[1]

Knowledge of ownership is a matter of hearsay, and local gossip, rather
than any statutory and central register of land ownership. A lovely anachronism of England. Long may it remain.
PETER WORMELL, Essex farmer[2]

A farmer ought not to be a rich man.
The Times, 1800[3]

Few people have eaten more taxes than farmers. Since the Second World
War, taxpayers have spent nearly £50 billion on supporting British agriculture.
Protecting it from foreign competition has probably cost twice as much again
in higher food prices. Farming is so stiff with subsidies and price-fixing that,
to all intents and purposes, it is a nationalised industry. It produces less than
one fiftieth of the national income, and employs only one in fifty people, but
it enjoys more favours than any other industry. Farmers even have their
own Whitehall department, the Ministry of Agriculture, Fisheries and Food
(MAFF), with an annual budget of over £5 billion.[4]

The modern British farmer is not the sturdy yeoman of tradition, but a
welfare dependant. In 1996–7 hand-outs from the taxpayer (£4.2 billion)
more than covered the bill for wages (£3.7 billion), which farmers are happy
to leave to a government body; indeed, they were upset when its abolition
was proposed. If the higher prices paid by consumers are included, half the

output of British farming is subsidised. Yet, after sixty years of government measures designed to make farmers rich, the share of farming in the national income has shrunk. Agricultural jobs have halved, and there are fewer farmers. Most are getting poorer, and many are angry.

In December 1997 hundreds of Welsh beef farmers marched spontaneously on Holyhead, threw forty tonnes of imported Irish beef into the sea, and mounted a picket to force lorry-drivers to take their cargoes back across the Irish Sea. Their example was copied by farmers in west Wales, Scotland and England. In the West Country, 250 farmers laid siege to a meat factory thought to be using Irish beef, and dozens more blocked major roads with their tractors.[5] Petitions were delivered to No. 10, and livestock let loose in Downing Street. By January 1998, the Welsh police were dispersing farmers with tear gas and batons.

On 1 March that year, 250,000 country dwellers and their urban and suburban supporters marched through London demanding that townies 'listen to us.' Beacons were lit, to warn the capital of the coming armada, and the government was rattled. Ministers were bullied into joining the Countryside March. Emergency aid worth £85 million was promised to farmers, followed by a further £120 million in the autumn. Foreign beef was banned, unless it was purged of offal. A commitment (firmly made in Opposition) to give ramblers a legal right to roam was postponed. Plans to carpet the countryside with 4·4 million new houses were withdrawn, in favour of refurbishing towns and cities instead. A private member's bill to ban hunting with hounds was allowed to die.

The events of the winter of 1997–8 testified to the formidable power of John Peel. But for farmers, the government had still not conceded enough: they wanted £1 billion in financial assistance, to compensate them for the ban on the export of British beef and the loss of income occasioned by the rise in the value of the pound.[6] This was the true measure of the moral insensibility of the farmer. Manufacturers, who account for a far larger proportion of the national income, complain about adverse movements in the rate of exchange, but they do not ask for compensation. Like most welfare dependants, farmers are more conscious of dues than duties. They are the chief citizens of Pauperdom, too long accustomed to public support to conceive of it as anything than a right.

Wise farmers blushed. They know their trade is unpopular; the average modern farmer is seen as greedy, and destructive and ungrateful. He and his like cram battery hens and broiler chickens into elongated sheds; inject cocktails of hormones into beef cattle; lock pregnant sows into wooden stalls; despatch veal calves in crates to Continental platters; rear migratory fish in densely-packed sea cages; slay indigenous plants and animals with chemicals and pesticides; and, in a final reproach to Mother Nature, drive their cows mad by feeding them sheep. Listeria in cheese, salmonella in eggs, E-coli in beefburgers, and Bovine Spongiform Encephalopathy (BSE) in cows have persuaded urban consumers that rural Britain bears little resemblance to Old Macdonald's Farm.

Opposition to the leisure pursuits of the farmer, from fox-hunting to shooting, is growing more militant. People were prepared to die (they said) rather than allow farmers to ship veal calves to Europe by air (the European ban on British beef made the final sacrifice unnecessary). Animal rights activists, hunt saboteurs, ramblers, 'New Age' travellers and self-styled 'eco-terrorists' are contemptuous of the property rights of farmers.[7] They want land, not to own it or to farm it, but as a public space in which to moralise about the evils of factory farming, seeding with genetically engineered crops, and the laws of trespass. Nationalisation of the landscape and of access to land (if not of land itself) is now a popular cause.[8]

Conflicts of interest between farmers and consumers are scarcely new. The latest clashes stand in a long tradition of animosity between the landed and the landless, and between the urban and the rural. What has changed is the balance of power. Every eco-terrorist and hunt saboteur knows that every consumer knows that subsidies and above-market prices add £20 a week to the household food bill, and that farmers are paid *not* to grow food. The 1992 reform of the Common Agricultural Policy (CAP), by shifting the burden of supporting farmers from consumers to taxpayers, has made these donatives more visible. Instead of guaranteed prices for their produce, farmers receive cash payments. Even consumers too parochial or lazy to notice that food costs less in America than in Europe can recognise a cash transfer when they see it. Money-for-nothing makes an easier read ('Farmer paid £14,000 to watch the grass grow') than the devaluation of the Green Pound.

When a Cambridgeshire cereals farmer, Oliver Walston, wrote in the *Sunday Times* how grateful he was to 'those generous taxpayers who make my life so pleasant' he received sackfuls of hate mail from his fellow-farmers.[9] 'Certain issues are best not discussed in public,' wrote one grain baron whose subsidy income Walston estimated at £1 million. 'Certainly when these issues are far too complicated for the average person even to start to comprehend.'[10] Frank Field, the MP for Birkenhead, has described how welfare dependency taxes honesty and rewards deceit among the urban poor. 'We're working the system,' his constituents tell him.[11] The grain barons of East Anglia are doing much the same.

Even the richest farmers can no longer imagine a life outside the system of subsidies and price supports. 'Whatever incentive is put there, I'll respond to it,' one Sussex farmer told the *Financial Times*. 'If there was a payment to build dry stone walls on the South Downs, I'd be out there doing it.'[12] This is the future which many farmers envisage: they hope that subsidies for growing can be swapped for subsidies for conserving. In other words, farmers want to join the Heritage Industry. In many parts of the country, they already have. Farmers are ceasing to be the Stakhanovites of the fields and orchards, overproducing more efficiently than any of their competitors in Europe. In the twenty-first century, they want to be the guardians of the lapwing and the hedgerow. A breed of men, who still proclaim their sturdy self-reliance, are pensioners of the state and playthings of the Greens.

Peculiar Economics

Dependence began with digging for victory. At the end of the last war, farmers were national heroes. By eliminating the threat of starvation by the encircling U-boats, they had saved the nation. The mistake was not to be grateful to them. It was to believe that the extraordinary conditions of the war should persist in peace. In wartime, the challenge is to produce enough for everybody to eat. At other times, it is to consume what is produced. Unlike other industries, there are natural limits to the expansion of agriculture. 'The rich man,' as Adam Smith wrote, 'consumes no more food than his poor neighbour. The desire of food is limited in every man by the narrow capacity of the human stomach.'[13] Scarcity, not plenty, is what makes farmers rich. This is the peculiarity of agricultural economics.

As economies industrialise, they can support more people. The demand for food rises, and the industrial economy supplies tractors and fertilisers which enable farmers to meet it. This is what happened in mid-Victorian Britain. Despite the repeal of the Corn Laws in 1846, which in theory exposed farmers to foreign competition, the thirty years from the mid 1840s to the mid-1870s were a golden age of British agriculture. Better drainage and breeding techniques, and breakthroughs in agricultural chemistry and mechanisation, enabled farmers to feed a growing industrial population. They got richer. It was not until the population grew more slowly, and new technologies such as steamships and refrigeration filled the shops with produce of the American prairies and the Argentine pampas, that farmers felt the pain of foreign competition.

Once a country is rich enough to feed its people, and the population stabilises, the consumption of food stagnates. Rising wealth is spent on other things. In 1947, when the Retail Prices Index (RPI) was first compiled in its modern form, food accounted for 35 per cent. It now accounts for only 14 per cent. Of course, as people get richer, they switch from carbohydrates to protein, and from fresh food to junk food, but the consequent increase in profit accrues to manufacturers rather than producers. In a mature agricultural economy, the sort of people who do well out of food production are Jack Eastwood and Bernard Matthews, who sell processed chickens and turkeys to the supermarkets. It is not the farmer who adds value by turning chickens into nuggets, or a pint of milk into a chocolate milk shake. Farmers can get richer only by displacing imports or exporting to countries where people are still hungry.[14]

For fifty years, British farmers managed neither. They simply got poorer. In the last quarter of the nineteenth century, shipments of grain and frozen meat from the Ukraine, the Americas and Australasia began to arrive in British shops. Grain prices halved. The price of livestock fell by a third. The value of land collapsed. Farming was plunged into a recession from which it did not emerge for several decades. By the time of the First World War, Britain was importing two thirds of its food. Urban consumers got cheap food, and farmers' incomes fell, but there were more votes in cheap bread than rich farmers. Britain stuck to industrial and financial exports, where it had a headstart over the rest of the world, and used the proceeds to buy food at low prices from countries which had yet to industrialise.

The Catalyst of War

The First World War shook British confidence in the case for free trade in food. Submarine warfare undermined it in the crudest possible way; by 1917, one in four ships which left the British Isles never returned. Farmland was brought back into cultivation, and farmers were ordered to plough it. They were guaranteed minimum prices for wheat, oats and potatoes, and began to prosper. When the war was over, a grateful nation let farmers keep the price guarantees which had rewarded them, and the Agriculture Act of 1920 promised they would continue indefinitely. In fact, they lasted only a year before succumbing to the public expenditure cuts of 1921, but an important principle was breached. For the first time since 1846, happy farmers had mattered more than cheap bread. Modern agricultural policy dates from the price guarantees of February 1917.

In the 1930s the government abandoned free trade altogether. A variety of quantitative restrictions and duties were laid on imports of food from outside the British Empire. Producer-controlled marketing boards were set up for milk, pigs, potatoes and hops, which guaranteed the price of whatever farmers could produce. They bought up surpluses and paid farmers the difference between market prices and the guaranteed minimum. These 'deficiency payments' remained at the heart of British agricultural policy until the country joined the European Economic Community in 1973. They benefited the farmer without increasing the price of food to consumers directly so the impact on public expenditure, initially at least, was slight. The charge to public funds, which had risen to £40 million by 1936, was modest by post-war standards, but farmers' incomes were relatively depressed throughout the 1930s.

The Second World War transformed the tentative collusion between farmers and the government into a lasting conspiracy against the taxpayer and consumer. Drawing on the experience of the First World War, the government did not wait for the U-boats. British agriculture was fortified with guaranteed prices, food rationing, retail price control and strategic stockpiles of essential foods. The National Farmers Union (NFU) and the Ministry of Agriculture forged a close partnership. Arable acreage was expanded by one half, and farmers were given strong financial incentives to concentrate on the production of staple foods – cereals, potatoes and milk.

The policy was an outstanding success. The British people survived the war better-fed than their continental allies and enemies. In a sense, the policy was too successful. It persuaded the politicians of the 1940s that state-financed and state-directed agriculture would work as well in peace. Food rationing continued for years after the war. On the world markets, food was scarce, Britain was short of foreign currency and it was pointed out that producing it at home would improve the balance of payments. Wartime success appeared to vindicate the ability of the planners to organise it, and farmers were in a powerful position to obtain concessions from a grateful nation.

By the Agriculture Act of 1947, the government guaranteed markets and prices for eleven major farm commodities, and obliged the Ministry of Agriculture to purchase all that farmers could produce. The food was sold to consumers at lower prices, protecting them from the rigours of the market. Conscious that the dearth would not last for ever, the NFU extracted a statutory pledge that farmers would receive 'proper remuneration' and 'an adequate return on capital'. These would be decided through an annual review of the financial condition of the industry, and prices paid by the government would be fixed accordingly.

By the time a Conservative government was elected in 1951, the worldwide shortage of food was abating. But the last Churchill administration was too reliant on rural votes to expose farmers to the cold winds of the marketplace. It scrapped the subsidisation of food prices, but retained the guaranteed prices to farmers. Farmers were invited to sell for the best price available in the market, then apply to Whitehall for a retrospective 'deficiency payment'. The pre-war agricultural marketing boards were revived, and equipped with monopoly purchasing powers over milk, hops, potatoes and eggs. In theory, the monopoly would enable the government to control the size of deficiency payments by manipulating the prices of the major agricultural commodities.

Farming for Farmers

These were generous arrangements. The agricultural industry was protected and subsidised, rescuing farmers from the realities of their profession in a developed economy. Instead of shrinking to allow cheap imports to feed a growing industrial economy, domestic agriculture was paid to expand specifically to displace imported food. It took British farmers some time to make their presence felt. As recently as the late 1950s, Britain was still importing half of the food it needed. Today, the country is 59 per cent self-sufficient in food and animal feed, and 76 per cent self-sufficient in foods which can be grown here.

This feat, conventionally portrayed as the greatest triumph of the mixed economy, is the closest Britain has come to running a Soviet-style nationalised industry, in which production is more important than consumption, supply is designed to exceed demand, over-investment and over-manning are rife, and wealth is destroyed rather than created. The effects on farmers were more pleasing. As their share of the domestic market increased, their incomes rose. But as Britain became increasingly self-sufficient in food, it became harder for them to increase revenues by increasing sales (because most imported foods cannot be produced in a British climate).[15]

The obvious remedy was to reduce their costs. Thanks to mechanical engineers, agricultural chemists, and crop and animal geneticists, this was achieved. Although the area of farmland has shrunk slightly since 1945, the number of cattle on it has increased by nearly two thirds. The number of sheep and poultry have both more than tripled, and the number of pigs has quadrupled. Milk yields have doubled since the war, and wheat yields have doubled in the last ten years. Since 1945, the number of people needed to produce this vastly increased output has fallen from 1,250,000 to 505,000.

These are the triumphs of the age of factory farming. Productivity could be increased further: farmers are now using computer and satellite technology to pinpoint the most fertile parts of a field. But rising productivity has made farmers the victims of their own success. A combination of rising productivity and guaranteed prices is designed to lead to over-production. Too much food puts market prices under downward pressure, making guaranteed prices expensive to taxpayers. The first gluts had appeared in the late 1950s, in eggs,

TABLE 18.1
Livestock Numbers in the United Kingdom

	1945	1997	% Increase
Cattle	7,237000	*11,609,000	60
Sheep	12,597,000	42,559,000	238
Pigs	1,732,000	7,992,000	361
Poultry	37,352,000	†126,960,000	240
Total	58,918,000	189,120,000	221

Source: *Agriculture in the United Kingdom 1997*, page 9, table 2.2.

* This figure is lower than in recent years, due to BSE. In 1996, the year the ban on beef exports was imposed, beef and dairy cattle totalled over 12 million, and they averaged 12 million in the late 1980s.
† 1995 figure. Comparable figures for 1996 and 1997 were not available.

milk and pigs. As over-production increased, price guarantees became hard to sustain politically. It became obvious that the price guarantees would work in the long run only if the government fixed the quantity as well as the price of food. In other words, the government had to decide who was to produce how much of what.

As the cost of price guarantees climbed in the 1960s, the government made the first attempts to fix the quantity of food by reducing the amounts paid to farmers for 'excess' production. British admission to the CAP in 1973 masked the problem temporarily, but eventually made it worse. Demand remained static, but the prices guaranteed by the CAP meant that, for instance, the price of British grain doubled overnight. Soon Britain and Europe were awash with butter mountains, grain hoards and milk lakes.[16] By 1985, *one half* of the entire European budget was spent on storing agricultural surpluses. It was only a matter of time before the European Commission would have to fix the quantities of food as well.

End of Farming for Farmers?

Milk was first. Production quotas were introduced in 1984. Farmers were fully compensated for loss of income, and bounties were offered to those prepared to give up producing milk altogether. The milk lake was drained by 1989. The cost of milk to the CAP budget shrank from one third in the 1980s to one tenth now. But milk quotas are still in place, unchanged, fifteen years later.[17] Consumers are still paying more for milk than they would in a free market. The most efficient dairy farmers cannot expand production, or develop export markets. Taxpayers are still funding mountains of butter and skimmed milk powder. The grain and beef mountains have not disappeared either, despite the most substantial reform of the CAP in its history, designed to reduce the dependence of farmers on price supports and storage of surpluses.

After some desultory attempts to tackle the problem with price cuts and even fines for 'excess' production, European agriculture ministers resolved in 1992 to bribe farmers to produce less. Guaranteed prices were reduced by between 5 per cent and 35 per cent over six years, and farmers were given cash payments for reducing production. The most notorious measure was the introduction of 'set-aside' payments, in which arable farmers are given cash for each acre of crops they grow provided they take 15 per cent of their land out of production.[18] The 1992 reforms were the first time the CAP had broken with price support since 1962. The beef, butter and grain mountains shrank over the next four years. The grain mountain fell from 33 million tonnes in 1993 to 3.5 million tonnes in 1996. Coupled with the world trade agreement of 1993, when major countries agreed to drastic reductions in agricultural import tariffs and subsidies, the price of farm commodities was set to move gradually towards market levels.

In fact, world shortages pegged grain prices at much higher levels than anyone had predicted. Cereal growers throughout Europe were overcompensated for price falls that failed to occur. In June 1997 the European Commission estimated European cereal farmers had received £5.9 billion more than they deserved over the previous four years.[19] In Britain, most went to the grain barons of East Anglia. Oliver Walston (see page 662) told readers of the *Sunday Times* how the system was working for him:

> I am a happy man. Not just because harvest has been easy this year, not because prices are higher than last year, but because by Christmas I will receive a little brown envelope. The postmark will be Guildford but the cheque inside, for almost £200,000, will come from Brussels. It is my share of the CAP . . . For every acre of cereals I grow, Brussels pays me £109. For an acre of oilseed rape I am paid £192 and for an acre of peas or beans £157. But there was a price to pay. We have to set aside 15 per cent of our farms and promise to grow nothing on this land. But even here Brussels was in a generous mood. I now receive £138 for every acre I set aside, which amounts to £40,000 on my farm.[20]

Two years later, Graham Harvey identified a dozen arable farmers in receipt of CAP cheques for over £1 million, and five who had pocketed more than £5 million each.[21]

By 1997, it was clear that the 1992 reforms had backfired. Output had started to respond to the higher-than-expected market prices. The cereal mountain was up to 15 million tonnes by the middle of 1998. The European Commission proposed a doubling of the amount of land taken out of production by set-aside, and cuts of 10 to 30 per cent in the intervention prices for dairy, beef and cereals.[22] Ultimately, set-aside, production quotas and price intervention are all doomed. The enlargement of the European Union to east and central Europe will bankrupt an unreformed CAP, because their farm prices are now so low. A fresh round of world trade talks, starting in 1999, will intensify pressure to remove all remaining forms of subsidy and protection.

British farmers reckon they are better-equipped than their European competitors to survive a genuine market in agricultural commodities. British farmers have agitated successfully for the winding up of the price-fixing British Wool Marketing Board (in 1993) and the Potato Marketing Board (in 1997). Dairy farmers secured the demise of the price-fixing Milk Marketing Board (MMB) in 1994. Its milk purchasing powers passed to a farmers' co-operative, Milk Marque, which sets the price of milk in two selling rounds in January and July each year. Two thirds of dairy farmers sell their output to Milk Marque, giving it over half the market and the power to dictate prices to major dairy processors such as Northern Foods and Unigate. Predictably, milk prices rose steeply after the abolition of the MMB; to secure supplies, the dairies bid for more milk than they needed, pushing prices up still further.

Because of the milk quotas imposed by Brussels, British dairy farmers could not relieve the pressure on prices by increasing the supply of milk. Quota-breakers face a fine of 29p a litre, and a possible two-year jail term, so milk quotas have become a valuable capital asset for farmers. They are traded eagerly by those who want to take advantage of rising prices (in 1995 a disagreement over the ownership of a milk quota ended in a shooting which left two men dead). The major victims of the new régime, however, were smaller dairy processors. Many went under or got taken over: Cricket St Thomas of Somerset, Lord Rayleigh's Dairies in Essex, and Scottish Pride, the processing arm of the Scottish Milk Marketing Board. Even Unigate and Northern Foods, under simultaneous pressure from the supermarket chains to cut the price of processed milk, found their profits squeezed.

They were rescued by the rising pound. The revaluation of the Green Pound pushed milk prices down. Milk Marque resisted, propping up prices by disposing of surplus milk for processing into cheese and butter abroad rather than in the domestic market.[23] It also began to acquire and build its own processing facilities, with the obvious intention of buying milk at artificially high prices and selling processed milk at artificially low ones. For the major milk processors, this was too much. Dairy Crest, the MMB manufacturing operation originally set up to process surplus milk for storage as butter and cheese, was separated from Milk Marque and floated on the stock market in August 1996 to prevent the farmers' co-operative exploiting its buying power.[24] In 1998 the major processors demanded and got a Monopolies and Mergers Commission (MMC) inquiry into Milk Marque. They boycotted the July selling round, saying prices for autumn delivery were too high. Milk Marque had to cancel the auction; later, it reached agreement at lower prices. The MMC, due to deliver its verdict in 1999, is expected to break the co-operative into a series of regional bodies, hand its control of the biennial milk auctions to an independent body, or order it to sell its processing capacity.

Milk prices have started to fall already. Dairy farmers, after a brief bonanza in the early years after the demise of the MMB, are angry and frustrated. The quota system prevents them expanding production, while the dairy processors and the supermarkets are taking advantage of lower prices. For the first time since the 1930s, the consumer (through the supermarkets) has begun to dictate the price of milk. Similar complaints, especially about the inflation of the price of peas and potatoes between the farm gate and the supermarket shelf, are being voiced by other farmers.

They will have to get used to it. The New Labour government is the first in eighty years openly to regard consumers as more important than producers. 'It took me six weeks to realise there was an entirely different philosophy,' admitted David Naish, president of the National Farmers Union. 'It was exactly the same argument but you had to start from the position of what the benefit to the consumer is . . . as opposed to what you produce for the consumer.'[25] The flagship of New Labour agricultural policy was a new and independent Food Standards Agency, a ministry for consumers to match MAFF, the ministry for producers. But the food industry refused to pay for it and the government baulked at breaking up MAFF to find the money. There is no doubt, however, that New Labour is less in thrall to farmers than any government since the New Liberals of the Edwardian period.

Farmers might have thought the last Conservative government hostile, but they did not know how lucky they were. In the 1980s and early 1990s MAFF presided over a series of food scandals, culminating in the BSE crisis, largely because its instinct was to protect farmers rather than public health. BSE was first identified in 1986. Yet the feeding of dead sheep to cows was not banned until April 1988, when BSE was first made a notifiable disease. A year later, offal was removed from cattle at slaughter, and brains and spinal cords banned from human consumption. In 1990, a BSE-type brain disease was identified in a cat, suggesting the infection could jump species. A link with pigs was confirmed in September that year. In March 1996, the European Union banned the export from Britain of beef from cows over six months old.

It was not until 1995, when people were dying from a new variant of Creutzfeld Jakob-Disease (CJD), that mechanically recovered meat was banned from meat pies. It was March 1996, ten years after the disease was first discovered, before government scientists admitted the possibility of a link between BSE and CJD in humans. All meat from cows over thirty months old was banned from sale.* It was too late; consumer confidence collapsed. The EU imposed a ban on the export of British beef, killing a trade worth £518 million to British farmers in 1995.

It was not lifted completely until November 1998, and left beef farmers to clear formidable veterinary and certification hurdles before consumer confidence was restored. The Phillips inquiry, set up by the New Labour government to investigate why the official response to the BSE crisis was so dilatory, has uncovered a predictable explanation. Officials and ministers at MAFF were terrified of the consequences for the beef industry: the culling of millions of cows, and an end to the export trade.[26] Both happened anyway. By the end of November 1998 the slaughter toll was 2·7 million cows. The EU ban had lasted two and a half years, and British beef farmers were receiving £1·5 billion a year in compensation.

The BSE crisis was a major policy disaster. Since 1995, twenty-nine people have lost their lives to new variant CJD. Hundreds of beef farmers are bankrupt. Thousands of people working in abattoirs, butchers' shops and food manufacturers have lost their jobs. The national income has shrunk. The British government has endured considerable embarrassment abroad. Taxpayers have spent a fortune on compensation. In July 1998 the NAO estimated the costs of the BSE crisis at £2·5 billion, and forecast they would hit £3·5 billion by 2000.[27]

Guardians of the Environment

Outside the looking-glass world of agricultural subsidy, a ministry could not survive a catastrophe of this kind. MAFF would be broken up. Its responsibility for food safety would be transferred to a Food Standards Agency; its

---

* A national cattle-tracking scheme, which would have helped to restore domestic and foreign confidence, was not introduced until September 1998.

industrial duties to the Department of Trade and Industry; its directorship of CAP subsidies to the Treasury; and its conservation and environmental work to the Department for the Environment, Transport and the Regions. In fact, MAFF is now re-inventing itself as the Ministry for Rural Affairs.

Farmers, like their patrons at the ministry, have long understood that taxpayers are no longer prepared to pay them for food nobody wants, or which may kill them. Their aim is to redefine the purpose of the subsidies. Instead of being paid to produce, they will be paid to employ, conserve and protect. One bumper-sticker 'Keep Britain Farming' is giving way to another: 'Conserve the Countryside: Support British Farming'. This is now the aim of official policy, at European as well as national level. The EU wants to wean farmers off price-fixing, set-aside and quotas, and pay them to open caravan parks, maintain the landscape and look after habitats. The British government, alarmed by the rural rebellion, is talking about the need to combine the economic regeneration of the countryside with a proper respect for the environment. As a Conservative White Paper of October 1995 said, expanding food production is 'no longer an overriding imperative'.[28]

It is hard to believe that protecting the rural economy and environment will be any cheaper. The European Commission says it may cost 10 per cent more to pay farmers to grow jobs and wildlife rather than wheat and cows. In Switzerland, where farming is already a paid-up member of the Heritage Industry, environmental aid accounts for four fifths of the value of crops produced. British farmers are also the least probable custodians of the natural environment; nobody has done more to destroy it. Farmers have grubbed up hedgerows; poisoned wild animals with pesticides; polluted surface and ground water with agro-chemicals; sacrificed meadows of wild flowers and field ponds to the production of subsidised crops; drained wetland habitats, and injected cows, pigs and chickens with antibiotics and growth hormones. They have turned farms into factories. Far from spoiling the countryside, cheap food from abroad may improve it. But it is more likely that production subsidies will be labelled as employment and environmental allowances.

In parts of the country designated as Environmentally Sensitive Areas (ESAs), farmers are already being paid to forgo intensive farming methods. Even outside ESAs, farmers can claim equivalent subsidies under the Country-side Stewardship scheme. The sums involved are not yet substantial (about £75 million in 1997–8, against the £3–4 billion MAFF spends on production subsidies) but the ministry is not the only source of public money for farmers. Preserving stone walls and hedgerows, letting native flowers colonise fields, planting native broad-leaf trees and keeping cows out of environmentally sensitive areas all attract subsidies from the Countryside Commission. The reappearance of poppies in cereal fields is only the most visible sign of the grants for *not* using herbicides. In 1998, the government introduced the first grants for farmers prepared to give up income to farm in ways which encourage wildlife habitats.[29] The same year, the NFU signed a co-operation agreement with English Nature to lobby for extra grants to run SSIs.[30]

Farmers have good reason to hope that the CAP can be turned into a rural and environmental welfare state. At the time of the 1992 reforms, European governments pledged themselves to make the environment a weightier consideration. That urge has intensified since. It would be comparatively easy for officials to rechristen set-aside payments as conservation grants since environmentalists are already warning that set-aside is vital to the preservation of wildlife. Farmers will be happy to adapt – provided the cheques keep coming.

Organic farmers are lobbying hard for public money. In 1994 the Conservative government agreed to pay five year 'conversion' grants to help farmers through a period of plunging yields as they wean themselves off fertilisers and pesticides so as to be able to label their produce 'organic'. The government, whose chief constituency is well-heeled urban consumers who can afford organic produce, is sympathetic. There are serious objections to organic farming, but they are not taken seriously.[31] Organic farmers are pressing the government for permanent maintenance grants to protect them against falling prices when there are more of them. Ministers have made reassuring noises, and the Treasury is now all that stands between consumers (already paying high prices for organic produce) and another subsidy for farmers.

What Farmers Earn

It is all richly ironic. Twenty years ago, farmers got subsidies for taking hedgerows out, draining marshes, grubbing out woodland, and ploughing up rough pasture. Nowadays, any farmer who grubs up a hedgerow without informing the local authority is liable to a fine, and councils can issue a preservation order if it is more than thirty years old. Farmers do not mind, provided there is a subsidy attached. They long ago identified heritage and environment as the coming gravy-train, and are now eager to board. Most farmers had a thin time in 1996 and 1997. The BSE crisis decimated the beef industry. The rising pound put the price of milk, grain, sugar, eggs, lamb, pigs and potatoes under strong downward pressure, sucked in cheap imports of commodities traded freely (peas and potatoes), and reduced the subsidies given to those that are not (mainly cereals).

By 1997–8, average farm incomes were down by a half on the boom years of 1995–6. In real terms, they have fallen even more dramatically.[32] But most farmers had three exceptionally fat years between 1993 and 1995. According to MAFF, average farm incomes more than doubled between 1991 and 1995, to their highest level for twenty years. Good farming, a run of fine weather apart, had little to do with it. The CAP compensation payments, both for set-aside and guaranteed prices, erred on the generous side. In 1995–6, arable area aid payments via the CAP totalled £1·3 billion, or £24,000 to each farm. World grain prices, which were expected to fall, rose.

The withdrawal of the pound from the Exchange Rate Mechanism (ERM) in September 1992 gave British farmers a second windfall. As the value of sterling fell, subsidies (translated into pounds at a fixed rate under the Green Pound régime) rose in value. Interest rates fell, reducing the burden of debt for farmers as they did for householders. And there were some other unexpected bonuses. Potato farmers had two freakishly good years in 1994 and 1995, when low yields drove prices up to £360 a tonne; prices did not slip below three figures until the summer of 1996. Pig and poultry farmers also had a boom year, as consumers switched from beef to pork and chicken in the wake of the BSE panic. Dairy farmers were able to use the BSE compensation payments to replace ageing herds with productive new heifers. Though many beef farmers were in serious difficulties before the compensation package was agreed in 1996, they received £1·5 billion of financial support in 1997–8.

The fat years did not make farmers rich – or at least not all of them. Even in 1995 the average man who owned his farm earned only £297 a week, or about £15,000 a year, well below the average for non-manual male workers (£23,000).[33] But averages make even less sense in agriculture than in other industries. Farming is not one industry, but many. The fortunes of a farmer depend on where his farm is, how big it is, and what kind of farming he does, even before differences in ability are taken into account. It is impossible to make generalisations about the wealth and income of farmers as a single group. According to the Inland Revenue, in 1995–6 one third of farmers had an annual income of less than £6,000, and four fifths of less than £20,000. But 12,000 had an income of over £50,000 a year.[34]

The inequalities in farming are immense. In 1996–7, a small lowland cow or sheep farmer made about £5,000 from his farm. The average English cereal baron, with 500–1,000 acres planted, made well over £100,000. On the same type of farm, the biggest farmers never earn less than two or three times as much as the smallest. In some cases, they earn more than seven times as much. But on even the biggest farms in the richest farming areas, the general cropper is always better off than the cattle rancher, because cereals are more valuable than cows. Short of collectivising the agricultural economy, nothing can be done to eradicate these massive differences in earnings. After sixty-odd years of agricultural support, farming still embraces those who are rich and those who are dirt-poor. Whatever achievements can be ascribed to agricultural subsidies, the equalisation of incomes is not among them.

The low, unequal and unpredictable nature of farmers' incomes was one of the main justifications for subsidising agriculture. But it was bound to backfire. In a system where subsidies are paid per tonne of wheat or even per acre of wheat, the farmer who produces 200 tonnes will get ten times the subsidy of the farmer who produces 20 tonnes. Unlike most subsidies, agricultural support was designed to reward rich farmers without helping poor ones. In fact, by raising land values, subsidies fossilised inequalities in farming. A higher price for land enriches large landowners, but makes it harder for small farmers to expand by buying more land. Smaller farmers who do buy land are forced to raise mortgages, increasing their debt. In 1996–7, the average British farm had borrowings of £28,000, and total external liabilities (taxation, rent arrears, credit accounts) of £48,000.[35]

Too Many Farmers

Subsidies also raise costs, by encouraging farmers to use fertilisers and pesticides wastefully, and to invest in new tractors and fancy buildings. Combine harvesters costing £100,000 are used for six weeks of the year. Staff were cut dramatically as the industry recapitalised at public expense, with over 500,000 jobs disappearing since the Second World War. Most of those who remain are permanent, not part-time, making it hard to adjust costs in a cyclical industry. This is why British farming is so unprofitable. The return on assets averaged just 5·5 per cent in 1995, which was an exceptionally good year. With inflation running at 3 per cent, British farming was scarcely in the black. Only the grain barons and horticulturists (who grow carrots and beans for the supermarkets) are enjoying even double digit returns, against the 20 per cent and more which investors seek in other industries.

On Welsh and English sheep-farms, where nominal returns are as low as 2·5 per cent, the owners are engaged in subsistence farming. The only thing keeping them in business is the inelegantly named Hill Livestock Compensatory Allowance (HLCA), which costs taxpayers over £120 million a year. This is paid to 60,000 farmers rearing sheep or cattle in 'less favoured areas', mainly in Wales, Scotland and the Lake District. The HLCA is, to all intents and purposes, a heritage grant. Its specific aim is keep uneconomic forms of farming, and the towns and villages and dry stone walls which depend on it, alive for the suburban tourist to gawp at. 'There is no other way, and certainly no cheaper way of achieving what the public wants in terms of landscape,' admitted Leon Brittan, the European Commissioner for Trade, to the National Sheep Association.[36] The average small sheep-farmer on a hill had a net farm income of £17–18,000 in 1996–7, but received subsidies of over £28,000.[37] The New Labour government has promised to end the pretence, and re-brand HLCAs as an environmental allowance.[38]

Scottish and Welsh hill-farmers are only the most extreme example of an industry packed with uneconomic producers. Average farm incomes have declined steadily since the early 1970s; the boom years of the mid-1990s were a blip. In any business where demand is stagnant, and rising productivity is putting prices under downward pressure, the only way that profitability can recover is if marginal producers withdraw from the market. Yet the number of farmers at work in Britain increased until the 1960s. Even now, there are more farmers (345,000) than in the 1930s (277,000).[39] Subsidies have created not only an oversupply of food, but an oversupply of farmers.

How do Farmers Live?

Subsidies are still valuable, but farmers are diversifying their sources of income. They rent cottages and stables, or undertake contract work for other farmers. Tourism (caravan parks, camping sites, farm museums, children's farms, zoos, bed and breakfast), shopping (farm shops and craft workshops) and catering (restaurants and tea rooms) are increasingly important sources of income. Enterprising farmers now provide passers-by with the opportunity to shoot real and clay pigeons, fish for trout, ride horses and ponies, eat venison, and stare at exotic animals. Llamas, war games, golf courses and motor-cycle races are now as much a part of the English country scene as nitrates and slurry. Some farmers have become property developers, converting barns and cottages into houses for sale or holiday lets, or turning farm buildings into offices for light industrial and commercial businesses.

The fruit and vegetable stall on the trunk road, and the hand-scrawled advertisements for everything from eggs to manure, suggest that untaxed sales of produce are not an unimportant source of cash. When the authorities set up a fraud hotline inviting farmers to report one another for exceeding the milk quota, it was besieged with allegations that the neighbouring farmer was selling milk on the sly to local cheese producers. Many farmers have second jobs. These range from driving a lorry at one end of the income scale to full-time jobs in industry or the City at the other, with the farm left in the hands of a manager. Perhaps one fifth of farmers are part-timers, many on small holdings which they run for pleasure (or tax losses). In addition to earned income, most farmers have an investment income from savings or pensions. At the highest income levels, earnings from the farm are relatively unimportant.

TABLE 18.2

Taxable Income of Farmers in 1995–96

Income Range	Number	Farming	Other	Pensions & Investments	Total Income
Up to £5,999	112,000	2,140	2,820	3,060	8,020
£6,000–9,999	75,000	4,810	8,490	4,070	17,370
£10,000–19,999	89,000	9,320	11,580	6,970	27,870
£20,000–49,999	57,000	20,820	23,270	7,710	51,800
£50,000+	12,000	46,230	84,810	54,560	185,600
Total	345,000	9,190	17,090	6,910	33,190

Source: *Farm Incomes in the United Kingdom 1996/97*, Table 2.5.

Farmers as Land Owners

One reason farmers have a high level of investment income is that they own most of the land. By selling a few acres with planning permission, and re-investing in financial assets, they can diversify their sources of income. One of the deepest curiosities of this near-nationalised industry – where there are statistics about everything from the price of a tonne of spring wheat to the nutritive value of cassava – is that nobody knows which farmers own what parts of the country. Farmers have resisted pressure for a full survey of ownership or even the compilation of an accurate register of who owns what.

The last time such an exercise was undertaken was in the 1870s, when the country was still owned by the great aristocratic families. Farmers, who were the prime beneficiaries of the break-up of the great aristocratic estates, have never suffered any such intrusion. A century ago, most farmers had to rent the land they farmed. With just 7,000 people owning four fifths of the surface area of the British Isles, and a quarter of England held in estates of 10,000 acres or more, nearly nine acres in ten were let. The crumbling of the great estates during the first half of the twentieth century gave tenant farmers the opportunity to buy the land they farmed. Today, perhaps one farm in four is still rented. Though many larger and wealthier farmers have set up trusts or companies to own land, which they then rent back from themselves, it is reasonable to assume that at least three quarters of the privately owned agricultural land of the United Kingdom is now owned by farmers.

Best estimates are that around nine tenths of agricultural land (45·2 million acres) is owned by private individuals rather than private companies and institutions or the public sector. Once large landowners are excluded, farmers are left with just over 30 million acres: a figure almost exactly equivalent to three quarters of privately owned agricultural land. When farm buildings are included, the physical assets which farmers own are probably worth nearly £40 billion.[40] With an acre of English farmland with vacant possession fetching over £5,000, any farmer with 200 acres is a millionaire.

The Farmer as Millionaire

On the face of it, farmers ought to feel richer than they do. But in the last decade and a half, farmland has proved a poor investment. During the thirty years to 1979, protection and subsidies ensured that its value increased by 4 per cent a year in real terms,[41] but land values have struggled since. Despite modest recoveries in 1988–9 and 1993–7, the price of agricultural land fell in real terms throughout the 1980s and 1990s. The market is illiquid, there are large fluctuations in price by size, type and area, and every transaction has peculiarities of its own. But one fact is incontrovertible: in real terms, the value of all agricultural land is below its 1979 level.

Farmers are feeling wealthier only because land prices are above the lows of the mid-1980s. The value of land and buildings, which are two thirds of a farmer's assets, is the prime determinant of the 'feelgood factor' in farming. When land values were booming in the 1970s, richer farmers were wealthy enough to enrol as Lloyd's Names. They could pledge the farm against underwriting losses, allowing their largest capital asset to earn its living twice. In the same way, the plunging land values of the mid-1980s caused a chorus of moans across the agricultural counties of England. But land prices began to rise again in 1992, and the value of tenanted farmland in England and Scotland doubled between 1993 and 1996 and with vacant possession rose by a third.

The driving force was farmers, who are always the biggest buyers of farmland – some for speculative purposes, but most to hold, not to trade. Many are sitting tenants looking to acquire their farms. As their incomes rose in the wake of the ERM débâcle, and interest rates stayed relatively low, they took the opportunity to raise a mortgage. Total borrowings rose by more than a quarter in the first half of the 1990s. But the demand of farmers for land was not the only factor pushing up the price. There is also a shortage of land, at least of the right kind, with farmers scrambling after what is often a one-off opportunity to

TABLE 18.3
Major Owners of Agricultural Land in 1997–98

	Acreage
Foreigners	*2,600,000
Aristocracy	2,297,225
Forestry Commission	2,085,565
National Trust	597,765
Ministry of Defence	588,109
Regional Water Companies	442,350
Crown Estate	371,061
Local Authorities	337,556
Pension Funds and Life Offices	135,000
Colleges of Oxford and Cambridge Universities	178,688
English Nature, Scottish Natural Heritage, and Countryside Council for Wales	154,830
Royal Society for the Protection of Birds	139,093
The Church Commissioners for England	129,061
Duchy of Cornwall	128,189
Duchy of Lancaster	48,506
Woodland Trust	39,840
Church of England Dioceses	†33,000
Co-operative Wholesale Society Agriculture	28,000
Society of Merchant Venturers as Trustee of the St Monica Trust	23,217
Coal Authority	‡21,500
Lands Improvement Holdings	16,000
Church of Jesus Christ of Latter Day Saints	14,000
Smith's Charity	8,000
Total	10,681,555

* Author's estimates. Foreign ownership of farmland is not recorded in official statistics. Nearly half of the land owned by foreigners is Scottish estates, but much of what they own in England is farmed.
† Author's estimate. Glebe land which used to support rural vicars has passed into the control of Anglican dioceses. In some rural dioceses, like Lincoln, Peterborough and Norwich, the acreage is significant.
‡ The 21,500 acres represents the residue of non-operational land, previously owned by British Coal, which is now being sold by the Coal Authority.

extend their fiefs. Just 1·5 million acres comes on to the market in England and Wales in an average year; in other words, only one acre in 20 is for sale at any time. Which tends to raise the price of the right land.

Land is becoming more valuable for other reasons too. The most controversial is the increasing appetite for land to erect houses and factories. The
Council for the Protection of Rural England (CPRE) estimates that 27,000
acres of countryside a year disappears under tarmac and concrete. Since the
Second World War, over a million acres of England have succumbed to
suburban sprawl. As planning restrictions tightened in response to concern
about the disappearing countryside, house builders bid up the value of virtually any land within sight of a town and with planning permission granted.
Until a government succeeds in loosening the Green Belt, residential land
prices will continue to rise, with an indirect effect on the price of farmland.
As urban and suburban house prices rise, successful industrialists and financiers are increasingly re-investing sale proceeds in a farmhouse with a few
dozen (or even a few hundred) acres attached. When *Prospect* magazine surveyed the income and expenditure of high-income earners in the City of
London in 1995, it found they spent nearly half their income buying houses.[42]
Privacy and spaciousness are the principal criteria, but many City bankers
and industrial Fat Cats claim to 'farm in a small way'. The price of agricultural
land in the Home Counties has lost touch with its value as agricultural
land.

Return of Institutional Money

The lifting of excessive security of tenure for tenant farmers has encouraged
the return of corporate and institutional money to farmland. This followed
the reversal of tenancy policy in 1995. One of the concessions the NFU
extracted in the Agriculture Act of 1947 was lifetime security for tenant
farmers. In 1976 another Labour government raised security to three generations, provided they farmed the same land. This meant landowners could
lose control of their property for 100 years or more. Unsurprisingly, the
supply of tenancies dried up.[43] Landowners farmed the land with advice from
land agents, or sub-contracted the job to a farm management company.

The three-generation rule was finally scrapped in 1986, but the tenanted
market did not revive. Young farmers without capital were finding it increasingly hard to get a start, so the government agreed to abolish the lifetime
rule as well. The Agricultural Tenancies Act of 1995 freed landlords and
tenants to make whatever agreements they liked, for as long as they liked,
via a new class of 'business tenancies'. It also gave newly let land exemption
from Inheritance Tax, putting it on the same footing as owner-occupied
farmland.

Easier tax and tenancy arrangements are now bringing corporate and institutional money back into the agricultural land market. One of the best-known corporate buyers is Lands Improvement Holdings PLC, a Victorian company revitalised by the easier tenancy laws. It first came to prominence when it bought the 5,493-acre Sutton Bridge estate in Lincolnshire from the Ministry of Agriculture (one of the first privatisations of the new Conservative government). The Lands Improvement estate peaked at 27,000 acres, after it acquired 19,500 acres from the Royal Insurance Company in October 1995 for £55 million.[44]

This was the most expensive purchase of agricultural land since 1979, when the Prudential spent £20 million to acquire the 16,600-acre Guy's Hospital estate in Hertfordshire from the family of Sir Charles Clore.[45] Other significant institutional owners include the Mormon Church and the Co-operative Wholesale Society (CWS), whose agriculture division is looking to enlarge a freehold acreage which is now over 28,000 acres. CWS Agriculture farms over 80,000 acres in total, including Castle Howard in Yorkshire, and sells a large proportion of its output to the Co-op.

Institutional Landowners Now

The pension funds and life offices, which alarmed farmers in the 1970s by investing heavily in agricultural land, are unlikely to return. As the population ages, pension funds are increasingly mature, and need liquid assets rather than long-term investments. Since 1985 the forty-odd institutional landowners monitored by Savills have sold more agricultural land than they have bought. Their involvement peaked at about 850,000 acres in 1984, but they were disappointed by the low returns from agricultural property, and by the steep fall in land prices in the mid-1980s. They sold as soon as land prices stabilised later in the decade.

Total institutional ownership of agricultural land in England probably stands at about 135,000 acres today – less than a quarter of one per cent. The proportion is higher in Scotland, where one estimate is that the ten largest institutional owners controlled 105,167 acres in 1995.[46] If institutions own land at all today, it is usually in the hope of developing it as a residential housing estate. Eagle Star owns 10,000 acres around Micheldever in Hampshire, which it bought for its life fund in 1975. Its plans to build a new housing estate on 870 of its acres helped to unseat the Conservative MP for Winchester.

Institutional ownership is some way short of the almost five million acres the Northfield Committee predicted financial institutions would own by 2020.[47] The Committee, set up in 1977 to 'examine recent trends in agricultural land acquisition and occupancy as they affect the structure of the agricultural industry,' began work in an atmosphere of alarm. Farmers were worried about the increase in institutional buying of agricultural land. The committee (chaired by former Labour MP Donald Chapman, newly ennobled as Lord Northfield) reported in July 1979 that the financial institutions owned a mere 530,000 acres, or less than one hundredth of agricultural land in the United Kingdom. It was difficult to portray ownership on this scale as a threat to the British way of country life, or even as a takeover of the natural heritage by finance capital. Foreign companies and capitalists, another target, owned little more. Northfield reckoned foreigners owned just over 1 per cent of farmland in Great Britain – the bulk was held in the Scottish Highlands, where the Dutch, the Danes and the Arabs had bought heather and hills for sport and forestry rather than farming.

Nowadays, financial institutions and foreigners probably own about 2·7 million acres of British farmland (about one agricultural acre in sixteen), the bulk in Scottish sporting estates. The Highlands are uneconomic anyway, and ought in theory to welcome investment. But farmers have always disliked outsiders. They fear competition and resent the tax advantages enjoyed by foreign exiles and pension funds.

But the unspoken fear in the 1970s was that creeping institutional ownership would lead to nationalisation by the back door. (The Old Labour government was seriously considering the nationalisation of life office and pension funds.) This was why the campaign against institutional ownership of agricultural land saw farmers at their most sanctimonious. 'It must be accepted,' intoned the president of the Country Landowners Association, 'that the essence of the difference between the institutional and the private landlord is that the former is accountable to his board, the latter to his conscience, his family and the community.'[48]

The Rise of the Grain Barons

Twenty years later, the claim sounds ironic. 'Modern farming is no longer a way of life,' says a Lincolnshire land agent. 'It is big business. Farms are getting bigger, and the people who run them are both better-advised and better-financed.'[49] One client had recently made £1 million profit in less than three years by buying a 600-acre farm at the bottom of the market and selling at the top. Another had collected profits of over £1 million in each of the previous three years from a mixture of cereal and livestock farming. Farms are certainly shrinking in number and getting bigger in size. At the turn of the century, the average farm was 63 acres; today it is 178 acres. But the acreage managed by a single farmer is often larger than 178 acres, once joint farming agreements are taken into account.

Power is passing inexorably to the biggest farmer: 500 acres is now considered the minimum size for a viable arable farm, and 1,500–2,000 the minimum acreage needed for a decent profit. Institutional owners and rich individuals use farm management companies – Velcourt, Broadoak (a subsidiary of CWS), Sentry Farming – which master the best techniques, cut overheads, strike better deals with buyers and use sophisticated strategies to protect farm incomes against adverse market movements. Tenant farmers, naturally, are finding it hard to compete. A recent episode of *The Archers*, in which the Grundys nearly lost their tenant farm to the control of a professional manager, was fanciful only in the happiness of its conclusion.

Old Macdonald's, with its few acres of cereals and vegetables, and a scatter of pigs, cows and ducks, is struggling. The grain barons, with their thousand-acre farms, are scooping the bulk of the subsidies. Their heavy demand for fertilisers, pesticides, chemicals, tractors and land itself deeply influences the price of all these things. Above all, they are more efficient at managing their costs. Accountants Deloitte & Touche Agriculture in Cambridge reckon the net income of their East Anglian clients averaged £147 an acre at the top of the boom in 1995–96; the top quarter was making £290 an acre. The average client produced a tonne of wheat for £89, but the top quarter are bringing the harvest home at just £79 a tonne.[50] Tomorrow belongs to them.

Marginal producers are finally being driven out of farming. The survivors will be large agricultural businesses serving world markets. As farmers are weaned off welfare, they must respond to the demands of the marketplace or fail. Not all British farmers are capable of this. All of them are convinced they are efficient, and some probably are. But many are not. Effective competitors have to innovate as well as cut costs, and virtually all innovation in British agriculture has come from outside the farm. It was Bird's Eye which introduced farmers to the idea of growing peas, sprouts and beans of uniform shape, colour and size, and freezing them quickly to preserve freshness. Farmers did not ask for less harmful methods of pest control-chemical companies developed them. Today, food processors and supermarket chains are encouraging farmers to meet the standards their increasingly eco-conscious customers demand.

In the recent past, bacon producers, strawberry farmers, apple-growers and potato producers have all suffered at the hands of foreign competition. In each case, they refused to provide the varieties, sizes or shapes the modern consumer wants. British apple farmers preferred to rely on the belief that Cox's are the best apples in the world, so French, Canadian, South African and New Zealand producers filled British shopping trolleys with new, cleverly named alternatives. Upset at what they saw as unpatriotic behaviour by consumers, British apple-growers decked their tractors with posters ('Save Our Orchards: Buy British Apples') and declared 21 October 1997 as National Apple Day.

Decades of subsidisation and protection have produced autarkic thinking of this kind. They have sapped the energy of farmers and blunted their imagination. For sixty years, the taxpayer has assumed market risk on their behalf. The shortcomings of British farming are to some extent a reflection of an era in which taxpayers paid farmers to grow whatever they wanted, but they are also aspects of a deeper human problem. A lot of farmers are not in farming for the money. One of the things they dislike most about institutional buyers of farmland is their emphasis on financial returns.

For many farmers, farming is so much more agreeable a way of life than commuting to a job in the city that it is worth financial sacrifice to enjoy it. The work and the life of a farmer are well-integrated. The house doubles as the office, the land as the garden, and the children work in the business. Modern machinery relieves them of having to employ much labour. Their tax position is favourable. The farm buildings are exempt from local authority taxes; they have full exemption from Inheritance Tax, and roll-over relief from Capital Gains Tax on the sale of business assets. They are free to average their taxable profits over two years. Most agricultural products are zero-rated for VAT. It is never hard to manufacture 'losses' to keep taxable earnings down in the good years.

Most farmers cannot imagine a life outside agriculture. They went to the local school, did a spell at agricultural college, returned to the family farm, and eventually married a local farmer's daughter. They have usually inherited the farm, and selling it would represent sacrificing the family heritage. Being reduced to taking a job would be a massive blow to their independence and prestige. Few farmers believe they have much value outside agriculture anyway. Although most earn relatively little, the farm provides them with all manner of benefits-in-kind. There are few travel-to-work costs. Most farmhouses are spacious and comfortable. Milk, eggs, meat and potatoes cost farmers much less than supermarket shoppers. Unlike an unemployed labourer on an inner city housing estate, it is possible to survive as a farmer without any income at all.

Farming can be a lonely life (it has a notoriously high rate of suicide). But the psychological benefits are immense. It enables natural countrymen and women to pass their lives in the open air, hunting, shooting and fishing as well as ploughing and spraying. But it is not a way of life which encourages progress and change. As an industry, farming is intrinsically hostile to new ideas. The sons and daughters of farmers reproduce endlessly the prejudices and failings of their fathers and mothers: few venture abroad to learn of new ideas or innovative techniques. Farmers seem to adapt only in response to a stimulus from outside. To that extent, the life of the farmer bears a closer resemblance to that of the rest of us than farmers would like to admit.

CHAPTER NINETEEN

MIDDLE ENGLAND

Why are you so disparaging about the middle class? You're middle class. I'm middle class . . . My roots, my background and the way I act is working class, but it would be hypocritical to say I'm anything else than middle class now.

JOHN PRESCOTT, explaining New Labour on Radio 4[1]

The traditional company man with his confidence in annual increments and a growing pension is as extinct as an eighteenth-century clergyman.

ANTHONY SAMPSON[2]

The labour market is the one where the Adam Smith doctrine of Natural Liberty has made least headway and the doctrine of the just reward has lingered longest. Wages above market-clearing rates give corporate executives a quiet life and a reputation among the less thinking as good employers.

SIR SAMUEL BRITTAN[3]

Neither so many inheritors and possessors of land are elsewhere as in England.

SIR JOHN FORTESCUE, Lord Chancellor to Henry VI[4]

In November 1990 friends of John Major were casting around for an idea of what he stood for. They came up with the classless society. 'In the next ten years,' their candidate told the nation, 'we will have to make changes that make the whole of this country a genuinely classless society.' If this glib phrase meant anything at all, it was reaffirmation of the traditional British trust in meritocracy. One of the great myths about the British way of life, put about by mischievous foreigners and their domestic admirers (but shared by almost everybody in Britain) is that it is class-bound.[5] Nearly 800 years have passed since William the Marshal rose from the dust to become regent of England.

Throughout that time, no office was denied to a man by reason of law or blood.

Yet two recent analysts of modern Britain reckon the country 'cannot be understood apart from its class system'.[6] Sampson quotes approvingly the former German chancellor, Helmut Schmidt: 'As long as you maintain that damned class-ridden system of yours, you will never get out of your mess.'[7] Ironically, it was German thinkers (Hegel and Marx) who taught the British to think of the different social ranks as classes condemned by material interest to mutual antagonism. Since the death of socialism the British have reverted to an earlier but truer self-image, where the difference between rich and poor is vast, but the source of social tension is not the gap between top and bottom: it is the distinction between people adjacent to each other.

Who is Middle Class?

The British are obsessed by the earnings of the man at the next desk. Differences in income and wealth, unimportant when the rich man is in his castle and the poor man at his gate, become irksome when the Smiths find that they have fallen behind the Joneses. Oddly, this is largely the consequence of the meritocratic society. Unless they mothered or fathered John Prescott, or are participating in a sociological investigation, virtually everyone in Britain says they are middle class. This reflects a rising standard of living, which is a great engine of upward mobility and solvent of social differences. But it has one major disadvantage. Once breeding, accent, education and dress are subtracted from the social equation, money becomes the rod by which people measure their place in the race for power and status.

It is a race in which there are few losers and even fewer winners. Most of those who take part are also-rans. Between the plutocrats at the top and the inner-city underclass at the bottom obtrudes Middle England – a term which encompasses the great bulk of the British people. Just 126,000 people, or less than half of 1 per cent of all taxpayers, earned more than £100,000 in 1995–6.[8] Perhaps half a million workers, out of a total of twenty-five million, pay no tax at all. Nearly two out of three people at work in Britain are earning between £10,000 and £50,000. Once the Fat Cats and the highly paid City and other professionals are excluded, it is policemen, bank managers and commercial travellers who are at the top of the earnings league. They tend to keep this to themselves.

For them, being middle class means having a good income, a secure job, an annual pay rise, a generous pension *and* the expectation of promotion. This last need is crucial. The prospect of advancement is the defining charac-

TABLE 19.1
Who Are the Middle Classes?

Social Group	Heads of Household %	Social Status	Occupation(s)
A	3	Upper-Middle	Higher managerial, administrative and professional
B	16	Middle	Middle managerial, administrative and professional
C1	26	Lower-Middle	Supervisory, clerical, junior managerial, administrative and professional
C2	26	Skilled-working	Skilled manual workers
D	17	Working	Semi-skilled and unskilled workers
E	13	Residual	State pensioners or widows with no earner, casual and lowest grades of worker

Source: *National Readership Survey*, NRS Ltd, July 1992–July 1993.

teristic of the true bourgeois. As the importance of background fades, people are differentiated by what they buy rather than where they came from. It is an apt measure of the triumph of affluence that their personalities are expressed mainly by their taste in clothes, food, furniture and amusements. This is why pollsters and marketing men abandoned conventional class analysis. Marketing experts divided the population into occupational groups labelled A to E as long ago as the 1950s, and sociologists use a similar system. Most reckon the middle classes extend as far as the C1s, so nearly half the population is now *officially* middle class.

The C2s, regarded by pollsters and political parties as 'crucial' to electoral success, are important because they are the point where Mr Pooter gives way to Alf Garnett. Their tastes and attitudes – not their incomes – exclude C2s from the burgeoning ranks of the middle classes. But any definition of the middle class is arbitrary and narrow. It is probably true to say that all but the inner-city underclass are middle class, aspire to be middle class, or expect their children to be middle class. In the United States, nine tenths of adults describe themselves as middle class. Far from being trapped in 'that damned class-ridden system', rising incomes and a broad spread of the good things of life are propelling the British people towards the same self-image.

There is more money in Britain today, spread more liberally across the population, than at any previous time in history. The national income increased from about £2·5 billion in 1914 to nearly £800 billion in 1997: the

TABLE 19.2
The Ten Best-Paid Ordinary Jobs in 1997 (£)

Men	Per week	Per annum	Women	Per week	Per annum
Police inspector	687	35,724	Systems manager	563	29,276
Systems manager	683	35,516	Personnel manager	498	25,896
Bank manager	681	35,412	Sales manager	498	25,896
Sales manager	673	34,996	Pharmacist	481	25,012
Personnel manager	669	34,788	Bank manager	470	24,440
Fire station officer	596	30,992	Engineer	470	24,440
Production manager	572	29,744	Computer programmer	440	22,880
Pharmacist	543	28,236	Scientist	432	22,464
Scientist	533	27,716	Police officer	428	22,256
Engineer	527	27,404	Production manager	396	20,592
All manual occupations	314	16,328	All manual occupations	201	10,452
All non-manual occupations	484	25,168	All non-manual occupations	318	16,536
All occupations	409	21,268	All occupations	297	15,444

Source: New Earnings Survey, April 1997.

All these figures are *average* earnings for full-time work. They exclude company directors, senior civil servants, doctors, City bankers and insurers, lawyers, university and school teachers, accountants and architects; these are covered in Chapters 15, 16 and 17.

amount of money generated by economic activity has increased sevenfold in real terms. Real disposable incomes, or what people have left to spend after inflation and taxes, have grown at slightly over 2 per cent a year since the last war. Even at this stately pace, living standards double every thirty years or so. As people earn more, they own more. In the 1950s, only one person in three owned a house; one in four a television set; one in twenty a fridge; one in six a washing machine; and one in seven a motor car. Central heating was the preserve of the rich.

In the 1990s, two in three houses are owner-occupied; nine people out of ten have central heating; four in five have a video recorder; nine out of ten a washing machine; three in four have a car. Only one in a hundred does *not* have a fridge.[9] Forty years have passed since Harold Macmillan told a Conservative Party rally: 'Most of our people have never had it so good.' Despite relative economic decline, militant trade unionism, two oil shocks and growing competition from abroad, most British people have carried on having it better since then. When Macmillan spoke, the British people owned assets worth an estimated £66 billion.[10] The Inland Revenue now estimates that they own 'marketable' assets (which can be sold or cashed in) worth £1,955 billion. When the accrued value of occupational pension rights (£743 billion) and the notional value of the state **pension** scheme (£930 billion) are added, total personal wealth rises to £3,628 **billion**.[11] This is nearly £79,000 for every adult aged over sixteen, and £62,000 for every person in the country, and it does not even include consumer durables such as cars, televisions and washing machines.

Consumer durables are not unimportant. Though they depreciate, and have a low secondhand value, they are the means by which most measure their standard of living – and are not a bad proxy. Their price, and the effort involved in their acquisition, have both decreased dramatically, and their quality has improved beyond recognition. A Ford Fiesta is more reliable, less uncomfortable and cheaper to run than a Ford Anglia of thirty years ago. The British people now earn more, own more, and buy more than they have ever done. Yet they seem more miserable than ever.

Why Do People Seem Miserable?

One reason is that most people work to live, rather than live to work. Significant minorities dislike their jobs so much they skive off as often as they can, especially in the public sector. A Cabinet Office study reckons the average public sector employee spends one third more time on sick leave (10–11 days) than his private sector counterpart (7–8 days).[12] The Treasury estimated absenteeism was costing the taxpayer £6 billion a year, and the Confederation of British Industry (CBI) thinks the figure for the private sector is £11 billion.[13] The Trades Union Congress (TUC) says one in seven white-collar workers and one in ten blue-collar workers suffer bullying at work.[14] Significant numbers of people cannot face the day without drink or drugs. The Chief Medical Officer estimates that one in twenty-eight men and one in twelve women are on anti-depressants. Drunk and drugged employees cost business £3 billion a year, according to Alcohol Concern.[15]

Indiscipline in the public sector is so rife that the government has set every Whitehall department a target to reduce absenteeism (by 2003). In the private sector, employers have adopted special disciplinary procedures (sacking the idlest first). But absenteeism is scarcely new: the British preference for idleness and drink (over work and money) faced eighteenth-century industrialists too. Saint Monday, when the first day of the working week was passed in drunken revelry, was celebrated deep into the nineteenth century.

What is new about unhappiness at work is envy. If the standard of living has risen for everyone, it has risen faster for some. Most people think they are asked to do too much for too little, while their colleagues are overpaid and idle. The feeling has some basis in fact. Since Thatcher took office in 1979, the incomes of the richest 10 per cent of the population have risen more than twice as fast as the average. The second tier raised its income 1·75 times, and the fourth 1·25 times as fast. The fifth is brushing the average. It scarcely matters to the middle classes that the bottom half of the working population are altogether worse off. The greatest threat to the happiness and dignity of the middle classes has become a reality: inequality is rising between adjacent classes.

Resentment is increased by ignorance. Although most people working in the same firm have no idea what their colleagues get, they do not doubt it is more than they are getting. People with salaries of £30,000 describe themselves as middle-income, but they are richer than 92 per cent of taxpayers.[16] Many would be surprised to know how well-off they are by comparison with the mass of their countrymen. The reason the surprise is not pleasant is that bank managers are not interested in what waitresses are earning.

In 1998 the general secretary of the National Association of Head Teachers stated his belief that headmasters should receive the same financial reward as senior police officers.[17] At bottom Middle England believes that everybody who looks, sounds and dresses the same – or bears a similar burden of responsibility – ought to be earning roughly the same. This is especially true of the public sector, where the absence of a proper labour market makes comparability more important than price. But it is true of the private sector too. On Acacia Avenue there is more support for equality, and less sympathy for the market economy, than even Old Labour dared to think, and it was certainly one of the reasons New Labour was elected in 1997.

Who Is Not Middle Class?

If most people are not as rich as they feel they ought to be, a substantial minority are genuinely worse-off. Government statistics show that the standard of living of the poorest 10 per cent has *fallen* since 1979. There are reasons to doubt the accuracy of the figures, but not that the gap between rich and poor has widened since the Conservatives came to office in 1979; one study estimated that by 1992 the average income of the top tenth of households was *thirty* times that of the bottom tenth.[18] A 1997 study reckoned that the richest 10 per cent had as much income as the whole of the bottom half of the working population put together.[19]

Incomes from work are not distributed as unevenly as savings and wealth, but there are now large gaps between top earners and what Adonis and Pollard call the 'new servant class'.[20] In 1997, the mythical average man earned £21,268 and his equally mythical wife £15,444. But the averages conceal large differences between the top and the bottom of the earnings league. The gap in earnings between a main board director at a major PLC and a waitress is now about £9,850 a week.[21] One of the many sound-bites which helped to unseat the Conservatives in 1997 was the claim that the differential between the highest earners and the lowest was wider than at any time since the first records of wages and salaries were compiled in 1886.[22]

Some inequality of income is of course essential to economic efficiency. If everybody were paid the same, irrespective of skill, effort or intelligence, nobody would invest time and money in the acquisition of specialist knowledge or skills. Many people would not show up for work at all. It was in the belief that it would increase economic efficiency that the Conservative governments of the 1980s acquiesced in the growing inequality of incomes. To some extent they fostered them deliberately. The trade unions, whose influence over the distribution of income between capital and labour peaked

TABLE 19.3
Distribution of Income in Britain (%)*

Percentiles	Share 1979	Share 1994–5	Change in Real Income†
Top Tenth	21.0	27.0	+68
Second	14.0	16.0	+51
Third	13.0	12.0	+42
Fourth	10.0	10.0	+37
Fifth	10.0	9.0	+33
Sixth	8.0	8.0	+28
Seventh	8.0	6.0	+21
Eighth	6.4	5.7	+12
Ninth	5.6	4.1	+6
Bottom Tenth	4	2.2	−8

Source: Department of Social Security, *Households Below Average Income: A Statistical Analysis 1979–1994–95*, 1997, p. 116, table A1; p. 119, table A3.

* Including self-employed and after housing costs.
† If the self-employed are excluded, the fall in the real income of the bottom tenth falls from 8 per cent to 4 per cent. There is no equally significant change in the other percentiles. The disproportionate number of self-employed among the ranks of the poorest groups is thought to be statistically unreliable.

in the 1970s, were emasculated by six successive acts of Parliament. The employment protection legislation enacted by the Labour government of 1974–79 was weakened. The pay of young people under twenty-one was excluded from the recommendations of the statutory Wages Councils in 1986, and the councils were abolished in 1993.[23]

State support for the unemployed was also reformed. The Re-start programme obliged every unemployed person to attend an interview (sparking the sharp fall in unemployment from its peak in 1986). Unemployment benefit, which was paid indefinitely, was replaced by a time-limited Job Seeker's Allowance. Earnings-related supplements to unemployment and sickness benefit were abolished in 1982, and child additions for unemployment and sickness in 1984. All the main out-of-work benefits were subjected to tax. But the most significant change was made in 1980, when the value of social security benefits and pensions was tied to retail prices rather than to average earnings. This decision, which has shaved an estimated £8 billion a year off the value of the state pension alone, was bound to widen income inequalities. Earnings always rise faster than prices.

These measures forced people to lower their expectations of both work and welfare, and increased the size of the gap between rich and poor. That is why the voters did not care for them. One of the main reasons Labour was elected in May 1997 was the popular consensus that the gap between the rich and the poor had become too large. According to the last British Social Attitudes survey taken before the election, nine people in every ten thought it needed to be narrowed. It did not matter that perception outran reality, or that the inequalities were exaggerated by a reliance on the measurement of cash incomes alone. About £2 in every £3 earned by the poorest households comes from means-tested benefits. They also benefit, as everyone does, from what Harold Wilson used to call 'the social wage': free schools and health care, as well as social security benefits and pensions.

In 1995–6 the 'social wage' was worth £3,950, or nearly half their final income, to the poorest fifth of the population. Despite the penny-pinching rhetoric of the Conservative years, expenditure has not fallen on any of these benefits-in-kind. Between 1979 and 1998, public expenditure on social security (84 per cent), health (75 per cent) and education (27 per cent) increased in real terms. Even in the Blairite Britain of the late 1990s, with its emphasis on the duties of the poor as well as their rights, this still amounts to a massive redistribution of income from rich to poor.[24] In May 1997 Middle England did not vote for further redistribution. It voted against those symptoms of inequality which it found uncongenial: beggars on the streets and burglars in the bedroom. It had little sense of who the poor actually are, or how they live.

It is not surprising. Politicians, civil servants and poverty lobbyists have bombarded one another with literature and statistics on poverty for a century, but the poor remain elusive. Apparently hard information dissolves into charts and tables, and mathematical formulae. It is further debauched by its reduction to the slogans and half-truths which lobbyists sell to politicians. The Dutch economist Jan Pen invented an imaginary, hour-long parade of the entire working population, with the heights of the marchers corresponding to their incomes. Dwarves marched until the last few seconds, when a race of mile-high giants finally made their appearance. It is an ingenious idea, used to good effect by Will Hutton and others to question the present dispensation.[25]

Effective lobbying for political action to relieve poverty has long depended on striking imagery and disturbing statistics of this kind. Charles Booth (author of *Life and Labour of the People in London*) invented the 'poverty line' a century ago in order to claim (with bogus statistical precision) that 30·7 per cent of the population of the capital was poor. Simply by moving the poverty line up or down, or changing the definition of poverty, it is possible to enlarge or reduce the scale of poverty at will. This is why, as the twentieth century has aged, the measure of poverty has mutated: from a basket-of-goods to the state minimum, via the state minimum plus a margin, to the numbers living on benefit. Recently, it has alighted on the numbers living on less than average incomes, or even the numbers excluded from participation in the dominant lifestyle. In 1990 the Breadline Britain list of 'social necessities' denied to the poor included a home computer and a meal at a restaurant once a month.[26]

It is easy to lampoon relative measures of poverty, but they are not superfluous. The expectations of the poor, like those of everybody else, are subject to change. As their neighbours get richer, they do feel poorer. This is why the official measure of poverty by the Department of Social Security (*Households Below Average Income*)[27] remains a relative one. The objection to relative measures of poverty is not that they change, or are invalid. Nor is it that the figures are inaccurate or misleading (though they are).[28] The chief objection is that they treat the poor as an abstract, undifferentiated and static mass of people.

In fact, the poor are not a homogeneous mass. Like everybody else, they are individuals. Like other individuals, their incomes change as their prospects improve or deteriorate. The British Household Panel Survey, which monitors the incomes of thousands of households over several years, has found that only one or two in a hundred of their sample remain in the poorest tenth of the population throughout the period of study. Just one in ten remain in the bottom third throughout.[29] Of course, for some the escape from poverty is temporary. But the Panel study also found that many of the lowest-paid employees were at the beginning of their working lives, and earn more later. Some were still living with their parents, in a household whose total income was well above average.

Taken over an entire working life, the incomes of individuals are more equal than they appear when a snapshot is taken during a particular month or year. 'Lifetime incomes are much more equally distributed than annual incomes,' concluded John Hills, chief author of the influential Rowntree Inquiry Into Income and Wealth. 'Depending on the measure, the inequality observed on an annual basis is reduced by between a third and a half.'[30] He reckoned that the top tenth are six times richer than the bottom tenth in any one year, but only two and half times as rich on a lifetime basis. The people who tend to get trapped in poverty are pensioners, single parents and the long-term sick and disabled. None of them, for obvious reasons, finds it easy to work. This denies them access to the obvious route out of poverty: getting a job.

The Poverty Trap

But even the able-bodied confront a system of taxation and social security riddled with perverse incentives. Social security benefits, being means-tested, do not pay people to work, or educate themselves, or save. They discourage people from taking low-paid jobs by the generosity of the benefits they receive when they do not work, and by the high rate at which means-tested benefits are withdrawn when they do. In 1995 Hermione Parker estimated that 600,000 working families faced effective marginal tax rates of 80–98 per cent. Three years later, the government estimated that 740,000 families faced effective marginal tax rates of 70p in the pound.[31]

Despite a comprehensive reform of social security in 1988, designed to make it worthwhile for everyone to take a job, the Conservative government failed to clear the five perverse incentives Mrs Parker identified in the tax and benefit system: not to work full-time, not to work part-time, not to acquire new skills, not to get married, and not to save. The only positive incentives offered by the Welfare State, she reckoned, were to stay poor or become an invalid. (The number of people on invalidity benefit certainly grew exponentially.) Mrs Parker estimated in 1995 that 10·5 million people of working age and 5·5 million pensioners were 'at risk' from one or more of the traps she identified.[32]

Frank Field has criticised the morals as well as the economics of the system. It rewards people, he says, for being lazy and deceitful.[33] Benefit fraud is running at £4 billion a year, and tax evasion might be six or seven times this figure. This is what enables the poor to spend more than they earn. In 1995 the Institute of Fiscal Studies found that, far from declining in line with official measures of their income, the real expenditure of the poorest tenth of the population actually rose by 14 per cent between 1979 and 1992.[34] Even the official statisticians found some of the people in the poorest categories for *income* were in the highest categories for *expenditure*. Almost all of them also had a fridge or freezer, a video and a car.[35]

The paradox is easily explained. The earnings of the poor are not static. They earn more at some times than others, and have savings to draw on. They also fail to declare all their earnings to the Inland Revenue or the Benefits Agency. The black economy, estimates of whose size range up to £90 billion, is largely their creation. From time to time, governments promise to eliminate it. This would be a mistake. The main reason many jobs are found in the informal economy is that they are not economic in the formal fully-taxed economy. Most people lose somewhere between one third and two fifths of their earnings in taxes and National Insurance contributions, even before employers' contributions are added. Employees naturally look to recoup some of that lost income through higher pay. Once the cost of private pension contributions, sick pay, work space, other non-wage costs and the burden of workplace regulation and tax administration are added to the price of labour, it is not surprising that so many people are out of work.

The chief cause of unemployment is the cost of employing labour on a fully-taxed basis. People are reluctant to believe this. Labour, they say, is not a commodity. Unlike bananas, the quantity which is bought does not fall when the price goes up. Of course, unemployment tends to rise and fall in line with the trade cycle, and governments can enlarge or reduce the amplitude of the cycle. To that extent, unemployment periodically reflects a lack of demand, and governments need to ensure that demand is not deficient. But the persistent rise in the level of unemployment, through each revolution of the trade cycle since the 1970s, has only one plausible explanation: pay and other labour costs have made workers unprofitable to employ. After all, people sell their labour in a market, and the cost of labour accounts for two thirds of the costs of production.*

---

* Once it is recognised that most of the cost of what companies buy, in terms of raw materials, finished goods and services, are the labour costs of others.

True and False Causes of Unemployment

High labour costs prevent jobs being created in the formal economy, either by making investments unprofitable, or diverting them into labour-saving machinery, or shifting the work into the black economy. The recent growth in self-employment, and in temporary and part-time work, are different aspects of the same phenomenon. Self-employed and temporary workers do not attract sick pay, holiday pay, pension contributions or redundancy payments, all of which are statutory obligations on employers in the formal economy. In 1998–9, for example, it cost an employer £1,817 a year less in tax and National Insurance contributions to employ two part-time workers on £6,000 a year than one full-time worker on £12,000 a year.[36]

The high cost of labour is one reason why more women work too. Well over half of all adult women are now 'economically active', as the statisticians call it, and they account for two in five people at work. As the number of working women has risen, the number of working men has fallen. This gradual feminisation of the workforce is expected to continue, until the number of working women overtake the number of working men some time in the twenty-first century. Many women want to work. But others are forced to work, because they are married to men who are unemployed or badly paid or over-taxed. In a minority of cases, the father of their children has abandoned them. There are also more opportunities for women to work.

As the economy has shifted from traditional activities such as manufacturing and construction towards shop and office jobs, the number of jobs which women can do has expanded. Women rarely lay bricks, but they are often bank clerks and lawyers. They are popular with employers, being more flexible and diligent than their male counterparts, and keener to work part-time. But the main reason more women can work is that they are cheaper than men. Women cost less than men in almost every category of work in every region of the country. This is partly because they are less educated, or less experienced, than men. Most of the jobs they do are also unskilled and poorly paid – working at the check-out or in a factory. Men refuse these tasks as 'women's jobs'.

This misplaced dignity has rendered men, and especially those without educational qualifications, vulnerable to competition from more productive machines and cheaper workers. Jobs once done slowly by unskilled men are now done quickly by machines. Assembly-line workers were replaced by robots; compositors by computers; laundry men by washing machines; and cobblers by sewing machines. Any repetitive task can be automated. Bank tellers can be replaced by Automatic Teller Machines (ATMs); telephone

TABLE 19.4
Average Weekly Earnings of Men and Women (£)

| | Manual | | Non-Manual | |
Region	Male	Female	Male	Female
Greater London	351.0	232.6	614.0	402.7
South-east	320.5	215.7	494.1	323.0
East Anglia	320.0	207.2	463.6	313.2
South-west	297.7	189.4	450.3	293.2
West Midlands	311.7	193.1	441.4	290.3
East Midlands	311.0	191.5	429.1	284.4
Yorkshire & Humberside	305.0	189.9	424.6	287.7
North-west	311.2	198.3	455.7	294.3
North-east	306.3	201.2	423.3	286.4
England	315.6	202.4	489.3	321.6
Wales	312.3	196.2	420.2	289.5
Scotland	303.3	193.9	449.8	293.9

Source: New Earnings Survey, April 1997.

operators by computers; postal workers by address-reading machines; order-processing departments by electronic data interchange; secretaries and receptionists by voice-mail. This is one reason why the earnings of the poorest one tenth of the population have fallen, and why unqualified men are out of work often and for longer periods.

Another is that unskilled work – digging coal or working on a production line – is done by Asians and east Europeans in their own countries for a fraction of the wages. Unlike the service sector, where 'women's jobs' are booming, traditional male jobs are concentrated in the one third of the economy open to international competition. One of the first manufacturing businesses to relocate to Asia was the textile industry, and this has turned the remaining textile workers into some of the worst-paid people in Britain. In October 1996 the *Financial Times* found that some Asian clothes manufacturers in Birmingham were paying their staff just £1 an hour.[37] George Bain, chairman of the Low Pay Commission, admitted he was 'shocked at what we found in some places ... We are saying to some employers that you cannot compete by treating your employees as cheap labour in competition with the third world.'[38] But the alternative is to get out of the business.

If manufactured imports are displacing unskilled jobs in Britain (and they probably are) the obvious solution is service industries. Gardening, or looking

TABLE 19.5
The Ten Worst-Paid Jobs in 1997

Men	£ per week	£ per annum	Women	£ per week	£ per annum
Kitchen porter	167.2	8,694	Kitchen porter	150.3	7,816
Bar staff	187.0	9,724	Waitress	152.9	7,951
Launderer/dry cleaner	200.7	10,436	Hairdressing	155.8	8,102
Cleaner	214.1	11,133	Bar staff	157.0	8,164
Shelf-filler	219.4	11,409	Launderer/dry cleaner	167.7	8,720
Sales assistant	222.5	11,570	Cleaner	167.9	8,731
Hospital porter	225.3	11,716	Textile machinist	179.6	9,339
Fishmonger	239.2	12,438	Sales assistant	180.2	9,370
Tyre and exhaust fitter	239.6	12,459	Receptionist	195.4	10,161
Butcher	240.9	12,527	Typist	220.1	11,445

Source: New Earnings Survey, April 1997.

These figures are average earnings for full-time work.

after the elderly, or household cleaning, are three jobs which cannot be exported to Asia or central Europe (or be performed by machines alone). The main obstacle is the lingering belief that service sector jobs are not 'real' jobs. When Nigel Lawson told an International Monetary Fund (IMF) conference that 'we must not be seduced by the wonders of high-tech into overlooking the fact that many of the jobs of the future will be in labour-intensive service industries – not so much low-tech as no-tech,' he was vilified.[39]

Many politicians, and most business people, believe that manufacturing is inherently superior – that making things is the only true source of wealth. Services are neither tangible nor exportable, they say, and cannot raise their productivity. This is fallacious. Services, such as the film and music businesses, can be exported. Though productivity improvements in service industries are harder to measure, they undoubtedly occur. Nor is the distinction between manufacturing and services real. Computers are built in factories, but the people who design them, and write the programmes which run them, work in offices.

At the lower end of the income scale, service jobs can mean waitressing, carrying groceries to the car, and flipping hamburgers. This is why many people find them objectionable. It is what has sparked the (now platitudinous) call for more education and training, or what economists call 'investing in human capital.' Ministers have convinced themselves that the future belongs to skilled and educated labour; it is why Tony Blair describes his policy priorities as 'education, education, education' and Gordon Brown talks of 'equipping everyone with the wherewithal to complete in the modern market place.'[40] The need to invest in human capital lies behind the New Deal welfare-to-work programme, which offers the young unemployed retraining and re-education for success in the fast-moving, high-technology, global marketplace Anthony Giddens told Blair and Brown about.

The New Deal, in other words, is a proletarian version of a university degree or a professional examination.[41] Businessmen, ever-ready to declare 'our people are our greatest asset', and keen to appear socially concerned, have taken the idea to heart. They applaud the promise of public subsidies for their training programmes, on the grounds that workers trained by virtuous firms like theirs would otherwise be poached by firms who do no training at all. A government-funded training industry is now at work in both the public and the private sector, creating courses and auditing the results in ways designed to increase expenditure on education and training. But it is hard to avoid the conclusion that 'education and training' is a slogan rather than a policy. It is not easy to identify the connections between even-higher rates of education and economic growth, or between a large stock of well-educated labour and a higher rate of productivity.

The Rowntree Inquiry into Income and Wealth concluded that only one quarter to one third of the growing inequality between the high-paid and the low-paid was attributable to education and training.[42] Even this was probably a large exaggeration. Education obviously matters. Workers need to be literate, numerate and adaptable. But it is fallacious (and alarmist) to believe that the income and wealth of the next century will belong to a new 'cognitive elite'. Few jobs require a high level of educational attachment, or formal training and re-training. Many young people entering the labour market – especially those with a university degree – already have expectations of fulfilment of work which are bound to be disappointed. It would be wiser to reassure them that, provided they can read, write and add up, they will be able to do all but a fraction of the jobs on offer, and keep abreast of any changes in the knowledge and skills they need to keep doing them.

Is There an Underclass?

However, there is a growing political consensus that the education system is failing a significant minority of people, who seem to be trapped in a culture of worklessness. In 1989 the American sociologist Charles Murray provoked a storm of protest by dubbing them the 'underclass'.[43] He had identified a similar lumpenproletariat of permanently unemployed young men and rootless teenagers in the inner cities of the United States.[44] Certainly, every major city in Britain now has pockets of poverty, often council estates, characterised by unemployment, illegitimacy, single parenthood, low levels of home ownership and a high percentage of young males with time on their hands and an aptitude for crime and violence. Their problems seem to be complicated, though not explained, by racial factors.[45]

The underclass is not always poor. Some of its members often make a good living from crime and the black economy but more seem simply to have lost their appetite for conventional work and lack the ambition to rise in the world. Their neighbours often prey on them, as well as on the better-off areas around them. Many young men in particular are detached from all conventional ideas of family life and self-improvement. In fact, the 'underclass' (if it exists) is not a conventional social or economic problem at all. It is a moral and cultural problem, which cannot be rectified by cash alone.[46] This is certainly the view taken by the New Labour government.

At the 1997 Labour Party conference the prime minister proclaimed that a 'decent society is not based on rights' and that a reformed welfare system must encourage work rather than dependency. This threw into reverse the entire conception of twentieth century welfare. Since modern welfare began, with the introduction of non-contributory pensions in 1908, social security owed nothing to actuarial principle: it was a 'right' which could be claimed by anybody. Yet the dramatic nature of the change announced by the prime minister was scarcely noticed (except by fifty sociologists, who wrote a letter of protest to the *Financial Times*).[47] This was partly because it already seemed familiar. When Labour was in Opposition both Frank Field and the Social Justice Commission (set up by John Smith) emphasised the duties as well as the rights of welfare recipients.

In practice under New Labour, it has given welfare reform a coercive flavour. The new 'social exclusion unit' at Number 10 does not worry about poverty, but truancy, homelessness, and sink council estates. The New Deal welfare-to-work programme, funded from the windfall tax on the privatised utilities, offers all jobless eighteen to twenty-four-year-olds a choice of work or training. But they must take one of the options on offer. By the autumn of 1998, 1,352 young unemployed had lost benefits for refusing to take part.[48] Single mothers with children of school age are now obliged to visit the local Job Centre. £300 million of public money has gone into creating a network of after-school child-care clubs to encourage single parents back to work, and another £200 million into after-school homework clubs. The budget of March 1998 included tax incentives designed to coax the sick and disabled into work. During his tenure as minister for welfare reform at the Department of Social Security Frank Field even advocated a compulsory second pension.

The one concession to Old Labour was the Low Pay Commission, set up to advise on a new national minimum wage. Chaired by George Bain, vice chancellor of Queen's University, Belfast, and a veteran of the Bullock committee on industrial democracy in the 1970s, it eventually recommended a minimum rate of £3.60 an hour for every adult over 21 from April 1999, and a lower rate of £3.20 for people between 18 and 20. These recommendations were accepted, with slight modifications, by the government.[49] The prime minister made no secret of his personal scepticism about the efficacy of a minimum wage. It is certainly an ineffective way of alleviating poverty, since the overwhelming majority of those affected by it are women earning a second income in otherwise well-off households. The poorest of the poor are not in work at all. It might even make them worse-off, by reducing their opportunities to work. Poverty is best tackled by setting a national mimimum income through the social security system, but this would raise the tax burden on Middle England to politically dangerous levels.

The Death of the Job-for-Life?

New Labour was invented to persuade Middle England that it was safe to vote for a left-of-centre government. It succeeded triumphantly, largely by playing on the guilt and fear of the middle classes. The first of the Blairite sound-bites ('tough on crime and tough on the causes of crime') encapsulated both in a single phrase. Asked in 1996 to define New Labour, Peter Mandelson and Roger Liddle placed guilt and fear at the top of their list.

> People feel increasingly insecure. This is caused by rapid economic and technological change throughout the world and a breakdown of society in Britain. The fundamental question for Britain today is whether we can compete successfully in the new global market-place and still live in a decent society. New Labour believes that we can, and that everyone should have a stake in the country's success. It rejects the view that the solution to people's anxiety is to create more insecurity in order to promote competitiveness.[50]

This message played on the middle-class fear of being mugged or burgled by an alienated teenager from the local council estate. But it played with even greater success on another of the threats to the middle class way of life: the impending death of the job-for-life.

By 1996 every middle class family knew of a friend or a friend-of-a-friend who had lost his job and was unable to find a new one. His presence hovered in the suburbs like a poltergeist, threatening the comfortable existence of generations of bank managers and sales directors the length and breadth of the land. When news arrived of a friend reduced to selling soap door-to-door, or water filters to housewives, shame drove out pity. Everywhere, expectations were being disappointed. A degree no longer led to a job. A job no longer matured into a career. Company cars were going back. School fees were unpaid. Neighbours were embarrassed. The insecurity to which the working classes had long since grown accustomed now stalked the bourgeoisie. 'The middle-class of salary earners', as Harold Perkin wrote in 1996, 'are being proletarianised.'[51]

How true was this? The answer is not very. Fear of getting the sack far exceeds its incidence. In 1968, a survey found that 37·7 per cent of men were in their tenth year of employment with the same organisation. In 1993, a follow-up survey found the equivalent figure was 36 per cent. In 1973 the average executive was forty-four, in his fifth year in his present post, and in his thirteenth year with the company. In the mid-1990s, the position was unchanged.[52] The average stay in any job remains as it was in 1979: eight years. Executives who lose their job can expect to find a new one in less than five months. Around half the new jobs created in Britain since the economy emerged from recession in 1993 were professional, managerial and administrative positions. A 1995 study by the Institute of Employment Research at Warwick University found that one million professional and executive jobs were created in the 1980s, and another 600,000 would be created during the 1990s.[53]

Middle-aged, middle-ranking executives have much less reason to be anxious about their future than the young and unskilled or those approaching retirement. The number of part-time jobs certainly increased in the 1980s and 1990s, but not to the extent or for the reasons that people fear. The majority of jobs are still full-time, and the overwhelming majority of part-time jobs are permanent. Surveys also show that nine out of ten part-time workers do not want to work full-time. Likewise, the number of people on temporary contracts has not increased since the 1980s. In short, the executive classes are not being proletarianised. Most of them have kept not only their jobs and pensions but the company car and the free BUPA subscription.

A managerial post in a large corporation is a comfortable way of life. Even the lowliest male middle manager can expect to earn one and a half to two times average earnings. On top of this, actuaries Towers Perrin reckon they share £50 billion in non-salary benefits such as pensions, company cars and paid holidays.[54] Businessmen enjoy faster check-in times, speedier reservations, members' lounges, valet car-parking, and business-class seats. At his or her destination, the average executive finds that the price of the hotel and the gimmicks it offers are designed exclusively to enlarge his or her pleasure at the expense of the shareholders. If he flies regularly, he accumulates enough air miles to take his wife and children free on their annual paid holiday.

The coy phraseology of the executive recruitment columns (45k, plus usual package) conceals a range of valuable benefits-in-kind, like free life assurance and health care. Share options tend to be monopolised by the boardroom, but most companies offer Save As You Earn (SAYE) share schemes to junior executives. By 1997 the Inland Revenue knew of 1,201 employee share schemes covering shares worth £4·2 billion; 1,517 savings-related share option schemes covering shares worth £14·3 billion; and 14,553 profit-related pay schemes covering over 4 million employees.[55] Because the benefits were going to better-paid executives, the government decided to phase out profit-related pay. In any one year, junior executives can expect to attend several major sporting events and theatrical occasions at the expense of the shareholders (or their clients' shareholders). But the most cherished benefit of all is the company car.

This extraordinary creation of the incomes policies of the 1970s has survived every attempt to tax it out of existence; of the 26 million vehicles on the road, about 2.3 million are company cars. There are now virtually no tax advantages to driving a company car, but executives value it more highly than cash (two thirds of companies offer a cash alternative, but only one in ten employees takes it).[56] This is partly because the company car is a palpable sign of rank and status. Broadly speaking, the chairman will drive a Jaguar, the £60,000 a year managing director a BMW, and the middle manager on £40,000 a year will make do with a Ford. Company car drivers do not have to pay for servicing, or ring around for repair estimates when they crash into a wall. They do not have to sell when they want a new car, and nor do they have to insure the car or pay the road tax. In many cases, they do not even pay for the petrol and the car telephone. People who lose the right to a company car are often shocked by the cost of buying, insuring and running their own. Pathetically, personal contract hire has become the fastest-growing sector of the car leasing market. Carless executives are attempting to mimic the benefits of the company car.[57]

Why Middle England Voted Labour

It is precisely because this life is so comfortable and secure, and subsidised so heavily by shareholders, that Middle England fears for the future. Opinion polls consistently record an increased level of anxiety. This is because insecurity is a state of mind, rather than an analysis of what is happening in the labour market. It owes something to the political ambitions of New Labour; a lot to the ambition of managers to cheer up their shareholders by portraying routine redundancy programmes as major cost-cutting exercises; a little to a portentous report on the future of work from the Royal Society for the Arts and Manufactures (*Redefining Work*); and a great deal to the alarmist advertising strategies of the insurance industry ('there could be trouble ahead'). But it owes most to the writings of management gurus such as Charles Handy (*The Empty Raincoat*) and William Bridges (*Jobshift*).

Management books are all the average manager reads. Most build an edifice on a grain of truth, enabling the reader to share the fear and excitement of extrapolation from their own experience. To the extent that the senior managers of the 1990s are less complacent and work harder, and concentrate on cutting costs and making money rather than empire-building, a job with a major employer is less comfortable than it was twenty years ago. But writers like Bridges and Handy have persuaded most junior and middle managers that their working lives will pass in a succession of short-term contracts and cash flow crises. Handy has forecast the replacement of the solid companies and stable hierarchies of the past with 'virtual companies' and 'portfolio careers' since he published *The Age of Unreason* in 1989. Subsequent books have amplified this theme. They depict a world of massive, continual and accelerating change, in which individual managers must adapt to new technologies and new methods of working with bewildering speed, or court corporate and personal disaster. 'Only one half of all paid workers,' Handy writes, 'will be in what, today, we would call "proper" jobs.'[58]

Despite his commendable efforts to portray classical corporate life as the enemy of creativity and innovation, and the portfolio career as a liberating release from the stifling embrace of the status quo, Handy tends to make his readers afraid. Men and women dread freedom, as Bernard Shaw pointed out, because they fear responsibility. This fear of change and responsibility played a large part in the electoral success of New Labour in May 1997. People did not vote New Labour to modernise Britain or embrace change, but to put an end to both.

Is Company Man Extinct?

Of course, change is not entirely imaginary. The shrinkage of the large corporate bureaucracies of the sixties and seventies began in the United States in the early 1980s, and spread across the Atlantic later in that decade. In recent years, a number of household names have cut middle management. In 1994

British Telecom excised five thousand middle and senior managers in a single year, halving its layers of management from twelve to six. Among those to go were thirty-five managing directors earning between £50,000 and £100,000 a year. W. H. Smith sacked six hundred store managers the same year, reducing its management layers from four to two. In 1995 Shell dismissed twelve hundred executives at its head office, put its famous 'downstream' building up for sale and dismantled a thirty five-year-old 'matrix' organisation which was once the blueprint for a thousand corporate organograms. Two years later, it subjected its European operations to similar treatment.

The mergers of the last fifteen years have spawned a second wave of executive redundancies. In 1996, after Lucas Industries merged with Varity Corporation, one hundred and sixty executives were forced to compete for a hundred jobs at the merged enterprise. That same year, the chief executive of ICI announced that he wanted to fill forty top posts in the company with outsiders rather than ICI career men. The idea, he explained, was to 'widen the gene pool'. The phrase, which he may have extracted from a popular exposition of neo-Darwinism by Dr Richard Dawkins, was ironic. In the 1990s, Darwinian ideas are used to justify the dismantling of corporate bureaucracies in much the same spirit that the 'the survival of the fittest' was used to justify the amalgamations which created them in the first place (ICI split itself in two in 1993). Charles Handy was tempted to use a biological metaphor on the front cover of *The Age of Unreason*. 'If you put a frog in water and slowly heat it, the frog will eventually let itself be boiled to death,' he wrote. 'We, too, will not survive if we don't respond to the radical way in which the world is changing.'[59]

Every generation believes it is in crisis, and that its difficulties are unprecedented. At the beginning of the twentieth century, Joseph Chamberlain considered protectionism the only way to save British industry from obliteration by the Americans and the Germans. At the end of the century, cutting out layers of middle management is not the work of macho managers who have read *The Selfish Gene*. It is an overdue reduction of costs. Profit, as the masters of the obvious reiterate, is the difference between revenues and costs. It can be enlarged by cutting costs as well as increasing revenues. This is why the 'endemic elephantiasis' of the great business corporations which Anthony Sampson denounced more than thirty years ago has given way to 'delayering.'[60] Technology has changed too. Just as computers, digital telephone exchanges and voice-mail eliminate the need for receptionists and secretaries, so they eliminate the need for people to manage them.

Modern communications have multiplied the number of people one manager can supervise effectively. Companies used to believe that nobody could cope with more than ten subordinates, encouraging the creation of a caste of middle managers, to be managed in turn by an expanded number of senior managers. Today, companies believe that one manager can handle thirty people. When he was chief executive of BP in the early 1990s, Bob Horton dismissed his middle managers as 'message carriers'. Today, the messages are carried by telephone, fax, and e-mail, making it easier for senior managers to keep in touch with the shop floor without layers of middle managers, and for different parts of the same organisation to keep in touch with each other without the need for dozens of meetings. The middle managers who used to keep the top half of the company in touch with the bottom half are genuinely redundant. Getting rid of them was sensible both for them and for shareholders.

Unfortunately, like American generals, the modern chief executive has developed a vocabulary of sinister euphemisms to cloak defensible decisions. Sacking middle managers is 'down-sizing' or 'de-layering'. Changing the working methods of those who remain is 'process re-engineering'. Increasing their responsibilities is 'individual empowerment'. The new corporate organogram, its boxes and dotted lines sensibly reduced, becomes a 'flat hierarchy', and subcontracting work to outsiders is known as 'out-sourcing'. Shrinkage of the company is 'focusing on core competencies'. The terminology makes the ordinary seem extraordinary.

It is not surprising that managers, even at companies which have not fired anyone at all, have begun to believe that they are the potential victims of vast, impersonal forces over which they have little or no control. In a minority of cases, the caricature comes to life. Senior managers are persuaded that their job is to make economies, not money. They cut gingerly, again and again. Like a botched execution, successive sounds of redundancies are inflicted. The morale of those who keep their jobs, like the survivors of the trenches, is damaged: they are plagued by guilt, and wearied by stress. The flat hierarchy begins to look like a plot to diminish their prospects of promotion. Empowerment feels not like liberation from an overbearing boss, but the stress of additional responsibility. The boardroom ceases to be the goal and becomes the enemy: the seat of the Fat Cats, reaping the rewards of cost-cutting in lavish salaries and share option schemes. Middle managers stop thinking in terms of 'us', and conceive of their career in personal terms. When a better offer comes along, they take it.

Even at companies where managers take 'downsizing' less seriously, the predominant emotion is cynicism rather than fear. There is no better measure of this than the lengthening of the working day. People do not go home on time, partly because markets are more competitive than they were in the sixties or seventies, and partly because there are fewer layers of management, but mainly because nobody is expected to go home on time. At the average

PLC, commitment and performance are measured not by results but by presence at a desk (or absence from it, if the firm has adopted the American practice of 'hot-desking', where there are more people than desks, to ensure executives spend time with customers rather than colleagues). As a result, junior and middle managers are putting into reverse a century-long decline in the length of the working week.

Many clerical staff are already working less than forty hours a week. The government recently implemented a European directive which makes it unlawful for anyone to work more than forty-eight hours a week. But most managers are already working at least fifty hours a week, and often more. The more senior a manager is, the longer he stays at work. Unlike a manual worker, whose overtime raises his standard of living, the business executive reduces the value of his salary. His quality of life declines as well, not least because he spends less time with his family. Executive overtime costs employers nothing, so it is consumed wastefully. Much of the creativity and experience of the company is squandered too, as executives retire, exhausted, in their early fifties. 'We seem,' writes Charles Handy, 'to be cramming the one hundred thousand hours of a traditional lifetime's work into thirty years instead of the traditional 47 years.'[61]

End of the Middle-Class Welfare State

Longer hours, routinely portrayed as the chief symptom of the leanness and the meanness of the modern corporation, are in fact quite the reverse. Only organisations which are rich and fat can afford to consume time and energy so wastefully. The chief architect of the anxiety of the middle classes is not the PLC at all. It is the government, which has spent much of the last twenty years dismantling the middle-class Welfare State without compensating reductions in the burden of personal taxation. The rates of taxation may have fallen, but the overall burden of taxation has gone up, and the generosity of benefits has declined.

Universal benefits collected by the rich as well as the poor – like the old age pension and child benefit – have fallen in value. Inflation, the friend of the heavily indebted *bourgeois* of the 1970s, is scotched. Modern mortgage borrowers are paying real rates of interest of five or six per cent on mortgages whose value may never be diluted by a renewed surge of government-induced inflation. The cuts in income support for mortgage-holders who lost their jobs punched another hole in the middle-class safety net.[62] Getting to work, on crowded roads and rundown railways, is expensive and disagreeable. Education is increasingly burdensome: state schools have declined to the point where some middle-class parents are forgoing holidays and cars to educate their children privately. Most of these go on to university, but they no longer receive tuition fees and a means-tested grant on top. The Conservatives introduced student loans, and New Labour added £1,000 a year in tuition fees. Crime has risen dramatically. Property is no longer secure. More is spent on insurance and burglar alarms.

The divorce rate, high and rising, is dividing incomes and inheritances. 'No, I am not rich,' Peter Hall told the *Daily Telegraph* in 1996. 'I have spent over three decades in the subsidised sector. Then there are a lot of marriages, a lot of children and a lot of alimony . . . I live comfortably, but if I stopped working tomorrow, it would be quite serious. I have some pensions, but I have been a working, underpaid director all my life.'[63] Families are economic as well as social units. As they disintegrate, they spread earnings and wealth across more wives, husbands and children. The average cost of divorce is about £10,000. The Child Support Agency, set up in 1993 to pursue errant fathers (most divorced) unwilling or unable to support their children financially, collected £400 million of maintenance in 1996–7.[64] This is another measure of the tax divorce levies on family life. But the costs of the crumbling family are not restricted to alimony. Divorce, single parenthood and the social problems which flow from them are one of the main causes of the steep rise in public expenditure on health, social security and law and order.

This has increased the burden of tax borne by married middle-class couples with children, best measured by the shrinkage in the value of the personal tax allowance. In 1950 a married man with children on average earnings paid no income tax at all. In 1998–9 he paid income tax after earning less than one third of average earnings. Today, married couples with children are losing more of their earnings to income tax, national insurance contributions, VAT and excise duties than they were in the 1970s.

Oddly, the burden imposed on single people and married couples without children has fallen in the same period. Most of the tax privileges which sustained the middle-class families of the last generation are truncated or gone. Tax relief on life assurance went in 1984. Taxation of company cars has trebled. The value of Mortgage interest relief, which used to be granted on the full amount of the loan at the highest rate of tax was eroded and finally abolished from April 2000. The value of mortgage interest relief peaked at £9·2 billion in 1990–1, and had fallen in real terms to less than £2·5 billion by 1996–7.[65] In its first two budgets, New Labour quintupled the stamp duty payable on houses worth more than £250,000, and increased it seven-fold on those worth more than £500,000.

It also continued the Conservative assault on the last of the great middle-class tax shelters: pension funds. New rules were introduced in 1986 to limit the surpluses which can accumulate, tax-free, in pension funds; tax-free lump sum contributions, and fast accrual pension schemes, were capped in 1987, as was tax relief for pension contributions. The tax-free dividend income received by pension funds was trimmed in 1993, and abolished in 1997. New Labour has also replaced Tax-Exempt Savings Accounts (TESSAs) and Personal Equity Plans (PEPs) with less generous Individual Savings Accounts (ISAs).[66]

Old Labour replaced child tax allowances with child benefit in 1978. Its value has not kept pace with inflation, and it was frozen between 1987 and 1990. New Labour pondered taxing it, and funded an increase in its value by reducing and then abolishing the married couple's allowance. This had already withered under the Conservatives ('a bit of an anomaly,' as Kenneth Clarke called it). In its last years, the married couple's allowance was worth less than £300 a year. The tax system has now shifted decisively from the support of marriage to the support of children. This finds its chief expression in subsidies for single parents who work. One study found that between 1980 and 1992 lone parents at every income level were consistently better-off, after taxes and benefits, than married couples with children.[67]

Tax relief for workplace nurseries was introduced in 1990. In 1993, a £28 per week child-care allowance was introduced for single working mothers. The New Labour government has added tax breaks and child-care and home-work clubs, and has proposed a national Family and Parenting Institute to teach parents how to bring up children. The government encountered its first serious parliamentary difficulties in the autumn of 1997 when it implemented a plan to ensure that the benefits claimed by new single parents were no more generous than those paid to couples. But every other measure it has taken is designed to support children, whether their parents are married, unmarried, divorced or bereaved. A cheap method of doing this (the family) is giving way to an expensive one (the state).

This has increased the burden of taxation on ordinary families, forcing more women to work. But a standard of living based on two incomes is vulnerable to child-bearing. Some women postpone it, fearful of jeopardising their job or career and the income it brings in. But children cannot be postponed indefinitely, and many women struggle to balance the competing demands of work, children and parents. Some give up, their ambitions thwarted by employers uninterested in adapting their working methods to an economy in which half the workforce is female. There is less time for children; private life becomes cramped and disagreeable; meals are rushed; exercise is not taken; and fun is reduced to watching a video on Saturday nights.

In the face of these repeated assaults on their way of life and standard of living, the passivity of the middle classes is striking. In the 1998 budget, the government raised the threshold for National Insurance contributions, paying for it by raising the employers' contribution for the higher-paid. This was one of the tax proposals which was supposed to have cost Old Labour the 1992 general election. Six years later, it was introduced without a murmur of protest. But the New Labour government, unlike its blundering Conservative predecessor, is a pickpocket rather than a highwayman. In 1984, middle-class antagonism forced Nigel Lawson to abandon a comprehensive reform of the taxation of pension funds, and Keith Joseph was forced to ditch a plan to introduce tuition fees for undergraduates. New Labour has accomplished both without serious difficulty, though it has yet to be as bold on another issue which helped to sink the Conservatives: long-term care for the elderly.

In September 1997, the government appointed a Royal Commission under Professor Sir Stewart Sutherland to investigate the subject. Two years earlier, the Major government had provoked an outcry when it tried to force the middle classes to pay for their old age. For decades, they had assumed that their tax and National Insurance contributions entitled them to free long-term care, either in an NHS hospital bed or in a local authority or private nursing home subsidised by the DSS. In an ageing population, that promise had become steadily less affordable, and in 1995 the Department of Social Security (DSS) decreed that any pensioner in long-term care with an empty house (or other assets worth more than £8,000) would not be entitled to help from the taxpayer.

It was estimated that up to 40,000 middle-class people a year would have to sell their houses to pay for nursing and residential care, threatening children with the loss of their inheritance. *This* was not why the middle classes voted Conservative in 1992: John Major had told the party faithful of his vision of 'wealth cascading down the generations'. When it looked as if it would cascade instead into the maws of proprietors of private nursing homes, the government had to change the rules. It agreed to disregard up to £10,000 of assets for the purposes of the means test, and even more if insurance policies were taken out against the costs of long-term geriatric care. Polls continue to show that, irrespective of means, everyone believes the taxpayer should pay for old age.[68]

Positive and Negative Equity

Housing and inheritance, though popular targets of tax reformers, are the forms of wealth closest to the heart of the middle classes. The family home is the most valuable asset most people possess. Their natural expectation is that it, and any savings accumulated over a working life, should pass, undiminished and unencumbered, to their children. The bulk of the increase in the wealth of the middle classes since the war is attributable to the steady inflation of house prices. The prospect of spending that wealth instead of passing it on was unsettling, which was why the Conservative government raised the threshold for inheritance tax dramatically in its last years in office,[69] taking all but the most lavish houses beyond the reach of the Inland Revenue.

A house is the key to the financial psychology of Middle England. Just as the euphoria of the 1980s stemmed largely from rising house prices, so the gloom of the early 1990s reflected their decline. Between 1990 and 1994 house prices did not just stop rising; they fell. Some houses in the south-east lost as much as one fifth to one third of their value. Thousands of social aspirants, far from making a capital gain, ended up with a capital loss. If anything hung more heavily over suburban dining tables in the early 1990s than 'downsizing', it was 'negative equity'. Although the pain was concentrated at the lower end of the housing market – in the studios, one-bedroom flats and former council houses of the lowest ranks of the middle classes – all who owned their house felt threatened by sluggish sales, rising interest rates and falling prices. Everyone felt less rich.

It was an odd feeling. For most people, buying a house is synonymous with getting into debt. The asset on one side of the balance sheet is matched by a mortgage liability on the other. The mechanism which translates the assumption of a massive long-term liability into the principal means of making people feel richer is rising house prices, and especially house prices which are rising faster than other assets. Between 1969 and 1989, the value of residential housing increased at a compound rate of 17·8 per cent a year. This was faster than earnings (10·1 per cent) and retail prices (9·9 per cent) and faster than the value of financial assets such as stocks and shares (12·7 per cent): for twenty years the average house increased its earnings faster than the average price, person or share.

Since the cost of borrowing could be offset against income tax, and the capital gains were free of tax, housing enjoyed uniquely favourable treatment by the Inland Revenue. It was this combination of handsome returns and tax efficiency which persuaded people to devote an ever-increasing proportion of their earnings to house purchase. The average house cost three times an average income at the beginning of the 1980s. By the end of that decade, it cost four and a half times an average income. When the housing boom peaked in 1989, the average mortgage bill accounted for between two fifths and one half of gross earnings – a large proportion of household income. But it made sense; in effect, it cost nothing to service the borrowing.

Rising house prices persuade people that they can afford other assets – motor cars, furniture, video recorders, CD players, camcorders and computers all seem more affordable when the house is earning more than its owner. The easy availability of credit tempted many owner-occupiers to treat their houses not as a form of shelter but as a store of wealth which they could raid at will. Rising house prices fuelled a fivefold increase in unsecured personal borrowing during the 1980s, to over £50 billion at the end of the decade. The savings ratio (personal savings as a proportion of personal disposable income) fell steeply. From 13·4 per cent in 1980, it had shrunk to 5·6 per cent by 1988.[70]

Much of the debt was unsecured borrowing from banks, building societies, credit card issuers and major retailers. It was short-term and expensive by comparison with a mortgage, but householders soon recognised that mortgages were relatively cheap and tax-efficient. During the 1980s, they turned the use of mortgage finance for consumer spending into an art form. First-time buyers borrowed more than they needed to buy the house, and spent the rest on carpets and curtains. Established owner-occupiers remortgaged their houses and spent the money on a new car and a holiday. Elderly homeowners, who had paid off their mortgage, took out new ones on which the interest would be rolled up and subtracted from the value of the estate on their death.

As early as 1982 the Bank of England warned that 'a substantial part of mortgage lending does not ultimately finance new or improved housing but is available for the acquisition of other assets or other spending.'[71] This process, known to economists as 'equity withdrawal', enabled people to turn their most valuable asset into ready cash. The Bank of England has estimated that equity withdrawal increased twentyfold, from £1·3 billion in 1980 to £24·5 billion in 1988. Between 1987 and 1989 consumers borrowed an estimated £60 billion more on mortgage than they invested in housing, and most of this seeped into consumer spending on imported goods. It took three years of double-digit base rates, two years of negative economic growth, three years of rising unemployment, and five years of falling house prices to halt the boom, arrest inflation, and persuade people to save again.

House prices remain the biggest single influence over the national economy. Their steadfast refusal to rise during the early 1990s spawned a host of quack remedies to stimulate the housing market as the best way of resuscitating the economy: higher ceilings on mortgage interest relief, tax deductibility for capital losses on houses, the abolition of stamp duty, and subsidies for first-time buyers. Their advocates had a point. Two in three householders have bought their house, and its value looms large in their personal balance sheet. When it rises or falls, it is bound to affect their confidence. The level of owner-occupation in Britain, though unexceptional by Anglo-Saxon standards and modest by comparison with some Latin ones, has become too influential.

Owner-occupation: The Limits to Growth

With two thirds of households owner-occupied, the economic consequences of home ownership are increasingly ambiguous. House-price booms spawn periodic credit binges, amplifying the effects of the normal trade cycle. Reliance on variable rather than fixed-rate mortgages has exacerbated booms and busts still further. The excessive returns available in the housing market have diverted savings from productive investment in small private businesses and listed stocks and shares into bricks and mortar or even consumption.[72] Rising house prices redistribute resources arbitrarily, from productive capital and labour to *rentiers*, without increasing the national wealth. When the boom ends, winners increase spending on consumer goods, school fees and second homes, while the losers grapple with mortgage arrears, repossession or negative equity. Many have to be rescued by the DSS, pushing up public expenditure and taxation. Others press for pay increases to compensate, stoking inflation. Excessive levels of owner-occupation also inhibit the mobility of labour. Houses are slow and costly to sell. The wide disparities in prices between different parts of the country make it impossible for householders to move from a depressed area to a prosperous one without a pay rise, increasing either unemployment or wage inflation.

This greater propensity to inflation and inefficiency saddles the entire economy with interest rates higher than they need to be. Throughout the 1980s, interest rates in Britain were consistently above the average for the other developed countries. Higher rates of interest hurt everyone. Between 1982 and 1989 the *real* cost of borrowing for house purchase (mortgage rate less inflation) fell below 5 per cent only once, and averaged 7 per cent. This was close to the rise in earnings, which averaged increases of 7·5 per cent throughout the 1980s. The main reason mortgage-holders were prepared to pay was their belief that surging house prices would eclipse the cost of borrowing. People who did not buy their own house were thought to be missing out.

This was a reasonable assumption. Apart from dips in the mid-1970s and early 1980s, house prices had risen continuously since the 1930s. In only nine of thirty-five years since the end of wartime controls in 1954 to the peak of the housing boom in 1989 did inflation outstrip house prices. They were rising strongly when the Conservatives came to power in 1979 and continued to rise, at least in nominal terms, throughout the recession of 1980–1. The price of the average house in Britain rose from less than £20,000 in 1979 to over £60,000, a compound increase of about 12 per cent a year. To keep up, it was necessary to borrow money. There was no shortage of it. In the 1980s, for the first time; the clearing banks competed with the building societies for mortgage business, and the building societies' interest rate cartel disintegrated under the pressure. Traditionally, building societies relied on retail deposits to fund their mortgage lending. The cartel, by obliging societies to offer similar rates of interest to depositors and borrowers, prevented one lender poaching deposits from another.[73] The practical effect was to restrict the ability of the societies to lend. Mortgage credit was rationed, by what was known as the 'queue'.

Until the 1980s, the queue obliged house-buyers to save with a building society for years to accumulate a deposit. The size of an advance was limited to a low multiple of gross earnings (typically two and a half to three times gross salary). But when the cartel broke up and the building societies won the right to borrow in the capital markets, mortgages were no longer rationed. From 1985 onwards, they were sold by price alone. The need for a deposit disappeared. The 100 per cent mortgage was born, and a flood of easy money fuelled the rise in house prices. These were further underpinned by layers of tax relief. Until 1991, interest on the first £30,000 of a mortgage was relieved at the highest rate of income tax. Until 1988 this relief attached to the individual rather than the property, allowing sharers to secure substantial tax relief on the purchase of a house. Any profits from its sale were exempt from capital gains tax. (They still are.) Even the Business Expansion Scheme (BES), in its final guise, was diverted into tax breaks for investors in residential accommodation.

In 1980 the Conservative government gave council tenants the right to buy their home at a steep discount from its market value. Over 1·5 million former council tenants have bought since 1979.[74] This further unbalanced a housing market suffering from a severe mismatch of demand and supply. The baby boomers of the 1960s entered the labour market in the 1980s, and wanted to live away from home. But their choice was limited. They could join the waiting list for a council house, or buy a place of their own. Most chose to buy. One of the most extraordinary facts about the British housing market is the high level of owner–occupation among people under twenty-five. Although buying a house rarely suits the fluctuating incomes and peripatetic working lives of the young, many had no choice. In theory, housing associations, private landlords and private construction companies were meant to increase the supply of private housing for sale and rent, but this did not happen.

After eighty years of rent controls and generous security of tenure for leaseholders, private rented housing has shrunk to less than one tenth of the total housing stock. Forty years ago it was half, and a century ago it was nine tenths. There is, of course, a private rented sector, and some landlords have

TABLE 19.6
House prices in the United Kingdom by region, 1979–1998

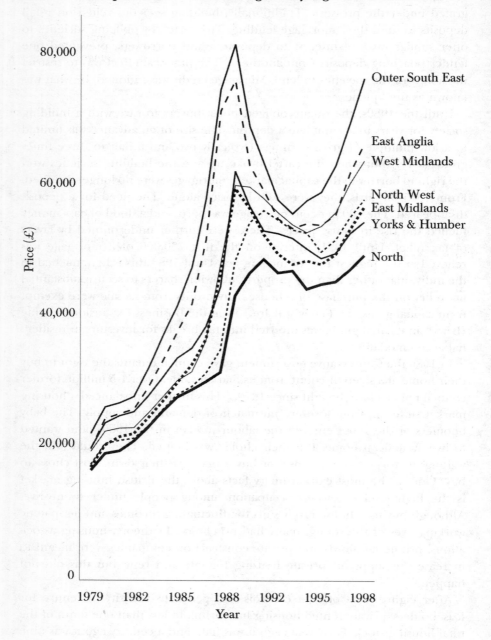

TABLE 19.6 *cont.*

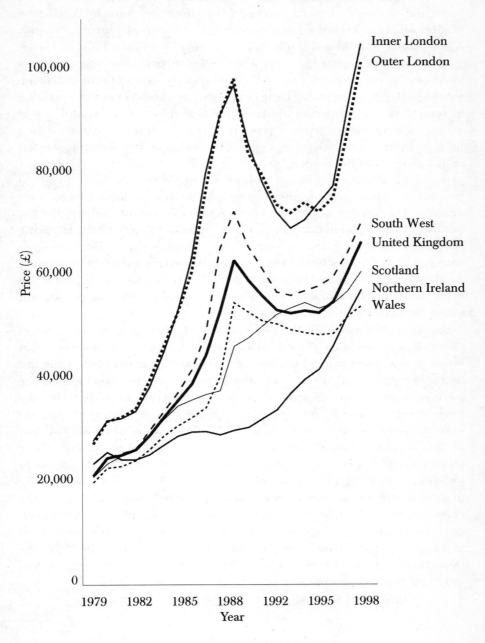

Source: Nationwide Building Society.

grown rich from it. But the sector is not only small; it is unpopular. When the Conservatives tried to revive it by restricting tenants' rights and freeing rents, they met with limited success. Other measures were taken. House-holders who rent a room are given the first £4,250 of rental income tax free. A new class of institutional landlord, the Housing Investment Trust, was given exemption from capital gains tax and invited to pay corporation tax at a lower rate. But the illiquidity of residential property means institutional inves-tors will never become enthusiastic landlords. Even companies that specialise in renting private properties dislike its political risks and the complexity of managing thousands of separate properties. After a series of measures dating back eighteen years, private rented accommodation still accounts for less than one tenth of the market.[75]

But if there are not enough houses to rent, there are not enough to buy either. House-builders and housing associations cannot keep pace with demand. The number of people under pensionable age living alone, and the number of single-parent families, have trebled since the early 1960s. An ageing population has multiplied the number of pensioners living alone to more than one in seven households. The government has estimated that the country needs another 4·4 million homes by the year 2016 because more people are living alone. But the supply of new houses is limited by planning constraints, which have reduced the availability of land.

Between 1968 and 1988 the price of houses rose twice as fast as prices generally, but the price of land for residential housing rose twice as fast as house prices. Land prices for housing have more than doubled in the last twenty-five years, and the cost of land now accounts for two fifths of the price of a new house. Successive Conservative secretaries of state for the Environment imposed ever tighter restrictions on the release of land for house-building, partly in response to the Nimbyism (not-in-my-backyardism) of their supporters but also as a sop to the environmental movement, whose influence was felt by the new government in 1998, when it was forced to withdraw plans to relax Green Belt restrictions. The government is now aiming to increase the proportion of new houses built on 'brownfield' sites in the cities, but the lack of building land remains acute, particularly in the over-crowded south-east of England. In the 1980s, the price of a hectare of land in Greater London rose from £390,000 to over £3 million. In 1992, the Department of the Environment estimated that planning controls had increased house prices in the south-east by 35–40 per cent.

From Bricks and Mortar to Stocks and Shares

By 1997, the shortage of land and economic recovery in London and the south-east was pushing house prices up again. Gazumping was back, prompting the government to launch an investigation into what Hilary Armstrong, the housing minister, called 'the root causes of delays and other problems which cause distress and misery to home buyers and sellers'.[76] It will focus on discouraging gazumping and simplifying valuation, surveying and conveyancing procedures. One idea is to make sellers bear the costs of survey fees. Another is to make buyers and sellers deposit an equivalent sum on agreeing a sale. Either might reduce the risk of gazumping, and so reduce the stress and unpleasantness of buying a house. But all reforms underestimate the British addiction to home ownership.

To some extent, addiction is unavoidable: the rented sector is too small to accommodate those who want to live on their own. But, like the company car, the owner-occupied house also seems immune to every attempt to tax it out of existence. Mortgage interest relief was finally abolished in the 1999 budget, but its disappearance is unlikely to disturb the British appetite for property.[77] The idea of owning property is too deeply rooted in the English psyche (though not, perhaps, in the British) to be swayed by purely financial considerations. For centuries, the English people have expressed themselves primarily through the ownership of land and buildings. It is now clear that even in the Middle Ages, when it was long assumed that virtually every inch of territory was owned by a feudal aristocracy, ordinary Englishmen and women owned, bought and sold land independently of any obligations they owed to a feudal landlord.[78]

When Sir Edward Coke (1552–1634), lord chief justice, declared that 'an Englishman's home is his castle' he was championing the rights of the individual under the Common Law against the arbitrary rule of the Stuarts. Important civic privileges, such as jury service and the vote, depended on the ownership of property (until 1918 anyone who had received poor relief within the previous year was not eligible to vote). The Act of 1430 which restricted the franchise to owners of freeholds worth at least 40 shillings remained in force until the Reform Act of 1832. After the Reform Act extended the franchise to new classes of householder, freehold land societies were formed with the objective of obtaining land and houses so that people could acquire the vote. Some of them – for example, the Abbey National – later developed into building societies. The property qualification was not abolished until the Reform Act of 1884.

Politically, it was thought that only those with a literal stake in the country could be trusted: those in possession only of money could flee abroad. As egalitarian democracy threatened to overwhelm property in the final quarter of the nineteenth century, the chosen antidote was to spread ownership. When Anthony Eden committed the Conservative Party in October 1946 to the creation of a 'nation-wide property-owning democracy', he was in a Tory tradition which stretched back to the time of Lord Salisbury.[79] Thatcher (who gave council house tenants the right to buy their home) and Major (who gave leaseholders the right to buy their freehold) merely continued it. But owner-occupation has reached its natural limits.

'The problem of the future,' said one late-Victorian thinker, 'is the solution of this difficulty: How is the individualisation of property to be brought about?'[80] In terms of home ownership, that difficulty is solved. The challenge facing the property-owning democracy now is to tilt the balance of ownership from real estate to financial assets. The British people own sizeable financial assets already, and the tax system is encouraging them to acquire more. In the personal sector as a whole, the value of cash deposits, life assurance policies, pension plans, unit trusts and stocks and shares (56 per cent of the overall balance sheet) now far exceeds the value of residential housing (32 per cent). Yet their saving and expenditure decisions are still more likely to be influenced by the price of their house than the price of their financial assets.

This is because, unlike their house, the bulk of their financial assets are institutionalised, abstract and remote. Most people can remember what they have in the bank or the building society, but few, even among the most sophisticated, know anything about the most valuable financial asset they possess: their pension fund. If Charles Handy is halfway right, people can no longer rely on the company, or the trade union, or the Welfare State, to underwrite their standard of living. They must learn to save, and to live off their savings. The future of ownership lies in stocks and shares, not bricks and mortar.

PART FOUR

BUSINESS

CHAPTER TWENTY

TRIUMPH OF THE PLC

If you come to grief, and creditors are craving,
(For nothing that is planned by mortal hand
Is certain in this Vale of Sorrow – saving
That one's Liability is Limited) –
Do you suppose that signifies Perdition?
If so you're a monetary dunce –
You merely file a Winding-Up Petition
And start another company at once!
Though a Rothschild you may be
In your own capacity
As a company you've come to utter sorrow –
But the Liquidators say,
'Never mind – you needn't pay,'
So you start another company tomorrow!

W. S. GILBERT[1]

Corporations have neither bodies to be punished, nor souls to be condemned, they therefore do as they like.

EDWARD, BARON THURLOW, Lord Chancellor (1731–1806)[2]

Shareholders are not, in the eyes of the law, part owners of the undertaking. The undertaking is something different from the totality of its shareholders.

LORD JUSTICE EVERSHED, 1947[3]

On 7 October 1893 a new musical by Gilbert and Sullivan was performed at the Savoy. Entitled *Utopia Limited, or The Flowers of Progress*, it told of a distant tropical kingdom whose people were so impressed by all things British that they became 'a Company Limited with Liability restricted to the amount of his declared Capital!' A century later, a nation composed entirely of limited liability companies seems closer to reality than satire. The company, run by insiders called managers but owned by outsiders called shareholders, is now the dominant form of business organisation in Britain. The domain of the company is now so extensive that it is virtually the only form of social and economic organisation which stands between the family and the state.

Most people get money by working for a company. They spend most of it in pubs and shops owned by other companies. If they manage to save, they generally entrust the money to corporate banks and insurers. These companies re-invest the savings by lending money to still more companies, or buying shares in them (perhaps even in the company which paid the saver his wages in the first place). Consumers now expect companies to assume social as well as economic responsibilities, and companies make much of their commitment to what they call 'good corporate citizenship'.[4] Part of the nineteenth century and almost the whole of the twentieth century were absorbed by the struggle between capital and labour. By the end of the 1980s, capital had won. The public limited company (PLC) dominates the life of the nation, in public and in private.

It is natural for a party as well attuned to the times as New Labour to make use of this. If the Conservative governments of the 1980s had a natural sympathy for business, the new government has made a fetish of it. In Opposition, it reorganised its party management on business lines, and switched its sources of funding from trade unions to companies, consumers and Fat Cats. In 1996, the shadow Cabinet attended management training sessions at an Oxford business school. In government, Blair has styled himself as the chief executive of Great Britain PLC, and treats his ministers like managing directors. He has recruited dozens of businessmen to serve in government, on committees and in various diplomatic and commercial ventures at home and abroad.[5] The administration is alive with image-makers charged with updating the British brand. The prime minister turned the opening of a Commonwealth conference into a movie première, arranged the furniture and the lunch for an Anglo-French summit at Canary Wharf, and approved the erection at Horse Guards of Rubens-like tents filled with British-designed gadgets and modern art. At Number 10, he has entertained designers, thespians, rock stars and celebrity chefs. His foreign secretary, Robin Cook, has appointed a panel of designers, artists and media babes to sell the 'new Britain' abroad.

The main purpose of the inordinately expensive Millennium Dome is to persuade foreign consumers that Britain is not a hidebound historical cul-de-sac but a creative, design-conscious and technologically go-ahead entrepôt for the ideas (and money and jobs) of the borderless world. But business is a partner as well as a model for New Labour. Companies were recruited to provide places for unemployed youths on the welfare-to-work programme, with bounty payments of £750 a head plus a subsidy of £60 a week (funded, ironically, by a windfall tax on privatised companies). They were given the added incentive of a mention in government advertising. The education secretary, David Blunkett, has created twenty-five business-subsidised 'education action zones', where private companies such as Nord Anglia, Capita Managed Services and the Centre for British Teachers can bid to run failing state schools. The action zones are also breeding grounds for a new class of business-funded specialist schools.[6] The prime minister has touched businessmen for donations to literacy summer schools and invited companies to provide libraries for employees and their children.[7] He has also appointed a Better Regulation Taskforce to reduce the regulatory burden on business and improve the efficiency of their dealings with the state, and set a target that a quarter of all transactions with government should be in electronic form within five years. He added, in a near-parody of the customer-conscious chief executive, that he wants government services to be available twenty-four hours a day, seven days a week, fifty-two weeks of the year.[8]

But the commercialisation of public affairs is not as new as it is made to seem. As trade secretary in the last Conservative government, Michael Heseltine styled himself as national chief executive (relegating John Major to chairman). He even called his 1995 White Paper on competitiveness 'the annual report of Britain plc'. An ostentatiously business-friendly government, however, grasps the spirit of the age. All alternative forms of ownership are prostrate before the PLC. Barely one person in ten owns their own labour (in the sense that they work for themselves). Most privately owned businesses no longer look to posterity but search for a sale as a necessary 'exit' from the anxiety and risks of ownership. Lawyers and accountants are preparing PLC-style accounts and pondering whether to turn themselves into companies with limited liability, and the great mutual societies, where savers and borrowers shared ownership, are fast disappearing. Building societies and friendly societies are free to incorporate, and many have. Even charities now ape the methods and manners of corporate life.

The state no longer contests the primacy of the PLC. Dumping the Old Labour promise of common ownership of the means of production marked the arrival of New Labour. All the great nationalised industries are now back in private hands; one hundred and forty separate parts of government have become PLC-style executive agencies. The triumph of the PLC over the state is as much a cultural phenomenon as a real one. Across the rump of the public sector, auditors, management consultants and business executives are briefing public servants on corporate accounting and professional management. Government departments are drawing up balance sheets for the first time. There is no part of Britain, either public or private, where the PLC is not the actual or ideal form of ownership.

What People Thought of PLCs

Yet the limited liability company feels least like traditional property. The true owners of a company – the shareholders – rarely work in it or control it, and most do not own their shares directly. They have entrusted their savings to giant insurance companies and pension funds, which employ fund managers to decide which companies to buy or sell. The companies are controlled on a daily basis by salaried managers who operate at two removes from the shareholders. This remoteness enables them to become Fat Cats, by treating the shareholders' money as if it were their own. Ultimately, the costs of Fat Cattery are borne by the shareholders, who can enforce their rights only through an elaborate structure of legal relationships which try to align the interests of managers and owners.

A right of property devised by lawyers, according to rules prescribed by acts of Parliament, is a distant, metaphysical thing. The bankruptcy of a fund manager, let alone a company, is often enough to rob people of everything they own. Yet neither managers nor fund managers feel the press of owners directly, making it easier for both to take the property of others guiltlessly and unnoticed. Owners know that they are waxing at their expense, but trust them to multiply wealth faster than they devour it. They usually do. Where they do not, it is too expensive and time-consuming for an owner to do more than sell his rights. It is not surprising that owning shares in a company, particularly through a fund manager, does not feel at all like ownership, and ownership through the great savings institutions is not true ownership at all. As the Jesuit economist Father Harbrecht dubbed it forty years ago, it is 'para-proprietorship'.[9]

The PLC is one half of a divorce between the ownership and the control of property which is testing the legitimacy and efficiency of capitalism precisely when it seems more secure than it has for one hundred years. The other half, the institutional investor, has generated an avalanche of literature and controversy about its systematic hostility or friendliness to investment and growth.[10] Even boardroom Fat Cats have become subjects of study by committees.[11] But the humble PLC, however, awaits its Boswell. 'We are', wrote a Nobel Prize-winning economist, 'appallingly ignorant about the forces which determine the organisation of industry.'[12] If it was of interest to classical economists at all, the PLC was studied as the enemy of competition, to be kept in check by vigilant government. Its behaviour could be influenced by changes in taxation or regulation, but was understood only as an urge to monopoly and the formation of price-fixing cartels.

In the sixties and seventies, the American economist J. K. Galbraith published several popular expositions of the monopolistic urges of the modern PLC. By the end of the 1970s, his clarity and wit had turned the private business corporation (especially of the American variety) into an object of near-universal fear and loathing. In *The New Industrial State*, he argued that private business corporations had attenuated competition to such an extent that their main interest was in expanding their empires rather than markets or profits. The standard text book of sociology courses assured its readers that 'a small number of giant corporations hold the keys of the economy'.[13]

In hindsight, the arguments of Galbraith and others were overstatements, based on a view of the company as a seeker of monopolistic power. Galbraith believed that once a company had reached a certain size it could not go bankrupt, but IBM, the Big Blue of blue chips, came perilously close to it in the 1990s. Philips, seen by Galbraith as the very model of the price-administering oligopolist in *The Age of Uncertainty*, has yet to recover completely from the onslaught of Japanese competition in the 1980s. British Airways may have sunk Freddie Laker, but they have yet to destroy Virgin Atlantic, even in the most highly cartelised industry of all.[14] There is a lot more competition about than Galbraith predicted.

What People Now Think of PLCs

This is why governments now fret about 'competitiveness,' not monopoly. Great Britain PLC, it is said, is uncompetitive against Europe SA or the United States Inc. Ministers are fond of this sort of language, finding it useful to blame declining prosperity on enemies abroad and to harness patriotic instincts to unpalatable policies. Businessmen find the idea of Great Britain PLC comprehensible, and a useful cover for pleas for protection or subsidy. But national competitiveness is a spectral challenge: it is companies, not countries, which compete. Nor can companies of one country grow only at the expense of those of another. The purpose of exporting is to import, as the purpose of production is consumption. The quantity of business which companies pursue is never fixed, but growing. British companies will fail only if their costs rise above their competitors, or they fail to diversify into new lines of business where they have a comparative advantage. This is why the government worries about the productivity of British companies, their research and development budgets, and the knowledge and skills of their workers. It has launched an array of tax and other policies to raise productivity and levels of investment in new machinery, innovative products and research and development.

In his first budget, Gordon Brown, the chancellor of the Exchequer, cut the rate of corporation tax on companies, abolished the dividend tax credits collected by pension funds, and reintroduced capital allowances for new plant and machinery. Theoretically, these measures would encourage companies to invest rather than pay tax or dividends. An extra £1 billion was poured into schools on the grounds that 'we cannot run a first rate economy on the basis of second rate education.'[15] In his second budget, he cut the rate of corporation tax and reformed capital gains tax to reduce the levy on long held assets. He also introduced a £50 million fund to help British companies reap the commercial rewards of British inventions, and launched an official inquiry into company spending on research and development.

Unfortunately, the productivity of the average British worker and the innovativeness of his company are determined by factors far beyond the reach of marginal changes in the tax system or the schools budget. Rhetoric about helping companies to compete is harmless, but where the government does affect the ability of companies to compete, it is making their position worse by implementing the European Union Social Chapter, Working Time and Parental Leave directives. These give employees the right to work no more than forty-eight hours a week; to refuse night and shift work; and to enjoy twelve weeks of parental leave, eighteen weeks of maternity leave and four weeks' paid holiday. Employees can claim unfair dismissal after one year, and the government has introduced a statutory minimum wage and automatic and statutory rights to union recognition.[16]

By the spring of 1998, the government had ten separate pieces of pro-worker legislation going through the parliamentary process, and more promised for 1999. Works councils for multinational companies are promised for the future. The informal tradition in British industrial relations, irretrievably damaged by the anti-union legislation of the Conservative years, has given way to a web of continental-style regulation which will add to costs and reduce the ability of companies to adapt quickly to changes in their competitive position.

Many union leaders, let alone businessmen, have failed to appreciate the scale of the reforms. 'Look at their deeds, not their words,' said the general secretary of the Trades Union Congress in September 1998. The heavier regulation of the labour market is not, as Margaret Thatcher might put it, a reintroduction of socialism by the back door. It reflects a tectonic shift in appreciation of the purpose of the PLC. For the management guru Charles Handy, companies are now so important to national wellbeing that they ought to belong to employees not shareholders. Their true purpose, he says, is not to make shareholders rich but to make employees happy and fulfilled:

Why is it sensible to think of an organised group of people as a piece
of property, to be bought and sold according to its market price? . . .
Organisations are nothing if they are not communities of people, and
a community is not a property. It does not make sense to say that a
community is 'owned' by outsiders. A community is not a commodity
to be bought and sold. . . . [It] has 'members' not 'employees' and it
belongs to its members . . . It could, conceivably, sell a share in the
future stream of net income – a form of equity – so that its financiers
could share in its fortunes, but such a share would give no other rights.
A community belongs to its members.[17]

The argument is tied closely to his belief that human capital is replacing
financial capital as the principal factor of production. If the principal asset
of a company is its people, the shareholders effectively own nothing.

The economist John Kay has enlarged the idea of the company-as-
community to incorporate shareholders, customers, suppliers, distributors
and the general public. In *The Foundations of Corporate Success*, he describes
the PLC as a set of contracts and trusting relationships among these various
'stakeholders'. In his view, it is the distinctiveness of its stakeholding arrangements which gives each company its competitive edge.[18] As Leader of the
Opposition, Blair endorsed the idea of the stakeholder company in a widely
reported speech in Singapore in 1996.[19] New Labour was still seeking intellectual distinction from the free-market capitalism of the Conservative government, and stakeholding spoke directly to fears of takeovers and the sack. It
was in harmony with a world in which competitive advantage stemmed from
human capital rather than the pursuit of shareholder value. Stakeholding
gave New Labour a new tune.

More interestingly, it appeared to answer the question: what is a company
for? Stakeholding imparts moral purpose to the type of organisation which
dominates the lives of most people in Britain. The stakeholding company is
no longer a machine for making money but a community of interest groups,
its purpose to secure its own existence in perpetuity, and so provide fulfilment
as well as a wage or salary.[20] It is an anthropomorphic view, endowing the
company with human characteristics it has lacked since experience disproved
the power urges described by Galbraith. Many companies, invited to state
what they are for, are reduced to banalities like 'Being Number One in the
World' or 'Attaining Top-three Status within Five Years.' Such ambitions have
a fragile hold on the imagination. But the answer to the question posed by
Charles Handy ('What is it all for? . . . What is this business for?') cannot be
found in metaphysics.

It is true that companies have a separate personality: they can be sued, damaged and libelled; and they have memories. Many companies trawl their archives in search of knowledge from the past. If a company dies, more than jobs are lost. Experience is dissipated, values evaporate, possibilities are cut off. But the utility of the PLC is reason enough for its existence. Its organisational and productive powers are immense. In its multinational incarnation, it comes close to fulfilling the vision of the Victorian statesman and campaigner for free trade, Richard Cobden: a beneficent capitalism abolishing war by the power of example. But it is fallacious to argue that the main purpose of the PLC is to give meaning to the lives of its employees. It is to make money. In theory, goods could be produced in a completely decentralised way by contracts between individuals, and in the early stages of the Industrial Revolution this was how production was organised. Entrepreneurs relied on armies of self-employed homeworkers using their own looms and tools to turn cotton, wool and iron into finished goods. But then they realised it would be cheaper to borrow money, build a factory, buy machines, hire workers and organise distribution directly. The costs of drawing up separate contracts, and maintaining relationships with dozens of different people, were too high.[21]

As the costs of employing relevant skills have risen, companies are now breaking themselves up. 'Out-sourcing' is endemic, in government as well as business. It enables companies and government departments to skip the management and social and overhead costs (especially national insurance contributions, office space and pensions) of employing hundreds of different people in dozens of different fields. The 'virtual company' predicted by Charles Handy (where teams of self-employed workers come together to complete a particular project) is displacing the highly integrated company of the past, but the origins of the virtual company do not lie in new-fangled ideas about stakeholding or the company-as-community. It is a creature of business economics.

The Alternative: Trade Unions

Far from changing the nature of the PLC, the virtual company affirms its essential purpose: it is nothing but a group of people who come together for the purpose of making money. The popularity of Handyism and stakeholding rests on resistance to this idea. Like the early socialist thinkers, their proponents hark back to the moral economy of the past, when capital had a duty to society as well as to its owners. In the Middle Ages, the love of gain was suppressed by the fear of hell, the usury laws, the 'just price' and the reciprocal obligations of rich to poor and poor to rich. The characteristic form of corporate organisation was not the PLC, but the guild. Unlike PLCs, guilds sought to make money by restricting trade, not advancing it; their descendant is the trade union.

British trade unionism grew out of the urban guilds of the Middle Ages, and especially out of the grievances of journeymen apprenticed to the masters of great craft guilds. Printers and bookbinders, joiners, engineers and cobblers founded the first Trades Union Congress (TUC) in 1868. Early trade unionism was the province of the skilled artisan, not the impoverished labourer desperate for a living wage. The aim of the skilled artisan was to monopolise available work and raise its price by limiting competition.[22] The paraphernalia of early trade unionism – oaths and initiation rites, feasts and entertainments, primitive forms of insurance against sickness, old age and funeral expenses – has more in common with a City livery company than a modern trade union.[23] In its aims, the modern trade union is no different from the Mercers Company which made Dick Whittington rich and powerful. Its goal is to raise the standard of living of its members. It achieves this by extorting wage increases from employers; resisting new machinery or changes in working practices which might increase the productivity of the workforce; and restricting the right of outsiders to compete for jobs. The role of the original trade unions, providing welfare services to their members, has long since passed to the state, but it is a role they must now recover if they are to survive in the twenty-first century.

The modern trade union movement is in crisis. At the heart of its difficulties is a simple truth: unions depend on members, but members no longer depend on unions. Most private sector employees – especially women and young people – think trade unions are irrelevant. As the economy has changed, the unionised heartlands of steel, shipbuilding, coal and large-scale manufacturing have shrunk. Firms and workplaces are smaller and working practices more flexible, which makes it harder and more expensive for unions to recruit members. Less than one worker in three now belongs to a trade union. Industry-wide wage deals are almost unknown outside the public sector, and so are strikes. It is not surprising that trade unionism exists now mainly in the public sector. The biggest trade union (UNISON) is sub-titled the Public Service Union, and the most vociferous (the National Union of Teachers) is also confined to the public sector. Perhaps three in four workers in the public sector belong to a trade union, against as few as one in twenty in parts of the private sector. In the fastest-growing industries, such as leisure and information technology, especially in the prosperous south-east, trade unionism is a bad memory.

Oddly, incarceration in the public sector means modern trade unionism is largely a middle class phenomenon. The average trade unionist is not a labourer or a miner or an assembly-line worker, but a teacher or a doctor or a nurse or a laboratory technician. The nursing union (the Royal College of Nursing) has the sixth biggest membership of any affiliated to the TUC, and the doctors' union (the British Medical Association) is the richest in terms of assets per head. Trade unionism is no longer a struggle for a living wage, or the workers-of-the-world uniting to cast off their chains. It is a facet of the struggle for wealth and power between the private sector and the public, in which the trade unions campaign for higher taxation and public expenditure not because they promise a new age of justice and equality but because their members want a pay rise. When the trade unions accuse the government of under-investing in the National Health Service or destroying the Welfare State, it is not the interests of patients or the poor that they have in mind. It is the interests of their members who work in hospitals and the civil service.

The members believe they suffered grievously under the Conservative governments of the 1980s and 1990s. The number of civil servants fell from 735,430 in 1979 to 455,000 in 1997. The majority now work in executive agencies, some of which were privatised. In local government, compulsory competitive tendering transferred jobs to the private sector, contracting union membership further. Many union members lost their jobs as contracts changed hands, or were re-engaged at wages which demonstrated the power-lessness of the unions. When Doncaster Metropolitan Council transferred its refuse collection to a private company, the Transport and General Workers Union (TGWU) was unable to prevent the contractors cutting the pay of a member by £50 to £135 a week; his holiday entitlement from twenty-five days to fifteen; abolishing his sick pay entitlement; and his exclusion from the local government pension scheme.[24]

Nor can public sector unions any longer appeal over the heads of national-ised industry managers to ministers. The major public utilities are in private hands, and the privatisations were accompanied by dramatic reductions in payrolls.[25] The Communications Workers' Union (CWU), which organised thousands of employees at the Post Office and British Telecom (BT) in the 1970s, lost half its members at BT, and the story was the same in the privatised rail, water, gas and electricity industries. The destruction of jobs before and after the privatisation of British Coal reduced to 10,000 members a union which once brought down a government.[26] By the 1990s, the National Union of Mineworkers (NUM was reduced to bloating its depleted membership rolls with retired miners and their widows, few of whom paid their dues.

When Arthur Scargill became president of the NUM in 1981, it had 350,000 members. By the time the industry was privatised fourteen years later, its membership had slipped below the thespians of Equity. By 1994 there were not enough miners left in Durham to fund their famous annual gala. But sponsorship was sought, and the gala was saved by a friendly millionaire. Mining unionism, like the coal industry, is now part of the heritage industry. The NUM has abandoned its prestigious headquarters in Sheffield, and moved into a modest building in Barnsley. Though its difficulties were exacerbated by the strike of 1984–85, and the formation of the breakaway Union of Democratic Mineworkers, the demise of the NUM owes more to the long decline of the coal mining industry than to Thatcherism or privatisation.

But the trade unions are partially right to blame their plight on the hostility of Conservative governments. Six successive Acts of Parliament between 1980 and 1993 made it harder for them to recruit members by organising and winning industrial disputes. The number of days lost to strikes fell from 29.5 million in 1979, the year of the notorious Winter of Discontent, to a low of just 278,000 days in 1994. This was a fall of 99 per cent, to the lowest level since records began in 1891. They have never reached their previous heights again. It is a convincing measure of the declining ability of trade unions to use their most powerful weapon. By the time the Conservative government passed its last piece of anti-union legislation in 1993, people had began to feel sorry for them.

Yet, in conjunction with the Employment Acts of 1980 and 1982, the Trade Union Reform and Employment Rights Act of 1993 did more to undermine the viability of the trade union movement than any of its five predecessors. The legislation of 1980 and 1982 undermined the closed shop (which forced all employees to join the union) while the Act of 1993 abolished the check-off system (in which employers deducted union dues from wages automatically). These were the keys to the buoyancy of trade union membership and finances. At the height of their power in the 1970s, the trade unions could rely on the closed shop to force workers to join the union and the check-off system to generate revenue without any effort on their part to recruit or retain members. One of the few Conservative reforms New Labour has reversed is the obligation on individuals to re-register their willingness to have their union dues checked off, but by 1997 much of the damage was done.

It was the curtailment of the closed shop and checking off, not the ban on secondary picketing or the requirements for strike ballots or even the lifting of legal immunity for union assets, which precipitated the massive decline in union membership. For decades, unions relied on the coercion of the closed shop and the inertia of the check-off system. In some cases, the effects of their disappearance were rapid and far-reaching. When British Rail abandoned its check-off system ahead of privatisation, the RMT rail union lost 20,000 members and 15 per cent of its revenues. In 1994 the National Union of Civil and Public Servants (NUCPS) had to cut jobs and services after a substantial minority of its members decided not to renew their subscriptions. The mighty UNISON had to shed four hundred staff as its subscription income dried up.

The abolition of the check-off system accelerated a decline in trade union membership which dated back to the election of Margaret Thatcher in 1979. Until then, membership had grown for a century. Of course, there were always periodic falls in membership, and occasional bouts of stagnation. The years between the General Strike of 1926 and the emergence of the economy from the Great Depression in the mid-1930s were particularly bad: the unions lost nearly a million members. In the 1950s, under a particularly unimpressive generation of union leaders, membership stagnated. But in four out of every five years of the twentieth century the trade unions had known nothing but growth in numbers, and in the power which numbers confer. Trade union membership peaked in 1979 at 13½ million people, or nearly two in every three workers. It has fallen in every year since.

Trade Unions as PLCs

Shrinking membership is financially debilitating. More than £4 in every £5 received by the trade unions comes from members' dues, but by 1996 membership had slipped below eight million. This was the lowest number of paid-up trade unionists since 1945. Between 1988 and 1994 the NUCPS spent all of its reserves as subscriptions dried up. In September 1994 it was forced into a merger with the Inland Revenue Staff Federation, to create the Public Services Tax and Commerce Union. In 1993 the Certification Officer disclosed that UCATT, the construction union, the RMT rail union and the Graphical Paper and Media Union had spent virtually all of their capital in a bid to stay afloat. UCATT had over-spent by nearly £2 million and was down to its last £400,000. It narrowly escaped bankruptcy. All three unions were forced to embark on massive retrenchment as a condition of continuing support from Unity Trust, bankers to the trade union movement.

It is the need for members to shore up their finances which accounts for the strength of the rivalry between unions operating in the same industries. Just as the members of the medieval guilds battled with each other in the streets, modern trade unions battle on the shop floor and in the classroom. No battle for members is more intense than the contest for teachers' subscriptions between Nigel de Gruchy's NAS/UWT and Doug McAvoy's NUT. But unions are making economies, as well as war on each other. Almost all trade unions have cut staff, sold assets, invested in labour-saving technology, and appointed managers far removed from the cloth-capped placemen of yesteryear. Like ailing PLCs, trade unions have even begun

TABLE 20.1
Trade Union Membership in 1996

Union	Membership
UNISON: The Public Service Union	1,374,583
Transport and General Workers Union (TGWU)	884,669
Amalgamated Engineering and Electrical Union (AEEU)	725,097
GMB	718,139
Manufacturing Science and Finance Union (MSF)	425,103
Royal College of Nursing of the United Kingdom (RCN)	307,094
Union of Shop Distributive and Allied Workers (Usdaw)	290,170
Communication Workers Union (CWU)	274,820
National Union of Teachers (NUT)	271,299
National Association of Schoolmasters and Union of Women Teachers (NAS/UWT)	238,472
Graphical Paper and Media Union (GPMU)	209,900
Association of Teachers and Lecturers (ATL)	166,793
Public Services Tax and Commerce Union	149,262
Civil and Public Services Association (CPSA)	116,681
Banking Insurance and Finance Union (Bifu)	116,165
Union of Construction Allied Trades and Technicians (UCATT)	111,901
British Medical Association (BMA)	101,334
224 Other Trade Unions With Less Than 100,000 Members	1,452,307
13 Unlisted Trade Unions	4,424
Total	7,938,213

Source: Annual Report of the Certification Officer 1997.

to merge. The 456 trade unions of 1979 had shrunk to 233 by the end of 1997.[27]

ASTMS, the white collar conglomerate created by Clive Jenkins, the first exponent of so-called 'business unionism', merged in February 1988 with TASS, the white collar engineering union, to form the Manufacturing, Science and Finance Union (MSF). The blue collar engineers of the AEU merged with the plumbers and electricians of the EETPU in April 1992 to form the Amalgamated Engineering and Electrical Union, and the National Communications Union merged with the Union of Communication Workers to create the CWU. Four trade unions now account for nearly half of union members. If the long-anticipated merger between the GMB and the TGWU takes place (merger talks were resumed in 1997), the figure will be three.

The argument for more mergers is strong. The inefficiency of British trade unionism stems from its fragmentation. GMB and TGWU officials often organise at the same plant. Both have large offices in the same town, and administrative costs are duplicated at national level. The chief obstacle to a merger is the fierce loyalty of trade union leaders to themselves: they are more interested in protecting their jobs than creating an efficient movement. Despite increasing white collar and female membership, union mind-sets remain predominantly blue-collar and male. The average employee is thirty-one, and often female, but the average union member is forty-six and male. As recently as 1998 a small but militant railway union (Aslef) elected as its general secretary a member of Arthur Scargill's Socialist Labour Party.[28]

The TUC has struggled manfully to persuade unions to think more con-structively. Relaunched as a businesslike organisation in 1994, the TUC has become the model of a socially responsible PLC. Its new general secretary, John Monks, is a technocrat who could pass himself off as a director of a merchant bank. He got rid of the seventeen committees which used to hold power at Congress House and replaced them with smaller teams reporting to an executive committee chaired by himself. In 1996 he announced that the TUC was cutting its full-time staff by 15 per cent, at a cost of £1 million in redundancy payments.[29] Proposing and managing mergers between unions would not be a great cultural shock for Monks's new model TUC.

But mergers between unions, as mergers between companies, are far from painless. When the local government and health service unions, Nalgo, NUPE and COHSE, merged to create UNISON in July 1993, it was followed by a £13 million redundancy programme in which one quarter of the staff lost their jobs. No trade union endured a sharper degree of 'downsizing' than the TGWU; its membership has halved since 1979, and assets had to be sold to cover a cumulative deficit of £23 million at the peak in 1991. Bill Morris was elected general secretary a year later. He called in the management consultants.

What followed was a textbook exercise in corporate restructuring. The number of regions was reduced from eleven to eight. One quarter of the full-time TGWU officials were fired, and sixty regional offices were closed. Transport House, the headquarters building near the Palace of Westminster which once housed the Labour Party, was evacuated and refurbished at a cost of £6 million. A central computer system was built and a finance director – Peter Regnier, formerly finance director at the Rover Group – was recruited as chief executive, to impose new disciplines on the finances. By the time he ran for re-election in the summer of 1995, Bill Morris could boast (like the chief executive of any PLC emerging from a distressing bout of restructuring) that 'we now have probably the strongest balance sheet in the trade union movement . . . We have no debts, no overdraft and we are cash rich.'[30] He omitted to say that the union was on the look-out for takeover opportunities; it undoubtedly was.

Limits to Business Unionism

Unlike their counterparts in the United States or Germany, British trade unions were never wealthy. The richest union in the country (UNISON) had net assets of just £80 million at the end of 1996, and the trade union movement as a whole has a net worth of less than £750 million. British unions were always run on a shoestring, with low subscriptions and limited services. Their strength flowed not from assets or income but from industrial muscle, which relied on weight of numbers. Where they were not forced to join a union by a closed shop agreement, people paid their subscriptions because they were persuaded that the union could win them a pay rise. As membership increased, so did income from subscriptions. Representation of the members, not services, is the traditional role of the trade union.

It remains a common view of their purpose today. 'Unions are not savings accounts but organisations that collectively represent our workers' interests,' says John Sheldon, general secretary of the NUCPS. 'Our financial health is important and is taken seriously, but it is only a means to an end, and not the end in itself.'[31] In the 1960s Sidney Greene, leader of the NUR, was considered a sell-out for investing union funds in private companies. Even today, investment income is less than 6p in every £1 received. This over-reliance on membership subscriptions, coupled with a failure to cut expenditure as membership fell, is at the root of the financial weakness of the trade unions; the problem is unlikely to be solved quickly.

Contempt for 'business unionism' means the administration of trade union finances is often chaotic where it is not corrupt. Union offices are filled with professional activists rather than people who work in the industries they represent. They neither know nor care about financial management, provided their salaries are paid: a job at union headquarters or in a regional office usually earns more than anything else they could do. In 1996 one quarter of trade union leaders earned more than £40,000 a year; another one fifth earned between £20,000 and £40,000. Many can count on cheap mortgages, company cars and expense accounts. This is one reason why trade unions still spend the bulk of their income on running costs. In 1996, trade unions paid £79 million in benefits to their members, but £571 million in administration and expenses. This bounty is spread more generously than the bare figures suggest, because the leaders of the smallest unions receive no financial

TABLE 20.2
The Wealth of the Trade Unions in 1996

Union	Net Income (£m)	Net Assets* (£m)
UNISON: The Public Service Union	(1.3)	80.2
Transport and General Workers Union (TGWU)	4.4	66.2
GMB	(1.6)	56.9
Amalgamated Engineering and Electrical Union (AEEU)	6.4	50.8
British Medical Association	5.5	43.1
Graphical Paper and Media Union (GPMU)	1.6	39.9
Communication Workers Union (CWU)	0.3	23.6
Union of Shop Distributive and Allied Workers (Usdaw)	1.1	19.0
Schoolmasters and Women Teachers (NAS/UWT)	1.4	16.2
Civil and Public Services Association (CPSA)	(0.4)	13.5
Public Services Tax and Commerce Union	0.3	10.1
Manufacturing Science and Finance Union (MSF)	1.6	9.6
National Union of Teachers (NUT)	0.1	9.0
Association of Teachers and Lecturers (ATL)	0.9	5.6
Banking Insurance and Finance Union (Bifu)	(0.05)	3.6
Construction Allied Trades and Technicians (UCATT)	(0.6)	0.4
Royal College of Nursing of the United Kingdom (RCN)	0	0.0
Trades Union Congress	0.4	5.6
13 Unlisted Trade Unions	1.6	49.1
224 Other Trade Unions With Less Than 100,000 Members	10.9	234.4
Total	33.8	736.8

Source: Annual Report of the Certification Officer 1997.

* Fixed investment and other assets net of liabilities. The net assets is equivalent to total funds at the year-end. Funds include general, contingency, pension and political funds.

reward, save their out-of-pocket expenses. The differential between the pay of union leaders and their members can rival the gap between Fat Cats and ordinary workers. The leaders of the teachers' unions earn twice as much as the best-paid teachers. Christine Hancock of the Royal College of Nursing earns three times as much as the highest paid nurse. For most modern trade union officials, managing a union is not a vocation but a career choice. The parallels with a political career are striking.

TABLE 20.3
Highest Paid Trade Union Leaders, 1996 (£)

Name	Union	Salary	Benefits	Total
Gordon Taylor	Professional Footballers Association	305,204	113,847	419,051
Mac Armstrong	British Medical Association	91,629	16,960	108,589
Christine Hancock	Royal College of Nursing	78,650	17,262	95,912
Peter Smith	Association of Teachers & Lecturers	77,122	14,853	91,975
David Hart	National Association of Head Teachers	72,994	10,437	83,431
Nigel de Gruchy	NAS/UWT	61,385	15,152	76,537
Doug McAvoy	National Union of Teachers	70,003	6,106	76,109
Roger Lyons	MSF	62,465	10,997	73,462
Chris Darke	Balpa	59,160	12,141	71,301
Bill Morris	TGWU	56,812	14,216	71,028
John Edmonds	GMB	57,000	14,000	71,000
Tony Dubbins	GPMU	55,167	14,373	69,540
Bill Connor	Usdaw	56,328	11,288	67,917
Alan Johnson*	CWU	58,367	8,405	66,772
John Monks	Trades Union Congress	56,096	8,875	64,971
Arthur Scargill	National Union of Mineworkers	55,032	9,814	64,846

Source: Annual Report of the Certification Officer 1997.

* Alan Johnson was succeeded in 1997 by Derek Hodgson.

British trade unionism has yet to uncover its Jimmy Hoffa. But unions on strike need money, and cannot always be particular about its origins or custody. During the miners' strike of 1984–85, the National Union of Mineworkers (NUM) not only received money from both Libya and the Soviet Union but placed much of the funds offshore to protect them from sequestration and receivership.[32] Many transactions were conducted in cash, and were reported neither in the accounts nor to the NUM executive. Years after the strike was over, its financing by NUM president Arthur Scargill and his general secretary Peter Heathfield became the subject of newspaper allegations. In March 1990 the *Daily Mirror* alleged that money sent from Russia had ended up in an offshore bank account, and that Scargill and Heathfield had taken money from Libya in the form of home loans.[33] The NUM called in Gavin Lightman QC to investigate. His report made criticisms of the conduct of the two men, but cleared them of the home loan charges. The NUM sued for the return of £1.4 million. It eventually settled out of court for half this sum. Inquiries by the police and the Serious Fraud Office came to nothing. The Certification Officer brought charges against Scargill and Heathfield for failing to keep proper accounts, but the case collapsed for lack of evidence.[34]

The NUM was an extreme case, originating in a need to protect union funds from sequestration during a prolonged and bitter strike, but the disbursement of funds by senior officials without recourse to the executive is common practice in union circles. In 1993 it emerged that the assistant general secretary of MSF had dispensed £300,000 of the members' money to retiring union officials without informing his colleagues. In the bitterly contested GPMU election of 1994, it was revealed that former national officers of the union had received 'excessive pay-offs exceeding £100,000'.[35] In the same year the TGWU uncovered a major fraud in its north-west region, dating back six years, which included misuse of strike pay and recruitment funds. A senior official resigned when it emerged that he had claimed £15,181 in expenses in a year (the TGWU paid only £32 a day in expenses, which implied he had worked more days than there are in a year).[36] This inability to control expenses claims is characteristic of the indiscipline of union finances. The Prison Officers Association (POA) was investigated and fined by the Inland Revenue over expenses claims by officials.[37] In 1998 the POA was censured by the Certification Officer for the same reason, and in 1996 two GMB officials were fired for fiddling their expenses.[38]

The Future of Trade Unionism

One positive effect of falling membership is a greater emphasis on financial discipline. Twenty years ago the veteran labour correspondent, Robert Taylor, was able to publish a definitive popular study of British trade unions which scarcely mentioned their financial condition. Today, unions can no longer afford to fritter income on local strikes, or tie it up in regional offices, conference centres and health spas.[39] Instead, a management centre has opened at Cranfield business school in Bedfordshire, where officials learn about strategy, marketing and financial controls.[40]

It is estimated that unions need to recruit one eighth of their membership once a year to counteract natural wastage, but only one union in four employs a full-time recruitment organiser. In 1997, the TUC estimated that unions spend less than 3p in every £1 of income on recruitment, whereas in the United States, some unions spend half their income on it. This is why fifteen unions agreed to invest £1 million in a new 'organising academy' based on the American example which will recruit and train organisers, especially among younger and female workers who traditionally shun union membership.[41]

Unions recognise that few will join for the traditional reasons: industrial action appeals to few employees outside the public sector. Nor is trade unionism an authentic vehicle of working-class political representation. The 1992 general election was the first where the TUC did not draw up a joint economic programme with the Labour Party. Five years later, the TUC did not even endorse the Labour Party; it ran an independent 'employee rights' campaign. In Opposition, Labour halved the voting power of the unions at the Labour Party conference, and warned that relations between the trade unions and a future Labour government would be based on 'fairness not favours'.

Since the election, Tony Blair has distanced himself still further from union leaders. None of the major Conservative legal reforms of the 1980s and 1990s will be reversed, and even the right to union recognition stops a long way short of a return to the closed shop. Labour has not resurrected the National Economic Development Council (NEDC), nor has it re-established the Department of Employment, once the unions' channel to the corridors of power. The government has made some concessions: it adopted the EU social legislation, and trade unions have returned to GCHQ at Cheltenham. The country now has a minimum wage. Unionised employees no longer have to insist that their dues are deducted by their employer automatically. But trade unionists are disappointed by continuing restraint of public sector pay, and appalled by privatisation and the Private Finance Initiative. They also think the minimum wage is too low.

Blair had earlier told the TUC that he was interested only in the 'persuasiveness of their arguments'. Since he became prime minister, he has sought to reduce their influence over the policies and direction of the Labour Party, and some of his close associates do not disguise their contempt for unions. Blair encounters little resistance from his MPs, because there is no longer any sizeable constituency for them on the backbenches. Only one Labour MP in twenty has direct experience of manual labour, despite most constituency Labour parties still being controlled by union officials. Irked by the over-representation of the bourgeoisie, the Amalgamated Engineering and Electrical Union (AEEU) decided in September 1998 to set up a £1 million fund to improve 'working-class' representation on the Labour benches. Today, union ties with New Labour are financial rather than sentimental, and even they are now fraying. During the 1992 general election, the unions met 90 per cent of Labour's costs; in 1996, they supplied less than half. Officially, it is now down to one third. Though union contributions to the running costs of the party at local level mean these figures exaggerate the independence of New Labour, the clearest thinkers on both sides recognise the need to terminate the relationship.

Percipient union leaders recognise that they can no longer rely on a friendly government to restore their fortunes, and that their survival now depends on meeting the needs and aspirations of potential members. Whether trade unions like it or not, individualism has penetrated the workplace, and they have to shed the collectivism of the past. There is no inherent conflict of interest between labour and capital any more and modern unions are prepared to trade pay for secure jobs. 'What is good for Ford,' Bill Morris told shop stewards at the Ford plant in Swansea, 'is good for the T and G.'[42] Headquarters now offers cheap household, car and life insurance, cut-price holidays, economic conveyancing and will-making services and discount credit cards. The Unity Trust Bank, founded in the mid-1980s by forty-four trade unions in conjunction with the Co-operative Wholesale Society, has developed a range of financial products, including mutual funds and pensions. Over one hundred thousand trade unionists already carry its credit card. Usdaw, MSF, the TGWU and the GMB are pushing money-purchase pension plans,[43] and the AEEU has formed an alliance with Friends Provident to provide a second pension to its members.[44]

These services mark a return by trade unions to their origins as mutual, self-help organisations. In 1993, the Institute of Directors suggested that trade unions lose their remaining legal privileges (including the right to strike) and become voluntary bodies servicing the needs and rights of individual workers.[45] Ian Duncan Smith, the Conservative social security spokesman, has suggested something similar. Before he left the government, Frank Field invited the unions to play a role in his plans for 'stakeholder' pensions. The Demos think-tank proposed that they might evolve into 'employee mutuals' selling their members' labour to third parties. But the trade unions already know better. They are appointing chief executives and finance directors, and installing computer-based financial controls. They are learning the black art of marketing, and the blacker arts of mergers and acquisitions. They have adopted new technology and trained management. UNISON shop stewards have hand-held computers, mobile phones, and hot line numbers to ring for advice.[46] A retired union leader is on the board of several public companies,[47] and the TUC has launched a study to examine how unions can contribute to industrial and commercial competitiveness.[48] Plans include training shop stewards on 'best practice' in working with employers.[49]

Modern union leaders such as Ken Jackson of the AEEU argue that productivity and profits are as important to his members as they are to shareholders. He even argues that the pound ought to join the euro as soon as possible.[50] Throughout the union movement, hostility to the EU has given way to admiration of the opportunities it presents to secure legislation, milk budgets, confer with colleagues abroad and embarrass enemies in the courts.[51] The European idea of 'social partnership', by which unions are entrenched in corporate life by law, has replaced the voluntary agreements of the age of Solomon Binding and the Social Contract, and the unions are learning to treat their members as consumers. The trade unions have become crypto-PLCs.

The First Companies

One sign of this is the refusal of the government to restore the lost legal immunities of the trade unions. Every corporation or combination of people for a common purpose enjoys legal privileges in return for fulfilling certain obligations. Thanks to a quirk of legal and political history, the trade unions were granted not privileges but *immunities*. The Trades Disputes Act of 1906, for example, granted trade union assets immunity from being sued for damages by employers whose revenues were hit by 'go-slows' and strikes. This made them a uniquely privileged form of human association, until the immunities were removed in the Employment Act of 1982. In common law, anybody can be sued for harming anybody else, and forced to make good any damage done. The idea is to shift responsibility for loss to the person who caused it.

Primitive forms of business organisation incorporated this principle of responsibility for losses in the most obvious way. The entire personal estate of an individual businessman was at risk if he failed to pay his debts. The members of a business partnership were fully responsible for any losses they caused. This principle (unlimited personal liability for any loss occasioned by error or wrong) is an admirable one. It corresponds exactly to popular notions of fairness; relates rewards directly to risks; and encourages prudence in the disposition of investment by obliging businessmen to back their judgment with their own money. Unfortunately, it is also quite unsuited to the practical demands of an advanced industrial economy, where the sums at risk are too large for one individual to bear.

The joint stock company, in which the capital and profits of a business venture are divided between several shareholders, was invented to reduce the risk of large investments. The earliest examples were the overseas trading expeditions of the Elizabethan era, like those undertaken by the Muscovy (1555), Eastland (1579), Barbary and Africa (1588) companies. All were established by Royal Charter, in which the monarch not only gave them a monopoly of the trade, but created corporate legal personalities capable of owning property and suing and being sued in the same way as a private individual. 'Private men,' wrote one seventeenth century trade expert, 'cannot extend to making such long, adventurous and costly voyages.'

The greatest and best-known of all the chartered companies, the East India Company, was founded on 31 December 1600. It has the best claim to be the forerunner of the modern business corporation. It is true that the 218 subscribers to the first issue of shares by the Company of Merchants of London Trading into the East Indies had signed up for one voyage only.[52] The business they financed lacked one essential feature of the modern company: its capital was not permanent, but subscribed only until the ship returned with goods which would enable shareholders to take their profit. The East India Company had no permanent office or staff either. To that extent, it was more like a medieval guild than a modern company; a regulator of trade, rather than a trading operation. Its original shareholders wanted minimum expenses and a quick profit, not ownership of a permanent capitalistic enterprise. They were punters, not proprietors.

It was subsequent shareholders of the East India Company who came to appreciate the virtues of continuity and permanence in the financing of business ventures. They agreed in 1613 to finance a fresh voyage every four years rather than consider subscribing for each one as it was proposed. In 1657, after its charter was renewed by Cromwell, the first real permanent capital was subscribed with the issue of New General Stock. The East India Company, in the words of one of its historians, 'cast its medieval skin, shook off the traditions of the regulated system and grew into one united, continuous and permanent joint stock corporation'.[53]

But not even the East India Company could claim to be a prototype of the modern, multinational PLC. Its incorporation was still seen primarily as a privilege granted by government, rather than as a form of business organisation. In their closeness to government, and their dependence on political patronage, the chartered companies were more like nationalised industries than private companies. The primitive state of economic thought encouraged the view that there was a fixed quantity of wealth in the world, which it was the duty of the government to assist its citizens obtain through the creation of trading monopolies.[54] These misapprehensions were reinforced by ties of political patronage. Most shareholders in the chartered companies were government officials or friends of government officials. Companies were expected to lend to the government and, with a monopoly dependent on political favour, were in no position to refuse the regular invitations which came their way.

For their part, the companies recognised that they also needed diplomatic and military support. Protecting their commercial interests abroad involved fighting, fortifying ports and refuelling stations, and knocking out commercial rivals – chiefly the French and the Dutch. After Plassey, the East India Company found itself governing vast territories and collecting taxes to pay for its administration. It was not surprising that the company ended up as an arm of the state. Though it did not lose its trading monopoly east of the Cape of

Good Hope until 1813, its Indian possessions were effectively nationalised as early as 1784.

Limited Liability

The excessively close relationship between the chartered corporations and the government prevented the modern PLC from emerging sooner, because their political influence enabled them to obtain legislation to suppress competition. After the Restoration, there was a boom in the formation of joint stock companies. Dozens of company promoters (or 'projectors', as they were known) set about turning ideas into money. By 1695, ninety-three joint stock companies were in existence, capitalised at £4 million. Most were founded to exploit a patent technique or machine or undiscovered part of the world and, because of their speculative nature, few came to anything. By 1712, only twenty-one were left, with the Bank of England and the Bank of Scotland among them.[55]

The second boom in the foundation of joint stock companies, in 1719 and 1720, ended in a virtual ban on company formation. This boom was ignited by the impressive but illusory success of the South Sea Company in refinancing the national debt.[56] The directors of the Company were greatly irritated by competition for the capital on which the ever-rising price of their stock depended, and were able to secure the passage of legislation banning all joint stock companies not authorised by royal charter. The only major company promotions to escape this ban were two equally well-connected insurance companies – the Royal Exchange and the London – but even they had to promise to pay the king £300,000 for the privilege of obtaining a chartered existence.[57]

The so-called Bubble Act was passed in 1720 not, as is popularly assumed, to prevent another South Sea Bubble, but to maintain the rate of inflation of the Bubble itself.[58] It effectively denied the British economy the benefits joint stock financing would have brought to the Industrial Revolution. A joint stock company could be founded only by special Act of Parliament, a route closed (on grounds of expense) to most ordinary forms of business. Though lawyers devised the unincorporated company as a way around the Act, most eighteenth-century industrial investment was relegated to the private sphere.[59] Exploitation of the coal mines was funded by landowners, or the miners, and the Cornish tin mines by partnerships. Other businesses relied on family and friends.

As Professor Mathias has pointed out, the early Industrial Revolution was funded by ordinary people bearing the burden of unlimited personal liability:

The Bubble Act . . . virtually outlawed the company form of enterprise in manufacturing industry. Because transferable shares, publicly-raised capital on the Stock Exchange, limitation of liability, were all prohibited, each partner in an enterprise was fully responsible in his private estate for the debts of the partnership to the last guinea, to the last acre. Anyone investing money in an enterprise and receiving profits as a reward for that investment, as opposed to making a personal loan to one of the partners at a fixed rate of interest, was deemed to be a partner in law and thus fully committed as responsible for any debts the concern made . . . The benefits of incorporation and limitation of liability were available to individual firms only by Royal Charter or special Act of Parliament, which were very seldom granted for a manufacturing industry.[60]

Adam Smith defended unlimited liability, arguing that joint stock enterprises were suitable only for capital-hungry undertakings such as canals and insurance companies. The diligence and vigilance required for success in ordinary business, he thought, 'cannot long be expected from the directors of a joint stock company.'[61]

It was a prescient observation. But, at the time Smith wrote, homeworking was the norm, and the most capital-intensive undertakings were the Royal Dockyards. In 1785 it cost £63,174 to build *HMS Victory*, as against £5,000 to build a cotton mill or £12,000 to capitalise an iron works. The capital value of the Royal Navy at the end of the eighteenth century is estimated at £2.25 million, or five times the sum invested in the West Riding wool manufacturing industry.[62] It was difficult for Smith to foresee the vast appetite for capital of the later stages of the Industrial Revolution.

The Bubble Act was not repealed until 1825. By then, the demands for capital in a rapidly industrialising economy had rendered its restrictions absurd. The construction of the railways absorbed huge amounts of capital, and a large number of unincorporated companies came into existence to build them. But their position in law was precarious: they could not be sued for damages except in the name of every shareholder. The principle of unlimited liability made people reluctant to risk their personal fortunes in a business where they might own only a few shares. The repeal of the Bubble Act, and subsequent steps to limit liability, sparked a boom in investment in capital-intensive industries: mines, banks, gas and water companies, docks, and especially railways. The abuse of railway company promotions to fleece people of their savings led to the establishment of an official registrar of companies, now known as Companies House. Companies which registered were given the privileges and status of incorporation, but the legislation of

1825 had not removed unlimited liability. This disappeared in the Limited Liability Acts of 1855 and 1862.

By these two Acts, the government sanctioned the creation of the modern PLC, an impersonal joint stock corporation, free to appeal to the public for capital, and run by a committee of directors responsible to external shareholders whose liability was limited to the value of their investment. Though the modern PLC was remarkably slow to emerge, this reform made its emergence possible. It marked the end of individual responsibility for the use of wealth, and the beginning of the separation of the ownership of wealth from its control.

The Privately Owned Company

The PLC, run by managers for the benefit of institutional shareholders, is now easily the dominant form of business organisation. In January 1997, the value of the companies listed on the London Stock Exchange passed £1 trillion, a figure equivalent to over one third of the net national wealth.[63] Most of this enormous sum is controlled by a small number of giant PLCs. The FTSE-100 companies account for nearly three quarters of the total value of the market.[64] It is often forgotten how few companies are quoted on the Stock Exchange. There are an estimated 3.7 million businesses in the country,[65] of which 1,184,900 were registered as companies in early 1998. Only 2,465 were quoted on the London Stock Exchange.[66]

The overwhelming majority of companies in Britain are still privately owned. Many of them are tiny enterprises. Few have more than a handful of employees from outside the family. A study by the TUC reckoned two out of three businesses had no employees, and that 86 per cent of all companies had no more than one to nine.[67] According to the Inland Revenue, only 372,759 companies paid the mainstream corporation tax in 1996–97. Less than 2,000 of them paid more than £1 million, and only fourteen more than £100 million.[68] The story is the same in terms of VAT. Slightly over 1.5 million businesses were registered for VAT in 1996–7,[69] which means only two in five companies even reached the £47,000 where VAT is compulsory. A great many businesses spend more than they get. The mortality rate among small companies is high. Between 1988 and 1997, between 158,000 and 266,000 enterprises registered and deregistered for VAT in each of the ten years. Most of the casualties went out of business. Over the decade until the recession in 1990, there was a net increase of 373,000 private companies registered for VAT, but 171,500 of them disappeared over the next five years.[70]

Disaster can strike even the biggest private companies. Heron, the property, petrol retailing and financial services giant built by Gerald Ronson, was the second largest private company in Britain. It ran into difficulties in the early 1990s (shortly after Ronson completed a six-month jail term for his part in the Guinness share ramp), and had to be rescued by a group of American investors. Yet, taken together, privately owned businesses account for two thirds of the total national income. So who are they?

Importance of Family

Most of them are family affairs: High Street shops, corner shops, jobbing builders, car dealerships, farmers, truckers, ironmongers, painters and decorators. They are the heirs of the shopkeepers, craftsmen and small manufacturers who accounted for the bulk of national output long before the Industrial Revolution. It was the bustling economy of the breweries and forges which formed the 'nation of shopkeepers' honoured by Adam Smith. Its importance to national prosperity and social stability was known long before the late Victorians discovered the property-owning democracy, or Margaret Thatcher first began to listen to the 'small business lobby'.

Most businesses begin as family-owned enterprises. In 1990 the accountants Stoy Hayward surveyed 8,250 of the largest companies in Britain. They found that over three quarters were still half-owned or controlled by the families which founded them.[71] The ownership of a large publicly quoted company such as J. Sainsbury is still dominated by members of the founding family, who control over two fifths of the shares. Smiths still own 11 per cent of W. H. Smith. At Barclays Bank, Pilkingtons, Whitbread and Pearson, members of the founding families have retained a boardroom presence and a psychological hold over the company long after their shareholdings have shrunk to a minuscule proportion. The quoted property sector is notorious for the number of individuals and families holding impregnable management positions through minority stakes.[72]

Private companies have the luxury of issuing non-voting shares to outsiders. The founding George family own only one tenth of the cereal manufacturer, Weetabix, but they continue to control the company through non-voting shares. Until 1993, when the non-voting stock was enfranchised, Great Universal Stores was controlled by only 2.2 per cent of its shareholders: the Wolfson family and the Wolfson Foundation.[73] Board meetings at the company were dominated for the first forty years of its existence by Isaac Wolfson; for the next twenty by his son, Leonard; and are dominated today by David, Lord Wolfson of Sunningdale. Likewise, the non-voting shares issued by the Savoy Hotel enabled its management to defy the Forte Group for years. Ironically,

Forte itself had issued trust shares whose voting power equalled the rest of the ordinary shares.

By retaining a grip on their patrimony in these ways, families have defied the implications of success far longer than they were entitled to expect. Virtually all successful businesses reach a point at which their appetite for capital exceeds the ability of the family to feed it, but family resources can run deep. The Vesteys pumped an estimated £145 million into Union International, the loss-making food and property arm of the family business, before conceding defeat and accepting liquidation. Their difficulties were exacerbated by borrowing from the banks rather than inviting outsiders to share the risk by selling a stake to an institutional investor.

Price of Privacy

It is not hard to see why families resist the sale of shares to outsiders. As ownership becomes more diffuse, control is harder to sustain, and privately owned companies can escape reporting full details of their activities to the Stock Exchange and Companies House. There is no need for them to comply with the cumbersome 'corporate governance' regulations devised by the Cadbury, Greenbury and Hampel committees.[74] Private ownership also offers some respite from prying journalists. But without issuing shares to outsiders by floating the company on the Stock Exchange, or tapping institutional investors for the funds to finance major investments or takeover bids, companies cannot expand quickly. Those which seek outside capital without being willing to cede control pay more because investors dislike non-voting shares, and pay less. Banks reserve their finest lending rates for public companies, and lenders of all kinds generally ask private companies for personal guarantees as security. Private companies always have to pay more for capital than public companies, which has an adverse effect on their rate of growth and financial performance.

Privacy also makes it hard to attract top managers. Families rarely sustain entrepreneurial flair, or even management ability, over several generations. 'From clogs to clogs in three generations' encapsulates the difficulties many family businesses have. Yet talented managers are not attracted by two-tier voting structures, or boards packed with family members. 'The family behaved as if it was still their private business, rather than being a public company with a Stock Exchange listing,' complained Ernest Saunders of his early days as chief executive at Guinness.[75] The family then owned only a quarter of the company, but it was still chaired and vice-chaired by Guinnesses. Six more were on the board, and two non-executive directors were family appointments.

TABLE 20.4
Thirty Largest Privately Owned Companies (£m)

		Net Assets	Sales	Pre-Tax Profits
John Swire & Sons Ltd	Transport	11,665	4,945	917
Littlewoods Organisation PLC	Pools and Retailing	978	2,309	97
Stadium City Ltd*	Property	749	60	(9)
National Parking Corporation Ltd*	Car Parking	493	309	25
Robert Stephen Holdings Ltd	Consumer Products	389	757	26
Linpac Group Ltd	Plastic Packaging	338	862	40
Emerson Developments Ltd*	Property	293	58	7
D. C. Thomson & Co Ltd*	Publishing	291	106	45
Midland & Scottish Resources PLC	Offshore Drilling	280	29	(1)
C & J Clark (Holdings) Ltd*	Shoes	279	722	25
Edwardian Group Ltd*	Hotels	255	65	10
Edrington Holdings Ltd	Whisky	252	98	29
William Grant & Sons Ltd	Spirits	219	254	27
Yattendon Investment Trust PLC*	Publishing	195	70	7
Fenwick Ltd**	Department Stores	174	231	25
Guardian Media Group PLC*	Newspapers	171	302	20
Charles Street Buildings PLC	Property	169	20	23
TJH Group Ltd*	Property and Leisure	166	36	7
Andrew Weir & Co Ltd*	Transport & Insurance	162	316	8
I. M. Group Ltd	Holding Company	157	180	10
Daniel Thwaites PLC*	Pubs and Hotels	154	88	8
Colaingrove Ltd	Caravan Parks	153	92	3
Weetabix Ltd*	Breakfast Cereals	148	271	37
Shepherd Building Group Ltd*	Construction	147	385	4
First Corporate Shipping Ltd*	Shipping	147	38	8
Automotive Products Group Ltd	Motor Parts	146	231	3
Cameron Hall Developments Ltd	Property	140	45	(11)
Bibby Line Group Ltd	Shipping	139	95	6
UGC Ltd	Motor Parts	139	86	3
Bloor Holdings Ltd*	Plant Hire & Property	133	211	1

Source: Jordans: Britain's Top Privately Owned Companies, 1997.

All figures are rounded, and are for the year ended December 1995 unless marked with an * (1996) or ** (1997).

At a Guinness wedding, Saunders found himself consigned to a distant table, with other family retainers. 'I suddenly realised how the family saw me,' he said.[76] In fact, Saunders was given a free hand in restructuring the company but, by the time he took over, the business was on the brink of disaster. Most family-controlled businesses are inclined not to seek outside help until that point is reached.

Union International was on the verge of collapse before the Vesteys agreed to appoint an outsider as chief executive. In January 1992, under pressure from a consortium of seventy-eight banks owed £420 million by the company, Terry Robinson was recruited from Lonrho to save the company. By selling scores of treasured assets, he brought Union International within an ace of salvation. But his subsequent fate was a lesson in why professional managers are reluctant to work for family-owned businesses. Robinson agreed to join Union International in return for a £14 million bonus if he saved the company. In March 1995, within £50 million of achieving that goal, the banks put Union International into the hands of receivers. By then, the Vesteys had bought a number of the remaining assets in the Union International portfolio at attractive prices, using the family voting power to exclude alternative buyers. Among them was Robinson, who had hoped to lead a management buy-out of some of the better businesses. Robinson was effectively isolated by the family. Yet the company had got into trouble while two cousins – Edmund and Samuel Vestey – ran the business. They ran it not necessarily because they were best-equipped, but because they were, respectively, grandson, and great-grandson of the founders. Even as disaster loomed in 1991, Edmund preferred to let his thirty-year-old son, Tim Vestey, try to solve the problems. It was the banks who insisted on Robinson.

Littlewoods, the football pools and retailing empire created by Sir John Moores is the second-largest private business in Britain. Yet the company found it tricky to attract high calibre managers from outside the family. It is not hard to see why. Sir John found it difficult to delegate to anyone. He fired one of his sons from the chairmanship and took charge again when he was well into his eighties, and spent sixty years at the top of the company before asking his first outsider (Desmond Pitcher, better known as chairman of North West Water) to become chief executive in 1983. Little changed as a result; the company missed the 1980s retail boom, under-invested in its businesses, and drifted into serious problems in the 1990s. As the problems mounted, new management was recruited from outside the company, but meaningful changes proved hard to effect. Like all outsiders appointed to run private businesses, the new managers found it hard to win and retain the confidence of the family shareholders.[77] Even today, Littlewoods is mired in the same mixture Sir John created in the 1930s: football pools, mail order shopping and high street retailing. But Littlewoods ought to have developed since the 1930s, shedding and investing in new businesses. Domination by the family was the reason it did not.

John Moores inhibited his children, and sowed dissent among them, partly because he distrusted their ability to run the business. The family shareholder–directors ended up neither running it nor owning it, but merely interfering. James Ross, current chairman of Littlewoods and another outsider, explained, 'If they made an announcement, was it a decision they would implement as managers? Or were they non-executive directors giving advice, or shareholders with ultimate power? They were confused, and that confused the professional managers. So, ultimately, you got a totally risk-averse management that wouldn't do anything.'[78] Being privately owned, Littlewoods lacked an external stimulus to change: the threat of takeover. Outside shareholders impose a constant pressure to perform.

Family ownership caused similar indiscipline at Union International. 'There were no financial controls,' Terry Robinson said, nine months after arriving at the company. 'No one knew why borrowings were increasing because no one knew who was spending what.'[79] Saunders found the same at Guinness: he had to hire outsiders to generate the most basic financial information about the business.[80] The Wolfsons ran Great Universal Stores without either a finance director or a treasurer until 1996. Like Littlewoods, the company held onto the declining mail order business which had been the foundation of its success. Unlike Littlewoods, the family produced a saviour. Since David Wolfson became chairman, Great Universal Stores has made a series of acquisitions (including Argos, the discount retailer) and used its mailing lists to build a financial information business.

Conservatism, stemming from a lack of external stimuli, seems to be innate to most family-controlled businesses. 'We have always done it this way' and 'If it was good enough for me, it is good enough for you' are the watchwords. It often manifests itself in the second and third generations. Once a company gets past the second generation, emotional commitment tends to cloud business judgment. 'The family and the company are disparate systems,' two students of family firms have said. 'The family invokes the idea of stability, caring, co-operation and fidelity; the company focuses on change, evaluation, competition and efficiency.'[81] A family business can easily become an heirloom rather than an asset, and once it is seen in this light, selling even a part of it becomes unthinkable.[82]

Is the Private Company Doomed?

The exceptions to this rule are the distant family shareholders who count on the dividends. Their primary concern is the protection of their investment. They want the money, not jobs or prestige. In that sense, they are the same as external shareholders. Several members of the Moores family sold their stock in Littlewoods rather than run the risk of losing it. Others insisted on fatter dividend cheques. John Moores made sure his family was comfortable, but was extremely frugal with pay-outs to shareholders. The cost of the dividend leapt from £2 million to over £30 million in the year after his death, as the incumbent faction tried to buy the acquiescence of family members restless about the custody of their huge but unrealisable fortune. The obvious restlessness of family shareholders encouraged outsiders to bid for the company. Littlewoods received two offers. One was from the former chief executive, Barry Dale, and a City consortium, and the other was a joint bid by Sir David Alliance and the Iceland frozen food chain. The Moores family rejected both bids. Yet, like any takeover proposal, they had a salutary effect. Family shareholders made it clear that their continued loyalty to the firm was dependent on an improved financial performance. In May 1996 Littlewoods hired James Ross, former chief executive at Cable & Wireless. His brief was to improve profitability, but the task is immense. He tried and failed to sell the High Street stores to Kingfisher (family shareholders demanded too high a price) and a bid for the Freemans mail order business was halted by the competition authorities.[83] Littlewoods is still the creation of Sir John Moores.

In recent years, several large private companies have floated their shares on the Stock Exchange to enable the family to realise the value they have created. Sir Graham Kirkham, creator of the DFS furniture manufacturing and retailing business, sold £130 million of shares belonging to himself and his family in 1993, and more followed in 1995. Steve Morgan, founder of the Welsh-based construction company Redrow, sold shares worth £62 million on the Stock Exchange in 1994. Fraser and Gordon Morrison, custodians of the Edinburgh-based construction company founded by their father, floated the business in 1995. The Moores family will probably float Littlewoods once the business is in better shape. C & J Clark, the shoe retailers, another private company with restless family shareholders, is planning a public quotation. Even the Vesteys have considered a public quotation for their surviving businesses.

It seems that the family company is yielding gradually to the all-conquering PLC. Certainly, the best-of-both-worlds solution (non-voting stock) is unsustainable. Whitbread, Greenalls, Austin Reed, Pifco and Liberty have all followed the example of Great Universal Stores and enfranchised non-family shareholders. As they subject themselves to the discipline of the market, much will be gained. Finance will be cheaper, and financial discipline tighter. Better managers will be attracted to the company, and they will be free to make difficult decisions. Making money will be more important than keeping control.

But the passing of a private company occasions loss as well as gain. A company which has no need to dance to the demands of outside shareholders can grow more slowly. Many companies have thrived precisely because they did not have to conform to the ambitions of outsiders. 'Being private is very important,' says Sir Anthony Bamford, chairman of J. C. Bamford. 'It has enabled us to plough our own furrow through the good and the bad times and not be swallowed up . . . All our capital investment would be looked at in a different light if we were a public company.'[84]

The chief characteristic of the outside shareholder is not the search for excellence, or innovation, but for the exit. It was the constant pressure to deliver shareholder value, irrespective of the nature of the business or its long-term strategy, which persuaded Richard Branson and Andrew Lloyd Webber to buy their companies back from outside shareholders. Alan Sugar tried to make Amstrad private too, though it turned out that the shareholders placed a higher value on his company than he did. Despite appearances, the private company is not simply a staging post on the road to a public quotation. There is a place in business for alternatives to the PLC. It is not yet a universal ideal, and will never be a universal fact. It just seems that way.

CHAPTER TWENTY-ONE

THE MULTINATIONALS

Surely it is better for the British people to buy Japanese cars made by
British workers than to buy German cars assembled by Turks?
Remark attributed to Norman Tebbit[1]

It is like coming over here and buying the throne.
ALFRED TAUBMAN, on buying Sotheby's[2]

I hope to give a lot of enjoyable annoyance to everybody. Wouldn't you?
'TINY' ROWLAND, on selling hotels to Colonel Gadaffi[3]

The multinational is the PLC in its most virulent form. It does not merely
divide ownership from control. Its owners are the fickle, faceless and often
foreign inhabitants of cyberspace, where Unilever is swapped for Procter &
Gamble if Ariel looks like selling better than Persil. Control is vested in a
new class of globe-trotting managers whose home is the first-class cabin of a
747 and whose only loyalty is to other members of their caste. The job of the
controllers is to increase the value of the capital invested in their companies
by the shareholders. If this means cutting costs by closing a factory in Bolton
and transferring production to China, neither patriotism nor conscience will
complicate the decision. The owners of multinationals are no longer proxies
for the countries they come from, and the people who manage their assets
take their decisions not in a national but in a global context. Multinationals
appear threatening not because they are foreign but, because they have shed
their nationality so completely, they seem to have no personality at all.

Thirty years ago politicians and commentators fretted that this non-
nationality made them indifferent to the prosperity of the economies where
they operated. In 1968, the French pundit, Jean-Jacques Servan-Schreiber,
predicted in *Le défi américain* that all important economic and financial
decisions would soon be taken by American multinationals, reducing the

great powers of Europe to servile dependency on American capital and technology. The book made almost as great an impact in Britain as it did in France. 'The time has come for governments everywhere to decide what to do about the great multinational companies that have grown up in the last twenty-five years,' wrote Christopher Tugendhat in the opening line of his award-winning book, *The Multinationals*, in 1971. Its second chapter was entitled 'The American Invasion'.[4]

British Multinationals

Ironically, the book appeared just as British multinationals began to invade America. The biggest, British Petroleum, was expanding aggressively in the United States even as Servan-Schreiber and Tugendhat were writing their jeremiads (BP began its gradual acquisition of Standard Oil in 1969). It was also during the 1960s, when successive British governments applied for membership of the Common Market, that companies such as ICI and Beecham began to compete with the Americans in the scale of investment in continental Europe. The sixties were the decade when the attention of British capitalism swung away from the old empire and towards North America and western Europe. In 1962 the ten most popular locations for British investment abroad were former Imperial or Commonwealth territories; twenty years later, only three were. The biggest destination was still the United States, but the remainder were members of the European Community.[5] Today, western Europe and the United States between them account for nearly three quarters of total British overseas assets and almost two thirds of net overseas earnings.

Interest in western Europe accelerated after Britain joined the European Community in 1972, and speeded up again during the single-market programme of the late 1980s and early 1990s and the prelude to the introduction of the single European currency in 1999. Investment by British companies in the United States surged as the pound strengthened against the dollar in the late 1970s and early 1980s, and rose particularly rapidly after the abolition of exchange controls in 1979. In the mid-1980s, British companies completed a series of audacious takeover bids in the United States: ICI acquired Beatrice Chemicals in 1985; Hanson Trust paid nearly $1 billion for SCM the same year, and added Peabody in 1990. Grand Metropolitan bought Pillsbury for nearly £3 billion in 1988, and BAT Industries acquired the Farmers insurance group for £2.9 billion. Even Robert Maxwell found £1.5 billion to acquire Macmillan, the North American publisher. In 1988 British companies spent over £13 billion on acquisitions in America. For a time, Hanson Trust was able to advertise itself on television as a genuinely Anglo–American company.

Despite all this activity, the net value of British corporate assets abroad is about the same as it was in 1914. The best guess is that corporate Britain had foreign assets worth £1.4 billion at the outbreak of the First World War, equivalent then to perhaps half the world total of overseas assets, but roughly the same in real terms as the present total of nearly £70 billion.[6] It is true

TABLE 21.1
Foreign Assets of British Companies, 1997 (£bn)

Country	Value	% of Total	Net Earnings	% of Total
European Union	95.8	42.7	9.5	32.9
EFTA	1.6	0.7	0.991	3.4
Other European Countries	2.5	1.1	(0.039)	(0.1)
UK Offshore Islands	2.7	1.2	0.223	0.8
United States	62.7	28.0	9.5	33.0
Canada	5.5	2.4	0.891	3.1
Bermuda	4.9	2.2	0.070	0.2
Brazil	2.2	1.0	0.386	1.3
Rest of America	7.2	3.2	1.2	4.0
Near and Middle East	0.923	0.4	0.478	1.7
Singapore	5.1	2.3	0.785	2.7
Hong Kong	4.4	2.0	0.617	2.1
Malaysia	2.3	1.0	0.319	1.1
Japan	1.6	0.7	0.267	0.9
Thailand	1.0	0.5	0.094	0.3
India	0.691	0.3	0.133	0.5
Rest of Asia	3.3	1.5	0.530	1.8
Australia	11.1	5.0	1.5	5.2
New Zealand	1.7	0.7	0.279	1.0
Oceania	1.2	0.5	0.175	0.6
South Africa	2.5	1.1	0.521	1.8
Nigeria	1.1	0.5	0.046	0.2
Zimbabwe	0.187	0.1	0.061	0.2
Kenya	0.247	0.1	0.072	0.3
Rest of Africa	1.9	0.8	0.274	1.0
World Total	224.4	100.0	28.8	100.0

Source: Office for National Statistics, Overseas Direct Investment 1997, 14 December 1998, Table 2.

that the official measures underestimate their worth, since they are based on book rather than market values. One study reckoned official figures underestimated them by 75 per cent.[7] But it is also true that it has taken Britain a very long time to recover the value of the overseas assets sold to pay for the First and Second World Wars.

The Influence of Empire

The bulk of those assets were in the United States, the principal British creditor in both world wars, and a country where the gradual imposition of import controls from the late nineteenth century had made direct investment the only route into the market. The two world wars claimed the bulk of the business assets and securities British companies had built up there: Courtaulds, for example, was forced to sell its American Viscose subsidiary to pay for Lend-Lease during the Second World War. Between the wars, rampant protectionism had diverted British investment towards imperial possessions. The empire accounted for over half the overseas assets of corporate Britain by the outbreak of the Second World War.[8]

The imposition of exchange controls in 1939, which were not lifted for forty years, reinforced this process by encouraging companies to invest within the sterling area.[9] But exchange controls were not entirely to blame. British companies reckoned it best to invest where they had a competitive advantage. British Leyland, for example, deliberately eschewed the rigours of the European motor-car markets in favour of Imperial and Commonwealth consumers. It was scarcely unnatural for British companies to follow the flag; investment abroad was pioneered by the East India and Hudson's Bay Companies, the precursors of British political as well as commercial involvement in Asia and North America.

The earliest multinationals of the modern kind were often domestic manufacturing or processing companies such as Dunlop (rubber), Lever Brothers (palm oil) and Shell and BP (oil), which relied as much on imperial power as their own efforts to control their sources of supply. Others, like Charter Consolidated and Burmah Oil, were effectively expatriate enterprises exploiting the rich resources of the colonies. They raised capital from shareholders and bankers in Britain only because it was cheap and available, and would just as happily have tapped American, German or French sources. The biggest company in Britain today, the pharmaceuticals giant Glaxo Wellcome, originated in New Zealand. It was a producer of dried milk until it took over the pharmaceutical manufacturer, Allen & Hanbury, in 1958.

Even today, the influence of the past over the shape of British capitalism is pervasive. Commonwealth countries still account for one fifth of overseas assets and a quarter of net overseas earnings. The business of British multinationals is tilted heavily towards the oil, mining, plantation and commercial banking industries which their Victorian and Edwardian forebears built on the back of the empire. Less than half of the twenty biggest British multinationals are engaged, even tangentially, in the industries of the twenty-first century: information technology, pharmaceuticals, the electronic media. Their efforts to re-invent themselves as 'multi-local multinationals' for the much-touted 'borderless' markets of the post-communist world have had mixed results. Midland Bank (now part of HSBC Holdings) and National

TABLE 21.2
Foreign Assets Owned by British Companies (£bn)

Year	Direct Investment Abroad*	Direct Investment in Britain†	Net Direct Assets
1979	31.4	22.0	9.4
1980	33.2	26.4	6.8
1981	44.9	30.0	14.9
1982	52.0	32.3	19.7
1983	57.8	37.2	20.6
1984	75.1	40.1	35.0
1985	69.4	44.3	25.1
1986	80.7	51.7	29.0
1987	85.3	62.6	22.7
1988	103.7	76.8	26.9
1989	122.4	99.8	22.6
1990	119.7	113.2	6.5
1991	125.3	120.7	4.6
1992	148.4	122.7	25.7
1993	169.0	127.9	41.1
1994	172.3	122.3	50.0
1995	202.8	131.5	71.3
1996	212.3	138.7	73.6
1997	236.0	161.6	75.0

Source: Office for National Statistics, UK Economic Accounts 1993, Fourth Quarter, Tables B14 and B15; UK Economic Accounts 1997, Second Quarter, Tables B18 and B19; UK Balance of Payments 1997, Table 8.1.

* Investment abroad by British companies in their overseas subsidiaries.
† Investment by foreign companies in their British subsidiaries.

Westminster squandered hundreds of millions of pounds on ill-considered American adventures, and Barclays spent almost as much on a failed experiment in international investment banking.

Despite this expenditure, no British bank has created an investment banking operation capable of competing with the Americans in the business of global money and securities trading created by that characteristic mixture of the late twentieth century: deregulation plus cheap telecommunications and computer power. At bottom, three of the Big Four British banks are just old-fashioned domestic money-lenders.[10] The largest and most successful (HSBC Holdings) is a former colonial bank forced to return home by the surrender of Hong Kong. Other businesses have also found it difficult to expand abroad. In 1997 British Telecommunications (BT) attempted to turn itself into a global business by offering £12 billion for an American company, MCI, but was out-manoeuvred and outbid by an indigenous rival. The biggest British engineering firm, GEC, is an enigma. Though financially successful, it is not known for innovation or technological prowess, and least of all for its international reach.

It is, however, easy to overdo the gloom. BP and Shell may be in old-fashioned industries, but they are global giants. Glaxo Wellcome is an unequivocal multinational success in an important new industry. And although Unilever is now undergoing massive restructuring after years of poorly managed international diversification, it remains the quintessential 'multi-local multinational'. Disparaging British industrial and commercial achievements is a habit hard to shake off since the British Disease made the country an international laughing stock in the 1960s and 1970s. But the political and economic reforms of the 1980s, and the destruction of militant trade unionism, transformed corporate Britain. Compared with its peer group, the growth, productivity, profits and job-creating record of the British economy since the early 1980s has put an end to decades of relative underperformance.

Fear of the Multinationals

There are many reasons why this longed-for economic success is not reflected in popular confidence. Among them are growing inequalities in income, volatile house prices and general insecurity. But one of the chief causes of inveterate British pessimism is the belief that international capital has the whiphand over domestic labour. A large part of the improved performance of the multinationals is experienced by their employees as longer hours and shrunken promotion prospects. The fear of redundancy is pervasive, as fac-

TABLE 21.3
The Twenty Biggest Companies in Britain, 1997 (£bn)

	Market Capitalisation	Turnover	Profits	Employees
Glaxo Wellcome	51.4	8.3	2.9	53,808
British Petroleum	47.2	44.7	3.7	53,700
Shell Transport & Trading	43.8	82.1	3.1	105,000
HSBC	40.9	9.6	4.5	109,298
Lloyds TSB	40.6	7.2	2.5	90,383
SmithKline Beecham	34.4	7.9	1.5	52,900
British Telecommunications	30.3	14.9	3.2	129,600
Barclays Bank	24.4	7.6	2.4	87,400
Diageo*	22.0	13.7	1.4	79,383
Halifax	19.2	n/a	0.893	30,349
Zeneca	18.9	5.4	0.975	31,100
Marks & Spencer	17.4	7.8	1.1	45,805
National Westminster Bank	17.1	3.3	1.1	79,100
BAT Industries†	17.0	7.2	2.5	81,039
Unilever	16.1	33.5	2.4	287,000
Abbey National	14.8	2.8	1.2	20,267
Prudential	13.8	n/a	1.6	22,187
Vodaphone	12.9	1.7	0.539	6,051
Cable & Wireless	12.2	6.1	1.4	37,448
BG	11.3	9.5	0.156	43,106

Source: London Stock Exchange Fact File 1998, FT 500, January 1998; Company Annual Reports and Accounts.

* In October 1997 Grand Metropolitan merged with Guinness to create GMG Brands, renamed Diaego. The turnover, profit and number of employee figures combine data for the year ended September 1996.
† In 1998 BAT Industries demerged its insurance and tobacco arms, and merged the insurance businesses with Zurich Insurance of Switzerland.

tories and offices are competed out of business or transferred to a cheaper location.

From a boardroom full of Fat Cats comes a message whose truth does not make it more palatable: the company is competing in a global marketplace. Cheap transport and telecommunications and increasingly powerful information technology are knocking down barriers to the free movement of people, capital and goods and services which even the deregulators were prepared to let stand. National governments, boasting of flexible labour

markets and low rates of corporate taxation to attract their share of inter-
nationally mobile capital, seem powerless to protect labour from the disrup-
tive effects of a genuinely global economy. Ordinary people sense that control
of their economic destiny has passed to an impalpable force known as *globalisation*.

This is why popular attitudes towards multinationals are so paradoxical.
They are welcomed as harbingers of investment and jobs and regions compete
to persuade them to invest[11] – the management guru Charles Hardy jokes
that the heads of the largest companies will soon be making state visits – but
they are also reviled as bringers of disinvestment and unemployment. They
are applauded as efficient disseminators of new technologies and management skills, and disparaged as builders of 'screwdriver factories' and
employers of the unskilled and the underpaid.

Newspapers pander to the insecurities of their readers by compiling lists
of the great British products which now belong to foreigners. Swiss-based
Nestlé owns Kit Kat and Smarties; French-based Gervase Danone has pocketed
HP Sauce and Lea & Perrins; Marmite, Bovril and Frank Cooper's Oxford
Marmalade belong to the Corn Products Company of America. Even Monopoly – thought of as the quintessentially British game, though it was invented
in the United States – is owned by an American toy manufacturer, Hasbro.
The editorial hand-wringing which greeted the decision of Toyota to build a
new car assembly plant in France rather than in Britain was almost as great
as that which greeted the sale of Rover, the last remaining British-owned car
manufacturer, to BMW of Germany.

In the popular estimation, the country is fast becoming the sweatshop of
the developed world, its industrial heritage in the hands of foreigners and
its people working for slave wages at foreign-owned screwdriver plants whose
managers are answerable to distant powers whose loyalties lie far from the
towns and cities where they have acquired businesses or built factories. The Fat
Cats share many of these fears. They are among the most gullible consumers of
fallacies like the belief that the only real jobs are in manufacturing rather
than services ('we can't earn our keep from hairdressing and hamburger-
flipping'); that no industrial country can survive without a steel or a motor
industry to call its own; and that nationality is more important than ownership.
They greet with alarm the revelation that Britain is reliant for half her export
earnings on foreign-owned enterprises, and record solemnly that there is no
British-owned motor manufacturer of size, or investment bank of influence,
and that only two of the regional electricity companies are still in British
hands.

Managerial Xenophobia

In April 1996 Sir William Barlow, formerly chairman of both the Post Office and of BICC, complained publicly that the 'strategic industries' of water, electricity and railways were 'in the hands of overseas masters . . . By losing control of our wealth-creating companies many strategic decisions affecting the future of manufacturing industry and the lives of British people will be made overseas. I don't like it.' He added, that the 'very idea of Texans supplying electricity to London sticks in my gullet'.[12]

The last comment was deliciously ironic. American companies played the largest part in the development of the British electrical industry in general, and in the provision of electricity to London in particular. The American-owned Utilities Power & Light Company Ltd led the creation of an electricity transmission network not just in London but throughout the southern part of England between 1925 and 1936. Electricity supply in London was entirely American-owned until 1936.[13]

Without American help, Britain would not have an electrical industry either: STC, GEC and EMI, whose beginnings can be traced to the 1880s, were all American, in terms of ownership, technology and management. Likewise, nearly all early telephone technology had to be imported from the United States.[14]

Another foreigner, the German William Siemens, installed the first electric lights in Britain, at Godalming in Surrey. Siemens became a British citizen and the company which bears his name, though German-owned, is still one of the largest forces in the British electrical industry. In 1995, it placed an advertisement in British newspapers. 'When the young William Siemens first came too the UK in 1843,' it read, 'Germans were still very popular. The Queen had even married one.'[15] Nothing made it so popular as the decision in 1996 to invest over £1 billion in a new semi-conductor plant in the north-east of England. Unfortunately, jubilation was short-lived; the semi-conductor market collapsed, and the Tyneside factory was closed in 1998.[16]

Disappointment was understandable, particularly as it followed a satisfying sense of economic schadenfreude. But the Siemens debacle was a reminder that the benefits of foreign investment in Britain should not be measured by jobs alone. The chief gains from foreign investment are competition, and the transfer of techniques, technology, and management skills. Fujitsu, for example, has transformed ICL from a problem-ridden mainframe manufacturer into a dynamic software and information technology services supplier which is scheduled to return to the stock market in its own right in the year 2000. A study by the National Institute of Economic and Social Research in

1993 estimated that a third of the productivity increases in British manufacturing were attributable to the power of foreign influence and example. This is most obvious in the motor industry, where the Japanese manufacturers, Nissan, Honda and Toyota, have achieved marvels of productivity with exactly the same British workers who drove Chrysler out of Scotland and British Leyland out of business.

In an earlier era, it was the Americans who brought new ideas and techniques to refresh British capitalism: Ford introduced the assembly line to its factories here in the 1920s; Esso pioneered productivity-based wage bargaining at its Fawley refinery in 1960; department stores (Woolworths), supermarkets (Fine Fare, and later Safeway), self-service petrol stations (Esso and Mobil) and fast-food restaurants (KFC and McDonald's) were all American inventions imported by American multinationals. As Japanese and European investment increased in the 1980s, different business cultures began to cross-fertilise in the British context. A *Financial Times* journalist, visiting a German-owned headlamp manufacturer in Banbury, was tickled to find British workers toiling under a sign reading *Genba Kenri*, the Japanese for 'workshop management'.[17]

But foreign multinationals make their biggest impact not by example but by competition. The competitive pressure they bring to bear on indigenous rivals and their suppliers forces them to transform their performance or go out of business. The decision by Toyota to manufacture in Derbyshire brought the Japanese components maker, Nippondenso, to Telford. The Nissan plant at Sunderland brought an American air-bag inflator manufacturer, TRW, to Peterlee. Samsung has attracted a brace of other South Korean companies to supply its television and microwave factories in the north-east. Pressure of this kind has led to such dramatic improvements in the quality of British-made motor components that British metal-bashers are now winning export orders from demanding manufacturers such as BMW and Mercedes Benz, and even from car makers in Japan.

Britain is now producing more cars than Italy, and more than at any time since the 1960s, but less than one hundredth of its output is manufactured by British-owned companies. The leading manufacturers are Japanese, German (Rover and Land Rover), American (Ford and Vauxhall) and French (Peugeot-Citroën). Britain is also the leading producer of television sets in Europe, making one in every three sold in the European Union. But five of the six biggest producers are Japanese (Toshiba, Sony, Hitachi, Matsushita, Mitsubishi) and the sixth is South Korean (Samsung). In 1997, Britain had a trade surplus of £500 million in TV sets.[18] Those made by the five British-owned companies which dominated television manufacturing twenty years ago – Rank, Decca, Fidelity, GEC and Rediffusion – are now found only in industrial museums.

Hostility to Foreign Takeovers

For some reason, the British find a lingering industrial death less troubling than a dramatic takeover of a native company by a foreign predator. Acquisitions of well-known businesses – Beecham (by SmithKline), Rowntree (Nestlé), ICL (Fujitsu), STC (Northern Telecom), Babcock International (Mitsui), Jaguar (Ford) and Rover (BMW) – were invariably accompanied by national lamentation about the loss of industrial prowess as well as jobs and major local employers. In 1985, the Thatcher government was surprised to find a vociferous group of its MPs opposed to the sale of Land Rover to General Motors or Ford. 'Continuing the negotiations under a blaze of publicity amidst enormous volumes of political claptrap was exceedingly difficult,' recalls the trade secretary at the time, 'and the hostility shown to GM and the anti-American hysteria of the Labour Party began to cause doubts in Detroit about the wisdom of increased investment in, and reliance on, the United Kingdom.'[19]

The purchase of Rowntree by Nestlé was also accompanied by deafening political opposition, based partly on grounds of reciprocity (British companies could not take over Swiss companies) but mainly on old-fashioned xenophobia (Nestlé was already a major employer in Britain). 'An outside observer would have formed the impression,' recalled Lord Young, the trade secretary, 'that chocolate was a strategic raw material.'[20]

The bid prompted an official government inquiry into takeover barriers in Europe, designed to pressurise European companies into opening their markets in corporate control. It concluded, unsurprisingly, that the British market was more open than those in the rest of Europe. But it did not conclude this was a bad thing for Britain.[21] A subsequent investigation by the Trade and Industry Committee made a number of detailed recommendations designed to make bids more difficult, but did not demand reciprocal access to foreign markets.[22] It was left to Sir Hector Laing, chairman of United Biscuits, to call openly in 1990 for British companies to be protected from takeover by continental predators: 'The chairman of a major French company told me recently that come what may, it would be inconceivable for his government to allow a takeover of his business from outside France – and that the "people of France" would not like it. What a contrast with our own attitude!'[23]

Sir Hector was right that the British market in corporate control is more open than its European counterparts, but it is not as open as he believed. The Thatcher governments retained a 'golden share' in most privatised companies, largely to deny foreign bidders. P & O used to insist in its Articles of Association that shareholders be British, on the grounds that its fleet was essential to national security in the event of war. In the 1920s GEC was one of a number of British companies to limit the size of foreign shareholding and to deny voting rights to foreign shareholders. Until the 1980s, Lloyd's insurance market and the London Stock Exchange excluded foreigners from membership. The Bank of England long made it clear that foreign bids for British banks were not welcome.

If all else fails, the Monopolies and Mergers Commission (MMC) has proved a trusty ally of governments looking to dislodge foreign buyers. It prevented an American company, Enserch, from buying Davy Corporation in 1981, essentially for nationalistic reasons. In 1988 the commission was used to make the Kuwait Investment Office (KIO) disgorge the massive shareholding it had acquired in BP. In the wake of the failing sale of BP shares in the autumn of 1987, the Kuwaitis amassed a stake in the company which peaked at 21.7 per cent. The proper response was to congratulate a substantial investor for playing much the same role Richard Whitney had played on the floor of the New York Stock Exchange in October 1929.[24] But this was not how it was seen at the time, by either the BP management or the British government. After massive political and diplomatic pressure had failed to persuade the Kuwaitis to reduce their holding, the issue was referred to the MMC. Its report (October 1988) gave the British government the respectable cover it needed to order the Kuwaitis to reduce their stake to 9.9 per cent, and BP bought an 11.7 per cent stake from the Kuwaitis for £2.4 billion in January 1989.[25]

Portfolio Investment by Foreigners

The KIO still retains a 4.5 per cent stake in BP, but the events of 1987 and 1988 left Kuwaitis feeling rather cross. 'Britain', thundered a leader in *Al-Rai Al-Aam*, a Kuwaiti newspaper known to reflect official opinion, 'has now proved it is not a friend we can rely on or trust.'[26] This proved to be a spectacularly premature judgment. Just over two years later, all the British assets of the KIO were frozen as British soldiers, sailors and airmen fought to liberate Kuwait from Iraqi occupation. But the Kuwaitis were right to wonder why they were singled out for special treatment. The scale of portfolio investment by foreigners exceeds the level of foreign direct investment by a large margin. In 1997 overseas investors owned British securities worth over £415 billion, more than three times the book value of the plant and machinery owned in Britain by foreign companies.[27] Yet there is rarely controversy over foreign ownership of British shares until a company is threatened with takeover.

This is understandable. A holding of a small proportion of the capital, unlike ownership of a factory or even a company, does not imply that foreigners have *control* of the assets. The Arabs are the one significant exception to this otherwise tolerant approach to foreign institutional investment. There are polite explanations for hostility to their purchases of shares in British companies. The distinction between private and public investment is unclear in Arab countries, where the state is often a fief of the ruling family, and the public investment funds are their playthings. British governments have protested against purchases of shares by state-owned companies based in France on similar grounds. But ever since the oil price rises of the 1970s, the British have worried about the sheer scale of Arab spending power. Augmented by the immunity from British taxes which is accorded to all state-owned investors, it is hard to ignore.[28]

The oil price hike of 1973 was thought to be putting between $50 and $60 billion a year at the disposal of Arab investors, which was more than enough to buy all of corporate Britain in 1974 or 1975. At their peak at the end of the 1980s, the resources of the KIO were estimated at £50 billion. The Kuwaitis sprang to public notice in September 1974, when they paid £107 million for the St Martin's Property Corporation. At various times the KIO owned large stakes in the Bank of Scotland, Morgan Grenfell, the Savoy Hotel group, Eagle Star, General Accident and Harry Ramsden's fish and chip parlours. Even the fear that it would not support a new issue was enough to guarantee exclusion of Jewish banks from the underwriting syndicate. Its secretiveness (it was entitled to use the Bank of England nominee account) meant its legendary wealth haunted every listed company. The appearance of the KIO on the share register of an investment trust was regarded as a sure sign of an impending takeover. In 1983 its stake in Anderson Strathclyde was decisive in delivering the company to Charter Consolidated, prompting fierce criticism by the chief executive of the defeated company. The Kuwaitis put the Royal Bank of Scotland in play in 1984 by selling its stake to Lloyds Bank, and in 1987 helped to precipitate Morgan Grenfell's sale to Deutsche Bank by selling its stake to the Australian arbitrageur, Robert Holmes à Court. They also supported the Forte bid for the Savoy group in 1981, and the Bells bid for Gleneagles in 1985.

But the Gulf War cost the KIO the fearsome status it enjoyed then; Desert Storm cost the Kuwaitis $22 billion, and the reconstruction of their devastated homeland another $20–30 billion. An estimated overseas portfolio of $100 billion in 1990 had shrunk within three years to $30 billion or less. In Britain, a Kuwaiti decision to sell a large stake in the Midland Bank just weeks before it was taken over by HSBC Holdings undermined its reputation as the feared initiator of takeover battles. (That one decision cost the KIO around £50–60 million.) Following retrenchment after the Gulf War, it now owns slightly more than one five-hundredth of corporate Britain. BP remains its only sizeable stake in a large public company.[29]

No other Arab investment fund has matched the status of the KIO. Its nearest rival, the Abu Dhabi Investment Authority, was damaged by the close and expensive association of Sheikh Zayed bin Sultan al-Nahyan with the Bank of Credit and Commerce International (BCCI). But in the 1970s, like the KIO, the authority was one of the mysterious 'Arab interests' which stalked the stock market. It was headline news when it helped to underwrite a Commercial Union rights issue in December 1974, and 'Arab interests' bought a 21 per cent stake in Costain, a construction firm which did a lot of work in the Middle East.[30] London has remained the centre of international financial wheeler-dealing by Arabs ever since, but as portfolio investors they are far less important than the Americans. Between them, the Kuwait Investment Office, the Abu Dhabi Investment Authority and the Saudi Arabian Monetary Authority owned a mere half of one per cent of corporate Britain at the end of 1997.

Other foreign investors popularly supposed to own large parts of corporate Britain own even less. The Singapore Monetary Authority held a quarter of one per cent of the London market. The legendary George Soros had British holdings worth just £121 million, or less than one hundredth of one per cent. The sultan of the oil-rich state of Brunei (now officially ensconced in the *Guinness Book of Records* as The Richest Man in the World, with a fortune of $30 billion) does not appear on share company registers at all. The Brunei Investment Agency, which he controls, is thought to have $45–50 billion to invest, but does not own even as much as George Soros. The falling oil price has forced the Agency to liquidate much of its portfolio. By the end of 1997 it had only one holding worth more than £5 million (in BT). The top half-dozen American fund managers alone, by contrast, control 5.5 per cent of the London stock market. The purchase of Britain by oil-rich sheikhs, genuinely feared in the 1970s, failed to happen. Even the US stake in corporate Britain, larger than that of any other foreign country, scarcely amounts to a stock-market version of *Le défi américain*.

Is Britain Losing Control?

Britain has more invested in foreign securities than foreigners have in Britain. The same is true of direct investment. At the very time the British government was asking the Kuwaitis to sell their shares in BP, and Sir Hector Laing was demanding protection from foreign predators, British companies made far more acquisitions abroad than foreign companies made in Britain. In that respect, 1990 was not unusual. The same is true every year. Between 1987 and 1997, the Office for National Statistics counted more then three times as many British acquisitions abroad as foreign acquisitions in Britain. But Sir Hector, like Sir William Barlow later on, had a point. If a company acquires foreign parents, decisions crucial to British jobs and prosperity tend to gravitate from London, Birmingham and Glasgow to New York, Frankfurt and Tokyo. The decision to close the Siemens factory on Tyneside, for example, was taken in Germany by German executives. In fact, the collapse of the semi-conductor market saw hundreds of British workers lose their jobs because of decisions taken abroad. In the autumn of 1998 National Semiconductor fired 600 workers at its facility in Greenock, Seagate Technology closed its plant at Livingston, and Fujitsu shut down its factory at Newton Aycliffe.[31]

TABLE 21.4
Merger & Acquisition Activity By British and Foreign Companies 1987–97

	British Acquisitions by Foreign Companies	Foreign Acquisitions by British Companies	British Disposals by Foreign Companies	Foreign Disposals by British Companies
Number	1,695	5,774	288	1,710
Value (£bn)	90.5	150.6	14.8	54.8

Source: Office for National Statistics, *Acquisitions and Mergers Involving UK Companies*, Third Quarter 1996, First Release; Third Quarter 1998, First Release

Despite oceans of talk about 'globalisation', most multinationals are still extremely nationalistic in terms of ultimate control of the company. This has occasionally persuaded British workers to believe they are being sacrificed to save jobs in the country of their foreign owners. Large parts of STC were sold after the company was acquired by Northern Telecom in 1990. ICL pulled out of personal computers in 1996, leaving the field clear for its new parent, Fujitsu. Leyland Vans nearly disappeared after its Dutch parent got into difficulties in 1993. In the same year there was an ugly dispute in Dundee when Timex Electronics, an American company, decided to sack and replace the entire workforce, following a failure to reach agreement with the unions on pay and working conditions. The plant was eventually closed.

Closures of this kind can be disastrous for small towns. When Nestlé closed the Crosse & Blackwell plant in Cumbria in 1994, five hundred workers lost their jobs. The closure of the Pirelli tyre-making factory at Burton-on-Trent was a blow to the town as well as the employees. When the Korean economy got into difficulties in late 1997, Samsung was forced to shut an excavator factory at Harrogate. One hundred jobs were lost. The same company later postponed a £450 million investment in a microwave, monitor and fax factory at Wynyard Park near Newcastle Upon Tyne. Another South Korean company, Hyundai, ran into difficulties financing its £3 billion semi-conductor plant near Glasgow. A third (LG) had to postpone a £1.7 billion investment in South Wales.

The sense of powerlessness these decisions conveyed stems from a loss of economic sovereignty. The French call it *délocalisation*. Although the British are much less sensitive about foreign control than the French, the same concern has lain at the heart of misgivings about foreign multinationals since they first arrived in Britain. In 1958, years before the hysteria about *Le défi américain* became widespread, one student of American investment in Britain reported popular anxiety about the 'danger of whole sections of UK industry passing into US hands – the implication being that this is necessarily a thing to be avoided'.[32]

The American Invasion

Ten years later the luridly titled *American Takeover of Britain* was published in London. In *Merger Mania*, published in 1970, William Davis recorded contemporary British fears about American economic hegemony.

> What would happen if the wishes of Detroit ran counter to British economic policy? What could anyone do if Ford or Chrysler decided that their British subsidiary should not compete with those on the Continent in key export markets? Would Leyland have been allowed to sell buses to Cuba if it, too, had fallen into the hands of an American bidder? Would anyone be able to stop Detroit if it was decided, at some future date, to close down plant in Britain and concentrate production in Germany and France?[33]

There were even allegations of 'white negroism', with American firms discriminating systematically against European suppliers.[34] But, if anything, discrimination ran the other way. In the post-war years, any American firm acquiring a company in Britain was obliged to pay in cash, and any American firm investing in Britain was required to prove that its investment would reduce imports, promote exports and add generally to the state of British industrial knowledge and technology.[35] These demands were totally ineffective. When Chrysler bought Rootes in 1964, assurances about jobs and management control were extorted from the Americans. By the time the company sold the business to Peugeot in 1978, the difficulties of running the company had overwhelmed its commitments on exports, jobs, investment and management control.[36]

But the demands were unreasonable anyway. By the 1950s, American businesses had a record of investment stretching back a century. Colt opened a pistol factory in Britain in 1852. An American-owned rubber factory was opened in Edinburgh in 1856, and the Singer sewing machine company built its first factory in Britain at Glasgow in 1867. It developed the Clydebank site into the biggest sewing machine factory in the world, and it was not closed until the mid-1970s. Ford sold its first car in Britain in 1903, and began assembling them at Trafford Park in Manchester in 1908. Heinz was manufacturing here before the First World War. Dunning estimated that some seventy American firms had invested as much as $100 million in Britain by 1914, and employed perhaps 15,000 people. By 1940, this had risen to two hundred and thirty-three companies and $530 million, as the Americans became the most significant investors in the new industries of motor cars, electrical goods and snack foods.[37]

Firestone opened its famous tyre factory in west London in 1928, where it was joined by the Hoover factory in 1931.[38] Nabisco (the makers of Shredded Wheat) arrived in 1929, Mars in 1932 and General Foods in 1938.[39] American brands – Kellogg's, Heinz 57 Varieties, Mars Bars, Vaseline, Daz, Ariel – were filling British shopping baskets as early as the 1930s. Vauxhall was purchased by General Motors in 1927. General Electric had an investment in Associated Electrical Industries (later merged into GEC) which varied between 25 and 40 per cent until 1953. Some leading British firms, including Boots, GEC and EMI, were bought by Americans, who sold them back only when the Great Depression set in. The usual lamentations erupted when Boots sold its pharmaceutical business to BASF of Germany in the 1990s. But the whole of the company was purchased in 1922 by Liggetts International of the United States, as the ageing and infirm Sir Jesse Boot began to worry about its survival. It did not return to British ownership until 1933.[40]

American firms accounted for two thirds of all direct investment in Britain in the 1960s. By 1970 about sixteen hundred were established, producing one in ten British manufactured goods and building dominant positions in the computers, electronic, motor and pharmaceutical industries.[41] Nearly thirty years on, US companies are still easily the largest investors in Britain, accounting for over two fifths of British assets of foreign companies. Indeed, American firms are so deeply embedded in the British economy that three of them – Ford, IBM and Motorola – rank among the ten largest British exporters.[42] (Half of the top fifty exporters in the annual *Financial Times* rankings are either wholly or partly foreign-owned.)

It is true that, because trade tends to develop between different parts of the same company around the world, firms such as Ford and IBM are also significant importers. But American investors not only add to the number of British jobs and the value of British exports; they run genuine manufacturing plants rather than merely assembly lines, and research, develop, design and market many of the products they sell around the world from British offices and factories. Their long experience in Britain disproves the gravest charge against foreign investment of all kinds: that it supplies only low-paid and insecure jobs in 'screwdriver plants' which are closed as readily as they are started up, while the value-adding design, engineering and research and development facilities remain abroad.

In the 1960s, as prime minister, Harold Wilson complained that *le défi américain* threatened the whole of Europe with an 'industrial helotry under which we in Europe produce only the conventional apparatus of a modern economy, while becoming increasingly dependent on American business for the sophisticated apparatus which will call the industrial tune in the Seventies and Eighties'.[43] Nobody talks about Americans like that any more, but the same arguments were rehearsed about Japanese investment in Britain. In the 1980s fear of *le défi américain* was replaced by fear of *le défi japonais*.

The Japanese Invasion

The pioneer of Japanese investment in Britain was a zip manufacturer, YKK Fasteners, which opened a factory at Runcorn in 1972. Later that year a company named Nittan started manufacturing fire alarms in Woking. When a manufacturer of plastic corrugated sheeting, Takiron, built a plant in Newport in Gwent towards the end of 1972 it became the first of dozens of Japanese companies to invest in Wales. But the investor everybody remembers is Sony. In May 1973 it bought an old factory at Bridgend and converted it into a television assembly plant. The story goes that Sony chose south Wales after an encounter in Osaka three years earlier between the founder of Sony, Akio Morita, and the Prince of Wales. Apparently the heir to the throne offered to open the new factory if the company came to the principality. With industrial relations in Britain at their nadir, Sony could not be accused of lacking courage.

The initial reaction of the natives was one of resentment, rooted in fear that the first industrial nation was now being overtaken by a country which had based its development on the British example. When Hitachi built the first entirely new television factory in the north-east in 1977, its welcome was less than ecstatic. Hostility to Japanese imports – especially motor cars, where import and local content quotas were imposed – persuaded many people

TABLE 21.5

Top Twenty Foreign Owned Companies in Britain, 1997

		Parent nationality	Exports (£bn)	UK Employees
Rover Group	Cars	Germany	3.9	37,761
IBM UK	Computers	USA	2.8	15,021
Compaq Computer	Computers	USA	2.6	2,173
Motorola	Electronics	USA	2.6	8,590
Ford	Cars	USA	2.5	28,700
Vauxhall Motors	Cars	USA	1.4	10,022
Nissan Motors	Cars	Japan	1.3	4,912
Texaco	Oil	USA	1.3	4,514
Esso UK	Oil	USA	1.0	3,399
Hewlett Packard	Computers	USA	0.760	5,578
Sony UK	Electronics	Japan	0.747	5,650
Kodak	Film	USA	0.715	6,154
Conoco	Oil	USA	0.641	1,104
Kvaerner	Shipbuilding	Norway	0.560	15,450
Cummins Engines	Engineering	USA	0.512	4,623
Rhone Poulenc	Pharmaceuticals	France	0.511	4,156
Caterpillar	Construction Equipment	USA	0.476	2,588
Polaroid	Film	USA	0.451	1,375
Exxon Chemical	Chemicals	USA	0.429	1,102
Inco Europe	Minerals	Canada	0.415	1,476

Source: *FT Exporter*, December 1998.

that Sony and Hitachi were likely to destroy as many jobs as they created. It is certainly true that one of the main reasons Japanese companies have invested so heavily in Europe (and in Britain in particular) is to find a way around the barriers Europeans have erected against Japanese imports. But much of the resistance was xenophobic.

After all, a quarter of a century after YKK came to Runcorn, Japanese assets in Britain are still one tenth the size of the American, and considerably smaller than those of Holland, Germany, France, Switzerland and even Australia. Yet as recently as 1991 the Trades Union Congress passed a motion condemning the 'feudal and alien' Japanese attitude to industrial relations. Their crime, it seems, was to prefer single-union agreements. The motion was not reversed until two years later. When a Japanese construction company acquired County Hall in London, topping a rival bid from the London School of Economics, it divided the Cabinet. Lord Plummer, a former leader of the GLC, exclaimed in the House of Lords: 'County Hall occupies a prime location in the heart of the capital and should not be allowed to lapse into an eastern bazaar.'[44]

Other critics have unearthed the Wilsonian charge of industrial helotry. Scottish academics and politicians are for ever complaining that Silicon Glen – the cluster of largely foreign-owned electronics manufacturers in southern Scotland, where the Japanese are strongly represented – is little more than a cluster of screwdriver plants piecing together the imported components of foreign laboratories. A Welsh Office report published in October 1997 complained that sixteen hundred projects and £11 billion of inward invest-ment in Wales since 1983 had failed to raise the standard of living because the jobs created were low paid and unskilled and the foreign companies did not use local suppliers or invest in research and development.[45]

In fact, many of the present Asian investors are gradually moving research and development, design, marketing and management functions to Britain. Engineers at the Komatsu plant in Birtley, for example, are now designing construction machinery for sale in Japan. Several of the leading Asian-owned television manufacturers – including Sony, Mitsubishi and Tatung – design and engineer sets in Britain as well as assembling them. The Korean giant Samsung, which recently moved its European headquarters from Frankfurt to London, has a research facility in Hampshire to test products for the entire European market. In 1998, as semi-conductor plants closed or failed to open in Britain, Cadence Design Systems of the United States began work on a semi-conductor design facility at Livingston.[46] It is true that much of the research and development work is simply the adaptation of products to the local market, but the American precedent suggests that more value-added work will be transferred as companies feel more comfortable in the British environment.

The initial commitment by Nissan at Sunderland in 1984, for example, was for £350 million. It has since invested another £886 million as it has increased production from one model to three. Honda has added £540 million to its initial investment at Swindon and promised a further £500 million to double production.[47] In 1994 Toyota pledged a further investment of £800 million on top of its initial £700 million.[48] Even when the company diverted another £400 million to a site in northern France in 1997, it promised to plough £240 million more into its engine plant at Deeside in north Wales.[49] Once foreign investors are entrenched as manufacturers, research and development tend to follow. In some industries, like pharmaceuticals and financial services, openness to foreign investment in the past has given Britain a comparative advantage today: the know-how it spawned attracts foreign investors.

TABLE 21.6
British Assets of Foreign Companies, 1997 (£bn)

	Value	% of Total	Net Earnings	% of Total
The Netherlands	15.7	10.0	2.0	15.3
France	14.1	9.0	1.2	9.4
Germany	10.3	6.6	0.569	4.3
Rest of European Union	9.4	6.0	1.4	11.0
Switzerland	10.4	6.6	0.277	2.1
Rest of EFTA	1.7	1.1	0.130	1.0
Rest of Europe	0.388	0.2	0.075	0.6
UK Offshore Islands	0.384	0.2	0.072	0.5
Canada	4.1	2.6	0.065	0.5
United States	69.8	44.4	6.5	49.5
Rest of America	2.9	1.9	0.225	1.7
Near and Middle East	1.5	1.0	0.096	0.7
Japan	6.5	4.1	(0.489)	(3.7)
Singapore	0.446	0.3	0.014	0.1
Rest of Asia	0.384	0.2	0.031	0.2
Australia	6.5	4.2	0.830	6.3
New Zealand	1.5	1.0	0.017	0.1
South Africa	0.743	0.5	0.046	0.3
Rest of Africa	0.210	0.1	0.009	0.1
World Total	156,9	100.0	13.2	100.0

Source: Office of National Statistics, Overseas Direct Investment 1997, 14 December 1998, Tables 5 and 6.

Clusters of Excellence

In 1970, it was thought worrying that 'of the top ten companies supplying the National Health Service with drugs, six are American, two Swiss, and two British . . . only one third of the market is in British hands.'[50] Today, Britain is the capital of the international pharmaceuticals industry. 'London', says John Zabriskie of Pharmacia-Upjohn, a US–Swedish pharmaceutical company whose headquarters are now in the capital, 'is the centre of the globe in terms of the pharmaceuticals industry.' Most of the leading pharmaceutical and biotechnology companies in the world have offices in London or the south-east for exactly the same reason. In 1997 the American company, Pfizer, announced it was investing £109 million in a new research and development facility at its existing site at Sandwich in Kent.[51]

But the City of London is the most obvious and influential cluster of international excellence. In 1997, five hundred and sixty-five foreign banks had offices in the Square Mile, two thirds of them from outside Europe. There are more foreign than domestic banks operating in the City, and more than half the total deposit base of the British banking system (or £1 trillion) is denominated in foreign currencies.[52] Despite a small domestic market, London dominates international lending, foreign exchange, and equity, bond and derivatives trading. Almost all the leading banks and trading houses are owned by foreigners, but the majority of staff are British, and local suppliers of legal and accounting services are in high demand. Two of the biggest German banks, Deutsche Bank and Dresdner Bank, chose recently to centralise their investment banking operations in London rather than in Frankfurt.

Of course, there are many accidental reasons why the City has thrived against international competition. One is that Britain, as the first industrial nation, once supplied capital to the world. Another is language. A third is its fortunate location in a time-zone neatly placed between Tokyo and New York. But the real secret of its success is its openness to foreign capital. A good part of the investment in Britain in the 1980s was by foreign banks and brokers establishing operations in the City to take advantage of the offshore Euromarkets and the liberalised capital markets of Europe. The City also helps to attract commercial and industrial companies. Its bankers, brokers and institutional investors offer multinationals ready access to finance, foreign exchange, derivatives, commodities, and insurance services.

The London-based financial markets, like the British market in corporate control, are open and lightly regulated. One reason the Japanese prefer Britain to continental Europe is that they are free to buy local companies, and are not expected to work with local partners.[53] No Japanese bidder was referred to the Monopolies and Mergers Commission until 1991.[54] The European markets, and France in particular, are much more hostile to foreign investment. In 1962 de Gaulle dismissed the Japanese prime minister as 'a transistor salesman'. When Nissan, Honda and Toyota started exporting cars to continental Europe, Jacques Calvet, chairman of Peugeot, complained that Britain was a 'Japanese aircraft carrier' (conveniently ignoring his own company's plant in Britain).

British labour is also relatively cheap, especially on a fully-taxed basis. For every £100 paid by an employer in 1997, Italy adds £44 in payroll taxes, France £41, Spain £34 and Germany £32, but Britain only £18. Labour is cheaper still in Greece and Portugal, but Britain has no serious union problems, few strikes, less bureaucracy, low corporate taxes, access to the European market (via, to the chagrin of the continental Europeans, a currency with a propensity to depreciate) and governments committed to capitalism in general and foreign investment in particular.

In fact, British governments are over-committed to foreign investment. Since 1979, Britain has sold herself shamelessly as the most desirable location in Europe for foreign direct investment. Three successive prime ministers have prostrated themselves before foreign potentates in search of factories and jobs for the voters at home. Dozens of regional agencies – Scottish Enterprise, the Welsh Development Agency, the Northern Ireland Industrial Development Board, the Northern Development Company, and others – compete against one another for projects.[55] Almost every local authority has some kind of economic development unit charged with attracting foreign investors. A string of other bodies – from the Rural Development Commission to the seventy-eight Training and Enterprise Councils (TECs) – compete for projects with funds dispensed by the Welsh Office, the Scottish Office, the Department of Education and Employment and the Department of Trade and Industry (the home of yet another agency, the Invest in Britain Bureau).

It is said that when, in 1990, Mercedes Benz indicated that it was thinking about building a car plant in Britain, it was inundated with one hundred and twenty offers of assistance from various regions and localities. It decided to keep production in Germany. Sir Colin Marshall, chairman of another inward investment body called London FirstCentre, has accused the agencies of 'gazumping' each other in their bids for foreign investment.[56] There were vociferous complaints in the autumn of 1997, for example, that the Welsh Development Agency had lured a Taiwanese computer manufacturer, Acer, away from the north-east by offering more generous financial incentives.[57] The English regions are convinced that their competitors around the Celtic fringe have more money to spend on bribing foreign companies. It may have cost £50 million to persuade Siemens to build its new semi-conductor plant in north-east England, but in 1996 the Welsh Development Agency was able to find £247 million to persuade LG of Korea to build a factory in Newport. This sum, equivalent to 15 per cent of the total cost of the project, was a subsidy of £40,000 a job.[58] (The project was later postponed.) Similarly, Locate in Scotland was somehow able to offer Hyundai £147 million to build its (now postponed) microchip plant in Fife.[59] The wide variety of agencies competing for inward investment are effectively bidding up the cost of subsidising firms which would have come to Britain without subsidy.

There is even evidence (most of it anecdotal) that inward investment agencies have started wooing established companies away from the English regions; in other words, taxpayers' money is being used to move jobs around the country. In some cases, the products manufactured are needed to supply prestigious foreign investment projects, like the LG factory in Newport. A company named Fenner was reputedly induced to close plants in Peterborough and Hull and move its operations to south Wales with the promise of grants worth £13 million.[60] Companies are increasingly aware that they can gain from moving locations. A 1996 study by Ernst & Young found that three of every four investment inquiries received by English local authorities came from other parts of the United Kingdom.[61]

By 1997 complaints of gazumping had become so vociferous that the government attempted to centralise the disbursement of grants and subsidies to foreign companies. It encountered strong resistance from the regions, and was forced instead to set up a committee of regional representatives to ensure the bidding process does not spiral out of control. The government believes the nine development agencies for the English regions, which began work in April 1999, will eliminate confusing competition between agencies of the kind which alienated Mercedes Benz.[62] But they could make competition between regions worse, especially if they prove to be the precursors to regional government for England as well as Scotland, Wales and Northern Ireland. The government already intends to make the agency for London answerable to the new mayor and assembly for the capital. Regional assemblies will naturally place their interests ahead of national taxpayers.

It would be better to scrap regional incentives altogether, but ministers fear unilateral abandonment might only drive companies elsewhere. After spending or committing £444 million to Siemens, LG and Hyundai to build semi-conductor plants, the taxpayer has little to show for his generosity. One plant is shut, and the others have yet to open. The taxpayer sank £30 million into the Fujitsu plant at Newton Aycliffe, a sum equivalent to £50,000 a job. The jobs lasted only seven years before the plant was shut.[63] Peter Mandelson, during his brief spell as trade secretary in 1998, reckoned the answer was to shift the balance from bribing foreigners to subsidising domestic entrepreneurs. He was impressed by clusters of excellence such as Silicon Glen and the City, and believed their example could be copied in other industries and regions. Clustering is not incompatible with foreign investment. Many smaller Japanese companies have opened factories in Britain to supply the major motor manufacturers: Honda, Nissan and Toyota. In fact, Toyota recently undertook not to copy the examples of other foreign-owned motor manufacturers and switch part procurement to cheaper suppliers elsewhere.[64] But there will always be more indigenous entrepreneurs than foreign investors.

Any change of emphasis would not be be dramatic. The taxpayer has already become a venture capitalist, but largely to foreign investors. His funds are also being committed by public officials working to political rather than financial agendas. Nowhere is this truer than in Northern Ireland, where politics holds economics in thrall. John de Lorean had toured Detroit, Puerto Rico and Ireland for taxpayers willing to support his plan to manufacture stainless steel gull-wing sports cars before a Dublin lawyer suggested he try Ulster, on the grounds, 'they'll invest in almost anything'.[65] By the time the project collapsed in 1982, British taxpayers had sunk £85 million into the factory in exchange for an investment of just £15 million. In their desperation to provide wealth and employment, the Ulster authorities provided incentives worth three times what de Lorean was offered south of the border.

But the dire economic condition of Northern Ireland after thirty years of The Troubles, and the need to undermine the extremists with investment and jobs, still tends to blind officials to the economic implausibility of many of the investment proposals put forward. The Hualon textiles company of Taiwan was given £61 million to assist its investment in the province, although it was known that the senior management of the company had faced criminal charges, and mainland textile manufacturers would be undermined by a subsidised competitor.[66] Likewise, a grant to build a glass bottling factory in County Fermanagh seemed to ignore the fact that the market for glass bottles was already suffering from massive over-capacity.[67] In 1997 the taxpayer found over half the cost of an Abbey National telephone call centre in Belfast.[68] In the previous year, Abbey National made pre-tax profits of well over £1 billion.

Foreign investors are equally adept at farming the British taxpayer. Ford, which has plants at Halewood, Dagenham, Bridgend and Southampton, has managed to tease increasing amounts of money out of British taxpayers by threatening to move production overseas. In 1994 it secured £9.4 million after threatening to move Jaguar production to Portugal. A year later, the company was back for another £80 million after threatening to build the new model in Detroit. In October 1995 it took another £10 million to finance the expansion of its engine plant at Bridgend (a factory which had already retrieved two fifths of its construction cost in various subsidies from the taxpayer).[69] In January 1997, Ford announced that it was cutting 1,300 jobs at its Halewood plant on Merseyside. A few weeks later, after some fruitful discussions in Whitehall, the company announced that it was asking the tax-payer for help to build a new production line there.[70]

When it emerged in early 1998 that the new Jaguar would be built at Halewood, the television news was filled with scenes of jubilant Scouses record-ing their gratitude to Ford. This was a tribute to the Ford spin-doctors, since the happy workforce should have thanked their fellow-taxpayers for advancing a £50 million subsidy.[71] In 1994, when Ford made its first bid for public assistance, it made profits of $5.3 billion. In 1997, when it made its latest application for help, Nissan was investing £215 million of its own money in the expansion of production at its Sunderland factory. Toyota built a whole new factory at Burnaston in Derbyshire without any grants at all. But the Ford example is obviously not lost on other foreign motor manufacturers. Vauxhall, a subsidiary of General Motors, made no secret of its intention to seek equality of treatment. When BMW wanted to build a new engine plant for Rover, it told the Department of Trade and Industry that it would cost the taxpayer £60 million to ensure it was not built in Austria or eastern Europe instead.[72] Two years later, dire warnings by BMW about low productivity at Longbridge and the damaging impact of the high pound were widely interpreted as a surreptitious pitch for a further tranche of public money.[73] It was forthcoming. 'We are in the business,' admits a Department of Trade and Industry official, 'of buying jobs.'[74]

Foreign Investment as Trade

Since the abolition of exchange controls in 1979, the value of foreign assets owned by British companies operating abroad has increased steadily to over £200 billion, and foreign companies operating in Britain have added to a hoard of assets now worth over £150 billion. Thirty years ago, both outward and inward investment of this kind was highly controversial. Overseas investment by British companies was thought to export wealth and jobs, and direct investment in Britain was thought to damage the balance of payments because profits were remitted to foreign jurisdictions. Blinded by neo-mercantilist thinking, nobody recognised direct investment for what it was: a form of trade. Companies invest abroad to gain access to markets which would otherwise be closed by barriers of distance, cost, or tariff. (In service industries, like law or banking or insurance, direct investment is often the *only* form of trade across borders.) They enter those markets because they believe they can supply something better or cheaper than the domestic product, or which indigenous companies cannot supply at all, or because they think it necessary to protect their global brand or franchise from erosion by competitors.

As with any form of trade, direct investment forces countries to specialise in businesses where they have a comparative advantage. This is why the most successful British multinationals tend to be oil or pharmaceutical companies, while the domestic motor and electronics markets are dominated by American and Japanese firms. Because trade also brings the discipline of competition, one effect of direct investment on the British economy is to put pressure on domestic firms to become more innovative and efficient – or fail. This discipline is not always borne with fortitude. Multinationals may no longer spawn hyperbolic essays by latterday Servan-Schreibers warning about the power of global capitalism, but people will always find it easier to believe that their job was destroyed by slave-labourers in foreign sweat shops or faceless men in foreign boardrooms. They need to confront the truth that it is they, as consumers, who are the true arbiters of the fate of companies. Most people still struggle to accept that consumption is the sole end and purpose of production. This is one of the paradoxes of an age in which people work largely to shop.

CHAPTER TWENTY-TWO

SHOPPING

The trouble with English towns is that they are all so indistinguishable one from another. They all have a Boots and W. H. Smith and Marks & Spencer. You could be anywhere really.

BILL BRYSON[1]

Consumption is the sole end and purpose of all production; and the interest of the producer ought to be attended to only so far as it may be necessary for promoting that of the consumer. The maxim is so perfectly self-evident that it would be absurd to attempt to prove it.

ADAM SMITH[2]

England is a nation of shopkeepers.

NAPOLEON[3]

The car, the furniture, the wife, the children – everything has to be disposable. Because you see the main thing today is – shopping.

ARTHUR MILLER[4]

In the spring of 1993 the burghers of Hampstead, long the preserve of the rich, the literate and the left-wing, were agitated. McDonald's, a fast-food chain which rivals Coca-Cola as the arch-symbol of capitalist rapacity and American hegemony, had applied to open a restaurant in the High Street. The cause of the offence was not the quality of the food, which is thought by some nutritionists to be the equal of most other things in the average diet. It was McDonalds' passion for uniformity: the *sameness* of its Big Macs and its Golden Arches. As the chairman of the Heath and Old Hampstead Society, saw it: 'McDonald's is representative of the homogenisation ... sweeping High Streets. Hampstead is idiosyncratic, and it is different, and if we clone Hampstead High Street people won't want to come. People will say: "Oh God, another McDonald's." '[5]

The uniformity of High Streets is a common complaint among nostalgics and snobs. They and their representatives have fought a long (and in some respects successful) rearguard action against the conquest of shopping by the ubiquitous PLC. It is only now that the corporate behemoths are overrunning the last bastions of idiosyncratic retailing: the chemist's shop, the village garage, the country pub, the old-world bookstore, the funeral parlour and the family butcher.

Most accounts of life in modern Britain agree that the chain stores and the transatlantic purveyors of fast food and motel bedrooms are expunging diversity, not only from the High Street but from pubs, restaurants and hotels. 'The country so proud of regional diversity and local autonomy, the family hotel and the corner shop,' wrote Sampson of the Britain of the 1970s, 'was now above all the home of giant corporations.'[6] Interchangeable High Streets are now the most visible symptom of the hegemony of the PLC. Daily confrontations with brand-name retailers, out-of-town superstores and shopping centres, and proliferating fast-food outlets, make it hard to remember a time when shops, pubs, hotels and restaurants were not dominated by a handful of business corporations advertising their formulaic products in newspapers, on hoardings and the airwaves.

That time is not so distant. Shopkeeping, long protected from foreign competition, was the last major economic activity to succumb to the ruthless PLC. Today, there are six retailers among the fifty largest companies in Britain.[7] But no retailer except brewers-cum-publicans were in this list until Great Universal Stores was admitted in the 1950s.[8] The lingering presence of the butcher, the baker and the candlestick maker, long after the rest of the economy had fallen into the hands of the giant corporations, probably accounts for the present nostalgia.

The uniformity of the High Street, though lamented by writers on British mores from J. B. Priestley to Bill Bryson, is of more recent provenance than it seems. McDonald's did not have a single outlet in Britain until October 1974, when it opened in Woolwich. J. Sainsbury, the epitome of the modern corporate retailer, became a public company in the same year. The first big edge-of-town shopping development, at Brent Cross in north London, was not completed until two years later. The real British retailing revolution occurred not in the 1930s, or even in the 1960s and 1970s, but in the 1980s. Nothing symbolises the ambivalent character of that extraordinary decade more completely than shopping. The unreflective mercantilism of years of popular journalism and sound-bite politics convinced the British people that they were victims of a false consciousness; that it was more sacred to work than to shop; that service industries were not industries at all; and that their country was no longer the workshop of the world. Nor was it even a nation of shopkeepers. It was nothing but a nation of shoppers.

In May 1997, the sense of release from self-disgust was almost palpable. The transfiguration of the economic character of the British people became flesh in the personality of the new chancellor of the Exchequer. His watchword is investment, not consumption. His ideal Briton is not the one who has never had it so good, but the one who has never worked so hard. In his first budget speech, Gordon Brown promised to restore to the British people their 'belief in hard work and self-improvement, the very qualities that made Britain lead the world in the eighteenth and nineteenth centuries . . . precisely the qualities we need to make Britain a strong economic power in the twenty-first century.'[9] But consumption is not the enemy of production. It is the purpose of it, and shopping rather than foraging for food is the hallmark of economic success. Only the rich can know the pleasures of work, and of investment for the future. Ironically, it was the British *consumers* of the Industrial Revolution of the eighteenth and nineteenth centuries, not the *producers*, who were the first to discover this.

Shopping in the modern mode was invented by the Georgian bourgeoisie, the main beneficiaries of the commercial capitalism of the era. Until then, the energy of most people was absorbed by the struggle for subsistence. In all primitive economies, survival is succeeded by rest, but the well-fed townsmen of Hanoverian England (like the wealthy burghers of Holland before them) were the first generation to prefer possession to repose, and they could afford it. The £40 or £50 a year which two in every five Georgian families enjoyed was twice what was needed for subsistence.[10] Well-stocked shops, trading from permanent addresses, gradually displaced the itinerant pedlar with his bundle of clothes and trinkets and readiness to adjust his prices. Permanent shops took trade from market stalls and annual fairs, both of which are now reduced to another aspect of the burgeoning heritage industry.

'The magnificence of the shops,' wrote a Prussian visitor in 1780, 'is the most striking thing in London.'[11] The commercial success of Georgian England saw the impulse to possess percolate through the middling classes, filling houses with glass, curtains, carpets, marble fireplaces, books, wallpaper and upholstered furniture. Clocks, porcelain, toys, mirrors, books and newspapers, bloated with advertisements for the latest fashions, became commonplace. Every town had its butchers and brewers and bakers, its shoe shops, ironmongers and booksellers. Shopkeepers sold not just eggs and bread, but the produce of far-flung corners of the globe: tea, coffee, sugar, ginger, molasses, cinnamon, and quinine. Mahogany, imported from afar, was fashioned into beautiful and elegant furniture.

The Rise of the Department Store

It took a mechanical civilisation to create shopping for the masses. Railways and trams brought ever-larger numbers of people within reach of shops. 'Now that the train service is so perfect between London and Bath it is quite possible to spend a day in town and return to Bath the same evening,' bleated the *Lady's World* in 1886. 'That is no small advantage when you have a day's shopping to get through.'[12] Cast-iron constructions, electric light and plate-glass windows meant shops grew larger and vulgar. Other technological advances – chemical dyes, electro-plating and the vulcanization of rubber – extended the range and colour of their fabrics and wares to include silver-plated cutlery, the MacIntosh (the name of its inventor misspelled as 'mackin-tosh') and the Aquascutum.

At the departmental (or department) stores which emerged towards the end of the Victorian era, even the different floors could be linked mechanically. The first passenger lifts were probably installed at the Army & Navy store in Waterloo Place in 1879. Harrod's disdained to purchase such new-fangled machinery, but did fit the first escalator in an English shop in 1898. An attendant was positioned at the top of the 'moving staircase' to revive women with a dose of smelling salts or a glass of cognac.[13] But, by moving customers between floors effortlessly, the escalator made a major contribution to the success of the department store, which was the chief contribution to shopping of the Victorians.

It emerged organically, as shopkeepers tried to increase sales by adding new lines. Harrod's grew into its present Edwardian terracotta emporium from a single grocery shop – acquired by an Eastcheap tea merchant in the village of Knightsbridge in 1849 – through acquisition of the surrounding buildings. Peter Robinson, founded in 1833, expanded from its original premises at 103 Oxford Street by buying numbers 104 to 108.[14] The only purpose-built department store, the Bon Marché at Brixton, never thrived. It was built by James Smith of Tooting, with £80,000 he had won at the races (he changed his name to Rosebery Smith in honour of the owner of the horse which won the Cesarewitch and Cambridgeshire Stakes at Newmarket in 1876). Opened in 1877, it had to be rescued from a mountain of debt in the 1890s.

The real creator of the department store was William Whiteley. His Bayswater store was closed in 1981 by its last owners, but his name lives on in the shopping centre built on the site by a group of property developers. Whiteley conceived the idea of a vast retail emporium after visiting the Great Exhibition. Starting with a single drapery store on Westbourne Grove, he gradually bought up most of the street, and moved eventually to the present site in Queensway. By 1872 Whiteley was styling himself 'The Universal Provider', able to supply anything from 'a pin to an elephant at short notice.' He eschewed advertising but, like Richard Branson, was a skilled and inveterate publicity-seeker. In 1896 Whiteley paid for Nelson's Column to be decorated with laurel leaves, bringing a steeplejack from the north of England to under-take the task. He even tried to persuade W. P. Frith (of 'Railway Station' and 'Derby Day' fame) to paint the customers of his shop. Unfortunately, Frith refused, but Whiteley created publicity enough by vexing his competitors. By crossing the traditional demarcations of the retail industry, he had become deeply unpopular with the surrounding shopkeepers, and Whiteley's was a regular target of arsonists. Whiteley himself was shot dead in 1907 by a young man claiming to be his bastard son.

Gordon Selfridge, the American creator of the neoclassical department store which opened in Oxford Street in March 1909, eclipsed even Whiteley in his talent for hyperbole. His primary weapon, as befitted an American, was the sheer size of his store, at the time the biggest building built solely as a shop. Selfridge's had one hundred and thirty separate departments, rest-rooms, restaurants, a soda fountain, a garden and even a post office. Its tempting, electrically illuminated window displays attracted the first window-shoppers, and scents and cosmetics have remained on the ground floor of every depart-ment store since Selfridge fetched them out from under the counter. He invented branding – staff uniforms, carpets, wrapping paper and delivery vans were all dressed in 'Selfridge Green' – and introduced the first bargain basement in 1912. Shopping was no longer a matter of necessity; it had become a leisure activity. Selfridge's, he boasted, was 'a social centre, not a shop . . . Why Not Spend a Day at Selfridge's?'[15]

The economics of department stores were simple. Their huge turnover enabled them to order in bulk, undercutting smaller retailers (one of the reasons Whiteley's went on being burnt down). The initial image of the department store was one of good value, not plenitude. David Lewis, founder of Lewis's in Manchester, advertised lavishly the discounted prices of the hats and fabrics he had bought from manufacturers. 'This is a very good thing for the public,' he averred, 'but not so pleasant for the middlemen.'[16] Prices plunged even lower in the annual 'sale', another innovation of the Victorian department store. But price was not their only advantage; the array of depart-ments offered choice and convenience. Peter Robinson was described as 'a hundred different shops . . . under one roof'. Kendal Milne, the Manchester 'bazaar' founded by John Watts of Didsbury, was not initially a single shop; it began soon after the Napoleonic wars as a two-storey building where retailers could hire a counter. These shops within a shop, like the 'Liberty departments' of the late Victorian era, were the pioneers of the modern 'concession': rented space in a shop belonging to others.

By placing goods on display, with price tags attached, department stores freed shoppers to circulate and examine the goods, without feeling any obligation to buy. The shops lost the opportunity to embarrass a customer into an unwanted purchase, but they could also economise on knowledgeable staff. The dim-witted 'shop girl' was discovered by the department stores. 'There are two very important changes which have contributed to the temptation of spending money nowadays,' wrote a contributor to the *Fortnightly Review*. 'One is the gathering together under one roof of all kinds of goods . . . nearly all the great shops in London are becoming vast stores, one of which, more enterprising than the others, is said to supply young men for dancing and coffins to bury them in. Many more people than formerly come to London, and to the large centres . . . where they can concentrate their forces and diminish fatigue . . . The other reason for the increased temptation to spend money is the large numbers of women which are now employed . . . they understand so much more readily what other women want.'[17]

Eclipse of the Department Store?

In the last thirty years the department stores have felt the pressure of competition from specialist retailers. With some exceptions – like Harrod's, which is now largely a tourist trap – they are no longer universal providers. Some have gone out of business, and others have merged. Four national groups now account for more than two thirds of all sales by department stores: the John Lewis Partnership, Debenhams, House of Fraser and Allders. The sector as a whole accounts for less than 5 per cent of the money spent in all shops.

Its troubles are typified by the unhappy story of the House of Fraser. Floated on the Stock Exchange a century after its foundation by Hugh Fraser in Glasgow in 1849, it consumed the Binns group and John Barker's of Kensington. Harrod's succumbed to its blandishments in 1959, bringing with it Kendal Milne (founded in Manchester in 1821), Dickins & Jones (Regent Street, 1790), D. H. Evans (Oxford Street, 1879) and Rackhams of Birmingham. In the 1960s and 1970s House of Fraser devoured yet more department stores – Cavendish House, Dingles, Jollys of Bath, Howells and the Army & Navy Stores. By 1980, it owned one hundred and ten stores, but could not contain the drift of consumers from its departments to the specialist retailers. By the time House of Fraser was taken over by the Fayeds in 1985, half its profits came from Harrod's, and the group as a whole was making losses. Half the stores were closed, and a slimmed-down collection of fifty-six stores was floated

successfully on the London Stock Exchange in 1994. But neither the decline
of sales nor the closure of shops was halted. In 1996 the managing director
resigned after issuing his fifth profits warning in two years. By 1997, the
number of stores was reduced to forty-nine, and House of Fraser was still
losing money.

TABLE 22.1
Major Department Stores, 1998

Brands	Owner	Outlets	Turnover 1997–8 (£m)
Debenhams, Browns of Chester	Debenhams PLC	90	2,474
John Lewis*	Staff Partnership	23	1,788
Harrod's	Mohammed Al Fayed	1	1,503
Various	House of Fraser PLC	49	812
Allders, Arding & Hobbs	Allders PLC	38	520
Selfridge's	Selfridge's PLC	2	294
Fenwick	Fenwick Limited	8	231
Harvey Nichols†	Dickson Concepts	2	129
Beatties	J. Beattie PLC	9	104
Bentalls	Bentalls PLC	7	104
Beales, Whitakers of Bolton	Beale PLC	7	62
Joplings, Robbs, Woodwards‡	Merchant Retail PLC	6	52
Heal's	Heal's PLC	3	27
Uptons	Upton & Southern PLC	7	11

Source: Companies; *Financial Times.*

* Eleven stores trade as John Lewis. The partnership also owns one hundred and seventeen
supermarkets trading as Waitrose.
† Harvey Nichols owns the Oxo Tower restaurant and stores in London and Leeds.
‡ Merchant Retail also owns forty-four branches of The Perfume Shop.

The fundamental problem is common to all department stores. They
seemed old-fashioned twenty years ago, when a department store was a fit
setting for a situation comedy (*Are You Being Served?*). Today, many still seem
trapped in a time-warp. Selfridge's recently spent £74 million refurbishing its
Oxford Street flagship in the (probably forlorn) hope of attracting younger
customers. But those which thrive make a virtue of being staid and reliable.
The success of the John Lewis Partnership depends on the traditional department store virtues of keen prices, good service, well-informed staff and a huge
range of goods. It is a difficult formula to copy, since its success is rooted in

the idiosyncratic ideas of staff involvement and profit-sharing introduced by Spedan Lewis during the First World War.

However, the worst seems to be over for department stores. Debenhams and Selfridge's are at last planning to open new stores rather than shut old ones. Even House of Fraser is planning its first new outlet since its flotation (at the Bluewater shopping centre near Dartford). The wave of mergers and closures has concentrated buying power, making it harder for specialist chains to undercut their prices. The population is ageing, giving the demographic edge to stores which cater to the middle-aged, and the department stores own their freehold sites, so that they do not have to pay exorbitantly for rented space in high streets or shopping centres. Inside the shops, anonymous goods have given way to brand-based displays and concessions, enabling them to compete with shopping centres, whose success depends on bringing specialists together at a single site. The time-pressed thirty-somethings, who appreciate a range of brands under one roof, a café and a clean lavatory to change the nappy, are re-discovering the benefits of the department store.

Own-label goods, in-store credit cards and real improvements to customer service (like clothing consultations for women) are also bringing back younger customers. Department stores have become the flagship tenants at some of the new breed of giant shopping centres. Existing stores are being re-invented as 'anchors' for smaller outlets at airports. Harrod's has opened 'signature shops' at Heathrow, on board the QEII, and in Vienna, Frankfurt and Hamburg airports. Selfridge's has a similar outlet at Heathrow, and has opened its first major store outside London at the new Trafford Centre in Manchester. House of Fraser has shops at the Metro Centre in Gateshead, Meadowhall in Sheffield, and at the Lakeside and Bluewater shopping centres in the south-east.

The changes have revived the enthusiasm of investors. Allders, House of Fraser and Harvey Nichols have all floated on the London stock market since 1993. Debenhams demerged from the Burton Group in January 1998, and Selfridge's has escaped the crumbling Sears retailing empire to become an independent entity. Allders sold its duty-free business to Swissair and reinvested some of the proceeds in eight former Owen Owen stores in the north-west.

The idea of the department store is even becoming glamorous again. Tim Waterstone, founder of the Waterstone's bookshop chain, has established the first department store for children. Called Daisy & Tom, its designers were instructed to create 'the correct level of opulence'.[18] Harvey Nichols opened a second shop in Leeds in October 1996, and has chosen Manchester as the site of a third. Not many people can afford to shop at Harvey Nichols but that is not the chief reason for rationing the number of outlets. The main limitation on the growth of the chain is its chief executive's belief that the 'image and prestige' of Harvey Nichols will not bear more than four outlets. However, it has extended its brand successfully into upmarket catering at the Oxo Tower in south London.

The Importance of Brands

A powerful, pliable brand is the single most important asset a modern retailer can possess. According to one recent survey, people trust Sainsbury and Tesco more than they trust the police or the judiciary.[19] The Harvey Nichols name is a brand in its own right; its shops consist almost entirely of concessions to other brands, where exposure does wonders for a clothing manufacturer or designer.[20] It is a successful formula, which other department stores would like to emulate. When the Hong Kong clothing retailer Dickson Concepts bought Harvey Nichols in 1991, the shop was losing money. Dickson Poon, having made a fortune selling Polo and Ralph Lauren T-shirts to the credulous nouveaux-riches of Asia, has turned Harvey Nichols into a successful business (with some assistance from Patsy and Edina, the champagne-swilling shopaholics of *Absolutely Fabulous*).

No retailing brand is better attuned to the spirit of an age in which nothing seems to engage the sympathies of a certain type of woman more passionately than the wardrobes of the famous. Among younger consumers, the key to success is different: French Connection (which also trades as Nicole Farhi) runs a series of mysterious advertisements with nothing but four letters, FCUK, and was pleased to find they merited complaints to the Advertising Standards Authority. Likewise, the Italian fashion retailer, Benetton, has used contemporary concerns and images (birth, death, racialism, pain and violence) to make its clothes appear more interesting than they are.[21]

Branding is dominant everywhere. The Fayeds extended the Harrod's brand into hotel-keeping and a luxury residential complex. But even at lesser levels, branding is all-important. Disney and Warner Brothers have pioneered 'concept retailing' (theme stores), in which staff behave like actors and shoppers are the audience. Chain stores too have discovered the power of brands. They sell an increasing proportion of goods under their own names or in-house names such as George (Asda), St Michael (Marks & Spencer), Linea (House of Fraser), or No. 7 (Boots). Supermarkets have found that own-label goods sell as readily as well-known brands, because customers recognise and respect *their* names as a guarantee. Own-label goods obviously generate fatter profit margins (about 5 per cent higher) than the branded alternative.

The three major supermarkets are now using their brand names to sell financial services. It is a logical progression, from cash-in-the-till, through charge cards, to credit cards and deposit accounts. The customer who deposits cash with Tesco is less likely to spend it at Asda, especially if he or she can decant and replenish the account at the till, or receive interest in the shape of a discount on groceries. Retail banking is also extraordinarily profitable for supermarkets, which have no legacy of costly branch networks and inadequate computer systems. They can cherry-pick the most profitable products and offer a marginal price advantage over clearing banks. No supermarket is offering a costly-to-run current account.

But they offer almost everything else. Marks & Spencer Financial Services, which started in 1985, offers account cards, personal loans, deposit accounts, mutual funds, life assurance and pension plans. Both Tesco and Sainsbury's have banking licences, and offer deposit accounts and credit cards. They have joined forces with major life offices to sell pension plans, and the government has invited supermarkets to help in selling the new Individual Savings Accounts (ISAs). The retailers are embarrassing the banks, whose brand images are too tainted to compete. But banks are not unpopular for nothing. No shop has ever turned a customer away, but banks refuse one in two applications for a credit card or a loan. The supermarket which denies customers a credit card, or forecloses on their mortgage, is likely to lose their custom in the shopping aisles.

Beyond the loss of custom lies the destruction of trust, and the worst thing a retailer can do is to undermine public confidence in his brand. Nobody did this more effectively than Gerald Ratner, who said publicly that one of the products on sale in his chain of jewellers' shops was 'crap'. Liberty undermined its brand by opening a string of regional outlets crammed with goods far removed from its mixture of oriental textiles and arts and crafts furniture.[22] Brands can survive mishandling of this kind, but no brand is immortal. Laura Ashley has struggled for years to rejuvenate its image without destroying its essence. Despite repeated changes of strategy and management, the company has so far failed to do this.

Customer Pull vs. Producer Push

One clue to the apparent insolubility of the problems at Laura Ashley is that the business began as a manufacturing rather than a retail business, and did not shed the last of its factories until 1998. Brands used to belong to manufacturers, who decided what goods would be made and at what price they would sell. They also supported their products with mass advertising, and shops were happy to carry popular products without incurring the costs of promotion. Branded consumer goods emerged in Victorian times, and became commonplace during the inter-war years.[23]

The 1930s was the decade of Quaker Oats and Marmite, Kellogg's Corn Flakes, Horlicks and Ovaltine, John West salmon, Bird's custard powder, Del Monte tinned fruit, Crosse & Blackwell soup, the Bisto Kids, the 57 varieties of Mr H. J. Heinz and Harpic lavatory cleaner (a by-product of munitions manufacturing invented by one Harry Pickup). Sales of potato 'crisps' first passed one million packets in the year of the Great Crash, and Nescafé 'instant' coffee was introduced as the economy began to climb out of the Great Depression in 1932. By 1938, over £100 million a year was being spent on advertising by the major manufacturers, mainly in the newspapers.[24] The advent in the 1950s of commercial television multiplied the power of advertising many times over.

Today, brands are increasingly in the hands of retailers, not manufacturers. The consumer society is no longer driven by manufacturer 'push' but by customer 'pull'. Supermarkets in particular have such a large share of retail sales that they are more powerful than the manufacturers who supply them. They also know that consumers are apt to confuse brand leaders and own-label lookalikes. Sainsbury's clashed with Coca-Cola over the packaging of its own-label Cola. Tesco was drawn into a similar tussle with Kellogg's over the design of a packet of corn flakes, which is why Kellogg's now explains on the packs that 'if you don't see Kellogg's *on* the box . . . it isn't Kellogg's *in* the box.'[25] United Biscuits took Asda to court over a chocolate biscuit, and was pleased when the judge ruled that consumers might well mistake a Puffin for a Penguin.[26] At H. J. Heinz, losses to alternatives became so great that the company admitted defeat and began supplying supermarkets with own-label versions of its baked beans. Consumers who still thought that Beanz Meanz Heinz were reassured that the own-label versions were prepared to a 'different and lower specification'.[27]

When consumers cannot tell the difference between an expensive brand and an own-label alternative, a product is no longer a brand; it becomes a commodity. Commodities sell on price, not prestige. Both Unilever and Procter & Gamble have found the price of branded soap powders and washing-up liquids under strong downward pressure from own-label alternatives. Some manufacturers have tried to protect their brands by refusing to supply the supermarkets, driving the retailers into the so-called 'grey market', where they buy branded goods in other countries and import them for sale. Tesco has clashed with Adidas and Levi-Strauss, and Sainsbury's with Nike, for selling branded products obtained in the grey market at discounted prices. The European Court of Justice has now ruled against this practice by supermarkets.[28]

The need to compete with own-label products, and escape the threat of being discounted, is one of the factors driving the frenzy of innovation. In 1994, manufacturers tempted supermarket consumers with three thousand three hundred new food and drink brands, three hundred and twelve new flavours of yogurt, and three hundred and seventy-five new types of sauce.[29] In a typical year, a supermarket will try fifteen hundred new lines. Nine out of ten fail, not least because consumers are baffled by choice. Even those which do work no longer generate high profits, because of manufacturers' shared access to ideas and technology. Genuine novelties are few and far between, and enjoy only brief monopolies before profits are eroded by a host of lookalike competitors. The old staple of changing the ingredients and labelling it 'new and improved' simply irritates consumers, who dislike changes to establish formulae or packaging.

New product launches can backfire spectacularly. Unilever was so badly hurt by own-label washing powders it was driven into launching a new brand of detergent before it was fully tested. When it emerged that 'Persil Power' damaged clothes, the company had to write off £57 million worth of unsold powder. It is another measure of the power of retailers that the product survived a knocking campaign by Procter & Gamble, but never recovered from the decision by Tesco to take it off its shelves. A few weeks later the chairman of Unilever, Michael Perry, more or less admitted that retailers were in control. 'We go along to them with a simple question,' he said. ' "How can we work together to maximise sales and margins across a whole product category?" '[30]

Abolition of Resale Price Maintenance

The most important factor in the rise of the supermarkets was the abolition of Resale Price Maintenance. Prior to its abolition in 1964, manufacturers fixed the price of half of all consumer goods. Retailers were too fragmented to resist. Until the 1950s, two thirds of all retail sales were made by single-outlet retailers, and over four fifths through chains no larger than four shops.[31] These small shopkeepers had no option but to let the suppliers package and price the goods they sold, since the manufacturers also bore the costs of distribution and advertising.

To the extent that it protected small shops from the competition of larger retailers, which could otherwise buy in bulk at lower prices, Resale Price Maintenance was a conspiracy against the consumer between producers and middlemen. But for decades there was little or no pressure to break it. It kept local shops open – important in an age before most owned a car or a fridge. The authorities also saw price regulation as more agreeable than the

TABLE 22.2
Major Supermarkets, 1998

Brands	Owner	Outlets	Turnover 1997–8 (£m)
Tesco	Tesco PLC	595	17,779
J. Sainsbury, SavaCentre, Homebase	J. Sainsbury PLC	702	15,496
Safeway	Safeway PLC	483	7,494
Marks & Spencer	PLC	289	8,243
Asda	Asda PLC	223	8,220
Somerfield/Kwiksave*	Somerfield PLC	1,424	3,711
W. Morrison	PLC	95	2,297
Waitrose	John Lewis Partnership	117	1,672
Iceland	PLC	770	1,566
Budgen	PLC	183	386
The Co-op†	Co-operative Societies	1,135	n/a

Source: Companies; Annual Reports and Accounts; *Financial Times.*

* Somerfield (540 outlets) merged with Kwik Save (884 outlets) in 1998.

† There are 49 separate co-operative societies, of which the largest are Co-operative Retail Services (480 outlets), the Co-operative Wholesale Society (600 outlets) and the Midlands Co-operative Society (180 outlets). Between them, the 49 societies own a mixture of stores which total 4,649. They also own 800 funeral parlours. The figure given in this table is the total number of superstores and supermarkets only in 1998.

market alternative, where manufacturers owned the shops as well. In the margarine price war of the early 1900s, rival manufacturers had bought up chains of shops rather than let them sell margarine more cheaply than independent grocers.[32] (Despite the warnings of Adam Smith, Britain did not acquire a proper competition authority, in the shape of the Monopolies and Mergers Commission (MMC), until 1948). Collusion between manufacturers to fix prices was attacked in the Restrictive Trade Practices Act of 1956, which brought a partial end to retail price fixing. But it was not until the passage of the Resale Prices Act of 1964 that it became unlawful for individual suppliers to fix retail prices or to withhold goods from shops which discounted. By then, Resale Price Maintenance was breaking down, especially in the grocery trade, and the introduction of Green Shield stamps (a disguised form of discounting) made a nonsense of it. Tesco, one of the first retailers to push Green Shield stamps, was then no more than a would-be discount retailer – and the fiercest critic of price-fixing. 'We are declaring all-out war on Resale Price Maintenance,' declared Jack Cohen, chairman of Tesco, in 1963. 'We are not attacking the small trader. It is the manufacturer we are after.'[33]

But small shopkeepers were not fooled. The real reason for getting rid of price-fixing was that it hampered the competitiveness and efficiency of British retailing, and making shops more efficient meant replacing small shopkeepers by giant chains. Unsurprisingly, abolition was controversial. Chemists, motor dealers and small shopkeepers inundated MPs with letters and pamphlets. Backbench rebellion and rumours of rebellion forced the government to concede that the deregulation of each and every item of merchandise be subject to judicial appeal, creating a loophole which eventually enabled books and branded medicines to escape abolition.

The worst fears of small shopkeepers and their parliamentary supporters were justified, though not immediately. It is true that, in the aftermath of abolition, the prices of dozens of consumer goods – from cigarettes to tennis racquets – plunged. Yet progress was patchy. Maintenance of the retail price of books did not begin to break down until the 1990s, and the retail price of medicines is still regulated. In recent years the Office of Fair Trading (OFT) has investigated allegations of price-fixing and collusion between manufacturers and retailers to maintain prices of cars, petrol, sports equipment, and electrical goods.[34]

Manufacturers have also emasculated discount retailers by refusing to supply them. Costco and Cargo Club, two American-style discount warehouses which started in the early 1990s, had trouble persuading electrical manufacturers to supply them because they refused to adhere to recommended prices. Their difficulties, and the similarities between prices at different electrical retailers, prompted a two-year inquiry by the MMC. Its report advocated banning recommended retail prices.[35] In 1998 Margaret Beckett, secretary of state for Trade and Industry, agreed.[36] The likeliest victims are the small and independent electrical retailers. Competition in electrical retailing has already driven several sizeable forces (Rumbelows, Powerstore, Colorvision, and Escom) from the High Streets. Without profits made on extended warranties, an over-priced form of insurance against mechanical breakdown, many more would have succumbed.

Rise of the Multiples

It is only where retailing is still relatively fragmented (as it was in electrical goods) that manufacturers can dictate to shopkeepers, because they retain control of the leading brands. Clothing is now the last major market to support a large number of independent outlets. Thirty-five years after the final abolition of Resale Price Maintenance, the multiple retailers dominate almost every other aspect of British shopping.[37] The modern chain store is largely the creation of the end of price-fixing. One hundred years ago, multiple retailing was virtually unknown: only the railway bookstalls run by John Menzies and W. H. Smith had national coverage, though regional networks were sometimes large, and the first chains appeared much earlier than the 1960s. By the time Victoria died, Jesse Boot had a chain of one hundred and eighty one shops, and Thomas Lipton, a grocer, over sixty outlets in London.

Major chains of stores first emerged between the wars. The Vesteys built the Dewhurst butchers' shops to sell the beef they imported from South America. Hepworths and Burtons supplied cheap, ready-made suits to a growing white-collar workforce. Burtons had five hundred and ninety five outlets by 1939. Marks & Spencer opened or extended two hundred and fifty eight stores during the 1930s, a decade in which its turnover increased ten-fold.[38] The secret of the new chains was limited assortments of goods and huge turnover, which enabled them to negotiate discounts from suppliers. Unlike the corner shop, they offered no free credit. On the contrary, it was during the 1930s that hire purchase first put furniture, suits and wireless sets within reach of even poor households.

For J. B. Priestley, writing in the 1930s, the Woolworths chain store ('nothing over sixpence') was a potent symbol of the age. Long before modern lobbyists added 'exclusion from the dominant lifestyle' to the measures of poverty, Priestley recognised that it was the ability to shop, and not the right to vote or to claim the dole, that brought democracy and equality to life for ordinary people:

> You need money in this England, but you do not need much money. It is a large-scale, mass-production job, with cut prices. You could almost accept Woolworths as its symbol. Its cheapness is both its strength and its weakness. It is its strength because being cheap it is accessible; it nearly achieves the famous equality of opportunity. In this England, for the first time in history, Jack and Jill are nearly as good as their master and mistress; they may always have been as good in their own way, but now they are nearly as good in the *same* way. Jack, like his master, is rapidly transported to some place of rather mechanical amusement. Jill beautifies herself exactly as her mistress does. It is an England, at last, without privilege.[39]

The bounty of the mature industrial economy, on show on the racks and shelves of the chain stores of inter-war Britain, offered many people their first glimpse of the Good Life.

In the 1930s a combination of plunging prices, rising wages and hire purchase meant that, for most, money was no longer an obstacle to ownership.

Contrary to its popular image as a decade of distress, the Depression years saw shopping come of age. It was likely, thought another contemporary writer, George Orwell, that 'fish-and chips, art-silk stockings, tinned salmon, cut-price chocolate, the movies, the radio, strong tea and the football pools have between them averted revolution'. Orwell was more right than he knew. Yet by the time the Second World War broke out, the retailing revolution was far from complete. Most shops were individual or family businesses, without the protection of limited liability or even the dubious benefits of partnership, let alone chains hundreds of stores in length. In 1939, one-shop retailers still accounted for nine out of ten shops and £2 in every £3 of retail spending.

The astonishing survival of the 'little man' owed something to the natural conservatism and incompetence of shopkeepers, who were often more intent on earning a living than making a fortune, but it owed most to Resale Price Maintenance. The modern supermarket is the creature of its abolition. By putting an end to price-fixing in most goods, it allowed supermarkets to compete with the corner shop and the village store on price rather than convenience. In some areas, notably groceries, the effect was devastating. The share of grocery sales controlled by the major supermarkets has climbed from less than half twenty years ago to over four fifths today. Independent fishmongers supplied well over half the market for fresh fish as recently as 1982. Today, they have less than one quarter.[40] In 1980, when Dewhurst or Baxter's the butcher were as familiar in the High Street as Boots the chemist or Smiths the newsagent, butchers' shops met nearly half the demand for fresh meat. They now supply less than one fifth, while the supermarkets account for over two thirds.[41] According to one study, greengrocers, bakers, butchers and fishmongers now share just 6.6 per cent of total retail sales, while the multiples have over 70 per cent.[42] The story is the same in the distribution of milk. In 1981 there were 42,539 milkmen. The milk they placed on the doorstep accounted for over four in every five pints sold. Today, there are 25,589 milkmen, and they sell only two in every five pints.

In every case, the success of the multiples is cheapness. Even newsagents are suffering from the competition. The number of independent newsagents and confectioners fell from 51,700 in 1991 to less than 45,000 in 1996.[43] The supermarkets already have sizeable shares in newspapers and magazines, confectionery and tobacco, and they are pressurising wholesalers like W. H. Smith and John Menzies to give them keener prices. Like other parts of the national heritage, the survival of the traditional newsagent now seems to depend on the National Lottery, whose twice-weekly draws fill their premises with smoking and sweet-eating punters.

Fate of the Escapees

The supermarkets and the chain stores have now turned to the last bastions of the small shopkeeper: bookshops and chemists, both of which escaped the demise of Resale Price Maintenance, on the grounds that every citizen ought to have access to literature and to medicines. The Net Book Agreement (NBA), which obliged retailers to sell books at prices set by publishers, collapsed in 1995. The OFT had tried and failed to persuade the Restrictive Practices Court to declare it unlawful in 1962. It did not return to the issue until 1994, following a campaign of disparagement by Terry Maher, then the proprietor of the Dillons chain of book stores.

Maher and Tim Waterstone, who ran the Waterstone's chain of book shops before selling out to W. H. Smith in 1989, revolutionised bookselling in Britain in the 1980s. Their large, branded and brightly lit bookshops, stocking three or even five times as many titles as the average independent, gave them unprecedented purchasing power.[44] When they turned it on publishers, the target was weakened: publishers had bypassed the NBA for years through book clubs. But most did not withdraw formally from the agreement until the OFT threatened them with a legal battle to defend it.

Reed Consumer Books was the first to abandon the NBA, followed closely by Hodder Headline. Most major publishers had deserted it by the autumn of 1995; multiple bookshops and the supermarkets are now selling popular titles at one third or more off the recommended price. Independent bookshops have started to discount, and have formed purchasing co-operatives to obtain better prices from publishers. But they are bound to meet the same fate as the butcher and the fishmonger. By the end of 1996, the Booksellers Association was reporting a rise in the rate of attrition among its members.[45] This may increase as Internet-based booksellers – Amazon, Bookpages and The Internet Bookshop – increase their share of the market by discounting prices.

Non-prescription medicines are now the last bastion of retail price-fixing in Britain, but the legislative programme for 1999 includes a commitment to abolish Resale Price Maintenance in over-the-counter drugs. This followed a concerted campaign, orchestrated by the Asda supermarket chain (which did much to hasten the end of the NBA by discounting pulp fiction). In October 1995 Asda launched a public assault on the medicinal cartel by discounting branded vitamin and mineral supplements by up to 20 per cent. Its reward was a stream of legal missives from manufacturers.

It withdrew the discounts, but returned to the fray in June 1996, when it announced it would discount the price of Anadin, a branded paracetamol which sold at seven times the price of the own-label version. The manufacturer took out an injunction, giving the supermarket chain another blast of favour-able publicity. Archie Norman, then chief executive of Asda, made an unashamedly populist pitch for public support. Resale Price Maintenance of medicaments, he said, was 'a hidden tax of £280 million a year on the British public'.[46] A few months after he was elected Conservative MP for Tunbridge Wells, his successors made a third attempt to embarrass manufacturers by cutting the price of children's medicines by 25 per cent. By then the OFT had referred the price-fixing of 2,200 medicines to the Restrictive Practices Court. The Director General of Fair Trading put the cost to the consumer of artificially high prices at £180 million.

The main beneficiaries of the price-fixing are the pharmacies, which include giant retail chains such as Boots, Lloyds and Alliance Unichem, as well as thousands of independent chemists' shops. Two in three chemists are still independent or members of small chains. Organised as the Community Pharmacy Action Group, they claim the abolition of Resale Price Maintenance will put one quarter of them out of business. A torrent of cant about the importance of the local chemist's shop to the poor and the vulnerable failed to impress the government. But abolition will certainly put the multiples in a strong position: they have eroded sales of household goods by independent pharmacies for years, and dispensaries are now being added to supermarkets. By 1998, multiples of one kind or another controlled one in three pharmacies, and their share will increase. They are actually being encouraged to expand by government, which sees supermarket pharmacies developing into adjuncts to doctors' surgeries, or as centres for the treatment of minor ailments. Asda and Unichem have discussed adding doctors to the company payroll, building surgeries in the car park and selling their services to the NHS. It is not as outlandish as it sounds. NHS prescriptions already account for two thirds of the revenues of the average pharmacy.

Petrol Retailing

Another little man who is feeling the competition from the multiples is the independent petrol retailer. Although consumers have not noticed, because 80 per cent of the price of a gallon of petrol goes to the government in excise duty and VAT, he is being squeezed remorselessly by a vicious price war between supermarkets and the major oil companies. Before tax, the price of a gallon of petrol has fallen by one third in real terms since 1990, partly because the price of crude oil has fallen but mainly because the supermarkets have attached petrol stations to their car parks and sold petrol below the prices charged by the garages. The supermarket share of the petrol market rose from 5 per cent in 1990 to 23 per cent in 1998. Since most of the rest of the market (49 per cent) is controlled by three oil companies (Esso, Shell and BP), which have cut their prices to match those of the supermarkets, the net effect is a sharp fall in the real price of petrol.[47]

The price war started in January 1996 when Esso, the largest petrol retailer, introduced Pricewatch, which forced its company-owned outlets and the independents it supplied to match the lowest prices offered by competitors in the same area. By 1998 profit margins on a litre of petrol had slipped from 6p to 4p.[48] Save, the biggest chain of independent retailers, reckoned the three-year price war which followed the introduction of Pricewatch cost it 40 per cent of its sales. Like the oil companies, supermarkets could buy in bulk from refiners; unlike them, they do not have to split the proceeds with a tenant (most petrol stations are not owned by the brand they trade under). Supermarkets have also concentrated their efforts on high-volume outlets, leaving the oil companies to cover the village pumps and the B-roads. Naturally they found this uncongenial, so the oil companies started to concentrate on high-volume sites too. The number of petrol stations shrank from 20,000 in 1990 to 15,000 in 1997.[49]

The main victims were the smaller, independent retailers; the number driven out of business was between 2,000 and 3,000. MPs were lobbied, and the OFT came under pressure to investigate the market. It was not pleased. The OFT had studied the market in 1993 and found no evidence of anti-competitive behaviour. Nor did its second study, published in 1998. 'Competition . . . results in winners and losers,' concluded the director general of the OFT. 'The prices charged by independent petrol retailers . . . are, on average, more expensive than their rivals. The consumer, not surprisingly, has chosen lower prices . . . There is no reason to believe that supermarkets or oil companies deliberately set out to remove independent retailers.'[50]

One reason for his confidence was that the price war had hurt the oil companies as well as independent retailers. Their market share was down, and so were their margins. In late 1996 BP and Mobil merged their retailing operations, and all Mobil sites were re-branded as BP outlets. In December 1997 Gulf sold its retail outlets to Shell. All the big oil companies have had to launch expensive promotional and customer loyalty schemes. The free glasses and Green Shield stamps of yesteryear have given way to electronic cards, on which customers accumulate points. But they are not conspicuously more successful than their predecessors in creating brand loyalty.

It is almost impossible to brand a commodity like petrol, which sells mainly on price. This is why the supermarkets were able to increases their market share so easily. It is also why the oil companies have now decided that the best form of defence is to attack the retailing franchise of the supermarkets.

TABLE 22.3
Petrol Stations

Brands	Outlets	Company-owned Sites	Shops (Retail Alliance)*
Leading Oil Companies			
Esso	1,874	48.3	1,520 (Tesco Express)
BP	1,831	50.5	1,511 (Budgen/Safeway)
Shell	1,459	56.9	1,313
Texaco	1,147	39.1	935
UK	726	1.5	386
Jet	670	32.9	635
Total	568	72.5	548 (Alldays)
Save	524	78.4	501
Elf	499	77.1	336 (Somerfield)
Q8	439	23.5	313 (Budgen)
Leading Supermarkets			
Tesco	288	100.0	271
J. Sainsbury/Savacentre	205	100.0	130
Safeway	156	100.0	156
Asda	129	100.0	14
Morrisons	64	100.0	56
Spar	26	11.5	–
VG	19	28.6	–
Co-operative Retail Services	16	0.0	9
United Norwest Co-operative	13	n/a	–
Somerfield	8	100.0	–
National Total	14,824	42.6	10,248

Source: Institute of Petroleum, *UK Retail Marketing Survey 1998: Special Supplement.*

* At least 10 square metres in size and selling five lines other than cigarettes, sweets, lubricants and car accessories.

The traditional forecourt shop, selling cigarettes, confectionery and gnarled sandwiches, is giving way to mini-supermarkets, fresh and junk food, and the ubiquitous National Lottery terminal. Some oil companies have joined forces with supermarkets to create a shop stocking up to 2,000 lines. 'We feel we can enhance the forecourt brand by also establishing ourselves on the high street,' explains one oil company executive.[51] Selling groceries is also far more profitable than selling petrol.

Other New Territories

By inviting the supermarkets to create new shops on their forecourts, the oil companies are inadvertently helping their tormentors to conquer another fragmented retailing market: the so-called convenience stores. In a sense, these have always existed. One authority reckons there are 26,500 independent grocers in Britain, of which a substantial minority stay open late enough to count as 'convenience' stores.[52] It is unlikely that there will be as many in future. Supermarkets are not only larger, cheaper and more numerous; they have begun to stay open at night, and to open for six hours on Sundays. They are also attacking convenience stores directly.

Tesco opened the first Tesco Metro, a miniature version of a supermarket, at Covent Garden in 1993. Sainsbury's, ever-ready to copy its competitor but add a twist of its own, has a similar format, Sainsbury's Local, with the emphasis on fresh and convenience foods. In 1998 Budgens bought the fifty-seven outlets of the 7-Eleven chain, and rebranded them B2 convenience stores.[53] Ironically, given the weight of rhetoric expended on the disappearance of the traditional High Street retailer, the new stores are largely the creation of tighter planning restrictions. As out-of-town superstores have become less popular with planning authorities, the supermarkets have returned to the city centre – in a guise which will destroy the shops which remained.

Other forces are at work too. An ageing (and divorced) population appreciates the convenience of a neighbourhood shop and its willingness to deliver. Longer working hours, and the increasing number of women who work, are tempting younger customers to skip the huge weekly shop. Consolidation of convenience stores is already underway; several chains have emerged, and one major supermarket group is betting its future on the format. Somerfield, which recently acquired the High Street outlets of Kwik Save, describes its ambition as 'to build our stores into the fabric of Britain's local communities. We'll become a focal point in the neighbourhood, so that people think of us as '"my friends around the corner who have the things I need at just the right price"'.[54]

It seems there is no limit to the appetite of the multiples. Any market made up of a large number of smaller outlets is vulnerable. Multiples are making their presence felt in such arcane areas as horticultural retailing, as the independent nurserymen give way to the garden centres which major supermarkets are adding to their DIY and home improvement warehouses. There

TABLE 22.4
Other Major Retail Chains, 1996

Brands	Owner	Outlets	Turnover 1997–8 (£m)
B & Q, Comet, Woolworths, Superdrug	Kingfisher PLC	2,025	6,409
Boots the Chemist, Boots the Optician, Halfords	The Boots Company PLC	2,102	4,976
Dixons, Currys, PC World, The Link	Dixons Group PLC	754	2,774
Burton, Dorothy Perkins, Top Shop etc.*	Arcadia Group PLC	*2,081	1,451
BhS, Mothercare	Storehouse PLC	485	1,335
WH Smith, WH Smith Travel	WH Smith Group PLC	742	1,267
Waterstone's, Dillons, HMV, Daisy & Tom†	HMV Media Group	459	†1,146
Lloyds Pharmacy	Gehe AG	1,443	1,042
MFI, Howden Joinery	MFI Furniture Group PLC	248	794
Adams, Miss Selfridge, Richards, Wallis, Warehouse	Sears PLC	769	618
Dillons, M & W, Supercigs	T & S Stores PLC	983	549
H. Samuel, Ernest Jones	Signet Group PLC	598	352
Laura Ashley	Laura Ashley PLC	237	345
Bacons, Barratts, Hush Puppies, Instep, Saxone	Stylo PLC	546	324
New Look	New Look Group Ltd	409	323
Moss Chemists	Alliance Unichem	531	297
Carpetright, Carpet Depot	Carpetright PLC	307	269
Baker's Oven, Birketts, Braggs, Greggs, Thurston	Greggs PLC	1,057	266
Allied Carpets	Allied Carpets PLC	258	264
Burberrys, Scotch House	Great Universal Stores PLC	28	255
Harveys, Kingsburys	Harveys Furnishing PLC	369	190

Source: Companies; Company Annual Reports and Accounts; *Financial Times.*

* Arcadia Group includes shops in Debenhams (de-merged from the group in 1997) and shops within shops in the Group and outside it.
† HMV Media Group was set up by Tim Waterstone, an American venture capital firm Advent International, and the EMI music group, which owned some Dillons outlets. These will be re-branded Waterstone. HMV Media Group also owns the 271 HMV music shops. Turnover is the combined sales figures for Waterstone's (£189 million) and HMV (£956.7 million) in 1998.

are an estimated seven and a half thousand garden centres in Britain, but only half a dozen are organised in a chain longer than seven outlets. Wyevale grew from one centre in Hereford into a chain of over sixty outlets, and is the biggest garden centre group in Britain. Yet it is a minnow by comparison with the major multiples, which are now bringing their purchasing power to bear on the profit margins of the independent garden centres.

Car Dealerships

Car dealerships are undergoing a similar process of rationalisation, as companies and consumers tire of being overcharged. In Britain, the price of a new car is up to 60 per cent higher than elsewhere in Europe,[55] mainly because the manufacturers have retained control of prices. Governments have granted motor manufacturers an exemption from the normal competition rules on the grounds that cars are dangerous machines which have to be serviced by properly trained mechanics at a location near the owner's home. As a result, cars are sold by authorised dealers who are not allowed to sell other marques or expand beyond a defined geographical area. This makes it easy for manufacturers to impose recommended retail prices on dealers, by denying or threatening to deny them stock or marketing support, and by paying cash bonuses to dealers who maintain prices.

Unlike the electrical goods market (where similar practices were discovered), dealers could not escape the grip of the manufacturers by buying stock in a 'grey' market.[56] Until the New Labour government changed the rules, dealers were not allowed to import more than fifty right-hand-drive models from a foreign country, even though prices are much lower than those charged by the manufacturers supplying them directly. Those who import more than fifty can expect to be starved of stock. One manufacturer is even said to have told its dealers to charge grey import owners more for servicing. Others are warning darkly of inferior specifications, servicing difficulties and safety risks.[57]

The OFT is not impressed. In October 1998 it said it was considering referring the new car market to the MMC on the grounds that a 'complex monopoly' existed.[58] This was the second brush with the competition authorities in six years, the MMC having identified a complex monopoly in favour of car manufacturers in 1992. As the MMC report pointed out, the lack of competition in the new car market is reinforced by the peculiarities of British buying. The dealership structure not only denies the consumer choice, competition and information, but the ordinary car buyer lacks clout in a market dominated by large fleet buyers who get heavy discounts from manufacturers.

The ordinary buyer is forced to subsidise company fleets by paying more for cars designed, equipped and priced for the company market. The retail customer pays, on average, £2,000 more than a fleet buyer for the same car. The discounts secured by fleet buyers sometimes run as deep as 35 per cent.

Despite charging ordinary buyers premium prices, dealers still find it hard to make money out of new car sales. Car manufacturers are more interested in keeping their production lines busy than in preserving dealers' profit margins. When sales in the showrooms fail to keep pace with output, manufacturers invent them. New cars are 'pre-registered' and sold at a discount, as 'demonstrators' or 'ex-rentals' which are driven for two or three months (usually by their own executives) before being returned to the dealers for sale at a discount. Manufacturers have also taken to selling cars directly to fleet buyers, cutting out the dealers, and especially the 'main dealers' which used to distribute cars to smaller outlets. In April 1995 the Korean manufacturer, Daewoo, decided not to bother with dealers at all. It approaches buyers directly, and has sub-contracted servicing to Halfords, the hardware subsidiary of Boots.

The profitability of new car sales was dented further by the bunching of activity around the annual number plate change at the beginning of August. Reluctance to buy set in around May each year, and then about 25 per cent of new car sales took place in a single month. This was said by the motor trade to cost an estimated £1.5 billion in stockholding costs. The last Conservative government accepted that change was necessary, but decided to postpone a decision. New Labour introduced a biennial change in the number plate from August 1998, with regional and age identifiers to follow in 2001 when the rest of the alphabet is used up.[59] Dealers welcomed the change, but it may make their problems worse: the number plate change did at least encourage people to buy a new car.

Dealers have got used to thin margins on new car sales. Soon, they may have to get used to them on used car sales, servicing and repairs too. Modern cars are more reliable, so dealers are generating less income from their workshops, and many of the most profitable aspects of servicing – exhaust, oil and tyre changes – are being lost to specialist workshops like Kwikfit. Even the second-hand market is now facing unprecedented competitive pressures. It is much larger than the new car market, turning over about eight million used vehicles compared with two million new cars, and makes up a large slice of profits for the leading dealers. But they now have to compete with regular car auctions, specialist magazines, and the Internet, all of which put buyers in touch with sellers directly.

For a time in the mid-1990s it looked as if Car Group would offer the advantages of buying a second-hand car through a dealer (wide choice and a guarantee of reliability) without the disadvantage of his fat profit margin (up to 40 per cent). It bought cars in bulk at auctions, and from company fleets and pre-registrations, and sold them from vast open-air sites around the country. By mid-1998 Car Group had a public quotation, seven sites, and aimed to sell 20,000 cars a year from each. But it had expanded too quickly: its margins were too thin when the market in second-hand cars faltered. It ended up in the hands of the receivers.[60] But the idea was good, and an imitator, CarLand, opened its first site at Lakeside Retail Park in Essex in 1998.[61]

Similar car supermarkets selling a wide range of brands at keen prices are expected to emerge in the new car market. But there is not much sign of them yet. The top ten dealers average just 1.3 franchises per showroom. The new car market remains astonishingly fragmented.[62] The market leader (Pendragon) supplies only 2 per cent of it. Although the franchised dealership market is now consolidating, dealers are becoming more rather than less reliant on selling the most popular marques. Until a force equivalent to the supermarkets emerges in the new car market, manufacturers will continue to dominate how they are distributed and priced.

The Last Independents?

If there is one area of retailing which is even more fragmented than the car markets, it is clothing and footwear. This reflects its peculiarities. Retailing of any kind is less stable and more shapeless than other forms of economic activity, but clothes and shoe shops are especially evanescent and amorphous. Retailers of clothes have to be alive to the unpredictable shifts in consumer tastes and fancies. As a host of ruined retailers (from James Smith to Sophie Mirman) could attest, fashion and the economics of fashion change with bewildering rapidity. Men wear different clothes from women, and children from adults. The fat need bigger clothes than the thin. Old people dress differently from young ones. Buyers of clothes support chain stores, department stores, mail order companies, and boutiques. On top of the national chains, there are about 45,000 independent clothing stores in Britain selling a vast range of fabrics, colours and styles. This is why only Asda and Marks & Spencer, among the major multiples, have made any progress in clothing and footwear. Sears, the one PLC with a broad portfolio of branded shoe and clothing shops, performed so badly that investors forced it to break up.

But clothes are not completely immune to the homogenising influence of the PLC. The main enemy of diversity is fashion, which, by definition, is the popular or prevailing manner of dress. Whether the constant demand for novelty reflects the mind of the modern consumer, or the need of the manufacturer and retailer to keep busy and prosperous, fashion inhibits the progress of the excellent and the unusual. If the idle wives of rich men are prepared to pay immense sums for frocks bearing the imprimatur of an acclaimed designer, those at the lower end of the income scale are equally in thrall to brand names. In fact, the ubiquitous brand has infiltrated the markets in clothing and footwear so thoroughly that some manufacturers print their labels and logos on the outside of their garments. Fashion-conscious urban teenagers are prepared to mug their contemporaries to get trainers or a T-shirt bearing the logo of Nike or Reebok. (Sports clothes have become fashionable in their own right.) 'We will never sell anything other than brands, it's as simple as that,' says Dave Whelan, founder of the JJB chain of sports shops. 'It's what people want.'[63] Clothes shops which disregard his advice soon run into trouble. Olympus, a chain of shops selling sports clothes, failed because it offered own-label goods rather than well-known brand names. Dunn & Co, a venerable chain of men's outfitters founded more than a century ago, expired at Christmas 1996 after refusing to admit that the modern office worker wants branded jeans and sweat shirts, not tweed hats and pinstripe suits.[64]

Shops are undone by more old-fashioned shortcomings as well as failing to appreciate the importance of image over substance. When spending growth is strong, as in the late 1980s, virtually any shop can do well. When spending is tight, only the strongest survive. At the height of the consumer boom, in 1987, Sock Shop found its public flotation was *fifty-three* times over-subscribed. Its founder, Sophie Mirman, became a minor celebrity. At the peak of its fortunes, Sock Shop was valued at £72 million. In 1990, the rump was sold to a group of venture capitalists for just £3.25 million. Yet the brand has survived. It was money, not the idea, which brought Sophie Mirman down, just as it was finance rather than the idea which enabled another 'category killer', Tie Rack, to survive the recession unscathed.[65] Roy Bishko, who set up Tie Rack after witnessing the feeding frenzy at Harrod's tie sale, told the *Financial Times* that nothing irritates him more than being described as a niche retailer. 'By heavens,' he said, 'I've been trying to add products all the time. Tie Rack is now a design-led retail accessory business, with emphasis on neckwear.' It is a witty but not a snappy definition. Nor is there any need for him to feel resentful. Tie Rack (though no longer independent) is the most conspicuous of a number of specialist chains, ranging from Clintons birthday card shops to Thorntons chocolatiers, which were bound to thrive in the shopaholic culture of late twentieth-century Britain.

High Street: Death or Resurrection?

Other beneficiaries of the same culture are less nimble: superstores and shopping centres. £1 in every £3 spent in the shops has migrated from the High Street to the warehouses and shopping centres which litter the fringes of every urban conurbation. The first superstore was opened by Asda at West Bridgford in Nottingham in 1967; in the 1980s lighter planning restrictions turned them into the main avenue of growth in British retailing. The biggest in Britain, a Sainsbury's SavaCentre in south London, has 240,000 square feet of space, and shopping centres such as Metro at Gateshead or Merry Hill at Dudley outstrip Oxford Street in sales per square foot.

Until the mid-1990s, there were few planning restrictions on giant shopping centres or edge-of-town warehouse developments. The sites were cheap to buy or rent, and out-of-town sites offered retailers significant savings in labour, sales and distribution costs. Shoppers liked the wider choice of shops and goods, and the convenience of the car park. The traditional High Street began to die. The emigration of flagship retailers such as Sainsbury's and Tesco to the edge of town denied surrounding shops passing trade they had relied on. The shopping centres had an even more devastating effect. Merry Hill, which opened in 1989, killed High Street trading in nearby Dudley, and its effects were felt as far afield as Stourbridge. Meadowhall, opened in 1990, took one third of sales from Sheffield town centre. The biggest shopping centres now have their own post offices, pharmacies, dry cleaners, cash points, restaurants and hotels, cinemas and sports complexes. They are capable of shifting the centre of gravity of a town.

High Street retailers of all kinds have suffered from the exodus of shoppers. Sketchley the dry cleaners, which had earned a reliable living from dirty linen, closed one in three of its seven hundred and twenty shops and eventually abandoned the High Street altogether by selling the remainder to a rival firm, Mister Minit. Sears, the sprawling retail conglomerate created by Charles Clore, reduced its tally of High Street shops and concessions from three thousand seven hundred and fifty in the mid-1980s to a fraction of that number. Buyers were so hard to find, it was reduced to selling hundreds of shops to Facia, the gimcrack retailing empire created by Stephen Hinchcliffe. The company collapsed before Sears had even received its money. A business which once sold one in four shoes worn in Britain was by 1998 no more than an embarrassment to its shareholders, awaiting the dissolution of its remaining businesses by gathering asset-strippers.

By the early 1990s, the lamentations of High Street retailers were too loud to ignore. The secretary of state for the environment, John Gummer, put the deregulation of planning into reverse. 'I want town centres to be a lively place to live,' he declared. 'I am not opposed to the retail revolution but there's a lot more retail growth to come and I want to see most of that in city centres.'[66] Preference was given to city centre planning applications. The effects were soon felt. Opponents took the Trafford Centre in Manchester all the way to the House of Lords before the developers were given permission to start in May 1995. The Bluewater and Braehead shopping centres opened in 1999, but projects of a similar size and scale will no longer be indulged by the planning authorities.

TABLE 22.5
The Major Shopping Centres

	Number of Shops	Square Footage	Est. Visitors p.a.	Owners
Braehead, Glasgow	100	800,000	–	Capital Shopping Centres
Trafford Centre, Manchester	280	1,300,000	30 million*	Peel Holdings
Merry Hill, Dudley	250	1,800,000	24 million	Chelsfield
The Mall, Bristol	130	725,000	14 million	Prudential/JT Baylis
MetroCentre, Gateshead	350	1,800,000	29.7 million	Capital Shopping Centres
Meadowhall, Sheffield	270	1,200,000	28 million	Stadium Group
Lakeside, Thurrock	350	1,300,000	25 million	Capital Shopping Centres
Bluewater, Dartford	300	1,500,000	30 million	Lend Lease/Prudential

Source: *Financial Times.*

* Projections.

The long-term effects of planning constraints are likely to be mixed. Ways around the regulations will doubtless be found. Purpose-built 'factory outlet' centres, such as Cheshire Oaks in Chester and Bicester Village, are providing retailers with a means of bypassing planning restrictions and manufacturers with a way to get rid of unwanted and end-of-season stock. There were twelve in existence by the end of 1996. Ironically, the slower growth of out-of-town sites is one of the factors driving the multiples into markets they have not previously tackled: books, medicines, health and beauty, dry-cleaning, music and videos, newspapers and magazines, clothes, and petrol. Far from rescuing the High Street, tighter planning might accelerate its demise. Worse, it may also inhibit competition between the multiples.

The only part of the superstore sector to have experienced genuine competitive pressure is DIY. The multiples over invested on the back of a housing boom in a sector already crowded with builders' merchants and hardware stores: the number of DIY superstores rose from one hundred and seventy-five in 1980 to over a thousand in 1995. Many of the products they sold – pots of paint and claw hammers – were available as cheaply elsewhere. Brands also proved hard to create. Attempts to differentiate their outlets as heavy ('You can build a house at Wickes') or soft (Homebase leases concessions to Laura Ashley) failed to increase customer loyalty. In the end, Texas sold out to J. Sainsbury, owner of Homebase, and W. H. Smith and Boots sold their shares in Do It All. Wickes had to sell its Builders' Mate and Hunter Timber subsidiaries.

In the last decade, the big food retailers have increased their share of the market from one third to nearly one half. The OFT is conducting a review of the profitability of the major supermarket groups to assess whether or not there should be a reference to the MMC. An independent report commissioned as part of its inquiry confirmed the popular belief that supermarkets squeeze their suppliers without passing any of the gain to their customers.[67] Farmers and manufacturers gripe that the supermarkets are pressing them too hard (as part of its evidence to the inquiry, the Meat and Livestock Commission identified a significant enlargement of the gap between prices paid to producers and those charged to consumers).[68]

Supermarkets have invested heavily in technology, which enables them to keep levels of stock closer to the volume of sales, and thus move the cost of holding stock to the manufacturers. These savings are not passed on to consumers either. Since the *Sunday Times* launched its first campaign accusing the supermarkets of profiteering, many other newspapers and television programmes have made similar allegations.[69] David Sainsbury, then chairman of Sainsbury's, conceded: 'The major food retailers in the 1980s concentrated heavily on meeting the increasing demands of customers for convenience, service and quality, and in so doing we allowed the prices on some basic commodities to drift upwards. This provided an opportunity for discounters to undercut us.'[70]

It seemed for a time that a new breed of discount food retailer was capable of embarrassing the major supermarkets. Archie Norman of Asda warned: 'We are planning on the basis that the halcyon days in the UK grocery industry in terms of profitability are over. The superstore industry will not be able to sustain the number of new openings planned without having some effect on margins and sales growth.'[71] But the discounters proved to be a recessionary challenge; they waned quickly in the mid-1990s. Shoprite had to sell to Kwiksave, which struggled on for five years before selling to Somerfield. Safeway abandoned Lo Cost, and Budgen closed down its Penny Market chain. Brown & Jackson's two hundred and thirty Poundstretcher discount stores had to be rescued by South African investors. Winners, another chain of discount retailers, went out of business. The three Cargo Club stores were sold to Sainsbury's after barely a year.

The demise of the discounters was a reminder of the ruthless instincts of the major supermarkets. They cut their prices to cripple the challenge, and then used the planning laws to hobble the Cargo Clubs. When Nurdin and Peacock and Costco, an American firm, announced their intention to set up warehouse clubs, the supermarkets launched a legal action to prevent them acquiring sites.[72] Competition between multiples themselves can be just as relentless. When Tesco offered to redeem money-off vouchers issued by any other supermarket, Asda flooded the areas where it had no stores with vouchers offering shoppers £10 off every £20 they spent.[73] In 1994 Sainsbury's had to apologise to Tesco after over-zealous superiors instructed store managers to remove Tesco vouchers from copies of *Radio Times* sold in its shops.

But the competition is rarely as fierce as it seems. Since the retreat of the discounters, the major chains have reverted to competing on 'service' rather than price. Expensive research had revealed, it is claimed, that customers are less concerned about prices than a smiling face at the checkout, extra bag packers, packaging that can be opened, carrier bags that do not split, and trolleys that do not have minds of their own. Tesco spent £4 million re-fitting two hundred thousand trolleys with a self-steering device.[74] After spending eighteen months and £9 million researching its falling market share, Sainsbury's invited Ulrika Jonsson to launch a new 'customer service commitment' in the late summer of 1995. At its heart was a 'one in front' rule, which promised 'checkouts that open on cue if there's more than one shopper in front of you'. Unfortunately, the promise ran so far ahead of reality that the supermarket was censured by the Independent Television Commission, and the advertisements had to be withdrawn. Sainsbury's, borrowing a line from British Rail, blamed the problems on 'staff illness'.[75]

Safeway had a better idea for beating the queues. It equipped shoppers with hand-held scanners, enabling them to scan their own shopping and charge it to their debit card as they went around the store. Asda relies heavily on gimmicks: at one stage it claimed to roll out a red carpet for its biggest shoppers; on rainy days, umbrella-wielding shelf-packers chaperone house-wives to their cars; there were 'pet stops' for dogs and cats who could not bear to be parted from their owners; and 'singles nights' when unmarried shoppers wre given name-badges and a map of the 'erogenous zones' around the store to search for sexually adventurous contemporaries. 'Colleagues', as Asda employees are known in the boardroom, get free use of a company Jaguar for a month if they can think of a new way to cheer up customers.

But if customer service at Asda has odd angles, the Woolworth approach to selling seems Orwellian. During the Christmas period of 1995, the company suffused its stores with the smell of mulled wine, reasoning that the 'seasonal aroma' would have a positive effect on sales. Its sister shop, Superdrug, has used the smell of baby powder and chocolate to the same end.[76] Subliminal influences do appear to work. Scientists showed that consumers buy French wine under the influence of accordion music, and cans of lager when the music changes to bierkeller tunes. British Oxygen now supplies synthetic odours, from the smell of new-baked bread to clean linen, Christmas trees, sandalwood, and a non-specific 'clean smell'.[77]

Technology

Retailers have used odours to influence shoppers since Gordon Selfridge put scents on the ground floor. But separating consumers from their money is now more of a science than an art. Modern retailers use technology to understand the behaviour of their customers, as well as influence it. Information from point-of-sale scanners is processed and analysed, not only to decide what to stock, but to tell manufacturers what to make. Weather forecasts are dissected to predict demand for salads, ice-cream and charcoal. Browsing shoppers are recorded on film, which is trawled for patterns and clues to better presentation. Loyalty cards are a form of information-gathering. By studying the buying patterns of card-holders, a supermarket can judge which goods branches should stock; gauge the success of promotions and gear new ones to customers who have bought the product before; analyse which parts of a store are unpopular; make differential offers, and tailor mail-shots to vegetarians or wine-drinkers only. One ambition now close to realisation is the 'smart' loyalty card usable at more than one type of shop, enabling retailers to build up a picture of individual lifestyles and spending patterns.

'Clubcard will enable us to recreate the old tradition of a shop manager knowing all the people who shop in his store,' claimed Sir Ian MacLaurin, who introduced loyalty cards at Tesco. If the manufacturers of Felix pet food are to be believed, supermarkets can even get to know their customers' pets. The Felix Club has assembled the names and addresses of one hundred thousand cats, who now get mail-shots inviting them to recommend other cats for membership.[78] In future, retailers will expect to know the names, habits and lifestyles of everybody who shops with them regularly. As Ian MacLaurin recognised, it is a dream of the past as well as the future. The multiples will rediscover the virtues of the village shop, which were thought to have gone for ever.

It is a re-discovery the supermarkets needed to make. Although they now seem omnipotent, their hold over the nation is tenuous. Power, having shifted from manufacturer to retailer, is moving from retailer to consumer. The main force for change is information technology. Theoretically, the consumer can decide what goods he is prepared to look at, and instantly compare the prices offered by different retailers. In those markets where the Internet is making an impact, the competition on price is already fierce. Anything in digital form – software, videos, music – can be distributed electronically, and what cannot be delivered down a telephone line can be ordered electronically. All of the major supermarkets have begun home deliveries.

Of course, there is nothing novel about shopping remotely. Catalogues and mail order have existed since the Victorian department stores despatched lists of goods around the Empire (the telegraphic address of Harrod's was EVERYTHING, LONDON). The change wrought by information technology is not that people can buy goods without visiting shops, but that shops are redundant. The main job of the shopkeeper is merchandising, or choosing what goods to offer for sale, and at what price to offer them. Before the age of computers and telecommunications, consumers were too short of time, knowledge, and buying power to purchase anything anywhere except at a shop. Technology has now solved those imperfections. It will never eliminate intermediaries altogether (somebody has to aggregate the orders and collect the cash) but they could just as easily be telephone companies or manufacturers as shops. But the chief benefit of technology is to reduce the random element in shopping. Deprived of the sights and smells of the modern shop, consumers will start to behave more intelligently. The survival of the retailers depends on their ability to make shopping for the many what it already is for the few: not a chore, but fun. Shopping has to become a leisure pursuit.

CHAPTER TWENTY-THREE

LEISURE

It is commonly believed that happiness depends on leisure, because we occupy ourselves so that we may have leisure, just as we make war in order that we may live at peace.

ARISTOTLE (384–322 BC)[1]

To be able to fill leisure intelligently is the last product of civilisation.

BERTRAND RUSSELL, 1930[2]

One of the most important developments in twentieth century society has been the growth of leisure and recreation.

JOHN STEVENSON, 1984[3]

Leisure, like shopping, is a gift of prosperity. Only a developed industrial economy can liberate time from the struggle for survival to give people the freedom to do nothing. The Fourth Commandment ordained the Sabbath, not simply to worship God, but to break the incessant routine of work. The Sabbath apart, leisure was the preserve of the few in pre-industrial civilisation; only the aristocracy, living off the labour of others, had the time and the money to invent and pursue refinement and idleness. It was the leisured class which cultivated philosophy, science, the arts, games and sports, and the first plays and concerts were staged largely for their amusement.

Aristocratic time and money turned Brighton, Bath, Weymouth and Tunbridge Wells into the prototypical holiday destinations and spa towns, with hotels and amusement arcades and festivals of music and drama. The aristocracy pioneered the foreign holiday as the Grand Tour, on which its youth surveyed the art and architecture of France and Italy. 'What a happy period of your life this is!' wrote Lord Chesterfield to his son in 1751, in the middle of his Grand Tour. 'Pleasure is now, and ought to be, your business.'[4] It was this ability to live off their property without working which made aristocrats gentlemen of leisure. 'To the upper part of mankind,' wrote Henry Fielding of the eighteenth-century peerage, 'time is an enemy and (as they themselves often confess), their chief labour is to kill it.'[5]

It was the triumph of the twentieth century to spread this dilemma through all ranks of society. Modern Britons live longer and work less than their ancestors; they have paid holidays, smaller families and greater sums to spend on their amusement. In former times, work crowded out leisure. What fun there was to be had was bound up with work. Impoverished London contemporaries of the Grand Tourists left the city not to take the waters at Bath or bathe at Brighton, but to go harvesting or hop-picking. In the countryside, popular recreations – wrestling, cudgelling, quoits, baiting, cock-fighting, marbles, and even football – took place mainly around the festivals and fairs which marked the progress of the agricultural calendar.

It was not until the economy began to grow significantly, in the middle of the eighteenth century, that people started to consume time as freely as their aristocratic masters. Racing and prize-fighting, which attract large working-class audiences, date from the late eighteenth century. Mass-produced alcohol meant anyone could get drunk, every day. In Gin Lane, cheaply distilled spirits ensured that a man or a woman could be 'drunk for a penny and dead drunk for two pence'. But everybody worked until Saturday night. The 'weekend', the commonest measure of leisure time today, was not honoured widely until the closing years of the Victorian era. For most people, throughout most of history, the line separating work from play was not distinct. A mixture of evangelicalism, temperance and the long, regimented days and cramped living conditions of the early Industrial Revolution made the distinction stark. It put paid to the anarchic revelries of the rural fair or Holy Day, though not immediately. In the early days of industrialisation, rural habits lived on. Weavers, miners and cotton-workers took off the Monday after payday so often it was known as 'keeping Saint Monday'. It was common as late as the 1860s for Monday to be lost to drunken reverie, especially among the unskilled. Skilled workers had too much pride in their labour to follow their example; they made the British artisan famous for his hard work, craftsmanship and sobriety.

The unskilled workers of the first production lines were not insulated in the same way from the alienating effects of modern industrial organisation. By the turn of the century, the British working classes had rediscovered work as the means to life rather than its object. Edwardians blamed the declining productivity of the British economy on the British worker's absorption in the turf, the music-hall and the pub. The Tariff Commission of 1906 complained that the average British workman was 'less thrifty, takes less interest in his work, is fonder of outdoor amusements, is more addicted to drink and . . . generally is more interested in the next football match and the nearest public house than he is in his work'.[6]

Not much has changed since. Throughout the twentieth century, the British have squandered the time liberated by rising productivity on the banal pleasures of mass entertainment. By the inter-war years, the reduction of the working week (Saturday became a full day off in most manufacturing industries during those years) and the spread of paid holidays (over 11 million workers were entitled to one by 1939) had caused an explosion in commercialised amusement: twenty million people visited the English seaside resorts every year, Blackpool alone attracting seven million. Hotels and holiday camps were built to accommodate them – Billy Butlin opened his first holiday camp in 1937, at Skegness – and swimming pools, fairgrounds, pleasure beaches, cinemas and ballrooms appeared to amuse them.

Car ownership opened up unknown parts of the coast and hills to day-trippers, and other sports – tennis, golf and motor racing – became popular. A new culture of leisure, homogenous and cosmopolitan, was fostered by the spread of radio, newspapers, cinema newsreels, and (eventually) television. Sport and music no longer revolved around the factory or the pit, and holidays no longer meant the works outing. The age of organised leisure and mass entertainment, supplied by commercial companies, had dawned. Leisure had become a business.

Cinemas

The cinema – new, cosmopolitan, commercial – was the chief symbol of this transformation. Cinema-goers in John O'Groats could see the same Hollywood films as their Cornish counterparts at Land's End. Though the first cinema had opened in London in 1896, and there were about three thousand screens in Britain by 1914, it was during the inter-war years that architects provided cinema companies with branded outlets of the kind then sweeping the High Street.[7] The development of the 'talkies' (1927), and colour film in the 1930s, turned cinema-going into a mass entertainment industry. At the peak of their popularity, one third of the population was going to the movies at least once a week; in 1946, 5,000-odd cinemas enjoyed over 1.6 billion admissions.

Their attraction was obvious. Like television today, the cinema was a cheap alternative to a night at the pub. The cheapness of the cinema killed off the Victorian music hall, only to be itself undone by television in the 1950s. By 1960, cinema admissions had fallen to less than one third of the level of 1946, and the decline continued throughout the sixties and seventies. By the early 1980s, when modestly priced video recorders became available, the average Briton found watching movies over a TV dinner at home more agreeable than squeezing into an uncomfortable seat at the local cinema. In 1984 admissions fell to a post-war low of fifty-four million: the industry was in near-terminal decline.

But the obsequies were premature. In the second half of the 1980s cinema-going revived dramatically and unexpectedly, and by 1997 they admitted just on one hundred and forty million people. The cause was the 'multiplex', a vast edge-of-town complex with between eight and twenty-four screens. With lavish parking space, the multiplex is the leisure equivalent of the out-of-town superstore. Surrounded by bars, restaurants, night clubs, bowling alleys and shops, it offers people things to do as well as to watch. Their secret is not merely to divide a large cinema into a series of smaller screens showing different films (which dates back to the 1970s) but to stagger starting times, creating opportunities for all age groups to patronise the adjoining bars and restaurants.

TABLE 23.1

The Big Six Cinema Operators in the United Kingdom in 1997

Owner	Number of Cinemas	Of Which Multiplexes*	Total Number of Screens	Total Number of Seats	Share of Box Admissions (Per Cent)
Odeon Cinemas (Rank PLC)	80	19	410	108,817	20.0
UCI†	28	26	253	‡59,078	18.0
Virgin Cinemas§	28	23	208	50,320	11.7
Warner Village‖	17	17	152	40,612	11.5
National Amusements¶	15	15	197	53,194	10.0
ABC Cinemas§	73	2	206	67,580	7.5

Source: Dodona Research.

* A multiplex is defined as any site with five or more screens built since 1984.
† UCI is owned 50:50 by Viacom/Paramount and Universal/MCA, itself owned by Seagrams of Canada.
‡ Includes seats in the Irish Republic.
§ ABC is a management buy-out of ninety former MGM High Street cinemas from Virgin. Virgin bought one hundred and fourteen former MGM cinemas in July 1995 in conjunction with an American investment group, TPG, but sold ninety sites to ABC.
¶ Family cinema company of Sumner Redstone, the chairman of Viacom, trading as Showcase.
‖ The Warner screens in Britain are owned 50:50 by Time-Warner Inc. and Village Roadshow of Australia.

Since The Point was built at Milton Keynes in 1985, over one hundred multiplexes have opened around the country. They account for two in every five cinema screens in Britain, and Virgin Cinema is promising to build the first twenty-screen 'megaplex' at Sheffield.[8] Time Warner and United News & Media are scouring the country for a suitable site (and a sympathetic planning authority) to erect a vast production studio with a Movie World theme park attached.[9] Multiplexes have even reversed the triumphant progress of the video recorder: Blockbuster, the biggest chain of video shops in Britain, has had to reduce its network.[10]

Another reason people have returned to the cinema is that the films are more watchable. By the 1970s, film producers had destroyed the middle market on which they had thrived in the thirties and forties, and were presenting cinema-goers with a choice between sex-'n-'violence-'n-'swearing and Disney animation. With nothing in between, few people over thirty bothered to go. The reinvention of the broad middle market by film-makers such as Steven Spielberg and George Lucas, backed by massive advertising and milked through sales of promotional merchandise, has brought people of all ages flocking back to the cinema. Their success has prompted the usual grumblings by British film-makers about lack of public support, but the main victim of the Hollywood studios is not the British film industry. It is the independent cinema in the centre of town. The multiplexes, more or less controlled by the big American studios, are having the same effect on independent cinemas as supermarkets had on the High Street.

Pubs

Independent pubs are also disappearing. The free house, though often used as a cynical marketing exercise by major brewing companies, did mean that some pubs were free to buy whatever goods they liked from whoever they chose. Today, although there are over 600 independent brewers, eight out of every ten pints drunk in British pubs are brewed by one of four large companies: Bass, Carlsberg-Tetley, Scottish & Newcastle and Whitbread. The national brewers own only one in five pubs. Most are either managed on behalf of a regional brewer or specialist pub retailer, or are independent. But in the most successful pubs, irrespective of ownership, the brand managers and marketing men are at work. A combination of heavy discounts and massive national advertising budgets is homogenising the taste of beer as well as the names and look of pubs.

The major breweries tried to homogenise tastes as long ago as the 1950s, when the invention of long-life pasteurised or 'keg' beers meant they could sell the same product across the land, backed by television advertising. At one stage in the 1960s, Watneys painted its pubs red, filled their cellars with a pasteurised fizz named Red Barrel, and launched a campaign inviting drinkers to join 'the Red Revolution'. The attempt to force beer-drinkers to imbibe Red Barrel and Double Diamond provoked a massive consumer backlash, led by the Campaign for Real Ale (CAMRA). With over 50,000 members, and a greater range of real ales on sale in the pubs than ever before, CAMRA could reasonably claim to have achieved almost total success. Yet it is right to warn, as it regularly does, that the battle for real pubs and real ale is never won.

The major brewers would not attempt anything as crass as the 'Red Revolution' today. Instead, they have blurred the distinction between real cask-conditioned ale and the new breed of pasteurised beers, with their flavour-destroying chill and gimmicky, gas-induced cloudiness. The strength of nationally advertised brands – and especially the advertising of lagers whose flavours are hard to distinguish – makes it difficult for smaller brewers of flavoursome real ales to compete. Even the most independent publican wants his customers to have heard of the beers he sells, and he is tempted by the hefty discounts offered by major brewers. This is why the national brands owned by Bass (Carling Black Label, Caffrey's, Worthington), Carlsberg-Tetley (Carlsberg, Tetley), Whitbread (Boddington, Heineken, Stella Artois, Murphy's) and Allied Domecq (Tetley, Skol and Castlemaine XXXX) dominate British beer consumption today.

National brands are squeezing out the regional brands of the past and the breweries which owned them. A string of well-known regional brewers (Eldridge Pope, Gibbs Mew, Morrells, Ruddles, Vaux) have stopped brewing beer. The triumph of national 'brands' is equally evident in the changes to the names of pubs and their corporate owners. It is possible to be overly fastidious about names (an apparently venerable name like Pig and Whistle may as easily be the whim of a medieval sign painter as a corruption of the Saxon piggin and wassail) but the traditional pub sign is a rich repository of political and social history.* Local noblemen and heroes, battles and sports, are often commemorated in the traditional pub sign. It also incorporates the name of the brewer, recalling a time when every town had its brewery.

Today, pubs trade under whimsical names dreamt up in the marketing departments of the major chains: Fatty Arbuckle, Hedgehog and Hogshead, Harvey Floorbangers, Slug and Lettuce, Tom Cobleigh. At Bass, market data is fed into computers, which choose the ideal location for the made-up brands aimed at particular segments of the population: Harvester (families), All Bar One (yuppies), It's a Scream (students), O'Neill's Irish bars (live music fans).[11] Morland, a relatively small brewer in the Thames Valley, has retitled

---

* A piggin is an earthen vessel, while wassail is the liquor drunk at festive occasions, perhaps from an earthen wassail-bowl.

pubs as IceObar, Newt and Cucumber, Wig & Pen and Exchange Diner. Nicholas Winterton, the Conservative MP for Macclesfield, was so enraged by the disappearance of traditional pub names that he introduced a private member's bill to make changes subject to planning permission. But his cause is hopeless. 'Pubs are just like other High Street retailers,' says the founder of one new chain. 'One needs to focus on one format and roll it out. We want to be the Marks & Spencer of pub retailing.'[12] His chain, J. D. Wetherspoon, is named after a primary school teacher he knew in New Zealand.

Pub retailers like J. D. Wetherspoon, which sell beer rather than brew it, are the creation of a massive, government-induced change in the ownership of pubs in the 1990s. Twenty-five years ago, after a string of mergers, six companies owned two thirds of beer production and three quarters of pubs: Allied Lyons, Bass, Courage, Grand Metropolitan, Scottish & Newcastle and Whitbreads. They were staggeringly inefficient. In 1977 a Price Commission investigation found that they not only charged more money for inferior beer, but made less money from it than independent breweries. But because they owned most of the pubs and the breweries, giving them a guaranteed market, they had no incentive to improve.

The investigation brought the Big Six to the attention of the MMC, who eventually condemned the structure and ownership of the British beer market in unequivocal terms:

> We believe that [a] complex monopoly has enabled brewers with tied estates to frustrate the growth of brewers without tied estates; to do the same to independent wholesalers and manufacturers of cider and soft drinks; to keep tenants in a poor bargaining position; and to stop a strong independent sector emerging to challenge them at the retail level . . . the monopoly has served to keep the biggest brewers big and the small brewers small.[13]

The MMC recommended that the Big Six be required to dispose of two thirds of their estates, or about twenty two thousand pubs. Lord Young, trade and industry secretary, announced that he was 'minded' to implement the report. But he reckoned without the enormous pressure that the Beerage (a powerful force within the Conservative Party) was able to bring to bear on backbench MPs. He was told by the whips that the proposals would not get through either House of Parliament.[14]

After a great deal of acrimony, the result was a compromise. The Landlord and Tenant (Licensed Premises) Act and the subsequent Tied Estate and Loan Ties Orders of 1989 ordered the Big Six to 'untie' half of their pubs by 1 November 1992. The intention was to increase competition and choice

TABLE 23.2
The Biggest Pub Owners, 1998

Owners	Examples of Brands	Outlets
Grand Pub Company*	–	4,200
Whitbread	Beer Engine, Dragon Inns, O'Hagan's, Tut n' Shrive, Wayside Inns	4,000
Allied Domecq	Ansells, Carpe Diem, Firkin, Mr Q's, Pig & Truffle, Scruffy Murphy	3,600
Scottish & Newcastle	Finnegan's Wake, Rat & Parrot, T & J Bernard, Whole Hog	2,624
Bass	All Bar One, Fork & Pitcher, Goose & Granite, It's a Scream, O'Neills	2,500
Punch Taverns	–	2,273
Greenalls Group†	Ale & Hearty, Boddington's, Devenish, Finn M' Couls, Quincey's	2,200
Enterprise Inns	–	1,500
Pubmaster	Celebration Ale Houses, Local Pub Company, Stout Fiddler	1,500
Greene King	Ale Café, Countryside Inn, Hungry Horse, King's Fayre, Pickled Newt	1,110
Wolverhampton & Dudley	Banks's, Hanson, Lazt Word, Poacher's Pocket, Tap House, Varsity	990
Marstons	Pitcher & Piano, Tavern Table, Thirsty Scholar, Via Vita	875
Vaux Group	Bar Zanta, Bramwell & Co, Starvin' Sam's, Ward's	848
Ushers of Trowbridge	Hannah's Kitchen, Micawber's, Wishing Well Pub Company	558
Century Inns	Dr Brown's, Royal Freehouses, Tap & Spile, Vintage Pub Co	500
Mansfield Brewery	Lloyd's No 1, Lock, Stock & Barrel, Trading Post, Xtra	500
Burtonwood	Forshaw Alehouses, Top Hat Taverns	493
Inn Business	Hooden Horse, Marr Taverns, Sycamore Taverns, United Breweries	473
Avebury Taverns	–	471
Morland	Artists' Fare, Bar Beristo, Ice O Bar, Newt & Cucumber, Wig & Pen	424
Chains of 100–410 Pubs	–	6,284
Chains of 20–100 Pubs	–	3,073
Chains of up to 20 Pubs	–	755
Independents	–	22,991
Total	–	64,742

Source: ACNielsen.

* The Grand Pub Company was formed by Nomura, the Japanese bank, after it acquired pubs owned by Inntrepreneur (see text).

† In December 1998 Greenalls sold 1,241 tenanted and franchised pubs to Nomura.

for consumers by splitting retailing from brewing, and to give smaller brewers access to the major national chains as 'guest ales'. In theory, consumers would benefit from greater choice and lower prices; tenants would benefit from greater independence; and smaller brewers would gain access to major chains of pubs. According to the plan, the only losers would be the Big Six brewery companies. Unfortunately, reality ignored the plan.

Far from falling, the price of beer began to rise, because the Big Six decided to offset the loss of guaranteed sales by raising their prices to publicans.[15] Choice did not increase much either; the major brewers retained their grip on the pubs they sold, offering landlords cheap loans and long-term supply agreements at attractive discounts. Brewing (as opposed to retailing) became concentrated in fewer hands. Without guaranteed markets for real ales, the major brewers have dropped regional beers and closed local breweries to concentrate on a handful of national brands. The share of the market supplied by regional brewers has fallen from 22 per cent in 1990 to 15 per cent. The six hundred-odd independent brewers account for about 1.5 pints in every hundred drunk.

Tenants did not gain either. Two of the big brewers abandoned tenanted pubs for the managed theme-pubs which produce the highest revenues. Cross-subsidisation of less successful pubs was withdrawn. Publicans were put on longer leases at higher rents, and charged penalties if they did not reach agreed purchasing targets. In 1990 Grand Metropolitan and Courage put their pubs into a joint venture company, Inntrepreneur. To avoid selling pubs at low prices, they complied with the letter rather than the spirit of the law, intending to sell at a more attractive price later. But Inntrepreneur borrowed a great deal, and was forced to press its tenants to pay higher rents to meet interest payments.

A National Association of Inntrepreneur Licensees was formed. Its members were angry enough to picket the Grand Metropolitan annual general meeting in 1993 in protest at excessive rent demands. Inquiries – by the Department of Trade and Industry, the Agriculture Select Committee, the European Commission and the Office of Fair Trading – followed, but nothing changed. Angry tenants stopped paying rent or refused to buy from their landlord, so Inntrepreneur evicted the recalcitrant. The company was sold in September 1997 to a Japanese bank, Nomura.[16] After a brief spell as the largest pub landlord in the country, Nomura has sold many of the 4,309 pubs it inherited, most of them to the new breed of independent retailers.

The forced sale of 13,000 pubs by the Big Six created a string of them, of which the biggest is Enterprise Inns and the best-known is J. D. Wetherspoon. Surprisingly, the independent retailers have not widened the choice of beer much, proving as eager as any pub manager to profit from the discounted prices of the major brewers. They are not obliged to carry a 'guest ale' either, but they have transformed their average pub into a consumer-friendly enterprise. The floor and the air are cleaner; the decor more appealing; the choice of food and drinks wider and better; the cellar is managed properly; and the lavatories are usable by people not wearing wellington boots. Children are made welcome, and there are quiz nights and giant television screens to keep people coming. The competition has forced the major brewers into similar improvements.

Change is necessary: beer-drinking is in long-term decline. In early Victorian England, before the Temperance movement got going, one third to one half of a working-class budget might be spent on drink, and this continued right down to 1914.[17] Hard labour of the kind which demands quantity from refreshment is no longer common, and anti-drink driving measures have made a visit to the pub less agreeable than it was, but the main cause of the decline in beer consumption is the rising cost. Consumption has never recovered from the higher taxation, weaker beer and shorter pub opening hours introduced during the First World War. 'We are fighting Germany, Austria and Drink,' said Lloyd George, 'and, as far as I can see, the greatest of these deadly foes is drink.'[18] The consumption of alcohol continued to fall during the inter-war years, and has not revived. The range of alternatives has widened: the beer, darts and dominoes of the traditional pub have now to compete with the pizza parlour and the television. The modern consumer wants to meet girls, eat pasta, heckle the quiz-master, surf the Internet, and drink 'designer lagers' straight from the bottle.

Pub retailers know this. A visit to the pub, says the chief executive of Whitbread, is a 'leisure occasion' which must compete with other 'leisure occasions'. The ambience and decor of a pub is now geared to whoever is present in numbers: businessmen, students, unaccompanied women. Even the humble pub-crawler has found respectability among the marketing men; he is now known as a 'circuit drinker'. Whitbread has attached Charlie Chalk Fun Factories to its Brewer's Fayre family outlets, allowing children to play dodgems and computer games while their parents sample the delights of the carvery. Allied Domecq has built Wacky Warehouse 'play barns' next to over a hundred of its Big Steak House pubs. Scottish & Newcastle has invented the Funky Forest play area.

At the pub, change seems incessant. It is an article of faith at corporate headquarters that a pub cannot survive unless it is gutted and refurbished every five to six years, though it may cost £1.5 million to do it. In 1997, the beer industry spent well over £1 billion doing up pubs in good locations, without arresting their remorseless decline: fifteen thousand have disappeared since the 1950s, and another five thousand will go by the end of the century. The average walk to the pub will rise from five to thirteen minutes.

But the decline of manual labour, and the invention of the breathalyser test, are not entirely to blame. The number of off-licences has nearly doubled in the last forty years (to over fifty thousand) and the amount of beer drunk at home has increased tenfold. A visit to the pub remains the commonest activity outside the home, but is now running neck-and-neck with a meal in a restaurant.[19] This, rather than the television set or the off-licence, is the true successor to the pub.

Restaurants

The restaurant industry estimates that around thirty million people now eat out regularly. There is no better measure of prosperity. Throughout most of history, people have struggled to avoid starvation. Rickets, dental caries and anaemia, all of them caused by malnutrition, were commonplace in Britain as recently as the 1930s. Today, two in five people visit fast-food restaurants as a matter of routine.[20] Restaurants are big business, turning over £5 billion a year and employing a quarter of a million people. Yet they did not really exist before 1850. There were inns, hotels, chop-houses and pie-shops, but people ate at them out of necessity rather than choice. The culinary skill of the average inn-keeper was not high; the food they served was not pleasant.

Until this century, eating well was the preserve of the rich, and eating *out* well that of the extremely rich. In Georgian times, wealthy men relied on the coffee house; in Victorian times, they switched to gentlemen's clubs. Though few would now associate the clubs of Mayfair and Pall Mall with good food, in their heyday they served the finest to the wealthiest people in the richest capital city in the world. The legendary French chef Alexis Soyer was appointed at the Reform Club in 1839, and set such standards of culinary achievement that his advice was sought by the creator of one of the first great restaurants to be opened in London: Simpsons-in-the-Strand. But Simpsons served only mutton and beef until it came under the control of the Savoy Hotel in 1904.

During the late Victorian and Edwardian period menus responded to the first 'stars' of stage and screen, who patronised the new restaurants of Soho during these years. Thevenon opened the Café Royal in Regent Street in the 1860s, Joseph Lyons rebuilt the Trocadero as a restaurant in 1895, and Escoffier fed royalty at the Carlton Hotel in the Haymarket from 1899. The percolation through other classes of the habit of eating out was obstructed by rationing during the Great War, but the quest for enjoyment in its aftermath popularised it. 'Road-houses' appeared in the suburbs and on the by-passes, allowing courting couples the chance to dine, dance and fornicate without fear of the licensing laws or the prevailing moral climate.

J. Lyons and the Aerated Bread Company (ABC), whose cafés offered substantial meals at low prices, gave the working classes their first taste of commercial cookery beyond the fish and chip shop. The London Corner Houses furnished them with 'brunch' in a cake box for 2s 6d, and the chance to sample occasional exotica. The first American-style cafeterias, which dispensed with waiters and waitresses, appeared in Woolworths' stores. The success of milk bars, with their high stools, chromium interiors and milk shakes, was assured by officially sanctioned advertising ('Drink More Milk') McDonald's would kill for. The greatest catering fortune assembled in Britain had its origins in a milk bar Charles Forte opened in Upper Regent Street in 1935.

Progress towards a modern restaurant industry was brought to an abrupt halt by the Second World War. For fourteen years, from 1939 to 1953, food was rationed. But over the next forty years, a people supposedly notorious for the conservatism of their diet embraced the spring rolls and chicken chow mein of the proliferating Chinese restaurants and takeaways, and the biryanis and vindaloos of their Indian competitors. Holidays abroad fuelled the taste for foreign dishes. (In 1961 a party of Welsh miners visiting Spain took their own chef with them. They sent him home when they found they preferred Spanish food.)[21]

Trattorias, pizza parlours, tandoori restaurants, burger bars, cafés and *haute cuisine* restaurants are now thriving everywhere. Twenty years ago, 3p in every £1 of household income went into eating outside the home; now, the figure is over 10p. The main beneficiaries of this surge of spending are the new commercial restaurateurs, many controlled by giant PLCs. The best known is McDonald's, a fast-food chain whose chief *raison d'être* is ensure that its products look and taste exactly the same anywhere in the world. McDonald's opened its first restaurant in Britain at Woolwich in October 1974; the High Street now being saturated, its restaurants are sprouting at railway stations, airports, museums and hospitals.[22]

Burger King, its only serious rival in Britain, claims that people prefer the taste of the flame-grilled Whopper to the pan-fried Big Mac, and that its new, improved French fries will overtake the McDonald's chip as well. Cannibalising sales of rival firms may now be the only source of growth in the fast-food market. McDonald's has not introduced a successful new product since Chicken McNuggets in 1983, and its relentless expansion may be faltering. New forms of fast food are becoming popular. Pizza Express, the oldest pizza chain in Britain, opened its first restaurant in 1965. But almost all of its restaurants in Britain were opened in the last ten years.

Not all commercial restaurant chains sell junk food. Terence Conran pioneered the upmarket mega-restaurant, Mezzo, which opened in Soho in September 1995. It is capable of seating seven hundred and fifty diners. Robert
Earl, a graduate of the hotel management and catering course at the University of Surrey, made his name with a mock medieval banqueting hall for
tourists visiting the Tower of London. He also created a restaurant chain
which he sold for £63 million weeks before the stock-market crash of October
1987. Earl then went to America, where he turned the Hard Rock Café into
a global brand name, its best-known feature (rock memorabilia on the walls)
providing him with the prototype for a brief craze in catering: the 'themed'
restaurant – food, shopping and entertainment rolled into one.

At Planet Hollywood, which opened in London in May 1993, diners are
surrounded by branded merchandise and film clips from classic Hollywood
pictures. Its success spawned imitators, but themed restaurants have struggled
to retain their fragile grip on the public imagination. The Fashion Café in
Leicester Square failed in October 1998, and other themed restaurants have
degenerated into tourist traps. But they still symbolise a shift in popular
attitudes towards eating out. It is no longer a luxury reserved for celebrations:
it is a 'leisure occasion', which competes with a host of alternative claims on
the time of consumers.

Fittingly, the one company to have survived all these changes is now betting
its future on 'leisure occasions'. Whitbread, founded in 1742, has in recent
years bought or opened 'leisure facilities' almost as fast as it has closed and
sold breweries and pubs. It has bought the TGI Friday's franchise, the Costa
Coffee shop chain, the David Lloyd tennis centres, the Pelican restaurant
group (which incorporated the Café Rouge and Dome chains), the BrightReasons restaurants group (which brought with it the Pizzaland and Bella Pasta
chains) and tried to buy dozens of Little Chef and Happy Eater restaurants
and Travelodge hotels from Forte. Its new Brewers Fayre pubs, with their
Charlie's Chalk Factories attached, are, says the chief executive, 'more like
Disneyworld than a boozer'[23] – an apt slogan to enter the second century of
popular leisure.

Hotels

The modern hotel is more like *Brave New World* than Disneyland: the same
marble and foliage foyers, stale air and L-shaped rooms. They are designed
for the rootless life of that great contemporary nomad, the international
businessman. It took the genius of a Texan, Conrad N. Hilton, to grasp that
the thing commercial travellers like least of all is a surprise. One of many

TABLE 23.3
Major Restaurant Chains in 1998

Owner	Examples of Brands	Number of Outlets	Turnover in 1997–8 (£m)
Granada PLC	Granada, Little Chef	439	1,611.0
McDonald's Corporation	McDonald's	731	1,088.5
Whitbread PLC	Café Rouge, TGI Friday, Dome, Costa Coffee, Pizza Hut†	870	616.0
Tricon*	KFC (430 outlets), Pizza Hut (439 outlets)†	869	§514.4
Investcorp Group	Welcome Break	22	409.0
Diageo PLC	Burger King	530	‡330.0
City Centre Restaurants PLC	Garfunkel's, Caffe Uno, Nachos, Metro, Wok Wok	292	165.9
Pizza Express	Pizza Express, Café Pasta, Pasta di Milano	220	71.0
Pret A Manger (Europe) Limited	Pret A Manger	72	70.0
Group Chez Gerard PLC	Chez Gerard, Bertorelli's, Café Fish, Livebait, Richoux	21	27.4
Capital Radio (My Kinda Town)	Chicago Rib Shack, Henry J. Bean's, Pizza Pie Factory	54	23.2
Wimpy's International Limited	Wimpy	285	19.8
Aberdeen Steak Houses	American Burger, Angus & Highland Steak Houses	40	18.0
Baldwin PLC	Simpsons of Cornhill, My Old Dutch	18	14.0
Pizza Piazza Limited	Pizza Piazza, Firehouse	22	10.2
Nando's Chickenland Limited	Nando's Chickenland	15	10.0
Harry Ramsden's PLC	Harry Ramsden's, Henry Higgins	27	6.8
Belgo	Belgo, Daphne's, Pasha, Ivy, Le Caprice, J Sheekey	7	3.5

Source: Companies; Company Annual Reports and Accounts.

* Tricon is the former restaurants division of Pepsico, demerged in 1997.
† Pizza Hut is a joint venture between Tricon and Whitbread, which is franchisor for the chain.
‡ Author's estimate.
§ £272.0 million for KFC and £242.4 million for Pizza Hut.

myths perpetrated by modern hoteliers is that businessmen are their most demanding clients. In fact, their demands – for fax machines and laptop sockets, taxis to the airport, hairdryers, swimming pools, secretaries and mass-ages – are a plea for sameness, not variety. Conrad Hilton understood this. He made it his life's work to ensure that every city in the United States had at least one hotel which was the same as the one its guests had stayed in the night or the week or the month before.

It was a philosophy whose success impressed others. When Kemmons Wilson opened his first Holiday Inn in Tennessee, in 1952, it was his declared ambition to build a chain of hotels which varied minimally in appearance and levels of service. Inter-Continental Hotels, founded by Pan-Am, used the same architecture and décor the world over. At Marriott, a chain founded by Mormons, chambermaids are issued with a sixty-six-step guide to cleaning a room. In the United States, two hotel bedrooms in three are now provided by chains such as Marriott, Hilton, Holiday Inn and Sheraton. The proportion is not yet as high in Britain, but the average British hotel is more homogenous than it was.

The chief architect of homogeneity was Charles Forte, a Scottish–Italian entrepreneur who mastered the art of uniform presentation in mass catering long before he bought his first hotel (the Waldorf in the Aldwych) in 1958. Ten years later he merged his relatively modest collection of hotels with the two hundred-strong Trust House chain, a Quaker hotel group well-known (and much-patronised) for its refusal to make a profit on the sale of alcohol. The functional interiors of Forte hotels, and the celebrated 'portion control' of their dining rooms, became a favourite target for snobs. This was unfair. The assets of the Forte Group ranged from the Grosvenor House in London to the George V in Paris, the Ritz in Madrid and the Plaza Athenée in New York. Forte battled for years without success to add the Savoy to his collection of prestigious hotels. Asked why it meant so much to him, he replied: 'Mention the Savoy anywhere, the name alone, the Savoy.'

The mistake he made was to love hotels not brands. His collection became too extensive and confusing for consumers or investors to appreciate. Profits fell, and investors lost confidence. In January 1996, Forte was taken over by the Granada Group, a company better known for motorway stopovers and *Coronation Street*. Its chief executive, an energetic Irishman named Gerry Robinson, knew little of hotels but a great deal about the value of brands. He kept the Little Chefs and the Posthouses, and sold the upmarket hotels and the stake in the Savoy. When he sold the luxury Meridien hotels, he was careful to retain ownership of the brand name. He had grasped the essence of modern hotel-keeping: when one hotel seems much like another, owning brands is more valuable than owning buildings.

The largest hotel chains do not always, or even mainly, own their hotels. They have grown by managing hotels owned by others, or through franchising their brand name. Both methods use strong brands which tourists and businessmen recognise instantly. Once it is established in their minds, it can be exploited ruthlessly by offering discounts to regular guests and strategic alliances with other chains to plug geographical and product gaps. Tie-ups with airlines ensure passengers are bussed to affiliated hotels, and allow the ubiquitous air miles to be offset against hotel bills. Branding puts smaller, more individualistic, hotels under pressure. Only the biggest chains can afford the airline-style reservation systems which ensure that they do not take on business at any price when the computer predicts the rooms will fill at the full price. To survive, smaller hotels are being driven into marketing consortia – Relais & Chateaux and Best Western – or into alliances which allow them to pool technology costs.

TABLE 23.4
The Ten Largest Hotel Groups in Britain in 1997

Owner	Brands	Number	Rooms
Granada PLC	Granada Lodge, Meridien, Posthouse	284	24,937
Thistle HotelsPLC	Thistle	96	13,595
Whitbread PLC	Travel Inn, Marriott, Country Club	199	12,106
Ladbroke PLC	Hilton	41	8,589
Stakis PLC	Stakis, Country Court, Metropole	55	8,400
Queen's Moat Houses PLC	Moat House	51	7,035
Bass PLC	Holiday Inn, Crowne Plaza, Inter Continental*	45	6,363
Jarvis Hotels PLC	Jarvis	66	5,457
Regal Hotels PLC	Regal, White Hart	100	5,404
Choice Hotels Europe		61	5,000
Accor (France)	Novotel, Ibis	31	4,658

Source: The Hospitality Year Book 1998 and Pannell Kerr Forster Research.

* Bass did not acquire Inter Continental Hotels until February 1998, when it paid the Japanese retail group, Saison, $2.9 billion for the chain.

The modern international hotel, like any modern international business, is all management and marketing and machines. Its denizens talk glibly of their business as 'hospitality', oblivious that the impersonality of modern hotels makes a mockery of the term. A century ago César Ritz and Auguste Escoffier made the Savoy famous by catering for the whims of their distinguished guests. As recently as the 1980s, Hugh Wontner, chairman of the Savoy Group, saw no shame in living in one of his own hotels. He thought it the only way to maintain the standards his guests expected. John Jarvis, a former chairman of Hilton International, is more representative of the modern breed of manager. 'There are only three things in this business that really matter,' he says. 'Sales, marketing and distribution.'

The domination of the branded chain is, like the epidemic of McDonald's restaurants, a symptom of the democratisation of leisure. Middle England, as well as the rich and fashionable, can now stay at hotels. The fastest growing segment of the British market is the branded budget hotel, filled mainly with dirty weekenders on cut-price breaks distributed by middlebrow newspapers. They are likely eventually to overwhelm the private and family businesses which still account for more than three out of five hotel bedrooms in Britain, though a counter-culture of upmarket or eccentric country and town-house hotels is already evident. One of the more predictable side-effects of the democratisation of leisure is to spark a renewed search for exclusiveness.

Gambling

Gamblers have no such pretensions. Despite a long association with up-market hotels, gambling is the most democratic of leisure pursuits. Gentlemen's clubs, like Boodle's and White's, were founded as little more than upper-class gaming dens where fortunes changed hands at roulette or baccarat.[24] The working classes of the eighteenth century bet just as enthusiastically on the outcome of cock and dog fights and bull- and bear-baiting. Aristocrats patronised prize-fighting and cricket, both of which were also popular with the working classes, partly because they could bet on the outcome. The sport of kings, still the chief vehicle for popular gambling, has long depended on a mixture of aristocratic patrons and proletarian punters. It acquired a strong working-class following as soon as the spread of newspapers and the telegraph allowed people to bet without going to the course. By the 1880s, *The Sporting Life* was selling 150,000 copies.[25]

Victorian governments were so alarmed by the spread of betting that they tried to stamp it out. Betting on credit, or in cash at the racecourse, was never outlawed, though it was strongly discouraged. But efforts were made to ban the betting shops of the industrial towns. Laws were passed in 1853 and 1874, but had little effect. The bookies lived on, masquerading as tobacconists or chop-houses, or as 'virtual' betting shops at factories, pubs and homes. The main effect of the ban was to pass the trade into the hands of organised crime, exposing children to the pleasures of gambling.

The government eventually undermined its own high-minded position. It taxed bets on races from 1928, greyhound racing from 1934, the football pools from 1947, and off-course betting from 1963. In 1956 premium bonds were introduced, the first state-sanctioned lottery since 1824.[26] The Horserace Betting Levy Board (the Tote) was set up in 1928 at the request of the Jockey Club to ensure some of the money from betting was channelled into the development of the sport. It created a state-owned betting monopoly which continues even now to pass 1 per cent of the value of wagers back into racing.[27] By the time the first licensed betting offices opened in May 1961, under the more liberal régime sanctioned by the Betting and Gaming Act of 1960, the law against them had long lost its moral authority.

Echoes of a prim Victorianism remained. Under the 1960 legislation, licensed betting shops were sombre and dreary. Each was to contain only the counter, books, slips and a list of starting prices. Seats, stools, television and radio were banned, in an effort to prevent gamblers loitering on the premises. But the growth of betting shops could not be contained. They had an immediate impact on floodlit greyhound racing, imported from America, mainly as a more convenient way to bet than a day at the races. It flourished from the 1930s to the 1950s, but has never recovered from the legalisation of betting shops. Going to the dogs has declined sharply as a popular pastime, though the volume of betting has not. Most greyhound tracks are owned by bookies, who televise the races in their shops.

Commercialisation and consolidation were bound to follow the liberalisation of betting. When the legislation came into effect in 1962, the big four branded bookmakers of today owned less than a quarter of one per cent of all betting shops. By 1977, they owned one in four.[28] Today, the major chains control well over half the market, and they are still buying. Consolidation threatened to turn into near-monopoly in 1998 when Bass sold the third-largest chain of bookmakers (Coral) to the largest (Ladbroke). But the deal, which would have given Ladbroke's a one third share of the market, proved a step too far. The government, on the advice of the Monopolies and Mergers Commission (MMC), instructed Ladbroke's to sell Coral.

The bookies and their unofficial predecessors were never the only competitors for the gamblers' pound. The development of the football leagues provided the occasion for a different kind of betting: the pools. Long before the pools were commercialised, tip-sheets offered prizes for correct predictions of matches, and self-appointed bookmakers distributed coupons at matches. John Moores, a former telegraphist in Manchester, spotted the potential for growth, and set up the Littlewoods empire in a small office in Liverpool in 1922, with just £150 in capital. But if a pools business needs little capital, it has a huge appetite for labour. By 1938 an estimated ten million people

TABLE 23.5
The Ownership of Betting Shops

Brands	Owner	Number of Outlets
Ladbroke	Ladbroke	1,906
Nomura	William Hill	1,510
Coral	Morgan Grenfell Private Equity	833
Stanley Leisure	Stanley Racing, Gus Carter	564
Horserace Betting Levy Board	The Tote	213
Others	–	3,474
Total		8,500

were staking £40 million on the football pools, obliging Littlewoods and its Merseyside rival, Vernons, to build veritable factories to accommodate the hundreds of staff needed to check the coupons.

In twenty years, British football pools became the biggest privately owned gambling businesses in the world, and turned the Moores into one of the richest families in Britain. As the sums at stake on matches increased, the 'nobbling' which had plagued the early years of racing and greyhound racing threatened to spread to football. The Football Association was convinced that matches would be rigged, and tried to deny the pools companies advance notice of fixtures, making it hard for them to prepare and print coupons. The game was embarrassed by match-fixing at Sheffield Wednesday in the early 1960s, and again in the mid-1990s by unproven allegations of collusion between footballers and a Malaysian gambling syndicate.[29] But the game has proved much stronger than the gambling industry which feeds off it.

Football waxed in the 1990s, but the pools waned. The introduction of the National Lottery in November 1994 reduced enormously the sums of money staked on football results, from nearly £1 billion in 1993–4 to £319 million in 1997–8.[30] Racing, greyhound racing, fruit machines – all have suffered from the lottery. The Big Three bookies counter-attacked by launching 49s, a lottery-like betting game which earned them an (unsuccessful) law suit from Camelot as unauthorised competition. But if the National Lottery confirmed that gamblers are more interested in the wager than the nature of the risk, it had a positive effect for the private gambling industry: making a nonsense of the regulatory restrictions on gambling. Sixteen-year-olds were able to buy state-sanctioned scratch cards with top prizes of £75,000, but were not allowed to play fruit machines with a maximum prize of £15 until they turned eighteen.

Both the Conservative government and its New Labour successor, alarmed

TABLE 23.6
The Major Pools Companies

Owner	Brand Name	Stakes Received in 1997–98 (£m)	Market Share
Littlewoods	Littlewoods	257.3	81 per cent
Ladbroke PLC	Vernons	49.6	15 per cent
Zetters	Zetters	12.4	4 per cent
Total*	–	319.3	100 per cent

Source: The Pool Promoters Association.

* There are other pools promoters, including Brittens, but their activities are minuscule by comparison with the big three. Manchester United also runs its own football pools competition.

as much by a fall in revenue from gambling duties as the plight of pools companies and bookies, have liberalised the law.[31] Pools players were freed to collect their winnings from the shops distributing coupons. Bookies were allowed to install larger televisions, advertise in their shop windows, sell refreshments, put in fruit machines, take bets on Sundays, and advertise in newspapers. The casino industry was also deregulated, though not as far or as fast as casino operators would have liked. The time that must elapse between a member joining a casino and starting to play was halved to twenty-four hours; casino liquor licences were extended to 3.00 a.m. in London and 2.00 a.m. else-where; payment by debit card as well as cash and cheque was authorised; the permissible number of jackpot machines was increased (from six to ten) and the ceiling on the sum they can pay out was also doubled (to £1,000).

At the time of the General Election, the Conservative government was preparing a number of other de-regulatory measures, and the New Labour government has taken most of them up. Casinos are likely to be allowed to advertise their name and address and the nature of the games they offer, but only in the classified section of newspapers. Postal membership applications, and automatic membership of other casinos owned by the same company, will also be permitted. A Conservative plan to allow another twenty-one areas of the country to license a casino has run into local political opposition, but the government is expected to endorse a proposal to allow casinos to replace their fruit machines with high-stake, high-prize slot machines.

Casinos are a surprisingly big business. In 1997–98, the total amount staked was £2.75 billion.[32] Two thirds of this enormous sum is dropped in the twenty-three London casinos, most of it by the high rollers (many of them foreign) who never stake less than £1,000. The average visitor to a provincial casino

TABLE 23.7
The Major Casino Operators

Owner	Casinos	Number
Rank	Grosvenor Victoria, Grosvenor Casinos, The Claremont	30
Stakis	Regency, Chevalier, St Ann's Leisure, Stakis	20
Stanley Leisure*	Stanley	24
London Clubs International	50 St James's, Les Ambassadeurs, The Palm Beach, Rendezvous, The Sportsman, London Park Tower, Golden Nugget	7
Capital Corporation*	Crockfords, Colony Club, Cromwell Mint	3
Ladbroke	Maxim's, Barracuda, Charlie Chester, Golden Horseshoe, Ladbroke Sporting Casino	5
A & S Leisure	Napoleons	5
Apinalls Club Ltd	Aspinalls	1
Ritz Hotel Casino Limited	Ritz Casino (Aidan Barclay)	1
Others	–	20
Total		116

Source: The Gaming Board for Great Britain; British Casinos Association; Companies; *Financial Times.*

* Capital Corporation was acquired by Stanley Leisure in March 1999.

goes once a month, stays four hours, stakes about £100 and loses an average of £20. In the top London casinos, the average loss is £3,000 and a high roller might drop (or win) £1 million or more at a single sitting. Despite this reliance on the cosmopolitan rich, and occasional problems with fraudulent employees, the police and the Gaming Board inspectors, the major casinos have sold themselves successfully as orthodox businesses.

All of the biggest firms are quoted on the London Stock Exchange, converting the losses of the high rollers into dividend payments for pension funds. Inevitably, the owners of Crockfords (founded in 1828) describe the casino as an 'international brand-name.' Shareholders seem happy to accept this line of reasoning, and assess casinos like any other business. 'We are no longer considered an exotic and slightly suspect investment,' the chief executive of London Clubs International told the *Financial Times* in 1995. 'The investment community is only just beginning to recognise the cash generative advantages of our business.'

The same cannot be said of Bingo, where investors have become sceptical

about the ability of operators to generate cash. The number of Bingo clubs
has shrunk by one tenth since 1993.[33] Three major leisure companies have
sold their bingo halls to the management since 1997, and two of the new
enterprises have merged their operations. The one company to stay in the
business (Rank Group) has lost the confidence of its shareholders so completely that the chief executive was forced to resign in October 1998.[34] Yet it
seemed as if the game was enjoying a revival in the early 1990s. It originated
among the soldiers of the First World War, and its popularity exploded after
the legalisation of street betting in 1962, but it declined when the post-sixties
generation of wives and mothers shied away from its associations with lonely
grannies and run-down cinemas.

Efforts to rejuvenate the game by introducing 'new generation' Bingo in
purpose-built facilities with welcoming car parks have had some success, and
even drawn in younger people. The game has also benefited from the removal
of restrictions on advertising. But the main reason for its modest revival was
the improved possibility of gain. Though Bingo prizes vary according to how
many people turn up, players can usually win no more than a few hundred
pounds. But the regional games introduced in recent years yield five-figure
sums and the national games offer prizes capped at £100,000. Bingo operators
are pressing the government to lift the ceiling.

TABLE 23.8
The Major Bingo Clubs

Owner	Brand	Number of Clubs
Rank	Mecca	140
Management Buy In/Venture Capital*	Gala, Ritz	147
Management Buy Out/Venture Capital†	Riva	22

Source: Companies; *Financial Times.*

* Bass sold one hundred and twenty-seven Gala Clubs to a management buy-in team backed by
the venture capital arm of Prudential, which later merged them with the twenty Ritz Clubs sold
by Vardon to a company backed by the venture capital arm of Hambros Bank.
† First Leisure sold twenty-two Riva Clubs to a management buy-out team backed by NatWest
Ventures.

The main problem for Bingo clubs is the National Lottery, which has
undermined all forms of commercial gambling. Another source of competition is the adult slot machine. There are a quarter of a million 'gaming
machines' in Britain. Most cannot dispense a prize larger than £15, but since
1996 the government has allowed betting shops, pubs, clubs and other 'adult'
environments to install so-called 'jackpot' machines. These are entitled to

pay out up to £250. Inevitably, unscrupulous operators have installed them in what the Gaming Board calls 'inappropriate environments' such as motorway service stations. But the slot machine is still the staple of the most hellish environment of all: the amusement arcade.

Holidays

Like the rest of the tacky paraphernalia of a British seaside town, the amusement arcade is a creation of that mid-century interlude when people took holidays in Britain rather than abroad. During Wakes Weeks, northern factory towns decanted their populations into the cheap hotels and boarding houses of Blackpool and Morecambe or the Butlin's holiday camp at Skegness.[35] Aquariums, funfairs, summer pavilions and winter gardens, swimming pools and piers, were furnished by the earliest leisure entrepreneurs. They are all still there, and new attractions like Sea Life Centres, the elaborate successors to the aquariums of bygone days, are joining them. Vardon PLC (owners of the Dungeons in London and York) has built one in every seaside town from Blackpool to Hunstanton. The Butlins of today is the 'holiday village' pioneered by the Dutch company, Center Parcs. Rank, which bought Butlin's in 1972, has six of them, and recently opened the first £100 million mega-holiday village at Penrith.

Another remnant of the inter-war holiday, the trailer–caravan, has proved durable. The main impact of the huge expansion in private motoring in the years before the last war was on holidays. The Bank Holiday traffic jam had already become a familiar feature of British life by the end of the 1930s, as the motor car opened up the south and south-west coasts and North Wales to motor cars and caravans. The National Caravan Council, a pressure group made up of caravan manufacturers and traders, caravan park operators and local authorities, was formed in 1939. It reckons there are now five hundred and twenty thousand touring caravans and three hundred and thirty thousand caravan holiday homes on the road, four thousand two hundred and thirty-one caravan parks with six hundred thousand separate pitches to accommodate them, and ninety-six thousand caravans parked permanently by the seaside. The Caravan Club boasts a membership of over two hundred and eighty-five thousand people, and they and other caravan enthusiasts now make over seventeen million holiday journeys a year in Britain. More than sixty million 'holiday nights' are spent in caravans every year, making them the most popular form of holiday accommodation after friends and relations.[36] Activity on this scale has turned caravan parks into a business which now turns over £2 billion a year.[37]

The plague of caravanning has spread to continental Europe, where major park providers – such as Rank – have began to buy up pitches for caravan enthusiasts seeking more exotic sights and sounds than rain at Hastings or Skegness. But the hordes of caravanners fanning out across Europe from the Pas de Calais are dwarfed by those flying overhead. A generation ago it was not uncommon for people to pass their entire lives without flying in an aeroplane. If they travelled, it was by boat and train. In the year to March 1998, air tour operators carried 23.5 million people from Britain to holiday destinations abroad.[38] The speed (and relative cheapness) of air travel has brought the world within the reach of everyone. In his memoirs George Brown recalled the ingratitude of the steel men of Shotton when he visited the works during the 1970 general election. In his day, he told them, the works outing was a day at Blackpool, whereas they were going by aeroplane for a week in the Mediterranean. What more could they want? Lower prices, they said.[39]

In the 1960s and 1970s the high prices levied by scheduled airlines created a booming business in package holidays. Holidaymakers reared in the traditions of Billy Butlin and Fred Pontin adapted effortlessly to the horrors of the chartered airline, the bus to the concrete hotel, and the uniformed hostess to guide them through the perils of foreign food and languages. In 1951, the British took two million foreign holidays; twenty years later, that figure had doubled. By the mid-1990s British residents were venturing abroad on holiday over forty-two million times per year. This was twice as often as they had gone even ten years earlier.

Thomson, the biggest provider of package holidays, is part of the giant Canadian publishing and travel group. But an industry growing as fast as package holidays left plenty of room for British entrepreneurs to get rich. The *Sunday Times* reckons David Crossland, creator of Airtours, is worth £150 million. The De Haans, owners of the Saga holiday company for pensioners, are thought to be worth over £60 million. Jim Moffat, founder of the AT Mays travel agency, banked £60 million when he sold the chain to Carlson Travel Group of Minneapolis. Though competition for punters with little money to spare (expenditure abroad averages £374 a head) has led to some spectacular collapses in the package tour industry over the years, the price wars are mostly a sham. The discounts offered to early buyers are recouped in interest on the deposits, and even the bargain-basement prices offered to late buyers are covered by sales of over-priced insurance.

Far from becoming competitive, the package holiday industry is moving towards a monopolistic structure which has attracted the attention of the competition authorities on several occasions. The big tour operators control not only the travel agents which sell holidays but the charter airlines which fly

TABLE 23.9
Big Four Tour Operators

	Direct Sales	Travel Agencies	Airline(s)	Passenger Share	Foreign Package Share*
Thomson	Portland	Lunn Poly	Britannia	17%	24.6%
Airtours	Direct Holidays	Going Places	Airtours	13%	15.9%
First Choice	Eclipse	Building a Chain	Air 2000	12%	10.1%
Thomas Cook	–	Thomas Cook, Carlson Worldwide	Caledonian, Flying Colours	9%	4.2%
Others	–	–	–	49%	45.2%

Source: Civil Aviation Authority; Monopolies and Mergers Commission, Foreign Package Holidays, Cm 3813, December 1997, page 77, table 4.2.

* Share of foreign package holiday sales in 1996, excluding cruises starting and finishing in UK, estimated by the MMC. Acquisitions since have raised the share of the Big Four operators to an estimated market share of 80 per cent. This cannot be verified from the MMC data.

holidaymakers to their destinations. The major airlines have felt the pressure, forming charter and cut-price airlines rather than undermine their own exorbitant fare structures.[40] The independent travel agent is being squeezed by the chains of the major tour operators. All of them own at least one tame travel agency to channel holidaymakers into their packages. There was much bogus dismay in the industry when Going Places admitted that its first recommendation to holidaymakers was an excursion with its parent (Airtours) and Lunn Poly (owned by Thomson) refused to sell the holidays of a rival (First Choice) until it was given bigger discounts and sales commissions.[41]

The Office of Fair Trading (OFT) finally referred the package holiday companies to the MMC in November 1996. The outcome was surprising. The MMC was expected to agree with the obvious: links between tour operators and travel agencies are anti-competitive. One in four independent travel agencies have disappeared since 1990, as tour operators have acquired them to push their own package holidays. Naturally, discounts, sales commissions and shelf space at tied travel agents are geared to selling the packages assembled by their parent company. The five biggest operators controlled nearly 60 per cent of the foreign package holiday market at the time the MMC began its investigation. Yet its report did not oblige the tour operators to disgorge their travel agencies. Concluding that the industry was broadly competitive, it merely called for the links to be made more explicit.

In effect, the MMC declared open season on smaller tour operators and the remaining independent travel agents. In the year which followed the publication of its report in December 1997, Thomson bought Crystal, the seventh largest tour operator; First Choice bought Unijet and Hayes & Jarvis, two small tour operators; Thomas Cook bought the Flying Colours airline and holiday business, and merged with Carlson, adding over a thousand travel outlets to its network; and Airtours bought one tour operator (Panorama), a telephone sales operation (Direct Holidays) and an orthodox travel agency (Travelworld). First Choice, the only one of the Big Four without a travel agency of its own, was so alarmed by the possibility of discrimination against its holidays that it promised to invest £60 million in three years on a chain of seven hundred wholly-owned travel agents.[42] By 1998, the Big Four sold four in every five foreign package holidays.[43]

One reason for the consolidation is that maturity has brought a natural deceleration in the rate of growth of the package holiday market. There is also a discernible shift away from the Mediterranean beach holiday of sun, sea, sand and sex. Wealthier people are venturing further afield, as the spectacular success of Trailfinders (an upmarket travel agency specialising in exotic locations) attests. An ageing population, living off fat private pensions, does not want sand or sex; they want painting courses and archaeology lectures.

Work as Leisure

The package holiday business may be the first part of the leisure industry to be experiencing a fundamental shift in the psychology of recreation. The industry as a whole is still living, like the Blackpool illuminations, off a bygone era of Wakes Weeks and factory outings which harks back to the age of industrial capitalism, mass-production and an alienated workforce. The traditional view of work and leisure is rooted in this period, seeing work as an unpleasant activity undertaken for the sake of the goods and time it purchases. Work, in other words, is the means of purchasing life.

Socialist killjoys have always disputed this view. Karl Marx stole from Hegel the idea that work, far from being the means to life, was the purpose of it. 'Hegel,' wrote Marx, 'believed that Work was the *essence*, the true essence of Man.' Work, not leisure, was the means by which man turned hostile nature into a congenial place to live. Work, not leisure, filled his life with the tools and toys which imparted meaning to his existence.

It is undeniable that the Leisure Society is accompanied by a pervasive sense of *ennui*. People have never worked less than they do today, and material goods and sensual pleasures were never more abundant, yet dissatisfaction is the common lot. Social scientists fret that a rich and productive economy, capable of supporting millions of pensioners and unemployed, is producing too much spare time. A species programmed to work, they say, is alienated from its essence by a surplus of time. This may explain the depressing nature of much of the leisure industry. It organises play like discipline, and packages and sells it like any other consumer good. Human psychology seems to dictate that leisure should be as much like work as possible. Men and women are condemned to the two-week annual beach holiday, or the week in the mountains, in much the same way that they are bound to go to work.

In Orlando, Florida, the Walt Disney company has built what it calls the Disney Institute. It does not offer entertainment, like Disneyland, or obliteration of the senses, like a traditional British beach holiday. Instead, it offers the chance to do a job you have never done before. A visitor described it:

> Arriving from all over the US, and a few from Europe, they had checked in the night before at the Welcome Centre, a large New England-style clapboard building. They were then driven in electric golf carts to their wooden bungalows or town houses, scattered around fifty-eight acres of well-kept gardens and lakes and an eighteen-hole championship golf course. There are swimming pools, a state-of-the-art performance centre housed in another New England-style building, a cinema, a vast indoor sports and fitness centre, a restaurant and a string of classrooms, television and radio studios, and high-tech kitchens for the institute's culinary programmes equipped with enough cookware for one hundred and twenty-five average kitchens. In the kitchens, groups of mainly elderly Americans were learning to bake bread and cook spicy Mexican dishes. In the television studio, four hours were spent preparing and filming the Disney Institute television news. Later, it took another four hours to edit the programme under the supervision of TV professionals. Next door, students were broadcasting live on the institute's own radio network. Elsewhere, visitors were developing their golf skills . . . or working out on the tennis courts. Others were learning to build elaborate sand sculptures or again, in the darkness of a classroom, creating their own cartoon characters . . .[44]

Considered generously, the Disney Institute is the best kind of leisure: a series of self-improvement courses designed to hone skills and refine minds. On a more realistic view, it is a glimpse at a Soylent Green-like future, in which the productivity of technology is so prodigious, and the capacity of medicine so immense, that work is reduced to a form of entertainment for flocks of sheeplike pensioners and work-shy.

Utilitarian economics, which sees work as the means of purchasing life, has nothing to say of a world in which every material desire is so close to complete fulfilment that people are reduced to passing the time by pretending to work. 'One still works,' as Nietzsche foresaw, 'for work is a form of entertainment' (or, as Noël Coward said, 'work is more fun than fun'). It is probable that work is following orthodox economics – increasing in quantity in line with the productivity conferred by new technology, but being redistributed in time and space. Work is shifting from the old to the young, from men to women, from unskilled to skilled, from work-rich to work-poor, and from blue collar to white. The working week is certainly getting longer, especially for well-paid professionals. Most people with jobs are working longer hours, perhaps out of personal ambition or the need to escape problems at home or from fear of losing their job, but more often from the necessity to make ends meet or the desire for more of the electronic and other gadgets thrown up by the age of affluence.

The group of people with most time to spare are the elderly. Earning more, sooner, has enabled many of them to retire earlier on generous occupational pensions. Handy reckons modern working life crams the one hundred thousand hours of work into thirty years, rather than the traditional forty-seven. This explains not only why the modern working week is frenetic but why the weekend and the annual holiday – both crammed with movement, activity and, above all, commercially organised recreation – are more like hard work than relaxation. Thirty years of industrial discipline leaves even the most independent spirit ill-equipped to do nothing. The premature pensioners making sand sculptures are the most pathetic victims of this speeded-up way of life, in which people earn enough in five days to need two days to spend it, or enough in thirty years to do nothing for the next twenty, but do not have time to cultivate the wit and the spirit to make use of the uncluttered years their effort and money have purchased. They have to buy things to fill them, packaged and branded, instead. John Masefield thought the days that make us happy are the days which make us wise. If this is untrue of the manufactured enjoyment of the modern leisure industry, it is even less true of the newspapers which people read and the programmes they watch.

CHAPTER TWENTY-FOUR

THE MEDIA

If I were asked to put a date on when the rot in our society set in, I'd say without hesitation that it began with the introduction of commercial television.

GEORGE BROWN[1]

In your otherwise accurate article about talks between Live TV and Channel One, you stated that the weather forecast in Norwegian had been dropped in favour of a dwarf reading the weather while bouncing on a trampoline. This is not the case. They are both working for Live TV but at different times.

Letter to the Financial Times from Kelvin Mackenzie,
Managing Director, Mirror Television[2]

No way will I call a truce. No one else wants to call a truce. They insult me every day, so they can go to hell.

RUPERT MURDOCH, November 1997[3]

I would not even start a local newspaper now – they've had their time.

EDDIE SHAH[4]

I've no doubt that the day will come when people will be able to watch what they want, when they want, where they want.

JOHN BIRT, Director General of the BBC[5]

There are many combinations of wealth and power. None is more exquisite than the ownership of a newspaper, a radio station or a television channel. 'What I want is power,' said Lord Beaverbrook, the prototype of every aspiring press tycoon. 'Kiss 'em one day and kick 'em the next.'[6] In recent years, rich businessmen as various as Tony O'Reilly, Tiny Rowland, Robert Maxwell, James Hanson, Maurice Saatchi, Mohamed al Fayed, David and Frederick Barclay, Richard Branson and Andrew Lloyd Webber have either owned or sought to own a national newspaper. Rupert Murdoch, alone so far in making a lasting success of that ambition, understands what they sought. He told his biographer that power mattered to him more than money.[7]

Murdoch occupies a special place in the demonology of those who believe that the media are the most powerful shapers of public opinion. In Opposition, New Labour was so convinced that the Murdoch press was responsible for the quadruple defeat of Old Labour that Blair travelled halfway around the world to woo Rupert Murdoch. Since then, the prime minister has tailored his European policy to the Murdoch press; opposed efforts by his backbenchers to subject it to a more rigorous competition; emasculated a privacy law which might have protected several of his ministers from intrusion; and even inquired of the Italian prime minister whether a bid by News International for the largest commercial TV network in Italy would be opposed.

No aspect of New Labour *realpolitik* has tested the loyalty of Old Labour more. They convinced themselves decades ago that the capitalists who owned mass circulation newspapers were the chief obstacle to the electoral success of socialism. In the 1960s, Harold Wilson was obsessed with misrepresentation by the press; Richard Crossman accused television of alienating the public from politics; and George Brown complained that the 'press and television, all the mass media, have reached a lower level than I have known in my whole life so far'.[8] Brown blamed the plunging standards of print journalism on the pressure to compete with television, but Tony Benn had a more sinister explanation. In his view, a trivialised media was a weapon of class war, used ruthlessly by Big Business to defend its commercial interests and the policies which protected them. The media was the means by which capitalists translated money into power.

The process by which this was supposed to occur remains stubbornly obscure. It is more likely that newspapers follow public opinion than lead it. The *Sun* did not persuade C2s to vote for Margaret Thatcher in 1979 any more than they persuaded Middle England to vote New Labour in 1997. The voters had made up their minds long before. The opinions and ideas which go furthest, as T. S. Eliot pointed out, are those which flatter a current tendency, and the purpose of journalism is to do exactly that.[9] This was never more true than it is today, when the driving force behind most publications and broadcasts is not proprietorial ego but the dividend hunger of the institutional investor.

Thirty years ago the *Daily Mirror* and the *Daily Mail* were controlled by nephews of Lord Northcliffe. The *Daily Express* was the plaything of a Beaverbrook. *The Times* and the *Observer* were owned by the Astors, the *Telegraph* by the Berrys, the *Financial Times* by the Pearsons and the *News of the World* by the Carrs. 'I run the paper,' Beaverbrook told the Press Commission in 1948, 'for the purpose of making propaganda and with no other purpose.'[10] This indifference to profit destroyed the Fleet Street of Beaverbrook and North-cliffe. By the 1960s, the print unions had turned national newspapers into a byword for over-manning, pointless demarcation disputes, and endless strikes and mini-strikes over trifling infractions of 'custom and practice' or even articles or advertisements which union officials considered offensive. No news-paper was immune to periodic losses of production. In 1978, *The Times* dis-appeared for a year.

Typically, its competitors increased their own production. Lack of solidarity among newspaper proprietors increased the power of the print unions. 'Over and again, they made ridiculous demands of one newspaper or another, witnessed the failure of the industry to close ranks, and scored,' recalled Bill Deedes, of his time as editor of the *Daily Telegraph* in the 1970s. '*They had never lost.* They believed they could never lose.'[11] In those days even Rupert Murdoch had to kow-tow to the print unions: 'As soon as the *Sun* began to be a great success, the unions were all over us, squeezing us to death,' he recalled. 'Life became a misery.'[12] Many proprietors sold rather than endure it.

The National Newspapers

All the national dailies, except the *Daily Mail*, the *Guardian* and the *Financial Times*, have changed their ownership, often twice, since the 1960s. The new owners, unlike the press barons of the past, have more money and less patience, and are interested in profit as well as power. Newspapers run for profit are different in character from newspapers run for propaganda. Their contents are dictated not by personal or political visions but by the narrower need to sell as many copies (and advertisements) as possible. The pressure to sell is intensified by the decline in readership of national newspapers under the combined assault of radio and television. Sales of tabloids have fallen steadily for decades, obliging them to compete fiercely for readers through television advertising, price wars, promotions, and kiss-and-tell features bought at expensive auctions. Sales of broadsheet newspapers have not declined as precipitately, but even they have had periodically to resort to price cuts, special offers and promotional games.

While the tabloids have fought Bingo wars, *The Times* and the *Daily Telegraph* have battled for readers with Portfolio and Fantasy Football games. Even the *Financial Times*, once the epitome of tedium and inaccessibility, has invited its readers to collect money-off coupons for electronic diaries, shirts and ties, railway tickets and dirty weekends in country house hotels. Its 'lunch for a fiver' promotion has become an annual fixture. Sensing a less deferential atmosphere among its City readers, the *Financial Times* has even dared to run investigative stories of the kind it long eschewed for fear of causing crooked directors to choke on their cigars. Like most newspapers, the *Financial Times* has shed the distinctive aspects of its personality. It is managed and sold as a branded product, tailored for an identifiable group of consumers, differing from its broadsheet contemporaries only in the absence of competition. This has allowed it to lower its journalistic standards and cut costs without losing readers.

Nothing symbolises the end of the heroic age of newspaper publishing more completely than the broadsheet price war, started by Rupert Murdoch in the summer of 1993, when the cost of *The Times* was cut to 30p. The *Daily Telegraph* initially adopted a dismissive air. A year later it had lost so many readers to *The Times* that it was forced to cut its own price to 30p. *The Times* lopped another third off immediately. At one point the ancestral voice of the Establishment was selling for 10p on Mondays (less than the *Sun*). By the summer of 1995 the finances of the *Telegraph* were so unstable that Conrad Black, the proprietor, bought the shares of nervous outside shareholders.

The *Guardian*, with a solid readership among left-wing public sector professionals who would not allow *The Times* or the *Telegraph* into their homes if they were being given away, has escaped the consequences of the price war. But the *Independent* is damaged. In 1993 it haughtily raised its price to 50p, accusing Murdoch in its leader columns of trying to 'drive this newspaper, the *Independent*, and the *Independent on Sunday*, out of business'.[13] There was substance to this claim: the only reason the *Independent* had appeared at all was the decision to take *The Times* downmarket in the 1980s. A decade on, News International was paying to recoup lost readers.

The *Independent* was forced to admit defeat and cut its price, but the damage was done. Its management had foolishly convinced themselves that broadsheets were above the economics of the marketplace. 'What really drove them,' one of the founders of the *Independent* recalled of his former colleagues, 'was a belief that a paper of this sort had a *right* to exist.'[14] It is an argument made familiar by Labour and Liberal Democrat MPs and peers, who tried unsuccessfully in 1997 and 1998 to outlaw 'predatory pricing' by *The Times*, on the grounds that newspapers are too important to democracy to be left to the marketplace. Despite four separate investigations since the price war erupted, the Office of Fair Trading (OFT) has not found evidence that *The Times* is engaged in anything but normal commercial strategy.

Cutting the price of *The Times* has boosted sales, even if it has not restored the paper to profit. Within six months, *The Times* had pushed its circulation up from 360,000 to 515,000. By the first half of 1998, it was at 815,000. Sales

TABLE 24.1
Circulation of National Newspapers, 1997

Daily Newspapers

Sun	3,779,605
Mirror	2,324,109
Daily Mail	2,237,949
Daily Express	1,202,291
Daily Telegraph	1,098,440
The Times	792,151
Daily Record	685,039
Daily Star	619,553
Guardian	403,999
Financial Times	328,793
Independent	260,223

Sunday Newspapers

News of the World	4,425,708
Sunday Mirror	2,276,089
Mail on Sunday	2,219,430
People	1,895,121
Sunday Times	1,343,324
Express on Sunday	1,140,328
Sunday Telegraph	887,204
Sunday Mail	821,209
Observer	439,573
Independent on Sunday	287,543
Sunday Sport	275,246
Scotland on Sunday	102,917

Source: Benn's Media United Kingdom, 1998.

of broadsheet newspapers, as well as tabloids, are sensitive to changes in price, but even price reductions cannot arrest the decline of newspapers. Despite price cuts, the overall market has not increased, and profits have had to be earned the hard way: by cutting costs. Again, Rupert Murdoch (encouraged by the example of Eddie Shah) challenged the conventional wisdom. In 1986 he transformed the economics of newspaper publishing by shifting production of his titles to a union-free, computer-based factory at Wapping in east London. Once journalists and sales girls could set words on screens, printers could be fired, newspapers expanded and set in colour, and advertising revenues increased.

The massive productivity gains conferred by breaking the Fleet Street unions and introducing modern technology did not accommodate more newspapers. *Today*, a seven-day-a-week, full-colour tabloid launched by Eddie Shah after his victory over the print unions at Warrington, was closed by its third and last owner, Rupert Murdoch, in November 1995.[15] Two new Sunday newspapers had brief lives. The *European* was rescued from the administrators, and flirted with death continually until it finally expired in 1998. *London Daily News*, the evening paper launched by Robert Maxwell in 1987, closed within five months, partly because it was poorly produced, but mainly because the owners of the *Evening Standard* resurrected the defunct *Evening News* at half its price.

The main beneficiaries of new technology and rising productivity are the established titles. They have got fatter, sprouting supplements, colour magazines and extra sections, and soaking up the increase in advertising revenues. The one new daily which did threaten to capitalise on a union-free Fleet Street was the *Independent*, which was launched in October 1986 by three former *Telegraph Journalists* on a wave of post-Wapping and mid-Eighties euphoria. Backed by institutional rather than personal capital, it promised a break with old-style proprietors. Its advertising slogan ('It is. Are You?') encapsulated its idea of ownerless journalism. Its target audience was yuppies, the 'missing readership' who were thought to watch television rather than read newspapers.[16] No single investor was allowed to own more than 15 per cent, and the staff were given share options. Editorially, the paper adopted a lofty tone, banning its political correspondents from joining the Commons lobby, forbidding freebies from travel agents and other hucksters, and refusing to cover the antics of the royal family. Andreas Whittam Smith, its first editor, appointed himself custodian of media ethics by bringing together Fleet Street editors to devise a code of conduct.

The character of the *Independent* was too earnest to appeal. But its biggest mistake was to start the *Independent on Sunday*, mainly to spoil the prospects of the short-lived *Sunday Correspondent*. The losses of the Sunday undermined the financial stability of the daily, forcing the company into the grasp of Mirror Group Newspapers and Independent Newspapers of Ireland (a company controlled by Tony O'Reilly, former chief executive of Heinz). The founding fathers fell out. Whittam Smith resigned as chief executive in July 1993, and as editor in June 1994. The paper has had several editors since, and is still short of money. In 1998 Independent Newspapers bought the share held by the Mirror, and Tony O'Reilly promised to 'reaffirm the vision of the founders' and provide 'a home for very good writing, and very good writers'. It will cost the Irish billionaire a lot of time and money, but profit, he says, is 'not the ultimate determinant in our investment'.[17]

The *Independent* is not the only newspaper in trouble. The *Daily Express*, known on Fleet Street as the Living Dead twenty years ago, has continued to limp on ever since. It is an unforgivable decline for a paper once personified by Beaverbrook, and which taught Murdoch much that he knows of popular journalism.[18] After struggling under the ownership of Nigel Broackes and Lord Matthews (who launched the *Daily Star* in 1978) and Lord Stevens (who planned an abortive merger with *Sunday Sport*), the two Express titles are now part of the financial and communications empire of New Labour millionaire Clive Hollick.[19] The paper, once the mouthpiece of suburban reaction, now supports membership of the single European currency, single mothers and the lowering of the age of consent for homosexuals.

Ideas of this kind were once the preserve of the *Guardian*, though not until it abandoned its Manchester birthplace. In 1962 Anthony Sampson described it as the home of 'robust North Country common sense.'[20] Today, it is more North London than North Country. It has struggled to enthuse about New Labour, and obviously misses the easy targets of the Conservative years, like Neil Hamilton and Jonathan Aitken. Times have got harder for the liberals who run the *Guardian*. But it is the only national newspaper which is genuinely independent. Its ownership is vested in the Scott Trust, a body maintained by the descendants of C. P. Scott, who acquired the paper in 1905 from his cousin John Taylor (son of the founder). It is also a profitable newspaper, unlike the *Observer*, its Sunday bedfellow. The Guardian Media Group, which also owns the *Manchester Evening News* and a string of regional newspapers, bought the ailing Sunday from Tiny Rowland in 1993. Despite a succession of editors, and several overhauls, it continues to lose money.

Why Media Ownership Matters

Newspapermen have always believed that the press has a higher duty than profitability. Unlike television, newspapers were leaders in the fight for freedom of expression. It was because a free press is the chief guarantor of democracy that it was written into the constitution of the first democracy. Its authors were well acquainted with the efforts of the eighteenth-century British state to muzzle the press. Even after the demise in 1695 of the Licensing Act, which empowered the government to censor newspapers before they were published, the government retained a formidable armoury of weapons to control the press: officials bribed journalists, subsidised journals favourable

TABLE 24.2
Ownership of National Newspapers

National Titles	Owner
Daily Mail, Mail on Sunday, Evening Standard	Daily Mail & General Trust PLC*
Glasgow Herald, Evening Times	Scottish Media Group PLC
European, Scotsman, Scotland on Sunday, Edinburgh Evening News	David and Frederick Barclay
Guardian, Observer, Manchester Evening News	Scott Trust
Daily Mirror, Daily Record, Sunday Mail, Sporting Life, Racing Post	Mirror Group Newspapers PLC
Times, Sunday Times, The Sun, News of the World	Rupert Murdoch (News Corporation)
The Independent, The Independent on Sunday	Tony O'Reilly (Independent Newspapers)
Sunday Sport, Daily Sport	David Sullivan (Sport Newspapers)†
Financial Times, The Economist (50%)	Pearson PLC
Daily Telegraph, Sunday Telegraph, The Spectator	Conrad Black (Hollinger)
Daily Express, Sunday Express, Daily Star	United News and Media PLC

Source: Benn's Media United Kingdom, 1998; *Financial Times*.

* Lord Rothermere and family hold 50 per cent of the equity and 75 per cent of voting shares.
† David Sullivan owns 50 per cent, and David and Ralph Gold 25 per cent each.

to the government, and prosecuted and jailed publishers for libel (bribing jurors where necessary). Taxes were imposed on the number of pages and the advertisements they carried.[21] The tax on advertisements was not lifted until 1853, and Stamp Duty lasted until 1855.

It took another century to end state censorship of lewd or violent material, and bad language. The journalism of today is restrained by nothing save laws against obscenity, defamation, blasphemy and sedition; these are rarely invoked. The debate about freedom of the press is no longer about state censorship, but corporate ownership and control. Freedom of expression, some say, is too important to be left to the spontaneous order of the market-place, and that if readers and viewers determine what is published and broad-cast, tastes and ideas will narrow to suit the interests of giant media corporations, such as News International. 'It is a mistake to suppose that what most people want is necessarily what is high quality . . . I do not want . . . a McDonalds culture, in which television provides the international fast food of the mind,' wrote a former editor of *The Times*.[22]

Advertising is identified as the main source of corruption. The need for revenue compels publishers and broadcasters to attract as many readers and viewers as they can, placing limits on their appetites for material about the condition of man.[23] For the liberal conscience, the consequences are paradoxical. Democracy says Jack has as much right as his master to choose what he watches, listens to and reads, but can Jack be trusted to choose the right things? Watching media personalities wrestle with this contradiction is hilarious. In the end it is reconcilable only through public ownership, subsidy or regulation, and history makes subjection of newspapers to the state unthinkable. The same is not true of broadcasting.

Commercial Television

'Newspapers,' as Lord Rees-Mogg has pointed out, 'were born free, but television was born in chains, a monopoly created by the state, dependent on the state and in every country regulated by the state.' Ironically, Rees-Mogg ended up in the chair of the Broadcasting Standards Council, set up by Thatcher to guard against plagues of sex and violence on the airwaves – a clear illustration of the contradictory impulses of Thatcherism. The Conservative governments of the 1980s and early 1990s did more to break state regulation of broadcasting than their predecessors, but their appetite for commercial freedom was not matched by eagerness for its moral and social liberation.

It is a contradiction written into the history of the relationship between Conservatism and broadcasting. In 1926, a Conservative government created a state monopoly of wireless broadcasting because it feared the power of the wireless to excite and corrupt its listeners.[24] Ten years later, another Conservative government assigned the first television broadcasts to the BBC for the same reasons, despite an offer from a consortium of private companies to provide the service. When a third Conservative government sponsored development of the first commercial television in 1955, it imposed a tight system of regulation. An Independent Television Authority (ITA) was set up to own the transmission system, award regional broadcasting monopolies to private companies, and ensure quality of programming. Time limits were imposed on the duration of advertisements, and the sponsorship of programmes by commercial companies (the dominant mode in the United States) was forbidden.

When this system failed to produce the expected results, regulation was tightened. Regional monopolies gave the companies no incentive to compete; soon they were producing programmes jointly and broadcasting them simultaneously. Their quality was depressingly low, because the companies faced no threat from one another or from the BBC. In 1963 the government gave the ITA control over the quantity, timing, distribution and quality of advertising, but it also imposed on independent television a BBC-style duty to broadcast edifying current affairs and religious programmes, and to cater for children. A year later, in a pointed snub to ITV the BBC was given a second channel to disseminate the higher cultural forms.

When ITV was given a second channel in 1984, it was established as a statutory corporation and given a specific remit to broadcast educational and multicultural programmes. Nobody thought these would attract sufficient advertising to enable Channel 4 to cover its costs, so the ITV companies were obligated to meet any shortfall in return for the right to collect any surplus. The new channel proved surprisingly popular with advertisers, and ended up paying £70 million a year to the ITV companies. One of the earliest decisions taken by New Labour was to abolish the funding formula. But lifting the ITV tax on Channel 4 had another familiar aspect to it: giving the government an excuse to intensify the public service obligations. Channel 4 is now expected to broadcast even more educational and multicultural material. Channel 5, a private company which began broadcasting in 1997, has similar requirements.

'Positive programme requirements', as the Independent Television Commission calls them, are a reminder that government never loses its appetite for deciding what people should watch. Until the arrival of satellite television in the late 1980s, the BBC–ITV duopoly made it relatively easy for them to interfere. Neither the BBC (which monopolised public funding) nor ITV (which monopolised advertising revenues) had any incentive to challenge it. Though the ITV companies were obliged to reapply for their franchises every ten years, the application process was notoriously opaque, and the incumbents were rarely disappointed. As recently as the mid-1980s, the government was told that a fifth terrestrial television channel was technically impossible.

The earliest cable operators were confined to remote or inaccessible areas where cable was the only way of delivering pictures of tolerable quality, and restricted to broadcasting of existing BBC and ITV channels. As coverage by BBC and ITV transmitters improved, the cable industry went into decline and was in danger of disappearing altogether when government decided to deregulate the industry in the Cable and Broadcasting Act of 1984. This allowed cable operators to compete with the BBC and ITV, and set up a cable authority to award local monopolies. As distributors rather than programme-makers, cable operators did not pose an immediate threat to the duopoly. Cable television also developed slowly. Five years after the industry was deregulated, cable franchises were operating in only eleven localities. The one company with the telecommunications network in place and the financial muscle to make rapid inroads into the terrestrial television market, was BT. But the government banned it from entering the market until the independent cable operators were able to compete. A decade and a half after deregulation, they are not strong enough yet.[25]

Protected from competition, journalists and programme-makers could produce what they liked. Lack of competition also freed the television trade unions to build a web of restrictive practices which raised costs and inhibited the use of new technology. Thatcher decided to take a hand. 'You gentlemen,' she told a seminar of television executives in 1987, 'are the last bastion of restrictive practices.' But change was already in hand. Two years earlier, after yet another battle over whether to increase the BBC licence fee, the government had established a Committee on the Financing of the BBC under the chairmanship of a liberal economist, Sir Alan Peacock. Its deliberations ranged far beyond the question of how the BBC should be funded. Its members understood that satellite, cable and pay-per-view technology was undermining the duopoly, and that their recommendations had to invite the government to encourage a genuine broadcasting market.

Because the Peacock Report did not recommend the BBC take advertising, it has become commonplace to argue that it changed nothing. This is wrong. It shifted the terms of debate decisively, from the paternalistic values of the broadcasting establishment to the marketplace:

> British broadcasting should move towards a sophisticated market system based on consumer sovereignty. That is a system which recognises that viewers and listeners are the best ultimate judges of their own interest, which they can best satisfy if they have the option of purchasing the broadcasting services they require from as many alternative sources of supply as possible.[26]

The spirit of the Peacock Report, and many of its ideas, found their way into the Broadcasting Act of 1990.

Franchise Auction Disaster

The centrepiece of the Act was the introduction of an auction of ITV franchises, taken directly from the Peacock Report, which recommended franchises be awarded to the highest bidder. Unhappily, this suggestion was warped by the political process. The old system by which ITV franchises were awarded was overgenerous to incumbents. The Peacock Report recommended that the ITC accept the highest bid for each franchise, or explain why it had not. But during the passage of the legislation, the government set a 'quality' threshold. This allowed the incumbent licensees to extract an 'exceptional circumstances' clause, which freed the ITC to disregard the highest bid if a lower bidder proposed to make programmes of exceptional quality. It introduced a subjective element which was bound to favour the familiar over the untested.

The Peacock Report had also envisaged a straightforward competitive tender, in which each bidder committed himself to regular payments to the Treasury. This would have extracted an appropriate rent for the taxpayer, and avoided the awkwardness of calculations based on advertising revenues. Instead, the government decided to ask for a single advance payment *plus* a proportion of advertising revenues. Theoretically, each bidder would pass an initial quality threshold. Franchises would go to bidders who offered less in advance, but stable finances and better programmes in the future. The taxpayer would not lose out, because his take was geared to the buoyancy of advertising revenues. In practice, the results were capricious. The ITC ensured that the invitations to apply for a franchise gave the incumbents an advantage; only four out of sixteen lost their franchises.[27] Two incumbents, Scottish Television and Central Television, bid laughably small amounts because they faced no competition. Central Television won despite offering to pay only £2,000 a year (plus 11 per cent of advertising revenues) for one of the most lucrative franchises in the network. But TVS, TSW and HTV, which faced serious competition, overbid. But only HTV retained its franchise. The highest bidder won in only five areas. Two of the winning contractors (Granada and LWT) bid only a quarter of the sums offered by their rivals while two others (Yorkshire and Tyne-Tees) overbid so wildly that they ran into serious difficulties and were forced to merge. GMTV has not made money since it started broadcasting in 1992.

The perverse results of the 1991 auction added to the problems of an ITV network suffering from a shrinking (and ageing) audience, and to the consequent restlessness among its advertisers. Lavish bids left little money to invest in programmes which might have gained audiences and regained advertisers. With the network split between sixteen separate franchises, it was hard to compose a competitive broadcasting schedule. Predictably, independence was followed by consolidation. All but two of the franchises auctioned in 1991 are now controlled by one of four large media groups. Granada Group added the merged Yorkshire-Tyne-Tees and LWT franchises to its existing licence; United News & Media added HTV to Anglia and Meridian; and Carlton Communications acquired WestCountry TV. Scottish Television took over Grampian TV in 1997 and tried to add Ulster later the same year.

Financial pressure encouraged eleven of the sixteen to take up their option

TABLE 24.3
Ownership of the Terrestrial Television Franchises

Region	Licence-holder	Major Owner(s)	Total Payment in 1998* (£m)	Total Payment in 1999† (£m)
Breakfast	GMTV Ltd	Various‡	50.5	20.0
Borders	Border Television PLC	CN Group Ltd (13.9%)	0.06	0.5
Channel Five	Channel 5 Broadcasting Ltd	Various§	22.0	*22.7
Channel Four	Channel 4 TV Corporation	H.M. Government	n/a	n/a
Channel Islands	Channel Television Ltd	Lapwing Investments (28%)	0.001	*0.001
Central Scotland	Scottish Television PLC	Scottish Media Group	0.002	*0.002
East Anglia	Anglia Television Ltd	United News & Media PLC	29.5	29.0
London Weekday	Carlton Television	Carlton Communications PLC	8.7	*8.9
London Weekend	LWT Ltd	Granada Group PLC	81.5	72.0
Midlands	Central Broadcasting	Carlton Communications PLC	31.5	49.0
Northern Ireland	Ulster Television PLC	Various¶	1.0	2.0
North East	Tyne Tees Television Ltd	Granada Group PLC	18.5	11.0
North of Scotland	Grampian Television	Scottish Media Group	0.823	*0.847
North West	Granada Television	Granada Group PLC	10.3	*10.6
South & South East	Meridian Broadcasting Ltd	United News & Media PLC	64.0	58.0
South West	Westcountry Television Ltd	Carlton Communications PLC	9.0	6.0
Wales & The West	HTV Group Ltd	United News & Media PLC	25.5	9.0
Yorkshire	Yorkshire Television Ltd	Granada Group PLC	52.0	35.0

Source: ITC; Companies; *Financial Times.*

* Payments consist of an index-linked annual sum plus a percentage of advertising and sponsorship revenues ranging from 0% to 15%, agreed with the ITC (see text).
† Payments for 1999 are based on projections of advertising income, but this is not available for companies which did not renew their licences. The figures marked with an asterisk refer to the annual sum only.
‡ Carlton, Granada, Scottish Media Group (each 20 per cent), Disney Company (25 per cent), Guardian Media Group (15 per cent).
§ United News & Media PLC (20 per cent), Pearson PLC (20 per cent), CLT-Ufa (36.9 per cent) and Warburg Pincus (23.1 per cent).
¶ CanWest Communications (29.9 per cent), directors (11 per cent).

to apply for renewal four years before their licences expired, in the hope of more favourable terms. The ITC was sympathetic, cutting an estimated £71 million from the value of payments to the government.[28] For once, it was not a conspiracy against the taxpayer between regulators and licence-holders. The fall in payments reflected the intensification of competition in the broadcasting market since 1991. The case for awarding franchises to the highest bidder had rested on the belief that regional television was part of a natural duopoly: there was no room on the airwaves for more than two terrestrial television networks. By the late 1990s, technology had made a nonsense of that idea.

Satellite and Cable Television

The BBC–ITV duopoly delayed the introduction of satellite broadcasting for a decade. Of the five Direct Broadcasting by Satellite (DBS) channels awarded to the United Kingdom by the World Administrative Radio Conference in 1977, two were awarded to the BBC, which did nothing with them until 1995.[29] The government decided that any satellite used by British broadcasters had to be high-technology and all-British, which led to further delays. In 1984 it proposed the joint DBS 'Club of 21' venture between the BBC and ITV companies. This collapsed in a welter of recriminations and lawsuits. In 1986, a contract to broadcast three channels by satellite was awarded to a consortium called British Satellite Broadcasting (BSB). The biographers of this unfortunate enterprise call it 'one of the greatest commercial disasters in British history, and certainly the greatest in the history of the British media'.[30]

The main shortcoming at BSB was that marketing hype ran ahead of the technology. Glitches in the development of its so-called Squarial forced it to concede a fifteen-month headstart to Sky TV, and eventually caused losses of a magnitude sufficient to drive the two companies into a merger in late 1990. That an uninvited and privately financed satellite channel broadcasting from outside the United Kingdom outperformed the BBC and the franchise-holder chosen by the regulators dealt a mortal blow to the old ways of thinking. BSB was chosen by the authorities on traditional grounds: a supposed technological superiority, coupled with a promise to broadcast three channels of 'quality' programmes ('Toffs' telly,' as the *Sun* mocked it). In the end, it was only because News International was under pressure from its bankers that BSB was even offered the face-saving solution of a merger with Sky; it would undoubtedly have lost any competitive duel. The merger left News International with a minority shareholding in BSkyB, but bringing Rupert Murdoch into the closed world of British broadcasting broke the duopoly for good.[31]

The failure of BSB also gave BSkyB a near-monopoly of pay-television, which lasted for over a decade. The one technology capable of competing with BSkyB was cable television. Though expensive to build, cable networks deliver a sizeable audience (more than one in two homes are now passed by a cable network) and a wide range of services in addition to television: telephone, electronic mail, Internet access and inter-active services like shopping and banking. Unfortunately, the cable companies squandered this strong position. They proved extraordinarily inept in their negotiations with programme suppliers in general, and BSkyB in particular.

Sport and movies were their undoing. Nobody would subscribe to a satellite television service without Sky Sport and Sky Movies and nor would anyone to a cable television service. BSkyB was more or less able to dictate the terms on which the cable television companies carried the two channels. Two of the leading cable companies were so anxious to secure Sky programmes that they signed ten-year contracts and agreed not to talk to alternative suppliers. BSkyB charged the cable companies a price which made it impossible for them to compete profitably with satellite technology, and insisted that they could not take on new customers without forcing them to subscribe to all Sky channels through the so-called minimum carriage rule.[32] This made cable television more expensive than buying a Sky satellite dish, and forced subscribers to pay for channels they did not want. This made it hard to sell.

It is true that the cable companies had little choice but to entreat with BSkyB. The alternatives were few in number, and unappealing. The chief highlights of Live TV, created by Mirror Group Newspapers especially for cable transmission, were a trampolining dwarf, topless darts players and weather forecasts read in Norwegian. In addition to the thirteen channels offered by BSkyB, ITC has licensed another two hundred and twenty-nine local and national satellite and cable television channels, of which one hundred and eleven were broadcasting by 1998.[33] The material ranges from 'adult entertainment' to Christian propaganda. The Rainbow Television Network offers the possibility of 'light entertainment for a gay audience'. But few cable companies make their own programmes, and few programme-makers produce for transmission only on cable and satellite. In programming terms, cable and satellite television have provided depressing confirmation of Amis's law: more means worse.

The poor quality of the programmes has not helped the cable companies persuade people to subscribe to their networks. Of the eleven million homes passed by the cable companies by the middle of 1998, one in five subscribed to the television service.[34] This poor rate of penetration was coupled with high 'churn', in which two in five persuaded to subscribe failed to renew after sampling the wares. With few television subscribers – and BSkyB squeezing them on price – the cable companies came to rely on selling telephone and Internet services. This helped to raise the rate of penetration to one home in three, but even telephone sales did not progress as rapidly as the cable companies had predicted, mainly because there was no objective way of knowing how their prices compared with Mercury or BT. Until 1995, when a Monopolies and Mergers Commission (MMC) report forced BT to let cable customers keep their existing telephone numbers, there was also a strong disincentive to change suppliers.

Unfortunately, the cable companies did not help themselves: the marketing of cable services was weak. The minimum carriage requirement, and the inability to undercut satellite access to Sky channels, meant selling cable television was bound to be difficult. But the cable companies were inept: weeks of disruption while the streets were dug up was followed by a knock on the door by a scruffy salesman. The first national advertising campaign, starring Dawn French and the slogan 'Get Connected', was not launched until 1996, and even the cable operators thought it a poor effort. Now that their networks are complete, the cable operators have promised to concentrate on marketing. Helpfully, the ITC has forbidden minimum carriage requirements in all new distribution contracts and existing contracts broadcast in digital form, and all contracts will be free of them from 1 January 2000.[35]

It will help even more that the cable networks are nearing completion. By 1998, the cable operators had invested £9 billion in building their networks, and they expected the bill to rise by at least another £1 billion before they were finished. Companies which invest billions and receive millions tend to struggle financially. By 1995, shareholders had tired of the losses, and the industry began to consolidate. Bell Cablemedia, Nynex CableComms and Videotron merged with Cable & Wireless, owners of the Mercury telephone service; Telewest has acquired SBC Cablecoms and General Cable; and NTL has taken over Comcast, ComTel and Diamond Cable. The twenty-four cable companies of 1993 have shrunk to seven, and the three largest control all but a fraction of the market. For the first time since the cable industry was deregulated in 1984, it can negotiate with programme-makers from a position of strength.

The Coming of Digital Technology

Digital technology, available on terrestrial and cable as well as satellite television, is loosening the stranglehold BSkyB has exerted over pay-television since 1989. Digitally broadcast signals are compressed, so they occupy less space on the airwaves than analogue signals, and hundreds of channels can

TABLE 24.4
The Main Owners of Cable Franchises

Operator	Owners	Homes Controlled*	Homes Passed†	Homes Connected‡	Market Share
NTL	NTL Incorporated	6,051,904	3,469,285	907,738	36.8%
CWC	Various§	6,049,567	3,850,308	780,206	31.6%
Telewest	Various¶	5,198,998	2,993,799	652,564	26.4%
Others	–	1,224,944	724,422	129,246	5.2%
Total		18,525,413	11,037,814	2,469,754	100.0%

Source: *Who's Who in Cable and Satellite UK*, Edition 25, July 1998, Phillips Business Information Ltd.

* Homes under the control of the management rather than the shareholders, since franchises are sometimes shared with other operators.
† The number of homes under management control passed by a broadband cable network.
‡ The number of homes connected to a broadband cable network.
§ Cable & Wireless PLC (52.6%), Nynex Corporation (18.5%), BCI (14.2%), Public (14.7%).
¶ Telecommunications Incorporated (26.75%), US West (26.75%), Public (26.5%), SBC (10%), Cox Communications (10%).

be broadcast where only a handful were before. This creates space for a massive expansion of competition, but digital technology does more than expand capacity: the sound and pictures are better and more varied. It creates room for pay-per-view, movies-on-demand, single channel subscription and inter-active television services, such as home shopping and banking, which make the consumer, not the producer, the arbiter of what is broadcast.

Under the BBC–ITV duopoly, regulators and programme-makers decided what was good for viewers, and trade unions decided the cost of the programmes. Satellite and cable television did little to expand choice. BSkyB used its rights to broadcast popular movies and Premier League football matches, insisting that subscribers buy all channels while spending virtually nothing on programming. 'I think it is fair to say that we haven't talked to at least half the population of this country for many years,' admitted Mark Booth, chief executive of BSkyB, in 1997. With the arrival of digital television, sellers of movies and sports rights can sell them to individual consumers on a pay-per-view basis.

Rivals to Sky Movies, offering recent and classic films on a pay-per-view basis, are already operating, and several leading football clubs are exploring the scope to sell Premier League matches in this way. Which is why BSkyB was willing to pay £624 million to acquire Manchester United. It recognises that the Premier League football clubs will not sell television rights in one block when the present contract expires, and the company wishes to show matches involving the best-known football club there is. BSkyB also knows that cable companies are less compliant; they have established a pay-per-view movie channel (Front Row) and rebelled against channel-bundling and high subscription prices. BSkyB is now producing programmes of its own.

The company has not, however, abandoned monopolistic ways of thinking. Few people are able to receive digital broadcasts without a set-top box to decode the signal. The BSkyB decoders are designed not to decode digital transmissions of rival broadcasters. BSkyB also had a share in ONDigital, the consortium which won the main terrestrial franchise, until the competition authorities insisted it withdraw.[36] This was followed by a race to decide whether BSkyB could start a digital service before ONDigital. It did, by a matter of weeks. By the end of 1998, BSkyB, ONDigital, the BBC, Channel 4 and all the ITV stations (including Channel 5) were each broadcasting in digital formats, most offering a combination of subscription and pay-per-view for the first time, in addition to their free-on-air channels.[37]

Digital television – and the pay and pay-per-view possibilities it opens up – is unlikely to transform the British broadcasting market until the government decides that broadcasters can switch off their analogue signals. Faced with a definite cut-off date, most consumers would be forced to buy a decoder or a digital television set. Which is why the government has refused to set one: there are no votes in forcing people to throw away perfectly good television sets or spend hundreds of pounds on a decoder. Though the Treasury is excited by the possibility of selling the right to use parts of the radio spectrum freed by the switch to digital transmission, the government has refused to commit itself to a date.

Commercial Radio

Uncertainty over the end of analogue broadcasts is greater still in commercial radio broadcasting, where digital transmission was to start in 1999. When the first national licence was offered by the Radio Authority in June 1998, it attracted just one bid.[38] Local licences are now being auctioned, but there is little excitement about digital technology in radio circles, mainly because few listeners will invest hundreds of pounds in a digital set to yield only a marginal improvement over existing FM transmissions, and the market for digital information on radio frequencies is already sewn up by paging and mobile telephone operators.

Unlike commercial television or BBC Radio, commercial radio lacks the money for speculative investment in digital technology. Collective profits amount to only £70 million a year, so a degree of caution is understandable. The financial fragility of commercial radio reflects its relative novelty and fragmentation. The first legal commercial radio stations were not established in Britain until 1973, when the Heath government ended the BBC monopoly. Until then, the only commercial radio stations were piratical broadcasters like Luxembourg and Caroline. Their legitimate successors grew slowly, largely because the BBC continued to broadcast pop music and chat shows. National and local stations run by the BBC captured most of the ordinary listeners, driving commercial stations into the esoteric and local areas that advertisers dislike. They entered the 1980s as carriers of cheap local advertising, attracting about 2p in every £1 of advertising. The indifference of advertisers was not overcome until the mid-1990s, when a group of leading commercial stations set up the Radio Advertising Bureau, which offered advertisers the chance to buy national campaigns spread across dozens of national and local radio stations. This transformed the economics of commercial radio. For a time, its revenues grew faster than any other medium, and now account for 5p in every £1 of national advertising expenditure.

The Broadcasting Act of 1990 completed the liberation of commercial radio, allowing three new national networks to establish themselves and a number of local stations to develop. Since they use little space on the radio spectrum, and are relatively cheap to set up, commercial radio boomed. The number of stations has increased from ninety-two in 1990 to over two hundred now. The growth of commercial radio was helped by disastrous programming changes at the BBC. Radio 1 lost an estimated three million listeners in two years. In mid-1994, commercial radio was able to claim that it had more listeners than the BBC. The stations were more in touch with what listeners wanted, and less encumbered by management and bureaucracy. Classic FM, for example, identified a gap in the market, created a brand and built an audience large and rich enough for advertisers to notice. As cheaper technology lowers the barriers to entry, the BBC has found it hard to compete.

Shrinkage of the BBC and unpopular changes to its schedules have led to accusations of a loss of seriousness and diversity in British radio. Commercial radio certainly concentrates on music, talk and news, unleavened by the drama, comedy, current affairs programmes and documentaries which characterised BBC radio in its days of monopoly. The one relatively serious new station broadcasting on a national scale, Talk Radio, struggled consistently to make money. In October 1998 it was taken over by a consortium led by Kelvin Mackenzie, former editor of the *Sun* and chief executive of Live TV.[39] It is now expected to be popular, not serious.

The Radio Authority, set up under the 1990 Broadcasting Act to issue

commercial licences and regulate broadcasters, is more to blame for indifferent quality than the downmarket tastes of the listeners. This is partly because
it continues to over-regulate broadcasts and advertisements, and because the
criteria it uses to award licences (like winning the support of local people
and broadening the range of programming in a locality) tend to encourage
reversion to the mean. Virgin 1215, a national station set up by Virgin Group
in April 1993 to broadcast a mixture of 'classic album tracks and the best
new music' to ageing hippies, is a measure of the failure of the system. The
station attracted huge audiences despite being denied an FM frequency, and
it was sold for a good price to the Ginger Media Group against a rival bid
from Capital Radio. In 1994, the Radio Authority effectively closed down the
popular LBC station in London by giving its franchise to a new broadcaster,
London News Radio (LNR). Listeners made their views known by shunning
the new station until LNT revived the LBC name and even brought back
some of the LBC presenters.

Since the 1996 Broadcasting Act, which switched the emphasis of regulation

TABLE 24.5
The Big Five Commercial Radio Groups

Group	Brands/Stations	Turnover 1997–98 (£m)*
Capital Radio PLC	Capital, Fox, Invicta, Ocean, Power, Red Dragon, Southern, Touch	92.9
GWR Group PLC	2CR, 2-TEN, Chiltern, Beacon, Broadland, Classic, GEM, GWR, Hereward, Horizon, Leicester Sound, Mercia, Northants, Ram, Severn Sound, SGR, Colchester, Trent, Wyvern	73.0
EMAP Radio Ltd	Aire, Radio City, Hallam, Key, Kiss, Magic, Metro, Piccadilly, Red Rose, Rock, TFM, Viking	70.3
Scottish Radio Holdings PLC	Radio Borders, Clyde, Cool, Downtown, Forth, Moray Firth, Northsound, South West Sound, Tay, West Sound	43.7
Chrysalis Radio Ltd	Galaxy, Heart	18.3

Source: Radio Authority Pocket Book, June 1998; Company Annual Reports and Accounts.

* Commercial radio activities in the United Kingdom only.

from broadcast mediums to market share, a number of sizeable groups have emerged through acquisition of multiple licences.[40] The industry has begun to consolidate: over two thirds of advertising revenue is now garnered by the five biggest groups, all of which are PLCs quoted on the London Stock Exchange. GWR is now a £250 million company confident enough to challenge Carlton Communications for the ownership of Westcountry TV. Capital Radio, one of the earliest successes in the 1970s, is a £400 million enterprise.

By comparison with BSkyB (£8 billion) or Carlton Communications (£3 billion) these are not large enterprises. Commercial radio is still developing, but its largest companies have acquired the chief instrument of success in modern business: brands. Stations such as Capital (Capital Radio), Kiss (EMAP) and Jazz FM (Golden Rose Communications) have become brands in their own right, capable of extension into merchandise, television and additional radio stations. Capital Radio has acquired a chain of restaurants (My Kinda Town) to ally with its Capital Radio Cafés, and Golden Rose Communications has launched Jazbar theme-bars. With the government pressing the industry to invest in digital technology, the consolidation of commercial radio broadcasting is not yet at an end.

Regional Newspapers

Regional newspapers are undergoing the same process of consolidation and commercialisation. Three in four of the regional dailies have changed hands in the past four years, leaving twelve hundred regional newspapers in the hands of ten major groups. Family-owned regional newspapers were once as common as local breweries, but they are now falling under the sway of the ubiquitous PLC. They are not the familiar or expected names. Almost all national newspaper groups grew out of regional papers or acquired them as an extension of their business, but the only ones now committed to the market are the Daily Mail & General Trust PLC and Mirror Group Newspapers PLC, both of which have expanded their interests in recent years. All the other major newpaper publishing groups – EMAP, Pearson, Reed, Thomson and United News & Media – have sold their regional newspapers to concentrate on other media.

The newspapers they sold have fuelled the growth of a new type of PLC: the specialist regional newspaper publisher. Previously obscure or even unknown companies – Johnston Press, Midland Independent Newspapers, Newsquest, Southern Newspapers and Trinity International – became the dominant forces in regional newspaper publishing. Some are the product of management buy-outs from major national groups. Midland Independent Newspapers, which was acquired by the Mirror Group for £297 million in 1997, began as a buy-out from the Birmingham Post group in 1991. The managers of Newsquest, bankrolled by American financiers, bought the foundation of their business from Reed Elsevier in 1996. The company has since acquired additional titles and floated on the Stock Exchange.

Trinity International, the biggest regional newspaper publisher, is not a buy-out, but a regional publisher which took advantage of the dislocation of the industry to expand from its Merseyside base (it still publishes the *Liverpool Echo* and *Daily Post*). In the last decade it has devoured a string of regional newspapers, but its greatest coup came in 1995. In a deal whose price was one and a half times the market capitalisation of the company, Trinity paid Thomson Regional Newspapers £328 million for all its newspapers outside Scotland.[41] By 1998 the company was large and confident enough to make an offer to buy a national publisher: Mirror Group Newspapers. The third largest group, Johnston Press, has also expanded by acquisition from a relatively small regional base in Scotland. It did not enter the market south of the border until 1978 but, after floating on the London Stock Exchange ten years later, Johnston was able by 1996 to pay EMAP £211 million for one of the largest portfolios of regional newspapers in Britain.

Specialisation and consolidation have attracted a new and more entrepreneurial class of manager to regional newspapers, as well as altering their character. In an age before the railways made it possible to disseminate London newspapers all over the country, and well before the invention of the broadcast media, the provincial newspapers were the main source of information. Today, the provincial press is driven less by news than by advertising. Over four fifths of its revenues of nearly £2.5 billion come from advertising, the bulk of it classified. During a period of retrenchment in national newspapers, this has allowed regional titles to increase, and the regional market is now larger, in terms of advertising revenues, than the national market. There is a fluctuating total of up to fifteen hundred regional titles, with a circulation nudging fifty million. Most of the new titles are weekly free sheets depending on cheap advertising. The weekly titles which charge a cover price have shrunk in number as rapidly as their national counterparts. Though they charge more for advertising, on the grounds that they are more likely to be read, they are more expensive to produce, employing journalists to fill the space between advertisements. Most regional groups publish a mixture of free and paid-for newspapers.

Their advertising support has the twin advantages of being immune to erosion by national competitors and less sensitive to the trade cycle. Classified advertising is also easy to convert into new products like local telephone directories and Internet advertising services. Yet they have remained sufficiently local to extend into new ventures of a more provincial kind: football fanzines, news bulletins for local radio stations, and premium rate telephone services. The local franchises of both Channel One (the failed cable channel owned by the Daily Mail & General Trust) and Live TV (the Mirror Group equivalent) depended on the branding, news and advertising support of local newspaper groups. 'People are not interested in massacres in strange-sounding places a very long way away,' explained Kevin Mackenzie, when he was running Live TV. 'If you have someone talking about their prize tomatoes being ruined by vandals, it makes great television.'[42] Live TV opted for local rather than national news.

Triumph of the Consumer

Similar trends are discernible throughout the media. Everywhere, news has shifted from foreign affairs to domestic concerns; from politics to people; from issues to stories of human interest; and from information to entertainment. The only popular news programme on television is on Channel 5, where news is treated as entertainment. News at Ten, despite repackaging as an electronic tabloid, was shifted from its traditional slot because it obstructed the flow of entertainment. Some broadsheet newspapers employ cheap young reporters to cover the domestic crime and sex scandals their readers enjoy, and the rest of the newspaper is filled with signed columns of opinion – the cheapest copy of all. Better-class newspapers dispense passionate opinion rather than dispassionate news, and especially not foreign news.

This is odd, when foreign news was never easier to obtain. One of the curiosities of global communications is its failure to enlarge human understanding or sympathies. The 'global village', which media analysts have predicted since Marshall McLuhan broached the idea in 1962, has certainly come about, but in an unexpected form. Television pictures unite the world in horror (crash of an airliner) or sympathy (floods in Honduras) or grief (death of the Princess of the Wales) only where the larger story can be told on the local or human scale. The 'journalism of attachment', deployed with ambivalent results by Jonathan Dimbleby in Ethiopia and Martin Bell in Bosnia, panders to urges raised by tug-of-love, near-death and crime-and-punishment stories in local electronic villages such as Kelvin Mackenzie tried to create at Live TV, or those of the imagination, like *EastEnders* and *The Archers*.

Soap operas are depressingly representative of real life (with the understandable exception that nobody in them seems to watch television), making it hard to tell where television ends and life begins. Newspapers report the lives of characters in soap operas as if they were real people, and the lives of real people as if they were characters in a soap opera. Sportsmen and women, pop stars, 'It' girls, celebrities and publicity-seekers of all kinds have begun to act in real life as well as on the stage. Gazza wept; Amanda de Cadanet got pregnant; Liz Hurley wore a see-through dress. 'I did a lot of the things the tabloids said,' Chris Evans admits, 'but I always knew I was doing them.'[43]

In pursuit of the same life-as-news scoops, modern documentary makers eschew commentary in favour of recording the comments and actions of people as they do their daily work or vent their opinions. Entire programmes are now built around clips from police and CCTV cameras recording drunken drivers, bankrobbers and muggings. *Crimewatch* reconstructs crimes with an attention to detail just short of detective series such as *Poirot*. In so-called 'documentary soaps' (the trials of O. J. Simpson and Louise Woodward, for example) the difference between information and entertainment is deliberately blurred. The trials ceased to be judicial inquisitions and became metaphors for the state of race relations in America and the tensions between working mothers and their nannies.

Even viewers have become actors. One recent fly-on-the-wall documentary recorded a husband and wife shredding their marriage on prime-time television. Another recorded the moment of the death of a man. Several day-time shows rely entirely on the willingness of the audience to share their problems and grievances. The invention of the camcorder has allowed viewers to record the news themselves, and pass it to the broadcasters for transmission. The BBC has created an entire series, *Video Nation Shorts*, where people record and transmit their doings or opinions to the rest of the nation. On the Internet, people now broadcast their daily lives.

The consumer, not the producer, is taking control. A combination of technology and deregulation is shifting the balance of power from producers, editors and regulators to readers, listeners and viewers. In most industries, the shift would hardly be seismic, but ministers, regulators, producers and journalists are uneasy. The media is an industry where the authorities have limited the power of the sellers (until 1996, joint ownership of newspapers and television stations was banned) and restrained the appetites of the buyers. The liberal values of the British establishment have never extended to the creation of a marketplace in ideas, information and entertainment. Even Margaret Thatcher, reviled by both the television establishment and part of her own party for her addiction to the market, was not an advocate of free trade in the media. She was close in spirit to John Reith when she urged the BBC to 'uphold the great institutions and liberties of this country from which we all benefited' and set up the Broadcasting Standards Council to police the moral content of television programmes.[44]

Official control of the media remains extensive. When the European Commission explored media ownership in Europe in 1992, it found in Britain that
the two largest suppliers in each market controlled 89 per cent of television
broadcasting, 96 per cent of radio broadcasts, and 58 per cent of the newspapers: a relatively free press alongside a broadcasting market divided between
a monolithic, publicly funded broadcaster and a collection of privately owned
but publicly licensed advertising monopolies.[45] Not much has changed since.
Half the broadcasting market it still controlled by two public corporations
(the BBC and Channel 4); the rest is regulated heavily by the ITC. Public
officials still determine the content and timing of a large proportion of broadcasts. As recently as 1996, they effectively nationalised the transmission of
major sporting events by insisting they be shown on terrestrial television.
Television news still adheres to the public insistence on impartiality and
access, which accounts for its tedium.

These constraints, defensible in an era of wavelength scarcity, are now
nonsensical. Cable, satellite, telecommunications and digital technology have
multiplied the amount of room on the airwaves, and made it impossible to
exclude unwelcome interlopers. When the authorities gave BSB a monopoly
of satellite television (largely to safeguard 'standards'), News International
bypassed it by broadcasting into Britain via a Luxembourg-domiciled satellite.
Technology has also broken down the traditional distinctions between different forms of publication, making it impossible to exclude publishers from
television and broadcasters from newspapers. Information, entertainment and
communications can be converted into digital form, the language of computers. A digitised newspaper or feature film can be sent down a telephone
line and read or watched on a computer screen. A regulatory framework
designed for an era of wavelength scarcity and analogue technology no longer
corresponds to reality.

The Broadcasting Act of 1996 recognised this. It authorised the most sweeping changes in the ownership and structure of the media since the establishment of the BBC. The legislation shifted the emphasis of regulation, from
restricting companies to one technology to restricting their share of the total
market.[46] In theory, this would allow companies to merge and compete abroad
without diminishing competition or diversity at home. A string of takeovers
and mergers followed, especially in the television industry. For the first time
since the invention of the wireless, the means of delivery became irrelevant
to regulation. One gauge of the changes was the hostility of Rupert Murdoch.
'You come and nationalise me,' he told *The Money Programme*. 'I don't care,
you know, if you say get out of Britain, give the world to the BBC. What sort
of society do you really want?'[47] The old restrictions on media ownership,
though theoretically draconian, had not prevented News International from

accumulating a 40 per cent share of national newspaper circulation without any regulatory interference. Building the largest satellite broadcaster was even easier; he faced no restrictions at all on ownership.

Murdoch was not the only newspaper proprietor to find the British market more welcoming in practice than in theory. Although all major newspaper acquisitions were meant to be reviewed automatically by the MMC, only the purchase of the *Observer* by Tiny Rowland in 1981 ever suffered that indignity. In television, the rules were equally brittle. In the early 1980s, Robert Holmes à Court was allowed to purchase ACC (owner of the Central TV franchise) because it might otherwise have collapsed. In 1992 Yorkshire Television took over Tyne Tees because both companies were in financial difficulties. Yet it was not until November 1993, under pressure from Europe, that the government allowed an ITV contractor to own two franchises. Granada, Carlton and United News & Media then bought the major regional franchises which have given them their dominant position today – starting years before the rules relaxed in the 1996 Broadcasting Act.

The results of the restructuring are puzzling. In theory, a smaller group of larger media companies competing in a market expanded by new technologies ought to satisfy a broader range of tastes. Competition between them ought also to improve their contents, as publishers and broadcasters battle to retain an audience no longer captive. Instead, both broadsheets and red-top tabloids seem to be converging on the middle-class, middle-market, Middle England mean exploited by the *Daily Mail*. Commercial radio is little more than a cacophony of competing platforms for pop music promoters. The inflation of channels and broadcasting hours seems to have reduced television to a medley of game shows, compered by celebrity hosts dispensing gaudy prizes for answers to ludicrous questions.

The conventional explanation for this plunge downmarket is Rupert Murdoch. He brought to the British market an approach its traditional practitioners could not allow themselves: giving people what they want, rather than what they ought to want. He was able to buy the *Sun* from the owners of the *Daily Mirror* for virtually nothing because they did not know what to do with it. The *Mirror* then sold eight times as many copies as the *Sun*, but it has not out-sold the *Sun* since the mid-1970s. Murdoch achieved this by applying a simple formula. He and his first editor, Larry Lamb, grasped what readers were interested in – sex, television, sport and scandals. The *Sun* was the first British newspaper to be driven entirely by its readers.

To the extent that this is now true of British radio and television, Rupert Murdoch is the best explanation of the relentless low-mindedness of the media. But this is a short-sighted view, which ignores the fact that half of the broadcasting market is still under the direct sway of the state, and that television continues to reflect the values of the traditional broadcasting élite. Only television producers believe that women are the feistiest characters in life, or that court rooms are crammed with female barristers, or that every police station has at least one black or Asian PC. They have even injected a strong dose of metropolitan social realism into soap opera, with neither *Brookside* nor *EastEnders* shying away from frank portrayals of modern sexuality. When Jeremy Isaacs handed the chairmanship of Channel 4 to Michael Grade he told him: 'I am handing on to you a sacred trust. If you screw it up, if you betray it, I'll come back and throttle you.'[48]

Giving the readers, viewers and listeners what they want is the antithesis of this (bastardised) Reithian tradition. It has driven the high-minded into nostalgia for the days when the *Daily Herald* sought to elevate the working classes and television pursued a mission to explain rather than entertain. 'Thirty years ago,' wrote Christopher Dunkley, television critic of the *Financial Times*, 'television felt like the logical electronic outcome of an age of reason following centuries, even millennia, of superstition. Everyone knew that there was a lot of rubbish on the box – game shows, variety, soap operas – but that was seen largely as packing around the more important material, the sort of material which might create a uniquely well-informed society.'[49]

Humankind has nursed similar hopes since the spread of printing in the eighteenth century created the possibility of enlarging the popular mind through knowledge. But the high-minded are condemned always to be disappointed. As literacy has spread, the interests of the great mass of the public remain sex, sport and crime. The *News of the World* was thriving on tales of randy vicars and queer house-masters in the 1930s, and every inter-war household understood that the length of *The Times Law Reports* reflected the interest of readers in crime and sexual misdemeanours.

Cecil King, who ran the *Daily Mirror* in the 1960s, is regarded as a 'good' tabloid proprietor. But his 'mission to educate' the working classes, by filling the pages of the paper with patronising articles about the arts and sciences, was a contributing factor to the success of the *Sun*. Oddly, King had no illusions about what his readers wanted to read. 'Of course you have got to give the public what it wants, otherwise you go out of business,' he observed. 'The trouble is the critics imagine the great British public is as educated as themselves ... it is only the people who conduct newspapers and similar organisations who have any idea quite how indifferent, quite how stupid, quite how uninterested in education of any kind the great bulk of the British public are.'[50]

Broadcasters did not discover this until the 1990s. Where competition is absent, profits can still be earned without the need to subscribe to grubby commercial values. For decades, it made for a happy conjunction of material

self-interest and public duty in British broadcasting. But a combination of
Rupert Murdoch and new technology is demolishing the self-important world
of public service broadcasting. 'Much of what passes for quality on British
television really is no more than a reflection of the views of the narrow élite
which controls it and which has always thought that its tastes are synonymous
with quality,' Murdoch told an audience at the Edinburgh Television Festival
in August 1989. 'My own view is that anybody who, within the law of the land,
provides a service which the public wants at a price it can afford is providing
a public service.'

There is no need to be downcast at this reinterpretation of the meaning
of public service. One benefit of the absorption of consumers in the trivia
and tittle-tattle of popular newspapers and television is a truncation of the
power of the press. Despite the unforgiving opposition of virtually every newspaper in the country, John Major survived as prime minister for over six years.
It is true that he lost a great many ministers and MPs in a bewildering variety
of circumstances, but the obsession of the newspapers with petty parliamentary sex scandals and financial corruption is a measure not of the power of
the press but of its obeisance to the interests of readers, listeners and viewers.
Tony Blair was elected in 1997 by a landslide not because the *Sun* gave him
its support, or because the media had dissected and explained what New
Labour stood for, but because he looked and sounded the part and the public
wanted a new set of faces at the top.

The widespread ignorance of the public about matters of state is the fault
of the media, but marks a return by newspapers and broadcasters to their
true purpose. For much of the twentieth century, journalists and producers
worked to satisfy their own vanity and the power urges and self-esteem of
politicians and regulators. Today, the media is no longer a tool of the Establishment. It is the vehicle neither of despotism nor enlightenment; rather, it
is the reflection of a nation which has returned to the age of ignorance, in
which people know little of the world, and care even less about it. 'As to
politics, we were like the rest of the country people in England,' wrote William
Cobbett of his Surrey childhood in the 1760s. 'That is to say we neither knew
nor thought anything about the matter. The shouts of victory, and the murmur of defeat would now and then break in upon our tranquillity for a
moment, but I do not remember ever having seen a newspaper in the house,
and most certainly that privation did not render us less free, happy or industrious.'[51]

THE SPORTS BUSINESS

When I first came into football thirty years ago, it was all about eleven men kicking a ball. That was very nice but it isn't like that any more, it can't be.

REG BURR, chairman, Millwall FC[1]

I have not invested in a football club. I have invested in a company which owns one.

ALAN SUGAR[2]

Mr [Member] was strongly against coloured clothing and did not enjoy Sunday League cricket. He felt that the issue should continue to be raised on a regular basis in the hope of ultimately achieving the abolition of coloured clothing.

Minutes of AGM of Kent County Cricket Club, 4 March 1996[3]

You can't measure winning and losing on the enjoyment factor alone; it comes in the number of pound notes.

SCOTT GIBBS, Welsh Rugby Union Centre[4]

It is commonplace to describe sport as Big Business. There are reasons to doubt that it is big, but not that it is business. Sport is not merely the latest province to be annexed by the ubiquitous PLC. In its dependence on human capital, it rivals investment banking as the most up-to-date business of any quoted on the London Stock Exchange.[5] Sport is where the value of human capital is at its most elemental. The Fat Cats of the boardroom and the City may earn a lot of money, but consumers do not see or judge them at work. In sport, the performance of the players is judged ruthlessly and continually. Infinitesimal differences in ability or performance translate into massive differences in rewards. A thousandth of second, or a putt on the last, or a tie-break in the fifth, marks the difference between the also-ran and the star.

Best-Paid Sportsmen

Stars attract crowds of readers, viewers and spectators, and crowds attract advertisers and sponsors. In their working lives, sportsmen and women operate at the cusp where the worlds of business, media and entertainment meet. Like any booming market, their activities have attracted a horde of gold-diggers, in the shape of rich men, middlemen and marketing men. It is also making sports stars rich.

In 1997 Pierre van Hooijdonk, a Dutch international footballer playing for Glasgow Celtic, explained why he was turning down a new contract with the club worth £7,000 a week. 'That might be good enough for the homeless,' he explained, 'but it is certainly not enough for a top international striker.'[6] He had a point. Unlike Fat Cats, leading footballers are bought and sold in a genuine international marketplace. To lure the Italian striker Fabrizio Ravanelli to the north-east of England for the 1996–7 season, Middlesbrough paid £7 million and £42,000 a week.[7] The German striker, Jurgen Klinsmann, cost Tottenham Hotspur a relatively modest £24,000 a week during the 1994–5 season.[8] His two-year contract included a controversial opt-out clause which allowed him to spend the next two seasons at Bayern Munich. He returned to Tottenham at the start of the 1997–8 season, having let it be known that he expected £50,000 a week and his own helicopter before he would be tempted to return to the Premier League. He was reported finally to have agreed to play for Tottenham for £2.5 million a year (£48,000 a week). Defenders are almost as expensive. At Chelsea, the French international Marcel Desailly is said to earn £1.8 million (£35,000 a week).[9]

According to Deloitte & Touche, wages in the Premier League in 1997 *averaged* £193,000 a player. Today, a regular first-team footballer earns at least £300,000, and many twice as much, even before their earnings from product endorsements and corporate sponsorship. Until recently, Manchester United found it hard to attract top men because it capped its players' earnings at £23,000 a week. At neighbouring Liverpool, the England striker Robbie Fowler was said to have asked the club for £50,000 a week. As Alex Ferguson, the manager of Manchester United, has admitted: 'For most Premiership players, a year's pay is like a pools' win and for the top men it's just about a lottery win.'[10]

Exorbitant demands are understandable, for a football career is not long. Forwards such as Klinsmann, and even midfielders, are usually finished by the age of thirty-three. Defenders can last longer, but even goalkeepers rarely continue beyond forty. 'At the age of sixteen, you have to decide to abandon your studies and stake everything on a profession that offers no guarantees and no safety net it you fail,' says Frank Leboeuf, the 30-year-old Chelsea defender. 'You have to bet on your own qualities and, while the rewards are massive if you succeed . . . Injury can destroy your career in an instant and many do not have qualifications to do anything else.'[11]

The rewards may be understandable, but they are not economic. Wages and salaries now consume one half to two thirds of the income of leading football clubs. In recent years, they have risen faster than revenue, pushing all but a handful of clubs into chronic losses.[12] Alan Sugar, owner of Tottenham Hotspur, calls it the 'prune-juice effect': rising revenue from broadcasting contracts, merchandising and marketing goes straight through the bank accounts of clubs into the pockets of the players. Football really is like investment banking: a new form of capitalism in which the employees get so much money there is nothing left for the shareholders.

Yet the earnings of all but a handful of footballers are dwarfed by the incomes of successful boxers, golfers, tennis players and motor-racing drivers. When Damon Hill was asked to sign for another year with the Williams motor racing team, his price was £6 million. 'It's satisfactory,' he explained, 'I wouldn't call it more than that. It reflects my worth.'[13] *Forbes* magazine estimated that Michael Schumacher earned $45 million in 1997, and the world heavyweight champion, Evander Holyfield, made $54.5 million. This is partly because individual sports have an intrinsic advantage over team games. The money is spread over fewer competitors, with a handful of global superstars winning most of the prizes and scooping most of the endorsement income. In some sports – boxing and motor racing – the participants also collect danger money. Individual performances can also be measured easily, by the computer rankings, the Formula One league table or the decisive knock-out.[14]

Individual sportsmen and women are the clearest exemplars of winner-takes-all economics in the business of sport, because they translate a sometimes marginal superiority in ability into massive superiority in earning power. No spectator, viewer or corporate sponsor wants to pay for the second-best, when he can have the best. A tennis player can be one of the top fifty in the world without attracting a single corporate sponsor. To get on to the European golf tour, a player has to compete against four hundred others to play in the pre-qualifying tournaments. Once pre-qualified, he has to compete against another one hundred and eighty aspirants for the forty places on the tour. Yet the difference in ability among all of them can be measured in a handful of strokes.

The introduction to boxing of pay-per-view television, where viewers pay directly to see the best boxers fight, has persuaded promoters that big-name fighters will be able to demand $50 million every time they fight. The successful British boxer, Naseem Hamed, has signed a six-fight contract worth $12

TABLE 25.1
Britain's Best-Paid Sportsmen

		Est. Earnings* (£m)
Lennox Lewis	Boxing	6.4
Naseem Hamed	Boxing	5.8
Damon Hill	Motor Racing	5.3
Alan Shearer	Football	3.5
Nick Faldo	Golf	3.4
Johnny Herbert	Motor Racing	2.5
Ryan Giggs	Football	2.1
David Coulthard	Motor Racing	2.0
Colin Montgomerie	Golf	1.9
Paul Ince	Football	1.8

Source: Radio Five Live Sports Yearbook, 1998.

* Figures are for November 1996 to November 1997.

million with an American cable TV company. But then boxers have become rich from fighting and product endorsements ever since fisticuffs gave way to professional prize-fighting in the eighteenth century.[15] In other sports, lavish earnings are a relatively new phenomenon. Roger Bannister earned nothing for running the first four-minute mile. Jack Brabham was paid a retainer of £10 a year in the 1950s to win the equivalent of Formula One. In his best year – 1961 – Stirling Moss competed in fifty-five races and won only £32,700. Thirty years ago, the total prize pool at the first open Wimbledon was £26,150. Rod Laver received £2,000 for winning the men's singles, and Billie Jean King £750 as ladies' champion. In 1998, the pool was £7.2 million. The winner of the men's singles collected £435,000, and the ladies' champion £391,500.[16] In the 1930s and 1940s, a football legend, Stanley Matthews, travelled on a bus or train to a First Division match, carrying his own boots. Until 1961, professional footballers were paid a maximum wage of £20 a week in winter and £17 a week in summer. When the ceiling was lifted, the footballing public was shocked to discover that Johnny Haynes, leading star of the triumphant Fulham Football Club, thought he was worth £100 a week. Today, strikers drive to the match in a sponsored BMW and use their salaries to sledge pushy defenders in the penalty area. ('A mortgage?' runs one insult, 'What the fuck's that?').[17]

Rise of Player Power

Several factors have contributed to this explosion in earnings. The first is the discovery by players of player power. In football, the maximum wage was overturned in 1961 by Jimmy Hill and Cliff Lloyd, then chairman and secretary of the Professional Footballers' Association (PFA). Two years later the Victorian master–servant transfer system, in which footballers remained the property of their clubs even after their contracts expired, was ended when George Eastham successfully challenged Newcastle United in the courts. This freed footballers to sell their talents, and created the modern transfer market. Complete freedom of contract was achieved in 1995 when the European Court, in the Bosman judgment, prevented clubs from hampering the movement of players by demanding transfer fees for those whose contracts had expired.[18]

Although lawn tennis professionals have existed for many years (the late Dan Maskell was a professional throughout his career), tennis players did not make a serious attempt to wrest control of the game from amateurs and promoters until the Association of Tennis Professionals (ATP) was formed in 1972. It took another eighteen years before the ATP secured control of the international game. Cricket and rugby union players had to wait for outside intervention before they could demand a higher price. Cricketers were so badly paid that Kerry Packer was able to sign them by the dozen for his World Series Cricket in 1977. They were all promptly banned from playing Test cricket by the International Cricket Council, which took the issue to court rather than concede the principle of player power. Packer was poised to do the same for rugby union when the International Rugby Football Board suddenly decided in 1995 to let the game go professional. In athletics, underhand payments were so pervasive by the early 1980s that Sebastian Coe complained of a 'situation which makes honest men dishonest'. The authorities caved in and allowed athletes to be openly professional.[19] Even the staid world of chess was not unruffled by the rise of player power. In 1993 the World chess federation, Fide, accepted a bid for the match between Nigel Short and Garry Kasparov which the players thought too low. They set up their own Professional Chess Federation, and signed a £1.7 million sponsorship deal with *The Times*.

The Football Transfer Market

The effects of free movement of labour on the value of footballers was immense. In 1947 Blackpool could secure Stanley Matthews for £11,590 and a bottle of whisky; fifty years later Newcastle United had to pay Blackburn Rovers £15 million for Alan Shearer, and the player a signing-on fee of £500,000 and a guaranteed annual salary of £1.5 million for five years.[20] But not only superstars can exploit the value of their talents: in both 1992 and 1996 members of the Professional Footballers' Association used a strike threat to boost the share of television revenues to clubs in the lower divisions.[21] It cannot be long before football hosts its first American-style strike by millionaire players against multi-millionaire owners.[22]

One in five professional footballers change clubs every year through transfer or loan.[23] Mobility is the distinctive characteristic of human capital; it cannot be monopolised by a single employer. This presents all professional team sports with a dilemma. Unlike individual sports, their economics have a peculiarity: competitors do not seek complete domination of their opponents. Audiences demand matches where the contestants are evenly matched, and the outcome is uncertain. To prevent the richest teams monopolising the most talented players, the sports authorities traditionally restricted remuneration and freedom of movement of players.[24] The abolition of the maximum wage, freedom of contract and the Bosman ruling of 1995 have made this impossible. The changes ought to have put an end to massive transfer fees, and encouraged clubs to sign players for longer periods at higher salaries.[25]

In fact, the transfer market has continued to grow. The top clubs in the Premier League, who lavished £68 million on new players in 1995, spent £80 million in 1996 and over £100 million in 1997. But most of the traffic was between clubs in the Premiership, and between Premiership clubs and their counterparts abroad (especially in Europe). By 1998, one hundred and forty-one players from thirty-six different countries were registered. On an average Saturday, perhaps seventy out of two hundred and twenty players who take the field in the Premier League are neither British nor Irish. This is worrying for the smaller clubs in the Football League, which have long relied on nurturing players they can sell to larger clubs for a fat transfer fee. They have not only lost transfer fees for out-of-contract players, but have to compete with clubs abroad to sell their talent to the Premier League.[26] Unless the price of foreign stars persuades Premiership clubs that cheaper domestic players are better value, the football authorities will have to find another way of redistributing income between the Premiership and the lower leagues.

A booming transfer market has also heightened interest in ways of valuing

TABLE 25.2
The Twenty Most Expensive Transfers in British Football

	Seller	Buyer	Price (£m)
Alan Shearer	Blackburn Rovers	Newcastle United	15.0
Dwight Yorke	Aston Villa	Manchester United	12.6
Juninho	Middlesbrough	Atletico Madrid	12.0
Jaap Stam	PSV Eindhoven	Manchester United	10.6
Stan Collymore	Nottingham Forest	Liverpool	8.5
Andrei Kanchelskis	Everton	Fiorentina	8.0
Dennis Bergkamp	Inter Milan	Arsenal	7.5
Faustino Asprilla	Parma	Newcastle	7.5
Kevin Davies	Southampton	Blackburn	7.5
Stan Collymore	Liverpool	Aston Villa	7.0
Paul Merson	Middlesbrough	Aston Villa	7.0
Marc Overmars	Ajax	Arsenal	7.0
Fabrizio Ravanelli	Juventus	Middlesbrough	7.0
Paul Ince	Manchester United	Inter Milan	7.0
Andy Cole	Newcastle United	Manchester United	7.0
Les Ferdinand	Queen's Park Rangers	Newcastle United	6.0
Les Ferdinand	Newcastle United	Tottenham Hotspur	6.0
Henning Berg	Blackburn Rovers	Manchester United	5.5
David Platt	Aston Villa	Bari	5.5
Paul Gascoigne	Tottenham Hotspur	Lazio	5.5

Source: *The Times.*

players. Ahead of its flotation in 1991, Manchester United invited the accountants Touche Ross to produce an independent valuation of its players. The
number-crunchers came up with a figure of £24 million, which increased
steadily in line with the rising performance of the team to a peak of £35
million before the Bosman judgment temporarily depressed values.[27] Other
quoted companies have had to make similar valuations, which are not as
arbitrary as is popularly supposed. About £4 in every £5 of a transfer fee can
be accounted for by objective factors like age, position and international
experience, the timing of the transfer, and the respective performances in
the league of the club buying and the club selling. The rest depends on
subjective assessment.[28] This is especially true of younger players, where prices
reflect expectations as well.

Spectactular mistakes can be made. In 1979 Manchester City paid Wolverhampton Wanderers £1.4 million for a player, setting a new record for transfer fees. Fifteen months later, the club sold him to the Seattle Sounders for just £300,000.[29] But as players get more expensive, and football clubs become PLCs, it is important to eliminate errors of this kind. In 1997, for example, three Brazilians cost European clubs £12 million (Rivaldo), £16.5 million (Ronaldo) and £22 million (Denilson) respectively. These are sums large enough to imperil the survival of a club if they prove unrealistic. When Alan Shearer was stretchered off the pitch during a match against Chelsea in 1997, it wiped nearly £10 million off the market value of Newcastle United.[30] In November that year, an investment bank reckoned that Tottenham Hotspur, a quoted company, had destroyed £13.5 million of shareholder value by buying too many older players at inflated prices.[31] A year later the club reported a £1 million deficit due to a £7.1 million loss on trading players.

How Sportsmen Became Brands

The players (unlike the shareholders) were unaffected. Their worth is no longer set solely by their performance on the field. All leading sportsmen and women employ agents, whose job it is to maximise their value in the market for products and services seeking their endorsement. (When he joined Newcastle United, Alan Shearer was already collecting £4 million in product endorsements.)[33] Agents are relatively new in sport. The prototypical agent was Mark McCormack, whose pioneering efforts earned him the dual accolade of a Harvard Business School case study and a place in *The Times* list of the thousand makers of the twentieth century. His first client was the golfer, Arnold Palmer, a sensible choice. Golf was commercial even before the last war, as equipment manufacturers battled to sell clubs and balls to wealthy golf club members. Prize money in the PGA Tour was more than $1 million in 1958. McCormack alighted on Arnold Palmer because he had noticed that golfers made most of their money from appearance fees and product endorsements. He realised that Palmer was a *brand* as well as a sportsman. By 1967 he could write of his first client:

> There is no precedent for a sports figure becoming the centre of the kind of merchandising empire that now surrounds Arnold Palmer . . . It is now possible not only to play your golf with Palmer clubs, while dressed from cleat to umbrella tip in Palmer clothes . . . but to have the Palmer image at your elbow in countless other ways. You can buy your insurance from a Palmer agency, stay in a Palmer-owned motel, buy a Palmer lot to build your home on, push a Palmer-approved lawn mower,

read a Palmer book, newspaper column or pamphlet, be catered to by a Palmer maid, listen to Palmer music and send your suit to a Palmer dry cleaner. You can shave with his lather, spray on his deodorant, drink his favourite soft drink, fly his preferred airline, buy his approved corporate jet, eat his candy bar, order your stock certificates through him and cut up wood with his power tools.[34]

In the 1960s this was new. The legendary baseball player, Babe Ruth, was a sporting millionaire – but from earnings as a player. When a cunning entrepreneur launched a candy bar called Babe Ruth, the great man saw not a cent of the profits.[35]

Today, the sportsman as brand is commonplace. The basketball player Michael Jordan, the tennis players Fred Perry and Bjorn Borg, and the golfer Greg Norman have all had ranges of clothing and accessories named after them. Ayrton Senna, the Brazilian motor racing driver killed in Italy in 1994, has achieved immortality by lending his name to a range of luxury goods far removed from the race track: his martyrdom to his sport has merely increased his selling power. To be a successful sporting brand, it is not good enough simply to win. Frank Bruno found that, with a winning personality, even a relatively unsuccessful heavyweight can secure valuable endorsements. Gareth Southgate, briefly notorious for missing the deciding penalty in the Euro 96 semi-final against Germany in June 1996, found advertisers flocking to make use of his unfortunate mistake. Tony Underwood, the England wing three-quarter brushed aside by Jonah Lomu in the semi-final of the 1995 rugby World Cup, turned his embarrassment to commercial advantage by making it into a television advertisement.

Different characters are needed to shift different products. Nick Faldo told Stephen Aris that his earnings increased much more slowly than he had expected after winning the British Open in 1987. 'I think the sponsors were waiting to say how I turned out as a personality,' he explained. 'They look at everything – it's frightening really. They want to see how marketable you are.'[36] Someone like Faldo is perfect for selling Bourbon sweaters and tassled golf shoes, but hopeless for selling lager and sportswear. The television advertising of a popular brand of crisps depends on mocking the wholesome image of the former England striker, Gary Lineker. Eric Cantona's value to sponsors rose after a conviction for assault.

The market in which stars like Lineker and Cantona are sold is vast. In 1996 (admittedly an Olympic year) corporate sponsorship of sport totalled £10 billion. Unsurprisingly, the success of Mark McCormack in a market of these dimensions has attracted a host of imitators. The number of sports agents and marketing firms has exploded from less than a dozen in the 1980s to about five hundred today. The International Management Group (IMG) founded by McCormack is still the largest, employing a staff of thousands in fields which now extend far beyond those of sport. It turns over $1 billion in a good year and its two main rivals, Interpublic and Marquee, the same between them. They operate everywhere, in every sport. Like most middle-men, they are regarded by players and sports authorities alike as parasitic, exploitative and corrupting. Conflicts of interest are certainly an everyday part of their work – taking fees from both stars and sponsors is routine. Their responsibility to deliver a star to a sponsor is often more valuable than their duty to their client. In football, clubs are known to have paid agents to persuade their stars to stay (or leave).[37] Agents also invent 'events' to reward their clients.

TV Makes Them Rich

What makes this possible is television. Televised sport delivers massive audiences, which makes it valuable to companies. Television enables everybody to see the best sportsmen and women in the world, every day. The World Cup football finals attract television audiences measured in billions. The 1966 World Cup finals generated just over £2 million, almost all of it from ticket sales. Thirty years later the smaller Euro 96 football championships generated revenue of over £150 million, and only one third came from ticket sales. The bulk was supplied by eleven official corporate sponsors, each of which paid £3.5 million for the privilege; the rest came from a list of second and third tier sponsors. Yet another company purchased sole rights to manufacture official T-shirts, baseball caps and other merchandise associated with the competition. The price of a thirty-second television commercial during the England games started at £50,000.

Formula One motor racing is entirely the creation of television and corporate sponsorship, and would cease to exist without it. Twenty-five years ago, hardly anyone watched it. Though it defies the peculiar economics of sport (the McLaren drivers always win the races), a Grand Prix now rivals the Olympics and World Cup football in its ability to command the attention of a worldwide television audience. Formula One has made Bernie Ecclestone rich precisely because he was astute enough to secure the sale of broadcasting rights when they were cheap. His organisation now claims a cumulative global television audience of over fifty billion, with over five billion people watching the races – three hundred and fifty million viewers per Grand Prix.[38] Because the races happen every year, Formula One attracts £1 in every £3 of corporate sponsorship. It is a natural host for car manufacturers and oil companies, and has given the tobacco companies one of their few television outlets. In 1993 ITV paid £70 million to poach the rights to Formula One races from the BBC. Four years later, when Ecclestone investigated the possibility of selling his interest in the worldwide broadcasting and commercial rights, estimates of its value ranged up to $4 billion.

Competition for broadcasting rights has injected more money into sport than any other factor. Until the 1990s, the BBC and ITV shared football, and ITV left golf, rugby union, tennis and cricket exclusively to the BBC. This allowed the BBC to take a high-minded view of advertising and sponsorship. It restricted the amount of perimeter advertising, and refused to screen a football match where players wore advertising slogans on their shirts. In 1987 it was confident enough to ban all tobacco-sponsored sport from its screens.[39] In the days of the BBC–ITV duopoly, ordinary league football matches were not shown live (it might reduce gate receipts) and *The Big Match* was shown at a different time from *Match of the Day*. Without competition from satellite or cable television, football had no means of forcing either company to try harder, let alone pay more. When ITV finally broke ranks and made an abortive bid for exclusive broadcasting rights in 1979 (the tabloids called it 'Snatch of the Day'), it was ruled against the public interest by the Office of Fair Trading (OFT). Subsequent efforts by the Football League to force ITV and the BBC to compete further reinforced the duopoly: there was no football on television through the first half of the 1985–6 season.

It was not until 1987, when the now-defunct British Satellite Broadcasting (BSB) offered to double the £3 million a year the BBC and ITV were paying to televise football, that the League realised the true value of the game to television. The Football League pushed up its price to £11 million a year for the next four years[40] and, when that deal expired, the duopoly snapped. In 1992, BSkyB and the BBC paid £304 million for the right to broadcast two matches a week for four years. By 1995, the price of a four-year contract had risen to £670 million from BSkyB for live matches and £73 million from the BBC for the right to show highlights. Even these sums are said to be about half the value of the rights to broadcast matches on a pay-per-view basis.[41]

Other sports have made similar discoveries. In 1994 the BBC and BSkyB struck a four-year deal with the Test and County Cricket Board to broadcast home Test matches and domestic games. At £58.5 million, it was worth nearly four times as much as the previous contract. In 1998, when the government lifted the requirement that all home Test matches be shown on terrestrial television, BSkyB and Channel Four raised the price to £103 million. The rights to broadcast the forty-two one-day matches of the 1999 cricket World Cup, being played in England, cost BSkyB and the BBC another £9 million.

In 1996 (and again in 1999) the English Rugby Football Union (RFU) found itself temporarily expelled from the Five Nations tournament after the Scots, Welsh and Irish unions objected to its general share of revenues from a five-year exclusive deal to broadcast all England international matches at Twickenham on BSkyB. The contract was worth £87.5 million, or three times the £27 million the BBC had paid for its previous five-year deal. England was not allowed back into the Five Nations until it agreed to share the loot with other countries: it proved difficult to agree an appropriate division of the spoils, and the row rumbled on for three years. Nearly £90 million was a large sum of money for a sport whose genuine following is measured in the hundreds of thousands rather than the millions, but its value to advertisers lies less in the size of the audience than its quality. Rugby Union delivers the highly desirable A and B groups of professionals, as Allied Dunbar confirmed in a £12 million sponsorship deal with English rugby in April 1997. The company explained that it had 'looked at golf, cricket and the arts but found rugby has the right ABC1 profile.'[42]

Television Corrupts Sport

Sport has struck a Faustian pact with television. By moving major sporting events from the terrestrial channels, it has sacrificed fans for cash and drawn the government into regulating the transmission of sports events. (There is now a list of so-called 'national' events – like the Derby and the FA Cup Final – which the government insists are shown on terrestrial television.) More worryingly, television broadcasters and the corporate sponsors and advertisers they rely on for revenue now 'own' the sports they broadcast in a way they did not when televising the First Division cost the BBC–ITV duopoly £3 million a year. They screen entire events dreamed up to meet the needs of corporate sponsors. Through skilful editing, television detects the 'hand of God', the sand in the pocket, and the foot in touch. It manufactures personalities to produce synthetic excitement. Television is turning sport into a branch of the entertainment industry, in which topless darts players and meaningless contests are all part of the fun. Television values are showbiz values, and they are changing the nature of sport .

   The penalty shoot-out is bad football (it is usually preceded by two hours of playing-for-penalties) but great television. In tennis, the tie-break and the abolition of the advantage rule are both designed to produce quicker results. In cricket, the qualities which make it fascinating to play (the slow pace at which a game unfolds, coupled with sharp changes in fortune) and the virtues it rewards (discipline, intelligence, patience) are those which television abhors. One-day matches, played in pyjamas, at night and under new rules, with coloured balls and microphones in the stumps, were invented solely to meet the demands of broadcasters. One reason English cricket is getting a two-division county championship from the year 2000 is the need to increase their interest.

In rugby union, the televisual need for continuity has persuaded the authorities to adjust refereeing techniques to allow the team in possession to keep the ball, if necessary by infringing in scrums, line-outs and rucks. Rugby union matches are coming to resemble their rugby league counterparts, with players strung out across the field as the man with the ball attempts to batter his way through the defence with little risk of losing possession. Television has also persuaded the rugby authorities to authorise inflation of the number of international matches, introduce a European competition in 1996, and propose the creation of a new British league which takes in Welsh and Scottish teams.

Sam Chisholm, the former chief executive of BSkyB, is reported to have tried to change the rules of football to produce more goals.[43] But no sport has sold its soul to television more completely than rugby league. In April 1995 the Rugby Football League scrapped the entire structure of the game in favour of a new Super League funded by an £87.5 million five-year contract with BSkyB. This entailed creating brand-new teams in Paris and London, amalgamations between existing teams, a switch from a winter to a summer season, and traffic in matches and players between Britain and Australia. In effect, Rupert Murdoch took ownership of the sport. Despite his millions, and funding from other tycoons, the game has failed to broaden its appeal and the television contract was re-negotiated on less generous terms in 1998.[44]

Athletics, too, has experienced the destructive power of television. There never was much money in the sport, but it enjoyed remarkable popularity in Britain in the late 1970s and early 1980s, especially after it became openly professional in 1982. The success of household names encouraged broadcasters and corporate sponsors to pour money into athletics. In 1984, it abandoned a longstanding relationship with the BBC and signed up with ITV, quadrupling its income with a five-year deal worth £10.5 million. This sum, five times the £2 million the BBC had paid for the previous contract, was described by the general secretary of the Amateur Athletics Association as 'the biggest sports deal ever in Britain'.[45] Three sponsors (Pearl Assurance, Kodak and Peugeot-Talbot) chipped in another £5 million to plaster their logos over twenty-odd televised athletics events and an audience estimated at one hundred million viewers.[46] Leading athletes of the time – Steve Cram (Kellogg's), Sebastian Coe (Horlicks) and Daley Thompson (Lucozade) – found manufacturers queueing for their endorsement.

The wave of commercialisation was lucrative and exciting, but it cost athletics its innocence. Organisers of meetings had to pay appearance fees to attract the big names to interest the broadcasters, so that the broadcasters could interest the sponsors.[47] Middle-distance races proliferated because television likes contests neither too short, nor too long. The authorities were indifferent about the use of performance-enhancing drugs. Bogus events were staged, purely for the cameras. In 1985 Zola Budd was paid £90,000 to race Mary Decker Slaney at Crystal Palace, in an unsavoury attempt to capitalise on television footage of Budd tripping the American in a race at the Los Angeles Games a year earlier. Little of the money which poured into athletics was invested in nurturing the athletes of the future. Britain won a solitary gold medal at the Atlanta Olympics of 1996, and one at the World Championships a year later. Television, having exploited athletics in the good times, abandoned it in the bad times. By the time ITV relinquished the broadcasting rights in 1996, it was screening just seven athletics events a year. Channel Four took over, but offered only £4 million for a four-year contract. In October 1997 the British Athletic Federation went bankrupt, its largest liabilities being unpaid appearance fees owed to athletes. Athletics officials have now promised to reduce the number of meetings, heats, disciplines and winners, cut out uninteresting events like triple-jump, and remove the clutter of high-jumpers, hammer-throwers and shot-putters which crowd the television screen during a middle-distance race. What money athletics attracts now goes largely to subsidise coaching and training world-class athletes, in the hope of creating a new generation of television stars. It may work. Britain won nine gold medals at the European Championships in Budapest in 1998 and television has already fallen in love with the comely heptathlete, Denise Lewis.

This concentration on a handful of telegenic stars is characteristic of every sport now. Television viewers and advertisers are interested only in the best, not the second-best. They want to see Linford Christie and Sally Gunnell at the Olympics, not A. N. Other on a windy afternoon at Gateshead. Money gravitates towards the stars. The same is true of team-games. Most of the broadcasting revenues pouring into rugby union go to the Premiership One clubs and players. But in no sport is the divide between the stars and the also-rans wider than in association football. The Premier League is effectively the creation of television. The leading clubs of the old First Division had often threatened to break away from the Football League unless they were given a larger share of the proceeds of broadcasting rights. It was when ITV was excluded from the first satellite deal for football television rights in 1988 that the idea of the Premiership surfaced as a serious proposition. Its chief advocate was the television mogul and Manchester United director, Greg Dyke, then at London Weekend Television. In a bid to guarantee some football for ITV, he tried to persuade the leading clubs to extricate themselves from the deal the Football League was concluding with BSB and give exclusive rights to broadcast their games to ITV.

'What hadn't been foreseen,' remarked Gordon Taylor, secretary of the PFA, 'was that when we broke up the television cartel, any loser in that cartel would turn round and try to break up the League.'[48] In the event, the Football League readmitted ITV rather than see the league break up. But the idea did not go away: the Premier League was set up in 1992, the year the television contract came up for sale. This was not a coincidence.

Commercialisation

In 1989 Stephen Aris suggested to Mark McCormack that his influence over tennis and golf was ruining the games. 'All these evils they talk about: the conflicts, the guarantees, the signing of young players, the wild cards, whatever,' he replied. 'You've got a sport that has sky-rocketed, higher prize money, bigger attendances ... What's everybody complaining about? I tell you what: the same sort of thing should happen to British football.'[49] Eight years on, it has.

At the time McCormack spoke, football was in steep decline. At the height of its popularity after the last war, in the 1948–9 season, the members of the Football League sold 41.3 million tickets to football fans. Forty years later, they were selling just 18.5 million. Television, scruffy facilities, hooliganism and tragedies like those at Bradford, the Heysel Stadium and Hillsborough, had all contributed to a catastrophic decline. By the end of the 1980s, four out of five clubs in the Football League were technically insolvent. The most successful club in Britain today, Manchester United, was severely in the red.[50] A decade later, everything and nothing has changed. Manchester United certainly makes money, and the smaller clubs which share a public quotation on the London Stock Exchange certainly lose it, but it is hard to tell whether any or all of the pack of clubs at the top of the Premier League are profitable or not. The Premiership clubs as a whole reported collective pre-tax losses of £66 million in 1996, and over £4 million in 1997.[51] Even Tottenham Hotspur, the most consistently profitable club in the Premiership, reports occasional losses which force it to pass a dividend.

In the lower divisions, which have to share barely £1 in every £3 which flows into modern football, the seventy-two clubs in the Football League are almost all in serious difficulties.[52] The Division One clubs reported a collective loss of £19 million in 1996 and £27 million in 1997.[53] Many of the smallest clubs in Divisions Two and Three are teetering on the brink of financial collapse, and some have fallen over. Bournemouth went into receivership in January 1997, and had to be rescued by its supporters. A month later, the accountants Coopers & Lybrand declared another forty clubs technically insolvent.[54] Many are so poor that the PFA (the players' trade union) subsidises the wage bill.

An ability to lose money is about all that football clubs have in common today. There is now a vast and growing differential between the incomes of clubs in the Premier League and those in the three divisions of the Football League, and between the most successful and the least successful clubs in the Premier League. Since its formation in 1992–3, the average turnover of the clubs in the top flight has more than doubled. The rising revenues from television are being diverted from the game as a whole, towards its exceptional clubs. The cause of the diversion is television. Payments under the BSkyB and BBC contracts are tilted not only towards Premier League clubs, but to the most successful clubs within it.[55] Sunderland reckoned its income from television had fallen by at least £1 million after relegation from the Premier League, even after the £1.7 million 'parachute' which the Premier League pays to relegated teams for their first two years in the First Division. When the club lost a play-off match against Charlton Athletic the following May, condemning it to a second year in the Football League, the Sunderland share price fell by almost as much (20 per cent) as the Charlton share price rose (23 per cent). As Sunderland chairman Bob Murray said at the time, 'the play-off was a lottery with a £10 million jackpot.'[56]

'The base of the pyramid is eroding,' admits Gordon Taylor, head of the PFA. 'Unless we are prepared to strengthen it there is no use throwing money at the apex. We must control the commercialisation of the game.'[57] This is unlikely to happen. The best guess is that the inequality between Premiership and Football League clubs will get worse. Only the top clubs can aspire to compete in Europe, where the rewards from television and the accompanying corporate sponsorship are higher still. The Premiership champions and runners-up qualify for the European Champions' League, whose lucrative structure guarantees at least three home games even if a club is knocked out at the first hurdle. The competition was worth £60 million to the sixteen clubs (now twenty-four) which took part in it in 1997, and they shared about half its gross revenues of £155 million a year later. One measure of its value is the £25 million fall in the market capitalisation of Manchester United the day after it was knocked out of the competition by AS Monaco in March 1998.[58] Other leading teams take part in a knock-out competition organised by UEFA, and the winners of the FA Cup contest the European Cup Winners' Cup. Both these lesser competitions pay less than the European Champions' League, mainly because it is not possible to tie sponsorship and advertising to a match which is not certain to take place. Winning either of them is, however, worth at least £3 million in extra revenues.

Participation in European competition matters because it delivers additional revenue from television. The sale of television rights alone can make progression to the semi-finals of a European competition worth as much as £10 million to a Premier League club. Yet the leading clubs reckon they could collect even more if UEFA did not share the proceeds of the Champions' League with its marketing agency, the national football associations and the clubs knocked out in the earlier rounds of other European competitions. This was why Manchester United, Arsenal and Liverpool were prepared to talk to Media Partners, a Milan-based sports marketing agency which proposed a breakaway European Super League involving the top thirty-six clubs in Europe. Fearful of losing its flagship competition, UEFA agreed to expand the Champions' League to thirty-two teams and to merge the UEFA and Cup Winners' Cup competitions to create a second competition for another one hundred clubs. The financial forecasts suggest that the two competitions will be worth £350 million, but Media Partners reckoned its proposals could generate £1 billion a year.[59]

A European Super League would not be welcome to lesser-known Premier League teams. 'Manchester United do not want to play Wimbledon,' the Wimbledon chairman Sam Hammam told *Sun* readers in 1996. 'They want to play Real Madrid, Barcelona or AC Milan. . . . There are hundreds of Wimbledons – do we really want those clubs to disappear? The game has become obsessed with money and power.'[60] It is an iron law of sporting economics that fewer and better games raise revenue. The original impetus behind the reform of the Football League was that too many games were either minor events or non-events. Liverpool versus Arsenal was a national event; Torquay versus Exeter was a regional event; but Torquay versus Carlisle was a non-event. This was why the top twenty-two teams in the English first division broke away from the Football League and formed the Premier League. Their counterparts in Scotland followed and set up a Scottish Premier League.

In England, the original aim of the Premier League was to reduce the size of the First Division and introduce regional football leagues in the lower divisions. The new top flight would stage fewer but better matches in more comfortable surroundings, and so attract more income from the sale of seats, television rights, corporate sponsorship, books, videos, replica kits and conference and catering facilities. Although it did not at first appear to change anything at all (despite the BSkyB slogan, 'It's a Whole New Ball Game') the Premier League has achieved this. The problem is that the first, second and third divisions have not adopted regional leagues. They are playing more matches, in the hope that higher gate receipts will compensate for lower subsidies.[61] 'You cannot possibly kid yourself that the country needs ninety-two football league clubs,' the late Matthew Harding, part-owner of Chelsea, told a journalist in 1995. 'What is wrong with regional leagues and semi-professionals? Clubs need to live within their means and be properly under-pinned.'[62]

In 1997 fifty-eight out of seventy-two clubs in the Football League lost money. To rescue them, plans for a smaller number of national leagues or a larger number of regional leagues are advanced from time to time, without agreement being reached on a solution. An alternative is to turn the smaller clubs into subsidiaries of the major clubs, nurturing younger players for eventual elevation to the Premier League. Clubs in the lower divisions have long relied on transfer fees from selling players to the top clubs to balance their books; they already act, in a sense, as human capital factories for the leading clubs. The rising salaries of foreign stars are rejuvenating interest in home-grown talent, and turning the Football League into a nursery is one way of ensuring rising revenues from broadcasting contracts, sponsorship and the sale of merchandise would be redistributed.

Retailing of replica kits, mugs, scarves and other paraphernalia is the most rapidly growing source of revenue for Premier League football clubs.[63] Although sales of replica shirts have dipped in recent years, *Match* reckons fans spent £8 million on them at the height of the boom in 1995. When Newcastle United signed Alan Shearer in 1996, the club sold five hundred replicas of his No 9 shirt in the first couple of hours, at £44 apiece. Arsenal sold ten thousand Dennis Bergkamp shirts at £50.89 each before the Dutch striker had played a single game for the club. The fan-as-shopper is at least as important as the fan-as-supporter.

Thirty years ago, gate receipts accounted for virtually all the income of football clubs. Today, a Premier League club such as Wimbledon can get by with virtually no fans. Those who watch live football account for only £2 in every £5 earned by the game. Even at Old Trafford, where the crowds are the largest and every home game yields a profit of £1 million, Manchester United earns only one third of its revenues from ticket sales. The rest comes from television rights, sponsorships, merchandising, catering, and conference suites. There is a gigantic store alongside the stadium, selling replica kits, bedspreads, videos, bibs, even Manchester United whisky, wine, chocolate and crisps. The club is now pondering a chain of Red Cafés modelled on the original at Old Trafford, and there is a museum, which attracts one hundred and fifty thousand visitors a year. Manchester United, Glasgow Rangers, Aston Villa, Leeds United and Chelsea have all built or plan to build hotels adjacent to their stadiums. Some sell credit cards, car and home insurance and even investment plans to fans.

Clubs such as Newcastle United have become international sports brands in their own right. Their followers (like their players) are drawn from around the world, and it is purely a historical accident that they have any connection with large industrial cities in England or Scotland. Manchester United has over three million fans around the world. Their loyalty to the brand is not in doubt. Trevor Phillips, former commercial director of the Football Association, says football clubs have a 'brand loyalty that firms in most other industries would die for,' and Alan Sugar describes football as a 'genetic brand, passed from father to son.'[65] This has persuaded some politicians that football clubs need government regulation to prevent them from exploiting their fans with higher ticket prices and over-priced merchandise. 'Football', as Hugh McIlvanney of the *Sunday Times* puts it, 'is one of the few areas of business that give scope for the legal exploitation of addiction. Fans, by definition, are . . . captive customers.'[66]

One of the earliest measures taken by the New Labour government was the establishment in July 1997 of a Football Task Force, chaired by former Conservative minister and football pundit David Mellor, to explore whether people were being priced out of the People's Game. It examined the effects of clubs becoming PLCs, whether replica kits are overpriced or changed too frequently, and especially whether match-day and season ticket prices are too high. To encourage voluntary change, the government issued a veiled threat to set up a new regulatory authority. It is right to doubt whether the bodies running British football are independent custodians of the public good, when they have become businesses in their own right. The first division of the Football League is sponsored by Nationwide; non-League football calls itself the Vauxhall Conference; and the Isthmian League has become the Ryman League. The Premier League is sponsored to the tune of £36 million over four years by Bass (brewers of Carling lager). There are Premier League publications, a Premier League breakfast cereal, and even Premier League crisps. The Football Association, which has retained control of the FA Cup and the England team, earns £50 million a year from television rights and the FA Cup Final – but also from five corporate sponsors. Even the FA Cup, that sacred symbol of the openness of British football to allcomers, is now the Littlewoods FA Cup.

Football Clubs as PLCs

The growing commercialisation of football has attracted the interest of the City. Investors want a slice of the (as yet elusive) profits generated by top-flight football, while clubs welcome their money to invest in players and facilities. All the leading City fund managers have invested directly in football shares. When the Singer & Friedlander merchant bank launched a mutual fund specialising in football, it received 800,000 applications for the prospectus. 'Manchester United is probably one of the strongest brands in the UK, right up there with Marks & Spencer or Heinz,' say the stockbrokers to the club.[67] Twenty-five British clubs are traded publicly, with their number being swelled by Continental rivals and other British clubs. The Sunderland issue was nearly three times over-subscribed; Newcastle United, which followed in March 1997, was over-subscribed sevenfold. But the City was not always so enthusiastic. When Manchester United floated in June 1991, less than half the shares were taken up. Investors had good reason to be cautious. The first football club to float on the stock market (Millwall) ended up in the hands of the receivers and the second (Tottenham Hotspur) had to be rescued by Alan Sugar.

The change in City sentiment reflects more than the financial potential of the Premier League. Investors are impressed by the new type of owner-managers who can treat a football club as a business as well as a personal enthusiasm. In 1981 Martin Edwards caused general hilarity by describing himself as 'chief executive' of Manchester United. Football is now filled with successful businessmen who see the sport as a sensible (if long-term) invest-ment opportunity. In 1989 Edwards was willing to sell his stake in Manchester United to Michael Knighton for £10 million. By 1997, with the Premier League in its fifth season, a much-reduced personal stake was worth £64 million.[68] David Dein was assured by the Arsenal chairman Peter Hill-Wood that the £330,000 he put into the club in 1983 was 'dead money'. A decade later Hill-Wood admitted the investment was worth as least ten times as much.[69]

Business benefits radiate beyond the value of the club itself. Sugar saw Tottenham Hotspur as a useful marketing device for his other businesses, which include satellite dishes for BSkyB, the biggest underwriter of British football.[70] The property developer, Sir John Hall, treated Newcastle United as an engine of growth in the north-east, where most of his business interests lie. But he also saw the potential to make money from sport. For a time, his interests encompassed not just a football club (Newcastle United) but a rugby club (Newcastle), an ice hockey team (Durham Wasps), a basketball team and a motor-racing team. He has invested a considerable part of his fortune in the players and the facilities they need and has recouped part of his outlay by floating the football club on the stock market. Others have followed his example. Chris Wright has bought a football team (Queen's Park Rangers), a rugby union club (Wasps) and a basketball team (Sheffield Sharks), and collected a sizeable profit by floating the business.

Football clubs are attracting impersonal pools of capital too. Southampton was acquired in a reverse takeover by Secure Retirement, a supplier of old people's homes. Chris Akers, head of the Caspian media group which took over Leeds United, has plans to build the renamed Leeds Sporting group

TABLE 25.3
Publicly Quoted Football Clubs, 1998

	Market	League	Value (£m)
Arsenal	Ofex	Premier	145.6
Aston Villa	Main	Premier	78.4
Birmingham City	AIM	First	16.5
Bradford City	Ofex	First	19.7
Burnden Leisure (Bolton Wanderers)	Main	First	19.7
Celtic	AIM	Scottish Premier	95.2
Charlton Athletic	AIM	Premier	16.7
Chelsea Village	AIM	Premier	121.4
Heart of Midlothian	Main	Hearts	9.0
Leeds Sporting	Main	Premier	52.2
Leicester City	Main	Premier	12.4
Loftus Road (QPR)*	AIM	First	7.6
Manchester City	Ofex	Second	54.0
Manchester United	Main	Premier	580.7
Millwall Holdings	Main	Second	10.3
Newcastle United	Main	Premier	144.6
Nottingham Forest	AIM	Premier	13.5
Preston North End†	AIM	Second	7.1
Rangers	Ofex	Scottish Premier	168.4
Sheffield United	Main	First	23.5
Silver Shield (Swansea City)	Main	Third	5.0
Southampton Leisure Holdings	Main	Premier	11.3
Sunderland	Main	First	48.8
Tottenham Hotspur	Main	Premier	73.5
West Bromwich Albion	AIM	First	8.4
Total			1,743.5

Source: *Soccer Analyst Weekly Bulletin.*

* Loftus Road also owns Wasps RUFC, which shares the stadium with QPR.
† Preston North End own Chorley Rugby League club; they share the ground.

into 'a European conglomerate with interests in a broad spread of sports clubs, media properties and entertainment brands and rights'.[71] One of its first targets was the nearby rugby league club. A disappointed suitor for Leeds United, the Conrad leisure group, owns the Coq Sportif sportswear brand

and the Bobby Charlton football schools. In December 1996 it paid £9.9 million to acquire Sheffield United from Michael McDonald, a Manchester businessman who had bought the club a year earlier for one third of the price. The Enic investment trust, partially owned by the Bahamas-based billionaire Joe Lewis, has bought AEK Athens, Vicenza and Slavia Prague football clubs as well as a 25 per cent stake in Glasgow Rangers.

Football finally arrived as a fully-fledged corporate business in September 1998, when BSkyB offered the shareholders of Manchester United £623.4 million. Why the satellite broadcaster was prepared to pay so much is clear: its four-year deal with the Premier League expires in May 2001, by which time a combination of digital television and new payment technology will make it possible for clubs to sell their matches directly to viewers on a pay-per-view basis. BSkyB introduced pay-per-view to British sport on 16 March 1996, persuading six hundred thousand households to pay to watch three rounds of boxing between Frank Bruno and Mike Tyson. It reckoned its earnings from live football were bound to fall once clubs could work with its competitors to sell games directly to fans. The present deal between BSkyB and the Premier League was also under investigation as a potential cartel: a hearing began in the Restrictive Practices Court in January 1999. If the Court decides that the Premier League is a cartel, clubs will be free to sell rights to televise their matches separately. BSkyB had also helped Manchester United establish its own television channel (in conjunction with Granada) and knew that Arsenal, Leeds United, Sunderland and Hearts were following suit. For similar reasons, the cable TV company NTL stalked Newcastle United.

For top clubs like Newcastle, pay-per-view is potentially lucrative. Manchester United may have over three million million fans, but there are only fifty-five thousand seats at Old Trafford. If all the fans paid £10 to watch every game, pay-per-view would be worth £1.2 billion to the club. If all seven million households which watch Premier League football watched all the games played by their favourite club, domestic pay-per-view income would be worth £2.6 billion to leading football clubs. But revenues are bound to be more modest. Not everybody will watch every game, and clubs will want to broadcast some games on terrestrial or subscription television, to reduce financial risk and avoid alienating the public. Nor will they want to put live attendance at risk by making pay-per-view a cheap alternative to going to the game. Earnings from pay-per-view will have to be shared between clubs, just as they are today, if the game is not to be undone by the peculiar economics of sport. The most comprehensive study reckoned pay-per-view would be worth £450 million a year to the Premier League clubs by the 2003–04 season.[72]

But, if the potential of pay-per-view is often exaggerated, it will tilt the balance of power from broadcasters to football clubs and their fans. Doubts

TABLE 25.4
Ownership and Income,
English Premier League Football Clubs, 1996–97 (£m)

	Main Owners (%)	*Turnover 1997**	*Pre-Tax Profit/(Loss) 1997†*
Arsenal	David Dein (24); Daniel Fiszman (27); Richard Carr (26)	27.2	(1.6)
Aston Villa	Ellis Family (40); Institutions (25); Private Investors (30)	22.1	(3.9)
Barnsley	Local families and individuals	3.7	0.346
Bolton Wanderers	Board of directors (57); Institutions (18)	7.7	(3.3)
Blackburn Rovers	Jack Walker (99)	14.3	8.1
Chelsea	Ken Bates (33); Matthew Harding Estate (27); RHK Nominees (25)	23.7	(0.376)
Coventry City	Offshore trusts (70); Geoffrey Robinson	12.3	(10.5)
Crystal Palace	Mark Goldberg (85)	7.9	(0.486)
Derby County	Lionel Pickering (69); Electra Investment Trust (25)	10.7	(3.5)
Everton	Peter Johnson (68); Board of Directors (30)	18.9	(2.9)
Leeds United	SBC Warburg (13); Schroders (11); Martin Currie (8)	21.8	(9.7)
Leicester City	Ken Brigstock (21); Roy Parker (17); John Elsom (15); Martin George (15)	17.3	(3.6)
Liverpool	David Moores (57); Steve Morgan (5)	39.2	7.6
Manchester United	Edwards Family (13); Marathon (6); Friends Provident (4); Mercury (4); Abu Dhabi (4)	87.9	27.6
Newcastle United	Douglas Hall (50.8); Freddy Shepherd (8); NTL (6.3)	41.1	(10.9)
Sheffield Wednesday	Charterhouse Development Capital (360); Board of Directors (7)	14.3	(3.2)
Southampton	Roger Everett (18); Mercury (8); John Corbett (8)	9.2	(3.6)
Tottenham Hotspur	Alan Sugar (41); Public	27.9	7.6
West Ham	Terence Brown (34); Charles Warner (25)	15.2	(5.5)
Wimbledon	Kjell Inge Rokke and Bjorn Gunnar Engelsk (80); Sam Hammam (20)	10.4	(0.111)
Total		432.9	(11.927)

Source: *Soccer Analyst.*

* Excluding transfers.
† After transfers.

about whether Newcastle United Sporting Club could be a paying proposition evaporate once it is grasped that the club could fill hours of television time with games of football, rugby union, basketball, ice hockey or motor-racing supplied by its own teams. Bernie Ecclestone is certainly convinced of the long-term value of pay-per-view; he has invested in equipment which will allow viewers to watch Grand Prix at different points by hopping between cameras. This will give him a larger share of income from the sale of television rights and clear the main obstacle to a further enlargement of sponsorship income: that conventional television follows the leaders of a race only, reducing the price of sponsoring a lesser team. 'It costs more to lose than to win,' as Ecclestone puts it.

Rugby Union: Gentlemen Become Players

The win-at-all costs philosophy has overrun the last bastion of amateurism in sport: rugby union. In 1995, after years of shamateurism, the game became openly professional. The effects were not edifying. Professionalism launched a series of incomprehensible rows between the rugby unions which had run the game in its amateur days and the clubs which would like to run it in the professional era. The differences between them are partly cultural, as the dismissive comments about union officials by Sir John Hall of Newcastle ('I cannot have amateurs running my business') and the England captain Will Carling ('old farts') suggested. But they are also about money. By the start of the 1998–9 season, the rich businessmen who subsidise most of the top clubs had sunk £40 million into them without return or likelihood of return. It is natural for them to seek a degree of control over which matches are played and when.

Until 1995, anybody who wanted to be paid for playing rugby had to go north and play rugby league, which broke with the union exactly a century earlier, when northern clubs were refused permission to compensate their players for time off work.[73] The administration of rugby union was performed gratis, mostly by former players. They were raised in an era of pure amateurism, when players skipped a match if they were busy at work or did not feel like playing. Competitive leagues were an impossibility. Clubs had no money to travel, players were not always available, and grounds had little or no accommodation for fans. The first competitive knock-out competitions were not introduced until the 1970s, and introduction of league rugby was postponed until the 1980s. Even now, amateur clubs chafe at the cost of travelling to away fixtures in the regional and national leagues.

Professional rugby union is different. It is organised in two national div-

isions sponsored by the Allied Dunbar insurance company, with annual promotion and relegation for two clubs in each division. Far from skipping
matches, leading players find themselves in forty or fifty games a season in
an era when the size, pace and power of the players in an intensely physical
game were never greater. The salary bill of the fourteen clubs in Allied Dunbar
Premiership One is £24 million a year, nearly half the revenues of the sport
in England as a whole. In 1996–7, the year Wasps won the first professional
league, the club lost £540,000. In 1997–8, when they lost the title, it cost the
shareholders £1.5 million.[74] The top clubs lost an estimated £15 million in
the first full year of professionalism in 1996–7, and another £20–25 million
in 1997–8. It is impossible to be exact because the clubs work hard to conceal
the losses, but it is not hard to determine the cause: the rising cost of recruiting
and retaining talented players at home and abroad.

Club competition is now seething with New Zealanders, Australians, Canadians, South Africans, Frenchmen and Pacific islanders hired to win their
clubs a larger slice of the television and advertising money pouring into rugby
union. The race to recruit was started by Sir John Hall, who hired the former
England stand-off half Rob Andrew on a contract said to be worth £750,000
over five years, and told him to build a team to win the championship. The
£500,000 price of one of his signings – the former All Black Va'aiga Tuigemala
– eclipsed the rugby league record of £440,000 which Wigan paid for Martin
Offiah in 1992. In the first season of professional rugby union, the going rate
was £50–100,000 for an international; £40–70,000 for the best of the others;
and £20–40,000 for people who might not even play every week. In the
fifteen-man game, where players are injured constantly, the wage bill had lost
touch with reality even before looking at the limited size of its following.

For all its virtues, rugby lacks a mass following. Perhaps four hundred
thousand people watch Premiership rugby union, rather less than the number
which support the leading Rugby League clubs. Bath, the most successful
rugby union team in England before the advent of professionalism, attracted
regular crowds of around three thousand spectators. Leicester, the biggest
club, has less than eleven thousand members even now. Saracens, which has
made a bigger effort than most to sell itself to north London, breaks records
when it attracts a crowd as large as ten thousand. To get on television at all
in 1997–8, the Premiership clubs (in conjunction with the Rugby Football
Union and Carlsberg–Tetley) had to meet the production costs of the *Rugby
Express* programme broadcast on Channel 5 on Sunday afternoons. Obviously,
rugby union has too narrow a base to sustain more than a handful of professional sides. When rugby league was the only form of professional rugby,
it was able to sustain only two. Yet there are now twenty-eight clubs in the
two divisions of the rugby union championship.

This is one reason why all clubs are losing money. Some, including historic names like Coventry, Moseley and Neath, have collapsed. It is not surprising that the clubs would like a larger share of the burgeoning television and sponsorship revenues controlled by the English Rugby Football Union (RFU) in particular. When the Union sold BSkyB exclusive rights to broadcast international matches from Twickenham for £87.5 million in 1996, it sparked a dispute with clubs (and the other British unions) which has rankled ever since. The RFU was eventually persuaded to share the money with the clubs and the Celtic unions, but it did not provide enough to settle the dispute with either. The Celtic unions threw England out of the Five Nations Championship twice in pursuit of a larger share of the broadcasting revenues, and the top clubs are in perpetual conflict with the RFU. They reckon they supply international players at an annual cost of £2–3 million, but recoup only £500,000 from the BSkyB deal. The RFU feels that the bulk of the earnings from television should pay off the loans raised to rebuild Twickenham (it borrowed £35 million to create a state-of-the-art concrete stadium in the early 1990s), and to nurture and sustain the eighteen hundred-odd clubs of the amateur game. It hoped at one stage to resolve the problem by paying the players directly, saving their clubs the cost and putting a cap on earnings

TABLE 25.5
Allied Dunbar Premiership One Rugby Clubs in 1998

Club	Members	Main Backer	Operating Profit/(loss) in 1996–7 (£m)
Bath	4,000	Andrew Brownsword	(1.5)
Bedford	700	Frank Warren (95%)	n/a
Gloucester	2,200	Tom Walkinshaw (73%)	(0.4)
Harlequins	3,000	NEC (Sponsorship)	(1.7)
Leicester	10,500	Peter Tom	n/a
London Irish	1,800	Anglo Irish Bank	(0.9)
London Scottish	–	Anthony Tiarks (79%)	(0.7)
Manchester Sale	1,200	Neil Black	n/a
Newcastle	2,000	Sir John Hall (76%)	(3.0)
Northampton	2,500	Keith Barwell (67%)	(0.6)
Richmond	2,500	Ashley Levett	(2.9)
Saracens	2,800	Nigel Wray	n/a
Wasps	2,600	Chris Wright/Loftus Road PLC	(0.5)
West Hartlepool	500	Andrew Hindle and Philip Yuill	(0.03)

Source: Annual Reports and Accounts; *The Times, Financial Times.*

overall by suppressing the effects of the transfer market. But the argument has now moved beyond money. The clubs in particular want control of the structure of competition, the sale of broadcasting rights, and sponsorship.

A season in which club encounters are suspended to accommodate international games which fill the coffers of the four unions is not sustainable. Unlike the football leagues, supporters are not always sure when and where a game will take place. In England, the clubs withdrew leading players from a tour of the southern hemisphere in the summer of 1998, on the grounds that they needed rest and recuperation. They also refused to participate in a putative European competition. If the fixture list and distribution of spoils are not resolved soon, the split between the leading clubs and the three unions may prove unbridgeable. The Scottish Rugby Union (which had an overdraft of £17 million by 1998) has already forfeited the support of the clubs after an ill-conceived plan to create two new district sides which incorporate all the best players. In Wales, Cardiff and Swansea have broken away from the Welsh Rugby Union in search of better opponents in the English Premiership. The English clubs (now organised as English First Division Rugby) may well have to follow their example. In the twenty-first century, rugby union is likely to have one feature in common with association football: a small group of large professional clubs leading a long tail of starving minnows.

Why Cricket Is Not Working

Fear of just such an outcome postponed a long-overdue reform of the game of cricket. For decades, the viability of English cricket has depended largely on international one-day matches and five-day Tests. Virtually all international matches sell out, attracting generous sponsors to both the Tests (Cornhill Insurance) and the one-day matches (Texaco). The Lord's Test against the Australians in June 1997 was the most heavily oversubscribed cricket match played in England. The sums the international matches generate from gate receipts, broadcasting rights and sponsorship have allowed the England and Wales Cricket Board (ECB) and its predecessors to give each of the eighteen county cricket clubs at the top of the national game around £1 million a year each. In most cases, the subsidy is half of its income or more, relieving the members of any serious need to raise revenue. It also made them immune to plans to make county cricket more competitive, for fear that successful clubs would monopolise the best players and the bulk of the revenues. As a result, county cricket has for years undermined the effectiveness of the England team on which its viability depends.

In 1996 Leicestershire won the County Cricket Championship. 'They won

TABLE 25.6
County Cricket Clubs

Club	Members	Sponsors	Turnover 1997–8 (£m)
Derbyshire	2,824	Wards, Williams Holdings, Don Arnott	1.5
Durham	7,015	Newcastle Breweries	2.8
Essex	7,442	Various, c. 250	2.6
Glamorgan	11.500	–	1.5
Gloucestershire	5,250	Merchant Investors	1.9
Hampshire	4,124	Greene King	2.4
Kent	8,000	Shepherd Neame	2.2
Lancashire	13,445	Energi (Norweb), ASICS UK	6.4
Leicestershire	5,500	Midland Mainline, Wm Younger	1.5
Middlesex	9,242	Hill Samuel Asset Management	1.8
Northamptonshire	4,300	R. Griggs Group, Doctor Martens	1.9
Nottinghamshire	4,600	BDO Stoy Hayward	2.9
Somerset	6,101	–	2.8
Surrey	7,500	Computacenter	6.7
Sussex	4,700	Dentilam	1.9
Warwickshire	14,100	Peugeot, Bass, Mitchell & Butlers	8.0
Worcestershire	4,761	Midlands Electricity	2.6
Yorkshire	10,000	Taylors of Harrogate	2.5
Total	130,404	–	53.9

Source: Clubs.

the Championship by using only thirteen players all season,' wrote Martin Johnson in the 1997 edition of *Wisden,* 'and were roared on to the coveted pennant by much the same number of spectators.' Because it is ignored by spectators, the County Championship is ignored by television. It has a sponsor (Britannic Assurance) but the rewards on offer are scarcely generous. After a five-month campaign, in which four-day matches against the other seventeen county clubs were interspersed with a series of one-day matches, Leicestershire won the princely sum of £65,000 for their 1996 efforts. Once a £1,000 bonus was added for each of the ten matches the club had won, and a series of other bonuses and sponsorships were totalled up, the thirteen players split £120,000. A boxer would not get out of bed for that sort of money.

It certainly deters talented cricketers from pursuing a career in the professional game. The England footballer Phil Neville is a gifted cricketer, who played for Lancashire before decided that fullback for Manchester United would be more rewarding. The entire income of the game of cricket in England (£75 million) is smaller than the turnover of Manchester United (£88 million). The total prize money available to the county cricket clubs from corporate sponsorship is about £400,000 – less than half of the £1 million Manchester United collected for winning the Premier League in the same year Leicestershire won the County Cricket Championship. Sponsorship earnings are similarly unequal. Even average Premier League footballers are earning substantial six-figure salaries, but journeyman cricketers on the county scene earn around £25–35,000 a year. For them, winter jobs, testimonials and the traditional 'benefit year' are important.

The low earnings of professional cricketers reflect the lack of interest by television in the main form of the game. Cricket is intrinsically difficult to televise. Even its shortest version takes up a whole day, and it is the only game which can be played for five days without deciding a winner. The nature of the game makes it dull-in-comparison entertainment, even at its best. But the traditional structure of county cricket ensures it is never played at its best. In the absence of a competitive league, most county cricket matches are meaningless 'non-events' of the kind the Premier League was invented to abolish. The effect is to lower standards, as well as devour revenues, making it even harder to attract spectators. English cricketers – especially the younger ones – play enough meaningless cricket to dull their appetites and not enough competitive cricket to sharpen them. When the best of them play for England, they find it hard to keep up with players from countries which play less but better cricket. A victory over South Africa in the summer of 1998 was the first England had accomplished in a full Test series for twelve years.

This record of un-success deters sponsors, broadcasters and the young players and spectators who are fuelling the growth of football and rugby union. Yet when Lord MacLaurin of Knebworth – former chairman of Tesco, who was appointed chairman of the ECB in 1996 – declared that 'winning is everything' and promised to reform the structure of the game to make it more competitive, the reaction of the cricketing establishment was disdain. Cricket is crammed with reactionaries who find comfort and tradition preferable to competition and success. The members of the Marylebone Cricket Club (MCC) voted to exclude women as recently as 1998. Gentlemen v.

Players was being played at Lord's as recently as 1962. Eton v. Harrow, and Oxford v. Cambridge still are. As Matthew Engel, editor of *Wisden*, has pointed out, cricket is 'widely perceived as élitist, exclusionist and dull'.

To his credit, Lord MacLaurin has ignored the grumbles of the élitists and dullards in the Pavilion at Lord's. In 1997 he persuaded the county cricket clubs to get rid of the Benson & Hedges one-day tournament and merge it with the Axa Sunday league to create a single two-division national league with promotion and relegation, to start in 1999. MacLaurin also persuaded the counties to scrap the county championship in favour of two divisions of nine teams each, with three counties relegated and promoted each year. The new championship, which begins in 2000, will mark the first real change in the main competition since 1890. To secure it, the major counties had to threaten a breakaway Premier League-style competition and the ECB had to guarantee that the counties would continue to receive grants of the same size (topped up with a performance-related element). Few clubs were confident they would win enough games to stay in the top flight, or attract people back to their matches.

Yet rebuilding an audience for county cricket is the most significant challenge facing the game. Membership of clubs and the MCC has remained static at roughly one hundred and thirty thousand people for years. But those counties which have embarked on reform have found it rewarding. Glamorgan woke to the possibilities of using the Welshness of the club as a marketing ploy, and introduced a credit card hotline to debit its new members. Surrey renamed themselves Surrey Lions for one-day matches, and introduced such daring innovations as a burst of pop music to greet incoming batsmen. Warwickshire and Surrey have experimented with floodlit matches, which people can watch after work. The ECB and some counties are developing the first ranges of cricket merchandise. Even in a game synonymous the world over with Corinthian values ('It's not cricket'), the myth of sportsmanship is being forced to yield to commercial realities.

Has Money Corrupted Sport?

English cricket, steeped in history and myth, has found it harder than most sports to surrender to commercial values. Even today, the Long Room is more museum than cricket club, and a frieze at the south-eastern corner of Lord's advertises the game with those lines from *Vitai Lampada* ('Play Up! Play Up! And play the game!') which make Sir Henry Newbolt so unfashionable a figure today. Ironically, his portrayal of cricket as a metaphor for the sterner tests of life is enjoying something of a revival, especially among those dismayed by the commercialisation of sport. In December 1994 the *Sunday Times* published an article by Hugh McIlvanney. The newspaper's distinguished football correspondent wrote:

> The struggle between morality and money in sport was bound to become more and more one-sided as the spoils available increased dramatically, something made inevitable by the incalculable impact of television. And in this country the glorification of greed in the Thatcher years was never likely to leave sport untouched. In fact, what we are witnessing may be quite simply the death of the cherished, though rather flimsily based, assumption that sport can remain permanently superior to the society it serves. If that belief is indeed shown to be a delusion, we are all in trouble. There is no relevant analogy in the principle that a society gets the politics it deserves. In politics, as happenings at Westminster are forever reminding us, idealism is a luxury. Without idealism, sport does not exist. Romance and honesty and fair play are not quaint, outmoded concepts but the basic apparatus of its survival. If sport ceases to be a slightly fantastic metaphor for life (one that accommodates wild notions of heroes and heroines, triumph and disaster) and becomes just another sleazy part of it, sport is a waste of time.[75]

Its passionate denunciation of the rise of money-mindedness in sport impressed no less a figure than Tony Blair, then recently elevated to the leadership of the Opposition, and anxious to empathise with the concerns of the ordinary football fan. The future prime minister, who would not normally expect to have his opinions coincide with those of Sir Henry Newbolt, did not hesitate to quote McIlvanney in an interview.[76] The idea of sport unsullied by money has provided his government with a slight but sufficient justification for the Football Task Force.

It is a common view, at all points on the political spectrum, that the commercialisation of sport is a regrettable development. Politicians and commentators are right to be worried about the character of sport, for sportsmen and women are the most influential of contemporary heroes. Sir John Hall thinks the example set by Alan Shearer and Kevin Keegan (for example) matters more to the young of the north-east than parents, policemen or teachers. The government is so convinced of this that it has persuaded Premier League clubs to run homework sessions at their grounds. Unfortunately, modern football and footballers could scarcely be more representative of the failure of sport to rise above the mores of contemporary society. Spitting, swearing, deliberate fouls, abuse of the referee and gamesmanship are rife in the professional game, and well-known footballers and football managers have filled the tabloids with addiction to alcohol, drugs and gambling, wife-beating, assault, indecent assault, and allegations of match-fixing and back-handers.

On the face of it, money has corrupted sport in the same way that it corrupts human beings in any walk of life. The penalty-seeking dive is one of the few ways to score in a modern association football match, professional defences having risen to the challenge of avoiding defeat. Virtually every sport has its own drugs scandal. Racing drivers shunt each other off the track. Tennis stars know that the fines for foul language and 'racquet abuse' will never be too onerous, because the organisers cannot afford to upset them. Even cricketers tamper with the ball, sledge each other mercilessly, send dismissed batsmen back to the pavilion with a volley of V-signs and foul language, and take money from bookmakers. Yet joylessness, rather than pleasure, is a feature of professional sport. A Grand Prix always concludes with a trio of bored racing drivers spraying one another with magnums of champagne, in a grotesque celebration of the triumph of money in a sport where even victory seems now to be for sale.

It is as good an illustration as any of how a money-minded culture informs people at play as well as at work. As Hugh McIlvanney points out, television is the link between money and cynicism in sport. Television needs audiences to attract advertisers. Audiences need excitement and aggression, and violence and even injury are a cheap way to provide it. In this respect, the Romans knew as much. Ironically, Corinth was a town of notoriously lax morals even by Roman standards, and Corinthian values, whose disappearance is often lamented, were developed not by the likes of Eric Liddle (who refused to race on Sundays) but by Regency bloods who had the time and money to drink, hunt, gamble, fight, duel and vandalise their way through the clubs, hedgerows, boxing rings and racecourses of Georgian England. Which is why they were called Corinthians.[77]

There was no golden age when sport in England was free of the taint of commerce. Sport became popular only because it was an occasion to bet.[78] Commercial sponsorship of sport goes back to at least the nineteenth century, when newspapers created events which they could then report exclusively. In cricket, most of the leading players were professionals from the outset. The game was promoted by entrepreneurs such as Thomas Lord (who established the cricket ground that still bears his name) and George Smith (who charged Victorian lager louts tuppence a day to eat, drink and wager their way through a game of cricket at the Artillery ground). In 1895 W. G. Grace was presented with £5,000, or over £300,000 in today's money, by the *Daily Telegraph*. In 1938 Paul Gallico wrote, in *Farewell to Sport*, that 'Championship tournament golf is no longer sport but business.'[79] Denis Compton, the Cavalier who played football and cricket for England, was also the Brylcreem Boy and the first British sportsman to appoint an agent.

Over thirty years have passed since Tony Kay, David 'Bronco' Layne and Peter Swan were jailed for fixing football matches, and over ninety since Billy Meredith, Manchester City captain, was suspended for trying to bribe his opposite number at Aston Villa. As J. H. Huizenga pointed out (in *Homo Ludens*, published fifty years ago), professionalism sucks the joy out of sport. 'The spirit of the professional,' he wrote, 'is no longer the true play-spirit; it is lacking in spontaneity and carelessness . . . In the case of sport we have an activity nominally known as play but raised to such a pitch of technical organisation and scientific thoroughness that the real play-spirit is threatened with extinction.'[80]

Fortunately, the consumers of sport place natural limits on the triumph of professionalism. The American experience suggests that where a sport has become too cynicla and materialistic (and its stars too spoilt) genuine fans start watching minor leagues and amateur games instead. British sport is nowhere near that point as yet. In fact, the average British sports fan of today is in search of success, not metaphors for success, and he knows that money can buy it. Elton John's millions took Watford from the Fourth Division to the First in just ten years. It cost Jack Walker £70 million, but he bought Blackburn Rovers their first Championship for eighty-one years. In 1992 Newcastle United came within an ace of bankruptcy and relegation to the third division. Five years and £50 million later, it is one of the biggest clubs in the Premier League, with a cable television company interested (for a time) in purchasing it. Manchester United had not won a championship since 1968 when it floated on the stock market in 1991. Since then, the club has won the championship four times and the FA Cup twice. Rangers had not won the Scottish league for nine years until David Murray spent £35 million on a new stadium and new players. They did not lose the championship for the next nine years.

Complaints by fans that proprietors are interested in sport only as a business, and not as McIlvanney's 'fantastic metaphor for life,' tend to be loudest at clubs likes Tottenham Hotspur, where a more businesslike approach is not allied to success on the field. 'I have been accused,' Alan Sugar once said of his stewardship at Tottenham, 'of buying Harrod's and turning it into Woolworths. In fact, we bought Del Boy's stall and have turned it into Marks & Spencer.'[81] Manchester United had the same trouble with fans before the club embarked on its astonishing run of success in the 1990s. In *Manchester United – The Betrayal of a Legend*, the chairman of the fan club and the journalist Michael Crick castigated Martin Edwards for his obsession with sponsorship and marketing rather than success on the pitch. Crick later orchestrated the campaign against the takeover of the club by BSkyB. But the name of his campaign (Shareholders United Against Murdoch) suggests that his views owe more to a love of politics than a love of football. It is also hard to believe that David Conn – whose influential *Football Business* is not about football as business at all, but a long lament for the golden-age-that-never-was – would feel quite so strongly about the loss of the essential spirit of the game if he supported Manchester United rather than Manchester City.

Fans, particularly of unsuccessful clubs, are apt to believe that nobody ever loved the club or the game as they do. It is also convenient for them to believe that metaphor matters more than money. They want success, but do not volunteer to pay for it through higher ticket prices: they would like the successful to pay for the unsuccessful. Conn recommends windfall taxes on the Premier League and the richest clubs, a wealth tax on their owners and the 'redistributive hand of regulation' by the state.[82] The Fabian Society wants friendlies for charity and 'fan forums', corporate sponsorship to cut ticket prices, and a new state regulator for football.[83] Ideas of this type are treated kindly by the New Labour government, which came into office armed with a Charter for Football, and a somewhat contrived affection for the People's Game. The Football Task Force is already at work, finding ways to do nothing about the grumbles of the traditional fan.

Certainly it cannot blame the clubs alone for the rising cost of a ticket to the match. In the wake of the Hillsborough disaster, the government forced clubs to replace their cheap terraces with expensive all-seater stadiums. Every major club has improved its stadium, and Bolton Wanderers, Sunderland and Middlesbrough have built entirely new ones in more convenient sites. Fans have met most of the cost. But it has bought them a seat, and seats have brought women and children back to the game. In fact, it is precisely because football is now comfortable, modern and safe that New Labour has allied itself with the game.

But money has bought more than comfort and respectability. Outside shareholders have imposed new financial disciplines on football clubs: to raise their income, control their expenditure and pay their taxes. Football had long operated in the half-world of the cash economy. Players, particularly in the lower divisions, could expect to be paid in cash from the bar or the gate. In 1992 the Inland Revenue recouped £10 million in unpaid tax from football clubs.[84] In 1990 the chairman of Swindon Town was jailed for failing to tax his players. Four years later Tottenham Hotspur was fined and expelled from the FA Cup for making interest-free loans to players which were never repaid. Players had come to expect tax-free gratuities of this kind. Transfers abroad provided opportunities for more sophisticated tax dodges – payments into offshore bank accounts, for instance. The Football Association spent five years investigating the so-called 'bung' scandal, in which various leading figures in the game received emoluments to lubricate the transfer market.

Kate Hoey, Labour MP for Vauxhall, claimed in the House of Commons in 1995 that corruption and tax evasion were so widespread in football that there needed to be an independent inquiry by government. 'I came to football from the property world,' agreed David Kohler, chairman of Luton Town football club in the early 1990s. 'I used to think the construction industry was bent, but I was shocked. Football is much worse, it seems to be bent from top to bottom.'[85] If football-as-business has sold its soul, it has at least brought a degree of probity to its financial affairs. It has also purchased a higher level of individual and team performance and a greater sensitivity to the comfort and safety of the fans – the direct consequence of a businesslike approach. There is a danger that, in reclaiming the soul of sport from business, nostalgics and reactionaries will merely re-create the traditional indifference of sport to the needs of its consumers.

The Financial Reality

For all of the changes it has occasioned, the impact of money on sport as a whole is exaggerated. The Sports Council reckons consumers spend about £10.5 billion on sport and sports gear, generating employment for half a million people, and £5 in taxes for every £1 of state subsidy.[86] That is perhaps 1.25 per cent of the national income; 2.5 per cent of the national workforce; and 1.25 per cent of tax revenues – not much for a business whose market engages thirty-six million people at one time or another during the course of the year. In fact, sport as a business is so unsuccessful it has to be subsidised by the taxpayer. Local authorities build most of the sports centres in the country with public funds, and in many cases lease grounds cheaply even to leading football and cricket clubs. Since 1974, sport has enjoyed the favour of a minister and a budget of its own. The Sports Council, set up in 1972 to promote development, has over £30 million to spend on sport each year.[87]

When football clubs had to build all-seater stadiums, the taxpayer paid, by forgoing a slice of his take from the football pools. Wembley Stadium, which was owned by a private company, will now be rebuilt at a cost to the taxpayer of £240 million. Another £160 million of National Lottery money is going to a new UK Sports Institute with headquarters in Sheffield and eight satellite centres around the country. Sport, as one of the 'good causes' eligible for lottery funding, collected £210 million a year from the National Lottery between 1994 and 1997. Few forms of public spending are as popular. Governments have long understood the narcotic and propaganda value of national success in sporting endeavours. Even serious writers are not ashamed to argue for the regulation and nationalisation of sport as a 'public good'.

Some identified in the gloom which enveloped the nation after the elimination of England from the World Cup in 1998 echoes of the 'togetherness' of 2 May 1997 and at the death of Diana. The ability of sport to transcend the personal (what Conn calls 'the spontaneous communal miracle') has mastered their imagination. But nostalgia for the feeling-of-belonging on the terraces is apt to find ugly political expression. The hooligans who wrecked Marseille during the 1998 World Cup never doubted that they spoke for England. In *Among the Thugs*, Bill Buford mixes with fans who sing 'Rule Britannia' and sell copies of *National Front News*. After England lost to Germany in the semi-finals of the 1990 World Cup, drunks poured out of pubs to vandalise German cars.[88] '*England. England. England. England,*' writes Buford of the English football hooligans. 'This chant . . . This declaration for England . . . These fools, despised at home, ridiculed in the press, incapable of being contained by any act of impulsive legislation that the government had devised, wanted an England to defend . . . They wanted a war.'

Since at least the Berlin Olympics of 1936, games have served as proxies for war: for clashes between countries and rival socio-political systems. Astonishing feats of athleticism by drug-drenched Russian and East German hermaphrodites were one of the constants of post-war Olympic Games, until the quadrennial meeting of the greats degenerated at Atlanta into a commercialism so complete that nobody cared who won or lost. In *The End of History and the Last Man*, his influential work on life after Communism, Francis Fukuyama suggested that in a world robbed of the traditional pleasures of war and conquest, winning football and cricket matches has replaced military aggrandisement as the chief expression of nationalism. This is not always welcome. In parts of Asia, Latin America and Africa, sport comes close at times to *casus belli*. On the whole, sport is safer as a consumer good than as a communal experience. Yet the official British view of sport seems rooted in a mixture of nationalism and eugenics. The Sports Council says: 'Sports and physical recreation have a vital role to play in today's society by giving a sense of pride, by helping to alleviate the consequences of social and economic disadvantage and by having a positive effect on the mental and physical well-being of individuals and the nation.'[89]

Harold Wilson linked the electoral fortunes of his party to the performance of the England football team. In the great industrial cities, it is said that productivity rises and falls in line with the performance of the local football team. Some believe a successful football team can bring investment and jobs. It may be true. Bidding for the Olympic or Commonwealth Games or the World Cup has become an integral part of the regeneration strategy of decaying British cities. Lobbyists, councillors and ministers apparently believe that a successful sporting event will attract the attention of foreign and domestic investors, but the benefits are invariably exaggerated. A study of the benefits of hosting the Euro 96 football championships in Britain found that the economic results were wildly exaggerated. The competition generated additional consumer spending of just £100 million, or less than £1 in every £100 spent by foreign tourists in Britain that year.[90] Even the biggest games in the most popular sport of all have only marginal economic effects.

Over one hundred sports are eligible for support from the Sports Council, but only a handful of clubs and individuals in a handful of sports are likely to get rich by playing them. Most people will only hear of baton twirling or sombo wrestling or unihoc because the Sports Council is paying people to play them. Even the sport of kings reckons it needs the taxpayer to survive, let alone thrive. Since the Aga Khan withdrew from British racing after a row with the Jockey Club over doping, racing in Britain has become dependent on the largesse of Sheikh Mohammed al Maktoum and his brothers, who are said to spend £20 million a year in Britain. When Sheikh Mohammed warned in December 1997 that 'this was a luxury we can no longer afford', the British Horseracing Board promptly submitted a plan to government for an annual subsidy of £80 million from the duty on betting turnover.[91]

Premier League football, the most nakedly commercial sport of any in Britain today, cannot pay its way unaided. Most clubs depend on wealthy benefactors whom football has enriched, but who have in turn enriched football. Even Sir John Hall, who regards Newcastle United as a business proposition, admits that a lost match fills him with gloom. 'If we lose a big match,' he says, 'I don't feel a commercial sadness so much as the sadness of the sports fan.'[92] Even Alan Sugar, apparently the most hard-nosed of the so-called soccer czars, has admitted, 'The bug, the buzz, the nervousness – I have fallen for the game, hook, line and sinker.'[93] Outside the Premier League, a string of clubs would disappear if their besotted owners stopped dreaming of winning the League or the Cup.

It is obvious that sport needs money more than money needs sport. Applications for funding from the National Lottery exceed fivefold the funds available. The lucky beneficiaries may include the Cleethorpes Scout Troop (which needed new kayaks) but they also include Hampshire County Cricket Club (which needed a new ground to play on). Manchester United may be big business, but most sport in Britain is still cottage industry. The Sports Council reckons that there are three times as many unpaid volunteers working in British sport as salaried employees. One and a half million people are working unpaid for an average of two and a half hours a week as coaches, referees, and administrators at sports clubs, schools and national sports organisations. They seem to enjoy it less than the John Halls and Alan Sugars of the world. Asked what their biggest problems were, the volunteers complained bitterly that not enough people were willing to help, and that most of the work is done by a dwindling band of enthusiasts.

Sport, even at the level of the village green, is not a fantastic metaphor for life. It is a faithful reflection of a life in which everybody is working (if only on their backhand or their swing), most are being asked to do too much, and nobody is being thanked. If they were being paid, says the Sports Council, the volunteers would be earning £1.5 billion a year.[94] Sport may be a cottage industry, but many of its enthusiasts would like it to be a nationalised industry. Which is exactly what charity, the other great voluntary industry in Britain, has already become.

CHAPTER TWENTY-SIX

THE CHARITY INDUSTRY

The proper duty of the philanthropist is to force society to do its duty.

B. KIRKMAN GRAY[1]

Britain has reached a curious stage in the evolution of social policy, where the government wants more from charitable institutions, while charities want more from the government.

FRANK PROCHASKA, *The Voluntary Impulse*[2]

Few trends could so thoroughly undermine the very foundations of our free society as the acceptance by corporate officials of a social responsibility other than to make as much money for their stock holders as possible.

MILTON FRIEDMAN[3]

Customers are increasingly looking through the front door of the companies they buy from. If they do not like what they see in terms of social responsibility, community involvement, equality of opportunity, they won't go in.

SIR ALLEN SHEPPARD, former chairman, Grand Metropolitan[4]

There is no clearer measure of the influence of the PLC than the spread of its manners and values into a world which once held them in contempt: charity. The organisation and management of a large international charity such as Oxfam is now virtually indistinguishable from the organisation of a large multinational company. It has a chairman, a chief executive, a finance director and a board of directors, many drawn from private industry and finance. Probably, one of them will have drafted a 'mission statement'. There will be separate operating divisions, including a 'human resources' department, and a marketing department whose denizens are familiar with all the latest sales techniques: branded merchandise, loyalty promotions, incentive schemes and products and services designed to reward people who give to the charity.

Far from being mere trustees or informal gatherings of worthy philanthropists, many modern charities *are* companies, incorporated under the Companies Act, registered at Companies House and in some cases enjoying privileges which exceed even those of limited liability.[5] A glance at the brass plates outside the headquarters of Shelter in Old Street, a few hundred yards from Companies House, yields the following corporate names: Shelter National Campaign for the Homeless Limited, Shelter Trading UK and Shelter Merchandising. 'The old voluntary ethos has gone, especially in the big national charities,' says an official at the National Council for Voluntary Organisations (NCVO). 'Doing good is not enough, though obviously that is what motivates people.'[6]

A new term, social entrepreneurs, has come into being to describe the modern, businesslike philanthropist. It was probably invented by Lord Young of Dartington, the ageing progressive who was known as the 'Charles Clore of the do-gooder business' thirty years ago (for his role in establishing the Consumers Association).[7] Unlike ordinary entrepreneurs, social entrepreneurs create 'social' rather than physical or financial capital. Michael Brophy, a former advertising executive and appeals director at the Spastics Society who is now chief executive of the Charities Aid Foundation (CAF), personifies the new breed. The organisation he runs, spun out of the eighty-year-old NCVO as a central marketing and financial management service for charities, is the very model of the charity-as-business. From spanking new offices near Tonbridge in Kent, the CAF sells research, tax planning and fund management services to charities and donors, and publishes a range of publications and statistics on the voluntary sector. Criticised for the opulence of his headquarters, Brophy was unapologetic. 'Wandering around looking shabby and shaking collecting tins is not our style,' he retorted. 'We are every bit as good as a bank, handling £400 million of charitable funds, and we must have decent premises.'[8]

The people who are doing well out of the charity industry have a strong incentive to claim that they are running multimillion pound businesses in a multibillion pound industry. Remarkably few are. The NCVO estimates that there are 135,000 active charities in the United Kingdom, sitting on net assets of £36.7 billion, with a total income of £13.1 billion, and employing nearly half a million paid workers.[9] But the big money and the best jobs are controlled by a small number of large charities. One tenth account for nine tenths of income, four fifths of assets and four fifths of salaried jobs. Barely one in a hundred charities has an annual income of more than £1 million, and most are making do with a few thousand pounds a year.[10] An elite group of about fifteen hundred charities is responsible for spending well over half the total income of all active charities. Most of it goes on the salaries of employees and the things they need to do their jobs. Though much of this outlay is put to good use (a hostel for the homeless needs food to eat and staff to prepare it), it means that social entrepreneurs have around £9 billion a year to spend on themselves and their suppliers. It is not surprising to find that expenditure on salaries, perks and office space has continued to rise while income stagnates.[11]

In 1998 the average salary for running a charity with an income of over £10 million was £63,000, and the average pay of directors was £43,000.[12] These rewards are not lavish, but nor are they miserly. A chief executive or finance director of one of the top fifty charities can expect to earn £70-80,000 a year, with a company car, private health insurance, a mobile telephone and a performance-related bonus. Seymour Fortescue, who joined the Imperial Cancer Research Fund on a salary of £70,000 after resigning as head of retail banking at Barclays in 1991, told Tom Lloyd, 'I don't take a taxi as readily because I know some old lady might be paying for it.'[13]

The dozen or so charities with a chief executive earning more than £100,000 may not be so scrupulous. They tend to be organisations like the Industrial Society, the Royal Opera House and the Chartered Institute of Public Finance and Administration, which do not always match the popular idea of a charitable undertaking. But Barnardo's, the British Red Cross, the Birmingham Royal Institution for the Blind, the Cancer Research Campaign, the National Society for the Prevention of Cruelty to Children and the Royal Society for the Protection of Birds all pay their chief executives more than £75,000. Those paying over £65,000 included Help the Aged and Save the Children.[14] The predictable protestations by charity professionals that they need to recruit the best financial and managerial talent have a whisper of Fat Cattery.

Need for Better Management

One reason salaries are rising is the need to recruit people from outside the industry. To the old hands, business values and methods are still abhorrent, but charities undoubtedly were badly run. In his seminal work of 1988, *Understanding Voluntary Organisations*, Charles Handy accused charities of 'strategic delinquency' (putting ethos before strategy) and 'servant syndrome' (making a virtue of shabbiness and parsimony).

Yet a charity is more in need of a sound strategy and good, well-equipped management than a company. Demands are unpredictable, and often unlimited. Income is irregular. The staff are mostly unpaid volunteers, who have a strong preference for collective rather than executive decision-making. Unlike companies, charities face no external disciplines, since they are effectively

unowned. 'It's much more difficult running Oxfam than running any commercial organisation of equivalent size,' says Joel Joffe, chairman of Oxfam.
'It's an enormously complicated organisation.'[15] The result is mismanagement, waste and occasional fraud.

Even after sweeping reform of regulation, the Charity Commission investigates one in four of the many thousands of cases which are reported to it
each year. In one quarter of cases surveyed in 1994 and 1995, the Commission
found evidence of deliberate malpractice.[16] The cover of charitable status has
for years provided small-time fraudsters with opportunities to extort cash
from an unsuspecting public. In 1997 David Valentine, the 'Singing Vicar' of
Merseyside, was jailed for four years after tricking the public out of £250,000 in
charitable donations, using a variety of genuine charities as cover.[17] Charity
fund-raising events organised by society hostesses are particularly vulnerable
to exploitation and even fraud, since the organisers of an event aiming to
profit from fun are liable to lose control of the expenses. In some cases, like
the notorious 'Lady' Rosemary Aberdour, the losses can be substantial. For
five years before she was jailed in 1992, this daughter of an Essex doctor
passed herself off as the daughter of a peer. She swindled £2.7 million out
of charitable events organised on behalf of the National Hospital for Nervous
Diseases, and spent the lot on extravagant living. Aberdour was a brilliant
example of a depressingly common occurrence. At one stage, fraud had
become so common in the charity industry that the Metropolitan Police
established a specialist unit to stamp it out.

Even the largest charities are guilty of naivety. In 1993 the Salvation Army,
whose expenditure of £97 million makes it the largest provider of social
services after the government, was the victim of a £6.2 million fraud. Officers
were persuaded that they could make unusually large profits by investing
$10 million in standby letters of credit, and made the investments, against
professional advice. The funds (after a circuitous journey) ended up being
invested, among other assets, in the Castle Inn at Dornie and a dog track in
Ayr.[18] Although the full amount plus interest (£8.7 million) was eventually
recovered, it took two and a half years and consumed a considerable sum in
costs.[19] In May 1991 two senior officials of the Spastics Society had to resign
after it was discovered they had placed community care business with a private
firm in which they had an interest.[20] Similarly, the London housing association
Circle 33 was defrauded of between £1 and £2 million by a greedy insider in
league with a building contractor.[21]

Maladministration, however, is a far graver threat to charities than systematic fraud. The Charity Commission identified more than twice as many cases
of maladministration as malpractice. In 1990 the campaigning charity War
on Want was declared insolvent. It had neglected the most basic financial

controls – budgets were over-spent; money held on trust was jumbled with money needed to run the charity; debts were uncollected; and membership records were inaccurate. Misleading accounts were published for five consecutive years. War on Want believed it had £1 million in the bank. In fact, it owed the bank over £41,000.[22]

The Charity as PLC

This was a telling insight into the old world of charity, where it was impertinent to question the motives or competence of charity managers and trustees, and embarrassing to treat income as seriously as expenditure. Such reticence allowed a cottage industry reliant largely on endowments to develop into a £13 billion a year multinational fund-raising business without either the donors, the beneficiaries, or the government daring to ask how the money was controlled or spent. At the time War on Want collapsed, charity was governed by an Act of Parliament passed thirty years before. The Charity Commission did not even have power to oblige charities to submit accounts. Just one in ten of the one hundred and seventy one thousand four hundred and thirty four charities then registered submitted them voluntarily. Many did not even reply to requests for financial information, partly because the Commission itself was working from a register which was inaccurate and out-of-date.

Charities had no incentive to help the Commission. Their ambition was to appear as poverty-stricken and pitiable as possible. Some officials refused to prepare accounts, or even tucked away assets and income where they could not be found by the auditors, for fear that contributions would dry up if they appeared too flush. At the Commission, files were prone to disappear. When Parliament passed a new Charities Act in 1992, its main goal was to give the Charity Commissioners the power to force charities to take their financial responsibilities seriously. All charities are now obliged to submit accounts to the Commission, audited by a firm of accountants if they are handling revenues of more than £100,000 a year.

This closer scrutiny by the state is another factor driving charities towards the corporate model of organisational life. Being a trustee of a charity used to be an unexacting honorarium. Now it means reading boardroom papers, scrutinising accounts, supervising the implementation of decisions by a board of directors, and reporting to the Charity Commission. As investment funds have increased in size, trustees are more conscious of their unlimited personal liability for losses. Working for a charity is now little different from working for a company, and people even plan careers in charity.[23] The London School of Economics and the Open University offer courses in charity management, and there is a visiting professorship in charity finance at the South Bank University.

The internal dynamics of a charity also have much in common with office life, even down to the politics. The average charity worker has about the same level of interest in the beneficiaries as the average corporate employee has in the customers. Their real energy is reserved for raising their own status and rewards. 'Whenever you talk to anyone in the organisation,' says one employee of a large charity, 'the first thing they mention is their car, the second is their line manager. About fourteenth down the list come children. Lots of people would like to leave, but their car is a golden handcuff.'[24] One reason why there are so many unflattering newspaper stories about the way charities are run is that the staff (like the employees of any large organisation) think they are being asked to do too much for too little money by managers they do not respect. Sane, the Terence Higgins Trust, the Charities Aid Foundation, Shelter and even Amnesty International have all had to contend with embarrassing stories of office life appearing or threatening to appear in the newspapers.

The management writer, Tom Lloyd, thinks charities are now so much like companies that the two species will eventually become indistinguishable, giving rise to an organisational hybrid he calls the 'comparity'.[25] This is not so far-fetched. In 1994 the management consultants of the Boston Consulting Group (BCG) offered to review the activities of a leading charity, Save the Children, for free. After much cogitation, their report concluded that the charity 'compares favourably to many corporate organisations with which we have worked. Indeed, we think there are some important lessons for the corporate world in the way it operates and thinks about itself.'[26]

The Charity as Huckster

The consultants meant that charities have ethical purpose, while companies have no purpose beyond survival. Yet this charitable ethic is being corrupted by the commercialisation of charity and the professionalisation of its management. The modern charity operates in a competitive marketplace. It must compete against other causes (and the National Lottery) to secure revenues. Charities are being dragged ever more downmarket as they battle to establish or retain a grip on the public imagination. What they are selling is compassion, but as a *product* or *service* rather than a moral *duty.* 'We're the market leader in first aid courses,' says the executive director at the St John Ambulance, without a trace of irony. St John Ambulance appears to make its services available free, but it expects donations, and often specifies how large they should be.[27]

Even charitable products and services need packaging. The Wishing Well Appeal for Great Ormond Street Children's Hospital was the first to make use of the entire armoury of media manipulation, branding and marketing techniques. Its tear-drop motif, created by an advertising agency, appeared in bus shelters and newspapers, and on Mars Bars, Hula Hoops, Skips, Comfort conditioner, Kodak films, Pudgies Baby Wipes and Wendy Wools.[28] The appeal, though facilitated by its focus on children, has become the charitable equivalent of a Harvard Business School case study of how to manage a major fund-raising appeal. Markets are researched, hoardings plastered, newspapers hired, and donors junkmailed. Fund-raising campaigns are subcontracted to professional firms of cold-callers and 'events' are staged for the media. Appeals on the lunch-time news, disguised as news items, have become notorious.

The modern charity-monger is proving – as newspaper editors and television producers before him – that an audience can be bought with sensational advertisements. Greenpeace (only part of which is a charity) recently ran an advertisement entitled 'You're not half the man your father was.' It claimed that chemical wastes were not only reducing sperm counts but shrinking penis sizes too. In a cinema advertisement, the NSPCC claimed that an argument between parents disturbs a foetus in the womb. None of these claims was scientifically verifiable.[29]

In 1995 the Royal Statistical Society criticised charities for using unreliable surveys and studies to support their claims, including small samples and out-of-date figures. Several charities were criticised by the Advertising Standards Authority for exaggerating claims, exploiting the trust of the public and damaging the credibility of the advertising industry.[30]

Other campaigns have relied, like Benetton, on shock value. One animal charity compared people who kill rabbits and squirrels for fun to a notorious American Serial Killer. The RSPCA used a photograph of a pile of dead dogs to campaign against the scrapping of the dog licence. But charities have always liked to shock consciences as well as prick them. Eglantyne Jebb, founder of Save the Children, was fined £5 for publishing a picture of starving Austrian children during the First World War. She knew that publicity-seeking is an essential part of the fund-raising process. Thomas Coram, who established the Foundling Hospital for orphans as long ago as 1741, knew it too. He solicited donations shamelessly from the great and good, making it fashionable for a politician (Walpole) artists (Hogarth and Handel) and leading professional men such as Sir Hans Sloane to give time and money to the Hospital.[31]

The Earl of Shaftesbury was not so much a philanthropist as a philanthropic brand name. As with Princess Diana, the knowledge that he was involved with a charitable project could transform its fortunes. This was why he could operate over an astonishing range of causes: mental health, blindness, education, housing, public hygiene. Over two hundred separate charities were represented at his funeral. Shaftesbury's protégé, Thomas Barnardo, was a brilliant publicist and marketing man, who raised around £3 million for children's homes in his lifetime. He was the first charity-monger to use photography, selling pictures of children 'before' and 'after' in the same way development charities do today. The first national street collection, Waif Saturday, was his idea. He organised house-to-house collections, leaving envelopes for collection later, and used parades and spectacular events at the Albert Hall to generate fund-raising publicity. Similarly, the revivalist Salvation Army meetings of William Booth, which used loud music and singing as much to raise money as to bring sinners to God, ante-dated Live Aid and Band Aid by a century.

The passion of the individual, and his or her willingness to use any methods, confront any interest and offend any opinion in pursuit of a cause, is where the life of any charity begins. On the face of it, the survival of these traits into the age of charity-as-business is encouraging. But there is also a risk that *caritas* is being corrupted by commerce. In a marketplace where thousands of images are jostling for the attention of a public whose sensibilities are numbed by the endless profanities of television and advertising, both companies and charities are finding that the only way to attract the attention of commuters and couch potatoes is to increase the dose. The charity industry has come to rely on the power of television to propel the image of a starving African child or a weeping Bosnian mother into the living-rooms of British suburbia. It was television which alerted Bob Geldof to the plight of the starving children of Ethiopia, and television which enabled him to do something about it.

Television is one of the reasons why charity, like football, is spawning a Premier League of giant charities which hog the headlines and win the prizes. The large medical and international disaster relief charities most easily marketed by television (such as Oxfam and Save the Children) tend to attract the bulk of voluntary donations. Starving children, unlike disabled children or wounded soldiers, make impressive television. Television may be a bad judge of the justice of a cause, but its unerring eye for the lowest common denominator has given charities access to audiences the Earl of Shaftesbury would not even have wanted to reach. Other media are following where it led. National and local radio stations and regional newspapers have all become part of the charity marketing machine.

This is changing the nature of charitable giving. Both the BBC (Children in Need) and ITV (Telethon) devote hours of television time to persuading viewers that giving money to charity is a form of entertainment. Comic Relief, a biannual charity-*fest* invented by a firm of professional fund-raisers, makes extravagant use of television time and television celebrities to raise money on its Red Nose Day. The National Lottery, where greed meets giving twice a week on prime-time television, has added 'good causes' to the lectionary of sound-bites. Charity is no longer rooted in biblical injunction or moral duty. It is a product people buy to make them feel good.

Charities as Brands

This is what makes charities valuable as brands. 'The secret of life is honest and fair dealing,' Groucho Marx said. 'If you can fake that, you've got it made.' Companies know that by securing charitable endorsements, or pledging sales proceeds to charities, they can increase sales by making themselves or their products seem virtuous. 'Cause-related marketing', as it is known, relies on the willingness of charities to sell their reputations for cash. 'Commercial organisations should recognise the benefit of using a charity as a brand name,' says a Mencap executive. 'Because of the "feel good factor", they can increase their market share at the same time as giving the charity a percentage in return.'[32]

Charities sometimes endorse particular products, imparting to the buyer an apparently objective testimonial as well as a feeling of wellbeing. But it can be a dangerous strategy to adopt, as the World Wide Fund for Nature (WWF) found out. In the 1980s the WWF allowed Procter & Gamble to put its panda logo on Ariel Ultra washing powder and Pampers nappies. This helped the company to persuade consumers its products were environmentally friendly, but damaged the WWF when it emerged that Ariel Ultra was tested on animals. Charities have made similar use of the Royal Family to add lustre to their causes. According to the Charities Aid Foundation, royals ranging from the Queen at the top to Angus Ogilvy at the bottom now patronise one thousand two hundred and fifty charities. The Prince of Wales is president of Business in the Community. Princess Anne is president of Save the Children. And Princess Diana, who wanted to be 'Queen of People's Hearts,' is probably doing as much in death as she did in life to turn charity into a fun-filled, television-based, celebrity-driven, mass-participation activity. Royals reach broader audiences than conventional celebrities. The prospect of their presence at a charity ball or gala evening pushes up the price of a ticket, and their powers of persuasion exceed those of professional fund-raisers. Patronising charities is not a new role for them: Queen Victoria's Indian famine fund of 1897 raised £2 million. According to the historian of the voluntary sector the extensive involvement of the royal family in charitable work is what has saved the country from republicanism.[33]

A strong brand is almost as good as royal patronage. Major national institutions – the RNLI, the RSPCA, Oxfam and Save the Children – enjoy the kind of instant brand recognition Guinness enjoys in the pub or MacDonald's in the High Street. Others, the Imperial Cancer Research Fund (ICRF) and the Cancer Research Campaign for example, struggle to differentiate themselves. Cancer is also a subject people prefer not to think about. As a marketing executive at the ICRF explains: 'We don't want to sell doom and gloom. . . . We need more optimism – the positive, not the negative, thinking.'[34] Some charities have changed their names in pursuit of a more positive image, rather as drab or failing companies sometimes do. After toying with Options, Link, Vanguard, Adapt and Excel, the Spastics Society eventually changed its name to SCOPE. Research showed that spastic had become an insult (though one used only by politically incorrect Conservatives such as Alan Clark). The Marriage Council and the National Society for the Parents of Backward Children did not face such a severe problem, but their names were distressingly to-the-point. They are now known, respectively, as Relate and Mencap.

For a charity such as SCOPE, an appealing public image is far from academic. It runs a chain of over three hundred shops generating annual sales of nearly £28 million and profits of over £8 million. It is competing against hundreds of other charity shops, not only for customers but for donated goods. One of the most noticeable changes in the British High Street over the last ten years is the replacement of electrical retailers and small supermarkets by the charity shop. In 1998 the annual survey of charity retailers by *NGO Finance Magazine* identified over six thousand charity shops around the country – or more than twice as many as on its first survey seven years earlier.[35] They are scarcely Big Business (turning over just £356 million) but powerful enough to upset their commercial neighbours. High Street retailers complain that charity shops compete unfairly, using unpaid labour, and selling new as well as donated goods with full relief from VAT and 80 per cent relief from business rates.

Oxfam has become a sophisticated retailer. It moves secondhand clothes between shops, tailoring its supplies to local demand to minimise disposals to rag merchants. It sells a high proportion of new but 'Fair Trade' and 'No Logo' goods to capitalise on mistrust of supermarkets and manufacturers, and is now experimenting with stand-alone *Fair Trade* shops, specialist book stores and branded Origin outlets to attract fashion-conscious secondhand buyers. But as the shops have become more adept at sourcing, distribution and stock control, they have also become more expensive to run. In London, a shop manager can now expect to earn up to £20,000. The head of retail trading for Help the Aged told *NGO Finance* in 1996 that 'the charity shop sector can now start to pay market salaries, thus improving the quality of management at all levels.'[36] A recent advertisement for head of retail operations at the British Heart Foundation boasted that the charity was opening a new shop every ten days.

TABLE 26.1
Top Ten Charity Retailers, 1997–98

	Shops	Staff		Sales	Profit	Goods
		*Full-Time	Volunteers	(£m)	(£m)	Donated (%)
Oxfam	873	448	22,588	60.4	16.5	80.9
British Heart Foundation	350	–	–	34.4	9.5	–
ICRF	468	–	14,000	30.5	3.2	73.1
SCOPE	302	764	3,432	27.8	8.5	90.3
Help the Aged	362	989	4,500	27.3	6.6	95.4
Barnardo's	332	†644	5,952	21.9	5.8	81.1
Cancer Research Campaign	255	354	5,000	18.5	4.6	100.0
British Red Cross	425	363	6,102	14.0	4.4	96.2
Sue Ryder Foundation	585	–	–	13.6	3.4	–
PDSA	110	299	1,702	9.1	2.5	98.2
82 Charity Retailers Surveyed	6,238	†5,400	92,500	356.0	91.0	86.4

Source: *NGO Finance Magazine*, July/August 1998.

* Plus full-time equivalents.
† Estimated.

Success at retailing has not arrested the decline in income from the general public. The NCVO reckons that the value of personal giving by all means, from buying a dinner jacket at a charity shop to signing a covenant form, fell from over £5.5 billion in 1993 to about £4.5 billion in 1996. The most visible forms of fund-raising – church collections, raffles, jumble sales, sponsored fun runs and street collections – are still the largest source of income.[37] But the amounts raised from individuals are not large, and are getting smaller. The average donation (much distorted by a few large givers) is £4.13 a week. Two out of three people give nothing to charity at all.[38]

There are occasional spectaculars. In 1992 Eugénie Boucher, a yachtswoman, left the RNLI £4.2 million. In 1996 Arthur McCullagh, a Dorset miser, left £1.2 million to four charities.[39] Some of the richest people donate sums of this magnitude, usually through a personal charitable foundation, but their gifts are unimpressive as proportions of their total income or assets. One study of the charitable giving of the five hundred wealthiest people in Britain reckoned that the richer people become, the smaller the proportion of their income and wealth they give to charity.[40] The rich, it seems, share the popular cynicism about charity, believing that the money they donate never reaches people in need, that too many charities have plush offices, and (paradoxically) that most charities are run by disorganised amateurs. The cynicism is obviously convenient, but research shows that people give more to local charities, or to projects they are involved in, which is why the biggest national charities are trying to build long-term relationships with their supporters.

Selling Charity to Companies

An increasingly important audience for the modern charity salesman is the corporate sector, which is certainly under-exploited. CAF puts total corporate giving by the top five hundred companies in 1996–7 at £305.6 million, or less than 2p in every £1 earned by the voluntary sector.[41] Though corporate support given in kind (free office space and staff on secondment) is not recorded properly, in the first half of the 1990s company giving fell slightly.[42] It has since recovered but still amounts to less than one quarter of one penny of pre-tax profits at the large companies monitored by CAF. Its present modesty is the main reason business giving is the source of charitable income most likely to grow. Companies are conscious of the sales value of charitable associations; they call it 'cause-related marketing'. Many company directors are also impressed by 'stakeholding' ideas, which oblige them to bankroll national charities and invest in the 'communities' where they have offices or factories. Corporate Community Involvement or CCI, as it has become known, now fills a few pages in every annual report; there is also an organisation, Business in the Community, persuading companies to give time and money to 'good causes'. Three out of four companies in the FTSE-100 belong to it.

Business in the Community was founded in 1982, after the industrial holo-caust of the previous two years had sparked riots in the inner cities. Its declared intention was to create small businesses in places like Toxteth and Brixton. But that seems to have lapsed. In 1986, Business in the Community set up the Per Cent Club: companies whose members promised to give not less than half a per cent of pre-tax profits or 1 per cent of dividends to community projects in cash or kind (mostly staff secondments). The moving spirit behind both organisations was Sir Hector Laing, then the chairman of

TABLE 26.2
Most Generous Personal Givers

	Annual (£m)	% of Personal Wealth	Foundation
George Soros	100.0	14.0	Open Society Fund, Soros Foundations
David Sainsbury	11.1	0.8	Gatsby Foundation
Sainsbury Brothers	10.4	2.2	Linbury, Headley, Monument Trusts
Peter Beckwith	5.0	12.3	Beckwith Charitable Trust
Martyn Arbib	4.1	2.1	Arbib Foundation
Sir Kirby & Maurice Laing	3.6	10.2	Laing Foundations
Robert Edmiston	3.0	1.0	Christian Vision
J. Paul Getty	3.0	3.0	J. Paul Getty Trust
Vivien Duffield	2.8	7.0	Clore Foundation
Moores Family	2.8	0.6	Moores Foundations
Paul Hamlyn	2.7	1.3	Paul Hamlyn Foundation
Sir James Goldsmith*	2.5	0.5	Goldsmith Foundation
Cameron Mackintosh	1.9	0.9	Mackintosh Foundation
Lord Rayne	1.8	2.2	Rayne Foundation and Rayne Trust
Benzion Freshwater	1.6	0.8	Mayfair Charities
Prince Charles	1.5	1.0	Prince of Wales Charities
Wates Family	1.4	1.7	Wates Foundation
Richard Branson	1.2	0.2	Healthcare Foundation
Sir Andrew Lloyd Webber	1.2	0.2	Various
David Thompson	1.2	0.2	Thompson Charitable Trust

Source: *The Millionaire Givers*, Directory of Social Change, 1994.

* Sir James Goldsmith died in 1997.

United Biscuits. 'I used to suggest to my business friends and acquaintances that they should get involved because if we have a rundown society our profits too would run down,' Laing told Tom Lloyd.[43] It marked the beginning of a concerted effort by Big Business, at a time when it was popularly supposed to be sacking people by the thousand, to win legitimacy on other grounds.

Companies see a number of other advantages to supporting charitable activities. At its crudest, sponsoring a charity ball or concert is an opportunity for directors and their wives to meet VIPs. Supporting a particular charitable cause can also deflect begging letters, disarm demonstrators, and impress hostile local and national politicians. More importantly, funding charities creates what Lloyd calls 'reputational assets'.[44] According to MORI, in the course of a year, three out of ten consumers will boycott a company or its products for ethical reasons.[45] This is why BT advertises its commitment to disabled groups and community projects on prime-time television ('You were always on my mind') and Tesco told shoppers it was devoting a proportion of its profits to buying personal computers for schools. Tesco claims the promotion increased sales. Inevitably, the first attempts are being made to gauge the value of CCI in terms of additional sales and profits.

Naturally, it will be helpful to charities if they can uncover a direct link between philanthropy and profit. But it is not necessary (the causation could just as easily work the other way) for businessmen to believe that the benefits of CCI are so concrete before they become involved. One reason BTR struggled to take over Pilkington was the contrast between its reputation as an 'asset-stripper' and the traditional commitment of the glassmaker to the town of St Helen's. Local and national politicians naturally find it hard to refuse meetings, subsidies and planning applications to companies with a strong charitable record. Journalists find them harder to attack. Consumers trust brands associated with good causes, and employees like to feel they are working for a company with a conscience. It is even said that ethically-minded graduates prefer to join the company with the biggest community programme rather than the biggest salary. Some companies claim seconding staff to charitable projects is a valuable aspect of staff training. Allen Sheppard has described a secondment to a charity as 'better than a thousand management courses. It's playing the game for real.'[46]

There seem to be less tangible rewards for staff. The life assurance and pensions company, Allied Dunbar, has encouraged employees to volunteer for charity work for over a decade. It reckons this has encouraged staff to stay with the company.[47] People who sell life assurance probably have an unusually high need to feel they are doing good (the sales techniques at Allied Dunbar have earned the firm the nickname of Allied Crowbar) but virtually every company in the country has found adopting a charity a useful antidote to the soullessness of life in the modern PLC. According to Geoffrey Mulcahy, chairman of Kingfisher, soulfulness is not purchased at the expense of the shareholder. 'We have four guiding principles,' he wrote in 1993. 'The first and firmest is that any issue we support must be relevant to our mainstream corporate objectives. . . . We support crime prevention because this ties in with the high street environment. . . . We support women's issues, because two-thirds of our employees are women. We are also active on critical health issues and education, because these too affect our employees.'[48] By using criteria as broad as this, companies can justify supporting any cause they care to name.

Enthusiasts for corporate giving believe that CCI marks the beginnings of

TABLE 26.3
Most Generous Corporate Givers (£m)

Company	Total
British Telecommunications PLC	15.6
National Westminster Bank PLC	15.0
Boots Company PLC	12.8
Barclays Bank PLC	10.0
Marks & Spencer PLC	9.8
B. A. T. Industries PLC	8.8
SmithKline Beecham PLC	7.4
Glaxo Wellcome PLC	7.0
British Petroleum Company PLC	6.2
Seagram Distillers PLC	5.5
Scottish & Newcastle PLC	5.0
Unilever	5.0
Grand Metropolitan PLC*	4.9
Shell UK Limited	4.3
Bank of Scotland	3.9
Cadbury Schweppes PLC	3.8
Halifax PLC	2.9
Tesco PLC	2.9
Esso UK Limited	2.8
BG plc	2.7
Total Support by CAF 500	305.6

Source: Charities Aid Foundation, *Dimensions of the Voluntary Sector*, 1998 Edition.
All figures are for 1996–7.

* Grand Metropolitan merged with Guinness in 1997 to create Diageo PLC.

a new social movement, comparable with the industrial benefactors of the Victorian age. They anticipate a time when companies will cease to be the exclusive property of the shareholders and become a social organism whose importance ranges beyond share prices and dividends. The difficulty with this prognosis is that the modern PLC, unlike its Victorian predecessor, divorces control from ownership. The paternalistic industrialists of the last century – Salt, Rowntree, Cadbury and Lever – owned all or most of the companies whose funds were diverted into better housing or working conditions for employees. Their employees did not just work for the company but lived in a company house, visited the company doctor, and attended company-organised night schools, debates, sports matches and holidays. The Victorian paternalists were industrial examples of a kind many would find intolerable today.

There is also a fundamental awkwardness, pointed out by Milton Friedman thirty-five years ago. The money the managers of a modern PLC give to charity does not belong to them:

> A major complaint made frequently against modern business is that it involves the separation of ownership and control – that the corporation has become a social institution that is a law unto itself, with irresponsible executives who do not serve the interests of their stockholders. This charge is not true. But the direction in which policy is now moving, of permitting corporations to make contributions for charitable purposes and allowing deductions for income tax, is a step in the direction of creating a true divorce between ownership and control and of undermining the basic nature and character of our society. It is a step away from an individualistic society and toward the corporate state.[49]

Although it is convenient for directors to believe that charitable giving adds value, and even more convenient for the charity industry to convince them it does, it is extremely hard to substantiate connections between corporate giving and corporate profitability. This is the main reason why corporate donations to charity remain at a low level.

Investment Income

For charities, investment income is much more important than corporate giving. Income from interest payments, share dividends, property rents and capital gains from the sales of assets account for one fifth of the income of the charity industry, or nearly £2.5 billion. The NCVO estimates that charities own total assets worth £39.8 billion and net assets of nearly £36.5 billion. These consist largely of stocks and shares (£25.2 billion) and cash (£5.4 billion) but include a surprising amount of land and buildings (£7.1 billion).[50] Some charities – the National Trust, the RNLI, the Salvation Army, Barnardo's and the Royal Society for the Protection of Birds – have to invest heavily in land and buildings to discharge their duties. The National Trust owns nearly six hundred thousand acres, and the RSPB nearly a quarter of a million acres. But £2 in every £3 owned by charities is invested in securities – a proportion which has increased since government relaxed restrictions on the assets charities are allowed to buy.

These enormous investment funds have made charities attractive to City fund managers. When the Wellcome Trust invited fund managers to look after its £2.75 billion portfolio, two hundred and thirty-seven firms applied. But the distribution of wealth within the industry is beginning to cause controversy. Unpopular causes tend not to attract generous benefactors or donations (with the exception of AIDS, which has benefited from its popularity among artists and thespians) while popular causes like cancer, children, animals, international relief and the environment tend to be heavily overfunded. In 1994, for example, the Charity Commission investigated why Guide Dogs for the Blind was still advertising for donations when it had reserves of £160 million. Meanwhile, the Royal National Institute for the Blind is chronically short of funding for medical research, education and publishing activities.

Inefficiencies of this kind are fuelling demands for mergers in the charity industry, which is highly fragmented; of more than one hundred and eighty-seven thousand charities registered in England and Wales and another thirty thousand in Scotland and Northern Ireland, 98 per cent have an annual income of less than £1 million.[52] 'The British in particular are ferociously individualistic about the way they approach problems,' Princess Anne, president of Save the Children, told the *Financial Times*. 'There is always an inclination to set up another fund.'[53]

As in other parts of the corporate economy, the bigger charities are getting bigger; in the first half of the 1990s, the income of the wealthiest charities grew twice as fast as the average, while many smaller charities experienced a decline.[54] The government has tried to encourage consolidation, by allowing smaller charities to wind up and transfer their assets to larger ones; some leading charities even talk openly of taking over their smaller rivals to eliminate the clutter of competing brand names. 'Why are there so many cancer charities?' asks Seymour Fortescue, the finance director of the Imperial Cancer Research Fund. 'Mergers would help the reputation of charities generally. There are . . . far too many.'[55] A merger wave would be an apposite way of celebrating the triumph of the values of the PLC in the charitable sector.

Nationalisation of Charity

But in terms of income, charities are more like nationalised industries than PLCs: they are increasingly dependent on the taxpayer. The state – as Whitehall, town hall, health authority, quango and European Union – now provides nearly one third of the income of the charitable sector.[56] The taxpayer is the largest single contributor to its income, and charities sell almost as many goods and services to the government as they do to the general public.[57] Modern governments have always given money to charity, in terms of tax

TABLE 26.4
The Richest Charities, 1997* (£m)

Charity	Net Assets	Investment Income
National Trust	509.3	40.4
Salvation Army	297.3	6.4
Royal National Lifeboat Institution (RNLI)	238.5	10.7
Guide Dogs for the Blind	196.1	7.1
Barnardo's	183.8	6.0
Royal Air Force Benevolent Fund	137.5	5.2
British Heart Foundation	109.9	6.5
Royal Society for the Prevention of Cruelty to Animals (RSPCA)	119.0	4.3
Council for World Mission	102.9	3.4
Imperial Cancer Research Fund	97.5	2.9
Leonard Cheshire Foundation	93.4	2.2
National Trust for Scotland	89.6	4.5
British Red Cross	88.1	3.5
Royal National Institute for the Blind	87.0	2.2
Royal Masonic Benevolent Institution	84.1	2.2
NCH Action for Children	78.9	2.1
St Dunstan's	77.5	5.9
People's Dispensary for Sick Animals	64.1	1.8
RUKBA	55.9	5.2
Institute of Cancer Research	45.7	2.3

Source: Charities Aid Foundation, *Dimensions of the Voluntary Sector*, 1998 Edition.

* Excluding Christ's Hospital (Chapter 7) with net assets of £154 million; Church of England Pensions Board (Chapter 4), net assets of £57 million; Anchor Trust Housing Association, net assets of £82.4 million; Methodist Homes for the Aged, with net assets of £49.7 million.

relief and cash grants, but they now sub-contract to charities responsibilities once regarded as core services of local or national government. This has given rise to a 'contract culture' far removed from traditional ideas of philanthropy.

This is especially true of the large charities. According to the Charities Aid Foundation, fees paid by local and central government accounted for 14 per cent of the income of the top five hundred charities in 1996–7. When grants from various public sources are included, the state is the source of £1 in every £4 they raise. In 1995 the foundation discovered that some charities were receiving almost their whole income from the taxpayer. Even household names such as Barnardo's (40 per cent), the National Children's Home (57 per cent) and SCOPE (50 per cent), were receiving income from the state sufficient to raise serious doubts about their independence.[58]

Charities collect about £3.5 billion a year from the government in fees, grants, tax relief and assistance in kind. The money goes to job creation programmes in the inner cities, conservation and environmental projects and campaigns against racialism and drug abuse, as well as to more orthodox charitable causes. But it is at the local rather than the national government level that public support is having the most significant impact on the charitable sector: charities are among the chief beneficiaries of a shift in local government from providing services to procuring them. This is especially true of social services. 'Care in the community', where local authorities are obliged to buy 85 per cent of their needs from private and voluntary groups, is the best-known example. But children's homes, meals-on-wheels, nursing care for the elderly, special education schemes for children and the rehabilitation of prisoners are all provided on contract by the charity industry. Over two thousand housing associations, many of which are charities and all of which are non-profit making, receive £3 billion a year in loans and grants from the taxpayer. Charities also benefit from business rate relief, staff secondments, peppercorn rents and other assistance in kind.[59]

Value of Tax Relief

But no subvention from the state is more valuable to charities (or more controversial) than their tax privileges. Every charity benefits from tax relief, and would benefit more if people used tax-efficient methods of donation.[60] Charities can reclaim the income tax paid on donations through Payroll Giving (where employees nominate charities to relieve a proportion of their pay), Deeds of Covenant (where people give a specific sum for a specified period for nothing in return) and Gift Aid (where people give lump sums). In the 1998 Budget the threshold for Gift Aid was lowered to £100, and extended to overseas as well as domestic charities.

Like pension funds, charities could reclaim the income tax deducted from their investment income until Gordon Brown abolished Advance Corporation Tax (ACT) in his Budget of July 1997. Though the government has since agreed to phase out relief for charities over the five years to April 2004, loss of the tax credit will damage one of the few sources of charitable income which is buoyant. Having warned during the Election campaign of 1997 that the Conservative aim of reducing the basic rate of income tax to 20p would cost the voluntary sector £30 million in lost tax relief, the chief executive of the NCVO was forced to complain after the election that the abolition of

ACT would cost the sector up to £250 million.[61] The effects will probably be harsher: the Inland Revenue has estimated that the loss of the dividend tax credit will cost the charitable sector £350 million a year when it takes full effect.

Charities were consoled by a government promise to review the structure of charitable taxation, and for a time nursed hopes that the tax credit would be switched to donors. This would undoubtedly increase the number and value of charitable donations, and was advanced energetically by the culture secretary, Chris Smith, who saw it as the ideal answer to gripes that promises of cash by the government in Opposition were not being fulfilled. But the proposal was dropped when it was realised that the tabloids would not take kindly to subsidising luvvies (and public schools). The hopes of the industry now rest on relief for irrecoverable VAT. Charities pay about £400 million a year in VAT which they are unable to claim back because they do not charge VAT on the non-profit-making goods and services they supply. It is an old ambition, which is unlikely to be fulfilled.

The government has further weakened the financial position of the charitable sector by exacerbating the already harmful effects of the National Lottery. Next to bingo halls and pools companies, no sector of the economy has suffered more from the National Lottery than the charity industry. Research suggests that spending on lottery tickets is the main source of stagnation in individual donations. It is true that charities are also one of the main beneficiaries of the National Lottery. By 1998, charities had received £638 million from the National Lottery Charities Board; the sector is expected to collect £1.8 billion over the seven-year life of the Camelot contract. But the addition by the government of a sixth 'good cause' will divert resources from charities to mainstream health and education projects.

In 1997, £150 million originally intended for charities, the arts, heritage and sport was diverted to the New Opportunities Fund set up by the government to tackle social deprivation. It left the National Lottery Charities Board £60 million worse off. Another £400 million of Lottery money is now going into after-school clubs and 'healthy living centres.' Once the Millennium funding comes to an end in 2001, health and education are expected to consume a third of all Lottery funding. Much of it will go to projects (like homework clubs, breast screening, scanners and hospices) which charities were assured would continue to be funded by the taxpayer in the normal way. Charities, with their well-developed sense of where the money now is, reckon the only way to recoup the lost revenues is to offer to run some of the Sixth Good Cause projects themselves.

Corruption of Charity

It is a reminder of how dependent charities have become. Many of the larger charities are now nationalised enterprises in all but name. There is growing concern, both inside and outside the world of charity, about the effects of reliance on public funding on the autonomy and the ethics of the charity industry. 'The issue,' as Frank Prochaska has written, 'is not that the voluntary sector has become a state within the state, but that so many charities have become *agencies* of the state ... It is no longer obvious that a charitable institution is not a government body ... The two sectors have become entangled.'[62] Charities are no longer performing tasks they choose, or which the state cannot fulfil, but are charging the taxpayer to deliver services which the state ought to be providing.

The underlying purpose of a charity is no longer sacrosanct once public money is invested in its work. Robert Whelan cites the example of two charities in the East End – the Mildmay Hospital and the Mayflower Centre – whose original purposes and Christian ethic were undermined by their reliance on state funding. Similarly, public subsidies forced Barnardo's to abandon its fierce Protestant evangelicalism for a 'statement of Basic Values' fit for a multicultural society. Charities dependent on income from contracts with the state have a strong incentive to encourage the view that public services are in a permanent state of crisis, surviving only through subsidies supplied by the voluntary sector. This puts taxpayers in the curious position of subsidising anti-government propaganda. Shelter, for example, accepts over £3 million in government grants while blaming the government for homelessness.

'We still work hard on increasing our voluntary income,' a Mencap official told the *Financial Times*. 'We make use of government money but it doesn't in any way stop our hand in campaigning on issues that are important to us.'[63] In fact, a great deal of money and ingenuity is thrown into campaigns for expansion of the tax privileges of charities. The Conservative government was persuaded to waive VAT on Live Aid in 1985, and in 1997 the New Labour government was bullied into returning the VAT on sales of *Candle in the Wind*. In 1995, when three hundred charities formed a Charities Tax Reform Group to campaign for an end to irrecoverable VAT, they took full page advertisements in the broadsheet newspapers, saying 'charities are having to use donated money – your money – to pay tax.'[64] The review of taxation has heard from almost all the major charities, and from a newly formed Charities Joint Fiscal Working Group.

Dependence on public money is bound to alter the behaviour of charities. In providing services to national and local government, charities work to budgets and targets set by ministers and officials, and standards are enforced by formal contracts. Even Lottery funding comes with objectives defined and conditions attached. Charities are losing their independence. One of the first great charitable institutions in Britain, the Foundling Hospital, discovered this as long ago as the eighteenth century. As state funding rose to half its income in the 1760s, the government insisted that the trustees sell assets and reduce the cost of keeping the children by apprenticing them to local tradesmen. It was to re-capture their ability to do what they thought best for the orphans in their care that the trustees developed their estate in central London, creating a valuable rental income. Most modern charities have no such windfall to cash in. Some would collapse if the state withdrew its favour. But the greatest loss is the shrinkage of diversity and innovation in social policy. Many of the better ideas developed by the voluntary sector die because charity managers know that the state will never give them a subsidy.

Grant-Making Trusts

Growing dependence on the state is magnified by the failure of the British voluntary sector to develop large, independent grant-making funds of the kind common in the United States. The endowments of foundations like Ford and Rockefeller make them unique in being able to decide what causes to support. They do not depend on the whim of public opinion, the dictates of a contract, or the caprice of voluntary giving. Britain has some nine thousand grant-making charitable trusts, only one of which measures its assets in billions; between them, they make donations of less than £2 billion.[65] A proposal to use the grants dispensed by the National Lottery Charities Board to establish a trust of American dimensions has yet to be taken seriously. Meantime, the British foundations will remain dependent on the enthusiasms of a few rich men.

The modern charitable trust is the successor to the many secular foundations endowed by rich men in the centuries after the Reformation. Henry Smith's Charity, which dates from the endowment of his trustees in 1627 with sufficient money to buy eighty-four acres of what is now South Kensington, is still one of the largest charitable foundations in Britain. Though the remains of the estate were sold in 1995 to another charitable fund (the Wellcome Trust) for £283 million, Henry Smith (Estates Charities) dispenses £15 million a year. Its survival and expansion owes much to luck, but it is also a good measure of the scale of post-Reformation philanthropy.

The second Elizabethan era has seen a comparable flourishing of plutocratic investment in charitable foundations; this time the motivation was not religion, but taxation. Modern foundations are set up when a rich man decides to sell some or all of his stake in the business he has created. Rather than pay capital gains, or even income tax on the revenue from investing the sale proceeds, the rich prefer to retain a measure of control over the wealth they have created by shifting a large portion of the proceeds into a tax-free charitable trust. One study found that the peak period for the establishment of charitable foundations was between 1950 and the mid-1970s, an era of exceptionally high rates of income tax. It seems that the rates of income tax are now too low to encourage them.[66]

Their value is probably shrinking anyway, as the ownership of companies becomes increasingly institutionalised. Foundations did not flourish solely because they were tax-efficient; they were also a useful device for retaining control. Most of the charitable foundations in Britain today were endowed, initially at least, with a large block of shares in the company created by the benefactor. The Wolfson Foundation was endowed with shares in Great Universal Stores, the Tudor Trust with shares in Wimpey Construction, the Leverhulme Trust with shares in Unilever, the Garfield Weston Foundation with shares in Associated British Foods, and the Wellcome Trust with shares in Wellcome pharmaceuticals. In 1993 David Sainsbury gave the Gatsby Foundation (he is a Scott Fitzgerald fan) stock worth £200 million.

This level of exposure to a single company has its drawbacks. One reason the Nuffield Foundation has shrunk is that it failed to disinvest from the motor industry before British Leyland went bust in 1975. Similarly, in the early 1990s the Baring Foundation was one of the most generous grant-making trusts in the country. In 1993 it disbursed over £9 million; two years later, with all but one sixth of its assets as shares in Barings Bank, it was virtually bankrupt. The Wellcome Trust and the Tudor Trust have diversified their assets to reduce exposure to a single business, but it is not easy for trustees to defy the will of a founder. Wellcome had to go to court to overturn the will of Sir Henry Wellcome, who laid it down in 1936 that shares should not be sold without 'good and unavoidable reason'.

The Wellcome Foundation is now the richest charitable trust in the world. Its total assets of £8 billion make it more than twice as wealthy as the Church of England and richer than the giant American foundations of Ford, Hughes and Kellogg. Its grants, in accordance with the will of the founder, fund medical research projects 'which may conduce to the improvement of the physical conditions of mankind'. This is a relatively narrow focus which has seen the Wellcome Trust spend more on medical research than the government-funded Medical Research Council. It has funded research in epidemiology, malaria, BSE and AIDS, which large pharmaceutical companies did not consider sufficiently profitable to pursue.

TABLE 26.5
Richest Grant-Making Charitable Trusts in 1997 (£m)

	Founder	Income	Grants	Assets
Wellcome Trust	Henry Wellcome	344.9	234.9	7,995
Leverhulme Trust	William Lever	19.5	12.6	650
Wolfson Foundation	Isaac Wolfson	21.3	18.3	533
Henry Smith (Estates Charities)	Henry Smith	21.1	14.9	503
Gatsby Charitable Foundation	David Sainsbury	18.4	16.9	447
Bridge House Estates Fund	City Corporation	34.1	14.5	395
Tudor Trust	Godfrey Mitchell	16.2	17.9	331
Esmee Fairbairn Charitable Trust	Ian Fairbairn	12.4	11.4	292
Shetland Islands Council Charitable Trust	Council	13.7	4.9	227
Joseph Rowntree Foundation	Joseph Rowntree	8.6	8.8	199
Nuffield Foundation	William Morris	7.9	6.5	179
Aga Khan Foundation (UK)	Aga Khan	52.7	32.8	173
Rank Foundation	J. Arthur Rank	9.1	7.0	169
Linbury Trust	Sainsburys	7.9	7.4	152
City Parochial Foundation	City Parishes	9.5	6.9	134
Joseph Rowntree Charitable Trust	Joseph Rowntree	4.3	3.7	115
Monument Trust	Sainsburys	4.5	6.1	99
Gannochy Trust	–	4.8	5.2	95
Henry Moore Foundation	Henry Moore	5.9	0.855	88
John Ellerman Foundation	John Ellerman	4.0	3.4	85

Source: Charities Aid Foundation, *Dimensions of the Voluntary Sector*, 1998 Edition.

This is one of the most important functions of charity: to serve as a forum for experimentation, not only in medicine but in all spheres of human endeavour. Charities are an important mechanism for discovering new needs, and a major source of ideas and techniques for achieving them. They can try new methods immediately, and drop them if they do not work. Institutions reliant on public money have no incentive to innovate, or even to spend money wisely. Ironically, this was foreseen by Sir William Beveridge, the founding father of the Welfare State. In *Voluntary Action*, published in 1948, he warned that the nationalisation of the activities of charities and other voluntary societies would destroy a valuable laboratory of social experimentation. 'In a field already made into a state monopoly, those dissatisfied with the institutions that they find can seek a remedy only by seeking to change the Government of the country,' he wrote. 'In a free society and a free field they have a different remedy; discontented individuals with new ideas can make a new institution to meet their needs. The field is open to experiment and success or failure; secession is the midwife of invention.' In the contract culture which now permeates the charitable sector, secession is no longer an option.

Decline of the Charitable Ethic

As dependence increases, the charitable ethic withers. Reliance on state funding and state contracts has robbed it of moral energy and the courage to discriminate. 'Private charity can give more to the more deserving,' John Stuart Mill said. 'The state must act by general rules. It cannot undertake to discriminate between the deserving and the undeserving indigent. It owes no more than subsistence to the first, and can give no less to the last . . . Private charity . . . in bestowing its own money, is entitled to do so according to its own judgment.'[67] The state dispenses charity not as a moral duty, but as a civil right. This was why the Evangelical conscience, which spawned the modern charity industry, opposed the expansion of the Welfare State.

'Are you zealous to redeem the time?' asked John Wesley, and many were. All the great Victorian philanthropists – Wilberforce, Shaftesbury, Barnardo, Booth – were zealous Evangelicals. They are only the best-remembered advocates of an urge to give which bordered on obsession. A survey conducted in the 1890s found that the average middle-class family devoted one tenth of their income to charitable causes – more than they spent on any other item except food. The Royal Commission investigating the Livery Companies of the City of London found that they were responsible for over a thousand charities, with a total income of nearly £4.5 million.[68] But the important difference between charity then and charity now was not scale, but ethics. The people who ran Victorian charities were not attacking poverty, disease and ignorance only but eliminating sin. Social evils were not a reflection of the structure of economic and social life; they were a measure of the moral shortcomings of individuals. The Victorian charity-worker argued there could be no permanent escape from destitution, and therefore no lasting social improvement, without moral elevation of the individual. Moral improvement could not be achieved by money alone, which would encourage people to live at the public expense if it were given without expecting anything in return.

It was the creed of the Charity Organisation Society, set up in 1869 to weld the explosion of charitable endeavours in London into some kind of system, that poverty could not be abolished without investigating and curing the causes of the poverty of the individual. (For this reason the society pioneered the 'casework' of the modern social worker.) Octavia Hill, housing reformer and co-founder of the National Trust, was a leading figure in the society.[69] 'The people's homes are bad, partly because they are badly built and arranged; they are ten-fold worse because their habits and lives are what they are,' she wrote. 'Transplant them tomorrow to healthy and commodious homes, and they would pollute and destroy them.'[70]

Octavia Hill believed that people had to learn the self-respect to fit them for decent housing, so she opposed the construction of houses on a non-commercial basis. She expected her tenants to pay a commercial rent (her charity was what the housing historian J. N. Tarn called '5 per cent phil-anthropy').[71] Hill was fiercely opposed to publicly-owned housing. She attacked Joseph Chamberlain for advocating the construction of council houses, and later refused to serve on the Royal Commission on Housing, set up in 1889. Her method was to despatch lady visitors to collect the rent and check that the tenants were keeping the place clean. Improvements to the property were conditional on prompt and regular payment of the rent, and on keeping the house spotless[72] – a rough and ready measure of moral character.

Such views are deeply unfashionable today. The Victorian distinction between the deserving and the undeserving poor (it was diluted to 'helpable' and 'unhelpable' in Edwardian times) is anathema to the modern charity worker. Today, the poor are not the authors of their fate. They are, as the Church of England has it, the victims of the 'unjust structures of society'. On this view, offering direct help to the victims of poverty, ignorance and disease is either pointless or actively damaging, in that it helps to prolong a system which cannot be redeemed except by the state. This is why so many charities have become lobbyists for changes in the law, or higher public expenditure, or some combination of the two.

Charities as Lobbyists

In 1995 Church Action on Poverty listed its achievements as commissioning six national poverty consultations, the opening of a parliamentary office, running Unemployment Sunday, organising conferences and training events, convening meetings with ministers, giving evidence to parliamentary commit-tees, and briefing the press. Robert Whelan comments:

> Modern Christian charities . . . seem to regard life on welfare as a valid
> option, and even offer training for it. Projects for the homeless tend to
> be based on the assumption that the ideal solution is to get the sufferer

on to the right combination of welfare benefits. Whereas William Booth used to boast of the numbers of homeless men he had been able to get off the booze, on their feet, re-united with their families and back into the workforce, the annual reports of some modern charities for the homeless, including the Christian-based ones, are more likely to detail the numbers who have been helped into council flats and on to income support.[73]

This view of charitable work is characteristic of the modern campaigning charity. 'We are not in the business of spending money to house the homeless,' a Shelter official explains, 'but on advice and lobbying to improve their general welfare.'[74] The equivalent of the Bible and the temperance tract is the Child Poverty Action Group guide to means-tested benefits.

It is an understandable order of priorities. Modern charities face a dilemma which did not confront their Victorian forebears: except in the developing world, where poverty is a daily, life-threatening reality, there is little more pressing for them to do. At the beginning of the twentieth century, the income of charities tackling poverty far exceeded total government expenditure on the same problem. Today, state spending on poverty, education and health far exceeds any sum which Oxfam or Christian Aid or even Band Aid could dream of. The total assets of the industry are about one tenth of annual public expenditure, and its income even less. Before the Welfare State, the relief of poverty, ignorance and disease was seen as the responsibility of private conscience and organised charity. The motives of the charitable were often debatable – charity was what some did to restrain the mob, or the free-spending state – and expectations of private enterprise were higher. Hill and Shaftesbury built model houses for rent in the full expectation that private builders would follow their example.

'Such interposition,' Shaftesbury said of state involvement in social welfare, 'must not take place until every effort has been made, every expedient exhausted, and indisputable proof given that, if the state does not do the work, it will never be done at all.'[75] Today, charity defines itself as doing only those things which are not done by the state at all. Over the last one hundred years, the state has aggrandised whole spheres of charitable endeavour familiar to the Victorians: housing, health, education, the elderly, children. Donations fell as taxes rose; the right to claim became more important than the duty to give. Charity was driven into ghettos like medical counselling (the Terrence Higgins Trust, set up in memory of the first British victim of AIDS) or suicide (The Samaritans, set up by Chad Varah in 1953) or modern missionary work (Voluntary Service Overseas, set up by Alec Dickson in 1956). Two in three of the top five hundred charities are now engaged in the arts or recreation, education and research, or social services, plugging the gaps in an otherwise all-embracing Welfare State.[76]

Much of the moral energy which once went into charitable work is now dissipated in political activities whose principal aim is not to alleviate suffering but to change government policy. In theory, charities are forbidden to campaign politically. Many of the most vociferous voluntary groups in Britain – Action on Smoking and Health, the Child Poverty Action Group, Compassion in World Farming, Greenpeace, the Joseph Rowntree Foundation, the National Council for Civil Liberties – have abjured charitable status in order to engage in political campaigning. Others – Christian Aid, Oxfam and Shelter – defy the ban more or less openly. In May 1991 Oxfam was formally censured by the Charity Commission for its openly political Free Front Line Africa, anti-apartheid, and anti-Khmer Rouge campaigns. Even the RSPCA has taken advantage of its unique constitution (it was set up by its own Act of Parliament in 1824) to campaign politically against abolition of the dog licence, export of veal calves and intensive pig and chicken farming. In 1996 Interpal, a charity for Palestinian refugees, was investigated by the Commission after newspaper allegations that it part-funded the Hamas terrorist group. It cleared Interpal of these charges.[77]

The traditional idea of charity is now under severe strain. An industry reliant on the taxpayer for the bulk of its income is using public money for political purposes. Services which could easily be supplied by ordinary companies on normal commercial terms are being supplied by charities armed with a variety of grants, fees and subsidies from the taxpayer. The legal definition of what is and is not a charitable cause is unchanged since the Statute of Charitable Uses of 1601: the relief of poverty, education, the spread of religion and any purpose deemed beneficial to the community. But the application of this outdated formula in modern conditions is arbitrary. A public school or religious cult can obtain charitable status; the village rugby club or Greenpeace cannot.

Some say a new definition is needed. In 1998 the Charity Commission began a comprehensive review of its register of charities. It is certain that some charitable causes will lose the coveted status and the tax privileges it brings, and that more fashionable causes will win them. Others argue that charitable status should not be redefined, but abolished.[78] In 1993 an official report on the future of voluntary action argued that charities delivering public services should lose their tax privileges and compete for public contracts without the benefit of subsidies:

Charity is a medieval concept that has no place in the modern world . . . A compelling financial argument for the abolition of charity is that it makes *no economic sense*, even in its own terms. From the point of view of value for money in the contracts culture, charity has no merit. It is a category that attaches itself to organisations not to action, and ... only a proportion of what a charitable organisation does is in fact charitable ... Providing services could be a candidate for charitable activity. The remainder relate to organisational matters such as planning, public relations, fund-raising, staffing and other management and logistical functions that have nothing to do with any charitable output.[79]

Loosely translated, the author was arguing that many charities are PLCs in every respect except their tax status.[80] He wants charities pared back to organisations which identify needs, relieve them and campaign for change. The rest would be stripped of their tax privileges, and set the same performance targets as any other supplier of services to the government. His view was endorsed by the Duke of Edinburgh in his 1994 Arnold Goodman lecture, but it was too explosive for the politicians. John Major disowned the report; it will be surprising if the present government dares even to rob the public schools of charitable status.

Like the public schools, charities are discovering that taking the Queen's shilling means taking the Queen's orders. The consequences reverberate beyond the shriven ethic and shrinking autonomy of the charitable sector. True charity is a vital moral force, which goads the fortunate into considering and addressing the plight of the poor, the sick, the destitute and the lonely. The Duchess of Gloucester once remarked that it was impossible to be a volunteer in her native Denmark because the state had left no meritorious works undone. The opportunity for doing good in Britain is not yet extinct, though it is much reduced. Only the opportunity to moralise has disappeared. But charity is not alone in the alterations which it has adopted or endured, and the inducements it has lost. Its reshaping by the machinations of the state, its growing commercialisation, and the accompanying loss of moral purpose, echo uncannily across a world where the PLC is obliterating all other forms of ownership: the world of money itself.

PART FIVE

FINANCE

CHAPTER TWENTY-SEVEN

BANKS AND BUILDING SOCIETIES

I sometimes joke that I am the man who went into banking because the law was unpopular.
> LORD ALEXANDER, Chairman, NatWest Bank[1]

To the average customer, mutuality means nothing other than irritation. If building societies didn't exist, they wouldn't be invented today.
> ANDREW LONGHURST, Managing Director, Cheltenham and Gloucester[2]

If we fired everyone who made a bad loan, we would be a very small bank.
> PETER WOOD, Finance Director, Barclays Bank[3]

I am absolutely astonished that what seem to me to be ordinary management principles are not yet established in this industry.
> MARTIN TAYLOR, Chief Executive, Barclays Bank, 1993[4]

We're in the risk business. We take positions. We lend money. We get most of it back.
> MARTIN TAYLOR, Chief Executive, Barclays Bank, 1998[5]

If I'm with a gang of people, and admit to being a banker, I get boxed around the ears. This does not happen in other countries. In other countries, bankers are well respected.
> SIR WILLIAM PURVES, Chairman, HSBC[6]

In February 1991, at the bottom of the deepest recession since the war, the chief executive of Lloyds Bank delivered a lecture at the Chartered Institute of Bankers in Lombard Street. 'We are facing the upheaval that manufacturing has already gone through,' Brian Pitman told his fellow bankers. 'Think of what happened to the engineering industry and the coal industry in the 1980s. We will go through the same thing because we have the same problems ... The whole idea that we must save our people, therefore we have to diversify, is wrong. We must cease to be workers' co-operatives and become successful businesses.'[7] The lecture was imbued with a characteristic demand for realism. Pitman had long cut an unusual figure in British banking: he believed that banks should be run for the benefit of their owners not their employees. A clearing banker born and bred, he had risen to the top of an industry whose ethos was closer to a nationalised industry than a commercial business. Only that year, Lord Alexander, patrician chairman of the National Westminster Bank, had described his organisation as 'part of the fabric of society'. It is a self-image the clearing banks have yet to shake off.

Why People Loathe Banks

For decades, banks had little incentive to pursue profits by pleasing customers. Until the 1980s, the clearing banks did not even pay interest on current accounts, giving themselves the cheapest funding of any business. They were insulated from competition by layers of laws and regulations, which they reinforced with self-imposed cartels. Employees joined the bank from school, as Brian Pitman had, with the justifiable expectation of securing a job for life. (It was not until 1994 that Barclays Bank made its first compulsory redundancies.) Customers were equally loyal, two thirds staying throughout their lives with the bank which first won their business, mainly because they saw no point in changing.

It was not surprising that one in two people, surveyed as recently as 1992, thought that the clearing banks were owned by the state: it matched their daily experience. Like nationalised industries, banks treated consumers with contempt. As customers used to associate British Telecom with strikes, queues for residential lines and broken public telephones, most people now associate their bank with random and unpredictable charges, 'till closed' notices, punitive rates of interest and pens that do not work. The clearing banks are the last major industry where the staff still strike regularly in pursuit of pay claims. The average branch even looks like a social security office.

From the 1930s, the banks operated a cartel which fixed the rate of interest on deposit accounts and overdrafts at unvarying margins below and above the Bank Rate at which they could themselves obtain funds.[8] They were not compelled, and felt no compunction, to publish the charges levied on personal accounts. They did not even inform customers, either in advance or after the event, that they were being levied. Cartelisation made it pointless for consumers to shop around, so banks confined their opening hours to 10.00 a.m. to 3.00 p.m., and in 1968 decided not to open at all on Saturdays.

Free banking for accounts in credit – introduced with great flourish in the mid-1980s as the flagship of a customer friendly service – encouraged banks to make exceptional charges. In 1993 the Royal Bank of Scotland was criticised for paying bonuses to staff who managed to increase the number of charges levied on customers.[9] 'It would make a great deal of sense if private customers were charged every time they cashed a cheque,' said Dr George Mathewson, the chief executive of the bank.[10] 'Free banking,' agreed Brian Pearse, then chief executive of the Midland Bank, 'was one of the two biggest mistakes ever made by high street banks.'[11]

To pay for it, banks have resorted to increasingly ingenious expedients. In 1994 a small businessman in Brighton who took his bank manager out to lunch found he was charged £110 for the manager's time. Yet banks are still enjoying a free lunch, even if their customers are not. Whenever a payment is made by cheque or standing order, banks debit the account of the payer immediately but collect three days' interest before crediting the account of the payee. It is not unknown for overdrawn accounts to endure longer delays, so as to maximise the charges levied. Once bank charges are included, the real rates of interest on an overdraft or a loan make usurers seem like saints. In 1994 a Sunday newspaper calculated that, once charges were added, an overdraft at the Midland Bank had cost one of its readers the equivalent of 9,000,000,000,000,000,000,000 per cent a year.[12] When the banks threatened

TABLE 27.1
Complaints to the Banking Ombudsman

Year	Telephone	Letter	Total*	Investigated
1987	–	1,682	–	223
1988	–	1,966	–	254
1989	–	2,537	–	305
1990	4,237	3,548	7,785	475
1991	7,972	5,898	13,870	746
1992	12,923	9,425	22,348	956
1993	16,858	9,578	26,436	1,111
1994	18,529	8,027	26,556	833
1995	18,667	6,723	25,390	717
1996	22,793	7,264	30,057	736
1997	26,561	8,818	35,379	674

Source: Banking Ombudsman Scheme, Annual Reports.

* Only a small proportion of complaints can be investigated by the Banking Ombudsman. Most are dealt with by the banks themselves.

to charge any account which fell below a specified threshold, there was uproar. Banks have a knack of making even good customers feel unwanted.[13]

Small businesses, a new group of customers wooed assiduously by the clearing banks over the last decade and a half, have suffered from a similar lack of discrimination. In the depths of the last recession, the financial pages of newspapers were filled with tales of small businesses ruined by their bankers. As the economy contracted, the banks increased margins on lending to small businesses, reduced their overdraft facilities, raised transaction charges, demanded additional security for outstanding borrowings and tipped businesses into receivership rather than formulate rescue plans. 'We may be a bank but we are also a business,' protested Lord Alexander, chairman of the biggest lender to small businesses.[14]

The behaviour of the banks now became a major public and political scandal. The Office of Fair Trading (OFT) took an interest, and the Treasury Select Committee of the House of Commons launched an investigation. In June 1991 the then chancellor of the Exchequer called the chairmen of the clearing banks into the Treasury for an official dressing-down. They promised to be more sensitive in the future, but by the autumn of the following year were back at the Treasury, explaining why they had not passed on to small businesses the full benefits of the cuts in interest rates which followed the ejection of sterling from the Exchange Rate Mechanism (ERM).

The banks were eventually investigated (not for the first time) by the OFT. The inquiry found them guilty of 'hidden and opaque charging, lack of notice of changes, reduction of facilities at short notice, failure to act upon informal agreements or to meet customers' reasonable expectations, and other examples of insensitive or high-handed behaviour.'[15] Given the public mood, they were lucky to escape with no more than castigation. There was rejoicing in 1995 when Lloyds Bank was sued successfully for damages by a small business,[16] and Eddie George, governor of the Bank of England, declared that the deterioration in relations between the banks and small businesses was jeopardising the pace of economic recovery. The clearing banks eventually published a 'voluntary' Code of Good Banking Practice. For some reason, it applied to personal customers only, and had to be rewritten, its coverage extended to small businesses.

When New Labour came to office in 1997, promising to tighten the regulation of financial services, it had to be rewritten again. Banks had continued to exploit their depositors and their mortgage-holders. Rates of interest on new accounts were raised to attract depositors, while those paid to existing customers were maintained or even cut. Little or no effort was made by banks to tell existing customers to move their deposits to higher-yielding accounts. When Scottish Widows entered the banking market in 1995, its chief selling proposition was not to offer higher rates to new customers without offering them to old ones too. Yet in 1998 the Northern Rock was criticised by the OFT for forcing savers into lower-yielding accounts while preventing them from moving their funds, by insisting they gave thirty days' notice of intention to quit. A revised code of practice, introduced under the threat of statutory controls, now obliges banks to apply new rates to old accounts and give customers sufficient notice of changes.[17]

Why People Ought To Loathe Building Societies

Mortgage-holders are not as lucky. The Council of Mortgage Lenders introduced a similar code in April 1998 to prevent lenders subsidising new borrowers by exploiting existing ones, but new customers still get better deals. This reflects competition for business in a mature market, where growth can be secured only by enlarging market share. Buying new customers at the expense of existing ones is the special province of the building societies and ex-building societies rather than the banks. New borrowers are tempted with a plethora of initial discounts, cash-backs, deferred interest, starter mortgages and other 'special' offers. (In 1998 Alliance & Leicester was offering three years' free gas and electricity to new mortgage-holders). But the rates paid by existing borrowers are left unchanged, unless a customer threatens to defect, in which case the society will usually negotiate.

With a fixed-rate mortgage, many customers are trapped in expensive obligations by redemption penalties which can amount to as much as six months' interest.[18] Variable-rate mortgage-holders, by contrast, find the cost is governed largely by the differential between the rates paid to savers and those charged to borrowers. When interest rates fall, the interest paid to depositors falls much sooner than the interest paid by borrowers, and when rates rise, the interest paid by home-owners rises much faster than that paid to savers. At building societies and ex-building societies, boardroom decision-making is dominated by the need to maintain the widest possible differential between the cost of funds and the cost of mortgages.

Hidden techniques can widen it further. Many building societies do not count capital repayments until the year-end, effectively giving themselves a free loan until the end of the year. Most still insist that borrowers pay an extra fee for house valuations, though they were rebuked for this by the Monopolies and Mergers Commission in 1994. Societies almost always recommend endowment rather than repayment mortgages, in the hope of making a sale for their life associates or collecting commission from an independent insurer. They also charge borrowers a fee for not using the house insurers they advise (ostensibly to cover the costs of checking the insurance company but in reality to penalise customers who deny them commissions).

Paradoxically, building societies do not pay a price for their rapacity. Though the competition is scarcely stiff, surveys show that the public thinks building societies are friendlier and more trustworthy than banks or insurance companies. Relativity is all: like democracy, building societies are flattered by the alternatives. This is why the Abbey National, ten years after it abandoned mutuality and floated on the Stock Exchange, has yet to append the word 'bank' to its name.

Building societies usually attribute their favourable public image to mutual status. In September 1994 Donald Kirkham, a former chief executive of the Woolwich Building Society, then serving as chairman of the Building Societies Association, wrote to the *Financial Times* to protest about an attack it had made on the benefits of mutual ownership:

> Building societies offer a better service to their customers than other organisations. Market research ... shows that, compared with other institutions, building societies are much more likely to be perceived as dealing with their customers fairly, more likely to be understanding of their financial problems, more able to communicate with their customers, taking complaints more seriously, and not pestering their customers about their service.[19]

Curiously, these important findings did not prevent the Woolwich electing to incorporate as a bank less than two years later, indicating that the benefits of mutuality do not always outweigh those of incorporation. But, in a crowded marketplace, it is a convenient distinction for the handful of major societies clinging to mutuality. In 1996 they drew up a 'charter', highlighting why a building society was a better choice for consumers than a bank. Its chief message was that building societies pay dividends to members rather than shareholders. 'We are discussing how to get the message across that customers are everything to us, whereas for a PLC, customers are a means to an end,' explained Brian Davis, chief executive of the Nationwide.[20]

The evidence does not support this cuddly self-image. Despite a shrinkage in their number as societies are acquired or convert to banks, the number of complaints is increasing. Many are from disgruntled members who have lost out on windfall payments or free shares when a society converts to a bank, but the majority concern mortgages, current and deposit accounts, and investment products. At the modern building society, customers are everything in the sense that they were everything to Phineas T. Barnum ('There's a sucker born every minute.')

This was never more evident than in the sale of 'home income plans' in the late 1980s. Elderly people were persuaded to remortgage their houses and invest the proceeds in an investment bond, ostensibly releasing equity in their house in the form of additional income. As rates of interest rose and investment returns declined in the recession of the early 1990s, many people found they were paying more than they were receiving. The Investors Compensation Scheme (ICS) paid out a total of £54 million to people who purchased home income plans. It then tried to recover the money from the building societies. The ICS recovered over £14 million from the West Bromwich Building Society and six hundred and eight-five West Bromwich mortgage-holders were given cash compensation and a reduction in the rate of interest on the mortgages, which was retrospectively capped at 6.25 per cent.[21]

The larger societies are not immune. The Cheltenham and Gloucester (now owned by Lloyds Bank) paid compensation in 1996 to victims of home income plans sold in the 1980s by a society it had acquired (the Heart of England).[22] It was during the same decade that the major building societies acquired chains of estate agents to secure a captive audience for commission – generating endowment policies and house and contents insurance. All building society borrowers are now offered life cover and household insurance which can usually be obtained more cheaply elsewhere. It is not unknown for building societies to urge people to cash in existing endowment policies

TABLE 27.2
Complaints to the Building Societies Ombudsman

Year	Mortgages	Other*	Total	Investigated
1987–8	512	468	980	788
1988–9	699	883	1,582	888
1989–90	815	1,757	2,572	1,528
1990–1	938	1,639	2,577	1,226
1991–2	4,618	4,907	9,525	1,070
1992–3	4,859	4,543	9,402	1,382
1993–4	5,412	3,688	9,100	901
1994–5	5,859	4,572	10,431	1,079
1995–6	6,810	6,403	13,213	2,081
1996–7	5,803	9,130	14,933	1,692
1997–8	4,306	11,167	15,473	2,391

Source: Building Societies Ombudsman, Annual Reports.

* Includes investments, acquisitions or conversions, and miscellaneous items such as unsecured loans or foreign exchange.

and take out a new one, despite the fact that almost all the premiums they have paid are wasted as a result. Householders are often surprised to find that the mortgage indemnity premiums they pay are to protect the building society, not their right to carry on living in the house. In the depressed housing market of the early 1990s, building societies earned an unenviable reputation for exacerbating the difficulties of people who could not keep up their payments. Even now, some continue to fine those who get into arrears, though the Ombudsman condemned the practice years ago.[23] Many borrowers in default have found their repossessed house offered for sale at an unrealistic price while their arrears accumulated, or sold at a give-away price which increases their burden of debt. In August 1995, a London couple won the right in the High Court to sell their house rather than let it be re-possessed and sold more cheaply by the building society. A month later the Halifax was found to be offering its estate agents bonuses of up to £200 if they managed to boost sales volumes by persuading sellers to drop their prices.

The benefits of mutuality are a fiction. Building societies are ostensibly owned by their savers and their borrowers, yet savers are not told of higher rates of interest and borrowers are not told of lower ones. Both savers and borrowers are sold inappropriate and expensive insurance and investments. The windfall payments despatched to members when a society converts to a bank are funded from reserves, built up by withholding dividends from their predecessors. The realities of mutual ownership are illustrated by the Britannia Building Society, whose vociferous advocacy of the benefits of mutuality extends to paying annual cash bonuses to its members. In 1996 it was forced to suspend one in five of its insurance and savings products sales force. 'It doesn't mean customers have been given bad advice,' explained the chief executive, John Heaps. 'But the forms to show why they were given certain advice have not been completed properly.'[24]

Why Nobody Owns Them

The ethos of the modern Britannia, and of other building societies, is as far removed from the mutual self-help of its Georgian and Victorian forebears as it is possible to get. The first societies were *terminating* organisations, established to pool funds for their members to build a house. They were closed down when all investors had acquired one. This meant that the borrowers and the investors were the same people: all members contributed, and all gained. They knew and liked each other and ate and drank together regularly. Virtually all the earliest building societies – from the foundation of Ketley's

Building Society at the Golden Cross Inn in Birmingham in 1775, the first society for which records have survived – were founded in the village pub. The scale of their operations was correspondingly small, and local. In the first fifty years of the building society movement between 1775 and 1825, a total of two hundred and fifty societies built or bought only two thousand houses, or just eight apiece.[25]

Intimacy of this kind is not an option for a modern building society such as the Halifax, which had nearly twelve million shareholders when it converted to a bank. Anybody with more than £1 in an account is a member, and anybody with more than £100 on deposit can vote at the AGM, but perhaps three in one hundred will bother to go to the meeting to exercise it. Millions of members with one vote each have long since recognised that they can exert no control over the management, or influence over the direction of the society. If the average member takes any interest at all, it is usually to complain about the miserly flotation windfall, or to gripe to the Ombudsman that he was unfairly disqualified. This means that building societies are, to all intents and purposes, unowned. Being unowned gives their managers extraordinary discretion. The Nationwide was able to squander £200 million on a sortie into estate agency without a single director losing his job. 'We have a business to run. We have to make profits. We have to meet our financial ratios, otherwise our credit rating falls,' explained Tim Melville-Ross, then chief executive. 'To an extent these are incompatible with the interests of our members.'[26]

In 1995 the Nationwide tried to take over the National and Provincial building society and turn itself into a bank. It now poses as the guardian of the conscience of mutuality. In 1997 and 1998 the management of the society fought emotional campaigns against the incorporation plans advanced by the former royal butler and self-styled 'carpetbagger', Michael Hardern.[27] On the second occasion, Hardern failed by only 33,710 votes out of 2.2 million cast by the members.

Many members were obviously less convinced than the management of the benefits of mutuality. Although building societies are generally more competitive than banks, the value of their better rates never equals the value of a windfall payment. The cash bonus paid by the Britannia to its members averaged a princely £36 in 1998. 'Members have to be given a choice,' as Michael Hardern says. 'Eighty per cent of them would have to live for ever to get more out of mutuality than out of a conversion.'[28]

The truth is that building society managers are not much concerned about the interests of members. When they needed extra capital in the 1990s, they did not ask them for more, or even for permission to raise more. They simply issued permanent interest-bearing certificates (called PIBs) to outside investors, effectively selling income which belonged to the members without paying for it. When the Conservative government proposed that societies might like to invite members to serve on consultative committees, or reserve board-room seats for candidates appointed by members, the Building Societies Association more or less told the Treasury to mind its own business.[29] The building societies have now persuaded the government, which has an attachment to mutuality, to make conversion more difficult: the turnout required to approve incorporation was raised from 20 per cent of the membership to 50 per cent.

Yet voting for incorporation is the only way the owners of a building society can make their views known to the management. The principal defect of mutuality is that the rights of ownership are not tradeable. People who own shares in a bank can sell them, but members of a building society can cease to be owners only by taking their custom elsewhere. Naturally, this makes them behave more like consumers than shareholders. The gradual replacement of terminating societies by *permanent* building societies during the second half of the nineteenth century made this inevitable. Permanence was the key to rapid growth in the twentieth century, because it vastly extended the numbers of depositors and borrowers a society could attract; it also made a mockery of mutuality. Membership was restricted to holders of investment accounts, and denied to mere depositors and borrowers. Building societies ceased to engage in the building of houses, and became bank-like corporations for the investment and lending of money.

Ever since, the building societies have pursued profits just as remorselessly as the banks, but without the inconvenience of having to share their winnings with shareholders. When the Cheltenham and Gloucester tested in the High Court in June 1994 the legality of the payments Lloyds Bank was offering to its members to take over the society, the judge was unequivocal about the limited value of mutual ownership. 'Unlike shareholders of an ordinary public limited company, the members of a building society do not have a significant stake in the profits of the society,' declared Sir Donald Nicholls, the vice chancellor. 'In general they do not have a right to participate in the profits.'[30] In reality, this makes it easier for a building society to persuade its members to vote for incorporation; the members have nothing to lose. Although they do not share in the profits of a building society, they do own its reserves. Their moral entitlement is dubious (reserves were built up over a century or more, and belong as much to past members as to present ones), but building society rules invariably say that, in the event of a winding-up, reserves must be divided among members. This means any society which converts itself into a bank, or agrees to be acquired by a bank, is obliged to distribute free shares or cash windfalls to its members.[31]

These can be valuable. In 1989, members of the first society to incorporate (Abbey National) got £140 worth of free shares. It was the Lloyds Bank bid for the Cheltenham and Gloucester which exposed the true value of the reserves. Payments of up to £13,500 were made, and the pay-outs averaged £2,000 a head. By the time Abbey National merged with National and Provincial, pay-outs were riding as high as £4,250. The flotation of the Halifax was accompanied by average pay-outs of £1,290, and of the Woolwich by an average of £1,948; the average member of Northern Rock got £2,300.

Entitlements to these windfalls proved surprisingly arbitrary. So-called carpetbaggers who opened the right sort of account could get free shares, while members of long standing did not. Eight years after it became a bank, the Abbey National was still trying to retrieve over-allocated shares (and the dividends paid on them) from the undeserving.[32] Every year, the Ombudsman is inundated with complaints by account holders that they were unfairly denied shares. It took legislation to persuade de-mutualising building societies to give free shares to disabled people whose accounts were not registered in their own name.[33]

For some, the arbitrary nature of the pay-outs is an apt symbol of the way incorporation has destroyed the spirit of mutuality. 'It represents the triumph of selfish, short-term individualism over collective community concern,' lamented Leo Westhead, a Halifax member who voted against the incorporation of his own society. 'It is an act of social vandalism.'[34] The prospect of free cash or shares changed the debate between the advocates of mutuality and their opponents. In 1989 the Abbey National was dogged throughout its flotation by a ginger group, Abbey Members Against Flotation. Eight years later, the Nationwide was under pressure from Members for Conversion. But carpetbaggers are a symptom, not a cause; even without them, major building societies would still have had to turn themselves into banks.

The Coming of Competition

The core business of the building societies – mortgage lending – is mature. In 1914 only one house in ten was owner-occupied; by 1939, it was one in four; and by 1970 one in two; and by 1979 two in three.[35] In 1980 council tenants were given the right to buy their homes at a steep discount. Layers of cash hand-outs and tax relief – ranging from housing benefit to mortgage interest tax relief and exemption from capital gains tax – further subsidised owner-occupied housing. In the 1980s, building societies found themselves servicing a growth market.

Funding the rise in home ownership enabled them to grow quickly, especially when house prices rose rapidly, people felt richer, and owner–occupiers increased what they were prepared to borrow. For twenty years, the housing boom fuelled building society balance sheets, which inflated at a rate of 15 per cent a year. For most of those years, the building societies did not have to worry about where the money would come from to lend. The banks scarcely bothered to compete with them for retail deposits until the mid 1980s.

The banks then bid for the retail deposits on which the building societies depended for funding, partly by offering more generous terms on deposit accounts, but mainly by agreeing to pay interest on current accounts. A range of new or revivified savings vehicles (unit trusts, National Savings, PEPs, TESSAs, and even the stock market) began to attract the savers who had traditionally placed their money with the building societies. This increased competition forced the societies to compete on price for the first time.

Since the mid-1930s, the building societies had operated an interest rate cartel, akin to that run by the clearing banks, whereby they kept their deposit and mortgage rates at the same level. Designed to prevent destabilising flows of cash and mortgage business between societies, it froze the structure of the building society movement: larger societies were unable to obliterate their smaller competitors on price. It is true that the cartel was never completely stable. Smaller societies often found it hard to retain deposits by adhering to the recommended rates, and larger societies resented the constraint it placed on growth. The Halifax withdrew from the cartel for eight years between 1956 and 1964.[36] But it was not until the late 1970s that it began to break up. A number of major societies, including the Abbey National and the Leeds Permanent, ignored the recommended rates. By 1977, only two in three building societies were still paying them.[37] In June 1980 the Wilson Committee, commissioned to investigate the workings of the financial institutions, recommended the abolition of the cartel, but within five years competition from the banks had destroyed it anyway.

Once the cartel was gone, it was obvious that the bigger societies would get bigger, not least by devouring the smaller societies. During the 1980s, the banks began to poach assets as well as deposits from the building societies. Bank advances for house purchase increased from virtually nothing in the 1970s to a peak of nearly £11 billion in 1989. The building societies' share of the mortgage market fell from four fifths to a half, and they had to find new ways to grow. In 1983 they lobbied the government successfully to be allowed to borrow in the wholesale markets, and a year later the government gave them access to the sterling bond markets. In 1986 a new Building Societies Act allowed them to offer their customers cheque books and unsecured personal loans. The same legislation empowered them to turn themselves into banks, provided the members agreed to the change.[38]

Mutuals become PLCs

A wave of restructuring followed. The number of building societies shrank from three hundred and sixteen in 1978 to seventy in 1998. Most had merged, but some gave up altogether, especially after the Building Societies Commission put a heavier burden of regulation and capital requirements on the building societies. Even the largest societies felt compelled to merge. The Nationwide merged with the Anglia in 1987, the Northern Rock with the North of England and the Halifax with the Leeds in 1994. Others sold out to banks. The Cheltenham and Gloucester was taken over by Lloyds Bank in 1994; the National and Provincial by Abbey National in 1995; the Bristol and West by the Bank of Ireland in 1996; and the Birmingham Midshires by the Halifax in 1998.

Incorporation was the third possibility. The first building society to turn itself into a bank was the Abbey National, in a difficult and expensive flotation of 1989. Its experience was so bad that seven years passed before another building society dared to follow its example. A year after the Abbey flotation Jim Birrell, chief executive of the Halifax, was asked if he would be following suit. He replied:

> We like mutual status, and research tells us our members like it as well. It allows us to concentrate on the job in hand, rather than on the vagaries of the stock market. We have no doubt at all that the public has a far more positive attitude towards mutual building societies than joint stock banks ... We are a mutual and we wish to stay a mutual.[39]

Seven years later, after devouring not only the Leeds but the Clerical Medical insurance company, Halifax floated on the stock exchange. It joined the Alliance and Leicester, which floated in April 1997, and was quickly followed by the Woolwich and the Northern Rock.

In search of profits, the newly liberated building societies broke into a range of new markets in the second half of the 1980s. In 1987 the Nationwide became the first building society to offer a current account. It also plunged disastrously into estate agency, building up a chain of over three hundred outlets at a cost of £200 million which it sold to Hambro Countrywide in 1994 for just £1. The Halifax, the Woolwich, the Alliance and Leicester, the Britannia and the Bristol and West made the same mistake. Building societies began to sell credit cards, insurance policies, stockbroking services, offshore accounts and even conveyancing. But easily the biggest new business for building societies was unsecured lending to consumers. The volume of non-

TABLE 27.3
The Ten Biggest Building Societies, 1997*

Society	Assets (£bn)	Members	Branches
Nationwide	47.1	7,980,146	681
Bradford and Bingley†	18.8	2,491,123	235
Britannia	17.8	1,470,151	188
Yorkshire	8.0	1,000,000	133
Portman	4.7	1,144,731	115
Coventry	4.4	686,331	53
Skipton	3.8	352,159	75
Chelsea	3.5	279,818	32
Leeds & Holbeck	2.9	325,000	68
Derbyshire	2.2	323,962	63

Source: Building Societies Association and Building Societies Yearbook 1997–8.

* Figures are for year ending 31 December 1997 except Nationwide where they are to 10 June 1998.
† Members of the Bradford and Bingley voted to incorporate in April 1999.

mortgage lending by building societies soared from zero in 1986 to £2.9 billion ten years later.[40]

These new freedoms proved insufficient. Building societies chafed at the restriction on lending to companies. They disliked the ceiling on the funds they could raise in the capital markets, and were unable for obvious reasons to issue shares to institutional investors.[41] Finally, in 1993 they persuaded the Treasury to allow them to set up their own life assurance subsidiaries, and in 1995 secured the right to lend without security to companies and to sell general as well as life insurance products.[42] It was the grudging pace of deregulation which finally persuaded some of the larger societies that it was impossible to become a fully fledged bank while remaining a building society.

Do Banking PLCs Do Better?

Becoming a PLC is no guarantee of success. Companies which convert tend to be over-capitalised and over-eager. No bank illustrates this better than the Trustee Savings Bank (TSB), the successor to the labourers' thrift banks of early nineteenth-century Scotland.[43] Privatised in 1986, it began life as a commercial company with a huge endowment of £1.5 billion, the government having eschewed proceeds of the sale after failing to prove to the courts that it owned the TSB. The bank proceeded to diversify recklessly into insurance, mortgages, estate agency and – most disastrously of all – investment banking. It bought merchant bank Hill Samuel in 1987 at a price quickly rendered nonsensical by the Great Crash.[44] The TSB never recovered, and was eventually rescued from itself by Lloyds Bank.

Abbey National, too, made dreadful mistakes in its early years as a bank. It squandered £258 million on a disastrous foray into estate agency; another £94 million was lost on a commercial property lending business in France; and a ten-year sojourn in Spain cost shareholders £36 million in its last three years alone.[45] It set up a derivatives trading business with Barings, which promptly went bust.[46] Building societies are not immune to poor lending and investment decisions.[47] But most of their lending is at least well-secured and well-insured.[48] They are also insulated from the industrial and commercial borrowers who caused the clearing banks to write off billions of pounds in the early 1990s.

It was in commercial lending that the banks made their biggest mistakes. Their loan books ballooned from £314 billion in 1980 to £1,265 billion a decade later: in real terms, their loan portfolios doubled in size in ten years.[49] Between 1990 and 1993 alone, they wrote off some £25 billion of them in bad debts. With hindsight, it is clear that the major clearing banks got caught up in the economic euphoria which their creation of credit did much to foment. In June 1988, the month when interest rates began their sharp climb to 15 per cent, Barclays Bank raised £921 million in a rights issue to expand its loan book. The main purpose was to recapture from National Westminster Bank its status as the biggest bank in Britain.

Most PLCs are driven by prosaic ambitions of this kind, largely because they have no more compelling *raison d'etre*. But the Barclays balance sheet had doubled in size in the previous five years, and inflating it further required economic and financial optimism of an heroic order. 'It has turned out to be a super piece of timing,' was how the Barclays chairman, Sir John Quinton, described the rights issue in 1989, 'since it enabled us to expand the loan book and put the money to good productive use.'[50] In fact, just about every struggling or failed property company of the era – Heron, Mountleigh, Speyhawk, Rosehaugh, Stanhope, Olympia and York – owed Barclays money they could not repay. The bank had lent £422 million to an obscure and privately owned property company named Imry. Half of the debt had to be written off, even after Barclays bought its assets and occupied one of its developments. Quinton explained in 1991: 'We don't force money on anyone. Obviously there was an over-expansion of lending, but how far we can be blamed is arguable.'[51]

In April 1992, after making a provision of £1.5 billion for bad and doubtful debts, Sir John was forced to step down. His last duty was to announce only the second loss in the three-hundred-year history of the bank. His successor, Andrew Buxton, had to announce the first-ever loss by the bank at the pre-tax level in the following year. This followed provisions for bad and doubtful debts of another £2.5 billion for 1992. In two years, the bank was obliged to write off more than four times the sum it raised from shareholders in 1988. By 1993, shareholders were restive. They forced Buxton to cede the job of chief executive to Martin Taylor, a former journalist and textiles executive with no previous experience of banking. It was an apt commentary on the confidence of the board and the shareholders in the decision-making powers of his predecessors.

In truth, misplaced exuberance was not the only factor at work. Having spent much of the first half of the 1980s writing off billions on loans to developing countries, especially in Latin America after the Mexican near-default of 1982, the clearing banks were keen to increase their share of safer loans in the domestic market. Their entry into the mortgage market was one aspect of this; increased lending to companies was another. Unfortunately, the well-established companies on which they had previously relied were now more creditworthy than the banks. Multinational companies were able to borrow more cheaply by issuing securities directly to investors than by asking a bank for a loan. One effect was to force the banks to develop securities trading businesses; another was to tempt them to lend to less creditworthy companies.

The clearing banks increased their loans to the property sector between 1985 and 1991 at twice the rate they were expanding credit to the private sector as a whole. At its peak in 1989, lending to property accounted for a quarter of all loans to the private sector. Land and buildings seem to provide rock-solid security for loans, but property financed by debt is inherently unstable. An office block built on a mountain of debt will increase dramatically in value as rental income rises and interest rates fall, but plunges as fast when conditions are reversed. To this inherent risk, banks added some twists of their own. Loans were made to off-balance sheet subsidiaries on a 'non-recourse' basis, leaving the banks with resort to the developed property only, not to the full assets of the company which owned it. In some cases, interest on the loans was rolled up and became payable only when the property was sold or fully let.

The main alternative to the property sector was smaller companies. Unlike the multinationals, they could not raise money directly from investors. Bank borrowings by industrial and commercial companies increased by a quarter in real terms to £72.6 billion in the five years to the end of 1986. But after the stock market crash of October 1987, which made it difficult for companies to raise equity finance, borrowings exploded. Over the next four years corporate borrowing rose one and a half times in real terms, to a peak of £169.4 billion.[52] Over the entire economic cycle, which ran from 1981 to 1991, corporate indebtedness to banks doubled. As the decade wore on, equity shrank from a third to a fortieth of corporate capital. Debt increased from two fifths to two thirds.[53]

The banks helped to de-stabilise corporate balance sheets with their enthusiastic support for 'leveraged' buy-outs, where groups of ambitious managers used bank borrowings to acquire subsidiaries of major companies, or clubbed together to buy entire companies. Decisions to lend were not always based on proper consideration of the character or creditworthiness of the borrower, or even the quality of the security.[54] All four of the major clearers lent money to Robert Maxwell – at the time of his death he owed the National Westminster Bank alone £155 million. In the 1980s, the National Westminster had made no secret of its delight in overtaking Barclays as the biggest bank in Britain. Its hubris had a deliciously ironic conclusion: reduced by 1998 to a takeover target, National Westminster received an offer of marriage from Barclays.

The same conflation of size with strength had ruined the Midland Bank. For a brief period either side of the Second World War, Midland was the biggest bank in the world. Its subsequent decline was as tragic as the TSB, and more prolonged. From its foundation in 1836 as the Birmingham and Midland Bank, it was the most progressive, unsnobbish and business friendly of the Big Four. The Midland was founded as a joint stock bank in a growing industrial city, and remained easily the biggest lender to industrial and commercial companies until deep into the twentieth century. It did not bother to come to London until 1891, and was not fully committed to the City until the turn of the century.[55] Its chief architect, Sir Edward Holden, was the most acquisitive and inventive banker of his period, using mergers and acquisitions to enlarge the bank, and leading the charge into international markets against what he saw as growing German and American competition.[56]

Even as it was overtaken in the 1940s and 1950s by the rivals Holden had feared, the Midland sustained its reputation for innovation in the domestic market. It was the first bank to offer unsecured personal loans and mass-market cheque accounts, and to acquire a merchant banking arm. Even in the 1980s, it was the first to establish a telephone banking service, FirstDirect. But in the end the Midland was undone by its glorious past: in an effort to re-create the Biggest Bank in the World, its management took the fateful decision in 1980 to pay $595 million for a 51 per cent stake in the Crocker National Bank of California.

Crocker appeared to give Midland the means to overtake the giant Citibank, which was then embarking on its conquest of the world. Instead, it lumbered

Midland with hundreds of millions of dollars of duff loans. By the time Midland managed to sell the bank in 1986, its shareholders had lost around $1 billion, the largest loss ever incurred by a British bank. It crippled Midland throughout the 1980s, insulating the bank to some extent from the mistaken enthusiasms of its rivals, but exposing it to all manner of predators. The condition of the bank became so pitiful that Lord Hanson and Robert Maxwell took stakes in expectation of a takeover. The humiliation of the management was complete when the Saatchi brothers inquired whether shareholders were interested in selling to them. The Bank of England parachuted one of its favourite sons, Sir Kit McMahon, into the top job as chairman and chief executive. He sold businesses to raise money, sacked most of the top management, hired American whizz-kids to replace them, accepted their advice to 'brand' accounts and loans, and initiated an on-off romance with the Hong Kong and Shanghai Bank (HSBC).

But the cock-ups did not cease. The bank squandered £116 million on an ill-timed bet that interest rates were about to go down. In 1991, as profitability stubbornly refused to recover, Sir Kit was obliged to step down. A year later, after a courtship interrupted by an ill-conceived bid by Lloyds Bank, Midland succumbed to the blandishments of HSBC. 'Honkers and Shankers,' founded in Shanghai in 1865 to bankroll the great trading houses of south China, had survived serious setbacks in America and Australia (where it lent $1 billion to financier Alan Bond). But, by buying Midland, it did make the British clearing bank Part of One of the Biggest Banks in the World.

In Asia, HSBC has a smaller and less ambitious rival: Standard Chartered Bank. In Britain, it is known for only two things. The first is that it employed John Major as a press officer. The second is that, like the former prime minister, it is highly accident-prone. Even its chief executive, Malcolm Williamson, has conceded that the bank has an unusually 'bad reputation for banana skins.'[57] Its basic problem, stemming from its origins as a colonial bank in nineteenth century Shanghai, is an unstable mixture of sterling liabilities and foreign currency assets. A solution (buying the Royal Bank of Scotland) was blocked by the competition authorities in 1981. The alternative (lending money to British borrowers) was then tried. It drove Standard Chartered into lending to borrowers (George Walker, Asil Nadir and Alan Bond) which even the Big Four avoided. In 1992 and 1993, as it was shaking off the legacy of those mistakes with massive provisions for bad debts and a cut in the dividend, the Indian arm of the bank was caught up in a major fraud.

In April 1993 Standard Chartered made a special provision of £272 million to cover a fraud on its Bombay branch. A year later, its Hong Kong securities arm was censured by local regulators for various abuses.[58] Within weeks, embarrassment turned to farce when it emerged that a Malaysian minister had failed to return a $10,000 gold coin given to him by Standard Chartered as a 'trade sample'. An internal investigation found that the bank was buying business by similar means in the Philippines.[59] In 1997, a mixture of falling currencies, high interest rates and corporate bankruptcies in the Asian markets meant write-offs once more. It will probably take new management to eradicate the habit at Standard Chartered Bank. Both Barclays and Lloyds TSB have already offered to buy.

Lloyds TSB is looking to grow overseas, an ambition it eschewed after it almost went bust in the Latin American debt crisis. Sir Brian Pitman, chief executive from 1983 and now chairman, has secured a reputation as the greatest British banker since the war. Under his leadership, Lloyds has confined its ambitions to the domestic retail market, enabling it to avoid expensive accidents in commercial lending and investment banking. Instead, it has broadened the range of products it sells to domestic consumers by buying a life assurance company (Abbey Life) and a building society (Cheltenham and Gloucester). It also increased its geographic and social reach by buying the TSB, a downmarket bank with a heavy presence in the north. As a strategy, it has certainly worked better than those of its rivals. Lloyds TSB is now the fifth most valuable company in Britain and the most valuable bank in the world. Its share price has doubled every three years, and its return on capital regularly exceeds 35 per cent.

Shareholders are grateful, but then they gave Lloyds little choice but to stay at home. As Pitman took over as chief executive in 1983, the bank was writing off £2.6 billion of dud loans. The shareholders refused to repair the damage by buying more shares, forcing the bank to retrench. It withdrew from foreign markets, sold its international lending operations, and stood aloof from the craze for investment banking at the time of Big Bang. It bought the Cheltenham and Gloucester and the TSB because they offered scope to create value by cutting costs rather than growing businesses. Lloyds bid against HSBC for Midland in 1992 for the same reason. The bank enters the twenty-first century mired in the domestic market, earning most of its revenues from retail consumers. After years of high profits in a booming economy, its balance sheet is weighed down with more capital than it can spend. If Lloyds has made no mistakes in the last ten years, it has also taken no risks.

Only one bank is less ambitious than Lloyds. The corporate motto at the Bank of Scotland, founded one year after the Bank of England in 1695, is 'short arms and deep pockets'. Though this did not save it from lending to corporate disasters (like the Lowndes Queensway buy-out, led by the Scottish entrepreneur Jimmy Gulliver), its institutionalised caution did save it from the over-exuberant approach of its English rivals. In 1998 it sold its only sizeable international operation, the Countrywide Banking Corporation in New Zealand, to Lloyds TSB.[60] It is understandably concerned that Scottish devolution, and especially the power of the new Scottish Parliament to vary the rate of income tax, does not create a climate of hostility in England. Scottish bankers remember that union with England in 1707 was largely inspired by the need to get English money to repair the losses Scotland had incurred in the Darien ventures of 1698–9. In fact, the Royal Bank of Scotland emerged in May 1727 from a company formed to manage the securities issued by the English government,[61] and something of the spirit of William Paterson, the London-based Scotsman who promoted the Darien expedition, still resonates within its portals.

In recent years the Royal Bank has contrived to lose money in dud buy-outs (Lowndes Queensway), failed financial conglomerates (British & Commonwealth), the Spanish mortgage market (a joint venture with Banco Santander), American retail banking (a network on the East Coast) and securities fraud (the Wallace Smith Trust).[62] Macaulay said of Paterson that his friends described him as a missionary and his enemies as a buccaneer. The Royal Bank is neither. It is too big to be buccaneering, and too small to conquer new territories. Its likeliest fate is to be taken over, probably by the Halifax.

Why Are Banks So Badly Managed?

The modern banker is better-integrated but more bovine than William Paterson. Keynes described him as 'not one who foresees danger and avoids it, but one who, when he is ruined, is ruined in a conventional and orthodox way along with his fellows, so that no one can really blame him'. His friend Robert Brand, a director of Lloyds Bank, had explained to him why the clearing banks fuelled the boom of the 1920s with oceans of cheap credit. 'We ladled out money,' he said. 'We did it because everybody said they were making and were going to make high profits; and while you had an uneasy feeling yet you thought that while they were making large profits there could be nothing said about ladling out the money.'[63]

Every banking crisis since modern banking was invented in the seventeenth century originated in the same urge not to be left behind. In the early 1970s a ruined property developer explained: 'It is no exaggeration to say that we were having bank money thrust at us from all directions.'[64] Of all Hegelians, bankers are the most naïve; their inability to learn from the past is complete. Keynes, who took an interest in the ideas of Sigmund Freud, attributed this wilful ignorance to the nature of the banking personality and the demands of the trade:

> It is necessarily part of the business of a banker to maintain appearances and to profess a conventional respectability which is more than human. Lifelong practices of this kind make them the most romantic and the least realistic of men. It is so much their stock-in-trade that their position should not be questioned, that they do not even question it themselves until it is much too late. Like the honest citizens they are, they feel a proper indignation at the perils of the wicked world in which they live – when the perils mature; but they do not foresee them. A Bankers' Conspiracy! The idea is absurd![65]

It is witty and an intriguing passage, much quoted by bankers themselves, and fits the contradictory speculations of men like Sir John Quinton exactly. Yet the true explanation of the tendency of the banker to swing from blinkered optimism to unrelieved pessimism is more prosaic. It is the fact that the behaviour of bankers is not governed by the ultimate discipline of the markets: bankruptcy.

Banks are, in effect, publicly owned utilities. No private business is as intensely supervised by the state as the profession of banking. Though all businesses are officially regulated to some extent, only banks are required to tell the authorities everything they are doing. If a major bank gets into difficulties, its managers know that it will not be allowed to fail. There are good reasons why the hand of the state lies heavy on the banks. The apparent simplicity of banking – run, say the cynics, on the 'eight, ten, two principle': borrow at 8 per cent, lend at 10 per cent, and tee-off at 2.00 p.m. – cloaks its dangers. The greatest of these is that all the depositors may ask for their money back at the same time. A bank such as Barclays, for example, will keep only 10p in every pound in the form of cash and a bit more in short-dated securities which can be sold expeditiously for cash.

Bankers own what other people owe, and owe what other people own. It is this paradoxical quality which makes banking so dangerous. If the borrowers do not repay their loans, the bank cannot repay the depositors. If the depositors sense their money is at risk, they demand it back, and if they all demand it back at once, most will be disappointed, and the contagion spreads quickly to other banks. Banking is inherently unstable, because long-term loans are financed by short-term deposits; if just one bank gets the balance wrong, it can spark a financial collapse. Which is why the primary function of central banks, such as the Bank of England, is to act as 'lender of last resort' to those that cannot raise money to repay their depositors.[66]

Not until 1970 did the Bank of England allow the major clearing banks to publish their profits and reserves, fearing that adverse movements in either figure would undermine public confidence and ignite a run. Banking is based, after all, on a confidence trick. If the depositors see through it, the bank must sell what assets it has, and borrow all it can, but in the absence of help from outside, it must close its doors and confess it has no money. Nor is this possibility confined to the history books. It is exactly what happened to depositors at the Bank of Credit and Commerce International.

Yet there is a deeper mystery to banking, which magnifies the dangers. Most businessmen venture their own capital, or capital they have raised from others, and make money by selling goods or services. Bankers alone have uncovered the Philosopher's Stone, and learnt the art of making money out of nothing. They do not lend only the money deposited with them, but many times as much. And once banks cease to lend only their own money, or the money deposited with them, an increase in lending automatically increases the amount of money in circulation. Every time a bank lends money to a customer, and the customer uses it to pay his bills, the cheque he writes will create a deposit at another bank. It is an axiom of banking that every loan creates a deposit. Since banks can lend multiples of the sums they have on deposit, the new deposit enables that bank to increase its lending too.

This is the mechanism by which the provision of credit multiplies the amount of money in circulation.[67] Some wonder why this process of increasing loans and increasing deposits cannot continue indefinitely. The principal restraint is the danger of inflation: if the supply of money rises faster than the quantity of goods and services, prices will rise. Bankers, by advancing credit, are the principal authors of their own punishment: a decline in the value of money which must at some point be reversed. The first credit-induced inflation occurred at the end of the seventeenth century, as soon as modern banking was invented, and recent crises have the same origin. Yet bankers refuse to admit that they play any part in amplification of the credit cycle.

Asked in 1992 to explain why the National Westminster bank had written off the best part of £2 billion in the previous year, the chairman, Lord Alexander, offered no more than 'there were undoubtedly some departures from the principles of sound lending.'[68] A year later, after another £1.8 billion had gone, Lord Alexander travelled to Manchester to explain why banks lent too much in the 1980s and too little in the 1990s. This time he blamed the government:

> The UK economy has resembled a roller-coaster, and one on which the ride has become progressively more dangerous ... Our national culture needs a determination right across the political divide to maintain medium-term economic stability ... To achieve this solid and lasting

foundation is primarily the responsibility of our government and the Bank of England.[69]

The New Labour government has taken him at his word. The chancellor of the exchequer has more or less promised to abolish the trade cycle, and has set the Bank of England free of interfering politicians to do so. The prime minister has told businessmen that macro-economic stability is 'sexy.'

But banks must bear their share of the blame. Some politicians and economists continue to believe that the volume of credit advanced by the banks can and should be controlled directly, either by quantitative restrictions or by technical devices administered by the Bank of England. But in an open financial system, there is only one way to restrain the expansion of credit: make it more expensive to borrow by raising the rate of interest.[70] The truth, unacknowledged in many banking parlours, is that government gave the banks and building societies their freedom in the 1980s, and they abused it. For most of the twentieth century, they operated within a straitjacket which was partly imposed by government and partly self-imposed. Governments find it easier to manipulate the financial system through large banks, so they have encouraged mergers between banks. The Bank of England monopoly of joint-stock banking was lifted in 1826, with the aim of eliminating hundreds of small partnerships. By adding onerous capital and regulatory requirements, the government forced the joint-stock banks to get bigger too.

As the nineteenth century wore on, hundreds of partnership banks gave way to a few dozen joint stock banks with hundreds of branches. The modern Barclays Bank was created in 1896 through the federation of twenty Quaker-owned provincial banks into a single joint-stock company.[71] In 1825 there were seven hundred and fifteen banks in the United Kingdom with eight hundred and forty-eight offices; by 1913 there were eighty-eight banks with eight thousand six hundred and ten branches. Only twenty-nine private banks survived.[72] By the end of the First World War, five banks – Barclays, Lloyds, Midland, the National Provincial and the Westminster – controlled four fifths of bank deposits, and most of the private banks disappeared shortly afterwards. Coutts was purchased by National Provincial in 1920, and ended up as the private banking arm of the National Westminster Bank. Child & Co, named after the Restoration financier Sir Francis Child, was bought in 1924 by Glyn, Mills & Co., which later merged with the Royal Bank of Scotland. The only genuine private partnership bank which now survives is C. Hoare & Co. of 37 Fleet Street. Its seven partners – H. C. Hoare, D. J. Hoare, R. Q. Hoare, M. R. Hoare, A. M. V. Hoare, A. S. Hoare, and V. E. Hoare – are all direct descendants of the goldsmith banker who founded it in 1672. Every other British bank is a PLC, or part of a PLC.

By the 1920s, the authorities were worried that the merger process had gone too far, and was restricting competition. A parliamentary inquiry led to the establishment of an advisory committee, which extracted a promise from the banks not to merge any further without government permission. The policy did not change until 1967, when the Bank of England and the Treasury 'made it plain' that they were not averse to further amalgamations between the eleven clearing banks. In the rush to merge, the Royal Bank of Scotland married the National Commercial Bank of Scotland, and the Westminster merged with National Provincial. Barclays, Lloyds and Martins proposed a three-way merger but this was overturned by the Monopolies and Mergers Commission, and Barclays had to settle for Martins.

TABLE 27.4
The Major British Clearing Banks, 1997

Bank	Deposits*	Assets	Pre-Tax Profits
Barclays	152.9	234.7	1,716
National Westminster	117.9	185.4	1,011
Lloyds TSB	101.9	158.1	3,162
Abbey National	86.2	150.8	1,424
Halifax	86.5	131.1	1,631
Midland	70.2	102.1	1,625
Royal Bank of Scotland	52.9	72.6	760
Bank of Scotland	35.8	54.7	742
Standard Chartered	34.3	47.2	870
Woolwich	22.6	31.9	402
Alliance & Leicester	19.0	24.4	395
Northern Rock	11.7	15.8	195
Clydesdale†	6.4	7.9	146
Co-operative Bank	4.3	5.3	55
Yorkshire Bank†	4.3	5.1	155

Source: Annual Reports.

* Deposits by banks and customers.
† Clydesdale and Yorkshire are owned by National Australia Bank.

A marsupial relationship between big banks and big government suited both parties. Regulators could supervise the system by a reading a handful of balance sheets. A change in interest rates could be transmitted throughout the financial system simply by changing the Bank Rate, and the expansion of credit could be controlled directly.[73] For their part, the banks were relieved of the burden of competition. Agreements between them not to compete on price for loans or deposits first emerged in the 1870s, and lasted a century. Until 1975 the English and Scottish clearing banks maintained a reciprocal agreement not to compete with each other, and there was no foreign competition in the domestic market either. As recently as 1960 there were only seventy-five foreign banks in London, and they did little or no business in sterling.

Protection from predators was complete. No matter how inefficient or incompetent a clearing bank became, it could not be taken over, let alone fail. In 1981, HSBC was told that its ambition to disturb an agreed merger between the Standard Chartered Bank and the Royal Bank of Scotland would be unwelcome, on the basis that a 'foreign' bank could not be trusted to own a British clearer.[74] When the 1987 Banking Act was going through Parliament, both the clearing banks and the Bank of England lobbied hard for a provision giving the government power to block overseas bids for British banks.[75] No clearing bank dared make a hostile bid for a rival until 1992, when Lloyds made its half-hearted lunge at Midland. The only truly foreign bank to have broken into the British clearing system is the National Australia Bank, which bought the Clydesdale and Northern banks from Midland in 1987, and the Yorkshire Bank (owned by the Big Four clearers) in 1990.

The government reinforced this lack of competition by entrenching the division of labour between banks (unsecured loans and cheque books) and building societies (mortgages and interest-bearing deposit accounts) in both law and the tax system. Until the 1980s, the interest earned in building society accounts was taxed on a 'composite' basis which made it hard for the banks to compete. Unlike the banks, building societies could merge with each other. The number of societies shrank from two thousand two hundred and eighty-six at the turn of the century to nine hundred and fifty-two in 1940, and two hundred and eighty-seven by 1979,[76] but mutuality protected building societies from unwelcome approaches just as surely as the authorities protected banks.

The Building Societies Act of 1986 made it more difficult to incorporate or take over a building society by insisting that a large majority of members had to approve the change. The legality of the mergers between the Cheltenham and Gloucester and Lloyds and the Halifax and the Leeds were tested in the courts. In the Lloyds case, the judge ruled that the legislation was designed to facilitate the organic development of the building society movement, not to allow an outside institution to take over a building society by tempting members with a cash windfall.[77] Any society which floats is protected from takeover for five years, and the directors may reject an approach without referring it to members. When the Abbey National wanted to buy the National and Provincial in 1995, it was provoked into making its wishes public because the management refused to tell the membership it was interested.[78]

In one sense, this protection worked: the last serious financial crisis in Britain occurred in 1866 and the last major banking failure in 1878, when both the City of Glasgow Bank and the England and South Wales District Bank went under. The banking system has remained remarkably stable throughout the twentieth century but, in another sense, the lack of competition was a disaster. Denied the ability to compete on price, the banks competed on distribution instead. Each acquired costly branch networks, crammed with expensive staff, putting every bank on every High Street. Innovation was stifled. The hire purchase industry, which emerged in the 1930s, developed outside the banking system. The Euromarkets, one of the biggest capital markets in the world, had to be invented by foreign banks in London. When Barclays began to sign up customers of other banks for Barclaycard, they promptly formed another cartel to issue Access cards.[79]

Within banks, there was no internal competition to make best use of capital. All banks had similar lending policies and their current and deposit accounts were indistinguishable, for there was no need for bankers to sell anything. 'When I joined the bank, I was taught it was bad form to tout for business,' a sixty-year-old clearing banker told Margaret Reid in the mid-1980s.[80] If her interlocutor was typical of his generation, he had probably joined the bank from school, taken banking examinations, and progressed steadily up the hierarchy. 'People who joined banks ten or fifteen years ago are often not very comfortable selling things,' said Richard Orgill, deputy chief executive at Midland Bank, in 1995. 'Those we are recruiting now are different, but we have still got some of the old variety around.'[81]

Until recently, membership of the board of directors of a clearing bank owed little to ability. Most directors secured their positions through nepotism, or the machinations of a politico-financial nexus which has long provided a steady stream of jobs for superannuated civil servants and impecunious aristocrats. At Barclays Bank, a squirearchy of Quaker families has managed to maintain a presence in the boardroom while controlling less than one hundredth of its capital. The present chairman, Andrew Buxton, is a member of one of the founding families. 'My progress in the bank has always surprised me,' he said; it surprised no one else.[82] His successor, Martin Taylor, was only the third non-family man to run the bank. He lasted less than five years.

The National Westminster had a longstanding preference for toffs over talent. When Anthony Sampson visited the bank in 1982, one earl, two viscounts, three barons and a baronet were on the board.[83] The bank still has a penchant for figures whose achievements lie far outside the field of banking. Recent recruits include Sir Geoffrey Littler, a former Treasury official; Sir Charles Powell and Dame Pauline Neville-Jones, both former Foreign Office officials; and Baroness Young and Douglas Hurd, both ex-Foreign Office ministers. Until 1998, the bank was chaired by Lord Alexander, a barrister. At the nadir of its fortunes in 1991, he admitted that 'the quality of management needed in other industries is now necessary for banks.'

Free to Make Mistakes

It was a wise observation. Poorly led, unused to competition and burdened with costs, it was inevitable that the clearing banks would make mistakes once they could make their own decisions. The first attempt to liberate the financial system, by the Heath government, ended in the secondary banking crisis of 1973–5. The banks agreed to scrap their interest rate cartel in return for an end to direct government control of lending, in the hope of recouping business from 'secondary banks' outside the cartel. But the retention of limited controls nourished the new class of fringe banks. The Bank of England and the Big Four clearing banks had to spend an estimated £150 million to rescue a number of them from failure, but the problems were not confined to the fly-by-nights: in 1974 the National Westminster Bank had to deny that it was being helped by the Bank of England.

Direct controls over credit were reintroduced, and supervision of the system was formalised for the first time by the Banking Act of 1979.[85] Lasting liberalisation had to wait until the 1980s. By then, conditions had changed. Britain had become a major oil producer for the first time, producing a generous dollar income which, if it was not balanced by a countervailing outflow of capital, would have led to a massive balance of payments surplus, an overvalued exchange rate and a deterioration in the competitiveness of British exports. Abolition of exchange controls, achieved in three stages between June and October 1979, was an economic necessity. It was the first of a series of deregulatory measures by the Conservative governments of the 1980s.

Nigel Lawson has identified ten specific acts of deregulation during the decade.[86] Once exchange controls had gone, attempts to control the volume of bank lending became ineffective: banks had only to shift their sterling lending offshore. The government acquiesced in the collapse of the building societies' interest rate cartel, and, as controls over credit disappeared, the banks and building societies embarked on an orgy of lending. Consumer credit ballooned to over £50 billion by the end of the 1980s, and by 1997 the amount had reached over £88 billion.[87]

The abolition of hire purchase controls in July 1982 sparked off frenetic competition between clearing banks, finance houses, mail order firms, retailers and manufacturers. Offers to borrow money crowded bank branches, became available in chain stores and showrooms and tumbled like confetti from newspapers and magazines. By the mid-1990s a host of competitors were offering credit cards, whose choice now has expanded to over twelve hundred. The number of credit cards in issue more than tripled in twenty years to well over thirty million by 1978. Banks have cut fees and interest rates, and given free gifts to new customers. The volume of credit outstanding on credit cards increased at a compound rate of 17 per cent a year.[88]

No form of credit promotion was more shameful than mortgage lending. Until the mid-1980s it was difficult for a home-buyer to borrow more than he needed to buy or repair a house. The total debt secured was rarely more than 80 per cent of its value, and no mortgage exceeded two and a half times the earnings of the borrower. All these rules were abandoned in the 1980s. The banks and building societies tempted young people with 100 per cent and low-start mortgages (which guaranteed their debts would increase irrespective of house prices and interest rates) and the elderly with 'home income plans'. Lenders were indifferent whether the extra debt went into bricks and mortar or motor cars, television sets, dishwashers and camcorders.

Consumers were not the only beneficiaries of the money being pumped into the economy. As blue chip clients turned to the securities markets, the banks increased their lending to small businesses and property companies, and at the peak of the credit boom they found an even riskier form of lending: the leveraged buy-out, or LBO. These transactions, usually the purchase of an unwanted subsidiary by its managers but sometimes the purchase of an entire company by outsiders, are entirely dependent on bank finance. The market in them has grown rapidly, from £14 million in 1979 to £10.5 billion in 1997. One of the earliest was the privatisation of the National Freight Company in 1982.[89] Woolworths, re-born as Kingfisher, was the subject of a £310 million buy-out in the same year.

Buy-outs and buy-ins became more ambitious. Some collapsed under the weight of their own pretensions. Lowndes Queensway – acquired in a £450 million LBO in 1988 – provided a sad conclusion, when it failed, to the distinguished career of Jimmy Gulliver and his Scottish backers. The Gateway food company, now much reduced in size and living under an assumed name (Somerfield) has never fully recovered from a £2.37 billion LBO in 1989. That year, the banks put up much of the £13.4 billion Sir James Goldsmith raised for his abortive assault on BAT Industries. The readiness of the banks to lend unlimited amounts of unsecured credit made such grotesque transactions possible. At the height of the boom, the average LBO consisted of six parts debt to one of equity.

Humiliated by Big Bang

Deregulation of the stock market, culminating in October 1986 in the event known as the Big Bang, drew the banks into further errors. Big Bang broke the monopoly the member firms of the Stock Exchange had enjoyed in the broking and trading of domestic bonds and shares. In the three years between the opening of membership of the Stock Exchange to all-comers and Big Bang, three of the Big Four clearing banks and all the leading merchant banks invested heavily in the securities industry. All but one of these investments were disastrous. Only Midland Bank, whose stock-broking and merchant-banking businesses were merged successfully with HSBC to form HSBC Investment Bank, is earning the 30 per cent return on capital which ordinary banking delivers routinely in the good times. Every other securities venture by a clearing bank was an expensive mistake.

Barclays created BZW through a three-way merger between Barclays Merchant Bank, the stock-brokers de Zoete & Bevan and the stock jobber Wedd Durlacher Mordaunt. After serious setbacks in the United States and Japan, and repeated restructurings, BZW in 1997 earned a return of 8 per cent on the capital Barclays had invested. This was one fifth of the 37 per cent the bank earned from retail banking the same year, and less than it could have made by investing the money in government bonds. In the autumn of 1997, Barclays gave up the struggle. The equity and corporate finance divisions of BZW were sold to Credit Suisse First Boston for less than their book value. Once trading losses were included, the sale cost Barclays shareholders well over £500 million and perhaps as much as £700 million.[90] The debt trading and derivatives remnant of BZW, re-named Barclays Capital, was retained but lost £325 million in Russia, and ran into further difficulties in the junk bond markets.[91]

National Westminster fared no better. Its first attempt to establish a serious investment banking business destroyed one merchant bank (County Bank), two stock-brokers (Fielding Newson-Smith and Wood Mackenzie) and a stock-jobber (Bisgood Bishop). It mired the bank in a scandal (Blue Arrow), cost it a chairman (Lord Boardman), a chief executive (Tom Frost), three directors, a £50 million provision and acres of bad publicity when three employees were convicted of misleading the market.[92] The firm was reinvented in 1992 as NatWest Markets, and bolstered by the purchase of two corporate finance firms (Gleacher & Co and Hambro Magan), a bond broker (Greenwich Capital Holdings) and a fund manager (Gartmore). It did not work either. The corporate financiers lost their appetite, and the fund manager lost many of its clients. After an options pricing débâcle cost the bank £77 million in 1997, the chief executive resigned and the equity and derivatives arms were sold for a loss of £535 million. The corporate financiers agreed to stay on only if they were allowed to keep *half* the profits they made. Having sold their firms to NatWest shareholders once, they were able to do it again.

Lloyds-TSB was the only one of the Big Four to escape involvement in the investment banking saturnalia, but largely because the shareholders refused to fund its ambitions. It is now forgotten how grandiose the ambitions of its rivals were. Sir Peter Middleton, chairman of BZW, told the *Sunday Telegraph* in 1993: 'We see ourselves as a big player in the world league, rivals to American houses such as Goldman Sachs and J. P. Morgan.'[93] In 1995 Martin Owen, chief executive of NatWest Markets, declared: 'The overall aim is to be in the top ten investment banks in the world. It is essential if we are to attract and retain our clients' business.'[94]

What Happened to the Merchant Banks?

Among the many disasters clearing banks have inflicted on themselves in the last twenty years, none has exposed their managerial shortcomings more pitilessly than investment banking. It was reasonable to expect the aristocrats of the City, the merchant bankers, to do better. 'You live on your deposits,' Lord Brand had famously mocked the clearing banks. 'We have to live on our wits.' By the time of Big Bang, they did indeed seem to be abreast of financial modernity in ways denied the lumbering clearing banks.

When Anthony Sampson visited the City in the early 1960s, he was told by Jack Hambro that the merchant banks were 'like the British Empire. There's nothing more to gain and quite a lot to lose.'[95] The firms he visited, with their titled partners lingering over the port in mahogany-lined luncheon parlours, struck him as characters in a Victorian play or a left-wing farce. Twenty years later, he found them quite transformed. They were making fortunes by advising companies in hostile takeover bids, trading in Eurodollar bonds and traversing the five continents in pursuit of other lucrative deals and financings.[96] There was every reason to hope that merchant bankers would succeed where clearing bankers had failed. The doubters were dismissed on the eve of Big Bang by the then chancellor of the Exchequer. 'A great prize is within our grasp,' he said. 'I do not share the pessimism of those who fear that British players will account for a disproportionate share of the casualties.'[97] Five of the six leading merchant banks had bought broking and jobbing firms, and looked forward to a future as American-style investment banks, or, as a wit said at the time, 'an Old Etonian version of Goldman Sachs'.

A decade and a half later, not one of the merchant banks had succeeded. Barings went bust and was sold to a Dutch clearing bank for £1. Hambros made so little money that its shareholders insisted it sell its businesses and return the money to them.[98] Morgan Grenfell never recovered from its involvement in the Guinness scandal of 1987, and closed its securities operation before selling out to Deutsche Bank. Kleinwort Benson was bought by Dresdner Bank. Rothschilds sold its interests to Merrill Lynch. S. G. Warburg came closest to success, but its businesses were eventually bought by a combination of Swiss Bank Corporation (SBC) and Merrill Lynch.

Ten years after Big Bang, the City can boast not a single successful indigen-

TABLE 27.5
Present Ownership of Merchant Banks

	Founded	*Current Owner(s)*
Arbuthnot Latham*	1833	Secure Trust Banking Group PLC
Barings	1763	ING Group
Charterhouse†	1880	Crédit Commercial de France
Brown Shipley	1810	Kredietbank SA Luxembourgeoise
Guinness Mahon	1836	Bank of Yokohama
Hambros	1839	Dissolved in 1998
Henry Ansbacher	n/a	First National Bank of South Africa
Hill Samuel‡	1831	Dissolved
Kleinwort Benson	1830	Dresdner Bank
Lazards	1870	Pearson plc (50%) and Limited Partnership: M David-Weill (18%) and Partners (32%)
Morgan Grenfell	1838	Deutsche Bank
N. M. Rothschild§	1804	Rothschilds Continuation Limited (Family)
Samuel Montagu	1853	Hong Kong & Shanghai Bank, via Midland
Rea Brothers	1919	PLC (Salomon family has 51.91%)
Robert Fleming	1932	PLC (Fleming family has 9.2%)
Schroders	1804	PLC (Schroder family has 42.5%)
Singer & Friedlander	1907	PLC
S. G. Warburg	1946	SBC/UBS

Source: Annual Reports.

* This is not the original bank, but a revival of the name. General Accident sold the various assets of the original Arbuthnot Latham after failing to sell the bank as a going concern.
† Charterhouse was owned jointly by Crédit Commercial de France (CCF) and BHF-Bank of Germany, but BHF sold its 50 per cent to CCE in 1997.
‡ Lloyds-TSB closed it down in 1997.
§ Royal and SunAlliance has a 20 per cent stake in Rothschild Continuation Holdings.

ous investment bank. In a sense, it does not matter: investment banking is a uniquely cosmopolitan business; British bankers hold prominent positions in foreign-owned firms, and foreign-owned firms are committed to the City. Its long-term success depends less on native ownership than history, law, language and location. In another sense, the lack of native champions matters. If they are not underwriting and trading securities, it is hard to see what the clearing banks will be doing in the twenty-first century. The traditional bank – taking short-term deposits and turning them into long-term loans, in a well-protected and highly regulated domestic market – will find it hard to grow.

Lloyds-TSB, which has stayed closest to the traditional idea of a bank, has already found this. There is overcapacity in the domestic market; too much money is chasing too little business. Most of the traditional banking services are being provided by specialists, many from outside the banking industry. If the investment banks have taken their biggest and best corporate clients, poorer clients are abandoning the banks for credit unions. These not-for-profit mutual lending societies bear a considerable resemblance to the early building societies. Six hundred and twenty-four were registered by September 1998, with nearly a quarter of a million members and total assets of £124 million. At the upper end of the market, some top customers are decamping to the new banking arms of life assurance companies (Friends Provident, Prudential, Scottish Widows and Standard Life) and supermarkets (Marks & Spencer, Tesco, and J. Sainsbury). Telephone, television and computer technology has made it easy for them to attract customers and, lacking the costly branch networks of the banks, they offer better rates of interest.

Credit rating agencies have usurped the banks' role in assessing creditworthiness; money market funds are assuming their role as deposit-takers; manufacturers and retailers are plundering their leasing businesses; electronic data interchange and collateralised computer systems are supplanting them as risk-takers in the payments business; and smart-card technology, which stores money in electronic form, will eliminate the banks even as managers of cash. Banks are facing the question which confronted the building societies in the 1980s: what are they *for*?

What Are Banks For?

They start from an awkward position. People dislike them. Bankers have for centuries occupied a unique position in the demonology of western civilisation. Lawmakers and theologians condemned banking: Aristotle described the lending of money at interest as 'unnatural'.[99] His condemnation passed into Christian teaching, where usury was tainted with the sin of avarice and constrained by the notion of the 'just price'. Interest was treated by Thomas Aquinas as inherently unjust, because it charged twice for the same thing. The moneylender dragged to hell with a bag of gold around his neck, and the 'shitter of ducats' are among the most powerful images of the Middle Ages. The great religions imposed formal prohibitions on usury, because lenders at interest get something for nothing and break the Golden Rule – that a man should help his neighbour without reward.

The moral qualms of the theologians were, however, no match for the needs of business. Merchants needed complex systems of credit. The monarchs of medieval England circumvented the problem by exempting Jews from the usury laws, and Jewish financiers mortgaged the estates of spendthrift aristocrats, financed the building of many of the monasteries and cathedrals of the early Middle Ages, and bankrolled a succession of ungrateful kings. In 1275 Edward I made usury unlawful for the Jews too, and finally expelled them from the country. This did not obviate the need for usurers. The moneylending monopoly passed first to the Knights Templar and, after the suppression of the order, to the wealthy Italian merchants of Lombardy, who gave their name to Lombard Street in the City. The first of the English bankers, and the man who began the process of making usury respectable, lived there. Sir Thomas Gresham, mercer and benefactor, took deposits and made loans. But his seminal contribution was to emasculate the usury laws. In 1545 he helped to persuade Henry VIII to authorise the levying of interest up to 10 per cent,[100] a liberalisation of the law finally confirmed by Elizabeth I in 1571. Easy credit made a significant contribution to the economic advances of the Elizabethan era, but the ceiling was lowered progressively, to 5 per cent in 1714. The last remnants of the usury laws did not disappear until 1854.

Nowadays, people understand more readily the need for banks to levy interest. They appreciate the risks of inflation and default. The usurer, in the popular estimation, is now the firm which levies *exorbitant* interest. Credit card companies enjoy this status – interest rates on credit cards have at times exceeded 100 per cent, and even in the competitive market of today have yet to fall to single figures. The inertia of consumers and lack of competition on price between banks and building societies have combined to make retail banking one of the most profitable businesses in Britain. In 1997 Lloyds-TSB made a 36.8 per cent return on capital, which is why banks are valued highly by the stock market, and why other firms, such as supermarkets, are investing in financial services. Six banks are among the twenty biggest companies in Britain.[101]

But lack of competition for consumers in the banking industry has failed to excite opinion-formers. Most are still mesmerised by the traditional idea of a bank as the chief source of capital for industry. Blaming the banks for the decline of British manufacturing is one of the oldest saws in British politics. Endless books and articles have compared them unfavourably with their German and Japanese counterparts, which are reported to have formed long-term relationships with industrial companies, shielding them from premature takeover while they invest in new products and technologies, and helping them to survive periods of distress rather than tip them into bankruptcy. In his best-selling polemic, *The State We're In*, Will Hutton argued that the 'disengagement of the banks, their obsession with short-term lending and their unwillingness to support companies in trouble' is one of the primary causes of the failure of British industry to invest in new products and technologies which could raise the rate of economic growth.[102]

Have the Banks Failed Industry?

This charge is more serious than that of usury. It accuses the banks of subverting the standard of living, and ignoring opportunities to increase their profitability. But it is difficult to substantiate. Institutions whose primary source of funding is short-term deposits are not in a strong position to advance long-term loans. The cardinal error in banking is to borrow short and lend long, which is why over four in every five loans advanced to companies by the major banks are repayable within a year or less.[103] This craving for liquidity pains Will Hutton, but conventional banks cannot lock up short-term deposits in long-term industrial and commercial ventures. They would have to raise funds of comparable maturity, yet long-term finance can be raised more cheaply by large multinational companies, whose credit ratings are often better than those of their banks.

The real opportunity for the banks lies not in taking a stake in GEC or ICI, but in funding small and growing businesses. Ironically, it is an opportunity which the banks have tried to seize for over fifty years. After the Second World War, the seven clearing banks and the Bank of England set up a venture capital business, known as the Industrial and Commercial Finance Corporation (ICFC), and later as Investors in Industry. The banks equipped it with £1 million in capital, and underwrote its ability to borrow £30 million more for lending to small and medium-sized businesses. The banks retained stakes in the enterprise until the mid-1990s, when the company was floated as 3i.[104] If anything hampered its contribution, it was the unwillingness of the government to guarantee ICFC's debts, not lack of support from the banks. A succession of official reports have exonerated the banks from the charge of failing to support growing companies. Recent research has also shown that their much-lamented indifference towards companies in financial difficulties is exaggerated. The banks nursed a large number of their industrial clients through difficulties in the 1930s, and sponsored the rationalisation and consolidation of the steel, cotton and shipping industries.[105] Banks also played a major part in helping stricken companies survive the recession of 1980–81.

There is a much sounder criticism of the banks than their indifference to the destruction of British industry. It is their chronic inability to design, price and distribute financial products which individual consumers and small businesses would like to buy. This shortcoming stems from their long hibernation as an arm of the state. They built up large, wasteful and costly branch networks which they are only now pruning and replacing with Automatic Teller Machines (ATMs). They failed to develop new techniques for measuring risk and pricing loans, perpetuating their traditional reliance on illiquid forms of security such as bricks and mortar, and little effort was made to distinguish between sound and unsound banking propositions. 'I feel a degree of discomfort,' said a Bank of England executive director in 1987, 'when bankers tell me that rising delinquencies do not worry them so long as margins compensate for the growing incidence of loss.'[106] It is precisely this rigidity which caused the banks to squeeze both viable and unviable businesses in the recession of the early 1990s.

Modern clearing banks are too big and too centralised to act more imaginatively. In the 1950s and 1960s, branches retained something of the ethos of the partnership banks of the nineteenth century. Many bank managers were close to their clients, often encountering them socially as well, and knew who they could trust. George Carr Glyn, senior partner of Glyn, Mills and Co, warned Victorian parliamentarians that giant PLCs would never uphold the 'duty of a private banker to become acquainted with his customers.' But successive governments continued to encourage banks to merge, and the banking industry gradually became centralised. An ironic result was to cut bankers off from industrialists. By the time Barclays raised £921 million from shareholders in the summer of 1988 to expand its loan book, most bank managers were no longer expected to make judgments about who should have the money. Their job was to ensure that Barclays inflated its balance sheet. In that respect, they were successful. But the shareholders never saw their money again.

The clearing banks could do worse than reinvent the nineteenth century private banker, whose primary role was to channel the savings of the provincial rich into local businesses. At the outbreak of the First World War, four in every five British companies were private, rather than public.[107] They financed their activities mainly from retained profits. Private funding was easy to obtain

TABLE 27.6

Staff of Clearing Banks, Branch and ATM Networks

	Staff		Branches		ATMs	
Bank	1987	1997	1987	1997	1987	1997
Abbey National	–	20,500	677	816	295	*2,074
Alliance & Leicester	–	5,300	–	319	–	539
Bank of Ireland	600	†6,300	–	200	11	†90
Bank of Scotland	10,900	11,400	545	349	302	561
Barclays	84,600	63,600	2,767	1,975	1,384	3,189
Co-operative Bank	4,400	3,900	92	109	56	243
Clydesdale	7,300	5,000	355	297	280	366
Halifax	–	27,000	–	897	–	1,952
Lloyds-TSB	78,200	61,700	3,736	2,878	3,590	4,219
Midland	47,000	44,000	2,127	1,681	1,397	2,659
National Westminster	81,400	55,900	3,101	1,754	2,342	3,128
Northern Rock	–	2,800	–	120	–	39
Royal Bank of Scotland	18,300	19,400	835	693	575	1,425
Woolwich	–	7,900	‡518	414	–	447
Yorkshire Bank	5,300	6,000	245	262	187	396
Total	338,000	340,700	14,998	12,794	10,419	21,327

Source: British Bankers' Association, Annual Abstract of Banking Statistics, May 1998.

* From 1996 includes ATMs previously operated by National and Provincial Building Society.
† Including Bristol and West.
‡ 1993 Figure.

locally, since the tax burden was light, and local banking partnerships were efficient at putting rich men in touch with needy ones.[108] As progressive taxation destroyed private wealth and sheltered institutional forms of saving, they were forced to seek a public quotation. The chief authors of the short-termism and para-proprietorship of which Hutton and others complain are not the obtuseness of bankers or the myopia of fund managers, but government-inspired centralisation and the system of progressive taxation.

Attempts to resurrect the wealthy private investor – initially through the Venture Capital Scheme, and latterly through the Business Expansion Scheme – had mixed results. The continuing shortage of private equity for small and start-up businesses is an opportunity for the banks, They could provide an effective and practical service to smaller companies, if they were prepared to transform their dowdy branches into autonomous businesses. The Bank of

Scotland says it avoided most of the bad loans of the early 1990s because its managers in Scotland still assess businessmen face to face. It was in England, where the bank expanded its loan book by electronic means and failed to get to know the local business establishments, that it experienced problems. 'Everywhere I go,' admitted Brian Pearse, chief executive of the Midland Bank, in 1994, 'customers, professional advisers and the media bewail the fact that good experienced people are no longer available locally to discuss problems and seek solutions.'[109]

This lament is for the experienced and authoritative bank manager of old. Long after the amalgamations of the nineteenth and early twentieth centuries, the branches remained the ultimate authorities on local business, and the manager was entitled to commit the bank to lend virtually any amount. Russell Taylor tells the story of approaching Henry Coe, manager of the Norwich branch of the Midland Bank, for a mortgage in the 1950s:

> Coe was certainly no saint, which perhaps helped him deal with difficult people. He never paid for a meal or a drink at any of my father's hotels but, equally, my father never expected him to; business in the community is about mutual help, particularly so in those days of high marginal taxation. Nor did Coe rely on his manager's salary. When I was sent to him, a completely green graduate with no idea of what a mortgage was, let alone whether I needed one, to discuss a loan for converting a tumbledown cottage, I reported back that Coe seemed willing enough, but very concerned about my health. 'You bloody fool!' said my father. 'Don't you know that's just Henry telling you you can have the loan, but you've got to take out a life assurance policy through him!'[110]

Midlands bought out the insurance earnings of its managers in the 1960s, and set up a centralised insurance-broking business. By then, the clever scions of the lower middle classes had started to go to university, where they developed higher ambitions than processing mortgage applications. Bank managers have become less competent. The clerical drones they once supervised have given way to machines, and especially to the Orwellian ATM. Branches have ceased to be independent fiefs with a sound knowledge of local citizens and businesses, and have become sales outlets for financial products dreamt up at head office for sale at a single price the length and breadth of the country. The classic branch, where queues of bad-tempered people snake up to a row of tills barricaded behind apparently soundproof glass, is giving way to comfortless showrooms where consumers are supposed to sit on sofas to buy mortgages and unit trusts in much the same way that they buy a fridge or a TV.

Banks and building societies have bought or set up insurance companies to prepare for their hoped-for future as financial supermarkets. Lloyds acquired Abbey Life, and Abbey National bought Scottish Mutual. Barclays and the Royal Bank of Scotland have set up new life assurance subsidiaries. National Westminster, after struggling for years in the unlikely role of insurance broker, has followed suit and set up NatWest Life. But the banks enter the insurance and saving markets with a significant handicap: companies with established brands are already entrenched. Savings and investment plans are dominated by branded fund managers such as Perpetual, Jupiter and Fidelity. Discount brokers like Charles Schwab offer cheap services in securities dealing and investment management. Independent accountants and lawyers dominate the markets in tax and financial advice.

In theory, banks do have an advantage: established relationships with their account holders. But cross-selling new products to existing customers is one of the great fallacies of modern business life. Consumers do not buy financial products any more than they buy hair-care products or breakfast cereals; they buy *brands*. Banks know this: Midland rebranded its accounts after varieties of fruit and trees. The Royal Bank of Scotland has developed a branded financial services business, Direct Line. NatWest has appointed its first marketing director, whose declared ambition is to create a 'truly admired financial brand – the sort people talk positively about in the pub.'[111]

It will be hard work. The only bank to have made a success of re-branding is the Co-operative Bank. In the 1990s it has reinvented itself as an 'ethical' bank for greens and *Guardian* readers by promising not to lend money to Saddam Hussein or a Master of Hounds. It is difficult to think of a more pointed reminder of the popular image of a bank than a bank which sells itself by promising to be less like a bank. In a world dominated by brands, banks have the worst in the world. Most consumers would rather deal with anything but a bank. Banks belong to a producer-driven past which over-capacity and deregulation have destroyed. The future belongs to the fund manager, not the banker.

CHAPTER TWENTY-EIGHT

THE RISE OF INSTITUTIONAL INVESTORS

I used to frighten clients by telling them they could fit their crucial shareholders into the first row of an auditorium. Nowadays, you can sometimes fit them in the loo.

CITY CORPORATE FINANCIER, 1996[1]

You are a great estate of the realm. Ministers are only too well aware of your importance.

KEITH JOSEPH, to National Association of Pension Funds (NAPF) Conference, 14 November 1979[2]

We could conceive of a society in which men practically never meet face to face – in which all business is conducted by individuals in isolation who communicate by typed letters or by telegrams, and who go about in closed motor-cars. (Artificial insemination would allow even propagation without a personal element.) Such a fictitious society might be called a 'completely abstract or de-personalised society'. Now the interesting point is that our modern society resembles in many of its aspects such a completely abstract society.

KARL POPPER, 1945[3]

On 19 January 1996 Carol Galley had two meetings. The first was with Gerry Robinson, the chief executive of Granada, the company which makes *Coronation Street*. The second was with Rocco Forte, the chief executive of his family hotel business. For both men, their meeting with this little-known woman was the latter-day equivalent of a bankrupt American railwayman making obeisance to John Pierpont Morgan, the Great Financial Gorgon. As vice-chairman of Mercury Asset Management, Carol Galley manages the investment of nearly £90 billion in the financial markets. At any one time, she and her colleagues will control 4–5 per cent of the London stock market, and usually more of the biggest companies. This is a larger slice of corporate

Britain than any other fund manager. As both Robinson and Forte knew, it was enough to make Mercury the leader of City opinion. And at the beginning of 1996, its 14.6 per cent shareholding in the Forte hotel group was more than sufficient to decide the ownership of the company.

When Galley voted her stock in favour of Gerry Robinson, Rocco Forte lost control of a business built up by his family over six decades. Hotels were sold. Jobs were lost. Granada ceased to be a soap-and-services company; it became a great international hotelier as well. This ability to decide the fate of great companies has encouraged journalists to label Galley one of the most powerful people in Britain. She enjoys neither the fearsome public reputation nor the massive personal wealth of the Great Financial Gorgon himself. Yet, as was once said of Pierpont Morgan, her power is not to be found in the number of her millions, but in the billions of which she is the trustee.[4] She owns none of the £90 billion; most belongs to pension funds, which hold it in trust on behalf of millions of past, present and future employees of the great industrial corporations. Yet such is the division of wealth and power in a modern economy that even as the trustee of trustees she commands the respect – though rarely the affection – of every chairman and chief executive in corporate Britain.

Death of the Banker

The corporate takeover battle, as between Forte and Granada, is the most vivid symbol of where ownership (and the economic and social power it confers) can now be found. When Charles Forte started his hotel and catering business sixty-odd years ago, the merchant banker rather than the fund manager controlled the destiny of public companies. Until at least the 1960s, the merchant banker alone could bridge the world of the company boardroom and that of the great institutional investors. Institutionalised money meant the great insurance companies. The merchant banker often served as a director of both, using his contacts and inside knowledge to mobilise capital, sack chairmen, encourage friendly mergers and discourage unwelcome takeovers. It was one of the unwritten rules of the City that any deal between two companies was broached not by an offer to buy shares in the market but between the financiers of the great banking houses of Baring, Hambro, Lazard, Rothschild, Kleinwort, and Morgan. These names were once synonymous with wealth and financial power; in 1962 Anthony Sampson reckoned the great merchant banking dynasties the 'princes of the City'.[5]

Yet even he recognised that their reputation exceeded their influence. Thirty-odd years on, one is bankrupt, another dissolved, two owned by the

Germans and one by the Swiss; the remaining pair are shadows of their former selves.[6] Sampson wrote shortly after the workings of that antediluvian City were opened to public scrutiny for the first time through the proceedings of the Bank Rate Tribunal of 1957, an official inquiry into the leak of an impending increase in interest rates which resulted in a number of City firms making a lot of money. Lord Kindersley, then managing director of Lazards, appeared before the tribunal on 11 December 1957. This was the opening exchange between him and the attorney general:

> You have been a member of the Court of the Bank of England for ten years? – That is correct.
> And managing director of Lazard Brothers for the past thirty years? – That is correct.
> And chairman of that company since 1953? – That is correct.
> Have you been a member of the Court of the Royal Exchange Assurance for the past twenty-nine years? – I have.
> And its governor since 1955? – Yes.
> Have you been chairman of the British Match Corporation since 1953? – I have.
> I think you are also chairman of Rolls Royce Limited? – Yes.
> And a director of the Bank of London and South America Limited? – For nineteen years.
> Also a director of S. Pearson & Sons Ltd.? – Yes.
> And of one other non-trading company? – That is correct.[7]

His subsequent interrogation revolved around the intimate relationship he enjoyed with Lord Bicester, chairman of Morgan Grenfell, over whether the rise in interest rates would necessitate the postponement of a capital-raising operation Morgan Grenfell was underwriting for Vickers, the arms manufacturer. 'Morgans and ourselves are probably closer than any other two issuing houses in the City,' Kindersley told the tribunal. 'We discuss intimate details of every kind and description. I do not think Lord Bicester would find it in the least surprising that I should come to him and say: "Look here, Rufie, is it too late to stop this business or not?"'

Unlike Gerry Robinson and Rocco Forte, for whom discussions with institutional shareholders are an everyday part of their working lives, it would not have occurred to Lords Kindersley and Bicester to appeal over the heads of the management of a company to its shareholders. This is why the first merchant banker to do so was not a member of the City Establishment at all but a German-Jewish refugee named Siegmund Warburg. In a complex but seminal takeover battle of 1958, known to posterity as the Aluminium War,

British Aluminium succumbed to an Anglo-American consortium advised by Warburg. The turning point was the revelation that British Aluminium had refused to tell their shareholders that the bidder was prepared to pay a premium of eighteen shillings a share to win control. When the company eventually fell Warburg found himself blackballed by the City Establishment for his act of *lèse-majesté*.

'I will never speak to that fellow again,' said Kindersley. (With great ostentation, he once left a reception at the Austrian embassy rather than risk an encounter with Warburg.)[8] Olaf Hambro, one of the merchant bankers who advised British Aluminium to ignore its shareholders, wrote to *The Times* to express his indignation that the City editor had backed the bidder rather than incumbent management.[9]

It is said that Hambro 'never accepted the stock market as the arbiter of corporate fate'.[10] It took an outsider like Warburg to recognise that shareholders were not the milch-cows of the management but the owners of the company. And it was the investment department of his bank – S. G. Warburg & Co., Ltd – which later became Mercury Asset Management. Carol Galley began work there in 1971. The investment department was the only place most merchant banks would have dared to hire a woman in those days. Fund management was a Cinderella business, run either on sufferance to keep the corporate clients sweet for more lucrative deals or as part of the means of controlling companies. Warburg had little time for fund management, preferring the risk-free and fee-earning excitement of brokering deals between companies to the workaday task of investing savings. Twenty-five years later, it is ironic that the power and influence he prized should have passed to his former library assistant.

It is also understandable. The purpose of the capital markets is to channel savings from people who have them to people who need them. In the heroic age of merchant banking, shareholders were small and dispersed. In the 1950s, two thirds of the ordinary shares in public companies were owned by individuals. The great institutional investors owned less than one fifth. Companies owned almost as much of each other. Managers could afford to treat their small and fragmented shareholders with minimal respect. Annual reports were sparse and uninformative. The *Financial Times* was little more than a list of share prices. There were no laws against insider dealing, which was practised on a lavish scale by company managers and their merchant bankers. It was easy for the hereditary princes of the City such as Kindersley and Bicester to direct the fortunes of corporate Britain through influence and inside information rather than the fairer but cruder machinations of the price mechanism. 'I've sacked a dozen chairmen in my time,' an anonymous merchant banker confided in Anthony Sampson in 1962.[11]

Birth of the Fund Manager

Today, the shares of corporate Britain owned by individuals and institutions are neatly reversed: individuals own one fifth, and institutions two thirds. The power which the anonymous banker enjoyed has passed to a new breed of financial intermediary – the fund manager. One of them – George Soros, the hedge fund manager who broke the Bank of England in the summer of 1992 – is a global celebrity on a par with Pierpont Morgan in his heyday. But the fact that his views are sought owes as much to his wealth, philanthropy and politico-intellectual enthusiasms as to his investment expertise. One of his alumni, Nick Roditi, is almost as famous in Britain simply because he is reputed to earn £1.5 million a week. Few fund managers earn as much, but the best in the City can expect substantial six and seven figure salaries.[12] One reason major pension funds sub-contracted the management of their assets to independent fund managers is their inability to match the salaries now demanded in the Square Mile.

Yet even the rising earnings of the best fund managers scarcely do justice to the range of their power and influence. If any group of people can be said to control the wealth of the country, they do. The top fifty fund managers control around two thirds to three quarters of the London stock market: corporate assets worth well over £800 million by the end of 1997. That those who wield this enormous power are almost unknown beyond the City (and a small part of Edinburgh) reflects the deep conventionality of their careers. Unlike the merchant bankers, whom they have succeeded as the arbiters of corporate Britain, their stars tend to evanescence. Of the 'Ten Men Who Control the Destiny of UK PLC' named by the *Independent on Sunday* in February 1991, only one is still where he was. Several have retired. The fund manager, unlike the merchant banker, is a functionary; it is the office, not the man, that matters. One conspicuous exception to this rule is Nicola Horlick of Société Générale Asset Management, who briefly captivated even the television news and the tabloid newpapers after parting unhappily with Deutsche Morgan Grenfell Asset Management in January 1997. But, as the title of her book suggests (*Can You Have It All?*), the public interest revolved around her life rather than her work. A former colleague at Morgan Grenfell, Peter Young, later attracted some press interest by appearing at a court hearing dressed in a frock. But, despite considerable effort, journalists have struggled to infuse other fund managers with similarly alluring human qualities. In 1989 a colleague of Paul Whitney – then chief executive of the Coal Board pension fund – was asked by a national newspaper for some insights into the man in charge of £11 billion. None sprang to mind. 'Frankly,' he confessed, 'he is rather unmemorable.'[13] The following year Whitney was useful to the press as the working-class hero taking on the City establishment, which was their version of a cheeky but otherwise dull bid for an investment trust.[14]

Traditionally, fund managers are actuaries. The actuarial profession, in the old joke, appeals to those who find accountancy too exciting. Dullness is the *déformation professionnelle* of the actuary, which is only to be expected of a mathematician whose responsibility, after six years of rigorous training, is to prepare the tables of mortality life assurance companies use to set their premiums. The boards of insurance and life assurance companies are packed with English FIAs (Fellows of the Institute of Actuaries) and Scottish FFAs (Fellows of the Faculty of Actuaries). Their chief duty, as they see it, is to provide policyholders and pensioners with a good return on their investments, and they are constantly surprised by their own importance. In 1989, when the electronics giant GEC was fighting to acquire Plessey in a bitterly contested takeover bid, an anonymous fund manager confessed to the *Financial Times* that he scarcely knew which way to turn. 'Part of our problem is that our marketing departments build us up into creatures of fantastical prescience,' he complained. 'Our real expertise is in buying and selling bits of paper, and sometimes I feel overawed by the stature we are supposed to have.'[15]

One of the chief criticisms of the actuarial profession in recent years, from within as well as from without, is the reluctance of its members to seek status commensurate with their importance. This may come about, but not because actuaries seek it. As Dermot Morrah wrote in 1955: 'The instinct to manipulate the fortunes of their fellow-subjects is somewhat foreign to the character of the kind of men who are attracted to a career in industrial assurance . . . [They] are modest cobblers who are content to stick to their last. In discharging their responsibility for the investment of life assurance funds, they cannot afford to look beyond the obvious, material, perhaps rather humdrum considerations. If their business is to prosper – and prosperous it is – they must never lose sight of the primary motives: to secure the capital against risk of loss, and to obtain as high an interest yield as is consistent with this cardinal principle of security.'[16]

Like the fund managers of today, J. Pierpont Morgan was accused by his detractors of 'Morganization' – the creation of great systems of business and finance with himself at their helm. Yet Thomas Lamont, a partner in the House of Morgan, remarked that 'he never knew a man who addressed himself more exclusively than Mr Morgan to the ad hoc situation and the ad hoc job that lay before him. All this talk about him devising or building up systems is perfect tosh.'[17] It is by the same, steady accumulation of minor and unrelated decisions that the great institutional investors exert their power

TABLE 28.1
The Top Twenty Fund Managers, 1997

Fund Manager	Owner	Funds Managed (£bn)
Prudential	PLC	91
Schroders	PLC	88
Mercury Asset Management	Merrill Lynch	87
Morgan Grenfell Asset Management	Deutsche Bank	69
Commercial Union*	PLC	68
Flemings	PLC	58
Invesco	PLC	58
PDFM	UBS/SBC (Switzerland)	57
Gartmore	National Westminster	51
Standard Life	Mutual	48
AMP Asset Management	AMP (Australia)	45
Legal & General	PLC	43
Norwich Union	PLC	40
Royal & Sun Alliance	PLC	40
Barclays Global Investors	Barclays Bank	35
J. P. Morgan	J. P. Morgan & Co.	34
Hermes Pensions Management	BT Pension Fund	31
Threadneedle Asset Management	Zurich Insurance	31
Hill Samuel	Lloyds TSB Group	28
Foreign & Colonial	Hypo Bank (Germany), (65%); F&C (35%)	27

Source: Citywatch Institutional Investor Yearbook, 1997; Companies.

* Commercial Union merged with General Accident in 1998. This raised total funds under management by the combined group (CGU) to £115 billion in 1998.

over the British economy today. Nobody argues that fund managers are impotent, or that their actions are innocuous. They are the wielders of a great and concentrated financial power, which they did not seek. They are the accidental inheritors of a long revolution in the way that the surplus wealth generated by capitalism is saved and invested.

The First Institutional Investors

Material progress depends upon investment, but investment depends upon savings. Through most of history, men and women have barely grown or earned enough to eat, let alone to save. Only industrial economies, armed with the machinery which enables people to produce more goods for less effort, are capable of generating a surplus which can be invested in further wealth-creating activities. As the British economy industrialised between the 1790s and the 1840s, investment increased from about £1 in every £20 earned by firms and individuals to £1 in every £10. Today, the public and the private sectors between them invest around £1 in every £5–6 they earn. In 1997 the money saved by the personal sector generated a flow of over £34 billion into long-term bank and building society accounts and another £1.5 billion into National Savings certificates. Bank and building society accounts give people a measure of control over their savings not very different from the cash they stuff into the mattress. Shares and bonds would also give their owners a measure of control, but in recent years individual savers have usually sold more than they have bought. The overwhelming bulk of the money which people save – two thirds of net savings – finds its way into a series of faceless savings institutions: life assurance companies, pension funds, unit trusts and investment trusts.

There is probably no country on earth today where savings are more heavily institutionalised than Britain. By the end of 1997 the four main groups of institutional investors managed nearly £1.6 trillion of assets on behalf of millions of employees and pensioners, insurance and life assurance policyholders and small investors.[18] The institutions own well over half the shares listed on the London Stock Exchange, most of the corporate debt issued by companies, and nearly £2 out of every £3 of debt issued by government to finance its borrowing.

Superficially, the power to direct savings is still widely dispersed. There are over eight hundred insurance companies registered in Britain; well over a thousand occupational pension funds; roughly seventeen hundred unit trusts (with over eight million account holders); and several hundred investment trusts. But control of British savings is, in fact, highly concentrated. Nearly half the funds managed by life offices and insurance companies are controlled by the ten largest companies. Two thirds of the pension funds invested by independent fund managers are controlled by just five firms.[19] Three quarters of unit trust funds are managed by the twenty largest providers, and the ten biggest investment trusts account for well over half the total market. An astonishing power over the corporate economy and the state is now concentrated in the hands of a few dozen people. Between them, they have effective

TABLE 28.2
Where Personal Savings Go (£m)

	National Savings	Bank Deposits	Building Society Deposits	Gilts	Company Securities	Life Ass. & Pensions
1979	1,062	6,384	5,833	1,919	(3,290)	10,503
1981	4,182	3,978	7,082	2,088	(2,145)	13,318
1983	2,907	2,903	10,250	1,707	(1,383)	15,120
1985	2,467	5,139	13,314	1,531	(3,129)	18,973
1987	2,439	7,989	13,577	1,668	(1,257)	19,950
1989	(1,519)	21,500	17,580	(2,212)	(18,925)	26,510
1990	783	17,195	17,959	(1,023)	(9,119)	25,928
1991	2,169	6,088	17,345	568	(3,507)	26,093
1992	5,019	5,382	10,802	(1,053)	471	28,090
1993	3,020	1,872	9,596	5,339	(3,206)	29,056
1994	4,597	2,727	8,540	1,170	4,536	28,086
1995	3,264	13,067	14,233	2,547	(7,707)	32,183
1996	6,867	15,007	11,091	(3,236)	(3,112)	37,630
1997	1,550	16,532	17,738	(7,829)	(265)	41,028

Source: *Financial Statistics*, Sources and Uses of Funds of the Personal Sector, Table 9.2 (later 10.7B).

control of every major public company in Britain, and a right of veto over the ability of the government to tax and spend.

It all began with insurance. Insurance is now such an everyday feature of life that people forget how extraordinary a business it is (the customer pays a great deal up-front, usually in exchange for nothing in return) and how unnecessary it was throughout most of history. Roughly two in every three households have house, motor and life insurance; three in four insure the contents of the house as well; and one in five is contributing to a personal pension plan. In all, 7 per cent of the total expenditure of British households goes on insurance. Protecting the house, its contents, the motor car and the lives of its occupants costs the average household £490 a year. Another £710 goes on life assurance, mortgage protection plans and personal pensions.[20] Yet as recently as a century ago, it was the preserve of the rich. Insurance is practicable only when the necessities of life are secure, and the value of life and property is great enough to be worth protecting. This is why the insurance, life assurance and pension fund industries (the institutional investors) did not emerge in anything like their present form until the British economy began to

TABLE 28.3
The Control of Corporate Britain

Fund Manager	Share of the 250 Biggest Companies (%)	Share of the 100 Biggest Companies (%)	Share of the Total Stock Market (%)
Mercury Asset Management	4.2	4.0	3.9
Prudential Portfolio Managers	3.7	3.7	3.6
American Institutional Investors*	2.5	4.2	3.5
Schroders	3.6	2.6	2.8
Legal & General	2.1	2.1	2.1
Standard Life	2.0	2.0	1.9
Barclays Global Investors	1.9	1.7	1.8
PDFM	3.3	1.1	1.6
Gartmore	2.1	1.3	1.5
Royal & SunAlliance	1.3	1.3	1.3
Hill Samuel	1.2	1.2	1.2
AXA Sun Life	1.1	1.5	1.2
Hermes	1.2	1.1	1.1
Norwich Union	1.1	1.1	1.1
Morgan Grenfell	1.3	1.0	1.1
Flemings	1.1	0.9	0.9
Scottish Widows	0.8	0.9	0.9
Threadneedle Asset Management	0.8	0.9	0.9
M & G (Prudential)	1.5	0.6	0.8
Foreign & Colonial	0.8	0.8	0.8
Top Twenty Fund Managers	37.8	34.1	33.7

Source: Citywatch, January 1998.

* As measured by American Depository Receipts (ADRs), dollar-denominated receipts issued to American institutional investors in lieu of shares listed on the London Stock Exchange.

industrialise. And they did not grow rapidly until Victorian times, when ordinary people were finally earning enough money to set some aside.

The impetus behind the foundation of the industry was the Great Fire of London in 1666. The value of the property destroyed was put at £10 million (perhaps £100 billion in modern prices). The Royal Exchange, the Customs House, the halls of forty-four livery companies, St Paul's Cathedral, eighty-seven parish churches and thirteen thousand houses were destroyed. A loss of £10 million amounted to perhaps a quarter of the national income, and it was uninsured.[21] After various failed attempts, the first recognisably modern insurance company received a royal charter of incorporation in 1688. It was named, with commendable directness, the Fire Insurance Company, but later changed to the more marketable Phenix Fire Office.[22] Phenix was not the first company to sell insurance against disaster. A lottery-like form of insurance, in which individuals funded hazardous sea voyages in the expectation of losing everything if the ship was lost but making spectacular gains if it returned safely, dates back to classical antiquity (though this kind is hard to distinguish from unsecured lending – what the Emperor Justinian called 'nautical usury'). The Lloyd's insurance market, which began meeting in Edward Lloyd's coffee house in Lombard Street at around the same time as the Phenix was founded, offered a form of insurance the Romans would have understood. The famous *Lloyd's List* of ships sailing and docking in London, and the equally famous *Lloyd's Register of Shipping*, began life as news-sheets for wealthy Georgian merchants who fancied a flutter over their coffee and biscuits.

The relatively short duration of a voyage by sea was well-suited to private underwriting. The protection of buildings and their contents requires a much longer-term commitment from a permanent institution than short-lived groups of rich people, and the building up of substantial reserves in the good years against claims in the bad. This was the opportunity the Fire Insurance Company of 1688 was designed to exploit. The moving spirit behind the new venture was Nicholas Barbon, son of the Cromwellian MP Praise-God Barebones, who gave his name to the Commonwealth Parliament.[23] For eight years Barbon's company shared an alternating monopoly with the Friendly Society for Securing Houses from Loss by Fire. Both this company, and the Phenix, disappeared eventually, but a third company, the Amicable Contributors for Insuring Houses from Loss By Fire, retained its independence from its foundation in 1696 until its acquisition by the Commercial Union in 1905. One reason it survived was its grasp of an essential feature of the insurance business: insurance is sold, not bought. In fact, the company was better known as the Hand-in-Hand, a name drawn from the badge (or 'fire-mark') it pinned on the buildings it insured. Modern marketing men call it a logo or brand.

The fire-mark was used chiefly as a form of advertising, but it also identified which buildings the company firemen should attend first. Insurers were expected to supply their own firemen and firefighting equipment, such as ladders, leather buckets and 'fire engines'. (In 1830 the Alliance Insurance Company owned a six-horse-power steam fire engine capable of hurling a stream of water 90 feet).[24] Though the insurers were supposed to douse the flames at insured properties only, they soon discovered there was not always time to check the fire-mark, and formed joint firefighting establishments. These private organisations continued to cover Londoners until the catastrophic Tooley Street blaze of 22 June 1861, the worst between the Great Fire and the Blitz. It destroyed property worth £2 million and took the life of the chief superintendent of the Sun, Royal Exchange and Phoenix establishment, James Braidwood – killed by falling masonry when a saltpetre warehouse exploded.* In the wake of the Tooley Street fire London local authorities formed fire brigades of their own, but several provincial fire offices did not relinquish firefighting duties entirely until the 1920s.[25]

Insuring goods against fire, as well as buildings, developed quickly. The Sun Fire Office – founded in 1710 by an irascible and litigious coal merchant, Charles Povey, but still known today by its badge of a smiling sun – insured contents as well as houses from the outset.[26] The Sun was one of a handful which survived the South Sea Bubble, but the chief beneficiaries of that first stock-market crash were the London and the Royal Exchange. Both were founded in the 'Bubble' years as funds 'for insuring ships and merchandise at sea' (which included slaves).† The Royal Exchange was headed by Lord Onslow and the London by Lord Chetwynd, and several of their directors were also directors of the South Sea Company. (Sir William Chapman, sub-governor of the London, was among those arrested after the Bubble burst.)[27] The promoters were also astute enough to offer the prime minister a bribe. They agreed to lend £300,000 apiece to the government – exactly the right amount to enable Walpole to clear a £600,000 deficit on the Civil List. They then bribed the attorney general to grant them royal charters, which gave them exclusive rights to conduct marine, fire and life assurance. Walpole doubled his money by prudently investing £2,550 in both companies before the grant of their royal charters was made public. Only the taxpayers lost out. The Bubble ruined the subscribers to the companies, and the government got only half the promised £600,000 after a two-year delay.[28]

The Bubble Act of 1720 had a profound effect on the way institutional investors evolved in Britain over the next two centuries. By forbidding incorporation except by royal charter, it prolonged the life of one unincorporated insurance enterprise far beyond its natural lifespan (Lloyd's of London) and fostered the growth of another unincorporated form of ownership (the great

---

* Braidwood became a posthumous hero. Queen Victoria sent a message of condolence to his widow; the popular novelist Dinah Craik composed his funeral oration, and hundreds of thousands of cards bearing his portrait were printed and sold. Braidwood's funeral cortege was 1½ miles long. Trebilcock, *Phoenix Assurance* 1985, p. 426.

† London Assurance became a heavy insurer of ships engaged in the slave trade, meeting claims for slaves thrown overboard as 'loss of cargo'. Barry Supple, *The Royal Exchange Assurance*, Cambridge University Press, 1970, p. 12.

mutual life assurance offices).[29] It was not until the end of the twentieth century that either form of organisation was found wanting.

Insurance against personal accidents arrived with the railway boom of the 1840s. The premiums charged by the first railway insurance companies – $3d$ for £1,000 in first class, $2d$ for £500 in second class, and $1d$ for £100 in third class – reflected the greater risk of injury from travelling in the roofless carriages.[30] One of the railway insurers – the General Accident & Compensation Company, founded in 1855 – retained its independence until 1998, when it merged with the Commercial Union to create CGU. Curiously, insurance against theft did not become commonplace until the 1890s, largely because insurers were convinced that most claims would be fraudulent. Motor insurance was not really necessary until 1896, when the government finally lifted the 4 mph speed limit and scrapped the requirement for a man in front waving a red flag. The first cars were insured by the Scottish Employers' Liability and Accident Company; with a sharp eye for publicity, it agreed to insure the competitors in the first London to Brighton car run on 14 November 1896. The run was actually a political protest against the Locomotives Act of 1896 (which had banned motor cars from the roads) and the insurance cover wisely excluded accidents 'caused by frightened horses'.[31] The first specialist motor insurer was formed in 1903, when Frederick Thoresby established the Car & General (now part of the Guardian). Thoresby correctly anticipated the surge in interest following an increase in the speed limit to 20 mph.[32]

Motor insurance now rivals buildings and contents as the largest source of premium income for composite insurance companies. Though third party insurance was not made compulsory until 1930, the growth of the market was driven by fear of ruinous claims from third parties run over by careless motorists. George Bernard Shaw wrote to his friend, Mrs Patrick Campbell, in 1913:

> Something really important. Attend ... Stella: is that car insured? If not, insure it *instantly*. Send up at once to the Car & General Insurance Corporation, 1 Albemarle Street, Piccadilly, and say you want 'cover' at once. It will be anything up to £18 or so for a whole year ... What is urgent – what you must have above all is insurance against 'third party claims'. If you get killed you are dead. If the car is smashed, *it* is dead. But if it runs into a motor bus or a beanfeast, everybody in it can take action against you, and even keep on taking actions against you until the end of their lives every time they have a fresh nervous symptom, and get enormous damages. You may have to support them and their children for ever. And you will have to buy a new bus for the company.

TABLE 28.4
Composite Insurers as Institutional Investors, 1997 (£bn)

	Ownership	Total Assets	Funds Managed
Axa Sun Life	Axa (France)	40.0	–
Commercial Union†	CGU PLC	54.4	65.0
Cornhill Insurance	Allianz	3.5	2.7
Eagle Star	Zurich Insurance*	16.2	31.0
General Accident†	CGU PLC	28.2	25.0
Guardian Royal Exchange‡	Axa (France)	18.8	16.5
Legal & General	PLC	45.9	44.3
Norwich Union	PLC	41.7	40.0
Royal & SunAlliance	PLC	55.7	48.5

Source: Citywatch Institutional Investor Yearbook, 1997; Annual Reports.

* BAT Industries centralised the management of the investment funds of Eagle Star and Allied Dunbar in a single entity, Threadneedle Asset Management, prior to the merger of its insurance businesses with Zürich Insurance of Switzerland in 1998.
† General Accident and Commercial Union merged in 1998 to create CGU.
‡ Guardian Royal Exchange was acquired by Axa, the French insurance group, in February 1999.

Your salary will be attached; you will be reduced to beg on the streets. This always happens in the first five minutes with an uninsured car. And you must insure your driver. Otherwise he will sprain his thumb or knock out his eye, and live on you for the rest of his life.[33]

The litigious society is clearly not an American import. Nor is 'road rage'. In 1936 one major insurer, complaining of its losses, blamed 'excessive speed . . . cutting in, discourtesy, wilful ignoring of dangers . . . [and] sheer carelessness' for the 'slaughter' on the roads. 'It is almost impossible', its historian decided, 'to escape the conclusion that the average motorist's attitude towards modern road transport is fundamentally wrong in some vital factor.'[34]

The Second Institutional Investors

By the end of the nineteenth century the modern 'composite' insurance company – which sells fire, burglary, accident, motor, marine, commercial and life cover – was established. But composites are not the largest source of institutional savings. Although risks oblige insurance companies to build up reserves of cash and securities against unexpected claims or bad years, it is the life assurance and pension funds controlled by composites and the specialist life offices and pension fund managers which control the biggest pools of savings. Composite insurers keep a relatively high proportion of their assets in cash, short-dated securities and gilt-edged securities, whereas life and pension funds keep four fifths of the assets they manage in long-term investments such as shares.[35] This is because life policies and pension plans are *investments* rather than insurance.

The managers of life and pension funds aim, by re-investing premiums, to create a pool of assets large enough to pay a substantial lump sum to the holder when the policy matures or the holder reaches retirement age – or dies unexpectedly. The longer-term nature of the contracts means that life and pension providers can buy long-term and less liquid assets, such as property and shares, rather than short-term investments which need to be turned into cash quickly. However, striking the right balance between premium income and the investment returns required to deliver a guaranteed minimum or 'assured sum' requires an encyclopaedic knowledge of rates of mortality, an understanding of when investments look cheap or expensive, and the ability to make heroic assumptions about likely rates of return. It requires, in short, an actuary.

The slow development of actuarial science is the main reason why life assurance (as opposed to fire insurance) took so long to become established. Actuarial knowledge developed in the seventeenth and eighteenth centuries, but remained crude until deep into the nineteenth. When London Assurance started offering *one-year* life policies in the 1720s, it refused people who had not had smallpox.[36] 'Be pleased to inform me,' the Royal Exchange actuary wrote to one of his agents in 1799, 'whether Mr Thomas Wardle is known to be a temperate man: if he is corpulent or inactive, mention it; when a life to be assured is an innkeeper, these matters are worth particular consideration.'[37] Under the management of Samuel Bignold between 1818 and 1875, 'diseased or intemperate persons' were excluded by Norwich Union, credentials checked with local surgeons, and agents sacked if clients died sooner than expected.[38]

At the Legal & General in the 1840s, the check for tuberculosis consisted of a single question: 'Do you spit blood?' Heavy drinking was defined as 'drinking brandy in the morning'. The company made Queen Victoria pay £9 extra on her life policy to cover her first pregnancy.[39] The Quaker life offices in England, and many of their Scottish competitors, were founded by abstainers convinced that excessive drinking was the shortest route to an early grave.[40] This view was not universally held. The United Kingdom Provident Institution was started in 1840 by Robert Warner, a teetotaller refused cover

by another life office on the grounds that not drinking was bad for his health.*
It was not until the end of the nineteenth century that Sir George Johnson, the
first chief medical officer to the Equitable, introduced 'testing the proposer's
water'.[41]

This was too late for many of the friendly societies formed by the working
classes to pay for health and unemployment insurance, and especially for
funerals. Their actuarial methods did not extend much beyond excluding
drunks, smokers, gamblers and blasphemers from membership or benefits,
on the grounds that they were likely neither to pay their premiums nor to
enjoy long and healthy lives. The Watermen paid nothing to members who
suffered from 'any illness got by lying with an unclean woman, or is clap't or
pox'd.'[42] The Independent Order of Rechabites admitted only teetotallers,
and fought recidivism by circulating improving tracts such as *Remarkable Deaths
of Drunkards* and *Teetotalism in Cockermouth*.[43] By the end of the nineteenth
century many friendly societies were in severe financial difficulties, increased
because most working-class people were too poor to make adequate contributions.[44]

The earliest life offices – for example, the Society for Assurance of Widows
and Orphans, founded in 1699, and the Amicable Society for a Perpetual
Assurance Office founded in 1706 by John Hartley – did not have that problem. Their clients were the prosperous upper and middle classes. But they
used equally crude actuarial methods. Hartley simply divided the annual
premiums among the relatives of those who had died. This led to wild fluctuations in the value of the pay-outs, and did little to improve the reputation
of the nascent life assurance industry.[45] Actuarially speaking, it was like betting
that people would not die sooner than expected, and for a time life assurance
was more or less synonymous with gambling.[46] Defoe thought it an incitement
to murder, denouncing it as fit only for Italians, among whom 'stabbing and
poisoning is so much in vogue'.[47]

Though the eighteenth century English were less likely to stab and poison
each other than their Italian contemporaries, they were inveterate gamblers.
(When George II led his troops against the French at Dettingen in 1743,
punters could get odds of four to one against his being killed.) This added
urgency to the search for scientific methods of calculating odds. Some of the
greatest minds of the early Enlightenment – Pierre de Fermat (he of the Last
Theorem), Blaise Pascal, Johan de Witt, Isaac Newton, Edmund Halley and

---

* Warner used Bands of Hope as his sales force. United Kingdom Provident policyholders who
broke their pledge and started drinking were fined 10 shillings for every £1,000 insured, and
expelled altogether if they became unrepentant recidivists. Unhappily, there were not enough
teetotallers for growth. See Withers, *Pioneers of Life Assurance*.

others – had worked on the laws of probability in the late seventeenth century, and the first usable table of mortality for setting life assurance premiums was completed in the 1750s. It was drawn up by James Dodson, a master at the Royal Mathematical School, from London Bills of Mortality for 1728–50. There was no official source to draw on: the government register of births and deaths was not introduced until 1837, the existing insurance companies wrote little life business, and virtually no policy lasted more than a year.[48] Dodson apparently began his calculations in a fit of pique after the old Amicable Society turned him down because he was over forty-five.[49] But he was also alive to the commercial possibilities; shortly after completing his work, he placed an advertisement in the *Daily Advertiser* calling on anybody interested in a 'scientific' approach to life assurance to meet him at the Queen's Head pub in Paternoster Row, near St Paul's Cathedral, on 2 March 1756. This was the first of a series of meetings which led to the foundation in 1762 of the Society for Equitable Assurances on Lives and Survivorships. Dodson did not live to see it, but his creation is still going strong – better known as Equitable Life.[50]

His mortality tables proved less durable. The London Bills of 1728–50 covered a time and place in which premature death was exceptionally common. The predictable result was excessive premiums, and the Equitable switched shortly afterwards to the celebrated Northampton Tables. These were prepared by Dr Richard Price from the records of the parish of All Saints, Northampton, between 1735 and 1770. Price was a far more interesting figure than the titles of his epoch-making works of actuarial science – *Observations on the Expectations of Lives* of 1769 and *Observations on Reversionary Payments* of 1770 – might suggest. A Unitarian minister and amateur scientist, as well as a gifted mathematician, Price was the very model of Enlightenment Man. He was a friend of Benjamin Franklin, Adam Smith and Joseph Priestley, the acquaintance of David Hume and Tom Paine, and protagonist of Edmund Burke in matters of revolution, both American and French.

But his tables of mortality were also not good enough. Death rates in mid-eighteenth-century Northampton were closer to the mean than those in contemporary London, but still under-recorded unbaptised births, over-recorded unburied deaths, and made no allowance for lower rates of death among the naturally cautious people likely to buy life assurance. Charles Babbage, father of the computer, actuary to the Protector Life Office, and a stern critic of the actuarial methods of the older life offices, reckoned the Northampton Tables had 'proved to be erroneous throughout a large part, in the proportion of two to one.'[51] No lasting solution was devised until the Institute of Actuaries published the first official Life Tables in 1869. The result, familiar to the modern buyer of life assurance, was massive profits for the life offices. The Equitable was embarrassed to discover, on its first valuation on the Northampton basis in 1776, that it had overcharged its clients by such a wide margin that it gave 10 per cent of the premiums back, inadvertently pioneering the reversionary bonus.[52]

Equitable Life was the inadvertent pioneer of something else as well. Today, it makes much of the fact that it is a mutual organisation, owned by its policyholders rather than outside shareholders. 'It is fashionable to knock the concept,' claimed the managing director of the Equitable in 1994, 'but a society run on mutual grounds concentrating wholly on benefits to members and not answerable to outside interests and influences can be one of the most effective forms of incorporation.'[53] But the Equitable did apply for a royal charter of incorporation at its foundation. The application was refused by the attorney general on the grounds that its business plan was 'a mere speculation never yet tried in practice, and consequently subject, like all other experiments, to various chances in the execution'.[54] Ironically, Equitable thrived, by concentrating on meeting the needs of the wealthy metropolitan élite. It still prefers to deal with the affluent managerial, professional and self-employed classes. (In 1994 a *Financial Times* reporter was shocked to hear the marketing director refer, without a trace of irony, to 'the proletariat'.[55])

But the incorporated life assurance companies were no more democratic. Clients of London Assurance included Pitt the Elder, Charles James Fox, the King of Poland, Emperor Napoleon III, the Kings of Norway and Sweden, the Queen of Spain, Queen Victoria, Edward VII, George V, Robert Baden-Powell, the Marquess of Salisbury, Pierpont Morgan, Sir Charles Hallé and virtually every duke in Britain.[56] It was left to the friendly societies, and to the non-conformist consciences of northern England and lowland Scotland, to provide life assurance for the mass market. They were mutuals rather than incorporated companies and, as a result, mutuals dominated the life assurance industry in Britain for the next two hundred years.

The Origins of the Scottish Life Offices

Almost all the great mutual life offices of Scotland were founded in a last burst of energy at the tail-end of that period when Edinburgh could claim with justice to be the Athens of the North. The oldest is the Scottish Widows' Fund, founded in the Scottish capital in 1812 by a writer, David Wardlaw, and an accountant, Patrick Cockburn. Their aim was to provide annuities to widows of Scottish clergy. Despite securing the approval of just about the entire Scottish aristocracy (every life office recognised the sales value of aristocratic endorsement), it took the Widows' Fund three years to get underway and ten before the directors could pay themselves. Their chief problem, it seems, was that sin-conscious Regency Scotsmen considered life assurance a form of gambling. 'I met some worthy men,' recalled the Reverend John McLean of his youth in the 1840s, 'who would have shrunk as sternly from counselling their sons to take out a policy of insurance as any prudent father among ourselves would from encouraging his son to visit the tables of Hamburg or Monte Carlo.'[57] But the Widows did persuade the Borders novelist, Walter Scott, of their soundness. They paid out £3,360 at his death in 1832.[58]

TABLE 28.5

Mutual and Ex-Mutual Life Assurance Offices (£bn)

	Ownership	Total Assets	Funds Managed
Britannia Life*	Britannia	4.9	3.3
Canada Life†	Mutual (Canada)	6.0	6.3
Clerical Medical	Halifax	13.9	16.2
Equitable Life	Mutual	19.7	19.3
Friends Provident	Mutual	15.9	17.9
National Mutual	Mutual	3.4	3.4
National Provident Institution	AMP‡ (Australia)	10.0	10.0
Norwich Union	PLC	41.7	40.0
Old Mutual	Mutual	47.5	–
Scottish Amicable	Prudential	12.9	14.2
Scottish Equitable	Aegon (Holland)	13.0	12.6
Scottish Life	Mutual	5.7	5.3
Scottish Mutual	Abbey National	6.1	7.9
Scottish Provident	Mutual	7.2	9.3
Scottish Widows	Mutual	24.2	23.2
Standard Life	Mutual	49.5	48.0

Source: Citywatch Institutional Investor Yearbook 1997; Annual Reports.

* The Life Association of Scotland was bought by the Britannia Building Society from ING group of Holland and renamed Britannia Life.
† Canada Life includes Albany Life, which it acquired in 1996.
‡ AMP had earlier acquired another mutual, London Life.

The biggest life office in Britain – and the largest mutual organisation in Europe – is the Standard Life Assurance Company, also of Edinburgh. It was established in March 1825 as the life arm of a fire insurance company set up by Edinburgh lawyers and merchants, and known as the Life Insurance Company of Scotland. By 1832, the partners had concluded that the name was insufficiently distinctive, though it is doubtful if the new name was an improvement. Another life office started up in Glasgow a year after the foundation of Standard Life: once the third biggest in Scotland, Scottish Amicable recently surrendered its independence to the giant Prudential Assurance. It began as the life arm of a Glasgow fire office set up by an accountant, James Johnston Duncan, who suffered the indignity of being refused as its first risk, on medical grounds, and died of his ailments whilst seeking a cure in Australia. The unfortunate Duncan is remembered mainly for an extraordinary vendetta he maintained against the Scottish Equitable (started by a group of businessmen in Edinburgh in 1831[59]). Foremost among his protagonists was one William Braidwood, an entrepreneurial ironmonger whose massive losses in various property speculations made him take his own life within a year of the foundation of the new enterprise. The Equitable, in keeping with the high moral tone Scottish fund managers have adopted ever since, refused to pay out on his policy.[60]

An equally typical blend of high- and low-mindedness persuaded James Cleghorn to join forces with a printer, William Fraser, to found the Scottish Provident Institution in 1837. Cleghorn, a self-taught actuary and journalist, had (like Dodson before him) convinced himself and his partner that the mortality tables being used resulted in the charging of excessive premiums.[61] He died a year after founding the company, and the £320 paid out on his life sorely tested the finances of the young office; it was insufficient for his sister to buy an annuity.[62] Scottish Provident nevertheless managed to survive, and even to breed: a former salesman with the Scottish Provident, David Paulin, founded Scottish Life in April 1881.

But even his legendary moral earnestness was outshone by Adam Keir Rodger, the founder of Scottish Mutual. He established his life business in Glasgow in 1883 specifically to insure the (generally longer) lives of teetotallers. Rodger had inherited from his father, who combined brewing during the day with teetotalism at night, a rare talent for living with the contradictions which must sometimes arise between sound business and uncompromising morals. He was able to sell life assurance with exactly the same zeal he brought to the Bible classes and Sunday schools he ran in his spare time. Prospective employees were asked only three questions: 'Do you smoke? Do you drink? Do you go to church?' What would now be called the company logo showed a woman standing on top of a globe holding a scroll which read 'Length of Days' – a quotation from one of the sterner passages in Proverbs, doubtless familiar to Rodger's contemporaries. This was underscored by the motto *Temperantia Vincit.*[63]

But there was method in Rodger's morals. Offering discounts to teetotallers had the happy consequence of improving the quality of the risks Scottish

Mutual assumed and increasing the ability of its largely working-class clientele to pay the premiums. 'Insurance,' as Rodger ingenuously said, 'is a very close relative, and also a dependant upon, Thrift.' Given the severity of his rectitude, it is hard to believe that Rodger understood the lifestyle of his company's most famous risk, David Lloyd George. In 1910 the future prime minister insured his life with Scottish Mutual for £4,000. As a man who managed to combine his duties as chancellor of the exchequer and prime minister with insider trading, adultery and an ample alcoholic intake, it could not be said that Lloyd George was completely at one with the company motto. (One of the few pieces of evidence that he had a conscience was his confession to Scottish Mutual that he had resumed drinking.) Though the spirit of Adam Keir Rodger lives on at Scottish Mutual, in the shape of discounts for the abstemious, moralising is a poor sales strategy in the age of moral relativity. The company stopped advertising its preference for teetotallers in 1952, and the scroll-bearing schoolmistress has given way to a friendly looking reindeer. In the end, even *Temperantia Vincit* must yield to *Pecunia Obediunt Omnia.*

Contribution of the Quakers

Rodger had his counterparts in England, where Quakers played almost as large a part in mass-market life assurance as the Scottish Presbyterians. Nonconformity was the best school of business in early industrial England. Denied access to the civil and military offices of the Old Corruption (and to Oxford and Cambridge, though they could of course attend the Scottish universities), the Non-Conformists were obliged to engage in commerce of all kinds, and to develop their own schools and universities.[64] Their goals in life and religion were also different, emphasising work, duty and saving over idleness, pleasure and expenditure. Eighteenth and early nineteenth-century Quaker letters and diaries portray a business culture whose denizens never escape the parable of the talents. They allied the peasant virtues of personal abstention and thrift to capitalistic energy and enterprise. (The advertisements of the National Provident Institution, which even today depict squirrels hoarding nuts, are characteristic of this outlook.) In an age before ownership became divorced from control, when owners and managers were one, spending less meant more to invest and, as the British economy industrialised, there was no group in England better equipped to usher in the age of institutionalised saving. In Britain, the Presbyterians and the Quakers are to life assurance what the Jews are to banking and finance.

The largest of the Quaker life offices to have retained its independence is the Friends Provident, founded in Bradford in July 1832 by Samuel Tuke and Joseph Rowntree, two prominent Yorkshire Quakers who were at school together. Like Adam Keir Rodger and teetotalism, they recognised that the abstemious habits of their brethren meant good life assurance risks. Membership of Friends Provident was confined exclusively to Quakers until 1915, when the chairman, Henry Priestman, delivered himself of the verdict that 'we are of the opinion that selected lives outside the Society of Friends are about as good as the lives of Friends.' The Quaker market was by then saturated, of course, but Friends continued to enjoy a discount even after allcomers were admitted to membership. It was another forty years before the company gained its first non-Quaker chairman, and sixty years before non-Quakers constituted a majority on the board.[65]

Friends Provident has since taken over another Quaker life office: the United Kingdom Provident Institution, founded in November 1840 as the United Kingdom Temperance and General Provident Institution.[66] The London offspring of Friends Provident, the National Provident Institution, also put itself up for sale in 1998, and was acquired in December that year by AMP of Australia. It was established in 1835 by the London agents of the Yorkshire parent, who were frustrated by the restriction of the business to Quakers.[67] A century ago its secretary was Samuel Smiles, author of those quintessentially Victorian self-improvement manuals, *Self-Help* and *Thrift*. No mind was better attuned to the demands of building a life assurance business. Smiles deplored the willingness of even the poorest labourers to go without food, let alone saving for the future, in order to fill their dwellings with trifles,[68] and declared that 'extravagance is the pervading sin of modern society.'[69] The greatest extravagance of all, and one he roundly condemned, was the 'respectable' funeral.

The one event for which even the lowliest member of the Victorian working classes was prepared to save was his own funeral. In 1870 it cost £5 9s to bury a London adult and £2 2s to bury a child. To these sizeable sums had to be added the cost of what Smiles called the 'worthless and extravagant mummery of the undertaker's grief': flowers, headstone, funeral cloaks, hatbands and scarves, gilded hearses and mourners' coaches. Smiles reckoned it was not uncommon to spend £40 or even £50 on the funeral of a mere tradesman.[70] Since an unskilled labourer earned perhaps £60 a year at the turn of the century, a complete funeral cost as much as forty times his weekly pay.[71] Few had the personal savings to cover the cost; nine out of ten Britons left so little property that the tax authorities did not bother to record their assets.

The Friendly Societies

The friendly societies were called into existence mainly to cover the cost of funerals, but they became and remained the chief savings institutions of the working class until deep into the twentieth century. They are a downmarket derivative of the guilds of the Middle Ages, when the superstitions of Catholicism required not only a lavish funeral but the singing of masses for the dead.[72] Like the guilds, they drew on the central insight of any system of insurance: 'the loss lighteth rather easily upon many than heavily upon few.'[73] Insuring against an expensive funeral drew attention to the other costs of a premature death, like depriving a family of its bread winner. Indeed, the sale of life assurance still relies on grotesque evocations of the penniless widow on the morning of the funeral.[74]

The burial or 'box' clubs of the seventeenth century, which locked cash contributions in a wooden chest or strong box, drew on their assets to meet the costs of widowhood, ill-health and sickness as well as funeral expenses.[75] They were spontaneous and highly localised, and the friendly societies were organised on much the same basis – around a pub, a church, a school, a workplace or a trade. Total membership grew rapidly from the second half of the eighteenth century. They had six hundred and fifty thousand members in 1793, over seven hundred thousand in 1803, nine hundred and twenty-five thousand in 1815, and probably as many as four million by 1872.[76] As the nineteenth century wore on, national federations of affiliated friendly societies emerged. Some, such as the Independent Order of Oddfellows (Manchester Unity) and the Ancient Order of Foresters, had hundreds of local branches and membership running into hundreds of thousands. Others, like Hearts of Oak, ran extensive postal operations. Unity was maintained across large distances by initiation rituals, curious handshakes and pass words of a kind normally associated with Freemasonry. In 1910, the last year before the government began displacing the friendly societies with the Welfare State, nearly twenty-seven thousand registered societies had a membership of over six and a half million;[77] by the eve of the Second World War, which ushered in the Welfare State, total membership was nearer nine million.[78]

The friendly societies built up substantial holdings of financial assets. Even today, after fifty years of the Welfare State, they have nine million policyholders and total investments of £12 billion.[79] One or two are sizeable by any standards. The Liverpool Victoria has over £3 billion under management, and was confident enough to spend £188 million in 1996 on acquiring Frizzell, the Bournemouth-based personal insurance provider, from Marsh & McLennan. Both Royal Liver and Family Assurance have over £1 billion under management, though Family Assurance was set up only in 1975 (unlike Liverpool Victoria and Royal Liver it does not collect door-to-door, but uses newspaper advertising and direct mail). Some societies, such as Tunbridge Wells Equitable, have drifted up market, but the overall image remains stolidly cloth-cap, and behind the success of the top few lies a story of unalloyed decline over the last fifty years. Under three hundred registered friendly societies are still active, compared with over two thousand seven hundred in business in 1945, and the number of branches has dwindled to less than eight hundred and fifty. Some of the great names of the Victorian heyday of the friendly society – like the Oddfellows and the Foresters – are as much social clubs as financial institutions, and many more are moribund, running off existing business or waiting to be taken over. The survivors look like abandoning mutuality altogether, and becoming orthodox PLCs.

The Man From the Pru

The chief cause of their decline is that the state provides comprehensive (if inadequate) insurance against unemployment, ill-health, old age and funeral expenses. This eventually drove the friendly societies into their present ghetto, where they survive as providers of small-scale savings, insurance and health plans of a tax-exempt nature. Their demise was retarded by Lloyd George, who decided to use the friendly societies and life companies ('approved societies', as they became known) to collect the premiums and administer the benefits of the first national health insurance scheme in 1911. Civil servants did not finally take over these duties until 1946, but the 'approved societies' began to decline long before that. Throughout the twentieth century, they were overtaken steadily by their partners in the Lloyd George scheme: the giant 'industrial' assurance companies – the Prudential, the Refuge and the Pearl.

These incorporated, profit-driven enterprises brought what was once a middle-class preserve – ordinary life assurance – to the C1s, C2s and Ds living in the slums of the great industrial cities (hence their classification as providers of 'industrial' assurance). They achieved this by using the oldest sales technique of all: knocking on the door and offering what was (until expenses were taken into account) a cheaper price. 'The working classes are peculiarly situated with regard to life assurance,' said the *Morning Advertiser* in 1854. 'It is only by small and frequent payments that they can effect and keep up their premiums. They must be collected weekly or monthly at considerable expense and even risk, from the character and the pay of the collectors, and thus a high premium, if the office is honest, must be charged.'[80]

This was why Lloyd George reluctantly agreed to rely on the 'approved societies' to collect his prototypical national insurance contributions: people had to be forced to save by weekly collections. The difficulty of persuading people with little money to set any aside still vexes the government today, but it was the secret of the success of the Prudential. The Man from the Pru began collecting weekly insurance premiums from working-class homes in the Potteries and the industrial north-west in the 1850s. A century and a half later, the Prudential Assurance Corporation is the largest fund manager in Britain, investing over £90 billion on behalf of nine million insurance and pension plan policyholders around the world.

But the Prudential was not an instant success. It was founded in May 1848, the year of revolution, at an inconspicuous solicitor's office in Hatton Garden (only a few yards from Alfred Waterhouse's gothic revivalist extravaganza of 1879 at Holborn Bars, which now serves as the company headquarters). The founders were a leather merchant, a retired naval officer, a surgeon, an auctioneer and a man describing himself as Bluemantle Pursuivant at the College of Heralds. In its early years, the joint enterprise came perilously close to disappearing. The initial ambition of pursuing respectable risks like clergymen proved unsustainable: by 1856 the Prudential was in deep financial trouble. Its initial capital of £2,500 was quite used up, the shareholders refused to subscribe any more, and the company was forced to borrow £35,000 to keep afloat.[81] Necessity rather than choice drove the Prudential into the business which made its fortune: the despatch of an army of collectors into the new industrial towns to collect the millions of tiny weekly premiums which made up the largest block of savings in the land.

'As a question of £. s. d., it is far more prudent to take the pick of the small policies than to have the crumbs which fall from the rich man's table,' reckoned Sir Henry Harben (1823–1911), first secretary to the Prudential, and the man largely responsible for its survival and subsequent success.[82] The first Men from the Pru, John and Thomas Clark, were appointed in September 1854. Their despatch to Coketown pitted the Prudential against the friendly societies, and its earliest rivals were from the friendly society movement. The Refuge Assurance was founded in Manchester in October 1858 as the Friend in Deed Life Assurance and Sick Fund Friendly Society. Its initial capital was £22 12s 6d, an apt measure of the difficulty impoverished Lancashire Methodists faced in insuring against the workhouse, ill-health and a pauper's grave. The Refuge was not incorporated until 1864.[83] The Pearl Assurance also had origins in a friendly society organised around an East End pub. It was founded in July 1864 by two undertakers, the splendidly-named brothers Hurry, who merged their loan-sharking operation with a friendly society run from the Royal Oak in Commercial Road.[84]

Edwin Balding, who founded United Friendly Assurance in London in 1908 was a former salesman with the Royal Liver friendly society, and the company, which opened for business above the White Hart pub in New Cross Road, was capitalised by the sale of his Royal Liver agencies. But not all industrial assurance companies are overgrown friendly societies. Britannic Assurance, best known for its sponsorship of the County Cricket Championship, opened for business in Birmingham in 1866 as the British Workman's Mutual Assurance Company Limited.[85] The London & Manchester Industrial Assurance Company Limited (now owned by Friends Provident) was incorporated in 1869. Co-operative Insurance Services, sponsors of Blackburn Rovers, was established in Manchester in 1867 to insure co-operative shops against fire and theft, and entered the industrial assurance market in 1886.[86] The Pearl was bought by AMP of Australia for £1.1 billion in 1989, and Britannic, the last of the classical industrial assurance companies, lives with the constant threat of being taken over. In December 1996, Refuge was forced to merge with United Assurance, but the stock market values their joint enterprise at barely one eighth of the giant Prudential.

TABLE 28.6
The Industrial Assurance Companies

Name	Ownership	Total Assets (£bn)	Funds Managed (£bn)
Britannic Assurance	PLC	6.8	6.5
Co-operative Insurance	Co-operative	12.7	14.2
London & Manchester	Friends Provident	4.9	3.7
Pearl Assurance	AMP (Australia)	13.8	13.2*
Prudential Corporation	PLC	78.4	91.0
United Assurance	PLC	7.3	8.0

Source: The Citywatch Institutional Investor Yearbook; Annual Reports.

*AMP now manages the assets of London Life and Pearl Assurance centrally, through AMP Asset Management, which has total assets under management of £45 billion.

The extinction of the mutual ethic which gave rise to the friendly society movement was embodied in the founder of United Friendly. 'The British working man,' Edwin Balding told his son and successor, 'is the salt of the earth. To serve him and his family is an honour and privilege.'[87] Yet his thinly capitalised and shaky enterprise was unable to meet its first claims. Staff went unpaid, and at one stage Balding was reduced to pawning his watch. The company was saved by his one outstanding gift: salesmanship. Victims of Zeppelin raids were paid in person, in cash, and when the Luftwaffe dropped a bomb on the United Friendly offices in 1940, Balding prevented a colleague shutting the door. 'Don't do that, old man,' he said. 'People will think we're closed.' Once, long after he had become rich, Balding was crossing Southwark Bridge in his chauffeur-driven Rolls Royce. A costermonger's barrow had toppled over in the tramlines. Balding told his driver to stop, got out, and asked the man if he was insured. He was not. Balding took him back to his office and paid him as if he were. United Friendly had little trouble attracting business from London costermongers after that.[88]

Happily, industrial life assurance of the kind which made Edwin Balding rich is in chronic decline. Regulators have rightly made it awkward for companies to recommend such anachronistic, uneconomic and tax-inefficient forms of life assurance as door-to-door collection. (In 1997 the Pearl had one hundred and sixty thousand customers paying less than £1 a month.)[89] The spread of bank accounts, with their standing orders and direct debits, has made visits unnecessarily expensive. The Prudential ceased to write new business in January 1995. The Pearl withdrew in April 1997, after discovering that many homes were contributing less than the costs of collection. 'If you are going to be committed to providing products that are good value for money, you can't sell industrial branch business,' admitted the head of industrial assurance at the Prudential in 1994. 'The right advice to most of those people is to open a bank account.'[90]

With some forty-five million industrial life assurance policies still outstanding, the business will not disappear for years, but it will never regain its dominant position of the first half of the century. At its peak in 1948, around eighteen thousand Men from the Pru 'walked the debit', calling on five million homes once a fortnight to collect small sums of cash housewives had hoarded in biscuit tins and lavatory cisterns. The Prudential insured one in three households. Today, the only area of growth in door-to-door sales and collection is lending, not insurance. Companies like Provident Financial, Cattle's Holdings and London Scottish Bank lend to poor and unemployed people denied credit from other sources – at the three-digit interest rates needed to cover the overheads. 'We perceive it as good news,' said the managing director of Provident Financial, when presented with evidence of growing inequality of incomes.[91]

Descendants such as these are unflattering to the pioneers of industrial life assurance. Yet men like Edwin Balding achieved what the friendly societies had failed to do: sell life assurance to the working class. When the Clarks started work for the Prudential in the 1850s, the poorer inhabitants of the industrial towns were either uninsured or reliant on friendly societies for unemployment, sickness and funeral insurance. As the industrial assurers tramped the streets, the number of paid-up industrial life policies climbed steadily, from less than seven hundred thousand in 1870 to twenty million in 1900, and to sixty-three million by 1936.

This was the making of the Prudential; the funds controlled by it and its competitors climbed over two-hundred-fold between 1880 and 1936 to a total of £317.1 million. Friendly societies, which had managed nearly one quarter of working-class financial assets at the beginning of the twentieth century, controlled barely one eighth by 1936. In the same period, the proportion of working-class assets managed by industrial assurance companies climbed from less than a fifth to nearly two fifths.[92] The Prudential towered above all others. By 1935 it controlled more than £1 in every £5 managed by the life offices.[93] People worried for the first time that an institutional investor had too much power.

Waking Up to Institutional Power

In 1937 a book entitled *Industrial Assurance: An Historical and Critical Study*, was published. The intelligence behind it was Dr Hermann Levy, a refugee from Nazism whose earlier work, *The New Industrial System*, had severely criticised the modish industrial concentration of the 1930s. Somewhat improbably, it was co-authored by a Conservative MP and apologist for Hitler, Sir Arnold Wilson.* Neither man is much remembered today. But their analysis of the rising power of the institutional investor was prescient:

> The salient characteristic of industrial assurance is the existence of vast aggregations of capital in a very few hands, with unlimited power, exercised in secrecy, and uncontrolled by any external agency, to give or withhold financial assistance in any country, at home or abroad, to any industry or trade. Without in any way reflecting upon the probity and skill of those who direct this great business – and it is seldom that either one or the other is questioned – it is submitted that under modern conditions they have become a repository of power greater by far than the banks, and less under effective social control . . . Investing, as is now the custom, in a vast variety of industries and trades, irrespective of the

---

* Lieutenant-Colonel Sir Arnold Talbot Wilson was educated at Clifton College and RMA Sandhurst before joining the Indian Army in 1903. At the outbreak of the Second World War he joined the Royal Air Force as a gunner, with the rank of pilot officer, and was killed in action. His decision to volunteer for active service at the age of fifty-five was remarkable in the light of his earlier support for the fascist regimes of Italy and Germany.

consequences to society at large, the boards of the great companies exercise to-day a greater influence on industry and trade than any other body of men.[94]

Levy and Wilson detailed the involvement of the insurance companies in the reorganisation of the steel and electricity industries during the 1930s, and their domination of the gilt-edged market. They also warned that fund management was superseding insurance as their most important function. 'From being regarded as an incidental necessity of a life-insurance business,' they wrote, 'it may come to be regarded as a desirable object in itself.'[95]

The policy-makers at the Trades Union Congress drew heavily on Levy and Wilson in drawing up their joint policy declaration of January 1949 with the Labour Party.* They argued that 'these accumulated and increasing funds were social funds, subscribed by the public, largely from working class pockets, and it was indefensible that such accumulations should be left in private hands.' Herbert Morrison even drew up plans to nationalise the fourteen largest industrial assurance companies and friendly societies. His proposals found their way into the 1949 policy document, *Labour Believes in Britain*, and its successor of 1953, *Challenge to Britain*. 'A service designed to meet the contingencies and adversities of life ought not to be a service that gives profit to anybody,' declared James Griffiths, minister of national insurance in the Attlee government. 'It is the bobs and half-crowns they collect and when money collected from the people is invested, that money ought to be publicly controlled and invested in the interests of the whole of the nation.'[96] Labour lost office, and did not regain it until 1964; but the spectre of nationalisation by a Labour government haunted the insurance companies for the next forty years. As recently as 1983, the Labour Party was committed to the nationalisation of institutional investors.

Six years earlier, in January 1977, the Labour prime minister, James Callaghan, had sought to relieve the pressure from the left of the party by inviting his immediate predecessor to chair a committee charged with reviewing 'the role and functioning, at home and abroad, of financial institutions in the United Kingdom and their value to the economy; to review in particular the provision of funds for industry and trade; to consider what changes are required in the existing arrangements for the supervision of these institutions, including the possible extension of the public sector.'[97] A month after Sir

---

* The policy debate was reopened by the veteran left-winger, Ian Mikardo, who proposed the nationalisation of the insurance companies in *The Second Five Years: A Labour Programme for 1950*, a pamphlet he published in 1948. Mikardo argued that industrial assurance companies like the Prudential invested in 'many types of commercial venture, not all of which are equally in the national interest'.

Harold Wilson and his colleagues began work, the *Financial Times* forecast the death of capitalism. As it turned out, the chief achievement of the Wilson Committee was not to bring capitalism in Britain to an end, but to discover that the Labour left was worrying about only half of the problem. The fastest-growing funds were no longer the life assurance offices and the industrial assurance companies but the pension funds. 'The pension funds are sitting very pretty,' concluded Sir Harold. 'They are so powerful that they do not know how powerful they are. They could well be, for example, transforming the nature of our society more than any government would ever dare to do even if it had a large majority in parliament.'[98]

The pension funds were little known or understood until Wilson and his colleagues identified them as a powerful source of capital in urgent need of proper public supervision. All the allegations which have afflicted the pensions industry in the 1980s and 1990s – particularly 'short-termism' and the allegations of inadequacy of regulation – are prefigured in the Wilson Committee Report. 'A gradual increase in the institutionalisation of savings has been taking place for many years,' it concluded, 'but it is only recently, and in particular during the time of this Committee, that it has reached the point where it has become an issue of general concern ... the implications for the rest of the financial system are far-reaching, and ... many of those concerned appear not to have come fully to terms with them.'[99] Over the previous thirty years, the market value of the assets of the pension funds had increased in real terms from about £10 billion to £40 billion; over the next twenty years, they increased to over £550 billion. The un-anticipated arrival of the pension funds was followed by unprecedented growth.

Rising Without Trace

The main reason why pension funds are a phenomenon of the post-war period is that few people had needed a pension before. This was not because the old and the infirm were seeing out their days in the bosom of the family. It is a myth (albeit an enduring one) that people once lived in extended families in which the young looked after the old. If it were true, it might explain why pensions were unnecessary. But it was not. The reason pensions were a rarity is that there were not that many retired people until the second half of the twentieth century. The need for pensions is created by longevity, but most people died long before they were eligible for retirement. Even in Edwardian times, a working-class man or woman could expect to die before he or she was fifty. Their middle-class contemporaries might reach the modern retirement age of sixty-five.* Most people simply worked until they died or, if they were too frail to pursue a physically demanding occupation, took a menial job as nightwatchman or washerwoman. In the worst cases, they went to the workhouse or received outdoor relief under the Poor Law. Today, only one man in ten over sixty-five is at work; three out of every four were a century ago.

One reason the non-contributory state pension for the over-seventies introduced by Lloyd George in 1908 was expected to cost so little (Asquith anticipated £6–7 million a year) was that there were not many over-seventies about.[100] In 1926 Neville Chamberlain replaced it with a contributory state pension of ten shillings a week payable from the age of sixty-five, ostensibly financed out of national insurance contributions. The structure of the basic state pension has remained unchanged, except in detail, ever since.[101] It is now collected by over nine million pensioners at a cost of over £30 billion a year, but the state pension is not funded. Contributions are not collected and reinvested in a separate fund, but transferred through the tax and benefits system from people still at work to people who have retired. It is, in the jargon, a pay-as-you-go system. This has not stopped people describing the right to a state pension as a property right. Once state pension rights are included, the distribution of personal wealth appears somewhat less unequal.[102] The economic effect of funded or unfunded pensions is the same: the pensions of retired people have to be funded out of the current national income, whether the money is derived from taxes or dividends. But those at work have greater confidence in the investments made by their pension fund managers than in the promises of politicians. The state pension is at best a civil or political right, earned through a combination of citizenship and national insurance contributions, though there are doubts about its enforceability.[103] It is not something which holders can cash in or sell to others.

Nor, until the passage of the Social Security Act of 1985, did occupational pension schemes give their beneficiaries any meaningful rights of ownership over their savings. Occupational pensions are funded out of contributions by both employers and employees, and paid out of investment income rather than on a pay-as-you-go basis. But it was not until 1985 that employees changing jobs were entitled to take with them the cash equivalent of pension rights they had accrued. Until then, so-called 'early leavers' from occupational schemes found the value of their pension frozen with their previous employer

---

* The retirement age for men was reduced from seventy to sixty-five in 1928, and to sixty for women in 1940. Following a European ruling that the different retirement ages discriminated against men, it was raised to sixty-five for women born after March 1955.

until they collected it at the age of sixty-five.* It was a stark reminder of who owned the pension fund: the employer, not the employee, because occupational pension schemes were not introduced as company-sponsored savings for the staff (or even as deferred pay) but as a form of industrial discipline. Their purpose was to tie useful employees to the firm by giving them a non-transferable stake in the enterprise, and to provide a ready pool of assets from which to finance the redundancy or retirement of their useless colleagues. This had the happy effect of keeping the cost of pensions down, as the contributions of early leavers subsidised the pensions of those who stayed. However, it also built into the system the tensions which exploded in the personal pensions débâcle of the 1980s and 1990s.[104]

Companies found the peculiarities of English trust law, developed for the benefit of rich families and charities, admirably suited to their purpose of keeping tight control of the pension fund. Employees were made beneficiaries of a trust, and the assets were placed under the control of trustees, who often as not were the board of directors. This built another conflict of interest into the system, which detonated spectacularly in the Maxwell defalcations of the late 1980s. Leslie Hannah traces the use of trust law to the pension scheme set up by Colmans, the mustard-makers, in 1900. There were of course advantages to a trust-based pension scheme: it kept the assets of the fund off the company balance sheet, thus guaranteeing that pensions would be paid even if the company went bankrupt.[105] It is not surprising that trade unions initially opposed occupational pensions as a management tool for controlling labour. Between the wars, Ernest Bevin also found that workers disliked occupational pension schemes because they would lose means-tested benefits.[106] The trade unions eventually overcame their hostility and came to regard pension funds as a useful bargaining point, especially in times of statutory pay restraint. In 1976, white-collar workers at Vickers went on strike for improved pension benefits. Employers began to use them for the same purpose. Two years after the Vickers strike, the Sun Alliance insurance company was carpeted by the government for giving staff a concealed pay rise in the shape of a pension contribution holiday.[107]

But occupational pension schemes did not become commonplace until well into the twentieth century. For most of the nineteenth century, the middle classes relied on life assurance policies to buy an annuity for their retirement or to provide for their widows. The earliest private-sector pension

* People who took their pension rights with them could buy into an occupational scheme operated by their new employer or a personal pension from a life assurance company or fund manager. The 1985 Social Security Act also obliged employers to uprate by the lower of 5 per cent or the annual increase in retail prices the value of any pensions left with them by previous employees.

TABLE 28.7
Ten Largest Private Sector Pension Funds (£ billion)

Name	Assets
Universities Superannuation Scheme Ltd	17.2
Lloyds TSB Group PLC	10.3
Barclays Bank PLC	10.0
The British Petroleum Company PLC	9.5
Shell Pensions Trust Limited	8.4
National Westminster Bank PLC	7.9
Imperial Chemical Industries PLC	6.6
Stanhope Pension Trust Limited (GEC	5.8
Midland Bank PLC	5.2
Prudential Corporation	4.3

Source: National Association of Pension Funds Yearbook, 1999.

schemes, such as those provided by the East India Company and the Bank of England, were organised on life assurance principles.[108] Hannah has identified only one nineteenth-century friendly society (the Northumberland and Durham Miners' Permanent Relief Society) which paid pensions.[109] Large utilities – waterways, railways, gas companies – pioneered funded occupational pension schemes in the nineteenth century, but these were not always soundly financed. In the 1840s, the London and Birmingham Railway financed pensions from the sale of lost luggage and newspapers.[110] The Gas, Light and Coke Company introduced a contributory scheme for salaried staff in 1842, and a second for manual labourers in 1870; London and North Western Railway started to pay pensions to ex-employees in 1854. Some other large manufacturing companies followed suit: the Siemens pension fund dates from 1872. The Prudential paid its first pension to the widow of a salesman in 1866, and introduced a retirement allowance for all its salesmen in 1872.[111] Predictably, the social conscience of the non-conformist firms was pricked sooner than most: Lever Brothers introduced a scheme in 1904, and Rowntrees in 1906.

Pensions for civil servants began rather earlier. In the days of the Old Corruption, senior civil servants secured their retirement by selling their offices for cash. Buyers could look forward not only to a salary but to a measure of the rake-offs which control of public money afforded. In some cases, incumbents were persuaded to pay a pension to their predecessor rather than a lump sum: Samuel Pepys paid one to his predecessor at the Admiralty. HM Customs and Excise, then the largest government department, started a contributory pension fund for its staff in 1712, which obliged them to donate 6d out of every £1 earned. The scheme was actuarially unsound, and by 1725 the fund was bust and had to be rescued with taxpayers' money.[112] Both that and the first non-contributory scheme introduced for civil servants in 1810 paid pensions to those unable to continue work. Central government has remained a generous provider ever since. Though there were brief interludes when civil servants were expected to contribute, the reformed scheme introduced in 1859 remained non-contributory until 1972, when inflation-proofing was added to the already excellent benefits. No separate pension fund was ever created: taxpayers, unlike companies, do not go bust.

TABLE 28.8
Ten Largest Local Authority Pension Funds in 1998 (£ billion)

Name	Assets
Greater Manchester Pension Fund	5.4
Strathclyde Pension Fund	5.2
West Midlands Metropolitan Authorities Pension Fund	4.1
West Yorkshire Superannuation Fund	3.3
The London Pensions Fund Authority	2.6
Metropolitan Borough of Wirral	2.5
Lancashire County Council	2.2
Northern Ireland Local Government Officers Superannuation Committee	2.1
South Yorkshire Pensions Authority	2.0
South Tyneside Metropolitan Borough Council	1.9

Source: National Association of Pension Funds Yearbook, 1999.

The first properly funded scheme in the public sector was introduced in 1922, when local authorities were allowed to set up schemes which matched a set of official criteria. These were made compulsory in 1937. Even today, local authorities remain the only providers of funded pension schemes anywhere in the government machine. Funded schemes for the police, firemen and school teachers were introduced but abandoned in the 1920s.[113] Postmen were not given the security of funded pensions until October 1969, when the Post Office ceased to be a government department and became a public corporation.

Typically, the motive for setting up the fund was to save public expenditure, which meant it was established on an insecure basis. The only asset the government was prepared to endow it with was a collection of the notorious 2½ per cent government bonds issued under the chancellorship of Hugh

Dalton twenty-odd years before (by 1997 inflation had eroded their value so completely, they could be bought for 40 per cent of their face value).* The actuarial deficit was put at £604 million, and the Post Office was told to make up the shortfall from its own resources. As inflation pushed up the wages of postmen, and pushed down the value of 2½ per cent Consols, the cost of earnings-related pensions spiralled out of control. By 1978 the Post Office pension fund had a deficit of nearly £2 billion. The Treasury refused to make good the shortfall, so the Post Office put up the price of telephone calls instead.[114]

The nationalised industry pension funds – coal, railways, water, gas – preceded their actual nationalisation. The same was true of the redbrick universities, where dons were given funded pensions in 1913, long before the system was effectively nationalised. The Universities Superannuation Scheme escaped public ownership and is now one of the largest in the country.[115] The other nationalised industry funds survived until the industries were privatised in the 1980s and 1990s, but the security of their pensions was badly eroded during their time in the public sector. The coal, electricity and railway funds all entered the 1980s with serious funding deficits. The British Railways pension fund was used by its trustees (the British Railways Board) as a source of cheap loans for the crumbling rail network. By the early 1980s the shortage of assets was such that the fund had to be put partly on a pay-as-you-go basis. The staff side of the electricity fund had to be topped up with a £52.8 million grant from the taxpayer in 1981.[116] Even local authority funds have suffered, mainly because councils have used them as a painless way of making staff redundant. In 1989 the then secretary of state for the environment, Nicholas Ridley, also ruled that they should take a contribution holiday so as to keep the poll tax down, and it was clear by 1996 that they were seriously underfunded.[117] Thanks to the abolition of funded schemes in the 1920s, local councils are also funding the pensions of firemen, policemen and teachers on a pay-as-you-go basis. Teachers' pensions, though shared with central government, are set to increase significantly, and in London pensions for retired firemen now consume a fifth of the total budget of the fire service.[118]

The same urge to restrain public expenditure lay behind the spectacular growth of the occupational pension fund industry after the First World War. One important government decision was to pay flat-rate rather than earnings-related pensions when the first state pension schemes were introduced either side of that gruesome conflict. Naturally, this increased reliance on private

---

* If the loss of purchasing power of the pound since 1945 is taken into account, the Dalton 2½ per cents have lost nearly all their value. See also the distaste of contemporary investors for these instruments in Chapter 29.

TABLE 28.9
Ten Largest Nationalised and Privatised Industy Pension Funds in 1998
(£ billion)

Name	Assets
British Coal Pension Schemes	22.9
British Telecommunications PLC	22.7
Electricity Supply Pension Scheme	18.8
The Post Office Pension Schemes	15.0
British Gas PLC	12.9
Railways Pension Trustee Company	12.7
British Airways (Pensions)	8.9
British Steel PLC	8.3
British Broadcasting Corporation	6.0
British Railways Board	4.3

Source: National Association of Pension Funds Yearbook, 1999.

schemes. Even when the government introduced earnings-related state pensions, first in 1959 and then again in 1975, companies were allowed to pay a lower rate of national insurance in return for providing equivalent pensions from their own funds. But the most influential subsidy to private pension funds was agreed much earlier.

In 1921 the government, after intensive lobbying by companies, exempted from taxation both the contributions to pension funds and the investment income from them.* The subsequent rises in income tax made pension contributions more attractive, for both employees and employers, than wage and salary increases. In fact, the tax concessions of 1921 probably did more than any other factor to boost pension funds, especially after the tax privileges given to occupational schemes were extended in 1956 to the private pensions of the self-employed. They were even given exemption from capital gains tax, provided they did not trade actively, making institutionalised pensions the most tax-privileged form of investment. From the turn of the century to 1956, membership of occupational schemes rose from one in twenty workers to one in three; by 1979 it was one in two.[119] Between 1956 and 1979 contributions to pension schemes increased threefold in real terms, to over £9 billion a year.[120] By 1997–8, the income of occupational pension schemes was running at over £14 billion a year, and the cost of tax relief had risen to £8.9 billion.[121] By then, the industry was so large and powerful that successive governments had

---

* Life assurance premiums already enjoyed tax relief.

tried for years to claw back the privileges they had accorded to this newest estate of the realm.

Power Without Responsibility?

In retrospect, it was during a single year in the 1950s that the power of the fund manager over governments and companies became plain. In 1956 Bank Rate reached 5.5 per cent, its highest level for twenty-five years. This was the year in which Harold Wilson talked of 'gnomes of Zurich' making their dispositions in sterling, but the real cause of the rising rate of interest was that domestic institutions had elected to buy shares rather than government bonds. That same year, the institutions publicly sacked a company chairman for the first time, taking on the role performed until then by the merchant banks. The victim was Sir Bernard Docker, the chairman of the BSA Company. Although he was a large shareholder he did not own as many shares as the Prudential, and his mistake was to carry on treating the company as a personal fief when its ownership had passed to the institutions. He used its money to buy himself a gold-plated Daimler, a luxury yacht named *Shemara*, and a plentiful supply of rosé champagne for his wife. The final straw was a £7,910 bill for Norah Docker to re-equip her wardrobe for the Paris Motor Show. His wife, one of the first of the publicity-seekers in an age still relatively innocent of them, had delighted the tabloids by sharing her yacht with partying coal miners, and arguing in public with policemen in Capri and casino-owners in Monte Carlo. 'I've only fallen for three men in my life,' she once said, 'and fortunately all of them were millionaires.'[122]

The Prudential sought Sir Bernard's resignation at a shareholders' meeting on 1 April 1956. He was deposed, complaining publicly that his institutional detractors had no right to leak details of his *modus operandi* to shareholders, and no doubt privately that the *modus vivendi* of his wife was irrelevant. But he had misunderstood the new dispensation: his demise was the first public instance of what a later generation calls investor activism, where the institutions behave like proprietors rather than punters. Its significance was not lost on the most astute financial journalist of the time, Harold Wincott of the *Financial Times*:

> You've got to face the fact, you personal shareholders, that the institutional investor is here to stay. We may not approve of the taxation trends that have brought this about. We may hope for and work towards a revival of the personal shareholder. But the Pru and the Pearl, the ICI and the miners' pension funds are here to stay and they're going

to grow bigger and bigger and bigger ... Do you want them, when they learn or discover that something is going wrong with one of your companies, just to slide quietly out of their shareholdings, leaving the basic trouble untouched and you holding the baby? Or would you rather they acted as the Pru acted on this occasion? ... You can take it from me, you personal shareholders, that there are companies in existence today, flourishing companies, companies which earn good profits and provide good employment, which would have been sunk without trace but for the intervention and help of the institutional investor.[123]

The Prudential, unaccustomed to the publicity which surrounded the case, was reluctant to assume the responsibilities of ownership. 'The action which the company took was in no way sponsored by the Prudential,' said a spokesman. 'It is our clear policy in the Pru not to interfere in the management of industrial companies in which we invest. In this case, when there were no other large shareholders whom we might consult, we came to the conclusion that we had a duty to all the shareholders as well as ourselves to take some action.'[124]

Leslie Brown, chief investment manager at the Prudential at the time of the Docker affair, confessed later that 'such incidents are essentially repugnant to the board and the policy is to avoid them, not at any cost, perhaps, but by appropriate foresight.'[125] The institutions have claimed ever since that their best work is done out of public view and have resisted repeated invitations – from the Wilson Report to the great corporate governance debate of the early 1990s – to take as close an interest in their financial property as the landowners of old took in their broad acres or the householder of today takes in his bricks and mortar. But this retiring position was absurdly at odds with their real power. As early as 1951 Professor Sargant Florence had astonished the City with his revelation, in a study entitled *Ownership, Control and Success of Large Companies*, that the Prudential was one of the twenty biggest shareholders in forty-seven (out of ninety-eight) large companies, the Pearl in thirty-three, the Royal London Mutual in twenty-seven, and the Refuge in eighteen.[126] By the 1970s, with the rise of the great occupational pension funds, the further division of ownership from control predicted by Levy and Wilson was also apparent. Richard Minns estimated that in 1980 two thirds of the assets of pension funds were controlled by independent fund managers.[127] He thought this meant that the merchant bankers, through their fund management arms, were still running British capitalism as they had when Barings were the Sixth Great Power and Pierpont Morgan and his son were Morganising the world.

The book, published in the same year as the Wilson Report, appeared at a time when memories of the role played by the institutions in the crises of the mid-1970s were still fresh. In 1974 the *Financial Times* index sank to an all-time low of one hundred and forty-six points. At the end of that year, an investor could have bought quoted corporate Britain for £17.3 billion. Courtaulds was embarrassed to find that the company pension fund was worth more than the company. The reason for this state of affairs was the refusal of the institutions to buy shares. A combination of soaring inflation, rising taxes and price controls had destroyed their confidence in the ability of British industry to make profits. Yet in the first five weeks of January 1975 the index shot up unexpectedly: five institutional investors, led by the giant Prudential Assurance, had met and decided to buy again. Years later, it emerged that the institutions had saved the banking system as well as the stock market by relieving the hard-pressed secondary banks of millions of pounds' worth of property they had acquired from bankrupt borrowers.

Likewise, the seemingly constant mini-budgets and interest-rate hikes which marked the chancellorship of Denis Healey between 1974 and 1979 were sparked by the refusal of institutional fund managers to buy government stock. In the autumn of 1976, it was the so-called Gilts Strike which prompted the intervention of the International Monetary Fund. In the spring of 1977, the fund managers again refused to buy government bonds unless the Treasury agreed to pay a higher rate of interest. Vilified by ministers for their irresponsibility, and attacked by businessmen for driving up the rate of interest, the institutions held firm. The taxpayer had to cough up.

It is salutary to remember, in an age when 'globalisation' has replaced 'capitalism' as the principal fear of the political left, and George Soros and his fellow international financiers are denounced routinely as unwelcome and dangerous, that governments could not pursue a monetary policy which offended professional fund managers twenty years ago. Minns was wrong to read the events of the 1970s as the reappearance of the banker in a new disguise. Far from confirming that the bankers were in charge, the Gilts Strike was the clearest possible sign that the balance of economic and financial power had shifted from the merchant banks to the institutional investors. In 1931, the fate of the government hinged on the contents of a telegram from the Morgan bank. In 1976–7, London fund managers did not even act in concert. They had simply concluded, quite independently, that the then combination of monetary and fiscal policies was unsustainable.

It is true that the wider significance of the Gilts Strike was not lost on the institutions, or on the Bank of England, or on the politicians. In October 1978, Peter Moody, joint investment manager at the Prudential, told the Institute of Actuaries that institutional investors should now accept their place as one of the great estates of the realm.[128] Shortly afterwards, his chief executive, Brian Corby, was invited to serve on the Court of the Bank of England. He was the first institutional investor to enter the hallowed portals of Threadneedle Street, where the Kindersleys and Bicesters had once held undisputed sway.

It was not surprising that the Gilts Strike also breathed new life into the campaign by the Labour left to put the great savings institutions under state control. In the 1970s the major institutional investors, already starved of income by dividend controls, considered themselves in serious danger of being nationalised. The trade unions, which enjoyed a degree of influence in Whitehall and Westminster unthinkable today, were convinced that the institutions were too busy investing in art, property and foreign countries to provide the funds to create new industries, jobs and services at home. They favoured a national investment bank, and several union leaders penned a note of dissent in the Wilson Report advocating exactly that.[129]

The British Rail Pension Fund, which had embarked on an art-buying spree which was making the British railwayman the greatest patron of the arts since the Medici, gave their dissension palpable shape. 'Is it totally fanciful to imagine a situation where pension funds not only hold the equity capital but also most of the commercial property and land in the country, rivalling central and local government?' asked a trade union leader in 1978.[130] Company directors found their abilities questioned by shareholders with massive stakes in their businesses. In the countryside, farmers found themselves outbid at land auctions by faceless money men from the City. A rash of hostile articles and books warned that the institutions were buying up the forests and heather of Scotland and the green acres of England, and would soon be the biggest landlords in the country.

In *The Irresponsible Society*, an essay first published in 1960 but rich in foreboding, the left-wing sociology don Richard Titmuss (who had worked briefly in an insurance company) attacked this concentration of power in the hands of a small group of institutional fund managers for its irresponsibility (or what is now called its lack of 'accountability'). 'It is a power,' he wrote, 'a potential power, to affect many important aspects of our economic life and our social values . . . It is a power concentrated in relatively few hands, working at the apex of a handful of giant bureaucracies, technically supported by a group of professional experts, and accountable, in practice, to virtually no one.'[131]

In his first *Anatomy of Britain*, published two years later, Anthony Sampson quoted these words when he identified the 'para-proprietors' of the life assurance and pension funds as a new and irresponsible centre of power: men who controlled vast aggregations of property without being burdened with the responsibilities of ownership. Sampson borrowed another phrase from the Jesuit economist, Father Paul Harbrecht, who had earlier compared the institutional investors to the Great Domains of medieval Europe:

> We might describe the change that has taken place in these terms. Where once the concepts of property served the function of attaching things to men, they now serve the function of assigning power over things. The thing itself is not given to a man, power over it is. The objects exchanged in such a system are not the things themselves but power over things. This is why we can say that our society has passed from a property system to a power system.[132]

In 1960 the economist Adolf Berle declared that the 'divorce between men and industrial things is becoming complete . . . a Communist revolution could not accomplish that more completely.'[133] What did he mean?

Capitalism Without Ownership

Berle was co-author, with Gardner Means, of *The Modern Corporation and Private Property*. Published in 1932, it is credited with uncovering the central problem of twentieth-century capitalism: the divorce between *ownership* and *control*. The emergence of the institutional investor has made final the divorce between the people who own companies and the managers who control them. In the earliest days of industrial capitalism, ownership and control were vested in the single personality of Gradgrind and his like. In that respect, the earliest industrial companies were little different from previous forms of private property. It is the sale of shares in a company to outsiders which splices ownership and control, and cuts the owners off from the things they own. A house bears the imprint of its owner, in the shape of its appearance, condition and contents, and cannot be sold without considerable expense and feelings of regret. But a share is just a piece of paper which can be bought and sold anonymously, on price alone.

As share certificates are replaced by electronic registers, it is now not even that. Karl Popper described the world of fifty years ago as an Abstract Society, in which men and women were cut off from each other by formal structures of law, and by forms of transport and technology, which allowed them to trade and to communicate without any personal contact. The decentralised stock and bond markets of today – their actors bound only by money, computer and telecommunications technology and the laws of contract and tort – have raised that abstraction to a state of near completeness. As property,

securities* have no precedent. Ownership of a security depends not on physical possession or the investment of labour but on an elaborate web of legal
relationships by which the holder can lay claim to a share of the income (and
the assets, in the case of a winding-up). The fact that courts will affirm
ownership on the basis of a name entered on a register, the possession of a
piece of paper, or a name on an electronic database, marks the final mastery
of Abstract Mind over Earthy Matter.

A modern security can even be broken up into its constituent parts, with
the income sold to one group of investors and the capital to another. The
work of mathematicians and economists has made it possible to create entirely
synthetic securities – futures, options, swaps and swaptions – which are not
things-in-themselves but merely *derived* from things-in-themselves, or *derivatives*. Like shares and bonds, these can be pooled into vast agglomerations of
capital in which the personal savings of thousands are reduced to mere units
in a greater whole whose individual parts may never be known to their owners.
As share and bond certificates disappear into mutual funds, and into the vast
electronic databases of the banks which monitor who owns what, the holders
of government debt and the owners of companies are shuffling off the last
connection with older forms of property: physical possession. The lawyers are
hard at work on new law, in which possession is not nine tenths but no part
at all. People will own nothing but a fungible right to part of a pool of
interchangeable financial assets.

The fund managers inhabit this abstract territory more completely than
anybody else. In 1964, EFS 'Plum' Plumridge of the Pearl Assurance, one of
the leading fund managers of his day, told Brian Waterhouse that 'all investment is essentially a matter of using your nose. Statistics and logic follow
afterwards to tell you your nose is right.'[134] His method was not greatly different from the approach of the great merchant bankers. Like them, Plumridge
relied on hunch and personality rather than the analysis of reams of financial
data. For Pierpont Morgan, the basis of credit was neither property nor
money, but character. 'A man I do not trust', he told the American Congress,
'could not get money from me on all the bonds in Christendom.'[135] Siegmund
Warburg thought the humble tie a guide to personal probity, reckoning its
loudness in inverse proportion.

Leonard Licht, described by no less an authority than Nicola Horlick as
'the most outstanding fund manager of his generation'[136], learned his trade
at the bank founded by Warburg. (Its corporate culture was famously strong
and influenced by the methods of its founder.) Unsurprisingly, Licht's

---

* The shares and bonds fund managers control, attesting to the ownership of debt and equity
issued by governments and companies.

method of choosing shares was not very different from Warburg's quixotic way of choosing clients:

> An excessive private life is a warning sign. I do not mind if a chairman is married three or four times, but he should keep quiet about it . . . A lot of not-so-nice people are handicapped from the start, and tend to go down quicker when times are hard. A mega ego is always worrying . . . You look at what we are good at in this country – retailing, the drinks industry, and the drugs industry – and you invest in those things. If you want engineering stocks, generally speaking you go to Germany, to Japan for consumer electronics, and for other high tech companies to the USA. . . When a share is under-performing, there is usually some good reason, and it is always an excellent warning signal.[137]

But Licht has retired now, and the Warburg style is increasingly unfashionable.

There was a time when all fund managers worked like Leonard Licht, analysing the assets companies owned and the sales and profits earned from them, and trying to forecast whether the share price was going to go up or down. This did not put ownership and control back together, but it did entail getting to know the management of the company and the businesses they ran, and making judgments about what their assets were worth and whether they were any good at their jobs. The trick, in essence, was to decide whether the share price was a true reflection of the value of the company and its management. This was much easier for the merchant bankers of old, who were privy to inside information. The laws against insider-dealing have made it much more difficult to understand a company from the inside, so fund managers have turned to mathematical modelling on computers, in the hope of discovering patterns in the publicly available information which will tell them how prices will go.

It is this turning away from fundamental analysis towards mathematical techniques which has increased the abstraction of owners from controllers. It began innocently enough in 1953, with a paper delivered by a distinguished statistician, Maurice Kendall, to the Royal Statistical Society. Behind the dull title – 'The Analysis of Economic Time-Series, Part 1. Prices.' – lurked an astonishing discovery. Kendall had discovered that share prices did not follow a regular pattern or cycle; they followed what statisticians call a *random walk*. In other words, they were just as likely to go down as up, in the same way that a tossed coin is just as likely to yield heads as tails. The behaviour of share prices could not be predicted by a fundamental analysis of the business and finances of companies. Fund managers might just as well choose shares by tossing a coin or throwing a dart at the back pages of the *Financial Times*.

This explains why even professional fund managers often get it wrong, and amateurs sometimes get it right. But there is a reason why fund managers refuse to accept that they may be redundant. They earn handsome fees from investors for their ostensible expertise in picking shares, and they are not willing to give them up. Surprisingly, they have a good case. In any market, prices are best established by open competition between as many buyers and sellers as possible. In the financial markets, competition among fund managers to buy the shares likely to increase in value and sell the shares likely to fall in value means that stock market prices always reflect a company's true value.*

Prices change only in response to new information, and it is the competition between fund managers to uncover fresh information about the business and finances of a company which ensures that share prices reflect *all* known and relevant information. Rises in profits or even forecasts of rises tend to be reflected in share prices almost immediately. This still leaves fund managers with an embarrassing dilemma. If share prices incorporate all available and relevant information, it is impossible for any fund manager to achieve consistently superior rates of return. Every now and again he or she will achieve higher rates than competitors, but this will be due to a lucky investment or the taking of an unusually high risk. Fund managers cannot beat the market regularly because they *are* the market.

Surveys of fund management performance prove that this is indeed the case. Above-average returns are rarely sustained. Investors who choose fund managers on the basis of strong performance in recent years are more or less guaranteed a few years of under-performance. It makes more sense to sack a fund manager who is performing well, than one performing badly, but few are brave enough to do that.† By the time they have charged their fees and paid commission to brokers for buying and selling shares, most fund managers earn a lower rate of return for their clients than they would by buying every share in the market without discrimination. In other words, most fund managers achieve worse results most of the time than they would if they did nothing at all.

A growing band of fund managers have drawn the obvious conclusion. Instead of picking stocks which they believe will rise in value faster than the market, they have settled for buying everything. They are called index fund managers, because they buy portfolios of securities designed to follow the

---

* The stock market price reflects the 'true value of the company' in the limited sense that the price incorporates all information known about the company at the time.

† This is partly because it is expensive. Changing fund managers can cost as much as 2–3 per cent of the value of a fund, so this decision is not taken lightly.

performance of a market index (like the *Financial Times* All-Share Index) as closely as possible.* They do this either by buying every share in the index in the same proportion, or by assembling portfolios of sample shares and derivatives which achieve the same effect. One of the biggest fund managers in Britain, Barclays Global Investors, now sells itself exclusively as an index fund manager.† It is estimated that one fifth of British institutional equity portfolios are now indexed.

This has a number of technical effects. The most important is that liquidity in stocks outside the main indices, and especially in smaller company shares, is drying up. Indexation also imposes further alterations in the relationship between *owners* and *controllers*. Stocks are bought and sold not because the shareholders think the assets and management of the company are good or bad, but because they are or are not in the index. This makes institutions less like owners and more like (fatalistic) investors. When Queen's Moat and Maxwell Communications failed, virtually the only major investors still holding the stocks were the index fund managers. 'I am violently opposed to indexed funds,' argued Graeme Knox of Scottish Amicable in 1992. 'The idea that a company should be bought and sold simply because it is in the index seems to me to negate the spirit of capitalism.'[138] Dick Barfield, his opposite number at Standard Life, agreed. 'One reason for eschewing indexation is the danger that you do not exercise your rights and responsibilities as a shareholder,' he said. 'I think that poses great dangers.'[139] One group who approve of indexation are the *controllers* in the company boardroom. If investors are going to buy their shares anyway, the controllers can do what they like without having to worry about shareholders. 'Perhaps the indexed fund manager will prove to be the best friend of management,' admitted the chief executive of one large company.[140]

Indexation is the most visible form of capitalism without ownership. But since the mid-1980s a new breed of fund manager, the quantitative analyst (or 'quant') has taken the process of abstraction still further. Armed with unprecedented computer power and an array of sophisticated mathematical and statistical techniques developed in other fields, quants aim to dispense with the search for fresh information. They process vast quantities of historical price data in search of patterns which will enable them to make predictions about price movements. This may seem self-defeating, since share prices are on a random walk. But these 'rocket scientists', as the City knows them, draw

* A market index gives the average value of the prices of securities expressed as a percentage of the average value at some base period.
† Indexation does not solve the performance problem. Even indexed funds incur management and transaction costs, which guarantee that they will under-perform the index.

heavily on chaos theory – discerning patterns where none seem to exist. Their work is sometimes criticised as 'data-mining', a pointless process in which anybody looking hard enough for a correlation will eventually find one, but many institutional funds are willing to entrust at least a part of their assets to the quants.

'The decisions in our organisation are made by a computer system,' explains Barr Rosenberg, the leading proponent of quantitative fund management. 'And the only way an individual can add value to the firm is to improve the computer system or the data that goes into the computer system. Our human – i. e. qualitative – effort is to make the models better.'[141] This approach to investment could scarcely be more different from the nose of Plum Plumridge or the ties of Siegmund Warburg. Its practitioners have cut themselves off from the need to make any judgments at all about the assets they buy.

But its significance is easily exaggerated. Most fund managers are neither indexers nor quants but highly conventional 'balanced' fund managers, who invest in a broad range of bonds and shares at home and abroad. All of the top managers of pension funds – Morgan Grenfell, Schroders, PDFM, Gartmore and Mercury – fall into this category. Yet their portfolios, ostensibly compiled with great forethought to achieve a respectable performance without taking unnecessary risks, are no more than a form of closet indexing. Any portfolio with twenty randomly selected blue-chip shares in it will tend to match the performance of the market, irrespective of the decisions of the people who manage it. Like bankers, fund managers have good reason to fear being seen as unconventional. It is consistency and not flamboyance which secures a steady flow of new business, and the safest way to win a place among the top ten fund managers is to copy what the other nine are doing.

'You might think that the job of the institutional investor is to forecast which of the assets will perform best in the future rather than simply reflect the past,' thinks Alastair Ross Goobey, chief executive at Hermes Pensions Management. 'But the pressures investment managers are subject to makes them relatively cowardly when it comes to taking an independent stance.'[142] Owners but not controllers, abstracted rather than involved, it seems the modern fund manager is also bovine. They all want the same things.

CHAPTER TWENTY-NINE

WHAT INSTITUTIONS OWN

Keynes once remarked that if investment is the by-product of a casino, the job is unlikely to be well done. Is it likely to be better done if it is a by-product of the pensions industry?

SIR SAMUEL BRITTAN[1]

The issue at stake is simple. Who manages the fund? Is it the investment manager or is it the trustees? I have said if they want they can see us in court.

ARTHUR SCARGILL, 1982[2]

On 26 March 1984 the National Coal Board (NCB) took the National Union of Mineworkers (NUM) to the High Court. One of the most surprising aspects of the miners' strike, then entering its fourth week, was the reluctance of the Board to use the law to curb flying pickets. But the occasion marked no change of policy: the NCB was seeking to prove that the NUM-appointed trustees of the mineworkers' pension scheme had breached their fiduciary duty to retired miners by refusing to endorse the investment proposals put forward by fund managers. The judgment which followed was remarkable.

Sir Robert Megarry, the vice chancellor, ruled that even the trustees of a pension fund – the men and women charged with looking after the savings of the people who contribute to it – have no right to place restrictions on the power of fund managers to buy and sell whatever they like. This was because (Sir Robert reminded the court) trustees have a statutory obligation to act always in the best interests of the current and future beneficiaries of the fund:

When the purpose of the trust is to provide financial benefits for the beneficiaries, the best interests of the beneficiaries are normally their best financial interest. In the case of a power of investment, the power must be exercised so as to yield the best return for the beneficiaries, judged in relation to the risks of the investment in question; and the prospect of the yield of income and capital appreciation both have to be considered in judging the return from the investment . . . In considering what investment to make the trustees must put on one side their own personal interests and views. Trustees may have strongly held social or political views. They may be firmly opposed to any investment in South Africa or other countries, or they may object to any form of investment in companies concerned with alcohol, tobacco, armaments or many other things. In the conduct of their own affairs of course they are free to abstain from making any such investments. Yet if under a trust investments of this type would be more beneficial to the beneficiaries than other investments, the trustees must not refrain from making the investments by reason of the views that they hold.[3]

Arthur Scargill and his fellow NUM trustees took a different view. They thought they should have the right to tell the fund managers to invest the savings of British miners in British industry and to disinvest from competing industries like oil and gas. But all they succeeded in proving was the all-encompassing nature of the discretionary power at the command of the modern fund manager. The managers of British savings can invest in virtually anything – financial or real, cash or derivative – at home or abroad. They can buy company shares and government bonds, old masters and gold ingots, deposit money at a bank, or invest it in futures contracts and traded options. With a few exceptions, they are free to buy as much or as little as they like of anything they like.

In practice, they buy mainly company shares and government bonds, and the proportions vary according to the type of institution and the imminence of its liabilities. Unit and investment trusts which offer investors income tend to buy bonds; those which offer them capital growth tend to buy ordinary shares. (In practice, both tend to own a higher proportion of ordinary shares than any other institutional investor.) Insurance companies, on the other hand, have to keep a lot of their money in cash or other investments which can be cashed quickly; they would otherwise not be able to meet claims as they came in. Life offices can make longer-term investments, but are constrained by the unpredictability of premium income and by the returns they have guaranteed to buyers of endowment policies. As a result, they prefer predictable investments such as government bonds, and use shares only to add a little excitement.

Pension funds are much heavier buyers of ordinary shares. Their responsibility to pay pensions can lie as much as forty years ahead, and their cash flow is relatively predictable, so they can take more risks. This is especially

TABLE 29.1
Gross Investment Assets of Institutional Investors in 1997

Asset Class (£bn)	Pension Funds	Life Offices	Insurance Companies	Investment Trusts	Unit Trusts
Cash and Near-Cash	26.4	38.9	5.4	1.2	5.0
Gilts	80.5	107.8	15.7	1.1	3.2
Local Authority Debt	0.156	0.914	0.016	–	0.014
Ordinary Shares	339.7	283.2	15.0	29.1	86.9
Other Company Securities	5.6	53.4	3.4	1.4	7.8
Foreign Company Ordinary Shares	104.2	68.8	3.5	17.8	42.9
Other Foreign Company Securities	3.9	4.7	3.1	0.421	3.2
Foreign Government Securities	13.1	8.5	8.2	0.498	–
Unit Trust Units	*21.9	50.2	0.415	0.202	–
Loans and Mortgages	0.2	8.0	1.3	–	–
Real Estate	†27.4	42.3	2.8	0.086	‡4.1
Other Assets	33.8	11.1	38.5	2.1	–
Total	656.9	677.8	97.3	53.9	149.0

Source: Financial Statistics, January 1999, Tables 5.1A to 5.2E.

* Includes £13 million invested by local authority pension funds in the local authority mutual investment trust.
† Includes £3.2 billion invested in property unit trusts.
‡ Market value of property unit trusts.

true of young pension schemes, which have many employees contributing and few retired pensioners. With high income and a need for long-term capital growth, they sometimes invest as much as £9 in every £10 in the stock market. Mature pension schemes, by contrast, have few contributors and lots of pensioners. With less income and heavier outgoings, they need the certainty of cash and bonds. Because the population is ageing, most British pension funds are now relatively mature. This means a shift in the balance of pension portfolios from shares to bonds. There are always exceptions: in 1994, the ICI pension fund had four times as many pensioners as contributors, but still had £4 in every £5 invested in equities.[4] But recent government decisions to remove a tax credit from the dividend income of pension funds, and to impose a minimum funding requirement (obliging them to keep a fixed proportion of their assets in liquid instruments) will help to persuade even the exceptions that they should buy more bonds.

Cult of the Equity

It is often forgotten that fund managers are aiming not to invest for the highest return, but to find the assets best suited to meet the liabilities the fund has incurred. This means the allocation of capital between companies and investment projects is not the *raison d'être* of the fund management industry, but a by-product of its responsibilities to trustees, pensioners and policy-holders. This is the source of most of the controversy which surrounds institutional investment today.[5] It is also explains the herdlike behaviour of the fund management industry. Since fund managers know that it is impossible to out-perform the market consistently, they aim only to do no worse than their competitors. The similarities between investment portfolios are far greater than the differences. The most striking similarity, and one peculiar to Britain, is the heavy exposure of long-term institutional investors to the equity market. British fund managers are said to worship a Cult of the Equity. This almost religious faith in the efficacy of equity investment has conferred on them the enormous power they now wield over the chief source of income and wealth in modern Britain: the PLC.

The leading evangelist of the Cult of the Equity was George Ross Goobey, actuary and investment manager to the Imperial Tobacco pension fund from the 1940s to the 1970s. When he joined Imperial in 1947, life offices and pension funds invested almost exclusively in government bonds (which pay a fixed rate of interest) and preference shares (which pay a fixed dividend). This was poor strategy. Between 1918 and 1998 government bonds yielded a real return of only 2.46 per cent a year. In the same period shares yielded a real annual return of 8.0 per cent. Between 1947 and 1997, the real yield on gilt-edged securities was *negative*: for fifty years, investors in gilts actually *lost* money.[6] These differences compound over time, so the effect on the wealth of investors is astonishing. In real terms, £100 invested in gilts in 1918 was worth £667 in 1998; but the same sum invested in equities had risen in value to £47,195.* The calculations ignore the effects of tax and the costs of dealing but, on the basis of past performance, an investor looking only to maximise his return would be well-advised to invest all his money in shares.

George Ross Goobey did not have the benefit of hindsight; he simply compared the yield on gilts with the yield on shares, and found shares were cheaper. He also recognised that unless the Imperial Tobacco pension fund changed its investment policy, the company would soon be paying its pen-

---

* Calculations made using data drawn from the Barclays Capital Equity and Gilt Study, published annually.

sioners out of corporate profits. Hired to help the chief accountant interpret the advice given by the consulting actuaries, he recognised immediately that the company pension fund could never fulfil its commitments by sticking to fixed income investments. But he had some difficulty persuading the trustees to agree:

> When I got to Imperial to run their pension fund I found that the company were guaranteeing the fund 5 per cent per annum. And yet, the year before, when Dalton issued his 2½ per cent Treasury at par the company bought a great dollop... Absolute madness. At that time the yield on British government securities was 2½ per cent, and you could buy the shares of leading industrial companies such as Imperial and ICI on an initial return of about 5 per cent ... The first thing I recommended was that they should sell this wad of Dalton 2½ per cents, which by that time had dropped to 83 ... I was almost shown the door. I mean, they were being asked to admit a mistake. But I was able to persuade them eventually to sell all the gilts they had got and buy nothing but equities.[7]

Only one Imperial director – Cambridge-educated mathematician and former wartime minister, Sir James Grigg – was supportive, but his influence was decisive. By the early 1950s, Imperial Tobacco pension fund owned no bonds at all; it was wholly invested in shares.

It took Ross Goobey rather longer to persuade his fellow fund managers of the merits of equity investment. He wrote the standard paper on it for the National Association of Pension Funds (NAPF), but found himself barred by the Institute of Actuaries from teaching students about investment. Like most professionals, actuaries are deeply distrustful of novelty. After all, the profession had first became respectable during the 1840s, a decade which coincided with the first great share speculation of the modern era: the railway boom. It was a period in which, as one contemporary stockbroker put it, 'a solicitor or two, a civil engineer, a parliamentary agent, possibly a contractor, a map of England, a pair of compasses, a pencil, and a ruler, were all that was requisite to commence the formation of a railway company.'[8]

The railway boom was accompanied by a great amount of parliamentary corruption, much wasted money, and a good deal of conscious fraud. George Hudson, the 'Railway King', went bankrupt in the same year that the Institute of Actuaries was founded. No wonder Griffith Davies, actuary to Guardian Assurance, told a House of Commons select committee in 1843 that railway shares were 'decidedly undesirable and incompatible' with the high reputation of an insurance company.[9] That said, the railway boom did lead to the creation of a sizeable market in industrial securities. Scottish Provident bought shares in 'established' railway companies throughout the boom of the 1840s, and by the 1850s the fixed interest stocks of the more respectable companies, such as Great Western Railway, had achieved a status comparable with government bonds.[10]

The Government Bond Market

By then, government bonds had been the staple fare of the first great institutional investors – the life offices – for over a century. Companies have sold pieces of paper called bonds (or 'notes' or 'bills of exchange') promising to repay the holder at some later date since they were used to finance overseas expeditions in the age of Drake and Hawkins. Once banks emerged to buy the bonds at a discount, allowing holders to realise most of their value before the ship returned or the goods were paid for, a thriving bond market developed. But company bonds were repaid within a few months or a year, and life offices need much longer-dated securities. Here, the influence of government was decisive.

Governments always need money, but have none of their own. Before the development of the Welfare State, their most expensive responsibility was the waging of war, and Britain was at war with France (and allies of France) almost continuously from 1689 to 1815.[11] Chronic conflicts require a standing army and navy, dockyards to build ships, barracks to house soldiers and sailors, forts to protect and victual them, armaments factories, and a vast bureaucracy to raise taxes and administer what John Brewer has called 'the fiscal-military State'.

According to Brewer, military expenditure accounted for over one tenth of national income and between two thirds and three quarters of total public expenditure throughout the eighteenth century.[12] Much of the sums required could be raised through taxation, but the immediacy of the demands of war obliged successive governments to borrow large sums from private investors. The public debt rose at a prodigious rate during the eighteenth century, from £16.7 million at the end of the Nine Years' War to £245 million in 1783.[13] By the time of Waterloo, the national debt had ballooned to a staggering £820 million.[14] This was a greater burden than the mountain of debt which provoked a revolution in France in 1789. But George I and his descendants had one advantage over Louis XVI: an efficient and reasonably fair system of tax collection. This not only distributed the burden on a fairer basis than the Bourbons managed, but convinced foreign and domestic investors in British government securities that they would get their money back with interest.

At first, borrowings were made by short-term expedients. The government issued irredeemable annuities, organised lotteries, and sold corporate privileges. The Sun fire office invested in state lottery tickets on five occasions between 1712 and 1719.[15] But its ability to mobilise the savings of the country could not compare with the Bank of England (1694), the New East India Company (1709) or the South Sea Company (1711), all of which began as little more than incorporated bodies of people willing to lend money to the government in exchange for commercial privileges. Intense competition developed among them to manage the public debt, because it gave holders access to a large and secure income to finance private enterprises. The South Sea Company, whose name is indelibly associated with the first great City scandal, was formed ostensibly to prosper from a monopoly of British trade with South America. It financed two voyages before the outbreak of war with Spain put paid to its South American ambitions. But investing in trade with South America was never its real purpose anyway.

The principal goal of its promoters was to wrest management of the public debt from the Bank of England and the East India Company. This it sought to achieve by persuading investors to swap their holdings of government debt for shares in the South Sea Company, whose promoters promised extravagant possibilities of gain. As more government debt was surrendered to the company, the directors issued more shares, inflating what posterity knows as the South Sea Bubble. The ultimate effect was a massive transfer of wealth from the latecomers to the earliest investors. Most stockholders acquired their shares at inflated prices and, when the Bubble burst, suffered grievous losses.

The South Sea Bubble could have smothered the nascent government bond market. The Amicable Society for a Perpetual Assurance Office[16] lost £13,000 when the Bubble burst. Both the London Assurance and the Westminster had to carry South Sea shares in their portfolios until 1854, when the outstanding securities were finally converted into Bank of England stock.[17] But the Bubble was the making of the government bond market, rather than its undoing. In its aftermath, the management of government borrowing was taken out of the control of private financiers and put on a proper footing. Although they were not admired – legislation was passed in 1734 against 'the infamous practice of stock jobbing' – the sheer volume of government debt led to the creation of new men who dealt in government bonds.

Brokers (who acted on behalf of investors) and jobbers (who guaranteed investors could always sell) increased the number and range of investors in government debt, and created new techniques for structuring and pricing long- and short-dated bonds. They developed margin trading, invented put-and-call options, set up the first registers to record changes of ownership, and altered the way that payment of interest was calculated. Astute City intermediaries such as Samson Gideon, financial adviser to Henry Pelham in the 1740s, made a fortune from dealing in government bonds; by 1744, he was rich enough to buy nearly one fifth of a government bond issue of £1.8 million, purely for his own account.[18] The development of a sophisticated government bond market also facilitated the issue of bonds by companies, which could use the rate of interest paid by the government as the benchmark for their securities – as they still do today.

The South Sea Bubble and the Equity Market

The principal victim of the South Sea Bubble was the market in shares. The Sun life office, which had shares in the Sword Blades Company as well as the South Sea Company, did not buy equities again until 1889. The first ordinary shares do not appear on its records until 1900 and, as recently as 1939, they made up just 11 per cent of its total assets.[19] This was not entirely a matter of choice. The Bubble Act of 1720 banned all joint-stock companies not authorised by royal charter, and this prevented the development of an active market in shares until the limited liability legislation of the 1850s and 1860s.[20] However, the government bond market did put in place the infrastructure for an equity market. The 'infamous jobbers' (a term which then encompassed all dealing in securities), banned from speculating in government debt, took to meeting in coffee houses, where they carried on much as before. Their principal haunts were Jonathon's and Garraway's, both adjacent to the Bank of England.

Samson Gideon was the dominant figure at Jonathon's. His importance and influence ensured that it soon supplanted Garraway's as the market of choice. Terms familiar today – 'bull,' 'bear' and 'stock' – entered common usage.[21] The British government bond market became surprisingly well integrated with the capital markets of Paris and Amsterdam, with money flowing easily across the Channel and the North Sea. The success of the rogue 'jobbers' was so unstoppable that by 1773 they opened the first proper trading floor at the corner of Threadneedle Street and Sweetings Alley (moving to its purpose-built home, on its present site, in May 1801). Although the exchange continued to deal mainly in government bonds until deep into the twentieth century, the emergence of a fully functioning capital market by the beginning of the nineteenth century created the community of expertise on which the modern equity market was eventually built. The most important function of the Stock Exchange was to provide a forum where investors could channel their savings into the coffers of the government, or into business ventures which could make use of them.[22]

In 1709, roughly ten thousand people bought government debt. Ten years later, thirty thousand did. By the outbreak of the Seven Years War in 1757 there were sixty thousand holders of government bonds.[23] This new class of rich and confident investors diluted the power of the chartered companies which had profited from the South Sea Bubble: they were too numerous to fall under the sway of groups of City financiers. Aristocrats, landowners, trustees of estates, Jewish and Huguenot businessmen, City and provincial merchants, clergymen, bishops, lawyers and (mostly corrupt) civil servants all bought government bonds. Thousands more invested via corporate bodies. Traditional agglomerations of wealth – livery companies, Oxbridge colleges, Christ's Hospital, even Queen Anne's Bounty – were prominent buyers. The new class of private banks, such as Child's and Martin's, recycled deposits through the government bond market. There were foreign buyers too, particularly the wealthy bourgeoisie of the Netherlands. However, the appearance on the first registers of bondholders of institutions – the Amicable Society for a Perpetual Assurance Office, the London Assurance, the Royal Exchange Assurance and the Sun fire office – was the true portent of the future.[24]

Even as the number of institutional investors increased during the nineteenth century, one asset they would not buy was shares. An analysis of the balance sheets of the Phoenix, Sun and Royal Exchange assurance companies between 1782 and 1875 found no equities, but plenty of bonds and mortgages.[25] A measure of the continuing wealth and power of the aristocracy was the appetite of the life offices and insurance companies for mortgages on the great landed estates. Land and its rent rolls remained the predominant source of wealth until well after the Industrial Revolution, and the mortgages were satisfyingly large. When the second Duke of Buckingham and Chandos went bankrupt in 1848 he owed the institutions £1.5 million, two thirds of which he had borrowed in to six years between 1839 and 1845.[26] By 1878, the Butes owed Equitable Life £550,000. The loans were long-dated, sometimes embarrassingly so. A loan of £6,500 from the Sun to the fourth Duke of Marlborough in 1816 was repaid by the seventh Duke in 1877.[27]

Bagehot commented in 1879, as the astonishing concentration of land ownership uncovered by the New Domesday survey seeped into public consciousness, that 'a large part of the titles of our richest landowners are mortgaged ... to insurance offices who have much money constantly to lend.'[28] In 1936 the historian of the Legal and General wrote of the archives he had perused that 'one must not betray the confidence of these most discreet leather-bound books, beyond writing that the descendants of some of our great English families today would be very astonished, and pained possibly, on reading them.'[29]

When interest rates fell towards the end of the nineteenth century, the institutions did not buy shares instead of mortgages and British government bonds.[30] They began to buy foreign government bonds. The value of foreign government securities owned by life offices climbed from £1.2 million in 1870 to £24.6 million in 1913. Most were listed on the London Stock Exchange, after an introduction by a merchant bank which would not have dreamt of underwriting an issue of industrial shares.[31] Few companies were quoted on the exchange; in a list of 1906 David Kynaston could identify only five stocks out of over two hundred, which were classified as 'home industrials'.[32] These were in a separate section tellingly entitled 'Miscellaneous', and consisted largely of safe options such as brewing companies whose directors had made it to the House of Lords.[33]

In 1913, ordinary shares accounted for just 3.5 per cent of assets of all life offices in Britain. The rest of their funds, bar a few property holdings, was in various forms of debt, and mostly in government bonds and mortgages.[34] British government bonds returned to favour only when the life offices were forced to buy them during the First World War as a matter of patriotic duty. Gilts were only one hundredth of life office assets in 1913, but one third by 1918.[35]

The Beginnings of Equity Investment

The disproportionate interest in debt was not entirely the work of bullying governments or snobbish merchant bankers. The institutions had persuaded themselves that shares were unsound largely on the basis of traditional actuarial advice. It took George Ross Goobey to challenge it. But if he was the evangelist of the Cult of the Equity, he was not its first apostle. H. E. Raynes, sometime actuary to the Legal and General and later historian of the insurance industry, had delivered a paper in favour of equity investment in 1928.

The chief argument of *The Place of Ordinary Stocks and Shares in the Investment of Life Assurance Funds* – which Ross Goobey read while studying for his actuarial examinations – was that ordinary shares were a valuable hedge against inflation because, as a claim on real economic growth, their capital value tended to appreciate.[36] To a profession which had traditionally pursued security and income rather than capital growth, this was a revelation. But its timing was unfortunate. A year after it was published the Wall Street Crash precipitated a fall in the stock market which did not stop until the middle of 1932. The economy deflated, money got cheaper, and 1932 turned out to be the best year in which to own gilt-edged securities since 1921.

A study by *The Economist* shortly before the Second World War found that life offices held 5.1 per cent of their funds in ordinary shares in 1932. This had risen to only 7.5 per cent in 1935 and 9 per cent in 1937, although the economic recovery was by that time far advanced. Friends Provident, which had owned no shares at all in 1924, had raised its holding to £1 in every £10 by 1939.[37] Pearl Assurance, pursuing a policy thought to be greatly daring, increased its commitment to equities from 4 per cent of assets in 1930 to 11 per cent by 1938. Yet by the time war broke out, life offices still had almost twice as much invested in real estate as in equities, and the overwhelming bulk of their funds remained in gilt-edged and company bonds.[38]

National Mutual Life, which is famously supposed to have pioneered investment in shares by insurance companies during the chairmanship of John Maynard Keynes, was not exceptional in this respect. One maxim of his – 'Life assurance societies must stand or fall mainly with the success or failure of their investment policy' – was certainly novel in placing fund management skills ahead of actuarial calculations.[39] But the chief innovation of his chairmanship, which ran from 1921 to 1938, was not to plunge headlong into equities. According to the company history, shares as a proportion of total assets actually declined during his chairmanship, and never rose above 21 per cent, which they reached on the eve of the Great Crash, in which Keynes lost nearly all his money. The Independent Investment Trust, which he had established with his friend and fellow-director Oswald Falk, was heavily invested in equities; it lost virtually all the £1 million they had sunk into American shares. Amid considerable embarrassment, its management was surrendered to a merchant bank, which cut its equity exposure from 54.8 per cent in 1930 to 25.88 per cent in 1933.[40]

At National Mutual, Keynes faced considerable resistance to equity investment among his fellow-directors, but he had more success at the Provincial, another insurer he advised: one third of its funds were invested in equities by the late 1930s. His greatest success was with the funds of King's College, Cambridge, which he managed without reference to others.[41] His disparagement of conservatism ('When I can persuade the Board of my insurance company to buy a share, that, I am learning from experience, is the right moment for selling it') was at least as important to his reputation as an innovator as anything he did. His lasting contribution was the introduction of an active approach to fund management. He introduced life offices to cash and gilt arbitrage, in which decisions to buy or sell government bonds were based on his views of whether interest rates were going to go up or down.

The reluctance of the directors of the National Mutual to indulge the enthusiasms of one man was understandable. It was not until April 1937 that Raynes delivered a second paper to the Institute of Actuaries, based on the performance of share prices over the previous ten years, which proved that his argument had survived the Great Depression. When Raynes sat down, the chairman, Leslie Brown, rose to declare that 'sufficient evidence is now available to support the contention that Ordinary shares deserve to take an important place in the portfolios of Life Assurance Companies.'[42] It was as Leslie Brown FIA, company secretary and chief investment manager to the giant Prudential Assurance Company, that he later carried the Cult of the Equity to the heart of the life assurance industry. 'Leslie Brown is sometimes talked of as the most powerful man in the City,' Anthony Sampson noted in 1962. 'In the stock exchange his name is a legend: for a new issue can depend on the raising or the falling of his eyebrow ... The importance of Mr Brown and his counterparts has grown steadily since the war, firstly because their share in investment has grown, secondly because they have put proportionately more into industrial shares and property and less into "gilt-edged." '[43]

But ordinary shares did not become even the second biggest asset owned by life offices until 1954 and, when Sampson spoke to Brown, equities made up less than a quarter of their portfolios.[44] The decision to buy shares was always momentous, and not one encouraged by the authorities.[45] George Ross Goobey was rebuked by the Bank of England for encouraging institutional investors to avoid government bonds, and other fund managers received the same treatment. Some did not have the confidence or expertise to buy shares – the Refuge did not have fund managers based in the City until 1953.[46] Scottish Mutual did not appoint any until 1956; its investment department was not fully formed until the 1970s.[47]

With the obvious exception of Imperial Tobacco, the pension funds were slower still to increase their holdings of shares. In 1960 Ross Goobey was being asked by the Imperial Tobacco board to give 'serious consideration to the question whether there ought not to be at any rate a temporary halt in the policy of buying (for keeps) only equities'.[48] As trustees, they were anxious to avoid being sued for imprudent investment. It was not until a year later that the Trustee Investments Act officially widened their powers of investment to include ordinary shares; until then, local authority pension funds were not allowed to invest in equities at all. When the Manchester Corporation pension fund decided to buy some in 1956, it had to secure permission by a private Act of Parliament.[49] It was inhibitions of this kind which exposed so many pensioners to the ravages of inflation. The only beneficiaries were the managers of investment trusts.

Rise and Fall of Investment Trusts

Investment trusts were invented as a less risky way for individuals to invest in the stock market. The original prospectus for Foreign and Colonial promised 'to provide the investor of modest means with the same opportunity as the rich capitalist'. Since the 1960s, like every other form of saving, they have become thoroughly institutionalised. Confusingly, they are not trusts at all, but companies which invest their capital in the shares of other companies. Investment trusts first become popular in the 1880s, when interest rates fell below dividend yields for the first time and it was possible to borrow money and reinvest it profitably in shares.[50] Equity investment remained their speciality. Glasgow's Guide to Investment Trust Companies of 1935 lists seventy-six Scottish and one hundred and twenty three English companies, all of which were already half to two thirds invested in equities.[51] By the mid-1950s, this had risen to 90 per cent or more.

For life offices and pension funds who knew little or nothing about companies and their shares, investment trusts were a godsend. They did not have to do any research, and the wide spread avoided the risk of investing in only a handful of companies. The number of investment trusts peaked at nearly three hundred and fifty in 1964, the very time when institutions were keen to increase their holdings of equities but lacking the expertise to choose them and the nerve to hold them in quantity. Ten years later, when the investment trusts had become reliant on institutional shareholders, the institutions began to withdraw their patronage. By the 1970s, the life offices and pension funds reckoned they could spread the risks of equity investment by buying the stocks themselves, or by hiring specialist fund managers to do it. Their withdrawal plunged investment trusts into a crisis from which they have never recovered.

It left them with no natural source of funds to manage. In London, they had originated among the metropolitan rich. A separate investment trust industry developed in Scotland among the solicitors and accountants equally wealthy Scotsmen appointed to manage their savings. Three of the most important fund management houses in Edinburgh – Ivory & Sime, Martin Currie and Baillie Gifford – were all late Victorian or Edwardian accountancy partnerships. Alexander Henderson founded half of Henderson Touche Remnant to manage his own family fortune; the other half was founded by an accountant from Edinburgh named George Touche. Only Robert Fleming of Dundee, whose name lives on as one of the last merchant banks to remain both British and independent, was not an accountant. He started the Investment Trust Corporation in his native city in 1888, moving to the City in 1900.

TABLE 29.2
The Ten Largest Investment Trust Groups

Name	Owner	Funds Managed (£bn)
Henderson Investors	AMP (Australia)	4.7
Fleming Investment Trust Management	Robert Fleming & Co	*4.0
Foreign & Colonial Management	Hypo Bank (65%)	3.5
Dresdner RCM Global Investors	Dresdner Bank	1.4
Mercury Asset Management	Merrill Lynch	1.3
Gartmore Invest Limited	NatWest	1.3
Schroder Investment Management	Schroders PLC	1.0
Morgan Grenfell Trust Managers Limited	Deutsche Bank	0.9
J. Rothschild Capital Management	J. Rothschild Assurance	0.8
AIB Govett Asset Management	Allied Irish Banks	0.7

Source: Association of Investment Trust Companies, September 1998.

* Robert Fleming & Co Ltd also has a joint venture with Electra Investment Trust which has a further £1.3 billion of trusts under management.

By fawning on institutional investors, the investment trusts alienated themselves from individual investors, who defected to unit trusts.[52] They also became corrupt. Dense networks of cross-shareholdings and interlocking directorships protected them from outside influences. Given their incestuous nature, it was not surprising that they became the playthings of a small cross-section of men drawn from the City and Scottish financial establishments. Nor was it surprising that they paid themselves generous fees for managing the assets – in many cases incompetently. The investment trusts owned the fund management companies, so it was impossible for the shareholders to sack them without severe embarrassment (or paying massive compensation for loss of the contract).

These conflicts of interest were built into the industry from the outset. An investment trust is set up to invest in other companies, but they often began as job-creation schemes for the well connected, and did not change for the better. 'We cannot help thinking', wrote *The Economist* during the investment trust boom of the 1880s, 'that the existence of a good many recent trust companies is due partly to the desire for easy directorates.'[53] In the 1960s, intricate webs of trusts were used by financiers like Harley Drayton to control business empires. The Drayton Group, which was one of the most important forces in the City of that era, was essentially a collection of seventeen investment trusts. These owned, and were owned by, major industrial companies – BET, BICC, United Newspapers and Consolidated Gold Fields. They shared common directorships and an invulnerability to outside influences in general and hostile takeover bids in particular. If they needed additional capital, they issued new shares to one another rather than seek outside shareholders. Sampson wrote that Drayton, chairman of twenty-three companies and custodian of no less than forty-eight, was 'omnipresent' in the City.[54] Among the corporate creatures to which the Drayton Group gave life were Tiny Rowland's Lonrho and Jim Slater's Slater Walker. In such complex and impenetrable corporate webs, a self-serving ethos is almost bound to develop. As Drayton was dying in 1966, it emerged that two of the investment trusts in the group were providing directors with highly geared share options. The Drayton Group lived on until it was rescued by Midland Bank, in the 1974 fringe banking crisis. The fund management which was at the core of its power survives as an independent fund management house, Invesco MIM, which still uses the Drayton name for its investment trusts.

Empires such as the Drayton Group flourished in that curious interlude before institutional investors had truly come into their inheritance, when the City needed the money of the great industrial companies more than the great industrial companies needed the money of the City. It was a moment when British capitalism might have developed along German or Japanese lines, with industrial companies answerable not to independent shareholders but to a claque of director-fund managers. The rise of the great institutional investors stymied that eventuality. Admirers of European and Asian business cultures might regret it, but it was a merciful deliverance, for the character of the investment trust industry was essentially nepotistic and protectionist. Apart from a brief revival in the 1990s on the back of speculative interest in emerging markets, their number has shrunk steadily since the 1960s through a mixture of liquidation, corporate takeover and unitisation.

The chief cause of their difficulties is simple, and ineradicable: the increasingly wide gap – known as a discount to net asset value – between the share price of the investment trust and the value of the stocks and shares it holds in other companies. In other words, investment trusts are worth less than the sum of their parts, which makes them unusually vulnerable to gold-diggers. Except for a brief period between the wars, when shortage of trust stocks drove net asset values to a premium, investment trust shares have always traded at a discount to net asset value. In the mid-1970s the discount widened to as much as 40 per cent; now, most trade at double-digit discounts, some as deep as 30 per cent. The discounts attract predators who recognise that they can purchase the underlying assets cheaply by taking over the investment trust. Paying 70p for assets others are valuing at £1 will always make sense.

In the 1980s Ian Henderson, an investment manager at the London and Manchester life assurance company, became a hate-figure to investment trust directors. He took over and unitised a succession of trusts trading at a discount. Based in Exeter, he was sufficiently remote from the City establishment to ignore complaints of unsportsmanlike behaviour. 'Management groups had forgotten whose business it was they were managing,' he told the *Financial Times* in 1984. 'They didn't regard themselves as accountable to their shareholders.'[55] His example inspired not only Robert Maxwell, who developed a strong taste for buying investment trusts in the 1980s, but created a whole new breed of so-called 'fund-busters' or 'vulture funds.' These are fund managers who buy large stakes in investment trusts, then try to persuade fellow-shareholders either to break up the fund or appoint new fund managers (usually themselves). Success in these endeavours was elusive until 1993, when the London Stock Exchange insisted that a majority of the directors of an investment trust should be independent of the fund managers. In 1996, the directors of the Kleinwort European Privatisation Investment Trust broke with the past by dismissing Kleinwort Benson as fund manager. A year later, the directors of the Murray European Trust dismissed their creators, Murray Johnstone. Battles to change the management of investment trusts are now everyday occurrences in the City.

The Battle for Globe Investment Trust

But it was the decision to turn on them by their pupils, the pension funds, which hurt investment trusts the most. In 1977 two nationalised industry pension funds – British Rail and British Coal – shocked every investment trust by launching takeover bids for the Edinburgh and Dundee and British investment trusts. Until then, it was regarded as unthinkable for a fellow institutional investor to attempt such a thing. The British Coal pension fund developed a taste for it. Between 1977 and 1988 it devoured the British for £100 million, the Drayton Premier for £158 million and the Touche Remnant Industrial and General for £560 million. For a giant institutional investor, this was a cheap way of buying shares in large quantities without moving the price against itself. But for the directors of the Globe Investment Trust, to which British Coal turned its attention in the summer of 1990, it was presumptuous. Globe was not just any old investment trust; it was the flagship of the industry, with a market capitalisation of £1 billion.

The takeover battle which ensued was remarkably ill-mannered, and given added venom by the clear distaste of David Hardy, the blue-blooded descendant of Kiss-Me Hardy and last chairman of Globe, for Paul Whitney, the bearded former research chemist who ran British Coal investment strategy.[56] Hardy's opinions of his opponent read like a page from an early *Anatomy of Britain*. 'One had bent over backwards to give him assistance, opportunities, recognition,' he told the *Investors Chronicle* in June 1990. 'He has a very big job and I think he's behaved despicably . . . He's a collector, a trophy collector.'[57] His distress was understandable. The British Coal pension fund had a large shareholding in Globe before the bid was launched. The ructions were not confined to the main protagonists. Globe sold its shares in Barclays Bank in protest at the decision of its investment banking arm, BZW, to advise British Coal.

The propaganda against British Coal from the industry trade body, the Association of Investment Trust Companies, was apocalyptic. It bore the stamp of its director general, Philip Chappell. Chappell, formerly a merchant banker with Morgan Grenfell, was a libertarian lobbyist with a passionate enthusiasm for individual savings and investment. (He had, in conjunction with Nigel Vinson, helped to invent the personal pension and the Personal Equity Plan). One of his propaganda sheets called on shareholders to lobby their MPs to demand the referral of the bid to the Monopolies and Mergers Commission (MMC). It claimed that the Coal Board Pension Fund bid 'removes direct ownership of shares from individuals and limits public participation in equity ownership . . . concentrates further the power of unaccountable and fiscally privileged pension funds . . . paid for by public subsidy and tax privilege, which is unfair and contrary to natural justice.'[58]

This was a fair point. Most people are more or less forced to invest in their pension fund, and the fund (until recently) paid no tax on its income or capital gains. Why should a captive hoard of unowned, tax-privileged savings rob private investors of their property and lumber them with a large bill for capital gains tax to boot? 'I know for a fact,' said David Hardy, 'that Mrs Thatcher is very keen that forty-four thousand shareholders do not disappear.'[59] Whatever Mrs Thatcher thought was irrelevant. Globe lost its battle for independence long before British Coal launched its bid. Investment trusts have not bothered for years to sell themselves to retail investors. When Chappell tried to interest his members in an advertising campaign, they refused to pay. The investment trusts which survive are owned largely by the institutions, which will always sell happily to other institutions if the price is right. David Hardy knew it even as Philip Chappell was calling for his crusade: 'Our lovely private shareholders will stand by me, I'm sure,' he said, 'but there are not enough of them.'[60]

However, the chief victims of the decline of the investment trust are not the lovely private shareholders: they are the people who manage them. They have lost their captive hoards of institutional money, to a takeover or to external fund managers appointed by independent directors more interested in investment performance than in sinecures for friends and relatives. The independent fund managers of the City (and Edinburgh) have suffered as a result. Henderson Investors, still the largest manager of investment trusts in the City, was forced to merge with a rival in 1992 (Touche Remnant). Four years later it was taken over by AMP of Australia.

Invesco MIM, the last echo of the sixties' adventurer Harley Drayton, was forced to wind up Drayton Consolidated investment trust and give the management of its successor to Foreign & Colonial. In the autumn of 1992 compensation was paid to the shareholders, after revelations that the fund managers had sunk £43 million into a troubled company which had failed without even the Drayton directors knowing about it, let alone the share-holders. Invesco MIM also lost the management of the Drayton Asia invest-ment trust. The company had found old habits hard to shake, and its funds had a distinct partiality towards companies with which the chairman, Lord Stevens, had connections.

Invesco MIM did not always keep the best company either – Robert Maxwell was a substantial shareholder from 1988 until his death. Although this helped Invesco MIM to retain management of the Mirror Group pension fund, it also helped Maxwell to remove its assets for use elsewhere. Fined £75,000 in October 1991 for maladministration of Personal Equity Plans, Invesco MIM was stung for another £750,000 and a further £1.6 million in costs by the regulators in June 1993 on *fifty-five* separate charges of breaching investment management rules. Three of them related to its handling of Maxwell pension fund assets,[61] and over fifty executives, including the chairman and the chief executive, were fired.[62] The company is now seeking a new future with fresh management and a new American partner, AIM Management, which it bought for $1.6 billion in November 1996.[63]

Travails of the Scottish Fund Managers

The lingering death of the investment trust troubles nobody more than the fund managers of Scotland. Once, Edinburgh was to London what Boston was to New York: a fund management centre in its own right, far removed from the frenetic deal-making culture of the Square Mile. For a time, Charlotte Square – a spacious Georgian townscape at the western end of the famous Edin-burgh 'dumb-bell', where many of the fund managers congregated – was a syn-onym for a peculiarly Scottish style of imaginative but prudent investment, heavily dependent on investment trusts. They make up two thirds of the funds managed by Ivory and Sime (the last of the great fund management houses to operate from Charlotte Square) and half the funds managed by Edinburgh Fund Managers. In Dundee, Alliance Trust is wholly dependent on investment trusts, and even Martin Currie, which has diversified more successfully than most, still relies on captive monies for over a third of its funds.

TABLE 29.3
The Ten Biggest Scottish Fund Managers

Name	Owner(s)	Funds Managed (£bn)
Baillie Gifford	Private Partnership	11.9
Edinburgh Fund Managers	Hermes (8.5%), M&G (5.5%), American Trust (5%)	7.6
Martin Currie	Institutions (16%), Directors and Staff (80%)	5.9
Murray Johnstone	United Asset Management (US)	4.1
Ivory and Sime	Friends Provident (68%), Caledonia Investments (9%), Sumitomo Life (4%)	3.2
Aberdeen Asset Management*	Scottish Provident (41%), Phoenix Life (14.9%), Philadelphia International (14.8%), Equitable Life (9.2%), Shell Pension Fund (4.3%), Scottish Amicable (3.7%)	2.8
Stewart Ivory	Scottish American Investment (24%), Directors and Staff (76%)	2.6
Alliance Trust	Alliance Investment Trust	1.8
Aberforth Partners	Private Partnership	0.6
Scottish Value Management	Directors and Staff	0.4

Source: Annual Reports, 1997–98.

* The London-based fund managers trade as Abtrust Fund Managers.

All the Edinburgh fund managers are now anxiously soliciting fund management business from pension funds, charities, insurance companies and overseas investors, especially in the United States, where they have long enjoyed a warm reception. Baillie Gifford, the largest of the Edinburgh fund managers, has had considerable success. Well over half the funds it manages belong to pension funds, and less than one fifth to investment trusts. Others have found the switch from managing captive money more painful. Edinburgh Fund Managers took over a local rival (Dunedin Fund Managers) but narrowly escaped takeover itself after inviting the British Coal pension fund to acquire a large stake. It was a form of protection which could not survive the privatisation of the coal industry. Murray Johnstone, based in earthier Glasgow, began the search for a partner to rescue it in 1991. It was finally sold in 1993 to a Boston-based public company called United Asset Management.

Ivory and Sime has had chronic managerial difficulties since the last Ivorys left in the 1970s to set up Stewart Ivory. In 1991 it lost the support of its largest shareholder, the Merchant Navy Officer Pension Fund, whose replacement by the Cayzer family investment vehicle, Caledonia Investments, prompted a further spate of internal ructions.[64] In 1996–7, another seven executives quit, and the chief executive resigned. The biggest institutional client, the BAA pension fund, took its business elsewhere. In November 1997 Ivory & Sime merged with the mutual life office, Friends Provident.[65]

The Unit Trust Industry

Investment trusts will probably disappear. Their likeliest fate is absorption, with unit trusts, into the single brand of Euro-friendly mutual funds: the inelegantly titled OEICs, or Open Ended Investment Companies.* Investment trusts were bound to flourish temporarily, thanks to a unique concatenation of circumstances. In the 1950s, life offices knew little of equity investment, investors were less conscious of performance, and the regulators of British capitalism overlooked even the most glaring conflicts of interest. Equally, they were bound to have problems once unit trusts offered serious competition for retail savings. The unit trust industry did not get going until the 1970s; in 1972, investment trusts were worth three times as much as unit trusts. Although the first British unit trust was formed in 1868, the earliest attempts to create a mutual fund based on units rather than shares did not succeed, and the idea did not reappear until 1929, when American unit trust providers tackled the British market.

The first indigenous unit trust was established in 1931, when Municipal and General Securities (M & G, now owned by the Prudential) launched the

---

* The dual pricing structure of funds (they buy units at one price and sell at another) was unpopular in Europe. This was not surprising, given that the 'spread' between the bid and offer prices can be as large as 7 per cent. It forced British unit trusts from January 1997 to transform themselves into a new type of fund called an Open Ended Investment Company (OEIC). All new unit trusts structure themselves as OEICs, and existing funds can change themselves into OEICs provided the holders vote in favour. Most unit trusts are expected to convert to OEICs over the next five to ten years, encouraged by a special government tax holiday into 1999. Unlike unit trusts, OEICs operate under company law and issue shares rather than units.

First British Fixed Trust. By 1939, there were ninety-six unit trusts, managing assets worth £80 million.[66] In the 1970s life offices and insurance companies finally grasped that unit-linked life assurance policies, with more emphasis on *investment* than *insurance*, might be easier to sell than the traditional with-profits variety. It was not until the 1980s that they decided to combine the best of both in the unitised-with-profits contract, in which bonuses were added to the value of the units. This left the market open to imaginative newcomers such as Mark Weinberg, and the later generation of bankers, merchant bankers and independent fund managers who still dominate the unit trust market.[67]

End of the Cult of the Equity?

One of the main reasons insurance companies and life offices were unenthusiastic about unit trusts was their heavy emphasis on equity investment. In the 1950s, even a major life office such as Standard Life preferred to buy the investment trusts managed by the Charlotte Square mafia rather than dip directly into the equity market. Once they understood the case for switching from bonds to equities, they soon found a more efficient method of investing. In 1961 the Cult of the Equity became the official religion, with the passage of the Trustee Investment Act, which allowed general trust funds to place up to half their funds in equities.

By the early 1970s, both pension funds and life offices reckoned gilts were the riskier element in their portfolios. This was undoubtedly correct. During the 1950s and 1960s the bastard Keynesianism pursued by successive governments led to a steady acceleration in prices. Governments had inadvertently stumbled on a way of reducing the real value of their debts, at the expense of the holders of their bonds. The Ross Goobeyites reasoned that equities, with their claim on real growth, would enable their funds to keep up with inflation in a way that fixed interest securities could not. 'I think,' George Ross Goobey told the Imperial Tobacco pension fund trustees in 1960, 'in this world there is no long-term future for a fixed interest security.'[68]

Financial commentators and journalists have periodically declared an end to the Cult of the Equity ever since. The first occurred when Ross Goobey wrote to his trustees. In 1959 the yield gap between government bonds and equities had disappeared. The trustees of the Imperial Tobacco pension fund began to lose their nerve and wonder, in the words of the regulatory cliché, whether the fact that equities had out-performed bonds in the past was an accurate guide to their performance in future.

'Investors may be fully aware of these facts but invariably say "this may

TABLE 29.4
The Twenty Largest Unit Trust Groups
(By Funds Under Management, £bn)

Fund Manager	Owner	Funds
Schroders	PLC	11.9
M & G	PLC	9.5
Fidelity	Fidelity (US)	9.0
Perpetual	PLC	7.8
Mercury Asset Management	Merrill Lynch (US)	7.5
Threadneedle Asset Management*	Zurich Insurance (Switzerland)*	7.1
Gartmore	Nat West Bank PLC	6.2
Barclays	Barclays Bank	6.1
Lloyds TSB†	Lloyds TSB PLC	5.4
Standard Life Trust Management	Standard Life (Mutual)	5.1
Friends Provident	Friends Provident (Mutual)	4.2
Save & Prosper	Robert Fleming	3.9
Aberdeen Prolific	Aberdeen Asset Management	3.4
Axa Sun Life	Axa Insurance Group (France)	3.3
Legal and General	PLC	3.3
Prudential	PLC	3.1
Hill Samuel†	Lloyds TSB PLC	2.9
Midland	HSBC	2.6
Morgan Grenfell Asset Management	Deutsche Bank (Germany)	2.6
Equitable Life	Equitable Life (Mutual)	2.4

Source: Association of Unit Trusts and Investment Funds, December 1998.

* Fund managers to Eagle Star and Allied Dunbar, now part of merged businesses of Zurich Insurance and BAT Financial Services.
† Lloyds TSB also owns Abbey Life, which manages unit trusts worth another £2.3 billion.

have happened for the past 150 years but it is not going to happen again",' Ross Goobey responded. 'This has certainly been my frequent experience during my short investment experience of the past thirty years.'[69] Unlike most of his trustees, he was still around thirty years later when the Cult of the Equity was pronounced dead for a second time.

In late 1991 and early 1992 the Norwich Union made a well-advertised switch from equities to bonds, and there was animated debate about whether it would be wise for other funds to 'do a Norwich'. The reasoning was that, with the pound in the Exchange Rate Mechanism (ERM), inflation was dead. The government would have to repay its debts, rather than inflate them away;

real economic growth would decline, and dividend growth and share prices would falter. Of course, everyone soon forgot these arguments once the pound was bounced out of the ERM in September 1992; interest rates fell, and the long stock-market boom resumed its steady upward course. It later emerged that the Norwich Union had not really changed its policy anyway. It was simply overweight in equities and property at a time when the real rate of interest was exceptionally high.[70] There was much less excitement in 1993 when it began to switch from bonds to equities.

These periodic changes of direction, though apparently abrupt, are a reflection of the chief curiosity of actuarial science: its practitioners value shares not by their price in the stock market on one particular day, but by discounting anticipated dividend income to arrive at a 'net present value'. Provided that companies pay dividends which rise in real terms, and share prices climb in parallel with dividend growth, the combination of income plus capital appreciation will always enable the assets of the pension funds to increase faster than their liabilities, which are usually linked to slower-rising wages and salaries. As George Ross Goobey wrote in 1955:

> In a Pension Fund the market value position is certainly not the prime consideration. The life blood of a Pension Fund is the interest earned on the investments, and one is only concerned with the market value in so far as this reflects the improvement in the interest income, which of course it does when a large proportion of Ordinary Stocks and Shares are held.[71]

This emphasis on dividend income rather than share prices insulates the institutional investor from the gyrations of the markets. The institutions more or less ignored the crash of October 1987, for example, because dividends carried on rising despite the fact that market prices had fallen sharply.

The theological foundation of the Cult of the Equity was the belief that the overall return on equity investment would always beat inflation. This is why its founder was able to reassure the Imperial Tobacco pension fund trustees that it was wise to continue buying equities, even though gilts were yielding more. 'If our view is that over the years the dividends on average of Industrial Ordinary Shares *will not go down on balance,*' Ross Goobey told them, 'then we must admit that the sort of equities we are buying will be better investments in the long run for our Fund than Gilt-edged.'[72] This argument held good throughout the 1950s, and for the first half of the 1960s, then began to break down. In every year between 1964 and 1974, the increase in dividends paid by companies failed to match the increase in the retail price index. Inflation was rising steadily; the performance of British industry was dismal; governments of both persuasions imposed price and dividend controls. In 1973, after the first oil price increase, the British economy was introduced to a new phenomenon: a combination of high inflation and deep recession, or 'stagflation'. With wage-related pension liabilities accelerating at between 15 and 25 per cent a year, and investments showing negative real rates of return, pension funds began to go into deficit. Life offices wondered how 'with-profits' endowments could deliver any profits at all. In March 1975 the chief executive of Commercial Union (now part of CGU) warned that pension contributions were likely to match salary costs within five years. Open-ended pension commitments, he said, were a 'high road to bankruptcy'.[73]

Desperate remedies were applied. It was at this time that the British Rail pension fund began to dabble in art as a hedge against inflation. Its first purchase, in 1974, was an illustrated book of Italian architecture dating from the seventeenth century, acquired by Christopher Lewin, the actuary who then ran the fund, on the advice of Anna Maria Edelstein of Sotheby's. Over the next five years, Edelstein convinced Lewin to invest over £40 million in no less than 2,200 *objets d'art* including Canalettos, Dalis, Gauguins, a Gainsborough, Tiepolos, Monets, Panninis, Renoirs, Pissarros, van Goghs and Picassos. Egyptian bronze heads were acquired, and antique furniture, silver, books, manuscripts, Ming vases, and French porcelain. But buying art was highly controversial for a nationalised industry pension fund. Union leaders grumbled that the savings of railwaymen ought to be invested in industry. Journalists and politicians complained that the fund was denying the public access to art. Museums griped that the fund was driving prices up, and preventing them acquiring significant pieces for national collections. Actuaries wondered about the wisdom of investing in assets which yield no income and cost a fortune to store.

But Lewin had the full support of the pension fund trustees, who were more or less synonymous with the directors of British Rail. They reckoned art offered both an inflation-proof return and a useful hedge against a fall in the external value of the pound. Their mistake was to be excessively gloomy about the prospects for the equity markets; the fund was so embarrassed by the soaring stock markets of the 1980s that it began to dispose of its art collection much earlier than expected. The first items were sold in 1987, with a real return of well over 3 per cent – better than bonds and property, but lower than equities. However, the fund did particularly well selling into the Impressionist boom of the late 1980s. A collection which cost £3.5 million brought in £38.3 million, and its Chinese porcelain, bought for £1.75 million, went for seven times as much to Asian buyers.

British Rail was not the only institutional investor to make esoteric purchases in the 1970s. Commercial Union underwrote the art dealing activities of two firms, Agnew's and Colnaghi's, and bought copper for its policyholders. Postel bought up thousands of acres of forest. The pension fund of Ciba-Geigy dabbled in Krugerrands. After such a prolonged bull market, it is hard to remember the scale of the crises afflicting British capitalism in 1974 and 1975, but the Cult of the Equity came nearer to extinction in the mid-1970s than at any time before or since. By 1974, even George Ross Goobey had apostatised. He reckoned undated government bonds, yielding 17 per cent, were the best buy. He had, however, given up buying equities much earlier, and turned to commercial property, his appetite for controversy undimmed. Of all the assets which institutional investors buy, none is such a fertile source of chagrin as commercial real estate.

Commercial Property

In 1997 institutional investors had nearly £77 billion invested in property (see Table 29.1). This is a substantial sum by any standards but property is by far the smallest of the three major classes of asset the institutions own. Its capacity to anger and excite stems not from its size, but from its visibility. As the historian of institutional investment in property wrote: 'Property development is a sphere of human achievement with a history as great as it is short. Unlike other fields of human endeavour and achievement, mistakes cannot be hidden or buried; they remain there for all future generations to see.'[74]

In the 1960s and 1970s institutional money transformed many British townscapes, usually for the worse. One of the few popular measures of the first Wilson government was a ban on office developments. By the 1970s, institutional buying of agricultural land was causing such consternation in the countryside that another Labour government was forced by fretful farmers to set up an inquiry into the ownership of farmland.[75] There is no clearer illustration of the sometimes melancholy consequences of institutionalised ownership. Unlike the Grosvenors, the Portmans or the Russells, property developers and their institutional backers do not make money as a by-product of providing congenial places to live or work. They make money pure and simple. Institutions fund; developers develop; PLCs occupy. Institutionally owned buildings are located, designed and built solely with that sequence in mind. 'Non-clients', complained Anthony Sampson in 1971, 'lead to non-buildings.'[76]

Many of the non-buildings to which he referred to are still standing. The Empress State Building in Earl's Court, the creation of Felix Fenston, stands tatty but defiant amid a flat, west London townscape. His Royal Garden Hotel, adjacent to Kensington Palace, is grimly recognisable after a comprehensive refurbishment. The life of Harry Hyams, the most notorious property developer of the post-war era, is twice commemorated – by the twenty-eight storey Draper's Gardens block in the City and by the grey concrete of Centre Point at the east end of Oxford Street (described by Erno Goldfinger as 'London's first pop art skyscraper'). Three of the chief architectural horrors of the early 1960s – Millbank Tower from which New Labour controls the airwaves of the nation, Bucklersbury House in the City, and the headquarters of the Department of Trade and Industry in Victoria Street – await friendly bombs. The finance for all three was supplied by the Legal & General Insurance Company, which still occupies Bucklersbury House.[77] The Euston Centre, the bathetic climax to a development which took Joe Levy four years and three hundred and fifteen separate deals to complete, still stands on Euston Road. Britannic House, the up-ended box which served for thirty-odd years as the City offices of BP was recently refurbished.

Norwich Union did not hold back even in the desecration of its home town. Its life office financed construction of the first multi-storey car park in Norwich. The Bull Ring, the inhospitable centre of Birmingham financed as a sale and leaseback by the ICI pension fund in the 1960s, was finally scheduled for demolition in the late 1990s. The Elephant and Castle shopping centre in south-east London is a continuing rebuke to those who believe in the need for a strategic planning authority in the capital. It was conceived by the London County Council, and differs from the Bull Ring only in its preference for shovelling pedestrians on to walkways as well as subways.

But if the buildings are ugly or nondescript and the clients faceless, nothing could be less true of the institutions' partner in crime, the property developer. For those who write about them – Alastair Ross Goobey, Anthony Sampson and Oliver Marriott – the great property entrepreneurs are theatrical, Kane-like figures with giant egos, whose acts of will transform towns and cities and yield gigantic fortunes with shocking speed. Their names have clogged the lists of the rich for decades: Charles Clore, Jack Cotton, Felix Fenston, Harry Hyams, Max Rayne, Harold Samuel, Maurice Wohl, Bernard Sunley, Nigel Broackes, John Ritblat, Godfrey Bradman, Stuart Lipton, Tony Clegg, Sir John Hall, Trevor Osborne, the Richardson twins, the Beckwith brothers, the Reichmann family. Any one of them is better known than businessmen who built enterprises which have added rather more to human knowledge and happiness.

Politicians, trade unionists, architects and journalists have hammered their deeds into the public consciousness, and spat on the fortunes they assembled from the destruction of picturesque high streets, bustling markets and medieval town centres. When Fenston demolished the St James's Theatre in 1957, Vivien Leigh was dragged screaming from the gallery of the House of Lords after interrupting a debate to protest. When Harry Hyams – described by

Oliver Marriott as the 'Howard Hughes of British business' – left Centre Point empty for years, waiting for its value to rise, it was a national scandal.[78] Today, a charity for the homeless has adopted the name.

The 1980s saw the rise (and occasional fall) of a new generation of property entrepreneurs. They ranged from urbane Harrow– Cambridge professionals such as the Beckwith brothers to genuine working-class heroes – the Richardson twins (the 'new Earls of Dudley') and Sir John Hall (now the owner of Wynyard Hall, once seat of the Marquess of Londonderry). The Beckwiths showed uncanny foresight in selling their company, London and Edinburgh Trust, to a Swedish mutual insurance company just as the market peaked in 1990. They collected £40 million apiece. Tony Clegg, who turned a textile company called Mountleigh into the most successful property trading business in Britain, had long since retired by the time the company collapsed in 1992. Elliott Bernerd, another successful property trader, sold out early enough to return to the property market as a developer in the mid-1990s. Others were not so lucky. Trevor Osborne, a former Middlesex County Council surveyor, came close to selling Speyhawk to the Swedes in the summer of 1990 but the deal fell through. 'Sir John,' he told the chairman of Barclays Bank a year before his company collapsed with debts of over £350 million, 'we owe you more than we can ever repay.'[79]

Godfrey Bradman, the most intriguing of the developers of the 1980s, also lost his company in the recession of the early 1990s. Twenty years earlier he was an ingenious tax accountant, and later the source of a £2.4 million offer to persuade coal-miners not to strike. A vegetarian teetotaller, he has deployed his modest fortune in a variety of causes related to his interests in health and hygiene. He has funded battles against the use of CFCs, cooling systems which incubate Legionnaire's Disease, and abortion. He has also chaired Friends of the Earth, presided over the Society for the Protection of the Unborn Child, and bankrolled the campaigns of the victims of the Opren anti-arthritis drug and the supporters of Freedom of Information, Parents Against Tobacco and CLEAR, which sought the removal of lead from petrol. But he will be remembered for Broadgate, a gigantic office development on the former shunting yards of Liverpool Street station: the most successful property development in the City since the Second World War.

The Eighties Property Boom

Broadgate is one of two developments which will always be associated with the vaulting confidence of the property boom of the 1980s. By the time it was opened in 1991, it had ruined Bradman and infected his co-developer

Stuart Lipton with financial maladies which obliged him to sell *his* company to John Ritblat of British Land, the most prominent survivor of the property crash of 1974. Rosehaugh, the company Bradman headed, finally went bust in December 1992.

Ironically, Broadgate is now an unqualified financial triumph, owing much to its location on the northern fringes of the City, but more to its utilitarian construction. Its buildings have furnished investment banks with the prairie-like dealing rooms they crave. Lipton was reluctant to accept this, arguing that Broadgate was good architecture as well as good business. But the character of Broadgate owes more to the accountant in Bradman than the artist in Lipton. What art there is, is the servant of business. In that sense, it is a fitting monument to the spirit of the age. The weakness of the other great symbolic development of the eighties' property boom was animated by an equally utilitarian spirit. Its weakness was its location.

Canary Wharf is named after a warehouse for the storage of tomatoes from the Canary Islands. Its transformation during the 1980s and 1990s into American-style office blocks, housing refugees from the high rents of the City a few miles to the west, began in the fertile minds of Archibald Cox and Michael von Clemm. Cox was then chairman of Morgan Stanley International, and von Clemm of another investment bank, Crédit Suisse First Boston (CSFB). In 1984 the planning restrictions of the City forbade buildings of the size and type they needed to house securities dealers and their electronic paraphernalia, and the rents charged by the owners of the few suitable buildings in the Square Mile were exorbitant. This seemed to provide an opportunity to turn London Docklands into a downmarket version of the City.

In June 1985 a Morgan Stanley–CSFB consortium acquired an option over a seventy-one acre site at Canary Wharf. The basic outline of the development which now stands there was drawn by the splendidly named G. Ware Travelstead, a Texan property developer. Unfortunately, his backers pulled out of the project before a single brick was laid. They had balked at the cost, then set at £3 billion, and at the prospect of ruthless competition from the City. In March 1986 the Corporation of London, alarmed by the threat emerging at Canary Wharf, loosened its planning restrictions. A further eleven million square feet, equivalent to a quarter of the office space previously available in the City, was released. Between 1988 and 1992 the Square Mile and its environs became a giant building site. In the ten years which followed Big Bang in 1986, one third of the City of London was redeveloped.

In the middle of this period, the Canary Wharf development acquired a new parent in the shape of Olympia and York. The company was the successor to the Olympia Tile Company founded in Toronto in the 1950s by a Jewish Hungarian refugee from Vienna named Ralph Reichmann. The York stemmed from a property development business founded in the same city in the 1960s by his brothers Albert and Paul. By the time they took charge of Canary Wharf, the Reichmann brothers had developed a formidable reputation for successful developments in unlikely locations. They did indeed complete one third of the vision of G. Ware Travelstead before Olympia and York collapsed under $15 billion of debt in 1992. Their spectacular demise left Canary Wharf in the control of the eleven banks which had agreed to fund the project. They managed to steer it out of administration (but were still owed £770 million) via a holding company named Sylvester Investments (so called, in what passes for humour in banking parlours, after the cartoon cat that chases Tweety-Pie, the canary).

Against all expectations, and thanks to greatly improved road and rail links, Canary Wharf continued to be built and to attract a steady stream of quality tenants. The Reichmanns, in conjunction with others, bought the development back for £800 million in October 1995. Months later, Docklands achieved the ultimate accolade of success; South Quay was blown up by the IRA. The message, which marked the end of the IRA ceasefire, was not lost on the beleaguered Major government. Nor was it lost on the Corporation of London, which was at one stage encouraging Trafalgar House to build a striking Millennium Tower to outdo the fat pencil at Canary Wharf. By the end of 1997 the City planning authorities were so agitated about the competition from Docklands that they liberated another thirteen million square feet of space in the Square Mile for redevelopment, and the deputy City surveyor made it clear that even designated conservation areas were no longer immune to the money-men and their developers.[80]

Making Property Developers Rich

Canary Wharf, which the Reichmanns lost and regained, is a potent reminder of the cyclical nature of the commercial property business. For those who can ride the cycle, it is remarkably lucrative – of the eleven hundred people who appeared in the pages of the *Sunday Times* lists of the rich between 1989 and 1998, no fewer than one hundred and seventy-three made their millions in property trading or development. Their success reflects the singular advantage property trading and development enjoys over most other forms of commercial enterprise: gearing. Office blocks are expensive to build, but banks are willing to lend large sums of money against them. The Broadgate development in the City of London cost £2 billion, the developers subscribing just over £1 million in equity capital. The rest came from the banks.

'The art of development,' according to the archetypal eighties merchant-developer, Trevor Osborne of Speyhawk, 'is to develop on someone else's site using someone else's money.'[81] By the end of the 1980s property boom, bank loans secured on land and buildings totalled £41 billion. Escaping this avalanche of credit at a profit depends upon the ability of the developer to find a tenant and to sell the completed building at a price high enough to repay the bank loans and earn a margin. This is where the investment institutions have proved valuable to the property moguls. Institutions are not interested in the cost of a development, only in its ability to produce a steadily rising rental income, and they will pay handsomely for a building which promises to deliver this. 'There are few more astonishing collaborations', wrote Sampson in 1962, 'than those between the cautious insurance bureaucracies, preoccupied with trusteeship and security, and the flamboyant self-made millionaires who, by borrowing huge sums . . . have changed the face of the cities, and made their fortunes.'[82]

Of course, the gearing effect can work in reverse. If tenants and buyers do not appear, and buildings have to be sold at a loss, the bank loans cannot be repaid and the developer is ruined. William Stern, a spectacular victim of gearing in reverse, could recall its consequences vividly: 'I believed property would hold its value and I was geared up to, in round terms, £180 million . . . [The crash of 1974] was equivalent to walking out of the house and, before you reach the corner, there is an earthquake. It was not capable of being foreseen. Some buildings were sold soon afterwards at 40 per cent of their previous values and sites for only 20 per cent or so.'[83] Cyclicality is intrinsic to property development. Developers have to undertake hugely expensive projects on the basis of their best guess at demand three to five years ahead. This would lead to uncomfortable lurches from dearth to glut even if banks were not egging developers on with oceans of credit.

Gearing lays a downward swing of the credit cycle on top of the downward swing of the property cycle, greatly accentuating the amplitude of both. Though the 1990s property slump was exacerbated by government policies which inflated the supply of land for development – the deregulation of planning, and the creation of enterprise zones and urban development corporations free of the usual restrictions – banks seem to have a congenital weakness for bricks and mortar. In many cases, the bank loans were made on a non-recourse basis. In other words, if disaster struck, the banks had recourse to the building only and not to the assets of the developer. 'The ability of banks to read investment cycles,' quips Alastair Ross Goobey, 'makes institutional investment managers appear relatively clairvoyant, and the banks' enthusiasm to lend to exactly the same areas as their rivals makes investment managers look like free-thinkers; by comparison to both, lemmings seem positively rational.'[84]

The institutions entered the property development business at a remarkably early stage, initially through variants of the mortgages they had pioneered with the aristocracy. Sun Insurance advanced £20,000 to Thomas Cubitt (the early Victorian developer of Belgravia and Pimlico) in 1827. It was secured on property around London, and backed by an assurance from Cubitt that he would also insure the buildings with the company.[85] The Guardian, the London and the Phoenix all advanced Cubitt mortgages on similar terms.[86] The London and the Phoenix bankrolled other developers, and the Royal Exchange helped to fund the building of Regent Street by John Nash and the Crown Estate by advancing £300,000 in two tranches at 5 per cent (plus the usual requirement to insure with the Royal Exchange).

Equity investment was much slower to develop. Life offices bought ground rents occasionally, but only as a trouble-free investment requiring little or no management. The Prudential opened an Estate Account to manage its property investments as early as 1864.[87] But most of the assets it managed were either leases of unwanted space in its own branch offices or mortgaged properties where the company had foreclosed. Mortgage finance remained the staple method of investment in property until the Cult of the Equity became properly established in the 1950s.

Much of the ribbon development of the inter-war years was funded by institutional mortgages advanced on blocks of flats and shopping parades in the expanding suburbs. The 1930s saw a flat-building boom, financed by mortgages from the likes of Eagle Star and the Royal Liver. Sir Cyril Black, the teetotalling prude, Conservative MP and laird of Wimbledon, was one whose fortune stemmed from running up cheap apartments for the middle classes between the wars. Dolphin Square, built by Costains in the 1930s, was at its completion the largest block of flats in Europe. The Prudential at one stage owned twenty-five blocks of flats, and countless more above the shops and offices it purchased between the wars.

But the popularity of residential property was shortlived. Flats and houses tend to hold their value better than the commercial alternatives but, like most private landlords, the institutions were driven out of the residential sector by rent controls. There were other deterrents too: large numbers of properties with separate tenants are expensive to manage, and residential leases are onerous. (Unlike commercial property, residential landlords have to repair and maintain the buildings they let.) The institutions have never returned to the residential market, despite various tax inducements designed to rekindle their enthusiasm.

After the war, the institutions still shunned equity in property. But they did agree to purchase fixed rate bonds issued by developers, who used the proceeds to repay loans and the rental income to meet interest payments. Although the institutions were aware that increases in rent (or the value of the building) would accrue to the developer, and tried with occasional success to lay claim to a share of its increase, they were slow to press their case. 'We supply the money,' claimed an institutional investor to the Institute of Actuaries in 1961, 'and I don't see why they should make the profit.'[88] But, on the whole, they did.

As lending became prohibitively expensive in the late 1950s and early 1960s, and developers could not raise a bank loan, they had to invite the institutions to take a direct equity stake in large-scale office developments for the first time. They sold completed buildings to institutional investors, who then leased them back to the developer in exchange for a fixed rental income. It was during these years that one of the most extraordinary features of the commercial property market became commonplace: the twenty-five year lease with *upward only* rent reviews every five years. This extraordinary device is entirely the product of institutional pressure for protection from the ravages of inflation. One of the main obstacles to institutional investment in property in the 1950s was the prevalence of ninety-nine-year and even nine hundred and ninety-nine-year leases with no provision for rent review, allowing tenants to occupy properties for sums made nonsensical by inflation. To the extent that it enabled institutional landlords to live with inflation, the upward-only rent review was an integral part of the Cult of the Equity. But the homogenisation of the High Street is its most lasting effect: small retailers cannot compete for space with giant multiples willing to sign long leases on such onerous terms.

Institutions liked the idea of an investment income which would keep pace with rising prices, and tenants were prepared to pay as long as their incomes kept ahead of prices. This ceased to be the case in the early 1990s, when upward only rent reviews became highly unpopular with retailers in particular. In May 1993, the government was driven to publish a consultation paper on the need for reform. Under the threat of legislation, the property industry agreed in 1995 to publish a voluntary Code of Practice. There is some evidence that leases are getting shorter, but the upward-only rent review remains a standard feature of the institutional market.

The upward-only rent review is a near-perfect example of the harm done to the allocation of resources by inflation, even of modest proportions. Institutional savings which should have flooded into productive industry were diverted into purchasing rental incomes secured against rising prices. It is true that even upward-only rent reviews cannot overcome economic reality, but if a tenant failed the institution still owned the property. Unlike shares, where dividends are paid semi-annually in arrears net of tax, rents are paid quarterly in advance without deduction. Life offices found twenty-five year leases a good match for twenty-five year endowment policies. Pension funds, which pay no income or capital gains tax, were spared the trouble and expense of reclaiming taxes paid on dividends. But the chief attraction of commercial property to pension funds and life offices in the 1960s and 1970s was its ability to hold its value in an age of inflation.

Debauching the currency was not the only way in which successive governments stoked the property booms they later came to deplore. The Second World War had damaged or destroyed over three million properties, a large proportion of them in London.[89] When the war ended, there was a huge shortage of property, and a shortage of money to replace what was destroyed, but the shortages of both were exacerbated by three deliberate acts of policy. The first was the maintenance until 1957 of the tight rent controls introduced in wartime. The second was draconian planning regulations in the Town and Country Planning Act of 1947, a measure which came as close to the nationalisation of land as Britain has ever known. The third was the imposition of a 100 per cent tax on the gains from property development (not lifted until 1953). There was also a great shortage of building materials, the distribution of which was controlled by licensing until 1954. A large mismatch between supply and demand is precisely the circumstance in which fortunes can be made, and they were.

'It's really quite simple,' Jack Cotton said in 1962. 'At one end of this table is an insurance company, which wants to invest its money, or a big concern looking for a safe investment for its pension fund. At the other end is a company we are associated with ... which wants money for development. And there, in the middle, sits Jack Cotton, who brings them together and works it all out.'[90] He created the biggest property company in the world, City Centre Properties, with the Pearl, the Legal and General and the Prudential as it biggest shareholders. Cotton sold his stake to Isaac Wolfson in 1963 for a fabulous sum.

The deal between Cotton and his institutional backers was the most brilliant of a series of partnerships formed between property developers and life offices. The Co-operative Insurance Society helped Harry Hyams to make his fortune; the Eagle Star helped the Freshwater family to become the biggest residential landlords; and the Commercial Union bankrolled Nigel Broackes. The partnerships between developers and institutions were not, however, exclusive. Plumridge of the Pearl dealt with Sidney Mason of Hammerson as well as Jack Cotton, and Cotton worked closely with the Legal and General. Eventually the life offices began buying property development companies as well as properties and development ideas. In 1958, Norwich Union acquired shares in Leslie Marler's Capital and Counties. A year later the Prudential bought a stake in Town and City Properties – one of the most spectacular casualties of the 1974 property crash. Standard Life developed a liaison with

Hammerson, fortified by a 23.6 per cent stake and seats on the board, which has lasted to this day. (They are now the joint owners of the Brent Cross shopping centre in north London.) In 1988 the ties were strong enough to persuade the life office to protect its charge by increasing its stake at an inflated price.

In the 1970s, the insurance companies took to swallowing property companies whole. Commercial Union tried to buy MEPC, then reeling from the collapse of a proposed merger with the Hill Samuel merchant bank, but had to make do with Holloway Sackville instead. The Prudential bought Edgar Investments; Royal Insurance acquired Sterling Estates; Legal and General bought Cavendish Land; and Eagle Star took over the Bernard Sunley Investment Trust in 1981. The larger pension funds soon joined in. Cotton formed a joint development company with the ICI pension fund in July 1960, and struck similar deals with the Imperial Tobacco and Unilever pension funds. The Shell pension fund formed a partnership with Harold Samuel of Land Securities.[91] The property assets of the pension fund industry climbed from £44 million in 1957 to £330 million ten years later, and to over £5 billion by the end of the 1970s.[92] They too were buying entire property companies: the Post Office fund bought English and Continental for £95 million, and BP paid £19 million for Western Ground Rents in 1969.

The results were not always pleasing. John Plender chronicles in loving detail the large number of property investments backed by the ICI pension fund which ran into difficulties in the 1970s. The Unilever pension fund also became involved in speculative ventures with property developers in continental Europe, and the Post Office pension fund was embarrassed by the unexpected withdrawal of Sir James Goldsmith from a Paris property development. In 1980 two senior staff at the Electricity Supply fund retired early, following criticism of their management of certain property investments.[93] The fund had to write off £80 million on failed property ventures. It lost more on the re-development of the Trocadero in the 1980s.

Illiquidity and the Search for Liquidity

Mistakes are hard to put right in the commercial property business. Unlike shares and bonds, property is by its nature an illiquid investment. Commercial buildings are expensive, so there are few buyers – and once they become obsolete or even obsolescent, they are unlettable. A building can become worthless overnight if existing tenants depart. These factors make the price at which properties change hands unusually dependent on professional valuations rather than market forces. But valuations are rarely carried out more than once a year, and tend to be based on comparable properties rather than the intrinsic value of the buildings. In a rising market, astute buyers like Tony Clegg of Mountleigh or Elliott Bernerd of Chelsfield found they could make millions overnight by buying buildings and jobbing them on at a higher price a short time later.

But in a falling market, valuations prepared in a boom can look nonsensical. In 1991 Weatherall Green Smith valued the Queen's Moat Houses hotels at £2 billion. A year later, Jones Lang Wootton reckoned they were worth only £861 million. In other words, the company balance sheet shrank by £1.1 billion in twelve months. 'The back of the envelope unfortunately remains a basic tool of the trade for many valuers,' a chartered surveyor admitted in 1994.[94] By then, the Royal Institute of Chartered Surveyors (RICS) was so concerned by the inability of its members to put sensible values on commercial property that it promised to publish firm guidelines on valuation procedures. It is not clear how much this helped: the RICS valuation manual, known to the profession as the Red Book, contains no less than ten separate definitions of value, and the client can choose whichever technique suits his purpose. Bankers are still complaining that chartered surveyors do too little to alert them to the possibilities of obsolescence.[95]

The transaction costs of buying and selling buildings are also high. Chartered surveyors are not the only charge; the ubiquitous lawyer takes his cut, and bankers and accountants get involved as well. A commercial property transaction will usually cost the buyer 2.75 per cent and the seller 2 per cent before legal costs are included. At a time when the costs of dealing in shares and bonds are measured in tenths of one per cent, transaction costs of 5 per cent do not encourage institutional involvement in the commercial property markets. Another deterrent is the difficulty of creating a diversified portfolio of properties. Because they are forced to buy a relatively small number of large properties, institutional owners are vulnerable to technological change (like the need for raised ceilings to accommodate fibre optics) or alterations to planning requirements (like pedestrianisation).

There are many reasons why the institutions have steadily reduced their exposure to property over the last decade and a half, but illiquidity and transaction costs are certainly among them. At the beginning of the 1980s, property claimed around 15 per cent of new investment by insurance companies and pension funds. Today, insurance companies are investing between 5 and 10 per cent of new monies in property, and pension funds about 2.5 per cent. During two spells, in 1989–90 and again in 1993–4, the pension funds were net sellers of property.[96] The total property holdings of life offices fell from 17 per cent in 1988 to 7 per cent in 1996, and those of pension funds from 7 to 4 per cent in the same period. There is something of a crisis of institutional confidence in commercial property.

Dwindling institutional interest has forced property men to depend much more on a mixture of their own resources, bank finance, and foreign buyers. Their resources, being largely dependent on institutional interest and bank support, are meagre. The main effect of the banks, whose interest in property lurches from exuberant overlending to self-destructive underlending, is to amplify the property cycle; foreigners are a much more reliable source of funding. Until 1987, they accounted for less than one in a hundred property deals in Britain. But for the last ten years they (particularly the Germans and the Dutch) have put more into British commercial property than pension funds and insurance companies between them.

However, property men know that foreign buyers are no substitute for a

TABLE 29.5
New Money Into Commercial Property (£m)

Year	Pension Funds	Insurance Companies	Bank	Property Companies	Overseas Buyers*
1980	948	855	72	147	100
1981	847	1,074	469	97	70
1982	983	1,061	822	263	120
1983	680	865	934	83	85
1984	997	744	963	237	65
1985	590	815	1,691	344	90
1986	434	830	2,220	737	150
1987	197	832	4,005	2,401	290
1988	272	1,424	7,990	761	1,897
1989	171	1,892	10,606	1,647	3,217
1990	(660)	1,298	7,052	178	3,271
1991	485	1,665	688	1,269	1,607
1992	977	678	(1,726)	279	1,283
1993	155	274	(3,715)	1,957	2,094
1994	(325)	2,527	(2,068)	1,889	837
1995	91	265	(1,449)	1,271	1,677
1996	(735)	579	158	1,911	1,987
1997	166	1,188	3377	1,350	2,400

Source: DTZ Debenham Thorpe Research.

* Prior to 1987, foreign buyers accounted for less than 1 per cent of property transactions in Britain.

serious revival of institutional interest. This is what is driving their desperate search to make commercial property investments more liquid. The obvious solution is to buy shares in property companies, and no market in the world has as many as the London Stock Exchange: those listed soared from thirty-five worth £30 million in 1939 to a peak of one hundred and eighty-three worth £730 million in 1964.[97] At the end of 1997 there were one hundred and nineteen companies listed on the main market, capitalised at £27 billion. Paradoxically, there is too much choice: with the biggest worth only £5 billion and the smallest less than £2 million, there were too many small companies. Most British institutional investors would welcome some consolidation of the quoted property sector.

Property shares are not only fragmented; like investment trusts, they tend to trade at a discount to the assets they own. An alternative is to buy units in a property unit trust, which were invented in the 1960s for the convenience of tax-exempt pension funds (they cannot work for private investors or tax-paying institutions, since they are liable to capital gains tax on any profits).* The first was the Pension Fund Property Unit Trust (PFPUT), founded in 1966 by Norman Bowie, a partner at Jones Lang Wootton, and Cecil Baker of Hambros Bank, with the backing of the Esso and Hoover pension funds. Its success encouraged merchant banks and insurance companies to start dozens more.[98] Though property unit trusts allowed the institutions to spread their risks across more properties, they had to keep a large proportion of their assets in cash to meet redemptions.† When the market was especially weak, the only assets they could sell were their best properties, and this meant that they too trade at a discount to the value of the assets they own. Like investment trusts, the discount exposed property unit trusts to predators who sensed that the parts were worth more than the whole. Mountleigh paid £271 million to take over PFPUT in 1987, and sold much of what it acquired. The North American Property Unit Trust fell to a £191 million bid from MEPC in 1995, and Scottish Provident paid £204 million for the Fleming Property Unit Trust the same year. In each case, acquisition was followed by sales.

In the last ten years, bankers and surveyors have squandered a great deal of ingenuity on various schemes to 'securitise' commercial property. This involves breaking the rental income and capital value of properties into their constituent parts, and selling them as tradeable securities. The pages of the

---

* Retail property unit trusts are now available. The first retail funds were authorised by the now defunct Securities and Investments Board in 1991.

† Hermes, the fund management arm of the Post Office and BT pension funds, is developing a listed Property Unit Trust, which will enable investors to sell shares rather than redeem units. If there are no buyers, assets will have to be sold to redeem units.

property press have filled with a succession of acronyms – SPOTS (single property ownerships trusts), PINCS (property income certificates), SAPCOs (single asset property companies) and PICS (property index certificates) – which have done little more than chart the near-impossibility of the task. Europe and the United States, with a $130 billion market in real estate investment trusts, and Australia, where listed property trusts (ALPTs) are traded, were trawled for novel approaches to the disaggregation of commercial buildings. But every attempt at securitisation has ultimately foundered on a mixture of tax and legal complications, the intrinsic illiquidity of property, and the persistence of discounts to asset values.

The most promising area of research is said to be property derivatives, entirely synthetic instruments which would enable institutions to increase or hedge their exposure to the property market without anyone having to buy and sell the buildings. But the omens are not good. The London Futures and Options Exchange offered index-linked property futures until 1991, but they were withdrawn due to lack of interest.

Even if commercial property was securitised successfully, most of the commercial and industrial real estate scattered around the country would remain in private rather than institutional hands. Popular accounts of property booms sometimes give the impression that property developers and their institutional backers rarely stray beyond the M25. It is true that the capital and its surroundings are easily the most successful part of the British economy, giving its property markets a size and value denied to even the largest provincial cities. Provincial property invariably sells at more generous yields than large office developments in London and the south-east. Institutions naturally prefer a big building in a city like London, which offers a reassuring combination of scale, security and (in so far as it is achievable) liquidity.

Outside the capital, it is mainly the larger office buildings, giant shopping centres and business parks which offer something similar. In fact, the shopping centre is a provincial invention: two Bradford-based developers, Arnold Hagenbach and Sam Chippindale, popularised it through their chain of so-called Arndale Centres. (They built their first shopping parade at Jarrow, of all places, in 1958, using money supplied by the ICI pension fund.)[99] Not until the 1970s was institutional money, in the shape of Standard Life, drawn into a major shopping centre development in the south-east, at Brent Cross in north London. But their generous rent rolls have now made them an integral part of the average institutional portfolio. Capital Shopping Centres is now one of the biggest property companies in the country, but funds buy them directly too. Fort Dunlop, the big new retail park outside Birmingham, is owned by AMP Asset Management, Clerical Medical and the British Airways pension fund.

Two of the mega shopping centres of the 1980s and 1990s were also the work of regional developers, though both now belong to metropolitan property companies. The Richardson twins built Merry Hill and Sir John Hall developed the Metrocentre at Gateshead. The Manchester-based property company, Peel Holdings, introduced institutional investors to the joys of the edge-of-town retail warehouse in the 1980s. Landscaped light industrial estates – or business parks, as they have become known – were pioneered at Stockley Park near Heathrow, where the Universities Superannuation Scheme put up £50 million. The Electricity Supply pension fund financed the curiously named Aztec West site between the M4 and M5 motorways in Bristol.

The institutions also acquire exposure to property when they buy shares in commercial and industrial companies. Most sizeable businesses own factories, warehouses, offices and greenfield sites of various shapes and sizes all over the country. The Department of National Statistics valued industrial and commercial buildings in Britain at over £300 billion in 1996, of which roughly two thirds belonged to the corporate sector. Less than one tenth of this enormous sum is reflected in the market capitalisation of the property companies listed on the London Stock Exchange.[100] In other words, at least £9 in every £10 worth of real estate in Britain is owned by industrial and commercial companies rather than property specialists, and property of various kinds makes up between one third and two fifths of the balance-sheet assets of the PLCs.[101]

Most companies are maladroit at managing their property, which they tend to regard as an evil necessity rather than an asset to be exploited. Until recently most did not think about property from one year to the next unless, as in the mid-1970s, they needed to raise cash urgently by sale and leaseback deals with the institutions.[102] This indifference is one reason why landlords were able to get away with upward-only rent reviews. The threat of being taken over has encouraged many companies to manage their property more aggressively, and privatisation has had a similar galvanising effect on those which previously languished in the public sector.

Overseas Investment

In its ability to create ill-feeling, property is unrivalled. But one other form of institutional activity shares its ability to generate controversy: investment abroad. Throughout the 1980s, institutional investors which bought shares in foreign companies, or bonds denominated in a foreign currency, were accused of starving British industry of investment, exporting jobs and generally behaving unpatriotically. Arthur Scargill's major complaint in 1984 was that the Coal Board pension funds were investing in foreign rather than British companies, and throughout the 1980s the Labour Party was committed to the reintroduction of exchange controls and the direction of investment. Hostility to overseas investment has subsided since, as other countries have gradually liberalised their regimes.

It was scarcely an issue before it erupted in the early 1980s, because purchases of foreign securities were subject to exchange control from 1939 until 1979. Admittedly, investment abroad still took place: the staff pension fund of the Bank of England, responsible for operating exchange controls, had 15 per cent of its assets invested abroad before exchange controls were lifted.[103] But it was not easy to invest abroad because the authorities were anxious not to undermine the stability of the pound by allowing institutional investors to sell sterling for foreign currencies. The composite insurance companies and the Lloyd's insurance market were obliged to apply for special licences to hold the foreign currency assets they needed to match overseas liabilities. Other institutional investors had to apply for a slice of a special pool of foreign currency controlled by the Bank of England, paying a fluctuating 'premium' for the privilege. If they sold foreign currency securities purchased with funds from the pool, they had to convert a quarter of the proceeds back into sterling.

The only other way an institution could raise foreign currency to buy overseas investments was to retain foreign currency earnings abroad. This was always an option for an occupational pension fund attached to a multinational company like ICI or Unilever. Borrowing in an overseas capital market was less attractive. On the whole the institutions did their patriotic duty; ahead of the devaluation of the pound in 1967, most dutifully obeyed the instruction of the prime minister not to increase investments abroad. Ironically, doing their duty did more harm than good. Interest payments, dividends and capital gains on foreign currency assets make a large contribution to the balance of payments. One analyst has estimated that overseas capital gains alone exceeded £80 billion in the 1980s, which was more than enough to offset a cumulative current account deficit of £17 billion.*

Scargill had a point, however. Institutions would not invest abroad if they did not believe that foreign companies (and economies) would be more profitable. To that extent, the institutions do favour foreign industry over British companies. But most fund managers who invest abroad are seeking

---

* This estimate includes direct as well as portfolio investment abroad. Direct investment abroad consists largely of the investment by British companies in their foreign subsidiaries; assets of this kind tend to increase in value over time, creating capital gains for their British-based owners. See Cliff Pratten, *Overseas Investments, Capital Gains and the Balance of Payments*, Institute of Economic Affairs, February 1992, p. 10. See also *The Economist*, 30 May 1992, p. 30.

TABLE 29.6
Overseas Portfolio Assets of the United Kingdom (£bn)

	Assets*	Liabilities†	Net Assets
1979	12.6	10.4	2.2
1980	19.1	11.8	7.3
1981	25.8	12.3	13.5
1982	40.9	15.2	25.7
1983	59.7	18.2	41.5
1984	84.3	21.9	62.4
1985	99.3	33.0	66.3
1986	140.1	48.9	91.2
1987	112.9	67.9	45.0
1988	145.6	86.6	59.0
1989	215.2	110.7	104.5
1990	189.6	109.6	80.0
1991	240.9	135.0	105.9
1992	302.9	181.9	121.0
1993	438.8	257.4	181.4
1994	401.6	269.9	131.7
1995	472.4	316.4	156.0
1996	521.9	354.1	167.8
1997	574.3	415.3	159.0

Source: Office for National Statistics, UK Economic Accounts 1993, Fourth Quarter, Tables B14 and B15; UK Economic Accounts 1997, Second Quarter, Tables B18 and B19; UK Balance of Payments, Table 8.1.

* Portfolio investments abroad belonging to UK investors.
† Portfolio investments in the UK belonging to foreign investors.

to reduce risk rather than enhance returns. By spreading their money across a range of markets, they can to some extent insulate their portfolio from the ups-and-downs of British companies and the domestic economy, and gain access to growing industries (such as information technology) not well represented in corporate Britain. Of course, overseas investment increases some risks as it reduces others: institutions which own assets denominated in a foreign currency when virtually all of their liabilities – in the shape of endowment policies and pensions – are denominated in sterling, are exposed to a rise in the value of the pound when they convert to the home currency. Overseas investments are also harder to value, and carry political and other risks which domestic securities do not, which explains why the overwhelming bulk of institutional funds are still invested in domestic equities and bonds. Pension funds have about one fifth of their assets invested in foreign equities, with more in foreign bonds.

But present institutional holdings of foreign securities are well below the levels of the first half of the century, when investors preferred the debt of foreign governments to the equity of British companies. It is estimated that in 1914 Britain had some £4 billion of foreign investments, from which it derived a dividend income of £200 million – more than sufficient to cover a mounting deficit on visible trade.[104] Most of these assets had to be sold to pay for the First and Second World Wars. In 1915 the Prudential alone sold forty-four thousand American bonds worth £8.75 million, partly to fund payments to the families of those killed in the war but also to ease the foreign exchange difficulties of the government. Another £7 million went in 1916. Most of the cash received was reinvested in British government debt: in 1917 the Prudential subscribed £25 million of an issue of War Loan. By the time the conflict came to an end, one third of its assets consisted of British government bonds.[105] At its rival, the Pearl Assurance, holdings of gilts increased from 1.5 per cent of the portfolio in 1914 to over 40 per cent by 1920.[106] By the end of the First World War, the government had purchased or borrowed all the American securities owned by the Commercial Union, and the company ended the war invested in nothing but government bonds.[107]

The British might have remained the first truly international *rentiers*, had the catastrophe of war not obliged them to sell their overseas assets. The Cult of the Equity might also have developed much sooner had the exorbitant cost of modern warfare not filled the great institutional portfolios with oceans of government debt. It has taken the rest of the twentieth century for the British people to rediscover both possibilities.

CHAPTER THIRTY

THE INSURANCE INDUSTRY

When people take in money today and pay it out later, it is easy to delude yourself.

NELSON ROBERTSON, general manager, General Accident[1]

To go into my local pub on Saturday night, and people would say, don't stand too close to him, he'll sell you some insurance – it was quite intrusive.

SIR PETER DAVIS, chief executive, Prudential[2]

As chairman of the Maxwell Group of companies' pension funds, I am addressing you today for the purpose of persuading you that it is in your and your family's best interests to remain a member of whichever pension scheme you are a member of in our group, i.e. the Mirror, BPCC, Pergamon or Hollis.

ROBERT MAXWELL[3]

The common strand is the complacency and arrogance that we didn't have a problem.

JOHN ELBOURNE, managing director, Prudential[4]

In 1962 an exiled South African named Mark Weinberg spent a week collecting brochures from insurance companies. Much to his surprise, not one of the people he met tried to sell him an insurance policy.[5] A great deal that has gone wrong in the British insurance industry in the last ten or twenty years can be traced to that unfamiliar experience.

In the 1960s insurance in Britain was dominated by the cautious mathematicians of the Institute of Actuaries, who hardly ever met a customer. Their boards of directors were crammed with impecunious aristocrats, superannuated admirals and descendants of the founding fathers. Actuaries and directors shared the view that any change would undermine public confidence in the rectitude and security of their company. Insurance was driven by its producers, not led by its consumers.[6]

It was an industry ready to be ravished by anybody who knew, in the old adage, that insurance is not bought but sold. When Weinberg loosed his commission-driven salesmen, he built a company which raced from nothing to assets of £100 million in just nine years. After selling Abbey Life in 1970, he started Hambro Life, which grew even faster. Weinberg became rich, and joined the ranks of the Great and the Good. From that lofty position he wove his ideas of commission-driven salesmanship into the constitution of the insurance industry. If the industry he inherited was dominated by producers, the one he bequeathed was not dominated by consumers. Its rulers were salesmen.

Influence of Mark Weinberg

Weinberg had more in common with the rumbustious pioneers of the insurance industry in Britain than with the dull functionaries whose world he transformed in the sixties and seventies. Men like Nicholas Barbon, Charles Povey of the Sun, James Dodson of the Equitable and Thomas Bignold of the Norwich Union were all difficult, angry, impatient, and entrepreneurial. Povey sold coal, published a magazine, advocated turning London theatres into alms-houses, and hatched plans to eliminate both drunkenness and courtly living. A convicted crook (indicted for tax evasion and selling coal in short measures), he had the effrontery to denounce as swindlers the men to whom he transferred his insurance business in 1710.[7] Thomas Bignold was equally impetuous and irascible, and fell out so badly with his directors in Norwich that in 1815 he was obliged to move to London. His association with the Norwich Union ended at an angry meeting of policyholders in a Bishopsgate pub on 25 September 1818, where even his three sons voted against the purposal that he should continue as secretary.[8]

The men who succeeded to the leadership of the insurance industry in the nineteenth century were less colourful. Entrepreneurial founders gave way to those for whom suspicion of the new and reverence for the tried and trusted were the chief axioms of success in business.[9] The two most important innovations in insurance between the establishment of the Equitable Life in 1762 and the personal pensions boom of the 1980s – the assured corporate pension scheme, and unit-linked assurance – came from abroad. Assured corporate pension plans were introduced between the wars by an American company, Metropolitan Life, which had followed American industry across the Atlantic.[10] Unit-linked life policies were the innovation which took Mark Weinberg to fame

and fortune. Unlike a traditional life policy, which offers a sum fattened periodically with annual or terminal bonuses, the value of unit-linked life policies
fluctuates in line with the value of the unit trusts in which the premiums are
invested. Weinberg emphasised investment rather than insurance.

The new product had the happy knack (until Nigel Lawson abolished life
assurance premium relief in 1984) of making the units tax-exempt as well.
This gave them an advantage over ordinary unit trusts and traditional life
policies, in that they offered not only life cover but tax-deductible premiums.
The combination proved successful enough for Weinberg to sell Abbey Life
(the name was invented, to sound old and respectable) to an American buyer
three years after it was founded.* The second life assurance company he
started was sold after fourteen years to BAT Industries. The established
insurance companies paid a heavy price for their conservatism.[11]

The Stagnation of the Insurance Industry

By the time Weinberg came to England, the British insurance industry had
stagnated for a century. Companies were steered not by entrepreneurs or
even managers, but by a combination of cautious actuaries and wealthy aristocrats. In the Victorian period, when company directorships were more or less
synonymous with fraud, it was argued that directors with no independent
means might want to enrich themselves rather than make the policyholders
rich. The poverty of this argument was accurately lampooned by W. S. Gilbert
in *The Gondoliers*:

> In short if you'd kindle
> The spark of a swindle
> Lure simpletons into your clutches
> Or hoodwink a debtor,
> You cannot do better
> Than trot out a duke or a duchess.

The cynicism can be overdone. At the University Life Assurance Society,
formed in 1825 to sell life cover to Oxbridge graduates, directors were

---

* Abbey Life was sold initially to a joint venture between Georgia International Life and ITT.
ITT bought its partner out in 1970. The company is now owned by Lloyds TSB. Hambro Life
was started by Weinberg with Hambros Bank in 1971. It was sold to BAT Industries in 1985 for
£664 million, and renamed Allied Dunbar. It now belongs to Zurich Insurance. In the 1990s,
Weinberg started a third life assurance company in conjunction with Jacob Rothschild, J. Rothschild Assurance, in which the Prudential has a one third stake.

expected to take no salary and live off their private incomes.[12] But the purpose of the titled directors on the letterhead – to boost sales – was plain.

Their successors are still to be found in insurance company boardrooms. The Duke of Westminster is a director of Royal & SunAlliance. Sun Life is chaired by Lord Douro, and the Guardian (recently acquired by Axa of France) by Lord Hambro. Lord Camoys is deputy chairman of National Provident Institution (now owned by AMP of Australia). But by comparison with a generation ago the insurance industry is now largely the preserve of professionals who rely more on junk mail and pushy salesmen than social deference. There is not a single toff on the board of the Norwich Union today. Yet in the early 1960s it abounded with figures such as Sir Hughe Knatchbull-Hugesson and Charles Mott-Radclyffe. They were parties to one of the greatest *faux pas* in British business history in 1963, when the board sacked one of their number for being Jewish. Lord Mancroft, a highly respected politician and businessman, had connections with Israel which were said to be costing the Norwich Union valuable business in the Arab world. Even in 1963, kow-towing to Arabs by sacking a Jew seemed bigoted and cowardly. A furious public row developed, which ended in the board being forced to admit its mistake and offer Mancroft his seat back. Understandably, he declined.

The real victim of the Mancroft affair was Sir Robert Bignold, the president of the company, who resigned shortly afterwards. The fact that a great-great-grandson of the founder was still running Norwich Union one hundred and fifty-five years after its foundation spoke volumes about the sclerotic condition of the insurance industry when Weinberg set up Abbey Life. Jobs were virtually hereditary. Four generations of Laurences served the London Assurance and four generations of Brownes the Westminster.[13] The Anson family had an honorary seat on the board of the Clerical Medical from the time the Earl of Lichfield sold the company its headquarters in St James's Square in 1856. George Nathaniel Curzon was a director until he became viceroy of India in 1898.[14] At the Royal Exchange Assurance – which, like the London Assurance, had relied since its inception on aristocratic patronage – Lord Bicester served as a director for sixty-two years, from 1894 to 1955, finally retiring when he was eighty-seven. When the chairman of Britannic Assurance died in harness in 1956, it was his thirtieth year in the top job. His successor had joined the company forty-five years' earlier, and he was succeeded by the son of his predecessor.[15]

Outsiders were unknown at the head of a company. Richard Gamble, the British Airways executive recruited to run the Royal in 1990, was the first outsider ever appointed to a top job at the company, as was David Prosser, who succeeded Joe Palmer as chief executive at the Legal and General in 1990. The Guardian did not appoint an outsider to any top job until it was in its two hundred and seventieth year, and certainly not as chief executive until John Robins joined in 1994. Women were even rarer than outsiders. In 1975 the National Provident finally removed the requirement that its directors be what the corporate constitution described as 'male members'.

The Insurance Disasters of the 1980s

The appointment of women and outsiders to top jobs at the end of the 1980s was a belated recognition by some of the largest and best-known insurance companies that they had reached the limits of their competence. When the Royal and the Sun Alliance merged in 1996, the deal was portrayed as a bold and far-sighted triumph of commercial logic which would create an insurance company capable of competing on the world stage. It was more like the final round between two horizontal heavyweights. Six years earlier, each had announced the first loss in the history of the company. Sun Alliance wrote off £180 million in 1990, £466 million the following year, and another £130 million in 1992. The Royal lost £187 million in 1990, and £373 million in 1991. The dividend had to be dropped, the share price collapsed, and the company nearly dropped out of the FTSE-100.

The nemesis of these two companies was a humble domestic business – mortgage indemnity. At the top of the housing boom, on the threshold of a deep recession, both had insured dozens of banks and building societies against a fall in the value of houses. Royal and Sun Alliance were not alone in making such an elementary mistake; Eagle Star was so badly damaged by its mortgage indemnity business that it cost the chairman and chief executive their jobs. It would have broken any company with a less generous parent than BAT Industries. In 1991 Guardian Royal Exchange recorded the first loss in its two hundred and seventy-one year history, as did Legal and General. But the humbling of the Royal and the Sun Alliance symbolised the end of flaccid management and failure to compete in British insurance.

When the Royal acquired the Liverpool, London and Globe Insurance Company in 1918, it created the largest composite insurer in the world.[16] As recently as the 1960s the Royal was the largest insurance company in Britain, and one of the biggest companies in the country: its market capitalisation exceeded even that of the great Prudential Assurance. Sun Alliance yielded nothing to the Royal in terms of prestige. It was founded by Rothschilds and to a large extent run by them since 1824. When the Alliance merged with the Sun in 1959, it allied the oldest name in British general insurance with the most prestigious. The company later devoured a trio of other great and innovative names – the London (1965), the Phoenix (1984) and Swinton

Insurance (1993). When the chairman, Lord Aldington, was libelled in a book by Nikolai Tolstoy, the idea of refusing to pay for his lawyers was unthinkable.[17] Sun Alliance and its directors were part of the Establishment. Subsidising a libel action launched by the chairman was also a trifle by the standards of the average insurance company in the 1980s.

In finding ways to spend money unwisely, their ingenuity was inexhaustible. No disaster was more typical or more complete than the decision of several leading composites and life offices to invest in chains of estate agents. Reared in a culture where market share (rather than profit) was the measure of success, the insurance companies assumed that house-buyers would be a captive audience for endowment policies and house and contents cover. The Prudential began buying estate agents in 1985, and built up a chain over eight hundred offices long at its final extent. The average price per shop was £250,000. It eventually cost Prudential shareholders £340 million to sell or close the lot. The Royal assembled an estate agency business of similar size at a cost of over £200 million, which struggled to make money even after a drastic pruning of the network. In September 1990, only weeks before the Prudential announced it was pulling out of the estate agency business, Scottish Widows paid £48.3 million for nearly one hundred and fifty outlets in the Midlands and London.[18] In 1996 the remnants of the chain were sold for £3 million.[19] Don Shore, deputy managing director of life products at Royal Insurance, was invited to comment on securing new outlets for insurance by buying estate agencies. 'It would have been cheaper', he said, 'to pour the money down the drain.'[20]

Estate agents were not the only extravagance. The return of Commercial Union to the American market bore impressive witness to the Bourbon-like qualities of its management. 'To go into America and do a large fire business,' explained John Trotter, the chairman of the company in 1905, 'is a very dangerous thing for anybody who has not got a long purse.'[21] The company was then paying the bill for its reckless expansion in the United States in the last quarter of the nineteenth century. Yet Commercial Union returned to lose money in the 1920s and the 1930s, and again in the 1970s and the 1980s. One of the few memorable advertising slogans in the history of the insurance industry ('We won't make a drama out of a crisis') was not the confident claim it appeared; the advertising campaign reflected the desperate need of the Commercial Union to break out of its loss-making commercial business into more profitable personal insurance.

Its rivals did little better in foreign climes. A joint venture in the Italian insurance market made Guardian Royal Exchange look fabulously go-ahead (and *communautaire*) in 1989, but within a year it had became an embarrassing and expensive accident. A year earlier, the management of the General Accident of Perth suddenly threw off the incubus of a century of Scottish conservatism. In the previous one hundred years, the company had made one domestic acquisition. But in 1988 its managers splashed out £264 million on a 51 per cent stake in the NZI Corporation, an insurance company based in New Zealand. Its banking operations immediately delivered a nasty loss, forcing General Accident to buy the rest of the company too. Eighteen months and one chief executive later, the company closed down what was left.

'Insurance companies tend to be such drab, hierarchical institutions,' said the managing director of Royal Insurance in 1987, at the start of a major restructuring of management which saw the company recruit a cadre of inexperienced and incompetent insiders who more or less broke it. 'We want business people here. That's part of the change I would like to see.'[22] The half-a-billion pounds the new generation wrote off in 1990 and 1991 was not what he had in mind. It cost him his job, and Richard Gamble was prised from British Airways to clean up the mess. He was surprised to find his predecessors had placed greater emphasis on reducing the expense ratio (costs as a percentage of premium income) than increasing the profits. Since the expense ratio was easily reduced by writing new business, the Royal did not pay much attention to profitability. 'I was horrified when I came into this business,' Gamble said two years later, 'and found it so driven by market share.'[23]

Lack of Competition

Gamble should not have expected otherwise. Like the clearing banks, the insurance companies did not face effective competition until the 1980s. Their quest for revenues, like their Parkinsonian management hierarchies and unionised workforces, was a symptom of an industry packed with companies which knew nothing of the fear of failure.

Two companies – Royal Exchange and London Assurance – shared a monopoly of marine insurance with the Lloyd's insurance market for over a century, from 1720 to 1824. In practice, Lloyd's cornered nine tenths of all marine business, and left fire and property to the chartered companies, which put buyers of both types of insurance at a distinct disadvantage. In 1782 a group of London sugar refiners had to set up their own insurance company (the Phoenix Assurance) because existing insurers refused to cover a business which used fire. It took Rothschild money (and the support of the free trade-minded President of the Board of Trade, William Huskisson) to break the Lloyd's–chartered company duopoly in 1824.

Competition increased briefly, but it was not long before the first price-fixing arrangements were made. Tariff agreements – cartels in which all insurance companies agreed to charge the same premiums – appeared as early as the 1830s and 1840s in fire insurance. The first industry-wide tariff deal was agreed in 1842, following a period of fierce competition to insure cotton factories.[24] By 1846 fifty offices were adhering to it, and from 1860 tariffs were agreed each year by a nationwide fire offices' committee.[25] The premiums were raised to absurd levels in the wake of the Tooley Street fire of June 1861, prompting a group of London businessmen to found their own insurance company; Commercial Union.[26] The new tariffs, they complained to the Lord Mayor of London, would 'convert an extraordinary calamity into the basis of a permanent source of excessive profits.'[27] The Royal too is the product of a quartet of companies – Royal, Liverpool, London and Globe, and London and Lancashire – set up in Liverpool between 1836 and 1862 by local businessmen who refused to pay the excessive rates charged by London insurers.[28] 'Business transacted at moderate rates' was the initial boast of one of them, the London and Lancashire.[29] There followed a price war, concluded with a fresh tariff agreement encompassing the new companies as well. By 1897 the burghers of Glasgow were again looking to escape tariff rates by setting up their own insurance business, the National Insurance Company of Great Britain.[30] In the Edwardian period, agreed tariffs even spread to marine insurance after the commercial companies had attacked the Lloyd's monopoly.

Tariff agreements remained a curse until they began to break up in the 1960s and 1970s. Even in life assurance and pensions, competition was virtually unknown. Life offices which belonged to either the Life Offices Association or the Association of Scottish Life Offices (ASLO) subscribed to a maximum commission agreement which obliged them to pay the same rates of commission to all independent brokers selling their policies. When Scottish Equitable decided in the early 1980s to pay its agents a higher rate of commission, the company was thrown out of ASLO and forced to dismiss its general manager.

The commission cartel did not give bank managers, building societies and independent financial advisers an incentive to push the life assurance and pension products of one company rather than another, but simply to make as many sales as possible.[31] There was no disclosure (by either insurance companies or intermediaries) of the costs of commission until January 1995. The result was life assurance and pensions markets in which companies did not compete on price or investment performance (buyers knew too little of costs and returns to shop around effectively), only for distribution. Most life offices had networks of local branches and regional offices where intermediaries could process the paperwork. Like the clearing banks – whose branches stood foursquare in every High Street, offering identical accounts – the insurance companies made money from higher sales, not greater efficiency.

In these cartelised, non-competitive markets, customers could be treated with contempt. The simplest motor insurance claim would take weeks to attract an initial reply. Buyers of life assurance policies or personal pension plans who failed to keep up the payments, or tried to cash the policy or pension in early, usually lost all their contributions. The insurance companies knew their policyholders had no alternative. If economic conditions deteriorated, or there was a run of bad weather or a crime wave, they simply made some risks uninsurable.

Shareholders suffered too. Price cartels led to cross-subsidisation, which made it hard for insurance company managers to tell which of their products was profitable. Shareholders received miserly dividends and endured regular calls for extra capital to cover unprofitable businesses or the cost of buying another slice of the market. The share prices of the composite insurance companies consistently under-performed the rest of the stock market in what was supposed to be a growth sector. When Peter Wood, the creator of the Direct Line insurance-by-telephone business, was asked how such a simple idea could have led to such phenomenal success, he replied: 'To be average makes you good in the insurance industry'.[32]

Competition Comes – and Fraudsters

Direct Line is the most visible of a series of competitors that broke into the British insurance markets in the 1980s. Foreigners came first. Liberty Life of South Africa (headed by Donald Gordon, sometime mentor to Mark Weinberg) first acquired a stake in Sun Life in 1980. After a series of corporate manoeuvres over the next fifteen years, the company was acquired by UAP of France, who later merged with its domestic counterpart, Axa-Midi, which had bought Equity and Law in 1998. The effect was to place three British insurance companies – Equity and Law, Sun Life and Provincial – in the ownership of a single French company. In January 1999, Axa added Guardian Royal Exchange as well.

Winterthur of Switzerland bought Provident Life in 1981. The giant Allianz insurance company of Germany acquired a stake in Eagle Star in the summer of that year, provoking a prolonged battle for control of the company, which ended in the sale to BAT Industries in December 1983 for the then-breathtaking sum of £968 million. Three years later Allianz bought Cornhill, sponsors of Test cricket in England for the last twenty years. Australian Mutual Provident had bought both the ailing London Life and the Pearl Assurance by the end of the 1980s and added the National Provident Institution in 1998. Zurich Insurance bought parts of the failed Municipal Mutual in 1992, and merged with the insurance businesses of BAT Industries (Eagle Star and Allied Dunbar) in 1998. Aegon of Holland acquired Scottish Equitable in 1993. The banks and building societies followed the foreign predators. For decades, they were content to act as distribution outlets, collecting fat commissions for recommending that borrowers buy house and contents insurance when they took out a mortgage. What changed their thinking was the invention of the interest-bearing current account (which made their core banking services unprofitable), their decision to sell mortgages and, above all, the growing popularity of the endowment mortgage. At the beginning of the 1980s four out of five mortgages were ordinary repayment loans, but by 1988 four out of five house-buyers were choosing endowment mortgages. The banks and building societies resented sharing the commission they earned on the sale of endowment policies with the insurance companies and life offices, and bought or set up their own insurance subsidiaries. The Abbey National bought one life office (Scottish Mutual) and tried to buy another (Scottish Amicable). The Britannia Building Society acquired the Life Association of Scotland, the Halifax bought Clerical Medical, and Lloyds TSB bought Abbey Life. Although their methods differ little from those of traditional insurance companies – forcing existing customers to buy insurance and endowment policies with their loans – the banks and building societies are competing seriously with the likes of the Prudential and Standard Life for the first time.

However, it was not competition from foreigners or banks and building societies, or even the gradual breakdown of the tariff agreements during the 1980s, which had the biggest impact on the British insurance industry.[33] (There were always companies which refused to join the cartels: 'non-tariff' companies, as they were known.*) The real catalyst for change was technology. A mixture of cheap telephone charges, computer power and television advertising gave birth to a new breed of telephone-based, advertising-driven insurance companies such as Direct Line. The result is cheaper insurance, and a more efficient service. Contrary to popular perception, Direct Line was not the first company to sell insurance over the telephone. That honour belongs to Preferred Direct, started by Friends' Provident (51 per cent) with a group of European insurers (49 per cent) some years before. It was soon eclipsed by the peep-peeping of the wheeled red telephone.† 'Never be a pioneer,' according to Mark Weinberg. 'It's better to be second or third.'[34]

---

* Eagle Star earned its reputation for innovation early in this century precisely because it stayed outside tariff agreements. 'We've always been buccaneers,' Sir Denis Mountain, the last member of the founding family to run the company, said in 1981 (*Sunday Times*, 7 June 1981).

† Preferred Direct was sold in July 1997 to Eagle Star, which has merged it with Eagle Star Direct.

One reason Direct Line established itself so quickly was the refusal of existing insurers to compete, fearful of upsetting brokers on whom they relied for new business. When General Accident began to sell motor insurance through the Ford dealer network in 1990, it was blacklisted by independent advisers for daring to sell direct. It was not surprising that the Royal gave its direct-writing subsidiary a name (The Insurance Service) quite unconnected with its own brand. Sun Life named its direct-writing business Prospero, and Zurich Insurance chose Churchill. But the real reason for the success of Direct Line was not the half-hearted competition of the established firms. It succeeded because it beat existing providers on both price and service. By parking telephonists in front of computer screens it cut its expense ratio to 15 per cent, against an industry average of 25 to 30 per cent. By cutting out the broker, and using computers rather than clerks, it can despatch documents and meet claims in hours or days. In marketing terms, Direct Line has created a powerful, instantly recognisable and trustworthy brand name of the kind essential to success in modern business.*

This combination of instant brand recognition and cheap computer power and telecommunications has enabled telephone-based insurance companies to succeed where previous cut-price insurers failed, often spectacularly. None failed more spectacularly than the Fire, Auto and Marine Insurance Company (FAM), which left four hundred thousand British motorists without insurance cover when it collapsed in July 1966. FAM was the brainchild of one of the most outlandish figures to grace the financial pages: Dr Michael Marion Emil Anacletus Savundranayagan, better known as Dr Emil Savundra, a Sinhalese fraudster of extraordinary persuasiveness and ingenuity. By the time FAM was exposed as fraudulent, and unpaid staff set about trashing its expensive offices on the North Circular Road, Dr Savundra had fled to Switzerland. From there, he claimed he had retired from the business after selling the company to its managing director: a reference to Stuart De Quincey Walker, a former marine engineer with a background in Mediterranean shipping. Walker was the fall-guy, Savundra claiming he was a drunk who had squandered the revenues of FAM on the purchase of a nudist colony at Hastings.

But it was always clear that Savundra was the principal character in the fraud. He was an established international fraudster by the time he secured his operating licence from the Board of Trade in 1963,[35] having profited from scams involving oil to Red China and coffee from Costa Rica. He had served

---

* Some of the established insurance companies' brand-names are now tainted by the personal pensions scandal, giving brands established in other fields an opportunity to get into financial services. Marks & Spencer, Virgin and Kwik Fit are finding that their brands enjoy a degree of public trust which the best-known insurance companies forfeited in the personal pensions scandal.

time in a Belgian jail before he turned up at the Board of Trade, but ensured that the police would have disposed of his files by publishing his obituary in the Belgian press.[36] He paraded an exaggerated respect for all things British, and used his money to purchase the support of influential MPs and aristo-crats. (He made a cameo appearance in the Profumo Scandal as the 'Indian doctor.') Savundra bought a mansion on millionaires' row in Hampstead, a country retreat on the Thames, boats and a fleet of cars – two Aston Martins, a Rolls-Royce and a Jaguar. But neither wealth nor influence counted for anything when his fraud was exposed.

When he returned to England in 1967 to face his creditors, he ostentatiously registered as unemployed, and invited himself on to *The Frost Programme*, where he delivered a performance of breathtaking arrogance before an audi-ence consisting largely of former FAM customers. The natural hostility of the audience allowed Frost to savage him. 'I'm not going to cross swords with the peasants,' protested Savundra. He was arrested after the programme and jailed for eight years. Released in October 1974, he died of heart trouble two years later. In the weeks before his death he was hatching a plan to sell his wife's family estates in Sri Lanka to the American military for use as a nuclear weapons base.[37]

Savundra was an old-fashioned conman who thought he could talk his way into and out of anything. But if the fall of FAM owed everything to his lack of scruple, its rise owed as much to the system of price cartels which had bedevilled British insurance for over a century. All Savundra had to do to win a substantial slice of the British motor insurance market was charge half the premium of the established insurers, and pay a relatively lavish com-mission of 20 per cent to independent brokers. Such an obvious opportunity was bound to be exploited by others. The mammoth Vehicle and General, whose rates were only just below the tariff rates, crashed in March 1971 leaving twice as many motorists uncovered as Savundra had done.

Though its managing director, Tony Hunt, was already associated with one failed insurance enterprise, Vehicle and General was not fraudulent. Indeed, it was a member of the prestigious British Insurance Association. (Ironically, Savundra had tried to sell FAM to Vehicle and General in 1966, prompting Hunt to tell a Board of Trade official that he ought to 'do something' about FAM on the grounds that 'this bloody rogue Savundra . . . [is] queering the pitch for the real pioneers'.[38]) But the actuarial methodology of Vehicle and General – selecting good risks, offering high no-claims bonuses to deter claims, and under-reserving – was fundamentally unsound, and proved uncompetitive when the motor cartel collapsed in 1969. By the end, it was paying motor claims by borrowing from its life funds. Typically, the insurance establishment had failed to notice anything was amiss until too late. 'While

... the company were at one time sailing pretty near the wind, there now appears to be a genuine desire to go "respectable",' was how the chairman of the British Insurance Association assessed Vehicle and General shortly before its collapse.[39]

A Brief History of Insurance Frauds

Insurance has always had an understandable attraction for gamblers, fraudsters and crooks: people pay cash in advance, and receive nothing in return save a paper promise to pay an unspecified sum if something unfortunate happens. The queue of insurance frauds stretches from the promoters of the West Middlesex General Annuity Assurance Company of the 1830s to the six bogus insurance companies fingered by the Department of Trade and Industry in 1993. Savundra did not improve on the techniques of either. The fraudsters of 1993 simply placed advertisements in the newspapers offering insurance at cut-price rates. The promoters of the West Middlesex, whose directors made off with £200,000 of the policyholders' funds, recognised that illusion could be as valuable as reality nearly a century before Savundra was born. The founders were a journeyman shoemaker-turned-smuggler and a bankrupt tallow-chandler, and their fellow-directors were a drunk, a boy of sixteen and a porter (who acted as auditor). They had the sense, however, to put posh names on the letterhead and open an account at the Bank of England. They proclaimed a capital of £1 million and adopted a lifestyle – complete with large houses, carriage and six, servants and entertainment – to persuade the uninformed that it was true.[40] Anybody who suggested otherwise was sued for libel.

The West Middlesex became something of a *cause célèbre* in early Victorian England. Thackeray re-created it as the West Diddlesex Fire and Life Insurance Company in *The Great Hoggarty Diamond*, a story published in 1841, and Dickens lampooned it as the Anglo-Bengalee Disinterested Loan and Life Assurance Company in *Martin Chuzzlewit* (1843). A parliamentary inquiry into the West Middlesex led to passage of the first companies legislation in 1844 but did not prevent other dodgy insurance ventures. Of over two hundred life offices founded between 1843 and 1870, no less than one hundred and seventy collapsed.[41] In 1852 the manager of the Scottish Equitable told the President of the Board of Trade that most of the new life companies were 'rotten; and are, in effect, though not perhaps in design, fraudulent'.[42]

One of the biggest and best-known failures was The Albert. After growing rapidly by acquisition, it collapsed in 1869, eight years after the death of the eponymous Prince Consort. A year after its demise, parliament passed the first legislation regulating the industry. The Life Assurance Companies Act of 1870 obliged insurers to deposit £20,000 of 'caution money' in the public funds before registration and incorporation; to separate the assets of the life fund from the general business of the company; and to keep proper accounts. Two years later, this did not prevent the collapse of The European, which had grown fat on a string of forty-six acquisitions. Even if an insurance company was not consciously fraudulent, actuarial science and management skills were too crude to prevent companies running into difficulties. The finances of the Prudential remained extremely precarious until the closing decades of the nineteenth century; the secretary, Henry Harben, was obliged at one stage to take his salary in stock rather than cash. In 1864 Gladstone criticised him personally in the House of Commons, hinting that the Prudential was insolvent and probably fraudulent.[43]

That same year Gladstone, horrified by the low morals and high prices of the commercial insurance industry, passed legislation allowing the Post Office to sell life assurance. The life companies, led by Harben, lobbied successfully for its remit to be limited to assurances worth between £20 and £100. This was high enough to prevent its damaging the life companies, and ensured the long-term failure of the Post Office scheme.[44] By the time the scheme was closed in 1928, the Post Office had sold less than thirty thousand contracts, worth only £1.72 million, of which fewer than ten thousand had remained in force; their value was less than half a million pounds. By then, the industrial life assurance companies had seventy-three million policies outstanding, worth £1.15 billion.[45] By the turn of the century the Prudential alone had ten million policyholders and Harben, once shamed in the House by the Grand Old Man, became not only rich but a pillar of respectability. He also knew something Gladstone did not: insurance is sold by salesmen, not bought at a post office.

The Expense Ratio

In 1990 the Office of Fair Trading (OFT) was pressing for life assurance salesmen to be obliged to declare how much commission they received for selling life policies. The response of Mick Newmarch, who as chief executive of the Prudential was the lineal successor to Henry Harben, is one Gladstone would have recognised.

To say that Sir Gordon Borrie at the OFT does not understand insurance would doubtless be impertinent. But insisting everyone selling insurance should show the commission they earn will discourage people from taking out investments – and so hit personal savings. At a time when all the talk is about raising the savings ratio, it's nonsense. The idea is somehow that people will pay fees for financial advice – to avoid all the bias that commission will bring. Once again, it is a romantic myth. Most of them have to be prodded into saving – and are not likely to pay salesmen or advisers to do the prodding.[46]

Newmarch knew his history. The Prudential succeeded where the Post Office did not precisely because the Man from the Pru collected the premiums in cash. Door-to-door collection was effective, but it was not cheap. Between one third and two fifths of every pound handed over to the man from the Pru was used to pay his salary and defray his administrative expenses: the 'expense ratio'.

A scheme by the Co-operative Insurance Society to sell life assurance through Co-operative stores failed for the same reason as the Post Office. By the 1880s, the society had accepted defeat and started selling door-to-door, using part-time co-operators rather than salesmen. The then chairman, William Barnett, deplored the 'paradox that working people have to pay 30 per cent more for life assurance than the middle and upper classes'.[47] The 'expense ratio' has remained the chief criticism of the industry ever since. In 1911, Lloyd George was attacked in the House of Commons for using the industrial assurance companies to collect National Insurance payments and distribute state benefits (a job they retained until 1946). He blamed the savers rather than the companies:

It is true that they are expensive, but that is not their fault. You cannot collect twopences from door to door without the expenses of administration being enormous; but the fault is not theirs. You cannot get the working classes voluntarily to insure without collection, whatever the benefit . . . You cannot get it done. This is the only machinery which has been devised up to the present for the purpose of collecting.[48]

When Sidney Webb advocated nationalisation of industrial assurance companies in 1915, his main argument was that the state would cut an expense ratio then running at 44 per cent. 'The fact that industrial assurance enables a few hundred shareholders to derive colossal profits, a few thousand directors, managers and superior officials to draw large salaries . . . does not seem to us to justify the perpetuation of so wasteful a system,' he wrote. 'We think it clear that public intervention is not only justified but imperatively required.'[49] Will Hutton thought much the same eighty years later.

The subject was revisited twice between the wars. The Parmoor Committee of 1919 discovered an industrial life assurance company, City Life, with an expense ratio of 60 per cent. It considered all the big names – Britannic, the London and Manchester, the Prudential, the Pearl and the Refuge – consumed well over 40 per cent of premium income.[50] 'It seems to be a business,' Lord Parmoor lamented, 'which you have to go and get.'[51] But he was not persuaded of the case for nationalisation. Nor was a second investigation of 1931, which found that expense ratios of 40 per cent were still common, and that only the Co-operative Insurance and the Salvation Army Assurance Society were interested in making administrative economies.[52] In 1937, Wilson and Levy put the industrial assurance expense ratio (30 per cent) at nearly six times that of the state pension (5.4 per cent).[53]

When William Beveridge came to write his Report of 1942, the expense ratio provided the clinching argument for replacing the industrial assurance companies with an Industrial Assurance Board. He thought that only public corporations could significantly reduce the costs of insuring people against the vicissitudes of life.[54]

The review of the savings industry launched by the New Labour government elected in May 1997 – initially under the generalship of Frank Field, minister of state at the Department of Social Security until the summer of 1998 – was a reminder to the great insurance companies that they operate in too sensitive and important an area to escape the threat of state intervention. An even sharper reminder was delivered by Helen Liddell, economic secretary to the Treasury, almost as soon as the new government was elected. Within weeks she had publicly criticised two insurance companies – Legal and General, and Sedgwick – for failing to understand the urgency of compensating people to whom they had mis-sold pensions. 'I am not convinced,' she said, 'by the objections of Legal and General to well-merited criticism of the industry's performance so far.'[55] The following month she named twenty-four companies, including other household names such as Prudential, Royal and Sun Alliance and Norwich Union, for the same transgression.[56]

It is estimated that between 1988 and 1994 over five million personal pensions were sold. By the autumn of 1997, six hundred thousand of those were under review, for being based on inadequate or misleading advice. The cost to the insurance industry of compensating the victims could exceed £14 billion.[57] The major life offices are unlikely to be major beneficiaries of any pensions reforms enacted by the government, and they have only themselves to blame, as one of their number has pointed out. 'It is the life assurance industry itself which has, by its unprincipled disregard for the interests of the public, earned its present appalling reputation,' said Joel Joffe.[58] The life offices dismissed such attacks; and there is certainly something of the Damascene about Joel Joffe. In conjunction with Mark Weinberg and Sidney

Lipworth, he helped to invent modern life assurance sales techniques. But Joffe has now banked his fortune, taken the chair at Oxfam, and begun to fret about the plight of the disinherited. 'The life assurance companies,' he told the *Observer* in 1992, 'have so complicated things that consumers do not know they are being exploited. They are sitting ducks . . . Higher commissions have increased the incentive for a salesperson to steer the consumer to buy an insurance policy rather than a rival savings product, regardless of the consumer's needs. Financial advice has become skewed.'[59]

Commissions

Yet these were precisely the principles on which Abbey Life, Hambro Life and J. Rothschild Assurance – the three life assurance businesses founded by Weinberg and his colleagues – were established. Weinberg never made any secret of his methods:

> Life assurance has always been a very difficult product to sell. People do not come to you. You have to go to them. And people do not want to think about death or old age. So even broaching the subject is not terribly easy. So you have got to motivate the salesmen so that they can accept lots of people saying no to them, which can be a difficult blow to take, time after time.[60]

The motivation consisted of strong financial incentives to make a sale. Weinberg companies stayed outside the maximum commission agreement, so that they could pay fat sweeteners to independent financial advisers. Like Mick Newmarch, Weinberg understood the necessity of financial incentives so well that, when he was deputy chairman of the Securities and Investments Board (SIB) in the mid-1980s, he did more than anyone to persuade the board not to insist on full disclosure of commissions paid to salesmen. He was the chief author of the extraordinary doctrine of 'polarisation', a mistaken approach to consumer protection which led to most of the problems the life assurance companies created in the 1980s, including the mass mis-selling of pensions.

Polarisation obliged banks, building societies and financial advisers of all kinds to choose between selling the products of one company or the products of all companies. Of the larger institutions, only National Westminster and the Bradford and Bingley opted not to tie themselves to a single provider, and National Westminster has since abandoned its independence. Most banks and building societies immediately reached an exclusive arrangement with a single insurance company, which they ditched for an in-house provider as soon as they could set one up.[61] Many previously independent financial advisers opted to become tied agents of major insurance companies, partly to escape the costs of complying with the investor protection provisions of the Financial Services Act of 1986. Smaller life offices, and independent fund managers, lost an important source of distribution.

The result reduced consumer choice. It also forced banks and building societies to switch their customers from the products of a possible market-leader to the products of a wholly-owned but potentially less attractive alternative. The change may have given the banks and building societies the commission on sales but it landed the customer with an investment which was often inferior. But the effects of polarisation were not merely perverse – consumers also got little protection against unscrupulous salesmen. In theory, it protected them from paying excessive commissions because all life offices adhered to an industry-wide ceiling on the maximum level which could be deducted. But this was no more than a *quid pro quo* for concealing from their customers how much the commission was.

The best protection for anybody buying a life assurance policy or a personal pension is full disclosure of commissions paid to intermediaries, and their effect on returns, or what the industry calls 'full transparency.' It would have given buyers the information they needed to choose between different life offices and fund managers, and prevented salesmen from recommending products with the highest commissions. This was precisely why the industry opposed transparency. Both the West Diddlesex and Dr Savundra built their fraudulent operations quickly by paying independent intermediaries higher commissions.[62] Even the majority of 'independent' financial advisers – who ostensibly recommend the best life policy or pension plan after a thorough and objective assessment of the costs and likely returns on offer – rely on commission from life offices to make a living. No 'independent' adviser ever recommends an index-linked gilt or Equitable Life, because neither the government nor the society pays commission to third parties. Their 'best advice' is almost always the best commission-paying life policy.

The refusal to disclose commissions was indefensible. But the insurance industry defended it with remarkable tenacity. The OFT took a dislike to the maximum commission agreement which underpinned polarisation as soon as the Financial Services Act of 1986 came into effect. In April 1988 the Trade and Industry secretary, Lord Young, told the insurance industry to scrap it by 31 December 1990. The Securities and Investments Board (SIB) introduced commission disclosure rules for the first time that year, but the insurers did their best to blunt the effects. (Commissions were not disclosed until after the sale was complete, and then only in percentage rather than cash terms.) It was not until 1993, after years of further investigations and rule changes by the SIB and a further damning report from the OFT, that the government ordered full disclosure of sales commissions and management and administration charges. Even then, the industry managed to stave off the reality until January 1995, arguing that costs were too complicated to calculate and the regulations too expensive to administer. Disclosure was not imposed on unit and investment trusts and PEPs until a year later.

It is not hard to understand why insurance companies and fund managers were shy. Once the figures were published, policyholders were staggered to know that between one fifth and one third of their contributions to the average twenty-five-year endowment were swallowed in costs (mainly administration charges rather than commission) and that it would probably be cheaper to have an ordinary repayment mortgage. In 1997 one major insurance company announced that its charges had eaten into endowment contributions so severely that many policyholders would have insufficient funds to pay off their mortgages. In the worst cases, the company agreed to make up the difference by adding £70 of its own for every £100 the policyholders had contributed.[63] A survey of the impact of charges on a typical twenty-five-year pension plan found that, in the worst case, 37 per cent of contributions disappeared in the first five years.[64] No wonder the property developer Godfrey Bradman could finance the start-up costs of his first business from commissions earned on policies on his own life.[65]

The Scandal of Surrender Values

This heavy 'front-loading' of commissions, as it is known to insurance insiders, is a nasty shock for anybody wanting to cash in a life policy or pension early. Less than half of with-profits endowments reach maturity. A 1991 SIB report found that 23 per cent of with-profits policies and 37.1 per cent of unit-linked policies were cashed in within two years of being started. Six years later, nothing had changed. In 1997, the Personal Investment Authority (PIA) estimated that one third of personal pensions and a quarter of life policies are surrendered within three years. At one industrial life company, more than two in every five pension plans lapsed within three years.[66] No policyholder cashing in a policy as early as that can expect to get even his contributions back, once the commissions are subtracted – many get nothing at all. The Treasury reckons that savers squander £250 million a year in commissions on lapsed policies,[67] and the Treasury itself probably squanders twice as much in tax relief on personal pensions which lapse within three years. One of the little-noticed features of the life and pensions scandals of recent years is that the taxpayer is subsidising the salesmen.

An OFT report of 1994 on sixty large life offices concluded that some offer such poor terms for early surrender that customers would be better off keeping their savings in cash.[68] In 1990 Hugh Scurfield, general manager and actuary at the Norwich Union, upset his fellow insurers by using his inaugural address as president of the Institute of Actuaries to attack the low values the industry placed on policies surrendered early:

> The impression given by these poor surrender values is one of indiffer-
> ence to the saver, who may want his money back even after the contract
> has run for a good few years . . . This is not the evidence of an industry
> that wishes to be taken seriously in a savings market in which there are
> an increasing number of players.[69]

Ironically, shortly afterwards the Norwich Union was attacked by the financial press over a 'return of premium' pension plan it had sold to one Rex Waring. Mr Waring had already suffered one heart attack when he bought the policy, making a return-of-premium policy highly inappropriate. When he died, his widow got £3,900: less than one tenth of the market value of the assets his contributions were used to purchase.[70]

The life offices have no real incentive to give a fair share of the common fund to people who cash in their policies prematurely or die too soon. General Accident was feted in 1993 when it became the first to guarantee the return of all premiums on an endowment policy surrendered early. It was an apt measure of how unscrupulous life offices were; few have followed its example. Salesmen and independent financial advisers sell life policies not on surren-der values but on maturity values, and low surrender values are essential to subsidise high maturity values. It is because there are plenty of league tables of maturity values but none of surrender values that cutting the annual bonus is a regular occurrence (usually justified by reference to lower investment returns expected in the year ahead) but a reduction in the terminal bonus is never adopted except *in extremis*.

On only three occasions this century – in the 1930s, the 1970s and the early 1990s – have life offices cut terminal bonuses. In the 1970s they decided not to advertise the fact that bonuses were being cut by between 40 and 50 per cent, and it was not until a disgruntled Scottish Widows' policyholder took his story to the press that the truth came out.[71] In the early 1990s a string of life offices tried to escape adverse publicity by selling unit-linked policies (whose value depends purely on market values) rather than with-profits policies (where the value of the terminal bonus is crucial). As in company pension plans, where the frozen benefits of early leavers subsidise the index-linked and final salary-related pensions of the long-stayers, savers who cash in their policies early are used quite openly to subsidise the final bonuses of those who keep up payments.

This is nothing new. It was not until 1878 that the Prudential offered so-called 'free' policies in which maturity values were reduced to take account of missed payments. Missing a payment was so common among their impoverished customers that agents were paid commission only on the *net* increase in business, not on the number of policies sold.[72] When Gladstone introduced legislation allowing the Post Office to sell life assurance, he cited the example of the Friend in Need life office. It had signed up eighty-six thousand policyholders, but eighteen thousand of them had missed a payment and lost all their contributions.[73] Even today, the life offices are so indifferent to the plight of early leavers that they have allowed a separate market in secondhand endowment policies to emerge, in which people who need to cash in their policies early can get a much better price from a third party, who can afford to keep up the payments.

This combination – front-loaded commissions and low surrender values – is one of the main reason why the hard-selling culture of the life assurance and pensions industry has proved so durable. Because they bear little or none of the cost of lapsed policies, insurance companies pursue new business at the expense of existing policyholders in much the same way as banks and building societies offer their best borrowing and deposit rates to new customers at the expense of the old. Yet overselling is the main cause of lapsed payments and early surrender – and polarisation encouraged it. The SIB found that life policies and pension plans sold through tied agents and directly employed sales forces were nearly twice as likely to be terminated early as sales made through independent financial advisers.[74] The PIA found a modest change when it investigated five years later, but essentially confirmed the SIB finding.[75] Even the Equitable Life – which has not paid commission to any third party since it turned away its first would-be commission-farmer, one Jacob Sypnut, in 1765 – was by 1997 investigating over eleven thousand suspected cases of mis-sold pensions.[76]

Selling Eighties-Style

The problem of mis-selling is not confined to tied salesmen. In fact, the unstable economics of commission-driven sales had their most spectacular impact on a firm of ostensibly independent financial advisers: the Levitt Group, which collapsed at the end of 1990. The main cause of its demise was the need to re-pay to the life offices front-loaded commissions earned on life and pensions policies not maintained when the economy tipped into recession. By the late 1980s, competition for sales was not only forcing up the size and timing of the commissions insurers were prepared to pay but making insurance companies indiscriminate about who they signed up and who collected their commissions. Roger Levitt, with his bowties, gold cuff-links and gargantuan appetite for cigars and champagne, even looked like a crook. But, as his opening line at sales meetings made clear ('I've sold £5 million of insurance – what have you done?'), he had an appetite for selling life assurance. He also had a talent for it.

Levitt seduced a string of otherwise respectable characters – including squeaky-clean athlete Sebastian Coe and a wholesome pop star, Adam Faith – into securing introductions for him among the rich and famous. It is a measure of his persuasiveness that Michael Winner, Frederick Forsyth and Lennox Lewis (none of them noted for naivety) became his clients. When the police charged him with stealing £513,000 from the novelist, Levitt protested through his solicitor that he was 'particularly concerned and unhappy about these charges because Frederick Forsyth is a close friend of his and was one of the first people to comfort Mr Levitt's wife when he was initially charged'.[77]

Most alarmingly of all, Levitt managed to persuade Commercial Union (4.9 per cent), General Accident (4.9 per cent) and Legal and General (4.9 per cent) to become shareholders in his business. Between them, the three insurance companies invested £20 million in a financially shaky and fraudulent enterprise, with a clear view to encouraging Levitt to place business with them. For this blatant violation of the spirit (if not the letter) of polarisation, the companies were later fined by Lautro.[78] Levitt was convicted of fraudulent trading and sentenced in November 1993 to 180 hours' community service. He now lives in the United States, where he works as a boxing promoter. Since convicted bankrupts are not supposed to act as company directors, the British authorities are keen to put him on trial again. 'I am not a conman, I am a very capable salesman,' said Levitt at the time of his conviction for fraud. 'I was most unlucky to lose a £150 million business.'[79]

Roger Levitt was only the most conspicuous of many life assurance salesman whose greed eventually obscured their judgment. The willingness of respectable insurance companies and life offices to risk their reputations by selling through intermediaries was comprehensible (hard-selling firms of financial advisers like the Levitt Group produced large volumes of business) but dangerous. Policies were sold not only to home-owners, but to pedestrians in the street and over the telephone to people at work. (One firm was bold enough to cold-call staff at the *Financial Times*.) By the end of the 1980s, independent financial advisers could barely keep up with the demand. One firm took to advertising for sales recruits on television.

For the life offices and insurance companies, the legacy was bitter. As the recession bit in the early 1990s, the market for life assurance contracted.[80] Schemes to guarantee domestic and commercial property values, which had earned salesmen a fortune in commissions and bonuses when the property markets were rising, proved costly when prices fell.[81] Some companies found over-stretched intermediaries had collapsed or disappeared, taking clients' money with them. Others, often recruited in haste without proper checks, turned out to be old-fashioned fraudsters.[82] When the sales boom ended in the early 1990s, hundreds of disputes broke out between insurance companies and salesmen over unpaid commissions.

Individualism is an ineradicable part of a commission-driven sales structure. A century ago the Prudential had to obtain a special Act of Parliament to force salesmen to hand back their commission books rather than keep 'walking the debit' and pocketing their share of the premiums after they had left the company.[83] As early as 1851 *Post Magazine* characterised life salesmen as 'keen fellows, sharp as needles, who would get the teeth out of your head if you were to open your mouth in their presence.'[84] In 1864 Gladstone disparaged the Men from the Pru as 'preachers and denominational missionaries, who, animated by the golden vision of 25 per cent on the premiums paid, find their way into every cottage in the country.'[85] Even the official history of Britannic Assurance confesses that their Victorian founders were 'businessmen first and philanthropists second' and that their agents were guilty of 'over-enthusiasm'.[86] In a commission-based system of remuneration, they could be no other.

'I will lead you', the founder and chairman of one firm of financial advisers is said to have told recruits, 'to the land of milk and honey'.[87] A salesman at an insurance company introduced 'seminar selling', in which he radiated friendship and objectivity by jotting notes on a pad rather than filling in a form. Another salesman described his pitch to wives: 'Back up the hearse and let them smell the flowers.'[88] In the over-heated atmosphere of the 1980s, these techniques were exploited by a breed of young people who were inexperienced as well as cynical. Recruitment was indiscriminate; turnover high. Technique was all. This is how a recruit described working on the road for Norwich Union as a commission-only salesman:

> As I had no insurance or investment knowledge, I thought I would not stand a chance of getting a job with Norwich Union. But at the first group interview it was obvious the company was happy to take on anyone who could string more than two words together and look as if they could tie a tie. Like myself, some of the other recruits seemed to be in some degree of financial difficulty. As a result, I am sure I was not alone

in being under pressure to earn a crust ... It was exactly how one imagines double-glazing salesmen are taught. We were instructed in the tricks of the trade necessary to break down customer resistance and to persuade them to sign on the dotted line.[89]

Some of the techniques – spilling beer over people in the pub to get to talk to them, or sending blank sheets of paper to wives to indicate what they would get if their husbands died – made time-share salesmen look altruistic. Training was minimal. A former saleswoman admitted to the *Financial Times* that her only qualification for selling life assurance was a 'half-an-hour test that a monkey could have passed'.[90] The rewards for success – and the punishments for failure – were even easier to understand. At one firm, the positive incentive was the right to borrow the boss's Rolex for the day. The penalty for failure was a run around the block, dressed in women's underwear or an out-size nappy.[91]

The Great Personal Pensions Scandal

This was the frenzied, commission-driven culture which was released, from 1 July 1988, on the greatest sales opportunity in the history of the life and pensions industry. From that date, eleven million employees gained the right to opt out of their occupational pension scheme to buy a personal pension. In the three months that followed, the insurance industry sold five hundred and fifty thousand personal pension plans, the Prudential alone selling well over two hundred thousand. Over a million personal pensions were sold in the first year, and a total of four and a half million by the end of 1991, when the scale of the mis-selling became apparent. But selling personal pensions between 1988 and 1990 was the easiest job in the world: for fifty years, occupational pension schemes had worked hard to make themselves unpopular.

It is often forgotten that the decision by the Conservative government to personalise pensions had its origins not in a drive towards individual responsibility and popular capitalism (though that was certainly part of it) but in the swindling of early leavers by occupational pension schemes. Norman Fowler, the Secretary of State for Social Services at the time the personal pension was conceived, had a memory of his father, who worked for the same engineering firm for thirty years. 'He had always set great store by the company pension,' his son wrote in his memoirs. 'However, he made the great mistake of not living to collect it. There was no widow's pension – only a return of contributions ...'[92]

Until 1988 those who changed jobs could not take the full value of their pension contributions with them; they had to be left behind to subsidise the pensions of former colleagues. Norman Fowler himself, on leaving *The Times* for the House of Commons, was given an unenviable choice: his contributions back, or a 1970 value pension in the year 2003. It took government legislation to secure protection for deferred pensioners (former employees who leave pension contributions with their former employer) against inflation, and then only to a ceiling of 5 per cent. The enormous scope for actuarial discretion which remains in place means that people who change jobs are still getting lower transfer payments than the combination of contributions and investment performance warrants. In a market economy, where job changes are frequent, it was never going to be hard for life assurance salesmen to persuade people of the merits of personal, portable pensions. One of them described his sales pitch: 'You get a guy and say to him, "Do you see yourself staying in the same job for forty years? How many jobs have had so far?" [You] then tell the prospective client that unless he planned to work for the same employer for the rest of his life, he needed a personal pension.'[93]

If the customer had doubts, the Conservative government helped to soothe them by promoting personal pensions vigorously as part of its remodelling of the economy. They were launched with a series of advertisements depicting people once shackled by their occupational schemes being set free to roam the labour market, coupled with an incentive to those prepared to opt out of occupational schemes – an extra 2 per cent rebate of National Insurance contributions for the first five years. This was not much in itself but, when it was added to the existing rebate offered to those who opted out of the State Earnings-Related Pension Scheme (SERPS), it enabled buyers of personal pensions to hand over to a life office up to 8 per cent of their salary without any immediate effect on their standard of living.

The chief cause of the holocaust which followed was familiar: commissions. As early as 1984, the National Association of Pension Funds (NAPF), the mouthpiece of the occupational pension fund industry, warned that it was essential for insurance companies to disclose in full the commissions salesmen earned on the sale of personal pensions. A year later, it warned in its response to a government Green Paper that 'stringent investor protection is essential if the proposals for personal pensions are to gain any semblance of public acceptability'. Its recommendations again included the full disclosure of commissions and of penalties for early surrender of personal pension plans.[94]

These arguments did not impress Norman Fowler, not least because he had invited Mark Weinberg and the Life Offices' Association to act as 'assessors' of his pensions reforms.[95] The case for transparency in commissions was unlikely to impress a former life assurance salesman and the trade body of the industry. Its self-appointed leader, the Legal and General, shocked even its fellow life offices by urging the government to encourage individuals (as well as companies) to opt out of SERPS by offering them a National Insurance rebate. In April 1984 the company published a document highly supportive of government plans. It had the Friedmanesque title, *Freedom to Choose*. An internal NAPF paper, leaked to the press, described it as 'a skilful composition designed to persuade the uninformed and inexperienced into believing that there are easy answers to a subject already made too complex by legislation'.[96]

Nobody can blame Legal and General for spotting a sales opportunity. All the life offices can be blamed, however, for failing to adjust a remuneration structure which did not pay a salesman to tell people to stay in an occupational pension scheme – even where this was manifestly the right advice. His lust for commissions saw people transferred out of the generous, earnings-related, index-linked pensions of the old nationalised industry schemes, and the government-guaranteed schemes for teachers, policemen, doctors, nurses and local government officials. Comparable benefits were not available in the private sector. Likewise, it was lust for commissions which saw people advised to opt out of company schemes, foregoing guaranteed earnings-related benefits, a measure of index-linking, and free death and disability benefits. What the buyers of personal pensions acquired was a personal investment fund, with no guaranteed return, which they could use to buy an annuity at an unspecified price some time in the future.

With an estimated forty-two thousand victims, the National Health Service (NHS) has the greatest number of people mis-sold personal pensions.[97] In a report published in December 1993, the SIB reckoned that in the first three years after personal pensions became available, *only one transfer in twenty was justifiable.* In the following two and half years, even as the regulators pressed the insurance companies to behave responsibly, the SIB estimated that nine out of ten pension transfers were made on the basis of advice which was either contrary to regulatory requirements, unsatisfactory, suspicious or actively misleading.[98] In October 1994 the SIB ordered the life assurance companies and other sellers of personal pension plans to review all those sold between 29 April 1988 and 30 June 1994. Where they found evidence that the sale was based on bad advice, they were to pay compensation from their free reserves or shareholders' funds, and they were to start with an urgent list of three hundred and sixty thousand cases who were either at or near retirement, or dead.*

The subsequent failure to act quickly in response to the SIB turned a

* The stipulation was made to ensure that the costs of compensation were met by shareholders rather than pension plan and life assurance policyholders.

serious embarrassment into a crisis for the life and pensions industry. The eventual cost of compensating everyone who was mis-sold a personal pension is put at £14 billion or more.[99] But by April 1996 the insurance companies had paid just £6.5 million in compensation.[100] Treasury figures leaked to the *Independent* in October that year showed that, after two years, twenty-six leading life offices and banks had assessed only nine thousand out of the three hundred and sixty thousand priority cases. They had resorted to every delaying tactic (including the courts). Public perceptions were not improved by the fact that the PIA, responsible for monitoring its progress, was chaired by Joe Palmer, chief executive of the Legal and General when it published *Freedom to Choose.*

'Patience is running out,' declared Sir Andrew Large, chairman of the SIB, in November 1996. He promised 'huge progress', but by February 1997 less than one in a hundred of the cases under review was resolved. By September 1997, the scope of the investigation had widened to include non-priority cases, and between one and one and a half million were still outstanding.[101] Amid this palpable reluctance to make progress Helen Liddell decided to begin shaming the life offices by naming the worst laggards. She then warned that individual directors, managers and sales staff would have to register with the PIA, and would be liable to fines, reprimands and restrictions on the type of work they could undertake if they did not speed up the review process.[102]

The Prudential Takes a Pasting

On 21 October 1997 the mighty Prudential Assurance Company was singled out by the SIB for special criticism. After listing a string of unfulfilled commitments and unmet deadlines, the Board said of the largest institutional investor in the land:

> The SIB believes that failure by the Prudential to meet an agreed target in the pensions review timetable reflects serious shortcomings in its conduct of the pensions review. The Prudential has failed, notwithstanding the resources that it has deployed in relation to the pensions review, to exercise the requisite due skill, care and diligence required of it in its conduct of the pensions review. The Prudential, on its own admission, has failed to manage the pensions review as a major project and has placed too much faith in its line managers and their reassurances. The Prudential has accepted that it has departed from the basic tenets of clarity of accountability and responsibility, and robust management information. The SIB takes the view that the Prudential's conduct, as

TABLE 30.1
Pensions Mis-selling: The Guilty Companies

Company	Priority Cases for Review	Priority Cases Further Investigation (%)	Cases Completed by November 1997 (%)
Prudential	70,800	84	40
Lloyds TSB	48,028	85	45
Co-operative Insurance	43,603	95	34
Pearl Assurance	40,863	95	43
Legal & General	35,094	62	60
Sun Life of Canada	25,850	80	29
Allied Dunbar	17,754	87	37
Britannic	17,484	84	34
Abbey Life	16,801	79	39
Barclays	16,739	65	71
Royal & Sun Alliance	15,278	90	34
National Westminster	13,849	76	43
Lincoln National	12,808	92	18
United Assurance	12,282	94	38
Equitable Life	11,054	49	70
Royal London	10,860	92	45
GAN	10,200	97	9
Sedgwick	10,175	74	41
Guardian	8,697	92	45
Windsor Life	8,279	84	21
Colonial	7,977	77	40
London & Manchester	7,826	93	31
Commercial Union	7,374	87	47
Norwich Union	7,081	71	54
Friends Provident	6,521	88	29
Standard Life	6,523	94	39
Hill Samuel	5,916	88	37
Canada Life	5,439	97	26
Midland Bank	4,740	93	46
Wesleyan Assurance	4,307	92	52
AXA Equity & Law	3,846	83	64
Albany Life	2,844	84	41
Countrywide	1,889	87	15
Hogg Robinson	1,896	67	54
Godwins	1,358	97	35
DBS Financial Mgmt.	545	98	12
Burns Anderson	413	93	26
Financial Options	276	74	29
M & E Network	269	45	68
IFA Network	229	81	47
Berkeley Independent	72	44	60

Source: H. M. Treasury, 1997.

described above, contravenes the requirements imposed upon it . . .
[by] the SIB Statements of Principle.[103]

That was about as rude as it gets when regulators are cross. But behind the
lawyerly prose of the SIB statement lay a long story of truculent behaviour
by the senior management of the Prudential in general, and by the rumbustious Mick Newmarch in particular.

The Prudential had expected to take a large share of the market in personal
pensions, and did. 'We are going,' Mick Newmarch promised, 'to take the
pension fund market apart.'[104] He was then chief executive of Prudential
Portfolio Managers. 'We can set standards and a pace that others cannot
easily keep up with,' he added. 'Everyone is going to want to sell everything
to people. So clients will want to cling to the timbers of the name they
know.'[105] He was certainly right about the pace. The Prudential sold nearly
two in every five personal pensions in the two years after the market opened
in July 1988. Newmarch was also confident that they were not being purchased
at the expense of standards. In 1990 he told the *Sunday Telegraph*:

> I found myself reading *Barbarians at the Gate* about the American
> takeover of RJR Nabisco the other day. On the outside of the book
> were what a man had called the rules of Wall Street – never play by the
> rules, never pay in cash, never tell the truth. It's a world we all know
> exists, but it's very sleazy all the same. It's easy to come over as pompous
> and paternalistic, but we are in the business of looking after long-term
> savings and not making a quick buck. The City will do itself no favours
> if outsiders get the impression investment is a get-rich-quick game with-
> out any rules.[106]

Even as he spoke, hundreds of commission-driven salesmen were making the
sales which would later give tens of thousands of 'outsiders' exactly that
impression. By 1990, the Prudential had sold eight hundred and seventy
thousand personal pensions, one sixth of the entire market. Success on this
scale encouraged Newmarch in his belief that it would be *infra dig* for the
Prudential to be regulated by the PIA, then being set up to protect private
investors. He demanded, in accordance with the status of his firm, direct
regulation by the SIB. It was a decision his successors had cause to regret.

Within three years, it was clear that the sale of personal pensions was maturing
into a major financial and political scandal. Journalists naturally concluded that
the Prudential, as the biggest single provider, might have made a few mistakes
and – even if it had not – the independent financial advisers it used might have
oversold its merits. But Newmarch would have none of it:

> An [IFA] is sorting products from a whole variety of providers on the basis of his view of the best advice for his customer. If my contract is the best in his eyes and he chooses to use it, that's presumably good. If he misuses it, I can't be held responsible for that, can I? . . . At the margin – I hope it's the margin – some companies have been uncontrolled in taking advantage of what they saw as a market opportunity, and the regulator's job is to stop that.[107]

That same month, the SIB published the results of the survey which indicated that nine out of ten pension transfers were based on incorrect or misleading advice. Newmarch took the trouble to write to the *Financial Times* to say that 'we have taken and continue to take a prudent and responsible approach to such transfers and do not accept the results of the survey apply to pension transfer policies arranged through Prudential representatives. Nevertheless we shall of course be happy to discuss any concerns our customers may have.'[108]

A few months later this message was reinforced by Steve Bee, pensions manager at the Prudential. 'We always advise against opting out of employers' schemes and we do not recommend transfers to customers,' he said. 'However, we will accept transfers if customers wish to make them and have no intention of withdrawing from the market.'[109] Until Newmarch resigned in January 1995, the company was alone among the major life offices in refusing to make financial provision for mis-sold pensions. The official explanation for his resignation was exasperation at the burden of regulation. His relations with the regulators were certainly poor.[110] When Kit Jebens, chairman of the Life Assurance and Unit Trust Regulatory Organisation (Lautro), suggested to Newmarch that lack of provision might be imprudent, there was what a leaked Lautro memorandum referred to as 'a sharp telephone exchange'.[111] A public statement was issued by the Prudential. 'We have always behaved properly with regard to the selling of pension transfers and therefore we have felt no need to make specific provisions against possible mis-selling of these products,' it read. 'No contact we have had with Lautro would indicate to us we ought to change our view.'[112]

It was not until Peter Davis took over in March 1995 that the company announced it would be setting aside money to compensate victims of pensions mis-selling. Ironically, when Lautro finished an eighteen-month investigation into sales abuses in October 1995, it decided not to take any action against the Prudential. But in June 1997 the SIB ordered the company to re-test its entire direct sales force, following a routine inspection visit, and to investigate mis-selling accusations at its Sheffield office.[113] Two months later the finance director of the Prudential (the splendidly named Jonathan Bloomer) announced that the company had doubled its provision for mis-selling to £450 million.[114] By then it was apparent that the Prudential had more cases of mis-selling to review than any other insurance company; the total exceeded seventy thousand. The number was so large that the company would never meet the self-imposed deadlines it had agreed with its regulator. SIB officials must have enjoyed drafting the press release of 21 October; but their successors at the Financial Services Authority (FSA), set up by the new government as successor to the SIB, were not content to leave it at that.

On 16 December 1997 the Prudential announced that, after missing its first two deadlines for resolving the mis-selling cases, it had managed the third. A week earlier, the company had agreed to fall into line with the rest of the industry and be regulated by the PIA. 'No pressure was brought to bear,' claimed a company executive at the time[115] – a generous interpretation of the SIB press release of 21 October. Just in case the Prudential had genuinely misunderstood its message the FSA released a second public statement about the company to coincide with the Prudential announcement. It was the most excoriating attack on a single company ever launched by financial regulators:

> The gravity, extent and nature of the contraventions identified to Prudential Assurance . . . indicate:
>
> 1. a deep-seated and long-standing failure in management which prevented Prudential Assurance from recognising its own shortcomings;
> 2. a failure satisfactorily to address and remedy defects previously identified to Prudential Assurance;
> 3. a cultural disposition against compliance which filtered through Prudential Assurance's branch offices, their managers and advisers;
> 4. that unsuitable sales have been made;
> 5. a failure to establish and maintain adequate systems, procedures and controls so as to ensure compliance with regulatory obligations. Such failing has necessitated a fundamental restructuring by Prudential Assurance in the areas of compliance and training and competence;
> 6. that Prudential Assurance had an organisational structure which allowed the cost of its own compliance arrangements to take precedence over the interests of its investors . . .
>
> The FSA is satisfied that Prudential Assurance's conduct has fallen substantially below the standards that the public have a right to expect from a regulated firm.[116]

'The Pru has had one hell of a shock,' admitted John Elbourne, managing director of Prudential Assurance. 'This is the worst experience it has had in its history.'[117]

It was not. After all, Sir Henry Harben was once denounced by the prime minister. But if the Prudential could rewrite its history, it would doubtless have preferred a fine by the PIA to public humiliation. A public dressing-down made the Prudential's new television advertisements more than usually disingenuous. They starred Peter Davis himself as the Man from the Pru, newly knighted in the 1996 New Year's Honours list for his services to training and industry. As he wandered through a downpour, and promised pensioners a beach-bound early retirement, the Prudential and its customers looked like inhabitants of parallel universes. Sir Peter thought his resurrection of the Man from the Pru would 'build on our traditional values of security, reliability and individual service, and . . . add the more modern attributes of efficiency, flexibility and investment excellence.'[118]

Paying for the Excesses

'For a salesman,' wrote Arthur Miller, 'there is no rock bottom to the life . . . He's a man way out there in the blue, riding on a smile and a shoeshine. And when they start not smiling back that's an earthquake.'[119] For the life assurance and pensions industry, that earthquake has started. The number of new life and endowment assurance policies fell from over three million a year in the mid 1980s to just one million in 1996. The number of personal pensions sold fell from well over four million in 1989 to just over half a million in 1995 and 1996. The number of people employed in the insurance industry fell by nearly fifty thousand in the six years to 1996.[120]

Among the principal victims of the shake-out was the untrained, commission-driven salesman of the 1980s. Under severe pressure from the regulatory authorities, all the major insurance companies have re-tested their sales staff to check they know enough to do their jobs. Those that failed were fired or retrained. In July 1993, Norwich Union sacked a third of its direct salesmen on grounds of incompetence. Nine months later, it was forced by the regulators to suspend the remaining eight hundred for retraining. The company was eventually fined £300,000 – then a record sum – for failing to meet industry standards in the training, recruitment and supervision of salesmen.[121] Norwich Union has now abandoned commissions, and put its salesmen on salaries; Allied Dunbar, the second creation of Mark Weinberg, has retrained its sales staff and switched them from commission-based remuneration packages to a combination of salary and annual bonuses; Sun Life salesmen now receive salaries.[122]

Most life offices have spent the 1990s atoning for their behaviour in the 1980s. Since 1991 dozens of life offices have paid regulatory fines and legal costs for varying degrees of incompetence and bad behaviour. Almost every well-known name in life assurance has committed some misdemeanour. Near the top of the PIA league table is Friends Provident, once the prince of the Quaker mutuals, now fined £450,000 for 'extremely poor progress' in sorting out its cases of pensions mis-selling. In March 1997, the Fraud Squad began investigating the possibility that some personal pensions were mis-sold deliberately rather than accidentally. Many household names have made massive provision for compensation: Lloyds Bank has set aside £165 million, United Assurance £150 million, and Eagle Star £123 million.[123]

End of Mutual Life Offices

But the pensions scandal has cost the industry more than money: it has damaged their reputation, perhaps beyond repair. How to save the life assurance industry from itself is now one of the great unanswered questions of British business. Mutual ownership is enjoying a revival in New Labour circles as an acceptable private sector alternative to the Prudential and Legal and General. But it is probably too late to bring mutuality back to life. As recently as the late 1980s, mutually owned life offices dominated long-term savings and investment in Britain just as the mutually owned building societies dominated deposit-taking and mortgage-lending. A decade on, both are succumbing to incorporated predators or to the temptation to incorporate themselves.[124]

Scottish Mutual was bought by the (demutualised) Abbey National in 1991. Scottish Equitable sold itself to Aegon of Holland in 1993, Confederation Life went to Sun Life of Canada in 1994, Provident Mutual to General Accident in 1995, Clerical Medical to the (demutualised) Halifax in 1996, Scottish Amicable to the Prudential in 1997, and National Provident Institution (NPI) to AMP of Australia in 1998. The mighty Norwich Union floated on the Stock Exchange in June 1997, delivering an average windfall payment of nearly £1,500 and a sheaf of free and discounted shares to its policyholders. Mergers with other mutuals have offered no escape from pressures to incorporate. United Kingdom Provident Institution was acquired by Friends Provident in 1986, but its new parent is subject to constant bid rumours from corporate predators. In August 1989 the thirty-four thousand members of tiny FS Assurance of Glasgow accepted a £14 million offer from the Britannia Building Society. Its new owners have made much of mutuality, but the lure of a

TABLE 30.2
Fines Levied by Regulators of Life Offices

Company	Date	Amount
Sun Life of Canada	April 1998	£600,000
Britannic Assurance	March 1998	£525,000
London and Manchester	January 1998	£525,000
Friends Provident	September 1997	£450,000
DBS Financial Management	September 1997	£425,000
Financial Options/Investment Options	June 1998	£400,000
Albany Life	December 1997	£375,000
Irish Life	December 1994	£300,000
Norwich Union	April 1994	£300,000
Premium Life	April 1994	£300,000
Countrywide Independent Advisers	February 1998	£250,000
IFA Network	October 1998	£250,000
Minet Consultancy Services	July 1998	£250,000
Aegon	March 1994	£225,000
Royal and Sun Alliance	November 1998	£225,000
Independent Order of Foresters	June 1994	£200,000
J. H. Marsh & McLennan	June 1998	£200,000
Legal and General	February 1994	£180,000
Interdependence	November 1998	£175,000
Interlife	April 1993	£160,000
Cornhill	May 1994	£150,000
Life Association of Scotland	January 1994	£145,000
Crown Life	January 1994	£130,000
Colonial Mutual	March 1993	£130,000
Homeowners Friendly Society	December 1994	£125,000
Scottish Widows	December 1992	£120,000
Combined Life	February 1996	£110,000
Commercial Union	December 1994	£105,000
Guardian Royal Exchange	November 1992	£100,000
M and E Network	August 1997	£100,000
J. Rothschild Assurance	August 1994	£100,000
Sedgwick Noble Lowndes	October 1998	£100,000
Canterbury Life	October 1993	£80,000
London & Manchester	November 1992	£80,000
Liberty Life	February 1993	£80,000
Prosperity Life	May 1993	£75,000
Laurentian Life	January 1994	£70,000
Manulife	April 1994	£65,000
Norwich Union	May 1992	£50,000
General Accident Life	June 1992	£50,000
Commercial Union Life	June 1992	£50,000
Cannon	October 1992	£50,000
NM Financial Management Limited	May 1993	£45,000
Ideal Benefit Society	December 1994	£25,000

Source: Personal Investment Authority.

* Figures are accurate to 10 November 1998. By that date, 222 fines worth a total of £5.6 million were paid. In some cases, firms had to pay substantial costs as well.

four-figure cheque from a bank is likely to prove more persuasive than two-figure cheques from a building society once a year.

The policyholders of London Life, which sold themselves to AMP in 1989, know already that marrying a mutual is no guarantee of fidelity. Eight years after the sale, London Life was closed to new business as AMP prepared itself to demutualise and float on the Sydney Stock Exchange. In 1997 AMP was among the bidders for Scottish Amicable, whose messy sale to the Prudential marked the moral passing of the age of mutuality in much the same way that the flotation of the Norwich Union signalled the demise of its economic viability. The sale of Scottish Amicable was prompted by the announcement of a complicated management plan to demutualise and float on the Stock Exchange in three to five years' time. This was quickly exposed for what it was: a jam-today plan for management, facilitated by a jam-tomorrow plan for policyholders. The obvious greed of both, preferring an instant windfall over continued independence, was an apt commentary on the decay of the mutual ethic.

The active participation of members in the life of mutual life offices has certainly declined since Thomas Bignold was disowned by his sons and seats on the board of the NPI were so eagerly sought that candidates bribed delegates to the AGM to vote for them.[125] In 1863 the NPI was forced to introduce voting by proxy after revelations that candidates were bussing in supporters, plying delegates with drink, and inviting reluctant supporters to 'name their price'.[126] The typical annual general meeting of the modern mutual attracts virtually no one who is not invited. But then the managers of the average mutual life office have not treated policyholders like owners for decades. Instead, they have chased new business with an alacrity indistinguishable from their incorporated competitors, driving up costs at the expense of existing owner–policyholders and making a nonsense of the new argument that mutuals can be more generous to policyholders because they do not have to pay dividends to shareholders. Consulting policyholders on management decisions? They were not even sent copies of the report and accounts.

Even the windfall payments policyholders collect when a mutual life office is sold or incorporated are not all that they seem. They are funded from reserves accumulated over decades by denying the owners the full value of their investment, and distributed for policyholders in ways which often seem arbitrary and unfair. The unspoken truth about demutualising life offices is that their owners would get far greater rewards than a windfall if the fund was closed to new business and its assets managed for their benefit. But that would deny managers the Fat Cat salaries and share options which are the lot of every man and woman who runs a PLC.

Of course, the urge to shed mutual status is not purely a reflection of the greed and ambition of life-office managers. There are genuine economic reasons for it. A mutual cannot sell shares, so writing new business is its chief source of fresh capital, but new business is expensive to obtain. As costs rise, the returns to policyholders fall, and it becomes harder to win. To maintain their place in the league tables, the managers dip into the reserves, which saps the financial strength of the fund. In the years before it was acquired by General Accident, Provident Mutual was a classic case of a fund being squeezed by shrinking levels of new business, forcing it to run down its reserves to maintain bonuses, and adopt conservative investment policies as its solvency deteriorated. The UK Provident Institution, by contrast, tried to maintain its bonus rates by making risky investments in unquoted American oil and gas companies. They did not pay off, and the company lost its independence.

Lack of access to outside capital also inhibits innovation. One reason mutuals were slower to develop unit trusts was a lack of capital. For a mutual like Norwich Union, with a capital-hungry general insurance business as well as long-term life and pension funds, the problem became acute. Because the owner–policyholders were effectively underwriting ordinary insurance risks, the life and pension funds could not be invested adventurously, and the overall financial strength of the Norwich Union was not appreciated by regulators or financial advisers. The purpose of the flotation of the company was fourfold: to put a proper valuation on the general insurance businesses, liberate the investment strategy of the life and pension funds, free up existing capital, and raise an additional £1.75 billion to spend on expanding the business.[127] Clerical Medical came to similar conclusions. Its managers believed they lacked the capital to expand or to convince independent financial advisers that the business was rock-solid.[128]

The remaining mutuals are under severe pressure. Scottish Widows has become a PLC by proxy, starting a bank and forming a variety of joint ventures with the Royal Bank of Scotland, its Scottish Assurance and Direct Line subsidiaries, and one of the major clients of the bank, the Tesco supermarket chain.[129] In the annual report the chief executive boasts, in the best traditions of modern Fat Cattery, of the society having 'taken out over one third of its cost base', re-engineered 'business processes' and created a new organisation which is 'customer-driven'.[130] Standard Life and Equitable Life have elected to play a role not unlike that of Nationwide, at the top of the dwindling band of building societies, emphasising the benefits for policyholders of mutuality rather than incorporation.[131] Their reports to members are full of timely reminders to windfall-chasers and carpet-baggers that mutual life offices do not accumulate vast reserves or pay dividends but deliver all save administrative costs to the policyholders and pensioners.

'It is fashionable to knock the concept,' says Roy Ranson, managing director of the Equitable, 'but a society run on mutual grounds concentrating wholly on benefits to members and not answerable to outside interests and influences can be one of the most effective forms of incorporation.'[132] The Halifax building society argued in the same vein before it became a bank, as did the NPI, before it was taken over by AMP. (Though its stated determination to remain mutual was not enhanced by the decision to appoint as chief executive a man who led the demutualisation of the National and Provincial building society.) One of the largest of the remaining mutual life offices, Friends Provident, has featured strongly in the financial pages in recent years as both predator and prey, and part of its business is listed already.[133] 'We are not wedded to being a mutual for ever,' said chief executive Michael Doerr in 1995. 'If demutualisation would help us achieve our objective we would certainly consider it.'[134]

The Passing of the Friendly Societies

Several friendly societies have already made their decision. In 1992, finding themselves unable to compete with banks and insurance companies, they secured the passage of legislation allowing them to incorporate. This has freed them to sell a wider range of financial products, including unit trusts, PEPs, household insurance, bank accounts and pensions.* By 1998 thirty-five societies, including the ten largest, had incorporated.[135] The Family Assurance Society became the first to do so in April 1993, and a year later pioneered the first takeover by a friendly society when it paid £1.75 million for Templeton Life Assurance. It is now planning to supply its members with electricity, via a joint venture with Northern Electric.[136] The Tunbridge Wells Equitable, an upmarket society with a reputation for innovation, also incorporated in 1993. Three years later Liverpool Victoria (slogan: 'We are here for our Members') took advantage of its new status by paying Marsh and McLennan £196 million for the Frizzell home and motor insurance and banking business.[137]

The chief difficulty the societies faced without incorporation was public ignorance of their existence, let alone their advantages. The two main trade associations, the National Conference of Friendly Societies and the Association of Collecting Societies, merged in 1995 to launch a joint marketing campaign. It is unlikely to reverse the shrinkage in the number of societies:

---

* Until the 1992 Act, friendly societies were unincorporated associations whose property was vested in their trustees. This, in tandem with European Union legislation prohibiting life and general insurance companies from engaging *directly* in other activities, meant they were unable to establish subsidiaries to compete outside their core insurance markets.

The five hundred and forty of 1975 had shrunk to under three hundred by 1998, as smaller funds have closed to new business or merged with larger brethren. E. P. Thompson was right to see the friendly societies as 'authentic evidence of the growth of independent working-class culture and institutions',[138] but he would be disappointed by them now. The people who run them are more like Fat Cats than nascent Bolsheviks. In 1994 members of the sizeable Lancashire and Yorkshire and Rotherham friendly societies were surprised to discover that many contributions were invested not in cash and government bonds but in property speculation.[139]

Lloyd's: Death of an Anachronism?

Nowhere in British boardrooms have the interests of insiders prevailed over those of outsiders to more destructive effect than at an institution once synonymous with the application of the mutual tradition to modern business: Lloyd's of London. Lloyd's was never a true mutual (indeed, in 1990 the members specifically rejected mutualisation as a way out of their difficulties); it is an incorporated market in which syndicates of individuals underwrite different risks. 'Individually,' goes the old Lloyd's saying, 'we are underwriters; collectively we are Lloyd's.' But the unlimited liability of its members (down to their last waistcoat button, or their last collar stud, depending on which romantic history a journalist has read) springs from the same pre-PLC traditions as partnership and mutuality.

Originally, of course, the underwriters meeting in Edward Lloyd's coffee house assumed risks in their own name only. It was not until 1771 that the structure of the Lloyd's market was formalised, with the subscription of £100 each by seventy-nine brokers and underwriters and the election of a governing committee. It did not need to change. Throughout the eighteenth century the only possible competitors were the two chartered companies, the Royal Exchange and the London, and they did not bother seriously to contest the dominant position of Lloyd's in the shipping industry. The market was sufficiently closed to make John Julius Angerstein, a Russian-born merchant who underwrote risks in the coffee house from 1756, one of the richest people in the country by the time of his death in 1823.

His successors were untroubled by competition for another fifty years. The market finally incorporated in 1871, but the underwriters elected to preserve individual liability. The modern syndicate of outside 'Names', which caused so much grief among the upper-middle classes in the 1980s and 1990s, was invented by Frederick William Marten in the 1870s to save Lloyd's from the potentially ruinous effects of corporate competition. Shortly afterwards, the market also ventured beyond marine insurance for the first time: the pioneer was Cuthbert Heath, who was elected to Lloyd's in 1880, when the market was still almost entirely concerned with insuring ships. He started by underwriting fire business supplied by his father (a director of the Hand-in-Hand), later adding a broking operation which channelled burglary, motor and aviation business into his operation.[140] By becoming a broker as well as an underwriter, Heath initiated the egregious conflicts of interest which all but destroyed Lloyd's in the 1970s and 1980s.

He also spawned imitators. Names coagulated into specialist syndicates, and were required to pledge all assets as well as 'utmost good faith.' But Lloyd's has always lacked capital by comparison with insurance companies. In 1997 its total resources to meet claims amounted to just over £15 billion. This is one reason why the market has shrunk throughout the twentieth century. In 1900 Lloyd's underwrote a tenth of the non-life and half the marine risks of the world. Today, it underwrites a fiftieth of the global market.[141] The strongest markets at Lloyd's – marine and aviation – are growing slowly, and are fiercely contested. It has a minimal presence in life assurance, the fastest growing area, and struggles to compete in motor and property insurance because it relies on brokers rather than direct or telephone-based sales. Today, it is effectively a specialist general insurance business, with a strong position in marine, oil, satellite, large catastrophe and reinsurance risks. It is mainly a market for companies; motor insurance is its only sizeable retail business. It was the decision of the underwriters one hundred and twenty-five years ago to retain their unlimited status which drove the market into its present ghettos. However, members are finally seeking to remedy the chief cause of their failure, which was reliance on individual Names rather than permanent corporate capital. In 1994 Lloyd's admitted corporate underwriting capital for the first time.

To attract it, the market has had to undergo drastic financial restructuring, designed to insulate the new members from the old claims which caused bad publicity and litigation in the early 1990s. As recently as 1995 newspapers were speculating whether Lloyd's was going bust, prompting questions in Parliament and rumours that the Bank of England was mounting a rescue attempt. A year later the market managed to reinsure all pre-1993 claims with a new company, Equitas Reinsurance Limited. Equipped with assets of over £12 billion, of which roughly half are investments,* Lloyd's hopes that the

---

* The formation of Equitas inadvertently created a sizeable institutional investor, with £5.995 billion in financial investments. It assumed responsibility for the pre-1992 claims of approximately 400 Lloyd's syndicates comprising over 740 open years of account, but it may take forty years for these claims to be finalised. Equitas Report & Accounts, year ended 31 March 1997.

TABLE 30.3
The Financial Resources of Lloyd's

Year	Premiums Trust Funds*	Members' Deposits†	Personal Reserves†	Special Reserve Funds†	Personal Wealth‡	Central Fund§	Net Assets of Corp. of Lloyds¶	Total Assets
1985	6,839	1,582	242	254	2,591	147	120	11,775
1986	8,200	2,092	273	240	3,330	301	132	14,568
1987	8,096	2,621	330	215	3,256	269	146	14,933
1988	8,655	2,831	465	226	3,492	313	168	16,150
1989	10,388	3,333	626	298	3,700	404	248	18,997
1990	9,318	3,504	621	293	3,036	377	279	17,428
1991	11,765	3,744	600	308	2,643	445	263	19,768
1992	15,834	3,718	601	178	1,880	1,147	252	23,610
1993	19,032	3,760	841	117	1,749	904	252	26,655
1994	20,059	4,227	778	73	1,487	738	259	27,621
1995	19,686	4,696	748	55	1,259	541	246	27,231
1996	7,888	4,477	722	57	1,017	236	57	14,454
1997	7,988	5,429	588	66	726	144	75	15,016

Source: Association of British Insurers Statistics Yearbook 1985–1995, Table 117, page 66;
Lloyd's Global Results 1997.

* These assets, representing premiums received from policyholders, are called on first by the Managing Agents in the event of a claim. They are invested in cash and securities at home and abroad, and investment income is added to the total.

† Names are required to deposit at Lloyd's readily realisable assets in proportion to their overall premium limit. The proportion rises from 25 per cent of overall premium limit for Names who participate in the market through a Managing Agent to 50 per cent for individual Names and corporate Names. The assets are placed in three trust funds: the Lloyd's deposit fund, the special reserve fund and the personal reserve fund. The special reserves allow Names to deposit part of their profits as a reserve without paying tax on them.

‡ Each individual Name has to show minimum personal wealth of £250,000 (excluding the house) in addition to assets held at Lloyd's in the Lloyd's deposit, special reserve and personal reserve funds. This minimum will rise to £300,000 in January 1998, and £350,000 in January 1999. Names are still liable to the full extent of their personal wealth.

§ All Names make an annual contribution to the Central Fund of the Corporation of Lloyd's. The Council of Lloyd's can draw upon it to meet claims where Names cannot meet their obligations, and to provide hardship assistance to ruined Names.

¶ These are the net assets of the Corporation of Lloyd's, now much reduced by the sale and leaseback of the Lloyd's building and the sale of the Lloyd's of London Press Ltd, which includes publications like *Lloyd's List*. The 1986 Lloyd's building was sold for £167.5 million, and the old building was mortgaged. If a syndicated five year bank loan of £276 million taken out to fund the Equitas reinsurance company set up to take care of pre-1992 claims is included, the Corporation has a negative net worth of £201 million.

investment of this sum will be sufficient to cover all claims prior to 1992. The largest are the long-running American pollution and asbestosis claims which caused most of the £8 billion of losses Lloyd's incurred between 1988 and 1992.

The restructuring has left Lloyd's stronger financially, but with a drastically reduced capacity to write new business. The £12 billion came from a transfer of reserves, the early release of underwriting profits, a special levy on Names, a sale of corporation assets – including the Lloyd's of London building – and a large loan. But by insulating the post-1992 Lloyd's from all past claims, Equitas has enabled the market to attract a shoal of limited liability companies as members. In 1998 just over four hundred companies were underwriting risks at Lloyd's, compared to nearly seven thousand individual Names, but they have virtually taken ownership of the market. In just five years, the corporate share of underwriting capacity has risen from zero to nearly two thirds.

With the impudence characteristic of Lloyd's in recent years, the leadership made the admission of corporate capital sound like the gift of statesmen blessed with foresight rather than desperate necessity: Lloyd's needed corporate capital because individual Names were quitting the market in droves. Since membership peaked in 1988, three in every four Names have left and it is not hard to see why. The lunch tables and dinner parties of upper-middle class England are agreed: Lloyd's destroyed more of their wealth than half a dozen Labour governments. Over the five years from 1988, it racked up losses of between £8 and £9 billion, a sum equivalent to four fifths of the underwriting capacity in 1988.*

Much to their surprise, Names found they were no longer receiving cheques, but writing them to pay their share of a succession of natural disasters and unexpected but massive claims for faraway asbestosis and pollution damage. The newspapers filled with heart-rending tales of country houses, farms and family heirlooms going under the hammer. Eventually, there were suicides. Adam Raphael, himself a sufferer, tells of the wife of a Name finding her husband hanging from a noose tied to the banister in their London home. He continues with the stories of Norbert Mallett – forced to sell his fifteenth century farmhouse; Clive Francis – a property millionaire living in rented accommodation; Rick Gratwick – his farm, business and car all gone; and Julian Tennant – who had to sell his Grade II listed Georgian manor

* The losses recorded by the market between 1988 and 1992 totalled £7.9 billion, but this figure was net of (a) claims made against Lloyd's losses on policies written in the Lloyd's market and (b) a premium of £859 million paid by all members to Equitas to re-insure their losses to 1992 (losses do not all come in during the year in which they are written).

house and move into a rented cottage. 'Remember this face,' a ruined Name spat at the Lloyd's chairman, David Coleridge, in 1992. 'I hope you have nightmares over it; you have ruined me.'[142]

TABLE 30.4
Lloyd's Membership and Underwriting Capacity 1979–97 (£m)

Year	Names (Number)	Capacity	Corporates (Number)	Capacity	Global Profit/(Loss)
1979	17,279	3,049	–	–	229.0
1980	18,552	3,415	–	–	352.7
1981	19,137	3,562	–	–	248.3
1982	20,145	4,111	–	–	161.7
1983	21,601	4,381	–	–	119.6
1984	23,436	5,090	–	–	278.2
1985	26,019	6,682	–	–	195.6
1986	28,242	8,511	–	–	649.5
1987	30,936	10,290	–	–	509.1
1988	32,433	11,018	–	–	(510)
1989	31,329	10,956	–	–	(1,863)
1990	28,770	11,070	–	–	(2,319)
1991	26,539	11,382	–	–	(2,048)
1992	22,259	10,046	–	–	(1,193)
1993	19,537	8,878	–	–	1,084
1994	17,264	9,303	105	1,595	1,013
1995	14,884	7,834	140	2,360	1,005
1996	12,798	6,949	162	3,044	574*
1997	9,959	5,823	202	4,500	366*
1998	6,825	4,105	435	6,064	–

Source: Association of British Insurance Statistics Year Book 1985–1995; Key Facts: Lloyd's of London; *Ultimate Risk*, appendix.

* Projected profits.

Anecdotes of this kind have fuelled the belief of the *haute bourgeoisie* that the Lloyd's losses of 1988 to 1992 were an unprecedented private holocaust. But hard cases make bad economics as well as bad law. In 1996 the total net worth of the personal sector was £2.9 trillion,[143] of which £8 billion is about a quarter of 1 per cent and about 1.5 per cent of the wealth of the wealthiest 1 per cent of the population – from which it is reasonable to assume the Names were drawn. Losses incurred amounted to an average of £250–280,000 per Name, or about 3 per cent of the personal wealth of the Names as a group. They were only writing an average of £340,000 in 1988, and could limit their liability with a stop-loss insurance policy or by placing assets. A minority of Names were ruined.

Many had become Names when they did not have the resources – not only because they were persuaded by commission-seeking recruitment agents, but because Lloyd's had relaxed its admission criteria. Into the 1980s, Names were allowed to include the value of their house in their statement of personal assets. As recently as 1990 a Name had to show minimum liquid wealth of only £100,000, and in practice as little as half of this. Two out of three relied on bank guarantees. In exchange for pledging a sum, quickly rendered trifling by the process of inflation, a Name could underwrite policies three or even five times the value of assets which did not have to be cashed or invested at Lloyd's. This is leverage of a kind rarely available outside the more arcane segments of the derivatives markets. Combined with the heavy taxation of unearned income in the 1960s and 1970s, it is easy to see why the number of Names shot up from six thousand in the early 1960s to over thirty thousand by the mid-1980s.[144]

Nor is it surprising, amid this influx of capital, that Lloyd's underwriters became careless about the risks they took on and the premiums they charged. 'I have no sympathy for Names who regularly get lousy returns from their syndicates,' wrote Robert Hiscox, a leading managing agent responsible for managing underwriting syndicates supported by Names. 'As Eli Wallach said to Steve McQueen, "If God had not meant them to be sheared he would not have made them sheep." '[145] One of the many indefensible curiosities of the unreformed Lloyd's was that Names put up the capital to enable the market to work but acquired no rights of ownership. If more Names were admitted to a syndicate, the share of profits was simply diluted. Syndicates were not even permanent undertakings: they were dissolved and re-started every year. There was no market in which Names could buy the right to participate in a particular syndicate, making it easy for insiders to assign outsiders to the worst-performing syndicates or party of syndicates.

In 1969 Lord Cromer had recommended that Names ought to be able to enjoy 'the same degree of accountability and consideration as is generally extended to the shareholder'. But not until August 1995 did Lloyd's institute regular auctions of underwriting capacity. Even now, the auction process falls far short of creating a genuine market in rights to underwrite risks. Prices are high; in the first auction, places on syndicates were going for up to £25,000.[146] And there are only nine auctions – all in the second half of the year, which means the information on which prices are agreed is inadequate or out-of-date. Nobody makes a market in the right to underwrite: indeed, trading is specifically prohibited. The Corporation of Lloyd's admits that

Names may well get a better price by exchanging their rights for shares in one of the new corporate members.[147] There is a suspicion that Lloyd's insiders would not be too sad if the traditional Name with his unlimited liability disappeared, to be replaced by shareholders in limited liability insurance companies. 'I just don't think you should have two classes of share-holder,' Hiscox admitted. 'Every thirty years or so we have blown Names out of the water. I just don't want anybody in future to have to sell their homes to meet losses.'[148]

The takeover by new corporate members of the managing agencies which run the underwriting syndicates is creating a series of embryonic insurance companies within the Lloyd's market which combine broking of risks with underwriting capital. The buyers are domestic and foreign insurance and reinsurance companies and a new breed of investment trust designed to enable retail investors to participate in Lloyd's through their ownership of shares in the company rather than by becoming a Name. As Hiscox says, the present blend of Names (with unlimited liability) and corporate members (with limited liability) cannot last. A corporate investor is risking only the assets the company puts up to support its underwriting activities. If the losses exceed the value of the assets, it is the personal wealth of the Names which will make up the difference. The bespoke portfolio of syndicates owned by individual Names is fading. Nearly two thirds of the total capacity supplied by them now comes to the market through the Members' Agent Pooling Arrangement (MAPA), a sort of unit trust in which Names have limited exposure to as many as fifty different syndicates. This spreads their risks, but reduces the gearing effect of being a Name. With rates of tax on unearned income now far below the 98 per cent of the 1970s, unlimited liability is no longer subsidised by the Inland Revenue either. Three hundred years of unlimited personal liability at Lloyd's is coming to an end.

Like the life offices and the building societies, Lloyd's was an association of individuals; corporate capital is abstract and anonymous. That said, de-mutualisation may have changed little at the life offices and building societies but the death of the Lloyd's Name is leading to overdue changes in the way Lloyd's is run: the market is being forced to adopt the reserving methods and the risk-assessment and actuarial techniques used by its commercial com-petitors for decades.

The difficulties of the Lloyd's market are self-inflicted, but its amateurish approach to risk-taking had at least as much to do with its problems as the morals of its members. In the early 1990s Adam Raphael spent a day with an underwriter named Reg Brown on the floor of the Room. He describes an exchange between Brown and a young broker:

A nattily suited broker from Fenchurch, a large broking firm, approached syndicate 702's box with a line slip for an indemnity policy underwriting a financial company operating offshore. 'These fellows,' said the broker encouragingly, 'have had only two small incidents [potential claims].' Reg Brown would have none of it. 'Only two,' he responded tartly. 'They're all crooks running tax avoidance companies out of Jersey.' The proposal was rejected smartly: 'Nice try.' The young broker walked away shaking his head sadly.[149]

The exchange was one which Edward Lloyd would have recognised. An insurance market looking to attract corporate capital, and to compete with giant commercial insurers, cannot expect to succeed if it is run by bookies living on their wits even if they are upper-class. A market can run on trust – the *Uberrima Fides* of the Lloyd's motto, which bound all parties to an insurance contract to reveal all material facts – but, after the events of the last twenty years, it would be laughable even to mention the word in the same context as Lloyd's insurance market.

Is Mutuality Dead?

A revival in mutual ownership is only marginally less remote than a revival of public confidence in Lloyd's. Perhaps twenty-five years hence, when share prices are low, some PLC will have the bright idea of buying out its shareholders. After all, this is exactly what some PLCs did thirty-odd years ago. Clerical Medical mutualised in the early 1960s to escape the threat of nationalisation by a Labour government. Scottish Life mutualised in 1968, primarily to escape the attentions of John Bentley, an ambitious asset-stripper trained at Slater Walker Securities.[150] Bentley had noticed that the value of the reserves vastly outweighed the value of the share capital. Standard Life had encountered the same problem in the 1920s. A PLC for the first hundred years of its existence, it switched to mutual status in 1925 to obviate being taken over by a predator.[151] Scottish Mutual was also a PLC until the 1920s; its mutualisation did not take legal effect until the passage of a private Act of Parliament in 1952, when the threat of nationalisation was at its height.[152] As recently as 1981, a senior City Editor suggested that Eagle Star could escape being taken over by the German insurer Allianz by opting for mutualisation.[153]

Takeovers may yet see a large PLC return to mutual ownership, but a revival in mutuality is most likely to occur on the smaller scale, where people known to each other provide a modest range of simple financial products. Hundreds of credit unions are operating on exactly that basis. 'There is something', says Clive Trebilcock, 'that is mutual about all insurance companies, whether or not they are formally titled in that way.'[154] This was much more obvious to the Georgian or Victorian mind than to its modern successor, and in 1762 (when Equitable Life was founded) or 1832 (when Scottish Amicable mutualised) the differences between mutuals and corporations were minimal anyway. In neither case was a third party involved, and gains and losses were split among subscribers who were effectively partners with unlimited liability. As Augustus de Morgan put it in 1838, life assurance was 'based upon self-interest, yet it is the most enlightened and benevolent form which self-interest ever took. It is ... the agreement of a community to consider the goods of its individual members as common.'[155] A Scottish newspaper declared in 1852 that 'the only practical socialism which can ever exist is an insurance company.'[156] These assessments do not read well today, but the problems created by institutional investors are not confined to the activities of over-enthusiastic salesmen. Institutionalised ownership of incorporated companies is raising awkward questions about the nature of capitalism itself.

CHAPTER THIRTY-ONE

PROBLEMS OF INSTITUTIONS

There has been a chronic tendency throughout human history for the propensity to save to be stronger than the inducement to invest. The weakness of the inducement to invest has been at all times the key to the economic problem.

JOHN MAYNARD KEYNES, *The General Theory*[1]

Disengaged, uncommitted and preoccupied with liquidity, the financial system has been uniquely bad at supporting investment and innovation ... Herein lies the chief reason for Britain's disappointing performance.

WILL HUTTON[2]

The pension funds are not 'owners', they are investors. They do not want 'control'; indeed, they are disqualified from exercising it. The pension funds are 'trustees'. It is their job to invest the beneficiaries' money in the most profitable investment. They have no business trying to 'manage'. If they do not like a company or its management, their duty is to sell the stock.

PETER DRUCKER[3]

It is a terrific act of arrogance for the institutions to think that they have anything other than money to contribute to British industry.

COB STENHAM, finance director, Unilever, 1982[4]

Britain is one of the richest countries on earth. About two hundred years ago, its peoples were the first to subjugate the forces of nature to the will and purpose of man, breaking the stubborn cycle of dearth and plenitude, and unravelling the secrets of abundance. They discovered, as no generation before them, how to make the national income rise faster than the number of people consuming it. Incomes rose. Wealth accumulated, not to be hoarded against perennial disaster but to breed more of its own kind. Ever since, few questions of politics or morals have seemed more compelling than this: how can we make the economy grow faster still?

In its capacity to liberate man from his environment, and to multiply the possibilities of human existence, nothing is more important than an economy which grows. Only a growing economy can provide more jobs, better wages and higher savings. This is why every government since the war has come to power armed with a new set of nostrums to reverse the relative economic decline of Britain, and each volume in the vast and various literature of British economic retardation – from *Lectures on the Great Exhibition* to *The State We're In* – has had that same purpose. It has seemed at times as if politics – indeed, public discourse as a whole – is concerned solely with identifying how the British people and their institutions can be induced to undertake activities which cause the economy to grow and desist from those which cause it to shrink.[5]

As the present chancellor of the Exchequer pointed out some years ago (in his clumsy praise of 'post neo-classical endogenous growth theory'), what makes economies grow is investment. Investment depends on savings, and most of the savings of the British people are now controlled by the fund managers of the savings institutions. This is why the important questions about the distribution of wealth and power in Britain today are asked not of the rich, the chief repositories of both in all previous epochs, but of the savings institutions and the companies they own.

In 1997 the total national income was just over £800 billion.[6] At the end of the same year, the 2,465 British companies listed on the London Stock Exchange were valued at £1.25 trillion.[7] The stock market was worth one third more than the total national income. As state-owned industries are privatised, mutually-owned companies turn themselves into PLCs, and companies raise fresh funds for new projects, the stock market is aggrandising still more of the wealth of the nation. Even where government business cannot be privatised, ersatz PLCs have sprung into being within the public sector.

No aspect of public policy is any longer immune to the advice and insights of the great captains of industry. Some – like Lords Young and Simon, and the unlucky Geoffrey Robinson – even make policy today. The current pre-eminence of the PLC in national affairs has justified at last the fears of those present at its premature birth. 'The wealth of the nation,' wrote Jonathan Swift at the time of the South Sea Bubble, 'that used to be reckoned by the value of land, is now computed by the rise and fall of stocks.' In 1733 Samuel Madden predicted, in his unpublished *Memoirs of the Twentieth Century*, that three centuries after his death neither Crown nor Parliament would reign supreme in the British Isles. Instead, the national fortunes would be directed by two giant public corporations.[8] As futurology goes, it was not a bad guess:

the PLC has become not only the dominant form of collective organisation but the chief source of income and wealth.

The Problem of Short-Termism

It is not surprising that politicians and journalists indignant for change should now be demanding the reformation of the PLCs and their institutional owners, just as their predecessors sought a redistribution of wealth and power from Crown and aristocracy to Parliament and Commons. Will Hutton tied the shortcomings of the British political and financial systems together in an ingenious critique of capitalist-conservative hegemony that ends with a call for the 'republicanisation of finance'.[9] Beneath the hyperbole lay a familiar argument: the British economy is suffering from a complex of maladies known as 'short–termism', or what Hutton calls the 'liquidity fetish'. This is the argument that institutional investors have a systematic bias against companies which *invest* in long-term growth.

Instead of rewarding companies which train their employees well, work patiently to build their market share, and research and develop innovative products and services (runs the argument) the institutions reward those companies which invest in projects to produce the highest returns quickly. The chief discipline which enables them to impose their will in this way is the stock market. It is fear that institutions will sell their shares, perhaps to a corporate predator, which forces companies to disgorge as dividends to shareholders the earnings which could be reinvested. This raises the cost of capital, discouraging investment in any but the most immediately profitable ventures, reducing the rate of growth of the economy, and lowering the standard of living.

If it is even half-true, it is a devastating critique of the structure of ownership in Britain today. For ultimately it holds the institutional investors responsible for the worst ills of contemporary Britain: ignorance, joblessness and poverty, and the crime which feeds off them.

Hunger for Dividends

It is true that the institutions like their dividends high and steady. Around one third of the post-tax profits of industrial and commercial companies in Britain are distributed in dividends – a much higher proportion of profits than those in Germany or Japan. Although it may seem obvious that dividends should rise and fall in line with profits, it is also true that a cut in the dividend is such a drastic step that companies will do almost anything to avoid it. In 1980, the mighty ICI shocked the City by cutting its dividend, in an act which became symbolic of the savagery of that recession. The company never recovered the confidence of investors; it was a takeover target for years before splitting itself in two.

This is why, even in the depths of a recession, companies are loath to cut the dividend. Dividend payments rose 21.5 per cent between 1990 and 1992, at the bottom of the last recession.[10] In the summer of 1992 the BP board had to replace its chief executive before they could secure consent to halve the dividend. As soon David Simon took over from Bob Horton, the BP share price fell 14 per cent in anticipation of a dividend cut, and another 5 per cent when the cut was implemented. It is a fact that several of the major companies which cut their dividends in the 1990–92 recession (Midland Bank, Lonrho and Royal Insurance) were subsequently taken over, merged or broken up. Those which maintained their dividend despite being in dire financial condition (like Rolls-Royce) retained independence.

It is not surprising that dividends soar during takeover booms. During the 1980s, when takeover activity was rife, dividends roughly doubled.[11] A survey of finance directors found more than half agreed that 'any cut in dividend payout sends adverse signals to markets and should be avoided.'[12] If the dividend is cut, shareholders are effectively being told that management have lost confidence in maintaining the earnings of the company. It is an invitation to look for new management.

In 1990, as the recession began to bite, Paddy Linaker of M&G, then one of the best-known fund managers, wrote to three hundred companies, telling them that 'we do not think cutting dividends is the solution to cyclical trading difficulties.'[13] He later argued in a paper to the Trade and Industry Select Committee that high dividend payments were a necessary form of compensation to the institutions for the poor growth rate of corporate Britain.[14] His critics were not slow to point out that Linaker had an obvious self-interest; M&G was running a number of income funds whose holders would be disappointed if the promised income did not materialise. But he was also confirming the centrality of the dividend in an economy where ownership is separated from control.

Shareholders accept that the managers of the companies they own will always take the detailed investment decisions. The only way they can ensure that the managers do not squander their capital on pet projects is to force them to make a strong case for retaining profits. If they cannot, say the institutions, they should return the cash to the shareholders for investment elsewhere. Some managers agree. 'They stop us doing marginal low-return business,' said Martin Taylor, former chief executive of Barclays Bank, of his decision to return cash to shareholders by buying their shares. 'And there is plenty around if you want it.'[15] The same applies to ordinary dividend payments. Institutions claim this does not starve companies of capital; if an enterprise identifies a profitable opportunity unexpectedly, it can recoup the money by selling new shares to investors in a rights issue – though this obviously has a cost in terms of fees.[16]

But is this true? In theory, it makes no difference to shareholders if earnings are paid as dividends or reinvested in the firm. Profits not distributed as dividends will eventually show up in a higher share price instead;[17] the total return to shareholders is the same. But this is not how the institutions see things. Instead of treating a rising share price as a substitute for a rising dividend, the actuaries advising pension funds and life offices rely on income alone. They make no reference to the stock market value of their shares. Instead, they extrapolate a rising dividend income far into the future, then discount that income back to today at an arbitrarily chosen rate of interest to decide what the shares are worth.[18]

There are good reasons for taking this view. It is cheaper to collect the return on an investment in the form of a dividend than pay a stock broker to realise it by selling shares. Apart from having to pay a fat commission, institutions can rarely sell large blocks of shares without moving the market price against themselves. This concentration on income has the further advantage of rendering them immune to market fluctuations, even of the most extreme kind (they more or less ignored the crash of October 1987). If the institutions were forced to recalculate their liabilities every time the stock market moved, the investment decisions of life offices and pension funds would become increasingly random.

But actuarial assumptions none the less remain a highly artificial method of valuation. The rate of growth of dividends and the rate at which they are discounted are no more than informed guesses. Nobody knows how fast dividends will grow at any one company, let alone across hundreds operating in different industries and markets. Minor alterations in either assumption will make the difference between a call for higher pension contributions and premium payments or a recommendation that these be cut.

This is one reason why company directors cannot absolve themselves of blame for high dividends. They discourage actuarial assumptions which are likely to oblige them to increase the company contribution to the pension fund, and the best way to ensure the assumptions remain favourable to their interests is to pay a high and rising dividend. These days, directors are almost always shareholders themselves. Any cut in the dividend, and a subsequent fall in the share price, affects their net worth as surely as that of any institutional shareholder. Traditionally, pension funds have had only one further incentive which directors lack: freedom from income tax on the dividends they receive.[19]

Trimming Tax Perks

This gave the institutions a direct incentive to demand dividends rather than allow companies to keep funds for investment. They paid no tax on dividend income but paid tax on profits retained by the company, because these were liable to corporation tax. Under these conditions, it made sense to pay high dividends even if the company needed the money. It was cheaper to borrow (interest payments, unlike dividends, are tax-deductible) or recoup dividends by issuing new shares in a rights issue. In 1991 both T&N and Costain launched rights issues while paying a high dividend.

Absurdities of this kind provided the last Conservative and the present New Labour government with respectable reasons to attack the tax privileges of the pension funds. In 1997, through a technical sleight-of-hand, Gordon Brown put an end to the payment of dividends free of tax to institutional shareholders. 'The present system of tax credits encourages companies to pay out dividends rather than reinvest their profits,' he told the House of Commons on 2 July 1997. 'This cannot be the best way of encouraging investment for the long term.' Though the first Labour chancellor for eighteen years was naturally sympathetic to the critics of institutional short-termism, the truth was more prosaic. The government, confined by its election promise not to raise rates of income tax, was raising revenue in a politically painless way. In that sense, Brown was completing the work of his Conservative predecessors.

Norman Lamont, in his 1993 budget, had first reduced the tax which pension funds could reclaim on dividends. A year later Stephen Dorrell, then financial secretary to the Treasury, had wondered aloud whether the government should go further in taxing the dividend income of the pension funds. His musings prompted the veteran Conservative industrialist, Lord Hanson, to accuse Dorrell of 'sounding like a socialist'.[20] The idea was reportedly dropped after Hanson wrote to John Major to complain, but traces cropped up in a trade and industry committee report of 1994 and the infamous White Paper on 'competitiveness' published by the Department of Trade and Industry (DTI) the same year.[21] In October 1996, Kenneth Clarke restricted the payment of tax credits on share buybacks (no more than another form of dividend payment) and some types of special dividend. After the 1997 election his former tax adviser, Edward Troup, agreed that abolition of the dividend tax credit was 'a reform whose time has come'.[22]

The chief appeal of the 'reform' was undoubtedly its promise of a higher tax yield from one of the greatest sources of (non-voting) wealth in the land: the pension funds. This became obvious immediately. Pension benefits are a product of contributions and returns on those contributions. To the extent that returns are reduced by tax, contributions have to go up or benefits down, unless investment performance is so dazzling that the extra tax makes no difference. Straight after the Lamont budget, Rentokil and Unilever announced they would be raising their dividends to compensate investors for the reduced tax reclaim.* A substantial part of the £1 billion infusion the BT pension fund received from its parent company over the next two years was intended to make good the valuation shortfall which resulted.[23] After the Brown budget, one actuary estimated that the loss of tax credits would add about £70 billion to the cost of pension schemes. This implied an extra £5 billion in contributions in each of the next ten years – a figure equivalent to half again what companies were already contributing – and some lower figure thereafter.

Another firm of actuaries reckoned it would cost the FTSE–100 companies between £1 and £2 billion, with BT being forced to contribute another £166 million, and ICI £62 million.[24] Funds already under pressure to meet their obligation under the 1995 Pensions Act to make good any deficits by 2007, found they were even less adequately funded than before. In August 1987 the engineering firm Glynwed International became the first company to make a special provision for the abolition of dividend tax credits on its pension fund.[25] One authority reckoned the abolition of the credit cost the pension funds £1.2 billion in the second half of 1997, or the equivalent of £2.5 billion in a full year.[26] The Securities and Investments Board (SIB), then advising life offices on how to calculate compensation payable to victims of pensions mis-selling, was able to raise discount rates to take account of the fall in value of pension funds.[27] The victims of pensions mis-selling will now attain less in compensation than before the Brown budget.

The Sub-Underwriting Rip-Off

If the attack on the dividend income of the pension funds had any happy consequences, it was to draw attention to the enormous fees institutional investors charge for underwriting new issues of shares. It was often argued in defence of dividends that, if companies found a profitable investment,

---

* Companies did the same as the basic rate of income tax fell during the 1980s, since this also had the effect of reducing the value of the tax reclaim.

they could always recoup the capital from the institutions by issuing new shares. But this is to ignore the costs, as Dorrell pointed out. In 1994 he asked a Confederation of British Industry conference whether tax-driven dividend payments were not only a cause of 'under-investment' but of 'churning' by institutional investors recycling them in the form of expensively underwritten rights issues:

> A long term rise in dividend payout ratios necessarily implies reduced availability to a business of its retained earnings, and greater reliance on its ability to raise new capital from the markets. It undeniably increases the cost of capital if the system requires a business to employ professionals to secure access to capital which it has just distributed.[28]

There was some truth in this. Although the cost of dealing in shares fell after the Big Bang of October 1986, the cost of raising share capital did not, because new issues of shares are underwritten.

Most companies want to be sure that they will receive the money they need, so they pay institutions to guarantee they will buy the shares if nobody else will. This 'underwriting' of the risk of failure will usually cost 2–2.5 per cent of the value of the shares being sold, of which roughly two thirds is payable to the institutions.[29] The cash sums can be immense. When Trafalgar House bid for Northern Electric in January 1995, it put the costs of underwriting its £1.2 billion offer at £30 million. When North West Water bid for Norweb, its £567 million rights issue cost £14 million in underwriting fees.[30] The Inland Revenue became so excited by the immensity of the sums the institutions were making that it tried to tax the pension funds on the grounds that underwriting was 'trading' rather than investment. (The plan was grounded by the Special Commissioners of the Inland Revenue.)*

Fund managers are unapologetic about the costs. 'You're going on risk,' says a Scottish fund manager. 'Sometimes it's money for old rope; sometimes you're left holding the baby. We would never underwrite something we were not prepared to own.'[31] Yet the risk institutions assume is slight. Shares are sold at a discount to the prevailing market price, usually of between 10 and 20 per cent; underwriters are rarely called upon. The BP share issue of October 1997, which coincided with the crash, is the one major occasion when they had to take up unwanted stock. Even then, the investment banks

---

* *Financial Times*, 23 December 1997. The judgment applied only to the British Telecommunications and Post Office pension funds, the two institutions involved. They underwrite issues only where they already hold shares in the company, and it is thought the judgment may not apply to funds which underwrite issues by companies in which they own no shares. The Inland Revenue appealed against the decision and won, but the case will now go to the Court of Appeal.

which acted as primary underwriters tried to renege, citing *force majeure*. It earned them a stinging rebuke from the chief investment manager at Scottish Amicable in Glasgow, one of many institutional investors which assumed their responsibilities uncomplainingly. 'In some cases,' Graeme Knox said, 'greed has motivated certain houses to retain unacceptably large quantities of new issues for themselves and it would be quite scandalous for these people to avoid their legitimate losses in the face of the huge profits previously extracted from the country.'[32]

Pre-Emption Rights

Knox was being slightly unfair. Unlike the investment bankers, institutional investors would have bought BP shares anyway. They buy shares every time any major company issues them, partly to maintain their weightings in the stock but mainly because shares acquired cheaply in rights issues, company flotations and takeovers are one of the chief drivers of investment performance. Companies are also obliged by law to offer new shares to existing shareholders. These pre-emption rights, as they are called, are controversial. On the face of it, they raise the cost of capital to companies by denying them access to investors around the world who might be prepared to pay a higher price for their shares. Companies can ask the permission of shareholders to sell stock to outsiders, but if they were allowed to admit new shareholders to the company at will, they would dilute the value of the stake which existing shareholders own: they would be transferring wealth from old shareholders to new ones without paying for it. 'What sort of cheeky question is that?' responded Knox, when asked if existing shareholders should retain the right of first refusal. 'Who else owns the companies? Why should their ownership be unilaterally taken away from them?'[33] This argument is incontrovertible, but makes it hard to understand why investment bankers and stock-brokers should be paid handsome fees to sell shares to institutions which would have bought them anyway, or why institutions are taking a fee for underwriting their own share subscriptions – particularly since it is at their own expense.

Where issues of shares are so large that overseas investors have to be involved, companies have had some success in reducing the underwriting fees charged by banks and brokers. The government gradually reduced them in major privatisations. But no company has succeeded in reducing the underwriting fees earned by institutions. Yet it was proved nearly twenty years ago, in a classic study by Professor Paul Marsh of the London Business School, that underwriting commissions were not worthwhile. After studying a series of rights issues, he concluded that underwriters charged twice what their services were worth, and when the Office of Fair Trading (OFT) looked into the underwriting cartel in 1992, it asked Professor Marsh to update his findings. He proved that getting on for £9 in every £10 spent on underwriting fees was unjustifiable and that, between 1986 and 1994, institutions had earned excess profits of £490 million.[34]

Despite this, in 1995 the OFT decided not to refer underwriting commissions to the Monopolies and Mergers Commission (MMC). The onus was placed on companies to shop around for better terms, and institutions to show willingness to be flexible. But it was not until the autumn of the following year, after the OFT had again threatened the institutions with an MMC referral, that institutions agreed for the first time to *tender* to underwrite stock. The reduction in costs was trifling.* The patience of the OFT finally ran out. In November 1997 the director general, John Bridgeman, referred the sub-underwriting cartel to the MMC, having found that the traditional fee structure was still being used in over half of all rights issues. 'The industry has had long enough to behave more competitively,' he said, 'and the time has now come for a full MMC inquiry.'[35]

What was puzzling about the MMC referral was the apparent inability of companies to persuade their investment banking advisers and shareholders to change of their own accord. It is often forgotten (amid the plethora of critiques of a malign 'financial system') that decisions to raise capital for productive investment are taken by company managers not institutional investors. Twenty years ago, when a Labour government was last in office, there were similar mutterings about a lack of investment. The then prime minister, James Callaghan, invited his predecessor, Harold Wilson, to chair a committee of inquiry into the functioning of the financial institutions. After an exhaustive investigation, spanning more than three years, the Wilson committee concluded that the problem lay not in a shortage of capital but in a shortage of sufficiently profitable opportunities to invest.[36]

It was scarcely surprising, at a time of high and chronic inflation, that the institutions demanded a high price for finance. What is surprising is that industrialists do not seem to have adjusted their expectations downwards now that inflation is under control. A Bank of England survey in 1994 found that the *average* rate of return demanded by company managers from new investment was 20 per cent, at a time when inflation was running at about

---

* In October 1996 Schroders merchant bank organised a rights issue for the Stakis hotel group in which investors tendered to underwrite stock at a lower fee. It saved Stakis £400,000. (*Financial Times*, 1 November 1996). In October 1997 the competitive tendering to underwrite a £125 million rights issue for the Berkeley Group reduced the institutional fee from 1.25 per cent to 0.3 per cent. But the shares were also issued at a discount of 26 per cent to the share price. (*Financial Times*, 15 October 1997).

one tenth of this figure. This was four or five percentage points above what institutions actually expected companies to deliver.[37] If bankers are prone occasionally to what Keynes called an 'error of optimism', it seems businessmen are equally likely to succumb to an error of pessimism.

The Lack of Venture Capital

One whose pessimism is not overdone is the genuine entrepreneur. The institutions are notoriously reluctant to back people starting new businesses or looking for support to make a small business bigger. 'We are not interested in venture capital at all,' was the blunt riposte of a Scottish fund manager in 1992. 'Unquoted companies, like property, are bloody risky, and the returns do not justify it . . . I do not mind risk, but I do not like speculation. It is the balance of risk and reward that is not right in venture capital.'[38] Another Edinburgh life office was no more enthusiastic. 'Our experience of venture capital and business start-ups has not been very good,' he said. 'I imagine that is true of most institutions. We would rather someone else took the risk and the first 20 per cent, and then we would come in. Obviously, that leaves the problem of where people get start-up capital but we do not see that as our primary function.'[39]

The institutions certainly had a number of bad experiences channelling funds into smaller companies with the mercurial Charles Gordon in the 1960s and early 1970s,[40] and more in the late 1970s after the Bank of England bullied them into supporting the establishment of Equity Capital for Industry in 1976. The fund, intended to back small and medium-sized companies, was founded solely to head off the threat of state direction of investment by a Labour government. Seven Scottish life offices and a handful of English insurance companies had argued against its foundation on the grounds that their responsibility was not to British industry but to their policyholders and pensioners. The major pension funds did not support it until they were told to do so by the National Association of Pension Funds (NAPF).[41] A plan to raise £500 million had to be scaled back drastically to £40 million, of which the pension funds provided £15 million and insurers and unit trusts the rest.[42]

The sceptics were swiftly vindicated. The first investment made by Equity Capital for Industry, a carpet manufacturer called Bond Worth, disobligingly went bust. In 1979 a second investment, in a paper manufacturer, Brittains, was also lost. In the end, more than half the funds raised by Equity Capital for Industry went unused, and its income came from placing what was left on deposit at the bank. But the main obstacle to institutional investment in smaller companies and start-up ventures is not a history of bad experiences.

It is the sheer size of the funds: a large pension fund or life office finds it hard to justify the expenditure of time and effort to find and monitor suitable small investments, especially as it risks divergence from the strategy of their peer group. Larger funds are under pressure not to risk their position in the performance league tables. This gravitation towards the mean reduces the institutional appetite for taking risks, even in return for lavish rewards. Larger funds also dislike the illiquidity of smaller investments by comparison with the securities issued by major quoted companies. Many pension funds are now maturing, and need easily realisable investments to meet immediate liabilities. But the institutional distaste for new and growing ventures goes back much further than the ageing of the population.

One of the hardy perennials of Labour government is the launch of an investigation into why the City is not investing in productive industry. In November 1929 Philip Snowden, the chancellor of the Exchequer, set up a committee on finance and industry under the chairmanship of Lord Macmillan.[43] Among its conclusions, published in 1931, was the recognition that 'great difficulty is experienced by the smaller and medium-sized businesses in raising the capital which they may from time to time require, even when the security offered is perfectly sound.'[44] During its deliberations, Lord Kindersley of Lazards, a merchant bank which introduced companies to institutional investors, confessed that illiquidity was the chief deterrent to investment in small and growing enterprises.[45] The Macmillan report led eventually to the foundation in 1945 of the Industrial and Commercial Finance Corporation (ICFC), forerunner of the largest venture capital provider in Britain today – 3i.*

The creation of ICFC followed a number of failed private sector initiatives, all of which had little capital to invest, and none of which was prepared to fund start-ups. They advanced only loans, and not equity, with the aim of gearing up well-established businesses. The goal was to make a substantial profit within three to five years by selling the company or floating it.[46] The so-called venture capital industry has not tried anything more ambitious since.

Venture Capital is a Misnomer

The Bolton Committee of Inquiry on Small Firms, set up in 1969 by another Labour government, reported two years later that the 'Macmillan Gap' (as it has become known) still existed. 'We cannot anticipate any significant improve-

* The clearing banks and the Bank of England owned ICFC (later 3i) until its flotation in June 1994. They retained stakes, but sold further shares in 1995. See Chapter 27.

ment in the provision of equity capital for small business,' read its report of November 1971. 'It will remain available only to the most promising and successful.'[47] Pension funds did invest in smaller companies in the 1970s, but by 1979 they had sunk a grand total of just £33.6 million in slightly over one hundred small businesses, most of them well-established companies rather than start-ups.[48] A year later, the Wilson Committee report confirmed that 'the financial system does seem to have a degree of difficulty in meeting the demands of small, and especially new firms, and in financing investment involving an unusually high degree of risk, particularly where there is a lengthy period before positive returns can be expected to accrue.'[49]

It is sometimes assumed that the venture capital industry which emerged in the 1980s has plugged the Macmillan Gap. One reason Nigel Lawson reduced the generosity of the tax reliefs available under the Business Expansion Scheme, and why Norman Lamont replaced it altogether with the less generous Enterprise Investment Scheme in 1993, was the belief that the venture capital industry was mature enough to fund small and growing businesses without excessive support from the taxpayer. It was too sanguine a view. The venture capital industry is small, investing only £2–3 billion even in a good year. It has invested less than £19 billion in *total* since 1984. This is unimpressive by comparison with the sums invested by so-called Business Angels – rich individuals, who back business start-ups, and usually become directors – without any institutional support.* The venture capital industry is also, despite its nomenclature, distinctly unadventurous. After some discouraging experiences with genuine business start-ups in the 1980s, venture capitalists now spend most of their time and resources on funding management buy-outs (MBOs) and buy-ins (MBIs).[50]

The venture capitalists, like the institutional investors before them, reckon most business start-ups are too small to warrant their attention. In recent years, only 1p or 2p in every £1 has gone into genuine start-ups. James Dyson, inventor of the ballbarrow and the dual cyclone vacuum cleaner, found the industry unwilling to back his invention even though he had a product and a track record. 'I couldn't believe it,' he recalled. 'I'd spent £4.5 million of my own money. I had working prototypes with ten years of research and development behind them. And I already owned a profitable product development company. But they said they didn't like backing designers.'[51] It is not hard to understand why the venture capitalists prefer MBOs and MBIs:

* Inland Revenue figures show that just over fifteen hundred companies had received £182.4 million under the Enterprise Investment Scheme by end of the 1997–98 tax year, of which £22.8 million came from just under a thousand Business Angels. But the Revenue figures do not measure the scale of angelic activity. It is estimated that Business Angels have more than £10 billion invested.

Dyson owned too much of his company, and knew too much about it, for the venture capitalists to reward themselves well. MBOs and MBIs not only have the advantage of being well-established businesses (greatly reducing the risk of failure) but tend to be sold by their corporate owners at bargain-basement prices to managers without much money of their own (greatly enriching the venture capitalists).

This transfer of value from institutional shareholders in large corporations to a small claque of Home Counties venture capitalists has not occurred without controversy. The managers of a business bought out of its parent company have a clear advantage over the shareholders in their ability to gauge its longer-term value: the very people the shareholders were relying on to manage the business change sides and try to buy the assets for less than they are worth. Occasionally, the institutions resist. In 1989, they rebuffed an attempt by the management of the Molins engineering group to take the company private. Later the same year a group of institutional shareholders criticised the £630 million MBO of Magnet on the grounds that management was trying to profit at the expense of the owners.

'We are very unhappy that directors of a company in which we are a long-term investor should use their time to work out a deal that could be to their own advantage and one that involves tremendous conflicts of interest,' said Geoffrey Browne of Sun Alliance Investment Management.[52] 'We are being done out of opportunities for the long term . . . We're not concerned whether the company has a bad year next year. Over the next ten years it will make an attractive investment.'[53] The deal, which went through despite institutional misgivings, became one of the most conspicuous financial disasters of the late 1980s.*

It is more common for the price of the buy-out or buy-in to prove spectacularly generous to the venture capitalists when they take their 'exit' by selling the company or floating it on the stock market – usually between three and five years later. The gap between the price at which the managers of Eversholt and Porterbrook bought the railway leasing companies and the price at which they sold them shortly afterwards caused considerable political embarrassment.[54] The £608 million MBO of Reedpack from Reed International (funded by the former venture capital arm of the Coal Board pension fund, CINVen) was sold just two years later to SCA of Sweden for £1.04 billion, yielding a compound annual rate of return of 31 per cent. Vero, bought by its management from BICC for £33 million, was floated on the stock exchange at £133 million eighteen months later. This large expropriation of shareholder value was one of the

* The deal carried excessive debt, as the institutions had also warned, and came unstuck within a year.

deals named by Robin Morgan, chief executive of fund managers M&G, when he wrote a letter of complaint in February 1996 to four hundred companies where their funds were invested. 'The speed of the return and the scale of the uplift in value,' he wrote, 'have, in many cases, been astonishing and galling for shareholders in the original vendor companies, and highly rewarding for the management and venture capitalists who financed the management buy-out.'[55]

Morgan was describing an industry far removed from the high hopes and good intentions with which the modern venture capital industry began in the 1970s. The transformation of the venture capital arm of the Coal Board pension fund into CINVen is a useful guide.[56] Today, CINVen is itself owned by its managers, who bought it from the Coal Board for £10 million in October 1995, and who long ago lost interest in funding business start-ups in the coal fields or anywhere else. Selling themselves through a series of smug advertisements on the front page of the *Financial Times* ('Our directors have worked 19,686,000 minutes in the venture capital industry – up to midnight

TABLE 31.1
Investment in Britain by Venture Capital Firms (£m)

Year	Start-Up	Early Stage	Expansion	MBO/MBI	Total
1984	25	13	73	*29	140
1985	32	18	120	*107	277
1986	58	28	124	*174	384
1987	75	45	301	513	934
1988	70	60	435	733	1,298
1989	86	129	338	867	1,420
1990	76	52	396	582	1,106
1991	35	23	387	544	989
1992	43	39	362	807	1,251
1993	34	35	393	769	1,231
1994	45	31	480	1,112	1,668
1995	26	59	495	1,560	2,140
1996	41	90	592	2,083	2,806
1997	58	101	907	1,999	3,066
Total	700	727	5,403	11,880	18,710

Source: British Venture Capital Association.

* Includes investment in acquisitions as well as MBOs and MBIs.

last night, it's a CINVen fact'), the fund now concentrates mainly on MBOs of £10 million or more. One deal it helped to fund in the summer of 1997 was worth over £1 billion. A second, completed with much self-congratulation over the Christmas holiday, was worth £860 million.[57] Bashfulness, rare enough among investment bankers, is virtually unknown among venture capitalists. Even investment bankers are known to complain about how they milk uninvested funds for management fees and invest on their own account in the projects which they back, being careful in each case to choose only the most lucrative parts of each transaction.* It is hardly surprising that the institutions have a jaundiced view of investment in new and rising enterprises.

Hostile to R & D?

The main reason small companies win plaudits is that they are thought better than larger companies at the one form of investment everybody agrees is crucial to economic growth: innovation. The Austrian economist Joseph Schumpeter assigned innovation a central role in his theory of economic growth. 'The fundamental impulse that sets and keeps the capitalist engine in motion comes from the new consumers' goods, the new methods of production or transportation, the new markets, the new forms of industrial organisation that capitalist enterprise creates,' he wrote. 'This process of Creative Destruction is the essential fact about capitalism. It is what capitalism consists in and what every capitalist concern has got to live in.'[58] The relentless discovery under capitalism of cheaper and better ways of doing and making things enables companies to outwit their competitors by producing more for less, and producing more for less is what makes an economy grow.

Innovation is of course preceded by research and development (R & D), and this is precisely the area where the British 'financial system' is thought to be at fault. International surveys show consistently that Britain invests less in R & D than other developed countries. In the 1980s Britain was unique among the member-states of the Organisation for Economic Co-operation and Development (OECD) in reducing expenditure on R & D as a pro-

---

* Venture capitalists typically collect management fees of 1.5 per cent of a fund before any money is invested. They also retain a 'carried interest' of 20 per cent of the eventual sale proceeds, though this is paid only if the fund achieves a (relatively low) target rate of return. In so-called 'co-investment schemes,' outside investors provide the bulk of the finance in return for fixed-dividend preference shares, while the venture capitalists supply a smaller sum in exchange for ordinary shares. This guarantees the venture capitalists the whole of any increase in the capital value of an investment in return for a relatively modest outlay. Understandably, they have found co-investment schemes increasingly difficult to arrange.

portion of the national income. 'British companies' priorities,' laments Will Hutton, 'are overwhelmingly *financial*.'[59] Company managers agree. 'UK companies distribute a relatively high proportion of earnings as dividends, putting pressure on the company to earn high rates of return and reducing the internal funds available for reinvestment (in times of recession, surplus funds can be eliminated completely),' griped the engineering company GKN to the Trade and Industry Select Committee in the early 1990s. 'Consequently, UK companies are relatively risk averse and tend to seek growth primarily through acquisition. There is also pressure, particularly during a recession, to reduce discretionary costs, such as R & D, in order to protect the dividend; a reduced dividend can have serious consequences in terms of lower share price and possible predatory takeover.'[60]

It is true that while dividends rose by 21.5 per cent between 1990 and 1992, expenditure by companies on R & D fell by 8 per cent in real terms.[61] But there is no innate conflict of interest between the institutional demand for dividends and corporate investment in research and development. Fund managers will support any investment that promises to increase profits and dividends. A study published in 1997 by the City University Business School (funded, admittedly, by the National Association of Pension Funds) found no correlation between high dividends and low investment in R & D. One economist has even identified a correlation between share prices and R & D expenditure which suggests that the institutions rate firms which invest more highly.[62] In some cases – notably biotechnology and Internet stocks – the rush to invest has run far ahead of commercial realities.

But institutional investors are right to recognise that innovation is not itself the source of growth. Growth stems from innovations which increase *efficiency*, and R & D is only one of the ways companies can achieve that. Expenditure is an exceptionally crude measure of virtue: what counts as research and development is a subjective decision. Pharmaceuticals, the one research-based industry in which British companies are conspicuously successful, has an obvious interest in exaggerating its expenditure to underpin the high price of drugs. As soon as the British and American governments put downward pressure on the price of drugs in the early 1990s, dire warnings emanated from the pharmaceutical industry about the deleterious impact on R & D budgets. As it happens, R & D expenditure by pharmaceutical companies nearly doubled in real terms between 1989 and 1996.[63]

The best test of investment in research and development is the ability to turn new knowledge into a saleable product; it is not a good in itself. A large budget is a waste of money if it is not matched by marketing and management skills. This, rather than a short-term approach to investment by the institutions, is probably where the British economy is genuinely weak. British

companies are famous for failing to exploit indigenous inventions. Examples
are legion. The first computer in the world was built at Cambridge University
in 1949; IBM turned it into a commercial product. An EMI scientist invented
the CAT scanner, but an American company developed the technology into
a saleable machine. Contrary to popular myth, this failure to exploit new
technology is not exclusively a British phenomenon. Philips, the Dutch electronics company, invented audio cassettes and compact discs but could establish market leadership in neither. It lacked the marketing skills to identify
and exploit the sales opportunities the technology presented. A successful new
product, like the Sony Walkman, may not even be technologically advanced; it
may be based on the transfer of existing technology to a new area, such as
adapting lasers from telephony to compact discs.

'A common business mistake,' as John Kay has pointed out, 'is to believe
that innovation can compensate for competitive disadvantages in other areas.
Such a strategy is almost never effective . . . The return to innovation is . . .
a return to a combination of competitive advantages.'[64] Britain led the world
in expenditure on R & D in the 1960s, but nobody would describe those years
as a great success for the economy. The relatively low level of expenditure by
companies today may not reflect short-termism at all but a proper appreciation by British managers of the limits of their competence.

'Companies often say big institutions don't encourage them to invest in
technology, R & D, and training, but it's not true,' Mick Newmarch, then
chief executive at the Prudential, told a newspaper in 1990. 'Often it's their
own natural inclination not to spend money for the long term; managers can
be very risk-averse.'[65] Politicians, officials and commentators, however, are
more inclined to believe company managers than fund managers, and fret
that institutional investors are starving innovative companies of funds. In the
same year that Newmarch spoke, the Innovation Advisory Board of the DTI
stated that short-termism was a major threat to investment. In October 1990
it published an 'R & D Action Programme', the chief result of which (in the
usual way of public bureaucracies) was an increase in its output of statistics.
The Office for National Statistics now publishes figures purporting to show
how much (or how little) sectors are investing in research and development.

These crude but unflattering comparisons with other developed countries
never fail to provoke a new outburst of national lamentation, orchestrated
by the large constituency created by the public and private subsidisation of
R & D projects, especially in Whitehall and the universities. A lobbying group,
Save British Science, has claimed regularly for over a decade that British
science is on the verge of extinction because of cuts, but expenditure by
government departments, universities and research councils rose by nearly
20 per cent in real terms between 1988 and 1996.[66] 'Science provides an

TABLE 31.2
Expenditure on R & D in Britain* (£m)

Year	State	Companies	Universities	Non-Profit	Total	% GDP
1986	1,212	5,951	1,288	317	8,768	2.29
1987	1,264	6,335	1,460	324	9,383	2.22
1988	1,360	6,922	1,575	179	10,035	2.14
1989	1,534	7,650	1,689	196	11,069	2.15
1990	1,566	8,318	1,873	234	11,991	2.18
1991	1,757	8,135	2,020	220	12,132	2.11
1992	1,846	8,489	2,129	224	12,689	2.13
1993	1,928	9,069	2,312	232	13,541	2.15
1994	2,051	9,204	2,623	168	14,046	2.11
1995	2,043†	9,254	2,696	177	14,172	2.02
1996	2,070†	9,301	2,792	177	14,340	1.94

Source: *Economic Trends*, August 1994, No 490, August 1996, No 514, August 1997, No 525 and August 1998, No 537, Office for National Statistics.

* In cash terms.
† Includes Research Councils.

exciting and rewarding life, and its practitioners deserve a larger share of the regard and rewards of society,' claims a former Master of Balliol. 'The next millennium will favour nations that have invested in basic scientific research. They will possess the ideas from which new industry will emerge.'[67] It is an unwittingly frank alignment of public and private interest.

Market in Corporate Control

Company managers make similar elisions, especially if their interests collide with those of their shareholders. When their control of the company is threatened they are prone to accuse the institutions of sacrificing the long term for the short and pursuing their private interests at the expense of the public good. When threatened with the loss of their jobs, even managers do not disdain to invoke the national interest. In 1990, after years of dismal performance, ICI became the subject of takeover speculation. Its chairman accepted that the company could be taken over and broken up but explained flatly that this would not be in 'the national interest'. Shortly afterwards, the company broke in two voluntarily. That, presumably, was in the national interest.

Smaller companies cannot claim an importance equivalent to a national icon such as ICI, but their directors are always free to plead for their own survival in the local interest. If a major employer is at risk of being taken over, the local and national media fill with forecasts of the dire consequences for jobs and businesses in the area. 'The Pru accepted the offer for reasons of commercial logic,' complained the chairman of Hillards after his grocery chain was taken over by Tesco. 'This is another example of the selfish and irresponsible attitude adopted by City financiers who put money before jobs.'[68] As the takeover boom of the 1980s drew to a close, having imperilled every quoted company in Britain for six or seven years, it seemed as if the entire business establishment was in open revolt against its institutional owners.

Sir Hector Laing, chairman of United Biscuits, compared the power of the institutional fund managers of the 1980s and 1990s to the trade union bosses of the 1960s and 1970s:

> Until their power was curbed, monopolistic representatives of working people – some trades union leaders – were not accountable to their millions of members and could cast their votes without consulting their wishes. That concentration of power was seriously damaging the economy and legislation was required to redress the imbalance between the trades unions and industrial management. Today there is a concentration of power in the hands of relatively few institutional fund managers ... In the buying and selling of publicly quoted companies they can cast the votes of millions of savers or pension fund beneficiaries without consulting their wishes. This too poses a threat to our future economic well-being ... By the time it becomes evident that our totally free market in corporate control is seriously damaging to the nation, it will be too late.'[69]

At the end of the previous year the director-general of the Confederation of British Industry (CBI), Sir John Banham, had denounced City fund managers as a 'lemming brigade'. 'The City attitude,' he said, 'is "Give it to me yesterday." '[70] A few months later his president, Sir Trevor Holdsworth, called fund managers 'punters rather than proprietors, using share certificates as betting slips operating on a Stock Exchange Tote'.[71]

The assumption that fund managers have wider social and economic responsibilities, including the support of long-term investment and the preservation of jobs from the boardroom to the factory floor, is obviously convenient for its proponents. It is not one which institutional investors would recognise, or would be entitled to recognise. 'There are clearly misconceptions about the duties and objectives of pension funds and a lack of recognition of their value to the UK economy,' explained Hugh Stevenson, chairman of Mercury

Asset Management (after his fund managers were criticised for selling shares in the Forte hotel chain to Granada). 'Pension funds are established to provide retirement incomes for their beneficiaries, the members of the schemes. When pension fund managers take on the stewardship of a company or local authority pension scheme they are accountable to the trustees of the scheme, to achieve the best possible investment performance. These clients, the pension fund trustees, have a duty to the beneficiaries of the pension fund. The trustees look for good long-term investment performance from pension fund managers . . . In turn, fund managers require strong performance from the managers of the companies in which they invest. If fund managers fail to provide good long-term investment performance, they can expect to lose their clients. And if company managers fail to maximise the potential of the company's assets, the management of those assets may be transferred to others.'[72]

This is an uncompromising message: the duty of the fund manager is to deliver the highest possible return on the savings entrusted to him, even if it costs incumbent managers and staff their jobs. It was precisely this narrow interpretation of the responsibilities of a fund manager to which Sir Robert Megarry gave the blessing of the law in the High Court in spring 1984.[73] That is why hard-nosed company managers believe (with militant trade unionists like Arthur Scargill) that the power of fund managers has increased, is increasing, and ought to be diminished. The *threat* of being taken over – and it is more often a threat than a reality – is the principal means by which managers are forced to experience that power; it is not surprising that they resent it. But it is also the means by which owners of companies overcome the divorce between ownership and control. If directors did not face the threat of losing their jobs, they would have no incentive to pursue the interests of the owners of the company. Those interests do not extend beyond maximising the return on the assets of the company. 'The best defence against a takeover', admitted Colin Hope, then chairman of T & N, 'is a well-managed company.'[74] A year after he spoke, T & N was taken over by an American bidder.

It is true that selling T & N to a foreign bidder was an expensive way of getting rid of its management. In theory, investors could simply deny capital to badly managed companies, and allow them to disappear. As a way of speeding up the process, takeovers are not a cheap alternative. The average merger or acquisition requires an army of lawyers, accountants, bankers, investment bankers, public relations firms, printers and institutional underwriters, all of them charging lavish fees. Sir James Goldsmith and his associates are said to have spent £140 million on their abortive bid for BAT Industries,[75] who spent £80 million beating them off. In 1995, the six bids launched for regional electricity companies were said to be worth £150 million to the variety of City professionals involved. The combined fees in the successful bid by Granada for Forte were put at £150 million.[76]

'In effect,' as John Plender has pointed out, 'the biggest shareholder in Forte, Mercury Asset Management, with 15 per cent of the Granada capital and 13 per cent of Forte, paid £22.5 million of its clients' money (15 per cent of £150 million) to get rid of the chairman and chief executive, Rocco Forte.'[77] Fees certainly give investment bankers a vested interest in stimulating bid activity. In 1989 Sir Paul Nicholson, chairman of the Vaux pubs and hotels company, accepted an invitation to debate the merits of takeovers with Sir James Goldsmith. 'The audience . . . consisted almost entirely of City people who make their living out of takeovers,' he recalled. 'Goldsmith's summing-up was brilliant, and he almost had the audience in tears by the time he had finished making his case about how wonderful contested bids were for regenerating British industry.'[78] When the vote was taken, only five people out of an audience of one hundred and twenty agreed with Nicholson that the number of takeovers ought to be reduced.

City v. Industry

It was at the tail-end of the great takeover boom of the 1980s that the debate about short-termism got under way in earnest. Companies and their institutional shareholders, driven apart by fee-hungry City intermediaries, had never seemed more out of sympathy with each other. No company felt safe from the threat of takeover. Even mighty ICI, flagship and bell-wether of British manufacturing industry, was being menaced by the archetype of the financially driven, short-term predator: Hanson. In 1989 Sir James Goldsmith had launched his £13 billion bid to 'unbundle' BAT Industries, with the backing of a horde of junk bond investors. A year before, Nestlé, the giant Swiss multinational, had taken over the York confectionery manufacturer, Rowntree, in a bitterly contested bid.

In 1990, Ernest Saunders, former chief executive of one of Britain's largest industrial enterprises, was jailed, together with two others, in connection with offences committed during the acquisition of the Distillers Company four years earlier. Saunders portrayed himself as the fall-guy for the sins of greedy City financiers, and won some sympathy from fellow-industrialists. Even the dry-as-dust Peter Lilley, appointed secretary of state for Trade and Industry in the summer of 1990, wondered whether 'deal-making in our open capital market has gone beyond the economically justifiable to become almost an end in itself'. By 1991 his complaints about an 'over-developed finance function vis-à-vis the production function' were positively Huttonesque.[79]

City *v.* Industry, Financiers *v.* Engineers and Gentlemen *v.* Businessmen are among the great staples of left-wing economic historiography. *The State We're In* knits the City, the Conservative Party, Oxbridge, the Monarchy, the Treasury and Home Counties rentiers into an ingenious conspiracy of southern financial interests against northern manufacturing industry.[80] It is undeniable that Britain has an exceptionally powerful and centralised financial sector, populated by men and women with strong ties to the social and political élite and the most tenuous links with the grimy realities of industrial Britain. This was a feature of the City even in medieval times; it has survived the Industrial Revolution to thrive amid the blinking abstraction of the City dealing rooms of the Information Age.[81]

When the first institutional investors emerged in London in the late seventeenth and early eighteenth century, they invested not in productive trade and industry but in government bonds and aristocratic debt. Some aristocrats used the borrowings to finance development of mines, canals, docks and harbours and towns and cities, but much was squandered on country houses, sybaritic lifestyles, declining agricultural projects and expensive dowries.[82] The historian of the aristocracy has accused them of diversion of middle- and working-class savings from urban and industrial Britain into their own unproductive pursuits.[83] 'The gentlemanly ideal reaches far back into British life,' alleges Will Hutton. 'It was the animating force in the rise of British capitalism . . . A gentlemanly income was necessarily one for which the recipient did not labour too obviously. Ideally it came from land, but the next best thing was income from interest, dividends and professional fees so that money made from finance and commerce in the City was nearly as good as acres in the shires. Manufacturing was less socially desirable, and although manufacturers and inventors were briefly celebrated in the middle of the nineteenth century the old values quickly reasserted themselves.'[84]

The nineteenth-century City was certainly not close to industry. In Victorian times, Britain effectively had two markets for capital: industrialists relied on local investors and retained profits, while City financiers bankrolled foreign governments and utilities. This division was reinforced by the social and political divisions between the industrial and City élites, and by the failure of the (mainly provincial) industrialists to make use of the London market.[85] In the City there were periodic booms in share prices: the American mining bubble of the 1820s (in which Disraeli lost a fortune); the railway company mania of the 1840s (which led to the demise of George Hudson, the 'Railway King'); the share-pushing of 'Baron' Albert Grant in the 1870s (Trollope's model for Melmotte); the electricity promotions of the 1880s (the 'Brush boom'); and the South African gold mining boom of the 1890s (the 'Kaffir Circus'). Each of these served to underline the ignorance of City stock-jobbers and brokers about the real prospects of industrial enterprises, and their tendency to exploit what little they knew to their own advantage. The reluctance of the respectable City to help industrial companies raise capital placed them at the mercy of unscrupulous promoters whose ambition was to puff up the price of shares. The blue-blooded merchant bankers, who might have offered industrialists more dispassionate advice, preferred to bring foreign governments and utilities to the London capital market. 'I confess that personally I have a horror of all industrial companies,' wrote Lord Revelstoke of Barings in 1911, 'and that I should not think of placing my hard-earned gains into such a venture.'[86]

In the Edwardian era, companies engaged in new industries such as electricity and motor cars complained about their difficulties in raising capital in the City on reasonable terms.[87] A suspicion of industrial shares became self-fulfilling, as the distrust of investors meant there was little activity in the few that were listed.[88] As early as 1909, the chairman of one electrical company was calling for 'the establishment of a strong industrial bank . . . on the lines of the Deutsche bank in Germany'.[89] Joseph Chamberlain advocated protective tariffs for manufacturing industry because he feared the greed and ignorance of the effete southern élite would destroy it in the name of Free Trade.[90] In the 1980s and 1990s, the acquisition of household names like Rowntree and Rover Group by foreign bidders seemed to be turning his fears into reality.

By 1990, the NAPF was so perturbed by the widening mental and social gulf between industry and the City that it commissioned a collection of essays to prevent 'misunderstanding between owners and managers of companies'. Published in February 1990 under the title *Creative Tension?*, most of the essays predictably prefigure the corporate governance movement of the mid to late 1990s. One of the essayists, Sir Adrian Cadbury, went on to chair a committee on the subject; another, Jonathan Charkham, to write the definitive text book on corporate governance ('required reading', said Sir Adrian) and develop a new career as a professional corporate governor. 'No one who talks to any of the protagonists,' he concluded in the book, 'has the slightest doubt that beneath the elegant logic and complex arguments, the basic dynamics are those of power. Everyone speaks their own book.' Yet he concluded blithely that 'there is a part for everyone to play – chairmen, boards, employees, the City, academe, shareholders, banks in creating a new system of corporate governance'.[91]

Better corporate governance promises a world in which institutional investors and companies talk to each other more often, and the responsibilities of the company are broadened beyond the Megarry formula to encompass employment and society as a whole. It is a fuzzy solution to fundamental problems: the divorce between ownership and control, and the concentration of economic and financial power in the hands of PLCs and their institutional shareholders. This may be why it has become, *faute de mieux*, the Establishment solution. Yet *Creative Tension?* is a striking record of how wide the gap which separates the worlds of the institution and the boardroom has become since the 1960s and 1970s, when there still was a recognisable Establishment spanning the worlds of Westminster, the City and Industry. Several of the industrial essayists complained of the concentration of power in the hands of a small group of fund managers, many of them young and most based in the south-east of England. 'A wedge is being driven between the providers of capital and its productive users,' wrote Sir Hector Laing. 'Each seems to be living and operating in a different world with a different timescale.'[92]

It was left to David Hopkinson, a former fund manager who had ascended to the chair of an industrial company, to explain how and why this great divergence had come about:

> Whereas two years ago the majority of people in the City were working primarily for their clients and only secondarily for their own profit, the reverse is now the case, with the majority putting self-interest first and the devil take the client ... The change in attitude of mind, which is particularly prevalent amongst younger people, has been accompanied by an arrogance that one does not meet elsewhere in public affairs. This arrogance seems to arise because people – like institutional investment managers, analysts and corporate finance men and women in merchant banks – seem often to have forgotten that they are the servants of their organisations ... But it is not just mental attitudes which have led to the decline in relationships, it is also a change in priorities and objectives. Whereas once upon a time analysts and merchant bankers were presumed to be advising clients with their interests in mind, they now seem motivated by the desire to create business and they seem not to be too fussy about how this is done.[93]

Much of this was imaginative nostalgia of the kind old City hands invented to cheer themselves up during a particularly brash period in the history of the Square Mile. But even in 1985, before the Big Bang of the following year had created the conflicts of interest now commonplace in investment banking, it was faintly shocking when a leading merchant bank agreed to act for a company bidding for one of its clients.[94] Today, it is not unusual for fund managers to hawk shareholdings around the corporate finance departments of leading investment banks in the hope of getting a takeover battle started.

Mercury Asset Management has acquired a considerable reputation for amassing large shareholdings in companies vulnerable to takeover and using them to tempt potential bidders and their investment banks. (Carol Galley is said to describe wasteful management of capital as a 'sin'.)[95] In 1990 Mercury topped a poll as 'the least loyal' shareholder.[96] In October 1994 it approached International Paper offering to sell to them its 25 per cent stake in a Swiss engineering firm called Holvis. A bid battle developed, eventually won by BBA, a British counter-bidder.[97] Another large fund manager, PDFM, accumulated a large stake in Ferranti in 1989 in the clear expectation of a bid. It had also accumulated a 25 per cent stake in House of Fraser by the end of 1995, and was well-known to be the 'key holder' if a predator wanted to bid. Of course, the identification of under-valued companies is an important part of the work of a successful fund manager. But a large position in any stock is hard to sell at a profit unless a bidder emerges to offer a premium to the market price. The truth is that fund managers now rely on takeovers to boost their investment performance.

Cynicism of this kind is not as recent as David Hopkinson appears to think. Nearly thirty years ago George Ross Goobey told the Imperial Tobacco trustees that 'no account in the comparison between equities and gilts is taken for the prospect of takeovers, when a little of the hidden fat in most companies is allowed to emerge.'[98] He deliberately sought out companies liable to be taken over: Ribena Limited found the Imperial Tobacco pension fund had bought a large number of shares before it was taken over by Beechams.[99] In retirement in 1992, Ross Goobey recalled selling a holding in Truman Hanbury and Buxton to Max Joseph at a premium to the offer price (there were then no takeover rules obliging bidders to offer the same price to all shareholders). 'Last week I went to a discussion at the Institute of Actuaries,' he explained. 'Chaps were getting up . . . and making their point that the rate of improvement in dividends was not as good as it used to be. None of them mentioned the fact that every now and again in the investment world we get a ruddy good takeover which bumps your performance up tremendously . . . I always liked a nice juicy takeover.'[100]

This does not mean fund managers will always sell if a bidder offers a premium to the current share price. Some institutions have a consistent policy of supporting incumbent management. In the 1970s, Britannic Assurance prided itself on taking large stakes in companies based around its Birmingham heartland and advertising that it never pledged its stock to bidders; its involvement was sufficient to block three takeover bids in 1979.* Both M&G, where Hopkinson was managing director, and the Prudential have long pursued a policy of supporting bid targets in all but the most extreme cases. 'We support incumbent managements,' said Mick Newmarch, who as chief investment

---

* The bids were by BTR for Bestobell, GEI International for Moss Engineering, and Armstrong Equipment for Jenks & Cottrell. See Minns, *Pension Funds and British Capitalism*, p. 107.

TABLE 31.3
Acquisitions and Mergers in Britain by British Companies

Year	Number of Companies Acquired	Total Value of Acquisitions (£bn)
1979	534	1.7
1980	469	1.5
1981	452	1.1
1982	463	2.2
1983	447	2.3
1984	568	5.5
1985	474	7.1
1986	842	15.4
1987	1,528	16.5
1988	1,499	22.8
1989	1,337	27.3
1990	779	8.3
1991	506	10.4
1992	432	5.9
1993	526	7.1
1994	674	8.3
1995	505	32.6
1996	584	30.7
1997	504	26.4
Total	13,123	233.1

Source: CSO Bulletin Issue 76/91, Acquisitions and Mergers Within the UK, Quarter 3 1991, 12 November 1991, table 8, page 16; Office of National Statistics, Acquisition and Mergers Involving UK Companies, Quarter 4 1996, 1 February 1997, Table 8 and Quarter 3 1998, 10 November 1998, Table 8.

officer at the Prudential was probably the single most influential fund manager in the City. 'It is not in any way to be *pro bono publico*. It is in our self-interest to behave as we behave.'[101] Between 1984 and 1989 there were nearly five hundred bids where the Prudential had an interest; it failed to support the incumbent management on only twenty-five occasions.

Under Newmarch, the company never sold shares to predators in dawn raids and never accepted tender offers for their stock. 'We build up big positions and run them in companies whose management is better than their peer group in the industry,' said Newmarch. 'If you transact regularly all you're doing is handing money to the brokers.'[102] The policy continued after he left: the Prudential backed ManWeb against a bid from Scottish Power in October 1995, and Northern Electric against CalEnergy in December 1996. Other institutions are less predictable, but support incumbent management if they consider a bid cheap or opportunistic. It is not unknown for the institutions to reject bids on the grounds that they will damage the *bidder* rather than the target. After all, they usually own shares in both companies. One survey found that fund managers invited to pledge their shares to one side or another in a bid usually fuss more about the long-term prospects than the short-term value of the bid.[103] Which is why shareholders rejected the Dixons bid for Woolworths in 1986, despite the fact that the bidder was offering a premium of 50 per cent to the share price before the takeover started. The institutions were also right to argue that Boots paid too much for Ward White in 1989, and that Farnell overpaid for Premier Industrial in 1996. In 1980 Imperial Tobacco bought the Howard Johnson motel chain in the United States against the wishes of its institutional shareholders, and the deal eventually cost the company its independence.

Are Managers Innocent?

Senseless and overpriced acquisitions are a reminder that most bids are initiated not by the institutions but by company managers. Some takeovers are genuinely strategic – they are the only way to reduce risks, eliminate potentially ruinous competition, or gain access to new markets or technology – but most are simply a better or quicker alternative to expanding through investment. A great many bids are driven by no more than overweening managerial ambition. Warren Buffett, the billionaire American fund manager, says: 'Many chief executive officers attain their positions in part because they possess an abundance of animal spirits and ego ... they won't disappear when he reaches the top. When such a chief executive officer is encouraged by his advisers to make deals, he responds much as would a teenage boy who is encouraged by his father to have a normal sex life. It's not a push that he needs.'[104] Buffett calls most Anglo-Saxon managers adherents of the 'gin rummy' school of management, where they see their role as pack-shufflers and deal-makers whose job is to buy businesses here and sell them there. Managers (as well as fund managers) talk of themselves as managing 'portfolios'.

The lure of the deal is undoubtedly an integral part of the Anglo-Saxon business culture, but it is reinforced by financial incentives. The costs of mounting (and resisting) bids falls not on the managers who conceive and prosecute them, but on the shareholders. Managerial rewards are usually tied in some way to earnings per share, and the quickest way to boost earnings is to buy them readymade rather than invest in a new factory which may not produce earnings for two or three years. In the 1980s (particularly after the crash of October 1987 made shares more expensive as a takeover currency) the quest for earnings per share also encouraged companies to finance acquisitions with borrowed money. It is an arithmetical truism that companies which borrow money to finance acquisitions can increase their earnings per share more rapidly than companies which pay for them with shares or cash (interest payments are also tax-deductible).

It is not unknown for a company facing depressed profits to make an acquisition with borrowed money purely to prop up its earnings per share, and tax considerations can also play a part. For many years, companies with insufficient domestic earnings to reclaim all the income tax they paid on dividends to shareholders had a strong incentive to buy the extra earnings by acquisition.[105] The GKN bid for Westland helicopters in 1994 was widely agreed to be driven almost entirely by a need to recover a mountain of unrelieved advance corporation tax.[106] After the deal is completed, acquisition accounting can provide further opportunities to enhance earnings, and the relatively favourable accounting treatment of takeovers has undoubtedly encouraged managers to buy assets rather than build them. 'Whatever accounting convention is used,' concluded one study of the subject 'acquisitions normally have a less unfavourable immediate effect on the rate of return of the acquirer than the investment of similar resources in internal growth.'[107] Reorganisation provisions – into which are poured every expense from sacking workers to re-painting the company vans – have helped bidders make accounting profits on takeovers even where the underlying reality was a serious loss.

The difference between the price a company paid for an acquisition and the actual value of its assets ('goodwill') can be written off immediately against reserves, avoiding the risk of reducing earnings per share by subtracting it from future profits. As Terry Smith has pointed out, when Coloroll bought John Crowther it managed to write off £11 million more than the total cost of the acquisition.[108] As if to prove that accounting profits and shareholder value are not the same thing, receivers were appointed at Coloroll in June 1990. Many other companies – from the whizzkiddery of British and Commonwealth, through the financial make-believe of Brent Walker and Maxwell Communications, to a venerable old stager like Boots – have suffered grievously, and sometimes fatally, from over-estimating the value of an acquisition or their ability to run it efficiently. When the accounting rules were changed in 1997 to make companies put goodwill on their balance sheets, this was expected to lead to a fall in takeovers. 'There has been a tendency towards overpayment over the years,' said the head of auditing at Coopers and

Lybrand. 'This will make people think a little harder about the prices they pay in acquisitions.'*

Do Takeovers Work?

The great paradox of the takeover is that even those acquisitions which do not end in financial disaster take a toll of profitability. Most research suggests that shareholders in the acquired company invariably do well, but shares in the bidder usually under-perform. This is partly because managers pay too high a premium for control, and partly because they are not good at making mergers work.[109] Even strategically sensible deals are often undermined by the process of integration. The obvious economies, like sacking people who do the same job at both companies, tend to be reflected in the price of the acquisition and so yield no benefits. 'The only consistent beneficiaries of the [takeover] process,' writes Plender, 'seem to be the shareholders in the acquired company, the City professionals who extract huge fees from the deals, and the individual managers of the acquisitive companies who can use the increased scale of their responsibilities to justify fatter pay packages.'[110]

This is scarcely surprising. Bidders are bound to overestimate their ability to run the acquired businesses better, because only the sellers understand what is for sale. Bidders will inevitably devote less energy to managing an acquisition than to making it because those who launch bids are in most cases looking to purchase additional earnings rather than opportunities to cut costs or invest in newly acquired assets. The wider economic impact of takeovers seems to bear this out: they are neither good nor bad for the rate of growth and the standard of living. Britain has the most active market in corporate control of any country apart from the United States, yet its overall economic performance is not conspicuously superior to that of Germany, France or Japan.

However, international comparisons miss the point. The British economy does not rely on takeovers to boost economic efficiency; they are simply the ultimate means by which owners of companies make their property rights effective. A failure to manage the assets of the company in the interests of the shareholders leads to lower earnings, reduced dividends and a falling share price. This attracts predators. In Germany, France and Japan, share-

---

* The Accounting Standards Board (ASC) struggled from 1980 to rectify the perverse incentive created by accounting for goodwill. In December 1997 it published new rules reducing management discretion over whether to put goodwill into the company balance sheet. See *Financial Times*, 4 December 1997.

holders are traditionally less important than financiers. This is changing – not least because European and Asian companies now have a larger number of Anglo-Saxon shareholders – but it is still true that managers of European and Japanese companies respond less to the demands of their shareholders than the promptings of their bankers, who often have a representative on the board. By contrast, institutional investors rarely sit on the boards of British companies. They may make their presence felt only by the constant threat to transfer management of the company to a new set of controllers. No amount of research can measure the effect this pressure has. It would be absurd to believe that managers of British companies consider nothing other then maximising returns to shareholders, but there is no doubt that they are the first priority of the senior management of every public company.

Returning to Private Ownership

It is because they are frightened of being taken over that British company managers make 'shareholder value' their priority. Companies which dislike the discipline are always free to revert to private ownership, and at the top of the last takeover boom a number of companies did exactly that. In 1988 Richard Branson took his Virgin group private just fifteen months after listing it on the London Stock Exchange. 'One of the sad things I notice,' he said at the time, 'is that if you create a company from scratch, which has always been the Virgin philosophy, you get very little credit for it in the City. Whereas if you buy and sell companies and lay off people, the City thinks that is exciting.'[111] A particular problem was institutional distrust of his burgeoning airline and travel interests. (Oddly enough, this did not prevent Branson listing Virgin Express on the Nasdaq stock exchange in the United States and the Brussels stock exchange in Belgium nine years later.)[112] The De Haan family – who took Saga Holidays public only to manage their liability for death duties – also took their travel company private, fed up with the pressure for steady profits in a highly cyclical industry. Anita Roddick of the Body Shop has complained that the City is full of 'pin-striped dinosaurs' and that 'finance bores the pants off me'. She pondered taking the company private and turning it into a charitable trust but its fading performance has instead forced it to become more a orthodox enterprise.[113]

Unorthodox businesses, like Andrew Lloyd Webber's Really Useful Group, have returned to private ownership partly because institutions find them difficult to value. Another factor which convinced Branson to go private was his belief that the institutions would never value Virgin properly. Shares floated at £1.40 in 1986 were trading as low as 85p when he decided to take it private. He was probably right to conclude that the City did not understand what he was doing.* Nor was their incomprehension necessarily to his disadvantage. The negotiation of the price at which a company is taken private, like the price at which managers can buy out a company subsidiary, illustrates the advantage managers have over shareholders in the absence of an external measure of value like a takeover. Branson bought out the Virgin shareholders for £90 million, and less than a year later was able to sell a mere quarter of the same company to Fujisankei Communications of Japan for £96 million. In less than twelve months, the company was worth more than four times the price the institutions had charged for selling it back. Like most managers, Branson knew a lot more about its prospects than they did. Andrew Lloyd Webber achieved something similar. He bought back the Really Useful Group for £77.5 million in 1990, and a year later sold one third of it to Polygram for £78 million, recouping his outlay on an investment worth three times the price he paid for it. The force of these examples was not lost on the institutions; when Alan Sugar tried to take Amstrad electronics private for £112.7 million in 1992, the shareholders refused. The shares were soon worth more than double his offer of 30p.

Long-Term Owners to Short-Term Institutions?

It is partly because institutions fail occasionally to appreciate the true value of a company that the takeover mechanism exists: the premium bidders pay to acquire a company brings market values back into line with real values. Naturally, the managers of companies which are acquired see it differently. They say the discount which attracted the bidder in the first place measures the lack of institutional understanding of innovative companies which invest for the long term. Takeovers, in other words, are the chief symptom of institutional short-termism.

This is one of the crucial points at which the debate about the nature of modern capitalism is joined. On one view, the institutional investors are punters rather than proprietors, robbing companies of the time and money they need to invest in new wealth and jobs, and stripping governments of their rightful sovereignty over the rate of interest and exchange. On the other, they are the guardians of economic growth and efficiency, supplying

---

* His biographer claims the under-performance of the share price was causing Branson personal embarrassment. A number of Virgin artists were shareholders and his neighbour in Oxfordshire had sunk £30,000 into the company. See Tim Jackson, *Virgin King*, HarperCollins, 1994, pp. 239–43.

the savings of the nation to those who can use them most effectively and denying them to wasteful and spendthrift politicians.

The choice between these points of view has moral, as well as economic, significance. Men and women struggle every day to strike the right balance between their natural prodigality and the need for thrift. Managers, investors, officials, ministers and economists struggle in the same way to establish the right relationship between spending, saving and investment. For John Maynard Keynes – who played all of these roles, sometimes simultaneously – the shortcomings of the economic and financial system became inseparable from human nature.[114] He embodied the contradictions between rational accumulation and spontaneous pleasure, arguing in 1923 that 'in the long run we are all dead' and in 1936 that 'speculators may do no harm as bubbles on a steady stream of enterprise. But the position is serious when enterprise becomes the bubble on a whirlpool of speculation. When the Capital development of a country becomes the by-product of the activities of a casino, the job is likely to be ill-done.'

In the 1920s, Keynes was a confirmed short-termist, speculating ruthlessly in stocks and shares according to a formula familiar to any addict of gambling. By the late 1930s, the speculative investments of his youth had given way to long-term industrial shareholdings in the same way that his economic ideas had crystallised against the mania for liquidity and the timidity about investing for the long-term:

> It is from time to time the duty of a serious investor to accept the depreciation of his holdings with equanimity and without reproaching himself. Any other policy is anti-social, destructive of confidence, and incompatible with the working of the economic system. An investor is aiming or should be aiming primarily at long period results and should be solely judged by these.[115]

One of the chief effects of the institutionalisation of share ownership since the last war is the elimination of the loyal individual shareholder of the kind Keynes had become.

As institutions have supplanted individuals, the tendency to buy and sell shares rather than hold them has increased markedly. Among the findings of the Wilson Committee was that the average length of time for which investors held a share had fallen from twenty-four years in the 1960s to between three and eight years in the 1970s. Today, institutions may be holding shares for as little as five years.[116] 'We buy shares because they look cheap and sell them because they look dear,' explains Dick Barfield, chief investment officer at Standard Life until 1996. 'That is basically what we do. That may mean we only hold some shares for a short period of time but, if they do us very well, it may mean that we retain a substantial shareholding for a long time. We are really neither short-termist nor long-termist. We have just got a philosophy of buying cheap and selling dear.'[117]

It is this loss of the sense of ownership which vexes company managers. Adrian Cadbury, former chairman of Cadbury Schweppes, recalled that in the 1950s the majority of the shares in the company were still owned by the family. At the time of the merger between Cadbury and Schweppes in 1969 over two thirds of the shares in Cadbury were owned by individuals and one third by institutions. Ten years later, the proportions were reversed. Sir Adrian thought this was the key to understanding short-termism:

> The basic change . . . has been the replacement of individual share-holders by institutional shareholders . . . [which] could be described as a move from ownership to investment. Institutional investors are placing funds belonging to others in a wide variety of financial instruments, while individual shareholders entrust their capital to a limited number of enterprises, of which they see themselves as part-owners . . . As owners they took a long-term view . . . They held on to their shares out of loyalty, because they still had family links with the management of the companies concerned, or simply through the lack of an open market for their shares. Their judgment on the balance to strike between profit now and profit in the future was usually much in line with that of those who ran the business. For whatever reason, they found themselves following Mark Twain's advice: 'There is a great deal to be said for putting all your eggs in one basket and then watching that basket carefully.'[118]

His solution was to make the institutional investors more like the family owners.[119] Within a year Sir Adrian was chairing the first of three committees on corporate governance, a managerially-inspired and politically-driven move-ment which aims to replace shareholders who sell with shareholders who understand and interfere.

Is Better Corporate Governance the Answer?

The leading figures in the corporate governance industry, like Sir Adrian, acknowledge the ineradicability of the divorce between ownership and con-trol. But they believe it can be bridged by a mixture of boardroom devices – splitting the roles of chairman and chief executive, appointing more non-executive directors, using a remuneration committee to set pay and perks, and encouraging regular dialogue between managers and their shareholders.

Jonathan Charkham thinks the process can be encouraged by changes to company law. 'The joint stock company is a legal construct, not a product of nature,' he says. 'It is not interventionist or *dirigiste* for governments to ensure that the balance of interests between all parties affected by companies is maintained. The Companies Act now creaks in some fundamental ways.'[120] He advocates separate company laws for owner-managed and public companies; tighter definitions of boardroom roles; less cronyism in the choice of non-executive directors; more inhibitions on hostile takeovers; and wider use of German-style two-tier boards. Attentive institutional shareholders are not fundamental to his reforms.

But those institutions which take corporate governance seriously are not prepared to confine their attention to the composition and duties of the board of directors. Its adherents believe that institutional investors should force badly managed companies to change their strategy as well as their structure. Institutional activism of this kind originated in the United States. In the 1980s the California Public Employees' Retirement System (Calpers), one of the largest pension funds, was finding it difficult to improve its investment performance: it was too large to sell holdings in failing companies without moving the price against itself, and its use of indexed fund managers meant selling the shares was not always an option. Calpers began to buy stakes in what it called 'crummy companies,' and tried to embarrass them into improving their performance by pushing for changes of strategy. It is now exploring taking this activism further by securing seats on the boards of badly performing companies.[121]

Some years beforehand, another American, Robert Monks, had established a firm called Institutional Shareholder Services (ISS). It monitors corporate behaviour and advises institutions on how to vote at annual general meetings (AGMs). Similar forces to the Calpers and ISS initiatives are now at work in Britain. UK Active Value, a fund manager in which Calpers has invested $200 million, is already picking off 'crummy companies'.* Hermes Pensions Management, the fund management arm of the BT pension fund, has set up a similar 'activist' fund and acquired LENS Investment Management, an American company set up by Robert Monks to invest in 'crummy companies.' ISS recently agreed to provide its services to the members of the National

---

* UK Active Value was set up in 1993 to make money by investing in under-performing companies and pushing for change. Its targets have included Scholl, Kenwood, Signet, Hambros Bank and Mirror Group. It is now looking to use the Calpers money to tackle companies capitalised at more than £250 million. See *Financial Times*, 13 January 1998 and 4 February 1999.

Association of Pension Funds (NAPF).[122] In 1996 an ISS-style company, Manifest, began issuing institutional investors with corporate governance briefings and advice on how to vote at company meetings. Its first big success came that autumn, when it successfully put the William Cook engineering group at the mercy of predators by drawing attention to its poor corporate governance record. The chairman, Andrew Cook, not only combined the role with that of chief executive but had awarded himself a five-year rolling contract worth £500,000 a year. In February 1997 Cook was forced to take the company private to escape a hostile bid from Triplex Lloyd.

The principal aim of Manifest is to make institutions behave more like owners and less like investors by embarrassing them into using their voting rights. Every ordinary share carries the right to vote at the AGM; it is one of the chief rights of ownership, but surprisingly few use it. When Jimmy Goldsmith and his associates bid £13 billion for BAT Industries in 1989, in the largest and most highly geared takeover offer ever made in Britain, only one third of BAT shareholders bothered to vote. About the same number of British Aerospace shareholders voted when the company sold the Rover Group to BMW of Germany. A survey by the National Association of Pension Funds (NAPF) found a quarter of pension funds had a policy of never voting, and that only one fifth made a point of voting at every AGM. It also found that unit trust providers and the fund management arms of merchant banks hardly voted at all.[123] This indifference would be understandable if voting rights were valueless but clearly they are not, as Alastair Ross Goobey of Hermes discovered. 'I have been approached by someone who wanted to pay us for us to vote our shares in their interests at an annual general meeting,' he has admitted. 'Whether or not this is either legal or ethical, it does demonstrate the value of a vote separate from the value of the other assets which a share certificate represents.'[124]

As the corporate governance bandwagon gathered momentum in 1991, the institutional investors came under increasing pressure to improve their voting records. *The Responsibilities of Institutional Shareholders*, a discussion paper issued by the Association of British Insurers (ABI) in March 1991, aimed to encourage insurance companies to vote their shares.[125] Nine months later the Institutional Shareholders' Committee reinforced this message in *The Responsibilities of Institutional Shareholders in the UK*. By 1993 the NAPF had set up a Voting Issues Service to monitor the agendas of AGMs of leading companies, and identify key issues where its members could be instructed to vote. The results of this burst of activity were discouraging. A 1995 survey found that just one third of institutional investors were voting routinely, and even the biggest funds voted only two thirds of the time.[126] Pensions Investments Research Consultants (PIRC) estimate that the average level of votes cast on resolutions at AGMs rose just 1.6 per cent between 1993 and 1996.

When the NAPF surveyed its members for a second time in 1996 it was embarrassed to find that only 28 per cent voted regularly; 32 per cent voted on contentious issues only; and 21 per cent never voted. Behaviour had scarcely changed since 1991. Exasperated, the association finally told its members they had a *duty* to vote, and this seems to have had some effect. Pension fund trustees have taken to drawing up and publishing corporate governance policies, which allow voting agencies and banks to vote automatically on their behalf according to certain guidelines. The RailPen voting policy, for example, includes an instruction to vote against the payment of dividends not covered by earnings. Nine out of ten fund managers have now published corporate governance guidelines.

It seems, however, that company managers take little notice of them in framing their resolutions. They obviously do not see institutional resistance as a serious threat to doing whatever they like. In 1997 the Commercial Union (of all companies) thought it could get away with a resolution preventing shareholders voting on its annual report and accounts.[127] In the event, the motion was withdrawn before it could be put to a vote, but it was a startling reminder of managerial indifference to institutional shareholders. The ABI claims its members now vote on more than nine resolutions out of ten, but this has made absolutely no impact on managerial power. No company motions were defeated at any AGM in 1996.

This gap between form and substance is symptomatic of the weakness of the idea of corporate governance. Conformity with its recommendations has become formulaic. Companies have split the role of the chairman and the chief executive; appointed non-executive directors; set up remuneration committees; and got rid of three and five-year rolling contracts for directors. Institutional investors vote more often, but their votes are being counted rather than weighed. Neither the workings of the average company board, nor the remuneration of its members, nor the overall strategy of the company, has changed in any material respect.

Fund managers are unperturbed. They claim that their best work is achieved by talking to managers behind the scenes. 'If we went about our business publicly, managements would soon be shy of talking to us,' said Mick Newmarch in 1990. 'But at any time there are between thirty and fifty companies you don't hear of which are receiving our constant and detailed attention.'[128] A Scottish fund manager agrees: 'It is surprising what can be done in a quiet way, without setting up a ginger group.'[129] Another Scottish fund manager reckons over-zealous monitoring of corporate strategies could backfire spectacularly. 'There is a potential downside to greater investor activism. Management may start trying to anticipate controversial issues and perhaps back off from backing their own judgment. In time, that may turn companies into more bureaucratic and less entrepreneurial organisations.'[130]

Hidden institutional pressure is not a myth. It manifests itself periodically, usually in changes of senior management rather than alterations in corporate strategy. In the early 1970s, the Prudential spearheaded a successful institutional coup to get rid of the head of Vickers, Sir Lesley Rowan. In 1983 the shareholders deposed Sir Peter Jay as chairman and chief executive of TV-am. That year, the senior management of the Rank Organisation was toppled in an institutional coup. 'It is not right to suggest we promote any particular commercial strategy,' contended Ron Artus, then the chief investment manager at the Prudential. 'At Rank Organisation we have not told the board there is a right way or a wrong way to deal with the . . . businesses . . . we told them that a successful management would have devised a better strategy, so we suggested they go out and find better management.'[131] In recent years, a whole string of top company managers have effectively lost their jobs to institutional pressure: Nicholas Wills at BET, Ralph Halpern at Burton, James White at Bunzl, Ephraim Margulies at Berisford, George Davies at Next, Derek Lewis at Granada, Philip Green at Amber Day, Terry Maher at Pentos, John Fletcher at Budgen, John Hardman and Graham Stow at Asda, Gerald Ratner at Ratners, Maurice Saatchi at Saatchi and Saatchi, David Plastow at Inchcape, Kit McMahon at Midland Bank, Desmond Pitcher at United Utilities and David Montgomery of Mirror Group.[132]

Occasionally, the institutions encounter serious resistance. An attempt in the first half of 1991 to replace the management at the pollution controls group, Tace, turned into a test of will between Mike Sandland, chief investment officer of the Norwich Union, and David Nicolson, the veteran industrialist recently appointed chairman of the company. Sandland led a group of Tace shareholders who were increasingly disgruntled by poor performance, corporate extravagance and the lack of a clear strategy, but when Sandland asked Nicholson why he had not discussed these concerns with the institutions, the Tace chairman allegedly replied, 'Why should I?'[133] Norwich Union was provoked into making an unprecedented public attack on the board, saying it had lost confidence in the management and required them all to resign. Nicolson was furious. 'Men like Sandland have spent their entire life in Norwich Union, have never been in industry and should not control industrial companies in this way,' he said. 'I think it is indicative of the short-sighted appreciation of industry among the institutions.'[134] He told the *Sunday Times* that 'Sandland wants to be seen as the white knight of corporate governance. It is politically motivated and it is vindictive . . . The institutions have become arrogant and they need to be regulated.'[135] The Norwich won the argument; the chairman and entire board of directors were obliged to resign at an extraordinary general meeting in June 1991.

The dismissal of the Tace management looked like the opening of a new front in corporate governance, with institutional shareholders forcing companies to change their strategy as well as their managers. 'The market does not allow you the easy option of just selling the shares and walking away,' said Sandland afterwards. 'You either sit and suffer or do what seems to be the morally correct thing and make representations for change.'[136] But in retrospect it was just an extreme example of a routine occurrence. Sandland was not suggesting that he knew how to run Tace better than Sir David Nicolson and his board, any more than Artus thought he could run Rank better than the directors dismissed eight years earlier. All Sandland secured was a change of management without going to the trouble and expense of supporting a takeover bid.

Provided directors' greed is not too conspicuous, and they keep the dividends up and the share price rising, the average board can do more or less what it likes. In 1986 Ernest Saunders, then chief executive of Guinness, reneged on a series of promises he had made about the management of the company during the takeover battle for Distillers. Yet both the Norwich Union and the Prudential supported him publicly when he asked the institutions for approval at an extraordinary general meeting. 'My only interest,' said a pension fund manager of the time, 'is my clients' property, and ensuring the Guinness share price does not fall.' The one fund manager, who dared to voice his misgivings earned himself a starring role in Ernest Saunders's *apologia pro vita sua*. 'The red-bearded Graeme Knox, who had been bellyaching for months, got his attack in first,' was how Saunders recalled the meeting.[137] But Knox, then chief investment officer at Scottish Amicable, lost the vote.

The Guinness EGM of 1986 was as good an illustration as any of the limits of corporate governance. Some years later Graeme Knox pointed out that a determined management will always argue that what they decide is in the best interests of shareholders:

> I thought I was dealing not with Saunders but with the Establishment. Plenty of people had tried to badger him behind the scenes. He had been pressurised by the Bank of England and others not to welch on his obligations, and he had said that he could do what he liked in the interests of shareholders. I was not prepared to put my name on the record as going along with that . . . Self-regulation was quite incapable of making him stick to his publicly stated obligations. A few very respectable people were, by going on the board, in effect supporting him.

Ironically, Knox later became an adviser to the Guinness pension fund. 'The company is now under new management,' he explained.[138]

Plenty of other companies – Burton Group, Saatchi and Saatchi, Midland Bank, Ratners, Fisons, Forte, P & O – have destroyed a great deal of shareholder wealth before the institutions questioned the decisions of the management. Typically, it was James Goldsmith who blurted out the truth about corporate governance. 'What is the real reason people want institutions to do it?' he asked in 1990. 'Because, basically, they realise this blasted capitalism is the right system, hate having to admit it, hoping we can have capitalism without capitalists. So if we could only hand over capitalism to a bunch of faceless folk out there, wouldn't that be lovely? We'd get the benefits of capitalism, without the irritation of capitalists.'[139]

The truth is that corporate governance is not a solution to the problem of divorce between ownership and control, but an aspect of it. Even in its most extreme forms, managers would still manage and owners would still own. This is why an increasingly influential body of opinion believes that the concept of 'the company', as a piece of property to be bought and sold by institutional investors, is in need of fundamental redefinition.

CHAPTER THIRTY-TWO

THE FUTURE OF OWNERSHIP

I want it to be as natural to deal in shares as it is to invest in a building society or a bank. It will take time. But that's the way this country must go.

JOHN MAJOR, February 1992[1]

While several million employees in the private and public sectors enjoy a form of property right by virtue of their pension scheme membership, the right amounts to little more than an impersonal claim on the revenue generated by industry and commerce, and it entails few responsibilities or obligations – and no power.

JOHN PLENDER[2]

On 8 January 1996 Tony Blair, leader of the opposition, delivered a widely publicised speech to a gathering of businessmen in Singapore. In it, he developed the idea of what he called the Stakeholder Economy:

The debate about corporate governance in Britain is still in its infancy and has largely been focused on headline issues like directors' pay and perks. We cannot by legislation guarantee that a company will behave in a way conducive to trust and long-term commitment. But it is surely time to assess how we shift the emphasis in corporate ethos from the company being a mere vehicle for the capital market, to be traded, bought and sold as a commodity, towards a vision of the company as a community or partnership in which each employee has a stake, and where a company's responsibilities are more clearly delineated.[3]

The prime-minister-in-waiting was giving his endorsement to the most fundamental assault on the traditional conception of the company since nationalisation: stakeholding.

Instead of seeing the company as private property controlled by managers but *owned* by shareholders, the stakeholders want managers to see themselves as the trustees or custodians of the assets and the liabilities of the entire enterprise. In that role, they manage the company not in the interests of the shareholders alone but on behalf of everybody and everything acquainted with it: employees, customers, suppliers, people living in the towns and cities where it has factories and offices, the nation and its people, and perhaps even planet Earth itself. Stakeholding, in other words, is a form of public ownership, but different from the orthodox socialist kind. It dispenses with the need for the public to own the company altogether; control, by the manager-as-philosopher-king, is enough.

Stakeholder Economics

This idea of the public company is not far removed from the revisionist socialism of Tony Crosland (who thought ownership irrelevant to economic success) or the old-style socialism of R. H. Tawney (who thought a rising standard of living was a question of technical expertise rather than financial incentives). But that was not why it appealed to Tony Blair. Unlike nationalisation, stakeholder companies cost the taxpayer nothing. Yet they offered Blair the semblance of a viable alternative to the economic individualism of the free market. Their argot of 'trust' and 'community' and 'social capital' is ideally suited to the Orwellian lectionary of New Labour. The stakeholder company is also the obvious economic handmaiden of the stakeholder society, itself rooted in the amorphous communitarian ideas Blair adopted in opposition to impart a sense of purpose to his urge to power.

Just as the citizens of the stakeholder society have responsibilities to each other as well as rights to claim from one another, so the owners and managers of the stakeholder company have duties to its employees and customers as well as claims to its earnings. In the same way that the idea of community offers respite from the contractual culture of free market capitalism, so the stakeholder company relies on the 'social capital' of a trusting business culture. It may even be more efficient, say its most enthusiastic advocates, since it can operate with much lower transaction costs than the lawyer-infested jungle of free market competition.[4] 'Competitive advantages', writes John Kay, a leading proponent of stakeholder economics, 'are generally based on stability and continuity in relationships.'[5]

The management guru, Charles Handy, has popularised the complementary idea that the conventional PLC is inappropriate to an economy in which the chief corporate asset is the knowledge and skills of its employees ('human capital') rather than the land, factories and machines they use ('physical capital'). 'I question', writes Handy, 'whether the idea of a company as a piece of property which can be owned by anyone with enough money to pay for it, or bits of it, a property which can be bought and sold over the heads of all those who work and live there, is still a valid concept in an age when people not things are the real assets . . . Ownership is not a valid or relevant concept, any more than property is. We ought instead to think of "membership".'[6]

Businessmen have a natural weakness for ideas of this kind. It flatters their self-importance and panders to their belief that shareholders are a nuisance. Airport bookstalls are lined with the works of Charles Handy; British businessmen buy them by the yard. When Anthony Cleaver, the former chairman of IBM in Britain, accepted an invitation from the Royal Society for the Encouragement of Arts, Manufactures and Commerce to chair a committee of inquiry into the future of the PLC, it was pre-ordained that *Tomorrow's Company* (as its report was called) would be a stakeholder company. It was more surprising to learn that the fund managers at Dresdner Kleinwort Benson were starting a fund dedicated to investing in companies which complied with the Royal Society criteria for being one of Tomorrow's Companies.[7] They were persuaded that the stakeholder-driven companies of tomorrow would deliver higher returns than the shareholder-driven companies of today.

Blair was not so naïve; he dropped the idea of stakeholding as soon as its rhetoric had done its electoral work. His spin-doctors were alarmed to learn that stakeholding had been taken up by Will Hutton, an Old Labour apologist who saw it as little more than a new label for old-fashioned policies of taxation, subsidy, public expenditure, state control and industrial intervention. (As John Plender has unkindly remarked, the popularity of stakeholding in New Labour circles waned as the popularity of its most enthusiastic advocate waxed).[8] But the idea of the company as public property rather than private refuses to die, chiefly because it corresponds to the everyday experience of ordinary people. The modern PLC is scarcely the valiant entrepreneur of the free market imagination. In fact, the free market stops at the entrance to the average corporate headquarters. Inside, jobs and money are allocated not by price but by politics.

As John Kay has pointed out, the fact that large PLCs are the most important institution in the modern economy is 'an awkward fact for advocates of the new right'.[9] To the people who work for a PLC – or buy from it, or supply it – the company does not feel as if it is *owned* by anybody. Individual shareholders are a small minority, and managers rarely encounter them in the flesh. They deal with intermediaries like fund managers, stock analysts and investment bankers, who are themselves (as often as not) the intermediaries of another intermediary such as a pension fund, a life office or a unit trust.

Individual owners exercise none of the traditional rights of ownership save the right to sell, and they rarely control even the timing of a disposal. They own nothing tangible save the right to income and to a return of capital if the company is wound up. As share certificates are replaced by electronic registers, which make extensive use of nominee accounts, many do not even receive a copy of the annual report and accounts. 'Shareholders', writes Plender, 'are not owners of companies, except in the most remote and intangible sense.'[10]

The modern shareholder has not only delegated control of the company to professional managers; he has delegated control of his shares to professional fund managers whose unwillingness to challenge the management of the companies they own is the hidden flaw at the heart of corporate governance. There is a flaw at the heart of stakeholding too. The company whose managers are in theory responsible to everyone are in practice responsible to no one. In modern capitalism, at least of the Anglo-Saxon variety, the divorce between ownership and control is bridged by the fact that ownership rights are tradeable. If the shareholders do not like what the managers are doing, they can sell their shares. If enough of them sell, the company will eventually lose money, go bankrupt, or get taken over by a more competent group of managers. Owners are the only people who have an interest in ensuring that the company and its assets are managed efficiently. It is only by making sure that sales revenues exceed costs by as wide a margin as possible that shareholders can increase the value of their shares. Other stakeholders have opposite incentives. The *customers* want the margin between costs and revenues to be as narrow as possible. The *suppliers* want costs to be as large a proportion of revenues as possible. The *employees* want to maximise labour costs as a proportion of revenues. It is only the shareholders who have any incentive to maximise the profitability of the company, and the only way they can make management pursue that goal is by withdrawing, or threatening to withdraw, their capital. It is the absence of this discipline in the European forms of capitalism admired by stakeholders which leads to costly corporate disasters such as Daimler-Benz and Crédit Lyonnais.

Companies as Public Property

It is also why stakeholding is so popular in British boardrooms: it promises relief from the relentless discipline of the marketplace. Businessmen free of responsibilities to shareholders could get on with empire-building and nest-feathering without worrying about irksome outsiders. This is why they are surprisingly enthusiastic about submitting their 'licence to operate' for approval by environmentalists, animal rights' activists, charities and other lobbyists. The more people who have a stake in the firm, the less control any of them will have.

Subjection to a wider range of social, political and ethical constituencies is not always comfortable. At some companies, annual general meetings (AGMs), which once were dominated by retired bores questioning minor discrepancies in the accounts, or blind loyalists who turned up mainly for the booze and biscuits, are turning into media events. The shareholder-protester dragged kicking and screaming from the hall, casting bloodstained fivers in all directions, became a regular feature of corporate life during the apartheid years, when companies with investments in South Africa found themselves under pressure to withdraw. Some, like Barclays Bank, were persuaded to sell their interests. In the early 1970s, institutional shareholders in Distillers were embarrassed by a press campaign which forced them to set up a trust fund for the victims of thalidomide. HSBC-Midland found a tank parked outside its 1995 AGM by protesters angry about its involvement in the arms trade. A year later, Lloyds TSB shareholders were treated to an 'ethical streak' by protesters against its Third World lending policies.[11]

In spring 1997 the AGM of British Aerospace was disrupted by the heckling and chanting of dozens of 'peace' demonstrators angry about the sale of Hawk jets to the Indonesian government. The *Financial Times* reported the scenes:

> Mr Bob Bauman, the chairman, was heckled and shouted down by more than a hundred peace activists who had bought shares in the company to gain access to the meeting. Points of order, chants and yelled questions continued for forty-five minutes . . . Security guards then started to drag anyone who continued to protest from the room. The directors remained on the stage while the riot continued, but the business of the meeting was effectively stopped. Some protesters had chained themselves to their seats with plastic ties which the guards had to cut with pliers. One activist tried to photograph the meeting, and had the film ripped from his camera in a struggle. Many threw photocopies of £5 notes spattered with blood into the air as they were dragged away. Protesters varied from young peace activists to elderly ladies, theologians to business studies lecturers.[12]

These protests are undeniably effective. A high-profile campaign can persuade consumers to boycott products, causing losses to shareholders and embarrassment to managers. In recent years, Shell has suffered two major public relations disasters: in Ogoniland (where it was portrayed as the lackey of the Nigerian dictatorship) and the North Sea (where it tried to sink a redundant oil platform). Both affected its sales of petrol. Pressures of this kind alarm shareholders, and encourage them and their fund managers to tell the management to change their policies. But they do not always wait for the protests to begin.

In 1986 a group of public sector pension funds, under pressure from their left and union-dominated trustees, founded Pensions Investments Research Consultants (PIRC). Its goal is to pressurise managers into taking ethical, political and social considerations seriously. In 1997 PIRC put down the first-ever shareholder resolution calling on a company to establish new procedures for dealing with human rights and environmental issues. (The victim was Shell, whose management was still smarting from the Brent Spar and Ogoniland fiascos.) PIRC also lobbied Yorkshire Water to cut its dividend and invest in a better set of waterworks. 'Our aim', says Anne Simpson, joint managing director of PIRC, 'is to promote socially responsible management.'[13]

An Ethical Investment Research and Investment Service was founded in 1983 to help the conscience-stricken saver find investments he could buy without doing the work of the devil. Fund managers seized the opportunity to boost sales. In 1984 the Friends' Provident life office launched a Stewardship Unit Trust, whose managers promised to avoid investment in arms manufacturing, alcohol, tobacco, gambling and South Africa. It did so well that Friends' Provident launched a version for the pension funds as well. In 1990, when popular enthusiasm for all things 'green' was at its peak, Clerical Medical launched a portfolio of pension and life policies pledged to invest only in environmentally friendly businesses. 'Selling is a last resort,' gushed a Norwich Union fund manager pushing his environmental savings products. 'Someone with less conscience than us might buy them.'[14]

The pressures on companies and their shareholders can be nationalistic as well as ethical. Fund managers have come under pressure not to sell their shares to foreign bidders. When Rowntree fell to Nestlé in 1988, Tony Blair, then Opposition trade spokesman, protested in the House of Commons that thirty or forty fund managers were not the people to decide the fate of a venerable British company. Scottish fund managers in particular have come under intense pressure to keep the ownership and management of companies in Scotland by refusing to sell to bidders from England – let alone Switzerland. When Standard Life bought the Barclays share in the Bank of Scotland for £155 million in 1985, many policyholders wondered whether they were investing to keep Scottish banks Scottish or to pay off their mortgages. But when Standard Life decided to sell its stake in 1996, Scots accused it of putting the bank at risk of a foreign takeover.

In the 1980s the Guinness bids for Bell's and Distillers, the Elders IXL bid for Scottish and Newcastle and the BP bid for Britoil all saw Scottish fund managers under pressure to be Scotsmen first and investors second. It is a pressure they seem to relish resisting. 'At the end of the day loyalty is a sentiment and there is no place for sentiment in running a commercial business,' says a fund manager at one Scottish life office. 'My clients would be very annoyed if they thought I was letting sentiment overrule my judgment . . . Most Scottish funds did not even own Distillers until the company was in play. I did not lie awake worrying about the impact on the company because I had watched these fat bastards do damn all to run the company properly for fifteen or twenty years.'[15] His opposite number at another Edinburgh life office took an equally unsentimental view. 'It does not matter what your personal feelings are,' he says. 'You have to look at things dispassionately . . . You have got to make decisions for the right reasons, and invest in companies that have the ability to grow, create wealth, and provide jobs elsewhere. . . . Securing good returns for our pensioners and policyholders is part of our social responsibility. If we look after their financial assets properly, they can have a comfortable retirement.'[16]

It was this narrow interpretation of their responsibilities that Arthur Scargill inveighed against in court in 1984.[17] 'You would have thought I had dropped a bomb when I said I was not accepting it,' he said of his refusal to endorse the investment plan offered by British Coal pension fund managers, on the grounds it offended the investment philosophy of the National Union of Mineworkers. 'All these people in pinstripe suits and red carnations – the shock on their faces should have been captured on camera.'[18] But the suits won the case. 'At the Coal Board, our criterion was very much to maximise returns, without any undue regard to the social obligations which the coal industry has inherited,' said Hugh Jenkins, chief manager of the funds at the time of the Megarry judgment. 'Maybe that's putting too hard an edge on it. But if you spoke to either the board of trustees or the pensioners, they'd always be looking for the best return. None of my people would have regarded themselves as performing a social service for the beneficiaries. That way, they did in fact perform the service.'[19] The Bishop of Oxford got the same dusty answer in 1990, when he sued the Church Commissioners for failing to invest in assets which matched the moral aspirations of the Church.[20]

But whatever the courts decide, stakeholders believe that the primacy of shareholders is bought at too high a price: cost-cutting and dividends are taking precedence over jobs and investment. A large part of the appeal of the stakeholder economy lies in its portrayal of contemporary capitalism as a cabal of cruel and overpaid Fat Cats firing defenceless workers to satisfy the money-lust of the financial markets. 'British companies can afford to provide job security, but in the face of changes in social attitudes and pressures from the capital market, they have chosen not to,' says John Kay.[21] He thinks Fat Cats would be more enthusiastic about preserving jobs if they were answerable to independent directors rather than shareholders,[22] an approach which would seriously erode the property rights of institutional shareholders. In some versions of his ideas, Kay seems to go even further and argue for a company responsive solely to *customers*; its success to be measured not by profits but by price cuts, and its capital to be subscribed in the form of index-linked bonds, not shares.[23]

This shows how difficult it is to translate stakeholder rhetoric into practical ways of organising and managing businesses. A company answerable to customers rather than shareholders could hardly be any friendlier to employees and suppliers than the orthodox PLC. Ultimately, job losses and terminated supply contracts are not imposed on defenceless managers by the capital markets. They are imposed on unsuccessful companies by their customers. The real masters of the modern PLC are not the shareholders but the customers. If a company exploits its customers, it will not sell to them for long. As sales revenues fall, shareholders lose their investment, employees their jobs and suppliers their contracts. It is hard to see how the stakeholder company improves on the conventional PLC, which exists solely to satisfy its shareholders. But it is easy to see how it might makes things worse. Entrenching management at the expense of shareholders is a recipe for economic inefficiency.

Who Owns a Pension Fund?

Stakeholding, like corporate governance, rests on the belief that the weaknesses of British capitalism can be addressed by changing the nature of the company. It would be more sensible to change the nature of the shareholder. The central problem is not that owners are forcing controllers to be short-termist but that, in the highly institutionalised form which saving takes in Britain today, the owners and the controllers are too often the same people. This is most obvious in the case of company pension plans, where the trustees are invariably directors of the sponsoring PLC, and the most important trustee is usually the finance director of the company.

The main interest of the finance director is to reduce the cost of the pension fund to the shareholders, so he looks for quick returns on its assets to persuade the actuaries to allow him to cut or cancel the company contributions. 'The chief executive of the company is usually a trustee of his pension fund, and if you put in a bad quarter you will find yourself being lambasted by the same person who has just been complaining about short-termism,' says an Edinburgh fund manager. 'If you retaliate by saying that his shares under-performed, you will be fired anyway. It may be true, but he does not want to hear it.'[24] In the 1960s George Ross Goobey used to tease the Imperial Tobacco director-trustees that he had turned the pension fund from an expensive liability into a profit centre. Today, all companies run their pension funds as profit centres.

This can be done only because employees and pensioners do not own their company pensions. Employees may think that their pension is a form of deferred pay, in which they have full rights of ownership, but the law stipulates that all they possess is a promise from the company to pay them a certain level of pension in retirement. The assets of the pension fund exist solely to underwrite that promise and – once they are sufficient to pay the promised pension – any surplus belongs to the company. Company pensions were introduced as a means of industrial discipline, and not to create an asset which belonged to the employee.[25] When the board of the Royal Exchange Assurance introduced a funded pension scheme in 1890, for example, the directors refused to allow employees to contribute on the grounds that 'contributions by staff might give them a legal right to a pension and would take away the free action of the Court of Directors.'[26] When a company goes into liquidation, any surplus in the pension fund goes to creditors, not pensioners. When the *News Chronicle* collapsed in 1960, shareholders sued to prevent pensioners being given their pensions. In 1997 pensioners of Ferranti, the electronics company taken over by GEC in 1990, were facing the possibility of having to repay millions of pounds in excess pension payments sent to them by mistake. The mistake was entirely the fault of the trustees, but there was no legal doubt that the company was entitled to ask for its money back.[27]

If a company is taken over, the new owners are not under any obligation to maintain the promised benefits. In fact, an over-healthy surplus can attract a hostile bidder; when BTR acquired Dunlop, the surplus was equivalent to half the purchase price. Companies are free to wind up a pension scheme altogether if they choose, restricting the benefits to those accrued to the date of closure. 'Employees', as the National Association of Pension Funds (NAPF) put it neatly a decade ago, 'do not understand the difference between rights and expectations.' But employees and pensioners are shocked when they discover the difference. In 1992 Lucas Industries was sued by its pensioners for taking £150 million from the pension fund. The company had used a surplus to pay for rationalisation costs and a maintained dividend; the legal challenge failed.[28] Many company pension funds now have similarly large surpluses, partly because actuarial and accounting conventions give directors enormous leeway in calculating whether a fund is in surplus or not. (In *Accounting for Growth*, Terry Smith entitled his section on pension fund accounting 'The Great Illusion'.) But quite a lot of the surplus is genuine. The heavy redundancy programmes of recent years have reduced the number of potential pensioners, and soaring stock markets have enabled assets to grow much faster than shrinking liabilities.

Since the government withdrew full tax relief from pension fund surpluses in 1987, a string of companies – Barclays Bank, British Airways, British Coal, Courtaulds, Grand Metropolitan, I C I, Lucas Industries, the Post Office, the Prudential and TI Group – have used a surplus as an opportunity to take a contribution holiday.* Although they could use the surplus to improve pension benefits for employees *and* existing pensioners, most companies choose to give shareholders a contribution holiday instead. Of the £28.5 billion in pension fund surpluses reported to the Inland Revenue between 1987–8 and 1997–8, only £1 in every £3 went on new or improved benefits: the rest went to shareholders in the shape of re-funds and contribution holidays.[29] When BT took a contribution holiday in 1989, for example, analysts predicted it could last for ten years and yield as much as £1.3 billion to shareholders over the next six years.† Only where companies face strong trade unions are they forced to share a surplus with their employees; in 1988, the British Rail Pension Fund used a £1.2 billion surplus to cut contribution rates and improve benefits.[30] British Coal did the same in 1990, sharing two thirds of its surplus with pensioners.[31] By contrast, it took legislation to force private companies to up-rate pensions in line with inflation before taking a contribution holiday, and then only to a ceiling of 5 per cent.

Company directors have found ingenious uses for pension fund surpluses. Hoover used one to cover part of its disastrous 'free flights' promotion.[32] Local authorities have found the surplus a relatively painless way of meeting the cost of redundancy payments. In 1997 the Audit Commission reported that so many council officials were retiring early that they were putting the viability of local authority pension schemes at risk. Over just five years, the cost to the funds had amounted to £5.7 billion. Only one in five council officials works until the usual retirement age of sixty-five (though many are re-hired instantly as 'consultants'). Privatised companies have used the surpluses for the same purpose. In the early 1990s, BT spent most of a £900 million surplus on redundancy payments for nearly thirty thousand workers.[33]

---

* The 1986 Budget stipulated that pension fund surpluses be reduced to a maximum of 5 per cent of liabilities or be subject to tax. Companies can achieve this by taking a contribution holiday (which boosted corporation tax receipts), paying higher pensions (which boosted income tax receipts) or by pocketing the surplus (in which case they paid a 40 per cent charge).
† The scheme developed a deficit of £750 million after dividends fell in the recession, redundancy payments increased and in the 1993 budget the government reduced the amount of tax the fund could reclaim on dividend income. See *Financial Times*, 14 May 1993.

Nuclear Electric spent £70 million of the Electricity Supply pension fund surplus on redundancies,[34] and the privatised regional electricity companies have also raided their pension funds for redundancy money.[35]

But there does not need to be a surplus to tempt company managers into raiding the pension fund. They see it as a useful source of finance when nobody else will give them credit. In 1976 a retired London Co-operative Society milkman, Robert Evans, took his old employers to court for borrowing large sums of money from the pension fund at sub-market rates of interest, claiming his pension would have been higher if they had not. The judge ordered the society to top the fund up.[36] The British Rail Pension Fund entered the 1980s underfunded through being obliged to make sub-market loans to the British Railways Board.* In 1979 the Post Office fund was obliged to lend the telecommunications arm of the parent company £50 million to cover a deficit caused by industrial action.[37]

Similar actions are far from unknown in the private sector. When J. Lyons was financially stretched in the mid–1970s, the management solved the problem by selling various properties to the company pension fund. At J. Sainsbury, the main tenant of the properties belonging to the pension fund throughout that decade was the retailer itself. In 1982 Plender found that James Goldsmith and Jim Slater had insisted that the pension funds under their control deposit surplus cash with their banking arms.[38] Ten years later Plender showed how Melton Medes had used pension surpluses in two companies it had acquired to make low cost loans to other parts of the business and to buy shares in acquisition targets. After a court battle, employees recouped £7 million in losses.[39] When the Belling cooker manufacturing company went into receivership in May 1992, £2.1 million was missing from the pension fund – it had been used to pay an 'advance fee' to a Newcastle-under-Lyme solicitor to arrange loans which never materialised.[40] In 1993 Dr Gerald Smith, former chief executive of a failed West Country construction company, was convicted of stealing £2 million from its pension fund to pay company debts. 'I believed the fund could properly be used to save the company,' he said.[41] Later that year, the director-trustees of the bankrupt Universal Computers Group were found to have siphoned off half the pension fund assets,[42] and Tony Cole, former chairman and chief executive of a collapsed conglomerate, Bestwood, misappropriated £900,000 in pension fund monies to finance his personal share dealings.[43]

These investments were usually made with the full authority of the trustees of the pension fund. The fact that the trustees usually double as directors of

---

* These were so expensive that in the early 1980s the fund had temporarily to be put partly on a pay-as-you-go basis. See Chapter 28, p. 1011.

the company creates an obvious conflict of interest, which the unscrupulous are free to exploit. Nobody exploited it more than Robert Maxwell: after his death, it emerged that £2 in every £5 belonging to the Mirror Group Pension Fund was invested in twenty companies, half having connections with Maxwell. No wonder he was keen to stop employees opting out of the company schemes into personal pensions.[44] During his trial, Kevin Maxwell told the court his father 'certainly believed – and said so in my presence and the presence of professional advisers – that any pension fund surpluses belonged to the company.'[45] One of the chief aims of the 1995 Pensions Act, largely inspired by the Maxwell scandal, was to give beneficiaries of pension funds some say over the appointment of trustees. Most funds had employee representatives before the Act, but these tended to be management lackeys. Now, if they are unhappy with the trustees chosen by their employer, they can elect one third of them.

Scandal of Self-investment

The Maxwell débâcle also persuaded the government to place restrictions on pension funds' investment in shares and other assets of their parent company. Self-investment is now limited to 5 per cent of the value of a fund. The NAPF had recommended (three years before Maxwell fell off his yacht) that self-investment ought to be banned. The recommendation had followed a string of scandals during the bitter takeover battles of the 1980s, when it was commonplace for pension funds to buy and hold shares in their parent company. During the Guinness bid for Distillers, the Guinness pension fund actually bought shares in its parent to help maintain the value of a bid where the shares were used as currency. The Distillers' pension fund was instructed to buy Guinness shares after the bid succeeded, even though it was obvious that the price would fall immediately. When English China Clays bid for the Bryant construction group in 1987, the Bryant pension fund bought shares in its parent company as part of its defence.[46] It helped to defeat the bid, but prompted an investigation by the NAPF.

The investigation found that three in five funds permitted some self-investment, though there were sharp variations in degree. Unsurprisingly, the rules tended to become more flexible if the company was subject to a takeover bid.[47] In practice, however, most funds avoided self-investment. Only three of those surveyed had more than one fifth of their assets invested in the parent company; less than one in twenty-five had more than 5 per cent invested; three quarters had no self-investment at all. The NAPF report nevertheless concluded that 'the potential for conflicts of interest, irresolvable pressures and argument is so great, that self-investment is an unhelpful and undesirable practice.'[48]

This is indisputable. Employees who rely on a company for their wage or salary should not also be expected to rely on it for their pension. As the judge said in the Scargill v. Coal Board pension case: 'The large size of pension funds emphasises the need for diversification, rather than lessening it, and the fact that much of the fund has been contributed by members of the scheme seems to me to make it even more important that the trustees should exercise their powers in the best interests of the beneficiaries.'[49]

It is not hard to see why companies resist this view. The trustees are almost always directors. Many pension funds were established with a grant of shares in the parent company, in some cases under a trust deed which forbade the fund to sell them. The Lucas staff pension fund, for example, entered the 1980s one third invested in Lucas shares.[50] In the 1970s, some of the contributors to the Wilson Committee argued that self-investment was a useful way of motivating employees and securing support for long-term investment.[51] The Wider Share Ownership Council voiced similar sentiments in 1987. Even now, directors of smaller companies can set up self-administered pension schemes entitled to invest up to half their assets in the company.

Pensioners Assert Their Rights

Self-investment is obviously unsound in principle: the whole point of a separate fund is to ensure that people can collect their pensions even if the company fails. A series of cases in which that promise was not honoured, of which the Maxwell scandal was the worst, have increased judicial and regulatory sympathy for the idea that pension funds ought to belong to the beneficiaries rather than the company. When Hanson sold Courage to Elders IXL in 1986 it tried to hang on to a £70 million surplus in the company pension fund, which the pensioners retrieved by taking Hanson to court. Four years later, Hanson was again sued successfully after trying to liberate a surplus in the old Imperial Tobacco pension fund by transferring the pensioners to a new scheme.[52] In 1993, when the Transport Secretary tried to seize the British Rail pension fund ahead of privatisation, by swapping its assets for a government promise to pay index-linked pensions to the beneficiaries, he was forced to back down.[53] In 1996 Hillsdown Holdings was censured by the pensions ombudsman for taking £18.4 million from the pension fund of a company it had acquired. The courts ordered Hillsdown Holdings to repay the money, plus accrued interest.[54]

Two other cases well-known to pensions lawyers – the Mettoy case, and that

of Barber *v.* Guardian Royal Exchange, which led ultimately to the equalisation of the pension age – have also encouraged the view that pension funds
are deferred pay which belongs to pensioners rather than company assets
which belong ultimately to the shareholders.[55] In a significant court judgment
against London Regional Transport in 1993, Mr Justice Knox ruled that
employers had to respect the increase in benefits implied by a surplus as well
as the actual benefits promised to pensioners: 'No doubt the larger the surplus
the livelier the expectation but in the majority of cases it remains an expectation rather than a right. That is not to say that it is either without value or
that the law will not protect it in appropriate circumstances.'[56]

This was the first clear sign that the rights of pensioners were coming into
line with their expectations. The judge had questioned whether companies
own the whole of any pension fund surplus, and had concluded that they
had a fiduciary duty to employees and pensioners.[57] Two years later, the
pensions ombudsman ruled that the British Airways pension scheme was
guilty of 'breach of trust' and 'maladministration' for failing to consider the
interests of pensioners (as opposed to people still working for the firm) when
it decided in 1989 to cream off a £186 million surplus and take a thirty-year
contribution holiday.[58] But the ruling related purely to the procedures followed by trustees, giving no definitive answer on the question of ownership.
The 1995 Pensions Act also left it to trustees to decide on the distribution of
surpluses.

Despite the legal uncertainties, it is increasingly clear that pensioners have
acquired rights of ownership beyond the benefits promised by the company.
In February 1999 the Court of Appeal ruled that National Power and National
Grid had acted unlawfully in using £350 million of pension fund surpluses
to fund a redundancy programme rather than improve benefits. Though the
case still turned on technical failings in the trust deed, the verdict overturned
an earlier decision by the High Court in favour of the companies, and backed
a 1997 ruling by the pensions ombudsman in favour of the pensioners.[59] The
National Union of Mineworkers took the coal industry fund to court for using
a £435 million surplus to subsidise transfer to the private sector. In 1997
the Transport and General Workers Union sued the government over its
appropriation of a £103 million surplus in the National Bus Company pension
fund when the bus industry was privatised in 1986. The one appearance
during the 1997 general election New Labour spin-doctors allowed the union
general secretary, Bill Morris, was outside Conservative Central Office, where
he unveiled a poster accusing the Major government of stealing busmen's
pensions.[60] In office, New Labour taxed everybody's.

Who Owns Life Office Reserves?

Savers have found it just as difficult to get at surpluses built up by those other great institutional investors: the life offices. Ever since their foundation, the life offices have consistently retained a significant proportion of the fruits of their investment success rather than return all of them to their with-profits policyholders.* 'The hazard having been run, and having turned out profitably, the proceeds belong to those who ran it, and to those who, by their own free consent, became their lineal successors,' an essayist complained of the Equitable Life as early as 1838. 'The general lesson taught by it (the history of the Society) is – be cautious; but . . . be cautious of carrying caution so far as to leave a part of your property for the benefit of those who are in no way related to you. If there be a Charybdis in an insurance office, there is also a Scylla: the mutual insurer, who is much too afraid of dispensing the profits to those who die before him, will have to leave his own share for those who die after him.'[61]

The reason so many life offices are financially strong today is that they have failed for decades (and some for centuries) to pay out a full and fair share of their investment success to policyholders. This is just as true of mutually owned organisations such as Equitable Life as of PLCs such as the Prudential. From its foundation in 1837 until 1959, the Scottish Provident Institution insisted that no policy holder was entitled to extract more than he had contributed.[62] Much of the initial caution of the life offices reflected the inadequacies of actuarial science, but later the acquisition of substantial reserves became deliberate policy. It enabled them to avoid wild fluctuations in the returns earned by investors, by using the good years to subsidise the deficits of the bad. The windfall payments made by de-mutualising life offices in recent years suggests this prudent approach was over-cautious.

Ordinarily, £9 out of every £10 of profits in a with-profits life fund is distributed to policyholders as annual and terminal bonuses. But in the early 1990s there was considerable controversy over the distribution to shareholders of so-called 'orphan assets', or reserves judged surplus to the 'reasonable expectations' of policyholders. The judge is the Department of Trade and Industry (DTI), which regulates the insurance companies. In June 1992 it authorised the London and Manchester (now part of Friends Provident) to distribute surpluses in its with-profits life fund to shareholders rather than policyholders, sparking controversy over the ownership of assets created by

---

* Holders of investments whose benefits are defined are not entitled to any surplus above what they were led to expect.

over-reserving rather than entrepreneurial energy. When the Legal and General secured permission from the DTI to begin distributing £1.5 billion to shareholders as well as to policyholders, Sir John Nott, former defence secretary, Lazards chairman and Legal and General policyholder, led a campaign against distribution to shareholders.[63] It was not successful.

In February 1995 United Friendly restructured its long-term life funds to distribute £275 million of surplus assets to shareholders rather than policyholders. When it later merged with the Refuge, Refuge shareholders complained that the terms of the deal forced them to share too much of their orphan assets with United Friendly shareholders. The terms of the deal were revised in their favour.[64] Pearl has yielded £1 billion in orphan assets to its parent (AMP) and Britannic is using a large slice of its with-profits life fund to underpin dividend payments. Sun Life has followed suit. Even when mutuals were taken over – as in the Aegon acquisition of Scottish Equitable, the purchase of Clerical Medical by the Halifax and the absorption of Scottish Amicable by the Prudential – a full share of the surplus assets was not paid to policyholders at once, although they were ostensibly owners of the business.

Broader But Not Deeper

There is a case for pension funds and life offices to favour shareholders over savers: the shareholders underwrite the risks of the bad years, so they deserve some reward in the good. The main weakness of institutionalised saving is not that it sometimes favours shareholders over policyholders; it is that it turns savers into investors rather than owners. The chief forms of institutionalised saving (pension funds and life offices) deny people a meaningful sense of ownership, cutting them off from the perils and rewards of owning the most valuable form property can take in the modern world – and so from the main source of income and wealth in an industrialised economy.

The problem (the institutionalisation of savings) and the solution (wider ownership of financial assets) are understood and accepted at almost every point on the political spectrum. At the 1997 general election, all three political parties pledged themselves to wider ownership. The left wish to confer riches and power on the workers; the centre to perpetuate themselves in office; the right to augment the legitimacy of private property. But reality has proved a stubborn opponent of rhetoric. Between 1979 and 1992 four successive Conservative governments tried to re-invent the property-owning democracy for a generation which already owned its own house or flat by resurrecting the private shareholder of the 1950s. By the end of their time in office, personal investors owned less of the stock market than when they started, and the institutions owned more. What went wrong?

The first mistake was an excessive (if understandable) emphasis on the individual ownership of shares over forms of collective ownership. This was intrinsic to the most significant part of the drive: privatisation. Contrary to revisionist histories of privatisation, which portray the sale of state-owned companies as an example of serendipity turned to opportunistic advantage, increasing the number of private shareholders was one of the central aims of the denationalisation programme. Sir Geoffrey Howe, chancellor of the Exchequer in the first Thatcher government, made this clear when he announced the sale of shares in BP in his first budget.

Unlike his Labour predecessor, who had sold BP shares to reduce public borrowing, Howe pledged that all privatisation sales would be structured and priced to attract as many investors as possible:

> Such sales are not justified simply by the help that they give to the short-term reduction of the PSBR. They are an essential part of our long-term programme for promoting the widest possible participation by the people in the ownership of British industry. This objective – wider public ownership in the true meaning of the term – has implications not merely for the scale of our programme but . . . for the methods of sale we shall adopt.[65]

Both Thatcher and Lawson, who played key roles in the origins and development of the privatisation programme, have confirmed in their memoirs that this was their ambition.[66]

In a sense, that ambition was fulfilled. The generous pricing of privatisation issues and the lavish marketing campaigns which accompanied them (headed by Sid for British Gas, and Frank N. Stein in the case of electricity) sold shares to the people in a way never attempted by ordinary companies. 2.3 million applied for shares in British Telecommunications; 4.5 million for shares in British Gas; 2.7 million for shares in regional water companies; and 7 million for shares in regional electricity companies. At its flotation in 1986, British Gas became for a time the company with the largest number of individual shareholders in the world.

These mass privatisations – followed by popular enfranchisements of account-holders and policy-holders at the Abbey National, Halifax and Woolwich building societies and the Norwich Union life office – did succeed in increasing the number of individual shareholders. When British Telecom became the first popular privatisation in 1984, only 7 per cent of adults owned shares. By 1987, after the sale of British Gas, British Airways, BAA, Rolls Royce and BP, that percentage had tripled. The privatisation programme

TABLE 32.1
Companies with the Most Shareholders

	Origin	Shareholders
Halifax	Incorporation and Flotation	5,000,000
Abbey National	Incorporation and Flotation	2,500,000
British Telecommunications	Privatisation	2,100,000
Woolwich	Incorporation and Flotation	1,600,000
Norwich Union	Incorporation and Flotation	1,300,000
British Gas	Privatisation	1,300,000
Alliance and Leicester	Incorporation and Flotation	1,200,000
Lloyds TSB	Privatisation & Acquisition	1,000,000
PowerGen	Privatisation	900,000
National Power	Privatisation	900,000
BAA	Privatisation	490,961
Scottish Hydro-Electric	Privatisation	441,547
British Petroleum	Privatisation	411,992
British Energy	Privatisation	390,000
Rolls Royce	Privatisation	381,030
Railtrack	Privatisation	349,400
Marks and Spencer	Ordinary PLC	307,600
Shell Transport and Trading	Ordinary PLC	300,000
Southern Electric	Privatisation	297,603
British Airways	Privatisation	240,000
Thames Water	Privatisation	240,000
Imperial Chemical Industries	Ordinary PLC	223,444
British Steel	Privatisation	183,000
United Utilities	Privatisation	158,684
Eurotunnel/Eurotunnel SA	Flotation	136,859

Source: Proshare.

and the incorporation and subsequent flotation of mutually owned building societies and life offices has raised the number of shareholders from around three million in 1979 to perhaps fifteen million now.

Yet in another sense privatisation was a failure. It broadened share ownership but did not deepen it. Most personal shareholders own only one or two shares, usually acquired at a privatisation or the flotation of a mutual. The Confederation of British Industry (CBI) Task Force on Wider Share Ownership, which reported in 1990, reckoned only 13 per cent of individual shareholders had acquired stock in the secondary market. Of the twenty-five companies with the largest number of shareholders, only two (Marks and Spencer and ICI) are not privatised industries or high-profile public flotations.

The new breed of shareholder got a misleading message from sales of that kind: assets were being sold cheap or given away free. 'Those privatisation issues', said Mick Newmarch in 1990, 'did nothing more than prove people will always look for a bargain.'[67] The number of shareholders has always decreased in the months and years after the sale as investors cashed in their bargain, despite the introduction of loyalty bonuses to long-term holders. In other words, privatisation created a nation of Stags, not a nation of Sids.* Sid, quip two analysts of the weaknesses of the privatisation programme, stands for Short-term Investment Dumper.[68]

The Tax System

Sid can be forgiven the shallowness of his conversion. The obstacles to buying shares – rather than pension plans and endowment policies, and even houses and flats – are formidable. The greatest is the structure of taxation. Anybody who owns shares directly pays income tax on dividends and capital gains tax on any appreciation in their value, while contributions to pension funds are untaxed until they are drawn in retirement. Home owners do not pay capital gains tax on any increase in the value of their house and enjoyed until recently a strong helping of tax relief on their mortgage payments. Large and long-term owners of shares face heavy capital gains tax costs if they sell, which the Conservative government attempted to alleviate by allowing indexation for inflation and the New Labour government to obviate by discouraging sales altogether.†

Pension funds do not face these constraints. Contributions are free of tax and, until recently, all income and capital gains accumulated within the fund free of tax. These privileges are gradually being eroded, and not replaced by compelling incentives to invest directly in the stock market. Though dividends and capital gains are allowed to accumulate free of tax in Personal Equity Plans (PEPs), these have to be financed out of post-tax income, and the annual limit on the amount which can be invested is low by comparison with pension plans. When they were first introduced in 1987, the government

---

* 'Stag' is a Victorian term for a person who applied for an allocation of shares in a new issue with a view to taking a profit immediately.

† In the 1998 budget the government withdrew indexation: instead, chargeable gains are now tapered according to the length of time an asset is held, falling to 10 per cent on assets held for ten years. The taper is intended specifically to discourage short-term buying and selling.

limited investment to individual shares listed in London; their scope was later widened to include foreign equities, bonds, convertibles, and preference shares. Predictably, the most important factor in their success was the lifting of all restrictions on investment in institutionalised savings vehicles: unit and investment trusts.

Although the annual investment limit for PEPs was raised from £2,400 in 1987 to £6,000 in 1990, investors did not take to them until the restrictions on investment in unit or investment trusts were lifted in 1992.* The amount invested in PEPs jumped tenfold over the next six years, but the proportion of funds invested in shares fell steadily from over two thirds at the outset to under a third. The institutionalisation of the PEP was the making of any unit trust fund manager with the sense to tie its marketing to their tax-free status. The change turned Martin Arbib, founder of Perpetual, into a multi-millionaire. Nigel Lawson, who introduced PEPs as a tax-efficient route to direct share ownership, appeared in an advertisement for M&G, another unit trust manager which waxed mightily on the back of the change. 'I must have been in a very generous mood,' Lawson joked about his 1986 budget, though his fellow-directors at Barclays Bank understandably failed to see the funny side of one of their number promoting a rival firm.

The other savings reform introduced by the Conservative government also failed to reverse the institutionalisation of savings: in fact, it did nothing at all for share ownership. The Tax-Exempt Special Savings Account (TESSA), introduced by John Major during his short stint at the Treasury, encouraged people to put their savings in the bank rather than the stock market. Holders of TESSAs enjoyed tax relief on interest earned from cash deposits, provided they left them in the bank or building society for five years. By the end of the first five-year period, over £28 billion was invested in over 4.5 million TESSA accounts.[69] In 1996, it was a fitting epitaph on the wider share owner-ship initiatives of the Conservative government to find PEP-based unit trust managers chasing funds liberated from their five-year penance in a TESSA.

It was a literal enactment of the fate to which all adjustments of taxes on savings are prone: the shifting of assets from one vehicle to another without any increase in the overall amount saved. But the savings plans of the New Labour government may reduce even that amount. Inhibited by its election pledge not to raise the *rates* of income tax, the government has more or less forced itself to tax savings rather than incomes. It has radically reduced the tax-free income of the pension funds by its reform of advance corporation

---

* From January 1992 investors were also freed to invest an additional £3,000 in a single company PEP which holds the shares of just one company.

TABLE 32.2
Personal Equity Plans (PEPs)

Tax Year Ending April	Invested in Unit Trusts	Invested in Bonds	Invested in Investment Trusts	Invested in Shares	Invested in Cash	Total Sum Invested in PEPs
1987*	65	–	5	300	70	440
1988*	95	–	35	490	100	720
1990	800	–	80	1,380	340	2,600
1991	1,450	–	180	2,440	450	4,520
1992	2,300	–	560	3,550	560	6,970
1993	4,520	–	1,070	5,710	590	11,890
1994	9,770	–	2,760	6,870	690	20,090
1995	13,430	–	2,010	7,650	710	23,800
1996	19,960	1,140	2,640	9,550	830	34,120
1997	29,320	2,840	1,360	12,830	1,380	49,530
1998	44,080	4,100	3,850	24,280	1,540	77,850

Source: Inland Revenue Statistics 1998.

* Figures for 1987 and 1988 are for December. There is no figure for 1989.

tax,[70] and replaced both PEPs and TESSAs with Individual Savings Accounts (ISAs) from April 1999. These offer continued protection from income and capital gains tax to savings in cash, stocks and shares and life assurance, but up to an annual limit of only £5,000,* much less than the £9,000 ceiling on PEPs.

The hope is that ISAs will attract a poorer class of saver as well as the relatively rich who have taken most advantage of PEPs and TESSAs. Although four in every five adults have a bank account, only one in eight adults owns shares other than privatisation stocks. One in seventeen has a PEP. Most of them are relatively wealthy, and the great bulk live in London and the south-east.[71] This is scarcely surprising. The poor not only have less money; the vagaries of their working lives mean they cannot tie up for years what money they do have. Direct share ownership, especially under the new capital gains tax regime, is bound to continue to be confined to wealthier people, who can defer consumption for longer. ISAs are likely to do nothing to reverse the institutionalisation of ownership; they may even accelerate it.

* In the first year of the scheme (1999–2000), the annual limit is £7,000, of which no more than £3,000 can go into cash and £1,000 into life assurance. Thereafter the annual subscription limit will be £5,000, of which only £1,000 can go into cash and £1,000 into life assurance.

Hostility of the Stock Market

The creators of the ISA, however, have understood that taxation is not the only obstacle to wider and deeper share ownership. Distribution, as life assurance salesmen have always known, is the most important single ingredient in the success of any savings plan. This is why the supermarkets, many of them already in league with the banks and fund managers to offer financial services at the check-out, were invited by the government to sell ISAs to shoppers.[72] A reason why few people buy shares in the secondary market is that the stock exchange is more like a golf club than a shop; the people who work there and the rules they apply might have been designed to prevent people joining. Ordinary investors bought privatisation stocks because the government made them easy to buy, as well as ensuring that they were cheap.

To some degree, it is now easier to buy shares. Most banks and building societies are prepared to deal at a fixed price without charging extra for unwanted advice, though the gap between the prices at which they buy and sell means the up-front commission is not as cheap as it looks. When Norman Lamont called for a 'share shop' on every High Street to help shift the last of the major privatisation stocks, the officially licensed 'share shop' became an established feature of the remaining state sell-offs of the 1990s. But they were not real shops; they were banks, building societies and retail stockbrokers pretending to be shops.

In 1997 the average commission paid by private investors trading shares (0.82 per cent) was more than *five times* that charged to institutions (0.16 per cent). It would be more expensive still, had cheap execution-only stockbroking services not been introduced. One cut-price broker, Sharelink, was so successful its founder became a millionaire even before the business was sold to Charles Schwab, the largest cut-price broker in the United States. Sharelink opened its first shop below its Birmingham headquarters in September 1996 – Brummie punters can now wander in and buy investments in much the same way as they buy Y-fronts and cotton socks at Marks and Spencer. The stock market, however, remains an alien place for most people. The only financial intermediary the majority of savers have encountered is a life assurance salesman, whose example has tainted the public image of stockbroker as well. Even at the top end of the market, stockbrokers are seen as snobs, or scions of rich families too stupid to earn their living honourably.

Most stockbrokers find it tiresome and uneconomic to deal in the small parcels of shares most people want to buy and sell. (This is what gave the banks, and Sharelink, their opportunity.) They find it easier and more lucrative to steer their clients into a unit trust, because collective investments yield higher commissions. Unit trust fund managers are also more adept at playing on the fear and greed of individual investors, continually launching funds which pander to the latest shift in public opinion. They can soup up the yield when people want income (usually by spending capital) and offer vertiginous rates when they want growth (usually by putting the fund at risk of total loss).

The overall structure of the stock market remains heavily biased in favour of the institutional investors, from which the biggest brokers earn their living. Unlike most markets, the London Stock Exchange continued until recently to rely on a quote-driven trading system, in which professional market-makers compete to offer the best prices for institutions to buy and sell shares. Individual investors are always better served by an order-driven system, where the orders of all buyers and sellers are matched at a single price, but the stock exchange did not introduce this until a competitor forced its hand in 1997. Stockbrokers and fund managers also exploit individual investors in less obvious ways. Institutional investors are informed first when a buyer is in the market offering a good price for their stock, and unwanted shares from an unsuccessful issue are more likely to find their way into private client portfolios than institutional funds.

Are Companies to Blame?

Companies collude in this process of discouraging individual shareholders, if only because they have effectively delegated the selling of their shares to stockbrokers. The one opportunity companies have to market their shares directly is the annual report, but most are too crammed with Companies Act requirements and the cautious but cliché-ridden prose of semi-literate or paranoid (about giving anything away) chairmen and chief executives to make sense to ordinary people. Instead of making the annual report less boring and more comprehensible, companies are cutting its distribution on grounds of cost. The growing use of nominee accounts makes it impossible for every shareholder to get a copy anyway.

Corporate contempt for individual investors is never plainer than at the annual general meeting (AGM), despite the fact that private shareholders (and single-issue fanatics) are often the only people who bother to turn up and vote. 'Many chairmen,' admits Henry Wendt, chairman of SmithKline Beecham, 'regard the occasion as a meaningless task to be dispensed with quickly.'[73] For chairman and chief executives, the important meetings with investors are not AGMs. They are the many private meetings with stockbroking analysts and institutional investors throughout the year. Virtually the only time they take individual investors seriously is when the company may be taken over, and the individual investors are suddenly deluged with newspaper advertisements, junk mail and freephone numbers where they can listen to a tape of the company chairman explaining why those who want to pay twice the current price for their shares are scoundrels or pirates. They become the foil for the faceless fund managers who are selling their company over their heads.

In the late 1980s, at the height of the last great bid fever, beleaguered boardrooms resurrected the individual shareholder as the saviour of British industry. The CBI's Task Force on Wider Share Ownership had a brief to recruit an army of loyal shareholders. It was led by Peter Thompson, the hero of the NFC worker buy-out, and John Harvey-Jones, the television personality.[74] Its report, *A Nation of Shareholders*, called for more generous tax breaks for retail investors, but made little impact. Its chief effect was the replacement of the existing Wider Share Ownership Council by the aggressive-sounding Share Ownership Movement. This militant body secured funding from all the FTSE-100 companies, the stock exchange and the DTI, and looked for a time as if it might encourage companies to take their private shareholders a little more seriously between bids as well as during them. But there was no crusade for changes to the tax system. ProShare (as the Wider Share Ownership Movement became known in 1992) seems to believe that the only hurdle between great companies and a horde of loyal investors is a lack of information. It offers stock prices over the telephone, churns out a monthly magazine (*The Investor*), and gives everybody who rings up a free copy of a portfolio management system, eight copies of the *Financial Times* and one copy of a book called *The Private Investor's Guide to the Stock Market*.

In August 1995, after five more years of institutionalisation, the London Stock Exchange set up a new committee on wider share ownership. It was chaired by Sir Mark Weinberg. His appointment coincided with the scrapping of a stock exchange rule which obliged any company issuing shares worth more than £25 million to offer some to the public, giving the process of institutionalisation a further boost by allowing companies to dilute the holdings of existing shareholders. The Weinberg Report, published in July 1996, reiterated the need for education and more generous tax breaks for direct investment. The government has never taken the idea of tax breaks seriously.

Listed companies do not want individual shareholders badly enough to demand tax reforms from the government. Far from battling to increase the number of shareholders, companies dilute the holdings of existing investors continuously with new issues of shares sold almost entirely to institutional investors; acquisitions financed with shares rather than cash; and periodic grants of new shares to the Fat Cats in the boardroom or (less often) the employees. Private investors rarely have the patience or skill to understand the documentation of a rights issue or a takeover, or time to arrange funding to maintain the value of their holding. The British Aerospace rights issue of 1991, for example, effectively halved individual ownership in a single transaction. According to one analysis, around two thirds of the decline in individual ownership is attributable to covert institutionalisation of this kind.[75]

Employee Share Ownership

There is one further sense in which companies have failed to back their rhetoric with action. Successive governments have offered tax relief to companies which offer shares to their employees, but boards of directors have used them largely as a tax-efficient method of increasing their own remuneration. Of the three types of tax-assisted employee share ownership scheme in Britain, the save as your earn (shares worth an average of £2,700 a head in 1996–7) and company share option plans (£24,000 at their peak in 1995) favoured by the directors are conspicuously more generous than the down-market profit sharing schemes they offer the rank and file (£680). By 1996 the exploitation of share option schemes had become so embarrassing that even a Conservative government had to introduce a ceiling on their value; discretionary schemes were eventually abolished in 1996.[76]

American capitalism has suffered from the same problem on an even grander scale, but its equivalent of the profit sharing scheme has become the vehicle for genuine employee buy-outs, even at large organisations such as United Airlines, TWA and Avis Rent-a-Car. At NFC, by contrast, once the most famous employee buy-out in Britain, institutionalisation has cut employee ownership to barely one tenth of the company. The most assiduous users of employee buy-outs since that flawed triumph are bus company managers – an easy way to profit from the certainty that the company will be taken over by using the company's own money to buy it from the state.[77]

Slow Death of Occupational Pension Schemes

By 1997, all three employee share ownership schemes had given a mere 1.75 million employees rights over shares worth £3.5 billion, or about £2,000 a head at most (there is a great deal of double-counting).[78] But giving employees access to shares was never intended to widen ownership. It was devised in the socialist era as a means of bridging the gap between workers and managers, rather than the gap between owners and managers. Since the Maxwell scandal, enthusiasm for entrusting savings and salaries to a single employer has wilted; employees want ownership of their own pension plans. This is not a demand which the closed and conservative world of pension funds has yet accepted. To a large extent, the unscrupulous behaviour of the life offices in mis-selling personal pensions has made it easy for them to ignore it. More than nine out of ten occupational pension schemes are still organised on classical lines, in which the employer guarantees that an employee will retire at the age of sixty-five on two thirds of his final salary, after forty years of loyal service to the company.

These 'defined benefit' schemes, as they are known in the jargon, were obviously appropriate to an age of minimal inflation, lifetime employment and corporate paternalism – the opposite of conditions most employees have experienced over the last thirty years. The famously 'flexible' labour markets are a euphemism for an economy in which it is cheaper to hire and fire people, where part-time and casual working is routine, and in which people change jobs many times in the course of a career. Defined benefit pension plans were not designed for people who work like this: they exclude the part-time and the casual; they penalise the redundant and the mobile. 'Early leavers,' as the actuaries call them, find that their pensions are worth less than those of luckier or less ambitious colleagues who stay on. In short, they subsidise the pension funds of their former employers.

The dirty secret of the occupational pension fund industry is that few employees ever receive the promised pension in full. Many leave, or are sacked, before they reach their forties. Many more are encouraged to leave in their fifties with a generous lump sum, usually drawn from the surplus in the company pension scheme, before they are allowed to enjoy their final salary. The heavy cost of salary-related pension contributions for relatively high earners in their fifties actually means they are more likely to be made redundant than cheaper colleagues. Even those who stay on until they reach sixty-five do not collect the full value of the pension fund, as most of any surplus now accrues largely to shareholders. Yet even employers – who might be expected to appreciate a system in which disloyal employees subsidise the costs of the loyal – are tiring of defined benefit pension schemes, because government is steadily increasing the cost of providing them. It has obliged employers to protect the pensions of early leavers against inflation (albeit only up to a ceiling of 5 per cent a year) and denied them full tax relief on contributions to the pension fund if it is running a substantial surplus.

In May 1990 the European Court of Justice ruled that occupational pension schemes must permit men and women to retire at the same age on the same pension, forcing companies to pay extra unless they raise the retirement age of women to sixty-five, which few have done for existing employees.* The adjustments to advance corporation tax, in 1993 and 1997, have also robbed company pension funds of much of their tax-free income.[79] The Pensions Act of 1995 has further increased the costs of providing pensions by imposing new liquidity requirements and regulatory burdens. In December 1997 the Occupational Pensions Regulatory Authority announced that it would bring *criminal* prosecutions against companies which merely pay their pension contributions late.[80]

The Authority is one of a number of forces which are gradually depriving companies of full ownership of the corporate pension fund. The law is increasingly sympathetic to the view that pension funds belong to pensioners and, as cases accumulate, it will become increasingly hard for companies to resist.[81] It is getting harder to run a pension fund as a profit centre. In 1988 the British subsidiary of Dow Chemical, the American multinational, became the first major employer in Britain to abandon a defined benefit pension scheme in favour of a defined contribution plan. Pensioners of a defined contribution plan receive back no more than their contributions to the fund plus any return which the fund managers have earned on them. The lump sum is then used to purchase an annuity, payable until the death of the pensioner, from a life assurance company (which is why they are also known as 'money purchase' schemes).

A number of leading British companies, including Barclays Bank, W. H. Smith and the British subsidiary of IBM, have now switched their pension funds to defined contribution plans, and the American experience suggests many more will follow. Yet it is an article of faith among pension experts that defined benefit is superior to defined contribution – partly because actuaries have made a handsome living out of defined benefit pensions. Unlike defined contribution plans, which transfer the risk from the employer to the employee, they require frequent and highly sophisticated valuations to gauge whether the fund is sufficient to meet its liabilities. But the weaknesses of defined contribution plans are significant. They are more expensive to run, and they have no employer standing behind them to guarantee the value of the pension: the costs and the risks of the scheme are borne by the individual, rather than his employer. There is also a risk that the fund manager will adopt an over-cautious investment strategy as the pension plan matures, to reduce the danger of having insufficient capital to purchase the retirement income which the plan-holder is expecting.

---

* A survey by NAPF found that 85 per cent of pension schemes had equalised the retirement age at sixty-five, but that 85 per cent also permitted retirement at the previous retirement age without a cut in pension. The state pension age for women is being raised to sixty-five over a ten-year period beginning in 2010.

These are valid criticisms, though they take no account of the ability of modern financial markets to assume much of the risk as retirement approaches. Research also suggests that the conventional belief about defined benefit plans being superior to the defined contribution alternative is flawed. This is scarcely surprising in an economy where people change jobs frequently and their earnings go up and down in a pattern far removed from the ever-rising salaries of the past. The Institute for Fiscal Studies found that a majority of the men and women it surveyed were better off in a defined contribution scheme, precisely because early-leavers and low-earners subsidised long-stayers and high-earners.[82] But there are strong arguments for defined contribution plans anyway: there are no cross-subsidies; the investment of the funds is not dictated by director-trustees who may decide, Maxwell-style, to use them for purposes of their own; nor do defined contribution pension plans require regulators to ensure they are solvent. Above all, everybody has an identifiable financial asset of their own, which they can take with them to another employer. Ideally, their owners would be free to draw on the funds before retirement, to buy a house, fund a business, meet the school fees or pay for any one of a myriad personal needs and enthusiasms.

Unfortunately, this is the one freedom the government did not concede in the pension reform plans it published in February 1999. However, its proposals could speed the demise of the defined benefit pension. Once they are enshrined in law, people both in and outside occupational pension schemes will be free to invest as little or as much as they like in unit and investment trusts (and the new breed of open-ended investment companies) with all the tax privileges (and contribution rules and ceilings) of traditional forms of saving for retirement. The funds they create will be fully portable, allowing people to change jobs without jeopardising their income in retirement. The introduction of a similar scheme in the United States has encouraged the majority of companies to switch their pension plans from defined benefit to defined contribution.

The displacement of the defined benefit pension will have the most profound effect on the structure of ownership, wealth and power in Britain since the invention of progressive taxation. For the vast majority of people, their pension is their most valuable asset after their house, and with a defined contribution plan, they will at last take full ownership of it. They will choose their own fund managers, receive regular reports on the value of their fund, and take it from job to job. Some people may even manage their own funds, investing directly in stocks and shares. But the vast majority will buy shares in collective savings vehicles: unit and investment trusts, or what Americans know collectively as 'mutual funds.'

Mutual funds pool the savings of many investors, and channel them into shares, bonds and other securities. The choice is wide: there are funds for income, and for capital growth; funds specialising in Europe, and others in Asia; funds which invest in commodities and derivatives; small companies and large; technology shares and gilt-edged bonds; and their managers offer indexed, balanced, bottom-up, or top-down investment strategies.* All an investor does is send a cheque to the managers of the funds which match his age, needs and preferences. He will then acquire his own blend of exposures to the risks and rewards of international capitalism. Unlike a pension or a life assurance policy, he can check their value and performance, every day, in the pages of newspapers and websites.

The great mistake of the Conservative administrations of the 1980s was to think that the future of the property-owning democracy lay in the wider ownership of stocks and shares. It actually lay in wider ownership of mutual funds, as the New Labour government has recognised. Only mutual funds can overcome the corrupted nature of corporate, institutionalised capitalism, and reconnect people with the risks and rewards of owning property directly. In the United States, where the mutual fund revolution has developed furthest, the assets already exceed the sums managed by either the pension funds or the insurance companies, and the total assets owned by the banks. One dollar in five is going into a defined contribution pension plan, and the proportion is rising by billions of dollars a month. The consequences for the occupational pension funds of corporate Britain are obvious. They will disappear, as employers cease to underwrite the pensions of their employees and contribute instead to savings which no longer belong to them.

The Slow Transformation of the Life Assurance Industry

The impact on the other great institutional investors – the life offices and insurance companies – will be almost as great. Though they sell mutual funds as well as pensions and insurance, the personal pensions scandal has tarnished their reputations so badly that few informed investors will be willing to entrust their defined contribution pension plan to even the biggest and best-known insurance companies. In framing the pension reforms around mutual funds, the government has publicised its own distrust of the life assurance industry. Its preference means that life offices will no longer be able to pursue unmeasurable investment objectives of their own, extracting usurious com-

* Top-down strategies choose investments on the basis of macro-economic data (e.g. buy Germany, or sell technology), while bottom-up strategies choose investments on the basis of micro-economic data (e.g., buy Unilever or ICI).

missions and piling up massive reserves for their shareholders, assured that their customers have no means of measuring whether what comes out bears any relation to what went in. The value of mutual funds – and their performance against their peer group – will be published in the newspapers and on the Internet each day.

The incessant, daily competition from hundreds of fund managers in dozens of markets will test the investment departments of the life offices and industrial assurance companies. The larger fund managers (until now confined largely to servicing occupational pension schemes) are already achieving stronger and more consistent results than the life assurance companies (which have dominated the retail market). By shifting power from the sellers of savings products to the buyers, mutual funds will make it hard for life offices and insurance companies to survive as fund managers. In a retail savings market dominated by mutual funds, specialist fund managers will have much the same effect on distribution-led life assurance as consumer-led competitors such as Direct Line have had on motor and household insurance.[83] Independent fund managers will appoint specialist administrators armed with computers to clear cheques, make payments, prepare valuations and despatch reports to investors. Instead of the Man from the Pru tramping the streets for captive clients, mutual funds will be sold on cost and performance over the telephone, through newspapers, television and the Internet.

Britain already has a mutual fund industry attuned to this new world. Unit trust managers have relied for years on newspapers, hoardings and junk mail. Fidelity, M&G, Perpetual and Save and Prosper have built brands at least as powerful as Scottish Widows or Friends Provident. Brands established in other fields, such as Marks and Spencer (which started a financial services arm in 1988) and Virgin (1995), have confirmed the power of trustworthy brands in this field as in every other. It was typical of the insurance companies that the first serious attempt by one of them to use mass-marketing techniques to sell mutual funds should end in disaster, thanks to less-than-stellar fund management. In 1987 Royal Insurance launched three international unit trusts backed by a £6 million marketing campaign, complete with privatisation-style TV and newspaper advertisements and junk mailings for 'The Royal Event of the Year.' Royal attracted 135,000 investors, and £240 million. But the funds, launched weeks ahead of the crash, did not recover from that setback. The Royal Event of the Year did lasting damage to the reputation of Royal Insurance as a fund manager, and the collateral damage reverberated through the life assurance industry.

But, if the unit trust industry is flattered by such comparisons, it is hardly ready to become the dominant force in British savings. Its total assets are one tenth those of the pension funds and life offices, and management is highly fragmented. The Association of Unit Trusts and Investment Funds (AUTIF) has one hundred and fifty-nine members, ranging from little-known fund managers such as Arbuthnot (managing £1.4 million) to giants like the Schroders investment banking group (managing £11.9 billion). Around one third of the funds are not independently managed, but sold to captive life and pension funds controlled by offshoots of major life and insurance groups. Another third is sold to captive customers of banks and building societies, leaving only one third to be sold in a genuinely competitive market on price and performance.

Dozens of incompetent and inadequate fund managers have survived, to charge fees and commissions at least as opaque as those of the life assurance industry and attracting nothing like the same level of scrutiny. The truth is that up-front charges of 5 per cent (rising to 7 per cent or more once the difference between bid and offer prices of units is taken into account) and annual management charges of 1.25–1.5 per cent are not uncommon in the unit trust industry. These are charges that can devour a large part of even the best investment returns (as newcomers like Virgin Direct recognised, by offering to scrap the initial charge rather than worry about choosing the right fund manager). Nor do unit trusts offer much feedback to their investors in the shape of valuations and investment reports – essential if a developed mutual fund industry is to succeed life offices as the chief custodian of personal savings. Philip Warland, director general of AUTIF, admitted in 1996 that the unit trust industry was 'among the worst service providers in the world'.[84]

But even a reputation for bad service is superior to the public image the life offices have earned. Fund managers are not spotless. Many have paid substantial fines to the regulatory authorities in recent years for a variety of misdemeanours. But the speed at which Morgan Grenfell Asset Management compensated investors in funds affected by the actions of a rogue investment manager – at a cost to its parent bank of £436 million – contrasted vividly with the dilatory approach of the life offices to pensions mis-selling. Virtually any fund manager uninvolved in the personal pensions débâcle is likely to be among those who will become the main providers of fund management products and services to individual investors.

Yet the problems of the insurance industry may not end there; insurance itself may have an existential problem. Its basic principle is the pooling of unpredictable risks. But risks are becoming increasingly predictable. Improved actuarial techniques, computer modelling and medical breakthroughs (such as genetic testing) are making it possible to predict the risks of premature death, disease, motor accidents, burglaries and hurricanes with greater precision than in the past. Once individual risks are understood, the case for pooling them begins to break down. The less susceptible demand lower premiums; the more susceptible have to pay higher premiums or become uninsurable. Insurers who take advantage of this new knowledge, and price risks accurately, will be more profitable than those who do not. They will need much lower reserves, at least as long as the good risks fail to realise they do not need to insure at all. Companies that continue to pool risks, by contrast, will suffer from the adverse selection of risks. They will have to maintain higher reserves, and their profits will fall. In the long run, many classes of risk will not be insurable commercially. The taxpayer will have to underwrite them.

In private health insurance, this is already happening. Elderly people, who are liable to clock up massive medical bills in their last years, are becoming virtually uninsurable. Most people die in the care of the National Health Service, not in a Nuffield Hospital at the expense of BUPA or PPP, and the cost of insuring the elderly against long-term residential care is also prohibitive. Smokers have paid more to insure their lives since 1971, when Scottish Mutual introduced lower premiums for non-smokers as a marketing gimmick. One in twenty-five life policyholders are already paying more to cover the cost of a perceived medical risk, and genetic knowledge, which is tracing an increasing range of fatal or crippling diseases, will spread this blight across a wider population. In the United States, insurance companies are already banned from making use of genetic data because it is encourages those most at risk to over-insure, driving up premiums. In Britain, Standard Life and Scottish Widows have said they will not ask people for results of genetic tests – but they are not yet widespread, so such piety is still costless. The reaction of the life assurance companies to AIDS is a more accurate barometer of their likely response once genetic testing becomes routine.

The insurance companies justified their efforts to exclude AIDS risks on the grounds that the exclusion of the worst risks keeps premiums down for the better risks. But actuaries, like most who read a newspaper or watched television in the mid-1980s, were convinced that the human race was on the threshold of a plague poised to claim more young lives than any since the Black Death. As AIDS mortality rates became better understood, and drug treatments improved, actuaries changed their opinion. By 1997, they were considering how to insure the HIV-positive. But the AIDS episode was a reminder that the insurance industry will always shun unmeasurable risk, which cannot be priced.

Modern insurance companies prefer pricing risks to pooling them. This has led to an overdue revival of the influence of the actuaries. In the 1950s and 1960s actuaries held most of the key positions at the large life offices, industrial assurance companies and composite insurers, but for the last thirty years marketing men and accountants have dominated their boardrooms. The great Nemesis which overtook the insurance industry in the 1980s and 1990s was largely their handiwork. It was they who insisted on widening the profit margins on premiums; expanded the underwriting book without regard to the risks being incurred; resisted the pressure for greater openness on sales commissions and management fees; connived at outrageously low surrender and pension transfer values; insisted on selling long-term savings contracts into a market where they made no sense; pumped up sales by projecting absurd rates of return; and, above all, tempted hundreds of thousands of uncomprehending people out of secure, generous occupational pension schemes.

The price these once-great institutions are paying is heavy. Their chance to profit from the coming dissolution of the occupational pension is forfeit. Their access to the new channels of distribution in the media and on the Internet is closed by the tainted nature of their brands, and a mixture of new knowledge and new technology is undermining even their original *raison d'être*: the pooling of risks. For British capitalism as a whole, however, the demise of corporate paternalism in pensions and the West Diddlesex Fire and Life Insurance Company removes the greatest obstacle to the restoration of true ownership. In the twenty-first century, if the government does not stand in his way, the British consumer will overrun the last redoubts of cartelised, paternalistic, institutionalised capitalism, and come into an inheritance which was once the sole preserve of monarchs and barons. He will live, as they once did, 'of his own'.

APPENDIX

Equivalent Contemporary Values of the Pound:
A Historical Series 1270 to 1998

This statistical series shows changes in the value of money over the past seven centuries and gives the amount of money required at December 1998 to purchase the goods bought by £1 at the dates shown on the table.

Thus, £78.29 would have been required in December 1998 in order to have the same purchasing power as £1 in 1690.

The figures are derived from the Retail Price Index, based at January 1987 = 100. There are no figures for individual years before 1800.

The RPI is based on the combined cost of a number of specific goods and does not take into account other factors relevant to a comparison of values: for example, the cost of real property or the level of wages. We know of no figures incorporating all possible factors.

1270 = £411.00	1420 = £411.00	1570 = £149.45	1720 = £74.73	1807 = £32.24
1280 = £411.00	1430 = £411.00	1580 = £164.40	1730 = £78.29	1808 = £31.02
1290 = £548.00	1440 = £411.00	1590 = £137.00	1740 = £78.29	1809 = £27.86
1300 = £411.00	1450 = £411.00	1600 = £117.43	1750 = £78.29	1810 = £27.40
1310 = £411.00	1460 = £411.00	1610 = £86.53	1760 = £68.50	1811 = £27.86
1320 = £328.80	1470 = £411.00	1620 = £86.53	1770 = £56.69	1812 = £24.91
1330 = £411.00	1480 = £411.00	1630 = £82.20	1780 = £56.69	1813 = £24.18
1340 = £548.00	1490 = £411.00	1640 = £78.29	1790 = £51.37	1814 = £27.86
1350 = £411.00	1500 = £411.00	1650 = £68.50	1800 = £28.84	1815 = £31.02
1360 = £328.80	1510 = £411.00	1660 = £68.50	1801 = £26.10	1816 = £34.25
1370 = £328.80	1520 = £411.00	1670 = £74.73	1802 = £33.55	1817 = £29.89
1380 = £411.00	1530 = £328.80	1680 = £74.73	1803 = £35.74	1818 = £29.89
1390 = £411.00	1540 = £274.00	1690 = £78.29	1804 = £34.98	1819 = £30.44
1400 = £411.00	1550 = £274.00	1700 = £71.48	1805 = £29.89	1820 = £33.55
1410 = £411.00	1560 = £182.67	1710 = £68.50	1806 = £31.62	1821 = £38.23

1822 = £44.33	1857 = £39.14	1892 = £51.37	1927 = £26.95	1962 = £12.27
1823 = £41.10	1858 = £43.26	1893 = £53.03	1928 = £27.40	1963 = £12.00
1824 = £38.23	1859 = £43.26	1894 = £54.80	1929 = £27.86	1964 = £11.66
1825 = £32.88	1860 = £42.15	1895 = £56.69	1930 = £28.84	1965 = £11.11
1826 = £34.25	1861 = £41.10	1896 = £56.69	1931 = £31.02	1966 = £10.68
1827 = £36.53	1862 = £42.15	1897 = £54.80	1932 = £31.62	1967 = £10.41
1828 = £38.23	1863 = £43.26	1898 = £54.80	1933 = £32.88	1968 = £9.96
1829 = £38.23	1864 = £44.43	1899 = £54.80	1934 = £32.24	1969 = £9.45
1830 = £40.10	1865 = £43.26	1900 = £55.03	1935 = £31.62	1970 = £8.89
1831 = £36.53	1866 = £41.10	1901 = £53.03	1936 = £31.02	1971 = £8.10
1832 = £39.14	1867 = £39.14	1902 = £51.37	1937 = £29.36	1972 = £7.58
1833 = £41.10	1868 = £39.14	1903 = £51.37	1938 = £29.36	1973 = £6.94
1834 = £44.43	1869 = £41.10	1904 = £51.37	1939 = £28.84	1974 = £5.98
1835 = £44.43	1870 = £41.10	1905 = £51.37	1940 = £24.91	1975 = £4.82
1836 = £40.10	1871 = £41.10	1906 = £54.80	1941 = £22.83	1976 = £4.13
1837 = £39.14	1872 = £39.14	1907 = £59.82	1942 = £22.83	1977 = £3.57
1838 = £38.23	1873 = £38.23	1908 = £48.35	1943 = £22.83	1978 = £3.29
1839 = £35.74	1874 = £40.10	1909 = £48.35	1944 = £22.83	1979 = £2.90
1840 = £35.74	1875 = £41.10	1910 = £48.35	1945 = £22.52	1980 = £2.46
1841 = £36.53	1876 = £42.15	1911 = £46.97	1946 = £22.52	1981 = £2.20
1842 = £39.14	1877 = £41.10	1912 = £45.67	1947 = £22.22	1982 = £2.02
1843 = £44.43	1878 = £42.15	1913 = £45.67	1948 = £20.81	1983 = £1.94
1844 = £44.43	1879 = £45.67	1914 = £45.67	1949 = £20.30	1984 = £1.84
1845 = £42.15	1880 = £43.26	1915 = £36.53	1950 = £19.57	1985 = £1.74
1846 = £40.10	1881 = £44.43	1916 = £31.02	1951 = £18.07	1986 = £1.68
1847 = £36.53	1882 = £44.43	1917 = £25.69	1952 = £16.44	1987 = £1.61
1848 = £41.10	1883 = £45.67	1918 = £21.08	1953 = £15.96	1988 = £1.54
1849 = £44.43	1884 = £46.97	1919 = £21.08	1954 = £15.66	1989 = £1.43
1850 = £46.97	1885 = £49.82	1920 = £18.27	1955 = £15.08	1990 = £1.30
1851 = £48.35	1886 = £51.37	1921 = £20.05	1956 = £14.30	1991 = £1.23
1852 = £48.35	1887 = £53.03	1922 = £24.91	1957 = £13.82	1992 = £1.19
1853 = £44.43	1888 = £53.03	1923 = £26.10	1958 = £13.48	1993 = £1.17
1854 = £38.23	1889 = £51.37	1924 = £26.10	1959 = £13.37	1994 = £1.14
1855 = £37.36	1890 = £51.37	1925 = £25.69	1960 = £13.26	1995 = £1.10
1856 = £37.36	1891 = £51.37	1926 = £26.52	1961 = £12.74	1996 = £1.08
				1997 = £1.04

Source: Bank of England

NOTES

CHAPTER ONE: *The Crown*

1 Anthony Sampson, *Anatomy of Britain*, Hodder & Stoughton, 1962, p. 41.
2 Anthony Sampson, *The Changing Anatomy of Britain*, Hodder & Stoughton, 1982, p. 12.
3 Ben Pimlott, *The Queen: A Biography of Elizabeth II*, HarperCollins, 1997, p. 249.
4 *Observer*, 13 February 1977.
5 Pimlott, *The Queen*, p. 381.
6 Bagehot had in mind not the Press, but the House of Commons. Walter Bagehot, *The English Constitution*, Fontana, 1973, p. 100.
7 Pimlott, *The Queen*, p. 389.
8 *The Times*, 1 September 1997.
9 *Sunday Telegraph*, 7 September 1997.
10 *Financial Times*, 8 September 1997.
11 Andrew Morton, *Diana: Her True Story*, Michael O'Mara, 1993, pp. 51, 165–6.
12 *Financial Times*, 6 September 1997.
13 ibid.
14 ibid., 10 July 1993.
15 Sampson, *The Changing Anatomy of Britain*, p. 11.
16 Bagehot, *The English Constitution*, p. 89.
17 Frank Prochaska, *Bounty: The Making of a Welfare Monarchy*, Yale, 1995.
18 Quoted in Tom Nairn, *The Enchanted Glass: Britain and Its Monarchy*, Vintage, 1994, p. (xxiii).
19 Bagehot, *The English Constitution*, p. 94.
20 Sampson, *Anatomy of Britain*, p. 49.
21 Nairn, *The Enchanted Glass*, pp. 213–322.
22 Will Hutton, *The State We're In*, Jonathan Cape, 1995, pp. 42–4.
23 Nairn, *The Enchanted Glass*, p. 85.
24 Sampson, *Anatomy of Britain*, p. 37.
25 Bagehot, *The English Constitution*, p. 111.
26 Ferdinand Mount, *The British Constitution Now*, Mandarin, 1993, p. 96.
27 E. F. Jacob, *The Fifteenth Century 1399–1485*, Oxford University Press, 1988 Edition, p. 78.
28 The Crown Estate Act of 1800.
29 On the demise of the 'Old Corruption', see Chapters 2 and 14.

30 Mount, *The British Constitution Now*, p. 88.

31 *Mail on Sunday*, 7 August 1994.

32 *Sunday Times*, 19 July 1987; Andrew Morton, *Theirs is the Kingdom: The Wealth of the Windsors*, Michael O'Mara, 1989, p. 147.

33 This marked a reversion to an earlier system. It was agreed by the Select Committee on the Civil List of 1971 that its value should be re-set by Parliament every ten years to take account of inflation. But the severe inflation of the 1970s made the arrangement unworkable, and the Civil List was revalued every year in the budget until 1990.

34 *The Independent*, 25 July 1990.

35 The Grant-in-Aid for the Maintenance of Occupied Royal Palaces in England, Annual Report 1996–97.

36 Philip Hall, *Royal Fortune: Tax, Money and the Monarchy*, Bloomsbury, 1992.

37 Jonathan Dimbleby, *The Prince of Wales: A Biography*, Little Brown, 1994, pp. 512–13.

38 Sampson, *The New Anatomy of Britain*, p. 226.

39 Emma Nicholson, who later defected to the Liberal Democrats. From Pimlott, *The Queen*, p. 534.

40 *Sunday Times Magazine*, 10 May 1992.

41 R. B. Pugh, *The Crown Estate: An Historical Essay*, HMSO, 1960, p. 16.

42 The Crown Estate: Commissioners' Report for the year ended 31 March 1997.

43 Maurice Powicke, *The Thirteenth Century 1216–1307*, Oxford University Press, 1988 Edition, p. 197.

44 May McKisack, *The Fourteenth Century 1307–1399*, Oxford University Press, 1988 Edition, pp. 73–5.

45 ibid., p. 482; B. P. Wolffe, *The Royal Demesne in English History: The Crown Estate in the Governance of the Realm from the Conquest to 1509*, Allen & Unwin, 1971, pp. 76–87.

46 Pugh, *The Crown Estate*, p. 9.

47 Wolffe, *The Royal Demesne in English History*, p. 188.

48 Pugh, *The Crown Estate*, p. 10.

49 ibid.; Shirley Green, *Who Owns London?*, Weidenfeld & Nicolson, 1986.

50 Simon Jenkins, *Landlords to London: The Story of a Capital and Its Growth*, Constable 1975.

51 *Survey of London*, Vol. XXIX, Parish of St James Westminster, Part One: South of Piccadilly, 1960, p. 26.

52 *Sunday Times*, 19 July 1987.

53 *Sunday Times*, 29 November 1992.

54 *Evening Standard*, 7 July 1993.

55 *The Times*, 29 June 1994.

56 'The Commissioners have made a policy decision to retain the agricultural estate at broadly its current acreage on grounds that the Crown has always had an extensive agricultural estate, but also so that they do not sell in a buyer's market. Other landowners are taking a different view.' *The Crown Estate: Report by the Comptroller and Auditor General*, National Audit Office, House of Commons paper 537, June 1988, p. 22, para. 4.13.

57 The other Royal Parks are now maintained by the Royal Parks Agency. For executive agencies, see Chapter 9.

58 *The Observer*, 11 December 1994.
59 Financial Statements of the Duchy of Cornwall for the fifteen months ended 31 March 1997.
60 Jonathan Dimbleby, *The Prince of Wales*, pp. 505–6.
61 ibid., p. 506.
62 Hall, *Royal Fortune*, pp. 56–7, 70, 263, 265.
63 *Sunday Times Magazine*, 6 April 1997.
64 Hall, *Royal Fortune*, p. 46.
65 *Sunday Times Magazine*, 6 April 1997.
66 The unoccupied Royal Palaces – the Tower of London, Hampton Court, the state apartments at Kensington Palace, the Banqueting House in Whitehall, Kew Palace and Queen Charlotte's Cottage – are treated as historic buildings, and maintained by the Historic Royal Palaces Trust. The Palace of Holyroodhouse in Edinburgh, where the Queen still stays, is maintained by Historic Scotland.
67 The Grant-in-Aid for the Maintenance of the Occupied Royal Palaces in England, Annual Report 1996–97.
68 The Royal Finances, Second Edition, 1995.
69 The Royal Collection Trust Annual Report 1996–97, p. 40.
70 *The Queen's Pictures: Royal Collectors Through the Centuries*, National Gallery Publications Limited, 1991, p. 10.
71 Andrew Morton, *Theirs is the Kingdom: The Wealth of the Windsors*, Michael O'Mara, 1989, pp. 172–3.
72 Hall, *Royal Fortune*, pp. 181–5.
73 Morton, *Theirs is the Kingdom*, pp. 170–3.
74 At a yield of 5 per cent, the going rate for farmland that year.
75 Revenue and Capital Accounts for the Duchy of Lancaster for the year ended 31 March 1997.
76 ibid.
77 *Sunday Times Magazine*, 6 April 1997.
78 Andrew Morton, in *Theirs is the Kingdom: The Wealth of the Windsors*, Michael O'Mara, 1989, p. 60.
79 This is the figure given in the *Dictionary of National Biography*, accepted by Phillip Hall. Andrew Morton, in *Theirs is the Kingdom* (p. 45) puts it at £250,000.
80 Hall, *Royal Fortune*, pp. 11–12.
81 Hall, *Royal Fortune*, p. 16; Morton, *Theirs is the Kingdom*, p. 42.
82 Hall, *Royal Fortune*, pp. 16–17, 20–32.
83 ibid., pp. 44–5, 70.
84 Edward VIII added Fort Belvedere in Berkshire to the royal house collection. It is now rented by Galen Weston, on a 99-year lease from the Queen.
85 Hall, *Royal Fortune*, p. 81.
86 Hall estimates that between 1838 and 1951 five successive monarchs saved a grand total of £67.3 million, p. 107.
87 Morton, *Theirs is the Kingdom*, p. 11.
88 *Sunday Telegraph*, 30 August 1992.
89 *The Economist*, 25 January 1992. This cited the *World in Action* documentary analysis of 1991, based largely on Hall's research.
90 *The Times*, 12 February 1993.
91 *The Sunday Times Magazine*, 4 April 1993; *The Sunday Times Britain's Richest 500, 1994*.

92 *Financial Times*, 12 February 1993.

93 *Financial Times*, 27 November 1992; Morton, *Theirs is the Kingdom*, p. 173.

94 Anthony Howard, *Rab: The Life of R. A. Butler*, Jonathan Cape, 1987, p. 356.

95 *Financial Times*, 23 January 1996.

96 Pimlott, *The Queen*, p. 546.

CHAPTER TWO: *The Aristocracy*

1 Jeremy Paxman, *Friends in High Places: Who Runs Britain?*, Michael Joseph, 1990, pp. 29, 31.

2 *Sunday Telegraph*, 3 December 1989.

3 Quoted in T. H. White, *Age of Scandal*, Penguin, 1962, p. 10.

4 *Sunday Times*, 28 February 1993.

5 *The Times*, 28 November 1997.

6 David Cannadine, 'The Landowner as Millionaire: The Finances of the Dukes of Devonshire', in *Aspects of Aristocracy*, Yale University Press, 1994, p. 182.

7 *The Times*, 26 April 1985.

8 *Sunday Times*, 16 November 1997; *The Times*, 4 December 1997.

9 Andrew Adonis and Stephen Pollard, *A Class Act: The Myth of Britain's Classless Society*, Hamish Hamilton, 1997, p. 132.

10 *Sunday Times Magazine*, 2 April 1989.

11 Andy Wightman, *Who Owns Scotland*, Canongate, 1996, p. 145.

12 *The Guardian*, 13 August 1994.

13 Hugh Montgomery-Massingberd, *Great British Families*, Debrett/Webb & Bower/ Michael Joseph, 1988, p. 12.

14 Graham Turner, 'New Life for Old Money', *Sunday Telegraph*, 26 November 1989.

15 Nicholas Coleridge, 'Why Lords Love a Lady', *The Spectator*, 22 October 1988.

16 'New Life for Old Money', 26 November 1989.

17 Paxman, *Friends in High Places*, p. 40; *Sunday Telegraph*, 3 December 1989.

18 Evelyn Waugh wrote to Nancy Mitford at the time that 'Bowood . . . is being demolished because its owner prefers privacy.' Paxman, *Friends in High Places*, p. 40.

19 Evelyn Waugh, *Brideshead Revisited*, preface, revised edition 1959, Penguin, 1981.

20 *Sunday Times*, 18 January 1998.

21 Peter Mandler, *The Fall and Rise of the Stately Home*, Yale University Press, 1997, p. 317.

22 Much of the northern part of the Bloomsbury Estate, including Woburn, Gordon and Tavistock Squares, was sold to the University of London. David Cannadine, *The Decline and Fall of the British Aristocracy*, Yale University Press, 1990, p. 641; Beard, *English Landed Society*, pp. 106–7; Simon Jenkins, *Landlords to London*, Constable, 1975.

23 Beard, *English Landed Society*, p. 105.

24 Roy Strong, *Lost Treasures of Britain: Five Centuries of Creation and Destruction*, Guild Publishing, 1990, p. 219.

25 B. E. V. Sabine, *A History of Income Tax*, George Allen & Unwin, 1966.

26 Beard, *English Landed Society*, p. 12; David Cannadine, *The Decline and Fall*, p. 97.

27 Cannadine, *The Decline and Fall*, p. 519.

28 *The Times*, 30 September 1997.
29 *Sunday Telegraph*, 3 December 1989.
30 *The Times*, 30 September 1997.
31 *Financial Times*, 22 November 1995.
32 Graham Turner, 'Heirs of Confidence', *Sunday Telegraph*, 3 December 1989.
33 Walter Bagehot, *The English Constitution*, Fontana, 1973, p. 122.
34 W. D. Rubinstein, *Men of Property: The Very Wealthy in Britain Since the Industrial Revolution*, Croom Helm, 1981, p. 219.
35 J. V. Beckett, *The Aristocracy in England 1660–1914*, revised edition, Basil Blackwell, 1989, p. 315.
36 Cannadine, 'Aristocratic Indebtedness in the Nineteenth Century', in *Aspects of Aristocracy*, p. 44.
37 Quoted in Paxman, *Friends in High Places*, p. 22.
38 Cannadine, *The Decline and Fall*, pp. 17–18.
39 'Heirs of Confidence', *Sunday Telegraph*, 3 December 1989.
40 *Daily Telegraph*, 30 March 1992.
41 *The Times*, 13 August 1997.
42 Quoted in *Financial Times*, 7 March 1992.
43 Cannadine, *The Decline and Fall*, p. 519; Doreen Massey and Alejandrina Catalano, *Capital and Land: Land Ownership By Capital in Great Britain*, 1978, pp. 77, 81; Douglas Sutherland, *The Landowners*, Anthony Blond, 1968, p. 85.
44 *Financial Times*, 12 March 1998.
45 ibid., 19 January 1998.
46 ibid., 14 October 1995.
47 Coleridge, 'Why Lords Love a Lady', *Spectator*, 22 October 1988.
48 Robert Hewison, *In Anger: Culture in the Cold War 1945–60*, Methuen, revised edition, 1988, pp. 75–6.
49 Cannadine, *The Decline and Fall*, p. 641; Lawrence Rich, *Inherit the Land: Landowners in the Eighties*, Unwin Hyman, 1987, pp. 20, 24.
50 Rich, *Inherit the Land*, pp. 14–35.
51 Lawrence Rich, *Inherit the Land*, Unwin Hyman, 1987, p. 167.
52 Mandler, *The Fall and Rise of the Stately Home*, p. 396.
53 ibid., p. 375.
54 Sampson, *Anatomy of Britain*, p. 10.
55 Quoted in Cannadine, *The Decline and Fall*, p. 695.
56 Montgomery-Massingberd, *Great British Families*, p. 58.
57 Mandler, *The Fall and Rise of the Stately Home*, pp. 10, 196, 201–4.
58 ibid., p. 378.
59 ibid., pp. 378, 189.
60 David Gilmour, *Curzon*, John Murray, 1994, p. 461.
61 'Redistribution to the Rich', *The Economist*, 5 November 1994.
62 See Chapter 3.
63 Cannadine, 'Portrait of More Than a Marriage: Harold Nicolson and Vita Sackville-West Revisited', in *Aspects of Aristocracy*, p. 234.
64 See Chapter 3.
65 See Chapter 3, for tensions which arise between the National Trust and former owners.
66 Earl Brownlow became a Jersey-based tax exile. *The Observer*, 21 August 1983.

67 Beard, *English Landed Society*, p. 161.

68 Montgomery-Massingberd, *Great British Families*, pp. 181–2.

69 Beard, *English Landed Society*, p. 132.

70 Mandler, *The Fall and Rise of the Stately Home*, p. 398.

71 Robert Hewison, *The Heritage Industry: Britain in a Climate of Decline*, Methuen, 1987, p. 67.

72 *Financial Times*, 3 October 1974.

73 Quoted in Hewison, *The Heritage Industry*, p. 68.

74 Cannadine, *The Decline and Fall*, p. 694.

75 CTT was the first tax ever imposed on life time gifts.

76 See Chapter 3.

77 *Financial Times*, 6 July 1991.

78 Salomon Brothers, reported in the *Financial Times*, 9 June 1990.

79 See Table 2.1.

80 *Independent*, 9, 22 February; 1 March 1990; *Independent on Sunday*, 29 December 1991.

81 Sunday Times Rich List, 1997.

82 Philip Beresford, *The Sunday Times Book of the Rich*, Weidenfeld & Nicolson, 1990, p. 198.

83 *Financial Times*, 16 December 1995.

84 *The Times*, 18 July 1997.

85 ibid., 17 May 1985.

86 *Observer*, 21 June 1992; *Financial Times*, 31 March 1992.

87 *The Times*, 5 April 1994.

88 Mandler, *Fall and Rise of the Stately Home*, p. 359.

89 *Financial Times*, 22 February 1992.

90 ibid., 10 December 1994.

91 See above, p. 56.

92 Inland Revenue Press Office; the figure is for 31 December 1997.

93 *Sunday Telegraph*, 11 December 1994 and *Sunday Times*, 18 December 1994.

94 *Sunday Times*, 24 June 1990.

95 See *Sunday Telegraph*, 11 December 1999.

96 *Sunday Telegraph*, 10 January 1993.

97 For a full account of farming subsidies, see Chapter 18.

98 *Sunday Times*, 1 December 1991.

99 English Heritage Annual Report and Accounts 1996–7, p. 10.

100 Mandler, *The Fall and Rise of the Stately Home*, p. 377.

101 Cannadine, *The Decline and Fall*, p. 660.

102 Nicholas Ridley, Environment Secretary, 22 November 1988.

103 Sir Frank Stenton, *Anglo-Saxon England*, Oxford University Press, 1987, p. 626.

104 Maurice Keen, *English Society in the Later Middle Ages 1348–1500*, Penguin, 1990, pp. 203–14.

105 Keen, *English Society in the Later Middle Ages*, pp. 38–40 and 171–2.

106 Quoted in W. G. Hoskins, *The Age of Plunder: The England of Henry VIII 1500–1547*, Longman, 1988, p. 121.

107 ibid., p. 147.

108 David Crouch, *William Marshal: Court, Career and Chivalry in the Angevin Empire 1147–1219*, Longman, 1990, pp. 133–4, 161–2.

109 Cannadine, *The Decline and Fall*, p. 333.
110 Quoted in Lawrence Stone and Jeanne C. Fawtier Stone, *An Open Elite?: England 1540–1880*, Abridged Edition, Oxford University Press, 1986, p. 23.
111 Sampson, *Anatomy of Britain*, p. 5; *The New Anatomy of Britain*, p. 211.
112 Montgomery-Massingberd, *Great British Families*, p. 14.
113 Hoskins, *The Age of Plunder*, p. 53; Joyce Youings, *Sixteenth Century England*, Penguin, 1991, p. 321.
114 Joyce Youngs, *Sixteenth Century England*, Penguin, 1991, p. 321.
115 This was too blatant even for James, who pointedly elevated Harington's cousin to a barony. See Lawrence Stone, *The Crisis of the Aristocracy 1558–1641*, Abridged Edition, Oxford University Press, 1967, p. 218.
116 Charles Wilson, *England's Apprenticeship 1603–1763*, Longman, 1975, p. 108.
117 J. V. Beckett, *The Aristocracy in England 1660–1914*, Revised Edition, Blackwell, 1989, pp. 486–7.
118 F. M. L. Thompson, *English Landed Society in the Nineteenth Century*, Routledge & Kegan Paul, 1963, p. 294.
119 See below, p. 77.
120 Cannadine, *The Decline and Fall*, p. 334.
121 ibid., p. 215.
122 Quoted in Kenneth Rose, *King George V*, Weidenfeld & Nicolson, 1983, p. 249.
123 Philip Knightley, *The Vestey Affair*, Macdonald, 1981.
124 Cannadine, *The Decline and Fall*, pp. 323–4.
125 Cannadine, *The Decline and Fall*, pp. 144, 184.
126 See Chapter 13.
127 Quoted in Beckett, *The Aristocracy in England 1660–1914*, p. 378.
128 ibid., pp. 168–71.
129 Frank McLynn, *Crime and Punishment in Eighteenth Century England*, Oxford University Press Paperback Edition, 1991, p. 257.
130 Ray Porter, *English Society in the Eighteenth Century*, Revised Edition, Penguin, 1990, p. 60.
131 W. D. Rubinstein, 'The End of "Old Corruption" in Britain 1780–1860', *Past and Present* No. 101, November 1983, p. 61.
132 Quoted in Sampson, *Anatomy of Britain*, p. 4.
133 Earl Cadogan, for example, retains the right to appoint the vicar at two churches on his London estate, Holy Trinity, Sloane Square, and St Luke's, Sydney Street. Robin Pearman, *The Cadogan Estate: The History of a Landed Family*, Haggerston Press, 1986, p. 110.
134 Cannadine, *The Decline and Fall . . .* , p. 273.
135 Harold Perkin, *The Origins of Modern English Society*, Routledge & Kegan Paul, 1976, p. 19; Beckett, *The Aristocracy in England 1660–1914*, pp. 194–205.
136 Porter, *English Society in the Eighteenth Century*, p. 57.
137 Trevor May, *An Economic and Social History of Britain 1760–1970*, Longman, 1992, p. 107.
138 Beckett, *The Aristocracy in England 1660–1914*, p. 198.
139 Porter, *English Society in the Eighteenth Century*, p. 57.
140 Cannadine, 'The Landowner as Millionaire: The Finances of the Dukes of Devonshire', in *Aspects of Aristocracy*, p. 174.
141 Beckett, *The Aristocracy in England 1660–1914*, p. 217.

142 Trevor May, *An Economic and Social History of Britain*, p. 72.

143 Porter, *English Society in the Eighteenth Century*, pp. 59, 66; John Rule, *The Vital Century: England's Developing Economy 1714–1815*, Longman, 1992, p. 47.

144 Perkin, *The Origins of Modern English Society*, pp. 19–21.

145 W. D. Rubinstein, *Men of Property: The Very Wealthy in Britain Since the Industrial Revolution*, Croom Helm, 1981, p. 194; Beckett, *The Aristocracy in England 1660–1914*, p. 290.

146 James Caird, *The Landed Interest and the Supply of Food*, 1878, quoted in Beckett, *The Aristocracy in England 1660–1914*, p. 134.

147 Introduction by David Spring to John Bateman, *The Great Landowners of Great Britain and Ireland*, Facsimile Edition, Leicester Press, 1971.

148 Cannadine, *The Decline and Fall*, pp. 9, 18–19.

149 The results of the official return were revised and popularised by an Essex squire, John Bateman, in his *Great Landowners of Great Britain and Ireland*, which ran through four editions between 1876 and 1883. The book was originally entitled *The AcreOcracy*.

150 From Robin Stewart, 'The Conservative Reaction', in *Salisbury: The Man and his Policies* (ed. Lord Blake and Hugh Cecil), Macmillan, 1987, pp. 110–11.

151 ibid., p. 99.

152 Mandler, *The Fall and Rise of the Stately Home*, pp. 118–27.

153 Montgomery-Massingberd, *Great British Families*, p. 81.

154 For the problems of Irish peers, see p. 85.

155 *Financial Times*,9 March 1991; *Sunday Telegraph*, 30 April 1995.

156 Cannadine, *The Decline and Fall*, p. 111.

157 Sampson, *Anatomy of Britain*, p. 14.

158 Beckett, *The Aristocracy in England 1660–1914*, p. 117.

159 Thompson, *English Landed Society in the Nineteenth Century*, p. 59.

160 Cannadine, *The Decline and Fall*, pp. 196, 206.

161 Beard, *English Landed Society*, p. 47.

162 Beckett, *The Aristocracy in England 1660–1914*, p. 46.

163 Rubinstein, *Men of Property*, p. 170.

164 Mingay, *English Landed Society*, p. 33.

165 Mandler, *The Fall and Rise of the Stately Home*, Yale University Press, 1997, p. 119.

166 Beard, *English Landed Society*, p. 40.

167 Cannadine, *The Decline and Fall*, p. 642.

168 ibid., p. 367.

169 Mandler, *The Fall and Rise of the Stately Home*, p. 243.

170 Beckett, *The Aristocracy in England 1660–1914*, p. 85.

171 Beckett, *The Aristocracy in England 1660–1914*, p. 475.

172 Douglas Sutherland, *The Landowners*, Anthony Blond, 1968, p. 48.

173 See Chapter 18. See also Beckett, *The Aristocracy in England 1660–1914*, p. 198.

174 Cannadine, *The Decline and Fall*, p. 64.

175 ibid., p. 110.

176 ibid., p. 105.

177 ibid., pp. 66, 110, 107.

178 Mandler, *The Fall and Rise of the Stately Home*, p. 463, *n.* 3.

179 Cannadine, *The Decline and Fall*, p. 61.

180 *Financial Times*, 26 August and 20 November 1992.

181 Gerald Cadogan, 'Dealing in Peppercorns', *Financial Times*, 4 April 1998.

182 Quoted in *Salisbury: The Man and His Policies* (ed. Lord Blake and Hugh Cecil), Macmillan, 1987. p. 99.

183 Andrew Adonis and Stephen Pollard, *A Class Act: The Myth of Britain's Classless Society*, Hamish Hamilton, 1997, p. 146.

184 Ferdinand Mount, *The British Constitution Now*, Mandarin 1993, p. 189.

185 Mandler, *The Fall and Rise of the Stately Home*, p. 383.

186 Rubinstein, *Men of Property*, p. 194; *The Great Landowners*, Sunday Times Magazine, 10 May 1992.

187 Cannadine, *The Decline and Fall*, p. 660.

188 Mandler, *The Fall and Rise of the Stately Home*, p. 105.

189 Quoted in ibid., p. 367.

CHAPTER THREE: *The Heritage Industry*

1 Peter Mandler, *The Fall and Rise of the Stately Home*, Yale University Press, 1997, p. 188.

2 Quoted in Jennifer Jenkins and Patrick James, *From Acorn to Oak Tree: The Growth of the National Trust 1895–1994*, Macmillan, 1994, p. 62.

3 *Financial Times*, 18 September 1997.

4 From Clive Bell, *Art*, Chatto, 1915, quoted in David Sawers, *Should the Taxpayer Support the Arts?*, Institute of Economic Affairs, 1993, pp. 10, 15.

5 Quoted in Roy Strong, *Lost Treasures of Britain: Five Centuries of Creation and Destruction*, Guild Publishing, 1990, p. 215.

6 Mandler, *The Fall and Rise of the Stately Home*, p. 101.

7 ibid., p. 104.

8 Martin J. Wiener, *English Culture and the Decline of the Industrial Spirit 1850–1980*, Pelican, 1985, p. 38.

9 Raymond Williams, *Culture and Society 1780–1950*, Penguin, 1975, pp. 139–52.

10 The book was published in 1894. Martin J. Wiener, *English Culture*, p. 119.

11 Mandler, *The Fall and Rise of the Stately Home*, pp. 144–5.

12 The chronology is a bit odd. Fiona MacCarthy has him in Burford in the summer of 1876, but dates the foundation of the SPAB to March that year. Fiona MacCarthy, *William Morris: A Life for Our Time*, Faber and Faber, 1994, p. 376.

13 Mandler, *The Fall and Rise of the Stately Home*, p. 160.

14 MacCarthy, *William Morris*, pp. 376–7.

15 Mandler, *The Fall and Rise of the Stately Home*, pp. 160, 170, 184–8.

16 ibid., p. 156.

17 ibid., pp. 187–91.

18 ibid., p. 274.

19 Department of National Heritage and the Welsh Office, *Protecting Our Heritage: A Consultation Document on the Built Heritage of England and Wales*, May 1996, p. 6.

20 Robert Hewison, *The Heritage Industry: Britain in a Climate of Decline*, Methuen, 1987, p. 24.

21 ibid., p. 24.

22 Quoted in Strong, *Lost Treasures of Britain*, p. 222.

23 *Sunday Times*, 11 August 1991.

24 Jenkins and James, *From Acorn to Oak Tree*, p. 325.

25 *Sunday Times*, 7 February 1993.

26 *Daily Telegraph*, 23 January 1992.

27 English Heritage Annual Report & Accounts, 1996-7.

28 *The Times*, 6 January 1995.

29 *Protecting Our Heritage*, p. 7.

30 *Financial Times*, 9 January 1993.

31 *Sunday Telegraph*, 28 February 1993.

32 English Heritage, Historic Scotland and Cadw Annual Reports and Accounts, 1997.

33 1996-97 Annual Report and Accounts of the Heritage Lottery Fund and the National Heritage Memorial Fund, p. 15.

34 See Chapter 2.

35 Mandler, *The Fall and Rise of the Stately Home*, p. 335.

36 ibid., p. 336.

37 The Lottery Fund had revenues of £71 million. Heritage Lottery Fund and National Heritage Memorial Fund Annual Reports and Accounts, 1996-7.

38 Quoted in Hewison, *The Heritage Industry*, p. 62.

39 For further details on executive agencies, see Chapter 9.

40 *The Times*, 19 July 1996; *Financial Times*, 8 October 1996; *Sunday Times*, 18 January 1998.

41 National Audit Office, *Protecting and Managing England's Heritage Property*, HMSO, July 1992.

42 *The Observer*, 9 August 1992.

43 *The Times*, 18 April 1996.

44 English Heritage Annual Report and Accounts, 1996-7.

45 On Branding, see Chapter 22.

46 National Trust Annual Report and Accounts, 1996-7.

47 *Daily Telegraph*, 26 March 1987.

48 National Trust Annual Report and Accounts 1996-7, p. 27.

49 Jenkins and James, *From Acorn to Oak Tree*, pp. 166-8.

50 ibid., p. 256.

51 For Charities, see Chapter 26.

52 *The Times*, 12 October 1993.

53 National Trust for Scotland Annual Report and Accounts, 1996-7, page 9, note 7.

54 Magnus Linklater, 'Save Us From Such Parodies of the Past', *The Times*, 4 August 1997.

55 Jenkins and James, *From Acorn to Oak Tree*, p. 173.

56 Paula Weideger, *Gilding the Acorn: Behind the Facade of the National Trust*, Simon & Schuster, 1994.

57 *Sunday Telegraph*, 19 December 1981.

58 *Sunday Times*, 2 September 1990.

59 ibid., 5 June 1988.

60 In a local radio broadcast, quoted in a BBC documentary in 1995.

61 Jenkins and James, *From Acorn to Oak Tree*, p. 170.

62 Letter from Lord Saye & Sele, 7 May 1993.

63 Hugh Massingberd, 'Time to Start Listing Families', *The Spectator*, 25 July 1992.

64 *Daily Telegraph*, 19 April 1984.

65 Charles Clover, 'Trust, But No Confidence', *The Spectator*, 2 November 1991.

66 The National Trust Annual Report and Accounts, 1996–7.

67 National Trust Facts and Figures Compendium, November 1997.

68 The National Trust Annual Report and Accounts 1996–7.

69 Landmark Trust Accounts for the year ended 31 December 1996.

70 Jenkins and James, *From Acorn to Oak Tree*, p. 189.

71 ibid., p. 259.

72 Robin Fedden, *National Trust: Past and Present*, Jonathan Cape, 1974; *From Acorn to Oake Tree*, pp. 213–14.

73 Jenkins and James, *From Acorn to Oak Tree*, pp. 298–301, 317.

74 *Independent on Sunday*, 4 November 1990.

75 *Sunday Times*, 23 December 1990.

76 *The Observer*, 24 August 1986.

77 Jenkins and James, *From Acorn to Oak Tree*, p. 20.

78 Matt Ridley, *The Origins of Virtue*, 1996, pp. 232–3.

79 Hazel Conway, *People's Parks: The Design and Development of Victorian Parks in Britain*, Cambridge University Press, 1991, p. 25.

80 Marion Shoard, *This Land is Our Land: The Struggle for Britain's Countryside*, Paladin, 1987, pp. 107–8, 408.

81 ibid., p. 109.

82 Richard Norton-Taylor, *Whose Land Is It Anyway? How Urban Greed Exploits the Land*, Turnstone Press, 1982, p. 51.

83 Shoard, *This Land Is Our Land*, pp. 413–15.

84 *Financial Times*, 8 July 1993.

85 See Shoard, *This Land is Our Land*, pp. 418–19.

86 *Sunday Telegraph Magazine*, 17 September 1995.

87 *Financial Times*, 25 September 1995.

88 Quoted by Colin Amery in *Financial Times*, 3 July 1989.

89 Jenkins and James, *From Acorn to Oak Tree*, p. 25; Fedden, *National Trust*, p. 24.

90 See Chapter 2.

91 It is estimated that between 1875 and 1975, 1,116 country houses were destroyed. See Chapter 2. See also Hewison, *The Heritage Industry*, p. 54; Lawrence Stone and Jean C. Fawtier Stone, *An Open Elite? England 1540–1880*, Abridged Edition, Oxford University Press, 1986, p. 308.

92 David Cannadine, *The Decline and Fall of the British Aristocracy*, Yale University Press, 1990, pp. 120–1.

93 Fedden, *National Trust*, pp. 40–3; Jenkins and James, *From Acorn to Oak Tree*, pp. 78–93.

94 Jenkins and James, *From Acorn to Oak Tree*, pp. 79–80.

95 ibid., pp. 219–39.

96 *The Independent*, 23 October 1990.

97 *The Observer*, 14 September 1986.

98 National Trust Annual Report and Accounts, 1996–7, p. 42, *n.* 14.

99 *The Guardian*, 16 February 1990.

100 *Sunday Telegraph Magazine*, 17 September 1995.

101 Peter Mandler, *The Fall and Rise of the Stately Home*, p. 271.

102 Jenkins and James, *From Acorn to Oak Tree*, p. 93.

103 ibid., p. 136.

104 Cannadine, *G. M. Trevelyan*, p. 175.

105 Cited in *Fifty Years of National Parks*, Council for National Parks, 1986.
106 In Scotland and Wales the work of the Countryside Commission was taken over by Scottish Natural Heritage and the Countryside Council for Wales. See p. 121 below.
107 Andy Wightman, *Who Owns Scotland*, Canongate, 1996, pp. 162, 186.
108 In 1991 the Nature Conservancy Council was split into separate bodies for England, Scotland and Wales. The Scottish and Welsh Councils merged with the local branches of the Countryside Commission, set up under the 1968 Countryside Act to strengthen the system of national parks. The Countryside Commission dispenses grants and advises government on National Parks, areas of outstanding natural beauty, national trails or 'Heritage Coasts'.
109 *Sunday Times*, 3 January 1993.
110 W. G. Hoskins, *The Making of the English Landscape*, Hodder & Stoughton, 1988 edition, p. 18.
111 Arts Council Annual Report, 1996-7, p. 11.
112 'Why arts need public money to flourish', *Financial Times*, 14 October 1993.
113 *Sunday Times*, 3 April 1994.
114 *Financial Times*, 2 October 1997.
115 Arts Council Annual Report, 1996-7, p. 11.
116 David Sawers, *Should the Taxpayer Support the Arts?*, pp. 10, 15.
117 *The Economist*, 27 November 1993.
118 Arts Council Annual Report, 1996-7, p. 6.
119 *The Economist*, 13 November 1993.
120 *Financial Times*, 31 October 1997.
121 Sawers, *Should the Taxpayer Support the Arts?*, pp. 22-3.
122 *Financial Times*, 13 November 1993.
123 From Andrew Sinclair, *Arts and Cultures: The History of the 50 Years of the Arts Council of Great Britain*, Sinclair-Stevenson, 1995.
124 *Financial Times*, 31 July 1997.
125 Arts Council Annual Report, 1996-7, pp. 5-6.
126 Jeremy Paxman, *Friends in High Places: Who Runs Britain?*, Michael Joseph, 1990, p. 303.
127 Anthony Sampson, *Anatomy of Britain*, Hodder and Stoughton, 1982, pp. 636-7.
128 Wiener, *English Culture*, pp. 157-66.
129 Hewison, *The Heritage Industry*, p. 9.
130 Paxman, *Friends in High Places*, pp. 332-5.

CHAPTER FOUR: *The Church*

1 The Right Reverend Richard Harries. In Terry Lovell, *Number One Millbank: The Financial Downfall of the Church of England*, HarperCollins, 1997, p. 131.
2 Quoted by Anthony Howard, *The Times*, 28 April 1998.
3 Quoted in Lovell, *Number One Millbank*, p. 166.
4 *Observer*, 3 April 1994.
5 National Heritage Memorial Fund, Annual Reports, 1981-1996.
6 Annual Report and Accounts of the Heritage Lottery Fund, 1995-6, pp. 17, 33.
7 See Chapter 2.
8 *The Economist*, 11 August 1990.

9 Canon Ronald Coppin of Durham Cathedral, quoted in *Observer*, 14 March 1993.

10 Interview, David Macey, receiver general, Canterbury Cathedral, 12 November 1992.

11 Robert Hewison, *The Heritage Industry: Britain in a Climate of Decline*, Methuen, 1987, pp. 98–9.

12 Ely Cathedral Accounts, 1991.

13 Letter to the author, 19 August 1993.

14 Letters to the author, 13 July, 1993 and 8 September 1993.

15 Danny Danziger, *The Cathedral*, Viking, 1989, p. 45.

16 *Heritage & Renewal*, pp. 154–5, 170.

17 ibid., p. 173.

18 Interview by the author, 12 November 1992.

19 ibid.

20 *Sunday Telegraph*, 18 October 1992.

21 *Heritage & Renewal*, p. 130.

22 ibid., p. 111.

23 'And Jesus went into the temple of God, and cast out all them that sold and bought in the temple, and overthrew the tables of the money-changers, and the seats of them that sold doves. And said unto them, It is written, My house shall be a house of prayer; but ye have made it a den of thieves.' Matthew, ch. 21, verses 12–13.

24 *Independent on Sunday*, 16 October 1994.

25 Letter to the author, 19 July 1993.

26 *Sunday Telegraph*, 19 July 1992.

27 *Church Times*, 19 January 1990.

28 Letter, *Financial Times*, 26 August 1997.

29 Interview by the author, 3 November 1992, and letter to the author, 15 October 1993.

30 English Heritage Annual Report and Accounts, 1996–7, p. 15.

31 The Church Commissioners for England Annual Report and Accounts, 1996, pp. 19–20.

32 ibid., p. 20.

33 ibid., 1988–96.

34 ibid., 1996.

35 Lovell, *Number One Millbank*, pp. 232–3, 237.

36 Owen Chadwick, *The Victorian Church, Part Two, 1860–1901*, second edition, SCM Press, 1972, p. 367.

37 Chadwick, *The Victorian Church, Part One, 1829–1859*, third edition, SCM Press, 1971, p. 131.

38 James Raitt Brown, *Number One Millbank: The Story of the Ecclesiastical Commissioners*, SPCK, 1944.

39 *Working as One Body: The Report of the Archbishops' Commission on the Organisation of the Church of England*, Church House Publishing, 1995, p. 85.

40 The veracity of Bede's claim is doubted, but in early 1993 excavations to install a new central heating system in Canterbury Cathedral uncovered the remains of a Roman church dating from the third century. *The Observer*, 7 February 1993.

41 Margaret Deanesley, *The Pre-Conquest Church in England*, A & C. Black, 1961, p. 115.

42 About one hundred priories, abbeys and bishoprics received a total of £19,200 in rent, a sum exceeded only by the collective wealth of the baronage. See Edward Miller and John Hatcher, *Medieval England: Rural Society and Economic Change 1086–1348*, Longman, 1978, p. 16.

43 Frank Barlow, *The English Church 1066–1154*, Longman, 1979, pp. 223–6.

44 ibid., pp. 175–6.

45 ibid., p. 129.

46 Dom David Knowles, *The Monastic Order in England*, Cambridge University Press, 1963, pp. 438 and 442–3.

47 Maurice Keen, *English Society in the Later Middle Ages 1348–1500*, Penguin 1990, p. 292.

48 J. H. Bettey, *Suppression of the Monasteries in the West Country*, Alan Sutton, 1989, pp. 18, 51–2.

49 Dom David Knowles, *The Religious Orders in England*, Volume III, The Tudor Age, Cambridge University Press, 1959, pp. 161–2, 470.

50 See Chapter 5.

51 See J. H. Bettey, pp. 12, 18, 48, 54, 81, 172–3.

52 Knowles, *The Religious Orders in England*, p. 260.

53 Hoskins, *The Age of Plunder*, p. 123.

54 A 'benefice' is a church appointment. See Alan Savidge, *The Foundation and Early Years of Queen Anne's Bounty*, SPCK, 1955 and A. G. Dickens, *The English Reformation*, Fontana, 1986, p. 197.

55 Knowles, *The Religious Orders in England*, pp. 387–8.

56 Knowles, *The Religious Orders in England*, p. 423.

57 Douglas McKean, *Money Matters: A Guide to the Finances of the Church of England*, Church House Publishing, 1987, p. 91.

58 The basic stipend is between £12,850 and £13,440, depending on seniority and responsibility.

59 *Working as One Body*, p. 77.

60 John Plender, 'Unholy Saga of the Church's Missing Millions', *Financial Times*, 11 July 1992.

61 Report to the Archbishop of Canterbury by the Lambeth Group, July 1993, p. 3; *Financial Times*, 14 July 1992.

62 Lovell, *Number One Millbank*, p. 73.

63 Coopers & Lybrand, *The Church Commissioners*, Review of Borrowings and Management Information, June 1993, p. 22.

64 Interview, 4 September 1992.

65 Lovell, *Number One Millbank*, pp. 54–7.

66 Coopers & Lybrand, The Church Commissioners, Review of Borrowings and Management Information, June 1993, p. 49; Lovell, *Number One Millbank*, p. 56.

67 In 1989 the Commissioners bought a one third stake in a Partnership with European Land and Imry to develop 1,500-acre Ashford Great Park, using loans advanced by the Commissioners. In 1992 the two property development companies failed, and the Commissioners took sole ownership of the site. From 'The Ashford Great Park Project: Briefing Note From the Office of the Church Commissioners', September 1993. See also Lovell, *Number One Millbank*, pp. 77–116.

68 *Working as One Body*, p. 84.

69 Lovell, *Number One Millbank*, pp. 179–80.

70 The Church Commissioners for England Annual Report and Accounts 1996.

71 Lovell, *Number One Millbank*, pp. 181, 192.

72 ibid., pp. 65–6, 174–5.

73 Quoted in *Financial Times*, 21 April 1995.

74 Lovell, *Number One Millbank*, pp. 66–7.

75 Lovell, *Number One Millbank*, p. 69.

76 Interview by the author, 4 September 1992.

77 Lovell, *Number One Millbank*, p. 117.

78 Interview, 4 September 1992.

79 The Church Commissioners publish a list of their larger investments in the annual report. The full investment policy was reproduced in the 1989 Annual Report and Accounts, pp. 26–7.

80 *Independent on Sunday*, 4 November 1995.

81 Church Commissioners, Reports Commissioned by the Archbishop of Canterbury, July 1993, p. 44, paragraph 1115.

82 *Financial Times*, 13, 16 June 1990.

83 Judgment, Chancery Division, Non-Witness List 121/91, p. 10. This mirrors the judgment given against Arthur Scargill in the British Coal Pension Fund case of 1984. See Chapter 29.

84 See Plender, 'Unholy Saga of the Church's Missing Millions'.

85 The Lambeth Group reckoned the Commissioners real annual yield over ten years was 6.2 per cent, against 9.7 per cent for the comparable funds. Church Commissioners, Reports Commissioned by the Archbishop of Canterbury, July 1993, paragraph 1103, p. 42.

86 *Financial Times*, 10 and 25 February and 3 October 1995.

87 Church Commissioners for England Annual Report and Accounts for 1993, 1994, 1995 and 1996. The sales consisted of £782 million of commercial property in Britain and the United States; £78 million of residential housing; and £89.23 million of agricultural land.

88 An invitation to respond to the Turnbull Report elicited only 33 responses from the 13,025 parishes and only 5 from over 900 deaneries. Half the dioceses responded. It did not help that interested parties had to pay £5.95 for a copy of the report. See Lovell, *Number One Millbank*, p. 227.

89 *Working as One Body*, pp. 24–33.

90 Lovell, *Number One Millbank*, p. 249.

91 *Financial Times*, 22 January 1998; *The Times*, 13 April 1998.

92 *Heritage & Renewal*, pp. 75–8, 5, 99.

93 *Sunday Times*, 11 December 1994, 5 April 1998.

94 *The Times*, 23 April 1998; *Sunday Times*, 5 April 1998.

95 Venerable Christopher Laurence, archdeacon of Lincoln, in Danziger, *The Cathedral*, p. 108.

96 Danziger, *The Cathedral*, p. 40.

97 *Church Times*, 19 January 1990.

98 *Daily Telegraph*, 20/21 July 1995.

99 *The Times*, 5 July 1996.

100 *Working as One Body*, p. 67.

101 Synodical Government in the Church of England: Summary of the Principal

Recommendations of the Report of the Review Group Appointed by the Standing Committee of the General Synod, 1998, p. 11.

102 Lovell, *Number One Millbank*, p. 164.

103 The Church Commissioners for England, Report and Accounts 1990, pp. 7, 12.

104 By the end of 1996, 338 clergy had applied for compensation. They include the former bishop of London, Graham Leonard, who defected to Rome in 1994. See The Church Commissioners for England, Report and Accounts 1996, p. 14.

105 *The Observer*, 20 February 1994.

106 *Financial Times*, 17 December 1994.

107 Each church pays a levy to its Diocesan Finance Board, which is known as the Parish Quota. Every church in a parish is assessed by the board to decide how much it is capable of giving, and the quota is then apportioned. The exact figure is calculated by multiplying the recorded membership of the church by an agreed factor (ostensibly to take account of absentees) and multiplying the result by an assumed average potential amount of giving per person – a sum which generally depends on the nature, wealth and religious enthusiasm of the congregation. In some cases, the diocese asks a congregation to state their personal incomes. Any investment or additional income a church enjoys – from benefactions, savings or rents – are included in the assessable income, and a small 'tax allowance' deducted from the total. The diocese then takes a proportion of the net result, keeping some for its own needs, and passing the rest to the Church Commissioners for redistribution as stipends, pensions and housing subsidies.

108 *Financial Times*, 24 December 1993.

CHAPTER FIVE: *Oxbridge*

1 Walter Ellis, *The Oxbridge Conspiracy*, Penguin, 1995, p. 11.

2 Andrew Neil, *Full Disclosure*, Pan, 1997, p. 453.

3 Ellis, *The Oxbridge Conspiracy*, p. 142.

4 Andrew Adonis and Stephen Pollard, *A Class Act: The Myth of Britain's Classless Society*, Hamish Hamilton, 1997, p. 59.

5 *Financial Times*, 24 October 1997.

6 Richard Norton-Taylor, *Whose Land Is It Anyway? How Urban Greed Exploits the Land*, Turnstone Press Ltd, 1982, p. 40.

7 Letter, *Financial Times*, 29 September 1997.

8 *Financial Times*, 24 October 1997.

9 See Chapter 2.

10 *Financial Times*, 16 December 1997.

11 Anthony Sampson, *Anatomy of Britain*, Hodder & Stoughton, 1962, p. 200.

12 Adonis and Pollard, *A Class Act*, p. 56.

13 Sampson, *Anatomy of Britain*, p. 200.

14 Neil, *Full Disclosure*, p. 453.

15 Ellis, *The Oxbridge Conspiracy*, pp. 148–56.

16 *Financial Times*, 31 January 1998.

17 ibid., 27 August 1994.

18 ibid., 22 February 1997.

19 See Chapter 6.

20 *Financial Times*, 25 March 1998.

21 Maurice Keen, *English Society in the Later Middle Ages 1348–1500*, Penguin, 1990, p. 246.
22 Quoted in A. L. Poole, *Domesday Book to Magna Carta 1087–1216*, Oxford History of England, Oxford University Press, 1955, p. 240.
23 V. H. H. Green, *The Universities*, Pelican, 1969, p. 168 and *The Victoria History of the Counties of England*, Volume III, ed. J. P. C. Roach: The City and University of Cambridge, Oxford University Press, 1959, pp. 150–504.
24 *The History of the University of Oxford*, Volume 1, p. 283.
25 Quoted in W. G. Hoskins, *The Age of Plunder: The England of Henry VIII 1500–1547*, Longman, 1976, p. 131.
26 *The Encyclopaedia of Oxford* (eds. Christopher Hibbert and Edward Hibbert), Macmillan, 1988, p. 272.
27 *The Victoria History of the Counties of England*, Cambridge, pp. 292, 306.
28 Timothy Mowl, *Horace Walpole*, John Murray, 1996, p. 32.
29 *The Encyclopaedia of Oxford*, p. 472.
30 *Report of the Commissioners Appointed to Inquire into the Property and Income of the Universities of Oxford and Cambridge and of the Colleges and Halls Therein*, Volume 1, Report, p. 23, HMSO, 1874, Session 6/2-5/8 1873, C-856, Vol. XXXVII.
31 *Report of the Commissioners* (1874), Volume 1, p. 24.
32 *Victoria History of the County of Oxford*, p. 33.
33 *The Victoria History of the Counties of England*, Cambridge, p. 282.
34 *Sunday Times*, 16 November 1997.
35 *The Victoria History of the Counties of England, Volume III*, p. 290.
36 V. H. H. Green, *The Universities*, Pelican, 1969, p. 186. *The Victoria History of the Counties of England*, Volume III, p. 290.
37 *Report of the Royal Commission on Oxford and Cambridge Universities*, March 1922, Cmnd 588, House of Commons Papers 1922, Volume X, and Extra Series Vol. IV (Appendices), pp. 334–5.
38 ibid., p. 198.
39 ibid., pp. 211–12.
40 ibid., p. 198.
41 V. H. H. Green, *The Universities*, p. 188.
42 See Chapter 6.
43 Dearing Report, Recommendation 74 and paragraph 19.46. Quoted in Commission of Inquiry Report, University of Oxford, paragraph 12.8, p. 219.
44 Total net HEFCE grant to Cambridge in 1998–99 is £88,991,997 and to Oxford £86,557,768. See Higher Education Funding Council for England, Recurrent Grants for 1998–99, Table 1, published March 1998.
45 Commission of Inquiry Report, University of Oxford, p. 217, paragraph 12.4.
46 University of Cambridge, The Cambridge Foundation, Annual Report and Accounts, Year ended 31 July 1997.
47 *Financial Times*, 23 February 1993.
48 Commission of Inquiry Report, University of Oxford, page 19, paragraph 2.35.
49 *Financial Times*, 4 March 1996.
50 University of Cambridge, The Cambridge Foundation, Annual Report and Accounts, Year ended 31 July 1997.
51 Quoted in Ellis, *The Oxbridge Conspiracy*, p. 62.
52 Commission of Inquiry Report, University of Oxford, pp. 223–4, para. 12-25–7.

53 ibid., p. 224, para. 12.30.

54 *The Observer*, 7 October 1990.

55 Letter to the author; letter to *The Economist*, 29 July 1989, from Sir Patrick Neill, vice chancellor of Oxford University.

56 Letter from John Bradfield, senior bursar, Trinity College, Cambridge, published in the *Financial Times*, 11 July 1991.

57 Letter to the author, 10 November 1993.

58 Letter to the author, 13 July 1993.

59 *Report of the Commissioners Appointed to Inquire Into the Property and Income of the Universities of Oxford and Cambridge and of the Colleges and Halls Therein*, Volume 1, Report, p. 24, HMSO, 1874, Session 6/2-5/8 1873, C-856, Vol. XXXVII.

60 For the South Sea Bubble, see Chapters 20 and 29.

61 Robert Skidelsky, *John Maynard Keynes: The Economist as Saviour 1920–1937*, Macmillan, 1992, p. 9.

62 At Oxford, university and collegiate income from securities climbed from £39,496 in 1871 to £124,773 in 1920, an increase in real terms of 46 per cent. At Cambridge, earnings from invested capital soared from £27,001 in 1871 to £78,409, an increase of 33 per cent. See Tables and *Report of the Royal Commission on Oxford and Cambridge Universities*, March 1922, Cmnd 588, House of Commons Papers 1922, Volume X, and Extra Series Vol. IV (Appendices), p. 358, Table IV, and p. 366, Table IV.

63 *Report of Royal Commission*, 1922, p. 358, Table V and p. 366, Table V.

64 *Report of Royal Commission*, 1922 (Appendices), p. 223.

65 *Financial Times*, 19 March 1993.
 Report of the Royal Commission, 1922, p. 221.

66 University of Oxford, Accounts of the Colleges for year ended 31 July 1997, Christ Church, p. 6.

67 Letter to the author, 15 November 1993.

68 *Daily Telegraph*, 21 October 1997.

69 *Financial Times*, 10 January 1995.

70 Paxman, *Friends in High Places*, pp. 173–4.

71 See Chapter 14.

72 *The Victoria History of the Counties of England*, Cambridge, p. 310.

73 In 1958 an appeal for £3.5 million was addressed to 6,500 companies in Britain. Two dozen founders gave more than £50,000. Seventeen others gave £50,000 each.

74 Paxman, *Friends in High Places*, p. 194.

75 *The Times*, 29 November 1997.

76 *The Times*, 29 June 1994.

77 The Cambridge Review, October 1987.

78 Gillings had done a short course in statistics at Cambridge before setting up a successful health care management group in the United States. From *The Times*, 15 December 1997.

79 *Sunday Telegraph*, 6 August 1995.

80 *Financial Times*, 21 July 1997.

81 ibid., 30 May 1997.

82 ibid.

83 *Daily Telegraph*, 29 June 1993.

84 *The Times Higher Education Supplement*, 1 October 1993, and subsequent letters, 8 and 15 October.

85 *Daily Telegraph*, 21 October 1997.

86 *Financial Times*, 26 September 1997. By 1997 Hitachi had invested £10 million in telecommunications projects at Cambridge. See *Financial Times*, 18 June 1997.

87 *The Times*, 27 December 1994.

88 Ellis, *The Oxbridge Conspiracy*, p. 271.

89 *Independent on Sunday*, 13 March 1994.

90 *The Observer*, 2 April 1995.

91 *Financial Times*, 1 March 1997.

92 ibid., 16 September 1996.

93 ibid., 12 December 1996.

94 Martin Wiener, *English Culture and the Decline of the Industrial Spirit 1850–1980*, Penguin, 1985, p. 22.

95 Sampson, *Anatomy of Britain*, pp. 202, 217.

96 Wiener, *English Culture and the Decline of the Industrial Spirit*, p. 23.

97 *Financial Times*, 21 March 1995.

98 ibid., 28 April 1998.

99 ibid., 18 June 1997.

100 ibid., 25 April 1998.

101 ibid., 4 November 1996.

102 *Sunday Times*, 27 March 1994.

103 An obvious risk is insider dealing in arcane knowledge.

104 From a review of *The Oxbridge Conspiracy*, in the *Financial Times*, 1 October 1994.

105 Ellis, *The Oxbridge Conspiracy*, pp. 275–6.

106 *Daily Telegraph*, 20 March 1992.

107 *Sunday Telegraph*, 12 November 1995.

108 *Financial Times*, 13 November 1996.

109 *Financial Times*, 18 June 1997.

110 *The Times*, 15 December 1997.

111 Ellis, *The Oxbridge Conspiracy*, pp. 186–7.

112 ibid., pp. 175–9.

113 Private letter.

114 See Chapter 4.

115 *Sunday Telegraph*, 10 October 1993. See also Ellis, *The Oxbridge Conspiracy*, p. 30.

116 *Financial Times*, 25 November 1996.

CHAPTER SIX: *The Redbrick Universities*

1 Elie Kedourie, *Perestroika in the Universities*, IEA Health and Welfare Unit, 1989, p. (xii).

2 Sir Douglas Hague, *Beyond Universities: A New Republic of the Intellect*, IEA, 1991, p. 71.

3 Speech at Llandudno, 15 May 1987.

4 Quoted in Walter Ellis, *The Oxbridge Conspiracy*, Penguin, 1995, p. 319.

5 The Higher Education Funding Councils for England, Scotland and Wales are located in Bristol, Edinburgh and Cardiff.

6 *Higher Education: Meeting the Challenge*, Cm. 114, April 1987. Quoted in Kedourie, *Perestroika in the Universities*, p. (xii).

7 Quoted in Sampson, *Anatomy of Britain*, p. 514.

8 V. H. H. Green, *The Universities*, Pelican, 1969, p. 182.

9 Anthony Sampson, *Anatomy of Britain Today*, Hodder & Stoughton, 1965, p. 221.

10 Green, *The Universities*, p. 117.

11 See Chapter 5.

12 Arthur Marwick, *The Deluge*, Second Edition, Macmillan, 1991, p. 276.

13 For the role of the City Corporation and livery companies in the creation of the City and Guilds of London Institute, see Chapter 8.

14 The Medical Research Committee became permanent council in 1920. The Research Councils are the Biotechnology and Biological Science Research Council; the Engineering and Physical Sciences Research Council; the Economic and Social Research Council; the Medical Research Council; the Natural Environment Research Council; and the Particle Physics and Astronomy Research Council. Supervision of these was moved from the Cabinet Office to the Department of Trade and Industry in 1995. For the origins of the Councils, see Marwick, *The Deluge*, pp. 269–71.

15 Higher Education Statistics Councils, Resources of Higher Education Institutions 1996–7, May 1998.

16 John Stevenson, *British Society 1914–45*, Penguin 1984, p. 252.

17 Between 1945 and 1968 another £797 million of taxpayers' money was dispensed in non-recurrent grants.

18 *Hansard*, 30 November 1945, Cols 1836–61.

19 Sampson, *Anatomy of Britain*, p. 514.

20 ibid., p. 210.

21 Green, *The Universities*, p. 182.

22 Sampson, *Anatomy of Britain*, p. 195.

23 Kenneth Baker, *The Turbulent Years*, Faber & Faber, 1993, p. 233.

24 Quoted in Noel Annan, *Our Age*, Fontana, 1991, pp. 509–10.

25 *The Independent*, 28 March 1991.

26 *Financial Times*, 1 October 1997.

27 Kedourie, *Perestroika in the Universities*, p. 15.

28 Baker, *The Turbulent Years*, p. 233.

29 Kedourie, *Perestroika in the Universities*, pp. 7–8.

30 *Financial Times*, 5 January 1998.

31 ibid., 1 October 1996.

32 ibid., 22 September 1997.

33 ibid., 30 April 1998.

34 Hague, *Beyond Universities*, p. 9.

35 For Gresham, see Chapter 30.

36 Michael Lynch, *Scotland: A New History*, Pimlico, 1992, p. 105.

37 Green, *The Universities*, pp. 94–5.

38 Dictionary of National Biography.

39 Funds were raised by donations and subscriptions in the form of £100 shares carrying a promised dividend of 4 per cent. A list published in June 1828 showed that £30,794 was collected.

40 Green, *The Universities*, p. 110.

41 Owen Chadwick, *The Victorian Church*, Part One, 1829–1859, SCM Press, 1987, pp. 545–50.

42 Chadwick, *The Victorian Church*, Part Two, 1860–1901, p. 442.

43 Quoted in Owen Chadwick, *Newman*, Oxford University Press, 1983, p. 56.

44 Quoted in Chadwick, *The Victorian Church*, Part Two, p. 439.

45 Quoted in Paxman, *Friends in High Places*, Michael Joseph, 1990, p. 184.

46 Anthony Sampson, *Anatomy of Britain Today*, p. 236.

47 Britain's Top 100 Universities, *Financial Times*, 29 April 1998.

48 He was best-known as the anti-Munich candidate in the Oxford by-election of October 1938.

49 *Dictionary of National Biography*.

50 Sampson, *Anatomy of Britain*, p. 209.

51 ibid., pp. 210, 217.

52 Quoted by David Starkey, 'Chasing Shadows', *Sunday Times*, 2 July 1995.

53 *The Times*, 1 December 1997.

54 ibid., 15 May 1998.

55 *Financial Times*, 8 November 1996.

56 ibid., 4 December 1996.

57 Britain's Top 100 Universities, *Financial Times*, 29 April 1998.

58 *Sunday Times*, 3 September 1995.

59 *Financial Times*, 15 December 1993.

60 Professor Alan Smithers, 'Students on the Road to Nowhere', *Sunday Times*, 3 September 1995.

61 *Independent on Sunday*, 2 October 1994.

62 *Financial Times*, 13 December 1996.

63 Baker, *The Turbulent Years*, p. 238.

64 Nigel Lawson, *The View From No. 11: Memoirs of a Tory Radical*, Bantam, 1992, p. 601.

65 *Financial Times*, 24, 28 November and 14 December 1995.

66 ibid., 14 March 1995.

67 ibid., 15 December 1995.

68 Susan Crosland, *Tony Crosland*, Coronet, 1983, p. 159.

69 *Evening Standard*, 30 September 1987. Quoted in Martin Holmes, *Thatcherism: Scope and Limits, 1983–87*, Macmillan, 1989, pp. 126–7.

70 *Financial Times*, 30 August 1995.

71 ibid., 29 April 1998.

72 ibid., 25 August 1994; 2 April 1996.

73 ibid., 31 January 1995; 1 September 1997.

74 Sampson, *Anatomy of Britain*, p. 199.

75 *Financial Times*, 9 November 1994.

76 ibid., 30 September 1994.

77 ibid., 29 September 1995.

78 ibid., 26 August 1995.

79 ibid., 6 and 13 February 1998.

80 ibid., 29 November 1994; 10 February 1995.

81 ibid., 24 April 1998.

82 'The Political Case for An Independent University,' published in *University Independence: The Main Questions*, edited by John MacCallum Scott, 1971.

83 Anthony Sampson, *The Changing Anatomy of Britain*, Hodder & Stoughton, 1982, p. 143.

84 *Financial Times*, 21 January 1994.

85 ibid., 30 December 1993; 7 March 1995.

86 Quoted in *The Economist*, 22 April 1995.

87 Edwin West, *Britain's Student Loan System in World Perspective*, Institute of Economic Affairs, June 1994.

88 *Financial Times*, 10 March 1997.

89 In 1997 a special purpose vehicle called Varsity Funding succeeded in re-packaging £49 million of existing university loans for sale in the bond markets. See *Financial Times*, 25 March 1995; 24 May 1997.

90 In 1996, a dozen universities were reported to be seeking £800 million to design, build and finance capital projects through the Private Finance Initiative. *Financial Times*, 27 March 1996.

91 *The Independent*, 19 July 1991.

92 The first holder was Howard Raingold, on the strength of his success at Oxford, but he moved on to Pembroke College, Cambridge. See *Sunday Times*, 24 April 1994, and Chapter 5.

93 Paxman, *Friends in High Places*, p. 173; Sampson, *The Essential Anatomy of Britain*, 1992, p. 75.

CHAPTER SEVEN: *The Public Schools*

1 Richard Hoggart, *The Way We Live Now*, Pimlico, 1996, p. 29.

2 The scold is Allison Pearson, who had reviewed his book unfavourably. Walter Ellis, *The Oxbridge Conspiracy*, Penguin, 1995, p. (viii).

3 Andrew Adonis and Stephen Pollard, *Class Act: The Myth of Britain's Classless Society*, Hamish Hamilton, 1997, p. 37.

4 Andrew Neil, *Full Disclosure*, Pan, 1997, p. 472.

5 Adonis and Pollard, *Class Act*, pp. 47–8.

6 Hoggart, *The Way We Live Now*, p. 199.

7 ibid., pp. 28, 199.

8 Neil, *Full Disclosure*, p. 458.

9 'For all the emphasis on meritocracy, the public school tradition remains strong – if understated. Few parents would want it otherwise: it is a large part of the product for which they are paying.' Adonis and Pollard, *Class Act*, p. 46.

10 'League tables on life?' asks an advertisement in *Financial Times*, 29 October 1997.

11 Hoggart, *The Way We Live Now*, pp. 26–7.

12 Adonis and Pollard, *Class Act*, p. 46.

13 Martin Wiener, *English Culture and the Decline of the Industrial Spirit, 1850–1980*, Penguin, 1985, pp. 10–22.

14 See Chapter 2.

15 *Evening Standard*, 30 November 1993.

16 Harold Perkin, *The Rise of Professional Society: England Since 1880*, Routledge, 1990, p. 368.

17 See Chapter 5.

18 Andrew Morton, *Diana: Her True Story*, Michael O'Mara, 1993, pp. 24–8.

19 FT 1,000 Schools, *Financial Times*, 11 October 1997.

20 Alisdare Hickson, *The Poisoned Bowl: Sex, Repression and the Public School System*, Constable, 1995.

21 Jeremy Paxman, *Friends in High Places: Who Runs Britain?*, Michael Joseph, 1990, pp. (ix)–(x).

22 Jonathan Gathorne-Hardy, *The Public School Phenomenon*, Penguin, 1977, pp. 88–94.

23 *Financial Times*, 22 November 1997.

24 See story of C. J. Vaughan above.

25 *The Times*, 1 September 1995.

26 Girls are now common enough for Rugby, King's Canterbury and Haileybury to have head girls, although in 1995 the boys at Rugby were sufficiently upset by the appointment of a girl as head of the school to boycott a chapel service and plaster the school with fly-sheets. See *The Times*, 14 June 1995. On the number of girls, see National ISIS Statistical Survey of Independent Schools, Annual Census 1998, p. 9.

27 *Financial Times*, 1 May 1993.

28 Paxman, *Friends in High Places*, p. 166.

29 ibid., p. 171.

30 *Sunday Telegraph*, 2 October 1994.

31 *Financial Times*, 11 October 1997.

32 National ISIS Statistical Survey of Independent Schools, Annual Census 1998, pp. 9, 3.

33 *The Times*, 27 September 1996.

34 Adonis and Pollard, *Class Act*, p. 31.

35 Susan Crosland, *Tony Crosland*, 1983, pp. 149–50.

36 Andy Beckett, 'Scenes from the Classroom War', *Independent on Sunday*, 27 November 1994.

37 *Financial Times*, 3 March 1998.

38 Peter Mandelson and Roger Liddle, *The Blair Revolution: Can New Labour Deliver?*, Faber & Faber, 1996, pp. 147–8.

39 Susan Crosland, *Tony Crosland*, p. 149.

40 *Ann and Nick Programme*, BBC Television, 1 December 1994.

41 *Daily Mail*, 24 January 1996.

42 Adonis and Pollard, *Class Act*, pp. 53, 55.

43 Anthony Sampson, *The New Anatomy of Britain*, Hodder & Stoughton, 1971, p. 141.

44 Nicholas Timmins, *The Five Giants: A Biography of the Welfare State*, HarperCollins, 1995, pp. 87–8. See also Adrian Wooldridge, *Measuring the Mind: Education and Psychology in England 1860–1990*, Cambridge University Press, 1994.

45 Anthony Sampson, *Anatomy of Britain*, Hodder & Stoughton, 1962, p. 188.

46 Susan Crosland, *Tony Crosland*, p. 148.

47 Donnison Report, 1970, paragraphs 27, 259. Quoted in Sampson, *The New Anatomy of Britain*, pp. 139, 145.

48 Margaret Thatcher, *The Path to Power*, HarperCollins, 1995, p. 171.

49 Sampson, *The New Anatomy of Britain*, pp. 148–9.

50 Letter to the author, 16 December 1993.

51 Brian Cox, *The Great Betrayal: Memoirs of a Life in Education*, Chapmans, 1992, pp. 147–8.

52 ibid., pp. 5, 142.

53 James Callaghan, *Time and Chance*, Fontana, 1988, p. 410.

54 Shirley Williams, *Politics is for People*, Penguin, 1982, p. 158.

55 Sampson, *Anatomy of Britain*, pp. 190, 191, 193.

56 Sampson, *The New Anatomy of Britain*, pp. 140–4.

57 See Ben Pimlott, *Harold Wilson*, HarperCollins, 1992, p. 512.

58 Adonis and Pollard, *Class Act*, p. 43.

59 There are problems of definition, but over sixty well-recognised public schools were founded during the reign of Victoria. See T. W. Bamford, *The Rise of the Public Schools*, Thomas Nelson, 1967, p. 18, Table 1, and Jonathan Gathorne-Hardy, *The Public School Phenomenon*, Penguin, 1979, p. 114; Appendix C.

60 Timmins, *The Five Giants*, p. 263.

61 Susan Crosland, *Tony Crosland*, pp. 148–50.

62 Adonis and Pollard, *Class Act*, p. 43.

63 This was obvious to Jonathan Gathorne-Hardy as early as 1977, when a Labour government was last threatening the middle classes with punitive taxation. See *The Public School Phenomenon*, p. 402.

64 Anthony Sampson, *The Changing Anatomy of Britain*, Hodder & Stoughton, 1982, p. 122.

65 National ISIS, Statistical Survey of Independent Schools, Annual Census, 1998, p. 3.

66 Adonis and Pollard, *Class Act*, p. 62.

67 Extract reproduced in the *Sunday Times*, 19 September 1993. He also called for an acceleration of funding by central government, to eliminate the local authority monopolies of secondary education, and open enrolment to allow good schools to grow and bad ones to die. See Neil, *Full Disclosure*, pp. 469–72.

68 Quoted by Anthony Sampson in *The Essential Anatomy of Britain*, Hodder & Stoughton, 1992, pp. 67–8.

69 Simon Jenkins, *Accountable to None: The Tory Nationalization of Britain*, Hamish Hamilton, 1995, p. 110.

70 See Chapter 10.

71 Baker, *The Turbulent Years*, pp. 166–7.

72 E. G. West, *Education and the State: A Study in Political Economy*, Third Edition, Liberty Fund, 1994, pp. 171–3.

73 W. K. Jordan, *The Charities of London 1480–1660: The Aspirations and the Achievements of the Urban Society*, George Allen & Unwin, 1960, p. 248. Jordan's figures are based on a sample of ten counties.

74 Gillian Avery, *The Best Type of Girl: A History of Girls' Independent Schools*, André Deutsch, 1991, p. 55.

75 *Victoria History of Middlesex*, pp. 308–10.

76 Avery, *The Best Type of Girl*, p. 327.

77 *Victoria History of Hampshire*, pp. 349, 359.

78 Brougham, a powerful advocate of educational reform, was also influential in the foundation of the University of London.

79 Clarendon Commission, Parliamentary Papers, Volumes XX and XXI and Volume XX, p. 47.

80 Some proprietorial schools, e.g. Stonyhurst, were Catholic. The private schools, such as King's College and University College School, were often founded by reformers dissatisfied with the public and grammar schools and opposed to sectarian education. They were also more likely to take up modern subjects.

81 Bamford, *Rise of the Public Schools*, p. 178.

82 The commissioners estimated that only 4.5 per cent of children of elementary school age were not attending school.

83 E. G. West, *Education and the State*, p. 178.

84 ibid., pp. 170–98.

85 Taunton Commission, Parliamentary Papers 1867–8, Column XXVIII, p. 110.

86 Bamford, *Rise of the Public Schools*, pp. 181–8.

87 Sir Robert Morant (1863–1920) is one of the founding fathers of the Welfare State. He began his civil service career in the Education Department in 1895, and served as permanent secretary of the Board of Education from 1903 to 1911. As chairman of National Health Insurance between 1911 and 1919, he effectively originated the present system of social security as well.

88 In 1997, 2,782 new pupils were children of parents or military personnel based abroad. See ISIS, Annual Census 1998, p. 18, Table 9.

89 *The Economist*, 6 June 1992.

90 ISIS, p. 17.

91 *Financial Times*, 27 November 1997.

92 *The Times*, 27 November 1997.

93 *Financial Times*, 9 December 1997.

94 *Financial Times*, 8 November 1995.

95 By the time Sutton died in 1611, he had endowed the foundation with properties worth £116,000. These were somewhat reduced when Sutton's nephew disputed the will, and James I made off with £10,000 to cover the costs of repairing the bridge at Berwick-Upon-Tweed. See W. K. Jordan, *The Charities of London 1480–1660: The Aspirations and the Achievements of the Urban Society*, George Allen & Unwin, 1960, p. 152.

96 Report of the Clarendon Commission, Parliamentary Papers, 1864, Volumes XX and XXI.

97 See Chapter 26.

98 ISIS, Annual Census 1998, p. 18.

99 *The Economist*, 29 July 1995.

CHAPTER EIGHT: *The Medieval Corporations*

1 J. H. Huizinga, *The Waning of the Middle Ages*, Penguin, 1990, p. 9.

2 Interview, 4 October 1994.

3 *Financial Times*, 18 August 1994.

4 Letter from Major General P. T. Stevenson, clerk to the Carpenters' Company, 9 July 1992.

5 Nigel Lawson, *The View From No 11*, Bantam, 1992, pp. 277–8. Under the Coinage Act of 1971, the officers of the Royal Mint must place in the pyx (or Mint Box) sample coins of currency manufactured for issue during the year. Tens of thousands of coins produced by the Royal Mint are then 'tried' over a three-month period for weight, composition and diameter by a jury of Goldsmiths. These are charged and sworn in by the queen's remembrancer, the senior judge in the law courts in the Strand, who presides over the Delivery of the Verdict (it is a formal court of law).

6 Jennifer Long, Pride Without Prejudice: The Story of London's Gilds and Livery Companies, Perpetua Press, 1975.

7 G. W. Whiteman, *Halls and Treasures of the City Companies*, Ward Lock Limited, 1970; Robert J. Blackham, *The Soul of The City: London's Livery Companies*, Sampson, Low, Marston & Co. Ltd, 1931.

8 Between 1480 and 1660 the average London merchant left estate worth £7,780, against £1,428 for provincial equivalents. Great merchants left an average of £13,605. W. K. Jordan, *The Charities of London 1480–1660: The Aspirations and the Achievements of the Urban Society*, George Allen & Unwin, 1960, p. 20 and Table 1, p. 423; and *Philanthropy in England 1480–1660: A Study of the Changing Pattern of English Social Aspirations*, George Allen & Unwin, 1959, p. 336.

9 See Chapter 27.

10 *The Royal Commission: The London City Livery Companies' Vindication*, Gilbert & Rivington, 1885, p. 175.

11 T. W. Moody, *The Londonderry Plantation 1609–41: The City of London and the Plantation in Ulster*, William Lullan & Son, 1939, pp. 123, 455.

12 *The Royal Commission: The London City Livery Companies' Vindication*, Gilbert & Rivington, 1885, p. 132.

13 I. G. Doolittle, *The City of London and Its Livery Companies*, Gavin Press, 1982, p. 91.

14 ibid., p. 94.

15 *The Royal Commission: The London City Livery Companies' Vindication*, Gilbert & Rivington, 1885, p. 158. Also quoted in Doolittle, *The City of London and Its Livery Companies*, p. 97.

16 Quoted in Doolittle, p. 98.

17 In 1874 the royal commission of inquiry into the property and income of Oxford and Cambridge estimated their combined total income at £672,789.

18 Letter, 26 February 1992.

19 See *The Observer*, 26 January 1992.

20 *Daily Telegraph*, 26 July 1992.

21 Pellipar Investments Limited, Reports and Financial Statements, year ended 30 June 1991.

22 Leathersellers Company Charitable Accounts, year ended 31 July 1991.

23 Oliver Marriott, *The Property Boom*, Hamish Hamilton, 1967.

24 G. W. Whiteman, *Halls and Treasures of the City Companies*.

25 Letter to the author, 21 January 1994.

26 Letter to the author, 10 July 1992.

27 Interview by the author, 30 July 1992.

28 Its first master, Sir Sefton Brancker, who was killed in the R101 disaster at Beauvais, left to the company the royalties from his memoirs. Long, *Pride Without Prejudice*, p. 167.

29 Hunting, *A History of the Drapers' Company*, p. 121.

30 W. K. Jordan, *Philanthropy in England 1480–1660: A Study of the Changing Pattern of English Social Aspirations*, George Allen & Unwin, 1959, p. 163.

31 Jordan estimates that between 1541 and 1660 wealthy London merchants and their families gave a total of £1,639,134 to the direct support of the poor and destitute, municipal improvements and the foundation of hospitals and schools in London alone. Another £1,889,211 – or nearly two thirds of total charitable benefactions made in a ten-county sample of the same period – also came from the City. See Jordan, *Philanthropy in England 1480–1660*, p. 247.

32 ibid., p. 423, Table 1.
33 ibid., p. 118.
34 Charities Aid Foundation, *Dimensions of the Voluntary Sector*, 1997 Edition, p. 90.
35 See Chapter 26.
36 Interview by the author, 2 September 1992.
37 Many properties are let to multiple tenants. The figure of 400 excludes the Leadenhall market lettings, and any properties let on long (2,000-year) leases.
38 B. R. Masters, Introduction to Chamber Accounts of the 16th Century, London Record Society, vol. 20, 1984, pp. (xxv), (xxviii).
39 B. R. Masters, *To God and the Bridge*, Exhibition Catalogue, 1972.
40 Doolittle, *The City of London and Its Livery Companies*, p. 10.
41 *Sunday Times*, 5 March 1995; *Financial Times*, 18, 21 August, 18 September 1995.
42 *Financial Times*, 1 November 1995.
43 ibid., 19 September, 18 November 1997.
44 ibid., 12 September 1997.
45 Interview by the author, 4 October 1994.
46 The site is owned by the Port of London Authority, and the Corporation sub-leases from Tower Hamlets Borough Council. The freehold to the site of the old market fetched £22 million.
47 Interview by the author, 11 October 1994.
48 *Financial Times*, 23 October 1995.
49 ibid., 19 April, 23 June 1995.
50 ibid., 6 October 1995.
51 Interview by the author, 11 October 1994.
52 Michael Cassidy, 'A City Marketing Challenge', *Financial Times*, 8 January 1996.
53 *Financial Times*, 12 June 1996.
54 Local authorities have to surrender business-rate income for redistribution on a per capita basis by the Department of Environment, Transport and the Regions. The Corporation of London generates an unusually large amount of money and is unique in having the right to retain part of its business rate. On a strictly per capita basis it would get back much less than £7.9 million. See Corporation of London, Annual Report 1997–8.
55 See Chapter 26.
56 See R. H. Coase, *The Firm, The Market and The Law*, University of Chicago Press, 1990, pp. 187–213.
57 Grosvenor, *Trinity House*, p. 107.
58 G. G. Harris, *The Trinity House of Deptford 1514–1660*, Athlone Press, 1969, p. 60.
59 Grosvenor, *Trinity House*.
60 Trinity House also owns half a mansion block on Cambridge Road in Battersea; Church and West farms around Goxhill in north-east Lincolnshire; Martines Farm at Hutton in Essex; The Trinity Homes at Walmer (£921,000) plus holdings of securities and cash (£4 million) account for the balance of the total assets.
61 See the account in Martin Short, *Inside the Brotherhood*, Grattan Books, 1989, pp. 457–63.
62 M. De Pace, *Introducing Freemasonry: A Practical Guide to Masonic Practice in England and Wales*, Lewis Masonic, 1983.
63 Charities Aid Foundation, *Dimensions of the Voluntary Sector*, 1997 edition, p. 174.
64 Martin Short, *Inside the Brotherhood*, Grattan Books, 1989, p. 454.

65 Stephen Knight, *The Brotherhood*, Panther, 1983, pp. 216–29.

66 Short, *Inside the Brotherhood*, HarperCollins, 1997, pp. 486–8.

67 Knight, *The Brotherhood*, pp. 227–8. The companies with their own lodges he names as the Basketmakers, Blacksmiths, Cutlers, Farriers, Feltmakers, Paviors, Plaisterers and Needlemakers – and 'etc., etc.'

CHAPTER NINE: *Central Government*

1 Sir John Banham, 'No Easy Birth for Regions', *Financial Times*, 28 November 1997.

2 Samuel Brittan, *A Restatement of Economic Liberalism*, Macmillan, 1988, p. 11.

3 *Financial Times*, 24 June 1998.

4 Simon Jenkins, *Accountable to None: The Tory Nationalisation of Britain*, Hamish Hamilton, 1995, p. 246.

5 *Observer*, 5 July 1998; Sunday Times, 8 October 1995.

6 *Financial Times*, 16 June 1998.

7 ibid., 30 July 1997.

9 ibid., 4 January 1998.

10 ibid., 29 July 1996.

11 Next Steps Report 1997, pp. 218, 226–7.

12 HM Treasury, Cm 2929.

13 National Audit Office, *Financial Auditing and Reporting: 1996–97 General Report of the Comptroller and Auditor General*, House of Commons Paper 251, February 1998. Corporate governance, see Chapter xx.

14 Next Steps Report 1997, Cm 3889, March 1998, p. (vi).

15 *Financial Times*, 19 October 1995.

16 ibid., 25 October 1995; 25 September 1997.

17 ibid., 18 November 1997.

18 ibid., 29 January 1997.

19 ibid., 2 July 1997.

20 National Audit Office, The Vehicle Inspectorate, 1992. According to Simon Jenkins, the National Audit Office fought for the right to review the policies as well as the performance of governments departments when was set up in 1983, but was overruled by the Treasury. See Jenkins, *Accountable to None*; pp. 232–3.

21 *Financial Times*, 16 April 1996, 29 February 1996, 30 January 1997.

22 ibid., 12 March 1998, 26 May 1998.

23 ibid., 27 October 1997.

24 National Audit Office, *PFI: The First Four DBFO Road Contracts*, January 1998.

25 The Blakenhurst contract went to a consortium, UK Detention Services. This was formed by the construction companies, Sir Robert MacAlpine and John Mowlem, and the Corrections Corporation of America, the largest provider of private prison services in the United States. Fazakerley was built and run by a consortium of Group 4 and Tarmac, and HM Prison Parc at Bridgend by a consortium of Costain and Securicor Custodial Services. Blakenhurst, which opened in May 1993, was the first to accommodate convicted rather than remand prisoners.

26 National Audit Office, *The PFI Contracts for Bridgend and Fazakerley Prisons*, October 1997.

27 The Harmondsworth contract was first awarded to Securicor, but Group 4 Security won its renewal in 1988.

28 In 1930 the English prison system consisted of 22 prisons and 7 borstals with a total capacity of 19,600 inmates: B. R. Mitchell, British Historical Statistics, pp. 12–14.

29 *Spectator* Allied Dunbar lecture, 18 September 1996.

30 *Financial Times*, 13 July 1998.

31 For compulsory competitive tendering in local government, see Chapter 13.

32 Norman Fowler, *Ministers Decide*, Chapmans, 1991, p. 195.

33 Quoted in Jenkins, *Accountable to None*, pp 68–9.

34 An American consultant Alain Enthoven published *Reflections on the Management of the NHS with the Nuffield Trust in 1985*. See Jenkins, *Accountable to None*, pp. 689.

35 Hutber's Law was coined by Patrick Hutber, sometime City editor of the *Sunday Telegraph*. It stipulates that a state-owned industry cannot be made to imitate private enterprise by following textbook rules or market simulations, any more than a mule can be turned into a zebra by painting stripes on its back. All attempts to improve public services without changing their ownership (like the creation of Executive Agencies and the writing of Citizens' Charters) are made in defiance of this law.

36 *Financial Times*, 2 and 3 July 1998, 21 July 1998.

37 'It is not my job to be an arm of the Department of National Heritage.' *The Economist*, 18 September 1993.

38 Audit Commission, *NHS Estate Management and Property Maintenance*, HMSO, March 1991, p. 13.

39 Scottish Office Annual Report 1994, HMSO, Cm 2514, p. 111.

40 NHS Estates Annual Report and Accounts 1994, p. 15.

41 *NHS Estate Management and Property Maintenance*, pp. 5, 10.

42 ibid., p. 24.

43 Audit Commission, *Trusting in the Future: Towards an Audit Agenda for NHS Providers*, HMSO, April 1994.

44 Cabinet Office Efficiency Unit, *Review of the Management of the Government's Civil Estate: An Efficiency Unit Scrutiny*, May 1994, Annex B, Table 1.

45 *Financial Times*, 6 June 1997.

46 *The Times*, 28 August and 3 December 1986, 17 June and 2 December 1988.

47 For an explanation of Trading Funds, see footnote on p. 334.

48 See National Audit Office, *The Sale of PSA Projects*, HC345, Session 1997–8, 26 November 1997, pp. 1–2. See also *Financial Times*, 26 January 1996; 3 June 1997, 20 January 1998.

49 *Daily Telegraph*, 8 December 1996.

50 Lawson, *The View From No. 11*, p. 314.

51 The £10 billion estimate excludes 50 sites yet to be valued. NAO, *Ministry of Defence: Identifying and Selling Surplus Property*, HC776, Session 1997–8, 17 June 1998, pp. 1, 9.

52 NAO, *Identifying and Selling Surplus Property*, HC776.

53 The married quarter's estate was sold to Annington Homes, a financial consortium led by the Japanese securities house, Nomura. Its members include Blackrock Capital Finance, Amec, Hambros Bank, Royal Bank of Scotland, Abbey National and HSBC. The company acquired 57,000 properties, with an agreement to lease them back to the Ministry of Defence for 25 years and 2,500 surplus homes for immediate disposal.

54 NAO, *Ministry of Defence: The Sale of the Married Quarters Estate*, HC239, Session 1997–98, 22 August 1997, p. 3.

55 NAO, *Ministry of Defence: Management and Control of Army Training Land*, HMSO, January 1992, pp. 8–23.

56 *Financial Times*, 23 April 1997.

57 Such interference with private property was so unprecedented that the government had to acquire the land by crown prerogative rather than parliamentary legislation. Arthur Marwick, *The Deluge*, Macmillan, Second Edition, 1991, p. 179.

58 Peter Hennessy, *Never Again: Britain 1945–1951*, Jonathan Cape, 1992, pp. 353–4.

59 Stephen Aris, *Arnold Weinstock and the Making of GEC*, Aurum Press, 1998, pp. 116–38.

60 Lawson, *The View From No. 11*, p. 513.

61 National Asset Register, p. 81.

62 The Government Art Collection includes 2,300 paintings, 1,800 drawings and water-colours, 200 sculptures, 50 tapestries, 235 photographs and 8,000 prints. It owns works by Henry Moore, Lucian Freud, John Piper, Paul Nash, Walter Sickert and Edward Burra, scattered across 500 locations and maintained by a £350,000 grant from the Department of Culture, Media and Sport.

63 *Financial Times*, 24 June 1998.

64 Ibid., 25 November 1997.

65 Ibid., 3 July 1998.

66 Paul Addison, *Churchill on the Home Front 1900–1955*, Pimlico, 1993, pp. 71–7.

67 See Chapter 18.

68 Welsh Development Agency Annual Report, 1996–7. For inward investment generally, see Chapter 21.

69 In 1996–7 the total grant-aid of English Partnerships was £164,048,000; Scottish Enterprise £434,824,000; the Welsh Development Agency £107,562,000; the Rural Development Commission £40,605,000; Highlands & Islands Enterprise £59,100,000; and the Development Board for Rural Wales £10,000,000. From annual reports, year ended March 1997. There were additional receipts from Europe.

70 Nicholas Ridley, who became Trade and Industry secretary in 1987, was an exception. In 1989 he ordered English Estates to sell everything it owned. Ironically, he was the grandson of the Second Viscount Ridley, one of the founding fathers of the EIEC. The order to sell shocked the management. See *Novel and Unorthodox: The Story of English Estates*, available from English Partnerships, p 33.

71 For Urban Development Corporations, see Chapter 13.

72 Marwick, *The Deluge*, p 288.

73 For a full account of the rise of agricultural protection, see Chapter 18.

74 This is the notorious 'set-aside' scheme. See Chapter 18.

75 The legislation passed before and after the war enabled local authorities to buy smallhold-ings of land. By 1914 there were some 15,000 holdings totalling roughly 200,000 acres. Many county councils still own sizeable farm estates; see Chapter 13. See also Cannadine, *The Decline and Fall of the British Aristocracy*, p. 68–9 and *Report of the Committee of Inquiry into the Acquisition and Occupancy of Agricultural Land*, HMSO, July 1979, Cmnd 7599, paragraph 520, p. 190.

76 Richard Norton-Taylor, *Whose Land Is It Anyway?* p. 45.

77 Shoard, *This Land is Our Land*, p. 121.

78 Hennessy, *Whitehall*, p. 444.

79 Oliver Rackham, *The History of the Countryside*, p. 27.

80 Samuel Brittan, 'Black Wednesday's Bill', *Financial Times*, 30 November 1992.

81 Quoted in Hennessy, *Whitehall*, p. 448.

82 *Financial Times*, 22 August 1997.

83 Trafficmaster Congestion Report, March 1997, quoted in *Financial Times*, 12 March 1997.

84 Terry Mulroy and Owen Simon, 'Way Out of the Traffic Jam', *Financial Times*, 22 August 1997.

85 Drivers were given £120 of electronic money to spend on getting into the city centre, and allowed to keep any money they saved. Coupled with a park and ride scheme, and bus lanes, one in five drivers used public transport all the time, and two in five did when the toll hit the peak rate. Reported in the *Financial Times*, 12 June 1998.

86 John Rule, *The Vital Century: England's Developing Economy 1714–1815*, Longman, 1992, pp. 218.

87 *Financial Times*, 27 April 1998.

88 *Financial Times*, 14 December 1995, 19 February 1996.

89 David M. Newbery, Memorandum on the Case for a Public Road Authority to the Transport Select Committee, February 1994.

CHAPTER TEN: *The Nationalisation of Industry*

1 Karl Marx and Friedrich Engels, *The Communist Manifesto*, Penguin, 1967, p. 96.

2 Quoted in Samuel Beer, *Modern British Politics*, Faber & Faber, 1982, p. 134.

3 E. F. Schumacher, *Small is Beautiful*, Abacus, 1974, pp. 120–1.

4 Quoted in Simon Jenkins, *Accountable to None*, Hamish Hamilton, 1995, p. 9.

5 Peter Mandelson and Roger Liddle, *The Blair Revolution: Can New Labour Deliver?*, Faber & Faber, 1996, p. 23.

6 Peter Hennessy, *Never Again: Britain 1945–51*, Jonathan Cape, 1992, p. 198.

7 Alan Sked and Chris Cook, *Post-War Britain*, Penguin, 1984, p. 29.

8 Robert Skidelsky, *Politicians and the Slump: The Labour Government of 1929–31*, Macmillan, 1994, pp. 254–9.

9 Peter Hennessy, *Never Again: Britain 1945–51*, Jonathan Cape, 1992, p. 201.

10 Anthony Wright, *R. H. Tawney*, Manchester University Press, 1987, p. 58.

11 Tawney eschewed prescription despite the fact that he had served on the government-appointed Sankey Commission, which recommended nationalisation of the coal industry in 1919. See R. H. Tawney, *The Acquisitive Society*, G. Bell & Sons, 1922, pp. 119, 140, 149.

12 Peter Hennessy, *Never Again*, p. 183.

13 Paul Kennedy, *The Rise and Fall of the Great Powers: Economic Change and Military Conflict 1500–2000*, Fontana, 1988, xxiv–xxv.

14 Linda Colley, *Britons: Forging the Nation 1707–1837*, Yale, 1992, p. 60.

15 John Brewer, *The Sinews of Power: War, Money and the English State 1688–1783*, Alfred A. Knopf, 1988, pp. 167–70.

16 Apart from the gains of trade itself, allowing other companies to compete for Asian trade was expected to broaden the Indian tax base, reducing the cost to domestic taxpayers. See P. J. Cain and A. G. Hopkins, *British Imperialism: Innovation and Expansion 1688–1914*, Longman, 1993, p. 325.

17 Robert Blake, *Disraeli*, Methuen, 1978, pp. 581–7.

18 Paul Addison, *Churchill on the Home Front 1900–1955*, Pimlico, 1993, pp. 156–7. The British National Oil Corporation was established in 1976. It was given the right to

buy up to 51 per cent of any oil produced in the North Sea, and first refusal over assets sold by private companies. It was equipped with £900 million of interest-free credit from the taxpayer and exemption from the special Petroleum Revenue Tax. It later acquired (at a price of £103 million) a majority stake in the North Sea oil operations of the Burmah Oil Company. Its operations were privatised in the 1980s.

19 The company was known as Imperial and International Communications Limited. The operating company was Cable & Wireless.

20 After the war, Labour added two further public airline corporations: British European Airways (BEA) and British South American Airways (BSAA). BSAA was merged with BOAC in 1949, and BOAC and BEA were merged as British Airways in 1972–74.

21 Hennessy, *Never Again*, pp. 267–8.

22 Alistair Horne, *Macmillan 1957–1986*, Macmillan, 1989, pp. 53–455. The Windscale incident of 1957 was the most serious accident in the history of the nuclear industry until the meltdown at Chernobyl in 1985. It rated 5 on the industry's own scale of seriousness, against 7 at Chernobyl. There have been seven level 2 accidents in Britain in the last six years, but only two in the last ten years that rated 3.

23 See Chapter 12.

24 In the run-up to the privatisation of the electricity industry, institutional investors pressed for details of the costs of decommissioning nuclear power stations. Estimates submitted by the (CEGB) rose from £3.7 billion in 1989 to £15 billion a year later. In 1993 the NAO reckoned it would cost £18 billion to decommission the nuclear power stations and other radioactive sites. Once the sites still owned by the UKAEA were included, the cost rose to £22–23 billion. These figures were more than sufficient to give the privatised electricity industry a negative net worth.

25 As Tom Wilkie has pointed out, the costs of nuclear power include the diversion of scarce scientific resources away from more productive purposes. The opportunity cost is incalculable. See Tom Wilkie, *British Science and Politics since 1945*, Blackwell, 1991, pp. 57–8.

26 ibid., p. 56.

27 Paul Addison, *Churchill on the Home Front 1900–1955*, Pimlico, 1993, pages 156–7.

28 Quoted in Arthur Marwick, *The Deluge*, Macmillan, Second Edition, 1991, p. 347.

29 Charles I opened the Royal Mail to the public so that his officials could read their letters. Oliver Cromwell halted a plan by John Hill to establish a private national penny post two centuries before Rowland Hill persuaded the government of its merits in 1840. When William Dockwra established a penny post in London in 1680, he was fined and his business suppressed. The state took over his receiving stations, and London was the only city to enjoy a penny post until 1765.

30 Quoted in Asa Briggs, *A Social History of England*, Weidenfeld & Nicolson, 1994, p. 317.

31 In telecommunications, technological changes, such as satellite and cable television and the Internet, mean that it is no longer a natural monopoly, and the privatisation programme of the 1980s uncovered a solution even where a natural monopoly remains intact. The network is separated from the suppliers, who are given franchises and allowed to lease the use of the network. See Chapter 11.

32 H. C. G. Matthew, *Gladstone 1809–1874*, Oxford University Press, 1991, pp 67, 119–20; Philip Magnus, *Gladstone*, John Murray, 1963, p. 66.

33 S. G. Checkland, *The Rise of Industrial Society in England 1815–1885*, Longman, 1989, pp. 174, 362.

34 Jay, *The Socialist Case*, Faber & Faber, 1946, p. 263.

35 Hennessy, *Never Again*, p. 204.

36 Martin Gilbert, *Churchill: A Life*, Heinemann, 1991, pages 184, 202, 906.

37 Quoted in R. Kelf-Cohen, *British Nationalization 1945–73*, Macmillan, 1973, p. 73.

38 *Hansard*, Volume 458, 15 November 1948, Cols 76–8.

39 ibid., Volume 457, 3 November 1948, Col 923.

40 See Norman Chester, *The Nationalization of British Industry 1945–51*, HMSO, 975, p. 1010.

41 ibid., p. 1018.

42 ibid., pp. 1019–23.

43 John Redwood, *Public Enterprise in Crisis: The Future of the Nationalised Industries*, Basil Blackwell, 1980, p. 4.

44 Chester, *The Nationalization of British Industry 1945–51*, p. 1025.

45 Margaret Thatcher, *The Downing Street Years*, HarperCollins, 1993, p. 676.

46 R. W. S. Pryke, *Public Enterprise in Practice: The British Experience of Nationalisation Over Two Decades*, MacGibbon & Kee, 1971, pp. 460–1.

47 Alec Cairncross, *Years of Recovery: British Economic Policy 1945–51*, Methuen, 1985, p. 471.

48 Quoted in Anthony Sampson, *The Anatomy of Britain*, Hodder & Stoughton, 1962, p. 534.

49 Quoted in Beer, *Modern British Politics*, p. 131.

50 'Social Democracy in Britain', reprinted in R. H. Tawney, *The Radical Tradition*, Pelican, 1966, p. 174.

51 'The Nationalization of the Coal Industry', Labour Party pamphlet, 1919, reproduced in *The Radical Tradition*, p. 126.

52 Jay, *The Socialist Case*, p. 278.

53 Quoted in T. E. B. Howarth, *Prospect and Reality: Great Britain 1945–1955*, Collins, 1985, pp. 113, 21.

54 For union involvement in the coal industry, see Martin Adeney and John Lloyd, *The Miners' Strike 1984–5: Loss Without Limit*, Routledge, 1988, page 11.

55 Jay, *The Socialist Case*, pp. 278–9.

56 ibid., p 258.

57 R. H. Tawney, *The Acquisitive Society*, G. Bell & Sons, 1922, pp. 140–6, 198.

58 Post-war legislation obliged nationalised industries not to make a profit but to break even, one year with another. This led to inefficiency, so the government tried to find ways of judging which activities were commercially profitable, so that uneconomic but socially desirable services could be subsidised at minimal cost. See Leo Pliatzky, *Paying and Choosing*, Basil Blackwell, 1985, pp. 97–8.

59 The most notable example of this was the ill-fated 'Buzby bond,' a 1982 plan to allow British Telecom to borrow directly from the public. There was a similar plan for a North Sea oil bond. In 1981 the Treasury also drew up the so-called Ryrie Rules, governing private investment in the nationalised industries. The rules were so tight, no private money was forthcoming.

60 Lawson, *The View From No. 11*, p. 204.

61 C. A. R. Crosland, *The Future of Socialism*, Jonathan Cape, 1956, pp. 479–80.

62 Sampson, *The Changing Anatomy of Britain*, Hodder & Stoughton, 1982, p. 365.

63 *The Time Has Come*, January 1987, p. 56.
64 Denis Healey, *The Time of My Life*, Michael Joseph, 1989, p. 580.
65 Pliatzky, *Paying and Choosing*, p. 88.
66 *Enterprise for Labour*, 6 July 1989.
67 Pryke, *Public Enterprise in Practice*, pp. 442–5.
68 The belief that debt is a sterner financial taskmaster than equity is one Pryke shares with the luminaries of the leveraged takeover market, e.g. Michael Milken and Henry Kravis. *Public Enterprise in Practice*, pp. 446–455.
69 Galloway, *The Public Prodigals*, p. 117.
70 R. W. S. Pryke, *The Nationalised Industries: Policies and Performance Since 1968*, MacGibbon.
71 Quoted in Kelf-Cohen, *British Nationalization*, pp. 9–10.
72 See, for example, Mandelson and Liddle, *The Blair Revolution*, pp. 23–4, 82–3; Anthony Sampson, *The Essential Anatomy of Britain*, Hodder & Stoughton, 1992, pp. 108–122.

CHAPTER ELEVEN: *The Privatised Industries*

1 Article in *News on Sunday*, 1 November 1987.
2 Cento Veljanovski, *Selling the State: Privatisation in Britain*, Weidenfeld & Nicolson, 1988, p. 81.
3 Quoted in Keith Boyfield, *Privatisation: A Prize Worth Pursuing?*, European Policy Forum, May 1997, p. 81.
4 Quoted in *Financial Times*, 5 December 1996.
5 Madsen Pirie of the Adam Smith Institute compared privatisation with the Dissolution of the Monasteries in *Privatization*, Adam Smith Institute, 1985. See Dennis Kavanagh, *Thatcherism and British Politics: The End of Consensus?*, Oxford University Press, 1990, p. 221.
6 *Enterprise for Labour*, 6 July 1989.
7 Boyfield, *Privatisation*, p. 10.
8 For Fat Cats, see Chapter 15.
9 The net wealth of the public corporations in 1979 was £79.2 billion (£227 billion at 1998 prices). What remained in public ownership was worth perhaps £50 billion in 1998. The figures are not accurate, but the orders of magnitude are correct. See UK National Accounts, 1997 Edition, Table 12.9.
10 Both BT and British Gas have underperformed the market since competition was introduced in the early 1990s.
11 Nigel Lawson, *The View From No. 11*, Bantam, 1992, pp. 210, 238.
12 Boyfield, *Privatisation*, pp. 13–14.
13 BT, and the water and energy companies for that matter, do pay rates on assets such as telegraph poles, gas pipes and sewers.
14 National Audit Office Report, DTI: *Sale of Rover Group plc to British Aerospace plc*, November 1989.
15 Committee of Public Accounts, Sixth Report, Sale of Rover Group to British Aerospace plc, HMSO, 28 February 1990.
16 Both buildings were given initially to Nuclear Electric, the English arm of what became British Energy. Bankside, an oil-fired station closed in 1981, will from May 2000 house the Tate Gallery of Modern Art.

17 Letter from John Caudle, Director, Rail Property Limited, 7 September 1998.
18 The fourteen stations are: Birmingham New Street, Charing Cross, Edinburgh Waverley, Euston, Gatwick Airport, Glasgow Central, King's Cross, Leeds City, Liverpool Street, London Bridge, Manchester Piccadilly, Paddington, Victoria. The stations have 455 shops covering 310,000 square feet and generating income of £30 million a year.
19 National Audit Office, *British Rail Maintenance Limited: Sale of Maintenance Depots*, HC 583, Session 1995–96, 19 July 1996.
20 The companies also paid the government a special cash dividend of £800 million, taking the total proceeds to £2.5 billion. See National Audit Office, *Privatisation of the Rolling Stock Leasing Companies*, HC576, Session 1997–98, 5 March 1998, p. 51.
21 Porterbrook Leasing Company, sold by the government for £527 million in 1995, was bought by Stagecoach just seven months later for £825 million. Eversholt Holdings, sold for £580 million, was sold to Forward Trust for £788 million less than two years later.
22 National Audit Office, *Privatisation of the Rolling Stock Leasing Companies*, 5 March 1998.
23 For discussion of the cost of underwriting, see Chapter 31.
24 This does not include the cost of the £5 billion 'green dowry' of debt write-offs and cash subsidies given to the regional water companies ahead of their flotation in 1989.
25 Simon Jenkins, *Accountable to None: The Tory Nationalisation of Britain*, Hamish Hamilton, 1995, p. 32.
26 Nicholas Ridley, *My Style of Government*, Hutchinson, 1991, p. 58.
27 These debts would have been added to the liabilities of the state if the company were allowed to fail. Committee of Public Accounts, Sixth Report, 1989–90 Session, Sale of Rover Group to British Aerospace plc, HMSO, 28 February 1990.
28 *Financial Times*, 4 and 5 December 1997.
29 *The Performance of Privatised Industries*, Centre for Policy Studies, September 1996.
30 *Daily Telegraph*, 16 September 1996.
31 For a review of the academic literature, see Boyfield, *Privatisation*, pp 49–50.
32 *Financial Times*, 22 and 25 March 1997.
33 ibid., 26 July 1997.
34 See Chapter 32.
35 Interview, *Financial Times*, 11/12 June 1994.
36 'The crucial difference,' Cento Veljanovski pointed out, 'is that in the privatised company there are tradeable property rights.' See Veljanovski, *Selling the States* p. 92.
37 In August 1998 the London Underground, which used to run its own electricity generation and transmission systems, sub-contracted the operation of its electricity supply, including its power stations at Lots Road and Greenwich and 150 sub-stations, to SEEBOARD. The contract will run for 30 years.
38 *Financial Times*, 16 July 1998.
39 ibid., 22, 24 and 30 April and 8 May 1998.
40 ibid., 21 March 1998.
41 See Sir Geoffrey Howe, *Privatisation: The Way Ahead*, Conservative Political Centre, August 1981.
42 Kenneth Baker, *The Turbulent Years: My Life in Politics*, Faber & Faber, 1993, p. 79.
43 The Water Authorities (Return on Assets) Order.
44 *Financial Times*, 4 July 1986.
45 Golden shares were questioned by the European Commission on grounds that they

contravened European law on equal treatment for all investors. See also *Financial Times*, 22 May 1998 and 13 March 1998.

46 See Chapter 10.

47 *Financial Times*, 3 June 1996.

48 Lawson, *The View From No. 11*, p. 781.

49 The government wanted to sell Land Rover, Range Rover, Freight Rover and Leyland Trucks to the Americans. Ford made a simultaneous offer for Unipart and Austin Rover. The greatest political sensitivity was over the sale of Land Rover to General Motors.

50 See Margaret Thatcher, *The Downing Street Years*, HarperCollins, 1993, pp. 437–41.

51 They are called statutory because they are incorporated under separate Acts of Parliament. They had remained outside the public sector when the rest of the industry was nationalised.

52 Both CGE and SAUR had acquired 19.5 per cent stakes in Mid Kent. Their ambition was to merge Mid-Kent operations with the contiguous water operations they owned in other parts of the south-east of England. See *Financial Times*, 24 May 1996; 22 January 1997.

53 The pumped storage business of the National Grid was also acquired by an American company, Mission Energy. *Financial Times*, 14 December 1995.

54 In 1997, there were complaints in 1997 that WCT had struck such good terms with Railtrack for access to the network that small freight operators were being squeezed out. *Financial Times*, 21 May, 22 July 1997.

55 See Chapter 20.

56 'The Nationalization of the Coal Industry', Labour Party pamphlet, 1919, reproduced in *The Radical Tradition*, Pelican, 1966, p. 140.

57 The Union of Democratic Mineworkers organised a scheme to buy more pits on behalf of miners, but the government was not convinced of its viability.

58 They raised £82.5 million to complete the purchase. *Financial Times*, 28 December 1994.

59 *Financial Times*, 16 December 1995, 24 April 1997.

60 ibid., 4 August 1997.

61 The median bill is the middle one if bills are arranged in order of size. This is thought to be more representative of the typical residential bill than the mean (average) or mode (most commonly occurring) bill. See 'The Telephone Bill of a Typical Residential Customer', Office of Telecommunications, January 1995.

62 British Waterways, which sells water to the regional water utilities, believes its 2,000 mile canal network could form the basis of a national water grid. But it is not a truly national network. See below.

63 *Financial Times*, 17 June, 14 August 1996, 17 December 1997.

64 *Financial Times*, 17 December 1997.

65 See Colin Robinson, 'Introducing Competition Into Water,' in *Regulating Utilities: Broadening the Debate*, Institute of Economic Affairs, August 1997, pp. 153–187.

66 *Financial Times*, 24, 25 and 27 August 1998.

67 The idea was judged technically impossible because some water types do not mix well, changing the taste; a national network would also create uncertainties over responsibility for impurities.

68 *Financial Times*, 11 September 1998.

69 Cecil Parkinson, *Right at the Centre*, Weidenfeld & Nicolson, 1992, pp. 264–5.

70 The National Grid Group plc owns the high voltage network which connects

generators to regional electricity companies. It also owns the 'interconnectors' which enable electricity to be transferred between England and Wales and Scotland and France.

71 Initially 10 per cent, the levy has fallen to 2.2 per cent. It was not called a nuclear levy because it was also used to subsidise 'green' electricity generation projects like solar and tidal power, landfill gas, copicing and wind farms.

72 *Financial Times*, 13 November 1997.

73 ibid., 24 October 1997.

74 Because the announcement of the review came a day after the Treasury sold the last tranche of shares in PowerGen and National Power, the government was accused of insider trading. There were calls, from the companies and disappointed shareholders, for the director general to resign.

75 In fact, direct competition is banned until September 1999, to allow the first rail franchisees to get established. Even then, new entrants will not be allowed to take more than 20 per cent of the revenues of existing franchisees.

76 The freight operations of British Rail were divided into six separate businesses. All save one were bought by Wisconsin Central Transportation, which trades in Britain as English, Welsh and Scottish Railways (EWS). EWS now owns the three regional freight operations of British Rail – Loadhaul (North East), Mainline (South East) and TransRail (West) – and both the Channel Tunnel (Railfreight Distribution) and Royal Mail (Rail Express) operations.

77 Railtrack, Annual Report and Accounts, 1997–8.

78 For a list of the sales, see *Hansard*, Written Answers, 27 November 1996, columns 273–276 and 20 February 1997, column 729. They raised about £2.2 billion.

79 M. E. Beesley, 'Rail: The Role of Subsidy in Privatisation', in *Regulating Utilities: Broadening the Debate*, Institute of Economic Affairs, 1997, p. 237 and Annexe 1, pp. 266–71.

80 *Financial Times*, 2 June 1998.

81 ibid., 2 March 1997.

82 Office of Passenger Rail Franchising, 1997–8 Annual Report, p. 28.

83 *Financial Times*, 27 November 1997.

84 Virgin Rail, Great North Eastern Railway, Connex and Stagecoach have all argued for an increase in the length of their franchises to justify investment in new trains, partly on commercial grounds but also that the leasing companies will not entertain loans of less than ten years, for fear a new franchisee will not want the stock. See *Financial Times*, 25 November and 24 December 1997.

85 *Financial Times*, 22 July 1998.

86 London was largely excluded from the legislation, though it directed London Regional Transport to put bus services out to tender. The ten subsidiary companies of London Buses Limited were privatised in 1994–5.

87 When the Council privatised the company in July 1994 it rejected a bid by Stagecoach in favour of Yorkshire Traction. Stagecoach retaliated by recruiting the Darlington drivers, offering them £1,000 golden hellos and a guarantee of three years' work. It then ran a free bus service on the Darlington routes. Yorkshire Traction withdrew its offer to buy the company, and Darlington Transport went into liquidation.

88 *Financial Times*, 29 April 1998.

89 ibid., 27 September 1997.

90 See Chapter 10.

91 Mercury Communications was originally owned by Cable and Wireless (40 per cent), British Petroleum (40 per cent) and Barclays Bank (20 per cent) but became a wholly owned subsidiary of Cable & Wireless. Following the merger of Cable & Wireless with three American-controlled cable television companies, Mercury became part of the newly named CWC Communications. Cable & Wireless owns 52 per cent of CWC, which has abandoned the Mercury brand name.

92 The four licensed mobile telephone operators are Vodafone, Mercury One 2 One, Orange Communications and Cellnet. BT has a 60 per cent stake in Cellnet. The balance is owned by Securicor (40 per cent). BT would like to buy the Securicor stake but Oftel will not allow it. Vodafone was founded by Racal (80 per cent), Millcom (15 per cent) and Hambros Bank (5 per cent). Vodafone was demerged from Racal in two stages, in October 1988 and September 1991, and is now a separately quoted company. Mercury One 2 One is owned by CWC Communications and Orange by Hutchison Telecom, a Hong Kong-based company.

93 For the cable television companies, see Chapter 24.

94 *Financial Times*, 16 April 1997.

95 *The Times*, 16 September 1998.

96 Office of Passenger Rail Franchising, 1997–8 Annual Report, pp. 8. The regulators have found it difficult to fulfil the simpler task of extracting financial information from the companies they regulate. See pp. 436–7 above.

97 Warburg Securities, May 1994.

98 *Financial Times*, 1 March 1997.

99 For the nationalisation of British Airways, see Chapter 10.

100 BAA plc is descended from the British Airports Authority, which was created in 1966 to own and manage the main city airports – then Heathrow, Gatwick, and Prestwick – run by the Ministry of Aviation. The three government-owned airports in Scotland – Edinburgh, Aberdeen and Glasgow – were added to its responsibilities in the 1970s. BAA presently owns and operates Heathrow, Gatwick, Stansted, Edinburgh, Aberdeen, Glasgow and Southampton airports.

101 *Financial Times*, 12 January 1993.

102 British Airways and American Airlines have formed the Oneworld partnership, which includes Cathay Pacific, Qantas and Canadian Airlines. It is one of four emergent global airline alliances. Despite deregulation, the airline industry has retained its fondness for cartels.

103 *Wall Street Journal Europe*, 8 September 1998.

CHAPTER TWELVE: *The Still-Nationalised Industries*

1 Speech at Corn Exchange, City of London, 7 April 1997, quoted in Keith Boyfield, *Privatisation: A Prize Worth Pursuing?*, European Policy Forum, May 1997, p. 207.

2 *Financial Times*, 3 November 1994.

3 ibid., 21 March 1998.

4 ibid., 22 June 1998.

5 For Golden Shares, see Chapter 11.

6 *Financial Times*, 12 June 1998.

7 The Mersey Docks and Harbour Board was founded as a public corporation in 1857. It had to be rescued from bankruptcy by the government in 1970. One legacy was a state holding of 13.9 per cent in the company. The Conservative government had tried

but failed to sell the shares in 1990, despite writing off £110 million of debts accumulated in the rescue. The New Labour government sold them for £70 million in March 1998.

8 The sale of the Commonwealth Development Corporation was a move the Conservatives explored in 1995, but did not dare. See *Financial Times*, 22 and 23 October 1997.

9 For the *National Asset Register*, see Chapter 9.

10 See Chapter 11.

11 Water and sewage services in England and Wales were placed in the control of 10 regional water authorities in 1973. In Scotland, they were provided by the nine regional and three islands councils until Scottish local government was reorganised in 1996, when the three regional water authorities were set up. For privatisation of the water industry in England and Wales, see Chapter 11.

12 Scottish Office, Water and Sewerage in Scotland: Summary of Responses to the Consultation Paper 'Investing For Our Future'.

13 For the reorganisation of local government in 1996, see Chapter 13.

14 *Financial Times*, 22 March 1995.

15 *Financial Times*, 15 January 1993.

16 The Self-Regulatory Organisations (SROs) set up under the Financial Services Act of 1986 are the Investment Management Regulatory Organisation (IMRO) for fund managers, the Securities and Futures Authority (SFA) for the securities and derivatives markets, and the Personal Investment Authority (PIA) for retail financial services.

17 Pym and Kochan, *Gordon Brown*, p. 97.

18 The fiduciary note issue is the issue of notes which are not backed by holdings of gold. The Bank Charter Act tried to limit this fiduciary issue to £14 million, but this ceiling was raised repeatedly and eventually abolished altogether. The Bank still holds gold reserves on behalf of the Government but they are valued at only £5 billion, against currency in circulation of over £231 billion in 1998. For gold reserves and the Royal Mint, see Chapter 9.

19 Bank of England Report and Accounts, 1998, p. 47.

20 All United Kingdom banks and building societies are required to deposit with the Bank of England a cash sum equivalent to 0.15 per cent of their 'eligible liabilities', or customer deposits, over £400 million. These interest-free deposits are invested to produce an income for the Bank, but play no part in the conduct of monetary policy in Britain.

21 The Bank also argues that its role as lender of last resort to the banking system is partly how it controls monetary conditions, since it can lend on its own terms. This enables it to set the rate of interest.

22 Margaret Reid, *The Secondary Banking Crisis 1973–75*, Macmillan, 1982, p. 190.

23 Bank of England Report and Accounts, 1994, p. 12.

24 There may also be cheaper and more effective methods of regulation. George Benston has advocated substantial capital requirements, periodic reporting of assets, liabilities and capital, and stronger incentives for central banks to intervene before a crisis is out of control. See Benston, *Regulating Financial Markets: A Critique and Some Proposals*, Institute of Economic Affairs, June 1998. For the various follies stemming from protection of the banking system, see Chapter 27.

25 See Lawrence H. White, *Free Banking in Britain: Theory, Experience and Debate 1800–1845*, Institute of Economic Affairs, Second Edition, 1995, pp. 144–6.

26 The 1844 Bank Act aimed to keep the supply of money in line with the amount of gold held at the Bank of England. Had the Act worked as intended, individuals and businesses

operating in a rapidly expanding industrial economy would soon have run out of money. It was the creation of bank deposits on which they could write cheques which allowed the supply of money to increase the growth of the economy.

27 Steven Levy, 'E-Money (That's What I Want)', *Wired*, December 1994.

28 Credit cards use unfavourable exchange rates and levy high charges on retailers. Some issuers also charge an annual fee, and all issuers force holders to pass a test of their creditworthiness. Holders of cash do not have to pass any tests.

29 Letter to the author, 18 October 1995.

30 For the independent television and radio companies, see Chapter 24.

31 *Financial Times*, 27 February 1998.

32 If the government fulfils its ambition to replace the telecommunications regulator with a new regulator for broadcasting, telecommunications and computers (Ofcom) the BBC is expected to be subject to it.

33 Digital technology turns conventional sounds and pictures into digits, the language of computers. This enables programmes to be compressed, so they occupy less space on the airwaves than analogue signals. This allows vastly more channels, and improves the quality of both sound and pictures.

34 BBC Annual Report and Accounts, 1997–8, pp. 33, 60. The BBC World Service is funded by the Foreign Office.

35 BBC Annual Report and Accounts, 1997–8, p. 33.

36 Four digital channels (BBC Choice, BBC News 24, BBC Learning and BBC Digital Text) will be funded by licence-payers.

37 BBC Worldwide Annual Report and Accounts, 1997–8, p. 2.

38 Castle Transmission Services is a consortium led by Castle Tower, a Texan transmission tower construction company. Its partners are Berkshire Partners of Boston, Candover Investments and France Telecom. Unusually, the proceeds of the privatisation (with the exception of the value of the World Service transmitters) went not to the government but to the BBC.

39 The BBC moved into Broadcasting House in Portland Place – the 'petrified dreadnought', as a contemporary critic called it – in May 1932. Sixty years on, it has no need to occupy a prime central site. The Television Centre at White City was opened in 1960, on a 13.5 acre site the BBC had acquired over ten years before. It cost the then astronomical sum of £10 million to build. See Asa Briggs, *The BBC: The First Fifty Years*, Oxford University Press, 1985, p. 326.

40 BBC Resources, list of properties prepared in 1995.

41 Michael Cockerell, *Live From No 10: The Inside Story of Prime Ministers and Television*, Faber & Faber, 1988, pp. 176–180, 207–8.

42 Will Hutton, *The State We're In*, Jonathan Cape, 1995, p. 40.

43 Quoted in Jeremy Paxman, *Friends in High Places*, Michael Joseph, 1990., p. 115.

44 *Prospect*, March 1996, page 64.

45 Asa Briggs, *The BBC: The First Fifty Years*, Oxford University Press, 1985, page 55.

46 Anthony Sampson, *Anatomy of Britain*, Hodder & Stoughton, 1962, p. 603.

47 Quoted in *The Economist*, 30 August 1997.

48 The Dutch, Swedish, Danish, German, American, French, Swiss and Belgian Post Offices all have operations in Britain.

49 *Sunday Telegraph*, 22 May 1994.

50 The Post Office employed an average of 197,712 people in 1998, according to the 1997–98 annual report and accounts.

51 The limited monopoly on handling letters costing less than £1 was suspended temporarily in 1971, 1984 and 1996.

52 *Financial Times*, 17 September 1998.

53 The Post Office plans to bid again in when the licence comes up for renewal in 2001.

54 Quoted in *The Times*, 11 March 1993.

55 *Financial Times*, 24 August 1994.

56 This is a surprisingly sensitive subject, causing almost as much dismay as the refusal by the European Union to create sufficient room for the queen's head on the British versions of the single European currency. Tony Benn tried to remove the Queen's head from postage stamps in the 1960s, but it had to be withdrawn.

57 Quoted in *Financial Times*, 3 October 1997.

58 ibid., 9 September 1998.

59 ibid., 28 November 1996.

60 They are the seven AGRs and one PWR at Sizewell previously owned by Nuclear Electric and Scottish Nuclear, which were extracted from the original privatisation of the electricity industry in 1990.

61 After an explosion at Dounreay in 1977, waste became trapped in the nearby cliffs. The cliffs are crumbling, and the UKAEA estimates it will take 25 years and £355 million to make the area safe. *Financial Times*, 1 April 1998.

62 BNFL Annual Reports and Accounts, 1998.

63 BNFL has 40 per cent of Westinghouse, and Morrison Knudsen of the United States 60 per cent. They bought the company from the CBS media group.

64 Nuclear power stations burned concentrated ('enriched') uranium fuel rods, which last about four years, at which point they are sent for 'reprocessing.' This involves removing the metal casing and dipping the spent rods in nitric acid. The acid separates waste matter from the uranium and the plutonium (burning uranium in a nuclear power station creates a small amount of plutonium) which can then be reused in nuclear power stations. Uranium from the Magnox reactors, for example, is being reused in the AGRs owned by British Energy. Plutonium was used mainly in nuclear weapons, so the end of the Cold War led to an abrupt fall in demand, but it is an even richer source of fuel than uranium so it can also be reused in nuclear power stations. The problem is what to do with the waste.

65 Science Policy Research Unit, Sussex University, 1997. See also report in *Financial Times*, 10 November 1997.

66 See Matt Ridley, 'Vested Interests and National Forests,' *Down to Earth*, IEA Environment Unit 1995, page 71.

67 Jennifer Jenkins and Patrick James, *From Acorn to Oak Tree: The Growth of the National Trust 1895–1994*, Macmillan, 1994, pp. 68, 195.

68 Forestry Commission Facts and Figures, 1996–97, and Oliver Rackham, *The History of the Countryside*, J. M. Dent Limited, 1986, p. 28.

69 See Douglas Sutherland, *The Landowners*, Anthony Blond, 1968, p. 116.

70 Forestry Commission Annual Report, 1996–7.

71 National Audit Office, *Forestry Commission: Timber Harvesting and Marketing*, March 1993, pp. 2–3.

72 Forestry Commission Annual Report, 1996–97.

73 For Next Steps Agencies, see Chapter 9.

74 British Waterways Annual Report and Accounts, 1997–8, p. 1.

75 British Waterways Annual Report and Accounts 1997–98, page 20.

76 See Keith Boyfield, *Pleasure and Profit From Canals: A New Plan for British Waterways*, Centre for Policy Studies, 1990.

77 The National Rivers Authority, which is now part of the Environment Agency, is responsible for building and advising on flood defences, controlling beach and river pollution, conserving water supplies, draining land, and supervising and licensing the use of inland and coastal waters by anglers, sailors and other water sportsmen.

78 The canals were nationalised with the railways and major haulage operators in 1948, and became part of the giant British Transport Commission. When the Commission was abolished, responsibility for canals and river navigation was passed to the new British Waterways Board.

79 The beginnings of the canal age are usually traced to the canal the Duke of Bridgwater built in 1761 to carry coal from his mines at Worsley to Manchester. It was the first true 'deadwater' link over a new route, incorporating difficult feats of engineering like a tunnel through a hill and an aqueduct over a valley. It also sparked a canal mania over the next 30 years, and by the 1770s all the major English river systems were joined by canals linking the new industrial areas with their suppliers and customers.

CHAPTER THIRTEEN: *Local Government*

1 Quoted in Peter Mandelson and Roger Liddle, *The Blair Revolution: Can New Labour Deliver?*, Faber and Faber, 1996, p. 192.

2 F. A. Hayek, *The Road to Serfdom*, Routledge, 1944, p. 174.

3 Quoted in Peter Hennessy, *Never Again: Britain 1945–1951*, Jonathan Cape, 1992, p. 139.

4 *Local Government Finance*, May 1976, p. 65.

5 *Local Quangos and Local Governance: Report of the LGA Urban Commission Hearing*, Local Government Association, 1998, pp 8–9, paragraph 2.1.

6 *Financial Times*, 9 July 1998.

7 *Financial Times*, 14 July 1998.

8 UK National Accounts Blue Book, 1998 Edition, Table 12.11.

9 A. J. P. Taylor, *English History 1914–1945*, Penguin, 1973, p. 326.

10 See Chapter 11.

11 Simon Jenkins, *Accountable to None: The Tory Nationalisation of Britain*, Hamish Hamilton, 1995, pp. 41, 59.

12 Quoted in Derek Fraser, *The Evolution of the British Welfare State*, Macmillan, Second Edition, 1984, p. 120.

13 This Act divided the 52 counties of England into 62 county council areas. London became a county under this legislation, carved out of parts of Middlesex, Kent and Surrey. The Act allowed any town with more than 50,000 inhabitants to establish a county borough council, and 82 towns took the opportunity.

   Parish, town or community councils are now the lowest tier of local government. They scarcely exist in the main urban areas of England or in any part of Scotland, and vary in size from a few acres to over 20,000, and in income from a few pounds to £100,000 or more. Their responsibilities include maintaining shelters, clocks, village halls, playing fields, open spaces, allotments, war memorials, street lighting, car parks, burial grounds, roadside verges, playgrounds, seats, litter bins, and lavatories. Their work absorbs an estimated 70,000 councillors and the larger ones employ paid staff. Between them, they spend over £100 million a year.

14 Alexis de Tocqueville, *Journeys to England and Ireland*, edited by J. P. Mayer, Transaction Books, 1988, pp. 58.

15 Report of the Royal Commission on Local Government in Greater London, paragraph 672. Quoted in Tony Byrne, *Local Government in Britain*, Penguin, 1994, p. 113.

16 Peter Walker, *Staying Power*, Bloomsbury, 1991, page 78.

17 The existing unitary authorities for Orkney, Shetland and the Western Isles remained unchanged. Responsibility for water and sewage was given to three independent state-owned public authorities. See Chapter 12.

18 Hansard, 2 March 1995, Col. 1183.

19 *Local Quangos and Local Governance*: Report of the LGA Urban Commission Hearing, Local Government Association, 1998, 4, paragraph 5.

20 For English Partnerships, see Chapter 9.

21 Quoted in Jenkins, *Accountable to None*, p. 258.

22 The taxpayer had to promise £100 million to persuade the tenants of council-owned tower blocks in Liverpool to vote in favour of a HAT.

23 pp. 176, 177–8.

24 M. J. Daunton, *Councillors and Tenants: Local Authority Housing in English Cities 1919–1939*, Leicester University Press, 1984, p. 107.

25 Private rents were controlled by the state from 1915, and most private rents remained uncommercial. The retention of rent control after the First World War began the destruction of the private rented sector.

26 One third are 'voluntary aided' schools, usually founded by the Church but supported for public funds.

27 For an account of the comprehensive experiment, see Chapter 7. Under the 1944 Education Act, the only compulsory element in the school curriculum was religious education. Everything else was delegated to local education authorities. In practice, teachers tended to followed a rough curriculum supported by the examination boards.

28 Margaret Thatcher, *The Downing Street Years*, HarperCollins, 1993, page 597.

29 Quoted in *Sunday Times*, 13 June 1993.

30 The Smallholdings Act of 1892 empowered county councils to buy small farms to lease to unemployed labourers and small farmers at a time of agricultural depression. By 1914 there were 15,000 holdings on 200,000 acres. After the First World War, councils were further encouraged to settle ex-servicemen on the land in the Land Settlement (Facilities) Act of 1919. The 1926 Smallholdings and Allotments Act of 1926 maintained the duty on councils to provide smallholdings for sale or letting for social rather than agricultural purposes.

31 See Chapter 11.

32 From April 1996 rules issued under the 1988 Local Government Act stipulated that 65 per cent of construction-related services; 45 per cent of legal services; 35 per cent of financial and personnel services; and 70 per cent of information technology work must be put out to tender.

33 See Hazel Conway, *People's Parks: The Design and Development of Victorian Parks in Britain*, Cambridge University Press, 1991.

34 Savings range up to 20 per cent. See, for example, *Realising the Benefits of Competition – The Client Role for Contracted Services*, Audit Commission, HMSO, 1993; *Competition and Service: The Impact of the Local Government Act 1988*, Kieron Walsh and Howard Davies, Local Government Research Unit, Birmingham University, July 1993; and Stefan Szymanski, *Fiscal Studies*, 1996, Vol. 17, No., pp. 1–19.

35 Speech to Labour Party conference, Brighton, 5 October 1995.

36 ibid., 13 October 1997.

37 ibid., 24 July 1998.

38 ibid., 4 March 1998.

39 ibid., 22 October 1998.

40 ibid., 30 October 1997; 22, 23 October 1998.

41 ibid., 1, 3 and 23 June 1998.

42 ibid., 2, 3 and 8 October and 20 December 1997. The decision was overturned on appeal.

43 *Municipal Journal*, 28 October 1993.

44 A. T. Peacock and J. Wiseman, *The Growth of Public Expenditure in the United Kingdom*, Oxford University Press, 1961, Table 11, page 100.

45 Three quarters of industrial property was exempted from rates. The idea behind the reform was to subsidise industry indirectly by shifting the tax burden to individual taxpayers at both the national and the local level.

46 Quoted in Byrne, *Local Government in Britain*, p. 385.

47 The Uniform Business Rate was introduced in 1990–91 to address the problem that business rates were half of rate income, but businesses did not have a vote. Under the new system, business rates were levied at the same poundage throughout the country, and the poundage was not allowed to rise faster than inflation. The proceeds are distributed to local authorities nationwide on a standard basis.

48 Margaret Thatcher, *The Downing Street Years*, HarperCollins, 1993, p. 645.

49 Danny Burns, *Poll Tax Rebellion*, AK Press and Attack International 1992, p. 10.

50 The council tax is not exactly like rates. It has a personal element: there is a 25 per cent discount for people living alone.

51 *Financial Times*, 26 January 1998.

52 Quoted in Byrne, *Local Government in Britain*, pages (xxviii)–(xxix), from *Public Administration*, Winter 1985.

53 Thatcher, *The Downing Street Years*, p. 642.

54 Peter Jones, 'Local Government', in *Anatomy of Scotland: How Scotland Works*, Magnus Linklater and Robin Denniston (eds), Chambers 1992, p. 185.

55 *The Observer*, 28 May 1995.

56 *Financial Times*, 4 March 1998.

57 ibid., 30 March 1998.

CHAPTER FOURTEEN: *The Rich*

1 Adam Smith, *The Wealth of Nations*, Penguin Classics, 1986, Book 1, p. 134.

2 J. K. Galbraith, *The Age of Uncertainty*, Andre Deutsch, 1977, p. 44.

3 Jeffrey Robinson, *The Risk Takers: Five Years On*, Mandarin, 1990, p. 364.

4 From *Tatler*, 27 July 1710. *Oxford Dictionary of Quotations*. Steele was the founder, with Joseph Addison, of *The Spectator*.

5 *Fortune* magazine in 1957 named Getty as the richest man in the world. He told his brother-in-law, Ware Lynch: 'I don't know how much money I have. I don't know how they would know.'

6 Redmond Mullin, 'Fundraising From the Rich', in Howard Hurd and Mark Lattimer, *The Millionaire Givers: Wealth and Philanthropy in Britain*, Directory of Social Change, 1994, p. 11.

7 Inland Revenue Statistics 1997, Table 13.1, page 130. The figures are for 1993, and

undoubtedly underestimate the number of millionaires in Britain then and now. Datamonitor, the market research consultancy, used the same data to estimate that there were 81,000 millionaires in Britain in 1995. See *Financial Times*, 11 February 1997.

8 See Phillip Knightley, *The Vestey Affair*, Macdonald, 1981.

9 Nicholas von Hoffman, *Capitalist Fools*, Chatto & Windus, 1993, p. 262.

10 *The Wealth of Nations*, Book 1, p. 134.

11 W. D. Rubinstein, *Men of Property: The Very Wealthy in Britain since the Industrial Revolution*, Croom Helm, 1981, p. 168.

12 See Chapter 2.

13 Anthony Sampson, *The Midas Touch*, Hodder & Stoughton, 1989, p. 49.

14 Michael Edwardes, *The Nabobs At Home*, Constable, 1991, pages 25, 31, 59.

15 Harold Perkin, *The Origins of Modern English Society 1780–1880*, Routledge, 1976, p. 46.

16 Rubinstein, *Men of Property*, pp. 71–2.

17 W. D. Rubinstein, 'The End of "Old Corruption" in Britain 1780–1860'. *Past and Present*, No. 101, November 1983, pp. 55–86.

18 Rubinstein, *Men of Property*.

19 Jose Harris, *Private Lives, Public Spirit: Britain, 1870–1914*, Penguin, 1994, pages 97–8.

20 In July 1996 the United Nations Human Development Report estimated that there were 358 billionaires in the world, whose combined assets exceed the total annual income of 45 per cent of the population of the world. *Forbes* magazine put the number at 447.

21 David Cannadine, *The Decline and Fall of the British Aristocracy*, 1990, p. 398.

22 Rubinstein, *Men of Property*, p. 89.

23 See Chapter 6 for the Dissenting Academies. See also David Landes, *The Wealth and Poverty of Nations*, Little, Brown and Company, 1998, p. 174–81.

24 Oliver Marriott, *The Property Boom*, Hamish Hamilton, 1967.

25 Aris, *The Jews in Business*, Jonathan Cape, 1970, pp. 226–42.

26 Alan Macfarlane, *The Origins of English Individualism*, Basil Blackwell, 1978.

27 Walter Bagehot, *The English Constitution*, Collins/Fontana, 1973, p. 122.

28 See Chapter 2.

29 *New Society*, 22 August 1986.

30 *Time*, 18 December 1995. When she died at the age of 101, Schreiber left her $22 million fortune to Yeshiva University, a Jewish university in New York City which she never attended.

31 A. B. Atkinson, *The Economics of Inequality*, Second Edition, Oxford, 1983, p. 179.

32 Rubinstein, *Men of Property*, p. 125.

33 Confirmed by a Datamonitor survey reported in the *Financial Times*, 4 October 1995.

34 Inland Revenue Statistics, 1997, page 117, table 12.4.

35 See Chapter 2.

36 J. A. Kay and M. A. King, *The British Tax System*, Oxford University Press, 1990, pp. 107–8.

37 For examples of the gearing effect in reverse, see Chapter 29.

38 Rubinstein, *Men of Property*, p. 237.

39 *Financial Times*, 31 July 1997.

40 *Financial Times*, 24 March 1998.

41 *Sunday Times*, 18 January 1998.

42 See Chapter 25.

43 Robert H. Frank and Philip J. Cook, *The Winner Take-All Society*, Free Press, 1995, pp. 29–30.

44 See Chapter 2.

45 Marriott, *The Property Boom*.

46 See Chapter 29.

47 *Financial Times*, 24 January 1998.

48 For the betting industry, see Chapter 23.

49 Alastair Ross Goobey, *Bricks and Mortals*, Hutchinson, 1002, p. 86.

50 Anthony Sampson, *Anatomy of Britain*, Hodder & Stoughton, 1962, p. 416.

51 Jeffrey Robinson, *The Risk Takers: Five Years On*, Mandarin, 1990, p. 433.

52 ibid., p. 375.

53 *Financial Times*, 24 September 1997.

54 Robinson, *The Risk Takers*, p. 33–4.

55 Aris, *The Jews in Business*, p. 241.

56 Sampson, *The Midas Touch*, p. 48.

57 Dictionary of National Biography.

58 Quoted in Roy Porter, *English Society in the Eighteenth Century*, Penguin, 1990, p. 81.

59 *Financial Times*, 22 November 1993.

60 Sampson, *The Changing Anatomy of Britain*, p. 327.

61 Robinson, *The Risk Takers*, p. 359.

62 Tim Jackson, *Virgin King*, HarperCollins, 1994, p. 300.

63 William Kay, *Tycoons*, Pan, 1986, p. 120.

64 Dictionary of National Biography.

65 The need for security is of course physical as well as psychological.

66 Sigmund Freud, 'Character and Anal Erotism,' 1908, quoted in *The Oxford Book of Money*, edited by Kevin Jackson, Oxford University Press, 1995, pp. 42–3.

67 *Sunday Telegraph*, 14 November 1993.

68 *Dictionary of National Biography*.

69 Edmund Burke, *Reflections on the Revolution in France*, Penguin, 1973, p. 140.

70 From *Lord Finchley*.

71 Robinson, *The Risk Takers*, p. 440.

72 See Chapter 25.

73 F. A. Hayek, *The Constitution of Liberty*, Routledge, 1960, p. 126.

74 Quoted in Robert Skildelsky, *John Maynard Keynes: The Economist as Saviour 1920– 1937*, p. 584.

75 F. A. Hayek, *The Constitution of Liberty*, Routledge, 1960, Note 7, page 447.

76 Skidelsky, *John Maynard Keynes*, pp. 524, 528.

77 Quoted in *The Economist*, 25 October 1997.

78 *The Independent*, 2 February 1993.

79 Howard Hurd and Mark Lattimer, *The Millionaire Givers: Wealth and Philanthropy in Britain*, Directory of Social Change, 1994, pp. (vii), (ix–xi).

80 Anthony Sampson, *The Midas Touch*, Hodder & Stoughton, 1989, p. 19.

81 In 1923, A. B. Atkinson reckoned the top 1 per cent owned 61 per cent of personal wealth in Britain. See *The Economics of Inequality*, page 168; Table 7.3, HMSO *Social Trends*, 1998 Edition, p. 104, Table 5.26.

CHAPTER FIFTEEN: *Fat Cats*

1 Gordon Gekko is the fictional corporate raider in the film *Wall Street*. Quoted in John Micklethwait and Adrian Wooldridge, *The Witch Doctors*, William Heinemann, 1996, pp. 208–9.

2 *The Sun*, 29 September 1992.

3 *Financial Times*, 27 June 1991.

4 F. A. Hayek, *The Constitution of Liberty*, Routledge, 1990, p. 321.

5 See Peter Mandelson and Roger Liddle, *The Blair Revolution: Can New Labour Deliver?*, Faber & Faber, 1996, pp. 23, 107.

6 This is a long-running theme on the left of British politics. In *The Acquisitive Society*, R. H. Tawney argued that the ownership of large companies by remote shareholders meant property rights were so attenuated that control of industry could and should be exercised by a new class of professional managers producing for 'the community' rather than profit. In *The Future of Socialism*, Tony Crosland argued that modern public and private enterprises were so alike that ownership was irrelevant; all that mattered was finding the most effective and efficient way to manage large organisations. New Labour thinks its chief economic task is to regulate private industry, not expropriate it. See *The Blair Revolution*, pp. 82–3.

7 See R. H. Tawney, *The Acquisitive Society*, G. Bell & Sons, 1922, pp. 108–9.

8 *Sunday Times*, 24 January 1988.

9 *Financial Times*, 27 July 1995.

10 See Chapter 11.

11 *Observer*, 14 May 1995. The article prompted defamation proceedings for implying improper conduct by directors of PowerGen. Six directors also received a written apology and undisclosed damages over a piece in *Today* alleging insider dealing in options on the basis of disappointing internal projections. See *Financial Times*, 12 June 1995.

12 Ownership of the National Grid was shared between the regional electricity companies when the electricity industry was privatised in 1990. See Chapter 11. See also *Financial Times*, 15, 25 May 1995.

13 *Financial Times*, 15 May and 21 July 1995.

14 *Times*, 19 August 1994.

15 Andrew Adonis and Stephen Pollard, *A Class Act: The Myth of Britain's Classless Society*, Hamish Hamilton, 1997, pp. 70, 72.

16 See below, pp. 560–63.

17 *The Times*, 3 June 1997.

18 *Financial Times*, 18 November 1997.

19 ibid., 29 June 1998.

20 ibid., 20 July 1997.

21 Survey by management consultants A. T. Kearney. *Financial Times*, 16 September 1996.

22 *Financial Times*, 16 July 1994.

23 Hoffman left Thames in March 1996, with compensation of £890,000. Thian was paid £398,400 by North West Water.

24 *Financial Times*, 1 December 1992.

25 See Chapter 11.

26 Similar forces were at work in the rush to de-mutualise at building societies and life offices. The Alliance & Leicester, for example, set up an executive share option at the time of its flotation. Less than a year after the society floated, the chief executive had

made a paper profit of nearly half a million pounds. Other societies have since set up share option schemes. For the de-mutualisation of building societies, see Chapter 27 and Chapter 30 for the demutualisation of life offices.

27 Directors' Pay Report, Incomes Data Services and Arthur Andersen, August 1998.

28 Quoted in *The Times*, 8 March 1995.

29 Anthony Sampson, *Company Man: The Rise and Fall of Corporate Life*, HarperCollins, 1995, p. 311.

30 *Financial Times*, 24, 25 February 1998.

31 *The Times*, 31 March 1998.

32 Quoted in *Financial Times*, 17 June 1998.

33 Namely, Polly Peck, the Bank of Credit and Commerce International (BBC1) and British & Commonwealth.

34 Quoted in Jonathan Charkham, *Keeping Good Company: A Study of Corporate Governance in Five Countries*, Oxford University Press, 1995, p. 4.

35 An apparently lavish pension for a limited contribution can neglect the transfer of assets from a previous scheme.

36 Most bonuses are performance-related. But special bonuses for completing transactions – selling a business or bringing a company to flotation – are also common. In 1998 Ken Hanna, chief executive of Dalgety, received a bonus of £554,912 for breaking the company into its component parts and selling them off. Also in 1998, Phil White of National Express got a one-off payment of £725,000 as reward for reorganising West Midlands Travel, a bus company National Express had taken over in 1995. Lord Simon of Highbury, now a government minister but previously chairman of BP, received a special bonus of £240,000 from BP purely in recognition of long service. See *Financial Times*, 12 April 1997; 7 October 1998.

37 *Financial Times*, 11 October 1993.

38 Sir Iain Vallance, 'Justice on Executive Pay', *Financial Times*, 25 January 1995.

39 *Sunday Times*, 22 January 1995.

40 *Financial Times*, 22 June 1995.

41 ibid., 18 December 1995.

42 ibid., 17, 22, 23, 27 June 1995.

43 ibid., 26 July 1996.

44 ibid., 9 January 1998.

45 Datastream/ICV Market Survey, published 23 December 1997.

46 As President of the TUC. Quoted in *Financial Times*, 15 September 1998.

47 It is said that the reason Michael Eisner, chief executive of the Disney Corporation, is so well-paid is that the 16-man board of directors includes his personal attorney; an architect who designed his house; the president of a university to which he donated funds; the head of the school attended by the Eisner children; two former Disney executives; and a former senator who was consultant to the company; *Financial Times*, 23 February 1998.

48 *Financial Times*, 11 February 1998.

49 ibid., 15 December 1995.

50 *Financial Times*, 29 June 1992.

51 Paper, *American Academy of Management*, by Martin Conyon and Simon Peck of Warwick Business School, quoted in *Financial Times*, 15 July 1998.

52 See Chapter 31.

53 *Financial Times*, 14 January 1995. They had until then bought the argument that his

departure would be disastrous for Saatchi & Saatchi, and they were probably right. Maurice Saatchi took several key people and clients with him and started a rival agency.

54 See page 574.

55 See Chapter 31.

56 Iain Vallance, 'Justice on Executive Pay', *Financial Times*, 25 January 1995.

57 Letter, *Financial Times*, 1 December 1994.

58 *Financial Times*, 9, 17 September 1997.

59 Sir Iain Vallance, 'Justice on Executive Pay', *Financial Times*, 25 January 1995.

60 A study of Australian companies by Melinda Muth, published in *Corporate Governance*, volume 6, number 1, in January 1998, found that returns to shareholders declined in direct proportion to the independence of the board, because the non-executive directors did not have time to concentrate on company affairs. See *Financial Times*, 9 February 1998.

61 *Financial Times*, 25 March 1998.

62 ibid., 15 October 1996, 8 April 1997.

63 Survey by New Bridge Street pay consultants. Quoted in *Financial Times*, 3 February, 11 March 1998.

64 In the twelve years following the 1984 budget, 6,515 share-option schemes covering shares worth £18,540 million were granted. See *Inland Revenue Statistics 1997*, page 70, Table 6.1.

65 Top Pay Unit Review, Incomes Data Services, March 1992.

66 ibid., 17 July 1998.

67 ibid., 23 January 1996.

68 ibid., 7 November 1995.

69 So-called out-of-the-money share options can give directors an incentive to agree to a takeover.

70 Economies and write-offs may of course enhance longterm value.

71 Paul Gregg, Stephen Machin and Stefan Szymanski, 'The Disappearing Relationship Between Directors' Pay and Corporate Performance', London School of Economics Centre for Economic Performance, November 1992.

72 *Financial Times*, 11, 18 May 1996.

73 ibid., 7, 8, 9, 11, 17 October 1996; 21 April 1997.

74 ibid., 8 November 1997.

75 ibid., 18 January 1995; 25 March 1995.

76 ibid., 5 June 1993.

77 ibid., December 1997, 4, 7, 9, 21, 31 January, 5 February 1998.

78 *The Times*, 17 January 1998.

79 *Financial Times*, 5 February 1998.

80 ibid., 26 March, 31 July 1996.

81 ibid., 7 October 1997.

82 ibid., 1 September 1995.

83 ibid., 1 March 1995.

84 ibid., 1 November 1996.

85 ibid., 4 April 1996.

86 ibid., 21 September, 16 October 1982.

87 ibid., 30 March 1982.

88 *The Times*, 31 March 1998.

89 ibid., 26 March 1996.

90 ibid., 13 August 1996.
91 The libel action was against Count Nikolai Tolstoy and a property developer, Nigel Watts. *Financial Times*, 22 April 1991.
92 *Financial Times*, 2 July 1998.
93 *Times* and *Financial Times*, 17 July 1998.
94 *Financial Times*, 31 May, 29 June 1991.
95 ibid., 20 October 1997; ISS Friday Report, 31 October 1997.
96 Conference Board/Monks Partnership survey, quoted in *Financial Times*, 27 September 1997.
97 Adonis and Pollard, *A Class Act*, p. 102.
98 Elisabeth Marx of NB Selection, quoted in the *Financial Times*, 7 August 1996.
99 Research for *Management Today*, published in *Financial Times*, 2 September 1995.
100 1 December 1994.
101 Iain Vallance, 'Justice on Executive Pay', *Financial Times*, 25 January 1995.
102 *Independent on Sunday*, 30 May 1995.
103 See Chapter 25.
104 Robert H. Frank and Philip J. Cock, *The Winner-Take-All Society*, Free Press, 1995.
105 Sir John Harvey-Jones, 'High-flyers and the Case for High Pay', *Observer*, 13 August 1989.
106 *Independent on Sunday*, 22 January 1995.
107 Quoted in *The Spectator*, 1 May 1993.
108 *Financial Times*, 12 June 1998.
109 *Independent on Sunday*, 30 May 1995.
110 *Forbes*, February 1992.
111 *The Times* and *Financial Times*, 16 April 1998.
112 Michael Shanks, *The Stagnant Society*, Pelican, 1961, p. 47.
113 *Daily Mail*, 19 May 1993.

CHAPTER SIXTEEN: *The Private Sector Professionals*

1 From *The Doctor's Dilemma* (1911), Act I.
2 Kurt Vonnegut, *God Bless You Mr Rosewater*, Dell, 1965, pp. 17–18.
3 *Bleak House*, Chapter 39.
4 The letter, from an investment banker at Deutsche Morgan Grenfell, denied 'false rumours' that he was defecting to a rival firm, and blamed rivals for 'attempting to stall our progress by spreading fear, uncertainly and doubt – many of you have been victimised by this phenomenon'. *Financial Times*, 17 March 1998.
5 The second letter – an E-Mail – announced he had left for a rival firm. *Financial Times*, 3 July 1998.
6 *Observer*, 8 December 1991.
7 *Sunday Times*, 18 June 1995.
8 *Financial Times*, 26 August 1997.
9 *Financial Times*, 19 September 1995.
10 The First Report of the Social Security Committee (1992–3), *The Operation of Pension Funds: The Recovery of Assets* (HC 189) stated that fees from all the firms involved totalled £34,118 million by December 1992 (paragraph 60). Further details in the Fourth Report in 1992–3, *The Work of the Maxwell Insolvency Practitioners* (HC835), which indicated that the costs of the same firms had risen to £51.6 million by the end of March

1993 (paragraph 14). The Committee gave its view at the time that the costs would rise to £100 million (paragraphs 1 and 14).

11 *Sunday Times*, 13 September 1992.

12 Fourth Report of the Social Security Committee in 1992–3, *The Work of the Maxwell Insolvency Practitioners* (HC835), paragraph 14, page (vii) and Third Report of the Social Security Committee in 1993–4, *The Work of Buchler Phillips on the Receivership of the Maxwell Personal Estate* (HC299). See also *Financial Times*, 27 July 1993.

13 Third Report of the Social Security Committee in 1993–4, paragraph 3. See also *Financial Times*, 31 March 1994.

14 ibid., paragraph 4.

15 *Financial Times*, 11 July 1997.

16 *Sunday Times*, 13 September 1992.

17 *Financial Times*, 3 February 1993.

18 One expert calculates that human capital accounts for 52 per cent of the national income today, against 15 per cent 100 years ago. Accountants have not yet decided how best human capital can be measured but its value is immense: it generates income. See Peter Lindert, 'Unequal English Wealth Since 1670', *Journal of Political Economy*, Vol. 94, 1986, p. 1131; Keith Bradley, 'The Value of Intellectual Capital', *Financial Times*, 26 July 1996; and Institute for Fiscal Studies, *Higher Education, Employment and Earnings in Britain*, in *Financial Times*, 21 May 1997.

19 Edward Heathcoat Amory, 'What They've Got, What They're Spending It On', *The Spectator*, 13 December 1997.

20 *Financial Times*, 27 August 1993.

21 ibid., 1 September 1993.

22 *Sunday Times*, 29 August 1993.

23 *Financial Times*, 27 August 1993.

24 *Sunday Times*, 20 February 1994.

25 *The Times*, 24 November 1994.

26 In *Financial Times*, 4 October 1995.

27 For the Oxbridge business schools, see Chapter 5.

28 Of the one million people in Britain who call themselves directors, only 400,000 work for companies large enough to have board meetings, and only 14,000 sit on the board of a PLC. About 1,000 directors a year are banned by the courts as unfit. At the end of 1997 the Institute of Directors proposed a specific professional title (Chartered Director, or Cdir). See *Financial Times*, 18 and 21 October 1997.

29 Maurice Keen, *English Society in the Later Middle Ages 1348–1500*, Penguin, 1990, p. 221.

30 The Old Corruption was the network of jobs in the gift of the government.

31 Quoted in Edgar Jones, *True and Fair: A History of Price Waterhouse*, Hamish Hamilton, 1995, p. 10.

32 Harold Perkin, *The Rise of Professional Society: England Since 1880*, Routledge, 1989, page 20.

33 There was 233,620 British qualified accountants at home and abroad in 1995. From Derek Matthews, Malcolm Anderson and John Richard Edwards, *The Priesthood of Industry – The Rise of the Professional Accountant in British Management*, Oxford University Press, 1998.

34 Andrew Adonis and Stephen Pollard, *A Class Act: The Myth of Britain's Classless Society*, Hamish Hamilton, 1997, pages 68–102.

35 D. M. Palliser, *The Age of Elizabeth: England Under the Later Tudors 1547–1603*, Longman, Second Edition, 1992, p. 261.

36 In his study of the wealthy, Rubinstein found London so preponderant that he concluded geography was more important than class in the distribution of millionaires. See W. D. Rubinstein, *Men of Property: The Very Wealthy in Britain Since the Industrial Revolution*, Croom Helm, 1981, p. 106; *Capitalism, Culture and Decline in Britain 1750–1990*, Routledge, 1993, pp. 25–44.

37 Inland Revenue figures show the mean income of the 12,000 taxpayers in the City in 1995–6 as at least £107,000, and perhaps £150,000. This is nearly ten times the average taxable income in the poorer parts of northern England. See Inland Revenue Statistics 1997, pp. 47–55, tables 3, 13 and 3.14.

38 City Research Project, *Revenues From the City's Financial Services*, December 1993, p. 6, Table 2.

39 Derivatives are securities that derive their value from another security. Some, like futures and options, are traded on formal exchanges. The terms now encompass interest rate and currency swaps.

40 *Financial Times*, 9 February 1995.

41 ibid., 26 February 1998.

42 For the demise of BZW, see Chapter 27.

43 Margaret Reid reckoned Big Bang cost the buyers £4 billion once they had recruited additional staff and bought the necessary office space and equipment. See Margaret Reid, *All-Change in the City: The Revolution in Britain's Financial Sector*, Macmillan, 1988, p. 72.

44 The Golden Handcuffs had taken the form of shares which could not be sold for five years.

45 *Financial Times*, 28 October 1992.

46 *Sunday Telegraph*, 2 April 1995.

47 *Financial Times*, 31 May 1997.

48 1996 Annual Report and Accounts for Lazard Brothers, Flemings and Schroders.

49 Paul Ferris, *Gentlemen of Fortune: The World's Merchant and Investment Bankers*, p. 181.

50 Morgan Grenfell & Co Limited, Annual Report and Accounts, Year Ended December 1994. Morgan Grenfell Asset Management Accounts, Year Ended 31 December 1995. Morgan Grenfell Group PLC, Reports and Financial Statements, Year Ended 31 December 1995.

51 Paul Ferris, *Gentlemen of Fortune: The World's Merchant and Investment Bankers*, p. 242.

52 *Evening Standard*, 8 April 1997.

53 ibid., 1 October 1996; *Financial Times*, 2 October 1996.

54 ibid., 9 December 1993.

55 ibid., 12 December 1995.

56 The exception is Cazenove & Co.

57 *Financial Times*, 20 January 1997.

58 ibid., 5/6 June 1996.

59 Ian Hay Davison, *A View of the Room: Lloyd's, Change and Disclosure*, Weidenfeld & Nicolson, 1987, p. 3.

60 Lambert Fenchurch Group and C. E. Heath PLC Annual Reports.

61 *Financial Times*, 27 July 1992.

62 See Chapter 30.

63 *Financial Times*, 25 June 1997.

64 Edward Miller and John Hatcher, *Medieval England: Rural Society and Economic Change 1086–1348*, Longman, 1978, p. 173, and Maurice Keen, *English Society in the Later Middle Ages 1348–1500*, Penguin, 1990, pp. 15–16.

65 Joyce Youings, *Sixteenth-Century England*, Penguin, 1991, pp. 175–6.

66 D. M. Palliser, *The Age of Elizabeth*, Longman, Second Edition, 1992, p. 123.

67 In the last 30 years the number of solicitors practising in England and Wales has trebled. By mid-1995 there were 82,828 solicitors on the Roll maintained by the Law Society, of which 66,123 are actually practising. There is another 9,743 on the register maintained by the Law Society of Scotland, of which 7,991 are practising. According to the Bar Council, there are 8,498 working barristers in England and Wales, and the Faculty of Advocates in Scotland has 614 names on its register, of which 378 are practising.

68 Telephone conversation, 12 September 1996.

69 See below, p. 602.

70 Letter from NHS Executive.

71 *Financial Times*, 21 July 1998.

72 Health authorities and hospitals pay the first £10,000 of any claim, and 20 per cent of any award up to £500,000. Anything above that is paid by the Department of Health.

73 *Sunday Times*, 10 December 1993.

74 *Financial Times*, 29 May 1995.

75 ibid., 22 November 1995.

76 ibid., 28 September 1996.

77 Subject to a 25 per cent cap on the proportion of damages which can taken by lawyers: the level recommended by the Law Society.

78 *Financial Times*, 28 September 1996.

79 According to the Law Society, Legal Aid payments to solicitors amounted to £1,117 million in 1995–6, 15.1 per cent of gross revenues (£7,415 million).

80 *Financial Times*, 31 January 1995.

81 Press Release, Lord Chancellor's Department, 28 April 1998.

82 The cases funded by the Legal Aid Board in 1996–7 included 'Baby C,' where the parents of a damaged child were seeking the right to end its life; an experimental claim for environmental nuisance in London Docklands; the Marchioness inquest case; and CJD allegedly caused by human growth hormone. General Council of the Bar, press notice, 28 April 1998.

83 *The Guardian*, 20 May 1995.

84 *Financial Times*, 5 October 1995.

85 Office for the Supervision of Solicitors, Annual Report, 1996–7.

86 *Financial Times*, 30 June 1998.

87 *The 1998 Legal Business 100*.

88 According to the Lord Chancellor's Department, barristers routinely submit exaggerated claims for fees to the Legal Aid Board. These are then reduced by a 'taxing master', encouraging barristers to exaggerate the numbers of hours worked to ensure that the fee is still generous after being cut. In 1994–95 fees paid were 69 per cent of those claimed. In 1995 and 1996 comparable figures were 44 per cent and 55 per cent.

89 *Financial Times*, 20 July 1993.

90 Review Body on Senior Salaries, 18th Report, No. 37, Cm 3094, Table 1.

91 See Chapter 17.

92 Joshua Rozenberg, *The Search for Justice*, Sceptre, 1994, pp. 90, 366.

93 Anthony Sampson, *Anatomy of Britain*, Hodder & Stoughton, 1962, p. 152.

94 *Financial Times*, 11 February 1994.

95 *Financial Times*, 19 June 1996.

96 *The Observer*, 29 May 1994.

97 *Financial Times*, 16 June 1995.

98 *Financial Times*, 28 February 1995.

99 Sampson, *Anatomy of Britain*, pp. 466–73. He did not discover the telegraphic address until 1965.

100 In 1996 the Institute of Chartered Accountants had 109,000 members in England and Wales. The Scottish Institute had 8,580 and the Irish Institute, which covers the whole island of Ireland, 9,690. The Chartered Association of Certified Accountants had 50,488 members, the Chartered Institute of Public Finance and Accountancy 12,360, and the Chartered Institute of Management Accountants 42,936. A total of 233,054 people are thus able to practise as accountants in Britain.

101 *Financial Times*, 10 April 1994.

102 Since 1991 all UK-qualified auditors have had to be licensed and regulated by one of the six bodies recognised by the Department of Trade and Industry. They are the ICA in England and Wales, Scotland and Ireland, the Association of Chartered Certified Accountants (ACCA, the Chartered Institute of Public Finance and Accountancy (Cipfa) for accountants in the public sector, and the Chartered Institute of Management Accountants (Cima). In 1998 the six self-regulatory bodies proposed a review board with tougher investigative and disciplinary powers. The plan was endorsed, on a trial basis, by the government in September 1998.

103 *Financial Times*, 19 October 1998.

104 The fee and partner figures are for the United Kingdom only, and are with three exceptions taken from surveys conducted by *International Accounting Bulletin*, 1 December 1997, published by Lafferty Publications. (For more information, contact Gerard Reilly at 353-1-671-8022 or fax 353-1-671-8240 or E-Mail cuservalafferty.ie or at their website, www.lafferty.co.uk). The exceptions are Pannell Kerr Forster, whose fee income figure is taken from their Annual Review of 1997; Moore Stephens, whose fee income figure is taken from *Accountancy Age*, 30 July 1998; and Kidsons Impey, whose fee income figure was supplied by the firm. Some Group A firms declined to participate in the *International Accounting Bulletin* survey. Bourner Bullock (JPA), Dixon Wilson (TAG) and Westbury Schotness (Fiducial) did not provide fee income but participated in other parts of the survey. Neither *International Accounting Bulletin* nor *Accountancy Age* is responsible for either the fees per partner nor the profits per partner calculations. These are the sole responsibility of the author. The profits-per partner calculation is made by assuming that costs, in terms of employing and training staff, renting and fuelling office space and equipment, and paying professional indemnity insurance premiums, are running at 66 per cent of gross fees at all firms. This is no more than an estimate. Costs obviously vary according to the number of professional staff employed. Nor is profit per partner the same as the profit share each partner takes home. Partners receive salaries, with profit shares of varying sizes payable on top, usually linked to age and length of service. Partners are also expected to contribute to the development of the business and to the partners' equity, depositing sums they cannot withdraw until they leave the firm or retire. On the assumption that partners reinvest around a third of their gross profits,

it is reasonable to assume that partners at Big Five firms are averaging £200–300,000 a year. Senior partners earn more.

105 *Financial Times*, 17 November 1994.
106 *Sunday Times*, 30 May 1995.
107 *Financial Times*, 8 July 1998; 28 May 1993; 9 June 1994.
108 See KPMG UK Annual Report, 1995, p. 38, note 2; KPMG Annual Report, 1997, pp. 42-3, note 2.
109 Ernst & Young, 1997 Annual Report and Accounts, p. 45, note 6.
110 BDO Stoy Hayward Annual Statement, 1996; 1998.
111 *Financial Times*, 11 June 1996.
112 The accountants were astute enough to waive fees of £750,000. *Sunday Times*, 18 January 1998.
113 Francis Fukuyama, *Trust: The Social Virtues and the Creation of Prosperity*, Penguin, 1996.
114 *Independent on Sunday*, 23 January 1994.
115 *The Times*, 13 September 1994.
116 *Financial Times*, 15 June 1994.
117 ibid., 21 April 1995.
118 Ian Hay Davison, *A View of the Room*, Weidenfeld & Nicolson, 1987, p. 5.
119 *Financial Times*, 17 November 1993.
120 *The Times*, 19 September 1995.
121 *Financial Times*, 23, 24 September 1998.
122 ibid., 24 January 1996.
123 ibid., 10 August 1994.
124 *Independent on Sunday*, 27 March 1994.
125 Medical Defence Union Annual Report and Accounts 1996.
126 *Financial Times*, 4 July 1996.
127 ibid., 3 June 1995.
128 Sampson, *Anatomy of Britain*, p. 457.
129 *Financial Times*, 12 November 1997.
130 *The Times*, 22 May 1996.

CHAPTER SEVENTEEN: *The Public Sector Professionals*

1 Harold Perkin, *The Rise of Professional Society*, Routledge, 1989, p. 10.
2 *Daily Telegraph*, 16 March 1992.
3 Margaret Thatcher, *The Downing Street Years*, HarperCollins, 1993, p. 45.
4 David Pannick, *Judges*, Oxford University Press, 1987, pp. 12–13.
5 Michael Lewis, *Liar's Poker*, Hodder & Stoughton, 1989, p. 30.
6 Andrew Adonis and Stephen Pollard, *A Class Act: The Myth of Britain's Classless Society*, Hamish Hamilton. 1997, pp. 93–6.
7 For the Redbrick Universities, see Chapter 6.
8 Harold Perkin, *The Third Revolution: Professional Elites in the Modern World*, Routledge, 1996; especially its attack on the Thatcher governments (pp. 667–76).
9 Architects cannot practise in Britain without being registered with the Architects Registration Council. In 1993, the Royal Institute of British Architects successfully resisted a government plan to end statutory registration, which would have allowed anyone to describe themselves as an architect.

10 *Financial Times*, 13 September 1993.

11 *What is RIBA?*, Royal Institute of British Architects.

12 *Independent on Sunday*, 5 December 1993.

13 1995 and 1997 Surveys of Professional Engineers and Technicians, Engineering Council, p. 66.

14 Anthony Sampson, *The Changing Anatomy of Britain*, Hodder & Stoughton, 1982, p. 223.

15 A survey by the Institute of Employment Research at Warwick University concluded that companies run by accountants were more successful than those run by engineers and accountants made better use of technology. Reported in *Financial Times*, 25 March 1997.

16 1997 Survey of Professional Engineers and Technicians, Engineering Council, p. 109.

17 Introduction, 1995 and 1997 Surveys of Professional Engineers and Technicians, Engineering Council.

18 *Whitehall*, Fontana, 1990, p. 512.

19 Jeremy Paxman, *Friends in High Places*, Michael Joseph, 1990, p. 134.

20 Margaret Reid, *All-Change in the City: The Revolution in Britain's Financial Sector*, Macmillan, 1988, p. 76.

21 Peter Hennessy, *Whitehall*, p. 374.

22 ibid, p. 34.

23 Sir Robert Morant was chief author of the Education Act of 1902, when the state took responsibility for secondary education, and pioneer of the National Insurance systems which initiated state pensions, unemployment benefit and the NHS.

24 Margaret Thatcher, *The Downing Street Years*, HarperCollins, 1993, page 48.

25 See Chapter 9.

26 Peter Riddell, *Honest Opportunism: The Rise of the Career Politician*, Hamish Hamilton, 1993, p. 9.

27 Quoted in Peter Riddell, *Honest Opportunism: The Rise of the Career Politician*, Hamish Hamilton, 1993, p. 8.

28 Private conversation, 7 July 1996.

29 The cost of political appointments to the Number 10 policy unit; in a written answer, quoted in *Financial Times*, 26 June 1998.

30 Quoted in Riddell, *Honest Opportunism*, p. 133.

31 Bill Deedes, *Dear Bill*, Pan, 1998, pp. 105, 121.

32 MPs' pensions accumulate at a rate of 1/50th of salary for each year of service. The contribution payable is 6 per cent of salary. MPs who lose their seats or retire can claim up to 4/3[rds] of the quarterly value of the Office Costs Allowance; 'a 'resettlement grant' to help them adjust to life outside Parliament is also paid, based on age and length of service.

33 MPs who are also members of the European Parliament (MEPs) get a third of their European Parliament salary in addition to their Westminster salary. Since this is equivalent to their Westminster salary, it amounts to £14,872. The office costs allowance is higher for members with a disability. MPs who represent constituencies in inner London get a supplement of £1,406 instead of the bed and board allowance, while those in Greater London can choose between the supplement or the additional costs allowance. MPs can claim motoring allowance of 50.1 per mile for the first 20,000 miles and 23.1p thereafter. The estimates in Table 4 are based on the assumption that the average MP drives 25,000 miles a year. Any MP claiming above 25,000 miles has to furnish full details. There is a bicycling allowance of 6.4p a mile. MPs can claim 9 free return rail

journeys a year between the constituency and Westminster for members of their personal staff. Spouses and any member of their family under 18 can also claim up to 15 return journeys a year between home and Westminster (though not home and constituency). MPs can claim one business-class air fare to visit a European institution, and two days' subsistence at £100–120 a day.

34 *Sunday Times*, 17 September 1995.

35 W. D. Rubinstein, 'The End of "Old Corruption" in Britain', in *Past and Present*, No. 101, November 1983, p. 73.

36 Review Body on Senior Salaries Report No. 38, Review of Parliamentary Pay and Allowances, Cm. 3330, Vol II, p. 11.

37 Michael Pinto-Duschinsky, *The Times*, 11 October 1994.

38 The Neill committee recommendation is likely to lead either to parties funded by the taxpayer or to parties owned by a handful of rich individuals.

39 David Cannadine, *The Decline and Fall of the British Aristocracy*, Yale University Press, 1990, p. 322.

40 *The Spectator*, 17 June 1995.

41 Quoted in David Pannick, Judges, Oxford University Press, 1987, p. 13.

42 Nigel Lawson, *The View From No. 11*, Bantam, 1992, p. 605.

43 See Chapter 16.

44 Review Body on Senior Salaries, 18th Report, No. 37, Cm. 3094, Appendix E.

45 Joshua Rozenberg, *The Search for Justice*, Sceptre, 1994, pp. 120–1.

46 *Financial Times*, 20 July 1995.

47 *Sunday Times*, 2 October 1994.

48 *Evening Standard*, 22 September 1994.

49 Pannick, *Judges*, p. 66.

50 *Financial Times*, 10 October 1997.

51 Rozenberg, *The Search for Justice*, p. 96.

52 Ironically, recruitment problems at some ranks are now so acute that enlistment and re-enlistment bounties are being reintroduced.

53 When regiments were merged in the 1990s, there were complaints about the loss of historic county regiments. In fact, the old regiments of the line were known by numbers, and did not recruit in any particular parts of the country.

54 Quoted in Cannadine, *The Decline and Fall*, p. 275.

55 Nicholas Timmins, *The Five Giants: A Biography of the Welfare State*, HarperCollins, 1995, p. 120.

56 David Green, *Reinventing Civil Society: The Rediscovery of Welfare Without Politics*, Institute of Economic Affairs, 1993, p. 99.

57 Guy Routh, *Occupation and Pay in Great Britain 1906–1979*, Macmillan, 1980, p. 13.

58 Nicholas Timmins, *The Five Giants: A Biography of the Welfare State*, HarperCollins, 1995, p. 411.

59 Norman Fowler, *Ministers Decide*, Chapmans, 1991, page 194.

60 For the White Paper reforms, see Chapter 9.

61 These were justified. 'We had further plans,' Thatcher recalls, 'to tackle restrictive practices and other inefficiencies in the medical profession, directing the system of merit awards more to merit and less to retirement bonuses, and we planned the general introduction of medical audit ... by which the quality of medical care provided by individual doctors is assessed by their peers.'

Margaret Thatcher, *The Downing Street Years*, HarperCollins, 1993, p. 613.

62 See Chapter 16.

63 *Financial Times*, 15, 16 August 1996.

64 He certainly earned £116,000 in 1997-8. See IDS Pay Review No 206, April 1998, p. 8.

65 Though see Iain Vallance, chairman of BT, in Chapter 15, who told a parliamentary committee he might find the hours of a junior doctor 'relaxing'.

66 Monopolies and Mergers Commission, *Private Medical Services: A Report on Agreements and Practices Relating to Charges For the Supply of Private Medical Services by NHS Consultants*, Cm 2452, February 1994, p. 46, table 7.3.

67 ibid, p. 55, paragraph 7.35.

68 ibid, p. 8, paragrah 3.13, table 3.1

69 ibid, p. 47, paragraph 7.12.

70 ibid, p. 46, table 7.3.

71 Dental Practice Board, Annual Report, 1996.

72 *The Times*, 21 January 1997.

73 Bernard Shaw, *Everybody's Political What's What*, Constable, 1944, p. 81.

74 Routh, *Occupation and Pay in Great Britain*, p. 70, table 2.8.

75 In 1996 the School Teachers' Review Body found vacancy rates of 0.4 per cent in primary schools, 0.3 per cent in secondary schools and 1.4 per cent in special schools. See School Teachers' Review Body, Cm 3095, 5th Report, 1996.

76 Timmins, *The Five Giants*, p. 327.

77 *Financial Times*, 2 April 1997.

78 Lawson, *The View From No. 11*, p. 605.

79 See Chapter 6.

80 *Financial Times*, 14 April 1998.

81 Association of University Teachers, *Efficiency Gains or Quality Losses: How Falling Investment Affects Higher Education's Capacity to Contribute to the UK's Economic Success*, Summer 1996, p. 21.

82 *Financial Times*, 18 August 1995.

CHAPTER EIGHTEEN: *Farmers*

1 *Financial Times*, 5 February, 1996.

2 Quoted in Richard Norton-Taylor, *Whose Land Is It Anyway?*, Turnstone Press, 1982, page 24.

3 Quoted in John Rule, *Albion's People 1714-1815*, Longman, 1992, page 60.

4 See Chapter 9.

5 *Financial Times*, 2, 6 and 8 December 1997 and *Times*, 10 December 1997.

6 A rising pound means that the subsidies payable to farmers through the Common Agricultural Policy (CAP) of the European Union fall when they are translated into subsidies paid to British farmers through the 'green pound' mechanism. A rising pound also makes imported farm goods cheaper than their domestic equivalent.

7 By the summer of 1998, twenty-seven sites where genetically modified crops were being tested had endured a sit-in or sabotage by 'eco-terrorists'. *Financial Times*, 23 July 1998.

8 See Chapter 3.

9 Oliver Walston, 'My Bumper Crop from Brussels', *Sunday Times*, 20 August 1995.

10 *Sunday Times*, 3 September 1995.

11 Frank Field, *Making Welfare Work*, Institute of Community Studies, 1995, page 9.

12 *Financial Times*, 7 December 1996.

13 Adam Smith, *The Wealth of Nations*, Penguin Classics, 1986, Vol. 1, Book 1, pages 268–9.

14 Food manufacturers, of course, can continue to grow as fast or faster by adding value to what farmers produce: frozen peas, yoghurts and semi-skimmed milk are three examples of this.

15 The introduction of milk production quotas by the European Commission in 1984 meant that Britain is no longer allowed to be self-sufficient in milk.

16 Being perishable, unsold milk was not poured into a lake, but turned into mountains of butter and milk powder. The CAP still guarantees minimum prices for milk powder and butter.

17 In 1998 the EC proposed a 2 per cent increase in quota levels, and a 15 per cent cut in prices; farmers would be compensated by cash payments related to the size of their herd. Young farmers would be given half the quota increase to encourage new entrants and the rest would go to farmers in mountainous regions.

18 Set-aside applies only to large farmers. Any farmer producing less than 92 tonnes of cereals can continue in full production. Nor are farmers free to keep their best land in production. The area set aside has to be rotated.

19 *Financial Times*, 10, 25 June, 18 November 1997.

20 *Sunday Times*, 20 August 1995.

21 Graham Harvey, *The Killing of the Countryside*, Vintage, 1998.

22 *Financial Times*, 10 June 1998.

23 Turning milk into butter and skimmed milk powder placed a floor under the price of milk, because they are subject to minimum guaranteed prices under the CAP. By selling milk into intervention, rather than to the major dairy processors, Milk Marque was able to resist the downward pressure on milk prices.

24 As part of the MMB, Dairy Crest belonged to dairy farmers. When the company was floated, two thirds of the shares, worth £120 million, were reserved for the 29,000 dairy farmers. The processing arm of the Scottish Milk Marketing Board was also sold separately, to 3,000 Scottish dairy farmers, as Scottish Pride.

25 *Financial Times*, 2 February 1998.

26 A junior agriculture minister was told in July 1987 that 'ill-informed publicity could lead to hysterical demands for immediate, draconian measures,' and to export bans by other countries. The Phillips inquiry has also heard attempts were made to suppress scientific research and journalistic coverage of BSE, and to manipulate official statements. See *Financial Times*, 2 June 1998.

27 *Financial Times*, 8 July 1998.

28 *Rural England: A Nation Committed to a Living Countryside*, October 1995.

29 *Financial Times*, 12 January 1998.

30 ibid., 26 January 1998. For Sites of Special Scientific Interest (SSSIs), see Chapter 3.

31 Organic food is contaminated by insects and fungi. The lack of animal hygiene increases the risk of tuberculosis and brucellosis (the reluctance to kill badgers is allowing tuberculosis to spread among cattle). Without antibiotics, E. Coli, salmonella and cattle bugs associated with serious conditions, such as Crohn's Disease, may enter the human food chain.

32 *Agriculture in the United Kingdom* 1997, Table 8.1.

33 New Earnings Survey, 1995.

34 *Farm Incomes in the United Kingdom 1996/97*, Ministry of Agriculture, Fisheries and Food, 1997, page 52, Table 2.5.

35 *Farm Incomes in the United Kingdom*, page 14, Table 1.8.

36 *Financial Times*, 25 October 1997.

37 *Farm Incomes in the United Kingdom*, page 19, Table 1.16.

38 *Financial Times*, 23 December 1997.

39 Guy Routh, *Occupation and Pay in Great Britain 1906–1979*, Macmillan, 1980, page 19, Table 1.6; Ministry of Agriculture, *Agriculture in the United Kingdom 1997*, page 52, Table 2.5.

40 MAFF put the value of owner-occupied and tenanted agricultural land and buildings at £50·95 billion in 1996. Three quarters is £38·2 billion. MAFF, *Agriculture in the United Kingdom 1997*, Table 7.3.

41 Christopher Johnson, 'Land of Hope and Glory', Lloyds Bank Economic Bulletin, Number 133, January 1990.

42 Douglas McWilliams and Mark Pragnell, 'The Rich – Are They Different?,' *Prospect*, October 1995.

43 There were tax disadvantages too. The rental income of landowners was taxed at the higher rates for unearned income; they could not reclaim VAT on purchases; Inheritance Tax was payable on sales.

44 Lands Improvement Holdings PLC, Introduction to the Official List, Beeson Gregory, June 1996.

45 Richard Norton-Taylor, *Whose Land Is It Anyway?*, Turnstone Press, 1982, page 64.

46 Andy Wightman, *Who Owns Scotland*, Canongate, 1996, page 150, 165, Table 10.

47 Report of the Committee of Inquiry Into the Acquisition and Occupancy of Agricultural Land, July 1979, Cmnd. 7599, page 10, paragraph 31.

48 Richard Norton-Taylor, *Whose Land Is It Anyway?*, Turnstone Press, 1982, page 66.

49 Conversation with Ian Walter, 1 November 1996.

50 Deloitte & Touche Agriculture, Survey of over 200,000 acres in East Anglia, released 26 September 1996.

CHAPTER NINETEEN *Middle England*

1 Quoted in Andrew Adonis and Stephen Pollard, *A Class Act: The Myth of Britain's Classless Society*, Hamish Hamilton, 1997, page 5.

2 Anthony Sampson, *Company Man: The Rise and Fall of Corporate Life*, HarperCollins, 1995, page 307.

3 Ian Gilmour, *Dancing With Dogma: Britain Under Thatcherism*, Simon & Schuster, 1992, page 278.

4 From Sir John Fortescue, *Learned Commendations of the Politique Laws of England*, written in exile in France in the 1460s. Quoted in Alan Macfarlane. *The Origins of English Individualism*, Blackwell, 1989, page 182.

5 Opinion polls consistently record large majorities in favour of the proposition that Britain is dogged by class war. Adonis and Pollard, *A Class Act*, pages 3–6.

6 ibid., page (ix).

7 Quoted in Anthony Sampson, *The Essential Anatomy of Britain*, Hodder and Stoughton, 1992, page 64.

8 Only 581,000 people, or one in forty-four taxpayers, reported earnings of more than

£50,000. Over three quarters of all taxpayers are earning less than £20,000 a year. *Inland Revenue Statistics*, 1997, Table 3.2.

9 Department of Social Security, *Households Below Average Income: A Statistical Analysis 1979–1994/95*, page 111, Table 8.6.

10 Central Statistical Office, 'National and Sector Balance Sheets 1957–1985,' *Economic Trends*, May 1987, page 98.

11 Inland Revenue Statistics 1997, page 134, Table 13.4. Figures relate to 1994. National value is set present value of anticipated future payments.

12 *Financial Times*, 11 February, 23 July, 14 September 1998. See also, Sedgwick Noble Lowndes survey in *Employee Health Bulletin*, Number 5, September 1998.

13 *Financial Times*, 14 September 1998.

14 ibid., 5 October 1998.

15 ibid., 10 September, 12 October 1998.

16 Inland Revenue Statistics 1997, Table 3.2.

17 *Financial Times*, 29 May 1998.

18 John Hills, Joseph Rowntree Foundation Inquiry Into Income and Wealth, Volume 2, February 1995, page 15.

19 Institute for Fiscal Studies, *Inequality in the UK*, 1997.

20 Adonis and Pollard, *A Class Act*, page 12.

21 See *Social Trends*, 1998 Edition, page 99, chart 5.17.

22 Low Pay Unit and Public Services Tax and Commerce Union, *Out of Poverty Towards Prosperity: A Report on Low Pay and the Minimum Wage*, page 6, Table 1.

23 The Agricultural Wages Council, which sets the pay of farm workers, is the only remaining Council.

24 *Social Trends*, 1998 Edition, Table 5.20, page 101.

25 See Will Hutton, *The State We're In*, Jonathan Cape, 1995, page 193, and John Hills, Joseph Rowntree Foundation Inquiry Into Income and Wealth, Volume 2, February 1995, pages 6–9.

26 Steven Webb, 'How Many Poor?', *Prospect*, November 1997.

27 See Table 3 above.

28 Richard Pryke has criticised official measures of poverty for failing to measure changes over time; double-counting; and ignoring free health, education and other goods provided free by the state. David Green also criticises the treatment of housing costs. See Richard Pryke, *Taking the Measure of Poverty*, Institute of Economic Affairs, 1995; David Green, *Benefit Dependency*, Institute of Economic Affairs, 1998, pages 19–30.

29 Department of Social Security, *Households Below Average Income*, pages 71–2, Table 8.6.

30 John Hills, Rowntree inquiry, Volume 2, February 1995, page 113.

31 *Financial Times*, 4 November 1998.

32 Hermione Parker, *Taxes, Benefits and Family Life: The Seven Deadly Traps*, Institute of Economic Affairs, 1995.

33 Frank Field, *Making Welfare Work*, Institute of Community Studies, 1995.

34 A Goodman and S. Webb, *The Distribution of UK Household Expenditure 1979–1992*, Institute for Fiscal Studies, 1995.

35 Department of Social Security, *Households Below Average Income*, pages 139, 110, Table 8.5 and 8.6.

36 An individual could earn £4,195 a year before paying income tax in 1998–9. He paid a rate of 20 per cent on the next £4,300 of income; 23 per cent on the next £22,800;

and 40 per cent on any income over £27,100. One full-time employee earning £12,000 a year pays £1,666 in income tax, but two part-time people earning £6,000 a year each pay only £722 between them. National Insurance contributions are not payable until a worker earns £64 a week, and the rate is levied at only 2 per cent of £64 plus 10 per cent on the next £421 of earnings. The full-time individual on £12,000 a year will pay £2,141 in employer's and employee's National Insurance contributions, but two part-time workers on £6,000 a year will pay only £634 each, or £1,268. In other words, it is £1,817 a year cheaper to employ two part-time workers.

37 *Financial Times*, 3 October 1996.

38 ibid., 19 June 1998.

39 Lawson, *The View From No 11*, page 428.

40 Hugh Pym and Nick Kochan, *Gordon Brown: The First Year in Power*, Bloomsbury, 1998, page 104.

41 See Chapter 16.

42 Rowntree Inquiry, Volume 1, page 20.

43 *Sunday Times Magazine*, 26 November 1989.

44 Charles Murray, *The Emerging British Underclass*, Institute of Economic Affairs, 1990; *Underclass: The Crisis Deepens*, Institute of Economic Affairs, 1994.

45 ONS, *Social Focus on Ethnic Minorities*, 1996.

46 See Norman Dennis, *The Invention of Permanent Poverty*, Institute of Economic Affairs, 1997.

47 *Financial Times*, 1 October 1997.

48 ibid., 5 November 1998.

49 The Low Pay Commission report also recommended the rates rise to £3.70 and £3.30 from April 2000. The automatic uprating for adults was rejected by the government. It was accepted for younger people, but will now be introduced at a lower rate of £3.00, rising to £3.20 in June 2000, and cover 21-year-olds as well as 18–20-year-olds.

50 Peter Mandelson and Roger Liddle, *The Blair Revolution: Can New Labour Deliver?*, Faber & Faber, 1996, p. 3.

51 Harold Perkin, *The Third Revolution: Professional Elites in the Modern World*, Routledge, 1996, p. 188.

52 David Shonfield, 'The Jobs Mythology', IDS Focus 74, April 1995.

53 *Financial Times*, 8 October 1997.

54 *Financial Times*, 10 November 1997.

55 Inland Revenue Statistics 1997, Tables 6.1 and 6.2.

56 *Financial Times*, 24 January 1998.

57 *Financial Times*, 30 October 1996.

58 Charles Handy, *The Age of Unreason*, Arrow, 1990, p. 24.

59 ibid.

60 Sampson, *The Anatomy of Britain*, page 426.

61 Charles Handy, *The Empty Raincoat*, Arrow 1995, p. 9.

62 Until 1995 mortgage-holders who lost their jobs could rely on the taxpayer to fund half the repayments for the first sixteen weeks, and the full amount thereafter. Mortgage payers now get no help for first nine months, and none then if they have savings of more than £8,000.

63 *Daily Telegraph*, 5 July 1996.

64 Next Steps Report 1997, Cm 3889, p. 192.

65 Inland Revenue Statistics 1997, Table 5.1.

66 TESSAs, PEPS, and ISAs all allowed savings to accumulate tax-free. Savers could place £9,000 a year in a PEP, but ISAs have a £5,000 annual ceiling. The government initially capped total contributions to ISAs at £50,000, but this was later withdrawn.

67 Patricia Morgan, *Farewell to the Family?*, Institute of Economic Affairs, 1995, Appendix, pp. 164–5.

68 *Financial Times*, 10 September 1998.

69 The threshold was raised from £150,000 in 1994–95 to £200,000 in 1996–7 and £215,000 in 1997–98. In 1998–9 it was £223,000.

70 *Economic Trends*, Table 1.6.

71 *Bank of England Quarterly Bulletin*, September 1982, p. 390.

72 Although it is true that equity in a house is the main source of collateral for business start-ups.

73 For the disintegration of the interest rate cartel and the deregulation of consumer lending, see Chapter 27.

74 See Chapter 13.

75 Compare with two fifths in Germany and nearly one third in the United States.

76 *Financial Times*, 6 August 1997.

77 No political party has dared to suggest imposing capital gains tax on the profit from selling a house, or re-imposition of income tax on the imputed rental income (the money saved by owning rather than renting) from owner-occupation.

78 See Alan Macfarlane, *The Origins of English Individualism*, Basil Blackwell, 1979; Susan Reynolds, *Fiefs and Vassals*, Oxford University Press, 1994.

79 Robert Rhodes James, *Anthony Eden*, Papermac, 1987, p. 328.

80 Thomas Mackay of the Charity Organization Society Quoted in Harold Perkin, *The Rise of Professional Society: England Since 1880*, Routledge, 1989, p. 151.

CHAPTER TWENTY: *The Triumph of the PLC*

1 From *Utopia Limited* (1893).

2 *Oxford Dictionary of Quotations* cites John Poynder, *Literary Extracts* (1844). Usually quoted as: 'Did you ever expect a corporation to have a conscience when it has no soul to be damned, and no body to be kicked?'

3 Quoted in Charles Handy, *The Empty Raincoat*, Arrow, 1995, p. 145.

4 The Future Foundation conducted a survey on public attitudes to social issues, and were surprised to find that large proportions of respondents thought companies had responsibilities for health, education, training and the environment as well as employment. See Future Foundation, 'The Responsible Organisation,' in *Financial Times*, 15 December 1997.

5 See Chapter 9.

6 The plan to have 450 specialist schools by 2001. The first, sponsored by Shell, is in Lambeth in south London, *Financial Times*, 5 November 1997; 23, 24 June 1998.

7 The electronics millionaire, Maurice Hatter, gave £1 million to the government literacy campaign in the summer of 1997. *Financial Times*, 29 August 1997 and 17 September 1998.

8 Tony Blair, 'Tough on Red Tape', *Financial Times*, 9 March 1998.

9 From *Pension Funds and Economic Power*, New York, 1959. Quoted in Anthony Sampson, *The Anatomy of Britain*, Hodder & Stoughton, 1962, p. 413.

10 See, for example, Will Hutton, *The State We're In*, Jonathan Cape, 1995; John Plender, *A Stake in the Future: The Stakeholding Solution*, Nicholas Brealey Publishing, 1997; National Association of Pension Funds Limited, *Creative Tension?*, 1990.

11 The Cadbury, Greenbury and Hampel Committees have all produced reports on better 'corporate governance'. See Chapter 15.

12 R. H. Coase, 'Industrial Organization: a Proposal for Research', in *The Firm, The Market and the Law*, University of Chicago Press, 1990, p. 63.

13 John Westergaard and Henrietta Resler, *Class in a Capitalist Society: A Study of Contemporary Britain*, Pelican, 1976, p. 150.

14 See Chapter 11.

15 Budget speech, 2 July 1997.

16 A White Paper published in May 1998, *Fairness at Work*, promised legislation to force employers to recognise trade unions if they can command the support of two in five workers eligible to vote in a ballot. Where a union already has more than half the workforce as members, recognition will be automatic.

17 Handy, *The Empty Raincoat*, pp. 152–3.

18 John Kay, *Foundations of Corporate Success*, Oxford University Press, 1993.

19 See Chapter 32.

20 Arie de Geus, a former manager at Shell, distinguishes between 'living' companies and 'economic' companies. *The Living Company*, Nicholas Brealey Publishing, 1997.

21 'Firms will emerge to organise what would otherwise be market transactions whenever their costs were less than the costs of carrying out the transactions through the market.' See R. H. Coase, *The Firm, The Market and the Law*, University of Chicago Press, 1990, p. 7.

22 Henry Pelling, *A History of British Trade Unionism*, Pelican, 1963, p. 22.

23 For City livery companies, see Chapter 8. See also E. P. Thompson, *The Making of the English Working Class*, Pelican 1968, p. 557.

24 *Financial Times*, 17 November 1997.

25 See Chapter 11.

26 Annual Report of the Certification Officer 1997, paragraph 4.7, p. 18.

27 Annual Report of the Certification Officer 1997, p. 6. There were in addition 107 employers' associations in existence at that date.

28 *Financial Times*, 8 May 1998.

29 ibid., 2 November 1995.

30 ibid., 22 May 1995.

31 Letter to the *Financial Times*, 24 May 1994.

32 Martin Adeney and John Lloyd, *The Miners' Strike 1984–5: Loss Without Limit*, Routledge, 1988, pp. 83–4, 173–6; *Financial Times*, 5 July 1990.

33 Paul Routledge, *Scargill: The Unauthorised Biography*, HarperCollins, 1993, pp. 199–231.

34 ibid., p. 230.

35 *Financial Times*, 5 December 1994.

36 ibid., 29 July, 5 and 20 October 1994.

37 *Sunday Times*, 16 May 1993. There was a libel action against *The Mail on Sunday* over this.

38 *Financial Times*, 20 May 1998; October 1996.

39 In the 1960s and 1970s the larger trade unions invested heavily in lavish headquarters buildings, regional and area offices, and a variety of country retreats. As recently as 1987 the EETPU bought Buxted Park, a Grade II listed health club with private

cinema and deer park near Uckfield. It is now sold. The TGWU still has a residential centre at Eastbourne. UNISON has a private holiday camp at Croyde Bay in north Devon, and rest homes for its members at Bournemouth, Bridlington and Lytham St Anne's.

40 *Financial Times*, 24 May 1995.

41 ibid., 5 September 1997.

42 ibid., 26 May 1995.

43 ibid., 15 December 1993; *The Observer*, 12 December 1993; 27 February 1994; *Independent on Sunday*, 9 January 1994.

44 *Financial Times*, 30 October 1997; 10 June, 22, 26 August, 7 September 1998.

45 ibid., 30 December 1993.

46 ibid., 6 April 1998.

47 Gavin Laird, the ex-general secretary of the AEU, is on the board of several companies in Scotland, including Scottish Television, Britannia Life, GEC Scotland and the Edinburgh Investment Trust.

48 *Financial Times*, 2 March 1998.

49 ibid., 15 September 1998.

50 ibid., 7 September 1998.

51 ibid. In 1993, for example, the TUC got £190,000 from the European Union to campaign for Works Councils in Britain. *Financial Times*, 13 December 1993.

52 John Keay, *The Honourable Company: A History of the English East India Company*, HarperCollins, 1993, p. 25.

53 ibid., 1993, pp. 99, 128.

54 This body of thought, which Smith dubbed the 'mercantile system,' emerged in the sixteenth and seventeenth centuries. Its practical expression was the encouragement of exports and the restriction of imports, primarily because a trade surplus increased the quantity of gold. The grant of overseas trading monopolies by Royal Charter was a perfect expression of its interventionist, nationalistic character.

55 Roy Porter, *English Society in the Eighteenth Century*, Revised Edition, Penguin, 1990, p. 203.

56 See Chapter 29.

57 Both companies still exist; the Royal merged with Sun Alliance and the Royal Exchange with the Guardian. See Chapters 28 and 30.

58 John Carswell, *The South Sea Bubble*, Alan Sutton, 1993, pp. 114–15.

59 Lawyers nullified the effects of the Bubble Act by the device of the 'unincorporated company', which could own property, issue transferable shares and even limit its liability, by using the law of equity. See Barry Supple, *The Royal Exchange: A History of British Insurance 1720–1970*, Cambridge University Press, 1970, p. 60.

60 Mathias, *The First Industrial Nation*, p. 145.

61 Robert L. Heilbroner, *The Essential Adam Smith*, W. W. Norton, 1986, p. 301.

62 John Brewer, *Sinews of Power: War, Money and the English State 1688–1783*, Alfred A. Knopf, 1989, p. 34.

63 By the end of 1997, the market value of domestic equity stood at £1,251,425 million. London Stock Exchange Fact Book, 1998, p. 41.

64 ibid., 1998, p. 59.

65 This is a Department of Trade and Industry Small Firms Statistics Unit estimate. Cited in Trades Union Congress, *The Small Firms Myths*, January 1997, p. 2.

66 The 'effective' number of companies (i.e. not in liquidation or in the course of removal

from the register) on the Companies Register at the end of the 1997-98 financial year. See also Stock Exchange Fact Book, 1998, p. 41.

67 Trades Union Congress, *The Small Firms Myths*, January 1997, p. 2, paragraph 1.3.

68 Inland Revenue Statistics, 1997, Table 11.6.

69 The number of 'registered persons' was 1,595,271.

70 HM Customs Annual Report and Accounts 1995-96 and 1996-97.

71 *Financial Times*, 20 August 1990.

72 One of the obstacles to the much-needed rationalisation of the sector. See Chapter 29.

73 The Wolfson Foundation, a charitable trust, at one stage owned half of the shares in the company. It has since reduced its stake considerably, in order to diversify its risk. The sales were accelerated after the collapse of the Baring Foundation, which held nothing but shares in Baring Brothers, the ruined merchant bank.

74 See Chapter 15.

75 James Saunders, *Nightmare: The Ernest Saunders Story*, Hutchinson, 1989, p. 75.

76 Ivan Fallon and James Strodes, *Takeovers*, Hamish Hamilton, p. 201.

77 *Financial Times*, 24 August 1995.

78 ibid., 26 July 1997.

79 ibid., 7 September 1992.

80 Saunders, *Nightmare*, pp. 59-61.

81 Alden Lank and Monica Wagen, 'Keep Family and Firm Together', *Financial Times*, 31 May 1994.

82 For many years, reluctance to sell reflected tax considerations as well as emotional attachments. Until the 1992 Budget gave private companies and family businesses exemption from Inheritance Tax, families who did not pass shareholdings on to their children at least seven years before they died paid Inheritance Tax at the full rate.

83 *Financial Times*, 1 July 1997.

84 ibid., 2 June 1993.

CHAPTER TWENTY-ONE: *The Multinationals*

1 Quoted in *Financial Times*, 29 November 1991.

2 *Sunday Times*, 28 June 1992.

3 'Why I'm Doing Business with Gadaffi', *Observer*, 3 May 1992.

4 Christopher Tugendhat, *The Multinationals*, Eyre & Spottiswoode, 1971, p. 1.

5 John M. Stopford and Louis Turner, *Britain and the Multinationals*, John Wiley & Sons, 1985, p. 81, Table 4.1.

6 See Table 21.6, p. 775, for the value of foreign-owned assets in Britain. The net value of British foreign assets was £67.5 billion in 1997. See also Stopford and Turner, *Britain and the Multinationals*, pp. 8, 52.

7 Cliff Pratten, *Overseas Investments, Capital Gains and the Balance of Payments*, Institute of Economic Affairs, 1992, pp. 85-6.

8 Stopford and Turner, *Britain and the Multinationals*, p. 61.

9 Until 1979 inward and outward investment was subject to exchange control, the purpose of which was to ensure that investment was financed by methods which protected official holdings of foreign currency. In practice, this meant the authorities discouraged investment outside the sterling area, on the assumption that sterling invested overseas was a net loss to the British economy, though the government tried to accommodate companies wanting to buy foreign assets. See Stopford and Turner, *Britain and the Multinationals*, p. 199.

10 For the failures of the British banks, see Chapter 27.

11 See below.

12 *Financial Times*, 29 April 1996.

13 John H. Dunning, *American Investment in British Manufacturing Industry*, George Allen & Unwin, 1958, p. 40.

14 ibid., pp. 17–18, 23–9, 42–3.

15 Example in *Financial Times*, 24 May 1995.

16 ibid., 1 August 1998.

17 Peter Marsh, 'Innovation Does the Rounds', ibid., 18 September 1995.

18 ibid., 26 February 1998.

19 Norman Tebbit, *Upwardly Mobile*, Weidenfeld & Nicolson, 1988, pp. 248–9.

20 Lord Young, *The Enterprise Years*, Headline, 1990, pp. 270–1.

21 Department of Trade and Industry, *Barriers to Takeovers in the Europe Community*, 1989, Volumes 1–4.

22 First Report from the Trade and Industry Committee, Takeovers and Mergers, 1991.

23 Sir Hector Laing, 'The Balance of Responsibilities', *Creative Tension?*, National Association of Pension Funds, February 1990, p. 63.

24 On 24 October 1929, Richard Whitney, vice president of the New York Stock Exchange and the Morgan broker, was instructed by bankers to go to the floor of the exchange and steady the market by buying stocks. See John Kenneth Galbraith, *The Great Crash*, Pelican, 1975, p. 124.

25 See Chapter 11.

26 Quoted in *Independent*, 7 October 1988.

27 See Chapter 29.

28 In 1993 the *Financial Times* alleged that the 21·7 per cent stake in BP ostensibly bought by the Kuwait Investment Office was actually bought by the Kuwait Petroleum Company, giving the Kuwaitis £600 million in tax credits to which they were not entitled. See *Financial Times*, 24 September 1993.

29 Its fall from power was symbolised by an undignified scuttle from a series of disastrous Spanish investments which cost the Office an estimated $5 billion and saw its reputation shredded in the Spanish courts. Its former partner in Spain, Javier de la Rosa, was arrested on fraud charges in October 1994. The legendary head of the Kuwait Investment Office, Fouad Jaffar, was mysteriously recalled to Kuwait in March 1990, later accused of mismanagement in the Spanish courts by his former employers, and named again in litigation in London. See *Financial Times*, 25 October, 1982; 23 July 1983.

30 Costain is still controlled by Arab interests. By 1997, after various shenanigans, they had a 19.7 per cent stake (down from 25.35 per cent), and the Saudis 9.7 per cent (down from 12 per cent). Costain is chaired by Dr Azman Firdaus Shafii, a Malaysian who is also vice-chair of Intria, a Malaysian construction group with a 37 per cent stake in Costain.

31 *Financial Times*, 4 September and 6 and 10 October 1998.

32 Dunning, *American Investment in British Manufacturing Industry*, p. 307.

33 William Davis, *Merger Mania*, Constable, 1970, p. 158.

34 Christopher Tugendhat, *The Multinationals*, Eyre & Spottiswoode, 1971, p. 214.

35 Dunning, *American Investment in British Manufacturing Industry*, p. 49.

36 Stopford and Turner, *Britain and the Multinationals*, p. 231. Some years before the sale to Peugeot, this blatant bad faith had not deterred the government from trying to persuade

Chrysler to keep its Linwood plant open with a package of cheap loans and an agreement to fund all its losses.

37 Dunning, *American Investment in British Manufacturing Industry*, pp. 36, 47.

38 ibid., pp. 38, 46.

39 Stopford and Turner, *Britain and the Multinationals*, p. 60.

40 Dunning, *American Investment in British Manufacturing Industry*, pp. 23, 42.

41 Davis, *Merger Mania*, p. 152.

42 Top 100 UK Exporters, *Financial Times*, October 1997.

43 Quoted in Stephen Thomsen and Phedon Nicolaides, *The Evolution of Japanese Direct Investment in Europe: Death of a Transistor Salesman*, Harvester Wheatsheaf, 1991, p. 125.

44 *Financial Times*, 13 December 1994.

45 ibid., 21 October 1997.

46 ibid., 5 May 1998.

47 ibid., 11 June 1998.

48 Invest in Britain Bureau, Successes by Country, Major Investments 1979–97.

49 *Financial Times*, 10 and 22 December 1997.

50 Davis, *Merger Mania*, p. 153.

51 *Financial Times*, 22 August 1995; 12 December 1997.

52 Bank of England, *Practical Issues Arising from the Introduction of the Euro*, No. 6, 10 December 1997, p. 9.

53 Thomsen and Nicolaides, *The Evolution of Japanese Direct Investment*, p. 16.

54 The unlucky bidder was Hamamatsu Photonics, which wanted to buy Thorn EMI's light-sensing business. See *Financial Times*, 7 August 1991.

55 See Chapter 9.

56 Letter, *Sunday Times*, 5 October 1997.

57 *Financial Times*, 6, 15 October, 16 December 1997.

58 ibid., 11 July 1996.

59 ibid., 22 October 1997.

60 ibid., 8 March 1996.

61 Ernst & Young, *Inward Investment Activities of Local Authorities in England*, March 1996.

62 There are regional development agencies for London, the South East, the South West, the Eastern region, East Midlands, West Midlands, Yorkshire and Humberside, the North West and the North East. It is likely that they will eventually absorb the budgets and responsibilities of the seventy-eight TECs, though these are not initially being devolved from the Department for Education and Employment. Separate arrangements are being made in Wales and Scotland, where the existing agencies are being merged into single entities. See Chapter 9.

63 *Financial Times*, 7 September 1998.

64 ibid., 13 October 1998.

65 Quoted in Stopford and Turner, *Britain and the Multinationals*, p. 159.

66 *Financial Times*, 31 May and 1 June 1994.

67 The grant was worth £13 million. *Financial Times*, 14 October 1997.

68 In all, Abbey National spent £5.8 million on the call centre. *Financial Times*, 5 November 1997.

69 *Financial Times*, 18 October 1995.

70 ibid., 17 January and 22 February 1997.

71 ibid., 7 January 1998.
72 ibid., 30 September and 2 October 1996.
73 ibid., 24 October 1998.
74 ibid., 13 January 1995.

CHAPTER TWENTY-TWO: *Shopping*

1 Bill Bryson, *Notes From a Small Island*, Black Swan, 1996, p. 39.
2 Edited by Robert Heilbroner, *The Essential Adam Smith*, Norton & Company, 1986, p. 284.
3 ODQ, p. 490:5.
4 *The Price*, Act 1.
5 *Observer*, 25 April 1993.
6 Anthony Sampson, *The Changing Anatomy of Britain*, Hodder & Stoughton, 1982, p. 308.
7 The six are Marks & Spencer, Tesco, J. Sainsbury, Boots, Great Universal Stores and Kingfisher. London Stock Exchange Fact Book 1998, p. 58.
8 Leslie Hannah, *The Rise of the Corporate Economy*, Second Edition, 1983, Appendix 3, pp. 185–192.
9 Budget speech, 2 July 1997.
10 Paul Langford, *A Polite and Commercial People: England 1727–1783*, Oxford University Press, 1989, pp. 62–3.
11 Roy Porter, *English Society in the Eighteenth Century*, Penguin, Revised Edition, 1990, p. 190.
12 Alison Adburgham, *Shops and Shopping*, Second Edition, Barrie & Jenkins, 1989, p. 231.
13 ibid., pp. 217, 234–5.
14 ibid., p. 142.
15 Michael Winstanley, 'Concentration and Competition in the Retail Sector, c. 1800–1990', in *Business Enterprise in Modern Britain*, edited by Maurice Kirby and Mary Rose, Routledge, 1994, pp. 236–62.
16 Asa Briggs, *Victorian Things*, Penguin, 1990, pp. 283–5.
17 Whiteley's was the shop which supplied young men for dancing and coffins to bury them. Adburgham, *Shops and Shopping*, pp. 235–6.
18 *Financial Times*, 21 December 1996.
19 ibid., 13 October 1997.
20 Harvey Nichols was founded in Knightsbridge in 1813 by Benjamin Harvey. At his death, Benjamin left the business to his daughter Elizabeth. She followed his advice to take the silk buyer, Colonel Nichols, into partnership. See Adburgham, *Shops and Shopping*, p. 161.
21 Its controversial advertisements, created by Oliviero Toscani, have featured the bloodied clothes of a dead Croatian soldier, a dying victim of AIDS, and a new-born baby attached to the umbilical cord.
22 Fiona MacCarthy, *William Morris*, Faber & Faber, 1994, pp. 430–1.
23 Asa Briggs, *Victorian Things*, Penguin, 1988, p. 16.
24 John Stevenson, *British Society 1914–45*, Penguin, 1984, p. 113.
25 *Financial Times*, 16 August 1996, 16 April 1998.
26 ibid., 19 and 25 March 1997.

27 ibid., 24 August 1995.

28 ibid., 25, 27, 28 August 1997; 17, 20 July and 1 October 1998.

29 ibid., 30 November 1995.

30 ibid., 8 July 1994.

31 Michael Winstanley, 'Concentration and Competition in the Retail Sector, c. 1800–1990', in *Business Enterprise in Modern Britain*, edited by Maurice Kirby and Mary Rose, Routledge, 1994, pp. 245–6.

32 Peter Mathias, *The First Industrial Nation*, Routledge, 1983, p. 360.

33 Quoted in *Financial Times*, 24 October 1995.

34 ibid., 22 January 1997.

35 *The Economist*, 31 May 1997.

36 *Financial Times*, 31 July 1997; 21, 26 May 1998.

37 Multiple retailers are those, like Marks & Spencer or Tesco, which trade from multiple sites rather than a single set of permanent premises.

38 John Stevenson, *British Society 1914–45*, Penguin, 1984, p. 113.

39 J. B. Priestley, *English Journey*, Penguin, 1977, p. 376.

40 The Sea Fish Industry Authority in Edinburgh estimates that in 1982 multiples accounted for 9.9 per cent of fresh fish sales, and fishmongers 57.8 per cent. In 1997 the proportions were 59.4 per cent and 23.8 per cent.

41 The Meat and Livestock Commission estimates that in 1997 butchers accounted for 16.2 per cent of total meat purchases, and supermarkets for 69.9 per cent. If freezer centres and the Co-op are included, the share controlled by the multiples rises to 77.3 per cent.

42 Research by Verdict, the retail consultants, reported in the *Financial Times*, 30 January 1997.

43 *Financial Times*, 11 September 1996 and 24 October 1997. Estimate by Verdict, the retail consultants. Nobody really knows how many newsagents there are in Britain. Keynote, another research consultancy, came up with an estimate of 33,225 in 1995.

44 Waterstone's is now planning to turn the old Simpson's of Piccadilly building into an American-style cultural superstore stocking 300,000 titles. *Financial Times*, 28 October 1998.

45 The Association claimed to have lost 119 members over the year, a higher rate of loss than usual.

46 *Financial Times*, 18 June 1996.

47 Office of Fair Trading, *Competition in the Supply of Petrol in the UK*, May 1998, p. 42, table 8.13.

48 Office of Fair Trading, Press Release accompanying publication of *Competition in the Supply of Petrol in the UK*, 18 May 1998.

49 The exact figures are 19,465 in 1990 and 14,824 in 1997. See Institute of Petroleum, *UK Retail Marketing Survey 1998: A Special Supplement to Petroleum Review*, p. 12.

50 Office of Fair Trading, Press Release accompanying publication of *Competition in the Supply of Petrol in the UK*, 18 May 1998.

51 *Financial Times*, 30 July 1996.

52 Keynote Report 1996, Convenience Stores.

53 *Financial Times*, 15 January 1998.

54 Somerfield plc, Report and Accounts 1997–98, pp. 4–5.

55 *Financial Times*, 28 and 29 October 1998.

56 Personal imports are restricted to people who bring their existing car from abroad or exercise their right to buy in the (usually left-hand drive) European markets.

57 *Financial Times*, 15 and 16 October 1998.
58 Office of Fair Trading, Statement, October 1998.
59 *Financial Times*, 10 June and 1 August 1998.
60 ibid., 20 October 1998.
61 ibid., 5 January 1998.
62 The £23 billion second-hand car market is even more fragmented. Transactions are divided among an estimated 14,000 Arthur Daleys.
63 *Financial Times*, 17 October 1996.
64 The 130 stores were later bought out of receivership by Ciro Citerrio, a menswear group.
65 *Financial Times*, 21 October 1996.
66 ibid., 21 June 1996.
67 ibid., 24 September 1998.
68 Meat and Livestock Commission, Press Release, 27 November 1998.
69 J. Sainsbury took a full page advertisement in the *Sunday Times* to rebut the allegations. See Andrew Neil, *Full Disclosure*, Pan, 1997, pp. 415–16.
70 *Financial Times*, 19 October 1994.
71 ibid., 3 July 1993.
72 The action was based on the fact that planning regulations are lighter for wholesalers than they are for retailers, and the warehouse clubs were classified as wholesalers.
73 *Financial Times*, 9 December 1995.
74 ibid., 3 October 1997.
75 ibid., 26 September 1995.
76 *Sunday Telegraph*, 8 March 1998.
77 *Financial Times*, 13 November 1997, 15 December 1995.
78 ibid., 11, 16 February 1995.

CHAPTER TWENTY-THREE: *Leisure*

1 *Ethics*, Quoted in Witold Rybczynski, *Waiting for the Weekend*, Viking, 1991, p. 21.
2 *The Conquest of Happiness*, Chapter 14.
3 John Stevenson, *British Society 1914–45*, Penguin, 1984, p. 381.
4 Lord Chesterfield, *Letters to His Son and Others*, Everyman Edition, 1986, p. 223.
5 From *An Inquiry Into the Causes of the Late Increase in Robbers*, 1751. Quoted in John Rule, *Albion's People: English Society 1714–1815*, Longman, 1992, p. 44.
6 Quoted in Jose Harris, *Private Lives: Public Spirit: Britain 1870–1914*, Penguin, 1994, p. 135.
7 See Chapter 22.
8 *Financial Times*, 30 September 1998.
9 *Financial Times*, 2 June, 19 November 1997, 2 October 1998.
10 Blockbuster was the creation of H. Wayne Huizenga, an American entrepreneur. From one store in Dallas in 1985, the chain now has 6,000 outlets worldwide. It first entered the British market in 1989, and currently has 670 outlets in Britain.
11 Vanessa Houlder, 'The Pub Should Be Round About Here, the Computer Says', *Financial Times*, 26 April 1998.
12 *Sunday Telegraph*, 24 September 1995.
13 *The Supply of Beer*, March 1989, Cm. 651, paragraph 1.23.
14 Lord Young, *The Enterprise Years*, Headline, 1990, p. 319.

15 Evidence submitted to the Agriculture Select Committee by the Office of Fair Trading, 1993. Increases in excise duty and VAT have also played a part.

16 *Financial Times*, 22–25 September 1997.

17 John Burnett, *Plenty and Want: A Social History of Diet in England From 1815 to the Present Day*, Methuen, 1983, pp. 61, 199.

18 Quoted in Arthur Marwick, *The Deluge*, Second Edition, Macmillan, 1991, p. 105.

19 Social Trends, 1996 Edition, HMSO, p. 221

20 ibid., p. 222.

21 Burnett, *Plenty and Want*, p. 348.

22 In 1996 McDonald's operated 21,022 company owned, franchised, affiliate operated or satellite restaurants in 101 countries: equivalent to a McDonald's for every 268,000 people on earth.

23 *Financial Times*, 9 February 1995.

24 Roy Porter, *English Society in the Eighteenth Century*, Penguin, Revised Edition, 1990, p. 238.

25 Mark Clapson, *A Bit of a Flutter: Popular Gambling and English Society 1823–1961*, Manchester University Press, 1992, p. 29.

26 Governments ran lotteries at various times from 1569, and operated one continuously from 1709 to 1824, applying the proceeds to what would now be called 'good causes' as well as bad.

27 The Tote operates a monopoly of totalisator or pool betting systems, in which all bets go into a single pot and the winners are paid out by dividing the pool. The bigger the pool, the bigger the potential pay-outs.

28 Clapson, *A Bit of a Flutter*, p. 72.

29 See Chapter 24.

30 Pool Promoters' Association.

31 One of the many hidden tax increases imposed by the government was a sharp increase in gaming duty in the 1998 Budget.

32 The Gaming Board for Great Britain, Annual Report 1997/98, Appendix 1.

33 ibid.

34 *Financial Times*, 30 October 1998.

35 The term 'wake' applied originally to the all-night vigils which preceded the great Christian festivals: it became associated with any festive occasion, particularly in the north of England.

36 National Caravan Council, British Caravan Industry Statistics, 1995.

37 The Sunday Times Rich List 1998 has identified three caravan park millionaires: Peter Harris (£60 million), John Cook (£32 million) and John Woodward (£35 million).

38 Civil Aviation Authority, *Atol Business*, Issue 12, July 1998.

39 George Brown, *In My Way*, Penguin, 1972, p. 263.

40 See Chapter 11.

41 *Financial Times*, 19 December 1995; 29 October 1998.

42 ibid., 29 October 1998.

43 ibid., 7 October 1998.

44 ibid., 22 June 1996.

CHAPTER TWENTY-FOUR: *The Media*

1 George Brown, *In My Way*, Penguin, 1972, p. 269.
2 *Financial Times*, 11 September 1996.
3 ibid., 13 November 1997.
4 ibid., 25 January 1996.
5 *The Economist*, 8 January 1994.
6 Remark to Rudyard Kipling.
7 William Shawcross, *Murdoch,* Pan, 1993, p. 550.
8 George Brown, *In My Way*, Penguin, 1972, p. 268. Brown suffered badly at the hands of the press, especially after backing the proprietors of the *Daily Mirror* in a takeover bid for the *Daily Herald* at a time when he was receiving a retainer from the newspaper.
9 T. S. Eliot, *Notes Towards a Definition of Culture*, Faber & Faber, 1962, p. 87.
10 Anthony Sampson, *The Changing Anatomy of Britain*, Hodder & Stoughton, 1982, p. 395.
11 Bill Deedes, *Dear Bill: W. F. Deedes Reports*, Pan, 1998, pp. 297–8.
12 Shawcross, *Murdoch*, p. 158.
13 The *Independent*, 2 September 1993.
14 Stephen Glover, *Paper Dreams*, Jonathan Cape, 1993, p. 72.
15 *Today* was owned for a time by Tiny Rowland. In 1995 his adversary, Mohammed al Fayed, made an offer to buy the newspaper.
16 Stephen Glover, *Paper Dreams*, Jonathan Cape, 1993, p. 27.
17 *Financial Times*, 6 April 1998.
18 Rupert Murdoch did a stint on the paper in the early 1950s. See Shawcross, *Murdoch*, p. 80.
19 Peter Chippindale and Chris Horrie, *Stick It Up Your Punter! The Rise and Fall of The Sun*, Mandarin, 1992, p. 227. The *Sunday Sport* was another beneficiary of new technology. It was launched with an initial staff of nine.
20 Sampson, *The Anatomy of Britain*, p. 124.
21 E. P. Thompson, *The Making of the English Working Class*, Pelican, 1977, pp. 791–800.
22 Quoted in Shawcross, *Murdoch*, p. 459.
23 Raymond Williams, *Communications*, Pelican, 1976, pp. 24–5.
24 For the BBC, see Chapter 12.
25 In April 1998 the government fulfilled a commitment made in Opposition by lifting the broadcasting ban on BT from 1 January 2001.
26 Peacock Report, paragraph 592.
27 Andrew Davidson, *Under the Hammer*, Mandarin, 1993, Appendix 1, p. 274.
28 See Table 3. Independent Television Commission Press Release, 25 November 1998.
29 Two satellite channels, BBC World and BBC Prime, began broadcasting into Europe in January 1995.
30 Peter Chippindale and Suzanne Franks, *Dished! The Rise and Fall of British Satellite Broadcasting*, Simon & Schuster, 1991, p. (xi.).
31 BSkyB floated on the Stock Exchange in December 1994. At the end of 1998, 34.75 per cent of the company was in public hands. The other major shareholders are News International (39.78 per cent), Pathe (16.91 per cent), Granada (4.29 per cent) and Pearson PLC (4.27 per cent) and still range up to 100 per cent in contracts between cable companies and other programme suppliers.

32 The minimum carriage rule specifies that eight out of ten cable subscribers must purchase all available channels. BSkyB initially insisted that all subscribers receive all channels, but the OFT reduced this to 80 per cent. Minimum carriage requirements are not unique to BSkyB and still range up to 100 per cent in contracts between cable companies and other programme suppliers.

33 Independent Television Commission, Factfile, 1998.

34 Who's Who in Cable and Satellite UK, Edition 25, July 1998, Table 1, p. 9.

35 Minimum carriage requirements were prohibited in all new pay-TV contracts from 1 July 1998, and from all existing contracts where material is broadcast in digital format from the same date. See ITC Press Release, 26 June 1998.

36 ONDigital is a 50:50 venture between Carlton Communications and Granada Group.

37 The BBC was allowed to keep the £244 million proceeds from privatisation of its transmission network, provided they were invested in digital technology. See Chapter 12.

38 The licence was awarded to Digital One, a consortium formed by GWR (57 per cent), the cable company NTL (21.5 per cent) and Talk Radio (21.5 per cent). *The Economist*, 27 June 1998; *Financial Times*, 24 June 1998, 13 October 1998.

39 *Financial Times*, 29 October 1998.

40 For the details of the 1996 Broadcasting Act, see footnote 46 below.

41 The Scottish titles, *The Scotsman* and *Scotland on Sunday*, were sold in a separate transaction to the Barclay twins, sometime owners of *The European*.

42 *Financial Times*, 25 September 1997.

43 *Financial Times*, 3 December 1997.

44 Margaret Thatcher, *The Downing Street Years*, HarperCollins, 1993, p. 637.

45 European Commission, Green Paper on Media Concentration in the Internal Market, COM (92) 480 of 23 December 1992.

46 The 1996 Broadcasting Act allowed newspaper groups to buy television stations up to 15 per cent of the total national audience, provided they had less than 20 per cent of national newspaper circulation, and local radio stations, provided they had no local paper with more than 30 per cent of local circulation. Television companies were allowed to buy newspapers and cable and satellite television broadcasters, provided they did not acquire influence over more than 15 per cent of the national television audience. Radio broadcasters were allowed to own thirty-five licences in place of the previous twenty, but only to the same limit of 15 per cent of the national audience. No media company is allowed to own more than 10 per cent of all media or more than 20 per cent of one medium.

47 *The Money Programme*, BBC2, 21 May 1995. Quoted in the *Financial Times*, 22 May 1995.

48 'When More Doesn't Mean Better', ibid., 22 January 1997.

49 *Financial Times*, 28 January 1997.

50 Quoted in Raymond Williams, *Communications*, Pelican, 1976, p. 104.

51 Quoted in Roy Porter, *English Society in the Eighteenth Century*, Second Edition, Penguin, 1990, p. 223.

CHAPTER TWENTY-FIVE: *The Sports Business*

1 *Financial Times*, 4 August 1993.

2 Jason Tomas, *Soccer Czars*, Mainstream, 1996, p. 21.

3 Kent County Cricket Club, Report and Accounts for 1995–96, pp. 11–12.

4 *Financial Times*, 21 February 1998.

5 See Chapter 16.

6 *The Times*, 10 April 1997.

7 Jason Tomas, *Soccer Czars*, Mainstream, 1996, p. 10.

8 David Conn, *The Football Business: Fair Game in the '90s?*, Mainstream Publishing, 1997, p. 23.

9 *The Times*, 31 July 1998.

10 ibid., 16 April 1998; 10 April 1997.

11 *The Times*, 24 October 1998.

12 Stefan Szymanski, 'Players' Wages and the Implications for Club Profits', *Soccer Analyst*, No. 2, 1997, pp. 2–5.

13 *Daily Telegraph*, 20 August 1995.

14 The same correlation between individual performance and reward can be observed (at a much lower level) in cricket, the most individual of team games, where the compilation of exhaustive statistics about batsmen and bowlers is part of the pleasure.

15 Georgian boxing stars – Tom Crib, Jim Belcher, Dutch Sam, Bill Stevens the Nailer and Daniel Mendoza – fought not only for money but to sell commemorative mugs and plaques and publish instruction manuals and memoirs. Their Victorian successors, such as Tom Sayers, also kept the potters of Staffordshire busy. See Roy Porter, *English Society in the Eighteenth Century*, Penguin, Second Edition, 1990, p. 237; Asa Briggs, *Victorian Things*, Penguin, 1990, p. 149.

16 Press Release, All England Lawn Tennis & Croquet Club, 28 April 1998.

17 Conn, *The Football Business*, p. 227.

18 A Belgian professional footballer, Jean-Marc Bosman, found that when his two-year contract with RFC Liège expired in 1990, he faced a choice of staying on at a quarter of his existing wage or transferring to Dunkerque. But the French club could not afford the transfer fee. The cost, worked out according to a complicated formula drawn up by (UEFA), put a BFr20 million price on his head against a notional value of BFr4.8 million. The transfer deal fell through. Bosman took his case to the European Court, which ruled in his favour. He also contested the 'three plus two' rule (no club could field more than three foreigners plus two 'assimilated' nationals on the field) and won on that count too. It had nothing to do with his case, but lawyers thought it would help to attack on two fronts. The aim of the 'three-plus-two' rule was to prevent the richest clubs buying all the best players, but the European Court ruled that it restricted the free movement of players.

19 It is said that by the mid-1980s, Steve Ovett could charge £5,000 a race and Steve Cram up to £12,000.

20 Conn, *The Football Business*, p. 228.

21 Alex Fynn and Lynton Guest, *Out of Time: Why Football Isn't Working*, Pocket Books, 1994, pp. 55–6.

22 There was a 232-day strike by major league baseball players in 1994–5.

23 Szymanski, *Soccer Analyst*, No. 2, p. 3.

24 See Peter Sloane, 'The Economics of Sport: An Overview', in *Economic Affairs*, Vol. 17, No. 3, September 1997, pp. 2–6.

25 Robert Simmons, 'The Implications of the Bosman Ruling for Football Transfer Markets', in *Economic Affairs*, Vol. 17, No. 3, September 1997, pp. 13–18.

26 The flow of transfer expenditure between divisions has fallen since the formation of the Premier League in 1992–3. See Bill Gerrard, 'The Economics of the Transfer Market', in *Soccer Analyst*, No. 6, 1997, pp. 1–4.

27 In 1993, two years before Bosman won his verdict at the European Court, Touche Ross reckoned the Premier League players were worth a total of £250 million and their First Division equivalents £80 million. See Gerry Boon, *Financial Times*, 30 September 1993.

28 Bill Gerrard, 'The Economics of the Transfer Market', in *Soccer Analyst*, No. 6, 1997, pp. 1–4.

29 Tomas, *Soccer Czars*, p. 27.

30 Matthew Glendinning, 'Transfers and Share Price', in *Soccer Analyst*, No. 6, p. 6.

31 *Financial Times*, 5 November 1997.

32 Ibid., 23 October 1998.

33 Conn, *The Football Business*, p. 228.

34 Quoted in Stephen Aris, *Sportsbiz*, Hutchinson, 1990, p. 16.

35 Ibid., p. 15.

36 Ibid., pp. 37–8.

37 Alex Fynn and Lynton Guest, *Out of Time: Why Football Isn't Working*, Pocket, 1994, pp. 207–9, 219.

38 These figures are probably optimistic. *Financial Times*, 6 March 1998.

39 Aris, *Sportsbiz*, p. 81.

40 Alex Fynn and Lynton Guest, *The Secret Life of Football*, Queen Anne Press, 1989, pp. 118–147; Aris, *Sportsbiz*, p. 148.

41 There are reasons to think this, too, may be optimistic. See below.

42 *Financial Times*, 18 April 1997.

43 Fynn and Guest, *Out of Time*, p. 82.

44 *Financial Times*, 16 July 1998.

45 ibid., 25 May 1985.

46 Aris, *Sportsbiz*, p. 123.

47 'What we were saying was that the top athletes have got to support the package,' the head of ITV sport told Stephen Aris. 'After all, they're the ones that put the bums on seats.' *Sportsbiz*, p. 121.

48 Fynn and Guest, *The Secret Life of Football*, p. 138.

49 Aris, *Sportsbiz*, p. 67.

50 ibid., pp. 144–5.

51 Stefan Syzmanski, 'Fields of Red Ink', in *Soccer Analyst*, No. 7, 1997, pp. 1–4; Deloitte & Touche Annual Review of Football Finance, 1998, Appendix 1.

52 Deloitte & Touche Annual Review of Football Finance, 1996.

53 ibid., 1998, Appendix 2.

54 *Sunday Telegraph*, 9 February 1997.

55 Of the revenue received from BSkyB, 50 per cent is shared equally between all clubs; 25 per cent is shared according to league position; and 25 per cent according to live matches shown.

56 *Financial Times*, 24 July 1997; 27 May 1998.

57 ibid., 10 August 1996.

58 ibid., 20 March 1998.

59 ibid., 21 August, 4 September, 7 and 16 October 1998.

60 Tomas, *Soccer Czars*, p. 186.

61 Fynn and Guest, *Out of Time*, pp. 46–7.

62 *Financial Times*, 21 August 1995.

63 Less surprisingly, they are also becoming a heritage item. A company called Toffs (The

Old Fashioned Football Shirt Company) recreates classic, 100 per cent cotton football shirts worn by players between 1885 and 1975, and sells them for £33.99 apiece. They are, tellingly, free of sponsorship logos. See *Financial Times*, 10 March 1997.

64 *The Economist*, 19 August 1995.

65 Comment at a Manchester United conference in 1997.

66 *Sunday Times*, 13 September 1998.

67 *Financial Times*, 26 February 1996.

68 Conn, *The Football Business*, pp. 38–48.

69 Tomas, *Soccer Czars*, p. 79.

70 ibid., p. 22; Conn, *The Football Business*, p. 19.

71 *Financial Times*, 8 July 1996.

72 Neil Bradford, 'Pay-per-view Football: Time to Choose,' *Soccer Analyst*, No. 7, 1997, pp. 4–8.

73 The regional nature of the division turned Rugby Union into a game of the upper and middle classes, except in South Wales. Football had a similar class-based row between the amateurs of the Football Association and the professionals of the Football League, but they were able to agree an amicable division of labour in which the Association set the rules and the League ran the leagues.

74 *Financial Times*, 3 October 1997 and 15 October 1998.

75 *Sunday Times*, 18 December 1994.

76 *Independent on Sunday*, 22 January 1995.

77 Philip Mason, *The English Gentleman: The Rise and Fall of an Ideal*, Pimlico, 1993, pp. 82 and 98.

78 See Chapter 23.

79 Quoted in Stephen Aris, *Sportsbiz: Inside the Sports Business*, Hutchinson, 1990, p. 14.

80 ibid., p. 102.

81 *Financial Times*, 15 November 1996.

82 Conn, *The Football Business*, pp. 292–7.

83 Fabian Society, *Football United: New Labour, The Task Force and the Future of the Game*, 1997.

84 Touche Ross Football Industry Team, *The Taxman Cometh! The Importance of PAYE to Football Clubs*, July 1993, p. 1.

85 Fynn and Guest, *Out of Time*, p. 343.

86 *What is the Sports Council?* Factsheet, Sports Council.

87 Figures supplied by the Sports Council. The Sports Council was until recently a byword for profligate bureaucracy. It was comprehensively reorganised in 1996.

88 Bill Buford, *Among the Thugs*, Mandarin, 1992, pp. 232, 305, 317.

89 The Sports Council Factsheet.

90 *Financial Times*, 14 April 1997.

91 Speech by Sheikh Mohammed to the Gimcrack Dinner at York, reported in *The Times*, 10 December 1997. See also *Financial Times*, 15, 17, and 30 January 1998.

92 *Sunday Times*, 17 September 1995.

93 *Financial Times*, 1 September 1995.

94 Sports Council, *Valuing Volunteers in Sport*.

CHAPTER TWENTY-SIX: *The Charity Industry*

1 In Philanthropy and the State or Social Politics, P. S. King, 1908. Quoted in Robert Whelan, *The Corrosion of Charity: From Moral Renewal to Contract Culture*, Institute of Economic Affairs, July 1996, p. 60.

2 'Let Charity Begin With Charities', *The Times*, 10 December 1997.

3 Milton Friedman, *Capitalism and Freedom*, University of Chicago Press, 1962, p. 133.

4 *Financial Times*, 2 July 1993.

5 Paul Voller, 'Incorporation of Charities: A Legal Perspective', in the 1997 Charity Finance Yearbook, pp. 118–121.

6 *Independent on Sunday*, 16 January 1994.

7 Quoted in Anthony Sampson, *The New Anatomy of Britain*, Hodder & Stoughton, 1971, p. 421.

8 *Sunday Telegraph*, 29 October 1995.

9 The income figure is for England and Wales only. If charities in Scotland (£0.4 billion) Northern Ireland (£1.4 billion) are added, it rises to £14.9 billion. See Charities Aid Foundation, *Dimensions of the Voluntary Sector*, 1998 Edition, p. 1; NCVO Publications, *The Overall Size and Contribution of the UK Voluntary Sector*, 1998.

10 Les Hems and Andrew Passey, *The UK Voluntary Sector Statistical Almanac 1996*, NCVO Publications, 1996, pp. (vi), 21, 25.

11 Growth in gross income levelled off between 1994 and 1997, but staff costs increased by 8 per cent in the same period, with the largest increases occurring at the largest charities. See NCVO PUblications, *The Overall Size and Contribution of the UK Voluntary Sector*, 1998.

12 NCVO Survey of Job Roles and Salaries in the Voluntary Sector, 1997–98.

13 Tom Lloyd, *The Charity Business*, John Murray, 1993, p. 160. His resignation from Barclays was reported in the *Financial Times*, 2 March 1991.

14 Caritas Data, *Baring Asset Management Top 3,000 Charities* 1997.

15 *Financial Times*, 18 March 1996.

16 Charity Commission Annual Report, 1995.

17 *The Times*, 13 August 1997.

18 *Financial Times*, 23 February 1993.

19 ibid., 31 October 1995.

20 Lloyd, *The Charity Business*, 1993, p. 35.

21 *Evening Standard*, 20 September 1993.

22 Andrew Jack, 'Spectres Linger at War on Want Battleground', *Financial Times*, 16 December 1993.

23 Lloyd, *The Charity Business*, p. 122.

24 Barry Knight, *Voluntary Action*, Centris, October 1993, p. 269.

25 Lloyd, *The Charity Business*, pp. 4–5.

26 Tim Dickson, 'Lesson From Charities to the Business Sector', *Financial Times*, 8 March 1995.

27 Lloyd, *The Charity Business*, pp. 169, 171.

28 ibid., p. 24.

29 *Financial Times*, 7 October 1995.

30 *Sunday Telegraph*, 27 August 1995.

31 Ruth K. McLure, *Coram's Children: The London Foundling Hospital in the Eighteenth Century*, Yale, 1981, pp. 41–2.

32 *Independent on Sunday*, 16 January 1997.
33 Frank Prochaska, *Royal Bounty: The Making of a Welfare Monarchy*, Yale University Press, 1995.
34 Lloyd, *The Charity Business*, p. 152
35 *NGO Finance Magazine*, Charity Shops Survey 1998, July/August 1998.
36 *NGO Finance*, June/July 1996, p. 24
37 Hems and Passey, *The UK Voluntary Sector Statistical Almanac 1996*, p. 42, NCVO Publications, *The Overall Size and Contribution of the UK Voluntary Sector*, 1998.
38 Charities Aid Foundation, *Dimensions of the Voluntary Sector*, 1998 Edition, p. 19.
39 *Daily Telegraph*, 15 October 1996.
40 Howard Hurd and Mark Lattimer, *The Millionaire Givers: Wealth and Philanthrophy in Britain*, Directory of Social Change, 1994, p. (xi).
41 The NCVO puts it rather higher for the sector as a whole, at 4.3p in the pound. See Cathy Pharaoh, 'CAF's Top 500 Corporate Donors in 1996–97', in *Dimensions of the Voluntary Sector*, 1998 Edition, Charities Aid Foundation, 1998, pp. 112–126.
42 Les Hems and Andrew Passey, *The UK Voluntary Sector Statistical Almanac 1996*, NCVO, 1996, p. 3, p. 44, Table 3.1; David Logan, 'Companies in the Community – Getting the Measure', in *Dimensions of the Voluntary Sector*, 1998 Edition, Charities Aid Foundation, 1998, pp. 105–111.
43 Lloyd, *The Charity Business*, p. 28.
44 ibid., p. 2.
45 Bob Worcester, 'The Ethics Business', in Business in the Community Annual Report 1998, p. 6.
46 *Financial Times*, 2 July 1993.
47 Lloyd, *The Charity Business*, p. 59.
48 Geoffrey Mulcahy, 'The Four Principles of Corporate Giving', *Financial Times*, 25 October 1993.
49 Milton Friedman, *Capitalism and Freedom*, University of Chicago Press, 1962, pp. 135–76.
50 *The UK Voluntary Sector Statistical Almanac 1998–99*, NCVO Publications, 1998.
51 Under the Trustee Investment Act (TIA) of 1961, charity trustees could invest only half of their funds in equities, as opposed to gilts, and then only in UK and Commonwealth companies with a five-year track record. This led to a severe under-performance by charity investments, as equities have consistently yielded higher returns than gilts. The restriction cost charities an estimated £400 million a year. In 1995 the TIA was relaxed, allowing charities to invest three quarters of assets in equities, and to invest in companies based in the European Union. Following lobbying by larger charities, in May 1996 the Treasury announced that all restrictions would be scrapped, and trustees were to be given the power to make investment decisions as if they owned the charitable funds. This legislation has yet to be passed, but investment performance has already taken many charities outside the TIA restrictions.
52 *Dimensions of the Voluntary Sector*, 1998 Edition, Charities Aid Foundation, pp. 9, 149.
53 *Financial Times*, 28 January 1994.
54 Hems and Passey, *The UK Voluntary Sector Statistical Almanac 1996*, NCVO, 1996, p. 25.
55 Lloyd, *The Charity Business*, p. 160.
56 Local authorities (£1.3 billion in 1996–97), central government excluding housing associations (£1.04 billion in 1995–96), the European Union (£0.170 billion in 1994–

95), National Lotteries Charity Board (£319 million in 1996–97) and tax relief (worth £824 million to the voluntary sector in 1996–97). See Charities Aid Foundation, *Dimensions of the Voluntary Sector*, 1998 Edition, p. 1.

57 The public supplies 35 per cent of charitable income, but this includes sales to consumers (15.4 per cent) as well as grants and donations (19.6 per cent). Sales of goods and services to the government account for 14.9 per cent of income. See *The Overall Size and Contribution of the UK Voluntary Sector*, NCVO, 1998.

58 Charities Aid Foundation, *Dimensions of the Voluntary Sector*, 1995 Edition, p. 144. All figures are for 1993–4.

59 Ian Mocroft, 'Local Authority Payments to Voluntary and Charitable Organisations for 1994–95', in *Dimensions of the Voluntary Sector*, Charities Aid Foundation, 1996.

60 Only 14 per cent of donations to charity are given in tax-efficient ways. See Hems and Passey, *The UK Voluntary Sector Statistical Almanac 1996*, p. 42

61 Stuart Etherington, chief executive, NCVO, letters to *Financial Times*, 4 April and 23 June 1997.

62 Frank Prochaska, 'Let Charity Begin With Charities', *The Times*, 14 December 1997.

63 *Financial Times*, 19 December 1996.

64 *Financial Times*, 24 November 1995.

65 Charities Aid Foundation, *Dimensions of the Voluntary Sector*, 1998 Edition, p. 87.

66 Howard Hurd and Mark Lattimer, *The Millionaire Givers*, Directory of Social Change, 1994, pp. (vi) or (ix).

67 John Stuart Mill, *Principles of Political Economy*, Books IV and V, Penguin, 1985, p. 335.

68 The Royal Commission: The London City Livery Companies' Vindication, Gilbert & Revington, 1885, p. 84. For the Livery Companies, see Chapter 8.

69 There is still an Octavia Hill Housing Trust in London. For her role in the foundation of the National Trust, see Chapter 3.

70 J. N. Tarn, *Five Per Cent Philanthropy: An Account of Housing in Urban Areas, Between 1840 and 1914*, Cambridge University Press, 1973, p. 78.

71 John Burnett, *A Social History of Housing 1815–1985*, Methuen, 1986, pp. 177–8.

72 Enid Gouldie, *Cruel Habitations: A History of Working-Class Housing 1780–1918*, George Allen & Unwin, 1974.

73 Robert Whelan, *The Corrosion of Charity: From Moral Renewal to Contract Culture*, Institute of Economic Affairs, July 1996, pp. 77, 85

74 *Sunday Times*, 2 July 1995.

75 Tarn, *Five Per Cent Philanthropy*, p. 113.

76 Charities Aid Foundation, *Dimensions of the Voluntary Sector*, p. 8, Table H.3.

77 Charity Commission Annual Report 1966, paragraphs 184–6.

78 See Matthew Parris, 'Uncharitable Thoughts', *The Times*, 12 December 1997.

79 Barry Knight, *Voluntary Action*, Home Office, 1993, p. 301.

80 In 1998 a trading subsidiary of the Royal British Legion, set up in 1927 to provide employment for ex-servicemen as security guards, announced it was seeking to float on the stock market. Royal British Legion Attendants Limited, now re-named Legion Security, was forced to surrender its charitable status after seeking and winning commercial security contracts.

CHAPTER TWENTY-SEVEN: *Banks and Building Societies*

1 *Sunday Telegraph*, 9 May 1993.
2 *Independent*, 6 November 1989.
3 *Financial Times*, 5 March 1993.
4 ibid., 11 March 1993.
5 ibid., 2 September 1998.
6 *Observer*, 4 December 1994.
7 Quoted in Russell Taylor, *Going for Broke*, Simon & Schuster, 1993, p. 195.
8 Technically, Bank Rate was the rate of interest at which the Bank of England would re-discount bills when called upon as lender of last resort. But its real importance was to influence the level of interest rates in the banking system and the financial markets.
9 *Financial Times*, 2 March 1993.
10 *Observer*, 9 May 1993.
11 *Financial Times*, 10 June 1993. Interestingly, the other mistake was failure to devise a common Automatic Teller Machine (ATM) network. This made it impossible for customers to withdraw money from any ATM in the country.
12 *Sunday Times*, 11 December 1994.
13 *Financial Times*, 10 February 1993.
14 ibid., 27 February 1991.
15 ibid., 25 October 1991.
16 *The Economist*, 9 September 1995.
17 *Financial Times*, 22 June, 14 September 1998.
18 ibid., 23 September 1998.
19 ibid., 9 September 1994.
20 ibid., 8 July 1996.
21 Joint press release issued by the Investors Compensation Scheme and the West Bromwich Building Society, 28 May 1998.
22 The Cheltenham and Gloucester paid £7.5 million to three hundred and nineteen investors. See *Financial Times*, 20 June 1996 and Building Societies Ombudsman Scheme, Annual Report 1993–94, pp 16.
23 Building Societies Ombudsman, Annual Report 1997–98, p. 28.
24 *Financial Times*, 26 July 1997.
25 Martin Boddy, *The Building Societies*, Macmillan, 1980, p. 6.
26 *Independent on Sunday*, 4 August 1991.
27 *Financial Times*, 24 July, 22 September, 17 October 1997.
28 ibid., 28 November 1997.
29 ibid., 5, 16 November 1994.
30 *Financial Times*, 12 July 1995.
31 Mergers between building societies, if they unlocked reserves, also saw windfall payments. When Cheltenham and Gloucester merged with the Guardian in 1989, in the first building society merger to unlock reserves, Guardian savers got £520 in cash and borrowers had £250 knocked off their mortgages. The merger of the Northern Rock and the North of England in 1994, by contrast, saw a pay-out to members averaging just £30.
32 *Financial Times*, 29 July 1997.
33 *The Times*, 18 October 1997.

34 *Financial Times*, 25 February 1997.

35 See Chapter 19.

36 E. J. Cleary, *The Building Society Movement*, Elek Books, 1965.

37 Martin Boddy, *The Building Societies*, Macmillan, 1980, p. 39.

38 The 1986 Building Societies Act allowed building societies to raise up to 40 per cent of their funds in the capital markets, and to make unsecured loans up to a fixed percentage of their total assets.

39 *The Observer*, 21 October 1990, 21 May 1991.

40 Office of National Statistics, *Financial Statistics*, Table 3.2A.

41 The ceiling was set at 40 per cent of total liabilities under the 1986 Building Societies Act. It was raised to 50 per cent from January 1996.

42 Changes foreshadowed in the Treasury document of 1994, *Review of the Building Societies Act 1986*, were given effect by parliamentary orders rather than primary legislation in 1995.

43 The first trustee savings bank is generally agreed to be the savings bank established by the Reverend Henry Duncan at Ruthwell in Dumfriesshire in 1810. Nearly ruined in their early years by defalcations and stiff competition from the Post Office Savings Bank introduced by Gladstone in 1861, the Trustee Savings Banks had by the late twentieth century become an impressive constellation of banks with a network of 1,600 branches. See H. Oliver Horne, *A History of Savings Banks*, Oxford University Press, 1947.

44 The TSB paid £777 million for Hill Samuel in October 1987; ten years later Hill Samuel was so dilapidated that the TSB could not even sell it. It had to be closed down.

45 Abbey National sold the three hundred and fifty-five-branch Cornerstone estate agency for £8 million in 1993. In 1998, it announced it was withdrawing from Spain. See *Financial Times*, 3 April 1998.

46 *Financial Times*, 25 August 1993.

47 In recent years the Cheshunt, Leamington Spa and the Southdown building societies were driven into mergers with other societies by bad loans. They merged, respectively, with the Bristol & West, the Bradford & Bingley and the Leeds. The Town & Country building society had to be rescued by the Woolwich.

48 Mortgages are secured on the value of the house or flat. Although there was a fall in house prices and a rise in mortgage arrears and re-possessions in the early 1990s, the building societies transferred much of the costs to the taxpayer (through the social security system) and the insurance companies (through mortgage indemnity insurance). The losses eventually became so immense that mortgage risk became virtually uninsurable. It was partly to enable building societies to self-insure that the government allowed building societies to set up their own general insurance subsidiaries in 1993.

49 Central Statistical Office, *Economic Trends*, Table B5.

50 Quoted in *Observer*, 29 July 1990.

51 *Financial Times*, 18 February 1991.

52 Central Statistical Office, *UK National Accounts*, Table 12.3.

53 Central Statistical Office, *Financial Statistics*, Table 8.2.

54 At National Westminster, much of the first half of the 1990s was taken up with rescuing National Westminster Bancorp, an American subsidiary which lost $1.1 billion by lending to American property developers such as Donald Trump.

55 A. R. Holmes and E. Green, *Midland: 150 Years of Banking Business*, Batsford, 1986, p. 85.

56 Edwin Green, *Dictionary of Business Biography*.

57 *Financial Times*, 28 December 1995.

58 ibid., 29 June and 3 November 1994; Standard Chartered PLC preliminary results, 10 March 1993.

59 ibid., 19, 20, 22 July 1994.

60 ibid., 14 September 1998.

61 *The Royal Bank of Scotland 1727–1977*, Royal Bank of Scotland 1977.

62 The Wallace Smith Trust was closed down by the Bank of England in May 1991, with losses of £100 million. Its proprietor, Duncan Wallace Smith, was jailed for six years in 1994.

63 Quoted in Robert Skidelsky, *John Maynard Keynes: The Economist as Saviour 1920–1937*, Macmillan, 1992, p. 39.

64 Quoted in Margaret Reid, *The Secondary Banking Crisis 1973–75*, Macmillan, 1982, p. 59.

65 Quoted in Russell Taylor, *Going for Broke*, Simon & Schuster 1993, frontispiece.

66 See Chapter 12.

67 In practice, of course, funds are transferred to the government (as, say, tax payments) and to foreign suppliers, so not all loans reappear within the banking system as deposits.

68 *Observer*, 1 March 1992.

69 Lord Alexander, Speech to Manchester Business School, 6 October 1993.

70 In practice, the short term demand for credit is influenced by factors other than its price, such as the likely return on investment made with it, and especially the possibility of a quick capital gain.

71 P. W. Matthews and Anthony Tuke, *History of Barclays Bank Limited*, Blades, East and Blades, 1926.

72 Michael Collins, *Money and Banking in the UK: A History*, Croom Helm, 1988, Table 2.4.

73 The last form of direct credit control, known as the Corset, was not removed until June 1980.

74 Stephen Fay, *Portrait of an Old Lady*, Penguin, 1988, p. 123.

75 Margaret Reid, *All-Change in the City*, Macmillan, 1988, pp. 157–8.

76 Building Societies Yearbook, 1996–7.

77 *Financial Times*, 9 June 1994.

78 ibid., 22 June 1995.

79 Access became the UK brand for MasterCard of the US. The shareholdings in the venture were divided. National Westminster, Lloyds and Midland took 30 per cent each, and Royal Bank of Scotland 10 per cent.

80 Reid, *All-Change in the City*, p. 123.

81 *Financial Times*, 20 February 1995.

82 ibid., 2 November 1992.

83 Sampson, *The Changing Anatomy of Britain*, p. 274.

84 Reid, *The Secondary Banking Crisis*, pp. 23–9.

85 The special deposits made by the clearing banks at the Bank of England, introduced in 1960, remained throughout the period of so-called Competition and Credit Control, which aimed to allocate credit mainly by price. The banks escaped the restriction by bidding for deposits in the wholesale inter-bank market and by issuing short-dated securities called Certificates of Deposit. The Banking Act of 1979 distinguished between reputable banks (lightly supervised) and so-called 'licensed deposit-takers' (heavily scrutinised). The distinction proved ineffective, since the first bank to get into trouble (Johnson Matthey) was not a licensed deposit-taker. See Chapter 12.

86 Lawson, *The View From No 11*, p. 626.

87 Financial Statistics, Table 3.2B.

88 British Bankers' Association, Annual Abstract of Banking Statistics, Volume 11, 1997.

89 See Chapter 11.

90 The 1997 accounts of Barclays Bank PLC record a loss of £469 million on the sale and restructuring of BZW. Trading losses are believed to have added another £200 million. *Financial Times*, 3 February 1998.

91 *Financial Times*, 2, 15 September 1998.

92 The convictions were overturned on appeal.

93 *Sunday Telegraph*, 27 March 1993.

94 *Sunday Times*, 25 June 1995.

95 Sampson, *The Moneylenders*, Hodder & Stoughton, 1981, p. 106.

96 Anthony Sampson, *The Changing Anatomy of Britain*, Hodder & Stoughton, 1982, pp. 278–281.

97 Speech, 26 October 1986. Quoted in *Sunday Times*, 2 July 1995.

98 *Financial Times*, 27 August, 5 November, 20 December 1997; 15 January, 1 May, 11, 24 June, 2 December 1998.

99 E. Victor Morgan, *A History of Money*, Pelican, 1965, p. 179.

100 For Gresham, the Mercers' Company and the City corporations, see Chapter 8.

101 See Chapter 21.

102 Will Hutton, *The State We're In*, Jonathan Cape, 1995, p. 134.

103 British Bankers' Association, Annual Abstract of Banking Statistics, 1997, p. 29.

104 3i was floated in June 1994. The banks maintained stakes after the flotation but these were found to inhibit liquidity of the shares, and were progressively sold. *Financial Times*, 23 June 1995; 7 June 1996.

105 Forrest Capie and Michael Collins, *Have the Banks Failed British Industry?*, Institute of Economic Affairs, 1993, pp. 45–59.

106 Reid, *All-Change in the City*, p. 132.

107 Leslie Hannah, *The Rise of the Corporate Economy*, Methuen, 1983, p. 24.

108 W. A. Thomas, *The Financing of British Industry 1918–76*, Methuen, 1978, p. 116.

109 *Financial Times*, 23 March 1994.

110 Russell Taylor, *Going for Broke*, Simon & Schuster, p. 212.

111 *Financial Times*, 4 May 1995.

CHAPTER TWENTY-EIGHT: *The Rise of Institutional Investors*

1 Quoted in *Financial Times*, 24 January 1996.

2 John Plender, *That's The Way the Money Goes*, André Deutsch 1982, p. 175.

3 K. R. Popper, *The Open Society and Its Enemies*, Routledge & Kegan Paul, 1984, Volume 1, p. 174.

4 Sereno S. Pratt, editor of the *Wall Street Journal*; quoted in Ron Chernow, *The House of Morgan*, Simon & Schuster, 1990, p. 68.

5 Anthony Sampson, *Anatomy of Britain*, Hodder & Stoughton, 1962, p. 378.

6 See Chapter 27.

7 Proceedings of the Tribunal appointed to Inquire into allegations that information about the raising of Bank Rate was improperly disclosed, December 1957, HMSO 1958, p. 185.

8 Ron Chernow, *The Warburgs: A Family Saga*, Chatto & Windus, 1993, p. 652.

9 Sampson, *Anatomy of Britain*, p. 390. Normally, was sold off in 1998 due to pressure from shareholders.

10 Chernow, *The Warburgs*, p. 652.

11 Sampson, *Anatomy of Britain*, p. 381.

12 See Chapter 16.

13 *Sunday Correspondent*, 29 April 1989.

14 See Chapter 27.

15 *Financial Times*, 6 September 1989.

16 Dermot Morrah, *A History of Industrial Life Assurance*, Allen & Unwin, 1955, p. 216.

17 Quoted in Chernow, *The House of Morgan*, p. 68.

18 See Chapter 29.

19 Mercury Asset Management, Schroders, PDFM, Gartmore and Deutsche Morgan Grenfell Asset Management.

20 *Insurance Facts, Figures and Trends, Association of British Insurers*, September 1996, p. 34. The figures are drawn from the 1994–95 Family Expenditure Survey.

21 Clive Trebilcock, *Phoenix Assurance and the Development of British Insurance 1782–1870*, 1985; P. G. M. Dickson, *The Sun Insurance Office 1710–1900*, Oxford University Press, 1960.

22 It was known as Phenix Fire Office from 1705.

23 Barbon was a 'projector' of various business enterprises, including a Land Bank and an Orphan Bank. He was also the first great property developer in British history. Simon Jenkins, *Landlords to London: The Story of a Capital and Its Growth*, Constable, 1975, pp. 38–42.

24 Sir William Schooling, *Alliance Assurance 1824–1924*, Alliance, 1924.

25 Hartley Withers, *Pioneers of British Life Assurance*, Staples Press, 1951, p. 22; Edward Liveing, *A Century of Insurance: The Commercial Union Group of Insurance Companies 1861–1961*, H. F. & G. Witherby Ltd (Printers), 1961.

26 Harold E. Raynes, *A History of British Insurance*, Second Edition, Pitman, 1964.

27 Bernard Drew, *The London Assurance: A Second Chronicle*, 1949, p. 26.

28 Barry Supple, *The Royal Exchange Assurance. A History of British Insurance 1720–1970*, Cambridge University Press, 1970, p. 32.

29 For the development of Lloyd's of London, see Chapter 30.

30 Liveing, *A Century of Insurance*. It succeeded to a merger with Commercial Union in 1998.

31 Raynes, *A History of British Insurance*, p. 304.

32 Supple, *The Royal Exchange Assurance*, p. 234.

33 From *Bernard Shaw and Mrs Patrick Campbell: Their Correspondence*, Dent, 1952, quoted in Supple, *The Royal Exchange Assurance*, p. 234, *n.* 1.

34 J. Dyer Simpson, *1936: Our Centenary Year: The Liverpool, London and Globe Insurance Company Limited*, 1936, p. 93.

35 *Insurance: Facts, Figures and Trends*, Association of British Insurers, September 1996, p. 50, Table 2.5.

36 Raynes, *A History of British Insurance*, Drew, *The London Assurance*.

37 Supple, *The Royal Exchange Assurance*, p. 100.

38 Robert Blake, *Esta Perpetua: Norwich Union Life Assurance Society 1808–1958*, Newman Neame Limited for Norwich Union, 1958.

39 E. P. Leigh Bennett, *On This Evidence: A Study in 1936 of the Legal & General Assurance Society Since Its Formation in 1836*, Baynard Press, 1936, p. 39.

40 See below.

41 M. E. Ogborn, *Equitable Assurances: The Story of Life Assurance in the Experience of the Equitable Life Assurance Society 1762–1962*, George Allen & Unwin, 1962, p. 253.

42 Quoted in E. P. Thompson, *The Making of the English Working Class*, Pelican, 1968, p. 258.

43 P. H. J. H. Gosden, *The Friendly Societies in England 1815–75*, Manchester University Press, 1961, p. 154.

44 By 1898 the Oddfellows had a reserve deficiency of 6*s* 6*d* in the pound, and the Foresters of 2*s* 5*d* in the pound. See Bentley B. Gilbert, *The Evolution of National Insurance in Great Britain: The Origins of the Welfare State*, Michael Joseph, 1966, pp 170; David G. Green, *Reinventing Civil Society: The Rediscovery of Welfare Without Politics*, Institute of Economic Affairs, p. 92–4.

45 Raynes, *A History of British Insurance*, p. 114.

46 This kind of insurance could survive once the usury laws were relaxed. See Chapter 27.

47 Quoted in Withers, *Pioneers of Life Assurance*, p. 43.

48 Dickson, *The Sun Insurance Office*; Ogborn, *Equitable Assurances*.

49 Ogborn, *Equitable Assurances*.

50 ibid.

51 Trebilcock, *Phoenix Assurance*, p. 578.

52 ibid.

53 Letter to *Financial Times*, 26 September 1994.

54 Raynes, *A History of British Insurance*, p. 125; Withers, *Pioneers of British Life Assurance*.

55 *Financial Times*, 2 July 1994.

56 Drew, *The London Assurance*.

57 Sir Herbert Maxwell, *Annals of the Scottish Widows' Fund Life Assurance Society: During One Hundred Years 1815–1914*, R. & R. Clark, Edinburgh, 1914, p. 55.

58 ibid., p. 95.

59 *SALAS 150: A History of Scottish Amicable Life Assurance Society 1826–1976*, Glasgow, 1976.

60 Charles Colquhoun McInroy, *Scottish Equitable Life Assurance Society 1831–1981*, Scottish Equitable, March 1981.

61 M. D. Steuart, *The Scottish Provident Institution 1837–1937*, Scottish Provident Institution, 1937.

62 Maurice Lindsay, *Count All Men Mortal: A History of Scottish Provident 1837–1987*, Canongate, 1987, p. 38.

63 Mamie Magnusson, *A Length of Days: The Scottish Mutual Assurance Society 1883–1983*, Henry Mallard, 1983, p. 108.

64 For the Dissenting Academies, see Chapter 6.

65 David Tregoning and Hugh Cockerell, *Friends for Life: Friends' Provident Life Office 1832–1982*, Henry Melland, 1982, p. 38.

66 Its founder, Robert Warner, had been refused by another life office on the grounds that abstention from alcohol was bad for his health.

67 Stanley Hazell, *A Record of the First 100 Years of the National Provident Institution 1835–1935*, Cambridge University Press, 1935.

68 Jose Harris, *Private Lives, Public Spirit: Britain 1870–1914*, Penguin, 1993, pp. 114–15.

69 Samuel Smiles, *Thrift*, John Murray, 1875, p. 233.

70 Paul Johnson, *Saving and Spending: The Working Class Economy in Britain 1870–1939*, Oxford University Press, 1985, p. 6.

71 Guy Routh, *Occupation and Pay in Great Britain 1906–1979*, Macmillan, 1980 p. 112, Table 2.24.

72 For livery companies, see Chapter 8.

73 Drawn from the preamble to a commercial assurance act of 1601, probably drafted by Francis Bacon. Quoted in Raynes, *A History of British Insurance*, p. 53.

74 See Chapter 30.

75 Unlike the early life assurance companies, they were commended by Daniel Defoe in his *Essay on Projects* of 1697. Quoted in Withers, *Pioneers of Life Assurance*, p. 43.

76 See E. P. Thompson, *The Making of the English Working Class*, p. 460; P. H. J. H. Gosden, *The Friendly Societies in England 1815–75*, Manchester University Press, 1961, p. 7.

77 A non-contributory state pension, passed by Parliament in 1908, came into effect in 1909. See David G. Green, *Reinventing Civil Society: The Rediscovery of Welfare Without Politics*, Institute of Economic Affairs Health and Welfare Unit, 1993, pp. 32, 42.

78 Paul Johnson, *Saving and Spending*.

79 Friendly Societies Commission Annual Report 1997–98, Appendix C, Fact Sheet February 1999.

80 R. W. Barnard, *A Century of Service: The Story of the Prudential 1848–1948*, Times Publishing Co, 1948, p. 37.

81 ibid.

82 ibid., p. 22.

83 Cyril Clegg, *Friend In Deed: History of the Refuge Assurance Company 1858–1958*, 1958.

84 *Pearl Assurance: An Illustrated History 1864–1989*, Pearl Assurance, 1990.

85 *Britannic Assurance 1866–1991*, Britannic Assurance, 1991.

86 Co-operative Insurance Services mutualised in 1899. Since 1913 it has been a wholly owned subsidiary of the Co-operative Wholesale Society, a consumer co-operative half-owned by shoppers and half by the retail societies. Membership is not an option offered to policyholders, so the Co-operative is a mutual.

87 *The First 75 Years: United Friendly Insurance*, 1985.

88 Richard Balding was the chief executive of United Friendly until 1994, when he became vice-chairman of the merged groups.

89 *Financial Times*, 18 April 1997.

90 ibid., 6 October 1994.

91 ibid., 9 May 1995.

92 Johnson, *Saving and Spending*; page 15 and Table 7.1.

93 Sir Arnold Wilson and Professor Hermann Levy, *Industrial Assurance: An Historical and Critical Study*, Oxford University Press, 1937, 383.

94 Sir Arnold Wilson and Professor Hermann Levy, *Industrial Assurance: An Historical and Critical Study*, Oxford University Press, 1937, p. xix.

95 ibid., p. 389.

96 R. G. Garnett, *A Century of Co-operative Insurance*, George Allen & Unwin, 1968, pp. 237–44.

97 Committee to Review the Functioning of Financial Institutions, Cmnd 7937, 1984, p. (i).

98 Quoted in Richard Minns, *Pension Funds and British Capitalism*, Heinemann, 1980, p. 8.

99 Committee to Review the Functioning of Financial Institutions, Report, June 1980, Cmnd. 7937, p. 371, paragraph 1404.

100 The hopes of cheapness were disappointed. By 1914 the pensions were costing £12.5

million. Bentley B. Gilbert, *The Evolution of National Insurance in Great Britain: The Origins of the Welfare State*, Michael Joseph, 1966, p. 230, *n.* 173.

101 Bryan Ellis, *Pensions in Britain 1955–1975: A History in Five Acts*, HMSO, 1989, pp. 1–2.

102 See *Social Trends*, 1993, p. 11, Table 5.21.

103 See Raymond Plant and Norman Barry, *Citizenship and Rights in Thatcher's Britain: Two Views*, Institute of Economic Affairs, 1990.

104 See Chapter 30.

105 Leslie Hannah, *Inventing Retirement: The Development of Occupational Pensions in Britain*, Cambridge University Press, 1986, pp. 18–19, 93–4.

106 ibid., pp. 6, 32, 44–5.

107 Minns, *Pension Funds and British Capitalism*, p. 5.

108 David Blake, *Pension Schemes and Pension Funds in the United Kingdom*, Clarendon Press, 1995, p. 27.

109 Hannah, *Inventing Retirement*, pp. 6, 32, 44–5.

110 ibid., p. 10.

111 Barnard, *A Century of Service*:

112 Blake, *Pension Schemes and Pension Funds*, p. 21.

113 ibid., pp. 24–7.

114 Plender, *That's The Way the Money Goes*, pp. 27–9.

115 The Universities Superannuation Scheme, founded in 1975, is the successor to the Federated System of Superannuation for Universities, set up in 1913 to provide pensions to redbrick university teachers without penalising them for moving between universities. A similar problem did not arise at Oxbridge, where fellows simply did not retire. See Douglas Logan, *The Birth of a Pension Scheme: A History of the Universities Superannuation Scheme*, Liverpool University Press, 1985.

116 *Financial Times*, 6 February 1981.

117 See Chapter 32.

118 *Financial Times*, 10 October 1997.

119 Hannah, *Inventing Retirement*; pp. 40, 66.

120 ibid., pp. 19–20, 44–5, 62, 72, 78.

121 Inland Revenue Statistics 1998, p. 75, Table 7.10.

122 The millionaires were Clement Callingham, chairman of Henekey's wine merchants; Sir William Collins, chairman of Cerebos Salt; and Sir Bernard Docker, chairman of BSA.

123 *Financial Times*, August 1956, reproduced in ibid., 20 December 1972.

124 Quoted in Sampson, *Anatomy of Britain*, p. 410.

125 Brian P. Whitehouse, *Partners in Property: A History and Analysis of the Provision of Institutional Finance for Property Development*, Birn, Shaw, London, 1964, p. 84.

126 George Clayton and W. T. Osborn, *Insurance Company Investment*, George Allen & Unwin, 1965, p. 176.

127 Minns, *Pension Funds and British Capitalism*, p. 146.

128 *Financial Times*, 24 October 1978.

129 'The Institutions and the Industrial Challenge of the Eighties: The Need For a New Investment Facility: A Note of Dissent by the Chairman, Lord Allen, Mr Jenkins, Mr Mills and the Rt Hon Lionel Murarry,' in Report of the Committee to Review the Functioning of Financial Institutions, Report, June 1980, Cmnd. 7937, pp. 274–287, paragraph 1404.

130 Ken Thomas, general secretary, Civil and Public Services Association, quoted in *Financial Times*, 5 February 1978.

131 Quoted in Plender, *That's The Way the Money Goes*, p. 19.

132 Paul Harbrecht, *Pensions Funds and Economic Power*, p. 280. Quoted in Clayton and Osborn, *Insurance Company Investment*, p. 242.

133 Quoted in Sampson, *Anatomy of Britain*, p. 413.

134 Whitehouse, *Partners in Property*, p. 820.

135 Chernow, *The House of Morgan*, p. 154.

136 Nicola Horlick, *Can You Have It All?*, Macmillan, 1997, p. 105.

137 *Sunday Telegraph*, 1 November 1992.

138 Interview, 22 July 1992.

139 Interview, 23 July 1992.

140 *The Independent*, 12 March 1990.

141 Barry Rosenberg, press release, 27 September 1993.

142 Alastair Ross Goobey, *Bricks & Mortals*, Century, 1992, p. 18.

CHAPTER TWENTY-NINE: *What Institutions Own*

1 *Financial Times*, 6 August 1992.

2 ibid., 7 September 1982.

3 20E–H and 22A–D. From Appendix II, pp. 30–1 of National Association of Pension Funds, *Investment Management: A Guide for Trustees*, 1992.

4 *Financial Times*, 2 February 1995.

5 See Chapter 31.

6 Barclays Capital Equity & Gilt Study: Investment in the London Stock Market since 1918, pp. 3–4.

7 Interview, 26 March 1992.

8 David Kynaston, *The City of London: A World of Its Own* Chatto & Windus, 1994, volume I, p. 153.

9 Barry Supple, *The Royal Exchange Assurance: A History of British Insurance 1720–1970*, Cambridge University Press, 1970, p. 326.

10 Maurice Lindsay, *Count All Men Mortal: A History of Scottish Provident 1837–1987*, Canongate, 1987, p. 60.

11 Wars occurred 1689–97, 1702–13, 1739–63, 1775–83, and 1792–1815.

12 John Brewer, *The Sinews of Power: War, Money and the English State 1688–1783*, Alfred A. Knopf, 1989, pp. 40–1, Tables 2.2 and 2.3.

13 ibid., pp. 115–16.

14 John Rule, *The Vital Century: England's Developing Economy 1714–1815*, Longman, 1992, p. 280.

15 P. G. M. Dickson, *The Sun Insurance Office 1710–1960*, Oxford University Press, 1960.

16 Founded in 1706 by the Fleet Street bookseller John Hartley. The Norwich Union bought the Society in 1866. See Chapter 28 and Robert Blake, *Esta Perpetua: Norwich Union Life Assurance Society 1808–1958*, Newman Neame Limited for Norwich Union, 1958.

17 Bernard Drew, *The London Assurance: A Second Chronicle*, 1949; E. A. Davies, *An Account of the Formation and Early Years of the Westminster Fire Office*, 1952.

18 P. G. M. Dickson, *The Financial Revolution in England: A Study in the Development of Public Credit 1688–1756*, Macmillan, 1967, p. 289.

19 Dickson, *The Sun Insurance Office*.

20 See Chapter 20.

21 The term 'bear' (or speculating that prices will fall) probably derives from 'selling the skin before you have caught the bear'. Presumably the term 'bull' refers to buying the bull before seeing it. The ancestor of the modern paper security or 'stock' was the 'tally'. In the seventeenth century, investors were issued with wooden 'tallies', made of hazel faggots. The amount owed to the holder was notched on the tally, which was then split in two. The investor was given the 'foil' and the Treasury the 'counterfoil'; by submitting the matching foil the holder recouped his advance with interest. The term 'stock' explained the grafting of new issues of debt onto the old. See Dickson, *The Financial Revolution in England*; p. 33.

22 ibid., p. 33, 498.

23 Brewer, *The Sinews of Power*, p. 126.

24 Dickson, *The Financial Revolution in England*: of pp. 300–3, 332–7, 452–3.

25 Clive Trebilcock, *Phoenix Assurance and the Development of British Insurance 1782–1870*, 1985, p. 653, Table 11.6 and pp. 733–4, Tables 13.8 and 13.9.

26 David Cannadine, 'Aristocratic Indebtedness in the Nineteenth Century,' in *Aspects of Aristocracy: Grandeur and Decline in Modern Britain*, Yale University Press, 1993, pp. 39, 44.

27 Dickson, *The Sun Insurance Office 1710–1960*.

28 For the New Domesday survey, see Chapter 2.

29 E. P. Leigh Bennett, *On This Evidence: A Study in 1936 of the Legal & General Assurance Society Since Its Formation in 1836*, Baynard Press, 1936.

30 Supple, *The Royal Exchange Assurance*, p. 336.

31 See Chapter 31.

32 David Kynaston, *The City of London: Golden Years 1890–1914*, Chatto & Windus, 1995, volume II, p. 460.

33 Kynaston, *The City of London: A World of Its Own, 1815–1890*, Chatto & Windus 1994 volume I; 1995, volume II.

34 Supple, *The Royal Exchange Assurance* p. 332, table 13.3

35 ibid., page 443.

36 George Clayton and W. T. Osborn, *Insurance Company Investment*, George Allen & Unwin, 1965, pp. 60–1, 63. The two papers by Raynes were published in the *Journal of the Institute of Actuaries*, volume LIX, part LXVIII, part iv, cover up the period 1912–36.

37 David Tregoning and Hugh Cockerell, *Friends for Life: Friends' Provident Life Office 1832–1982*, Henry Melland, 1982, p. 191, table 2.

38 *The Economist*, Insurance Supplement, 18 July 1936, p. 12.

39 Eric Short and Richard Glenn, *The History of the National Mutual Life Assurance Society 1830–1980*, National Mutual, 1980, p. 31.

40 Glasgow's Guide to Investment Trust Companies, Eyre & Spottiswoode, 1935.

41 Robert Skidelsky, *John Maynard Keynes: The Economist as Saviour 1920–1937*, Macmillan, 1992, pp. 25–6, 524, 526.

42 Quoted by G. H. Ross Goobey in *Pension Fund Investment Policy*, August 1955, p. 7.

43 Sampson, *Anatomy of Britain*, p. 408.

44 Supple, *The Royal Exchange Assurance*, p. 527.

45 'It seems clear that investment in risk capital is not inconsistent with the first responsibility of a life office – to safeguard its policyholders' money,' Sir John Benn told the annual general meeting of the UK Provident Institution in 1954. 'On the contrary, I

believe that such investments as part of a well-balanced portfolio are now the best if not the only means to achieve this objective.' Clayton and Osborn, *Insurance Company Investment*, p. 132.

46 Cyril Clegg, *Friend in Deed: History of the Refuge Assurance Co. 1858–1958*, 1958.

47 Mamie Magnusson, *A Length of Days: The Scottish Mutual Assurance Society 1883–1983*, Henry Mallard, 1983.

48 'Review of Investment Policy', a paper considered by Sir James Grigg, Mr A. Pym and Mr G. H. Ross Goobey on 7 April 1960.

49 The Trustee Investments Act of 1961 allowed them to invest half their funds in shares. This was widened in 1974 to three quarters. See Minns, *Pension Funds and British Capitalism*, pp. 24.

50 Theodore J. Grayson, *Investment Trusts: Their Origin, Development and Operation*, John Wiley & Sons, 1928.

51 Glasgow's Guide to Investment Trust Companies, Eyre & Spottiswoode, 1935.

52 See below, p. 1042.

53 David Kynaston, *A World of Its Own*, Volume 1, p. 409.

54 Sampson; *Anatomy of Britain*, p. 387.

55 *Financial Times*, 8 December 1984. Henderson lost his job at London and Manchester in May 1986 and started his own firm, Exeter Asset Management. See *Financial Times*, 24 May 1986.

56 See Chapter 28.

57 *Investors Chronicle*, 8 June 1990.

58 Association of Investment Trust Companies, 1990.

59 *The Observer*, 29 April 1990.

60 *Investors Chronicle*, 8 June 1990.

61 *Financial Times*, 4 June 1993.

62 *Independent on Sunday*, 6 June 1993.

63 *Financial Times*, 5 November 1996.

64 The Merchant Navy Pension fund owned a 28 per cent stake, which it sold in 1991. The Cayzer family investment vehicle, Caledonia Investments, acquired a 29.2 per cent stake in 1994, and merged its Clan Asset Management business with Ivory & Sime.

65 *Financial Times*, 8 November 1997.

66 E. V. Morgan and W. A. Thomas, *The Stock Exchange: Its History and Functions*, Elek Books, 1969, page 179.

67 For Mark Weinberg and Abbey Life, see Chapter 30.

68 'Review of Investment Policy', p. 6.

69 G. H. Ross Goobey, 'Memorandum on Investment Policy for the Pension Fund', Imperial Tobacco, July 1960.

70 The switch from equities to bonds was accompanied by a much less conspicuous unloading of property. The Norwich Union invested heavily in property in the 1980s, following a formula which had worked well in the 1960s and 1970s, when it had often preferred property to shares. As late as August 1988, with base rates rising sharply, it was promising to invest £300 million in property in 1988 and another £400 million in 1989. By then it had £4 billion in property, which made it one of the biggest commercial property owners in Britain, together with, Land Securities and the Prudential. See *Financial Times*, 10 August 1988.

71 G. H. Ross Goobey, 'The Effect of the Change in the Investment Policy of the Pension Fund', Imperial Tobacco, 1 February 1955.

72 'Review of Investment Policy', p. 2.

73 *Daily Telegraph*, 11 March 1975.

74 Brian P. Whitehouse, *Partners in Property: A History and Analysis of the Provision of Institutional Finance for Property Development*, Birn, Shaw, London, 1964, p. 146.

75 See Chapter 18.

76 Sampson, *The New Anatomy of Britain*, Hodder & Stoughton, 1971, p. 536.

77 Whitehouse, *Partners in Property*.

78 Oliver Marriott, *The Property Boom*, Hamish Hamilton, 1967, pp. 6, 254–5, 108.

79 It was a lucky escape for Midland Bank. Osborne had started banking with Barclays in the mid-1960s when the bank gave him a £5,000 advance which Midland had refused. Alastair Ross Goobey, *Bricks & Mortals*, Century, 1992, pp. 164–5.

80 *Financial Times*, 15 December 1997.

81 Ross Goobey, *Bricks & Mortals*, p. 164.

82 Sampson, *Anatomy of Britain*, p. 415.

83 Quoted in Margaret Reid, *The Secondary Banking Crisis 1973–75*, Macmillan, 1982, p. 106.

84 Ross Goobey, *Bricks & Mortals*, p. 20.

85 Dickson, *The Sun Insurance Office*.

86 Hermione Hobhouse, *Thomas Cubitt: Master Builder*, Macmillan, 1971, p. 324.

87 R. W. Barnard, *A Century of Service: The Story of the Prudential 1848–1948*, Times Publishing Company, 1948.

88 Whitehouse, *Partners in Property*, p. 70.

89 3,025,000 houses, 75,000 shops, 42,000 commercial or entertainment premises, 25,000 factories, 24,000 hotels, 26,000 farm buildings, 17,000 churches, 8,300 schools, 6,000 public buildings and 1,500 hospitals. One third of the damage was inflicted on London. See Whitehouse, *Partners in Property*, p. 14.

90 Sampson, *Anatomy of Britain*, p. 418.

91 Whitehouse, *Partners in Property*.

92 Richard Redden, *The Pension Fund Property Unit Trust: A History*, Franey Publishers & Co. Ltd, 1984, p. 49.

93 Plender, *That's The Way the Money Goes*, pp. 124–65.

94 *Financial Times*, 4 November 1994.

95 Norma Cohen, 'Overcoming the Obsolete', *Financial Times*, 31 October 1997.

96 DTZ Debenham Thorpe, *Money Into Property 1997*, p. 5, figure 2.

97 Marriott, *The Property Boom*, Appendix 4.

98 Redden, *The Pension Fund Property Unit Trust*.

99 Marriott, *The Property Boom*.

100 UK National Accounts, 1997 Edition, Table 12.1.

101 ibid., Table 12.3.

102 Angus P. Mackintosh and Stephen G. Sykes, *A Guide to Institutional Property Investment*, Macmillan, 1985, p. 22.

103 Plender, *That's The Way the Money Goes*, p. 196.

104 Peter Mathias, *The First Industrial Nation: An Economic History of Britain 1700–1814*, Methuen, Second Edition, 1983, p. 289.

105 Barnard, *A Century of Service*.

106 *Pearl Assurance*, p. 120.

107 Liveing, *A Century of Insurance*.

CHAPTER THIRTY: *The Insurance Industry*

1 *The Observer*, 16 May 1993.
2 *Financial Times*, 23 October 1998.
3 Corporate video circulated to dissuade people from opting for a personal pension. Quoted in *The Observer*, 26 January 1992.
4 *Financial Times*, 20 December 1997.
5 William Kay, *Tycoons*, Pan, 1985, p. 177.
6 Alan Parker, Life Assurance: the new deal, Economist Brief 12, 1969, quoted in Anthony Sampson, *The New Anatomy of Britain*, 1971, p. 525.
7 P. G. M. Dickson, *The Sun Insurance Office 1710–1960*, Oxford University Press, 1960.
8 Robert Blake, *Esta Perpetua: Norwich Union Life Assurance Society 1808–1958*, Newman Neame Limited for Norwich Union, 1958, pp. 20, 23.
9 Clive Trebilcock, *Phoenix Assurance and the Development of British Insurance 1782–1870*, 1985, pp. 676–708.
10 In the 1930s Metropolitan Life transferred its assured pension business to the Legal and General. See David Blake, *Pension Schemes and Pension Funds in the United Kingdom*, Clarendon Press, 1995, p. 29.
11 See David Cannadine, *The Decline and Fall of the British Aristocracy*, Yale University Press, 1990, pp. 406–20.
12 University Life was later taken over by Equitable Life. See Alan E. Campbell, *University Life Assurance Society 1825–1975*, anniversary booklet.
13 Bernard Drew, *The London Assurance: A Second Chronicle*, 1949; E. A. Davies, *An Account of the Formation and Early Years of the Westminster Fire Office*, 1952.
14 A. D. Besant, *Our Centenary: Being the History of the First Hundred Years of the Clerical, Medical & General Life Assurance Society*, 1924.
15 *Britannic Assurance 1866–1991*, Britannic Assurance, 1991.
16 J. Dyer Simpson, *1936: Our Centenary Year: The Liverpool, London and Globe Insurance Company Limited*, 1936.
17 See Chapter 15.
18 *Financial Times*, 26 September 1990.
19 ibid., 15 August 1995, Scottish Widows Annual Review 1996, p. 13.
20 ibid., 17 March 1995.
21 Edward Liveing, *A Century of Insurance: The Commercial Union Group of Insurance Companies 1861–1961*, 1961.
22 *Financial Weekly*, 21 May 1987.
23 *Financial Times*, 2 March 1992.
24 Trebilcock, *Phoenix Assurance*, 1988.
25 Barry Supple, *The Royal Exchange Assurance: A History of British Insurance 1720–1970*, Cambridge University Press, 1970.
26 For the Tooley Street fire, see Chapter 28.
27 Liveing, *A Century of Insurance*, p. 6.
28 J. Dyer Simpson, *1936: Our Centenary Year*; E. V. Francis, *London & Lancashire: History of London & Lancashire Insurance Co Ltd*, privately printed, 1962.
29 E. V. Francis, *London & Lancashire*.
30 The National Insurance Company of Glasgow was acquired by Commercial Union in 1917. See Liveing, *A Century of Insurance*.
31 See the story of Russell Taylor in Chapter 27.

32 *Financial Times*, 8 May 1993.

33 See above.

34 Kay, *Tycoons*, p. 178.

35 Savundra found that in order to set up an insurance company in Britain he had to produce nothing more onerous than evidence of £50,000 in liquid assets.

36 Jon Connell and Douglas Sutherland, *Fraud: The Amazing Career of Dr Savundra*, Hodder & Stoughton, 1978.

37 ibid., p. 233.

38 ibid., p. 160.

39 Richard Spiegelberg, *The City: Power Without Responsibility*, Blond & Briggs, 1973, p. 223.

40 Harold E. Raynes, *A History of British Insurance*, Second Edition, Pitman, 1964; Hartley Withers, *Pioneers of Life Assurance*, Staples Press, 1951.

41 Trebilcock, *Phoenix Assurance*.

42 M. E. Ogborn, *Equitable Assurances*, p. 236.

43 R. W. Barnard, *A Century of Service: The Story of the Prudential 1848–1948*, Times Publishing Company, 1948.

44 ibid.

45 Dermot Morrah, *A History of Industrial Life Assurance*, Allen & Unwin, 1955, pp. 33–4, and Paul Johnson, *Saving and Spending: The Working Class Economy in Britain 1870–1939*, Oxford University Press, 1985, p. 36.

46 *Sunday Telegraph*, 22 April 1990.

47 R. G. Garnett, *A Century of Co-operative Insurance*, George Allen & Unwin, 1968, p. 94.

48 Quoted in Morrah, *A History of Industrial Life Assurance*, p. 91.

49 Fabian Report on Industrial Assurance, published in the *New Statesman* of 13 March 1915. Quoted in Garnett, *A Century of Co-operative Insurance*, p. 233, *n.* 2.

50 Garnett, *A Century of Co-operative Insurance*.

51 Quoted in Wilson and Levy, *Industrial Assurance*, p. 166.

52 Garnett, *A Century of Co-operative Insurance*.

53 Wilson and Levy, *Industrial Assurance*, p.xii.

54 Morrah, *A History of Industrial Life Assurance*, p. 147.

55 *Financial Times*, 25 June 1997.

56 ibid., 17 June 1997.

57 ibid., 1 February 1999.

58 Letter to *Financial Times*, 18 June 1994.

59 *Observer*, 6 September 1992.

60 Kay, *Tycoons*, p. 180.

61 See Chapter 27.

62 Withers, *Pioneers of Life Assurance*; Connell and Sutherland, *Fraud*.

63 *The Times*, 18 October 1997.

64 Report of the Director General's Inquiry into Pensions, Office of Fair Trading, July 1997, Volume One, p. 75, table 4.5.

65 Ross Goobey, *Bricks & Mortals*, p. 45.

66 In 1989 Britannic won the PA Management Award for Marketing Success, its advertising campaign having secured a 5 per cent market share in the first year. *Financial Times*, 5 November 1997.

67 ibid., 23 July 1993.

68 Office of Fair Trading, *Surrender Values of Life Insurance Policies*, 1994.

69 *The Independent*, 1 July 1990.

70 *Sunday Telegraph*, 26 September 1993.

71 *Financial Times*, 4 December 1982.

72 Johnson, *Saving and Spending*.

73 Morrah, *A History of Industrial Life Assurance*.

74 Their cancellation rates were 45 per cent, against 22–32 per cent for sales through independent financial advisers (IFAs). See *Financial Times*, 24 January 1992.

75 Their cancellation rates were 36.3 per cent, against 22.4 per cent for IFA sales. See *Financial Times*, 5 November 1997.

76 Ogborn, *Equitable Assurances*.

77 *The Independent*, 19 July 1991.

78 *Financial Times*, 27 June 1992.

79 *Financial Times*, 29 November 1993.

80 ibid., 13 December 1990.

81 The biggest problems arose at companies which had sold mortgage indemnity insurance to banks and building societies.

82 *Sunday Telegraph*, 11 October 1992.

83 Barnard, *A Century of Service*, p. 58.

84 Supple, *The Royal Exchange Assurance*, p. 139.

85 Paul Johnson, *Saving and Spending*, p. 33.

86 *Britannic Assurance 1866–1991*.

87 *Financial Times*, 28 January 1987.

88 ibid., 11 December 1993.

89 *Sunday Telegraph*, 3 April 1994.

90 *Financial Times*, 24 March 1994.

91 Peter Marsh, 'When He Dies My Dear, All This Will Be Yours,' *Financial Times*, 11 June 1994.

92 Norman Fowler, *Ministers Decide*, Chapmans, 1991, p. 203.

93 *Financial Times*, 11 December 1993.

94 ibid., 1 February 1994.

95 Fowler, *Ministers Decide*, p. 205.

96 *Financial Times*, 2 July 1984.

97 ibid., 3 November 1997.

98 The study was conducted by accountants KPMG on behalf of the SIB and examined in detail seven hundred and thirty-five cases drawn from four hundred separate occupational pension schemes. See *Financial Times*, 17 December 1993.

99 *Financial Times*, 1 February 1999. See also footnote 57.

100 ibid., 18 April 1996.

101 ibid., 8 November 1996; 21 February 1997; 19 September 1997.

102 Helen Liddell, Statement to the House of Commons, 18 November 1997.

103 SIB press release, 21 October 1997.

104 *Financial Times*, 3 May 1986.

105 *Sunday Times*, 5 January 1986.

106 22 April 1990.

107 *Financial Times*, 9 December 1993.

108 ibid., 20 December 1993.

109 ibid., 26 March 1994.

110 ibid., 24 January 1995.

111 ibid., 19 July 1994, 24 January 1995.

112 *The Times*, 25 January 1995.

113 *Financial Times*, 4 June 1997.

114 ibid., 7 August 1997.

115 ibid., 19 September 1997, 16 December 1997, 10 December 1997.

116 Financial Services Authority, Public Statement, 16 December 1997.

117 *Financial Times*, 20 December 1997.

118 Sir Peter Davis, Group Chief Executive's Review, Prudential Corporation Annual Report, 1996, p. 8.

119 Arthur Miller, *Death of a Salesman*.

120 Association of British Insurers, Insurance Statistics Year Book 1985–1995, pp. 13, 19, 69, tables 15, 29, 122, 1986–1996, pp. 14, 20, 79, tables 14, 28, 123.

121 *Financial Times*, 30 April 1994.

122 ibid., 15 October 1997, 28 July 1994, 21 May 1994, 15 August 1994.

123 ibid., 18 March 1997.

124 See Chapters 7 and 28.

125 Blake, *Esta Perpetua*; p. 23.

126 Hazell, *First 100 Years of the National Provident Institution*.

127 Norwich Union Share Offer Prospectus, May 1997, pp. 26–7.

128 Proposed Transfer of the Business of Clerical, Medical and General Life Assurance Society to Halifax Building Society, Clerical Medical, May 1996, p. 8.

129 See Chapters 22 and 27.

130 Scottish Widows Annual Review 1996, pp. 9–10.

131 See Chapter 27.

132 Letter to *Financial Times*, 26 September 1994.

133 Following the takeover of Ivory and Sime, the merged fund management businesses have taken over its listing.

134 *Financial Times*, 28 December 1995.

135 For details of friendly societies, see Chapter 28; also Annual Report of the Friendly Societies Commission 1997–8, p. 7.

136 *Financial Times*, 29 October 1996.

137 ibid., 8 February 1996. Liverpool Victoria Group Report and Accounts 1996, p. 38.

138 E. P. Thompson, *The Making of the English Working Class*, Pelican, 1977, pp. 460–1.

139 *Financial Times*, 26 May 1994.

140 Dictionary of Business Biography.

141 Lloyd's Global Results 1996.

142 Adam Raphael, *Ultimate Risk*, Bantam, 1994, pp. 7, 198–9, 201–3, 210, 242.

143 UK National Accounts, 1997 Edition, table 12.2.

144 Godfrey Hodgson, *Lloyd's of London: A Reputation at Risk*, Allen Lane 1984, pp. 114–18.

145 Quoted in Raphael, *Ultimate Risk*, pp. 44–5.

146 *Financial Times*, 26 August 1995.

147 Lloyd's Capacity Auction 1997: Explanatory Guide and Rules, Council of Lloyd's, p. 12.

148 *Financial Times*, 2 December 1993.

149 Raphael, *Ultimate Risk*, p. 47.

150 James Denholm, *One Hundred Years of Scottish Life: A History of the Scottish Life Assurance Company 1881–1981*, Chambers, Edinburgh, 1981, p. 81.

151 Sir William Schooling, *The Standard Life Assurance Company 1825–1925*, Blackwell & Sons, 1925.

152 Mamie Magnusson, *A Length of Days: The Scottish Mutual Assurance Society 1883–1983*, Henry Mallard, 1983.

153 Kenneth Fleet in the *Sunday Express*, 14 June 1981.

154 Trebilcock, *Phoenix Assurance and the Development of British Insurance*, p. 7.

155 Garnett, *A Century of Co-operative Insurance*.

156 Supple, *The Royal Exchange Assurance*, p. 117.

CHAPTER THIRTY-ONE: *Problems of Institutions*

1 Quoted in Robert Skidelsky, *John Maynard Keynes: The Economist as Saviour 1920–1937*, Macmillan, 1992, p. 607.

2 Will Hutton, *The State We're In*, Jonathan Cape, 1995, p. 21.

3 Peter Drucker, *The Unseen Revolution: How Pension Fund Socialism Came to America*, Harper & Row, 1976, p. 82–3.

4 John Plender, *Thats the Way the Money Goes*, Andre Deutsch, 1982, p. 74.

5 Lyon Playfair published his *Lectures on the Great Exhibition* in 1852, calling for an increase in scientific education and training. Will Hutton published *The State We're In* in 1995. It called, *inter alia*, for the same thing. That investment in human capital is the key to economic growth in the modern world is a key theme of the New Labour government, popularised in the remark of the Prime Minister that his top three priorities were 'education, education, education.' Many of his Victorian predecessors had the same idea.

6 Gross Domestic Product at market prices, *Economics Trends*, Office for National Statistics, January 1999, table 2.1.

7 London Stock Exchange Fact File 1998.

8 Paul Langford, *A Polite and Commercial People: England 1727–1783*, Oxford University Press, 1989, p. 178.

9 'The financial system, in short, needs to be comprehensively republicanised.' Hutton, *The State We're In*, p. 298.

10 'Company Profitability and Finance', *Bank of England Quarterly Bulletin*, August 1993, p. 367.

11 ibid.

12 Dividend Policy, 3i, April 1993.

13 *Sunday Telegraph*, 13 January 1991.

14 John Plender, *A Stake in the Future: The Stakeholding Solution*, Nicholas Brealey, 1997, p. 61.

15 *Financial Times*, 22 September 1997.

16 See pages below.

17 M. H. Miller and F. Modigliani, 'Dividend Policy, Growth, and the Valuation of Shares,' *Journal of Business of the University of Chicago*, vol. 34., no. 4, October 1961, pp. 411–33.

18 See Chapter 29.

19 *Fiscal Studies*, Vol. 16, No 3, Institute for Fiscal Studies, August 1995.

20 *Financial Times*, 4 June 1994.

21 HMSO, *Competitiveness of UK Manufacturing Industry*, April 1994.

22 Edward Troup, 'Right Result, Wrong Reasons,' *Financial Times*, 27 June 1997.

23 Letter, Alastair Ross Goobey, *Financial Times*, 4 April 1997.

24 *Financial Times*, 26 July 1997, 29 August 1997.

25 *The Times*, 13 August 1997.

26 The WM Company, UK Equity Returns 1997.

27 'Pensions Review: Rates of Return,' Securities and Investment Board, press release, 1 August 1997.

28 *Financial Times*, 19 May 1994.

29 The investment banks who act as primary underwriters charge 0.5 per cent of the value of the shares being issued. They then lay off the risk with the institutions, using brokers who charge another 0.25 per cent. The institutions charge the company a fee of 1.25 per cent in exchange for a guarantee that they will buy a certain number of shares (and unwanted shares) during the first thirty days plus another 0.125 per cent for every week or part-week thereafter.

30 *Financial Times*, 11 January 1995, 20 September 1995.

31 Interview with the author, 24 July 1992.

32 *Financial Times*, 29 October 1987.

33 Interview with the author, 22 July 1992.

34 The study was first published in 1980. But Marsh is a strong supporter of pre-emption rights, arguing that 'to imply that pre-emption rights are a restrictive practice is akin to arguing that laws against theft are anti-competitive'. See letter, *Financial Times*, 17 June 1996. His conclusion that underwriters were charging twice what their service was worth was based on the supposition that sub-underwriting fees ought to equate to the price of a 'put' option in the shares (a right to sell the shares to a third party at a pre-determined price). After studying six hundred and ninety one rights issues between 1986 and 1993, Marsh concluded that companies had paid out somewhere between £240 and £480 million in 'excess returns' to underwriters. After another year, the excess returns had risen to £490 million. *Financial Times*, 10 and 17 November 1994, 1 and 4 November 1996.

35 *Financial Times*, 21 November 1997.

36 See Chapter 28. *Report of the Committee to Review the Functioning of Financial Institutions*, June 1980, Cmnd 7937, p. 257, paragraph 929 and p. 371, paragraph 1406.

37 John Plender, *A Stake in the Future: The Stakeholding Solution*, Nicholas Brealey, 1997, page 65.

38 Interview with the author, 23 July 1992.

39 Interview with the author, 24 July 1992.

40 Plender, *That's The Way the Money Goes*, pp. 75–84.

41 *Financial Times*, 8 June 1976.

42 Richard Minns, *Pension Funds and British Capitalism*, Heinemann, 1990, pp. 87–8.

43 Robert Skidelsky, *Politicians and the Slump*, Macmillan, 1994, pp. 117–18.

44 W. A. Thomas, *The Finance of British Industry 1918–76*, Methuen, 1978, p. 114.

45 ibid., pp. 137–8.

46 ibid., pp. 118–22.

47 ibid., p. 134.

48 Minns, *Pension Funds and British Capitalism*, p. 101, Table 3.4.

49 *Report of the Committee to Review the Functioning of Financial Institutions*, paragraph 930, page 257.

50 See Chapter 27.

51 *Financial Times*, 22 November 1995.

52 *The Times*, 27 May 1989.

53 *Financial Times*, 27 May 1989.

54 See Chapter 11.

55 *Financial Times*, 9 February 1996.

56 Minns, *Pension Funds and British Capitalism*, p. 93.

57 The first transaction was the MBO of the health care arm of Générale des Eaux, worth £1.1 billion, in 1997; the second was the purchase of IPC Magazines from Reed Elsevier in January 1998.

58 Joseph A. Schumpeter, *Capitalism, Socialism and Democracy*, George Allen & Unwin, 1957, p. 83.

59 Hutton, *The State We're In*, p. 8.

60 John Plender, *A Stake in the Future: The Stakeholding Solution*, Nicholas Brealey, 1997, p. 71.

61 Research and Experimental Development (R & D) Statistics 1995, *Economic Trends*, No. 525, August 1997, p. 29, table 2.

62 R & D Scoreboard, Survey, *Financial Times*, 26 June 1997.

63 Research and Experimental Development (R & D) Statistics 1996, *Economic Trends*, No. 537, August 1998, p. 61, table 8.

64 John Kay, *Foundations of Corporate Success*, Oxford University Press, 1995, pp. 111–12.

65 *Sunday Correspondent*, 17 June 1990.

66 Research and Experimental Development (R & D) Statistics 1996, *Economic Trends*, No. 537, August 1998, p. 55, Table 2.

67 Baruch Blumberg, 'The Importance of Basic Research,' *Financial Times*, 23 January 1995.

68 *The Guardian*, 16 May 1987.

69 Sir Hector Laing, 'The Balance of Responsibilities', *Creative Tension?*, National Association of Pension Funds, February 1990, pp. 60–63.

70 *The Observer*, 26 November 1989, 15 April 1990.

71 *The Independent*, 7 June 1990.

72 *Financial Times*, 26 January 1996.

73 See Chapter 29.

74 *Financial Times*, 28 November 1996.

75 Alan Peacock and Graham Bannock, *Corporate Takeovers and the Public Interest*, Aberdeen University Press, 1991, p. 13.

76 *Financial Times*, 23 January 1996.

77 Plender, *A Stake in the Future*, p. 68.

78 *Sunday Telegraph*, 10 January 1993

79 *Financial Times*, 25 October 1990, 11 March 1991.

80 Hutton, *The State We're In*, p. 42.

81 See Chapter 16.

82 Trebilcock, *Phoenix Assurance and the Development of British Insurance*, p. 653, tables 11.6; pp. 733–4, tables 13.8 and 13.9.

83 Cannadine, 'Aristocratic Indebtedness in the Nineteenth Century,' in *Aspects of Aristocracy: Grandeur and Decline in Modern Britain*, Yale University Press, 1994, pp. 48–9.

84 Hutton, *The State We're In*, p. 42.

85 See P. J. Cain and A. G. Hopkins, *British Imperialism: Innovation and Expansion 1688–1914* and *British Imperialism: Crisis and Deconstruction 1914–1990*, Longman, 1993.

86 David Kynaston, *The City of London: Golden Years 1890–1914*, Chatto & Windus, 1995, Volume II, pp. 456, 459.

87 ibid., pp. 461–8.

88 ibid., p. 459.

89 ibid., p. 462.

90 Cain and Hopkins, *British Imperialism: Innovation and Expansion 1688–1914*, p. 211.

91 Jonathan Charkham, *Keeping Good Company: A Study of Corporate Governance in Five Countries*, Oxford University Press, 1995, pp. 340, 342.

92 Sir Hector Laing, 'The Balance of Responsibilities,' *Creative Tension?*, National Association of Pension Funds, February 1990, p. 60.

93 David Hopkinson, 'Relations Between the City and Industry in the 1990s', National Association of Pension Funds, February 1990, pp. 47–8.

94 Morgan Grenfell agreed to advise Guinness in its bid for Arthur Bell & Sons in June 1985. See Dominic Hobson, *The Pride of Lucifer*, Mandarin, 1991, pp. 319–22.

95 *Sunday Telegraph*, 17 October 1993.

96 *Financial Weekly*, 28 September 1990.

97 Global M & A, Winter 1995/96, page 14.

98 G. H. Ross Goobey, 'Investment Policy for the Pension Fund at the Present Time', Imperial Tobacco, 30 April 1969.

99 Minns, *Pension Funds and British Capitalism*, pp. 78–9.

100 26 March 1992.

101 *Financial Times*, 8 August 1990.

102 *Sunday Correspondent*, 17 June 1990.

103 Alan Peacock and Graham Bannock, *Corporate Takeovers and the Public Interest*, Aberdeen University Press, 1991, pp. 59–60.

104 Quoted in Plender, *A Stake in the Future*, pp. 68–9.

105 See Peacock and Bannock, *Corporate Takeovers and the Public Interest*, pp. 34–5.

106 In the autumn of 1997 the Chancellor of the Exchequer announced that advance corporation tax would be abolished.

107 Peacock and Bannock, *Corporate Takeovers and the Public Interest*, p. 35.

108 Terry Smith, *Accounting for Growth: Stripping the Camouflage from Company Accounts*, Century, 1992, p. 23.

109 Peacock and Bannock, *Corporate Takeovers and the Public Interest*, pp. 49–62.

110 Plender, *A Stake in the Future*, pp. 67–8.

111 *Sunday Times*, 11 February 1990.

112 *Financial Times*, 22 October 1997.

113 ibid., 1 November 1995.

114 Robert Skidelsky, *John Maynard Keynes: The Economist as Saviour 1920–1937*, Macmillan, 1992, pp. 236–8.

115 ibid., pp. 525–6.

116 *The Economist*, 13 May 1995.

117 Interview with the author, 23 July 1992.

118 *Creative Tension?*, p. 27.

119 See Chapter 15.

120 Jonathan Charkham, *Keeping Good Company: A Study of Corporate Governance in Five Countries*, Oxford University Press, 1995, p. 341.

121 *Wall Street Journal*, 26 December 1997.

122 Institutional Shareholder Services, Press Release, 14 January 1998.

123 *Financial Times*, 2 March and 17 July 1991.

124 *Financial Times*, 20 September 1996.

125 Association of British Insurers, *The Responsibilities of Institutional Shareholders*, March 1991.

126 Warwick University survey reported in *Financial Times*, 10 February, 24 August 1995.

127 *Financial Times*, 3 and 4 April 1997.

128 *Sunday Correspondent*, 17 June 1990.

129 Interview with the author, 23 July 1992.

130 Interview, 22 July 1992.

131 *The Observer*, 27 March 1983.

132 *The Times*, 13 August 1997, *Financial Times*, 22 January 1999.

133 *Sunday Telegraph*, 12 May 1991.

134 *Financial Times*, 1 June, 15 June, 20 June 1991.

135 *Sunday Times*, 16 June 1991.

136 *Financial Times*, 11 June 1991.

137 James Saunders, *Nightmare: The Ernest Saunders Story*, Century Hutchinson, 1989, p. 191.

138 Interview, 22 July 1992.

139 *Financial Times*, 26 May 1990.

CHAPTER THIRTY-TWO: *The Future of Ownership*

1 *The Observer*, 19 July 1992

2 John Plender, *That's The Way the Money Goes*, André Deutsch, 1982, pp. 198–9.

3 Tony Blair, speech to Singapore business community, 8 January 1996.

4 See Francis Fukuyama, *Trust: The Social Virtues and the Creation of Prosperity*, Penguin, 1996.

5 John Kay, *Foundations of Corporate Success*, Oxford University Press, 1993, p. 367.

6 Charles Handy, *The Empty Raincoat*, Arrow, 1995, p. 131. See also chapter 20.

7 *Financial Times*, 18 November 1996.

8 John Plender, *A Stake in the Future: The Stakeholding Solution*, Nicholas Brealey, 1997, p. 14.

9 John Kay, 'The Good Market,' *Prospect*, May 1996. Will Hutton has said much the same thing: 'Stakeholder political economy has at last given the centre-left the confidence to take on the free market right on its own ground – the private company.' See 'Left with No Illusions', *Prospect*, March 1996.

10 *Financial Times*, 26 August 1995.

11 ibid., 12 April 1996.

12 ibid., 1 May 1997.

13 *Financial Times*, 1 May 1997.

14 *The Independent*, 14 May 1990.

15 Interview with the author, 23 July 1992.

16 Interview with the author, 24 July 1992.

17 See Chapter 29.

18 *Financial Times*, 7 September 1982.

19 ibid., 21 October 1989.

20 See Chapter 4.

21 Kay, *Prospect*, May 1996.

22 John Kay and Aubrey Silberston, 'Corporate Governance', *National Institute Economic Review*, August 1995.

23 'We must move away from the PLC structure, while retaining the advantages of managerial autonomy and commercial discipline in a framework focused on customers, not the capital market.' Kay, *Prospect*, May 1996. See also, 'Troubles Caused by a Lack of Legitimacy', *Financial Times*, 3 November 1995.

24 David Skinner, Martin Currie, interview, 24 July 1992.

25 See Chapter 28.

26 Barry Supple, *The Royal Exchange Assurance: A History of British Insurance 1720– 1970*, Cambridge University Press, 1970, p. 389.

27 *Financial Times*, 22 November 1997.

28 ibid., 1 and 2 September 1992, 10 November 1993 and *Sunday Times*, 18 October 1992.

29 *Inland Revenue Statistics* 1998, table 7.9, p. 75.

30 *Financial Times*, 14 October 1988.

31 *The Independent*, 28 April 1990.

32 *Financial Times*, 7 September 1993.

33 ibid., 28 April 1993.

34 *Independent on Sunday*, 23 January 1994.

35 *Financial Times*, 18 January, 8 February and 11 June 1997.

36 *Daily Telegraph*, 21 May 1976. See also Leslie Hannah, *Inventing Retirement: The Development of Occupational Pensions in Britain*, Cambridge University Press, 1986, p. 95.

37 *Financial Times*, 23 October 1979.

38 Plender, *That's The Way the Money Goes*, pp. 195–8.

39 *Financial Times*, 7 March 1992; 9 June, 22 June, 22 November 1993; 13 July 1994.

40 ibid., 16 July 1992; 4 October, 5 October 1995; 25 January 1996.

41 ibid., 29 July 1992; 12 September, 4 November, 25 November 1993.

42 ibid., 4 March 1993.

43 ibid., 27 April 1993, 21 January 1994.

44 See quotation at top of Chapter.

45 *Financial Times*, 17 October 1995.

46 *The Observer*, 25 January 1987.

47 National Association of Pension Funds, *Self-Investment By Pension Funds: A Report*, June 1988, p. 25.

48 ibid., p. 29.

49 From Appendix II, page 32 of National Association of Pension Funds, *Investment Management: A Guide for Trustees*, 1992.

50 Later reduced to less than 15 per cent. Richard Minns, *Pension Funds and British Capitalism*, Heinemann, 1990, p. 137; *Financial Times*, 7 September 1982.

51 Report of the Committee to Review the Functioning Financial Institutions, HMSO, June 1980, Cmnd. 7937, p. 95.

52 *Financial Times*, 5 December 1990; 19 January 1991; *The Observer*, 16 June 1991.

53 ibid., 21 May 1993.

54 ibid., 6 June, 13 July 1996.

55 John Cunliffe, *The Role of the Pension Fund Trustee*, Croner 1991, pp. 159–63.

56 *Financial Times*, 7 May 1993.

57 ibid., 25 October and 2 November 1994.

58 ibid., 15 September 1995.

59 ibid., 18 January, 8 February, 11 June 1997, 11 February 1999.

60 ibid., 13 March, 18 April 1997.

61 Augustus de Morgan, in his *Essay on Probabilities*, quoted in M. E. Ogborn, *Equitable Assurances*, p. 206.

62 Maurice Lindsay, *Count All Men Mortal: A History of Scottish Provident 1837–1987*, Canongate, 1987, p. 116.

63 *Financial Times*, 17 November 1995; 25 February 1995; 5 and 24 September, 1 October 1996.

64 ibid., 5, 24 September, 1 October 1996.

65 *Hansard*, Col. 249, 12 June 1979.

66 Margaret Thatcher, *The Downing Street Years*, HarperCollins, p. 677; Nigel Lawson, *The View From No 11*, Bantam, 1992, p. 238. See also Chapter 11.

67 *Sunday Telegraph*, 22 April 1990.

68 Matthew Gaved and Anthony Goodman, *Deeper Share Ownership*, Social Market Foundation, 1992, p. 26.

69 By December 1997, the total invested in the second generation of TESSAs, stood at £27.3 billion. Inland Revenue Statistics 1998, p. 85, Table 9.3.

70 See Chapter 31.

71 *Social Trends*.

72 For ventures between banks and supermarkets, see Chapters 22, 27.

73 *Financial Times*, 1 November 1993.

74 NFC was bought from the Government for £53.2 million in 1982, and floated on the Stock Exchange for £800 million in February 1989. See Chapter 11.

75 Gaved and Goodman, *Deeper Share Ownership*, pp. 35–6.

76 See Chapter 15.

77 For the privatisation of the bus industry, see Chapter 11.

78 *Inland Revenue Statistics* 1998, pp. 65–6, tables 6.1, 6.2.

79 See Chapter 31.

80 *Financial Times*, 22 December 1997.

81 See above.

82 Andrew Dilnot, Richard Disney, Paul Johnson and Edward Whitehouse, *Pensions Policy in the UK*, Institute for Fiscal Studies, 1994.

83 See Chapter 30.

84 *Financial Times*, 11 December 1996.

INDEX